The Cabin

Journal 1964 -1984

The Cabin

Journal 1964 -1984

William Heyen

H_NGM_N BKS
www.h-ngm-nbks.com

Copyright © 2012 William Heyen

All rights reserved. No part of this book may be reproduced in any manner without written permission from the publisher, except for brief quotations used in reviews or critical articles.

First Edition H_NGM_N EDITION, April 2012

ISBN: 978-1475044454

Front cover woodcut by John DePol from *With Me Far Away: A Memoir*, by William Heyen (Roslyn, NY: Stone House Press, 1994).

Back cover woodcut by Alice Wand from *Along This Water*, by William Heyen (Syracuse, NY: Tamarack Editions, 1983).

Book & cover design by Nate Pritts & Scott O'Connor, with thanks to Tom Holmes

Preface

I had just turned 24 when I began this diary—I thought of it at first as only a *diary* of quotidian jottings, but over the years hoped that it was becoming a *journal*. I didn't have much to say to it, and I blush easily now at the rube, the huckleberry I sometimes was. I came from a home where my three brothers and I had no music or art or serious discussion of issues. I never saw one of my hard-working parents read a book. After high school, I got into a small teachers' college where I remained more interested in sports than in the English education major to which, from physical education, I gravitated. I have excuses for this young diarist, but his worries/ambitions/gushings became a kind of compost for my sensibility now, which still often quails me. So what the hell.

My main question was whether or not to edit my thousands of entries down to the most interesting, the most literary, and edit these entries further. But poet Lucien Stryk speaks of "the hateful will to impress," and I've decided that I'd rather be on full record, even to my grandchildren, as fool and academic and puerile striver and only sometimes, in William Stafford's phrase, "worthy company," than as mature presence from the get-go.

There are dozens of closely-handwritten blank books filled with my days. (Because I sometimes talk about these, I'll identify each new one as it begins.) My journal has comforted me in hundreds of awkward situations. If for the first several years I had a hard time keeping it going, for decades now journal writing has usually seemed natural to me, a way to steady myself, to try to make clear sentences, as much as a record of events or a following of theme. I'm not going to change anything or leave anything out. Occasionally, I might bracket some extra information—in some cases to save a few poems I've referred to that were in magazines but which will never be in books. I'm not going to identify people or provide bibliographical information or add further memories to often skeletal notations or try to make the ampersand/and usage or other usages consistent, etc. I want to have the experience, over years, of typing the whole thing and revisiting myself, including my posturings and evasions, my pettinesses, my loyalties and decencies, my weaknesses and stupidities, my occasional intensities and discoveries.

I thought of waiting until I was in my '70s or '80s before publishing any of this journal, but my older brother, Werner, my childhood protector and lifelong friend, died in 2003 at 65, so I want to get to this now—the journal as a whole is voluminous and there will eventually be several volumes the size of this first one— in case the original is lost. In a brief preface to my book of stories, *The Hummingbird Corporation* (2004), writing in the third person I say about these fictions that "As echoes and asides, they would keep his other imaginings company, and the light they heard together would not be quite as lonely." I have the same hope for my journal.

William Heyen
Brockport, NY
February 2006

[#1: December 25, 1964-September 1, 1975]

12/25/64

Well then Diary, without further ado, be begun. It is Christmas. Hannelore and I and of course Billy Jr. are spending the holidays in Nashville, New York with Hanny's folks. Wolf and Ken, her two brothers, were here today with their families, Pat and Kurt, and Sandy and Kelly, their wives and children, respectively. There were many gifts and lots of good food. Ken, Wolf and I went up an old dirt road to shoot Ken's 22 pistol a bit and then we played some penny poker. I lost 20¢.
Called home at 5:30. The folks and my brothers in Nesconset are all fine. This is my first Christmas away from home, but this has become my second home.
Han and I and her folks exchanged gifts last night. Among other things, we gave her folks a set of wine glasses and just happened to bring three bottles of imported German wine along with us. Then the four of us played a few hands of pinochle.
One of my gifts was this book. Han knew I wanted to begin a journal. I read Pepys last night—rather last month—and have had the itch to record a few things for the pleasure of my old age, for the pleasure of my grand-children-fate-willing, and perhaps for publication a few centuries from now. I cannot write in code or live at the center of this country's political and social life or even be as racy as Pepys. But who can possibly tell what the future will find interesting? Twenty or thirty years from now I will probably look back at my own scrawling with a sense of disbelief.
There is much to enter but much time on other days to describe my life as I seem to be living it now. I am 24. My family, my poetry, my books, are my chief loves. Hanny and Billy and I are fine except for slight colds; I finished writing what I call my first "Song From the Folk" today; one of the things Han and I brought to store here for a couple of years was a big bookcase filled with things I won't be using until we get our own home. (We now live in an apartment in Cortland.)
The Diary has been begun. I'm sure I will never go blind and be forced to leave it. To all and everything, a good night.

12/28/64

Got up early to correct some papers and then finished "Lists and Things." It works well, I think, mixing seriousness and the comic spirit just enough. I've gone quite a while without writing much, but this poem and "Christ and the Choir at Smith Mills" and "Over Bare Oaks"—done last week in Cortland—mark a kind of comeback.
I like to think that after various academic bothers and pressures I renew myself here in Nashville, which isn't even a town, in this big, old house.
Went to see Kenny and Sandy and bought some tropical fish for Han's folks: two beautiful red swordtails, a leopard danio, a couple of platties, a couple of rosy barbs and a catfish. I cleaned the tank yesterday, adding a big chunk of slate, and it looks great now.
I'm getting a big kick out of this journal.

12/30/64

Wrote parodies this morning of Frost's "Stopping By Woods" and Williams' "Red Wheelbarrow." Will send them around, first to *College English*, probably.
Went to visit Sandy & Kenny last night. Sandy's step-father showed me some interesting things: a Civil War dress sword, a lantern handed down in his family since the Revolution, and a shotgun replete with notches that was used on the stage on the run "between Dry Gulch" and somewhere.
Billy is forcing me to play with the Popeye guitar he got for Christmas.

1/3/65

The three of us are back in Cortland after a hazardous, snow-bound trip from Nashville yesterday. Corrected the rest of the papers I had to do and got lots of poems ready to send out today. Haven't had an acceptance in a long time.

So ends a great vacation filled with laughs, presents, kids, and candles burning on the centerpiece. Han and I spent New Year's Eve—for the third year in a row—at the Kosciusko Club in Dunkirk—a small Polish club where our wedding reception was held on July 7, 1962. All our friends were there and we had a great time. They served a steak dinner at 1:00 when we were all about to go under. Even Han, after just two mixed drinks, almost left us. She absolutely cannot have more than a very little whiskey—as we have learned twice before. Wolf, Laverne Hall and I clicked glasses often, went around kissing all the gals after midnight, and in general made a lot of noise. We left about 2:30.

Next day was the second annual "Press Invitational Basketball and Card Tournament Held on Jan. 1 Each Year." Wolf, Laverne, Jimmy Muck and I play a few games in the Press's barn—staying warm with lots of booze—and then play pinochle and poker. We keep careful track of all scores and plan to do it every year. The ball court is short, one basket, and narrow—sided by a wall on one side and a hay bin on the other. Sentiment mixed with a loud time. The four of us have become good friends, although I think we are of four different breeds. Wolf's mother-in-law made us a big meal around 7 and we retired to cards, bowl games on TV, and more liquor. At 4 in the morning Laverne brought me home in a snowstorm which seemed to signal the end of 1964 for good.

Read Snodgrass' *Heart's Needle* today. Some fine things. I like the title poem and "April Inventory" best. Added another stanza to my own "Lists and Things" a couple of days ago. Now 80 lines, the poem is perhaps my best. *Lists and Things* would be a good title for my first volume that I'd like to publish in about 5 years. I find myself often writing poems that catalogue images.

1/4/65

Classes went well today. Talked about Eliot and "Prufrock" in two of them.... Got a nice letter from Bob Long who liked my "a certain party" in *The Southern Poetry Review* that I had sent to him.

Read Hemingway's *Moveable Feast* today, which is very interesting and a good source for anecdotes, but not too important, I think.

Heard just this moment that T.S. Eliot died today. What can be said when a great man dies? His achievement, I feel, was tremendous, but although a few of his poems are very fine I think he will go down in literary history more important for his influence than for his work. But who am I to say?

On a TV program today, Hanny tells me, Jayne Mansfield mentioned that she named her new poodle "T.S. Eliot." Curious conjunctionings, and ironic.

Han just came back from Syracuse where she bought me Lowell's new book: *For the Union Dead.* Will Lowell die next?

1/7/65

Finished Amis' *Lucky Jim* and have begun Cowley's *Exile's Return.* I heard him read a paper at Syracuse U. last year. So far his book is impressive and terribly interesting. The '20s are fascinating years of fascinating writers.

Got a letter from Jerry Mazzaro yesterday. He is adding a final chapter to his Lowell book and getting ready to go to Europe. His Guggenheim has given him a chance to turn out a lot of work this year.

Sent Bob Long a few more of my poems. Put together a few paragraphs on Melville's poetry last night and sent them to *Midwest Quarterly* along with the three sections of *Moby Dick* that I put into verse form.

Finished supervising my practice teachers today. Thank goodness. High schools depress me. Fraser Stokes and I stopped in a bookstore in Johnson City on our way back. I picked up a nice collection of three symbolist poets and a few other things.

Hanny has gone out to a faculty wives meeting. Billy, who is getting to be quite a boy, is sleeping. I'm going to get back to Cowley. Good night.

1/10/65

Han and I went to a small cocktail party last night at Ray Malbone's place. John Durrell was there and Doug Hill and Charlotte. Nice time.

Played poker at Lester's Friday night and lost $14. Have just not had the cards the last couple of months.

Began and almost finished my first verse play today. A half-fictionalized meeting between Cowley and James Joyce in 1923 Paris. I don't know yet if it is any good, but I wanted for some time to try a play.

Have begun smoking in earnest now. I've had the urge ever since the big cancer scares of a few months ago. It must be a death-wish or something. It would be funny if it wasn't so serious. All it can do is kill me.

1/16/65 Sat. 11:30

One comes home from a cocktail party pleasantly dizzy-drunk and notices that he writes larger than usual and with a careful strain toward precision. ---- Went to Wright Thomas' for a department party. Nice time. Dee West was a scream, embarrassing all the men, and later, at the Cortland Hotel, squeezing me around the neck violently enough to draw blood. She fell—chair and all—right on her back at one point.

Time goes by. Last day of classes of the semester yesterday and final exams begin Monday. One more semester and then back to being a student again.

Talked with Van Burd tonight who will have a book review on a collection of Ruskin letters in the *Times*.

I've completed a second section of "Lists and Things"—an attic movement. *Approach* is considering the first part. The poem will probably run 320 lines when done. Maybe a section on July 4th at the beach and Easter at a town dump.

After reading of Hart Crane in Cowley I'd like to write an article called "The Aesthetic of Booze."

1/24/65

I'm on mid-semester vacation now and enjoying it very much. Finished a couple of short poems. Read two powerful novels: Carson McCullers' *Clock Without Hands* and William Styron's *Lie Down in Darkness*. Styron's book is effortlessly constructed, the kind of book I would like to write someday. The Loftis family, unable to love, contrasted with the enduring faiths of the Negro, come alive.

Winston Churchill died early this morning. A man of courage. Perhaps the greatest man of the century, I guess. Locks of his youthful curls just flashed on the T.V. screen. Aah!—life, truth and things ineffable.

1/25/65

This morning Arnold Kantrowitz left Cortland for a half year off and some writing before he goes back to NYU I helped him move out along with John Durrell and Doug Hill. Arnold might be too nervous for teaching, unless he eventually finds a place that treats him a hell of a lot better than Cortland did. He's a good, if somewhat pathetic chap, and he promised to keep in touch.

Got a lot of work done today. Have two batches of poems ready to go out and that graduate paper, appreciative rather than critical, on Spenser's "Epithalamium." I know that I frequently try to rush into print without devoting solid scholarship to a project—maybe some day I'll have the time. I also send out poems and get them in very little magazines though they are good for only the circular file. But I do have about ten poems that I think are good.

Billy says "Oh No" to everything now, but is a very good boy. Han finally finished the jacket and skirt she has been working on since September. Surprisingly enough, she called my mother today, so I guess a reconciliation has been effected. --- I'm worried about my father—he has a hernia and will have to have an operation sometime. --- I had one when I was 5 or so. Ran behind an ice truck in Woodhaven that went too fast, and took a hell of a flop. Still remember turning over in my hospital bed and the pain in my groin after the operation. And remember watching at night the green and red blinking lights of planes as they flew over the hospital.

2/3/65

Saturday night Han and I had Marion Thompson and June Sprague over for dinner. It was a very pleasant evening. Today June called to say thanks and to tell us that Stu Dodge was seriously ill, was going to have an operation for a malignancy and would probably not teach next semester. Stu is a bull of a man and sickness has always seemed alien to him.

Finished a couple of short poems, "Danton" and "Rose ... Rose." Have things out to twenty places now in a "conspicuous consumption of stamps," a phrase Ciardi used. --- Jerry Mazzaro wrote that his Lowell book has been formally accepted by Michigan Press. He didn't think much of the three poems I showed him.

Registration procedures began today. I'm having a hard time forcing myself to work. Did read *Gulliver's Travels* and it should make good teaching. The parties are over and it's back to work. Never did get to the Stevens article I wanted to complete, but the poetry and some other little things accomplished themselves over the vacation.

2/10/65

Classes have begun again and Han and I are busy as hell. Billy is getting along fine next door when we are gone though.

Yesterday I went to Cornell with Karl Keller and spent the day in their library. Couldn't find the things I wanted, but read a lot of literary magazines. Saw Mark McCloskey's poem in *Contact*, a fine one. Mark is a friend of mine from graduate school. He is really rolling along now, having acceptances from *Virginia Quarterly*, *Saturday Review*, *Poetry*, etc.

My work remains out to all sorts of places. I'm getting hungry for an acceptance. Am working on an essay on the young poet as bread-winner now. Don't know if it will come to anything. Added a couple of sections to my Whitman poem and sent them to *December*.

Not much else new. Things in Viet Nam seem to be coming to a head. The sun still beats down on Egyptian pyramids. Somewhere, a baby cries. William Heyen sits in a Cortland, New York apartment scribbling in his diary.

2/16/65

Called home tonight. The folks are fine, except for Pop's rupture, and are planning a trip to Germany this July. Henry is going to New Hampshire with the YMCA for a few days. Earlier, Werner called to urge me to somehow subtly convince Pop to go in for his operation and get it over with. He said Pop has aged terribly lately.

Carl Keller went out of his way to praise the few poems I showed him. I was very flattered.

Not much else new. Lost $3.50 playing cards Saturday. Han gets her first check tomorrow, we hope. Kennedy and Wagner still in the news. I'd bet my life that Bobby will be president in '72—if we all last that long.

2/18/65

I received an acceptance today from *Prairie Schooner*, the best journal I have made. They took "Boy of Gull, Boy of Brine." I wrote the poem in a burst of energy one evening after reading two poems by James Wright: "To the Ghost of a Kite" and "On the Skeleton of a Hound." I'm very excited about the acceptance and look forward to seeing the poem in print.

To celebrate the occasion, Billy pooped on the couch and now he is nursing a sore behind. Some day I'm going to tell his fiancé about the incident. That will teach him!

2/25/65

Lester Hurt died at 10:30 this morning. A terrific shock and hard to believe. Something burst in his head Sunday night and we have since just waited for him to die, as we were told he inevitably would. He was a fine man. He sat on my left at a card game Saturday and after I bluffed him out of a pot with a $10 bet said that there would always be a job at Cortland for me because he would want his revenge. My diary is becoming an obituary column. I wrote what I think is a fine poem in memory of Lester and sent it to *College English*. I hope they print it. It will mean a lot to a lot of people.

Hanny and I will attend his interment in Homer tomorrow. He was quite a man and died before his time. I'll never forget him. His bookplate was a studious monk with glass in hand, and he often quoted Housman's lines: "I shall have lived a little while / Before I die forever." The only philosophy that makes any kind of good sense.

2/28/65

At Lester's burial Friday the snow and wind blew while Bob Rhodes read "Stopping By Woods On a Snowy Evening" and a selection from a Faulkner story. Then many of us went to a kind of wake at Ted Jocobus' place. I spoke with Torchy, Lester's wife. The whole thing is so damned sad. And I heard that Stu Dodge is really in tough shape with his cancer. A terrific pall has fallen over our department.

I got a nice letter from Bob Long yesterday. He wants to finish his degree but kind of itches to write a novel. Also, *Approach* took my garden section of "Lists and Things." I am awed by these last two acceptances.

3/3/65

My "Three Poems From *Moby Dick*" was accepted yesterday by *The Mark Twain Journal*. It is a minor thing, but I am very glad it was taken. I have things coming out in seven different magazines now.

Wrote a little poem: "The Man Who Drinks Brandy."

Beautiful weather today. Spring seems to be on its way. We will probably wake up to snow.

Finished Malamud's collection of stories: *Idiots First*. Fine. Am reading *Madame Bovary* now. Have not read it before. Don't have much ambition for school work though. Would like to start a short story and a couple of ideas are rattling around in my mind.

Got Jerry Mazzaro's translation of Juvenal in the mail yesterday. Very impressive. It promises to be the standard text in English for a long time. I hope he gets good reviews in good places.

I have been in the habit lately of taking a nap each afternoon. My dreams have been vivid, and in color. Wish I had the energy to record some of them here.

3/17/65

They have decided to use my "A Poem For Lester Hurt" in the yearbook. I'm glad and hope Torchy will like it. *College English* turned it down. I still think it is pretty good.

Got the first edition of *Harmonium*. Paid $35 for it. Perhaps my dissertation will concern Stevens' revision of his best book.... Got a nice letter from King at Ohio University guaranteeing me a contract in a month. Han and I have decided to take the whole summer off and stay with her folks. I'm going to do a lot of reading, writing, gardening, swimming and maybe baseball playing. Boy, do I look forward to it. I'll start at Ohio in the fall. The summer is now a cool, green space in my academically gray mind.

Studies in Short Fiction sent me John Cheever's *The Brigadier and the Golf Widow* to review. A nice surprise. I might do it by June or might put it off until summer.

Am reading *Crime and Punishment* now. Read Matthew Josephson's *Life Among the Surrealists.* Very exciting. Read Ross's *Portrait of Hemingway.* Comic.

Hanny and I now have $600 saved.

Heard from Arnold Kantrowitz. He seems to have settled down a bit—has his poems in the mail at last. Talked to Bob Long on the phone twice. I had him check on some Picasso lithographs and aquatints in New York for me. They were too much--$400-$800 each. Might see Bob the end of the month.

My brother Ed is going to study at Heidelberg University this summer. Great. My brother Werner is going to be a father again almost any day now. My brother Henry is raising hell as usual. Folks are fine. My mother was quite sick with some kind of flu for a while.

3/29/65

Have been neglecting my diary. Usually am too tired or too busy. A few things have happened.
1. Werner and Barb had a daughter, Deborah, a few years—wow!—I mean days ago. They are all fine. My folks really wanted a granddaughter. Can't wait to see her.
2. Got a nice note from Henry Rago at *Poetry* saying I should keep sending poems there.
3. Finished the Cheever review and sent it off to *Studies*.
4. Wrote a good story, "The Dreams of Edward Reiner," and have it off to *Kenyon Reviews*. I should be able to write several this summer that focus on the Nashville scene. I think I've learned something about story telling lately. I attempted too much in my first story, "Carl's Christmas Vacation."
5. Am teaching *Crime and Punishment*. Hanny is very busy, giving tests now. We look forward to the summer more every day.

4/8/65

Well, life has been hectic and all three of us really need a vacation. I did go out last night with Gene Hnatko and John Durrell. Saw "Last Year at Marienbad" and did some drinking.

Bought a cheap--$22—but very attractive Picasso lithograph today at an exhibition: "*a los toros.*"

Studies in Short Fiction accepted the Cheever review and *Trace*, after asking for a revision, took my essay, "Academia and the Young Poet as Breadwinner." A nice surprise and I look forward to seeing it in print. *Kenyon* rejected my story and it's off to *New Yorker.* Fat chance!

Billy has the chicken pox, but, luckily, a mild case. Hanny is out playing bridge tonight.

My contract for a teaching fellowship from Ohio came today, or rather (I hate to scratch things out), about a week ago. $3,200 and free tuition—a good-sized grant. I'm very fortunate—might even get a Ph. D. some day.

4/23/65

Well, the three of us returned from vacation at Han's folks' and school begins Monday. Hell of a nice holiday. Celebrated Billy's birthday the 17th. He was wide-eyed with wonder. He's now completely over the chicken pox.

Won $80 playing poker a couple of weeks ago.

Descant took a poem, "At Arlington." *Forum* took my Spenser article. Nice. Have 10 things coming out now.

Jerry Mazzaro is back from Europe. Heard from him yesterday.

Got my beautiful roll-top desk moved to Hanny's place.

Am smoking like a fiend now.

Have planned another story, "The Anti-Christ," to be written this summer.

Have lots of work until school recesses in June, as does Hanny.

My story, "The Dreams …", is now off to *Prairie Schooner*.

Arthur Mizener came over from Cornell to talk on Fitzgerald the other day. I cornered him at Alice's cocktail party and we talked about Wallace Stevens. He suggested that I get away from Stevens for a dissertation and get on to someone like Allen Tate.

Got a nice letter from Matthew Josephson. I had written him praising his *Life Among the Surrealists*. Can't wait to move out!

4/26/65

Monday. It is raining and it is going to rain. The gray day bends down.

5/2/65

Very warm today. A beautiful Sunday, but our 3rd floor apartment is too hot. Only four weeks remaining in the school year and they seem like forty. Hard to work in this weather.

Heard from Bob Long and again from Jerry Mazzaro. Both are fine, and busy.

Last night Hanny and I chaperoned a dinner-dance at the Cortland Hotel, along with another couple, Val and Fred Drake. Stayed up late talking about various in-law problems. They are English, and very pleasant folks.

Have no energy to do any writing at all—nor the time. Finished teaching *Moby Dick* and reading *For Whom the Bell Tolls*.

We loaned Kenny and Sandy $200 for a year. We'll go to Kenny's graduation in Cleveland next month.

Billy loves it outside.

Hope to play some golf next week.

6/1/65

Have been neglecting this diary, putting EVERYTHING off until summer vacation. We plan to leave Cortland in five days.

My Mom & Pop stopped by today on their way to Oswego. We all went to dinner and had a good time.... I give my only final tomorrow. Made out a good one.

Have several projects planned for this summer:
- a. beer, lots of it, and cold
- b. an article on *A Farewell to Arms* (syphilis)
- c. lots of poker
- d. all kinds of poems
- e. baseball
- f. a NOVEL, if possible, which I have been mentally planning and preparing for for a month. Can I do it?
- g. a tan
- h. an article on Tate's *The Fathers*?

James Farmer of CORE talked on civil rights here the other night.

Second U.S. Gemini flight scheduled this week.

We are pretty sure that Hanny is pregnant again. Perhaps some day a child of this child will read these words and get some sense of the past and of time passing. I have recently been fascinated by *The Sound and the Fury*. We are happily anticipating another child. I would like a boy again, but would not feel badly if we had a girl. Child, think of the evening your grandfather drew this star: ☼

10/5/65

Hell of a gap in this diary. Suggests not that my last four months were blank, but busy and all that.

What can I say? The summer was meteoric. I drank a lot, played baseball with the Forestville Merchants (played *some* good shortstop, got *some* good hits—but was not always proud of myself), played in some pretty big poker games in Dunkirk, Fredonia, and even in the back room of the Forestville Hotel. I don't know whether I got bored with the general decadence or whether I was sad to come back to school. I did write a short novel this summer, *A Cry of Pulleys*, which I must revise some other summer and get in the mail. One great thing happened: *The Southern Review* took one of my poems, "The China Bull." Got $30 for it, too.

I have courses in Old English, 18th Century & 20th Century lit, now have 2 or 3 articles and notes in the mail and am hoping. Things are going OK at Apt. #23 Wolfe St. I play a little intramural football.

Heard former president Eisenhower talk today. It was kind of exciting and names like Omaha Beach and Iwo Jima kept rushing through my mind. He didn't say much though. He concluded his talk by saying that being happy and having fun is part of being a good citizen.

11/2/65

Heard James Dickey read his poetry today. He was handsome, Southern, and impressive. Good voice and pleasant manner. One of his new poems, "Slave Quarters," seems to me to be striking and important. He discussed the motivation for each poem that he read and then raised the pitch and volume of his voice and went ahead. Wish I had had a damn tape-recorder.

I was 25 yesterday. Billy blew out the candles. I am working on a quarter-century poem. My folks called and then Werner. Southampton College is now on my mind more and more as Old English is getting me down.

Shenandoah sent me 3 novels for review. My Cheever review came out in *Studies in Short Fiction*.and poems in *Prairie Schooner* and *The Personalist*.

Billy and I have now found 150 golf balls. Will give some to Wolf for Christmas.

Got a letter from a lady in Texas who liked my *Trace* essay.

Hope to play some golf next week.

Jerry Mazzaro might be editing a collection of essays on *New Poets of England and America* and has asked me to contribute. James Wright? James Dickey? Would be a nice publication.

> Halloween just days ago;
> therefore was a pumpkin there,
> hollow-lit by candle light
> that night....

12/10/65

Damnit, things are going badly, I think. Hard to put my finger on what is wrong though: Old English, Pope—the greatest bore in the language—a lesson plan—Egads!—to write for some dumb woman—on a composition lesson on character analysis—freshmen, all kinds of boring busywork and a vacation to look forward to that will not be a vacation. The ranks of academia. The dung of it all. I sound to myself like some melancholy romantic.

Billy has been pretty sick. He seems to be O.K. now though, after much penicillin.

1/3/66

Well, we are back from a hectic vacation and all is well. I now plan not to take another trip until I finish up here. I'm just sick of packing and unpacking.... We had a nice Christmas and on New Year's Day the 3rd annual "P.I.T." was held. I got drunk and had, generally, a great time.

This will be a busy week for me. O.E. report and 20th Century Stevens paper to present. But the semester is fast drawing to a close. I did manage to write 3 poems over vacation. Had a lot of rejections waiting for me when I got back here, but Rago at *Poetry* and Lytle at *Sewanee Review* sent nice notes, at least.

Went to see a guy over vacation that I envy. He has 15,000 books in his cellar. I dream about a little bookshop or book-basement someday and a fine collection of modern first editions.

My diary is already a year old. I will leave it to Billy when I die, and if, eventually, I establish the kind of residence on L.I. that I think of, perhaps this volume will join my other books in an antique library and be passed down & down.

> Chicken Little,
> more than the sky.
> The world is falling ...
> with a heaviness,
> like Jack's giant who fell
> from heaven with a human thud.
> ... magic stalkfall.

Billy and Hanny are fine. Viet Nam is going badly. The U.S. and Russia are rushing to reach the moon. I would like to live until the year 2000. It will be a strange feeling reading these sentences then. Who was it, I will ask, who scratched these lines....

Two ideas for poems: 1/ Hanny's whacky step-father destroying our party hats last week. The 4 A.M. noises drifted up to us. 2/ A man drives into a New York City tunnel and comes out in a strange world that is like no New Jersey there ever was.

2/1/66

Somehow the semester is over. I just managed a B in Old English and received 8 hours of A. Have had a nice vacation of about a week and the grind begins again Thursday.

Have never seen it snow this hard in Ohio.

Hanny and Billy are fine. I put up the next one's crib today, and we are looking forward to him or her. We will leave here with a nice family—maybe a year from June, if I'm lucky.

Have been sending out lots of poems and getting lots of rejections. *Approach* came yesterday with my "Lists and Things," a poem I still like a lot. I've written several things since September and like one, "To Live in the World," a lot. It seems to me that in order for one to be a poet he has to say something about a way to live—after the deaths of the dozen old optimisms, faiths, beliefs. Something that begins with existentialism and transcends Sartre's increased awareness of nothingness. Hell of an order for a poet though. The poem, "To Live ...," just says that a man does go on after the death of a son—it isn't explicit about how he does "gather the glass of his life together."

You know, it is kind of frightening for me to write about my writing ambitions, because I do want my children and grand-children etc. to read this diary some day and, of course, the chances are that I will prove *not* to have the talent (for want of a better word) to be a poet of stature. And I do not want to be thought of as a failure. It seems to me that what a man can do is dedicate himself to the realization of his ambitions—and then—come what may. He can find a lot of happiness along the way. But, the fact remains, I want to become a recognized poet.

Have been reading Robert Bly (terrible!), Dylan Thomas (?—some great things), Ransom and Ruth Stone (both fine) and some Yeats plays.

The U.S. has resumed its bombing of North Viet Nam as of yesterday.

I'm kind of happy.

Why not?

2/7/66

Somehow, I've read too much the last few days and feel all washed out—bored, tired, listless, restless. Moods are odd things, and when I lose my enthusiasm even for poetry, I feel, truly, that the world is too much with me.

Found out I'll be taking my comprehensives this spring and am a little frightened. Have been reading Tennyson & Browning. If only the Victorian novel course I'm taking now was Victorian poetry, I'd be in good shape. I think I'll handle modern poetry pretty well though.

Jerry Mazzaro surprised me with a call Saturday morning. Had to do with his not getting to edit the Twentieth Century Views Lowell after giving, he says, Prentice-Hall the idea. And now he's asking Michigan not to allow Parkinson (?) to use part of his book.

Bob Long failed his comps at Columbia. Quite a shock.

There's so much snow on the ground that the slightest rainstorm ought to bring on another flood here.

Not much else new. I want out of here. The weeks are like watched clocks & pots.

3/7/66

Another month gone. Not much else new. Hanny is due any time now and I find myself actually looking forward to another child. They are the innocent and the hope of the world, as I once was.

Comprehensives April 9. I'm worried, but hope to do well. It will be one of the most important days in my life. If I fail I'm pretty sure I'll leave and not try again. Right now I'm busy as hell reading Victorian novels and reading for my two philosophy courses. Will have to do my final comps study over Easter vacation that begins the 26th here.

Jerry Mazzaro's book of poems has been taken by the press here at OU.

I got a nice notes from Rago at *Poetry* and Moss at *New Yorker*. Almost! I'm in a poetry slump now. Too many other things on my mind.

Billy is fine. So damn smart.

Two days ago it was 60° here. Today it snowed like hell. I would like to give Ohio back to the Indians.

3/17/66

Yesterday, a Wednesday, at 12:23 in the afternoon, our second child, a daughter, was born here in Athens at Sheltering Arms Hospital. Mother fine, and both will be coming home tomorrow. Hanny & I are very happy and pleasantly anticipating the difficulties of raising a girl. And Billy, 3 next month, is looking forward to seeing his little sister. All the grandfolks also happy. 6 pounds, 9 oz--20½". Strong, and, says her Mom, quiet. No name as of yet.

Our apartment will be filled up and things will be hectic for a while. I only hope I can get through my comps next month. It's getting to be quite a responsibility for me to get the Ph.D. now. This semester crammed with work and I can't work on other projects and papers until the comps are off my mind.

Approach, quite a surprise, took my long (160 line) "Such Was the Earth."

Daughter, a long and happy life. –Your father.

4/11/66

In two days, my orals. I'm nervous. The written exam went so-so. A question each on the drama, novel, and poetry. I did well, I'm sure, on the latter.

I have written one poem, "The Spring Come," a good one, I think. But school has kind of dried me up. I still feel the same tension etc., but the words and feeling will not come together into poems.

I have an immense amount of work to do this semester after the orals.

Kristen Hannelore is fine. A good baby. No trouble. Nice to have her around. Can't wait to leave here, get a steady job, and start paying off a piece of land and a home in which the four of us can learn to *live*.

Nice rejection notes from *Poetry* and *New Yorker* again.

The golf course is my haven. Walking around now in its scenery one or two hours every day. Finding lots of balls, too.

My next entry will be a happy or despondent one.

Jerry Mazzaro called yesterday to wish us happy Easter.

5/14/66

Egads, a month since my last entry. Time has gone quickly this semester—especially since the weather has turned spring.

Children fine. Hanny tired and headachy lately. Would like to take her on vacation after this semester, but hate like hell to drive any distance. I'd rather die some other way.

Oh, regarding my last entry. Passed the comps all right. Never did get full satisfaction: it was a strange letdown, once over—I'm not sure why. Hollis Summers was very pleasant, Roma King a little picky. I'm glad-------its over.

Semester fast drawing to a close. One more paper to type and then finals and then a couple of weeks off. I have a review of four volumes of poems to do for *Prairie Schooner*, and will do it then. Two other publishing things of note: *Twentieth Century Literature* took my note on the text of *Harmonium*; and, wow! the Borestone Mountain people took my "Boy of Gull, Boy of Brine" for their *Best Poems of 1965*. Best thing, and most unexpected, that has happened to me since I've been writing. Have written three other poems: "Epistemology," "What Love But Cries," "Kamikaze," the latter of which says my feeling, I think.

    Seeing all this, knowing
    I will never fully awake
    from such pilots.

6/20/66

---got all A's last semester
---am now fighting German, Eng. 4, Phil 391 (Mysticism)
---Hanny & kids fine; we all stayed here and had a nice vacation
---finished *Prairie Schooner* review; had another article accepted by *Forum*; had two poems, one good, in *Four Quarters*; some chap, Jerry Burns, is reading two of my poems over radio in Wisconsin
---am not getting any poems written
---got a great set of used golf clubs for Father's Day
---am currently taken with Roethke
---Eddie graduated from Oswego, will teach hs German, get married next summer, probably
---Gail Knauss still typing the 1st draft of my novel
---Viet Nam escalating
---dreamed all night of death

7/19/66

First summer session over today. Had a German test that went so-so. Not much new. The heat is punishing.

Kristen and Billy and Hanny are fine. Everyone holding up though the summer is a drag. We ought to be able to get away from here for a month or so in six weeks or so.

Am researching Roethke and am 100% certain my dissertation will be on him.

No recent acceptances or rejections.

8/6/66

Hanny and the kids flew to Buffalo for a couple of weeks but German kept me here. I wish I was doing more than I am. It isn't the heat. I'm just lazy. Bachelor life isn't bad, but I'm beginning to miss the family. Have played a lot—too much—golf.

Henry Rago at *Poetry* took a poem. Egads! I was elated. "Kamikaze". I was thinking of calling it "A Language of Gerunds". The poem, I think, really says what I feel, or felt when I composed it. I should have taken the whole summer off and done some writing, perhaps polished my novel, which is now all typed. Some parts strike me as sentimental, some fine. Lots of technical work yet to be done on it.

Wrote 2 comic poems last night, "Patsy" and "Clem." Finished a poem, "I Hung on Like Death." It might be a good one. I want to try something long one of these months.

Finished Roethke's *Collected Poems*. Somehow the later work disappointed me after the great early stuff. I may change my mine with further study.

TV filled with nonsense all day. Luci Johnson got married.

I've had a couple of pleasant talks with Jack Matthews, Steve Parker, and Mark McCloskey lately. I feel in, kind of. Hollis Summers and Matthews will also have poems in the 1965 Borestone anthology.

We are looking forward to two weeks on Long Island. A house is empty next to Werner. It ought to be great, even though we'll have to drive, even though every vacation with my folks has ended in—hate.

8/28/66

Summer session over, at last. I passed the German reading exam, after 11 weeks of worry. 15 out of 35 failed. The test was a greater ordeal than the comprehensives. Now I have 6 hrs, French and dissertation left, but I feel like I am over the hump.

We are leaving tomorrow for L.I. and what we hope will be a pleasant vacation. I don't look forward to the drive, but do want to see my folks and brothers again.

Also finished my minor this summer, with Grean's philosophy of religion course. Wrote what I think is a good paper on Roethke's "The Abyss" and sent it off to *College English*. Not much else new. Have been working on a long poem, as yet untitled. Am using my "Easter" poem for its first part. My favorite poets are so various—Eliot, Stevens, Roethke, Whitman, Frost, Cummings, Dickinson—that their influences on my work have not been dangerous. Some day I might look back on my poetic ambitions and smile—probably, in fact; but, I might yet be a poet. Sometimes I think I have it, sometimes I'm dejected.

Hanny and the kids are fine. Weather has been a little cooler.

Jack Matthews had his first novel accepted. McCloskey is off to Cortland. Steve Parker is one of the German victims, Jerry Mazzaro writes often and seems fine, though vaguely ill-at-ease, as always. I'm looking forward to Hollis Summers' course this fall—20th Century Poetry.

Graduation going on around here today. Maybe by next August ...

I am more composed right now than I have been since—leaving here with my Masters, I guess.

9/10/66

Vacation went nicely. All of us relaxed. Everyone at home fine but Henry seems to be getting to be a problem child. Young kids are all nuts though.

Decided against L.I. as a place to settle down. Just too crowded. Need land. Vermont or New Hampshire?

New York Times took one of my poems. Pleasant surprise. Reactions to my *Trace* essay appeared in *Trace* 60.

Classes begin Wednesday. Hang on for a couple more semesters, Bill.

Maybe someday I'll have the time and ambition to make this diary more than a scratch pad.

10/4/66

Not much new. We are all holding on, trying to take care of ourselves; things could be a lot worse, and vice versa.

I am enjoying Matthews' creative writing course. He is quite a chap, a human being, a genuine writer who came up the hard way. I've read his poems and his collection of stories, *Bitter Knowledge*. He said in class that he aims to confront an idea and this usually involves a semantic difficulty: when does a handicap become a handicap?, for example. I've written one junk story so far, a satire on the Miss America contest. Another is underway: "The Ballerina." But poems still make my world go round and I want to keep feeling this way. As an assignment for this course I may be allowed to organize my first (last?) volume.

Summers' course is all the worst. Nonsense. We waste periods on Yeats in ineffable ways. He ought not to be teaching an all graduate critical course as though it were a creative writing seminar. And he is strange as man. Odd, aloof, somehow rude though he effects a kind of old-South gentility.

Jerry Mazzaro called to say hello. He sounds fine and might make it down here or we might both go to the MLA meeting in NYC this year.

One more rough semester. Middle English is interesting but hell. French is easier than German. I'll get by and eventually smile at these difficulties.

Billy, Kristen and Hanny keep me happy.

My brother Ed was married this past weekend. Met his wife Jean just once and she seemed nice. Ed is solid and practical and will be a success, whatever that is.

Wrote 2 or 3 more poems: "I Move to Random Consolations"; "Fritz's Grace"; "Poem For a New Year";-- I'm still working on my "Such Was the Earth" (II)—seems to have enormous potential. My only poem, as I recall, that grew out of a short-lived experiment with automatic writing. Shades of the symbolists.

I am still pursuing the red-rose bordered hem.

10/8/66

I am putting together, little by little by little, my first book of poems, and it is quite an adventure. I suddenly discovered that I have enough for a volume, and will put it together over the semester for Matthews' course. I am confident that it will be publishable somewhere, some day.

Summers invited the class to his place for "a glass of punch" Sunday at 5:00. It ought to be interesting. I have a lot of work to do, but this semester, like all others, will slide by. Too many things to do at once; one large project would be much preferable.

I am teaching Hawthorne again—a master. The last paragraph of *The Scarlet Letter* has taken up my last two periods. My perception and my teaching are always improving, I think.

Received a nice note from Guy Owen. I'll want to try his *Southern Poetry Review* again soon. All my poems are out now.

We have money troubles. Just can't seem to get by on my pay. Hanny has taken on a recreation job for Saturday afternoons. I am looking forward to leaving here and getting out of debt.

10/17/66

Have just completed what I think is my finest poem, "Poem For My Daughter"—64 lines. Complex and meaningful I believe. The young poet has this problem: his tendency is to write as best he can, but he knows editors do not have the time to study a poem to ascertain just how meaningful it is. I can see an editor reading this poem quickly and saying "Nice, but what the hell is it about—why this? why that? And I know that I have in the past tried to simplify, to descend a couple of levels, until I've lost my poem. The problem is to attract attention. More people are writing poems than reading them. Perhaps I'll just have to write as best I can, and endure, as I am enduring this Ph.D. program. I dream of audience.

Finished a story, "The Ballerina." Not bad, but I have no illusions about being a fiction writer. My shorter "Such Was The Earth" is now in finished form. I want to get my volume together in time to try the Yale contest. Fat chance of winning!

Heard from Jerry. He is determined to have his *Changing the Windows* taken notice of. I hope he succeeds, but remember what Melville said about first volumes of verse.

10/22/66

I actually won the 1965 Borestone contest—received a first-prize check for $300 two days ago and haven't been able to sleep since. An amazing stroke of luck. I'm not sure yet whether the honor or the money means the most to me right now. We can finally pay off the hospital for Kristen and several other little bills. –In effect, that Borestone group considered my poem the best published in the English-speaking world in 1965. It is astounding to me that someone would send me $300 for a poem. Now I am girding my loins to try the Yale contest next year. –I'm sure "Boy of Gull, boy of Brine" is not as good as a half dozen other poems I've written, notably my last, "Poem For My Daughter." And this makes me feel pretty good. The effect of the whole thing is hard to explain: I've had faith in my poems and now someone else has manifested the same faith. Every aspiring poet ought to receive this same recognition at least once.

Otherwise, things are miserable. I have so much work I don't know what to do first. Also have a cold. But after the award these things seem minor.

11/7/66

Wrote "Mammoth"—I like it—and revised "To Live in the World"—which is kind of an important poem. If only I could explain the source of such courage—but then I would be God.

Not much else new. Passed age 26 the 1st of this month. Feel no different. Have job feelers out and got a nice reply from Brockport already. Somehow, it would be fun returning there.

Got Jerry Mazzaro's *Changing the Windows* as a birthday present. I like some of the poems very much and feel others are too personal or too prosaic, whatever that means.

Am trying *Poetry* and *Prairie Schooner* again.

12/2/66

Not a great deal new. I got a D in a Middle English test, which was discouraging as hell, but will hang in and survive. Turned in a first draft of my prospectus on Roethke. Finished a paper on Yeats's stylistic influence on Roethke for Summers.

Got the *Letters of Wallace Stevens* to review for *Shenandoah*. My *TCL* note on *Harmonium* appeared, as did the Borestone. Richard Wilbur and James Dickey won the second and third prizes. Nice to be in such company. Heard from Bob Long, Doug Hill--& hear from Jerry often. I've submitted some poems to a friend of his at *Salmagundi*.

Not much poetry in me lately. Did write "Eve's Is The Only Muse", which, right now, I like. Am teaching Emerson now. Am still job-feeling. Brockport, Oneonta, and Bennington College are interested in me.

A journal, of course, ought to be much more than a summary of superficial details—I mean to do something more with this once I leave here. But now I leave myself in my poems, or, fortunately but regrettably, in my teaching.

Kristen, Billy and Hanny are healthy after having colds. Billy has a pin-ball machine and one good friend, Tod. We are all looking forward to Xmas vacation. I'll do the review, put together my book of poems, drink, sleep, and play some cards.

1/3/67

Played some cards is right; I guess I lost about $150 over the vacation. Terrible luck. Full house in five cards once lost about $60 to four 4's. –Nice vacation. Quite a change from Athens for a change.

---Hanny went off the road with her Mom's Rambler. Nobody hurt though Billy bumped his head.
---No PIT this year. Wolf punked out.
---Nice interview at Brockport. They want me and I believe I'll go there. Chairman Gerber sharp.
---Finished review of Stevens's letters for *Shenandoah*.
---My "Boys Will Be Princes" appeared in the *Times*—12-17-66.

1/12/67

Took a job at Brockport for next September. Bennington took Jon Silkin. Some competition. I'm looking forward to the old Alma Mater.

Semester fading rapidly. I don't think I passed the French test. Too bad.

Bought the *Collected Auden*. Don't know him very well, and want to.

Took Billy to a basketball game last night. OU won by 1 pt. over Marshall.

Am teaching Whitman. Great stuff. One of a kind.

Am in one of those times when words & lines won't come together. A dissociated sensibility.

My prospectus on Roethke was passed first time through. Next semester ought to be my most enjoyable one in graduate school. French, one class to teach, dissertation. That's all.

The guppies on the shelf over my head are prolific as hell. Two batches within a week.

Jerry Mazzaro's *Lowell* got a nice review in *Poetry* and his *Changing the Windows* in *Times Book Review*. He seems to be arriving. More power to him. He has just one life, the literary.

Middle English danger over—A on second test, B or A on the one we just took. Pshew!

Bill Elkins just arrived for dinner. Ro's father died & she is spending a week with her mother in Kentucky. Bill was just the father of a boy about a month ago. I have two nice lines in mind:

> I know no other, better ways,
> to toll what the awkward heart says.

1/26/67

Another semester over, one I won't easily forget. I am now an AB.D—all but dissertation. My French prof dropped me enough hints to suggest that I passed the exam. My only responsibilities now are to teach one class and to write the dissertation. I feel a ton lighter.

Jack Matthews was kind enough to read my book of poems and to suggest four deletions. For the next couple of days I'm going to work on it and put it in final form. Will try Yale in March. --- Matthews also got me a job proofreading with the OU Press. Good experience and good money. I brought home my first galleys today. Dr. Grean's book.

Have written, and this is crazy, about 50 poems during the last couple of weeks. A new kind, I believe. A kind closer to me. I'm not clear on their achievement yet, but want to continue thinking about them (notebook #3). Poems with thematic centers and yet a sort of ungrammatical automatic writing.

No recent acceptances or rejections—oh yes, I almost made *Hudson Review*, from the sounds of the note.

Jerry Mazzaro called Sunday. Seems generally healthy and happy.

I wrote Mark McCloskey at Cortland to say hello.

Billy and Kristen are growing fast. Both are handsome, intelligent.

Not much else new. I look forward to Brockport. Hope we can find a house to rent there. Lots of those damn SUNY personnel forms to fill out.

2/6/67

Am clearing my mind to begin work on the dissertation. It is snowing and I wish it would snow for a couple of months—easy working then.

Heard from Mark McClosky. He sounds happy at Cortland and is continuing to make good at *Poetry*. I envy him.

Summers gave me an A. I didn't think he would. B in Middle English made me happy. A from Matthews.

My review is out in *Prairie Schooner*. Group reviews are terrible things to write. Also, *Southern Humanities Review* took two poems, "Written in Winter" and "She."

Am reading Lowell's new book, *Near the Ocean*.

Have finally finished *To Live in the World*, the book and the poem. Have written another short poem, "Epitaph."

2/13/67

Have finished reading James Joyce's *Letters*, Lawrence's *Collected Poems*, John Ashbery's *Some Trees*. Not much else new. I've been taking a vacation until I begin dissertation next week.

Book in <u>final</u> shape. Am done fiddling. Have written two poems for another volume: "The History of Civilization"; "But Another Mortal Country"; am reading Manchester's book on the assassination in *Look*, as is everyone else in the country. What comes through is the insidiousness of human nature—I do not want to hate people, but do hate the inhumane tendencies the human being has not yet suppressed. The hell with acting solely according to the passions and the arguments that can be mustered for this kind of action.

Got a letter from Jerry yesterday. I wrote him a couple of days ago, sincerely at the time, assuring him I value his friendship very much. I wonder, however, if I keep telling him this because his walking, talking ego is getting to be a pain in the butt? Or, am I envious of the reputation he is gaining? He didn't like my *PS* review; but he's right and I think this has nothing to do with the feeling I sometimes have that his acquaintance is almost oppressive.

2/16/67

Received official notice from graduate college that I've completed everything but dissertation.

I have the bad habit of getting nervous about nothing. Have always been restless, but so much graduate school has upset my stomach—I'll have to start pacing myself—I keep saying the word "pace" to myself. Sometimes I manage to achieve a calm when things are put in proper perspective.

Have written a short lyric, "Epithalamion", that I like.

Almost made *Harper's Magazine*. Am anxious to get some things to them again.

The folks called. All fine at home. Henry is going into the Air Force. Viet Nam still raging.

2/22/67

Completed "The Murder of Guttmann's Daughter" and "The Bear." Am working on a longer poem concerning the St. James windmill. So far—3 sections—so good.

I still haven't gotten down to serious work on the dissertation. Will.

I have two doubts about my book: "First Islands" and "Survivor." Will probably replace them when it comes back from Yale next fall.

Am teaching Poe now, again.

Kristen is beginning to take her first steps. She is very cute, if her father says so himself. Billy is smart as a whip.

I lay awake a long time last night thinking about a place that is home. Long Island draws me, but I think it is an Island that was. A sense of roots. I feel a very real nostalgia and need, and thought about my father, a German, perhaps visiting his son and grandchildren in Brockport. All of my feelings were, and are, of course, inexplicable. I would like to be home and grow old with my folks and brothers, and wonder if I can develop the feeling of "home" at Brockport. My conflict, perhaps, is simply with the reality that all things break up and divide. What of two raindrops in love? But this, too, for the optimist, implies an eventual theology of the transcendental oversoul. Babblings. Yeats was not among the last romantics. I am closer to Werther than any other character I could name.

2/26/67

"The China Bull" out in *Southern Review*; I'm very pleased with the appearance of the poem, and I think it's a fine one. Henry Rago at *Poetry* is sending me four books for review. "Kamikaze" is due out in *Poetry* next month.

Saw some terrible films of Viet Nam on TV yesterday. I don't know how I feel about the matter. I'm probably too politically ignorant to have an opinion, and perhaps humanitarian objections come too easily and unrealistically. I don't know. "Kamikaze" says it, though.

Am working on a longer poem, "The Windmill." Am having trouble deciding on or finding its thematic center. Will send out *To Live in the World* in a couple of days. Read "Climates of Opinion" in Carl Becker's *The Heavenly City* ... and am becoming confident that the last poems in my book are important.

Sent for four books of poems—two by James Wright and two by James Dickey. Wesleyan still has first editions left. If I had money I would have some collection of poetry. Sent for Tuckerman's *Collected Poems*.

Everyone fine here. March 1st I shall get down to <u>very</u> serious work on the dissertation.

5/7/67

Long time, no see. We are fine, although Kristen had a bout with tonsillitis and spent 2 days in the hospital. She's in great shape now.

First draft of ⅔ of my dissertation done. I still hope to graduate in August. Depends on how much revision I'll need to do.

Poem in *Poetry* out. Sent lots of copies to family & friends. Also did a review for Henry Rago that he very much likes. I hope to land another poem there in a month or two. *Southern Review* is sending me 16 books to chronicle! This is the way to build up my collection, and the publication won't hurt. Am writing an occasional poem. Just finished "Exhumation," which I like. Got up some energy & now have 10 things in the mail I'd let slide for a couple of months.

Heard from Jerry (often), Bob Long, Mark McCloskey. Mark now has books of poems out to Vanderbilt & Wesleyan Presses. I'm surprised & disheartened that he has had so much trouble placing his first book. My poems damn sure aren't hitting lately. Even *Four Quarters* turned 3 good ones down. My best dozen poems aren't being taken.

Am trying to cut down on smoking again. Am playing softball twice a week & hitting an occasional golf ball.

5/17/67

Am set to begin writing the last section of my dissertation. Have not seen the first two parts since I turned them in. Still hope like hell to finish the degree by August.

Bob Long writes that he was mentioned (concerning Hemingway) by Malcolm Cowley in *Esquire*.

Am enjoying softball. Have a hell of a hitting streak going, seven in a row.

Poetry Northwest (David Wagoner) took one of my poems, "No Elegy for My Father." Nice note. I think he wants to see more. Will come out in the fall. Am presently working on a five-part elegy on Theodore Roethke. Tough job. His is not my mode, but I hope to make it so, for one poem anyway. I don't think Lowell's poem on Roethke is anything to crow about.

We've gotten a $1200 loan for the summer. Only ½ to be paid back if I teach five years. Some deal!

Got the books from *Southern Review*. Must finish the review by the end of next month. Might, I think, make 3¢ a word, and I hope to do a good job.

Am teaching Whitman again. A pleasure. I'd like to teach a course on just him, or just him & Melville. Maybe I'll get the chance at Brockport.

We are all fine. Kristen occasionally cranky—cutting teeth. But she's a doll—loves to dance to radio music. Billy is a fine child: bright, kind, sensitive, athletic—a four-year-old now, already.

Have been hearing from Mike Stephens, a student who was at Cortland when I was. His letters are, as Bob Long writes he is, somewhat incoherent—but he's a good sort, and I much enjoy hearing from Bohemia.

We hope to get to Hanny's folks for a week & to visit Brockport some time next month. I hate long drives. Too damn dangerous.

Not much else new. Going away party Thursday night for the Hardings out at Club 33. Should be fun.

I'm nervous about getting started on Pt. 3. If I finish the damn degree and read this¶ in Brockport next year, won't I be happy as hell? What then to stop me? Poems to be written.

Heard Judson Jerome read today. Unimpressive.

5/23/67

    Han's 27th birthday today. I am still in love, more so all the time. We are happy, if occasionally nervous about one thing or another.
    Not much else new. Have started Pt. 3, have finished the Roethke poem & one on Bartleby, that I like a lot.
    Nice weather. Much work to do.

6/28/67

    I haven't mentioned yet that Grove Press will be bringing out a book, *What Happens in Fort Lauderdale*, that I wrote one weekend with Bill McTaggart. A piece of junk, but it might sell. I'm using the name Haines. Much deception involved. Hope we get away with it.
    Am working hard on dissertation. Still hope to graduate, but time is running out on me. Dissertation due, completed, August 2. Quite an order. Bill McTaggart's sister is helping me type the second complete draft. I don't know when or if I can squeeze in the *Southern Review* review.
    University of Tampa's *Poetry Review* took six poems.
    Hanny & the kids & I had a week at her folks'. We were actually able, under a land-contract deal, to buy a house in Brockport. Paying it off will be cheaper than paying rent. A lovely place four miles from the college. Clean, and very well-built, says my father, who met me there one day. I will finally be able to use my desk, and to get all my books together. We should all be very happy there.
    The garbage men stole my golf clubs. I have a witness, but still can't prove it. Bastards. I'm liable to bust a couple heads before I leave here.
    Hanny is teaching day school. I have the mornings to work. She takes Billy & Cindy Otto watches Kristen.
    We were actually ahead in a softball game 14-0 the other night and lost. Most difficult.
    Heard from Jerry. His second book of poems, *The Caves of Love*, is about finished.

7/1/67

    Bad day. House deal fell through; after we'd already made a lot of dreams on it. David Madden said he was too busy to serve on my committee this summer.

7/25/67

    Good day. It seems as though months have gone by since I last wrote here. Lots new.
    I'll graduate for sure. The final copies of the dissertation are out to my committee, on which Jack Matthews has so graciously consented to serve. Today he gave me a copy of *Hanger Stout, Awake!*, his first, a brilliant, novel.
    Heard from Mark McCloskey, and often from Jerry, who likes the few little poems I've sent him. Now he heard Rilke in my work—I've never read Rilke. The riots follow him from Buffalo to Detroit.
    Ann Arbor Review took "The Old Poet Is a Tramp." I'm now doing a review for Fred Wolven, the editor. My *Southern Review* review is done, and now needs typing. *American Scholar* took "The Bear," for which I received $35. A great acceptance, and things seem to be moving along. I have various things out to 16 different places now.
    August 26th, right after graduation here, the four of us will drive to Columbus and fly down to the Island. My 10 yr. high school reunion is being held that night. For many strange reasons, I look forward to it, and the trip, very much.
    Heard from Philip Gerber, my chairman at Brockport. I'll be teaching only nine hours—two sections of American lit and one of modern American poetry. Again, he told me that they want to give me plenty of time "to write your verse." This is much better treatment than I expected, or deserve, and I'm happy about the whole thing. Will get *To Live in the World* in final, final shape in September, I guess.
    Hanny & the kids are fine, all healthy & happy.

"How slowly dark comes down on what we do." "In Evening Air" is one of the half-dozen greatest lyrics I've read.

7/30/67

I give my lecture—on Roethke's mysticism—August 3rd. Then some odds and ends and I'll actually be done.

The *Southern Review* took my Roethke poem, which seems to get better each time I read it. *Prism International* took two of my poems, both interesting, but unimportant. This rash of acceptances is unbelievable. And I have lots of good things in the mail. *The Nation* took the same poem, damnit, as did *American Scholar*. A mixup. I'm probably messed up with *Nation* for good now. Review finally off to *Southern Review*. Have written two poems: Birds & Roses Are Birds & Roses"; "The Hangover".

Karl Otto's new axle might make him a million. He made me a beautiful mug.

My golf is getting pretty good.

Bill Elkins & Ro gone—East Tennessee State. We'll miss those good people.

Jack Matthews was kind enough to ask me for a poem for the *Ohio University Review*. I gave him two and hope he likes one. *One* of the reasons I started writing when I began graduate school was that I wanted to be someone, to be recognized as a little different here. I've made it. The professors don't know quite what to make of me. This sounds funny. It's hard to explain.

8/9/67

Somehow, it is all over. The talk went very well. Conover, Matthews, Summers, Purdum, all said nice things. Dissertation all filed. Now I just have to wait around for graduation. Hard to believe. The goal, when attained, becomes worthwhile. I hope to live long enough to make enough money to get the family in good shape.

Han has been sick, anemic, but is feeling better now. Kids fine. We are looking forward to the two events of the 26th.

Poet Lore took "Omens," a poem I continue to like. The last image, I think, is a fine one. I've completed "Case for the Defense" [of writing poems]. Will do the *Ann Arbor Review* piece today and tomorrow.

Got a nice note from Yates at *Prism*. Have not heard from Jerry for a while. By the way, the war in Viet Nam continues to be a farce, a horrendous one; and the country, with its racial situation, is going to hell. Blank.

8/15/67

I'm going through a father's pain. All morning three kids downstairs have been teasing Billy and saying they do not want to play with him. Impossible to give a young child a sense of independence, and every hour on the hour he ends up crying. I just had words with Sally Hass (her husband is an ass—she struts around like Queen Mary—both are pompous for no reason I can discover) about her brat. They check on their kids perhaps once a day, clothe them poorly, feed them worse (a piece of bread eaten outside is lunch). They've even gone to church and left their infant at home <u>alone</u> for hours. Subsequently, and ironically, their son, the same age as Billy, has grown up tougher. Perhaps we <u>are</u> over-protective. But I <u>know</u> that Billy plays nice, does not tease, and has a good time without starting trouble. His one good friend, Tod, is away, and this is half the problem. But those goddam Haas's are so stupid, hypocritical, falsely proper. I can't wait to leave this place, and very much dislike these social tensions.

Now that I have nothing to do, I'd better get involved with a long poem or some such thing. Maybe a *Dunciad* to vent my spleen.

Nice note from Goldman. That's all cleared up.

Did *AAR* review.

Heard from Jerry who called me a "masterful poet." Egads!

They're tearing down several houses across the street, including the one where Mark McCloskey stayed for a year or so.

Wrote Bob Long, finally.

We now have an address at Brockport: 165 Barry Street. Little by little we're packing our things.

Matthews had brief notices in *Time* and *Saturday Review*.

Hanny feeling weak. Will go in for a check-up this afternoon.

I went to see *A Man For All Seasons* last night. Fine picture. On More.

We finally won a softball game last evening. 12-4. I had a homer. Tournament begins next Tuesday.

Yes, I need to begin work on a longish poem, or on a story. I have a nice title for the latter: "The Water Is Always Greener (or Clearer) on the Other Side."

Yes.

10/2/67

---finally graduated, am now a "Dr"—Egads!

---upshot of the Haas affair is that I settled his hash, he pressed charges for assault and battery, I skipped town, forfeiting bail, per lawyer's instructions

---no new acceptances, much in the mail

---a couple new poems ("Indian Summer" a fine one)

---school hectic, but pleasant, and at last I'm making some money—but taxes are murder

---our house is roomy—have my big desk here, and we have a smaller roll-top we picked up yesterday, a lovely piece of furniture

---Jerry Mazzaro visited this weekend—nice seeing him again, though his presence becomes trying. Only one thing on his mind: publishing. He told a wonderful story about John Berryman's visit to UB. Berryman has since said "I'd rather go to hell than Buffalo." Jerry might get to NYC to see Lowell this month. Lowell, it seems, has let it be known in several quarters that he likes the *Poetic Themes*.

---Werner was in an accident—four Negroes, drunk and in a stolen car, rammed him—but he's O.K. now.

---Eddie lives only an hour from here—he might get here this week

---I don't know whether I want in or out of the creative writing programs here. The student poem depresses me, and teaching anything, even technique, is, I believe, impossible.

---sent *To Live in the World* to Wesleyan. Fat chance.

---Allan Seager was kind enough as to send me a letter Roethke wrote in 1942. A treasure.

---have been teaching Eliot & Taylor—quite a combo.

10/14/67

Last night the Grades and Gerbers visited. We all had a nice time. I made the folks some rum toddies.

Haven't been able to write a poem, or a line, that amounts to anything.

Will spend next weekend at some kind of creative writing affair.

We are finally settled, and comfortable. Rug for the living room came, cold winter coming. School is enjoyable. I'm now on cummings and Poe. Next semester I'll be teaching modern British poetry and the second half of the American lit survey. What I have to do is find out what subjects are most conducive to my writing my own poems. I'm not sure teaching poetry is.

Received $70 from *Southern Review* for the long review. Heard from Grove Press. They'll be bringing out *Lauderdale* 6 or 8 weeks before Easter.

Hanny's folks gave me a beautiful calendar watch for graduation.

One student, Lyle Akens, has been in to show me his poems. He shows a lot of promise.

Kristen and Billy are growing like weeds, and are fine children.

Eddie, I think, is going to get a fellowship in German at Berkeley. Mazzaro's friend, Arcuti, is friends with the chairman there, and connections have been made.

I've, after reading *Ancestors' Brocades*, become infatuated with Miss Emily again. "The name of it is autumn--/The hue of it is blood."

10/19/67

Finished a poem, "Existential," that I like a lot. I just wonder whether or not it ought to have this sort of title.

Wrote to Grove Press about an anthology idea.

Am ready to go to Cortland tomorrow for the creative writing seminar, probably the last one I'll ever attend.

I still feel a vague yearning for Long Island.

Heard from Mike Yates at U. of British Columbia. A wild man, and he makes me feel inclined to respond in kind.

Jerry called tonight, about nothing in particular. His eyes are bothering him. And my folks called. They sound hale and hearty.

It has been raining for two days.

I'm afraid to think about my book at Wesleyan. Wouldn't it be something if ... but no ...

My poetry seems to be coming very slowly. I feel the need for some change from school.

Applied for a faculty fellowship for the summer off to work on my poetry. $1500. I hope it is approved. The university patron fascinates me.

11/7/67

Grove Press is going ahead quickly on the "book." We just might rake in the dough. I've been in close touch with Bill McTaggart, who is sweating profusely as his comps approach.

Southern Humanities Review took two poems.

Han & the kids fine. We visited her folks this weekend and had a nice time. The snow almost kept us there.

Book of poems still out to Wesleyan. I have a hunch, since he knew my new address, that David Wagoner is reading it, but I'm not sure.

Have written "Bloodletting" and "Gravity." I think both poems do the job. The first is especially complex, a poem about permanence in violence.

11/12/67

Western Humanities Review took two poems, including my Bartleby poem, and I'm pleased. Lots of acceptances since August, but, yesterday, a rejection from *Poetry*, and this hurt. I was feeling just on the verge of something, and I was counting on Henry Rago, since I'd sent him seven (or six?) of my best poems. A nice note back, but alas!

I hear that Mark's book, *Goodbye, But Listen*, has been taken by Vanderbilt University Press. I'm surprised that I feel no envy, only gladness for him. I hope he makes it big. Actually, I've read only six or eight of his poems, and look forward to seeing the book.

I know that I've made nothing of this journal. I have so little imaginative energy lately, it seems, that I'd better save it for poems.

Werner and Barbara are coming to visit—should be here tomorrow. I'm supposed to hear James Wright read in Buffalo on Wednesday, but now don't know if I'll make it.

12/12/67

I didn't get to hear Wright. Last night Knute Skinner read his terrible stuff here. My idea of what a poem should be and do is confirmed when I hear such drivel. A very nice chap, but no kind of poet.

I'm pretty weary, just hanging on until Christmas vacation. I'm planning, primarily, to sleep.

Satire Newsletter took a little thing I did some time ago; no news on my book, and no definite plans on what I'll do with it when it comes back. I've completed a couple of good poems lately—"Contingency," "Windfall"—but am, by no means, burning with inspiration. I'm to give a reading here next month—am working on it. There are probably too many Ginsberg advocates among the students for any of my poems to strike responsive chords.

The kids have colds, but we remain pretty happy around here. I was depressed before I listened to Skinner, but it made me happy to listen to that garbage while repeating fragments of my own songs to myself.

Sent in the proofs of my *Poetry* review. It reads well, I think. My last two sentences on Huff may not be in good taste.

Ned Grade told me that Frost described to him how he'd fall in and out of love with certain of his poems. This is what happens to me.

Hanny remains a lovely wife. Where she gets her spirit and energy I have no idea.

Nothing new on the Lauderdale. I expect proofs in about a month.

12/28/67

Am right in the middle of a fine, relaxing Christmas vacation. My folks were here for just two days, and the weather held up long enough for me to pick them up and then get them back to the airport. Everyone was so showered with gifts around here that our house seems newly-furnished.

Proofs corrected already and back to Grove. March publication, and now *Evergreen Review* in March for sure.

I'm getting rested, organized, caught up. Reviewed Eliot's *Poems Written in Early Youth* for *Shenandoah*. Am working on a couple of poems. Wrote "Watermelon Time." *Poetry Northwest* took "Existential", a good one, but passed up "Magnifying Glass" and "Bloodletting", two perhaps better ones. Sent some poems to *Poetry Ireland*, my first overseas venture. Am still trying to be assigned a volume with William Martz' *Modern Poets Series*. Here's hoping.

We've all been fighting colds, but have so far managed to avoid the flu that is reaching epidemic proportions around the country.

Hanny has not yet managed—ha—to get out our Christmas cards. The pictures we wanted to enclose have not yet come.

The *Trace* controversy has started up again. It's time for me to answer with a long paper. Now, I think, I'm in a position to answer my original questions and to take stands on other issues that these questions seem to have generated.

I spent a couple of evenings with Knute Skinner, who read here before vacation. An engaging chap, but not much of a poet, I fear. We made a TV tape, with Greg Fitz Gerald, that we hope will be taken by the Rochester station.

It is pleasant to be here, relaxing in Brockport, rather than at the MLA convention in Chicago, to which several department members have gone. I would have liked to hear Lowell, and to have gone to the Iowa party Greg describes so glowingly, and to have visited the *Poetry* office, but am quite content here.

Almost forgot the best news of all. I was given a SUNY Faculty Fellowship ($1,500) for the coming summer. I'll actually have three months off to work on my poetry. A boon, indeed. Mark McCloskey had one at Cortland last summer, and Jerry Mazzaro has had a couple. Egads, the SUNY is supporting my poetry. A wonderful cycle: more time off to write (I hope) more and better poems which should lead to more money and more time off. The awards were scarce this year, too, and my hopes were not high. It means more to my writing, my teaching, than I can describe here. Peace of mind for not just three months, but probably for an entire year.

I'm still thinking about a long poem, which I can work on from time to time between shorter lyrics over the summer. A first line?:

What are the images, and why, that press?

1/2/68

This is the first time I've said it. I'll be glad when school starts again (tomorrow). The vacation has been delightful, but lately slow.

I'm still fighting for a title for my book of poems. The other revisions I have in mind will be much easier. Nothing, no phrase from any of my poems, strikes me as just right.

Evergreen Review has taken two of Pat Ryan's poems. I'm glad. There's a good chance that when he gets a book-length collection together Grove Press will take it. His voice is distinctive, if his poems are not my bag. I'm sure I'm the only one around here who has encouraged him.

I'm worried, as always, about a voice of my own. But I'll just write my poems and let someone else, if anyone ever becomes interested, worry about it. I'm now working on "Grape Arbor in Two Seasons"—it has a lot of promise, but I've got to find out what it's about.

My poetry reading is coming up soon. I'm a bit nervous, but looking forward to it.

1/23/68

Finals over, off for a week, but I'm staying plenty busy. Hanny and the kids are fine, and we are still avoiding the flu. After this next semester, three months off, and I hope to show Han and the kids a good time over the summer.

Texas Studies in Language and Literature asked me to tighten up my article on Roethke's mysticism and to send it back to them. I have it ready again, and will send it off tomorrow. It's a good one, and I want very much for them to take it.

Dabney Stuart at *Shenandoah* wrote me a very kind note, and accepted "Confessional" and "I Move To Random Consolations", two pretty good ones.

My book, now called *Depth of Field*, is revised again, and so extensively that I can send it to Wesleyan again when *To Live in the World* comes back. It's quite a book, and now moves from poem to poem with some authority, I believe. The title poem just won't be denied. When I read it at my reading (which went <u>very</u> well) it came alive, sang.

Promotions and raises are coming up quickly now, and I may be in for something. We could sure use the money. Before we're too old, I'd like us to move into a home of our own and escape this $200 a month rent. And our car is damn sure gasping its last.

I do want to work up some kind of essay for *The English Record*, whose editors have asked me for something on my own poems. My reading-talk might be the basis for it.

Not much else new. I love the cold, and hope the snow builds up some more. Took some time out from my esoteric musings yesterday to read Plimpton's *Paper Lion*. Delightful.

1/31/68

Jerry called yesterday. He's been promoted to full professor, at 33. Quite an achievement. Here, I've been recommended "first priority" for a "maximum" raise. Gerber wrote a very flattering note on the forms that now go to the president. I'm very happy, though lots of others here are not, with this treatment.

Am teaching Hopkins now. Learning much. I remember being taken with him several years ago. I wrote a poem called "Over Bare Oaks", a bad one, during that influence.

2/12/68

We spent the weekend with Hanny's folks. Kenny was on leave, and it was fine seeing him again. He'll be in Viet Nam in about a month. They'll visit us here in a week or so. The visit to Han's folks was nice, but tiring.

Not much new here. I can't, the last month or so, seem to write anything. Maybe it's an after-*Depth of Field* slump. I have lots of things in the mail and lots of things about to be published, but our mailbox is always empty.

W.S. Merwin is to be here the 27th. I'm reading his work now, preparing myself for the tape.

Nice note from Jerry on *Depth of Field*.

2/29/68

    W.S. Merwin spent two days here, and left today. I was quiet around him, and a bit awed, not so much by his poetry, which I've been cramming in in great gulps lately, as by the man. Completely self-possessed, complete equilibrium.

    His reading went well. His voice is deep and clear, and there's a trace of an (British, I guess, though he's not British) accent that jars a little, or complements his bushy hair, turtle-neck sweater, baggy brown-corduroy trousers, with its sophistication. After the reading Greg forced me to ask him a question, and I asked about the change in his voice that Stepanchev discusses in *American Poetry Since 1945*. But he seemed to think—he went on the defensive—that I'd said something derogatory about the clarity of his recent poetry.... A party at a student's last night, and much cordial talk.... Today, a TV tape, and I think it went well, as well as our format will allow. Greg wants conversations. I want poems.

    Well, Merwin was very cordial, kind, patient with us all. He may be the most intelligent person I've ever met. I'm not depressed by his accomplishments, just am more determined than ever to keep working at my poems land trying to make them live.

    The *Poetry* review is out. *Texas Studies LL* took my paper for publication sometime in 1970. I'm <u>very</u> pleased. *English Record* took a little thing, "Two Ideas and Two Poems", I worked up. More important, I've written a few poems, including some "quiet" ones that I like.

    I'm very tired, but will rest the next few days. Hanny and the kids are fine. I took Billy to see *Alaskan Safari* last night. Great. I don't think I'll ever get the image of that perpetual ice-traveler, the polar bear, out of my mind.

    I might be doing an essay on Snodgrass for an anthology Jerry is planning. I don't mind at all.

3/11/68

    Mark McCloskey and Barry Targan were here for a couple of days last week. I very much enjoy their company. Mark's *Goodbye, But Listen* is out, and I can't say I like it, competent as it is. But who am I to say? Greg Fitz Gerald and I made a tape with each of them.

    Jerry's book was rejected by Ohio. I don't know what the hell is the matter with me, but I don't like *The Caves of Love* either. Nor Bly's *The Light Around the Body*, nor anyone's poetry I've read lately. Usually, I'm uncritical and enjoy everything I read. Oh, an exception: an actor read some of Browning's dramatic poems at school today. I'd forgotten just how fine "My Last Dutchess" and "The Bishop Orders His Tomb ..." and "Porphyria's Lover" are.

    My review of Eliot's *Poems Written in Early Youth* just appeared in *Shenandoah*, and imagine my surprise when I found, in the same issue, Richard Eberhart's letter attacking my review of Stevens's *Letters*. I've answered, politely as I could. Eberhart is a strange chap. One of his ¶s (about Frost & Williams) had nothing to do with my review at all.

    The Lauderdale book is out. Now to see what happens. The second $250 sure is coming in handy.

    Ken Greiner left for Vietnam yesterday. I feel deeply about the wrongness and immorality of the war, but almost beyond expression.

    I've written lots of poems lately, including some good ones. What is taking shape is a volume of poems, or one long "poem" on Long Island. I read a few at The Crypt Friday night, and they worked well.

    Received a kind note from Robert Huff. He liked the *Poetry* review.

    Han and the kids are fine. Her folks might visit us this weekend. And my folks might show up for Easter.

3/14/68

    Werner's birthday today. We called to wish him a happy. He seems to be in good spirits.

Postcard from Richard Wilbur today. The press at Wesleyan has received *Depth of Field*, and he is, it looks like, going to send us a poem for *The English Record*.

Miller Williams at *New Orleans Review* took two of my poems, "Windfall" and "The Sentry", the latter not too hot.

I sent my second copy of *Depth of Field* to Knopf. Big chance.

Well, I'm giving exams and am about to get snowed under with papers. Ouch!

3/21/68

Received an angry letter from Ronald Johnson on the *Poetry* review.

The Far Point (Canada) took "Awakening in the Lord's Chambers".

John Malcolm Brinnin visited here for a couple of days. A delightful fellow. I've learned that he is one of the 4 members of Wesleyan's poetry board (with Wilbur, Aamons, & Weiss), that he's read *To Live in the World* (he says he likes it) and now has *Depth of Field*. Egads, the world of writers is small. I'm embarrassed by any such confrontation. I don't mind playing the literary game a bit as long as I can do it at a distance. But the very idea that my book was under his consideration stood between us. We talked about Roethke. He knew "Ted" very well.

Arrangements were ragged here, as usual. Han & I had him over for a couple of drinks after his lecture Tuesday night. All in all I'm glad that I met him. He's kind, articulate, patient, a true gentleman. And his presentation was excellent. Unfortunately, only about 20 people attended. Brinnin mentioned that Roethke once read at MIT to a grand crowd of 9. This is the kind of thing Brinnin would say to keep everyone at ease. He is the only person I have heard praise the architecture at Brockport.

Yesterday Kimon Friar was here. His presentation on Kazantzakis's *Sequel* was like something from *Master Plots*.

Sent for Snodgrass' *After Experience*; also the *Gallows Songs* volume. Also John Haines' *Winter News*, which Merwin especially recommended.

1968

ESSAYS
Howard Baker
Ben Belitt
Malcolm Cowley
Ian Fletcher
Jesse Hill Ford
Patricia Hutchins
J. C. Levenson
Marion Montgomery
Howard M. Munford
W. K. Rose
Walter Sullivan
Arlin Turner

POETRY
William Childress
Donald Davie
Jean Farley
John Gardner
Ann Hayes
William Heyen
Julia Randall
Louis Simpson
Ann Stanford
Mark Strand
Richard Tillinghast
Robert Wallace

FICTION
Robert Canzoneri
Harris Downey
Charles East
Pat M. Esslinger
Evans Harrington
Robert B. Kimber
Smith Kirkpatrick
David Madden
Willard Marsh
Joyce Carol Oates
Reynolds Price
John Hazard Wildman

REVIEWS
Frank Baldanza
Bernard Benstock
Bernard Bergonzi
Jay L. Halio
A. Sidney Knowles, Jr.
Leo B. Levy
Brita Lindberg-Seyersted
Karl Malkoff
Charles L. Sanford
Margaret Schlauch
Martin Turnell
Thomas Vance

U.S.A., Mexico, Canada
Overseas

The Southern Review

DRAWER D, UNIVERSITY STATION
BATON ROUGE, LOUISIANA 70803

1967

ESSAYS AND REVIEWS
Frederick Brown
Edward Callan
Murry C. Falkner
Kenneth Fields
Caroline Gordon
Robert Greacen
David H. Hirsch
Bruce King
George Lensing
J. C. Levenson
N. Scott Momaday
Ronald Moran
Richard J. O'Dea
Grosvenor E. Powell
Jeanne Richardson
George Santayana
Irvin Stock
A. M. Tibbetts
Frederick Willey
Yvor Winters

POETRY
Richard K. Bass
Stephen Browning
R. A. Christmas
Kenneth Fields
Ann Hayes
William Heyen
John Judson
Susumu Kamaike
Konstantinos Lardas
Douglas J. Livingstone
Samuel French Morse
Robert Pack
Dora Pettinella
Dennis Schmitz
Richard Schramm
Mona Van Duyn
John Williams

FICTION
Sylvia Beckman
Robert Canzoneri
William Childress
James T. Farrell
Shirley Ann Grau
John J. Iorio
Smith Kirkpatrick
James Prewitt
Anne Tyler

U.S.A., Mexico, Canada .... $4.00 for 1 Yr.
Overseas .... $5.00 for 1 Yr.

The Southern Review

DRAWER D, UNIVERSITY STATION
BATON ROUGE, LOUISIANA 70803

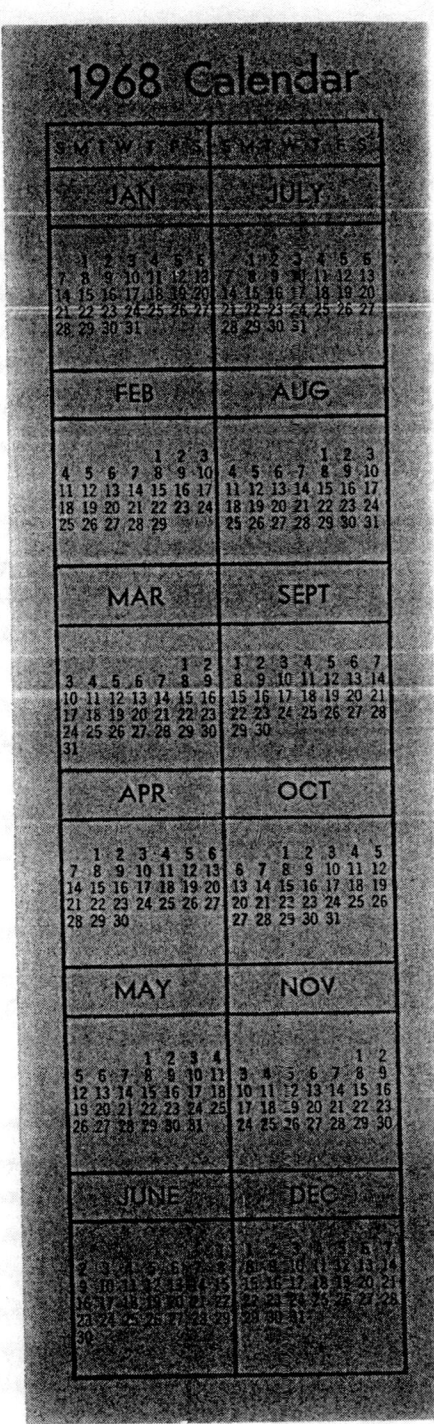

3/28/68

    James McConkey visited yesterday and talked on "Voice in Fiction". He seems to equate voice with vision and prophecy. In any case, I enjoyed him. Han and I had him over for dinner and then he and I took over Greg Fitz Gerald's workshop. I know I wouldn't mind teaching at Cornell, and unless I'm mistaken McConkey hinted about this. He did urge me to send something to *Epoch*, and I will, when I have a good group of poems to show him.

Spring seems to be here. The peepers are holding forth outside all day and night. Beautiful ring-necked pheasants appear on our back lawn and then disappear, as Stevens said poems did, into the brush. They're so nonchalant it almost seems as though they don't know there's a war on.

3/30/68

Han and I are going to The Crypt tonight to hear Barbara Fitz Gerald read, and look forward to it.

Michigan Quarterly Review took "Through the Passenger Pigeon's Eye", a little poem I like. He passed up a couple of better ones, but he's crowded, I think

I'm reading Hyatt Waggoner's *American Poets*. Hope to write some more quiet L.I. poems soon.
Finished "Nude in Search of a Pedestal". I like it. Reminds me of "The Mind as Green Thumb".

4/5/68

Last night in Memphis Martin Luther King was murdered. I'm reminded of a section in McConkey's *Crossroads*: at one point the narrator, during WWII, passes a pile of bodies—this has little or no effect on him; later, he passes a cow, a victim, and feels this poignantly. A man can comprehend only so much. I am staggered when I hear that after the murder Negro leaders received calls from people who simply laughed into the phone. What have we come to? I could be more sermonic did I not know that violence only rests in my own heart. Are King's dreams even remote possibilities? No. Does, should one stop dreaming? No.

W.H. Auden says it. We must try to live as E.M. Forster suggests:

"The people I respect must behave as if they were immortal and as if society
were eternal. Both assumptions are false. Both must be accepted as true if
we are to go on working and eating and loving; and are able to keep open a
few breathing-holes for the spirit."

Can one struggle against what he accepts? This is the thing Baldwin, I think, talks about in one of his novels. The supreme fiction.

The King is dead. The King's men will follow.

4/9/68

King's funeral on television today. The most touching moment: a woman sang, in a deep, strong voice, "I know the Lord watches over me." She did not waver or cry, although others around her were sobbing. I would like to work this singer into a poem.

Poems seem so foolish, so uninvolved today. I feel moved to an essay, but have nothing to say. A pessimist has no cause.

King, in his coffin, was drawn through the streets of Atlanta by a farm wagon drawn by mules.

5/15/68

Some time the beginning of this month Richard Purdum, my close friend and teacher from Athens, killed himself. I don't understand, and have made a couple of efforts to write about him, hoping the words, through some accident or inspiration, will let me in on why he did what he did.

School almost over—another week and a half. Can't wait. Jerry just called; his anthology has gone through and I want to get busy on the Snodgrass essay. Have a lot of other things to write, and hope to finish *Noise in the Trees* before school begins again in September.

I've received Roethke's letters for *Saturday Review*, and *Prairie Schooner* has accepted "To Live in the World". Not much else new. –Hanny and the kids are fine. Jerry is visiting us this weekend, and the next we'll visit Hanny's folks. We bought, or rather are buying for the next three years, a new car—Ford.

Henry visited us for a couple of days. He leaves for England and elsewhere the end of this month. He's a fine boy, but so goddamn young. We had some long, fruitless talks over the war.

The Paris talks are going nowhere fast. The poor are marching on Washington, D.C. McCarthy is on his way down in the primaries and joyful Hubert, I'm afraid, may prove to be too powerful for Kennedy.

I'm reading *Long Island Discovery* and some Stephen Crane pieces I've never read. Am getting things together for a literary issue of *The English Record*. Am teaching W.H. Auden and *The Sound and the Fury*, and need to make out some final exams.

Bob Long and Bill McTaggart will finish their degrees in June. The Lauderdale book seems to have caused some trouble in Athens and is being censored there.

I've gotten interested in coins again. Henry gave me his collection—a few nice things. And I've hooked up with a couple of softball teams—the good one plays in Rochester over most of the summer. I had to lay out ten bills for a pair of spikes.

We've had a fine, clear, cool spring. Sat outside tonight and breathed deeply. In general, it's good to be alive. At least, it's not too bad.

6/1/68

This is the day I've looked forward to for a long time. The whole summer off. Wonderful. I've even, as of today, given up smoking, I hope. Han and I are going out for dinner tonight to celebrate the vacation.

I have a great deal of writing to do and, as of next week, will get with it. First thing is the essay on Snodgrass for Jerry's anthology.

Was given a $1,280 raise for "extra merit" and usual increments for next year. We're pleased.

I have a yawn in the back of my throat—always happens when I write in this book. I wonder if anyone of my generation is keeping a daybook that is meditative rather than just random chatter.

6/23/68

Well, so far, so good. Am relaxing, playing a lot of softball, playing with the kids, but doing little else. Smoking again, of course. But I'm still convinced this is going to be a very profitable summer.

We visited the Otto's in New Jersey and my folks on Long Island. Trips to Princeton and the Bronx Zoo. Many ideas for poems, but no poems. I'm getting nervous about the essay for Jerry. Much spark, no flame.

Review appeared in *Saturday Review* and I look forward to their check—Han and I realized we'll have to take out another loan for the summer. *Cambridge Review* printed "Good Money After Bad". *New York Times* took two poems. Still lots of things to look forward to. No rejection from Wesleyan on *Depth of Field* yet. I read it over yesterday morning and was impressed. Most of those included are more difficult poems than I'd remembered.

I'm still arranging things for that one issue of *The English Record*.

The kids are great. We are, come to think of it, a close family. Han remains the same doll I married.

7/22/68

Well, another month of the summer gone. Han's mother suddenly went blind in one eye and was hospitalized. We've spent three weeks at her place, driving here and there, since the old man can't. I have managed to write three or four poems, somehow, and this pleases me.

But here we are, back in Brockport again, and to stay, I hope. The heat has driven me down cellar where it is cool. I'm tired. We've been on the go since school let out. No more.

The Nation will publish "Good Money After Bad".

Han and the kids are fine. We're getting along wonderfully, except financially.

Now to get going and, for a starter, finish the Snodgrass essay.

7/24/68

The summer is ending with a whimper, and in a welter of heat. Last night a frightening lightning storm, worst I've seen.

We're finally done visiting. We saw Han's folks again and helped them find a new car. I played some cards and Han kept Sandy much company. Half Kenny's tour is over.

Am trying to make up my mind on whether or not I want to stay at Brockport. Will talk to the President Monday morning and try to convince him that, for one thing, I'm being underpaid about $3,000. Lots of things to take into consideration. In general, SUNY is a good place to be. I like the security, though sometimes I wish I were part of the Ginsberg scene described in the current *New Yorker*. But not often. Have to go my own middle-class, steady way. And what the poems will be they will be.

Jerry likes the Snodgrass essay. I'm fairly satisfied. More and more I'm discovering that I don't have a mind for criticism. ---Jerry's own *Caves of Love* has been taken by Macmillan. He has a tremendous bachelor's energy.

Minnesota Review will probably take, though they dislike its length, my essay on Roethke's minimals. *Quarterly Review of Literature* took "For Wilhelm Heyen". Nice magazines to make. I used to wander around the stacks at OU determined to appear in just one of the magazines on their shelves. A lot has happened since then. Publicity, of course, is part of the drive. But only the poems are important. I've written one this summer that I especially like: "For Hermann Heyen". And, I guess, I've fulfilled my obligation to the State for this summer. Next year I'll try for the fellowship again and try to get to Breadloaf in some capacity.

The Republican convention, and its nomination of Nixon, and him of Maryland's Agnew, was very depressing. The Democrats get together next week and it seems highly unlikely, with Humphrey the strong favorite, that the country will have a choice in November. Robert Kennedy would have been the man to beat the machine. I don't think McCarthy can.

What is happening to the Czecks (sp) is incredible. I think the Russian show of force and the world's reaction dramatizes the tragic U.S. colonialism, or political insistence, in Viet Nam. We're not in much of a position to condemn the Communists.

Que sera. Wonder where we'll be a year from next month. Millions of Biafrans starving and I feel selfish whenever I think about myself. But maybe everything but my own existence *is* a fiction. I used to think this when I was in grade school, I remember.

9/21/68

I'm swamped with work, deluged; but I'm managing to maintain my equilibrium. Next summer and next year undecided, and this always makes for some anxiety.

Depth of Field has suffered another revision. LSU sent a nice letter, suggesting a reordering and lengthening. Done. But now I've sent the book to Macmillan. No word from Wesleyan on the 48 pp. version.

Have read Frost's *Selected Prose, Selected Letters, Interviews*. Many lessons from the master. About ten pages a year. An admirable aim. No way to worry yourself into a poem.

I've applied for a Faculty Fellowship to finish *Noise in the Trees* next summer. Should come through. About a dozen of the poems I have are fine, I think.

My poems came out in *New York Times* August 3 and Sept. 13. The latter works, though the diction is a bit stilted?

Kids have been sick on and off—they're scheduled to get their tonsils out Oct. 14.

Werner might visit this weekend.

Henry up and had to get married. We've never seen his bride. I think he's up against a lot of things now. Wish I had some money to send him.

9/28/68

Well, a lazy Saturday. I've caught up with my classes and decided to relax and watch Purdue whip Notre Dame today.

Visited Jerry Wednesday. Had a nice time. I enjoy his wheeling and dealing, his mild paranoia about the NYC literary establishment, his talk about John (Logan), Robert (Creeley), Jack (Barth), Leslie (Fiedler). Jerry is O.K. Han and I like him a lot. He can be overbearing, but he is a pleasant correspondent and has a good heart.

"Existential" came out in *Poetry Northwest*. Nothing else new with my poems, except that I wrote another Long Island one, "Where It Began".

My 2½ hr. Thursday night graduate course on Frost and Stevens is turning into a pleasant experience. Much participation. Many bright people. Times goes by quickly. I got through only half of my material last time.

"Things are not the same any more, / Maybe they never were." These two lines have been on my mind.

10/7/68

Probably, the more I write here the less I'm getting done elsewhere. I am at kind of a stale-mate. Don't seem to have any poems in me and I'm too lazy to work on the Bly article I have to do. And I should write something on Roethke: Seager's *The Glass House* is out. I read all day Saturday. A fine book, though there will be other biographies. And it tells a frightening story.

W.S. Merwin was here Oct. 2. His presentation was mysterious, but his new poems were excellent. He read one on a one-armed explorer that just exploded; another, a long one with the refrain "I am the son" that I want to see again when it gets into print. I had a nice talk with him later on at a party. He's a fine chap, but I'm too ill-at-ease around him.

Sometimes, like today, I lose faith in myself. I've always felt that I'd be writing poems my whole life. Today, I seem too far from even a line. I pray to whatever God that I'll be able to write poems, even bad ones, so long as they fool me, until I die. Not an unreasonable request.

George P. Elliott will be here Wednesday, and Snodgrass later in the month, the 23rd, I think. And Diane Wakoski soon, and Ihab Hassan, and Patsy Goedicke. John Hollander is also coming, and probably Richard Wilbur.

I have not heard from Wesleyan yet. The longer *Depth of Field* is at Macmillan (they ended up turning down Jerry's book) and LSU Press. The latter just might take it.

I got in kind of an argument with our venerable Dean Burke today, and Gerber is irascible as hell, for no reason. Ned & Bob Gemmett are also complaining.

I've just typed letters of application to four schools. On alternate days I want to leave here.

We are always broke, but, generally, happy. I have a lovely family. They are my sense of order in life.

Detroit won today, but has about as much of a chance to win the Series (against Gibson) as Humphrey.

Heard from Hollis Summers today. I'd sent him a few of my poems and asked permission to use some of his *Four at Wilmington* essay for the special issue of *The English Record* I'm putting together. I also wrote Hayden Carruth, who is sending us a poem.

My letter to Bill McTaggart c/o Neville Rogers came back. I don't know where the hell he is. We were supposed, by this time, to have heard from Grove Press on the Lauderdale. When I do I'll have to call his sister and try to get his address. It would be nice if we made even a little bit of money. I think we won't.

Bob Gemmett and I are going to put together a *Dictionary of Periodicals* to supplant the Gerstenberger & Hendrick.

I am living another life under the one of my self acting. Hard to explain. I feel, often, to use a corny word, "disembodied." I know, were I to let myself go, I would have an experience like Roethke's first. I remember a day—I was about 19—when I was going mad. I began running and concentrating only on not thinking. I ran the 3 miles to the Lake and walked back, happily, or unhappily, exhausted. My mother had driven me that close.

I have just read through many of the entries earlier in this book—"awed" by an acceptance from *Approach*, glad about *Mark Twain Journal*, pleased with a terrible story, etc. I'm certain none of the poets I admire were as unsophisticated as I was, and am. My only defense is that I feel as deeply as they do. Somehow, a poem like "For Wilhelm Heyen" is an excellent one. Where did it come from? I know nothing. Never became interested in knowing anything until it was too late. I have a mind like a sieve. But if I were any more sensitive to the air around me (maybe "sentimental" is the word), I'd be sick. I celebrate stupidity as a defensive measure. I know nothing because, by and large, I am unable to listen either to books or to people. I hear the felt sound of this pen. Time to get another sleepless night.

10/11/68

These are fine pens, and this is a fine day. For one thing, it's Friday, and I can do some of my own things. For another, the weather has been absolutely lovely.

Heard from Bill McTaggart and wrote him in return. He said he visited Grove Press when he was in NYC and that we might be getting some small royalties. We were to hear on Oct. 1st! Bill is at Oxford now.

An odd coincidence. I wrote ⅔ of an essay on Bly in a style unlike anything "critical" I've tried to write. I'm tired of the rules, though my methodological training still comes through here and there in the essay. In any case, I'm getting some of the world into the essay…. And the next day Ihab Hassan came here to talk on "metaphors of silence." I then made a tape with him and talked, in a sense, about the kind of criticism that is my Bly essay. I want to go on this way. I want to write an essay on Frost's "To Earthward" that throws out more of the usual approaches. I was particularly pleased to listen to Hassan's praise of D.H. Lawrence's *Studies in Classic American Literature*.

I'd sent Snodgrass my essay on him. He wrote me back a kind, and revealing letter. I now want <u>very</u> much to place the essay with a magazine before its appearance in an anthology. Time is a problem. It would have to appear before next fall. Snodgrass will be here the 23rd. I remember first being touched by his poems at Cortland, and I look forward to meeting him, though I was once, at Syracuse several years ago, group-introduced to him by Jerry…. This marks kind of a change in me. I'm no longer so afraid of meeting people, even important people.

I've run into a snag with Bob Blake on *The English Record*. Unless he agrees to allow me <u>the</u> disposition of poetry & fiction manuscripts, the final say, I resign. I can't really solicit the people I want if he is there hanging over my head.

10/15/68

I've been writing a few lines, and feeling pretty good about it. Wrote "The Deer". Working on "The War Is Over. Watch for These Things".

Kids had their tonsils out yesterday morning. Things have been hectic. Han's folks were here. Han's mom is always moody and miserable, and always over nothing. But Han and I manage to ignore her. It's all pretty tiring, really.

Have finished *Light Around the Body* and holding my breath waiting to have the last part of my Bly essay finish itself.

Am reading Robinson Jeffers' *Letters*. <u>He</u> is admirable. His poetry may be another story.

I've never done a better job teaching than I have this semester. I've learned to relax. The only regrettable thing is that I have to assign papers and give tests.

Have gotten to know Steve Dobyns, who teaches here, and writes well, though not my scene. He showed me a xerox of a recommendation George Starbuck wrote for him. Starbuck is anxious to see his first book finished so he—Starbuck—can recommend it to a publisher. Must be nice.

The weekends are so damn short, especially when I can't tear myself away from television when pro-football or, now, the Olympics is on.

10/19/68

Wrote "The Dark". Somehow, this poem and "The Deer" say a lot.

I remained aggravated all day yesterday. A couple of weeks ago I wrote *Saturday Review* asking to review Seager's biography of Roethke. Yesterday they sent me a letter saying they'd called me several weeks ago and left a message "at the University." They wanted me to do the book—a week went by and they assigned it to someone else. I never got the damn message. A real shame—money, the publication itself, but mostly the debt I feel I owe to Seager, who wrote me kindly a couple of times before he died last spring. I might turn this adversity into something better than a short review. *Letters* and *The Glass House* and some revision could turn it into a book.

Talked a lot with Ned Grade today about collecting books. Leslie Frost gave him, among other things, one of Frost's letters. He's quite an operator anyway.

I'm convinced, now, that Frost is not a major poet. And I'm disappointed that Jarrell could have liked some of the Frost poems he did. 90% of Frost is crap.

I'm convinced that Stevens is the greatest American poet of the century.

While I'm up to these kinds of statements:

1. A poem is not much of a poem unless it wants to be talked about, at least by other of the poet's poems.
2. Atheists are fools; agnostics are healthy fools.
3. It *is* possible for a human utterance to be completely formless.
4. My kind of poetry is a roll-top desk. My Long Island poems, so far, are only some little drawers and cubby holes. But the desk takes shape with each new one.
5. If scientists could vaccinate away our greed there would be no war.
6. Roses are dying, come back to me darling....

10/21/68

We had a homecoming party for some old friends. A fine time—showed slides, played my "oldies but goodies" tape, etc. Had a long talk with Sal Salorenzo, who is at Buffalo now.

Poetry took two poems, "The King's Men" and "Depth of Field". I feel great about the acceptance. I've always felt that anyone can make *Poetry* once, with their newcomers-only policy each summer. After this it's rugged. Daryl Hine (seems as though I've heard of him) is filling in for Henry Rago for a year. I was thinking "For Hermann Heyen" had the best chance. In fact, Rago rejected "Depth of Field" once.... So, at this time I have poems coming up in *The Nation, American Scholar, Ohio University Review, Quarterly Review of Lit., Southern Review, Poetry, Prism International, New Orleans Review, The Far Point, Prairie Schooner, Poet Lore.*

I want to write a third poem, "The Doors", to fill out the other two. And I must finish the Bly essay when the time is right.

Snodgrass comes Wednesday. Another of those nerve-wracking television tapes to make.

Henry's wife leaves for England, to join him, tonight.

Got a dark letter from Eddie, who dislikes his courses at Santa Barbara.... Werner seems to be doing all right.

The four of us here have had a fine, relaxing Sunday.

10/25/68

Snodgrass' visit was a great success. The only thing that didn't, I think, come off, was the videotape. I couldn't ask the questions I wanted to ask and finished, again, with the feeling that we really didn't get to the meat of his work. His reading was fine, quite a show, and his audience large and receptive. He was very kind to me, said he was in my debt because of the essay.

He came with Camille, a lovely woman. His wife? His beard was bushy and his features somewhat fleshier, more cherubic, than his picture on the *After Experience* jacket. He seemed in good spirits and gave a lot of himself to the students, et. al.; wrote kind notes in my copies of *After Experience, Gallows Songs*, and the wonderful 1st edition of *Heart's Needle* Hanny surprised me with just before the reading. A birthday present. I've been trying to find the book for years.

Tomorrow night Han and I go to a softball banquet. I get a best-batter trophy. Batted .511 last summer.

10/31/68

    Diane Wakoski read here last night. Terrible stuff, just terrible. There is nothing more to say.
    Tomorrow is my birthday. We're having a small party. Should be fun. And Jerry will be here this weekend.
    I WILL, as of <u>now</u>, stop smoking. Best birthday present I could give myself.
    The kids went out for tricks or treats tonight, but I had a class and didn't get to see them in their costumes. Han went along, of course.
    Bill McTaggart and I are corresponding regularly now. He's a fine chap, and I think we'll never lose touch with one another. I'm looking forward to a couple of books he said he's sending me. Bill gets the Ph.D, works under Neville Rogers, goes to Oxford on a Fulbright to work on Shelley, places a couple of articles with the *Keats-Shelley Memorial Bulletin*, and now he's burning to write fiction. Ain't this the way it goes!
    Have read Dickey's fine tribute to Roethke and Seager in *Atlantic Monthly*. It ought to stir up some noise. The notebooks will be published by Doubleday next year.
    Spent all day in Rochester Tuesday looking for books with Ned Grade. I found only a book of poems by Ramon Guthrie.
    Ned and I are working on the idea of putting out a special collector's item of a limited edition of about a dozen of my poems. I've chosen them—under the title *The Lord's Chambers*. Issue of 150 at the most. I hope it comes to pass. I also hope that I'll hear on *Depth of Field* one of these years, and on some other things I have in the mail.
    U.S. bombing halt in Viet Nam announced today. War might end soon. I hope so. But I'm so cynical I think that goddamn Johnson is pulling strings to influence the election, coming up soon.

11/10/68

    Sunday evening, and all's well. It's that hectic time just before the kids go to bed: the TV is on, the kids are playing ring-toss just past my feet.
    Nixon was elected, just barely. The life of the spirit ought to be more foreign in America than ever before.
    I've written "Nuances of a Theme by Williams and Stevens", something I've wanted to do for a long time.
    Macmillan sent back *Depth of Field*. Nice note from Arthur Gregor. My range is too limited, I'm told; but poetry is a damn serious business. I'm sending the book to Doubleday next.
    Called Werner today. We look forward to a trip to Long Island over Thanksgiving.
    Potsdam asked me—thanks to Lew Turco, probably—to read there in April.
    My seminar on Stevens is moving fine, even if I'm the only one doing any work. The students here, generally, won't do a damn thing unless threatened by tests to do so.
    Bill McTaggart now has 6 books on their way to me. I have no idea what they are. I've added Delmore Schwartz, James Agee, and Louise Bogan to my library lately. And Antoninus' book on Jeffers, which Jerry gave me. His visit here was brief and pleasant. The party seemed, to its host at least, pretty dull.
    Last night our electricity went off. For 3 or 4 hours, until the electricians came, we enjoyed an old fashioned evening. Dinner by candles, talk, stories. We're missing a lot these days.
    Will go into Rochester Tuesday with Ned Grade to price the printing job we want done on my twelve poems. It's going to be quite a little item.

12/9/68

    Egads, time is flying. Seems like yesterday I made the last entry here. Scratch these seventeen out-of-place words.

11/23/68

I've written a war poem, in four parts, no title yet. A pretty good one. In general though, I've been pretty dry lately.

What a hectic week: basketball games Monday and Thursday nights; a meeting Tuesday night; a party at Greg Fitz Gerald's last night (Fri); and Wednesday, went to Buffalo with Ned and Pat Ryan. Dinner at Jerry's, with Angus Fletcher, reading by serape-bedecked Robert Bly, a crowded party at John Logan's apartment afterwards.

Bly was impressive—recited, didn't read, his poems. And the ones I knew were more impressive than on the page. The war has become his obsession. It was nice meeting him—just long enough for him to sign my books—and meeting John Logan. Logan introduced me to a woman as "Bill Heyen, a fine poet, but he doesn't write enough." Jerry wandered around the party insulting people. Told Bly that more than anything else his terrific conceit came through at the reading. ---Leslie Fiedler was at the party—Pat's hero; and John Wieners; and Bob Haas, who is in the Carroll anthology. Fun, in all, but too damn intense. I found it impossible to relax. I want to go my own way.

Minnesota Review will print my Roethke article in their next issue. *Prism international* came out with two poems, and *The Nation* with one. Not much else new.

We're leaving for the Island Monday afternoon. I look forward to a few days with the kids and Han and my folks. I seem to be too damn busy around here to spend time with my own family. Got snow tires for the car today, so we're ready to roll. Han very much needs a vacation too.

12/2/68

The vacation was delightful, but exhausting. Two nights at my folks', one night at Werner's, one night at the Ottos' place in New Jersey—lugging the kids around.

The Island is frantic, all sand and frenzy. Each road seems to grow an extra lane every few minutes.

Truman Capote walked into the Southampton bookstore I was browsing in. I should have bought a few of his books and gotten him to sign them.

All in all, we had a fine Thanksgiving. My Mom put on quite a spread and things went happily. The folks seem to be getting along together O.K. now.

Played in an old-timer vs. varsity basketball game Saturday night. Threw in about 15. Felt pretty good, but terribly out of shape.

I'm tired, and this is going to be another one of those weeks.

OU Review came out with two poems, and *The Far Point* with one.

Have been reading Patsy Goedicke's *Between Oceans*. She visits here Wednesday and Thursday. A tape to make Thursday. Have been reading Nemerov's (ed.) *Poets on Poetry*. I enjoy these sorts of papers in a pseudo-aestheticians' sort of way. Am reading Louise Bogan's *The Blue Estuaries* and will review it for *Prairie Schooner*. My usual hit and miss, disorganized reading. If I had any sort of discipline I'd have finished a book on Roethke by now. The controversy in the current *Atlantic* is fun. Much inside information needed.

Jerry sent me his *Salmagundi* essay on Logan. We just seem to speak a different language, to have a different vocabulary. I've sent some more poems to *The Nation*. Will be interesting to see what happens.

The kids are a delight. I wish I had more time for them.

Christmas vacation looms. I must finish the Bly essay, do the Bogan review, get to the Roethke work, hope a couple of poems come along.

Now for a good night's sleep....

12/9/68

I'm pretty tired, but have classes and things under control. Han is running around here and there getting ready for Christmas. Han's folks sent us $40 and my folks $60, so we're getting along O.K.

Poetry Northwest took "The Deer" and "The Dark". I hope to complete this sequence—4 or 5 poems—maybe this summer. I'll find out soon about the summer fellowship. Makes the whole spring easier just looking forward to a summer off, and makes the fall semester easier, so I pray it comes through. I think it will, or I'll have Mark McCloskey to blame. ---He has a nice poem in the current *Western Humanities Review*, and several in *Literary Review*. Lew Turco has a haiku in the new *Nation*—something about sharks and ships.

I may be wrong, but I think I'm going to break out into something new this summer. I need a scheme, aside from the Long Island scheme, for a long poem, or long sequence of lyrics. Robert Bly rejected some of my L.I. poems for *The Sixties*—the poems had been there for 6 months—but wrote a nice note. Suggested I was too locked into memory, into the "bubble" of his talk. He may be right, but the poems written are all right—they may need others to balance them.

Played a ball game tonight—faculty team. We won. I got about 20.

Patsy Goedicke's visit was fine. We made a satisfactory tape, and talked long, after her reading, about Dr. Purdum. A sad story. I do miss the man. Patsy & I stayed at a student party until 2:30. She looks fine, seems happy and, if I'm any judge of what I've seen and heard, her second book is going to be better, much better than *Between Oceans*.

Benjamin DeMott here Wednesday. I want to read *A Married Man*. I've been collecting, also, the Writers Forum programs. Turning into quite a collection.

12/16/68

Heard today that my $1,600 Fellowship for next summer came through. Terrific. I hope I can write much.

Poetry Northwest took "The Deer" and "The Dark". Not much else new—many things out, including *Depth of Field*.

Sandy & Kelly visited.

We are all hoping that the Hong Kong Flu misses us. Epidemic proportions all over the country.

12/19/68

A nice break—school closed 4 days early because of the flu epidemic, and also because of various kinds of student unrest. In any case, a fine chance for me to rest and catch up with my work.

Finished my review of Bogan today. Will type it and get it off tomorrow. Then to Bly, and to a poem that's coming along. It begins: "They know, the neighbors of Loch Ness...."

"The Bear" has appeared in *American Scholar*. *Jeopardy* took "The Assassin"—I don't know if it's any good. I don't even have a copy of the poem.

We had a Christmas tree up, and presents under it. We are comfortable and happy. A party at the Gerbers tomorrow night. Right now Han is sewing a dress, floor-length. She's getting stylish in her old age.

Went into Rochester with Ned Tuesday. Picked up Galway Kinnell's *Body Rags* and Dickey's *Babel to Byzantium*. Kinnell's "The Bear" strikes me as first rate. Dickey's criticism strikes me as noisy.

12/22/68

Have read John Berryman's *His Toy, His Dream, His Rest*. The book has gotten me terribly restless to find a frame for a long poem. Idea after idea, but no flame. It will come unbidden, I suppose, if it ever comes.

Jerry called Friday night. The anthology is coming along quickly now. I'm looking forward to it. Wish I had a dozen essays like the Snodgrass one. I'd have a book.

Finished my review of Louise Bogan. Have worked on Bly. Have finished the Loch Ness poem, except for the title and a word here and there.

Rain, snow, sleet today—a good day to be at home—and all of us healthy despite the flu.

We have three men on their way to the moon! Egads! This is quite an age, though after the great poem of the world is one of boredom for me.

I am watching television. Custer is heading for destruction. This is something like life. We too well know the essential parts of the plot.

"The Idealist's Song":

A lizard can tongue its eye,
wash it clean. And so can I.

Always wanted to write a two-liner. I wrote down a realist's song too, but it escapes me at the moment. The way I feel now I'll finish out my days writing haiku and cinquains. Adelaide Crapsey's aren't half bad, come to think of it.

Custer is riding right into the thick of it.

1/4/69

New York Times took and already published "A Man Is a Forked Animal". I've written "In the Asylum" and "Dream Song".

We had a nice vacation at Han's folks. The next few weeks of school will be hectic as hell, but I'm well-rested.

Have been smoking a pipe, and enjoying it.

Han & the kids are fine. We're in good shape. Our one large anxiety, now, is moving out of here before summer. I hope we can manage to buy something, and something we like. We can't decide whether we want to live in or out of town.

"Plaque for a Bibliomaniac":
    Only edition.
    Boxed.
    Spine Broken.
    Skin foxed.
Nothing new.

1/22/69

My *Minnesota Review* essay on Roethke is out, and the *Prairie Schooner* poem, and the *Satire Newsletter* piece. *The Far Point* likes my Bly piece, and *Prairie Schooner* the Bogan piece. But I've been dry of even a start for a poem for weeks.

Still house-hunting. My folks are going to let us borrow $2,500 for a down payment.

No school for a week—great—but I seem to be too damn lazy to do anything.

Even write anything else here.

2/6/69

Ronald Gross, the "Pop Poet," read here last night. After reading *Pop Poems* I was proud of myself for anticipating just what he was going to say. But he was fun—fads usually are. We made a TV tape that went nicely, though Greg Fitz Gerald hardly let me squeeze a word in. Gross was pleased, and the interview ought also to see print.

Well, I think we've settled on a house, one about a block away. $27,000, no real estate broker, a terrific buy says Ned Grade who was a broker himself. 5 students will bunk in very separate quarters and pay most of the monthly mortgage. I think Han & I will once and for all get ahead. And I'll have that study I've desired for years. My folks have been terribly generous about the whole matter.

University of Windsor Review took 3 poems. I've not seen the magazine.... But I don't seem even to have much energy to send out my poems lately. No word from Wesleyan or LSU on *Depth of Field*. If I try the Yale contest this year I'll probably expand and revise the damn book again. No end to it. Organicism. Evolution. A book of poems. Fascinating, but enervating business.

For weeks I've been thinking about, reading about, working on a poem about Charles Darwin. The issues are complex and the poem can't make up its mind whether it wants to stop, or go on, and if so, in what direction.

Played another basketball game tonight. We won again. Tonight I was terrible. Missed everything. Legs were lead, though I'm in pretty good shape. An early game, and I ate too late. Wonderful to have excuses.

Han is out playing cards tonight. I'm happy to see her get away once in a while. The kids are fine. Billy got his first "report card" yesterday—everything fine. His teacher says all the kids look to him as their leader. He's very sensitive, and yet tough in his own way. He and Kristen, usually, play nicely together.

Good war film coming up. Think I'll watch it.

We've just lost our 1,000th helicopter in Viet Nam.

"Darwin pursues the pleasures of spiders."

2/13/69

John Hollander was here last night. He looks and talks like a younger version of Peter Ustinov. His shaped poems are interesting, but he doesn't write my kind of poem and has a hard time concentrating his line. This is an unstudied opinion, but he strikes me as terribly bright, but no poet. And this is my dilemma: either I'm the or one of the best damn poets around; or this is, psychologically, a thing I have to believe; or it's just that I like a certain music and a certain kind of imagery. I think I'll die, even if I never publish a book or gain any kind of reputation, thinking that I was a damn fine poet.

All four of us have heavy colds and are kind of miserable, but working hard at keeping our spirits up. I did the shopping today—second time since we've been married. 60¢ for a small can of asparagus? Absurd.

Jerry called. He's leaving soon for Detroit and then for about three weeks in Italy.

Sprained my ankle again last week and am still limping. The old animal will have to retire one of these years.

Campuses in turmoil all over the country. What I have noticed lately is a total lack of respect on the part of so many students, both for themselves and their classmates and for the faculty, or elders in general. I'm beginning to understand why Clarence Styza blew up at one student for coming to registration without a pencil and at another for walking into his office with a hat on; I'm beginning to see why Joe Jenks is tired of the long-hair set and tells them they make him sick. When students begin to demand that they establish curriculum, that they hire and fire faculty, it's time to tell them to go to hell. Students at U. of Chicago occupied an administration building for two weeks and the administration thought they'd finally go home, but no dice. Then the students disrupted meetings of faculty just trying to get together and talk the problem over. Hell.

3/4/69

We are still sick. Had to bring Kristen to Dr. yesterday for a shot, Billy having ear trouble, Han and I have colds. Damn, expensive medicines and all, we just can't seem to get better. I'm getting very impatient to get some work done, but this cold stops me. Contrary to what Housman said, I can't write when I'm out of sorts.

Well, we've applied for 95% FHA mortgage on the Ryans' house—hope like hell it goes through. If it does, a year from now the Heyens will have no financial troubles.

I'll have a terribly busy time from here to June. Lots of work to cover in my classes. Readings at Potsdam, East Tennessee, and here.

Ernest Gaines, a fine chap, was here last week. I've read and like *Of Love and Dust*. Had a nice talk with him. Jack Anderson, a jerk, charlatan, was here the week before. Tomorrow, Ahmad, about whom I know nothing. Next week Wilbur—I'm reading his new *Walking to Sleep* and preparing interview questions. It will be a bit embarrassing. That damn Wesleyan, after a year, still has my book. I wish to hell they'd rejected it months ago.

Fellow at *New York Times* took one of my poems, "Boys Will Be Princes", for his anthology. He should have taken a different poem. My Darwin piece is still hanging, but I think I've frinished the piece on Hieronymous Bosch that has occupied me lately. And I like it. Today, despite my cold, I'm excited about my poems & projects: the book of L.I. poems; the poem needed to complete "The Deer," "The Dark," "The Doors" sequence; anticipating revising my 1st book, *Depth of Field*, and fleshing out another for which I have some excellent poems; the Darwin poems. And I look forward to the Heyen interview, the Snodgrass essay. *Poetry* in April, etc.

3/10/69

Well, finally got up some energy today and sent out about 20 poems. Also, wrote "The Mist," the 4th poem of "The Deer" sequence. No, the Bosch poem is not finished, but will be a poem before too long.
    Found out we'll need 10% down on the house. Things will be tight.
    Think I'll find out very soon about *Depth of Field* from Wesleyan & LSU Press.
    I think I'll spend 2 weeks, the first two weeks in June, by myself with the folks on the Island, writing the L.I. poems. Things will be very hectic here as we prepare to move. This will give me a chance to get something done right at the beginning of the summer.

3/15/69

    Richard Wilbur read here Wednesday night. He's my poet, more so even than Snodgrass. I'd been teaching him, reading him, reading about him, and it meant a great deal to me to meet him. He believes what I do about poetry, writes the kind of controlled, yet sometimes irrational poem I want to write, even reads aloud the way I read. And he's very personable. The videotape was a great succeess though I didn't have a chance to ask a couple of questions I wanted to ask. This is corny, but he is my hero. Some of those poems, wow. He'd like "Depth of Field", "Windfall", "For Wilhelm Heyen". I mean he is this kind of poet. Though he is on the Wesleyan board he didn't, thank God, know me from John Doe, and I was glad. I warned Gerber, Fitz Gerald, not to mention a damn thing about my book.
    Talked with him at a party Wednesday night. He told one story I got a terrific kick out of: It seems he was having dinner and drinks at his home when—he was with some art critics—Gregory Corso and Jack Kerouac—he didn't know them—walked unannounced into his living room. Corso said: "Are you Dickie? I wanted you to see my Ben Franklin spectacles." Two cultures coming together like that. Beautiful. He laughed when I said that what they wanted was to sit down with him and get mystical.
    We also talked about Ihab Hassan, his boss. He was very frank, saying that Hassan's trouble was that he hadn't come into contact with life, the real world. Literature, art, is to Hassan, said Wilbur, real life, and not just a version of it. Wilbur said that Hassan left a lecture at Harvard in which the speaker had described a gang rape muttering: "that's what we need, more rape in this world." Wilbur said that he's witnessed a rape, that it is a terrible thing, that Hassan doesn't realize that words have real meanings for some people.
    Wilbur draws lines. There are Rod McKeun and Ronald Gross and there are poets.
    I was immensely impressed by the man, his work, his bearing, his large sense of life. Also, no doubt, by his reputation and the circles he moves in. Tuesday night, he said, he'd been in the Village at 2 in the morning pitching pennies with Kunitz. At his reading he mentioned that he'd read a certain poem in Moscow. But, most important, when he read "Love Calls Us to the Things of This World" I was very touched. I learned a lot, and I plan to write an appreciative essay on his work. I think I can do a good job. It may be the one piece of criticism I write this summer.
    House deal going through.
    Cindy and Karl Otto had a boy.
    New England Review took "The Inquiry", a poem that has potential, I think, but needs work.
    Played poker from 8 last night until 9 this morning. I'm crazy, of course.
    Have been working on "Academic". Trouble is, Snodgrass in "April Inventory" does it much better.
    I have a hunch I'm going to hear about *Depth of Field* next week.
    Sandy and Kelly arrived for a day or so today. Kenny leaves Viet Nam very soon now. Should be home in a few weeks.
    I've gotten behind in all of my classes and will have to sprint from here to June. And now the papers will begin rolling in.

3/28/69

Dwight Eisenhower died today, and television has had its instant biographies. He once, in Athens, had smiled at Han and little Billy and me. I didn't like his talk, and was fashionably indignant when he joked and didn't satisfy my serious and burning soul, but he was already very old. I saw a T.V. special some time ago in which Ike revisited Normandy and, over rows of crosses of Allied dead, reminisced. It was touching, and Ike was touched, warm, human, understanding the incredible sacrifice. The great tragedy is that we have gone to Asia for two wars since. "When will it ever end?"—as the song says.

Granville Hicks was here Wednesday. He read an introduction he's written for a Wright Morris *Reader*. Nice chap. Han and I had dinner with him at the Gerbers. I've just finished *Part of the Truth*, his autobiography. I learned, I think, quite a bit about the politics of the 30's.

New Mexico Quarterly took "After a War"—this acceptance is thanks to John Logan who told me to send it there and mention his name. *Depth of Field* finally came back from Wesleyan, with a very encouraging letter. This was only the shorter, much weaker version. If LSU does not take the longer I will not be disappointed. I think that with the summer off and the new poems I have I could put together one hell of a book. I finished a poem today, as yet untitled, that I'm excited about. It begins: "This evening's heavy air mutes / even the crickets...."

Jerry back from Italy. Heard from him yesterday. I believe he'll be here for my reading the 16th (moved up a week) of next month. My month will be a busy one. I don't even like to think about it. Arrangements are all made now for Tennessee and Potsdam. I do want, in the future, to give a lot of readings, but want to get a substantial body of work behind me first.

Well, Anne Sexton didn't like Steve Dobyns' work, so George Starbuck is recommending it to Stanley Kunitz, the new editor of the Yale contest.

Ed and Jean had a little girl, Kimberly, last week. I imagine I won't see the child for quite a while. On the phone Ed sounds a little depressed. He has his work at Santa Barbara cut out for him.

Han and the kids are fine. She took them out for about $25 worth of shoes tonight.

Richard Eberhart answered my answer to his answer to my review of Stevens' *Letters* in *Shenandoah*. Case closed. I was at least half wrong. Eberhart's replies were at least half irrelevant.

Spring is here.

4/20/69

Both the poetry reading and the lecture went over fine at Tennessee. I had a nice, if exhausting time. The Elkins haven't changed. Bill's colleagues are good folks. Johnson City is idyllic—rolling hills, picturesque brick homes, mild weather, intensely conservative. My visit was quite an eye opener. The objective correlative for the university: the words "Music"—"ROTC"—"English" incised on the building in which Bill has his office.

My reading here last Wednesday went beautifully. Jerry was here, and Sandy & Ken, and Sandy's folks, and many old friends. I think I was impressive, if I say so myself.

At Potsdam I felt that my reading went badly, though there were many compliments. Lew Turco was kind and funny and dynamic the whole time. I've really gotten to like him. He had a million stories, has published several million words. His wife is a doll. Richard Frost was also there, and I like him. Read his book when it came out in Athens, and now bought a copy and will read it again. The two of them interviewed me for a television tape, and I like the results. Glad to have gotten to know them. In general, Potsdam is a dead place. Not nearly as many interested students as there are here. ---Jane Cooper was sick and couldn't show. The 3 of us gave a group reading the last night and had a hell of a good time. ---Egads, I drove home in a snow storm.

Sandy and Ken left this morning. It will probably be a year before I see them again. Han will visit them in June while I go to the Island to write.

Richard Wilbur sent me a great pick-me-up letter.

Poems out in *Poetry, New Orleans Review, Michigan Quarterly Review, Poet Lord, Perspectives* (supplement). *Poetry Northwest* took the remainder of "The Deer" sequence. I finished a poem called "The Fourth Day" that I like a lot.

Must concentrate on teaching for the rest of the semester.

Han not feeling well. She'll be going in for tests Tuesday. I hope she gets back some of her old energy. Billy & Kristen are fine.

5/3/69

There was kind of a poetry workshop here yesterday and today. Dave Kelly gave a reading. Dreadful, verbose, propagandistic stuff, and Steve Dobyns was offended that I didn't like it. All very tiring. I went to one workshop this morning and then cut out. I'm bone-tired of talking about questions of aesthetics in regard to poetry. I know what I like. I know, in general, the kind of poems that mean something to me; and I think I'm developing my own style. I'm tired of the dreary business of talking about poetry, talking about poetry at lunch, at parties, in class. And I need to go my own way, get away from Kelly and his kind of sensibility. I whistled all the way home when I cut out today, and got some work done. I'm getting more independent all the time, surer of myself, more self-sufficient, have less of a need to blow my own horn or show anyone my poems or list my publications. I'm happy, and will be if I stay away from things as upsetting and depressing as Kellyish readings and workshops. I want to read more and talk less, associate with people with different interests.

Han is feeling fine again, and the kids are enjoying spring, which has finally sprung itself on Brockport.

I've just about finished a little poem on a lawnmower that has occupied me for a week or so. I see more unity in what my poems say, in their assumptions, all the time.

Bill McTaggart might still end up working here.

I've not heard from Louisiana on *Depth of Field*. I'm only 50% hoping they'll take it.

Jerry Mazzaro is definitely starting *Modern Poetry Studies*. He's going to print some of my work, perhaps feature it. Damn it, he is a good friend, but has so many hang-ups, monumental ego and insecurity. I hate characterization by antithesis, but that's Jerry.

Mark McCloskey was here yesterday and today. We really didn't talk and don't have much to say to one another. I do like and am impressed by this fellow David Lundy from Fredonia.

Han took the kids to Kurt's communion today, and had a nice time. I've relaxed since cutting out, once and for all, of the Workshop.

5/7/69

Well, I made a start tonight. Went to Dobyns' reading, started out for a party, turned around and came home. I have realized that what I need in my life, more than anything else, is discipline. I am too restless. Sit still.... Dobyns was okay. I was surprised at his elaborate explanations that preceded the poems, explanations usually free from explanation, I'm afraid: I just don't know what is going on in most of his poems. Not my type, to say the least. But certainly competent, not infuriating, like Kelly's.

Finished "The Mower". Added some lines to the first stanza that try to expand the theme, as in Stevens' "Domination of Black" when the planets gather themselves or, to push the idea a bit, in "Young Goodman

Brown"'s gradual expansion of the community of evil. The wind in my poem whirls the stars as mindlessly as the mower destroys the bees.... I think, also, what I've done on Darwin is better than I'd remembered it. "Bonsai" would be a fine title. Either I'll add a 3rd part or drop the 2nd and eventually just publish the first. Don't know yet. But what I have works, I think.... I'm again these days feeling a need to find a frame for a long poem. My discipline would come easier if I were at work on a novel. With lyric poems I have to wait until something happens. I could be writing some of my romantic criticism. I want to write, first, an essay on Roethke and, 2nd, one on Wilbur. I hope that by next May I'll have done both.

5/18/69

One more class, about 150 papers to read, grades to turn in, and I'll be through. The summer should be a fine one.

For two weeks Faulkner's *The Bear* has knocked me flat. Wow! I must write one great story. I've been thinking that an adaptation of my poem "Bloodletting" might make it possible to begin a story.

Have not heard from LSU yet.

We are all healthy again after assorted flus and colds.

I think Ed must be having some trouble. He's thinking of leaving before finishing the degree.

Astronauts heading for the moon again. A group is scheduled for the 1st landing in July. This no longer turns me on. Our cities & poor need the money more than they need the moon.

7/8/69

I spent 3 weeks on the Island and what I wrote I am pleased with. I added a few prose sections to the book and several poems including "The Tree of the Shore", "Clamming at St. James Harbor"; "Off the Hamptons." This last one has magic in it.

My folks fought like cats. My mother is lonely, frantic, mad, my father incredibly patient. All in all my visit was good for them.

We are now pretty well settled in our new home, our first home, and are as pleased as can be. At long last I have a room to myself to use as a study. My books surround me. We got quite a deal on this place. A week more of settling in and I'll have a good month to write and to get things in the mail.

Had a long talk with Jerry yesterday. He's going to print the Wilbur interview in the first # of *Modern Poetry Studies*. The interviews, in general, leave much to be desired, but I don't mind getting my name around as long as I don't come off as too much of a fool. James Wright is at Buffalo this summer and Jerry wants me to meet him. I'd like to. Also, I'm trying, with Jerry's help, to get Robert Lowell here for a reading and television interview in the fall. Not much else new in my literary life yet—I have to send things out. I haven't heard from LSU. Bread Loaf turned my scholarship down—I was surprised. I thought, for the qualifications they listed, that I was a shoo-in.

I had a chance to do some reading on the Island too, and this pleased me. This is my finest, most carefree vacation ever. Living in my own place means more to me than I can say. I don't have to leave this house, to pack and move again, unless I want to.

Minnesota Review took two poems. Henry Rago, at *Poetry*, died, and now Daryl Hine is the permanent editor. I'll try some things there in September, maybe my whole damn L.I. book.

Han having back trouble. The kids are fine. I have a card game to look forward to tonight. During the last 6 weeks or so before school let out I won about $1,000. We needed it, and, because of it, are in much better financial shape than we thought we'd be.

7/23/69 (Wed)

Monday morning we saw live, on television, men walking on the moon, where no wind blows. This is another event I am unable to talk adequately about. Very occasionally the enormity of the achievement strikes me. The accomplishment, for Americans, I think, is touched with sadness. What we can do while we are failing.

So far the moon remains pretty much the same, an object of wonder, mystery, romance. I don't think this will change. Were I to take a spaceship there I'd still stand in awe of the heavens. Again, the whole business shades off into the absurd. The country's priorities are absurd. Armstrong, the All-American boy, first set foot on the moon. People in the ghetto hear rats gnawing at their walls. And Science is hero. And all the businessmen are wondering how they can get a piece of the space action.

I've written "The Old Man of the Sea", have strengthened "The Polar Bear", have written a few more pages of prose for the Island book, have finally gotten some things into the mail, have been staying busy around the new house. Bought a book case for $30 the other day, replaced 2 panes of glass, and now have a lovely piece of furniture. I've discovered that I love to polish wood.

Han's folks were here for a few days.... I'm playing softball again—1st game tomorrow night.... Things in the department are sticky—Gerber might resign.... Heard, at length, from Bob Long.... Jerry is trying to help us bring Robert Lowell in for a reading and interview this year.

Han is feeling much better. Kristen is a little devil, but a delight. Billy has learned to ride his bike without training wheels. I want to teach him to swim. He's afraid of the water, but learns everything so damn fast that I'm not worried about him. I couldn't have a finer son, a finer family.

8/19/69

I wish I knew what the hell is the matter with me. I can't relax, can't get no peace of mind nohow. The kids, during this long and hot summer, are beginning to drive me nuts with all their damn yelling. One thing is certain. We've had too many visitors since we moved in. Every damn day. My mother was here for a week and this would drive the sanest man bats. I should be very content. Nice house. We're healthy. I've written several things this summer. But, I'm nervous. Maybe I'm worried about school beginning again.

Quarterly Review of Lit, *Minnesota Review*, and *New Mexico Quarterly* have appeared with my poems. Today I sent off a revised and <u>much</u> expanded *Depth of Field* to Wesleyan, though I haven't heard from LSU yet.

Jerry, who was here for a few days—so who was not?—said some outrageously nice things about my L.I. book. I'm going to sit on the book for another year, make it count when it gets taken.

9/18/69

LSU Press accepted *Depth of Field*. I thought long and hard on how I could possibly allow enough time to hear from Wesleyan before signing contracts, but I couldn't, and settled the matter yesterday, writing to Wesleyan and requesting the manuscript's return. My only concern now is that LSU publish the version I'd sent to Wesleyan.... Beyond this nonsense, I am happy, and a bit amazed. When, occasionally, the knowledge that a book of William Heyen's poems will, indeed, be published, becomes an emotional fact for me, I smile, blush, pat myself on the back with both elbows. Once just what it is they will publish is settled (editor sending me readers' suggestions) I won't at all mind the wait (up to two years). I have the Long Island book to work on, and it just might be a fine (great?) one, and a couple of essays I'd like to do. So, *Depth of Field* is going to be published!!

I have a dream schedule, and much time to read and write, this semester and next. Gerber has taken excellent care of me. I hope the next chairman is as understanding. I'm reading & thinking deeper in American literature than I have in the past, not as deep as I'd like, still.... Tonight I was reading, with fascination, Perry Miller's book on Jonathan Edwards, and some of Edwards' best-known pieces, and I realized, again, how much I don't know, how much of my personality is grooved toward (but I have resisted this) the scholarly life. Aah, the pleasure it must give a man to know one subject inside out, one subject better than anyone else. A victory over the forces of chaos. And much of me wants this. But it is too late, or I am not equipt, or the world (grass, trees, animals, family) mean too much to me. I want to read, study, digest everything I see. When I read something deep I skim, look for burrs to stick a la Frost's poet. But I am happy, sometimes feeling myself a great phony, sometimes having much confidence in my abilities. I am able to write poems, some of them fine. I am able to indulge in most of the tricks of prose composition, disguising superficiality. But lately another sense of self, another aesthetic has broken through. More and more, in the poems and prose, I find myself trusting intuition, feeling my way toward a conception of "rightness" or relevance. I just finished a poem, "The Sandshark." The word "love" comes up, almost from nowhere, in its final stanza. I trust it. I trust the explosion of syntax. I have many ideas. I'm not always sure what they are. I will write some fine lyrics that go as they have to go. This is not, I think, an evasion. I let my mind take me as far as it can. The intuition is a passing gear. It clicked in perfectly in "For Wilhelm Heyen," I now see. That poem's phrases say so much more than I knew at the time.

I am happy, more secure (except for the schizophrenia I've just outlined) than I have ever been. This house is a delight. We are going to make twice as much money this year than we ever have before. I feel respected in the department. I look at others and then count my blessings. I feel only slightly guilty about my own good fortune.

I finished a review, overly generous again, I'm afraid, for *Poetry*. Have enough things coming out to keep me comfortable until the book appears. Will try, before too long, to place some of the Long Island poems in good quarterlies. Some are at the *New Yorker* now, & I anticipate about my 30th rejection there. A rejection from *Atlantic*, and then I see the absolute trash in their last issue.

The kids are fine. Han is getting along with her teaching. The weather is fine. I don't anticipate a period of depression this year.

10/23/69

Well, the final (so far) version of *Depth of Field* is off to Louisiana. I want that book off my mind. Maybe it won't be until page proofs go in.

New Yorker actually took a poem, "Clamming at St. James Harbor." I'm pleased, and a little shocked, but am not as excited as I've been in the past. I have been excited about "Spirit of Wrath" for a couple of weeks now.

Suddenly, I'm review and criticism editor of *The Far Point*. Myron Turner (I've never met him) called me from Winnipeg a couple of weeks ago. So far, a pleasant job. I've been receiving books, and like this. Have already asked Jerry to review the Joyce Oates volume.

Miller Williams was here last week. He's unimpressive, to say the least, but is a nice chap. I guess he helped out on my book at LSU. Most people here thought he was kind of pushy, that he came on too strong. He really does seem to enjoy the role of Visiting Poet.

Galway Kinnell left here today. My God, what a powerful reading he gave last night—I mean he, his poems, knocked me flat. I couldn't talk. He read "First Song" and one or two other early poems, then "The Porcupine," then selections from his work in progress—incredibly good poems—maybe the best I've ever heard—then that tour de force, "The Bear." Kinnell has to be one of the best. He may be the best. Wilbur, yes, the control, the emotions held in check, the perfect lyric. But Kinnell is deeper, driving, a poet with subject matter and a remarkable imagination. He didn't read, he recited, brought those poems right up out of his guts.

We made a TV tape and it went well, I think. He was gentlemanly about trying to answer my questions about Ideas. Good interview. Well, I'll never forget him. He's one of the real ones. His next book will be a knock-out.... John Logan showed up for the reading and recited a poem. It was a warm night.

I look forward to Stafford, Bly, Creeley yet.

Jerry will probably be here for my birthday next weekend. I look forward to seeing him. He's in St. Louis today.

We are all fine. Hanny seems especially happy today. I, after listening to Kinnell, have never felt so humble. ---He published *What A Kingdom* when he was 33. If I can come into my own in my 40's the way he obviously has—I mean these new poems are going past "Avenue Bearing the Initial ..."—well, wouldn't that be something!

1/3/70

Sal and Ro and kids visited today. Hectic.

We're happy, cozy in our new home. This vacation has kind of made us appreciate what we have. One of the things we have is a new color TV. Great watching the ball games.

Went to Denver for the MLA. Met Charles East there, & Henry Taylor. Liked the place—my first time out west. Wide open city, clear, bright, clean, but pornography shops and what seemed to be a great many derelicts in the street.

I'm up for promotion—should make it.

Visited Jerry last week. Had a nice talk.

Signed up for a *Studies in Theodore Roethke* with Merrill.

Have finished one or two new poems since last entry, including "The Cat," a good one.

We got snowed in here, thank God, and didn't have to visit Han's folks.

I like my life. Too much to write here. Han & the kids are fine.

You know something? I just decided that I'm going to abandon this diary. It's been going just five years now, has been sitting on my shelf making me nervous, rather than anything else. I just never could get the hang of it. All of my invention being reserved for poems and good dreams. It was fun while it lasted.

4/10/70

You know something? I'll write a paragraph or two once in a while. It von't hoit, as the old Jew said while giving chicken soup to a corpse.

Depth of Field due very soon. It's not a bad book.

I've written several more poems for the Island book—"Worming at St. James Harbor," "The Mill," "Bailing," "Afternoon"—but the project grows bigger in my mind all the time. It just might take another five years for me to do it full justice.

Met Justice. We played poker all night after his reading—he won $150, I won $380—and we went straight to the television tape from the game. He's a fine fellow, his poetry kind of boring.

Met Bly. He put on a great show here, and flattered me by dedicating a poem to me and mentioning my article a couple of times. I like him very much. He's honest. He's 3/5s genius, 2/5s sheer fudge, as Lowell said of Poe, he's half bluster and half genuine. I sent him a few of my poems that he marked up in very predictable and authoritative style. I got a kick out of this. His visit here was a pleasure. Han's folks were here and heard him read, too.

Met Creeley. He was fine until about 3 hours after the reading, and then he went mad, with <u>no</u> provocation. We never made a tape. He left the same night with Paul Blackburn, and I thought of Bly's poem on him, the ending, that crows are only happy flying around the country together.

I've nothing in the mail. I've slowed down.

I'll direct—egads—the Forum next year. Should drive me nuts enough.

My library has been growing by leaps & bounds. I have 7 signed Lowell 1st editions now.

10/1/70

Why I should write something here tonight, when I have a million things to do, I don't know. Anyway:

The summer was too much. Trips to the Island, New Jersey, Tennessee. Then teaching 2nd session. Murder. And trouble with my teeth. More pain and more pain. I'd gotten in shape playing basketball, even stopped smoking 3½ weeks, then the teeth drove me back to dissipation. I am still living the life that always looks forward—to time off, rest, leisure, peace, health, time, something. I'll be 30 in a month.

Han and the kids are fine, wonderful. Han not teaching this year, thank God. We are a happy family, get along better, love one another more than any other family I know. Kristen began pre-kindergarten—3 times a week—loves it—is so cute & lively—a joy. And Billy is the smartest of the advanced second-graders & handsome, sensitive, a fine athlete. What a boy. I love them all.

Depth of Field out—no reviews out—anyway, I don't expect anything to happen. A nice note from Wilbur, some good words from friends. It was worth it except, at the same time, I would stop straining to write if I could, if I could live life as it should be lived, seeing things, loving, something beyond the ego that wants poems and recognition, wants to make a mark of some kind. I wish I could say I write for more romantic reasons. Hell, I don't want to exaggerate this. Certainly there is pleasure in lucking into getting something down right. But I always have the feeling that I'm missing something at the same time.

I'm not depressed about my writing. I've written some of my best poems in the last few months. Acceptance after acceptance: *Poetry, Southern Review, Prairie Schooner*, etc. *New Yorker* poem appeared; have done 3 reviews for *Saturday Review*. Have been meeting all kinds of people. James Wright, poor, scared man, here last week, John Berryman next. I seem to be in touch with more & more people about more & more things. Will read at Monroe, Ohio U, Marietta this month. Will interview Allen Ginsberg. My world is getting wider all the time, certainly. But I need a lull, time to gather myself together, somehow. Have applied for a Fulbright. God, how I'd like to leave Brockport for a year. But my busyness has become habitual. Teaching is becoming a real drag. That's a lot of my restlessness for something else. Dream Song #14.

I was promoted. Make $14,700+. We are well off while the world goes to pieces. This is all a kind of high comedy. The fool asks himself how he can be happy when he knows that someday he has to die and regrets the time spent writing even this while nothing else he might have done would have been more satisfying.

1/6/71

Here I am again. Another vacation, I suppose the best I've ever had—nothing on my mind, no pressures except the slight one of anticipating John M. Brinnin's visit the 27th. Dickey's reading went fine, and the television tape, I think, is exceptional. He was very kind to me, said he'd read some of my poems to his class, said he'd get me a Guggenheim if I said the word, asked if 25 grand would get me to South Carolina, etc. A lot of hogwash working, but he's a powerful man, to be sure. I liked him. We played some basketball outside— Dickey & Jim Hancock lost to me & Billy Jr. We drank. We had nice talks. He spent the night with some broad from Buffalo. She has a drug problem, he told me somewhat abashed, "and we're gonna try to pull her through." Anyway, I admire many of his poems, and he's at least as big in reality as is his image. I'm glad I met him. The Berryman visit was beyond words. If I hadn't kept notes somewhere else I'd write about him here. God, I don't think he's long for this world.

---Read at Ohio U, Marietta, Monroe, Memorial Art Gallery.

---Am working on L.I. book—wrote "Smith's Ride."

---Just went over proofs on the Roethke compilation.

---Only Mazzaro & Piccione reviews of *Depth of Field* so far.

---I'm trying to stop smoking—a new year's resolution—so far, so good. Murder. Wish I could go under hypnosis.

---Am working on a series of machine poems that has a great deal of potential—10 done, 9 good, the bad one was in the *Times*.

---heard from Jack Matthews, that fine man

---nice reactions on my Wms. pieces in *Sat Review*, except from the crazy Siegel crowd.

---family fine—we're happy.

---I might still get that Fulbright to Germany. I'm over the initial hurdles & find out, finally, in 2 months.

---got a $1,280 research grant from state. Will probably fly to Seattle this spring to see Roethke papers & work on the essay I've wanted to write.

---hear from Jerry often, have his Cornell book, an MLA choice

---We skipped holiday parties. I'm rested.

---have been listening to oldies but goodies on tape whole vacation

---cold as a witch's tit today

---I'm kind of lazy lately

---Han now has a dishwasher, we have new tenants downstairs, the D'Agostinos across the street have a St. Bernard pup

---a smoke, a smoke, my kingdom for ...

3/3/71

Al Poulin & John Logan were over the other evening after Poulin's interview here. We'd been reading poems. I shouted a Berryman song. Al said: imagine writing hundreds of those. Logan said: J.B. has a persona, I don't. I said, John, that's why you are so lonely.

4/17/71

A Saturday night, the night of Billy's 8th birthday. I remember the minute he came out of the delivery room in Athens. Now he's quite a boy. I'm glad the summer is here for him. And for Kristen, who needs to run more than any kid I've ever seen.

We've had a fine Easter vacation. Spent several days at Han's folks, including one lovely day the four of us took a long walk down Alleghaney (sp)—a dirt road across from the folks' house. I scrounged around in some 30-40 year old dumps in the woods. The kids picked up pretty rocks. How fine it is to get away from school, to spend a day like that.

Just before vacation Wm. Meredith was here for a reading. I had a nice talk with him later at Ned Grade's. I enjoyed the talk a lot more than the reading. His poems are better than he makes them sound, I think. His devotion to Frost is almost religious. Talking about "Robert" he seems almost to be praying. Anyway, I liked the man, and was amazed that I was neither shy nor embarrassed around him. It was easy for me to talk. I have come a long way.

Read and wrote a brief review of a book by Nathan Scott, *The Wild Prayer of Longing*. Book struck deep, my guts nodding assent, Scott's arguments affirming for me the world of my Long Island poems. The sacramental impulse, I think, is strong in my poems. Almost eerie the fact that I wrote "The Island" a couple of weeks before reading Scott ("Low tides, early mornings, / I'd walk the mudflats for nothing"). Also, "Dog Sacrifice at Lake Ronkonkoma." ... Now am trying *Physics & Beyond*—Werner Heisenberg. One of the delights of a vacation is the chance to read. Even went through the ghastly *Love Story* the other day. And read Cuummings' *Letters*. Didn't type up *Noise in the Trees*, as I'd planned, but there's no hurry for that. And I want to work on "The Witch," based on a direction in Scott, anyway.

My Roethke *Profile* is out. Looks good. Also *Poetry* & *WHR* with new poems. I can't decide about "Texts" in the latter. Kind of heavy handed at the end, but I might let it stand. The first stanza or so is as good as anything I've done.

Mark McCloskey & Lucien Stryk here next week. Brinnin, Kinnell, Snodgrass the weekend after. This is all fine but miserable, if you know what I mean.

7/15/71

Saw Wm. Stafford at U. of R. Monday night. Liked his reading a lot more than I did his Brockport one. I like the man. We had a couple of nice talks. He hadn't seen the piece I did on him, stuffed it in his bag. I got home late at night and on an impulse looked at it again myself. It was a bit heavier, more negative than I'd remembered it, but I'm sure he'll take it in the spirit it was intended. Lawrence—I've been teaching *Studies in Cl. Am Lit* again—has me jumpy, always thinking that what I've said says better and truer than I know.

We are getting ready to leave for Germany the end of August—my Fulbright is to Hannover. I am alternately frightened and pleased. A real drag to be packing, making arrangements to rent, leaving our comfortable home behind, etc., etc., etc.,--but if we didn't decide once and for all to go we might never, and I would always regret it. So, we're off on the Bremen—John Brinnin ordered us to <u>sail</u>—Aug. 30.

Noise in the Trees is done. I think it's a good one. I have a sense of personal satisfaction in it that I didn't or don't really have with *Depth of Field*. This is somehow a more necessary book. It goes way back into my feelings, and forward into other possibilities of feelings.

No reviews of *D of F* so far.

I've sold some notebooks & drafts to Boston University. Vain and satisfying.

New Yorker took "Four Songs." They should have taken "Smith's Ride" and "Refrain."

7/16/71

I am most restless when I have nothing to work on, as now. Jack Matthews—I heard from him today—used to talk about the pitcher needing time to fill up. Random consolation.

Mike Waters was back in town for a few days. I read the poems that he has coming out in a chapbook from some English press. Very strong. No question but that he's the best young poet I know. At least his taste and mine, our aims are awfully close.

Jerry & I have poems in the new *OUR*, which reached here today. I remember that he read me that poem over the phone when we were in Cortland. He's not been well—his left arm in a sling with bursitis.

I think I have an idea for a novel. I have, at least, three characters, and a strong setting. Maybe some day, with enough discipline, who knows? Also, a plot would help, or the beginnings of one.

7/20/71

A fine, cool evening. I'm outside on our back porch, pleased by the ash that rises above me and the maple behind it in the center of our back lawn.

The summer stutters by. Only 8 more teaching days. We've done so little in class, but have done so much, really, and every semester several of the kids really get caught up in what's going on. My "Emergence of America in Literature" course is a good warmup for Germany.

Packing today. Hell deciding which books I will try to take along. Which is the law that says they will prove to be the wrong ones, anyway?

Han's folks surprised us with a visit this weekend. It was Saturday morning. I had just given up smoking again and was mowing the lawn when they drove in. Nice to see them, and the old lady is lonely and frustrated about her job and worried about the future, but I was all nerves again as I am whenever any relatives (or anyone else) are around. Gerber, Piccione, anyone—I'm just ill-at-ease around people. Rock, Mirko,--anyone. Even absolute extinction will be something like heaven for me, for my idea of heaven is quiet. Probably a point in its favor, that old saw about my not being able to hear its silence.

I've been a little dry lately, but certainly have written enough and well enough since school was out so that I can feel comfortable with my deepest Puritan self.

7/28/71

It's the same old story. For three days I've been busting a gut on a poem called "The Catfish." It wants to resist, or I cannot let it become something, or I want to know what it wants to become, but something is wrong, and will be. But just now, in a few minutes, sitting here on our back porch, I wrote out "Maple and Starlings" and it's a good one and I'm happy. We have to learn to wait, but maybe the other poem got me ready. Something. It's a hell of a thing to be cryptic to your own self. But that book I read yesterday, *Zen in the Art of Archery*, and that Bly poem beginning "How strange to think of giving up all ambition!" There is so much involved in all of this. This is my whole life.

7/29/71

Bill Stafford sent along a nice photo and letter today. I'd asked him about R. Jeffers, and learned something in the letter, certainly, about them both.

Jeffers once said that he wasn't even born until he was thirty. My insides have felt so large the last few days, that this seems true of me. And I can live better with my stupidity and dullness that is apparent on every page of this journal—such conceit, such game-playing. I am thirty. I feel as though something is happening to me. I feel as though I am growing toward something. I can feel Billy as he plays a few yards away and as his voice carries toward me. Eight years old, and just what his father was. But something is happening, something, perhaps, part of this lovely evening out here on our porch.

8/9/71

Well, we are in the last stages of getting ready for Long Island and Germany. Still too much that we have to take with us, and packing is such a pain and is filled up with so many lousy memories. But we are really looking forward. I know that I couldn't imagine beginning courses here in the fall again. I need a change, and will learn a great deal.

Rocks, Gerbers, Mirko & wife, all threw a big bon voyage for us last night, replete with gifts—a travel bag for Han and a beautiful attaché case for me. Nice people, good friends. They are all threatening to visit us next year. A card game until 7 this morning. I won $90. Nice to win just before we leave.

Prose took the center section of the new book, and will pay $500. Wow. The money will sure help—more than I'll make on the whole book eventually, I'm sure. I haven't seen the magazine, but it must be fancy. I'm also pleased to have that piece-in-search-of-a-genre taken. Good things have happened this summer. I've been wondering if I could ever expand "Noise in the Trees" to something book-length. There are other things and places I'd like to get in there—Springville, Forestville, Cortland, a few more dreams, maybe a meeting (all dialogue) with the American Dream Girl. Maybe I'll just write things down as they occur, & in 5-10 years I'll have something.

We had to zip over to Forestville a couple of days ago. Han's step-father had an operation on his double-hernia. He seems to be recuperating all right. They both want to retire, the folks, and I hope they do. The hassle at work really gets the old lady down. They'd be happy in retirement, I think. And so would I.

8/14/71

I don't know why I submit myself to such torture, but I just read over the first 15 pp. of this book. What the hell did I have in mind? It all reads like a note intercepted in a high school class.

Worked four or five hours last night on "The Catfish." Can't get it right, but I have been beginning to experience some sort of masochistic pleasure in sitting straight-backed and working at something hard for a long time. Staying at it like that, there are moments of absolute absorption, almost non-conscious, but it seems hard to stay in that world for more than a few seconds. But I do think that there, way down, is where any great poem must come from if it's going to come at all. This is no denial of mind; somehow, a higher, or deeper mind is the thing. "The Catfish," over which I'm busting my back, and "Maple and Starlings," relatively untouched since it was written out—I wonder about these two and my ways to them and will think about them, pay attention to them over the years. I want to see which one, if either, is a real one.

8/30/71

Well, we are finally underway. I am in a deckchair on one of the upper decks of the *Bremen*. It is a beautiful day. Han and I are still anxious about being gone for a whole year. I know that I miss the comfort and security of knowing what is going on. Jesus, everyone on board except me seems to speak fluent German. I am determined not to become paranoid because of the inevitable embarrassments in front of us. People to talk to now....

The Ocean. Atlantic. I watched it roll by as the sun set, and I've been on deck late watching it, seeing it. I'm awed. I can't believe it. The sense of itself it has. Incredible. I'd always heard: "That's a lot of water. You can sail for 6 days and see nothing but water, etc." But this is something I had to see, the ocean itself under the stars as it was in the old days. Magnificent, so much more than I could have imagined, the whale road, Ocean. My God, this evening the sun left a slick, a gold wake on it, that stretched into a far horizon of haze; later, the moon's slick was sort of a gray silk. I have not felt like this for a long time. Its sheer grandeur and depth. I have to go out again tonight. And to think of the creatures under all that silence and darkness. I never could have known.

There was a small black bird with red-tipped wings flitting about the deck, delicate and nervous as a shrew. I doubt it could have flown back to land if it lost the ship, but it would hover astern, sail and bank off, and come back against the wind. No less a miracle than this ship, 1971, the miracle that got men here, or the ocean itself, the veritable *ding an sich*. Stevens, who never saw it here, I think of—it is not tragic-gestured—it doesn't gesture; Hart Crane, who leapt or was thrown into the Gulf; the wars out here in its immensity; the men who first crossed it. I don't know if I'll ever find any words for it. How could I have known? And whatever caused it to be, as Dickey said, is worthy of worship—and, somehow, fear. I would not want to die in it. Afloat alone in it I would go mad, like Pip. But I would be buried in it. I've seen the land all my life, I guess, have grown from it. But this is Ocean. I've never seen anything like it. I did not believe until I saw it.

9/2/71

We have veered away from Newfoundland now, and are in center ocean. Tonight the water is fairly smooth, swelling rather than chopping, but dark and foreboding. I seemed to be the only one on deck. I was on a low deck where a rail bows out. It was almost tempting, the water, but I was, of course, afraid, heeding Ishmael's lesson to all pantheists, *soi disant*.

We have been seeing small birds, sort of a cross between gulls and swallows, that are so much at home floating and bobbing in the waves, or gliding over the surface, a wingbeat or a quick flurry of wingbeats every thirty seconds or so. I've still not seen any other life, except kelp. I think I missed a whale yesterday that other people spotted when I was below. I wish I'd seen it.

We've not heard definitely about an apartment. I'll have to have our trunk forwarded to the university, I'm afraid. Tomorrow, we have that kind of business to take care of.

I am in my bunk, writing under the nightlight, curtain drawn. The wall on my left is against the ocean. The family is asleep. And this floating city is alone out here under the starlight and above the water. Wood seems to be rubbing against wood around us, creaking, almost like the sound of straining ropes. These are old sounds of hammocks in holds and of masts bending against the wind. I think I would have liked sailing alone, going out on a whaler or trader for two or three years. The retired captains of New Bedford and Southampton, rocking in front of their fires, must have had a wonderful sense of having been there, having known, having seen. And their own mortality, after seeing such depth and space, must have been especially poignant to them, as it is to me even now.

9/15/71

We are in Bremerhaven with Tante Sigrid and Uncle Helmuth, who met us at the pier and are wonderful people, warm and open and very unlike what my parents said they were. We spent our first two nights, as I wanted to, in a Bremerhaven hotel, because I didn't want to burden or bother the Wörmkes. Then he drove us to Hannover, where our apartment was supposed to be waiting for us, but no such luck. I've since made a couple of trips between Bremerhaven and Hannover and now we do have a place and will move in Sunday. *So geht es.* I don't know what we would have done without Helmuth here. The bill for two nights in the hotel was 233 marks alone. Another 10 days of that would have hurt, certainly.

I could have picked Helmuth out of a million people, he looks so much like me and my mother. And he has shown us all about and been very generous with time and food and all despite his busy bakery and unusual hours. Not a false note in his personality.

We visited the house on the old Nettelstrasse, just a few blocks from here, where my mother was born. So small and quaint, a small backyard with the inevitable German garden and a small arbor of sorts built by my grandfather fifty years or so ago. We drove past the house my father grew up in—though he was born in Aurich—and visited the carefully-kept cemetery where my grandparents (my mother's side) are buried, their graves covered with ivy, chrysanthemums, small evergreens. And I walked past the old church where all the Wörmke girls were confirmed. It will be hard, maybe impossible, to get into touch with any of my father's family—maybe when my parents come to visit us, perhaps in the spring.

Everything here seems rushed and orderly, cobblestones and orange-tiled roofs, small cars and prosperous shops, men in ties and jackets and trolleys all over the streets, American television programs and fast and clean trains, beer and bockwurst and a baker's shop or a cigar shop on every corner. The people I've met, here and in Hannover, seem honest and friendly. I miss home, but I like it here, am glad to be here and will be glad to get back.

9/21/71

It is 4:30 in the morning. I am down in the Wörmke kitchen. Helmuth has been up and working in his bakery for hours already, and Tante Sigrid has just come downstairs to begin her work. And last night we were all up until midnight talking and looking through old papers. They break their backs here. And they're always fun and warm and even-tempered. I don't know what we would have done without them here. Still, I'll be glad, tomorrow, to get to Hannover and get settled.

We found a letter last night that my father wrote in 1937—he was 28—to my mother's parents telling them thanks for their good wishes after my parents were engaged. I'll keep the letter. I wouldn't have recognized his writing, but there is something in the way he introduces himself and mentions his birthplace, as he frequently does to me, that marks the letter as his.

Three times in the past few days the cobblestones have rumbled and I've rushed outside to see tanks traveling the roads as casually as though they were Volkswagens. It's easy to see there was a war here, and there are still a lot of American soldiers in Bremerhaven, many apartments and barracks only a few blocks from here. Once in a while Helmuth says something about his days as a 15-year-old soldier, about rows of bodies piled—killed by bombs—where a particular shop is now, about the English first coming through this town. And Sigrid remembers Bremerhaven in flames.

I've not been able to write anything. It is never quiet here. I have worked at a poem about the ocean, but it has not reached the point at which I can say it will ever be finished. Dr. Hunold, at the University, would like to translate some of my poems, and I think this would be a good idea—especially my four "German" poems, the two from *Depth of Field* and "Men in History" and the "Letter to H. Greiner." But Hunold, and the others I've met in Hannover, strike me as peculiarly unliterary. They have not heard records of poets reading, have not been to a poetry reading. A literature of the dead hand. Something is very wrong somewhere. I happened to show Hunold Dylan's "The Force That Through the Green Fuse," and he was fascinated. I'd like, very much, to give a poetry reading in Hannover, but it would never occur to anybody there, I'm sure. So I will play scholar for a year, except in my better moments. And next to these people in their school *für Anglistik*, I'm an expert on American literature, to be sure. I am pleased that to prepare for some straight lectures I will learn a lot. Pray that the 3 boxes of books I sent to the University some 6 weeks ago arrive there, and soon.

9/26/71

A lot has happened quickly. Helmuth drove us over to Hannover again, and we are now settled in our apartment and trying to get used to things. My books are here. I'm beginning to work on an essay on Richard Wilbur.

I realized tonight when I walked out for cigarettes that this is liable to be a long year for us. It was only 10:00, and our apartment, where Han was ironing, was the only one lit up. We'll be pretty much alone all year, to be sure. This will be good for me and my work. Even television here is primitive by American standards. Our life will be quiet, reserved. Kind of scary. Somewhat lonely. No phone. Just what I asked for, and now I don't know if I want it. But now there's no choice. But I know this is good for us.

Our apartment is fine, comfortable, in a very nice neighborhood, convenient to everything, Billy's school only 2 or 3 blocks away, and some woods, and homes 1 & 2 hundred years old. We're lucky about our *Wohnung*, anyway.

This language thing. I don't think I can have my cake and eat it. When I put this journal down for tonight, I'll work on a poem or work on Wilbur when I could be studying German. Maybe the practical thing to do is to just say screw the language—we can certainly get along with the few things we've already picked up—and do my own work. That's the thing to do. Then why do I feel so stupid and guilty about the whole thing?

No typewriter. I might not even send over any poems this year. Having the book in the mail is enough, and maybe I can write some true poems, some things for their own sakes.

I'm uneasy about nothing. Ha, our big adventure. Already I miss Brockport's upcoming snow, our home, Christmas, friends, the poetry scene, the bitching going on over coffee from day to day.

10/16/71

Old time is flying for sure, and I think homesickness has already left us. My only apprehension now is teaching here. I'll begin next Thursday.

Two days at the orientation meeting at Bad Godesberg. I'm glad I decided to go, both for the information and for the people met. Six of us drove into Bonn one night to drink wine and talk, and both were good. I learned a great deal, heard some stories I'll not forget. I'll see those people again in Berlin during the winter, and one fellow, Joe Davis from Georgia, maybe sooner.

On the way down the train went through the outskirts of Köln and I began looking for the cathedral when it loomed up to my left out of the fog. No words for it. This next weekend we'll visit Bob Phillips in Düsseldorf and we might visit Köln. So much to do. An invitation from Freiburg today. I imagine I'll get around a great deal and will try to take Han as much as possible. Tonight Han finally talked to her 71 year old Aunt in Hildesheim. We must get there. Tübingen has been in touch, and the America Haus in Berlin. They want lectures, not my poems, but that's OK too.

So many ideas for poems. But I won't forget them. I need about a month's work on "The Wolf," too, which could be an important poem, at least to me. Its "shape" is occupying me now.

It was 3 in the morning in Bad Godesberg when we drove up to the peak itself where a restaurant has been built within and around the ruins of a 12th-century castle. Walking around there, everything spread out below us—I don't know. To think of the men who walked there, the sounds of their voices during the night, the same Rhine below them, the same tower rising above them. I'll be a long time defining my feelings, if I ever do. These experiences sort of temper <u>everything</u> else I know and feel. They nudge and adjust everything else I feel about myself and this world. If my soul, my being were a neighborhood, streets and trees and houses and all; and if I were used to certain colors and tones, a certain time and weather; and if a neighbor down the street got a new dog who barked every night and changed everything. It's something like this.

The Wilbur essay is done. I think it's OK, though it got away from its intention, became more rational. And "Letter to Hansjörg Greiner" is done. "The Wolf" next, and what prose I'm not sure. Freiburg wants a lecture on Cummings and Hunold wants a paper for a festschrift for Prof. Dr. Wilde's 65th birthday. Maybe 2 birds with one stone. I never thought about a Cummings essay for my book, but maybe now I will.

Heard from Richard Wilbur, Stan Plumly, Bob Long, Jerry, Phil Gerber. Han's mother writes long and often and is amazed we're really here.

I bought a beautiful old teapot for 300 marks. We love it, and wanted something just like it to take back with us.

The kids are doing better in school every day. They're happy and that's a relief. And Han says she really likes this life. So, *es geht gut mit uns, das ist die Wahrheit*. My little nervousnesses here, really, are no different, and maybe even less, than those groundless ones in Brockport.

10/25/71

About a half-page of energy tonight. We spent 3 days with Bob Phillips & wife in Düsseldorf, came back yesterday. Nice meeting them. They're good folks, if so different domestically from us. Neither is a poet to write home about. That's for sure.

We walked through the old city, boys turned cartwheels in front of us. We walked around the sole remaining tower of the old city's walls, and had a chance to see the inside of Saint Lambertus Church. We saw the Rhine at two different points, and toured Benrath Castle, and walked leisurely through oak and linden and maple and chestnut woods. Now Han and I are getting ready to travel all the way down to Freiburg. Should be fun, if the kids will be all right with the Mertens. I finished an essay on Cummings—it is basically inconsistent, but will do, I think. Will type it up tomorrow or so. Have written a poem called "Wakefield" which decided to say something different from what I thought it was going to say.

Received a welcome postcard poem from John Berryman. Lots of mail. We are sometimes a bit lonely for old Brockport, but are getting along. It's a good quiet experience for both, all 4, of us. Kristen seems to be maturing quickly. Billy is happy, I think; I try to play ball with him occasionally, & games. Han has been fighting some sort of sinus cold for a week now. The late hours at Düsseldorf didn't help, and there seems to be a lot of damp western Atlantic wind here in Hannover.

10/31/71

Tonight Han and I are off with the Mertens to hear the Berlin Philharmonic here in Hannover. Should be something.
Helmuth and family here Sunday for my birthday. I was 31 Monday, have stopped smoking, will not smoke, will stop goddamnit.
Time passing, we're very busy. I've about finished a poem called "The Train." Everything I hear from Phil Gerber or Al Poulin or Bill Stewart in Brockport makes me happy that I'm over here this year, working quietly, living so different a life. Teaching seems OK. I've just begun, really. Will begin finding out next week just how things are. This place also has its intrigues. Prof. Wilde is senile and somewhat paranoid: *zum Beispiel*: I mentioned to him that I would be lecturing in Freiburg on the 11th. He later told Hunold that it looked as though Prof. Weber (dir. of Lehrstuhl B here, formerly from Freiburg, I understand) has taken Heyen over, and in that case Wilde himself would have nothing to do with me. I've never met Weber, people at the U. in Freiburg & America-Haus got in touch with me. But it could have happened the way Wilde suspected, and I would have been a lost innocent (I may be anyway, for Hunold made me swear I would not mention anything to Wilde—Hunold is not supposed, of course, to visit me) abroad, caught in a spider web of hierarchy and pride and tradition. Aah, and then Wilde said to me that he'd heard from one of his students that in a lecture Prof. Heyen said the whole tradition of literature and scholarship was no good. What I had done, I told him, was to pass out poems by Bryant and Longfellow and explain what it was about those poems that dissatisfied the Imagists. Well, the situation is almost impossible. Jesus, I only spend about 6 hrs. a week at the University as it is. I don't know how to further disengage myself. The shame of it is that the other people seem all right, that Wilde's influence over 500 people is so pernicious. He runs the whole place, controls the whole atmosphere. Shame. But I really don't sweat any of this. Damn glad I don't depend on Wilde for my livelihood though.
Han just back from the post office where she was actually reduced to tears trying to mail some packages. Every day someone has told her something else. Bastards. I am not becoming endeared to the German people. What a hell of a scene this whole country would seem to me were it not for Helmuth & the Mertens.
But this has been a black page. All in all we're doing fine, are getting rid of our colds, are getting ready to see the police for our involved registration, are getting used to the bad air here and the lost sun. And last night Han and I realized we would have paid $15 for a pizza from Tony's in Brockport.

11/18/71

Middle of November and all is well. Han and I spent two days in Freiburg, visited the old cathedral twice, climbed it, were moved by it, saw so much else in that lovely town, had dinner one night in a Black Forest restaurant: pheasant for Han, venison for me. My lecture went fine. Only 2nd time in our 9 years of marriage that we've been away from the kids overnight.
Some bright spots, but in general teaching here is lousy. Today only 14 people showed up for a lecture on Eliot, and most of them I'm sure had not read "Prufrock" which I'd passed out and referred to for weeks. I'm going to teach as little as possible next semester. It is impossible around the Institute also—cold and austere. Cannot describe the tyrant Wilde here. Hope to write something about him. He is precisely the sort of man who could push people into ovens. Hunold would follow his orders.
We still, to be honest, miss home. But the kids are happy enough, as we are, and time is flying. I'm writing. Just about finished "Lines to My Father" this evening, have finished "The Train" and about finished "The Buried Man." Finished the Cummings essay—will start tomorrow a crash-project on Kinnell.
I've not smoked since my birthday. Really hope to stop this time. I walk a lot, rain or rain.

11/26/71

The Buried Man

I was the first
to strike bone.
I was somewhere

near his knees.
Then others ten
or twenty feet away

gave the same cry until
two hours later
we'd dragged his great bulk

above ground and washed it off,
and he was breathing,
and he was moving his hands in air,

and we couldn't believe him,
but stood in a daze
as he walked to nowhere,

or only he knows where,
that fleshyard, that
luminous man, our one

old one. Still, those of us
there that day meet
by the same clearing

where he lay, and ask:
why did he leave us?
remember his eyes big

as orchids? the barrel
that was his chest? his legs
stout as fifty-year oaks?

Listen, they were something,
the old days, when he
ran the earth like a bear.

They were something,
the old ones, before Leyden
entered the black cave

and walked out with all
our deaths. Heaven
help us to remember. Listen,

each foot was a mammoth's,
each hand a shovel. Listen,
I rubbed the dirt

from his blue face
with my thumbs.
Listen, his hips

stood taller than a man's head.
Next time we will tend him
night and day, buff

those limbs to a glow,
our wives will sew him
a silver suit. Listen,

we needed that great man
breathing in the dirt,
and found him,

and lost him. Pray
we will strike bone again. Pray
we'll hear his heart

beating in the ground. Pray
his dark eyes will break ground
again. Heaven help us to find him.

12/14/71

 I am at this moment in the offices kept semi-secret from the abominable Prof. Wilde who should, as the fellow above, run from all but the memory of those who knew him.
 The hundred strange songs and dances that go on around here, but all is well, time is moving quickly. Han and I and the kids are healthy and happy.
 Have met Klaus Burmeister. I think we will always be friends. A good man who has been through it. An occasional bit of shrapnel still surfaces on his neck and has to be cut out; an occasional bad dream keeps him jumpy. This after only 4 blessed months in Viet Nam in 1964.
 Have not smoked since Nov. 1.
 Southern Review accepted the Wilbur essay.
 Poetry poem arrived, & note on Gardons.
 Did brief review of Bob Phillips' book for *Saturday Review*.
 Klaus, Han, & I visited Bergen-Belsen, about which I am writing.
 Al Poulin, a driven man, writes often, is headed for unhappiness.
 Such warm letters from Dickey, Wilbur.
 I am the happiest person I know. I mean this.
 The Mertens attempt to keep us as furiously busy as they themselves are.
 I just bought Han a cute duck/bank for Christmas.
 Fine news from the Stewarts in Brockport: Bill's show selling out.
 Looks as though Henry & Liz & Matt will be in England by February.
 Fri. night to Marktkirche for Bach concert. Quite a setting.
 Saturday to Hildesheim.
 26th to Bremerhaven.

Probably 30th to Braunschweig.
Have been invited to lecture at Stuttgart. Will.
Will write an essay for delivery in June at Tübingen.

12/25/71

A nice Christmas. No snow, which I miss. The Bach concert, the first three parts of his "*Weinachtsoratorium*," was lovely. Yesterday at 5:30, *Heiligeabend*, Han and kids and I went over to Mertens to exchange gifts, then home so kids could open all theirs, then Han and I to Mertens' church for 11:30 service. All nice. A quiet day today. Tomorrow to Bremerhaven to see Uncle Helmuth et. al. for *ein paar Tage*.

The Hildesheim visit was pleasant. Klaus drove us there and back. One of Han's aunt's (Hanchen) daughter's husbands (I'm my own grandpa) took us around to the three beautiful and old churches—St. Michael's particularly moody & impressive to me—but we must get back again in spring. We came home with many of Han's father's things, and this whole story is so dizzying. Hansjörg Greiner's 1940 diary, when Klaus translates it, may tell us what he was, though I'm afraid I've a better idea now than when I wrote "Letter to" last summer. But at this moment he is still missing in action. His diary is partly poetry, his membership in the party lapsed, the obscene propagandistic anti-Semitic books are the ones that seem unread. And he suffered. But we will find out more about him. Eerie to have here his fraternity cap, books he read, mugs he drank from—one book even signed as present from Goebbels.

1/21/72

John Berryman a suicide Jan. 7. Hannelore and I felt/feel badly. We felt something for lonesome John. Hard it was not to like him. I'm very glad I had the chance to meet him, talk with him. Will write about his visit some day, I think. I think I could have listened to him read a hundred Dream Songs the night he read at Brockport.

Wilde's 65th birthday celebration today, replete with the pomp of pompous speeches, tears, bad champagne, the presentation of the festschrift. I took Hannelore to the Institute, gave her a glimpse of that life. Were it not for Klaus Burmeister, I'd be seahorse out of sea around here. No way to feel comfortable teaching. But the next 5 months in Germany should be whiz-bang. Trips also to England, Leipzig, Oslo. Still miss home. Still know this year will be a blood bank for many poems. A little one called "The Woods at Stöcken," seen now as one within a German sequence of sorts:

> For two months I have not put two lines
> together. Still, when I walk these woods, pigeons
> burst into the pine-green air like applause
> for something in my life that will always matter.

That something works as at least 3 things within the poem itself: nature; poetry; *beide zusammen* in the very act. A damn fine poem, if I say so myself. Have also finished one (I think) on Bergen Belsen. You're not dried up yet, Bill old Boy.

Waiting anxiously for two books from *Sat Review* so I can meet their deadline (Feb 1). I need that one hundred or so dollars—to buy books, if nothing else. A lot I'll have to catch up on when I get back home.

Am working on a poem on Jack Ruby: Jack Ruby? I think it will come to something. Jack Ruby?

1/31/72

Well, a pretty good evening of sorts. Will lecture only two more Mondays and then will be off. Plans solidifying for London and environs next month. January licked and we're on short time, as they say in the army. I think all the bad things about coming here—arrangements, new situations, housing, etc., etc.—are over—and we can coast into a good spring.

I've written out a draft of an essay on Miller for Tübingen. Now I'll see if I can make it say anything. Still awaiting, alas, the books (Roethke, Dickey) from *Sat. Review*.

In a dream last night someone said of *Depth of Field* (especially of "Boy of Gull") that I do "not mourn but pine." That's a damn good phrase and damn good distinction. I <u>know</u> that in sleep I have finished poems and then have relaxed to fall deeper and then, of course, have forgotten everything. So often I dream conversations I can't remember. <u>Those</u> would be worth reading.

Kristen seems fine all day and then coughs for hours when she goes to bed at night. Driving us nuts. This has been going on for a month.

News from Brockport is that Manny Mouganis, my old teacher and now compatriot/friend/fellow card player, seems to have recovered from what seems to have been a heart attack on New Year's Eve. The scene must have been frantic, and Manny must have been rushed to the hospital about the time I was watching rockets explode over the Hannover skies.

Han and I visited Loccum with Mertens last Friday. A deep, deep place is the 13th-cent. Cistersian monastery there. We were given a fine tour by one of Werner's friends from the days when he studied there. I imagined torchlight processions and the sounds of Gregorian chants echoing the passageways and chambers. They had a beautiful library, have. I am beginning, also, to get a real sense of the architectural romanesque. --- Hameln—town of Pied Piper, seen a few weeks ago. Lovely town.

Notations is all I will ever be up to in this journal. That's all right. I will use it myself to fill in between the lines when my memory needs a workout.

I wonder what the diary that Dr. Dr. Hunold has been keeping for years is like. Barbarous and sentimental, must be.

2/11/72

Reviewed journals/notebooks of Dickey (*Sorties*) and Roethke (*Straw for the Fire*) yesterday. What is all this talk about what poetry is, what it isn't, what it is, what it isn't? Even Henry James said that no standards could compete with what a person just plain liked. All that talk: what is behind it is Dickey saying or Roethke saying <u>this</u> is the kind of poetry human beings <u>should</u> like, <u>this</u> is the sort of sensibility human beings <u>should</u> have, one that can appreciate <u>this</u> kind of poetry, <u>my</u> kind of poetry. A wonderful sort of legislation. And a wonderful sort of self-justification: like what I like and believe what I believe and then you will be like me and then the world can't go wrong. Oh world, be a mirror to my feelings. Jesus, imagine a whole world of Roethkes, or Wilburs. I'm guilty, of course, of the same thing, suffer from the same syndrome. There are worse sins. But that old song declaring itself truer and truer through every new fog of taste and persuasion: please thyself, Bill old boy, please thyself—your heart vibrates to that iron string.

2/13/72

My desk here is in our living room behind the couch. I am leaning back on the back two legs of my chair with my feet up on the back of the couch. The sun is setting on what may be the warmest February day I've ever known. There is a streak of gold in our curtains (don't number the streaks on the tulip, said Dr. Johnson), and the poinsettias in our window are back-lit. It's five o'clock, late afternoon, and the room shines, now a redgold as the sun falls lower, now falling behind houses opposite our apartment building. This is a very beautiful world, made beautiful because I will not always be thirty-one and be hearing Han and the kids in another room; made beautiful because the sun is falling.

2/14/72

Klaus Burmeister has mentioned that he knew of many soldiers—his own men had told him this—in Viet Nam that had had an orgasm while in the act of killing, so primitive and exciting is it. Alan Watts in *Playboy* writes that "In the late Roman Empire, it was considered a great kick to go to the Colosseum and watch flatloads of pretty girls hauled around the arena, waving and laughing, and then suddenly they were surprised by wild animals who tore them to pieces while the spectators masturbated in the stands." And what to say or think of this, god knows.

Reading that *Playboy* made me write an odd poem called "Of Abortion." But, still, the idea for such a poem, at least feelings about what it could be, have been with me for several years. There is, first of all, no comparison between birth control and abortion, whatever case a philosopher or prophet could make. At least, it seems to me, whatever case a philosopher or mystic <u>could</u> make here too, control might at most be a sin of omission while abortion might be a sin committed, and I think I will always hold to great differences here. So, I've felt about birth control: of course. But abortion—Lord, that's something else, though every liberal seems to vote yes, yes. That's something else. Of course, there can be no law, except one that says that the matter must be between the woman and her—who?—doctor? pastor? Damn it, I will not believe every woman is fit to be her own judge as to whether or not she will have that child.... My poem—all I mean it to do is to give pause. All I want it to say is that the world is very beautiful, so beautiful that it had better be thought about for a long time before a fetus headed inevitably into the sunshine and air is eliminated.

2/15/72

After my lecture today, I walked to the trolley stop and waited for about ten minutes, barely noticing a little girl, maybe eight or nine, waiting beside me. Once on the trolley and half-way home, I finally noticed the miracle of this girl: she was dressed up as an Indian, painted cheeks and forehead, a headdress of feathers, beaded leggings. I had not even noticed her outfit while waiting for the trolley. That world is too much with me for sure. It would be all right if I was absorbed about something important, but I don't even know what was on my mind while the miracle of that little Indian was standing next to me. That's no way to live, in a blur I mean.

Kristen was also dressed up for a *Fasching* party today. Han made her a nurse's cap and outfit—she has a doctor's kit to go sort of with it.... Meanwhile, I dressed up as a university professor, Herr Professor Doktor Heyen, and talked about Ahab's fury to no one who has read a word of Melville. Kafkaesque, it is.

3/1/72

Walked London until the balls of my feet were sore and my calves seemed separated from their bones. It was a fine week, and the four of us played the worst sort of bright-eyed flashbulb-popping tourists at the Tower of London, St. Paul's, Westminster Abbey (the highlight of the trip: we spent two afternoons there), Buckingham Palace, Madam Taussaud's (the flop of the trip), etc., etc. We walked and walked, found things by accident, like the time we stumbled into St. James Church, where Blake was baptized, or over to Hyde Park where communists and homosexuals and blacks were damaging their causes at the Speakers' Corner. We saw "Hair" and Polanski's "Macbeth" and Kubrick's "A Clockwork Orange." We traveled up to Nottingham where I read and where we were guests at a long, fine party. I looked at a million books and came back with ten. We ate in all sorts of restaurants, were really taken in in a dive, visited a burlesque where girls maybe 16 years old made us so goddamned sad. We had fun fighting the periodic blackouts. My brother Henry arrived and it was great seeing him after four years. We went in and out of a thousand shops and walked around the famous circles and squares. All five of us had dinner at a place in Soho called Lord Byron's with Joyce and Ray Smith, who had made reservations. I think they enjoyed themselves as much as we did, even invited us to their flat afterwards, but I was smart enough to jump in and refuse. And all of us spent more money than we could afford, but it was worth it, and now I know the place well enough to get there again some time with Han, maybe stay right in the Kenilworth again, maybe have some time to spend several days at the British Museum, which we had to breeze through in two short visits. And, finally, it was wonderful to get back to Han and the kids and a bed I could sleep in again. That's one of the joys of any trip, I'm sure.

Only four months left in Europe now and we'll be on our way back home. We'll make the best of it. My work (whatever that means) will probably go sliding, but that's okay as long as I see some things now. All the week in London I didn't touch pen to paper, didn't even think of a poem. That was good. I feel like a new man. I think I'll try to get used a little more to the idea of wasting time.

3/9/72

Actually, I've nothing at all to say. I just thought that once I jotted down the date I would be forced to write something.

I've tried to stay in bed with my cold the past couple of days. Caught it from Han and now, I'm afraid, the kids have caught it from me.

We're heading for Leipzig, Han and I, Saturday, with the Mertens. Only for two days. But it should be an eye-opener. Already, filling out entry forms and making lists of all possessions, we're a bit apprehensive. This is the real thing we're heading for, a world without freedom, and we're a little scared. We've read and heard about it, and now we'll see some of it.

Southern Review took "Maple and Starlings." An unusual poem written in unusual circumstances. Its "test partner" I inadvertently left in Brockport, and will look at it again next summer. I mean "The Catfish."

Weather warming up fast here.

I've been too beat to do any work lately. Did type up the two new poems ("On a Snapshot of My Father" and "Of Abortion") this evening and they sound good to me. All I wanted to do in the latter was to say that it is an incredibly beautiful world and that we have to remember this before we deny it to anyone. Curious to see what the reaction will be. Hell, it could just as well be called "Of Suicide."

Now my old card-playing bum and buddy Bill Rock has taken a job in Washington. Will miss him, but suspect he'll fly in for poker once or twice a month, and will return permanently to Brockport after a year or two.

Have read through Parkinson's *Beat* casebook in bed these couple of days. The same old question I've been sort of worrying with half a mind since years ago at Cortland when Galway Kinnell borrowed my copy of Allen's anthology and read Ginsberg's "Sunflower Sutra." I guess I'm about in the same spot and would still like to write that poem over again for Ginsberg.

Have been reading Bewley's *The Complex Fate*. What I do know is that he just doesn't know what the hell poetry can be. I mean it. He's one of those chaps who wouldn't know a poem, as Ginsberg said, if it buggered him.

Okay, Bill, take a deep breath and fill up this page with something poetic. Some news to myself: "The Cat" is a great poem, as good as anything in Wilbur. [Keep going.] "The Lamb" is as good as Ransom's "Janet Waking," which I've always loved. [Keep going!] The Island book is a hell of a good book, may it R.I.P.

3/18/72

Our two days in Leipzig made as strong an impression as our visit to Bergen-Belsen a few months ago. It was really there, was no film or novel. The watch-towers at the border, the proliferation of police between the border and Leipzig and in Leipzig itself, the starkness of the lives we glimpsed in some of the small towns all boarded up, the attempt by the party to put forward its best foot while admitting how badly the country needs Western money. Children came up to us on the street and asked for a Western coin to use in the "Intershop." Leipzig striving for a monumental effect while apartment houses are falling apart and building materials and labor are non-existent for most of the population. A woman working in a ceramic shop whispering to me that she and all the other Easterners were Germans, too. The fact it takes years of waiting to get a car, if one can afford at least 8,000 marks for something ⅓ the quality of a Volkswagen. The four-hour lines (not during Messe, of course) for bananas. The fact that one of those women working in the freezing cold at parking cars makes maybe 150 marks a month. The musical director of a church crying when I gave him 4 marks for razor blades in the Intershop. Han leaving her sweaters behind after finding out the need. The slight traffic (and that Western) in a major city, and the frightening vision of what it must be like to live there when all foreigners are gone after the fair. Thomaskirche where Luther preached (probably in the pulpit I touched) and Bach is buried. The watery cola and orange juice, the weak and bitter Bulgarian wine, the paltry rumpsteak (a $1 steak sandwich in U.S.) that was a restaurant's most expensive meal at 9.80 marks. The massive Battle of the Nations monument, and the beautiful Russian church where the commander of the Russian forces is buried. The feeling I had that someone was following us. The girl we met who was #1 in her class but was turned down for study at the University for political reasons. Stepping inside Nickolaikirche at night, its massive columns. And the several people we got to know. And they know they cannot get out. We ate from old Meissen, a reminder of another time. And the people cannot get out.

3/25/72

Somehow, I've never been as exhausted by any trip as I was by our brief one to Oslo. Two good nights' sleep since, and I'm still tired. Wondering if I should see a doctor. Have had no energy since we arrived in Europe, actually, even though I try to walk a lot, even though I haven't smoked since Nov. 1. I find myself just killing time.

But the Oslo trip was wonderful! So different, from the moment Sigmund Skard met us at the airport. He's quite a man, my privilege entirely to have met him. Showed us around the library he has built up from scratch, was so modest, showed us around town and through Vigeland's park and the Rathaus, threw a party for us and raved about my lecture: which 200 or so attended, which was a pleasure because the audience was so warm and understanding, which, said Per Seyerstet (fellow LSU author) and Skard, was just what was needed. Skard: an unforgettable fellow—looks exactly like photos of Wm. C. Williams and seems to have as much energy. The man is a national treasure, but acts as though he's just a happy-go-lucky merry-go-round operator.

We also saw the Viking ships, the Kon Tiki, the Cathedral. Would be a nice city to return to, though all there say we should see Bergen, and Mrs. Skard tells us to try to get up North, way up, where in winter there's only an hour or two of daylight. The way I feel now, though, I just want to recuperate in Brockport for many years.

Skard: I must learn more about him. I have the feeling I have met a most rare man, one in many millions. I have one of his books to read, and one by his famous father-in-law, both signed, both of which I am so happy to have. Oh, Lord, it would have been lovely to work and teach in Oslo this year.

Have been invited for lectures in Rome. Must be Frank Judge's doing. Okay. Will see the world this year.
Bill Rock writes he has lost $2,000 at cards. I'd be less surprised to hear McGovern won the nomination.
Wonderful news from Brockport that that miserable bastard Ned Grade didn't get promoted.
Kristen six the other day, my little doll.
Bought an alabaster polar bear in Oslo for my desk.

4/2/72

Easter today. Rain this morning, and I leading the family to church, holding an umbrella in my right hand, holding a paper-wrapped bouquet of flowers in my left, looking down at the splashing cobblestones as the church bells begin echoing down the streets, a feeling of timelessness. I closed my eyes for a few steps at a time, and smelled the flowers, and felt the wet air, and heard the bells. A miracle, this life, and nothing less.

But church depressing, Kristen so saddened by the organ music that she began crying, other women crying, maybe 100 people in the pews and nine of ten women and old, old. Sunshine and air, sunshine and air, I kept repeating to myself to the tune of Berryman's "Tyson & Joe, Tyson & Joe." That old story now leading only to nostalgia for the time when it was true. It is a joy to walk the streets in the rain, to see the hedges beginning to leaf green, to draw air down into my lungs. It all has to begin there: in praise. We'll all learn too much of the dark, and soon enough.

So, April begins, and will be awfully busy.

Prose arrived yesterday, and I'm pleased to have published a little of my life. And the Borestone people took three (3) poems for their '71 anthology. Something to look forward to. Am I arriving anywhere? I'm not even sure what the question means. I haven't written anything in a month or two, but it's building up, and nothing will be lost, I feel sure.

Nice letters about my Dickey/Roethke review. I took a chance, and it worked. Would have liked more room for that piece.

Judy & Bob Phillips coming weekend April 22; sent a couple of photos to the Smiths in London; I owe Jerry a letter; Fitz Gerald getting Grade in trouble in Brockport; Mertens will visit this evening; our apartment definitely too small for domestic bliss, but we're not only surviving, but prevailing; I remain anxious for America.

4/6/72

Back yesterday from Saarbrücken. I was great. Spoke hard and fast and good for about an hour. Applause was, said the fellow who introduced me, "noticeably lengthy." So, okay. But my reception there at the evening dinner, in the way of a civil welcome, was cold. The goddamned unfriendly Germans. Such a contrast to Oslo. To hell with it. Tomorrow, I leave for Berlin, a week that can't miss. I've no responsibilities, I know some people, a program is all planned for us. I look forward. Am becoming proud of myself in the way I've been finding myself around strange cities.

4/16/72

My week in Berlin is over, and I'm now trying to catch up on some sleep. Han, too, is tired. But we had a very nice time. A sort of highlight was an evening of Mahler at the Philharmonic. Lovely music in a beautiful building. Later a party at Dora and Klaus Hausler's (sp?)—he plays a violin-cello in the Berlin orchestra, and we met them earlier here in Hannover.
Many lectures at the Amerika Haus. Many confusions. Viet Nam again in the news, and passing through borders again with accompanying indignities, it is difficult to say, simply, to hell with Viet Nam. The goddamned DDR, its propaganda everywhere, its guards guarding only they know what. The Brandt Ost-Politik enough to boggle the mind. The reality of the wall. Shut the bastards off! Or, kill them with kindness! Or, what! Werner Merten and I have argued about just what is on the minds of the guards. The debate is a long story.
Some rain, some fine weather in Berlin. A pleasure just to walk up and down Kurfurstendammstr—so much going on, including, at night, wide-open prostitution. Strange women so available is exciting. I am also smart enough to know how dangerous they are. Still, I'm fool-hardy. But I am also shy: of making arrangements; of syphilis.
Bought a West Berlin stamp album (how's that for a country boy leap?)
Billy's 9th birthday party tomorrow.
We're having a big party the 22nd.
Bly's *Seventies* #1 arrived. Getting to be quite a cloud.
Bob Phillips arriving Friday.
Not a cigarette for 5½ months.

4/29/72

Worked at a poem tonight, "Hawk," don't know if it will come to anything, but I've learned: I suppose I haven't worked at a poem for 2½ months, and this is the longest ever since I started, and I've learned: it can go away. It is easy to forget the sort of concentration and awareness I used to snap into. I used to know what the other words & lines were doing and saying—I mean it. But my brain is already going at different frequencies, and after just a couple of months. Hard to explain. I really am not concerned, I'll get it all back when life allows, but I have learned something, that I can forget how to snap into I suppose another sort of consciousness, one real and confident and alert and ready and more internal than the flash and bang and train-rush of this life here and now: Rome in a couple of weeks is next. It's okay, it's all okay, I'll take a thousand books of things back with me that I couldn't have read in the States.
Lovely day today. Han and I went out walking three times. Will we ever make it back to Brockport? Will I read this out on our porch, that nice maple rising into the evening above me?
Woke up dizzy the other morning. Not sure why. Am tired, of course, but it must be more. Sinus, maybe. Actually, I've been tired since we got here. I hope I get some of my energy back once we're home.
I think it's harder to write without smoking. But I will not smoke. 6 months *ohne* cigarettes tomorrow.
Han and kids fine.
I owe so many letters.

Borestone people took 3 poems for 1971 anthology; otherwise my reputation & achievement are in decline. Did get book in mail to LSU. Random House must have lost it.

Mike Waters getting married May 13.

Tony Piccione has new daughter: Sarah.

Bill Rock moving to D.C.

Writing this page was a heroic effort. I'm tired of being so damned tired. What the hell would I do if I had to work for a living? Poulin & Turco are dynamos. I'm going to sleep.

6/3/72

Since last entry, we've been to Rome and on the Rhine and the Gerbers have visited us here for three days. We are more than tired. We are anxious about getting back, worried about packing and cleaning up the apartment and travel and rent arrangements and car insurance and more visits and visitors. Surely, we'll get home, get our lives in order again.... But this was meant to catalogue, etc.

Book arrived at LSU.

A while ago I wrote one of my dizzy letters to Bly; he jumped on me, called me a blockhead, said I felt I was superior. I just wrote him back, a bit strong. I'm surprised that I don't really give a damn. I mean it: I'm going not to stop writing, but to pull out of the writing game. A fellow by the name of Anselm Parlatore hurt me a couple of weeks ago, too: sent a warm invitation to contribute to *Granite*, said he knew *Depth*, etc.; then rejected all 7 poems I sent him, including "Of Gatsby," "Fireman Next Door," "The Mailman." Those little things bother me inordinately. I might pull way away, getting the satisfactions I get from breathing deep after having stopped smoking. Wrote a letter not wholly praise to Poulin about his book, too. If he doesn't answer, I'll know what stuff he is made of. This sounds like a wonderful contradiction, but it's really not. Honesty, is its resolution, cutting ten ways at once.

What's new? I don't like kissing all these days goodbye without getting any work done. No hope of relief before September, it looks like. Will survive, prevail.

6/11/72

This meant to catalogue a miserable moment, one to look back on with a sense of relief. Tonight, a cold coming on full force; tomorrow, a regular lecture and then a special lecture for Wilde, climaxed by a reading. A bad time. Feel miserable & nervous. Heartening, though, to think we'll be flying back to a world I better understand in 18 days. A good year it's been, and it will be a good one to end.

Bly writes back apologies.

Terrible weather—has rained part of every day for about a week. Another time, another place and I'd like it.

Would be good to sleep for a couple of weeks.

9/18/72

If I wait for time to write a few pages, I'll never get to write a word. So. We are back in our country and our home. We've worked hard getting settled again. We're happy to be back and have so much to think back on.

I'm wonderfully busy, but have never, I think, been so content. I have a study now, downstairs, psychologically comfortable, color television and all, books all around me, a new flat-top desk to put my feet up on, the carpet from our living room. I've been wanting a room like this for ten years. Pictures & poems on the walls. Souvenirs from Europe. Perfect.

Have written a little. Have been getting things in order, filing, finding, carrying books around. Just got some poems & things in the mail though, and applications for grants to take next semester off.

Han and the kids are fine. Kristen is not exactly enjoying going to 1st grade, and turns us into nervous wrecks every morning so far, but we hope she'll learn to relax before too long.

Department politics raging—at a distance.

Note from Guggenheim people saying M.L. Rosenthal suggested I apply. I will. Next year. That made me feel fine, I tell you. Maybe he'll swing it for me for 74-75. Hope LSU takes the 2nd book. Or does *American Poetry in 1975*.

The Snodgrass's visited a month ago to ask about Germany. They're off to Europe for about 10 months. And he seems nervous already! Odd coincidence that he's writing about the last days of Hitler in his bunker and that I've been at "German" things for this past year.

So, what the hell, for better or worse this journal goes on.

1/30/73

Have been prowling around my study all evening and night, moving a book here or there, adjusting papers, looking for something to do. I'm restless, don't feel like any real work. I'm sort of marking time until after my D.C., Baltimore, Philadelphia trip coming up Feb. 7th. It should be a good one. Will see the Rocks, Elkins, Dick Lautz, will meet John Irwin, will probably record at Library of Congress (should look good on my record, as we academicians say) and read my Wilbur essay at Johns Hopkins. Etc.

Billy and Kristen are fine, lovely children. We're a lucky family, have everything, probably too much. Han has troubles, "women troubles" occasionally, but has been generally a lot healthier than last year. Winter keeping us at home now. I teach Monday nights, Tuesdays and Thursdays. I have a lot of time, but am often lazy. Spent all Christmas vacation doing a couple of lousy reviews for *Shenandoah* and *Poetry*. Then worked on the Miller paper for Tübingen. Somewhere in there I got lucky and wrote "The Pigeons." Was inspired to send it to Perishable Press, and Hamady is going to do it. I'm happy about that, and look forward to whatever lovely thing he makes. Can't think of much else new. As usual, my paragraphs, as this one, take the form of my ego, or obsession.

Have met Gary Snyder, Mark Strand, Paul Engel the past few months. Have gotten to know Al Poulin, sometimes a fine fellow, sometimes the penultimate Iowa Workshop Graduate Determined To Make It. In general, his poems are bad, weak, thin. But I'm losing faith in anybody's ability out there to read and discriminate. Jesus, Bill Davis' poems in *Poetry* and *Prairie Schooner* incredibly bad! Diane Wakoski is just awful, and she's pumped up all over as though she were the reincarnation of Sappho. I'm blind and stupid, or one poem like "The Cat" or "The Pigeons" or "Oak Autumn" is worth more than all of that shit! Or am I just dreaming of a world in which everyone has won through to the feelings about poems that I have? Or is it simply a matter of my taste being opinion, arbitrary? No, goddamnit, "The Pigeons" is better than Poulin's whole book. *In Advent*, indeed!

Now that I've written a page and have assuaged my conscience, I can settle back with an old film until 3:00 or so. And why not?

2/22/73

Read last entry. Had to laugh. Al was over here today & mentioned he thinks Helen Vendler is going to nominate his book for the National Book Award!

It's a Thursday night, my favorite. Whole days off. And I've been puttering around happily in my study all night.

Promotion to full professor came through. Done with all of that competitive horseshit and form-filling-out at last. At last? I shouldn't bitch. I may be the youngest full professor in SUNY. Anyway, wonderful. It is all over, that nonsensical Becoming. Now I can Be, and for a good many years, I hope. I have no desire to leave here lately.

Perishable now is also going to print a few of the new autobiographical sections. What a delight! Terrific! (I'm using as many exclamation marks as Robert Bly!) But I really am irrationally happy about these Perishable things. Something to hand down to the kids, to give to friends.

The trip to D.C., Baltimore, and Philadelphia just couldn't have gone better. I think the recording was a good one, and my other readings. I got to know John Irwin and Sandy McClatchy, and like them. I saw the Elkins, & of course the Rocks, & Dick Lautz & Jack Seydow. And made some money—about $500 profit. A short & sweet trip. Enjoyed Josephine Jacobsen's company & those hallowed halls at the Library. Enjoyed the hallowed Independence Hall in Philadelphia—I got choked up in there, I tell you.

This has been too happy an entry. Han goes into hospital Sunday night for probably a week, & will be laid up pretty much for a couple of weeks after that. But we sure do hope her pains go away at last after that.

3/3/73

Han in hospital recuperating from operation Monday. No more uterus. No more period. We hope that at last she will be healthy. She's had enough misery this past year or two.

I am playing father & mother. Getting along. I am on vacation, at least, and have been watching ballgames & doing nothing literary. Han should be home in a few days, but then will have to rest for a few weeks.

But we just heard from Jerry that Judy Phillips had a stroke, a cerebral hemorrhage. Very serious. Very sad. I hope she will get better, but I guess that the outlook is not good.

Billy and Kristen getting along fine without their mother. The week has gone quickly.

Long talk on phone with Stan Plumly. He's moving. Reports from Baton Rouge, where he's just been, are still good about *Noise in the Trees*. Wish to hell I'd hear for certain.

Can't think of anything new. Tomorrow is Sunday. Bullets vs Knicks to look forward to. I'm just sort of killing time until we get back to normal.

10/4/73

Why now? I don't know. The beat goes on. Egads, I've just picked this up for the hell of it, and have glanced at the entry above: and now Han is in the hospital again, recovering, this time, from something she did to her back a few days ago. We don't know yet what is wrong. Otherwise, things are okay. The newest member of our family is sleeping at my feet: Butch, a beagle, is about 6 months old now. Sometimes he's a terrific pain. I swear that if it were not for the kids I'd have gotten rid of him 20 times.

I have a Tuesday and Thursday schedule, and work hard on those days. Much rain lately—I look forward to the snow, the kids in school, Han home and healthy, a day off for me. That is the life.

Bobbs-Merrill will publish *American Poetry in 1976* once I get it edited. I'm pleased. Now I plan to get more young poets in on it than I originally did, but Bly, Stafford, Simpson, Rich, have said yes also.

Aah, but the big news is that Vanguard Press has accepted *Noise in the Trees*. They'll bring it out this spring already. I'm happy as can be about this. Bob Phillips had much to do with the acceptance. Even a $500 advance. Amazing. A lot off my mind. I was hurt by the LSU rejection, and won't leave myself open like that again. It is as though I now have packaged another part of my life, and have it behind or between hard covers, and can go on with the next phase. A good feeling, this second book. I am beginning to take myself seriously now.

I've applied for a sabbatical semester, and for all sorts of other grants to try to spring some time off. Fingers crossed.

I guess I keep writing, though I don't feel very prolific these months. But a wonderful letter from Richard Wilbur about a few of my new poems.

Met Anne Sexton & made a television tape with her. She was good here, not a crazy lady. David Ignatow here next week, and then Ginsberg again.

Han & I planning a big reunion party for old friends at Homecoming. I hope she's okay by then.

I'm having a blackjack party for the local boys, Billy's friends, tomorrow night. I sent out mysterious invitations to them.

Another argument with my mother when we drove down to the Island last summer. We're not talking again. I was defending Werner, actually. They're not talking, either.

Life sure has been hectic the past few days. Come to think of it, my whole life has been hectic.

1/2/74

A new year. Picked up this journal last night planning to write something in it, but became so engrossed reading all the Germany entries that I added nothing. It was good to write those things down. Delusion to think that I will always recall the most poignant moments of my life. This isn't true at all. Odd, too, how time for me begins to cover most things with a romantic haze. Once away from Stöcken, my long walks there all become moonlit and fragrant. I suppose that this is what happened to most of *Noise in the Trees*. We've never really had a poetry of the present in English.

That book is due out in May! I'm very happy about how things have worked out with Vanguard. The book will have to last me a long time—I seem unable to write now. I must say, without kidding myself, that I've not had the courage or ambition, in general, this past year. I hope I can come out of it. I have to stop planning a direction—thinking about a 3rd volume all on German themes—and just write. I'll be all right. I'm often, though, a little bothered thinking that at 33 already, my propensity for the image, my fund of imagery & my feeling for and talent for it and memory of it is already gone. I hope not. Is everything too fine, too secure in my life? I hope I can back to the rock before too many more months.... Have been working on *American Poetry in 1976*, which, as it turns out, is going to be an important book and be around for a very long time.

Han and the kids are fine. We had a fine Christmas. Not much is new. The family flourishes. Made up over Christmas with my folks, and with Bob Long. Tis the season.

World news is of constant crisis. We have gas heat. And I can walk to stores and work, so we're in good shape as far as that goes. This feeling of security will either lead to wonderful or awful poems.

Vacation for about 3 more weeks. We head for Forestville Friday—Han's mom having a gallstone operation.

Resolution for the New Year: will write more. Here and elsewhere. Will rely on law of averages and write more hoping that once in a while something deep and true will find itself there on the page in full glory in words.

1/3/74

I wonder if I can really do it. Can I do a section of "The Handbook of Heartbreak" every day for 26 days? I would like to, and will try. A & B done. So far, not bad. Something like this is imnportant to me now.

1/7/74

Sections through F are done. C, D, & E are very good, too, I think. I will keep trying here, keep trying.

We're back from Han's folks. Her mother is fine after her operation. It was good to get away, though I was tired from playing poker the night before until 4:30 in morning. Lost $200, too, but did win $250 week before. The beagle Butch had a fine time in Nashville, even found a twenty-foot high pile of manure that must have made his nose bloom.

Bill Matthews sent me E. Bishop's signed *Poem* as a gift. Very nice of him.

Bowled with the kids in Forestville. 180 & 179 in two games for me. Always had the feeling I could be a good bowler if I got out there more than once or twice a year.

I'm growing a beard—maybe only until Z day. But the poem may continue to fill in—I did 2 F sections today.

Just heard that the United States is a Cancer—born on 4th July. And heard that Scorpios will have rising reputations in 1976.

Nothing interesting to write down here. That's fine. G.

1/15/74

I am actually through the Q section of the *Handbook*. It's still good.

Something seems to have come up about my sabbatical. It has messed up my afternoon. It would be terribly unfair if it did not go through. I think it will, but my emotional rhythm is now messed up. Hope to clear it up tomorrow. I've been counting on having next summer and the following semester off.

Mirko & Irma coming home soon. We look forward.

Snow has stopped, alas. Rain. Rain.

1/28/74

Sabbatical still unsettled. I wrote a strong letter to the President. Am hoping it will be cleared up soon.

Handbook of Heartbreak actually finished. I think it is good, and I'm glad I did it. Actually, only section A bothers me. Will type it up next weekend, I hope, and send it off.

It looks as though we will get some sort of raise, 4¾%, from the State, retroactive to September. Maybe I'll get a bit for my promotion, too.

No snow at all lately. It's been warm, and raining, and raining. Miserable getting up in the dark to teach with this new Daylight Savings Time business.

Lost $50 at poker last night, but won $535 a week ago! Have sent for some books and generally needed the money.

Long talk with Jerry on phone yesterday. Seems that Ignatow is upset for silliest reasons over review Poulin did of his *Notebooks* for *Times*. God, imagine a 60-year-old poet giving a shit about a review! Postcard from John Logan, too, who complained about two reviews of *Anonymous Lover*. Maybe I'll change my tune, but I hope soon to get to the point where I don't give a damn about such things, not even, within easy reason, publication. Easier said than done, maybe, but we'll see. What hurts most is paranoia; also, friends worrying about, or asking about, or keeping up with one's "progress."

Mirko & Irma back. We've had some wonderful reunions and dinners and talks already. Love those people. Turkey dinner yesterday. Emmanuel told long hilarious story about bailing out of his bomber over Hungary in 1945. All eight of us laughed until exhausted.

Another depressing letter from Sandy McClatchy. On the other hand, my friendship with John Irwin is a joy—he's of high spirits. He's going to Athens, U. of Georgia, to run *Georgia Review*.

We're all in pretty good shape—just the usual colds land sniffles.

Really big show coming up here beginning of April: Howard, Bly, Kinnell, Simpson etc. will all be here in one week. It should only kill me.

Not much else new. I have actually been at this journal for almost ten years. Will try, for hell of it, to fill remaining pages this year.

1/30/74

Sabbatical came through today. A fine feeling to look ahead to about eight months off. I will have to accomplish some things during that time—then I'll feel fine about it. The Puritan ethic. That collection of essays! And some poems. And some regular exercise. Maybe a trip or two, but I'm not at all anxious to travel.

I read over parts of the *Handbook* today. Seems to be good. I hope it is substantial enough. Should it be a little heavier? Can it be a book?

Weather incredibly warm. Awful.

Nixon's State of the Union address was tonight. Same old story. I hope that as the whole impeachment mess works itself out, what happens is best for this country.

Han and I went to a basketball game last night—Brockport over Geneseo in overtime by three points. Poor Tom Pope, who was so close this time. Old Tom is a cool customer, though, as he was when we played soccer together.

2/2/74

Han and I stopped over at Belva Brown's today. Her husband Clyde died of cancer a few days ago. She's such a sweetheart. Belva worked in nurse's office back when I was in school here, and used to write out excuses for me for when I missed class. And then for a few years, before she retired, she was dept. secretary. I wish she still were. She's had it very hard with Clyde for the past few years. Aah, this life, so mysterious. I'm dazed whenever I begin to think. My head clouds and buzzes. There are occasional real flashes of illumination, and these are sometimes frightening and sometimes comforting. We have just begun to watch the river run.

At last, snow, and it's cold.

Publisher's Weekly announces *Noise in the Trees* at $7.95. That's quite a price for a book of poems. Page proofs should show up before long. But can't say how happy I am to have done the *Handbook*. January 1 I had nothing. Now, I have almost a whole book.

Ray Smith starting a new magazine, *The Ontario Review*.

My dear diary must be astounded by all this recent attention.

2/7/74

Much snow. I'm pleased.

A fine Thursday evening. Poker game to look forward to tomorrow night. A long weekend. Don't even feel like trying to write anything.

Lew Turco writes that Vanguard turned down his book of criticism. I still can't seem to get a copy of Bob Phillips' confessional book. I think I will do just that one critical book. That's all. I don't have the brains, and essays have to get lucky to be built entirely on intuition and appreciation.

2/16/74

Han took the kids to her folks' place for a couple of days. It is a Saturday night, cold, and I just took a long walk. Felt good. Not much sleep last night—won $170 playing poker—and I'm about ready for some now. Yes, I guess I really am.

3/3/74

Lost $115 last weekend at poker, but won $175 this Friday night. Have been winning fairly regularly, actually, but have been using up the money quickly. Food prices, etc., out of sight, but we should finally get ahead this spring & summer with an income tax return and my grant and the small retroactive raise.

New Yorker took section M (the mourning piece) from the *Handbook*. I'm pleased, and it will give the whole book a bit of a boost, but I sent many better pieces. Moss did say he wanted two others, but alas etc.

It's a lazy Sunday afternoon, a Knicks/Celtics game coming up on television, Billy bowling and Kris next door, the weather warming again and tough on my sinus condition and on Han's. But we are all warm and secure while the news is of crisis and dilemma.

Turns out I'll be reading here <u>with</u> Stafford on April 2. Nice of Al to set it up this way, though my new book will not be out by then. The dustjacket will have branches. It will look fine, although the box could have been eliminated. Hope the book does well, by which I mean well enough so that Vanguard is satisfied & might do another.

Got the big 6 months' food shipment in yesterday. It's a good thing because food went up 20% last year, and probably will again.

3/26/74

Old time flying. Back to classes today, but only classes Thursday and I'll be off for a week while 15 poets flood in here. Al and I have been on the phone constantly about arrangements, but today we talked only about dropping out, having only one or two, and fiction, writers here next year. Especially after reading in Pittsburgh last week—the reading went well: I think I outshone Appleman & Minty—I'm tired of meeting and dealing with so many literary people. Did spend two fine days in Pitt with Bill McTaggart; and did have some fine talks with William Meredith. It was good, though I think Sam Hazo had me there only so he could read here, and his secretary bugged Al Poulin even today. Thank God Al has to deal with this.

I've not been doing much. Sort of waiting for *Noise* to surface. Looking forward to May and the end of the school year. Looking forward to warm weather and to getting to a lot of things around the house. Looking forward again to auctions. Hope to take a week's vacation trip to Canada. I should really be able to relax, with only the *76* book to <u>have</u> to think about.

Strivers' Row has appeared and <u>is</u> lovely. I hope it stays afloat. In any case, John Irwin is a talented and ambitious and good friend. Glad to have gotten to know him. I can even talk to him on the phone without being nervous, and this is unusual, as I hate the phone.

"Watergate" goes on. Very interesting. Supremely important, and the cleansing is wonderful. Would like to hear a couple of the tapes. Would clear up a great deal.

Will get ready this weekend to make videotapes with Stafford and Simpson. Shouldn't be too bad.

4/10/74

That week is over, and we are still sort of high here in Brockport, but coming down now. Hard to believe all the readings, meetings, parties. I met Howard (briefly), Jong (briefly), Simpson, Jon Anderson, Carolyn Kizer. Renewed friendship with Stafford and Logan and Bly and Stan Plumly,. The Bly-Logan Friday night reading was the best I've ever been to, ending at maybe 1 in the morning, ending with all of us reading poems and then Logan and Bly finishing up. Big audiences (for this place) all week, including good crowds during the afternoons. The parties were all fine, especially the Saturday gathering with Bly & Logan & Plumly & Stan and all at Tony Piccione's.... Wouldn't begin to know where to begin entering the memories here: our dinner for Stafford, and the intensity of the Stafford and Simpson tapes made the next morning; the magnificent reading by Logan of "Spring of the Thief" and by Bly of his hockey prose-poem; Carolyn Kizer, drunk and exhausted and sad and lost in the back of my car complaining that Richard Wilbur was determined to be happy; Bly saying Berryman was just plain evil and that Annie Wright was killing James, wanted him to be an alcoholic like her father; my walk and talk with Bly around Tony's cemetery in Kendall; getting about a hundred books signed; Dick Lautz and Anne Maxwell and Julia up from Philadelphia; meeting Terry Stokes, a fine fellow but the sort of bippity-bop poet I dislike; Jim Hancock and Mike Waters here the whole time; Kinnell's wonderful reading; the whole spectacle billed as a celebration for the release of Heyen's book which was not (and is not yet) out; Arthur Furst snapping his photos and being moved by so much; Al and I drawing closer together as we kept trying to keep things together as we got more and more exhausted; Logan's drinking; so many people saying that Brockport was such a fine place for them to read; dishes undone here the whole week; meeting Stan's new girl Susan; late Friday night staring at Logan & Bly as I said "To Earthward"; etcetera. It all went on and on and will never be over. I learned a <u>great</u> deal, I surely did. Han held up, and the kids, though we had to ignore them. And now I am back to the prose of teaching. There's less than a month to go now, and I'll hang on. After that, eight months off! We're heading to Hamburg this weekend for a huge Easter gathering/dinner; two weekends later, we'll head that way again, where I'll read in Fredonia with Al & Logan & Simpson at the SUNY Blast. We're all in pretty good shape here now. In one month, bliss and ecstasy for me. Can't wait to get to work. Have even given up poker for a long time. Won $1,300 and then lost $700 and don't like the ups and downs, or wasting all the time or breathing in all the smoke and losing all the sleep.

4/19/74

To hell with enjoying the <u>present</u>! I have made it to the 19th now, and will be off after last day of classes May 9th. Will hold on. Need a rest, and need to stop meeting writers. Daniel Hoffman, a fine man, was here yesterday. I'm glad to have met him and hope to read all of his criticism, at least, one of these months. Some of his poems sounded good to me, others awful. What is happening is that I am less and less inclined to read other people's poetry, at least for now. Many reasons. One thing is that all these damned kids writing for *APR* and *Poetry Now* and all over sound very much the same to me, and say the same things, and their poems even look the same. There is a new Iowa poem now coming out of the workshop by the thousands. Sort of a cross between Terry Stokes and Dobyns and Marvin Bell & Jon Anderson—straight-forward and cynical and cute and forced and about poetry and employing metaphor in the same false way, filled with of's, not very closely connected with the real world (where the poem must begin) or the real heart (where the ladders must start). Still, I'm not very close to defining this hybrid poem all over the place these days. I just know I want to avoid it and not get infected. One can get to be a bad speller by reading bad spelling.... One thing is that so many of these people decided by about 18 that they would be poets. And that was it! I would rather trust confusion and accident. I never saw a poet until I was 27/8. Hell, good kids like Mike Waters and David Fraher have already heard Kinnell and Bly read a half-dozen times each! What the hell will this do to them, this overwhelming exposure, as they try to find their own poems? I don't think it's a good thing. I don't. A man has got to begin privately, I think. Yes, I think so.... I remember that when I first wrote that I didn't know if the things I sent out were even poems! I mean this literally. And when *Depth* was accepted, my reaction was, well, I guess I have written a book of things considered poems. This is true. And, for better or worse, those *Noise* poems are mine, or I have absorbed, from a distance and from careful love, some Frost or Roethke or Wilbur. Will Waters and Fraher be able to work their way through to something their own? God, it will be hard.... Now I seem to have met half the poets in the country, and I do scramble for their books and to get autographs, etc. But I read little, a stanza here and there. Not out of arrogance, not in the surety that I can do better, but I sure do distrust this poem in the air that everyone seems to be writing a piece of. Well, these things are on my mind in elaborate ways that I don't have time to get down here. Bill, get to your own work once mid-May rolls around.

House broken into while we were at Wolf's last weekend. Coin collection stolen, including the two gold coins my father gave me and the 4 Olympic 10-mark pieces, and all sorts of other silver coins and souvenirs. We're pretty sure who did it, but will never, it seems, be able to prove it.

Brockport is drying up at last. My poplars in the back, 5 of them at least, are coming out of the water and the winter. Still cold today.

5/3/74

Getting very close to the last week of teaching.... Ishmael Reed was here the other night. Meeting him was a pleasant experience in every way. He's quite a man, intelligent and warm, and with a discipline I admire.... Billy has begun playing soccer again.... Han and I went to our first auction of the year tonight—Parma Auction Barn. I bought a sheet of 4¢ stamps.... Billy and Kristen had perfect report cards again.... Al came over yesterday and read many new poems to me. He just doesn't have much sense of compression, of a line's energy, and he's still got that tinge of the melodramatic. But I'm glad he's writing.... I've written "This Father of Mine."... Still looking forward to *Noise in the Trees*.... Long talk with John Irwin the other evening. I like that man, and will give him my best things for *Georgia Review*.... Plan to mow the lawn tomorrow for the first time this spring.... Fine time in Fredonia last weekend with Al and John Logan and Louis Simpson et. al. A six-man reading. Egads!... Not much else new. Sweet summer on the horizon.

5/14/74

I've been working very hard the past several days reading journals. Now, I am done, and will turn in grades tomorrow. Will be done for eight months. Hard to believe. A last meeting of APT Committee, a few last details around the office, and done! I feel guilty already, but will work hard. I'm just glad to be done teaching for that long. I've been getting very stale. Have also been getting anxious to get busy with other things.

Actually heard last week that I've received an NEA Fellowship for poetry for $5,000. One applicant in about 10 was successful, and I'm still dazed. So much money. At last, we will have a little money in the bank. This money comes on top of a $1,400 grant for the summer, plus recent raises negotiated by the Union. At last, the pressure will be off. My salary should be about $19,000 by Sept.

John Irwin just called. He's trying to get someone to take on *Strivers' Row*, and I think he will. I might stay on as poetry editor. Right now I'm helping John gather for *Georgia Review*. John's book of poems coming out in Sept 75 from Georgia, too! Will edit Stafford & Sexton tapes for John, and give him my best poems.

Okay. This entry all business. The spirit getting ready to blossom. Looking forward to a wonderful gathering at Mirko's Friday.... Jesus, $5,000!

5/15/74

Han and I went to an antique show & sale. I bought a green Northwood vase for her birthday—she hasn't seen it and it will be a nice surprise. $25, but I'm feeling prosperous. It's very lovely. Another auction tomorrow night. I think I'll go. Some fun just sitting and watching.

Turned in grades today. Also, with APT Committee, interviewed a candidate for Dean of Graduate Studies. We were on the 16th floor of the new administration bldg., high over Brockport. A man's body in a space of the air. I can see myself hovering up there, buildingless. Somehow, the height is the thing that lends wonder.

5/21/74

Invitation came today to do the Connecticut Poetry Circuit this November. A pleasant shock. I don't think I applied. At least I don't remember. I must owe a big favor to Brinnin or Meredith or Wilbur. It will be nice. And there will be money, and some books will sell, I guess. Eight to twelve readings, and just when I'll probably be getting restless. --- I have the feeling that good things are happening too fast. I truly feel undeserving of the attention. Sometimes.

Dilemma about Butch, our beagle. We can't seem to live with him, and can't imagine getting rid of him.

Still very tired. Don't feel on vacation yet. Very busy, and there seems to be something to do every day: tonight all four of us went into Rochester to Billy's bowling banquet.

Al Poulin has been very sick. We got a doctor's appointment for him today. Looks like just a bad case of flu. He looks like hell and smokes like a smokestack and his coughing jags are getting worse.

Manny & Helen, Bill & Sis off to Greece today.

Tony and then Phil Gerber stopped in today.

David Fraher writes that Stan Plumly will be at Iowa next year.

Joe McElrath has quit here for a job at Florida State U. He's a very ambitious fellow, and will rise no doubt to the top of the scholarly heap. He's also damned smart. He's also, well, self-centered and selfish in many ways. He also has reason to be, what with the screwing he has taken around here.

I'll be getting together with Jerry soon, I'm sure. Am supposed to call him tomorrow or next day.

5/25/74

Bill Matthews was in Spencerport for a couple of days and came out here for dinner and long evenings and early mornings of talk. It's been fine getting to know him. We shot baskets one afternoon, then ate steaks and then Al & Boo & Tony & Sandi came over for good talk. Next evening Bill & Al & I ranked all poets our age. It was fun, and I played along though I haven't read all these people that Matthews has really <u>read</u>. Matthews heading for Colorado, Stan Plumly for Iowa. Stan called to ask if I were interested in a job at Ohio. Dear diary: I am beginning to feel like one of the boys. I mean, and this is important to me though it probably shouldn't be, I want to be one of the people of my generation who is talked about with respect when all these literary folk gather. Matthews, Plumly—those fellows get around. I don't want to be ignored. It seems as though 20 or 30 of the people of the Bly, Wright, Kinnell generation have become known, are anthologized, etc. Why shouldn't I be among the 20-30 of the next gang? I can be both together and write apart.

5/26/74

Two things: one, I'm sick and tired and run down and happy to be in bed today taking pills and watching television and reading; two, the other morning I woke up with a vivid idea for a novel, of all things. It would be good to try to write, and I will, some day. Will keep its two key moments in my mind. One is red and terrifying, the other cool and shadowy and literally otherworldly.

Read the new *APR* today. I wonder if the thing to do is to develop independently of the noise, rage, contradiction, theorizing, etc., etc., etc., etc. Once in a while I lean toward some exclusive view of what I ought to be about doing. Surely, this is wrong.

5/30/74 (1 a.m.)

About five hours ago, Billy's team was down 1-0 in a soccer game at half-time. In the 3rd quarter Billy scored a long one, and then knocked one in lefty, and then another one in on a corner kick, and then kicked a fourth goal. As he kicked the fourth one, some son-of-a-bitch hit him with a sliding tackle and broke his left leg. Jesus, what pain he had until it was set. He is in the hospital tonight, cast and all. Han and I are hurt for him. It was a very difficult experience for us all. We love him so much, and he had terrific pain. His whole summer will be fucked up. It will maybe make him a stronger person. We'll take good care of him. God take me before anything serious happens to the kids or Han.

6/7/74

Billy has been home for several days now and is getting along okay. Little pain. He'll just have to wait out the slow times. The neighborhood kids are going swimming & fishing already. So far, the days have gone quickly.

Can't believe how hard I've been working, inside and outside, on 101 things, from working on his essay with Ignatow to transplanting an ash tree to adding three shelves to our big oak cupboard to transcribing the Stafford interview for John Irwin to working on a poem at least a little every day to ...

Han and Kristen fine. Kris's guppy mother had 16 little ones, and she's delighted.

Calls from John Irwin & Sandy McClatchy & Dick Lautz today. I dug up some discarded L.I. poems and sent them to Dick at *Four Quarters*.

Book out any minute.

Reading *Doctor Zhivago*, at last. I love it.

Jerry Mazzaro was here for two days. Jesus, he's all right & means well and is sometimes even sentimental about our relationship, but he's often insufferable just the same, just too fucking habitually obsessed with Mazzaro. He can't even hold a conversation. Still, a friend. Oh, what a life, !, interesting for its imperfections, an optimist would say.

Still thinking about a novel.

My father called yesterday to say he was going over to England to see Henry this fall. I said maybe I'd go with him, and we could digress to Germany. I just have a feeling Mom will talk him out of it again.

Al still sick with some kind of flu. Tony still plagued with his in-laws out at the farm.

Enough. I'm beat and can't get to the bottom of the page.

6/20/74

New pen for Fathers' Day. A beauty! Sterling silver, no less, a damned <u>investment</u> these days.

Book still not out, and it's beginning to weigh on me. I've always, I think, exercised—I almost wrote "had"—a lot of patience. But this is a bit hard. A lot of people are really waiting to see it, even to buy it, ferchrissakes.

Pastan essay in. A bit thin. James Wright wrote to say <u>yes</u> to a piece, and to ask to get a copy of *Noise*! Will see him this summer. For some reason he's teaching in Buffalo.

Billy is getting along okay, went in for the last day of school yesterday, wheelchair and all.

Somehow, Han and I are working hard just cleaning up around here, just getting organized.

Auction season here for real. Went to one last night, will go to Parma Auction Barn tonight, to Bergen Grange Hall Friday night, and to that fine auction on College Street Saturday morning. Last night listened to the farmer selling off his machines etc. He's moving down to Tampa. As he talked about his machines and his land and the seasons, I realized that we are losing a breed of men, resourceful and independent, that we won't replace in this country—the Wenzels and Waxhams.

Back of my mind putters and simmers occasionally with the idea of a novel. Would need a complete month off; might then be able to manage a draft—a month <u>away</u>, I meant.

Barry Leeds & brother visited Picciones, and we stopped out there. David Fraher had just visited them, and Jim Mann, and the Petroskys, and many relatives. Tony may really break one of these times. It's too much.

Al still a little ill.

Finished the Stafford tape. Don't seem to have any poems in me right now, though I've looked at the mother poem from time to time.

6/25/74

Nothing new. Nothing. Zero. Ought. Maybe a poem called "Of Love," a long-lined thing. Otherwise, the days go by lazily. A poker game to look forward to tomorrow night at Bill Rock's.

New book somewhere in limbo.

Rain hovering above us.

Bought a box of things at the auction Saturday for $10. Turned out that a beautiful old blue bottle with hollow ground stopper was in it—this I did see; also a piece of Wedgewood, a tureen—ivory, ram's head, just lovely. Best bargain ever for me at an auction. Lovely things, which would have been auctioned off separately, usually, and brought a lot of dough. Also in the box were two oak frames. Some fun, too, this auctioning!

Manny coming back from Greece any minute. Mirko leaving for Ukraine soon. It will be, in many ways, a long summer. Somehow, it's hard to get to work because Billy is always at hand, no problem, really, but on my mind. Will have to get over this to get down to work. I've played a lot of euchre and hearts the past few days. Too much. How deep in my personality is this inability to relax?

7/1/74

The fifty special copies of *Noise* arrived a couple of days ago, and I've been sending many out. The book is just beautiful, I think, a pleasure to hold and read from. Well, I'm filled with doubts, but it's done, and the book as a <u>thing</u> will do much for the contents, as subversive as this may be. I'm happy, and it will give years of pleasure and, I hope, feelings of security. Vanguard has printed 2,500 copies. Seems like a hell of a lot. Book should be around for years. I don't know how many copies of *Depth* were printed.

Poker game tonight. Bill Rock picking me up. Han and the kids are visiting her mother for a few days. It's good to be along, even working alone, as I did yesterday, sealing the driveway, getting blisters and straining my back, but at peace, covering the asphalt with slick black shine.

Will have to get down soon to <u>serious</u> work on the *76* book. I can begin, I think, by drafting a preface that backgrounds the idea.

Still fooling around with a very long line, trying to finish up a second poem.

Letter from John Peck, who desires more time for the essay. Other essays should be drifting in now.

Long talk with Joe McElrath the other day. Reminds me of my own old ambition.

7/6/74

Worked all day mowing and raking and mowing the lawns. Still have a lot to do. It was a beautiful day, and my hands ache pleasantly. Han and I are relaxing this evening before our 12th anniversary. Tomorrow, I'll take it easy and probably go to an auction. Did take a short swim today in the Studiers' pool.

Pleasure of the new book still warms.

Jerry and the Wrights coming to visit next Friday. I hope we can make them all happy for a couple of days. Sandy McClatchy sent me a bunch of books to get signed, including *The Green Wall*, which I've been looking for for years!

Gave Al Poulin a ride to the airport yesterday. It was a shock to Han & me to hear that Al and Boo are "splitting," as Al put it. It's going to be a very sad and lonely scene for both of them. Ran into Boo in the post office yesterday and she burst into tears. He's been drunk for days and is now off to Boston. Very bad, all around.

David Fraher is around again, and seems happy. He's quite a man. Jason Poliner and Ken Venick, ex-students, visited yesterday. Jason is going far, in law. Galen Green writes that he's going into Vista.

My own book is my only new recent collector's item!

7/18/74

The Wrights' visit was a strain, but was fine. We all talked much and ate good and went swimming out at Picciones'. Annie & Jim (as they insist I call them) slept good and had privacy here. He looks fine and is not drinking, but is very tense, has emotional problems, as he told me.... He left a wonderful, very long prose collage for the '76 book. I hope it's not too long!

Lucien Stryk sent me such a letter about *Noise*! and Mike Waters, and Dave Smith. It warms. I hope the book does well. A guy from *Newsday* called and said they might run some of it. That would surely help. And Bob Phillips says it is prominently available in the NYC bookstores. Vanguard has done me well. Joyce Oates has several times written to say she loves Vanguard.... I'd like to get lucky with *Noise*, maybe have something very nice happen to it.

My folks visited in a whirlwind and are off again, looking, they say, for another home, one for summers, because they cannot use the pool where they are during summers because people would learn that my mother has that skin problem! They are absolutely frenzied people, my father almost as crazy as my mother, now. Nothing could possibly penetrate their heads except for their own ideas. And they talk every second, every second, every second.

I have to keep reminding myself that I have the summer off and should be happy and thankful and relaxed, because I get tense. Days slide into one another, and I've no clear sense of accomplishment. Should I take pleasure in the very anxiety? I don't know. That idea gets pretty complex and I'm pretty old-fashioned. I was reading Emerson's "Works and Days" and hold, still, to those "traditional" notions and goals, inner peace, and "Write it on your heart that every day is the best day of the year," and "He possesses nothing who does not own the day." Yes, not to glory, for me, in aggravation, but through Becoming, occasionally, to Being, and stillness. This may be hopelessly ... pastoral. Maybe the modern man should shudder acceptance and enter the screech of the day, sing to the blazing nerve endings, allow his knotted stomach to remind himself that he pains and is, a miracle. I can't do it. Keep yearning. That other genius, though, is around somewhere, even though I would want to read him even if I knew who he was.

7/26/74

A rainy day. Nice to be home. Han and Kristen went off to pick berries at Picciones', and I hope that between showers they managed.... *Newsday* review done. They sent me 67 books to write 1,200 words on! I picked five or six, and did, and will be paid $100. But all those books, so many I wanted and didn't have. I hope the guy at *Newsday* will do the same thing next year.

The Stafford essay came in. A fine one. So generous of all these people to respond as they have.

Al is busy fixing up his house, the back rooms, a kitchen stove, a new floor in the kitchen. He doesn't know if Boo will return in September. A mess. Sad.

Rocks, Mouganises, & Pylyshenkos really surprised me the other night. The eight of us went out to dinner, and Manny began a welcome home speech for Mirko, and it ended up that the party was for me for *Noise*. Mirko had drawn up a second "presentation," like the one for *Depth*. The eight of us are pretty close, all in all, and I hope we all stay healthy for many years.

Mazzaro, with his review of *Noise*, has really gone too far. An awful misrepresentation of the book, an egomaniacal job on his part, and badly written. Han is angry, too. We're through. Bob Phillips once wrote, simply, "What a shit Mazzaro turned out to be."

Raining hard now. Han & Kristen should be home soon. That little girl—she's really something with her gymnastics this summer. She's the busiest, liveliest, most constantly turned-on kid I've ever known. A sweetheart.... Billy's doing fine, playing soccer in our driveway even on crutches.

8/2/74

So many things. Am sitting on the back porch on a perfect early evening. Perfect. The lovely ash rises to my right. It is so beautiful. I tried to begin a poem saying that it is as though the ash and I could really talk right now. I love this simple beautiful tree. It does not have names for itself: greens, leaves, sunshine on trunk.... Well, the ash. Also, I've just read the essay Robert Creeley sent me for the 76 book. It's so beautiful. I was choked up all the way, and my eyes filled twice. The wisdom in it, the grain of the man's life-experience. Stately and deeply found. There is so much to it. That sonofabitch, what a man. I must study again, I think, Wms & Creeley. Or maybe the ash tree.... Also, Han and the kids are away, only until tomorrow, to Forestville, and when I am alone I am always very sensitive, inside myself, maybe for the better—why did I wonder: anyway I just am this way—and act differently in many ways.... I know the poles. Why can I not relax—it is, I think, a matter of turning off—into the kind of life that lives for these things, for the ash and for Creeley's moving words? The other part of me bought ten gold coins yesterday—but, hell, it really is for the kids, for Han's security, unless I am deluding myself and the deepest love I can give them is to become what I sense I should—and is nervous about business, in myriad forms. Maybe I can get that shit out of me. I do feel I underwent a major personality change at least once in my life, and maybe can again, or continue the straight road down the center of that life begun. However it is.

8/8/74

Robin & Mike Waters visited. We like them, we do.... Tomorrow we're off to Margie & Jack Polombellas' in Auburn for lunch, to Ed & Jean's in Cayuga for dinner & overnight, & we're off to the Island Saturday. I should be able to get away completely from literature for a while. A mental break from this 76 book which is always simmering.

President Nixon resigned tonight. I've so many feelings, ranging from compassion to anger. But, above all, all seems calm, this "orderly transition of power" so amazing, thanks to God. What a country!

Bob Phillips is staying in touch & sending me signed books and being, in general, a fine friend. Have I written earlier in this journal about Jerry Mazzaro's review of *Noise*?... Jesus, he's sick, and impossible. Now I do know what "academic," at its worst, means. I've written him a letter telling him just what I think. An awful review, gross misreading, egomaniacal, twisted, even badly written. Han was bothered, too, as she should have been. A couple of ideas took hold of Mazzaro and it was damn the text, full speed ahead. And he is supposed to be a friend. Well, hell, perhaps this is cruel of me, but, depending on how he reacts to my letter, maybe we're done with this ill and eccentric man we always humored and could never feel close to. We bear him, for christ's sake. He's impossible. Sad. Fuck him, the poor, poor bastard.

8/20/74

Back again, and back at work at the 76 book. The Rich and Reed things have just come in—Ishmael has turned my jargon back on me. The man has some head. I'm pleased to be in his new novel, even if indirectly.

Billy got the cast off his leg yesterday, at last. I trust his leg will limber up and fatten up again. He swam at a neighbor's pool for the first time this summer.

The Island, out Werner's way, isn't bad. Werner and I and the 4 kids fished at a channel near his place and caught, in about two hours, sea robins, eel, dogfish, blowfish, begalls, bass, and porgies. We all had a lot of fun, especially Kristen who was almost pulled in by an eel. Went fishing 12 miles out with Werner & a neighbor one day, and got seasick as hell, but survived. We caught only one tuna, while mostly trolling for white marlin. Spotted a big barnacle-backed turtle, but no sharks.... Well, the vacation was a good one. I even had a chance, at Ed's and later at Werner's, to scrounge various shops for books. Wonder if an American 1st of *Bambi* is worth anything. I know that the 1st of *Mosquitoes* I found is! Getting awfully tough, though, to find any decent books at auctions I go to.

Nothing very new. Good.

8/23/74

I spent most of today at Strong Memorial Hospital in Rochester where Al Poulin lay in shock from bloodclots outside the heart and lodged in the lungs. Tonight he underwent surgery, and is at this moment in the surgical recovery room in critical condition. I did not go in with Tony & Boo & David & Sandy & Annie (Al's 19 year-old sister) tonight, and will get another call soon when more is known. It's all awful and hard to believe, even though with his valium & whiskey & lack of exercise & lack of sleep & poor eating & chain smoking Al has been heading for it. I feel a hundred different ways about this. That poor son-of-a-bitch. Anger, because he seems to have consciously chosen this, grief of eighty angles, resignation. He's only about 36 & has the body of a 50 year-old man in bad condition. I don't know. May he pull out of it. And then, hopefully, some sort of will to see this life out to the end as best as he is able. So much strain on him this summer, with Boo's absence and with the things he's been doing with the house, but really, except for some increased drinking, his life this summer has been about the same as always: he's lived obsessively, abusing his body, driving himself. I hope the poor son-of-a-bitch pulls out of this one, but it sounds as though he's in for it. I don't know, I don't know. Was looking at some photos of Tolstoy in the biography by his daughter yesterday, the old man bearded white talking with grandchildren. Something noble about a man living long enough to be a comforting presence to grandchildren, being there. This is not the least love, living so as to survive for those grandchildren. Hasn't Al been essentially selfish? Hasn't he, also, been laboring under the delusion that his pain and grief & sleeplessness will lead to fine poems? Hasn't he chosen, another delusion, the ruined drunk god of poets that Bellow mentions in regard to Berryman? Also looking at photos of Whitman, one remarkable one taken in 1849 or 50 in the 1900 McKay edition I just picked up: what eyes! I see so much in them. Aah, that man, heading outward into whatever. Sometimes, of course, despair, but going on until something <u>else</u> and not your own demons takes you. Think of Jeffers in "The Deer Lay Down Their Bones." <u>This</u> kind of commitment. And why not? To read Whitman, Williams (writing, writing, affirming even between heart attacks), Stevens, Stafford, Wilbur, poets of life. To write poems of life. Al, my friend, may the Lord, and his doctors, help you this time. And then may you help yourself.

8/26/74

Saw Al last night: he was asleep in intensive care, hooked up to a respirator and sundry catheters. Frightening. A bandage over the massive incision. But, we understand, stable, and "as well as can be expected," as they say. We are all still holding our collective breath, and hoping he'll be all right. We'll see. So far, so good.

Tony rushing into the breach of the Forum for next semester, and I'll probably make a few tapes. If I had planned an extended writing project, I'd have to leave town, but all I plan to finish is the 76 book, most of which will be busywork. Still, it's a relief not to have to teach.

Billy's leg out of the cast and getting better now. Both kids sort of looking forward to school, a week or so away. I hope they stay healthy—I need some peaceful days this fall.

Labor Day

Und nichts gibt neues. Al improves, actually called Han the other day when I wasn't home, and may be home in another week. His personal life is still a turmoil, with Boo planning to leave for Boston with Daphne again, I think, as soon as she is able to extricate.

Today was a long & lazy day. Wolf & Pat & Kurt were here, and we all played cards and ate too much & played a little soccer & miniature golf. Weather has gotten cold fast, feels like fall & Halloween.

Have to work hard on the 76 book, little details and the big job of my own essay. Await late essays, also. Well.

Spent the day yesterday mostly with Kristen—we went to an auction in Rush together. She was sweet all day, and good company, a little lady growing up very fast.

Our new toy, our player piano is much fun, & good exercise for Billy's leg, which is getting stronger.

Han & I have turned down several parties & dinner invitations lately. We just want to stay home. I look forward to fine long days once the kids are in school.

Excerpts from *Noise*, my mother reports, in *Newsday* yesterday. Why the hell (though I know this won't happen) can't I get lucky and sell a lousy few thousand copies?

David Fraher here last evening. Quite a boy. Going far.

9/5/74

Han and I went in with Boo to see Al today, and it was depressing, but there was another dimension to it, something frightening about his demeanor, his apparent refusal to help himself come back, his smoking even now, his deep-set eyes and his comments about the joy of the whole experience of three lost days in his life as he hovered near death. Black & gloomy, it was, complicated by the fact that Boo has told him she is still determined to leave. I swear, though, that if he makes it home and throws his chances away with heavy smoking & drinking, if he doesn't change, there will be no tears from me, no trips to the hospital.

Applied for a CAPS grant. Never can tell. NEA & SUNY grants this year. Egads! I've managed not many poems and feel undeserving, but what the hell. There's no way to get away. I do putter with a poem here and there—actually got both the Erie Canal and the Pantheon in Rome in the same poem yesterday.

Turned down Chancellor's invitation to serve on the University-wide Committee on the Arts. Glad I did. It would have involved a 2-day meeting every month, in Albany or NYC or Cortland etc. And I almost put my foot in my mouth and said "yes." Praise the Lord I am getting smart. As Bill Rock says, "what's the pay?" Zero. No, those people, meetings, concerns are not for me.

Han in the other room putting up peaches. Nice smells.

Weather has been beautiful, but suddenly cold. Winter in the air, though we will probably ascend to Indian Summer.

Postcard from Pop in London who says Henry is showing him the sights & that the "wrong side of the road" traffic scares him.

Billy struggling in school with his crutches, having to go up & down stairs often. I'll be, as he will, <u>so</u> glad when he can walk again. It's slower going than I thought it would be.

Will take in a couple of auctions this weekend.

My own essay for the 76 book is a weight on my mind. Many other little things to do that I can't seem to get to.

Lew Turco writes that he has finished a 1,200 page book on witchcraft in America!

9/24/74

Long talk with Tony today about Al. Al seems headed right back to where he was. Smoking heavily now. Tony says he's sure Al will begin to drink again. No answers. Boo, too, is in an impossible situation. Al is hustling up new contracts for anthologies, getting two more phones installed. He was an inch away from death a month ago, and now this slippage. I hadn't known this, but Tony mentioned today, too, that Al's sexuality had been hovering between two worlds, that this was one of the things that was a problem between Boo and Al. What else? I'd hoped a psychiatrist would be brought in, but I think Al has abandoned the notion. Enough. We're heading right back.

Another beautiful autumn day, though I've been too busy, as usual, to fully enjoy it. I also realize that I use up a lot of energy just being anxious about work instead of <u>doing</u> it. I'll change. It may take another five years.

Have been taking such pleasure in my collection of books. Never lose interest in skimming catalogues, getting things in order. Why not? Many additions lately. Found a mint 1st of *The Old Man and the Sea* at the Seymour sale for 20¢, and now have bought a fine 1st of *For Whom the Bell Tolls* for $12. Many new 1sts of poetry. Hope to get MacLeish to sign several things next week. Han & I are to have a dinner for him.

Billy going to school without even a care now! Wonderful!

Ten readings in Connecticut are definite now, the first at Yale.

The 76 book is a pain, but will be worth it. Some essays will be coming in late. The bibliography occupies me now.... I have finished my own essay. I think it's pretty good. Written in one day, and this becomes part of its point.

Not much else new. Maybe I have too much time.

9/30/74

Archibald MacLeish arriving tomorrow. I have been reading him and reading him, finding that I care more for his prose in *A Continuing Journey*, in general, than in his poems. He is quite a man, has done so much, lived so truly and gracefully, lived so long. It will be a privilege to see him, speak with him.

Saw Al yesterday for 15 minutes—rode my bike over—and this time I swear he almost drove me crazy—so many ambitions, schemes, ideas, projects. It seems that he just can't turn off, can't make his affairs as one or two, as Thoreau advised. Han and I have promised ourselves tonight never to say anything about his smoking again. It just does not help, and sort of darkens the air. I don't know. Things in the Poulin household get worse rather than better.

Won $200 again at poker the other night. I've won a straight $1,500 now!

Mowed the lawn today, hopefully for a last time this year. I like our little property, the fine maple and two ash trees and one Dutch elm—still alive, still—out back; the flowering ash and two different maples, and one red maple out front, the last one in front of Kristen's window. This place is enough for us now, and maybe for always.

Went to Sunseri's the other day, as I do every week or so, and bought for $10 a large, beautifully framed, photograph of Benjamin Harrison, and cut into the mat below his portrait is his autograph. It's quite something, looks like it came out of a museum. Old man Sunseri didn't know Harrison was a president! I got lucky.

I haven't been sleeping very well lately. Either my 10 p.m. sandwich or my anticipation of the MacLeish tape may be keeping me up.

10/16/74

I just happened to open this journal to March 25, 1972, and the sentence: "The way I feel now, though, I just want to recuperate in Brockport for many years." So much exhaustion in so many entries. And I'm tired now. So much has happened the past couple of weeks.

MacLeish was just wonderful. We loved him. An old, tender, beautiful man. Many moments to remember: when on the way in to Brockport we talked about Mark Van Doren and he looked straight ahead and said "Gosh, I miss him."; when he told us at Al Poulin's that his and Ada's oldest son, Kenneth, was dying of cancer; his reading, and the standing ovation by 500 people who <u>loved</u> the man and his poems; his many attentions and kindnesses to all of us, adults and kids; his stories about Joyce and Hemingway and Stevens that I'll never forget. This man who has lost so many friends, whose son is dying, who wrote *J.B.* and endures. I'm so happy to have his signature & inscription in several books. His inscription in *A Continuing Journey* made us, Han and me, <u>part</u> of the journey. He has written us that he loves us. A sensitive man, a caring man, a wise man. The videotape he and Tony and I made is very fine. It was a privilege to meet him, touch his hand, break bread here with him. And we are glad that he is back now, safe at home, writing again. He is even reading my poems and promises to write, though I asked him to promise not to when I gave him *Noise* and the *Georgia Review* poem with his lines. I hope he is warmed by having meant so much to all of us. I hope, during any upcoming dark times, to dwell on him.

Anne Sexton is dead, a suicide, poor woman, poor woman. Al, who was on the phone with her many times during the weeks before her death, is setting up an *American Poetry Review* tribute to her, calling people all over the place about it. I was glad to meet her but, I guess, afraid of her, "her kind." I transcribed the interview we did with her here, and will write an introduction and use it in the 76 book—this is the best thing to do, I think. She seemed not terribly unhappy when she was here. John Logan was saying last night that Anne was the one poet of his generation he'd never met.

Logan was here for Richard Hugo's reading, yesterday, and looks terrible, red-faced and not a sloping gut but a bulbous and terribly unhealthy-looking bubble. He's drinking heavily, I gather, closing up Buffalo bars at four. He makes me nervous. Hugo said he has seen Logan's bad scenes. About Logan: Jesus, he's next as sure as hell. Depressing. There's sort of a blowsy geniality about him that upsets me, a feeling close to revulsion, the man killing himself and probably knowing it, and in, if this makes any sense, sort of a sloppy and soft way. I don't know. People now, it seems to me, avoid John. Hugo certainly did, and went back to his motel room early. John closed up a Brockport bar. I went over to Mirko's for a card game and won $72. This morning was a videotape with Hugo—only so-so. Han and I sure enjoyed Hugo—a decent and warm man who gave a fine reading. Brockport was his 7th reading on the NYS Circuit, and he was tired, but bearing up. He felt at home here, loved Han who seemed to remind him of his new wife. He's fifty and in love!, he said, and was anxious to get home. I'm glad to be going on the Connecticut Circuit, but will have to go slow, pace myself, take care of myself.

Han and I got back from Katonah the day before Hugo blew into town. Christ, what a hectic and exciting time. Met William Goyen, Naomi Lazard, Evelyn Schrifte (president of Vanguard), Tom and Elizabeth Woll, Seon Manley—what a woman!—and her delightful husband. I read well, I think, went over well. Seon urged me to strike while the iron is hot, to get another book to Vanguard in a hurry. I hope to, maybe in January or so.... And we got to know Judy and Bob Phillips again. She is all right, physically, now, pretty much—we argued like hell one evening about, of all things, homosexuality and masturbation and such things—she's some kind of strict radical fundamentalist Jesus freak. But Bob, he's amazing, a wonderful guy, so generous and warm. Christ, entertaining those Vanguard people even though they've just rejected a book of his poems and a book of his stories. He's a pianist, too, as it turns out. Most important, he's a real friend, true, loyal. We'll be close always, I'm sure. Han and I enjoyed the drive there over the Taconic as the leaves were turning their millions reds and yellows, and along the Thruway on the way back.... So, back again, after MacLeish, Katonah, Hugo. Happy and too busy to do all I have to do so, even, relaxed. Yes, my brow smoothes itself as I realize this is true. I have a hunch that tonight I'm going to get my first good sleep in a week.

10/21/74

Read William Goyen's *A Book of Jesus*. Here and there something broke through and struck me—the description of the entrance into Jerusalem on a pony, the language of the parable. Goyen is quite a man.... I was thinking today of the Christ, self-proclaimed, I saw in Hyde Park a few years ago. Pale, emaciated, dressed in a white gown and sandals, he stood there in his deep sad maybe drugged eyes saying that he had come again.

11/2/74

Yesterday was my 34th birthday. Stood at home, had a fine day.... Getting ready for the Connecticut jaunt day after tomorrow. I'm apprehensive, but the time will fly.... Han's back and arms have been hurting. I'm always sort of down, living life defensively, when she's not well.... We're going over to Manny's to play a little poker tonight.... I must get the 76 book into the mail about ten days after getting back from Connecticut, and this will be pressure. Essays are still dribbling in. It looks as though Logan has actually written one.... Not much else new. Will rake leaves tomorrow and try to relax.

[Schedule:
November 4   Yale University
November 5   U. of Connecticut, Storrs
November 6   Trinity College
November 7   University of Hartford & Central Connecticut State College
November 10 Connecticut College
November 11 Mohegan Community College
November 12 Manchester Community College
November 13 Wesleyan University
November 14 Mattatuck Community College]

11/4/74

(Kennedy airport waiting for a Pilgrim flight to New Haven). Never can sleep before a trip, even a trip down the Thruway to Buffalo. Last night no exception. Finally dropped off around five, up at seven when Billy came in to wake up Han as he does before he leaves for school. It's a nice day, the sun shines, but I'm generally apprehensive about this whole thing, these upcoming ten days. When I left for the West Coast last year I wondered why, as I do now before this jaunt. One thing is that planes always make me a little ill—takes me a day to shake it off. The sort of humming noise in terminals is enough to make my stomach flip-flop a little. Still, I am also glad to be heading out into the unknown territory of ten readings. Look forward to meeting the many kind people who have already been in touch with me; will also, no doubt, encounter many other characters "of death and blight," as Frost once put it. No doubt, too, that before long I'll feel displaced, daffy, begin to stutter and mumble, be unable to think because of tiredness. I should try to pace myself.... There's a birch tree in a pot across the lobby. An old woman sitting next to me just said (to her daughter?) I don't think that poor tree is going to make it in here. And she's right: the tree is already dead at the top, as its lower branches drain out of the soil the last sunlight it is likely to feed on.... Wondered what to pack: settled on just my one pair of black shoes, several sweaters, no suits or jackets, my old windbreaker. Don't want to look like a bum, but I can't bring myself to wear a tie and jacket.... Tried, on the plane to Kennedy, to think over a program of readings for tonight. I have a list of things, but will also play it by inner-ear.

11/5/74

(on a train from New Haven to Hartford, where someone from the U. of Connecticut will meet me). Discovered I can't write on a train!

11/6/74

(in a room in Storrs). I don't know about continuing this, but will, but with no special reason. To find out what I myself feel. Must be honest. Must not have the publishing of this in mind if it is to be honest.... Before the reading at New Haven, Sandy McClatchy and Richard Lautz (old friends both) and I checked out the room and moved chairs into it from an adjacent cafeteria. There were maybe twenty people at the reading, and wouldn't have been any if Sandy hadn't been buttonholing people for a long time, if he hadn't invited people to a party afterwards. I didn't care, really, about the lack of any attention, but was surprised the University couldn't find a decent room for the reading.... Met Holly Stevens, and we talked about her "Dad" and about my copy of *Harmonium* and about versions of incidents in her father's life. Met Richard Geller at Sandy's party and liked him immediately, could talk with him in a kind of intensity, right away. Met a man by the name of Ted who used to run Corinth Press and who promised me a package of books.... Sandy's introduction to my reading was wonderful, off-the-cuff, funny and kind, saying I once slaughtered (not true!) James Dickey in a one-on-one basketball game, saying nice things about my poems. Only one or two students at the reading, most of the other people, I guess I felt, just sort of putting in time before the gathering at Sandy's. I left Yale just sort of feeling I hadn't been there. It was more than fine to see Sandy and Richard again, anyway, and to visit Norman Holmes Pearson in his office in the afternoon. He'd written a nice letter to Vanguard about *Noise*, and a xerox had been sent me some time ago, out of the blue, and had felt good. Anyway, at eye-level on my left when I walked into his office was a row of books by John Berryman. I'd heard about Pearson's office, his books, so after just saying hello to him I fingered his Berryman books and said "I bet you don't have Stefanik A12," and, of course, he didn't: for one thing Stefanik isn't out yet, and for another, A12 is a sort of Christmas card limited to 1450 copies. Anyway, I told him I was a bibliomaniac, terminal case, and this got us talking. He broke out some sherry and a half hour went by on all sorts of things. He's warm and deep and I'm glad I met him.... Also saw the Beinicke, the central stack of rare books rising inside of it like the true path to heaven, shining and in all the tones of old leathers.... A student by the name of Dan and an English department member by the name of Loring Taylor met me at the Storrs train station for my University of Connecticut reading. I banged my head twice on the low roof of his (Toyota?) truck, but kept silent inside my own mild claustrophobia as we drove. We stopped at his house about 20 minutes from the university for coffee and cookies. His home is filled with antiques and conversation pieces, old Shaker chairs and spinning wheels, African carvings, et. al. He's just back with his lovely wife, Rosalie, from Romania, two years on a Fulbright. He's quite a man, and it was uncanny, I kept thinking, how he sounds just like Robert Bly, <u>exactly</u> like him, and shares some of the same gestures—the way he runs his hands through his hair. And the same smile just under his eyes. I finally mentioned this to some people, and they said that Allen Ginsberg had told Loring the same thing. Where was Loring from? I asked. Canada. But then someone remembered that Loring's father was from Minnesota.... Warmer here, friendlier, a few people who cared, not about my poems—Herb Goldstone had read *Depth of Field*, but no one else seems to have read a single poem (No, a young man name of Seon Golden said something to me about the diction in my poems), but that I was fed and entertained and comfortable. Nice folks around, with the exception of an insensitive and stupid woman who is picking me up in about ten minutes to drive me to Hartford—she is sort of half-responsible for the reading series here, but knows nothing about anything. She offended Jim Scully—I was at the opposite end of the table in a bar after the reading—and I soon found out why. I would say I hadn't happened to teach Charles Olsen in a modern poetry class last semester. She would say, from on high: "That's terrible. Students must be allowed to choose the poets they will read. (still 11/6—in a guest room at Trinity). She has a love-hate thing going for Robert Creeley, as I've just found out during an interminable trip from Storrs to Hartford with this woman. But, enough. She has problems, and knows it, told me she always offends people as she offended Scully and me. Enough to say that she'd planned on taking me to a restaurant for breakfast but it was closed when we got there and I was happy to get here, happy to be hungry but away from her.... The reading at U. Conn. felt pretty good—I read several different things from the things at Yale. I am beginning to notice that I am relaxed and my audience is relaxed and unselfconscious in direct proportion to how bright the lights in the place are. And when I am in the audience, I just want to relax, dream down into myself a little, and not meet the poet's eyes very directly and nervously. Ideally, I think, there should be no lights on in the audience.... Was up late last night about a dozen miles from Storrs at Ruth Daigon's (sp?) place. It was good talk, all around. I sure liked Loring Taylor and his wife.... Well, this is descending into I'm not sure what.... Trinity was ready to receive me. I was in my room three minutes after getting here. Hungry, waiting for Dori Katz to get out of class at 11:30, glad to be here. A shining, warm day. Fellow by the name of Peter who just showed me to my room—a fine suite, palatial compared to Storrs where the damned heat wiped me out (air conditioning wouldn't work, windows nailed shut, pipes hot)—said that Mark Twain said that if you don't like the weather in New England, just wait around a minute and it'll change. I like this change. Might see one or two friends at the reading tonight. No mention of the reading in the school paper, I see, though a boxed-in section on events tonight mentions a concert, an art exhibition, a musical and other things. Will there be about twenty people there again? I wonder, even though Vanguard has sent books to all these campuses, if I'll see a single copy of my book on this whole trip. Anyway, this is the third day and I feel pretty good. Called Han last night—she's painting our downstairs kitchen with Boo Poulin.

11/7/74

Trinity has been by far the best. Nice people around. Dori Katz has been thoughtful and warm, the students I've met have been sharp and tolerant. A decent bunch, maybe 40 or 50 at the reading. Met Bill Bedeker—I know him from LaSalle. Terry Stokes came over.... Crazy thing happened last night. At 12:30, exhausted, I was just getting to sleep when the phone out in the hall of my apt began ringing. Before I could fumble on a light and get out there, it had stopped. I was nervous, but was just drifting back to sleep again when I heard pounding at my door, someone saying "Security." It turned out that a campus security man had brought an old friend who'd been looking for me to see me. Bob Gumaer, who started with me on the old Brockport 5 in 1960-61, had seen my photo in the papers and gone looking for me. Haven't seen or heard from him in ten years—he's regional manager of a transportation company here in Connecticut—but one of those friends you don't have to hear from to be close to. So, it was good, but lord I was tired by the time I got back to sleep around 3. Then was jolted out of sleep at 6 by pounding & banging outside. Then sleep again until maybe 8. This is the hardest thing for me, this sleeplessness. I'm 34 and in decent shape, but it's still hard. Bly once told me that he was always weary in his 30's, but began to feel real energy when he got to be 40.... Had a nice breakfast, am waiting for a ride to U. of Hartford from a lovely woman by the name of Millie. I think I'm all set for the two readings today.

11/7/74

The one at U. of H. is over with—9 people showed up, but it was still, somehow, a good scene—the kids who were there were interested. But, still, 9 people—about $17.50 a ticket is what it would amount to. I read several things I've never read before, and it was good to hear them. I sat down, and was comfortable. Talked with Terry Stokes for a while, and will run into him Saturday in New York, hopefully.... Sitting at this moment in the hall at the English dept. at Central Connecticut, and feeling conspicuous. Mr. Burney should show up any minute. This is a clean, bright, busy place—all the classrooms seem to be humming. Brendan Galvin just stopped over. Heyen: "That's an awfully good book you've done." Galvin: "I think so. Now if I can just get some reviews." Will see him tonight. He looks a lot older than I thought he would. He is, to be sure, a fine writer. He sounded like my friend Barry Leeds from here, some inflection at the end of the sentence. I don't know what it is. Enough for now. Posters w. my name up on every board around here. How many tonight, ten?

CONNECTICUT POETRY CIRCUIT

Director
MRS. JEAN MAYNARD

THE HONORS COLLEGE
WESLEYAN UNIVERSITY
MIDDLETOWN, CONNECTICUT 06457

Telephone
347-9411, Ext. 260
Home: 347-4717

Friday and Saturday, November 8 and 9. No scheduled readings.

Sunday, November 10 — **Connecticut College**, New London. (442-5391)
* Mr. William Meredith, Department of English. Arrive by 3:30 p.m. for reading at 4:00 p.m. in the crypt of Harkness Chapel. Dinner and overnight accommodations to be provided. On Monday Mr. Heyen should be driven to

Monday, November 11 — **Mohegan Community College**, Norwich. (889-3391)
Mr. James Coleman, Department of English. Arrive by late afternoon. Reading at 8:00 p.m. Dinner and overnight accommodations should be provided. To be driven on Tuesday to

[handwritten: stay at Norwich — will be picked up a little after 5 for dinner.]

Tuesday, November 12 — **Manchester Community College**, Manchester. (646-4900)
Mr. James Gardner, Department of English. Arrive by late afternoon. Reading at 8:00 p.m. Dinner and overnight accommodations to be provided. To be driven on Wednesday to

Wednesday, November 13 — **Wesleyan University**, Middletown. (347-9411)
Mr. Morton Briggs, Director, The Honors College. Arrive by late afternoon. Reading at 8:00 p.m. followed by a reception. Dinner and overnight accommodations to be provided. To be driven on Thursday to

Thursday, November 14 — **Mattatuck Community College**, 640 Chase Parkway, Waterbury. (757-9661)
Mrs. Nancy Malone, Department of English. Arrive by 11:30 a.m. for lunch before reading at 1:00 p.m. Mr. Heyen should advise Mrs. Malone whether he wishes overnight accommodations. Please arrange to transport him to his place of departure.

[handwritten: tel. 354-0100]

*[handwritten: * Bill Meredith's home telephone: 848-8486]*

TOUR OVER

CONNECTICUT POETRY CIRCUIT

THE HONORS COLLEGE
WESLEYAN UNIVERSITY
MIDDLETOWN, CONNECTICUT 06457

Director
MRS. JEAN MAYNARD

area code - 203

Telephone
347-9411, Ext. 260
Home: 347-4717

Itinerary for William Heyen

NOTES: College representatives should write directly to William Heyen, 142 Frazier Street, Brockport, New York 14420, to advise him of precise meeting places and to arrange hospitality and overnight accommodations. Letters should reach Mr. Heyen at least one week before the tour begins, by October 28, 1974. As he will be arriving by public transportation, it will be necessary for each college to arrange transportation to his next reading engagement. It would be helpful if a campus map marked with his destination and other pertinent directions could be sent to him.

The check for the honorarium, $125, should be given directly to Mr. Heyen at the time of the reading. His social security number is 080-32-0836.

Monday, November 4
: Yale University, New Haven. (432-4454)
Mr. Dwight Culler, Department of English. Arrive by late afternoon. Reading at 8:00 p.m. Dinner and overnight accommodations to be provided. Leave by train on Tuesday for Hartford. Mr. Culler should call Joanne Akeroyd at the University of Connecticut Library to advise her of Mr. Heyen's arrival time in Hartford, where a representative of the University of Connecticut will meet him.

Tuesday, November 5
: University of Connecticut, Storrs. (486-2519)
Mrs. Joanne Akeroyd, University of Connecticut Library
Mr. Herbert Goldstone, Department of English.
Arrive by late afternoon. Reading at 8:00 p.m. in University of Connecticut Library. Dinner and overnight accommodations to be provided. On Wednesday Mr. Heyen should be driven to

Wednesday, November 6
: Trinity College, Hartford. (527-3153)
Ms. Dori Katz, Department of Modern Languages.
Arrive by late afternoon. Reading at 8:00 p.m. in Wean Lounge, Mather Hall. Dinner and overnight accommodations to be provided. Thursday morning Mr. Heyen should be driven to

Thursday, November 7
: University of Hartford, 200 Bloomfield Avenue, West Hartford. (243-4731)
Ms. Barbara Pfister, Editor, HOG RIVER REVIEW, Gengras Center. Arrive by 10:30 a.m. for reading at 11:00 a.m. Lunch to be provided. In the afternoon Mr. Heyen should be driven to

Central Connecticut State College, 1615 Stanley Street, New Britain. (225-7481)
Mr. William Burney, Department of English. Reading at 8:15 p.m. in Marcus White Lounge. Dinner and overnight accommodations to be provided. Mr. Heyen will advise Mr. Burney where he should be driven on Friday.

(continued)

Thanksgiving 1974

    I've been waiting to write in this almost-ten-years'-journal for a few weeks now. I've been busier than ever before in my life, I think; busier than during comprehensives at Ohio, even. But now *American Poets in 1976* (as of yesterday) is in the mail winging (or crawling) its way toward Indianapolis and, hopefully, my work on it from here on in will not be a burden. It's quite a book. I'm glad I did it. I would not do it again. The pressure built up because some of the contributors were late—my August deadline became an end-of-September deadline became a November 1 deadline became a <u>final</u> Dec. 1 deadline; and because the bibliography was a lot more time and trouble than I'd anticipated. Bly, Bill Matthews, and Plumly still not in, though I hope they can be added; some details of copyrights, photos, etc., to take care of. <u>But</u>, all 600 pages are in the mail, out of my study, largely off my mind. I hope everything goes all right and the book makes its way into print. I feel responsible for about 25 people, and this is a burden. I believe I will <u>never</u> do anything that requires a deadline again. <u>Never.</u>

    We are at Han's folks in Nashville for a few days. A sense of time is always intensified for me here, time passing, past. I haven't been here for, I don't know, maybe a year. The four of us walked down the dirt road during a light snow this morning. It was a good walk—good to breathe deep and to walk and to throw a few snowballs. A 22 pound turkey is in the oven now, the pleasant buzz of talk and play downstairs. I like this place. If bad things were to happen in the country, if I were to lose my job and a food crunch came or one of the thousands of versions of apocalypse predicted or rumored, the four of us would get out of Brockport and move here and we'd all somehow make it. This sounds sort of silly even to me as I write, but the general atmosphere in the country is of some kind of dark time coming. It's hard to think/believe, that during my lifetime, which has been easy and secure, I may yet have to live through something cataclysmic, through upheaval, storm. What will happen, will happen, and there is no conceivable way I can influence, beyond my family, what will happen to us all. Well, and how will disaster come--? Mom & Han & Pat are talking about the price of sugar downstairs, their strains of amazement coming up through the stove-grates of this hundred-year-old house.

    The ten readings in Connecticut came and went. So much to digest. The highlight was Wesleyan where Richard Wilbur introduced me in a way I couldn't believe and where several kids actually knew my poems. Wilbur is simply a beautiful man. He means a great deal to me. We talked, and I read well, I believe. I hadn't known he'd be there, and was gratified.... Spent much more time with William Meredith—saw his home within the same 24 hrs. I'd seen Richard Howard's apt. in NYC and James Merrill's in Stonington, Conn.—and learned to care for him, too. He "confessed," as he put it, until early into the morning, the two of us sitting in front of his fireplace, about his sexuality, his young present lover, etc., etc. McClatchy had told me about his various affairs with men, I'd visited briefly Howard (and his lover Seymour) and Merrill, and then the Meredith revelations made me feel further alone. But he is a kind and decent man, lives a life of integrity, close to the trees around him, his home rustic, without a driveway, and overlooking the Thames River. I saw his school, his office. We worked over his bibliography for the 76 book a bit. I like him, indeed I do. His life-style and Howard's—Howard, too, was <u>very</u> kind, pressing gifts of books on me, showing me around his apartment, leaving Stokes and Linda conspicuously behind, as I thought—a million light-years apart.... Spent a day in New York in the bookstores (Gotham, Strand, Scribner's, Brentano's) and bought many things, but needed more time. Saw the Olson archives at U. Conn., met James Scully, who came to my reading; met a fascinating guy name of Gardner at Manchester who said things <u>knowingly</u> about my two books; met Richard G—at Yale, and we talked, and he is real; saw Dick Lautz, who just sent *Four Quarters* with my sixteen throwaways. But, best of all, home. Han had labored to fix up the downstairs, which is now so comfortable and clean—I'm looking forward <u>again</u> to getting home in a couple of days. The next 6 weeks, now that the 76 book is "done," should be wonderful. Downstairs, now, to the love of this family of mine.

12/8/74

    Fine Christmas party at Gene and Phil's last night. Mirko and Bill & Manny and I and the wives singing old songs outrageously loud until two in the morning. Much love and warmth. Today, Sunday, has been lazy. I fooled with a couple of poems while Han & the kids went in to the War Memorial with the Poulins for the Ice Follies. Raining all day. Don't think I managed to do anything worth much.... Finished a pretty good series of twelve poems the other day though—Plants of Palestine. And finished "Brockport, New York: Beginning With 'And'", which is one of my best, I think. Then why do I feel restless? In part, because of details with the 76 book that hang around. Also, I feel this wonderful sabbatical running out! Also, because of the weather's indecision—I feel finest when it snows, but everything is melting.

Kunitz coming Thursday. I must prepare for the tape.

Al seems to me unhealthy, particularly so, the past week. Those clouds of smoke around him are depressing. Now he's planning to pick up his Ph.D. at Buffalo, his dissertation being an intro. to poetry text that he wants Houghton Mifflin to publish. Egads! He just can't turn off. And he continues to abuse his body, not slowly, as I do, not planning to get into shape one of these seasons, as I do, but mercilessly, as though it cannot fail him. Lord, and Tony Piccione is getting so Zen, as he says, but is suffering from frequent nightmares. I don't know. My anxieties seem localized primarily in my stomach.

12/9/74

Long cordial talk on phone with Tom Wittenberg of Bobbs-Merrill. He said everything looks in good shape on *AP76*, that from here on in it was pretty much a matter of routine. A relief. I still have some copyright things to clear up and other details. But things look good! Much work left, but things look good.

Southern Review accepted six poems today. They're from *The Handbook of Heartbreak*, a book I will turn to in maybe a year or so again. Anyway, I'm happy that six are taken care of. I have a good feeling about that book.... *Four Quarters* is out with my sixteen little things. Have I mentioned in this journal that Halpern will have 4 poems of mine in his under-40 anthology? (Avon)

I just rescued another baby from Kristen's guppy tank!

Snow may be on its way again.

Have been reading Kunitz today. Definitely care for his later work more than the metaphysical torque of the earlier.

Dec. 1974

Friday the 13th, I realize, but a good day (so far, says the conservative) nevertheless. It is about noon, I am home alone—Han is down at the bank selling Twig cookies—and unwinding after the Kunitz visit. He and Al and Han and I and Irma and Mirko had breakfast out at Mirko's this morning, and Kunitz is about now in the air back to Washington.

Everything turned out fine. He was easy to like, easy to talk to and interview, and the videotape, done yesterday, is a pretty good one, I think. It was nice talking to him, especially about his own 10,000 volume library—he happened to mention that he has not one but two copies of *Land of Unlikeness*! (so, it's that kind of library)—and once in a while he would say something, on other matters, particularly graceful, as it seems to me. He wears his position lightly, though there is still—as when he held me by the elbow just a minute before his reading yesterday evening to tell me that Tony, who was to introduce him might want to mention that he, Kinitz, was just elected to John Ransom's chair in the American Academy of Arts and Letters—there is still a bit of an ambitious edge to him. Oh, well, there are no saints. He was never pushy, but was happiest talking about himself. Oh, well. As far as his poems go—well, Wilbur's blurb on the back of K's *Selected Poems* disappoints. I have to be careful because of the way fashions change, but that constant metaphysical drone of his—it's in his voice, too—cloys. *The Testing-Tree* is better, though, for example, "Heart's Needle" so far outclasses "Journal for My Daughter," the same kind of thing come to by K. so late. An occasional real flash (of blue) as in "Robin Redbreast." Well, all in all I suppose K is an odd case. He's gone so slowly, has changed a little (or lot) only in the last 5-10 years. Made up his mind as a kid to be a poet. Not nearly, it seems to me, the raw talent of a Roethke or Wright or Bly or Kinnell or Wilbur or ... but a kind of tenacity that brings him, at 70, to where we must pay attention to the man he is in the light of his own peculiar purity. Well, what does this all mean? I liked him. I respect his poems—that sometimes non-committal word.

Had a little vodka at Mirko's. Am now tired. Mirko said a beautiful toast to the American poet who has done more than any other to make the work of Ukrainian poets known in this country. Mirko and Irma's table: a feast of Irma's current juice and blackberry & strawberry jams, Mirko's flapjacks, vodka and caviar.

Mid-month, and a fine month ahead.

12/18/74

I've been trying to get an overall view of *The Swastika Poems* book. It could be very strong. It seems to me to be important that "The Wolf," once I get to work on it, be excellent. This would be necessary if the conclusions are to be placed in a realm where they do not go flat. It is also important that any prose I use, from this journal or elsewhere, be thought out clearly. I'll use "Erika," certainly, and "The Owl" and "The Spire," but I don't picture a central section of prose as in *Noise*. Well, I plan to work on the book during all of 1975.

One day blurring into another lately. Feel kind of logey, haven't had any exercise at all, not enough fresh air. Went Christmas shopping last night. Wonderful and awful.

Tony just called to say that <u>at last</u> he got a State grant. I take the credit for getting him to apply. I wasn't eligible, but will take the summer off anyway! All's well. I <u>need</u> to get back to teaching. Well, for one semester, anyway. Al will be off next semester & the summer & maybe more.

12/25/74

It was an April or May afternoon in 1957, my senior year in high school. I was at home, shooting baskets by myself up against the old shop where a rim was mounted. It was a nice day, I remember, and I was enjoying myself when Mom called me in to the phone. It was Karen. She said that there had been a terrible accident. She was crying. She said that Ellen Wagner and Bob Lahahn had been driving around after school and there was some kind of terrible accident, that Ellen was actually dead. I went outside again and began shooting baskets again, but dizzily and in a kind of frenzy. My mother called me to the phone again. Karen said, oh God, that Bob was dead, too. Ellen and Bob were close friends of mine. I couldn't believe it.

That accident cast a pall over the last part of the last year of high school. Teachers couldn't console us. There were those empty chairs in our classes, there were kids breaking down and crying during exams. And I was only sixteen and couldn't comfort anyone, not even my girlfriend Karen who would suddenly remember and suddenly slump in a swoon against a locker.

Some of the details of the accident were too much reality for me, as when Joe Cravotta told me that when he arrived at the scene, the second car there, he'd had to put his jacket over Ellen's head, which was sliced open at the top, her brains strewn on the macadam. I went to Bob's funeral, saw his cosmetized face in the casket, my first such experience. I made it through that. But Ellen was a Catholic, and our whole class attended a mass for her, and I'd never been inside a catholic church before—the crucifix, incense, the Latin and dark strangeness, frightened me and broke me down completely. I wept, right there in the presence of my friends, who also wept. I remember thinking, as I knelt to the floor, that Ellen was gone, dead, that she had gone on a journey, was alone. Oh, Ellen, you're so young to be on such a journey, I thought. It was a pure moment for me, a moment of the apprehension of death, loss, absence.

Last night, seventeen years later, I dreamed I boarded a bus and walked down its aisle, its tunnel, to the back. I tried to squeeze into one seat, but it was too close, there were too many people. I moved one seat forward. Then there was an argument behind me—a friend of mine was involved with a tall man dressed in a black suit, a man handsome as Valentino. He was with a woman. I looked at her and then away and then back at her. "Is it you, Billy?" she asked. "Is it you, Ellen?" I asked. It was Ellen. She was about my age now, but still beautiful, as tall as ever, her auburn hair shining as always, her teeth white and even as always. We embraced, and because we knew one another the altercation between her escort and my friend was over. Ellen and I embraced.... Thank you, Lord of Death. It was a privilege last night, after seventeen years, to board that bus and to see Ellen again still journeying outward. Thank you, Lord of Dream. May I board that bus again, in this life and in the next. May I see all of my old friends again.

12/31/74

So, the last day of the year. This journal now a decade old. Ten years, a large part of my life. The life has come to something more substantial, I trust, than has this diary of fragments, spurts and dribbles, drivel and spoof, silliness and stupor. I don't know yet whether I'll begin another one. I should. For one thing, it is good to be able to look back at <u>details</u>.... It seems to me that my <u>material</u> lot has vastly improved over ten years: things—home, books, et. al.—now mine; love, too, has deepened with Han and the kids; now, to put energy into what it is I want to be and do. I want to accept and be calm about what I am. I want to work toward a habitual discipline, put most projects except for poems aside, come to a detente with my ambition, which dissipates energy. One definite resolution for the New Year: I want to get back into pretty good shape. Will walk more, eat less cake and candy, run more. I'm 34, never have been so far out of condition, but still have a good body only a dozen sessions away from lean condition.

Poulins & Picciones coming over for a small party tonight.

"Of Palestine" now finished—15 poems in all.

Very little snow lately, alas, although some is supposed to be on the way.

Daniel Hoffman listed *Noise* in a review as one of the best books of the year. That was nice of him. Philadelphia *Enquirer*.

The other $500 from Bobbs-Merrill came yesterday. We'll be able to put all of it in savings, and this feels good.... Gold now legal. Will be fun to watch prices, now, on our 12 oz.

Some fun the other night at the Studiers' party. We ended up at Waddams'. Ross Wicks got drunk and punched Doc Anderson in the mouth, and I helped wrestle Ross out of the room and up the stairs. It was some show, and has the neighborhood buzzing.

Read Louis Simpson's *Riverside Drive*, Curtis Harnack's lovely *We Have All Gone Away*, much of Bob Phillips' *Denton Welch*.

Soon, I want to put everything aside except for *The Swastika Poems*.

I'm ready to go back to teaching, I think.

I hope, with luck, to fill up this journal tomorrow.

Ten years. Does it seem like two or thirty? Well, both, I guess.

1/7/75

1/22/75

Nothing two weeks ago! Nothing now. School has begun again. Busy, a little nervous. I've been going over the Germany part of this journal, seeing what I can salvage or build on for a possible section of prose in *The Swastika Poems*. Sort of glum going back to teach after all that time off. Also sort of turned on to it.

9/1/75

I won't bother looking back at what I've written.

I kept planning to finish this journal (and buy another blank book), but wanted to finish adapting the German sections first, and that job dragged on, and I suppose I've been wondering about the whole possible place of a journal in my life. Jim Wright told me he could not live without his now, that it is his greatest writing pleasure, that he doesn't give a damn what happens to it after he's dead but that he would break the hands of anyone who should open it now. It's apparently an intensely private experience for him. Imagine writing with <u>no</u> regard to being read: This cannot be imagined? Anyway, I don't know. Maybe the journal would be a good thing for me, maybe not. If I begin another one, it will be different, a fresh beginning, perhaps, simply, an ongoing bound steady progression of all drafts of all writing in addition to other sorts of entries.

The summer is over. School begins in a couple of days. I guess I am ready. Where am I? I've sent off *The Swastika Poems*. Several of the poems came quickly a while back as I was gathering the project together. Problems with the central section, and I need some intelligent advice. The poems (26) I feel are strong. I have my fingers crossed that Vanguard will do the book.... Completed a poem this summer called "Fires." I hope it will hold up. It takes suburban risks. One inch more and all is mush, if it isn't already.

Now I see that eight months have actually gone by since I set this aside. No way, now, even to enter the names of the writers I've met, or my petty successes and defeats during that time. I'll probably regret this. It is true that I usually carry a poem around inside me and that it ends up being finished. But other things I might want to write in the future will suffer. There should be details here of the moving time I spent with Wright, Bly, Kinnell in Michigan this summer. I will write about those men, and other people there, and will not remember as precisely as I would/should have with journal entries. The problem is that I feel guilty doing a shoddy job with this journal—it was always filled with holes. I always wanted it perfect, Teutonic as I am. But if I could adjust to the notion that even my notes and sketches are better than nothing, that though this raggedy piece of shit took ten years, it is still better than nothing and helped me with *The Swastika Poems* and other things—then I could/would continue it, perhaps in the same way. Well, hell, yes, I should. And why not?

Hannelore is now sitting in our easy chair in my study to my left, sewing and watching television. She has two broken fingers from an accident this summer. She is 35 now, a lovely woman, kind and beautiful, occasionally depressed (and this is a new dimension in our lives) but generally on an even keel. We're very close, still, and hopefully our lives are going deeper. Bill and Kristen are such fine children, such unbelievably fine children, and have been healthy, and have had a summer of swimming, fishing, tennis, neighborhood games. We are all sometimes so happy, fulfilled, that ... well, it's hard to say. What is next. The world of traffic, cities, starvation, has seemed for me, except when I entered the *Swastika* book, far away this past summer. I've been thrown off the track by gnats' wings—as when I replied to that ugly review in *Poetry* of *Noise*—but am grateful for my life, nervous about settling too complacently into it—but grateful for it. Our home is filled with beautiful oak furniture, a pleasure to touch and age with; Han's flowers and "my" trees flourish, as do the children; my "fame" is something that should satisfy me, my career, and I am content most of the time, far better balanced (I believe) than most of my peers. I have loyal friends. I have been both lucky and deserving! Aah, this American suburban middle-class life, so clear and yet so odd because of forebodings and dreams. I got out of a state of half-sleep a week or two ago to write "The Trenches." No escape. We are all everything at once. Blood, bombast, bibliomania, boredom—as we dance on.

The Trenches

The trenches run
ankle-deep in piss, shit, garbage.
This is Verdun,
horizon of barbed wires
lit with flares.
Shudder of mortar on both flanks, and now
down the dreamed line the repeated scream:
gas. My thick fingers,
my mask unstraps slowly and heavily from my pack,
a fumble of straps,
buckles, tubes.
I try to hold my breath,
and now the mask is on,
smells of leather and honeysuckle vomit.
The poison smoke
drifts into the trenches,
settles, my neck
strains to hold up the mask.
I will.
Behind this pane of isinglass
I am ready,
my bayonet fixed for the first black shape
to fill trenchlight above me and fall.

I know that all my life one
German soldier has plunged toward me
over the bodies of the lost.
I am ready for him.
We are both wearing masks,
and only one of us will live.

>   William Heyen
>   Brockport, NY
>   Sept. 1, 1975

[#2: October 2, 1975-February 8, 1980]

10/2/75

I remember that I was being driven to Middletown. It was early last November, and the Connecticut autumn was wet but still shone yellow and red. Then there was a flash of recognition: looking to my right across a field, I saw a figure dressed in black walking against a line of woods. The person seemed to be wearing a gown, or graduation robe, but was too far away for me to see clearly. A few seconds later, we turned a corner and were in Bolton, driving past an old yellowish church. It was then I thought of Jonathan Edwards, and that this was Edwards country, these were the landscapes that sometimes, as he said, gave him "the idea of the taste of honey in [his] mind," and made him weep with love and adoration for his Lord. My host recited an old rhyme: "Bolton town, / strange people, / yellow church, / and no steeple." The church had no steeple, was sort of squared off: economics two hundred years ago, or non-ornamental piety?

Last night I was reading *Personal Narrative* again. This time my throat began to tighten from even his first paragraph, his uncertainty, his suspicion that some of the early light he felt was delusion, and from Satan—his constant theme. Later, his moments of deep peace and joy, sensible apprehension. I heard him mention, single out from other walks and other experiences, a time that must have been terribly important to him. He experienced, he said, certain deep hours: "particularly once at Bolton, on a journey from Boston, while walking out alone in the fields."

10/3/75

Word after word ("sovereignty," "affections"), line after line, reason and assumption after reason and assumption, image after image, Edwards' poetry (and it poured out of him, and had to) is stunning. His summary paragraph in "Sinners," this one, in which all the abstractions already have text behind them, in which his image reaches far back, surely, into his listeners' minds:

"The bow of God's wrath is bent, and the arrow made ready on the string, and justice bends the arrow at your heart, and strains the bow, and it is nothing but the mere pleasure of God, and that of an angry God, without any promise or obligation at all, that keeps the arrow one moment from being made drunk with your blood." --- Relentless, inexorable, rhythms of power, and the whole thing delivered steadily and level as he stared straight ahead of him, as the reports go. And that arrow must have terrified and disgusted Edwards' people—"being made drunk with your blood": even from the *Primer* drunkenness seen as vile and even Satanic, this arrow "being made drunk with your blood" must have been overwhelming even for those who had come to know the imagery of this poet of terror and glory.

Sun./Oct. 19

Today the four of drove out for dinner to Brighton with the Shapiros & with Patti & Jim Hancock. They are all old friends now, and it was a good time.

Had to use a car borrowed from Manny Mouganis: last Tues., Han was driving to Nashville to give her mother a lift to the hospital when she was pulled over, with three other cars, by a Trooper on the Thruway: as he was giving her a ticket for speeding, somehow the car in line behind her smashed into the back of our car: so, all's a mess, and we'd just had the car inspected & winterized & a new $45 battery: only 50,000 miles on our '68 Ford, and it was in fine shape & good for another 5 years: now we'll be offered way under what it's worth, I'm sure: well, we'll see: it might be time for the old whiplash trick: it's a pain in the ass, and we've no car and were 100% innocent & only wanted our car back: now we're getting angry & might get a lawyer....

Vanguard has actually accepted *The Swastika Poems* and is sending a contract. Early 1977 publication, a $750 advance—incredible, for a book of poems. Well, I do feel unworthy, do feel very strange to have written, I guess, another of these things called "books." But reading from it yesterday, I felt it to be <u>strong</u>, and I think I manage to read it "objectively" now, i.e., as though the "I" were someone I don't know.... Though I'm reluctant now to drown in the book any longer, I'll want, once or twice over the next 6 or 8 months, to get back into it, to get it just the way I want it, <u>maybe</u> to add a piece, <u>probably</u> to cut down the prose section. But the book is about done. Yesterday I found a spot for "The Trenches," I think, a strong poem but a WWI one, on the surface.

It may very well be that before this journal is filled up—it seems to have about a twenty-year heft—I will be entering sad tales of rejection, but right now I feel fortunate and blessed, among just ten or twenty poets with a definite publisher. And not only the Vanguard book coming up, but *American Poets in 1976* from Bobbs-Merrill in March, *Of Palestine: A Meditation* from Abbatoir/Cummington probably next year, and a small book probably to be called *Prose Dreams* from Perishable Press—these last two should be lovely things. I don't know how this has all happened. It was only eight or ten years ago when I was straining to get a poem accepted by a little magazine; now, invitations arrive often, and the thrill is about gone. Surely, it is not <u>all</u> a matter of merit and improvement. Still, so many young people would like to be where I am now, and won't get there, and many my age now who began as I did are still straining the same way and not getting closer even to their first book. Now the primary joy for me is to have done a poem like "Darkness" or "Cardinals" and to know it is a good one. Of course, this isolationist appreciation is probably only possible because my marketplace-reading-public-famehungry-statusseeking ego is satisfied in other ways, eh? As, it seems, at readings.

Han and I were at U. Maryland Oct 8—saw Dave Fraher & Carolyn Kizer & Rod Jellema (a sad man) and Ann Darr—and in Pittsburgh the next couple of days—Richard Wilbur, Sam Hazo, Gerald Costanzo, a guy by the name of Makuck, the beautiful Zimmer, Tony Petrosky, Jon Anderson, Ed Ochester, Bill McTaggart, Charles Simic—aah the world of poesy. The readings were good, Wilbur sort of distant as ever, Ernest Stefanik & Bill Lint & *The Mermaid* broadsides maybe the best part of the whole Carnegie show. My reading, I thought, good—I did include, after much worry, three of the *Swastika* pieces. And I found myself, all in all, getting <u>used</u> to the scene in a way I'm not sure I like. I was surprised that I was not moved by Wilbur's reading, not even when he read "Love Calls Us...." I'm surprised. Maybe it was that I was on the stage, & self-conscious. But I hope I do not lose that sense of wonder and love for the beautiful poem and for the man who has managed to live in the way that enabled him to write it. The whole country is filled with cynics, and I don't want to be one myself; at the same time, I will not struggle toward false enthusiasms. In truth, I've always suspected myself of this—when I allow the suspicion to surface to where I can catch it—in regard to Wilbur? I'm going to study his next book of poems, and decide some things for myself. This is difficult to enunciate for myself, but important for me. But it's something like this: I feel there are all sorts of riches and moving experiences in those (long) Stafford books on my shelves, that should I have the time, there is so much there for me, so much to breathe; I don't feel this way right now about Wilbur's books, or about the new poems he read; I do feel this way about James Wright's books and about the poems I had the <u>privilege</u> of hearing last July.... What does this all ramify?

10/26/75

Mirko, Bill Rock, Lou Hetler, Joe Winnick, and Manny are coming over in about a half-hour for a poker game. I pace around restless until the game begins and I can start picking up cards. Last Thursday at Chuck

Lang's on the Lake I won about $190. The game before I won about $185. So, I've had a good streak, somehow, though I've not felt particularly lucky.

A clear and bright day today. I was on the roof this morning, cleaning leaves out of the gutters and putting the cover on the air conditioner over the garage. I sat for a while on the higher house roof and looked out over the scene that is this town, the college in the distance, the town's church steeples closer, the woods behind our homes along Frazier Street all ablaze, and people along the street mowing or walking. A sense of space here, and Indian Summer, and the feeling in the air that everything is all right. This evening, too, the stars all sharp white—if only this life could go on forever. But, of course, it can't, and I know that even before I finish this diary, I could be on the run, or in trouble or danger, and this could come from anywhere.

I was invited to apply for a Bicentennial Fellowship to England, so I've typed up a "project." If, by any chance, it comes through, I'll, we'll spend a few months over there. I think I would love that, as long as Han and the kids stayed healthy and happy with me over there. I've also applied for a Guggenheim. I hope that if I do somehow get some time away from teaching, I have the discipline and imagination to do something with it. That old idea of writing a novel is persistent with me. If only I could have one ready for publication soon after *The Swastika Poems* appears in 1977—this would give me the chance, this sort of sandwich, to become known. But I don't feel right now as though I <u>could</u> write a novel. But I know that it would be possible to enter a flow and to surprise myself.

Three lines left to this page and not an image in mind. But I was reading Jeffers' *Letters* again, and Mark Van Doren or Anne Ridgeway mentions that Jeffers waxed absolutely poetic in his letters about his inability to write letters, and perhaps during the next 300 pages I could achieve some of this about this journal. And now it is page 6, #6, and perhaps I'll hit a 6 with 2,3,4,5 in my hand in a big game of double-draw. The players about to enter. The light of this journal dims. The stage is set. The play soon begins.

11/2/75

Yesterday I was 35. Gatherings with friends, family warmth. All is well. I should, I suppose, have serious thoughts about such a serious age, but I don't.

Poker game again tonight. At Mirko's. Emmanuel picking me up in twenty minutes, and Han will come, too, to keep Irma company and work on the quilt she's making. I've been winning quite a bit, $92 at the game mentioned above on this page, and $77 in a small game since then. Mirko winning more. Emmanuel and Bill Rock losing, and the others losing as usual. I've been restless lately, and would rather play poker than do anything else, it's true. Haven't written anything in a while, partly maybe because, and this <u>is</u> the one serious thought I have now that I'm 35, my life is so easy and comfortable; my poems have usually come from various strains. I don't like this, but it's true. I want it to be true that poems come at easy times, but they usually haven't; from Cortland to Athens to occasions in Germany to Brockport to Nashville, they have come when I was busiest & most anxious and thus <u>aware.</u> Well, and this bleeds into the problem that Snodgrass describes about the poverty in this country of a poetry of maturity. But I would rather be happy, which I am, than write poems, if these things are exclusive. But I may be exaggerating all this, and with a 3rd book done and ready to appear in a year or so I may just be relaxing. Enough on this.

I have other thoughts, but Emmanuel is about to pull in. I hope I break even: I need the money.

11/7/75

Unbelievably warm weather for November. In the 70's today. Walked around in the warm air this evening in a drizzle. Had to step over worms sliding along Frazier St. by the millions. When I mentioned this to Billy just now, he was disappointed he hadn't gathered some. He's been fishing the Canal lately and catching large suckers and small bass.

I didn't break even in that last game. I lost $125, but two nights ago I won $310. Played all night with Nelson Algren, who read that night at the Forum. He's a fine man, and played well enough among all the sharks to lose very little.

Han and I are going to Burlington up in Ontario tomorrow with Helen & Manny. We'll stay overnight with Lily & Alice, those incredible Greek women, & play cards for small stakes and laugh a lot and I'll drink some ouzo.

Paul Zimmer called and I'll be reading 6 or 8 manuscripts by people who have already published books with Pittsburgh. Jesus, what passion & desire is riding on those manuscripts I can imagine. Books by Minty & Herb Scott included. I've already read one by Thomas Rabbit that I can respect but not believe in or like. I'm supposed to rank them, & Paul says they'll be able to do maybe two. I don't know. Those books, I do know, are so important to their writers—Judith has told me about the rejection of her manuscript last year & hinted that at one point after the Festival in Michigan she'd thought of ending it; and, I know I'm going to like Herb's book—so, or but, I'm going to strain like hell to somehow name the best books to Paul. The fact that I am a reader will never come out, anyway. That's much for the better.... I'm worried, as I should be, about my ability to read & judge, but, Christ, who wouldn't be? I'll do my honest best. Am I, suddenly, part of the goddamned "establishment"?

I still feel too comfortable, middle-class, lazy, successful to write anything good, but things will change, maybe with the weather when & if. Right now I'd rather play poker.

11/12/75

I've been having fun sending out the Rook Press postcard of my "Dream Song." It's a good way to make up for letters I should have written.

Shreela Ray reading at the Forum tonight. Guess I'll walk up. She's been wanting to read here for years. The audience, I'm sure, will be scant, & she'll be nervous. I've always liked her, and have felt sorry for her. The story is that years ago Galway broke her heart....

We're still walking, but hope to have the old Ford soon.

I've been doing junk. Jesus, 13 letters of recommendation to different law schools for Jason Poliner now! I feel like telling him to cease and desist.

We had tremendous winds yesterday. This house, though, is bolted down, and I bet the wisteria vines along the garage help to anchor us, too. Anyway, I find myself waiting for winter & snow & sharp, clear air in my lungs.

11/15/75

Spent the day reading and dreaming about Marion Starkey's *The Devil in Massachusetts*. Came to the point where the younger Ann Putnam, years after she'd cried out against the "witches," including especially old Goody Nurse, stood up in church to be accepted within the flock of a new minister who strained to bring them together, and I choked up. Ann said, "And particularly as I was chief instrument of accusing Goodwife Nurse and her two sisters, I desire to lie in the dust and be humbled for it...." All too deep for tears. Ignorance and superstition so inevitable.... It is a powerful book, filled with words that bloom on my tongue, like its Salem's blue September asters, "smoky blue," she says: "red paragon," "garboils," "besom," "spadefoot frogs." I'd like to work up a poem. Maybe "The Tall Man of Boston?"

The movie *The Great Gatsby* begins with a Carraway spech, and now Nick is speaking to Tom Buchanan. I'll watch.

11/18/75

I have been mainly confused lately, but no, not. It is all of this noise, television, kids, domestic talk, phone calls, trucks, neighbors—the buzz of being in this time and place. And my life goes by. And I cannot hope to write what might otherwise be written. Unless I change my life. I know this. I know it does not have to be a radical change, divorce or flight; but it will have to involve the discipline, again, of work that I had years ago, and it will have to involve quiet, when available.... This has been on my mind for a long time, but what brings it up directly is an article today on Ted Hughes in *APR*. Yes. Something hard & rough & real. Something that knows, digests everything, & survives. Something that goes under. And my movement toward that hard poem actually has a start in *The Swastika Poems*, but the last couple of weeks I find myself pecking away at the softer left-over things, prose pieces like "The Pearl" and "The Bell," and poems like "This Father of Mine." If I could put them together, do a small book, and get them out of the way. Then, maybe, I could get on to wherever it will be.... Now I have to & want to see the 76 book into print, *Of Palestine* into print, must read manuscripts & do some readings & make that trip next summer. But, I think to myself today, maybe January 1, 1977 will be the day. Maybe. Can I, and in my Nordic way I need this, can I prepare and clear away and work toward this. I can begin that new life as I stopped smoking, as hard a thing as I've ever had to do. I will <u>not</u> have to deny my family or lose what is best and fortunate in this life. But I will need discipline, much exercise & control, and freedom from the warm-water companionship of television.... All in all, so far so good in my desire to become a <u>poet</u>—there, I have said it; but there is no question that within recent sloth & comfort I have been losing some kind of necessary <u>edge</u>. But I am aware of this, at least, and this awareness via Snodgrass & Hughes & others may be something new, necessitated by the 20th-century.... I <u>feel</u> I know what I need to do. This is the important thing, and not my rational articulation of it. All right, then, resolution. I will follow through where I am for now, father of young children, suburban husband, but that's not all there must be. I will need to work late & hard again. The time will come. I believe it will. The will that wrote those 3 books won't let itself down like this.

11/19/75

I will not read over the last entry until I finish this one, but what I felt is true and serious. Right now the kids are watching television again—it's 7:30 in the evening—and the dishwasher is swishing and rumbling upstairs. There never seems to be any damned quiet. Today in an afternoon class, I could hardly again hear myself think, what with a filmtrack coming through the walls, and a rattling radiator, and noise from the street and from the hall. I'm becoming more sensitive to this pollution all the time. No simple answer. But quiet is a necessity. Maybe, it occurs to me, I will start spending time in the library, but it would be lamentable to have to leave my own home which, after all, I'm sure, is quieter than most.

Christmas, 1975

It is almost midnight. Han and I are up in the kitchen. She's working with her new plate block album, mounting the blocks. It was what she wanted for Christmas, and she's going to have a beautiful collection.

I walked around the block this evening in a light snow—I've not been particularly sentimental, but have been happy. We are all healthy, if a bit frazzled by the usual Christmas rush. The Picciones, the most harried people in the world, stopped by yesterday with their kids, & Sandi promptly ran out to McDonalds for hamburgers though we wanted to feed them all. We were happy they stopped by, but it is always a scene beyond description. Tony, the individualist, would be amazed to know that he's exactly the person Thoreau is trying to save. He & Sandi make $25,000 a year, and never have any money. He has a farm & even a cabin on a pond, but can't stay at home, driven out by kids or his own restlessness. MacLeish will write an introduction to a volume of Tony's poems that Al Poulin will publish—I know this won't lift Tony's spirits for long. And what a sideshow (or, because Han & I seem to be audience, theatre in the round) the Poulin-Piccione relationship is!

Al, Boo, & Daphne were here for dinner today and all was very pleasant, Al sounding better than ever, knowing he has to curb his driving ambition to be happy, knowing he has to learn to slow down without feeling guilty. There's no question but that Han and I are much more comfortable around the Poulins than the Picciones. I hope Al will be all right. Next semester he'll have to deal with his own work, with a regular teaching schedule in the English dept., and with the demands of this crazy conglomerate of a press he's beginning.... The 29th we'll all get together—that should be a laugh—at the farm in Kendall. Tony & Patti Petrosky will be visiting from Pittsburgh. I like them.

A few evenings ago we had Rocks, Mouganises, Pylyshenkos over for drinks and slides of past parties and Christmas carols around the player piano and a late snack and poker. It was a warm gathering, and we all parted glowing.

Also, egads, the 27th Han & I will have the neighborhood party here, about 30 people. I actually look forward, and I know there will be many laughs. We've got kazoos ready for Ross Wicks & Pete DeToy, who had a fight last lyear.... O dear diary, my friend—for I have still after ten years found no voice, no audience for this journal—I list all these things to give a sense of the Heyens' suburban Christmas, whatever your impression may be.

I thought I had ambition to write a long entry, even, maybe, to enter the poem "The Chestnut Rain" which I seem to have finished. One of these days I will. One of the things that has relieved me immensely in regard to all my laments about time/noise/privacy, is that I did work on and finish a little book—17 poems & 7 prose pieces—called *The Chestnut Rain*. Have sent it to Vanguard, and then will send it maybe to a small press, or will just hold to it.

For Christmas Han got me a beautiful bookcase that Pete Mosher shipped over from England. About 7 ft. high, leaded-glass doors. Lovely. And she surprised me with a <u>signed</u> first edition of *The Lost Son*. It even has a dustjacket. A book I'll treasure, will learn from—I've learned a bit from it <u>today</u>, the way its poems feel as it stands alone, the tendril-like form on the jacket, Roethke's careful early signature—and will save for the future.

12/30/75

It's the morning after. Han's not well after the Picciones' party. She doesn't drink, but we were up late in all that smoke, and she's been terrifically busy. So, she's resting, & has kept down a cup of peppermint tea I made her....

And the heating man downstairs has just put in a new something to stop a leak, maybe a new circulator, and I just wrote a check for $52. And the other day a guy came to fix the pilot light on the stove--$18 for a minute's work. Yes, I know where I am here in the middle of the machines in the middle of the garden. I'm all right. I know this plastic despair, I mean the plastic and motor source of the empty purse & empty spirit. I'm all right, have enough money and enough humor, and when the time comes that I haven't, then I'll do without, as will I hope my children, if they have to, will do without, when the future becomes again the oil stove or coal stove in the rude kitchen.... Another way in which the future will remind us of the past.... And Bonnie Stewart was just here to pick up a punchbowl & a coffee-maker for her party tomorrow night—I hope we'll miss it!... But I am going to make 1/ a poetry out of this suburbia and 2/ a poetry despite this suburbia.... The pair of cardinals outside again this morning, clean & pure in their world as we are not in this world of cucumber-onion dips & whiskey punch & the goddamned cigarette-cigar smoke that covers everything. Still, I walk this lot and the outside air is clean and cold, blowing down from Ontario.... Hard to believe, though, the kind of life flowing within this entry: the water-meter man was just here to read the meter, upstairs Kristen is tooting her clarinet, & in the next room Billy, who is just back from basketball practice, is watching a game show on television. This is a time when I'll have to call on my maturity. Thank God that somehow I have written enough—*Swastika*, *Palestine*, *Chestnut*—to keep me alive for a while.... Unbelievable: the milkman is here....

1/2/76

I'm watching *Where the Lilies Bloom* downstairs with Kristen, my sweet little daughter, whose eyes have been wet since the opening. I love her. I still hardly know what to make of life, cannot help the children understand death, can only live and make them want to live and believe that we just keep going. Once in a while something poignant or dark happens around here, and there are bad things coming—deaths of grandparents. We will go on, I tell them.

A little ¶ & a little nudge: reading so much Thoreau & Whitman again, I felt I knew of an afterlife, dreamily conscious, of some kind.... Last night I walked around the block, at ease, but the stars <u>were</u> ice-cold up there. We keep going, with small satisfactions:

Poetry took "Fires." Important poem for me, and I'd rather have it there than anywhere. *Ohio Review* took "The Swastika Poems" and "Passover: The Injections"—so, the poems from *The Swastika Poems* are being picked up pretty quickly.

Irma & Mirko having a big dinner for the 4 couples on Sunday. Han & I look forward. Tomorrow Chris Kayser coming over & we'll trade German stamps. Next Thursday I'll take a bus—a 10-hr. trip—to Middlebury. Much time to think....

Time to take down the Christmas tree again.

I like filling up the page with news-notes, & will.

Tom Wittenberg called. *American Poets in 1976* on its way, & will be advertised, it seems. I hope it makes some money, but will have a long way to go to make up pre-payments of $6,000.

Finished the Mss-reading job for Paul Zimmer. Believe Herb Scott's *Groceries* was the best, most finished. I will love John Engels' book more when it's finished. Judith Minty—well, good, somehow "artsy-craftsy," rarefied, poetic. The other 4 books not very interesting to me, even Den Boer's.

Fine letter from Tom Woll today. I'm feeling (am I?) secure at Vanguard.

Bob Phillips writes that he won a CAPS grant. I'm happy for him.

Read a few Sherwood Anderson stories this morning, including "The Corn Planting." Lovely & deep. I got an idea for a little sketch I'm planning, started to write it, and the phone rang. So, this is the way it still is, but now that the report for Zimmer is in the mail, and I have no other pressing projects, I feel pretty much at ease.

Was in the back with the iron rake yesterday, busting up ice in the ditch, & looked up from the whiteness across our back yards—everything black & white, trees & snow—and realized how stark & beautiful a winter day can be.

Bill Stewart stopped over today. He's realized, too, that he's got to do his work at home. I wonder if he needs quiet. After the designs, is it all technical?

1/5/76

Monday, today, and Christmas really over, and Kristen home from her first day of school with the flu. So it goes.

The dinner was all right last night, but I got aggravated (ww) with Rock, again, his drunken ravings about starting/not starting a poker game with the wives, whether he & his were leaving or not, etc., etc. So Han & I left about 10:30, though we really wanted to play, and then that fucking Rock stuck around and probably played! I may hate the bastard, all these years of bullshit that I can't help swallowing and that always gives me a stomach-ache, as I have now, just thinking of it. But he's also heading for much trouble, the poor fellow, with his drinking day-in and day-out, and needs help.... Anyway, I stood up and read and wrote until 5 in the morning, did the sketch called "The Pool" I wanted to do, so ...

A ring-necked pheasant male and two females were strutting out in back this morning. I'm afraid all the sunflower seeds I put on a board yesterday were eaten by the squirrels our feedings have drawn. Today I'll spread the seeds widely, throw out a whole bag. I'd like to buy that land out back, maybe throw a small mobile home in the middle of the trees & plant wisteria around it and have a place to go back to. I wonder who owns it. Giff Mosher knows, I think, and is watching over it. I think a woman owns it, and she's sick.

Much snow last night, and it's still snowing this morning.

Ha, whose journal was it, did I read, that was five hundred pages of weather?

Tree at my window, window tree.

1/11/76

After a few days away, and after a long eleven-hour bus ride, my return home yesterday was lovely, the kids and Han so glad to have me back. Christ I was cold, too, in Vermont, and I took a hot bath last night, and Han and I made love, and I ate a sandwich and had some hot soup, and slept. I am a lucky man. Today was a fine day, relaxing. Snow all day, no place I had to go, the kids over their colds.

I can confide to this journal that my reading at Middlebury was a great success. Much applause, enthusiasm. I heard again and again that the students were knocked flat, that it was a while before they could get up to leave the room. And old Doc Cook even told me that I said Frost's "To Earthward" beautifully.... It seems to me, ahem, that I give better readings than just about anyone else I can think of. Enough. It was very rewarding, and I read that maybe the reason symphony orchestra conductors live so long is that they get much applause and a subsequent sense of well-being. So, the reading added a year to my life.

Peter Stitt, my age, has been denied tenure there. A sad story. He's in for a rough ride on the job market, I'm afraid.

I read Emerson both going and coming. Will continue. There's so much.

Met Robert Pack, had a friendly lunch with him. Impressed him, I think, but the bastard, I just know, will never invite me to the Bread Loaf summer thing. Too bad. I'd love a couple of weeks up there.

I think I'll stand in the snow for a few minutes and then—it's midnight—go to sleep.

Thurs. 15th

I've had some of the best several days I've ever had. I've worked an hour or two mornings on *The Swastika Poems*, have walked for good distances in the snow, have enjoyed working with my books and stamps. I've enjoyed the kids, and nothing has disturbed my equilibrium. Tomorrow should be another good day. We even had a good lunch with the Poulins the other day, and today Al called to say his two days here with one of his Houghton-Mifflin editors went beautifully—10,000 copies of his anthology sold this past year, and HM Co. will publish, after the Rilke, a book of his poems. So, he's high and I wish him well. I've been very kindly disposed toward him lately, and lately Tony has spooked us both! Tony, who believes he is perfect, the only completely honest man in the world.... Never mind. I'm <u>loose</u> inside, and it feels <u>good</u>.... Elvis is on television now for 90 minutes: he's the greatest. Only in America.

1/18/76

I wrote out a poem called "The Circle" this morning. I think it's a good one. I want to try to leave it alone—did I ruin the one called "Christmas Shopping in a Small Town" by tinkering with it too much? This happens on occasion, though I keep the faith that some conscious rational tinkering <u>can</u> improve even those poems that come very quickly.

It has been <u>cold</u>. 4 below zero right now, and dropping. Kristen and Daphne Poulin were skating down the ditch all afternoon. They've got nice ice now, and it does my heart good to see a bit of suburbia become a skating rink this way.

Today was Super Bowl (#10) Sunday. The Steelers won, leaving Billy and Dallas groaning.

I've been working a little bit every morning on *The Swastika Poems*. This morning I think I solved the little problem of what will be the "Notes" section.

Han working with her stamps. I'm about to assist.

2/1/76

Helen & Manny & two of the three Greek sisters arriving soon for some poker—I won $130 the other night in a dollar-limit game—and maybe I have time for a few notes here.

Have written out "Mare," which looks good. Got lucky again. Ernest Stefanik likes "The Circle" & will do a special printing of it. Does my heart good. The broadside "Cardinals" arrived. As I signed the 250 copies, I first got to like it. At first, the cardinal's beak bothered me. I think Ernest will also do "The Cardinal."

Han & I went to the stamp show in the dome at Monroe County Fairgrounds yesterday. Han picked up some plate blocks, and I picked up some West Germany & Berlin stamps. I'm still casting around lfor the collection that will most interest me. I think Germany will be it, and I'll begin to accumulate many sets of certain issues.

School has begun and seems all right. Tomorrow I'll read some poems to the new course called "Literary Potluck," which is supposed to demonstrate different faculty interests/obsessions. Maybe I should talk about stamps?

Judith Minty visited for a day or so. We talked little about poetry, took a long walk, discussed her problem with the rejection from Pittsburgh (egads, I didn't let on—Paul Zimmer called to say "sorry, man," a dozen times when he heard Judith was visiting!), got together for Michigan Rummy with the Poulins until 5 in the morning. We all laughed like hell, & I drank much ouzo. I don't know about Judith's poems. They're Poems; maybe that's the problem—POEMS. Exotic subjects & diction. They're too-too, and too often so.

2/15/76

A lazy Sunday. Very windy, very rainy all day. The four of us went out to dinner, to Lista's, the place where Han & I went on our first date, I guess about 17 years ago.

Finished another book on Germany today, this one on Weimar.

I've actually sold 3 boxes of letters under my desk to Boston U. for $2,500, a figure I quoted (out of my hat) to Gotlieb. A miracle—I'm glad to get all that stuff off my hands. I've kept the letters in my file, & those I'd laid into books. A miracle. Hope the boxes arrive in Boston safely! We'll be able to save the money for the kids, their college expenses being our only real financial worry.

Of the $316 we pay for mortgage (including taxes) every month, $40 is against the principal now. This sounds slight, but is much better than it was, and will get better.

John Irwin at *Georgia Review* turned back the poems from *The Swastika Poems* I'd sent him. Wonder what I can do with them. I'm thinking of trying *APR*, but maybe will stay away, because of Poulin's connection, & because maybe it would cloud my relationship with Steve Berg—I wrote him about *Grief*— quite a book. Don't know. It's not urgent. How could "Darkness" have been turned down by several magazines now?

Still working on "The Chestnut Rain." Have added a section.

Wrote a long letter to Arthur Oberg, but letters are getting to be a real drag. I think of myself as lazy, as becoming unexcited about "the literary life," unenthusiastic, but maybe it's good if I stay with the poems. I'll probably not fill up three boxes with letters again.

I was up drinking a couple of nights ago until 4 in the morning with Rod Parshall & Steve Bird & several students after an English Club party. About once a year this happens, & it's okay. I'm probably just discrete enough to stay out of trouble.

The television buzz getting to me again, & the kids will be off from school all next week. I'll stay cool, I hope.

Could use a good poker game. Mirko's been out of town, the rest of us pursuing our phantoms.

Back to *Kojak*.

3/3/76

A Wednesday, and I've been in bed all day. Missed school yesterday, and will tomorrow. Have had aches, pains, all the miseries of the flu. Haven't been sick in a long time. Can't complain. Have been thinking, in fact, of worse days, as in Athens. I am secure here in my downstairs study, couch pulled out, surrounded by books, pampered by Han. I'm a lucky man. It's no damned fun being sick. I'd forgotten what it was like, had lost the power of sympathy, to which I now hope to hold. Absences at the college have been very high. Billy's been home sick too—he was happy that today the local schools were closed because of the ice-storm. So it goes.

Had a quick call last week from brother Henry, back in this country again, due at his new assignment in Nebraska this week already. The four Heyen boys seem scattered, are scattered. Ed & I are the closest, but don't get together. Werner & I are really the closest. We'll visit them for a week next summer. The four kids are so close, too.

Creeley screwed me by publishing his essay first as *Sparrow 40* without any acknowledgment. He knew exactly what he was doing, knew, for months I believe, he was going to do this, and just went ahead. As a person, he's a creep, nothing but trouble the four times I've seen him, and other times I've heard about.... I do wish that damned book would appear. An inquiry from Ignatow today. I've dropped some postcards around, but not in a systematic way.

I sent off some *Swastika Poems* to Ernest Stefanik, & won't do anything else. The book is done. Sunday I went to my office & read through the book again & saw that it was done and came home after an hour and a half. Mss. ready to go back to Tom Woll.

There's a little place, #162 Barry St., that I've had my eye on for years, a little cinder-block place—no driveway, surrounded by trees, only a block away. Finally, Han tracked down the owner—the snow never seemed broken around the place—and I called him & wondered if he'd be interested in selling. He lives near Cortland, and may. It would be wonderful to have a place to walk to, just for writing, during the busiest time of the day—no phone or television or doorbells. Maybe it could save me, in the long run.

3/24/76 (Wed.)

Not much to enter here. The weeks are flying by, and I am in about the same place—the way things feel now.

Finished, yesterday, "The Chestnut Rain." Haven't done much else lately. Too fat a cat?... Ernest Stefanik continues to be my man, my ace, wanting to do limited edition pamphlets & broadsides of my poems. I love this, and don't feel much like sending poems out to magazines these months. He & Cis, his wife, also want to do a Heyen bibliography! I told them for, maybe, my 40th birthday. I think I would like to see everything set down like that. Yes.

Fly to L.I. Sunday. 2 days at Post, an afternoon at Hofstra, an evening with Werner & Barbara in East Quogue, and two days in NYC, with an overnight at Bob Phillips, is the way it all looks.... Recent flattering invitation to read at Wesleyan this summer. Will read at Ohio University next month. Starting to feel I should get an invitation to go somewhere to write. No word on #162 Barry.

American Poets in 1976 is out next month.

Have found and bought, at last, first editions of *The Beautiful Changes* and *The Green Wall*.

Warm the past two days, and I've played basketball outside with Billy & the neighborhood boys.

Is my ambition waning (and is this good or bad?), or is my energy waning? Don't know. Seem generally content to go slower.

Guggenheim: NO. Even with Wright, MacLeish, Brinnin standing up for me. On to freshman composition!

I'm tired.

Another slice of tree ruined!

"Give me a field where the unmowed grass grows."

4/5/76

Sunday, and I got back Friday from the Island and New York City. For two full days now I've had a deep feeling of relaxation, as I'd feel for maybe a half-hour after a good night's sleep before this, but I haven't felt this calm for so long a time for as long as I can remember. The city really made an impression on me this time, the four trips by train to and from Katonah and the traffic and the pavement and well-dressed people driving themselves and the general anxiety and the dreary lives of the commuters and the waitresses. At home now in this small town, all the spring's trees budding, all the kids bicycling the streets, I feel so fortunate to live here. Several evenings ago, crossing at a busy corner in the city, I had a sudden realization of the insanity & misfortune of it all.... Well, rural boy is overwhelmed by city and happy to be home: a cliché of a story, for sure. But something happened, this time, that sent me home so happy to be here.

It was a good trip—except for one nutty class at Post that workshopped my poems carelessly & anonymously (with me in the room!), "Dog Sacrifice at Lake Ronkonkoma" read badly & then dismissed—"I don't understand it," three people said. Otherwise, the classes I attended were fine, & the Post reading (Mom & Pop & Werner & Barbara showed up & enjoyed themselves), & the lovely gentle & graceful workshop with

Arthur Gregor at Hofstra, & my visit with Bob to Gregor's place, meeting the Krapfs, visiting Bryant's grave at Roslyn & seeing Patchin Place in NYC, visiting the Vanguard offices again. And finding some books & seeing Burt Britton by accident at the Gotham, & keeping Bob company. So it went. So good to be home.

Skimmed *The Swastika Poems* with Tom Woll. The book is finished, and I'm glad. It will be slim and hard. Now I can go on.

So much to do. Have to round my classes into shape.... Heading to Athens with Picciones in a couple of weeks. Letters of recommendation to write, books to order for classes, yearly Dean's report to report. But I'm still relaxed, even now, as I write, down inside, and it's amazing. I imagine that some people always wear this serenity beneath the breastbone.

4/23/76

Rainy morning. Driving back from dropping Billy off at Brockport Bowl, past Stull Lumber, is a beautiful drive—down Park and over the Canal, the streets empty, the early green of spring—and I was thinking: A man writes, and the older he gets the more he turns to the general, the more his eye turns to idea—I was seeing the scene widely—rather than to the pure power of the particular. To a certain extent this is natural, I think, but to think this, again, is the idea of the older man, thinking.

5/8/76

Sat for a while this evening up by the canal while Billy fished. It's like sitting in a postcard—the old canal, the bridge, boys fishing, the old warehouse off to the right. I'd known this place was there, behind Market Street, have driven by thousands of times, but never really knew this place, this little part of my home town. Will return there often. America's first reapers were built there where I sat, O industrial America branching past and out of Brockport....

American Poets in 1976 has been out for two or three weeks now. It's a pleasure to hold it, to have it all between covers at last. Bobbs-Merrill did a beautiful job with it, first responses have been fine, and I believe it will sell for two or three years. I hope so. The trade book, it seems, will not be advertised or reviewed—I can get no response from the B-M trade division, but I'm confident that word on the paperback text is getting around.

Hannelore is a member of the Brockport Quilters, and for a couple of days she had at home their Brockport Bicentennial Quilt. It's beautiful & moving to me, with its squares of Hartwell's tower, the canal, the Morgan-Manning House, Soldiers' Monument, etc. I'm glad Han has her name on it, her hours in it. I hope it is on display at the Morgan-Manning house for the Tricentennial, too, and that even then a few people remember a few of my poems.

Mothers Day today. The four of us went up to Lista's for lunch. It's been a fine day. Kristen has been catching pollywogs all day in puddles out back. She's a joy.

Ernest Stefanik called about a hundred projects. He and I are going to be close from here on in.... *Cardinals/The Cardinal* should arrive this week, and another broadside or two. Joseph the Provider (Ralph Sipper) in California has ordered ten copies, Ernest says, of the little pamphlet for his next catalogue.... Nice letter from Wm. Ewert (who has taken 2 of any Heyen items from Ernest) who was, is, it turns out, a real collector, a Frost collector, and wants a complete Heyen collection.... From Ernest I just get (and am glad to) many copies of things, but I actually got $223 from Vanguard the other day, royalties on *Noise*, and I think there will be another check in six months for that book. Amazing, the way things are, that a book of my poems can make some money. The money feels good.... Next, *The Swastika Poems*, and it's finished, and I need only wait for proofs.... I've done one or two new poems lately, one called "The Light," and one about the one experience I had with madness, maybe to be called "Anthem," is just about done.... Have just seen Archibald MacLeish's foreword to Tony Piccione's book. He says, "There is Bill Heyen who has made a poet's country of Long Island where nobody else since Whitman has been able to see the fields for the houses." I love that man, profoundly; it's as simple as this.... Nice letter from Herb Scott. He & Shirley might visit us next month.... My folks have made it down to their new home in Florida now, & Wern & Barb say, too, that the old folks' trailer on Long Island is a fine one in a fine spot. So, maybe now they'll have the best of both worlds, and be content. They may be on the Island when we go down to visit Wern & Barb & kids end of June. A busy summer planned for all of us.... Just recovering from bad muscle pulls in my right leg, just able to walk again after days—softball injury, but I beat the hit out, says the old jock!... A day of prowess, indeed.

5/20/76 (Thurs.)

Sunday morning Tony Piccione had a breakdown. He was out on his farm in Kendall, Sandi had just gone to audition for a play at the college, and he went berserk. I've just heard fragments of everything: he tried to force himself on a baby sitter, threatened to kill his children, wanted his guns, screamed and danced and ate grass and took his pants off and lay in the road, pounded on cars, kicked people, was finally taken away in handcuffs. He's in Strong, and under close scrutiny. I've seen him twice, Han has seen him once, and he seems okay, like Tony, but his main psychiatrist does use the word "psychotic" when talking about him. We are all afraid (and, indeed, physically afraid of him—Sandi fears they will let him out too soon, and if so, she'll have to leave home with the children), baffled, exhausted. Barry Leeds flew in, incredible little-old-lady that he is, and stayed here three days, and I drove back and forth to hospital & airport. I'd worked hard reading journals, too, and now I'm tired & want to relax. Tony has deep-rooted problems, hates his father, is ambiguous about his mother, is obsessed with death, detests his fat body, wants to be the liberated man but wants his wife at home and wants to be feudal lord, loves people about as much as I do but professes all-embracing love for mankind. Han & I have just been finding out what horror it's been for Sandi the past nine years. He has often affected a kind of happiness among his friends while he's gone home and raged at his wife. It will take time, surely, for Tony to make it to where he'll be okay. I don't know. I suppose we all should have seen it coming, but he was becoming so eccentric that almost nothing seemed strange. I have many other things on my mind about all this, but they are no doubt all too simplistic.... Otherwise, I'm all right. I need some time now, and have it.

Much joy lately for me with the things Ernest has been sending. *Cardinals/The Cardinal* arrived, and three broadsides: *Pickerel*, *Dusk*, and *The Trench*. Also, the Folio of 12 broadsides (of which *Cardinals* is a part) illustrated by Bill Lint. And he called and we had a long talk about all sorts of things. From now on I'm going to send my poems mainly to Ernie.... Have finished one called "Our Light" that I think is good, and I think I've finished "Anthem," though I've been looking for a better word for "opened." "Anthem": and I'm back to Tony.

Sometimes I've cared very much for him, and sometimes have been infuriated with him, his selfishness and moral righteousness. Should I be more grief-stricken than I am? I am what I am. I'm worried about him (for himself & his family, and for me & mine), but am not crazy about driving into Rochester often to see him. Well, this is all right, and he needs his doctors anyway. Sandi tells me to call, but Tony has always hated the phone anyway, and I told him to call me anytime. So it goes.

Helen & Manny leave next week for Greece and will probably be away till about December. We'll sure miss them. I hope they stay healthy.

5/24/76

Will see Tony again tomorrow. He's okay, has been okay, in general, since the bad scene.

Han's folks left today. Pshew, they talk loud & much, but it was generally a good weekend.... We went with them to the alumni dinner where I got an award, & they liked it.

Weather still bad, but I brought two more trees from the back to our property line, a maple and an ash. Hope they & the ones from last fall all take.

Wacky letter from Joe McElrath today. Wants me to be a nature writer and not, as he says, a fag like Ashbery.

Misquoted article on me & 76 book in *Democrat & Chronicle* today, but at least it was readable & meant well. Why can't people hear what's being said? I know what I said, and what comes back is usually some kind of mush.

Ali vs. Dunn fight on tonight from Munich. Jesus, what a battle!

The most sexual smell I have ever smelled is the flowering mountain ash this time of year—heavy, sickly sweet, disgust & wonder, an intensified honeysuckle, bloody period and perfume at once, the smell I imagine ambergris has.

Han's mother told a story about how their dog acted when they were dropping him off at the kennel. The big St. Bernard is a clown. Then she told the story again, and again. And this morning again. It's as though certain experiences so delight & reverberate that we keep saying them, angling in on them, maybe with different words & rhythms, but keep them at recall & want to share. Like those ponds of my childhood, the slime & scum & the sleek black backs of snakes in the water. I will try them again & again in poems. "The Return," and then years later "Pickerel." And other images: the bells of "Somewhere, Another Continent" and "Anthem." The deer of "The Deer" and "Our Light." But this just scratches the surface. Blue.

Went over to say goodbye to Helen & Manny tonight. They leave in the morning.

Card from Bob Gemmett today, who says Edinburgh reminds him of Brockport. I trust he jests.

5/31/76

Memorial Day today. A slow rain fell all day. We've had a nice day at home.

Tony home from hospital over the weekend—we were with them over at Poulins last evening, another dreary gathering—and tomorrow will go back to Strong to sign himself out, I understand. He tells me, in his suffocating way, that he feels wise now. He's the same Tony. I hope he'll be all right, will not break down again, will be his impossible self.... Han and I are still uncomfortable around those four people, who strain so hard to be "cool." And I'm tired of driving back & forth to the fucking hospital for my soi-disant friends.

Taking much pleasure in my new row of trees. There are eleven now, all but two ash. And the line is straight. Should I take it out to the road? There's a chance we'll be able to buy (from Giff Mosher, who hopes to buy the whole piece out back) the land behind our property, and maybe behind Vallones'. Oh, we'd love this! I'd put up a fence & spend years putting in lawns & rows of trees. That's all we'd ever want. I could even have a little shack back there, if I want. Fingers crossed.... In anticipation, I've planted in a flat about fifty red maple seeds from the little tree in front. I've got time, & it would be a pleasure watching them grow for the next twenty years. I'm not sure, though, how to start these seeds, have tried to imagine the wings spinning the seed to earth (are there one or two in each wing-nut?) and have only stuck them into the dirt shallow, the wings protruding. Should I have let the seeds dry? Well, I'll see. I've had a green thumb all my life. Also have a bunch of seeds in a jar of water. Maybe this will start them. The crimson maple is absolutely beautiful.

Always get a little nervous (about nothing) when I do nothing literary. Want to begin reading *The Freedom of the Poet* soon, & do that review for Ernest.... Am working on a rhymed poem about my father's father's drowning, the whole thing, almost, imagined.

We're having a big party, gulp, Saturday.

6/6/76

The big party was a disaster, as far as I'm concerned. Han is angry that I began playing poker with Bill & Mirko around midnight—I lost $95, but I've won three times these last couple months—didn't even say goodbye to guests. She's right, I guess, but how did it happen that we had a party (for a fucking 2 week trip the Gemmetts took) and had so many people over that I despise or am just absolutely bored by, from Gerber (the former) to Maier (the latter). Egads, what deadheads & assholes most of my colleagues are. It's true. It's true. That's why I wasn't more gentlemanly, I suppose. And my resolve, today, is to learn from this horseshit, to become more selfish, to stay home and stop straining to be more than cordial with such nerds. Paul Fergusson! Charles Napravnik! I must be crazy. And all because, really, Gemmetts sent us some flowers for our cabin on the *Bremen* years ago. Shit, I'll learn. Enough is too much. And because of all this I feel low today. No more. No more of these damned parties. I am so happy just to be at home. Also, Han worked like a dog—making me feel guilty—preparing food & cleaning etc., etc—for a few days getting ready. No more. Han thinks I've been too selfish. Hell, my resolve is to become more selfish. No more of this social nonsense! Enough.

I just about finished "The Ash" this morning. It's strong, one of my best, I think.

Phoenix vs. Boston in game 6 is about to start. Game 5, triple-overtime, was amazing.

Ernest called yesterday, and we had a long talk about most things. Now there's a guy I want to visit, someone to talk to about the things most important to me.

Billy's fishing, Kristen's playing with Daphne. Tony & Sandi were here last night, & it was good for Tony to put in an appearance, I'm sure.

6/8/76

Last night I hurt my right leg again playing softball, but not before I had two hits in two at-bats as DH. Felt good, and we won 4-0. It takes <u>experience</u> to hit those line drives in slow-pitch, indeed it does. Don't know about this goddamned leg of mine. Another game tomorrow night, and two on Friday. Don't know if I can play. In just two weeks we fly to Long Island for a week. The kids can't wait to get into Werner's new pool.

Got in mail today from Archibald MacLeish his new *Collected Poems*, inscribed at length. Such a pleasure to have such a book. Also, *Pembroke Magazine* arrived. My essay reads well, I think.

Went over to the high school today for Kristen's 4th Grade band concert. Kristen was cute, and was introduced as first clarinet. Parents proud, and even brother Billy. The four of us went out for ice cream later. I got home just before dark, in time to water the trees. The last couple of days have been hot and clear.

Presidential primaries over today, Reagan taking California, as expected, from Ford, Carter taking Ohio by more than expected. The conventions will be dogfights, it looks like.

6/13/76

Sunday. An hour or so ago Shirley & Herb Scott (and son Wally) left. They'd arrived from Toronto yesterday, are on their way to Boston where Herb will be in a seminar with Helen Vendler this summer.... Their visit was short, but exhausting, as always. Han again worked too hard, dinner & breakfast & beds, and I don't like this.... They're good folks. I didn't tell Herb that I was the reader for *Groceries*.

Literary talk, literary talk. And I showed off my book collection. And Herb & I talked about who is where, and how to sell books—that sort of thing. Do I rave on about such things because this is me and I care, or because it seems to be the thing to do, gossip & laugh & compare notes & paranoias & laments? Why do I feel drecklich after such a visit? I do not <u>want</u> to be this kind of person, clutching at straws from here and there that tell me my reputation waxes. But I guess I am; and I guess, with the 76 book, I've entered the arena, am not back in the woods effecting image as hermit, uncaring recluse, am in the arena where I will be talked about as salesman/businessman. What do I want? I want to be known (did I just shy from "famous"). I want to be known, but I want to be a man (and want to want being this man) who minds his business, does not enter the scramble. I want to be on hand when I arrive (as the Wilbur poem goes) as a <u>man</u>, not as some sort of fucking wheeler and wheedler. I feel <u>public</u> and don't want to be but do live in the suburbs & do teach literature & do collect books & do get pissed off as Wakoski & Simic et. al. keep winning prizes & giving prestigious readings. Well, what the fuck is wrong, and can I change my life, my being? These kinds of dilemmas: I wait for mail, & get it, and then answer, and then regret that I spend time answering mail, & wait for more, & think that some letters, as from young "poets" I don't know, or "whackos," should just be ignored, and think on the other hand that I should be gentlemanly enough to answer all letters, & it goes on, nothing ever quite satisfying....

Already I feel better. Billy & 4 friends were just here for a game of "trump." I lost, but that's the kind of real, domestic rhythm—<u>my</u> world. Hmmm.... I don't know what it is. I want to think well of myself, and <u>don't</u>, when I engage in "making it." But I do not want simply to bury or repress my urges in that direction; I want to lose them, & direct my energies into living my life/writing. But it's not this simple. For one thing, I want to be aware of what is going on. For another, I am alive and human, and fine poems and ambition are not necessarily exclusive of one another.

Perhaps I can live with my foibles, and tone down, discipline myself in company (a kind of repression) and letters to stop <u>chattering</u> about nothing, about crap, stop <u>advocating</u>. I sense I know what I mean now.

I have an opportunity like few of my contemporaries. There's Ernest, at Rook Society, to do about anything I want—he called the other day to say *XVII Machines* could be done letterpress, & some copies hardback, e.g.—and (probably) Vanguard every several years. I can mind my business & let others advocate, even apply for grants, etc., in a relaxed, low-key, low-profile manner. I sense I know what I mean.

It is, too, the time: men of sensitivity & talent praising shit, assholes attacking fine poets, poets being ignored because the community is looking for the next hotshot's first book—and, above all, the great American haze of ignorance & apathy. Enough.

I'm happy again, in my chair, Han & the kids swimming, the phone off the hook, a tennis match coming up on television, maybe a letter to Ernest to write, or a Berryman essay to read. All right.

6/16/76

I've just about finished another poem, one called "Witness." It's strong, I think. I love the rhapsodic, the repetition, even (gulp) rhetoric, a rolling rhythm & sound. It's what I want to do. And I keep in mind Stafford's shock at Auden's worry that he was repeating himself. This is not what Stafford has in mind in regard to the nature of art. And if I am back with Wenzel and the curve of light again, and if I roll into a very rhythmical long-line conclusion again, so what? This is what I want to do, & the poem is another part of a gradual discovery & a gradual updating of feelings to now. Come to think of it, "Wenzel and the Curve of Light" would be a fine title for another poem.

Ernest called last night to tell me Sam Hazo was upset about being left out of *American Poets in 1976*. Spare me! But this is all part of the choice I made, part of what I knew would happen when I went public. I'm secretly thankful, though, for all those poets I asked who said no or didn't answer. I think, had they known what the book would become, they would have done essays.

Al back, & he & Daphne & Boo stopped over.

The big food delivery is tomorrow. Much work.

6/19/76

The last several days have gone by the way my life should. I worked on "Witness" for an hour today, but that was about it. I even avoided literary talk when Al was here. Softball game this evening—I sat the bench but got tired enough just in workouts. Home to a cup of coffee & tucking the kids in. No bullshit. If, for example, Tony had stopped in today and if, again, I strained to talk about <u>something</u> during his silences, my day would have been fucked up again. I am 35 years old now, a serious age, and should be old enough to simplify. I have <u>wailed</u> to this diary lately, and the thing is that all the materials I need for my happiness & peacefulness are right here—the family, my study, luck on an occasional poem, a letter or book in the mail. Right now—it's about one in the morning—I'm tired and <u>really</u> content & will drop off soon, falling to sleep immediately. Then, what does this say about what does upset me when something does? Something about people. I want distance—not from Han & the kids or from Wern & Barbara (I love them & can't wait to see them next week)—but from the Picciones, yes, & the Poulins, yes, & other assorted assholes. This is not supposed to be the communal American song-of-the-open road impulse. It's not Whitman, anyway. But Thoreau knew, & Lawrence knew. Jeffers' was an entirely different context, but "Distance makes clean." I can <u>still</u> have my anthology & my books & my literary life, can have everything, as long as I avoid my neurotic acquaintances. And, shit, Al and Tony are just fooling around. "The Ash" & "Witness" are damned deep & fine. I can't help either one of them or, say, even Bob Phillips, a dearer friend. I'm even glad that <u>he's</u> too far away & busy to visit us. It was good, the rupture of my friendship with Jerry, who'd visit a few times a year & made me miserable, too. Yes, people. Spare me!

6/21/76

I think that's the date. Anyway, it's the first day of summer, a rainy Monday, and I'm home alone—Han at sewing, the kids in school—and don't feel like doing anything.

The morning after my last entry Tony stopped over. His mother in Texas had had a heart attack and he was about to train down there—he's afraid of airplanes—to see her. He's there now, & will stay until Wednesday, I guess. A bad time for him now, and I'm sorry. But when he stopped in he said several times that he didn't know what life means & went on in this dreary vein again.

I'm trying to finish typing up that whole list of my books by Thursday, when we'll leave for the Island. The kids are excited about our trip already, as I am.

Leg still hurting, but I played soccer with a bunch of kids yesterday and it's not getting any worse, so ...

Wonderful surprise the other day. That guy Bill I wrote in Michigan last summer <u>did</u> bind the Roethke <u>Profile</u> and <u>The Mower</u> in ¼ leather & boards. They're beautiful.... And good old Ernest is making plans to do a beautiful letterpress job on *XVII Machines*—some copies to be hardbound. The book will be too good for the poems within. But, so what?

Called Bobbs-Merrill to find out why, after two months, I couldn't get my 6 hardback copies of *Am. Poets in 1976*. Tom's secretary told me the 1st hardback printing was sold out, that she couldn't remember that this ever happened so early before. The bastards have not taken advantage of what that hardback could have been. I'm sure they only did one or two thousand at first. I'm glad they sold out, but I don't have one myself, and will be both pleased <u>and</u> pissed off if, when mine come, they are marked "2nd printing."

Called the folks in Florida yesterday, Fathers Day—they hate it down there, the dogs & birds & blacks moving in down the block & the "old fogies," as they keep saying, all over the place. They've already got their house on the market, & miss the Island, & my mother is already talking about a bigger trailer in another park on the Island. Is all this keeping them young or driving them to an early grave?

July 4, 1976 / 3:30 a.m.

"The best-selling poet in the history of the world."

We're back from the Island, glad to be home, but had a good week of swimming and fishing. We missed some terrible weather here, but not much else. Werner and Barbara deepen into their ways, as we do into ours. We all got along well. It's good to be home.

I brought back two seedlings from the woods behind Werner's house, a pine eight or ten inches high, and an oak still rooted half in its acorn. Will plant them today, to mark this day here in this small town, to do <u>something</u>.

As I've written these two paragraphs Rod McKuen has been on television singing and now talking. Oh, how awful and embarrassing "the best-selling poet in the history of the world" is. Oh, he's finished, and I'm blushing: "Because, God damn it, we're all we've got"—his last line. And Ed McMahon: "That's really something. I hope that gets published." America, and how to love her people? America, "Live from Fort McHenry." Surely, things will be the same at the Tricentennial? Much faith in that sentence, and there's the irony again: whatever the quality of her culture, America has been a free country for most of her citizens for two hundred years, maybe a luxury the world won't tolerate or can't afford for another century, but an Eden for most of her citizens next to those of the poor or jackbooted lands. And do its banal energies and life-affirming energies have the same source? In other words, who am I to complain? But will the country ever know, to choose a small example, that two of its great poems are the two David Ignatow just wrote out for me, "The Question" and "The Dream"? And everything I would have wished to be eloquent about, everything I feel deeply about this occasion—and I've choked up often the past day or two with the realization of this Indians'-despair-and-immigrants'-dream-of-a-country—is in these poems. The United States of America. The Republic. I am trying to learn, which is to say to witness. All in all, it still ends up in praise. I am grateful for the billions of intricate moral impulses and moves that allowed this home, this street and small town, this country to be. And this <u>is</u> my country, land of my one life within Time. Maybe we ought to direct our energies outward, toward the far points of light, some of which appear to be stars but which are vast galaxies of billions of planets, to the Lord of this. But, for today, America, the Republic. I'll plant those two trees, grateful.

7/8/76

Planted the pine out back, temporarily, until I find a permanent spot for it—maybe we'll be lucky enough to get hold of the land out back. Planted the oak where I hope it will live for two hundred years, outside our bedroom window.

Well, the 4th is fading away. And our 14th wedding anniversary was yesterday. And I played a bad softball game yesterday and my physical prowess seems to be fading away. A game tomorrow, and 3 or 4 Saturday, and 2 or 3 Sunday—maybe I'll begin to get into shape.

Have finished "The Ewe." Another good one.... Haven't heard from Ernest in a while. His last letter to me was down & unlike him. I should call, but hate the phone.

<u>Still</u> haven't gotten hardbacks of *American Poets in 1976*. Still am not absolutely sure about the boat trip. No answer at the woman who is supposed to arrange for my connection in Albany.

Joyce & Ray are to visit Sunday or Monday. I'm glad. They're good folks. I admit I can't seem to get myself to read Joyce's novels, and her poems are not usually really to my taste & feeling, but some of her stories are wonderful. She's quite a woman.... Read Kirst's *No Fatherland*.

Find myself getting a little restless these days, and actually, once that trip begins, my free time is about over for the summer.

7/13/76

Joyce & Ray were here and everything was pleasant. The Poulins came over for dinner, too. It rained like hell, but I was determined to cook out, and had the grill at the edge of the garage, steaks broiling, while lightning flashed (or so it seemed) right next door. Joyce wanted to talk & gossip about literature and writers. It was fun. She did not want to talk about her own work, kept praising mine. I like the Smiths, and she's a woman of great integrity, writing what she wants to write. And more and more I realize that she is <u>read</u>, that she has many people following her from book to book. I'm pleased to be her friend. The "Mr. Oates" thing is a bit of a problem, as when I ask her to inscribe books, but a small one. Joyce & Ray look fine, seem to have a solid marriage—she even nags Ray about not having another beer or more to eat. Han and I mentioned we'd be apart for a week this summer, and she said that she and Ray haven't been apart a day in 15 years.... They asked me, no exaggeration, about five times for poems for *Ontario Review*. I'll want to send them one or two or three of my best things.

I guess I about have the arrangements made for the trip, will fly to Hartford Thurs. morning, spend the night at Sandy's place, spend Friday in NYC, & fly from Kennedy to Albany that night. I hope someone is there to meet me. My "liaison" in Pittsburgh is a bit shaky.

I really wish I could just stay home for the next two weeks, play softball, mow the lawns. Well, I let myself in for it. I'm even going to miss those wonderful hours of watching the Olympics on television. Probably won't see anything in Montreal, but I'll breathe and remember the Olympic air.

Tomorrow will be hectic & nervous & I won't sleep much.

Hope to get into Gotham & Strand again & send some books home.

Talked to Giff Mosher about the land out back again today. We're sure anxious. I think everything will be all right. Fingers crossed.

7/26/76

I'm home! That whole damned trip, after Wesleyan & NYC, went sour. Only two towns came up with the dough, and I said <u>no</u> to traveling to Watertown & Dunkirk. I'm so happy, after being at Lake Sturgeon for a week with the family, to be home this week, watching the Olympics, relaxing.

Wesleyan went well. Stayed in New Haven with Sandy McClatchy. Saw Bob Phillips in New York, & Burt Britton, & stopped in at Vanguard, where I was warmly received. Flew to Buffalo where Han picked me up. Drove to Canada next morning for a wonderful week. The days blurred into one another there in a good way. No mail, no phone, swimming, golfing, fishing. One beautiful evening fishing out in the middle of the lake during showers, catching pike after pike, the four of us (Billy, Kurt, Wolf & I) happy under the canopy, gray gloom around us.

Joyce's *Crossing the Border* given to me at Vanguard, an appropriate book to read on the trip, as I did.... Found in the Strand Logan's *Zig-Zag Walk*, the copy John inscribed to his son John! For $2!...

Wrote a nasty letter to an ass, Alec someone, who wrote stupid things about *76* to B-M & then said "Quote me if you like and dare."

Things look excellent for the piece of land out back. Keeping my fingers crossed all the way. With luck, in ten or twenty years I'll read this out back, after we work that land, in a little cabin of my own, maybe under willows.... I wonder if this journal is, after ten years, finding its audience in a way that makes sense out of what is here: what is here is a sketch of happenings, and I'm to be the audience, maybe making poems out of memories that fill the holes.

7/30/76

The last several days have been beautiful. I've been clearing off my desk & getting ready for my summer class & watching the Olympics. Will go to a softball tournament in Perry tomorrow, alas (missing many Olympic finals), but that's okay.

Han & Kris went out shopping yesterday & brought back a baby beagle. Jesus, I hope he doesn't drive me crazy, as Butch did. I'm going to let Han do <u>all</u> the worrying. The cute little bastard already, though, woke me up 3-4 times last night with his whining. Worse than raising a kid.

Have read *The Mind-Reader* (fuck the critics—Wilbur is still doing some beautiful, inimitable poems), *Searching for the Ox* (a fine book, though the danger of the method is that it can turn into absolute shit in a hurry, and this often happens), Jim Harrison's *Farmer* (some good things, and I yearn to do a short novel like this one before I'm done); am reading, skimming, Lucien's *Heartland II*, which came today. Want to apply for a SUNY grant, and this will take some time, & want to apply for a Guggenheim: ditto. I will be off all next summer, & with some luck, maybe can spring a Guggenheim. What the hell, why not. I imagine myself in a trailer out back on our land writing that small novel. Even jotted down 5 or 6 ideas for chapters yesterday.

Have finally gotten hardbacks of *American Poets in 1976*.

Ernest going ahead with *XVII Machines*. There will be just 17 hardbacks, each with a holograph poem. I love the idea. 60 signed copies in wraps, I think, and he'll do a broadside of *Mare* to sell at the same time.

Kristen has named the puppy: Booter. She & Sue DeToy are out playing with him now.

Mon. 16th/Aug

I am in bed with a real bad groin injury. I can struggle out and shuffle along, but it's a bad injury. I tried to play hurt in a softball game at Warsaw yesterday, and tried to turn and run too fast, and heard something pop, and went <u>down</u> like I never have before. I don't know. I've had enough leg-pain and trouble this summer. I'm in decent shape, not overweight, still walk and bicycle a lot, but have had this bum right leg all summer. Well, now I'm done playing ball for this summer. And maybe I'll give the whole thing up in the future. Mahan's is a serious ballclub. Well, I was 12 for 25 this summer. We won $200 the other day. Next summer, maybe, I'll garden.

Republican National Convention is on now, Nancy Reagan waving to the crowd in her bright red dress. Looks like Ford, but something unexpected could happen. I'd vote for a Democrat in November even if King Kong were the nominee.

Ernest and family coming to visit Wednesday. I hope all goes well. He has two little kids, and they may stay until Sunday, which is a long time. I hope to go to a couple of auctions, and will take Ernest to my classes, and we'll talk books, of course. I'm counting on being able to walk a little by then. Will try like hell (and will manage) to get to class tomorrow.

Have been going nowhere with my poems lately, but am not worried about it. I have a body of work that will make up *The Chestnut Rain*—all I need is a concentrated time to begin to see it as a whole—and even have one or two pieces, including "The Ash," for a book past that one. Meanwhile, Vanguard is working on *The Swastika Poems*. It's no wonder I'm at ease, with this strong sense of ongoing career I have, rightly or wrongly.... I need the land out back, and a heavy summer. Next one.... I feel pretty good, despite the new semester rocketing toward me, the class now, the leg.... The new dog, Booter, is so far all right, not nearly as hyperactive as Butch was.... In bed today, reading more of *The Ascent of Man*.

"Fires" out in August *Poetry*. Joyce and Ray just took several of the swastika poems and want to feature them in *Ontario Review*.

9/6/76

I'm writing this while Wolf & Kurt & Billy & Kris are down here in the family room yelling about a U.S.-Canada hockey game. What noise. And Wolf just keeps talking to me, saying the same things again & again even when I'm not listening at all. Anyway, tomorrow (Labor Day) I hope to finish up the Guggenheim application, hope to get it into the mail on Tuesday, hope to prepare for my first classes Wednesday, and hope next weekend to be able to relax a little. Fat chance.

My leg has been healing much slower than I'd hoped. I'm still hobbling around, and every few days I seem to hurt it again, as today when I (carefully) tried to throw a football. If I can ever get back to being able to, I'm going to walk and bicycle like hell. Haven't done anything for a month now. I think I got hurt just four Sundays ago.

Saw Tony & Patti Petrosky out at Picciones' yesterday. I'm feeling closer to them. Will maybe stay a night with them when I make it to Pittsburgh first week in November.

Wrote a "Letter to Hugo from Brockport," a poem that got about everything into it of a week of reading I'd been doing & a summer's fascination with some things and more. Poured the kitchen sink in, & elephants, & my bad groin. I'm glad I did it, though one of those once in a while goes a long way. Doc Williams might have liked this one.

Summer class is over. One journal not in. Grades go in Tuesday. I've been leading a shallow life, I feel, the past few days, and worrying about the new semester, but do feel energetic, ready to begin again. This goddamned leg, leg, leg.

Actually bid (and lost the bid) $350 on a trunk of books at the MacVean auction last week. I'm sort of glad I didn't spend that much money. All historical books.... There's an auction in Bergen Wednesday night in Bergen that advertises many first editions—unusual, to say the least, for around here. We'll see.

Spoke to Tom Woll. Proofs on *Swastika* not far away. Should be a nice-sized book, pages 6 x 9.... *XVII Machines* going ahead now, and Harry Duncan sent proofs of *Of Palestine*. So, many things to look forward to.... Lucien coming the 15th. It's going to be a busy year for writers—Stay Rubin is ambitious. Rocks back from St. Lawrence & we'll go to their place for a welcome-back-from-Russia dinner for Mirko next Saturday.... Not the ghost of a profound thought or feeling in my body.... Poulin in bad shape after very bad luck with a backed-up chimney & other household problems & Boo away tending her mother who had an operation.... Not a hell of a lot of feedback on the 76 book, though I have a hunch I'll be pleasantly surprised by sales this next year, if Bobbs-Merrill's salesmen do a job, and if they advertise a little, etc.... Got some poems to *New Yorker* and *Poetry*. Have a hunch *New Yorker* will take at least one of those poems Moss wanted me to send back.... Ernest phoned again with half-a-dozen other ideas. He wants a 12 pp. supplement of my poems for *JBS*! I can't do it, but sent him "The Wolf" a few sentences of which I really like. He also just sent me a draft of the "C" section of the projected Heyen bibliography. Imagine that! It runs to 250-300 items. Will be published when I'm 40. I'll weigh it in my hands, and put everything away, and begin to write, maybe even a novel. I feel suddenly fine moving this flow of blue ink across the page. I would like to fill a book like this with a story, I would.... Also sent Ernest the middle Yeats-Roethke part of my dissertation for *JBS*'s last #. What the hell do I care. I'm interested in the piece, as I read it, insofar as what it tells me about what I was—not in regard to ideas but in regard to strategies & how I could (or could not) write. Whether anyone could be interested in what it says is another matter. I suppose I should guard a little this outpouring of Rook Press things, but I was so hungry for some small press to do my things for years, that I'll just keep letting Ernest go crazy. Things change fast in this world, so I'll just let those little items pile up.... I have 15 copies of the *Dream Song* broadside Ernie just published. Don't know what I'll <u>do</u> with a lot of this stuff. Maybe will sell all these things in New York in about ten years. Or, that dream of a bookshop in some future lifetime.... Party at Cal & Margie Rich last night. Much fun. I talked with Rod Parshall about *Noise* for quite a while. The kids in his class have really liked it, especially those from Long Island, I gather.

After one period: 3-0, Canada.... My next entry will be deep & mysterious. Ha!

9/15/76

I must/will change my life.

I will do this between now and the first of the year—some things to clear up by then, strings to cut, thinking to do; but I'll change my life, or I'll lose it.

Profound disgust, waves of disgust sweeping me all night over things that happened surrounding Stryk's visit. But mainly: after the reading last night, Poulin cornering him, dominating him, the two of them absolutely cutting me off in a way I've never been cut off/out before. And just a few weeks ago I was trying to persuade Poulin to include Stryk in the third edition of his anthology and Poulin would have none of it. Now Poulin coming on strong, bosom friend, talking offhandedly of "Dick" Wilbur's worry that Poulin's meter in the Rilke was not regular enough (or something) and Stryk saying "Oh, you know Wilbur!" And Stryk (I overheard) whispering to Al how wonderful his translations are—and the disgust, I realize welling up for years now—here Stryk & Poulin talking about translating a language they can't <u>read</u>. Poulin's aside to Stryk that the Rika Lesser translation from Cummington is "insensitive." And he can't even read the fucking language and his book's jacket will be filled with blurbs from Lowell & MacLeish and all. This unabashed drumming up of things. This has bothered me, and bothered Han, too, for two days with Stryk, too—the gushing, the constant rehearsal of his bibliography, the pitches. And I kept trying to tell myself that all this ego-based reference was of the right spirit, the Emersonian business-man-can-be-a-priest amalgamation, that the man was something more than—I'll say it—another one of these fucking people with no talent for life or the language who just hang on until who knows what, until a bunch of goddamned suckholes & sycophants like Piccione and me lose all sight of what is really there, the vapidity at the core, the self-serving, the emptiness at the center. Not a single reference to his wife or home in two days. No self-examination, such as I have felt after every reading. The absolutely unabashed glorying of being in the spotlight. Sickening. And Heyen telling him it was a fine reading, when it was too long, and monotonous—his voice low-level and dull & filled with melodrama. I hated it, and I had maybe fifty of my students there, who trusted me and went to see what poetry was about. No delight, just a kind of plodding and second-rate wit and sight like his "Fountain of Ammanati" poem. No short, shining things like some of the haiku. But this all somehow doesn't even touch what it was—surely, Ignatow's reading was dull a few years ago—that led to this real sense of soul-sickness I feel. Even the late talk at Piccione's about books coming out and all was okay. The reading—oh, hell, it was okay. But it was Poulin who rudely—Boo said she was worried that Al was dominating Stryk, and I didn't say anything, and she knew that again her husband's mania was in full play—forced people away from him and the two of them traded whatever the coin of the business is. Hot & heavy their palms & minds pressed together. To know Poulin—I am the only writer in the country who does know him, even while he carries on voluminous correspondence with everyone—is to know how sick he is. I can't tell him <u>anything</u>, or he tries to cut in and move me out. And he doesn't give enough of a shit about MacLeish even to send out—we've asked for years—the finished interview that wd. give the old man pleasure; but he'll immediately rush in for a Guggenheim recommendation from MacLeish, because I mentioned I had asked the man, that the man said he'd <u>see</u> about getting one for me next time. The whole Gray Wolf press episode. The way that ¶ in his anthology takes all information I gave him & then dismisses my work—and I <u>made</u> the fucking selections for three or four poets therein. Time after time after time the incredible overriding ambition that uses people with no sense of guilt. His feeling that he shouldn't have to teach at all. Stryk saying he's aghast & appalled about having to teach freshman composition. This, really, was below him, as he said straight out. Poulin with no home life, no natural life at all. Stryk saying that it is only the work that matters. He's crazy, too. Each of my sentences here needs much qualifying & detail, but <u>oh</u> when those two locked together in their revolting dance last night. Sure, I have done some steps in this dance, wanting to be known, esteemed, of "reputation." This is still the demon in the view. Now I will change, knowing full-well I have said this before, that my diary elsewhere waxes about this theme. Piccione is not well and can be of no help in this, is dazzled and tremendously confused (as he should be) by the ideal (which we share) and the blatant but disguised presence/talk of the hypocrite. We find it almost impossible to make up our minds about things, but I have made up my mind about this. I will not drop in, visit, call Poulin again. Will not. That's one thing. I don't give a shit what he comes to make of this. And all night I've been thinking of a radical break, *Swastika* being my last "public" book—I mean not carrying on correspondence with any writers, not having writers as friends. When I think of the lost frustrated unhappy souls: Mazzaro, Phillips, Poulin, Piccione often; when I think of the frequent humiliation and embarrassment that attends the desire for audience, for readings & books & recognition.... I am thinking (because, too, something wishy-washy has been happening to my voice), of getting away from teaching the contemporaries. I am thinking of not thinking again (or of vastly limiting my true preferences) of a new edition, should the chance come up, of the 76 book. I am thinking, in short, I guess, of halting the lying right now, of being true to myself, of finding my life where my happiness has been—the family & the ground here & the town & friends. Where will my bibliomania fit in? I might have to improve my taste. But I am sick of what happened last night, indeed I am. I have much thinking (thinking, shit, who can think things like this through) to do. No, I'm going to trust my emotions about this. I know what I know, what I felt. Some of the disgust was self-disgust. But Poulin is a sick man and a man of slime. His boldness & rudeness & ambition is an incredible thing to behold. He's poison for me, all knowledge of his activities is poison for me. Maybe Tony will be all right. I've not helped him. He's looking for a good man as I've looked for my next publisher. In any case, I'm going to somehow pull away....

    A full day of teaching coming up. I must write one clear page on all of this this evening, if I am able.

    I'm in class, my freshman class writing the first theme of the year. And here I am writing toward knowing this constant theme.

    Is it possible to tell the truth about what I feel? I constantly find myself, just to be gentle, just to be human, thanking people for books & praising poems and books that I don't think much of, really. What is this all about. Is it that I'm afraid to be honest, or is it that I want to be kind, or is it that I think aesthetics is relative and am reluctant to tell the truth of what I feel (and it would take too much time and breath, to say that something is no good)? And this is why the answer seems to be a break, away from writers. I will teach here at Brockport for the next, say, twenty or thirty years. I can teach courses in American literature and poetry without embroiling myself in the whole scene. It would be best, I even believe, for me to keep reading the classics.

    Oh, Lord, am I thirty-five and suddenly old? Do I want, truly, to mind my own business and write at my damned leisure over the decades remaining, to be forgotten as one of these creatures, the up-and-coming-poets-of-the-generation, or do I harbor a secret hope that such non-gregarious eccentricity will draw attention to me? There's no end to the ins and outs of this. Last night, literally, sickened me. I am all right now. It must be that I have learned something. I love some poems. This is true. I do. The country kid I was, the athlete, the naive bumpkin I still am does love many poems, and does wish to be lucky & good enough occasionally to write one. My life is all right, but too self-serving and public in the wrong ways. I wonder: can I be one of the few people in every generation who do, and maybe ought to be encouraged to, drop away from the ongoing body of society; or, do I need to find a forgetfulness of this quotidian of striving muck poetry scene in doing something of practical value for someone, in helping people. Maybe teaching is my answer & my way. Maybe it is right under my nose, right now. These kids, looking for their ways, looking for strength, the strength that is right there, if we can find it, in the language, in the story and poem. But does teaching have to be, semester after semester, an elementary discourse with nothing in it for me? I mean, do I have to have gentle discussions in class and then break away to my own work that will leave that elementary world for what really is on my mind?

    Everything comes to one. Where to begin, in this my desire, to be free. Maybe a few practical, outer steps are necessary. If I want to erase this desire of waiting for the mail (which is, of course, a desire to hear what the heart has always waited for: fame, in whatever manifestation within the next envelope), I have to discourage mail, and not write people (there will be exceptions: who are my friends) and not write my friends about our disease all the time. If seeing *Coda* & *APR* etc., etc. makes me nervous, then I ought to get my name off their fucking mailing lists. If I want readings, which take me away from teaching & turn me into a seeker, a grubber, then I ought to say no more readings. Do I have to cut things off the way I had to cut off smoking, or can there be a diminishment? How much poison does it take, anyway, to murder the soul.

    Yesterday afternoon, riding Billy's bike—my leg is getting better and I so much need exercise—I smelled something, a damp hay-fur smell, and a scene flashed back to me that I'd not seen in about 30 years—Werner and I discovered a litter of kittens in a barn on our property in Hauppauge. This, and the sense of time I have at this second, here in the room in Hartwell on the top floor where I sat many times as a student—the ghost traffic of the 1800s goes by outside. The mystery & clarity of all this will deepen, if I allow it. I think I would be happy. I want to get away from the mail, and the poetry scene. It will take courage. It might mean not having anyone to publish what I eventually bring together in books. Can I begin to look into people's eyes with real interest? Can I myself become, maybe without knowing it, the man I have been looking for. A disease, this homage to the person who is recognized. If only, if only I could become my own artist of the beautiful. I have every chance here, and if I can't, who can?

    later—it's about five o'clock. I'm waiting for Han to pick me up after her cheerleading session. She'll have Kristen with her, & Billy. Lord, what a world this is: I just had two very good classes, and feel fine, high. I'm off, too, until Tuesday. Everything is all right. What was everything about? All those things are, finally, trivial. Everything I said about Poulin is true—he can't help being the worst sort of shit. And I suspect that what I suspect about Stryk is all too true. But what are these things to me? It was very hard work, these past 2½ hrs. And that's another reason I feel fine. I need work. I mean it was even physical work, and I'm tired. Is it always the same: I'm unhappy about, or become unhappy when I'm around these people who disappoint me, humanists who act like cut-throats and assholes. Is this all hopelessly ideal? I still expect, though of course the poem is the thing that matters, that writing poems should help civilize a man or woman. When Tony says, "how can a bad man write a good poem?"—well, he's fucking A right, though we would have to talk about this for a long, long, long time before I got my terms right. And within the poem, if we can see it, read it clearly & truly, we would know the man or woman. By their language, which never lies, which always tells the truth, if we can only see it. Well, then, the essential weakness of a poem like "South"? I spent an hour in the last class talking about it, but, still, finally, it is thin, and we are better readers already than the poem is a poem. But now I've deflected my argument.... The change, maybe, does not have to be radical, but maybe there must be a certain cooling as time goes by, not to the production & sending out of my poems, but to the entangling of personalities that seems so often to result. I know who my friends are. I will no longer have anything (oh, a hello of course) of substance to do with that driven fuck Poulin. He makes me hate myself for how he makes me feel.
    I will put this away.
    Enough. Now for a quiet, steady, slow action on all this.
    Enough. Now it is time.

9/24/76

    Well, I feel pretty good these days. Have seen Al briefly once or twice, have been pleasant, will never tell him anything again, about what I publish, where I'm going, etc., etc. Will never have any news for him, or stop over there. Enough was enough. He's run up at school to show me the proofs of his Rilke, and I twice haven't mentioned that I have the *Swastika* proofs, and I'm glad. Nothing. That's it. I still can't think of that evening without getting sick. I almost, in writing Martin Booth—I did in fact write the letter but didn't send it—let it all go, too, about dear Lucien, but didn't. To hell with it. Nor do I have to change my life radically—I just have to stay the hell away from Poulin. I like my life of mail & little magazines & book catalogues and books & poems. I am mildly, even more than mildly interested in being known; but I was sickened that night. That was too much.
    Reading *The Swastika Poems*, I felt good, realized many things, e.g. that "The Uncertainty Principle," engaging as it does B's planned action of kneeling in the pond, deals with just what I do with the whole book, try to craft poems about the misery—something that worried me and that I wrote several discarded prefaces about. The book will be out in February, Tom says. That's a good time, early in the year, but 1977.
    What a pleasure, still, this friend Ernie Stefanik is, his enthusiasms mine. An issue of *Thistle* will be a Heyen number, with many *Handbook of Heartbreak* poems—I actually loved them when I read them today—and my "story" "The Wolf" and a few other poems. Ernie is doing so much for me.... He also sent samples of card advertisements he'll do on *XVII Machines*. So, then, there are all these Rook/Sisyphus things, the Abattoir book, maybe something from Martin Booth, & Duane Schneider has asked me about a pamphlet. No greater pleasure than these little things. The next big book will be *The Chestnut Rain*. I've written a few

poems lately, but they seem to be on odd, scattered, even surreal subjects. Can't even remember. I think one is called "The Tank."

Mike Waters will be here all next week, reading and "in residence." Should be fun. I've been working hard in my classes, trying to get them on track. Am getting, or have, a little cold. Played poker until 6 this morning at Rocks'. Won $68.... Han substituted at the high school today. I'm sure proud of her, the way she's jumped into this life of teaching/coaching/school again. It takes guts. The four of us are so busy, there are so many details just to keep the household going. So far, so good. Even the dog has been okay.

Many letters to answer—Phillips, Dave Smith, Peter Stitt, Vince Clemente, etc.—will catch up a little tomorrow. Don't mind—usually write notes/letters while watching a ball game. but it is true that I must by now have written <u>thousands</u> of letters in my time. Was it Lewis Carroll who kept a register of every letter he wrote or received?... Off now for a few days, and no freshman compositions this weekend. Wonderful.

9/28/76

Tried to sleep, couldn't, got up to watch the rest of a football game. It's after one in the morning, and I'm just sort of hanging around waiting to get tired enough to sleep.

Mike Waters stopped over yesterday evening and we talked a lot about Al & Tony. I admit pleasure when Mike said Stan Plumly referred to Al's disease as "creeping Poulinism." I think Mike knows most of everything. He's writing fine poems, it seems. It makes me genuinely happy when something good happens to him. Ernest is doing various things of his, too.

The New Yorker accepted "Mushrooms" today. I'd had several rejections from them, and for better poems. So it goes.

Han substituted again today. And again today, as yesterday, rain.

Bill McTaggart wrote to ask me about reading at his place. My week away in November should be a good one.

Herb Scott sent *Groceries* today.

Have gotten a copy of MacLeish's *Actfive*.

Announcement in *Times-Union* of Hannelore's appointment as Village Library Trustee. I asked her if she's trying to get to be more famous than I am!

The flowering mountain ash's berry's seed's husk seems to be hardening inside all that orange flesh. But I think I've done my poems on the ash.

I'm sleeping downstairs with my cold. Also slept down here with my injury this summer. Also sleep down here when I have a hard time sleeping. Don't know why, on occasion, as tonight, I suddenly tense up, neck & throat, & get nervous. Over nothing conscious. It just happens.... Maybe I'll turn to a poem. With luck it will put me to sleep and be <u>useful</u> for once.

9/29/76

Long talk with Tony today. We'd gone to Mike Waters' good reading, and he gave me a ride home. Talked about Al, Tony upset about being involved with Al again over Tony's *Anchor Dragging*. I don't blame him. It's lousy. I told him how I felt about things, how I would simply never talk with Al about literary things again, period.... Tony seems all right. We got a little drunk, talked about everything in the world. Lucien is very important to him. I was glad I never mentioned the reservations I'd been feeling.... Al's press: well, who knows if anything will ever come of it?

Mike will visit my 3:30 class tomorrow. I'm glad. Then he'll come over for dinner. He had a nice audience today, and reads beautifully. Han liked him too, though a few times there were flashes of slickness. But, shit, all these readings are performances, and there's no way around it. The poems are exhibitions.

In a soccer game with Greece yesterday, Billy's team was trailing 1-0 with only a minute left. They won 4-1. Now, that's scoring. He's doing well.

10/17/76

I'm much too tired tonight to write anything, but do wish to record in my diary that while watching Ford on television saying inane things from the back of a whistle-stop campaign train, I spotted behind him, clapping wildly and with a cat-that-caught-the-mouse smile, none other than—Rod McKuen!

10/22/76

David Ignatow and Richard Wilbur sent statements on *Swastika* to Vanguard, and Tom sent them to me. When I read them—I was home by myself—I cried. Many things were behind this cry, about the book and my work on it over the years, about its subject, about the recognition by these men of my own work. I'm very grateful.

I've been high as a kite the past few days. My letter to President Brown got results: I'm to have Room 224 in Hartwell for my office/classroom beginning next semester. It will be so comfortable, big enough for classes of 20-30, and for my desk & files & equipment, and the room is part of the old library and has high golden-oak bookcases. Brown came through for me, and I'm going to have the most comfortable teaching situation on campus. And the room looks over lawns and beautiful trees. I'm not saying this well. This is all deeply important to me, this place away from that damned Neff Hall and the English department, this place I can make warm for my students. I'll be a much better teacher because of this, and will be able to work at school now. Amazing. I can see myself at work there. It's a wonderful room. I'll get carpets and plants. And the room is at the center of my memories/future of and in Brockport. Just what I've wanted.

Patti & Tony Petrosky are in town & Han & I joined them at Picciones this evening. It was very pleasant. Just before we left, Tony Piccione cornered me to ask me again about Poulin & what happened to the MacLeish interview and whether Piccione should pull his book Mss. from Poulin's press, etc., etc. Again, I begged off on such questions. He'll have to confront Poulin himself, and, as I told him, I just won't talk to Al about literary matters again. I won't.

I actually went downtown today to a suit sale at Brockport Clothing and bought two suits for $78! So, from no suits I now have two suits. May even wear them occasionally in my new office!

Nice letter from Joyce Oates today, and she sent a little book to me and Han: it's called *Fertilizing the Continent* and seems to be limited to 12 copies! Beautifully bound in leather (red) and marbled papers.

I've got to read a lot of Nemerov this weekend to get ready for the tape next Thursday.

10/25/76

Dream

I went looking for my son
and found him in the grass,
prone, his chin in his hands,
watching a bull snake.
I said, "Be careful, anything can happen."
Beside him, somehow, a possum
rolled from under leaves, bared its teeth,
but licked his ear. I said
"Watch out." At that
a coon appeared,
touched my son's nose
gently with its pink fingers,
and lay down beside him.
I stood in my tracks, afraid.
A wolf rose from the grass,
and licked my son's forehead.
"He is only twelve, Lord," I prayed.

The gun was soundless when I fired.
The snake, the animals
began to shine, to shine, to shine.
My son and I walked home, holding hands.
He said, "I love you,"
but when I looked back he lay in the grass,
his chin cupped in his hands,
the snake and animals a shining circle around him.

10/31/76

All Hallow's Eve, & Kristen & Billy will dress up and wander the neighborhood. A rainy and cold evening, but when did that ever stop or even worry a kid?

Tomorrow, my birthday, I fly to Pittsburgh where Lauderdale Bill will meet me at the airport. Look forward to this trip because the arrangements are so simple and because I'll see many friends.

Harry Duncan writes that the two contributor's copies of *Of Palestine* are on their way to me. I don't mind that the book has not made it into hard covers, but will I get only two free copies?

Bill Rock's birthday yesterday, and we met the Rocks at Pylyshenkos'. Mirko's best friend, Roman, died a couple of days ago—a heart attack at 42—and Mirko is shaken, of course. A great loss for him. Childhood friends. He hasn't cried yet, but will. He and the other old friends buried Roman with a bottle of cognac and a deck of cards.

Gary Lepper's bibliography has arrived, and I've spent pleasant hours with it.... I think Ernest may have published more of my things by now, and I'm anxious to see them, and visit the Stefaniks, and look over Ernie's library. Will stay with Petroskys for a day or two, too.

This is starting to be my kind of weather. I've gone for a walk in the drizzle once today, and will again. But it's nice to have no work outside, to be cozy inside fiddling with books & ragging Billy about his Dallas Cowboys & generally enjoying our warm & comfortable home.... Han will be busy as hell when I'm gone. She needs a break from me once in a while.... Bis spater.

11/13/76

A lazy Saturday. Things generally fine. Billy has Ralphie over and Kristen has Sue DeToy. I'm watching Texas A & M take it to Arkansas.... Worked outside for a while. Brought Booter's house into the garage for the winter. It's been very cold. Once in a while some realization of what a winter without fuel to heat the house would be like. And I know that the supply is precarious. But, says the twentieth-century suburbanite, there's nothing I can do, and things will be fine this next winter, anyway.

The Pittsburgh trip was a good one—three high school readings and a reading & classroom visit at Westminster College with Bill McTaggart. The Petroskys were kind, and are warm folks who are becoming close friends. Saw the Zimmers, & Ed Ochester. Ed & Tony are both plotting strategies to gain tenure, & we had much fun talking about this, the visibility necessary and the wearing of ties.... The Stefanik place is kind of a madhouse, but they are lovely people, and I was glad to see the brain center of Rook Press. Ernest & Cis had printed several little things of mine, including *The Crickets* and *The Dogwoods*, which I'm fond of. Met wild Norman McWhinney, but Bill Lint wasn't around. All in all, a good trip.... Next time out it will be Long Island, in April, Stony Brook and, hopefully the same trip, SCCC.

Actually wrote two little poems while away, a piece called "The Manuscript," and a companion-piece to "Dream," this one purely fabricated, about Kristen. I want to see those two pieces face one another in print, some day.

Of Palestine is out. 275 copies. At first, I wasn't very excited about it. Now I love the little thing. Want to send many out for Christmas, so have sent $50 as an installment for 30 copies to Harry Duncan.

I don't know. I'm just sort of marking time, content with the things coming out and the other poems to place. I think I'll work next summer on seeing what *The Chestnut Rain* might want to look like. It is enough, now, just to be at home, family noises around me.

11/21/76

Harry Duncan sent back my check and said that 40 copies are on their way to me—author's copies!

Snow this evening, just a slow sift, and I went for a walk. Also went for a longish walk this morning with Billy & Kristen. Have spent most of the day correcting papers & clearing away school stuff. We'll leave Wednesday for Han's folks & Thanksgiving, and I don't even mind, this time, somehow. I'm going to go for long walks there, & eat a lot, and relax for those few days.

Week after week goes by, and I'm happy, but seem to do little writing. I would like to get tied up, say, with one longer poem this winter. Maybe something will turn up. Part of it, still, is this limbo I'm in with *Swastika* (and, in a smaller way, *Machines*, coming soon). Tom Woll says there will be copies in January already. He's actually still trying to arrange for slipcases for the fifty numbered copies. It's a very strong book, but I must expect nothing in the way of attention, or I'll be disappointed. Amazing that there's little chance that it will sell out the first printing of 2,500 copies quickly—so few copies. *Noise* has sold about 2,000 now. Why can't a damned book of poems by a commercial publisher sell 5,000 copies?... Beyond this, I have made this book, and it's done with, and I'm glad. When the enormity of the art-Holocaust business (terrible & maybe apt word!) strikes me, as it often does, I hope, pray, the book honors the dead, remembers, and keep telling myself that I am human and impure, and remind myself of something that is true: the poems were written naturally, as I had to write them, with no ulterior motive, no planned exploitation, though reading them from a stage I feel that I'm a manipulator. Anyway, the book is <u>done</u>.... And now I feel sort of written out.... Not just that, but as though it's not that important to me to write more. Is this happiness & maturity? And sanity? Or is this just unimaginative, too comfortable, middle-class malaise? Or both?

I'm reading Joyce's *Childwold*. It's quite a book, now that I'm into it. She's an amazing writer. How is it possible? I think I know. Those word-filled reveries I sometimes have when trying to sleep or wake up—well, this is the word-filled, story-filled, character-filled consciousness she must enter as she sits down to type her books.

12/7/76

Ned Grade died yesterday—a heart attack, and right while he was at the doctor's office with chest pains. He was 46 or 48—too young. I never liked Ned as much as I did the last year. He seemed to have mellowed. There was a time, in fact, when I detested him for his ambition & cheapness, but we'd become friends, I think, veteran members of the department, and I'm sorry we won't grow old together now. It's amazing, the way a person can disappear. His office was across from mine and now, with no warning, he's gone. Four children, the oldest about sixteen. Funeral home gathering tomorrow, services & burial the next day, right in the middle of a cold and dreary December.

12/12/76

Mary Anne Grade asked me to read Frost's "Directive" at Ned's service, and I did. It was all very sad. Terribly cold that day. The service was not as spooky as was Ellen Wagner's—this was only my second Catholic service—but there was still the incense, and communion, and the <u>words</u>. Three priests in attendance.... Now I find myself trying not to think of Ned or, when I do, thinking of him in his coffin in storage somewhere until the spring thaw.

We put up the Christmas tree this evening, though there are still many ornaments to add. It's snowing out, too. This is the season.

XVII Machines arrived, and it's a handsome little book. I'm grateful to Ernie & Cis for all their work. Also, the Christmas cards, with Kristen's illustration, arrived, and I sent out more than in recent years. I like the card very much. --- There's another one, too, that Rook Press is sending out, with "Christmas Shopping in a Small Town" on it.

My mind is as much mush as this entry these days. I did, however, sit down yesterday morning alone & in silence for a couple of hours and drafted a table of contents for *The Chestnut Rain*. No wonder I'm tired! The book is about done, & may be my best. Yes, it is. It will be a beautiful book. I'll stare at it next summer, but am confident that just the materials already on hand will make for my best book. No wonder I'm tired, too tired even to remember writing all those poems. Good night.

1/2/77

After a hectic two weeks—in-laws, parties, dozens of kids always around, Han frantic with cheerleading duties—the winter break is becoming calm, and I'm relaxing. Billy & Kristen will even go back to school tomorrow.... I've been moving into my new office—carpet down, shelves up. What a pleasure it will be! And my new office is the talk of the campus—everyone I run across has heard about it. Ha, it makes me a star around here. The room is quiet, and should be cool in summer. It's only a healthy walk away from home. It has an oak luster, has the spirit of the old school, and I want to hear the sounds of the old singers, want to read and study and learn again for the next ten years, move away from the contemporary little by little. Will have a good start with my courses the next couple of semesters.

Darkness and *The Carrie White Auction at Brockport, May 1974* are out, the latter a surprise. Cis & Ernie keep me happy with these little things.... *Swastika* out this month, I suspect.... Have about finished a new poem that could have been in that book, near the end: "The Jewish Children." Have sent about 5,000 words, *The Swastika Prose*, to Ernie.... The summer grant, $1,850, came through, and we needed the money to build again (after spending just about that much on the land out back) toward Billy's college.

Saw Joe & Sharon McElrath the other day, up from Florida. Gave Joe all the little things of mine, mostly Rook Press, that have accumulated. He's used both *Depth* & *Noise* in classes. Wish he still taught here.

Many letters to answer, & small chores to do, but I just have no ambition for these things. Just want to walk in the snow.

1/12/77

Still calm, inside, even though kids have filled up the house the past couple of days—school has been snowed out. Away from teaching, from necessity, I'm relaxed.... Tom sent the *Swastika* dustjacket. It's as fine as I hoped it would be. That book is going to make me known. It is. I'm glad I did it, feel, the last six months or so, not shy or apologetic about it as I once did. Aah, the "artist" has, finally, no scruples? No, it's not that: it's simply that a book is not a book, as Berkeley's falling tree is not a tree, until it's read, and the Vanguard packaging of this book will help it be seen, bought, read. I think, also, if nothing else, *Swastika* will send some young Jews into their histories, and there will be other such books.... Found out, today, that I have work in two anthologies. Quite a surprise. Jack Higgs used "The Stadium" in his sports anthology, and Joe Davis—I wasn't even sure he was alive—wrote to say that he used two in his new Scott, Foresman intro. to lit. anthology. Wonder if all these poems were free to the editors! Don't know which poems Joe used, but probably from *Depth of Field* also. I really like that son-of-a-bitch.... Han finishing long drapes for my new office.... I've had a cold, but am shaking it....

1/23/77

High school wrestling match last night. Wd. like to write a poem about it some day. So much there.... And we've been watching Billy's basketball games—he's the best kid on the floor, a guard getting 15-20 points a game, a wonderful shooter & ball-handler.

Call from a fellow at U. of R. the other day saying R. Howard wd. be reading there next Wednesday & when asked if there were anyone he'd like to know about the reading, mentioned me! With luck, the weather will keep me here. The son-of-a-bitch—no, really he's very kind—could mean a big award for *Swastika* or money or a year off for me.

I've been writing, working at different poems in my new office, and feel good about that place as a place to work. Hope to spend a few hours a day there this summer, <u>enjoying myself</u> writing; otherwise, I'll stay home and garden or shoot baskets.

Such a cold winter. Such a warm home.

I'm on a long winning streak in poker, and wish to record for posterity my last dozen games (since October): +12, +68, +68, +220, +93, +32, +30, -55, +69, +141, +194, +41. Eleven for twelve, and money for books, primarily, so gambling supports the arts around here. But I don't want to get too confident. But my new strategy of waiting, not pushing my cards until I have them, and watching Bill Rock, the tightest player who only plays with <u>cards</u>, is paying off. I've not really been <u>lucky</u> during this streak.... We might have some new blood in this game, too—a few new players floating around.

School, & seriousness, begins again in a week.

Mon. Feb. 7, 1977

My eye caught the number series above. I won $104 the other night.

Manny & Helen are back, and it feels good.

I've had a long, good weekend, fooling with my books.

Classes have begun, sort of raggedly what with weather conditions, but they've begun. My new classroom feels as comfortable as I thought it would, though it's crowded during the transcendentalism course.

38 of the 50 special copies of *Swastika* have arrived. I hope the other twelve are not lost in the mails, and I write this while waiting to see if the mailman will deliver.... Not today, alas.... But the book is perfect. I couldn't be more pleased. Slipcase and all! Though I <u>won't</u> be able to, I <u>should</u> be able to sit back and relax for a couple of years working slowly on *The Chestnut Rain*. I will. I've been working on a longish thing called "The Light," but might make this a section of the title poem. Also have a good one about a ewe's sad song going.

The folks from Vanguard even phoned last week, and we all had a mutual admiration talk. Evelyn said she thought "this one will <u>sell</u>!" They printed 3,500, and that's a lot for a hardback book of poems. I hope the book sells enough to satisfy them.... The book is so handsome that it's been a pleasure sending out special copies to friends.

2/20/77

Still winter. Today, Sunday, I was inside all day, except for one walk around the short block. Still winter. Only notations here.

Appt. for physical with Doc Sansocie yesterday. He found some red blood cells in the fluid he forced out of my prostrate—I've felt uncomfortable urinating. Will have more tests. I trust nothing serious is wrong. How would I take it if I knew I were going to die in a year or two? Hard, <u>hard</u>, but I think of this occasionally and do have some faith in myself. Not much! Some. I don't want to be tested this soon!

At last the kids will be back in school tomorrow!

Han & I chaperoned a high school dance last night, after the basketball game. What a way to kill an evening. Han will substitute teach for a few weeks beginning tomorrow.

My classes are all right now. The first weekly meeting with the creative writing class was generally painful, the second fine. I have all 3 classes in my new office now. A pleasure.

Am still working on the pricelist of my books for insurance purposes. Almost done.

Ernie sent a pamphlet of the poem "Riddle" he'd done in bright orange covers. Awful. I've written him to say I'm scrapping it.

Sent Steve Berg my poem "The Jewish Children" in a letter, & he wrote to accept it for *APR*. Meanwhile, I'd sent it to *The New Yorker*, and have a hunch Moss will take it (no doubt I'm wrong). Will see. Either way.

I'm buying the last 250 copies of *Depth of Field*. Don't know what the hell I'll do with them, but at least all rights will be mine for future printings. A buck each for the books.

Lovely letters from Mike Waters, Barry Leeds, Vince Clemente etc. about *Swastika*. In general, though the books fall into a silence, always waiting for a future (past rock groups and the advertising of flashy trash) that may never arrive.

2/27/77

Just spent a few fine and peaceful hours at my office at the school. Found out I could pound screws into the plaster and hang things up—put up the map of the Island, and the MacLeish broadside, just framed. Cut a couple more shelves, and brought over a small oak table for the record player I've checked out for the semester. That place is a home away from home for me—so private, even when school is in session; so beautifully available to students when I teach & have office hours.

And, with luck now, I might be spending a hell of a lot of time there writing next year: the Guggenheim people asked me for a financial statement, so I must be close to a fellowship. Within a month, I'll know. That would be amazing—a grant to write for a whole year. I want it badly, but don't think about it much, else the disappointment will be too much. One of the best things about it is that I wouldn't have to apply again. What a drag that is.

Warm & gracious letters coming in on *The Swastika Poems*. Odd how some of what should be the friendliest, supposedly from friends (Turco, McClatchy, Phillips) are the most distant, somehow. Unfriendly, even. I'm not talking about the lack of praise (this is there, in odd ways) but the lack of warm congratulations & a realization of what it means to me to have done the book. That fucking McClatchy asks me what the response has been, says I'm too lucid, somehow. Then I hear from Stan Lindberg at *Ohio Review* that Jack Matthews insists on reviewing *Swastika* for them. What a man he is, a wide soul if there ever was one. He makes old Bob Phillips, even, seem like such a prune.... And what a circle-jerk is going on over there in N.Y. McClatchy informs me that Merrill's Pulitzer will be announced in May. Wonder what Atheneum poet will win it next. Screw them all, that whole scene. McClatchy lives in one social whirl over there at Yale—Howard & Hecht just dropped in at him, party for Warren, house to buy with his lover Alfred & a beach vacation to take somewhere, Merwin & Simic on their way to him. I'm glad I live here. Will keep those words from MacLeish about my taking it easy now, giving my work a chance to breathe like wine, on my desk & in my mind. To write poems like Wendell Berry's "The Lilies"—that's the thing. Damned lucky I know wide souls like Wilbur, Stafford, MacLeish. So many creeps around.

My work is beginning to clear away. Have at last finished the list of my book collection for insurance purposes. Hope to get $50,000 in coverage. Then I can really relax. It was a big project, this list, taking up part of my study for a year.... Tonight I hope to finish the Gregor checklist for FPAA, then on to the Pastan one.... My classes are going along pretty well now.

Han finished a full week of substitute teaching, & finished doing the tax returns today. She put a lot of work into both! The kids are fine. Snow melting outside, & rain due. Very dark today. I feel good these days, calm, as though I arrived at the point of self-acceptance with my life, my self. I begin to see myself as some of my students see me. I'm generally kind, generally sensitive to them, manage to be polite even when I'd rather kick their asses. I work hard for them. I hope to grow old gracefully. Pshew, a Guggenheim would result in a lot of poetry for me, I know.... It's all right, this suburban, middle-class, spoiled-by-too-many-comforts, man with 2 kids & a wife who cooks & a beagle life of mine, voice of mine. I'll be what I am, with a bit of courage, with a bit less ambition.

March 5, 1977

Feel like I'm just marking time, waiting to hear about the Guggenheim—but I feel good, mainly because of the new office. Such a pleasure to teach in, and it's a quiet and psychologically right place to work in. I see more students there, too: they're around Hartwell on my teaching days, and drop in to see me. Yesterday I put up Ignatow & MacLeish holographs: "The Question" and "Mark Van Doren and the Brook."

Doctor's appt. in Batavia Monday, dentist Thursday. Such things make me nervous. I trust there's nothing serious wrong with me; I feel pretty good lately.

Tony Piccione has done a beautiful review of *Swastika*.

3/13/77

Just an infection, for which I'm taking ten days of sulfur tablets. I feel fine these days, only my sinuses acting up, but that's not news. I've been getting exercise, walking with Han this weekend and playing basketball with Billy and his friends.

The snow is gone now, and water has been running off through the ditch steadily. Trees have budded all around us while we haven't been looking. Han's crocuses are up. I sure look forward to working out back.

Packing up boxes of books to put on shelves at my office, I keep running into things I want to read/study again, or for the first time, maybe my well-underlined Pope, maybe Burroughs on Whitman; other times, feeling overwhelmed by all I'd like to know, I say to hell with it all and get on with my own work, with what I can do, the occasional poem & book of poems. I often find myself thinking that this is what the heavenly afterlife will be, full knowledge of everything, every story of every man & woman who ever lived, of every star, of God. It may be this way, too!

Stopped in to see Al a couple of days ago—it was sunny and I was walking and feeling high. It was about 2 in the afternoon & he was still in his bathrobe and sitting at his desk straining to become famous, in a cloud of chainsmoke, coughing. He is sick often—colds, flus. Will not take care of himself. Is still obsessed.

An ass by the name of Lyn Lifshin read here last week. She's so stupid, so engrossed with the idea of being a POET ON TOUR. The reading was grotesque, the "poems" unbelievable discharges of smelly juices. The message to me is always the same: Wm. mind your business, avoid writers, win your way through to freedom from lust for false fame.... I'm happy, and then read some flyer from Columbia, or *Coda*, and then all the circle-jerk stuff makes me feel competitive, and I get tight. Right now, Sunday evening, the house asleep, I'm peaceful, so happy, full. Tomorrow, as always, I'll look for the mail, and desire. This can be beaten. I only want to desire the poem, like "Witness," or "The Children," and hope many arrive....

3/17/77

Another Thursday night, teaching over again for several days, and I'm tired. I expend much energy. But I've gotten into touch with some kids this semester, and the strain, I think, is worth it. And my office is a tremendous pleasure.

I should hear about the Guggenheim any day now. Fingers crossed. If not, my world won't end.

180 copies of *Depth of Field* arrived today! I'll have fun giving them out for years.

Looks, again, like no review of *Swastika* in any of the big places. So it goes. Read, today, that Erich Segal just made 1½ million on his sequel to *Love Story*. So it goes.

Yesterday was Kristen's eleventh birthday. She's just a lovely kid.

Haven't written a word, or tried to, in a month or two. Feel relaxed. Waiting for the weather to break, too, to get outside. Much snow on the way, is the report tonight.

Watched basketball & boxing on television all evening.

Need a good night's sleep, and tonight's the night.

3/18/77

Sure enough: snow hit hard, it's blowing like hell outside this morning, and Frazier St. looks almost impassable. Yesterday I was playing basketball outside!

Back again. The street was passable and the mail came with the news that the Guggenheim people said YES. I'm very happy, cannot really imagine what it will be like to have all that time away from teaching. I know that it will be a central year in my life, a year during which I will become a man, I hope. I'll be working my way in this journal toward what I'll want to do during that time. It won't be easy. Ass that I am, some of my first thoughts were that I would get around, promote myself, give lots of readings. No. I will walk, write, and mind my business—what a difficult art!... O my lucky stars! I'm going for a long walk in the snow-storm.

Over the next month or two, I'll be making plans, knowing that too-rigid plans, of course, and too-grandiose goals will ruin the fellowship year. All in all, with the SUNY grant, fifteen months, which includes two summers. I don't feel guilty about it, but grateful and, when the facts sink in, will be ecstatic. No freshman composition next fall. No school paperwork. No bad student poems to hear & read. *The Chestnut Rain* to dwell on lovingly. Too much to realize right now. I can't believe it.

3/23/77

    I'm in bed, having a cup of coffee. Han is off teaching, the kids in school. The house is silent, only the hum, almost unheard, of appliances, maybe just the freezer. Deep snow outside again after the storm yesterday. In front of Hartwell the maples already had a reddish tint, their leaves unfolding, and then the snow hit. Well, they've been through this before, many times. On the 1907 postcard I have of what was the Normal School principals' residence and is now Alumni House, I can pick out a few of the same trees that I can see from my office window.

    Another good session with the creative writing class last night. I think much of my own energy/desire goes into that class, and I don't write myself—this is another reason the Guggenheim year will be <u>so</u> good for me. I still glow inside over the news. But the other night, thinking of projects I'd like to accomplish, I actually lost sleep because I felt myself pressed for time! No, this is ridiculous, and I'll do one or two things, and do them well.

3/30/77

    The weather has broken—over 70° yesterday, and more sun today. I'll soon walk up to the school. / Gary Lepper called to say he'd found five Heyen collectors if I'd cooperate. I sure will. / Argument w. two stupid students yesterday who knew all about Emerson & Thoreau without having to bother to read them. / Trimmed wisteria for an hour yesterday. But, no doubt, it will soon snow again. / Billy off to Washington with his class for a week & we miss him. / Han doing fine but working like hell at this substituting she's been doing. / Within the last week or so I actually put together the collection of my prose pieces which will be called (if ever published) *The Shine of the World: Essays in Appreciation of American Poets*. I've written to ask Tom if Vanguard wants to see it. I've surprised myself. The individual pieces are okay, though I'm worried about the range of the book as a whole. Will need to do a brief preface, with one or two "apologies" on my mind.

    Got the records I'd sent for—listened to Yeats yesterday, and a little Dylan Thomas. Will ease <u>slowly</u> into MacLeish & Wilbur & Graves & Stevens & Wms & Cummings, etc. Have M. Moore to hear, & Gertrude Stein & Edith Sitwell. Aah, technology! Have <u>2</u> Roethke records now.

    Lift Bridge party for *Swastika* Sunday. I think many people will be there. I don't <u>exactly</u> look forward, but look forward.

    Bob Phillips sent me another terribly written poem called "Decks." I hardly know what to say—so write him "slant"—and if I say nothing he badgers me for a response.

    My office at the college continues to be my <u>place</u>, my <u>refuge</u>, my calm center in this academia.... The fifteen months without teaching unfold before me. This will never happen again, I think. Sometimes students get to me—words used so badly, and bad logic, and terrible compositions—I do need to get away, to read and hear the clear sounds of the old masters.

4/5/77

    Teeth cleaned yesterday, so I'm all done with the dentist for a while! Appt. with doctor in Batavia yesterday—my prostate is now fine and my urine "nice and clean," as he says. Feel healthy! Okay, now for the spirit!

    Gathering at Lift Bridge was all right. I'd hoped more people would be there. I'm still learning.... Chased to Rochester today to do a short radio spot, and they want another. A possibility of national exposure for *Swastika*, so I will. This was all right, but looking through *Coda*, which arrived, and seeing (with some envy) a review of Poulin's *Rilke* in *Time*, makes me anxious, or depressed, or <u>something</u>—it's hard to define the feelings. But, I <u>have</u> learned something: that when I have time to decide something, I'll almost always or always decide the manly, right way—as when I decided <u>not</u> to attend the Howard reading in Rochester, <u>not</u> to read for Dale Davis, <u>not</u> (to mention something slight) to stop in at the bookstore & see if any of my books have sold. When I can think about it, I force myself to mind my own fucking business. What I'd like, of course, is an <u>instinctive</u> calm and manliness. Maybe, after much decision-making noble action, it will become habitual. As I learned not to smoke.

 Should have a fine time on L.I./NYC. Will leave the 15th.

 Oh, the weather is wearing me down, cold wind again knocking me over as I walked to school & back today. <u>Snow</u> this evening. Warm weather and the land out back and the physical work to do there will help me mature, I know…. Am I becoming Johnny-one-note about this? I would like, simply, to be less vulgar than my scrambling friends, and write, again, for myself, with the innocence of trying to write these things called "poems" that I once had. "Any man who wants to be famous can never be famous enough," as Louis Simpson said of Berryman. And shit, where's the pressure on me? Han couldn't care less, or the kids. Do I want to impress my "friends"? Family? It must be just for me. And the world's rewards seem to have little to do with quality. I'll win. Watch me, diary, as I learn (choose) to treat the mail (that metaphor of my gross life) cavalierly! Watch me. Thank you, Lord, for the Guggenheim. I need no greater gift than this <u>time.</u>

 Very happy to hear from Larry Gaffney that he's been offered an assistantship at Ohio University.

 Tony Piccione drunk twice this past week. I hope he's not slipping again, that this is just from the misery he's been through with the dentist.

 Bill Rock made an ass of himself, insulting Han, at the goose dinner at Mirko's the other night.

 Momentous day two days ago. Kristen's first period arrived! She handled it fine. And Billy is growing into such a fine, strong young man. Han and I so lucky…. One more day of teaching for Han. She's made a lot of money—a good feeling, what with the world falling apart. If the money is false security, it still feels good.

Easter Sunday, 1977

 The Greiners from Hamburg are here, and we've had a nice time. Sun today, and it's warm! After some breakfast and basketball this morning, I went walking out back on our new property with Wolf & Kristen. That land means so much to me, gives me a deep sense of peace. Dozens, hundreds of trees, ash and elm back there. Grapevine to cut from them. Everything budding today, and the ground drying, as it will for the next month or six weeks, everything spongy now. We'll have the property surveyed—it's about 156' x 186'—and probably put up a fence along the one side where all the houses are. Then I'll plant trees and bushes along it. I thought I could dig up & level the whole piece by myself, little by little, but there is a tremendous amount to do, and I might have to bring in a tractor, just once. But, maybe not. Han is in a bigger hurry, I think, to get things done than I am. This year, a fence, small garden, and clearing out directly behind our property. I'm in no hurry. I feel <u>free</u> back there. I love it. And I'll have time as I've never had it before. This break in the weather says everything is possible!... Mr. Wren, over there, called the other night and wanted to buy a piece of our new property, a piece behind his. Han said she'd ask me—she was being polite. <u>Never</u>, of course. It will be one of the good things we do before we die: we will keep our little acre and let trees grow. Something so ludicrous about this, a suburbanite waxing about his postage-stamp property while the world becomes a suburb of Detroit. But I can't do everything. But this I can do, walk from tree to tree over the years and touch them, and keep the asphalt away.

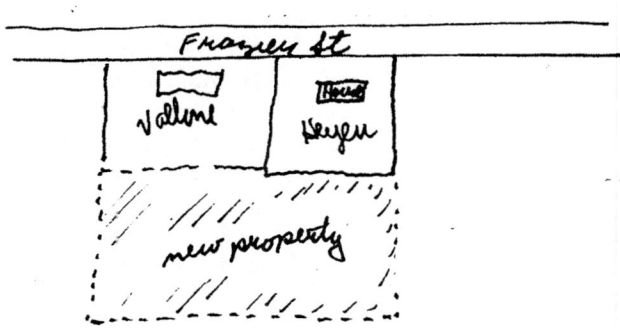

It's almost unbelievable that anyone now could be as free as I will, to work out back and then walk up to my big private place at school. I've decided that I will <u>not</u> write essays on American writers as I thought of doing, <u>not</u> fool with a novel, etc., etc., during the year off, but will write poems. Thought of a nice compromise that will satisfy other of my selves—will study & do research on Jonathan Edwards, hoping to draft a book-length poem. This I could do, with great pleasure. I would <u>learn</u>, about Edwards, about writing long poems. This would be excellent for me. I've discarded other project ideas, but this one has real staying power. I've been overwhelmed by Edwards, the pure power of his passionate speech, for years, his poetry, his soul. "Do I love the world"—this line came to me the other day as a beginning that begins everything. I want to know Edwards, to feel him, with the sweetness that he sometimes felt grace. Yes, there's the project, my personal narrative of him—but all strategies to be decided after a mountain of notes. I know that sometimes I'll be able to enter a flow when I write about him.... Telephone....

    Lew Turco called with all sorts of news abut Mathom Press--& congratulations on the Guggenheim. He's all right, if too frenetic.... Back there, on that land, my mind <u>really</u> is far away from phone and mail. Today the Lord rises and rises.

May 1, 1977

    Finally, a warm, even hot day, a true Sunday. It's early afternoon—I'm waiting for the 7th game of the Boston/Philadelphia series.... Mowed both lawns this morning, with Billy. And I've been out back on our new property, cutting & axing away crab apple and brambles. It's slow work, but a pleasure. The brambles are amazing things, the downcurved barbs going right through my work gloves, catching me even when I'm trying to walk away. Even their roots hold, to one more tough taproot under the clump, and then another, and a last one, and then another.... I'm not feeling a bit guilty that we have all that property back there to ourselves. Across the street Toby wants to expand his dining room onto his small front lawn, and add to his already double driveway! Wren, and other neighbors along our land, would just asphalt it!

    I've done no writing in months, but after this month I'll be free, and know I will.

    The reading at Stony Brook was disappointing, rushed and formal. SCCC was just right, warm & many kids interested in my poems, & several faculty friendly. Clemente quite a guy, doing too much for me. Jim Mattimore, Dave Axelrod, Dan Murray—quite a community there.

    My folks seem about as jumpy as always, Werner about as sour as always. Brother Henry blew through, and seems into his life in good ways. Folks can't wait to move out of Selden. Trying to sell their empty trailer, and now, we hear, their cemetery lot—in favor of cremation. I don't know.

    Went to Happy Hour at Barber's Friday, and there was Poulin, ready to pounce on me, to tell me how amazing it was, for the 30th time, that his review in *Time* was seen all over the world, & to show me the Gray Wolf little *Catawba* book of his, and to tell me how much attention Snodgrass' *Fuhrer* poems will get. It's not my imagination. He feels almost insanely competitive with me, phones Han to see what I'm doing, expanded his sabbatical to 12 months when he found out about my Guggenheim, will push the Snodgrass book to compete with my "German" book, etc., etc. Oh, well, I'm <u>very</u> happy away from him. While I was working out back this morning, he was no doubt at his desk & phone drumming things up. Fuck it all. I don't care what he does, as long as I can avoid him!

Saw Bob Phillips for only a few minutes in NY. He's been a real friend, has reviewed *Swastika* for *Partisan Review*, e.g.... Stopped into the Vanguard offices for a half-hour, and they were friendly as could be. Dropped off essay collection. Don't know if anything will come of it. Not terribly important to me. Bought 5 remaindered copies of Kunitz' essays: can't imagine that mine would sell any better, so won't be surprised if they don't publish it.... Not from Evelyn the other day on bottom of a royalty check for *Noise* saying she hopes they publish many more of my books past *Swastika*. I'm very lucky. Is anyone else my age in this good shape with a publisher of integrity? I suppose it would be good if they'd do a paperback. I'll think about this and see if I want to talk them into anything. But, no sweat.

Herb Yellin from California & Charles Seluzicke from Maryland have written me lately about collections of my things. I love fooling with this stuff.

The binding bill for *XVII Machines* a real sore spot, will even end things between me & Ernie—though the major thing is that so many things are not done well enough.... Allen Hoey in Potsdam will do a little pamphlet of my ash poems. I'll love this!

My hands, arm, shoulders so pleasantly tired from the work outside. I feel so at ease, even when considering the poetry business as in the last few ¶s. Labor outside not to forget that I want to write great poems & be known for them, but to put things in perspective, to clarify. And look at the energy of this entry.

May 12, 1977

Weather warm again at last. A fine weekend to look forward to. Next week classes end, and then a week of reading journals and getting grades in. And then!

Must clear things away here, clean out drawers. Want only to have my poems in front of me for a year, and nothing to do with school. Will still decide on a regimen for myself, at least to begin in September.

Have had no contact, except in passing, with Poulin lately—so, I've been happy.

Wonderful call from Rabbi Goldman. Looks like I'll read at his temple next month or so. I believe he'll help quite a bit get the book around.... But I've had few literary thoughts lately. Have played much poker—not getting good cards, but holding my own—lately, and trying to catch up on sleep. Just want the semester to end, and have not even been very conscientious preparing for classes the past week or two, though they've gone all right.

We'll pick up onion sets & tomato plants tomorrow, etc. Still wonderful to work out back, but I tire easily. It's this poker pace I've been leading, and I haven't slept well even when I do hit the sack.

Three more inscribed books back from MacLeish.

Packages of books to mail to Seluzicki & Yellin, who complained about Rook Press.... Wonder how Ernie is. Not too well, I bet. Haven't heard from him in a long time, but should. Have sent him $140 for binding of *Machines*. What a beautiful job Bill Gilmore did.... Have sent *The Light: Ten Poems* and *The Swastika Prose* to Harry Duncan, who said I should send something if I'm willing to wait two years. Twenty would be okay!

Han has substituted twice this week again. The money is <u>welcome</u>, and she's glad to be busy, also glad to be at home when she's not called in, so it <u>works</u> both ways.

Fine letter from Steve Berg, who says Sandra McPherson has done a good review for *APR* of *Swastika*.

Norton wiped up Bobick in the first round last night.

Will read at GCC next week, & do a workshop at Attica Prison soon after, with Frank Judge.

Nothing deep in my life lately—maybe a few moments in the dirt out back.

May 20, 1977

Classes ended yesterday. Today the letter came that officially gave me the leave of absence at the college. I'm surrounded by journals/papers to read, dazed, but happy, and only need some strength to finish up and get grades in. Will do. Then ...

Won $250 at poker last week. Lost $11 last night. Have won 20 out of the last 27 games, and losses have been small.... Rock made an ass of himself in the last two games in arguments with Manny & Joe. He's got real problems. I'm happy that I could stay out. Joe almost hit him!

My reading at GCC went well. Frank Judge wasn't even bad company! Will go in to Rochester for an interview with Bob Koch on Monday for WXXI Radio on *Swastika*, and then will have a workshop at the prison at Attica Monday night.

Han is still busy planting many things. Monday she begins teaching.

A copy of *AP '76* arrived the other day, a paperback, and was marked "Second Printing—1977." I'm not sure what this means, how many were printed, but this is a good sign. There's still a chance I'll clear a little money on the book, anyway.

Called Ernie Stefanik the other day. He's down in the dumps, teaching wiping him out.

I still feel way behind on my sleep. The spring has been frantic, but everything will change before long now. It's true I've played a lot of poker, into the wee hours, & this has thrown my whole nervous system off.

Did get to know Whitman the past few weeks, so teaching was not a complete loss.... Enough. My next entry will be written by a relieved man.

June 2, 1977

I was hit hard by Attica, going in past outposts of guards, the walls, the prisoners. The walls. And one young man in the workshop said he's been in for five years and is not eligible for parole until 1995. Overwhelming. Another prisoner mentioned how he has seen the sudden recognition on a prisoner's face that the prisoner will really have to spend 5, or 10, or 25 years there. It is like the sudden realization of death. We walked past the yard where all the killings took place. We were called "civilians." Outside that place the air was so cool, the grass so green.

De Snodgrass came over with Poulin Saturday, stayed through dinner and until about midnight. Camille is in Florida, De on his way back from Stratford. He looks good, seems happy, did most of the talking. We all had a good time. He made some wild statements ("suffering is never important") that shocked Al more than me—I know where he stands. But he is still a poet I admire, going way back to Cortland, and I'd be the last one to argue. Gave him a copy of *Swastika* because Al said he wanted one, and De seemed pleased. I hope he reciprocates with a hardback of his book upcoming from Al. De said it looked as though the two of us would corner the poetry market on this subject.

I didn't realize that Al is taking this whole press on by himself, that he'll have to pay for all the printing, etc., and worry about distribution himself. I don't know. A million headaches, and just when he & Boo are worried about money, since he'll be on half-pay for a year. I wonder how long the press will go on. I want to get a copy of each book—that's all I care about, I guess. Tony is putting the pressure on Al to get *Anchor Dragging* done, too.... When *The Führer Bunker* appears, Al & Boo & Han & I might travel to Erieville for the signing, etc. I'd enjoy that!

Sent a copy of *Swastika* to Tony Hecht: decided to stop being paranoid, etc. Got a very nice letter back from him today. I want to send a copy to Maxine Kumin, too, & Helen Vendler, when I get more copies. Why not? What the hell, maybe I can wangle a NBA nomination; if not, it won't break my heart.... Was finally invited to read in NY at the Donnell by Academy of American Poets. Everyone but Heyen has read there. I had the feeling it would be soon. The folks at Vanguard will enjoy this, I'm sure.... Might travel to Cincinnati this month; NY in the fall, I'd guess.... Jack Matthews' beautiful review of *Swasika* out in *Ohio Review*. Yesterday *Ontario Review* came with 4 poems & my picture. Next *APR* will have a review & a poem. This is quite a bit of attention, actually. Don't know if the book is selling at all.

Beautiful light rains the past couple of days. I can't believe how fast the vegetables are growing. I swear the corn grew an inch in a day. I dug up another small plot—a good-sized garden now.

Well, Manny in Greece, Rock up on the St. Lawrence, Mirko in Russia. No poker, but pleasant happenings go on. Family reunion in Hamburg last Sunday. We all had a great time. Wonderful competitions in horseshoes & basketball, me & Wolf against Billy & Kurt. All of us look forward to two weeks in Canada this summer.... I've been getting a lot of exercise lately, hours a day—biking, digging, playing basketball with the boys. I feel good.

Beginning to get school behind me.

SUNY $1,850 check came today. Wonderful. Han teaching every day, too. We're making money now, and hope to save some. I still have $350 coming from the GCC/Attica thing.

Party at Gemmetts Saturday, and I want to see the Peckinpah *Cross of Iron*, coming to town. And some great Portland/Philadelphia games upcoming. Life is fun these days.

June 5, 1977

Called Mom & Pop today—a barrage of news: they're renting out their Selden house & hoping to move back to Ridge & their retirement village; Mom having some kind of bladder surgery this month; Eddie was just there, & it turns out that he and Jean are not living together—a sad story; and Sepp, Henry's father-in-law, hanged himself—part of the heritage of the Afrika Corps, still.

Saw *Cross of Iron*—it was lousy, in bad taste in so many ways, confused.

Richard Lautz stopped in yesterday & went with us to the Gemmetts' party. It was good to see him, and he's been a warm supporter & good friend, but I can do without visitors, too.

Friday I spent 2-3 quiet, delicious, intense hours in my office at school working on "The Ash" sequence. It was good, again, to enter that swirl inside poetry as it gets written.

June 6, 1977

I just read over the six poems of my Ash sequence. I think I've done with it what I can. Morning, I'm home alone—Han off teaching & the kids in school—the phone is off the hook. I love this silence out of the world.... It's even overcast today, and it's good to be inside, for now. Coffee & quiet. June will unwind me.

6/12/77

Sunday, and overcast. Noon. Lazy. Cleaned out the garage with Billy this morning. Han is out to buy strawberries at a stand.

Bought a box of frames at an auction yesterday for $22, and inside, at the bottom of the box, unseen by me or by anyone else, were about a dozen WWII Office of War Information posters, all dated 1943—great big things, Norman Rockwells urging the buying of war bonds, a giant Uncle Sam with his fingers to his lips urging secrecy, sailors in a lifeboat with their ship going down behind them & a message about secrecy, a troop-train & a message saying troops were on the move and "Is Your Trip Necessary?" The posters are probably worth quite a bit, but I love them. We'll frame one for home, and I'd like one or two in my office at school. Bill Stewart & Mirko will flip when they see them. My father will remember them, no doubt—they must have been posted in the shipyards where he worked. Nora Studier says she remembers one with the motto something like "A Slip of the Lip Can Sink a Ship." I had great luck in getting these. Pete Mosher said that reproductions have been printed. But these are the real thing.

No one can believe how long it's been since we've had any rain here. At least we have water, & can water the garden.

Saw *Rocky*. Loved it. Han & the kids did, too.

Saw Tony Petrosky out at Picciones the other day, & then they all stopped in here. Tony seems solid—he & Patti have bought a new house in Pittsburgh, will move in in August. He says it's up high, up in good air. *Rapport* projects flourish--$4,000 in grants for the magazine lately. They've not seen Ernie Stefanik in many months, & Tony feels about the way I do about how Ernie has made many bad moves lately.

6/13/77

The two Tonys came over today. We sat in the shade out back and had a couple of beers. Lovely day today. My back hurts a little, so I haven't worked out back. Or anywhere! Took a bike ride along the canal this morning. Mainly, have just sort of been hanging around, as the number of my entries in this journal shows.

While we were sitting out back, a hummingbird flitted in and out of Han's flowers. Wish I knew what the beautiful bird was that Han & Irma & I saw out back yesterday. Will watch for it again. Maybe will put up some birdhouses in the future. So much to look forward to back there.

6/20/77

Al checked into Yaddo after running around in Wash., D.C., & maybe NYC, and after a day or two checked into the Saratoga Springs hospital with leg pains. A "superficial clot," a doctor said to Boo. We really don't know how he is, but probably okay, but if he does not change his life and get some regular fresh air and food and exercise, he's always going to have trouble. If I thought he'd change a little and try to take care of himself a little bit, I'd be very sympathetic. Well, he is still what he is.

I've been having great days, riding up to the school (bicycling) once a day, working out back for an hour or two a day, writing or gathering together *The Handbook of Heartbreak* for an hour or so a day. I want to "finish" it as a form into which I can pour everything, before I go on with *The Chestnut Rain*. I'm going over all my early poems to see if they can get into the *H of H*. Once & for all, then, I'll be caught up & can go on with new work. I think I have the frame lines now (thanks to another auction & things felt there & the 100s of farm journals I bought there) to expand the title poem quite a bit, & with good stuff. Months of rewarding work to be done there, & I'll have a good sense of accomplishment, I know.

A long letter from Wm. Ewert. He offered $200 for my drafts of "Fires." Sure! I sent the stuff to him today. He also wants to pay me $15-30 for handwritten poems. Amazing, that this fellow has found me. I love it!

My mother has her operation tomorrow. Trust she'll be all right. I'll probably fly to LI in July & help them move.

We've had some rain the past few days, at last.

Alaska Oil Pipeline opened today.... Supreme Court decision that states do <u>not</u> have to pay for or provide non-therapeutic abortions. Thurgood Marshall dissents saying he's appalled by the "moral bankruptcy" of those who thus condemn the poor women to unwanted children & the unwanted children to unhappiness & poverty. Shit—it's as easy to say that <u>he's</u> the immoralist. What of the children, their being & existence? My abortion poem, too ideal, talks to this point. Contraception, yes (though even this is hard to reconcile), abortion for non-therapeutic reasons, no. Public monies have to solve the problem in other ways.

My trip to Cincinnati Friday has me a bit nervous.

Garden's first crop, radishes, coming in.

Tony & Sandi complain of always being broke, but Tony spent $600 on some <u>beautiful</u> oak furniture at the auction the other day. Table, chairs, buffet (or sideboard, as they call it), & a china cabinet, wonderful stuff. If we'd had the room, I'd have wanted the stuff. The table has 9 leaves!... I do hope Tony will be all right. So many pressures. Now the Leeds are coming to visit Wednesday. Egads, & I haven't said Egads in a long time. They (Tony & Sandi) and Boo were over the other evening, and we all had a pleasant time.

I'm still raking rocks out of the ground by the hundreds the last few days. It's a lot like clamming.... My back has been a little strained, but okay. And the stone fence is looking pretty good.

Mon.—June 27

All went very well at Cincinnati. Rabbi Goldman is a <u>wonderful</u> man, a real man, who has built much with much love in his life. All the people I met were kind and gracious. Isaac M. Wise Temple magnificent, and the new school/center very impressive.... I read well, I think. The service was lovely. Many compliments, & about a dozen copies of *Swastika* sold afterwards. Amazing. What a life this is. And I just read a book by an Italian Jew, Levi, about Auschwitz. And I, a German non-Jew, reading my poems at a temple service. Amazing.

Have been happy, working hard outside (getting stuff to the road for town pick-up), and bicycling. Billy & Kristen finishing up school now, & Han to begin a class at the college soon. The land out back tempers my whole life, calms me, makes me feel at ease. Often I just stand back there, under trees or by the garden, leaning on a rake, listening to the birds and trying to name the shade of green light shining through the ash leaves. Han & I have planned, now, where our bigger garden next year will be, and where we'll plant some spruce trees this fall.

Poulin went to Strong in Rochester this morning, and they gave him some tests, and he has clots in his legs, and he's on anti-coagulants and will be in the hospital for a week or two. He won't change his life, it appears. I'm afraid I just don't care much. I wish him well, but don't want to drive to the hospital & visit, and won't. It's the same old story.

About writing I feel lazy.

7/2/77

A beautiful, windy Saturday, lovely family days to look forward to. Han will begin her class on Tuesday. I love the July 4th weekend here. So, my little July 4th, 1976 oak from Long Island has held on and now has six leaves. Maybe I should transplant it to the back in a year or two?

Al will have to be in the hospital until at least Wednesday. I called him Thursday and we spoke quite a while. Twice he asked me if I was sitting down, once to say that over $1,300 in royalties just came in on his Rilke, and once to say that Library of Congress (meaning Robert Hayden, who he just visited!) offered him $1,000 for a reading in March. For one book of poems (and a bad one) Poulin does pretty well. And a translation. He also got in the mail, anonymously, the Dead Ear Award for the worst translation of Rilke in history. It probably is, so little German does he know. I laugh to myself over all my emotions about Al. If he were to write something indisputable and fine, then I would admire him. But <u>everything</u>, from his NEA grant, to the publication of his anthology & Rilke, etc., etc., is from personal contact, phone calls, back scratching. He knows this too. The doctors say he won't change his life and stop killing himself until he thinks better of himself. And he's an ex-Catholic, if there is such a thing, haunted, guilty over how he milks everything, how money that he hasn't earned rolls in, how he has gotten even a full professorship without deserving it. I harbor some of the same feelings, and know what they're like. Enough.

Al just phoned, asking us to pick up maybe a plant for Boo, which we will. The poor guy. I like him. I ask this of myself (though I am not nearly as afflicted) as I do of him: why can't he mind his fucking business and write and stop the constant boosterism. The work first, first.

Boo & Sandi & Tony & Han & I went to see *End Game* last night. A fine production, directed by Dave Hamilton, who left us tickets. I kept thinking how the language of the play needed the body of the actors, how a lyric poem cannot do this. Hamilton caught so much, and Hamm was played brilliantly, I thought, by Derek Hill.

William Ewert sent me $240, a long letter, & copies of a Forest Notes magazine. How fortunate I am that he found me. He wants to buy another manuscript in a few months. Ahem, and I was talking of undeserved money.

Mom is home from the hospital, and mending.

A little magazine, a new one, *West Branch*, took three poems.

I'm still putting together *The Handbook of Heartbreak*. It's up to 69 poems now. Once and for all I'll catch up with where I am. Don't know if I'll send it to Vanguard. The poems are all endearing to me, but not, with a few exceptions, my very best.

Buzz of the mail truck outside.

Life should stay as it is, right now, for a few hundred years.

7/3/77

The ground out back just behind our glade of ash trees is rutted and hard, filled with stones and small stumps, so I'm digging it up and trying to level it. The first few minutes of digging and raking and banging the dirt from the mat of weeds are a drag, but I notice that after a while my mind turns off or smiles at the mush of its reveries, and the body works and enjoys and keeps going. After a while, I have to remember that I'm tired and should stop, or that the sun is too hot. The hard work eases and cleans, clears the mind, much of its pettiness, places me here again inside a better and truer life.

I spend a little time every day with *The Handbook of Heartbreak*. I'm going to be willing to let some things in, to allow them their eccentricities & weaknesses in a way I haven't before. It will be a big old source book filled with all sorts of stuff. Do I want Vanguard, say, or just a few hundred copies to be done? Maybe I'll write Tom & be honest & explain that I wanted to catch up with myself, & like the things in *H of H*, but *The Chestnut Rain* will be my next …… book—fill in the space with "good," "fine," "important," "big."

Gary Eddy might stop over today. He's thrilled about his Slow Loris chapbook. He's a good kid, and headed for graduate school at El Paso this fall.

I'll cook some steaks outside today.

Jury duty July 11th—hope like hell it won't drag on and fuck up the Canada trip.... Cousins Billy & Kurt Greiner will have a wonderful time when Kurt gets here Wednesday for a week or so.

Tony Piccione's birthday today. We got him a cactus.

Cleaned out the closet in this study yesterday evening. Have been wanting to do this for a long time.

July 4, 1977

Played blackjack with Billy & Dougie & Ralphie & Han yesterday evening until midnight. Made sure each of the kids went home winning a little.

Will go swimming later, and maybe play tennis—Billy just walked in to ask me if I would. Well, then, I'm off.

July 4th. What a day. I'm filled with the day!

July 11, 1977

I sure know this date. I leave this morning for jury duty in Rochester, which has been on my mind for months. I hate the drive into the city, the strain of even finding parking, but most of all hope that I won't get stuck for weeks—we leave for Canada in about ten days.

Beautiful days lately, and all passing quickly. Billy has been with Kurt in Hamburg, and we miss him around here. I miss the bunch of boys who are always around for cards, basketball, soccer when he's here. He'll be back Tuesday by bus, we guess.

Saw Al yesterday. He's back from the hospital, picking up his life again: he's smoking, and today Snodgrass will visit, and this will make him nervous as hell. I don't know. Nothing Boo can do, either. The smoking will be the big test. Boo has stopped, Al is doing about half-a-pack a day.

My mind leaps to the land! Han has picked four or five quarts of raspberries lately back there. The surveyor is about half done, told us he'd finish today. Then, a fence, and much pleasure planting trees along it. Found two catalpas on the lot behind Vallones. No tree reminds me more of my childhood. Our driveway in Nesconset was lined with them, big old broad-leafed white-blooming string-beaning trees. I'll make some room for my two finds to grow. What they will mean to me when I'm old! I'll visit them often.

Vanguard won't do *The Shine of the World*. It's a relief to me, for many reasons. I don't want to worry about the book during my year off. I should write an occasional essay, and maybe in 20 years put the book together again.

Heckman did a fine job of binding the manuscript and page proofs of *Swastika*. I have quite a collection of such Heyen items now.

Dear diary, whimsical friend, wish me luck as I set off on this jury adventure.

July 12, 1977

Yesterday was a full day, to say the least. I made it to Rochester, was herded here and there with about a hundred others, then talked to the judge alone and managed to be exempted ("permanently exempted," he said) from jury duty. What a relief. And when I found 490 West immediately on leaving the parking lot, I knew it would be my day.

When I got home the surveyor was there staking off our property. It goes deeper and wider even than I'd hoped. We called up right away about a fence, and the guy from Sears showed up within the hour. It will be put up right after we get back from Canada. Wonderful. Glad we have a little extra money right now. The fence will run along that one side of our property for about 190', and then about 35' on a right angle at the corner. If we ever want more, we can add to it.

Snodgrass was at Poulins' all day, signing and inscribing *The Führer Bunker*. Al smoked all day. Boo is going nuts. Al needs <u>rest</u>, and had a long and tense day—Snodgrass even stayed over. It's unbelievable. They wanted us to stop in, and we did, late, around ten, for an hour. I was glad to get paper & hardbound copies of the book, inscribed. De was nice, tried to compliment me a couple of times on *Swastika* & I shrugged & cut in, the way he does. Well, hell, all I want is respect.... But something must be wrong with him & Camille. When Han mentioned her, he changed the subject adroitly. Al said that De is in bad shape, needs deep therapy.... Anyway, the book is handsome. I read from it last night and this morning. The thrust of it reminds me of the "Men's Room in the College Chapel" poem, that whatever is twisted inside of us will out, will rise. The last poem, spoken by Goebbels, ends with this.... Apparently there are more poems and De will do even a bigger book with Harper & Row when the time comes.

I'm beginning work at clearing along the property line so that the men can put the fence in. In spots, it won't be easy. I hope to finish before we leave for Canada. It's hot & muggy now. An hour outside is a very long time.

Little Stephen Gemmett came over with Bob yesterday to see our stamp collections. He's at the maniac stage right now. I know what that's like & went through it many times myself. I gave him dozens of nice stamps, many commemorative mints, especially. He was thrilled. He'll never forget it, I know.

Sent off packages of inscribed things to Bill Ewert & Calvin Israel today, things they'd sent me.

A fine week to look forward to, meaning an empty one except for what I want to do, and then an auction Saturday.

Billy came back from Hamburg today. He had a fine time, played golf on two courses, looks good. I sure missed him.

7/13/77

Soon after my words about my empty week, I got a disconcerting call from this man Cuddihy from California who edits *Ironwood* and said I "promised" to do an essay on Wright. This is bullshit. I said I'd try, but told him not to count on me. But, somehow, he got me to say (because I'm so bad on the phone) I'd do it & get it to him soon. I worked last night, made progress, was dead tired, couldn't sleep, got up to write him a letter to tell him to go fuck himself, didn't send the letter, read for & worked on the essay again today, and it looks as though I'll be able to finish it, now, turning for a few pages to *Moments of the Italian Summer*. So, it may all work out for the best. If I finish it (I will) I'll be glad I did it.

Also worked hard for 3-4 hours outside today, clearing along the line. Found it easier to dig out the old apple trees than to chop them down. Made much progress. Have to lay the line through the raspberry patch tomorrow, I'm afraid. And I think some nice 10-12' ash trees may be <u>right</u> on the line. Today I found two small horse chestnut trees on the property. Wonderful! Will probably transplant them to give them more room somewhere.

Marvin Bell called, a friendly call from a friendly man, but one I could have done without. Maybe I'll go to his reading in Rochester tomorrow night.

7/16/77

Boo Poulin is picking me up in 20 minutes & we're going to an auction near Medina. It's <u>hot</u> today, but it will be fun.

Tony back. They stopped in for a minute. Sandi is covered with poison ivy. I worked out back in it, clearing it from trees, yesterday myself. I was careful. Hope I avoided it. Sandi said it takes 3-5 days for the "eruptions." Some of the poison ivy vines are as thick as my fingers. And I've found grapevines two inches thick choking trees back there.... I've just about got the line cleared for the fence.

And I've finished 9 pages of the James Wright piece, my usual quirky work. Will now write a few pages on *Italian Summer*.

Han and I have picked about a quart of raspberries a day from the patch out back. Nothing makes her happier than these berries, so much a part of her childhood, the more pleasant parts of her childhood, are they.

Tues. 19th July

It's been so hot that I only worked outside an hour today, scything around some fine ash trees being overwhelmed by morning glory and grape vines.

We'll leave Friday for Wolf's, Saturday for Canada.

Finished the piece on Wright and have it in the mail. It's pretty good, I think—I could improve it a lot if I had the energy & desire to work with it for a month, but I have neither. It's all right, I think (he says again).

Her clarinet teacher told Kristen today that he's never had a sixth grader as qualified as she is. I encourage her, want her to be the best. She's just a little better than average in most of her subjects, but she's a sweet, lovely girl.

Marvin Bell dropped in for a half-hour the other day. He's all right, friendly, but I can do without visits. Norbert & Katherine Krapf want to visit in August.

We'll watch the All-Star baseball game on television tonight.

Haven't touched *The Handbook of Heartbreak* in a few weeks, after working at it steadily for a while. Guess I'll plan on finishing in August, after our trip. Still can't believe that I'll be off for a whole year beginning Sept.... Now, diary, I'm going fishing.

Sun. Aug. 7, 1977

Back yesterday. Billy off today for basketball camp. Eddie, who is split up with Jean and in bad shape, will visit today. I hope he'll be all right.

So good to be home. The vacation was excellent, though being with Wolf, as unconscious and inconsiderate as he is, got wearing near the end. I wrote one silly & angry poem ("The Singer") but otherwise did no writing, sent only one postcard, to Mirko, who has sent me so many cards.

I caught one good bass and one good pickerel, shot an 85 in golf, did some swimming, played horseshoes and much volleyball. Don't know if I improved my soul any: find myself looking forward to the 2 weeks' mail the Vallones have for us, & they'll be back this evening. Read, on vacation, *All the President's Men*, *The Final Days*, and the terrible but fun Irving Wallace Novel *The Man*.

It's drizzling today, and I'm glad. Picked a few tomatoes this morning, and onions. Han and I took a walk, past Acetos', and they called us over and gave us some celery. I love this neighborhood—Joan Aceto showed me the tree line from the old farm, the big ash and elm (now stumps) that had marked one side and now can be traced from yard to yard and across the street.

Yesterday was the big parade. I caught the end of it. It's also the centennial of the Brockport Fire Department. The old equipment in the parade choked me up—there was, for example, an 1822 hand pumper, the oldest one in the state, that belonged to Weedsport Fire Department, and an 1876 steam pumper that belonged to Chili.... I rode up by bike yesterday evening, the bike I rode the kids on so much in Hannover, and drove past my secret places at the school. It's been twenty years, come this September.

8/9/77

Lovely day today, cool and sunny. Decided to spend a few hours at the school writing. I figured out that only two things could happen up there that could disturb me in my fine office: they could mow the lawn below my windows or, worse, could be clipping the hedge. Well, a guy was shearing the hedge, and the electric whine got to me. But, I put tissue paper in my ears, and managed to finish the poem "The Song" which turned out, I think, fine—subtle and indirect about the thing it's most serious about. It will be for *The Chestnut Rain*. All in all, my office and my comfort here are behind my not applying to Yaddo, though I was thinking of it. What the hell do I want to do over there? I'd miss home, and have a good life here.

Mowed the rest of the lawn, and trimmed the wisteria for an hour, will finish this evening.

Tom Woll wrote to say that *NYTBR* will review *Swastika* next Sunday. Six months after publication. I'm amazed. It will be the first big place I've been reviewed in. I hate to admit it, but if it's a negative review I'm going to be bothered quite a bit, upset and angry and sorry for myself. Everybody reads that damned thing.

My fingers are crossed. Tom sent a rave review that will be in *Choice*, and a negative one from *VQR* saying my emotion was "willed" in the book & that I wanted to do such a book. My feeling is that the former charge won't hold up, and I <u>know</u> that the latter charge is bullshit. "Laconic," the reviewer said, which means to me, again, a reviewer who can't hear what really is going on or the music of even apparently prosaic stanzas.

    Long talk with Eddie, who even tried suicide six weeks ago. I think, he sounds as though, he'll be all right now, is past most of the pain. He's a good man. Wish he lived in Brockport, actually. We could be fairly close, I think. Hope to see him before long again. Han and I don't think he'll ever get back with Jean again. And we don't know everything about the split.

    Well, Al did sell his books. Wilson from The Phoenix trucked away the collection. Al says he got good money. What good is the money? He doesn't need it. The books mean so much more. And I remember how he chased for autographs. Now, all that is gone. He's a fool.

8/10/77

    I had a good day, touched up and finished "The Song," took a couple of bike rides, but got sort of restless after supper, jumpy, looking for something to do, almost went out to B & B Stamps to buy some plate blocks. Anyway, wandering around out back, I spied the big ash stump in one of our paths to the back, and began digging, and got my ax, and dug, and axed, for about an hour. Worked hard, sweated. Now, after a shower, it's amazing how good I feel, how relaxed. The lesson comes to me again & again. I know, too, I'll sleep better tonight than I did last night. It's been hot & muggy mosquito weather, but I should work like that every morning.

8/22/77

    Eddie called. He & Jean will be getting a divorce. Ed asked to borrow $500, which I'm sending him. Hope he'll be all right, and is not making a mistake in wanting to buy Jean's half of the house, etc. He's got to watch out for himself a little bit. He seems to have a new girlfriend. Maybe they'll visit in a couple of weeks.

    Ralphie Matsko is staying with us 12 days while his folks are visiting relatives in Illinois. He's a great kid.

    The Krapf visit was <u>hectic</u>, but fine. Hannelore liked them very much, too.

    I wrote a whole bunch of little poems, called the group *Lord Dragonfly*, and sent it off to Ernie. Wrote another little one today: "I lean on my rake, / trusting the field." Also wrote a Christmas poem the other day called, come to think of it, "The Field." Bill Andrews will print it up. I feel good about these things.

    I've been clearing in the back, bulling the lawnmower through. And I've just been walking around, for hours, clipping something or leveling the ground a little. I'm so happy back there. And to think I don't have to begin school Friday (!) already when the college semester begins. I actually look forward 2-3 times a day to working back there.

    Irma & Mirko visited yesterday evening, and we had a good time. Walking around the property, we found a patch of black-eyed Susans, & dug many out, some for Han's beds & some we dropped off for Irma.

    It's funny how much the land can mean. And sometimes I only regret that I don't have another five, or fifty, acres. At the same time, when I see Mirko's place or Piccione's, I don't want all that either, could never take care of it all. This is one thing. But part of it is that I can have almost a personal relationship with, especially, particular trees, and <u>many</u> of them, on my property, while a much bigger place would somehow cost me everything good & deep that comes from this long-staring. Today I cut the high meadow weeds from around a group of three five-foot ash trees. I'll watch these trees over the years. I couldn't do this kind of thing with Tony's acreage, or even Mirko's six acres. We have enough. And now the fence makes me feel at ease. I hope I have 3-4 decades back there. And the person to inherit this property will find it beautiful, and care for it, I pray. I find myself saying all this about one acre! I write badly about all this here. The proof will be in the poems, the nature, yes, but the character of the man I can become back there.

Items:
1. First volume *FPAA* arrived.
2. Looks like I'll go to Athens for Mike Waters & a reading 1st week Oct.

3. My *Frescoes for Mr. Rockefeller's City* arrived back with an inscription, and a letter saying Ken MacLeish died—after "five years of unremitting pain and courage," as Archie puts it. A beautiful, moving letter.
4. M. Cuddihy from *Ironwood* called to say he loves the Wright essay.
5. Ernie doing *The Elm's Home* soon. And his Heyen bibliography has been accepted by whatever magazine it was he sent it to. I'm glad.
6. *NYTBR* review never did show up. Wonder what happened.
7. Elvis Presley died about a week ago. I'm irrationally sad. He was a good old boy.

8/26/77

Lord Dragonfly

i.
A friend dies.
Another,
forcing the lilac to flower.

ii.
Lord Dragonfly
sees me from all sides
at once.

iii.
Pear blossoms
sift the same air
as last year.

iv.
In the mowed field,
a million crickets for hire.
My steps are money.

v.
Inside the windfall apple,
tunnels of bees
singing.

vi.
Curves of the summer pepper
lit with every green.

vii.
Sunflowers
our lamps
on such a rainy day.

viii.
I lean on my shovel,
trusting the field.

ix.
When I look for him

he is away,
finding another home,
the borer that killed my poplar.

x.
Half the mantis still
prays on my scythe blade.

xi.

Breaking the field I find
a ring of round white stones,
gift of the glacier.

xii
One red cardinal,
one gray cardinal,
three cinnamon-spotted eggs.

xiii.
Arrow-headed
morning glory tendrils
attack the wire fence.

xiv.
Only the hummingbird's beak
and green breast-
feathers clear.

xv.
Outside at night
I close my eyes:
the dead elms' roots
luminous underground.

xvi.
Meteor shower—
a little more, or less,
of the Lord.

xvii.
In the autumn field,
my body,
a warm stone.

xviii.
With trees overhead,
where is the void?

    I've done some others, but I think I'll type up these eighteen as kind of a single poem and try *The New Yorker*. For a while, I've seen about all I can see back in my field? Anyway, probably the spate of little poems is over. It was fun. I don't want to strain for others. Glad I found them. Ernie or someone will probably do a little pamphlet.... Put five poems together for Duane Schneider who called. Will call it *fires*. He'll probably do it fast, maybe in time for my visit. I might go the first week in October.... Call from Patti Ross in Albany—there will be a SUNY poetry conference in November for a few days at Binghamton. Should be fun. I sure won't have any schoolwork on my mind.

Worked a lot outside again today, and will tomorrow, weather willing. We're going to Poulins' for dinner. Al now working with Tony on Tony's book with the MacLeish introduction.

Han and a <u>bunch</u> of kids & I went up to a college field and played soccer this evening. A good workout.

School beginning in a few days, and I'm <u>away</u> from it. The first $4,500 Guggenheim check has already been deposited in my checking account!

8/31/77

I've done a few more of the little poems of *Lord Dragonfly*. Would like to do a little book, with Mirko's woodcuts, one day. Hey, come to think of it, I think Vanguard might even want to do it.

My Guggenheim year begins in about an hour!

We had Emmanuel over for dinner yesterday. He looks good, and it was wonderful seeing him again. Helen will return from Greece in a couple of weeks.

Picnic at Hamlin Beach State Park today—Han's library people. It wasn't bad. I walked along the lake with Kristen picking up white, brown, green, and apparently scarce blue bits of glass worn smooth by the waves. Also, played a little soccer with the kids.

Town crazy again, filled with college kids.... I have two things on my mind: writing for blocks of time, and working the ground outside. Once the kids start school, I'll enter a routine. Hell, we've done so much outside already this year, much more than we thought we could. If I did nothing more before the snow, it would be no big deal, and I've got the fall months yet.

Han begins with her cheerleaders tomorrow.... It's supposed to be hot and humid as hell again.

Haven't seen Tony or Al in a few days.

Bought a field guide to insects, which are sort of tough, often, to identify specifically. But I've been learning some things about crickets & aphids & planthoppers.

The kids are getting excited about school. Han is the perfect mother. Today she took Kristen and several other kids to the school to show them their rooms, etc.

Let's see, can I remember any of the new poems?

>I am safe here,
>not a friend in sight.

>Light escapes
>the blackberries.

>Carrying a branch
>of silver maple
>I walk through the storm.

Well, my fingers are crossed as my year begins!

Sun. Sept. 11, 1977

Beautiful day today. Billy and I worked outside for a few hours, marking the places along the Mosher line where we'll transplant ash trees. We moved five little ones over. It did Billy good to plant a couple by himself, prune them, water them. Tuesday the nursery delivers fourteen evergreens that Han and I picked out—I've got the holes about ready along the fence line.... I've been puttering around outside, leveling here and digging out a stump or boulder there or hacking some weeds from around a tree. I spend much time just leaning on a shovel looking at the trees. A touch of winter is already in the air—too soon! too soon! I hope for a long Indian Summer next month.

The kids seem happy, are in good situations in school. Han is very busy with cheerleading again, but took the time today to can a dozen jars of thin-sliced pickles, which will be delicious all winter.

Had to make that little poem longer:

> In the far galaxies,
> collapsed stars,
> yes, but here,
> light escapes
> the blackberries.

Ray and Joyce at *Ontario Review* gave me their annual poetry prize ($100). Egads. Not much else new in my grand literary career. But as book collector, I ventured to an auction in Gates and made off with 1sts of *Seize the Day* & *The Floating Opera* for 25¢ each. A Serendipity catalogue lists the Barth book for $185! But I've got to play dumb about such things around here and not tell people about books & modern first editions & such—that way, I think, more finds will come my way.

One day flows into another. Serious work when weather drives me inside.

9/13/77

Bob Phillips called this morning to tell me that Robert Lowell died last night. Bob was sad, and I'm not happy about it, but I never knew the man or became emotionally involved with his poetry. I shook his hand once at the University of Rochester, and he signed three of my books before Anthony Hecht could spirit him away.

I told Al, and then stopped over to talk with him later. He'd called Snodgrass, who was hit hard. Snodgrass & Lowell go way back, of course. Then Jerry Mazzaro called—I wrote him last week, breaking a long silence. Jerry sounds about the same. He has yet another Lowell essay about to appear in *APR*.... A sense in which Lowell's death brought several of us a little closer together.

In rain today, I planted nine evergreens. The smell was indescribable, as I bent down into them.

9/17/77

And the day after, I planted five more trees and sprained my back. It's still stiff, though not very painful, and I'm only sorry I can't work out back. Otherwise, everything is fine. Han and I did walk around back there this evening. Lord, how we love it!

Looks like Han's mother has a blood clot in her neck and will need an operation next week. Han will probably spend a few days there with her. I hope the old gal will be all right. She's a good soul.

Ralph Sipper sent me several books today. Linda Pastan sent a broadside. My collection grows. I called up Chip's Books for a couple of items. This next year should be an especially good one for books. I'm going to splurge in NYC in November.

Han canned more tomato sauce today.

Much fun at the Kaysers' party yesterday evening. Then, at 2 a.m., the Pylyshenkos & Rocks & Heyens woke up the Mouganises to welcome Helen home. I had much brandy.... Two nights ago I won $148 at a poker game out at the lake at Chuck Lang's. Not bad for a $3 limit game.

9/22/77

It's a Thursday evening. Han has been away since Tuesday, and will be gone a couple more days, anyway—her Mom had a 6-hr. operation today for removal of a clot near the brain. Han called to say the surgeon said the operation was more difficult than he thought it would be, but that things went well. Instead of cheering Han up on the phone, I was glum, and needed a pep-talk. I'd hoped Han could make it home by tomorrow. Now she'll have to stay, & then come home, and then return again when her mother gets to go home in about eight days. I don't know. I should be more generous, certainly, but do get nervous when Han is driving around in Buffalo, and my back hurts like hell, and Kristen has a cold coming on, and Mom <u>is</u> in a hospital getting excellent care. I guess I resent the old man, who can't even drive and has usually been the worst sort of asshole since I've known him. And I resent stupid Wolfram, who gives a shit about no one but himself & no doubt is not straining himself over there in Hamburg to take care of his mother. Yes, I should be more generous at such a rough time, but I'm human. Fuck it, I'll mellow again when it is all over. Mainly, my wife is away and I need her, and my back hurts.

Lord Dragonfly is pretty close to its final form.

First *Manassas Review* arrived. It looks pretty good, and I'll try to get some good things into their Heyen #, and get it around a little.

Have finished Eric Sevareid's *Not So Wild a Dream*. A very great book. A great man. Yes.

Must get tickets for Athens trip.

Another gloomy day—it's been terrible here. I had a poker game the other night, lost $54, but had a fine time. But I guess it was no good for my fucking back, again.

Crazy details w. students are tying me still to school, but all these threads will break. The time off is still paradise, no matter anything else.

Monday

Han will be back today, I hope.... Terrific rainstorms again, the whole world flooding.

My damned back is still not strong. I'm careful just bending down to pick something off the floor.

Bob Phillips called to say the review of *Swastika* is in *NYTBR* this Sunday. It's by Wm. Meredith, is reviewed with Stan Plumly's, & is favorable. I'm glad. Should please the Vanguard folks & even sell 5-10 copies.

I'm still puttering with *Lord Dragonfly*—added a poem today, and reinstated one that I'd cut. I'm thinking of showing it to Vanguard, just in case (Harcourt Brace has done some little books like Berry's *Country Marriage* & Wilbur's *Opposites*, and *Lord Dragonfly* would be excellent for this), but Ernie will probably do it next year.... Duane Schneider sent the proofs of *Fires*—it's going to look good. 300 copies, 50 signed.

Kristen just walked in to say she'd heard a weather bulletin: heavy rain & hail for Brockport & vicinity!

Tues. A.M.

Han is home, getting some extra sleep this morning. I love her. And what a difference it makes having her home. It is as though it takes the two of us to balance this home, to keep the roof on the walls and the kids human. I was so nervous about them when she was away.... Her Mom seems to be recuperating okay, even better than expected.

The sun has actually appeared this morning.... I've puttered with *Lord Dragonfly* for an hour or two again. It's up to 33 poems now.

Will go to the school today to xerox a bunch of title pages for *FPAA*. Ben Franklin has been a friend, and will help me earn all the series volumes, I think.

Lord DragonflyI will conclude:

        Cosmos, planet, field—
        and the dead
        aware of everything!

Oct. 1, 1977

Another miserable day, as was yesterday, and more rain promised for tomorrow. Weeks and weeks without a single shining autumn day; record rains, and no end in sight.

Lost $140 playing poker the other night. Surely the worst luck in my life, losing with 4 of a kind, full houses, 6 lows all night. So, I'm $50 down over three games. Unusual. It doesn't feel good to lose.

"Mushrooms" appeared in *New Yorker* yesterday. In the issue, too, is a jolting article by Daniel Lang about the Germans today. One of his conclusions is, and it seems to me he earns it and will say it better than I will here, that the strange atmosphere of Germany (and I've felt it) is of millions who committed vast crimes that went <u>unpunished</u>, whatever else is said.... At one point he quotes Theodor Adorno: "To write poetry after Auschwitz is barbaric." Yes. And the opposite can be said. And I felt (maybe my wishful thinking & prejudicial predisposition to feel this way) that, again, whatever else (and I feel far from the book already) *The Swastika Poems* is not only psychologically right, but justified, and necessary, even (gulp) a fine thing to have done, that I might feel this way even from the outside were I not the author.

Will get ready for the Athens trip, and putter around inside today. Very tired. Couldn't sleep, & lost the whole night's sleep playing cards the night before.

10/14/77

Some sun yesterday, but cold. I did get some trees planted a couple of days ago. Han and I went out to Salmon Creek Nursery and picked out a scotch pine, two white spruce, and a white pine, the long-needled and soft beauty that grew beside the back porch in Nesconset. The four trees are about six feet already.... Yesterday I transplanted four small ash over to the Mosher line, and four maples to various places. Unless I've forgotten one, then, we have 13 maples (not counting a couple of tiny seedlings) on the property. For as many years as I can, I'll walk from tree to tree—a nice way to see the property. What the century has come to: the American suburbanite on his .95 of an acre visiting his 13 maple trees. And a hundred years from now?

The Athens trip was gratifying. Duane had *Fires* ready. Matthews had a fine dinner, as did the Summers. My reading filled the chapel. Bob DeMott & Sam Crowl & Wayne Dodd and all were very friendly. The videotape program with Sam went well, I think. Mike's performance for his dissertation went well, at least his reading of poems, but he was almost inarticulate when one or two token questions were asked. Mike simply does not seem to have the ability to talk about literature. Often he does not seem very intelligent. As stupid and ill-prepared as I am critically, I am a genius next to Mike. What this means in regard to his poems—well, who knows. Have I always sensed something lacking at the core, some intelligence that (I think) enters one of my poems, say a poem like even "The Crane" with its developing metaphor and the word soulful and, in general, the integrated mind (or voice) that holds it together? I like Mike, and wish him well. The "Dr." will fit him now more ungainly than it does me.

Have loved watching the playoff and world series games. There's one tonight. I'm pulling for the Dodgers.

My folks seem moved in & happy in their new place. Han's mom is home from the hospital and recuperating slowly. Han seems always to have various aches and arthritic pains. I'm fine, though the old body creaks. I hope the aging process slows down in my 40s.

10/19/77

Han has substituted the past few days, and loves to, apparently.

Some sun today—I mowed for a couple hours, then saw Billy's soccer game. His team beat Gates, 3-1. Paul Gaylord was one of the refs, and was a good one!

Duane Schneider called again. The signed edition of *Fires* is sold out, & he couldn't even give some shops all they wanted. And I guess Bill Ewert wants to buy the typescript from him, etc., etc. I'm gratified. He'll send me more copies of *Temporary Facts*. Now, I'll trade some.

I must write Sandra McPherson a long letter of thanks for her *APR* essay on *Swastika*. It's quite something. Hard for me to believe. It has relieved me, somehow, lifted me for two days since my copy arrived. And the book not only holds up for me, but has so much more to give than even she has space to give it. I guess the book has become the best-known book of poems by any poet of my generation? I think so. And the poem in *APR*, "The Jewish Children"—it actually choked me up the first time I read it again.... So many good things seem to have happened to me lately—all this exposure at once. But there will be many quiet years, and that's for sure. And, all in all, small potatoes anyway, this business of "poetry" in this country. But I can't think of any other skin I'd rather be inhabiting now.

Tony visited today. He's not very happy. But he will be, for a while at least, once his BOA book is out.

I haven't been sleeping lately, so can't get up as early as I'd like. Well, I'm sort of resigned to relaxing & doing little of anything except puttering in here and out in back until after the NYC trip. Nov. 20th, I'll <u>begin.</u> Or after Thanksgiving, whenever that is.

10/25/77

Played poker until 5:30 in the morning—won $75 after being down $80. Maybe I broke my bad streak. Played at Mirko's. Read sad letter from Irma to Mirko. Don't know why the hell he doesn't wake up a little.

Another beautiful day. I was too tired to work out back, but did walk around a while.

Han will leave tomorrow for a couple days at her mother's, getting Mom ready for the winter. I'll go to the Irving Feldman reading tomorrow night.

Long call from Ernie the other night. He's very happy these days, & will be doing three or four more of my things, at least, including *Lord Dragonfly*.

Just saw a television show on Preston Jones that followed his *A Texas Trilogy* to New York where, after great buildup, it closed after five weeks. At the end, paraphrasing one of his own characters, he said, "I don't know what I expected, but it sure wasn't a bunch of fat critics, leaning against a greasy city, smoking cigarettes, and thinking of ... nothing at all." Wink.

Sent for James Wright's new book. I bet I'll love it.

Hope I'm not too disappointed when I hear in a week how *Swastika* sold through June.

I'm only in mid-life, but have gotten very lazy about reading, studying, learning. I've lost (or it's in hibernation) my academic ambition. Unless this stops my poems from widening, or finding ways just to <u>be</u>, this is okay, though it makes me nervous. I am learning other things—never pulled corn stalks or seen their root systems before yesterday; never watched sap bead on a spruce tip before last week.

11/1/77

Thirty-seven today. Yes, I guess so. I feel just about that old.

I'm very happy, at ease, though doing nothing substantial lately. A mind full of jottings, so an entry of jottings.

Beautiful weather, but I'm tired of working outside. I really now "understand," for the first time, what emotion begins "After Apple-Picking."

Irma stopped over yesterday evening with gypsy Katja—seems the Pylyshenkos had a fire in their kitchen the other night. I gave her a copy of *Fires!*

Ernie sent his Heyen bibliography. He's gotten a kind of order into all my writing life, and I'm grateful. The bibliography will go through 1977, and I'll feel like I'm making a new start after that.

Tony stopped by with a birthday bottle of wine yesterday, and then called to say he'd probably go to that creative writing gathering in Binghamton after all. After that trip, and my New York trip, I'll be settling in happily for the winter.

Our big food order comes Thursday.

Beautiful letter from Tom Woll about "The Jewish Children" in *APR*. I started working on that poem about my grandfather & father yesterday. I think two parts are done.

I have a thousand feelings about the Sexton letters just published. She was quite a spirit, even valiant, that woman. But, again, there's something touching, yes, but disgusting about the striving for reputation, as always, and the business of finding fame. I'm half jealous and half repelled by, again, everything new I learn about that Snodgrass/Lowell/Sexton circle. Looks as though James Wright didn't want letters to be published now. The one letter to Summers is a scream, so perfect on his distance. Her letters from Europe are the most moving, the great struggle to get well, be well, so apparent there.... The whole book tinged by its commercialism, oh the desire to remember mom, yes, but also to make dough and promote the cult figure for future royalties....

Tillie Olsen here Wednesday. I've been reading *Yonnondio*.

11/2/77

Suddenly yesterday the noise started from across the street. Bulldozer and roller and other machines. Toby is having a double driveway added to his double driveway. Here in suburbia I am now located across from a fucking parking lot. Oxygen lost, beauty lost, more room for the noise of Toby's own machines—they are good people, Toby & Barb, but we sure could have gotten a lot luckier in neighbors. I'm going to take out (maybe not) the one small maple on our lawn across from the quadruple driveway, and plant a goddamned row of trees, thick evergreens of some kind there. So it goes. Thank God for the land out back. Talked to Harold Wren (senior) yesterday, and learned more of his sensibility (or my knowledge of it was solidified). Said, as I groaned, that he was to be credited with getting Frazier St. (once a dead-end) joined to the tract. As though I wouldn't wish my house were at the end of a dead-end street.

Maybe I'm stupid. I've become sentimentally attached to this place, its trees and new depth, when maybe I should look for a farm out in nowhere. Well, I won't let myself get carried away. It's usually very quiet here. I will make a fucking treed island of this place if I have to. Yes, Wren would have asphalted the back acre. And I spoke to my neighbor to the back the other day, Wieczorek, whose lot backs on mine. He's okay, is filling in with tons of leaves and prune pits, but he's not crazy about trees, and said he'll come right through my ditch line with his power saw in the spring, if I like. I declined, softly.

11/8/77

Mainly, I've been moving books around. The tall glass-doored bookcase is upstairs now, and I'll fill it with Heyen stuff, getting it all out of my study and to where I will look at that accumulation seldom. I was spending too much time sitting around and wondering whom I could sent what small item to.

Maybe If I did become a little more nervous about my writing I would write a little more. Have finished the poem that may be called "Brockport: The Language." It's a good one.... Have spent a little time here and there poking & prodding "Stories," which may some day turn out. It's taking a swing toward being about what Sandra McPherson said about my father (at least she heard this in *Swastika*) admiring the Nazis—I think not. His brothers were brothers to him, not Nazis, and he has always been very apolitical. She misreads the book, in that sense, I think—look at "For Hermann Heyen"—he wants his brother to bail out!

Arrangements about all made for my trip—two nights in Binghamton, two on the Island, one in Katonah, two in NYC & then home from LaGuardia. Should be fun, nervous, exhausting.

Dug up one good-sized pine and several small ones at Mirko's and planted them out back.... I've calmed down about Toby's driveway. Maybe it's no big deal, or maybe we get used too fast to the blacktopping of America.... Rain the last two days. I don't mind. Walked out back yesterday and ate some wet raspberries. Delicious. We still haven't had a killing frost.

11/23/77

Good to be back, clearing off my desk, looking forward to the four of us at home the next several days over thanksgiving, food and much love.... Binghamton (Simpson & Logan books signed, my reading, Turco & I hanging around together, & Vince Clemente, & Dan Murray's reading that broke me up, & so much more), Long Island (folks now settled in their lovely retirement community, Mom & I fighting about blacks et. al., but friends, the old man in his daily shopping, Wern & Barb & kids fine, train to Penn Station/New York (my reading at Donnell & seeing Bob & the evening/night in Katonah, & all Vanguard folks around, & so much book-hunting & an evening with Stan Plumly, & hearing *Swastika* has sold 1,539 copies now, & the love coming from Evelyn & Tom & all, & getting to Mrs. Cohn at House of Books & seeing Burt at Strand & Matthew at Gotham, meeting many people, walking Times Square & Rock. Plaza)—a memorable trip. Han & kids fine, the kids doing tremendous jobs in schoolwork, music, sports. Han & I so lucky. Seeing friends the past few days, Greek women visiting Mouganis' & much poker. Added 50-60 books to my library, packages arriving daily.... *Ironwood* & *West Branch* out, & card from Joyce asking for something for an *Ontario Review* postcard—I love this.... I'm only a little anxious about getting to serious work. Know I will, soon. Get away to get back to my life with more intense joy. Need a trip like that every year or so. Wd. like to be invited to the city more often. Stan writing much criticism, being genuinely generous to me, I think. Talk of Halpern & city life & all. Bob okay, so busy, so burdened with Judith the way she is, hideous eyebrows and all, the kid a brat of the first dimension. *Swastika* on shelves in Gotham, Brentano's & Scribner's! Read in Vanguard offices the 1st 5 pages of Joyce's upcoming *Son of Morning*. It reads beautifully, will be big, I'm sure.... Card from Maurice Sendak who will inscribe some books for us—will send him a package in January.... My study overflowing with books, but I'll get things in order, but this is a pleasure, all this stuff piling up.... Got beautiful Kinnell & Stafford items from Mrs. Cohn.... Met the legendary Elizabeth Kray. Well, that is a scatter-shot response to my trip. Seems to me I was the best reader and read the best poems in Binghamton & NYC. Warm responses. Hell, I'm grateful to sell a couple of books, gain some small measure of respect, see a book or two of mine on shelves. Now back to Brockport, the real world. Does NYC really exist, now, Grand Central Station & Times Square & the Vanguard offices over there?... My next book must be a big one. It will be.

11/26/77

Snow piling up now. I'm puttering around inside, still putting books in order.... Did finish "The Snake" (was called "The Language") today.... Heard from Joe Davis at last. Four or five of my poems will appear in his anthology, when it splits up into genres, next year.... Han and kids fine. We had a lovely Thanksgiving.... We're trying to send Christmas packages to Germany, but the dock strike is still on.... I'm planning on going into my office early Monday, for my first serious work-day, and a taste of what it will be like after Christmas. Will pack my lunch & stay there until close to supper-time, or until my energy is gone.... I've been invited to Jamestown for a reading, but Feb 3, but $3-400, so I'll try to make it. That's a lot of dough for a day.... Did Zimmer bibliography for *FPAA* & now have to xerox title pages.... I'm at ease.

12/1/77

The last few days have been fine. I've worked several hours each afternoon over in my office. Finished "Stories" & "Walking on Christmas Eve," have been typing and touching up prose pieces, reading. Now I have a taste of what some serious & steady work will be, what I'll be doing all winter. Han picks me up on the way back from cheerleading, about 6:00—so, I'm there a long time, will not begin early in the morning, but ease over there about noon or so each day.

Went to Nikki Giovanni "reading" for about 15 minutes, Ann Waldman reading for about ten minutes. Much fun at a party last night. And saw Billy play a beautiful game, JV though he's only a freshman, against Madison the other day, and will see a game tomorrow night. Lew Turco will visit tomorrow, I think.

My Yeats/Roethke piece is out in *JBS*—it reads okay, & what a contrast to my Wright essay, just out in *Ironwood*. In the old days I was logical, methodical, solid—now I say "I don't know why but I love Wright & if you don't you're just a dumb fuck." To see the two essays is to see the hundred ways in which I've changed.... I'm glad to be in the Wright issue. Dave Smith wrote me a nice note on my essay.

Tony in bed with a sore back the past few days. And Al seemed terribly tense after his Thanksgiving visit home, his hands shaking like hell. Hope he'll be all right. I really do. I've grown fond of the silly bastard.

12/3/77

Have to laugh at myself, now, about a half-day past my crisis & misery, which arose so unexpectedly. Yesterday, in the mail, just before Lew Turco arrived (with surprise! a pain-in-the-ass of a son ((reminding us, egads, of John Stefanik)) and wife Jeannie), a letter from Bob Phillips filled with grief—sick Judith, strange-acting Bill Goyen, etc.—and then with a list of National Book Critics Circle (or something like that) books that those who vote/nominate could use. This leads to about ten nominations, I think. *Swastika* was left off, inadvertently, I guess, because the poetry section seemed to include everything. No big deal, but Bob said that Wm. Cole, for one, thought my book was on the list, and confused it with the listed *Führer Bunker*. Bob said this confusion might help Snodgrass get nominated. How about that? Somehow, it didn't bother me until I got home from Billy's basketball game last night, exhausted. Then I began to fill up with bitterness against the world. Now I have my senses back again. Need a good night's sleep, anyway. Life has been so frenetic lately, and I know how emotional I get when I'm tired. Some residual anger against Al comes in, probably, though I've felt close to him & even visited him today. <u>He</u> knew how to get *Bunker* on the fucking list. Enough.... Turco was tiring, <u>so</u> self-centered. And Lew, somehow, just doesn't have any taste, from his scrapbooks with pasted-in broadsides etc. (!), to his badly self-bound books & Mss. that crack apart, to his own publications & way of putting things & bad puns. Well, in other words, a visit from Turco was like what a visit from Mazzaro used to be like, and a visit from old Bob Phillips. All life takes a back seat to egocentric activity. It's unhealthy. Aah, poets. I'm to blame, too, but am certainly more aware of this bullshit than most, & will grow away from it. How about a new year's resolution a month early?: no more of this showing of my book collection to people who can't/won't appreciate? There's something that leaves a bad taste in my mouth after I drag out treasure after treasure to someone like Lew. And I somehow strain & act so enthusiastic & hyper in such a presence. Why? Beats me. I'm not like that. Such wonderful days last week, at home & writing in my office, & then a literary friendship & some literary bullshit broke the rhythm, but good. I'll get it back again. As Han said, Lew would never even have visited if it weren't for the *FPAA* bibliography I said I'd maybe do on him.

12/4/77

Bob Gemmett here this morning to chain-saw our dead apple-tree. Good, cold fresh air, with a little snow. I feel wonderful. I have a secret.

This is not impulsive, really, but has been on my mind for quite a while. I want "The Chestnut Rain" to be a book-length poem. This would be right for my development, I know. So, I'm going to make a book (hoping Vanguard will do it, maybe next fall—I've written Tom & Evelyn) called *Fires and Other Poems* to give me a sense of having finished everything up to *The Chestnut Rain*. I have plenty of poems, and some of my best, at least my favorites. So, this will be my secret—I don't even want to tell Han or Bob or anyone until the book comes out. I do think they'll do it. Hell, it will be my best book! It's done—it's just the arrangement that will occupy me the next few weeks. It's the thing to do, for lots of reasons.... Then, a couple years of experimenting with, working on *The Chestnut Rain*. So, I hope this works out. Typing the prose pieces like "The Bell" & "The Pool" last week (vulnerable as they are) convinced me, too, that *Fires* could be quite a book. It will get me from the Island to Brockport, the sensibility of my 2 nature books, from the country to the suburbs of "Fires."... I'm going to keep the secret, as I type & work. And, should I get away from these poems (by having them in a book) like "Witness," "The Song," "Cardinals," etc., etc., I'll be able to devote myself to a book-length poem. A wonderful idea. Much typing to do. I want to have a good week or two, now, before Christmas, in my office.

12/6/77

My work on *Fires* is going beautifully. I realize, now, that my greatest writing pleasure is, once the poems are about done, gathering & arranging, staring until orders and progressions are seen. My poems are better within contexts of other poems—they become, then, part of a wider complexity. But there's more to it than this.... And these poems of *Fires* are so damned <u>unfashionable</u> that I am beset with doubts, but these doubts are not about the quality of the poems, but about their acceptance or salability in this fucking wild commercial plastic America. Hell, they're good. I care for them, & this is where it has to begin & end.

And if Vanguard does publish *Fires*, say, next fall, how will I be able to think of myself, as I have, as one of my admired poets who publishes a book every 6 or 8 or 10 years? Surely, it will mean that I am a prolific writer, for better or worse. Well, then, why not? I do feel that Tate and Ransom, for example, outsmarted themselves, became so critically conscious that this sense overwhelmed the poetry in their souls. The basketball player who fakes left & then right & then drives left but runs into the defensive man who hasn't moved. A certain naiveté & intuition necessary, not the slow painful accumulation of a poem over decades as Tate's Confederate ode—no, such procedure is based, consciously or unconsciously, on absolutes. I am responsible within my poem for its rhythms, images, and I know my poems in this inner way almost by heart.

The wider implications, wide as all the world through time (as when I read that primitive societies saw lightning as a snake in the heavens—and I think of the end of "Fires," etc.) just won't be mastered. So, I write, stare & dream my way into my poems, and then will let them go. I still feel like a slow writer, crochety, but the books seem to get written. *Fires* will have 20 poems in section I & eight little prose dreams in section II & 15 or 20 poems in section III, a decent-sized book. <u>This</u> is the book (with "Cardinals" & "Witness" & "The Song") I'll always read some poems from at readings the rest of my life, I know.

Snow storm yesterday, and it's still snowing today. The Brockport schools are closed, and the kids are glad to be home. Birds flocking to our feeder out back, including, the first time we've seen them, yellow grosbeaks, if this is what they are. Not a single dove this year—I wonder why.... Drifts in the driveway four feet high. I'll dig a little to get some air today, but won't worry if I can get the car out. Han is baking Christmas cookies and her cheerleading practice is called off for today, too.

The little pamphlet *Fires*, Duane Schneider tells me, was sold out (300 copies) in a month, is out-of-print. I'm pleased that Duane made a little money on my five poems in the pamphlet. "History of the Resurrection" is a poem I'll probably never get to use again, except in *The Handbook of Heartbreak* twenty years from now.... The little pamphlet *The Elm's Home* should be out any day now. My Yeats/Roethke essay is out in *JBS*—40 pages! It still reads solid, though done ten years ago. To compare that piece with my *Ironwood* Wright essay is to see what has happened to me (for better or worse) in ten years.

I've read over my second ¶ in this entry: Robert Penn Warren, on the other hand, never got caught in that trap, has written, even since *Audubon*, intriguing & tradition-breaking poems, deep books, because he <u>wrote</u> & felt his way along and distrusts (I think) his own formidable intellect enough to allow his pen to move!

12/9/77

Cold & driving wind & snow today. School, but both kids home with colds, but Billy's game and all other activities postponed, so he doesn't feel too badly, nor does Han, now that she won't have to make the long trip with her cheerleaders tonight. Kristen's concert called off, too, last night. And a major storm, we hear, is liable to hit soon. I'm glad to be home, writing out Christmas cards, staring at arrangements of *Fires*.

Tony stopped by yesterday with a copy of *Anchor Dragging*, which is handsome. I hope it somehow lightens his life a little. I was surprised to see that only 500 copies were done—I was sure that Al said he'd do 1,000. Tony will have a party at Lift Bridge a week from Sunday. It will be fun to watch him in that kind of scene.

Well, I'll get to the cards for the folks in Germany, I guess, and walk to the post office this afternoon.

12/11/77

Lazy Sunday morning, though I did mull the table of contents of *Fires* again. Guess I'll use "The Ash" in the 3rd section—it, with "Fireman Next Door" gives another dimension to the book—now, if only "Anthem" were good enough to be in the first section. I'll work on it.

Read *Rapport 10* in the bathroom this morning, the right place. I don't know. Everyone is writing the same poem all across America, the page-length ho-hum thing. As Dickey said, after a while one longs for something different. Hard to say what. Some mind-blowing, God-speaking, apocalyptic, all-embracing voice. Something different, not this poem, this mild lyric that everyone is writing. For better or worse (as the poem turns out), I'm 100% right to be thinking of a book-length poem. Whether it fails or not, it will at least be something a little different.... Hope to have a good week next week typing up *Fires*, finishing that & sending it to Vanguard. It will, I believe, have many of my best poems, if it is not my most unified "book."... Didn't really know Kristen's cassette player worked so well, but it does, and I played last night for the first time the tape of my reading (Wilbur's introduction) at Wesleyan in 1974. Jean Maynard sent it to me. Hell, it was <u>strong</u>. I read all poems from *Noise*. It was the best poetry reading, & poetry, I've heard in a long time. Maybe this means, simply, that I write the kind of poetry I most like. Whatever. But I liked my voice, & the poems, like "Cat & Star," seemed to me <u>fine</u>.

Usually something in each one of Phillips' letters lately that bothers me. In any case, the mail still is able to disturb what is otherwise a wonderful equilibrium, and I might be gearing myself up for a New Year's resolution on the matter. I'm not sure what.

Will I be bothered much if Vanguard doesn't want to do *Fires*? I think not, though I <u>do</u> want to do this book & might look elsewhere. I realize, now, that I <u>won't</u> be bothered much because I've told absolutely no one, including Han, except for Tom Woll of course & Evelyn, that I'm doing the book. This secret is a perfect device. I hope to keep it even after I sign, if it comes to this, a contract! There's absolutely no anxiety this way.

We (mostly Han, who has the best touch) put up the Christmas tree last night. Very cold out, & it's good to be inside. I have Han's Christmas present, a sweater. Two weeks away, and the year has flown.... I've been shoveling snow, for muscle work, & then walking & trotting a little around the block. My right elbow is in bad shape, & my groin is still bad, but all in all I'm not in too-bad shape for 37. I have a hunch that I'm going to start jogging, will be a jogger in years to come. Maybe I'll start this spring.

12/13/77

Long letter again from William Ewert yesterday. He wants to buy some manuscripts. I dug out two good ones for him—"The Song," & "Lines to My Parents" from *Swastika*, a Mss. that brought back lots of memories for me when I looked it over, memories of Germany & my work on the poem, my walks, the monument at Stöcken that sprung the poem, finally, the "meeting."... Ewert is a wonder, dedicated to me.

I'm still very pleased with the typing & juggling & writing I'm doing. I'm getting close to finishing the typing of *Fires*—wonder what Tom Woll will say after he gets the book—and today I saw how "The Mare" could become the beginning of "The Chestnut Rain." Hope to have a good afternoon tomorrow at *Fires*. A matter of decisions—I say <u>yes</u> & then <u>no</u> & then <u>yes</u> to "The Witch," e.g. And what about "Our Light"? Not theme, but the individual poem is what I've got to worry about. Unless I'm all wet, the eight prose pieces are okay.

A guy called today & said Jarold Ramsey had recommended me & offered me $85 for a reading this spring at Naples, about an hour and a half from here. I said no, and I'm glad I did. I told him to call Poulin & Piccione. Not for less than $200 anywhere, from here on in, & preferably more. Also, I worry about such things in advance, & it's not worth it except for plenty of money. If the weather allows, I'll make $300-400 for one day at Jamestown in Feb. With that much money I have fun buying books & dinners for me & Han etc. for months.... Otherwise, the writing is coming, my work is coming, and I'll work steadily until it's time to begin the garden again.

12/15/77

Well, I finished typing *Fires* today. It's in about final shape, and I'll xerox it & send it to Vanguard tomorrow. It seems to me to be a strong, tight book—30 poems & 7 prose pieces. I'm impatient, or at least excited to get busy with the book-length poem, and I still have the feeling that books of poems are books of poems & I want something different from the hundreds always flowing out (the short lyric has about reached the end of its possibilities?), <u>but</u> *Fires* is a good book. When I think of my favorite Heyen poems I think of "The "Song," "Witness," "Fires," "The Ash," and they're all in this book.

Typing up "Ellen" today, something came back to me. I began thinking of that day I attended the mass for Ellen, and remembered afterwards that we all piled on a bus to go back to school. I remember sitting near the back, on the right side, and looking at the church steps as we pulled away. <u>This</u> must be where the dream came from. I must have thought, as the bus pulled away, that Ellen should be with us, and not alone in her casket in the church.... How deep we are. Ellen, I <u>will</u> see you again, and I won't be so shy this time. I could have loved you. I remember when you and Dave & Karen and I went to the Catskills for a day. And I most remember Joe Cravotta talking about kissing you at Gaynor Park....

Since I was in about the 6th grade, I've been saying a prayer, and say it still, usually a couple of times a night before falling asleep. I remember learning this prayer by flashlight under my blankets in my room in Nesconset, found it in a church pamphlet & wanted to memorize it. Last night I wondered how much of an influence its rhythms must be on me, on my poems. I've heard or said nothing in my life nearly as much as I've said this prayer:

"In the name of the Father, and of the Son, and of the Holy Ghost, Amen. / I thank Thee my heavenly Father that through Thy dear Son Jesus Christ that Thou has graciously kept me this day, and I pray Thee that Thou will keep me from all my sins and where I have done wrong and graciously keep me this night. For into Thy hands I commend myself, my body, my soul, and all things. Let Thy holy angel be with me that the wicked foe may have no power over me, Amen."—that's it, written out quickly. There was a long series of prayers that I attached to this one, about my father doing well in his shop and about me doing as well in high school sports as I did in grade school, etc., but I've forgotten them. But I will of course never stop saying the one above—sometimes habitually, and sometimes with great deliberation as I try to make the words into pictures, the prayer into a cosmos.

Fires is still a secret. Maybe secrets are the secret. Wright has brought this up for me.

12/16/77

I have to laugh. The thing that has been happening to me for years, happened again today. I don't know exactly what to do about it, either.

I had such a good day. Got up early, got xeroxing of *Fires* done and got the book into the mail to Tom Woll (hoorah!) and got a package into the mail for Bill Ewert. Then *APR* came in the mail with Stan's essay that of course made me happy. Then I played cards with the boys and won $87. Home for supper, and looking forward to Billy's ball game. THEN a call from Poulin. He read me, very dramatically, a letter (even wanting Han on the other extension!—I'm glad she slipped out of that!) to the effect that the *Führer Bunker* has been nominated (1 of 5 books, I guess) for a NBCC Award. Well, I was gracious, & really am past that, and don't give a shit, in the end. How corrupt the whole fucking process is. Has the book had 3 reviews? THEN Poulin said he had a letter from Tom Woll saying they should talk about the distribution deal, I guess. Christ, can I do nothing without Poulin jumping in? Can I not even have my own publisher, or will I have to be followed around by a fucking BOA list. Amazing, that my day can be so wonderful, and then turn out bloated with bad juices. Why can't he just leave me the fuck alone and let me get on with my work? Phillips. Poulin. Son of a bitch. I will escape it all. But how? Phillips will be easy to ignore, to write different kinds of letters to. But Poulin! Isn't my spleen, after all my good days, incredible. And if Snodgrass were to win the Nobel, what the fuck would I care—my collection would just be worth that much more. It's Poulin bugging me all the time. And he's a failure, a loser, and I realize I'm either paranoid or half the reason he keeps laying this shit on me is to compensate for his feelings of failure as a poet. Yes, I guess I do believe this, & this is why I'm resentful, too. He's given up his own poems—Jesus, another Mushinsa edition of his *Catawba* just out, & Graywolf is doing 3-4 Rilkes!—but he's not a poet, & has turned to publishing! And made about 6 grand settling on his non-book with Dutton! And signed another contract for many thousands with H-M for a 3rd edition of his anthology. Well, I don't give a shit about these things, but when all this business overshadows the work of writing poems of integrity (how insufferable of me)—well, my stomach is at this instant a knot.... And I know how often I've written here that I've felt close to Poulin lately—probably trying to dissuade myself about my true feelings, to make me appear to myself less of a monster. Maybe I just hate the bastard and wish him dead. Him, Rock, the asshole Piccione. I detest them. I do. Now, what can I do about it? I'm sick of humoring Piccione. I'm sick of the Poulins, Boo too, who rushes to show me her latest trinket, never thinking to say congratulations on *Swastika* or anything else.

Is it true that if I became a man, had no desire for fame or recognition, this wouldn't bother me? No, because, well, he would still be phoning me, bothering me. Am I actually going to have to tell him to leave me alone, to never again under any circumstances tell me any literary news? I am not imagining things. The Poulins did not even give me a hearty word of congratulations on the Guggenheim. That's a fucking fact, should I ever doubt the validity of my feelings about all this. I am so overwhelmingly sick of whining in this diary over Poulin-related angers and upsets. In truth, I wouldn't give a shit if he dropped over (I'll say it, died) tomorrow. Forgive me, my lord. Forgive me my dirty humanity, my lord.

In perspective. Han is oblivious, doesn't care, none of it is important to her. Maybe Poulin & I are the only ones who know the stakes in this town! So, can't I maintain my equilibrium. Well, Poulin & Piccione are both so fucking sick, literally sick, and I'm soul-weary of smiling in their obsessive presences all the time.

But I'll get through this again, gracefully, or I'll bust. Will go to Tony's Lift Bridge party Sunday. Will go on with my own work, count my own blessings, and (so important) keep my own secrets. Much thinking & feeling to do.... I can't split in anger with them. Can't live that way. Will prevail. Will outlive my immaturity, if this is what it is, or that fucking desire, if that is what it is.

12/17/77

After writing all that last night, I talked with Han about all this for about an hour, and felt much better, and slept like a baby. For one thing, and she's right, poor Tony & Al are both, literally, sick. Maybe I can be human and grown-up enough to humor them both and go about my business. Tony, especially, is so insecure, needs so much, some recognition, is beset with problems even regarding his Poulin-published book. And Han says that Al & Tony think of me as having arrived, not as someone who needs an occasional pat on the back, or recognition. But we decided that I might have to tell Al that I just don't want, simply don't want to hear about all these political doings, that I can tell him I just don't want any news, especially during my year off as I write my own poems.... Well, the emotional upset was wearing off this morning as I sat sipping coffee, looking over *Fires*, and then the mail came.

An envelope from J. Walter Thompson Co. again. I was reading the enclosed xeroxed protest letter to the head of the NBCC awards, when I realized it was Joyce, not Bob, who wrote it. She is angry, mentions my book and hers, and resigns from the group. I felt/feel like crying because of her loyalty & guts. I also felt like weeping "Why don't they all leave me alone?" But I'm of course grateful to Joyce & wish the letter were an open letter, published somewhere. I toy with the idea of writing a letter myself, trying to get it into *APR*, ending with the line "Let this be known forever after as the Circle-Jerk Award."—something to that effect. Really, in truth, it's so disgusting, the prejudicial listing of books that haven't even had reviews, some that haven't even been published!... For a moment today I leaned toward going over to Poulin, unburdening myself, showing him Joyce's letter, etc. I might. I might not. But I won't lie if Al or Tony asks me how I like Snodgrass' nomination. Never mind the quality of the book—I think it's disgusting.... Now I'll write Joyce, thank her, and then hope all this will blow away, out of my chest where it is sort of lodged right now.

And another letter in the mail, which also has to do with my life, what I am up to, what I have to be doing. *The New Yorker* accepted "Stories," all 60 long lines. I'm very happy about this. I have to go about the business of writing my own poems, and somehow physically, emotionally distance myself from all the nonsense. I <u>will</u> keep this little secret, not mentioning "Stories" to anyone, except maybe Tom & Evelyn when I send them the four poems I'd like in *Swastika* some day.

Thirty-seven years old, and I'm still within this excruciating growing-up process. Maybe, as a writer, this is my adolescence.

Monday 19th

Han is off substituting and the kids are in school. I'm sitting down with my first cup of coffee, the phone off the hook, as it will be all day.

Went to Tony's party at Lift Bridge yesterday. Many people there buying his book. People from Kendall, & Al's friends from Rochester, & Tony's students, etc., etc. A great success. I was envious, of course, that the gathering for my third book was much smaller than this one for Tony's first—mainly due to Sandi, & to the million cards Al sent out. Tony glowed, and Sandi complained that more people, especially English Dept. people, weren't there.... Well, it should all hold Tony together for some time.... I won't even enter here the Sandi slight of Han, Sandi's weeping apology call right after we got home. What a melodrama. Some day, I will write a memoir of all this, maybe beginning with MacLeish's first ¶ in Tony's book.

My secret (alas/okay) about *Fires* is out. I wrote a long letter to Joyce, and Han wanted to read it, which was fine, but I'd forgotten that I'd mentioned *Fires* to Joyce. So Han knows, and this is fine. She would of course mention it to no one—it's just that now I might be tempted to talk about it with her once in a while between now and publication (which I am counting on--& I do think Vanguard will be happy with it) when all I want to be absorbed with is *The Chestnut Rain*.

The more melodrama in my life, the longer this diary gets.

I feel fine again, even selected my favorite coffee mug this morning. But I want to be left alone, and probably will talk to Al about all this, in a gentle way, in a few days, telling him that from Jan-June I'll be burying myself with my work and just don't want any news at all, that all literary news is just a distraction. Which it is. Yes, this will be good. Tony was already here this morning, dropped off a hardback of his book in the garage, and knocked on the door, but I didn't answer, only because I didn't want to sit a couple hours & rehash the party, etc., and smell his smoke. Poor guy—in a year I'll be entering here news of another Piccione crisis, or one of Al's. Or one of mine, if I can't manage to be left alone with my family & books & poems and interests wider than this local thing that gets me down or the political literary thing that gets me angry and competitive.

I won't spend much time, if any at all, at my office today, but will beginning again tomorrow. Have to write a letter for Stan Plumly to Houston (and there will be other letters when other depts. ask—poor bastard he is not to have a permanent job, & I hope something breaks for him that will make him happy for a decade or two instead of always on the run as he's been) today, and will putter around.

The mail truck is outside—I know its hum. What new emotional adventures today? Lord, let there be only bills and Christmas cards.

12/20/77

I really don't feel too sharp, have some sort of bug that keeps me coughing and my throat confused. Still, will go up to my office this afternoon.

Notice in the papers that Louis Untermeyer died, at 92. I had one or two nice notes from him.

About that mail yesterday. A lovely card from Joyce who called me a true poet. Wonder what she'll think of the long letter I just sent her. And a letter from, of all people, John Frederick Nims, who said he'd been reading me since Richard Wilbur twice told him not to forget William Heyen. It was a nice letter, though I sometimes wonder how poets in their 60s can still give a shit about such—well, such what?—games? trivia? the network of friendships etc? *Poetry* is important to me, as a place where the traditions over the century have streamed, and I'm glad Hine is gone, but I wonder about Nims wanting to be editor. This rambles. I don't know what I mean. But, again, with the *New Yorker* poem, the recent pieces in *APR*, and now this invitation, personal, from an editor at *Poetry*: ten years ago I couldn't have dreamed that I could make it this far. And much of it has been a matter of "making it." But, nothing can take the place of doing fine work. What good is all of this if I have nothing strong to send Nims?

Well, I'm going to look over *Fires*. Still don't know if "The Witch" should stay.

12/22/77

Nete Wicks just dropped off a copy of *Swastika* for me to sign for Ross for Christmas. I started leafing through, reading a little, feeling the book again. Unless I'm crazy, it's a great book. How it sustains itself! It's an amazing book. How did I do it? And I sensed that the addition, to Pt. I, of "Stories" will add a tremendous amount. After all, I never saw any swastikas on our steps, and this is just one example. I never talked to the Belsen caretaker. Art has a different kind of morality and range from that of empirical truth.

12/23/77

I wrote Tom Woll this morning about three things. 1/ I sent him "The Ash" sequence for *Fires* & new order of 1st 3 poems in Section III. 2/ I sent him the four last pieces for *Swastika* & mentioned where they'd go in the sections in case of any new edition in the future. 3/ I talked about the Poulin business, made excuses for talking about Vanguard's business, and told Woll to sign the bastard up, if they had to. Okay. That's about it on all these things. I can't do anything else. Now I hope to relax.

The Elm's Home came from Ernie yesterday. It's sort of nice.

Picciones stopped by yesterday when Han & Billy were away. I don't know, they seem so sad. They're off to Long Island today.

Judith Viorst just coming on Dinah Shore show. It never stops.

About ten things to get into the mail, recommendations etc., and I'll be free to turn completely to *The Chestnut Rain*. I think I'd like to go down to the Island for a couple of weeks—or is that too long—to get away a little.

House filled up with kids today. 16 or 8 here to make a film with Billy for a class of his. A little too nerve-wracking for Dec. 23rd. I went to the school, but came back too early, & was even driven out of my study. Tis the season to be jolly, but not <u>this</u> jolly.... Kristen and I walked up to see *Close Encounters of the Third Kind* last evening. Liked it.

Are the bad juices leaving my system? It all started with that NBCC stuff, continued through Poulin's BOA party, but now dissipates, I trust. I'm wishing for a calm, soul-relaxed 1978. Amen.

Christmas

Have had a wonderful day, and, just now, sitting in bed in my study, I was getting ready to enter a few things here, when Kristen came in, a little pale, but glowing: Han just pierced her ears upstairs, something Kristen has just yearned to have done (as have so many of her friends), and is proud and happy—a tiny step somehow into womanhood.

Poulins were here. <u>No</u> talk of literature, and this was good. And I said, very matter-of-factly with Han & Boo & Al there, to Al, that I wd. <u>bury</u> myself the next few months—so, maybe I won't be bugged & upset by nonsense. I paved the way for my disappearance from Poulin's life for a while.

A slow day. Too much food. The kids home. Calls to Wern & Barb, the folks, Han's folks this morning. Games & gifts. A day of love. Calm.

12/26/77

Another fine day. Dinner with Mirko & Irma—turned out the Poulins were there too, but this was okay: not a word about literature spoken—herring & smoked fish & turkey & salads & rum cake etc., etc. The kind of evening I always look forward to during this season.

Han & the kids are fine. I think more & more about the three of them lately. Day by day the kids grow & mature. Day by day, when I'm wise, I realize what a wonderful woman Han is.

And day by day I realize that if I'm any good over the next few months I might be able to write a beautiful long poem, *The Chestnut Rain*. Fingers crossed.

12/27/77

Spent a serious afternoon at my office working on "The Chestnut Rain." I felt good by the time I quit at 5:30. Stopped where I could start again, I think. I'm close to where I'll have to do all that reading I'll have to do. Looks as though the third section will alternate stanzas of what I thought were two separate pieces, but come together into another music.... It's an odd situation. I have the poem's ending already—it took me a long time to get that—and what I'm doing now is working toward that. I do feel, as romantic/traditional/unfashionable as the poem may be, that I'm experimenting & learning & taking chances as I haven't since the old days of my first poems. There's really no precedent—Whitman closest—for the kind of poem I sense out there waiting for me to come to it.

Billy has a basketball game tomorrow. I look forward. Would be nice if his team could win one.

Nice letters from Ida Sadoff & Vince Clemente today. I hope to hear from Vanguard!

12/28/77

Al called last night just at dinner to say something about his getting some group in Rochester to invite MacLeish for a reading, and to say that *Führer Bunker* was just bombed by Hugh Kenner in *NYTBR*. Nothing to bother me, but I thought maybe I could go through one day in my life without hearing about literary politics, especially from Poulin. Well, beginning Jan 1, really Jan 2, I'm really going underground, will not go to the phone. Might have to drop Poulin a note. He just won't get the message, and it's crucial now for me to mind my business while working on *CR*.

Worked in my office for a couple hours only, but good hours. I'm only at the beginning, but think I have the first five sections, and now is the point for the long "light" section, begun last January & looked at once in a while. I've worked in the poem "Our Light." I'm beginning to read all the bulletins. I'm worried about the whole *CR* becoming a kind of pastiche. But so far, so good. I like it myself. It is, will be an odd animal to be sure, but more than a batch of unrelated sections, more than a sequence—this must be what I will keep in heart: to make it <u>a</u> poem, a single poem, one with <u>long</u> rhythms and teasing digressions, but a center, felt if not understood completely. No hurry. I have years for this. But it will be important for me over the next few months to let the first drafts flow. Time for self-consciousness later. I'm biting off an awful lot, to be sure.

Billy's team lost by 55 pts today! He played lousy, didn't take shots when he had them. The other team, from Syracuse, was <u>much</u> bigger. But he's not depressed, is off to watch the varsity game this evening.... He needs to have some teeth extracted tomorrow, poor kid. He's a great boy, more mature than I am, I often think.

Snowing this evening.... I hope to spend a few hours in the office again tomorrow.

Want to send some poems to Nims at *Poetry* after his lovely letter.

Phone is off the hook, & will be until Han & the kids get back.

The black boy from Syracuse who stood last night with us wants to be a cop.

1/1/78

I wasn't in the mood for a party last night, but it turned out, really, to be fun, even moving in a sentimental way. About twenty neighbors first together at Studiers' for cocktails, then the main meal at Waddams', then dessert at Wicks', then drinks & piano playing & singing at our place into the new year. It was all very pleasant, and the tradition is a good one.

A new year. I have to laugh. I'm so happy. I count my blessings—family, home, security—all the time. But the year begins with the slight discomfort of knowing that Al wants us over to see Snodgrass who arrived yesterday. I was glad we were busy last night, and I don't at all feel like seeing them today. I don't know if we'll go over or not. Maybe De will go home early. In any case, I've decided to fade away from such things. Let them be. Let them talk politics & big deals & coups. Fuck it, I'm not going over. Should I lie & say I'm sick, or should I just say I'm busy, or not say anything at all, or take the phone off the hook.... It's funny: I notice that when I sat down to write this, I was almost completely at ease; now, my throat is tight & I'm nervous because of this simple nonsense.... I worked a couple of good hours at my office yesterday on the "light" section of *CR*, felt great, & when I got home Tony was here. He is often a lovable sad soul, but, shit, again, I want to disconnect with my literary friends. Will I just moan about this here in my journal, or will I disconnect?

1/2/77

Notre Dame is killing Texas in the first half of the Cotton Bowl.

Lynne Studier was here for lunch—a sweet smart girl. She's working in the museum at Oxford.

I feel lazy. Will try to force myself to do a little typing this evening, to get some poems ready to send to *Poetry*. I'm liking my old poem "The Train."

A good amount of snow has piled up outside again.

Jesus, a foul on Notre Dame as time ran out in first half, and then a Texas pass for a touchdown! Anything can happen in 2nd half.

I'll spend some time in my office tomorrow afternoon working on that "light" section. Some questions I have about it. Fun finding patterns, developments of meanings in it.

1/4/78

Good day's work today in my office, both on the "light" section and on making one or two other changes—changing the mare into a doe in the first section—that have brought the poem together. I sense its unity now. Now I only hope good things come to me for a few other sections in addition to the ones I have & the long one I know I'll read for & work on a long time. I think things, directions, will come to me.

Poulin called, but Han talked to him. I'm glad. He asked if I'm still underground & Han said yes. Guess the Poulins & Snodgrass went out to Mirko's on New Year's Eve. I'm glad.... My whole dilemma regarding seeing Snodgrass was solved just by doing nothing, by staying home.

Nice letter from Tom Woll, but enigmatic regarding *Fires*. He says he has an initial reaction, has passed the Mss. to Evelyn, & will get back to me soon. I hope they can see it's a good book. He said *Swastika* is selling well, & that he'll be cautious about Poulin & his fucking BOA books.

The minute Ralph Sipper's catalogue arrived yesterday I called California to get the Wilbur/Calder *Bestiary*, at last! A beautiful copy, too, & I won't even have to pay the $125, but will keep sending Ralph things, as I have in the past. Can't wait until the book arrives.

Must type up that bunch of poems & try *Poetry*.

Want to send off those books to Sendak.

Han is teaching this week, & enjoys it, & this clears my days beautifully. She's gone by seven, the kids soon after. I get up at nine, do some things around here, & then walk up to the school around one, & Han picks me up at 5-5:30 after her cheerleading practice. A perfect life.... I just have to guard against feeling badly because I don't make great (or any) progress every day on "Chestnut Rain."

I think Vanguard will take *Fires*. If they don't, will I be upset? I really don't think so, though it would clutter up my good plans.

1/6/78

Progress again yesterday on "CR". The piece about tasting the stripped chestnut down to Lincoln's time found the thin shape it wanted. It is somehow suited for the "Oak Spring" & "Oak Autumn" line, the stuttering revelation of the dream in this case, and the piece will definitely be a part of the poem, maybe section VII, maybe not. Maybe an easy-going narrative should be 7. I have an idea, too, involving my poem "The Summer," its beginning & pace, & the story of other tree blights. Will see. The two or three hours in my office each afternoon when I stare at the poem & touch up finished parts & maybe progress a little with a new section, tire me out. This morning I'm home & lazy.

Kristen & I will have a nice evening at home. I was nasty yesterday, accused her of opening a package of candy bars & eating one (she's such a sweet tooth, a junkie, & it's hard to get her to cut down), and I made a scene, & she cried & was hurt that I didn't trust her. So, I feel lousy about it. Han & Bill go to an away game this evening, and I'll try to make it up to Kris a little, ha, maybe won't nag her when she's on the phone for too long with her friends.

1/9/78

Cold, bad winds, snow—kids home early from school, & I stayed away from the office. Will get back there tomorrow. A lazy, easy-going day. Got the package of books off to Maurice Sendak for inscription, and hope they'll get back okay.

I think I've managed to drop away from Al & Tony, that they'll not bug me for a couple of months.... I gave Boo a ride over to her stuck Pinto today, but didn't see Al, or want to.

Began a little section, maybe, on *CR* today—telling the reader to picture a lone tree in a field & to say the name of his state. Will it come to anything?... No word from Vanguard on *Fires*. I'm not anxious, but it would be pleasant to hear, especially something good, of course.... The literary world seems blessedly slow, swirled in snow. I just want to keep staring at *CR*, & moving forward a little.

1/10/78

Storm again today, the kids home from school. I took a long walk anyway, stopped at Hartwell, which was about empty, and without planning to, wrote some good lines for the light section of *CR*, including ones about the "digression forward" that images the aesthetic of the section, & maybe the book-to-be.... Despite the weather, the office was cozy, & I'm going to spend much time there tomorrow, no matter what.

1/12/78

Wrote "The Snow Hen" section of *CR* today.

1/14/78

Saturday. <u>Much</u> snow falling. A good day to be inside with Han (who is getting better) and the kids. I'll watch soccer & basketball on television, & be lazy.

Fixed up "The Snow Hen" yesterday; otherwise, sort of a nervous day, beginning with the Incident of the Meter Men—I threw them out, then saw Police Chief Hare. It was all for everyone's good that I did this. I'm sort of proud of myself.

Long letter from Joyce. She's a sweetheart, understands everything, has been through it.

Billy scored 10 pts yesterday in a losing cause. Wish he'd take charge more. He passes too much. This will work later on with better players, but right now his teammates don't know what to do with the ball.... And this morning he bowled a 589 series, without handicap. The kid is some athlete.

1/20/78

Kids went to school this morning, but came home after two hours. Snow already, and a big storm on its way. Another ballgame cancelled for Han & Billy this evening.

Wednesday Tom Woll called, mainly about Vince Clemente's wanting to print all the prose of *Noise* in his anthology. But Tom mentioned that Evelyn has *Fires* now, but that he doesn't think it's nearly as strong as *Noise* or *Swastika*. I guess I'm disappointed, but don't really feel bad. It's not a matter of acceptance or rejection—Tom will no doubt suggest changes—it's a matter of having unfinished business on my mind while I'm working on the long poem. I believe in *Fires*, and I have to be on guard against people, like my gracious and well-meaning editors, who don't know as much about poetry as I do, can't hear it as well as I can. At the same time, maybe the book could benefit from some cutting. I keep seeing a book, small & tight, no prose, with a title like *Fires: XIX Poems*. But the main thing is that I be of such an emotional set, as I am, to continue working on the long poem.... Wrote the plum section this past week, finished the very risky & dangerous & <u>good</u> lovers section, and have begun the reading of bulletins I've wanted to do. Will walk to the school for several hours' work today.

1/21/78

I never remember this much snow. My driveway is buried. Han & Kris & I went uptown today, walked. I bought Kris a pair of earrings, as I'd promised. $28.50 for tiny things, but I'm glad. Also had a band put on Billy's identification bracelet, the one my folks gave me for my eighth-grade graduation from the old Nesconset School. I still remember that evening, the reception downstairs in the fire hall.

Walked by, on our way home, Poulins—stopped in for not more than two minutes, and I was lucky—Al was in the shower. Now, I'll work hard in my office the next couple of weeks, until Jamestown Feb. 3.

Yesterday, after writing in this journal, I walked to the school and stared at "CR" & <u>solved</u> my huge problem, which was how to get from the fellatio section to the rest of the poem. I turned it into a 1st person section, made the woman more mysterious, a muse, and decided to bring in the poem "The Song" as the following section. It even begins "Wenzel said 'Come,'—so <u>many</u> fine connections now that came in naturally—snow & vapor & sperm & rain & even the word "sip" in "Snow Hen" & fellatio section. A daring, successful move through to "The Lamb," if I say so myself.

Picked up the new & collected Stafford at Lift Bridge, & read the new part. Sort of disappointing, somehow. Just, often, a little too weak & diffident.

Tomorrow, Sunday, I'll read the papers & watch basketball. Monday, all day in my office.

Oh, I think I'm going to tear into the light section again, do some chopping & shaping. I have the confidence to do this, now that the poem's shape is just about determined. I'd like, anyway, to make the section I'm doing all the reading for, the real long one, the longest of the poem. And that reading, I hope, will suggest a few other things like "The Plum."

About Vanguard & *Fires*: I wrote a long letter, about lots of things. Hell, maybe the prose to Tony Petrosky and a solid little collection of 25 poems with Vanguard or someone else. I do know that *The Chestnut Rain* will someday be wonderful. Maybe, too, in terms of how I want a *Collected* to look like years from now, *Swastika* should be followed by a small collection, & then the book-length poem.

1/23/78

Yesterday I shoveled snow for a couple of hours, and then was just about to watch the Notre Dame/UCLA game when Han said "Guess Who's Here?" and Poulin came in. Just what I needed. Anyway, I listened to him for a couple hours, his myriad entanglements (his phone bill, he says, up to $200 a month now) and, I'm happy to say, nothing bothered me. Let him go.... His BOA party at the Gotham is Feb 13th, and I said I wouldn't see him until after that, so he should have a nice time. So, I've just about cleared weeks of mental space for myself again.... Stories of crises in the life of Sandi & Tony, of meetings with Gemmett & Fitz Gerald & Patti Ross & NYSC on Arts & groups in Rochester & this & that. Turns out Lowell won that NBCC Award & Snodgrass called Al to moan that his career was over. Oi Weh. So it goes. I just want to get on with my long poem, and will today.

1/25/78

Thought I'd carry this journal over to my office once, and write a little. It's wonderful over here, even though, somehow, I'm a little tired of working on the long poem now. Or tired out by it. All in all, what I have is fine, I think.

Once in a while, from somewhere, a tense sort of excitement builds in me during the morning, maybe gives me a slight headache. Today is one of those days. I'm a little tight back of my throat, & my temples pulse, for no good reason.

Iowa Review took "The Ewe" today. Sent back "The Song," and I'm glad, because it's the one piece I want to make part of "CR," and I don't want to send any of that out for a long time.

Jerry Ramsey called yesterday, invited me to read at U. of R., was so nice, offered $150. I said okay. It's about fucking time they acknowledged my existence, which is to say, the existence of Brockport.

Nice letter from James Scheville today on *Swastika*. Lovely note yesterday from a stranger in NYC. The book still gets around, strikes people.

Phoned in and got from Phoenix two firsts of Oates' novels I didn't have. Glad to be getting them. Glad I have a little extra money.

I don't think much about *Fires*. So much attention paid to *Swastika*, that maybe I should just hold off until *The Chestnut Rain*. Still, there <u>are</u> about twenty poems between those two books that <u>should</u> see light. Well, I'll just wait for old Tom's letter, & will go on from there.

Billy's team lost again yesterday. He played fine.

I've written a section of "CR" on butter-making.

Han will pick me up in about four hours. I'll turn to the poem.

Sat. Jan 28

Edward Field took "The Children" for his 1979 Bantam anthology. They will probably publish the most of anything I've ever been in.... And I guess things are all set for Vince Clemente to use sections of the *Noise* memoir in his anthology.... A conference at SCCC in April that I'll go to, with pleasure. April will be very busy, but I plan anyway not to write a lick then.

Called Tom Woll yesterday, and was glad I did. I wanted to tell him that I had a better idea regarding *Fires* than any others I'd suggested, and that I didn't want him to spend a lot of time on the book writing me about it. He said he was just about to call me, that he'd gotten the Mss. back from Evelyn that morning, and that they thought a limited edition thing selling for more would be a good idea. He said the poems would be published, one way or another, no question about it. A week ago I'd have been thrilled. But I had another idea several days ago, which might be best all around, for sales and for my sake. I wasn't going to tell Tom on the phone until I worked it up for a couple of weeks, but he urged me, and I did.

Long Island Light: Poems and a Memoir would collect all of *Noise* (it's almost out-of-print anyway), with some slight revisions, and integrate most of *Fires*, which I've always thought of as a sequel volume anyway. This would be a "big" book, would benefit from following *Swastika*, would satisfy my sense of catching up with myself, would gather all my L.I. stuff, and the Brockport poems, prepared for in the original memoir anyway. I've been thinking hard about this. It seems to be the right thing, could be the book that anyone interested in poetry on L.I. would read. So, I'm going to work up the table of contents & send it on to Tom. It could be a beauty.

Tom said they're going to publish Bob's gathering of Schwartz poems. And he said he was sure that in a year or two they'd have to reprint *Swastika*, and would include the four extra poems.

I'm a lucky man. Wd. like to see *Long Island Light* appear early in 1979. Adding poems like the cardinals poems & "Witness" & "Fires" to *Noise*: this is what I've always wanted to do anyway.

1/30/78

Working steadily on *L.I.L.*. I love it. 66 poems, & the 7 new prose pieces. So many fine things happening. Hope Vanguard will do it.

Han & Billy off to an away game.... I'm a little bit uneasy about Han as, not really wanting to, she pursues the Masters degree. She registered for a class today.

Poulin stopped over yesterday. Same old trivial stuff. I'd much rather be me.

Nice letter from Sandra McPherson today, & 3 items from Sipper. Was warmed to see my name in acknowledgments of proofs of Wright book.... The poetry community around the country knows my name. How could I have even hoped for this ten years ago?

We'll go to Kris's concert tomorrow evening. It was snowed out on her twice. This time, it will be, I think.

2/2/78

Manuscript of *L.I.L.* all ready to go. I love it. I wonder if there's a weak place of 3-4 poems in first section. Anyway, I love it, & hope Vanguard will do it.

Jamestown trip tomorrow. Purely for the $300. Looks like weather will allow it.

Han just went in to substitute, even at mid-morning.

Monday will begin in earnest again on *Chestnut Rain*.

2/4/78

My time in Jamestown was fine in every way—2 classes & the reading, the people (Bob Hagstrom, Doug & Donna Carlson, others), the good food, & even the successful selling of about a dozen books Doug had

Vanguard send. But the trips, especially return, were terrible, cold & dangerous. Car heater doesn't work, & I froze. Got back at one in the morning. Am still warming up.

My poems sounded good to me, all that I read, & I read a lot in the three hours.

Tomorrow, have to put together my application for a little of the merit money floating around at the college. I should get some. A few hundred bucks added on, every year, means a lot, what with the percentage increases. Monday I'll get back to my office & back to work on CR. Just for fun, counted the lines in Warren's *Audubon* the other day—it's only about 400 lines or so long. So, mine will be book-length. Hope I end up getting the "They are gone now" section right. It will take the rest of the winter, at least, to do the reading, & then get started.

So good to be home.

2/7/78

Kids home from school again today, Tuesday. Even the college is closed, & snow is still falling. I've walked a lot the past couple of days, and have gotten some strength-work shoveling.

Han had her first class last night. She's going to be as busy as can be.

Maybe tomorrow I can get back to work, at home in the morning & at my office in the afternoon. I've been reordering the poems in the first section of *Long Island Light*. Haven't heard from Vanguard yet—New York City is about closed down!

Kristen was happy yesterday to be named to All-County band, & a little upset that she was only second chair. She's some kid.

Dentist this morning. And in May/June I'll go a few times to get my front teeth fixed up so that I'll be able to smile.

Can't think of a thing else new. With everyone home, I just sort of walk around & kill time—darts, television, food, this American life of comforts that can't last forever, but oh what a lovely light they make right now.

2/8/78

Typed up the added sections of "The Deer" and "Tonging at St. James Harbor," and got the table of contents in order for *Long Island Light*. The whole first section seems very good now, in its movements. One weak place, a weak turn in 3rd section. I'll stare at it again tomorrow.... More & more I like the idea of that book.

I'm not really in the mood for the long poem this week. Don't want to force it. Will read for a couple of hours tomorrow.

Irma dropped off about 20 copies of *NYTBR* at my office. Today, I went through aversion therapy, as it's called, reading most of the issues straight through for a couple of hours. What a piece of shit it is, 90% hype, reviews & ads. And the criticism: I knew every angle of the theory ten years ago. Nothing to learn in the rag except what the commercial presses are priming their pumps for.

A nice first of *Marriages & Infidelities* arrived today from Phoenix. Little by little. Hope like hell I never have a fire, or some university's beautiful room filled with my collection is going to be lost, alas.

Looks like we have a break in the weather. It will be cold, but no snow. So, maybe Stephen Spender will make it here after all.

Letter from Bob Phillips today. Nothing on the surface, but some kind of hysteria underneath. Maybe it's what's missing: he mentions 3 books coming out (poems, Schwartz, Goyen), but seems joyless. Says he's writing a play now.

Called my folks yesterday. They're okay, despite record levels of snow on the Island—cars still buried by the hundreds on the highways. They said Eddie got married! Well, it appears that Ed just doesn't want anything to do with the family.... Pop might fly down this month to spend a week or two with Henry. I'll see them in April, will spend a few relaxing days with them.

Haven't seen Rocks, Pylyshenkos, Mouganises for weeks. I don't want to play cards, anyway, and want to avoid smoke. Summer, with windows open, is a big difference.

2/11/78

Saturday morning. Coffee. The family running wild, a hundred things to do, & this makes me nervous (3 phone calls in last 5 minutes); otherwise, a pleasant morning. Guess I'll head to my office this afternoon for a couple hours, or maybe not. Nice to lounge around in a bathrobe.

Now I'm puttering with the order of the third part of *Long Island Light*.

Wrote a longish letter to Bob Phillips. Said I was determined to grow up, become a man. Still am. Regarding the literary "scene."

Phone just rang again.... Han & Billy off to a game again in a half-hour. Kristen has 2 friends coming to stay overnight. Han & Kristen going to a play tonight, Billy just got back from bowling. Han has a class Monday night & hasn't done her homework. Etc., etc., etc. She substitutes next week, too. Well, I can't be worried about her pace, just have to stay aside and go about my own business. In truth, I sometimes wonder how nice it would be if my wife were different, calmer, less gregarious, could find more pleasure in less of this phone & committee life. But she is what she is, a warm & too-busy woman. I was looking at Han's high school yearbook the other day, & in the section of what-people-could-be-seen-doing, Hannelore Greiner could "be seen talking to someone." Han on phone twice more while I was writing this paragraph.... My life one of opposites: Monday morning the house will be empty again, I'll take the phone off the hook, and will have silence, here, & then at my office. One problem, usually just minor & occasional, though, is loneliness in the midst of this wild family activity.... Han has just made another call. Now she has about a half-hour to the time she has to get to school. Wild. Sometimes I jump from one mood to another and back again in a minute.... She is dialing another call. And the second she gets off the phone, Billy or Kristen will question her about some plan or ride or arrangement.... I'll stop this now. At least I know what makes me nervous. Will take a long walk today.... She's dialing the phone again.

Later: yes, it works every time: I had a nice long walk, and feel relaxed as can be. Even jogged a block. Will get a few things done while watching sports on television.

A beautiful first of Shapiro's *Selected Poems* (1968) came in the mail.

2/14/78

A busy few days. After the Forum's Spender dinner, the man came over here, sat in the chair where I sit now. He was very warm, charming. He liked me. Inscribed the few Spender books I had. I gave him a copy of *Swastika*. He asked me to inscribe it. Then, last night, before his reading (Gerber & others keeping him away from most of us, it seems, so I couldn't see him last night, wherever they went), he stood with me in the hall for a spell & we spoke, about *Swastika*, and about his Nazi play, which he's now revising. Said he wanted to send me one of the dozen xerox copies he'll have made up.... His reading was fine, a selection from the decades. His spirit is filled with light. Stephen Spender—I've met another of the grand old poets.

Auden once said to him, he said, that something like suicide just wasn't very gentlemanly.... Reminds me: I want to send him a copy of *XVII Machines* & inscribe it to one of the "Pylon boys"!

Ghastly scene after the reading with Shreela Ray, who marched up to me and asked if I were going to buy her book, then quizzed me about how much money she could get for a Guggenheim & when she'd hear, and then asked me again if I was going to buy her book, & when! Poor soul. What is this writing business doing to all of us? Liquor on her breath, so heavy.

Poulin in NYC. Will see Tom Woll today. Ha. I hope he keels over.

Fuck it. Was thinking yesterday of this journal. Will make it honest. It relieves me. And often, as this morning, I churn with shit like the Ray business.

Oh, I would like to win the Pulitzer, only so that all these local shits would kneel & back away.

David Fraher called & invited me to Wyoming for a week of readings in April. Yes, hell, why not. It should be some fun—he'll drive me and keep me company all week.

Lucien Stryk coming, apparently, next month, via bill Andrews' program/Piccione. I won't get caught up with his ego again like last time.

Talked and drank into the morning with Ken Venick & Bob Fox. Will read some of Fox's things & send a letter for him to Oswego, or somewhere.... Man by the name of Freeman asked me to talk to an Alternate College class. I get roped in, the disadvantage of staying home during this year.

I've only puttered with *Chestnut Rain* lately, but I'm amazed, & not fooling myself, with how much I've done & how good it is.

Made last revisions of *Long Island Light*. Vanguard's move. I hope they will do it. It's quite a book.

Again, it feels good to have noted these things down here. One other thing: Christ, Jack Wolf has gotten an NEA—who next? He's never done a fucking thing!

Han so busy, but will not go in teaching tomorrow, she says.

Billy playing fine ball these last games. Scored 14 in the last one. Just brought home a beautiful report card. Kristen seems happy these days.

We're using the garage as our refrigerator. The damned thing broke down about a week ago.

The sun shines today. I'll go for a long walk later.

Have the urge to send "Disco" to *New Yorker*. Haven't gotten proofs yet on "Stories."

Still no word from Ernie. Must call him.... Back in touch with my old pal Bill McTaggart. I'm lonely sometimes. Wish Bill Elkins or McTaggart lived next door.

I would like to fill up this second page of this entry and then go about the day's business, first looking at *Long Island Light* for an hour.

Letter from permissions person at *New Yorker* yesterday. Editors of a text in art appreciation want to use "The Colors," which came out in 1974. O fame!

Ali-Spinks tomorrow night. Poker game Thursday night. I hope to get back to *Chestnut Rain* in earnest soon.

Mom & Pop report that Eddie is married again.

Kristen did some nice drawings for the Banjo Press *The Ash*. Hope it turns out nice. Will never ask Mirko again.

2/17/78

Played poker until seven this morning. Had much fun, despite the smoke & despite losing $145. It's only paper money.

Harper & Row somehow sent me Donald Hall's *Remembering Poets*, which I've read. I wrote him. I like the book.

Card from Wilbur today. He's still the man who does everything right.

Professor from Old Westbury wrote to say he was using both *Noise* & *Swastika* in one of his classes this semester! Maybe I'll read there in April.... Can't be too many copies of *Noise* left. Rod Parshall is using it in his class again this semester.

Will browse *Long Island Light* for a while.... Look forward to Billy's game tonight.

I've been sitting here reading over the "Neighbors" and "Disco" sections of *Chestnut Rain*. They are so good. I mean, I love them, just want to keep reading them & see how they're made, don't feel like beginning new things. And several other sections of the poem, like "The Snow Hen" & "Butter" are just as good.... Bill, if you ever (and you will) complete that book to your satisfaction, you really will have something.... Lord, let me get lucky again & again.

Billy was terrible in first half last night—0 points & some mistakes—and then came out & scored 13 points in the second half & made some great plays. Most I ever got in a J.V. game was 12, & I was a junior! The kid can play, if he'd only take charge more, drive more, do more.

Will browse *L.I.L.* for a while now, & go to office this afternoon, since there's nothing in the way of sports on television that I'm anxious to see.

2/19/78

Kids are off from school this week. I'll spend afternoons at my office, reading toward the big section of *Chestnut Rain*. Han very busy with her class & cheerleading.

Wonderful news Saturday. Al is back from N.Y., & he called & talked to Han, & said he was at Vanguard, & talked to Tom Woll for ten minutes, that they liked each other but decided they couldn't do anything for one another. Christ, I'm glad he'll not follow me around at Vanguard, too! Maybe I'm wrong, but I don't think he can do anything to bother me from here on in. I'm wrong: it would bother me if he won the NBA for his Rilke pastiche. Past that, I think I'm done being bothered.

Finally got Ernie's number & called him. They're settling in now. He sounds all right.... Vince called—Street Press might do a little chapbook in time for my reading down there, & will send up some interview questions. Vince is one in a million.

.... I just read over my sound & fury 9/16/76 entry. Have I gotten any better in a year and a third. Yes, a little. Far to go but, yes, a little. After my last letter to Phillips, even, I'm at the point where I will correspond with him more about home & family & the land out back than about our disease.... Yes, it's a disease. And the cure: attention away from our own assholes; physical work; the ground under our feet.... So funny. Just heard the mailman outside! But, yes, I'm getting better. Always knew, somehow, it would be slow, but I'm getting better.

2/22/78

Note from Nims at *Poetry* saying he just got to my poems, likes them VERY MUCH, especially "Lord Dragonfly" and would like to see 4-5 others in the magazine, too. Don't tell me I'm going to get past that asshole Parisi! Not yet. Nims will let me know in about a week. I'd love to see all my tiny poems of *Lord Dragonfly* in that magazine.

Bill McTaggart sent *Poetry in Crystal*, one of 250 special copies.... Old Bill: he's a real friend.

Beautiful letter from a girl who must be a student at the Iowa workshop.

Am sending off a copy of *The Pearl* to Karl & Brenda Elder on the occasion of the birth of Seth Wade.

SUNY Buffalo called yesterday about a reading when I wasn't home. I'll call back later. I really have the sense, the past month or two, of arriving. Even the local bastards like Rochester & Buffalo are inviting me.

Well, the Wyoming thing is all set. I'll love it.

Just about finished with a new section (not the big one) of *The Chestnut Rain*, the "Foals" section. It's a good one.

Except for sending sections of *CR* to *New Yorker* from time to time, I'll keep the sections together, in general. Sent off the "Neighbors" & "Disco" sections. I like to keep my secret, keep these poems to myself, but do love to see poems in *New Yorker*—because everyone sees it, from the folks at Vanguard to local folks. Aah prestige. Otherwise, I will keep the thing together so that when the time comes I can send big batches to *Poetry* or *APR* or wherever. Disease or prudence? Both. Reminds me of Hall's story of the time Roethke pulled page proofs from his pockets saying to Hall that this was a book (*The Far Field*, I think) that would put Lowell & Wilbur in the shadows! *Chestnut Rain* is going to be a magnificent book. From my own point of view. Which is enough.

A little snow again yesterday & today. Goddamned cold.

I wrote Phillips a long letter about our disease. He'll answer at length, in length, he says. That should be an interesting letter.

Will spend a few hours at my office today. Han has some free time today. A miracle.

Played cards again—the Greek women were in town—and won about $40.

Note from Bob Mondy about his doing some bibliographical work on Wilbur & wanting to borrow my bibliography. Al wants to publish some ungathered Wilbur poems, I think, & Mondy's gathering would be just the start. Ha, this time I'm going to have some fun, & trade off the use of my collection for a copy of each variation of the eventual Wilbur book. Or they can go to hell. No more of that *CAP* screw-job.

2/23/78

All Han's cheerleaders were here yesterday for pizza. Nice girls this year. All the prunes gone, as Han says. Tonight, a group of people coming over too, a soccer board meeting. Sometimes Han drives me crazy. But I will allow her her world. I have my own hours to do my own work. Will spend as much time in my quiet office today as I like. Will putter with "Foals," and go on reading.

Worked all day yesterday on that interview for Vince. Rushed it, would like to type it again and add to it, but won't, want to get on with *Chestnut Rain*.

Daphne Poulin will be here from Friday-Wednesday while her folks are in NYC. I'm not crazy about the kid, but they had no one else to leave her with anyway. What price "friendship"? Maybe I'll get to like her. She's just so fucked up because of her parents. At least she'll get some food and care here.

Boo Poulin reports that Sandi Piccione has gone off to Toronto for a few days by herself. The Kendall farm must be a madhouse. Sunday Tony takes a train to the city & Al's Gotham party. He's scared, I know. Tony doesn't think he has our disease, but his case is almost terminal. Good thing, I suppose, he fools himself.

Will browse *Long Island Light* for an hour, & then pack a lunch and head up to school. Writing *Chestnut Rain* is a matter of realizing that I'm involved in a project that just won't get finished in a week or a month. Not easy for a German.

2/24/78

Fine day, relaxing & busy. Finished the poem "The City," which I like. Just happened to come across it again. Think I have it right. It's about growing out of my disease.

Poetry, <u>Nims</u>, took six poems, including "Lord Dragonfly." I love it! I want to write him, now, about *Western Wind*, & hope he'll use something of mine in the next edition.

Finished the "Foals" section.

No word from Woll on *Light*. "Anthem" & "The Crow" were two of the poems taken by Nims.

A pile of mail every day. Heady stuff. Too much. If I were teaching now, I'd be going nuts.

It's a small world, this world of contemporary poets, but I have become known in it to an extent I never thought possible. That's the truth. What do I want? I want to write beautiful poems, read them to people, & move people, & keep adding anthologies & magazines & books to my shelves & bibliography. Bill, you're a megalomaniac today, like the guy in the dirty joke who says he never gets enough. Six poems in *Poetry*? I want twelve!... Take aspirin and drink many soups & fluids.

2/28/78

Last day of the month already. Today may be the first day in weeks the temperature rises above freezing. I hope all this snow melts gradually, and not with lots of warm rain, which would make a pond out of the back. But we always worry about this, and then, in May, I'm back there mowing.

I spent yesterday just writing letters—Nims, Hall, Stefanik, Ewert. Looks like Ernie will do *Lord Dragonfly* after all, if he doesn't mind the previous appearance in *Poetry*.

About every day I look over *Long Island Light*. No word from Woll. The book is fine, and if they won't publish it, it <u>will</u> disrupt my inner-clock, which thinks of *LIL* in 1979, and then *The Chestnut Rain* in 1981 or 2 or 3. But if they won't do *Light*, I will feel a gap, and now I sure won't feel like tearing it all apart again and doing a smaller, limited-edition book with them, which Tom said "yes" to.... You know, diary, and this is the truth: Tom is sometimes slow on the uptake, so when I tell him I'd like to send him the Mss. of *Light*, he might very well think that I am sending it, and he may be waiting for it now, without telling me to send it.... Well, the order of the poems is all set now, and maybe I should send him the revised proposed table of contents.... Added a fine little prose piece the other day, written after a dream—a fine piece to end the memoir with.... It could be a beautiful, big book. Will look it over now.... Here's the little poem I've added to the "Lord Dragonfly" sequence:

Beetle's cargo:

> heaviness?
> happiness?
> Neither, nor
> both together.

Also, I revised my little preface, which is sentimental, but what the hell. I seem, at least, to be doing things different from what others are doing, and this is a good sign.

2/28/78 (evening)

Ten minutes ago I was just feeling sort of sour. Now I feel fine. A Buffalo-New Orleans game has begun on television, a Buffalo-Houston game will be televised tomorrow. I'll watch "Magnum Force" tonight. What I guess is bothering me is that I would like Vanguard to say <u>yes</u> to *LIL*. I've decided to type up the revised table of contents, & send a note to Tom. Just the thought of this action makes me feel better.

Poulins stopped over. They had a great time in the City. Al saw everyone, of course. Tony is still on his way home by train.

I guess the reason I'm stuck/bored with *Chestnut Rain* is that I'm not <u>writing</u> it, which is exciting, but <u>reading</u> for it. And I'm reading for it because I made up my mind that the next section, 16, would be the long catalogue. I still think this is the right strategy. I've written my way into some things <u>after</u> #16, but it's hard to anticipate. I'll keep reading. Am finding many things I'll use. No hurry. Guess I'd like to know that *Long Island Light* will be a book.

3/1/78

Played basketball today for about an hour and a half. Wore me out, but relaxed me completely. I have a locker now over at the college gym, and will get over there from time to time to sweat.... My old competitive instinct came out again when fat old Pat Smith started pushing, and my team won all three games.

I'd written to McCullough at Harper wondering if they wanted to see my essay collection. She said yes, so I'll send it along within the next few days. I doubt that they'll want it, but there's no way to tell.

Kevin Nolan asked me to read his thesis, a collection of poems, this semester. I don't mind.

I have some poems that are sort of surreal. Don't really know what to do with them, but if I ever found the right title, maybe I could gather them into a chapbook: poems like "The City," "The Red Pearl," "The Buried Man"—

Syracuse about to play St. Bonaventure. Pro game on later. Will have some ice cream.

Yesterday about fifteen little finch-like birds were at the feeder. Half had reddish breasts & red caps. I'd never seen them before. Found out that they're redpolls, & there are a lot around this year. Haven't seen them again. And those yellow grosbeaks are gone.

3/2/78

I've got *The Shine of the World* ready to send to Harper & Row.

Billy & Han will be off to a ballgame tomorrow evening. I think I'll take Kristen to dinner & a movie.

Yes, I'm really getting bored. Walking through the dirty snow. The cold. The realization that I've done <u>plenty</u>, for now, on *Chestnut Rain* & should let my mind & the poem breathe a little. So, I'm bored, but the month will go by quickly, anyway, & I'll be away for half of April.

4-5" of snow tomorrow, we're told. A drag. Han wants to go shopping with Nora to the Mall.

Was reading about egg incubation today. I'm gathering good lines. The material for section #15 will be all there. It will be a matter of crafting the individual lines to my taste, & building the catalogue's movements.

3/4/78

Jogged again this evening. I'm doing all right, increasing the distance, little by little. And I'll play basketball tomorrow & Monday & Wednesday. By the spring, when it will be fun to run in shorts & sneakers instead of in boots & heavy coat, I should be in decent shape.

"Neighbors" & "Disco" turned down by *New Yorker*. Now I'll send the "Butter," "Snow Hen" & "Deer" sections of *Chestnut Rain*, & except for any possible *New Yorker* acceptance, will otherwise, in general, keep the thing together, eventually for a try at *Poetry* or *APR*.

Letter from that fellow about the reading at Buffalo. It could be fun, if I could bring a few of the kids along to read—Venick, Jeff, Tom, maybe Gretchen.

Still haven't seen Tony since his venture into the lions' den. I think Stryk shows up soon. Didn't I just come in here?

Saw *The Goodbye Girl* with Kristen last night—it was okay, not as good as I thought it would be.

All's well, though I lack, these days, I'm afraid, the "inner resources" of Dream Song #14.

3/8/78

The days flow by. I'm not doing much writing, but am enjoying life. Will play basketball again today. Am getting into shape. As long as the ankles and groin hold up. My wind & legs are already pretty good.

Spent the last two days reading the Atlas biography of Schwartz. Quite a book. And the lessons, whatever they are, however simplistic my feelings & observations may be, are always the same. I know the excitement of wanting to bust that comes in the presence of the famous, or that comes when I've felt "on the way." This is the intense excitement of the young Berryman & Schwartz. But life is not one big literary gathering. Publications, fans, reputation do not sustain. And what did these poor bastards have going for them: 1/ fucked-up family backgrounds; 2/ the disastrous decisions at 5 or 10 or 15 to be poets!—nonsense; 3/ immense egos which, of course, may have worked in reverse, been defensive; 4/ no knowledge of or interest in the body—too late, Delmore, to stick with your Jersey jogging; 5/ no knowledge of loam, flowers, trees, animals, no first-hand <u>felt</u> knowledge; 6/ an aesthetic that believed art is rooted in suffering—Berryman praying, as Bellow said, to the ruined drunken God of Poets; 7/ above all, and whatever its ramifications, an overwhelming desire for fame, frustration & bitterness to learn (as though the writing were not on the wall) that America does not give a shit about poets.... They never grew up. They never grew up. So much more, of course. They wrote in the shadow of the great ones directly preceding them.

Bill, it's always right there in front of you, the lesson of those things that sustain. Know who you are. You are a country boy. You have a healthy lack of interest in all the fashionable knowledges. You know you are not dumb, but know that you read for rhythms & pictures, skim, cannot figure the world out. Know how far you are from the Ivy people. Shut your mouth & pick your openings. You are where you belong. Survive.

Home, family, the trees out back, and still the pleasures of small things—poems in *Poetry* or an anthology, a reading invitation, an occasional letter from someone who (a beautiful long letter from MacLeish the other day) has been everywhere, known everyone. Bill, you are right where you belong, and right on time. <u>Decades</u> ahead. You'll write something once in a while that you'll know is good, never mind the <u>literati</u>.

3/11/78

Letter from Phillips today with news of NBA nominees—Nemerov, Howes, Simic, Bell, Harper. I've been watching myself the last hour, but it's true that I hardly care! Oh, Lord, thank you, if it's true, and I think it is. I want to be a man. Ha, old Bob never for an instant replied to the serious questions I posed him about the lives we're leading of ambitious kiss-ass.... <u>Nothing</u>, I sense, will take the place of the weather warming to spring. What I have on my hands with Bob Phillips is another fellow just slightly less manic than Mazzaro (and with more cause, of course, with Judith's sickness).... I have this fantasy, that the cold weather keeps all ambitious poets Poulin-like at their PR phones & letters, that warm weather tends to disrupt this. I mean, who glances at a literary magazine in July?... I feel fine.

Billy bowled a 236 game today, the high league game of the year, and we're happy about it.

Brockport lost the big game at the War Memorial last night by one point. Sad. They were 20 points better, were completely out-coached. Corbin never let the kids play. Pressing (as they should have from the beginning) only the last 1½ minutes, they scored ten points. Second time this season (the only two losses) this has happened.

Much basketball on TV today.

3/13/78

Off to the gym in fifteen minutes to play ball. Seems warm today—won't be a bad walk at all.

Am writing a little prose piece about moments of sorrow. Bonhoeffer said something that struck me, and I'm trying to understand it. He was a whole man and another death of that April in 1945.

Lisa and Gretchen, two of my ex-students, stopped by yesterday. Sweet girls. And a letter from Larry Gaffney today: he'll stop by in a week or two. It's almost spring, and I'm lazy, and ready to come out of my shell! Had a fine time at the "dissertation burning party" at Fergussons' Saturday night. Many things crowding into the open weather ahead.

When I think of it, I am conscious of having grown up these past few months. I've probably not gotten any smarter during this Guggenheim year, have forgotten as much as I've learned, but I may have gotten a little wiser.

3/14/78

Called Werner today to wish him a happy birthday. And called Henry, who wasn't home, but talked to Pop who is visiting him. Got a nice letter from Eddie, & must write back one of these days.

Typed up my little prose piece called "Home." And wrote a little poem about Mickey Mantle that may become a real one.

Got hurt playing ball, hit in the chest. Don't know if I can play tomorrow, though I'd like to do some running, at least. Will see. <u>Definitely</u> have to play in a grad. assistant-faculty game in a couple of weeks.

Still no word from Vanguard on *Long Island Light*.

My father said that it was 49 years ago today that he sailed from Bremerhaven to America.

3/17/78

My chest still hurt today, but I went up and played basketball, anyway, and had a good workout, & still feel wonderful from it this evening. Should try to get more exercise this weekend.... Nothing much new. Still love the "Mantle" poem.... Ten of us gathered to read poems & drink wine in my office yesterday evening. I enjoyed it, & my own new poems sounded just excellent to me.

3/19/78

Palm Sunday. Sunny, but cold out. I'll have a lazy day watching boxing and basketball. Tonight, a gathering at Picciones for Stryk. I'm not crazy about going, but probably will. I don't think I'm wrong about Stryk as a human being.... Tony has been drinking a lot lately. I haven't seen Al, but Han has, twice, this week, & the Tony-Sandi stories are wild. Tuesday evening is Billy's basketball banquet, and I'll miss Stryk's reading, and don't mind. I will go to one or two of his lectures. Tony, who was behind having Stryk here for the lecture series, is probably nervous as hell. Han is so busy, but still, if Zimmer or some other decent ego were here, we'd have a dinner, and I'd go more out of my way to be on hand.

My chest still hurts, but has slightly improved. I hope to play basketball tomorrow.

I'm fixing up my office, hanging framed things, etc. When the big OWI posters are framed & up, that will make the office.

Read the Manley book on Dorothy & Wm. Wordsworth, a book for young people, I guess, and found I liked the Romantic voice—Wordsworth, Coleridge, Keats, less than I thought I did. Just read "Ode on a Grecian Urn" again, and (stupid & preposterous as I sound to myself) was not impressed. This probably doesn't have anything to do with the quality of the poem (I'd need to make myself its contemporary, enter the mind of its conventions, etc.) but with the slowly-being-defined kind of poem I want to write. *The Chestnut Rain* is, of course, the kind of poem I now believe in, desire.

3/20/78

Went out to Picciones with Al, in that new car of theirs that is always stalling. And it did, but we made it.

Small gathering. Not-quite-usual talk, because I brought up this business of our mutual disease. Made everyone nervous. Tony said, of course, that he is perfect, ever since especially nothing happened to his book.... Al knows what he is, it's true. And Lucien said some things that showed a little depth, anyway, that I've worried isn't there.... All in all, a good evening.

In a half-hour I'm off to play ball, though my chest still hurts quite a bit.... Larry Gaffney to visit at 2:30, & maybe we'll go to the Stryk lecture at 4:00. Will see. I actually have the car today to drive over to the gym.

3/21/78

Strange day yesterday. Heard Stryk two hours in afternoon, & then 1½ hours last night. He's still hard to figure. He is such a plodder, repetitious, keeps discovering the wheel, lacks intensity. He is, in short, dull, and still there is the never-ending turning-toward-himself-in-odd-ways of his speech. But he seems gentle, & seems to know himself to an extent. I can never seem to get toward it, no matter what I say about him. There's a kind of <u>pomposity</u> at the center, which is never justified or assuaged by flashes of depth or the excited recollection of a meeting with one of the masters, or the saying of a poem from memory, or anything. He is not a brilliant man.... I'll go to the seminar this afternoon, and say goodbye, thankful to be going to the basketball banquet tonight.

Good seeing Larry Gaffney yesterday.

Wine reception last night, & then I went with Greg & Bob Fox to Casey's for drinks. I probably talked too much, & feel oddly dirty? Bill, talk to yourself in this diary, tell the fucking truth. You are always talking with people who simply don't know anything, have not worked their way through things the way you have.... I never get anything from anyone else. No one has read (or heard of) the book on Schwartz, or Bachelard (Stryk mentioned him) whose book on <u>Space</u> (esp. the section on "Miniatures") I know, or knows the resolutions poets have come to on the questions raised. I've said this badly. It's not just the students, but the faculty people here seem so stupid. I just have a better mind, one that leaps much better than "Stryk's or Piccione's or Poulin's or Fitz Gerald's or Andrews', e.g. I'm always constrained to explain to them the real question they're asking, or the justification of something opposite, etc, etc. I know I sound compulsive here. Often, I say <u>little</u>, & this is an inner-dialogue. But Brockport is best for me when I stay home & mind my business. When I am out with the local literary folks, it's true that I'd be <u>much</u> better off around people with some brains & actual writing experience, people from whom I could get something.

> Layman Heyen,
> never a priest,
> but who knelt more?
> The thing itself is in the saying.

Turns on itself like a figure eight. No one in this town could hear it. I know how proud it is, and so does the fourth line. I tried, and just for fun because the poem was jotted out in fun last night, to explain it to Tony. He's so often befuddled. Oh, & his students: little Tonys everywhere.

Someone reading this entry would hear a strange, even sick mind. Oh, if my reader only knew Stryk & Piccione, & some of the tiny-mindedness mixed in with, especially, these great Zen texts these days. Enough.

Spring rain yesterday & this morning as I write. Again, such a joy to be having a cup of coffee, the phone off the hook, I in my easy chair in my sweater, warm & knowing, with bed-rock security & truth, how happy I am <u>away</u> from the scene I will again enter for an hour or two this afternoon. So be it. This will all pass, and

I'm still learning to become a man. I've made progress the past six months, though these pages do not suggest it.... One of the problems—oh, Bill drop it.... But it's another difficult balance: how, if I'm a "teacher," can I stop talking?

3/22/78

Just picked up Billy at the high school where he played basketball in an evening recreation program. A beautiful evening, a cold but clean-feeling rain falling. Billy is getting big, and strong.

The banquet was perfect last night, the food and the program. Han spoke very well about her girls. I talked a lot with Chaz Crawford, athletic director at the college, who has a boy in Billy's class.

I played ball again today. Ran a lot, & hit some shots, & a hot shower felt good, & real, as Mishima says in that *Sporting Spirit* anthology.... Then I made a tape on *Swastika* with Stan Rubin. It went well, and I'm glad to get some of those things on record. I'll help transcribe it, so that maybe I can clear up/flesh out my occasional inarticulateness.

Bruce Berlind invited me to read at Colgate, April 13--$250. A nice one-day jaunt again. I hope the car holds up. Many readings in April, more than ever before for me. I'll be glad to stay home all May.

I feel just fine, at ease. Han will sub tomorrow, & the kids will be in school, and I'll have one of my fine mornings & then take a long walk. I am so relaxed that it's hard to believe how many vile/confusing/bitter juices flow inside me around that Piccione/Poulin/Stryk connection.

Still tacking things up in my office, which is gaining in atmosphere.

Kristen brought home an honor-roll report card today.

The Bell & Berg books arrived from Hugh Miller. Traded for 6 copies of *Depth of Field*.... Nice letter from Vince Clemente. The student who burned *Swastika* is enjoying *Noise!*... No word from Vanguard on *Long Island Light*. I wonder why.

The snow is almost all gone, except for the densest ice-piles.

3/24/78

Fine day today. Basketball—took Ralphie & Billy & both played well against the old guys; a long walk; fussed with the Mantle poem. Tomorrow we'll travel to Nashville, & we all look forward. Will come back Sunday evening. This diary began in Nashville years ago.... Cold, but sunshine. I just took my first walk of the year around the back, still covered by frozen snow, but patches of earth showing here & there. Those maples in the corner, & all the pines along the fence, look fine—a few of the pines might need some straightening.

Han is off to the mall for an Easter dress and to buy Billy some weights for his birthday next month. He wants an early start.

The four of us will go to church in Nashville, where they have a congregation of about ten, where Han went to church when a kid, that old wooden church right next to the folks' place. I look forward.

3/28/78

Easter Sunday the four of us and Han's mom rose early and walked over the ice to tiny Nashville Methodist Church, about a hundred yards down the road. Counting the pastor and about five kids, Kristen counted sixteen people there. I sat right in the middle. A space-heater kept the little room warm. The floors were slanted this way & that with age. Everyone was happy that we were all there, & some of the folks hadn't seen Han in twenty years. The kids got a kick out of the service, too. Billy & I sang from the same hymn book. That little group is good for Han's mom, though she still acts so officious, as my mother would.... In the day's program was the note that a gift in remembrance of Walter & Elizabeth Müller of Hildesheim, Germany, had been made. That little church, Mr. & Mrs. Shevelin singing, the daffodils on the altar rail, the knowledge that Han went there as a girl, the 80-year-old woman who played the piano, the concrete steps that pitched inward, the friendly talk (not the hush-hush of St. James Lutheran) ...

Played ball yesterday, and will again today.

Han is off to her sewing class.

Two books, *Public Speech* & *The American Story*, arrived back inscribed by Archibald MacLeish today.

I've just read Eileen Simpson's *The Maze*, and Ross Feld's *Years Out*. Enjoyed reading fiction. Both books about a kind of city-intellectual-world/weary-scattered life I'd like not to lead.

Still fiddling with my Mantle poem, trying for a gently curved shape. But, I've not worked at writing lately. Spring is in the air.... My reading at U. of R. in two nights, & I want to give one of my best.

I get depressed sometimes because Han is not happy with having to take a course & everything that goes with it. Otherwise, I've been very relaxed lately, maybe too relaxed to write, but feeling no pressure. Life has a flow this past week that is easy to take.... Off to the gym. My chest injury is getting better.

3/29/78

Finished *The Nuremberg Mind*. Picked up some things.

Played basketball for a couple hours today. My left calf seems tender, but the pain in my ribs is almost gone, and I can begin to rebound. Until I sprain an ankle—long overdue!

Woke up from a dream this morning, of a railroad trip & great chestnut trunks, and got up to write it down. It will eventually, when extended & smoothed out, be a section, one of the last ones, in *CR*. It has a lot going for it, the natural long lines, & directions like "parallel," and the train/chestnut motifs. I'm glad. Something to work on. I've been lazy about getting to that 16th section.

U. of R. reading tomorrow night. I just made up a list of poems, spanning the books, though I'd like just to read all new things. I'll go on about an hour. I want, more than usual, to do well, so many local folks will be there.... Got a call today asking me to read 10 minutes in May in Rochester when the City Hall is dedicated.

Snow still melting, and weather report says <u>warm</u> tomorrow, and maybe even 60° by this weekend!

4/1/78

Rain all day, but warm. Supposed to snow this evening.

Ernie Stefanik called today, as he did yesterday. About the Tyler & Eddy essays, and about bibliographical matters. He sounds fine & is planning a June visit (I hope without his kids!). Projects going ahead.

Billy is at a party. I pick him up at 11:30. He's growing up.

Al called yesterday wondering if I had the new *Poetry*—seems there's a long review of his Rilke. He had a hard time talking to me through his coughing & gagging.... Picciones stopped in yesterday. Sandi has stomach pains lately.

Stan Rubin talked about *Swastika* & played a recording at a conference in Albany, & the people were stunned. He says he sold some books for sure.... Got an anonymous letter about *Swastika* from Kansas City the other day, one that warmed me. There has really been much response, & I think the book will be around for a long time.

U. of R. reading went well. Met Hollis Summers' brother Joseph & wife. Ramseys were warm, & the other couple, Frank & Kate. Dale Davis at reading, & Jim Hancock & Carol & Harriet from Monroe CC, & several Brockport people, & Frank Judge, & a Rochester nucleus that said good things. I especially like it when young people, grad. students etc., say sincere thanks & praise after a reading.

April should be much fun, with things here, & readings away, etc. Should arrange Monday for the L.I. trip.

Saw *Saturday Night Fever* last night. Fun, but not as good as I thought it would be.

Leah & Don Johnson here for pie & coffee today. And Nora Studier. A good day. I'm relaxed.

4/3/78

Letter from Acting President Wolin came today saying I've been given a $500 merit raise. I'm glad. This is tacked on for keeps, and future percentage wages figure in, etc. It will add up to quite a bit over the years.

Got the Guggenheim list of new fellowships, today. No Shreela Ray, who bugged me, & no Pastan or Minty whom I recommended, & no Poulin.

Made ticket decisions & arrangements for my L.I. & Wyoming trips. And things on L.I. are falling into place.

My left calf is bad, and it will probably be weeks before I can run & jump again, but I did walk quite a bit today, to give my body some air.

Han substituted today, & has a test in her class tonight. She'll be relieved when she gets home this evening.

I listened to Kristen play her clarinet for a half-hour just now. She's getting good, and I remember her when she first got the instrument and couldn't draw forth a sound.

4/4/78

Glanced at *Light*. Walked to school & worked an hour on the new section of *Chestnut*. Walked home & washed out the garage, and walked around out back. It's raining now, and warm, the blacktop threaded with worms. A beautiful evening. I'm a bit restless. Maybe will have a few drinks tomorrow night after the Walker reading.

Reading Shapiro's *To Abolish Children*: the repeated theme: poetry as we have known it is irrelevant & dead, the old classics creak. It's all over, folks. He's wonderful. He's probably right. But we "poets" will be the last to admit this.

4/9/78 (Sun.)

Wonderful weekend. Relaxing. Much fun with kids—cards & basketball. Much walking around outside, as spring comes on now, though it's cold these days.

Still reading Shapiro, the man who struggled to stay outside. Here he comes to Brockport, and nobody knows a fucking thing about him, except me. "Once upon a time there was a thing called poetry.... It died." Yes, he's right. And I'm just a sentimentalist, but doing the kinds of gorgeous poems, full bodied & romantic, I want to do. But I'm not fooling myself.... And, oh, the classics pale for me these months—though Yeats is not quite a graduate student for me, as Shapiro says.

Finished the Parini Roethke Mss, & wrote a general letter for U. Mass. Press. Shit, in general it was tiring, kept discovering the wheel, repetitious, and somehow boring as it went over the territory, diminishing Roethke, & dwelling on the poems, of course, that need explication & apparatus & myth/Jung/et. al. approach. I love the last poems of "N A Sequence," which he managed to write, to flow with, free as he had seldom been. But, all in all, diary, the body of Roethke is not enough for a poet's full career. Something is missing. Throw away the mannered poems, and there's not enough there. Maybe Creeley is right after all!: that R. never knew who he was. Diary, when *CR* is done, if it becomes what I hope it will, I will have done as much as Roethke—nothing as wild (I'm not interested) as the "Lost Son" sequence, but nothing in R. is within the realm of *Swastika*, either. And *Depth* is better than *Open House*, for a start, and my Island has been what his greenhouse was. And I have a long way to go, if I keep writing, which I will, if I want to, if I really want to, if I can come to know whether I want to or whether it is a habit fraught with tension & gloom. I have been thinking about this much lately, in these terms:

maybe, just maybe, say, if on my 40th birthday (*CR* behind me), I walked home from my office, say, with the resolution never to write again, to slide away from literary people, to answer the queries for a few years about various things by saying "No thanks, I just don't write any longer, & won't, & am not interested in writing & have given it up forever,"—maybe, just maybe a great weight would lift from my shoulders (the competition, & the ambition, & the nervousness when I don't write for a week or two). Maybe. Maybe to turn to something else, to widen my life for a couple of decades. Well, I think of these things. Perhaps poetry could become a natural & easeful part of my life, or maybe my relationship to it was the same as my smoking: it either seemed to be chain-smoking or stopping it. Would I feel lazy, guilty, worthless if I didn't give poetry everything or give it up? Well, there is nothing urgent about this, certainly not now, when I am quiet inside.

Will read tomorrow at Buffalo with the four students. Will stop with them early at the Lockwood, and then we're to be taken to dinner.

Han just about done doing the taxes, which has been on her mind for a while. Looks like we'll get about a grand back!

Talked to Vince yesterday, & Graham Everett, about the chapbook. Vince is too much, is making me the poet of Long Island. He keeps talking about Whitman, Wheelock, & Heyen.

Yesterday afternoon hundreds of birds on the back lawn against the ash trees, grackles & cowbirds &, and this is unusual, at least a hundred red-winged blackbirds. I have some lines in mind about them.

4/11/78

Noon, and calm. I slept until an hour ago, after the Buffalo trip.

We first went to the poetry room at Lockwood, where Karl Gay was gracious. They seemed to have all my things, and I signed/dated about a dozen. I looked over their Wilbur & Kinnell & Wright things.... Then a cocktail party at Mac Hammond's, sparsely attended, & then the reading, even more sparsely attended: I counted sixteen people. There was another reading, at a bar, by prize-winning student poets, & even Hammond & young people I saw at the party & John Logan had to go. I wished, for the Brockport kids' sakes especially, more people had been at our reading, of course.... Later we went to the other bar, a shitty scene with a young woman reading & reading & reading & no one paying attention. Then we went over to a quiet bar with John Logan—such an abysmally sad and lonely man now, it seems to me. He had <u>no one</u> with him, no one, and was all alone when we had to leave. He is about the saddest man I've ever known.... Driving home, I wondered aloud for an hour about this whole business of giving readings. I'm coming to some decisions, though I don't yet know what they'll be. I'm learning at every reading, though I'm not sure what.... Oh, that vast Lockwood collection, and who really gives a shit? Everything in this country is against poetry, the poet's happiness. I'm learning—ha, my constant theme.

Literary notes: *Ontario Review* postcard arrived; it's nice, though I don't know why I labeled my poem "After Rilke"—only one movement in it is from him.... Another card done with a crappy poem by Bob Phillips.... Lovely letter from Ernie Stefanik, & gifts of books, etc. He prevails.... Gifts from Donald Hall, too.... Phoenix Cat. #147 arrived, & seems to be the one with the many items Poulin sold, & many Writers Forum programs!... Well, another $150 yesterday, anyway, & if I can make it to Colgate & back day after tomorrow, that will be another $250.... Man from Southampton called & talked to Han & wants me to read for $50. I'll say <u>no</u> if he calls again—a <u>slight</u> bit of integrity therein.... Dave Fraher called & talked to Han. Now <u>there's</u> a sweet friend, & I'll have a fine time in Wyoming, as I will on Long Island with Vince. A lesson there, too: go to places where there are friends.

I love Han & kids more & more lately, & pray thanks when I get home, as from the world of Logan & Buffalo & poetasters.

Diary, you are a help when I am filled with indefinable bile. I usually leave you having written my way to ease. Still, there are some things I have to learn, though I don't know what they are. My disease has tricky symptoms. I still, of course, like attention, & maybe I could get to the point where I allowed things to happen to me when they do (without stopping everything) but did not at all hang on things, anticipate. I'm close to something here!... The fellow from Southampton did call just now, and I did say no.

4/12/78

A thought about the reading in Buffalo: so, I visited the poetry room at the Lockwood, where all my things were laid out on a table, all my books and fifteen or twenty small things, and I signed some things, and the library was interested in collecting me, and preserving me for the future: then, maybe twenty people showed up to hear me read: it was as though I was already dead.

Working on that poem about redwings.

4/20/78

I am in the folks' living room in Ridge, on Long Island. Will fly home tomorrow morning.

I feel like I've lived years since my last entry. The Colgate reading was pleasant—long drive, tiring, sparsely attended reading—Bruce Berlin & wife Mary warm. Saw many signed Yeats, Pound, etc. books, including a first of *The Waste Land*. Didn't get a chance to talk to any of the young people at the reading—Berlin whisked me away. He seems sad, in many ways. He has only published that one book, and a pamphlet, which he gave me, and his "career" stretched back to Berryman at Princeton.

SCCC reading went <u>very</u> well, including the "Light" & "Lovers" sections. Reading the latter took guts, but I'm glad I did. Wish they'd had *Noise* & *Swastika* on hand to sell. Vince & Ann Clemente warm & wonderful. Lubbers Oak awe-inspiring. Stood under it with Vince for a long time & have a piece of fallen bark. Renewed friendships with Pat Bizzaro, David Axelrod (& wife Joan who gave me a book of her poems), Dan Murray, and others. Met Allen Hoey. Only sour note was the terribly lurid, tasteless cover on the chapbook Graham Everett published, but it's no big deal, though it depressed me & Vince.... Went back to Roslyn with Katherine & Norb, to their lovely home perched up against the traffic. The Old Westbury two-hour class visit/reading went beautifully. A pleasure to see all those copies of *Swastika* around, & the response to the book. A fellow from *Newsday* there. Jon Collett a fine man who taught with Wilbur at Wesleyan.... Katherine took me to some bookshops. Found a copy of a Kumin novel for a buck, etc.... All in all, a fine visit, & a valuable one for *Chestnut Rain*, I know. But I'm tired of being away from home, & will have to leave Sunday for Wyoming, but after that will <u>settle in</u>.

My folks are fine here. We've not argued at all, & never will again. Will just avoid politics, etc. Pop & I have played some pool. Mom fusses over me constantly & cooks things that are too good.

Called Han last night. Her back still hurts. She really misses me now, & said "I love you," and we're realizing more all the time what we want & need. And it is called by two names: love, and home.

Kings Inn
777 East Second
POWELL, WYOMING 82435
(307) 754-5117

4/27/78

I did not carry my journal along on this trip, but thought that I would write this evening, and maybe staple this page in when (if ever!) I get home.... I've just finished my 4th (of 5) readings, here in Powell. They have all been about the same: four people as audience the first night, & fifteen to twenty the other nights. I've read well, I think, have done a good job for David. Our car trips have been fine, the landscapes unbelievable, from Cheyenne to Gilette (ugliest town in the world, a dirty boom-town) (or maybe spelled Gillette) to Caspar to Riverton to here (tomorrow to Sheridan). People have been sparse, but kind, and probably almost half the people at readings have bought the books, *Noise* & *Swastika*, that David has been lugging. I've had too much scotch to drink, have not run into anyone in Wyoming who cares much for contemporary poetry, have been wide-eyed with wonder seeing this country, Red Buttes on the Oregon trail, the canyon we passed through today, Teapot Dome! the other day, the sage brush & wandering herds of cattle & antelope, Shoshone, & Cody with its "Irma" & its historical center where I fell in love with two Bierstadt paintings. So much more. Seeing cowboys. The fences. The rock & range formations. The distances of purple & brown & sudden buttes. The vast ranches. The towns announcing populations of five or ten. A place called "Hell's Half Acre."... I guess I'm homesick now. I guess, too, I'm disquieted by the silence, the small groups at the readings. I guess I'm bothered, too, by this business of repeating the most effective poems, & of being a "performer," especially with poems from *Swastika*. I don't think Kinnell or Wilbur would have drawn better here. It's just sort of a vacuum. David says that when Keith Wilson was here, he lugged copies of one of his books, but didn't sell one, and I've inscribed/sold, let's see, about 25 books, anyway. What a world. I want to be home minding my own business. The great joy of this trip will be the looking back on it for the rest of my life, I know.... David is good company, but he's lonely, needs a woman, a wife. I think so often & with real love of Han & Billy & Kris. I'll call home again tomorrow.... My poems, as I keep feeling when I read them, are wonderful. I've done well. Fuck the future that will read this. I've written the poems I truly care for, and that is all there can be....

Before I left, a letter from Tom Woll saying yes to *Long Island Light*. This is quite a thing for me. I must write him right when I get back. It will be a big book. I don't know when, but maybe next spring.

It's only about 11:00, but I'm tired. Another 3-hr. trip tomorrow, & then a long one, five hours, on Saturday. Tomorrow night, my reading is at some kind of honors banquet. Egads, it's impossible to know what the fuck will happen from one reading to the next, and this is one reason it's difficult to play this goddamned role, or <u>not</u> to play some kind of role, or (whatever I mean) just to <u>relax</u> when I'm always putting my soul & dignity on the line, it seems....

———

Morning. I slept well. It's Friday. We've been departing these towns about 11:00 after a big breakfast, and I've felt fine.

I keep learning. And I keep growing up, it's true. It's fun, often, to be on the road, & the change is good, & I'll use the money for a tiller, etc., but I love to be home, and must reach the calm when it doesn't bother me when people ask what I did and where I've been lately. I'm getting close to being a man. Poetry: to write it, the best I can, and to let it go at that, to let <u>others</u> do the selling of small press things, to let <u>Vanguard</u> sell my books (if this is realistic—within reason, without feeling dirty, I can ask that sponsors have books available when I read). But to write *The Chestnut Rain* and mind my business—this is the thing. To get many things behind me, like the Wyoming Poetry Circuit, is a help, will let me be, with my garden & family & books, as the disease stays dormant, or even disappears.

4/28/78

Well, it just happened. I am back at the motel here in Sheridan watching the Denver/Milwaukee basketball game. And thank you, Lord, for the game. The reading was washed out. I was to follow an awards banquet at the Sheridan College. I prepared a list of poems, thought of how I'd begin by thanking the Wyoming folks for the privilege of touring their State. Then, no one was there for a reading. No one knew about it. No one. Two women, maybe, one Dave's contact. I'm glad the ball game is on, and I'll concentrate on it beginning with the second half. I'm a little sick at heart. What a way to end the trip. I just want to hold to a little dignity, want to avoid humiliation, and can't even do that. I have published three volumes of poems, edited two books, have impressive academic credentials, read well and have poems that could interest these people, but poetry is nothing in this land, and in five days I have read to maybe 40-50 people. Why shouldn't I feel hurt, even embarrassed? The lesson appears again, then, and this time in neon lights. Bill, remember, when you read this in Brockport, that as you wrote this in Sheridan, Wyoming, you felt empty, and you weren't sure what the exact lesson was—it is one, surely, and one with blurry edges—but it has something to do with self-sufficiency, certainly, <u>and</u> with not caring, <u>and</u>, certainly, with real care & even cunning in picking my spots. I expend a great deal of energy & nervousness, and guess I just won't do it until I believe maybe 50 people, anyway, will be listening. Usually, I think, I should be able to anticipate this. Of course it is part of my disease that I want recognition & attention, but I am human, and I believe in what I've managed to write. I am lucky to have a publisher that will now even do a 4th book, & a thick one. This must be enough. This incident, tonight, in Sheridan, Wyoming (Holy fuck: Larry Csonka has just come on television to recite a poem to sell deodorant: poetry in America is about dead, surely; I am alive during its death gasps, & if it will be taking new forms, electronic, plastic, whatever, for better or worse I'm not interested) is a key one in my maturation, my life, I know. It finally happened, all the way. A fucking reading actually called off! A couple hundred people filing past me on their way out, the college president remembering he was supposed to announce something at the end of the awards ceremony, and talking into a dead mike. Okay. I'll remember. And what it must do is make me write more intensely, and keep it to myself. I have about 30 years. And I will want/ought to want to spend it with my Art in a way different from the way I have. I have to stand tall, and alone, keep my head up and continue to care for myself & my poetry during a time when everything seems to want me to blush & stammer & apologize for what has become the thing that defines me. I will pick my spots from here on in. I imagine I will make a few mistakes, but I will pick my spots. I'm bothered by the 2 things coming up in Brockport, but the reading may not be bad, and maybe I'll cancel the Rochester City Hall thing. Anyway, the second half beginning, and now the trip home is close, and I called Han today & talked with her & Kristen, & I have a family that I love & need very much, & who need me.

5/2/78

So good to be home. I'm still very tired, and adjusting, and glad to be off the road.

That Wyoming evening when no one came for a reading was not really a big deal. Who cares. But I will pick my shots from here on in. Watch me!... David called today to say that a Casper woman sent him a check for seven more copies of *Swastika*, which she will donate to libraries. Again, this is one of the good things resulting from even a sparsely-attended evening.... Thurs. I read here, & next Tues. I'll talk to Billy's class, & next Wed. at that fiasco in Rochester. And <u>then</u> I will no longer commit myself to things I'd rather not do. A real turning point. I told Han that she'll never again hear me complain about agreeing to something over the phone that I wished I hadn't. "Cautious" will be my middle name.... What more could I want: one book to be published in the spring (talked to Tom Woll yesterday) and my other, *CR*, will be a pleasure to work on for years.

Trying to clear my desk off. Too much mail. It really is a drag, & is my fault, but I'm too polite not to answer. A pleasure to correspond with Ernie & Vince & Ewert & such, but not with many others. And this does take time away from the poems. Well, it's no big deal—I'll have my desk cleared soon. And I drafted what will be another section of *CR* today.

Haven't seen Tony or Al since I got back. They read, too, this week.

Lovely letter from Michael Cuddihy about "Witness."... Duane Schneider probably will do a Heyen hardback next year. I'll have plenty of miscellaneous poems.

Might as well press through to the end of this page!

Stafford's *Collected* arrived back safely with holograph & inscription. A treasure.... More small press things in the works: 1/ *Son Dream/Daughter Dream*; 2/ *Lord Dragonfly*; 3/ *The Ash*; 4/ *Manassas Review*.... I'm sending out cards for *Elm's Home* & *Praise*. Haven't gotten my signed copies of the latter, yet, and hope I will soon.

I think I'll be happy all year looking forward to *Long Island Light*. Told Tom that Han and I would drop it off in July, but I might send it along sooner, but I might not.

5/3/78

I've had a fine day. Am waiting, now, for Han to get back from softball practice so we can have supper, and then the Piccione/Katz reading is tonight.

A fine day, with a good royalty report from Vanguard and, more important, lovely notes from Evelyn. They will always be with me. I wrote her a letter about all sorts of things.

Stopped in to see Al Poulin. It's getting to be a joke. He sent manuscripts to Duane Schneider right after he saw *Fires*, and seems to have squeezed out poor Bob Mondy's manuscript, which I sent down. Now he tells me he's been on the phone several times with Ernie about various things! And he just called me to get Norbert's & Vince's addresses for who knows what. I wonder if I'll ever have anything in the world to myself, even one friend. Yes, I have Vanguard. Pure joy that he couldn't push BOA on them. And then he called again to say he was afraid that Fitz Gerald wd. get the Forum & the MFA Directorship, & might apply himself. I hope he does! Go to it, Alfred. I'll stick with my poems. It's fun to watch these fellows, Al & Tony.... I did write a letter to Ernie to subvert Poulin a little. Ha. No passion, just deliberate subversion. Ernie/Rook & Vanguard—I want these places for myself, whether this is selfish or not. I feel good about all things since getting back from Wyoming. I think I'm growing up. At last. I will just write subversive letters, & smile, & go about my life.

5/7/78

    I am close to finishing answering every damned letter that piled up, telling people I enjoyed poems/books I didn't give a shit about. Aah, human relations. For example: Pat Janus read the other night, and her poems were awful, the worst we've had here in ten years, and I avoided talking to her at the reception so I wouldn't have to lie, and then, late, Han and I were deciding whether or not to go to Fitz Gerald's party, & I thought the Rochester people wouldn't be there, and went, & Pat Janus rushed right up & gave us an inscribed poem, and her eyes were wet, and she told us how important we were to her, so I said something about enjoying the reading, & felt bad, & all arguments that said fuck the goodness or badness of poetry/let's worry about people came to the fore. And what's the answer?

    $130 in royalties for *Swastika*. Next check will be bigger.

    Al's reading had me blushing—he was so embarrassingly "dramatic"—god it was awful. I felt the way I feel when Miss America contestants answer questions. He read like a speech teacher, & I hate this.... Tony was okay, but went on forever. What a week. So glad it's over. My own reading made me nervous. I read only from *Chestnut Rain*. Well, shit, I was the best.... Heather McHugh was okay, is fun....

    We're so proud of Kristen. She stood up like a trooper & concentrated & played a beautiful solo the other night, under pressure. And she won two blue ribbons in Gates the other day in competitions.

    Phillips sent me 3 of the most absolutely awful poems. So bad that it's hard to believe. How can he show them around, those poems on beans & "Miss Crustacean?"

    Record snows in Cheyenne & Denver. I just missed them.

    Hope to get a tiller soon & break ground for garden out back.

5/10/78

    Almost wrote here last night. Decided to wait until another tense day passed. And it has. It's almost midnight, and I'm relaxing.

    Tony was supposed to pick me up at 10:30 this morning, but came at 9. The City Hall reading was stiff. All those folks. I like many, but guess I just feel uncomfortable during such social occasions. I read "Give Me the Splendid Silent Sun," Ignatow's "The Question," and "The Tree." Bob Koch mentioned that our radio program had gotten such a strong response that they'll put it on again.

    Kristen home from school for a few days now. She feels dizzy. Blood test results due tomorrow. I feel sorry for the little thing, & pray it's nothing serious. Billy & Han fine, though Han hates schoolwork & her upcoming exams.

    Son Dream/Daughter Dream arrived today. The woodcut is a bit grotesque, but grows on me. I called Ernie & we had a good talk. He'll probably visit for about a week when he arrives. I mentioned again the Poulin thing, & he's with me, says he's written me about this, saying Poulin is no poet.

    My reading to Billy's class & others went beautifully yesterday.

    Service-berry out. I'm going to give Jeff Schiff a special *Swastika* for graduation.

    Tomorrow, fun: Horowitz reading, drinking, probably a poker game at Mirko's.

5/15/78

    Han's folks surprised us with a few days' visit. It was sort of tiring, but okay. Han was really up against it with her schoolwork & other things, and wanted to keep her mother company, so was frustrated & anxious. But she got her class presentation over with tonight, and has a week to type up her final paper. But she's doing so many other things. But I know I just have to go my own way, and plan to work outside a lot.

    Alfred stopped over with his first Gray Wolf Rilke. It's pretty, but nothing terribly special. It should certainly have included a page mentioning the date of Rilke's text, a little about it, etc.

    Tomorrow I'll keep up my tilling in the afternoon. Tilling, weather willing. Morning, I think I'll take a last look through *Long Island Light*, and make the few last changes I've listed, and send it off. Have to get the *Son Dream/Daughter Dream* package off to Ernie, too. Look forward to his visit. He is a real friend. Hope he stays on top of things now, after his occasional depressions.

Played basketball today, & ran hard, & my muscles held up. Will get strong working outside. Now, if my bladder infection is cleared up, as I think it is, and after I get my teeth fixed this month, I'll be in good shape.

Sent my "Mantle" off to *APR*. They're jerks if they don't take it.

Finished the Goebbels book I began on my way to Wyoming. And read a little book by Robert Francis today called *The Satirical Rogue in Poetry*, which was fun. Got an $8.50 check from *Poetry* for a poem in May issue I look forward to seeing.

Hope to put in <u>some</u> work this summer on *The Chestnut Rain*. Want to get it typed up to the point I've finished it, so that it will be a solid entity in my mind as I go through the next school year. I did get enough done so that I <u>know</u> the poem will be a poem, eventually.

5/17/78

<u>Another</u> perfect day. Got *Light* ready to send off, wrote Vince & Bill Ewert, got a couple other literary things cleared away, and washed out the garage & worked out back spading for a couple hours. Minding my business, & getting strong digging, & staying in touch with <u>friends</u>. Love it. Tomorrow, again! It's days like these that seem usually impossible to come by.

May 19, 1978

Kristen's band concert last night was fun, and even touching. All those Brockport kids on the stage, including one of ours, and Billy down in front with his friends, and all those Brockport people—Nora & Lisa Studier behind us, and Roy & Caroline Schumacher & kids in front of us, & the Millers to our left—it's all sort of amazing, our lives in this town, amazing & blessed. After the concert, an art show in the gym, & punch & cookies. We talked to "Bubba," Frank Balling, my old co-captain & now Vice Principal at the Middle School. This is the kind of community I sense around us.

It's morning, the kids in school & Han to the dentist in Rochester. A beautiful day. I'll dig & till & mow this afternoon.

Yesterday I read closely over the first section of *Light*. It's so good. All my doubts vanished. Today I skimmed the third section. Little doubts (the phrase "way back past" in "Odor of Pear," the word "guts" in "the Lamb"), but the book is finished. Some larger questions (the book's overlapping time schemes, & the poems' various ((since they were written over so long a time span)) textures), but the book is finished, and I'll love it, and it's the right book to have upcoming now, as *The Chestnut Rain* grows in my soul, if not always on its pages.

Party tomorrow night for *Service-berry* at Tony's. Don't know if I'll go. Sandi sounds just haggard, at the end of her rope.

Han says that Sandy McClatchy called when I was in Wyoming. I wrote the last letter or two, and won't write again, despite his call. He was not much of a friend about *Swastika*, and has gone his own way, and is just the kind of correspondence I ought to drop anyway. I want <u>friends</u>, not fair-weather acquaintances, & my friends are with me & my poems until the end. Let Sandy go his sweet Ashbery/opera/New York way. I will trust myself. I know who I am. And this has little to do with McClatchy. As *The Chestnut Rain* will have little to do with that whole crowd.

Imagine, Mr. White, my 6th grade teacher, is still alive & kicking on the Island! Heard from Bets Vondrasek. Wonder if he has read *Noise*. He was old & gray-flecked & hunched over and constantly coughing even back in Nesconset. I still love him. Hope to see him again…. Another old man, Archie MacLeish, sent a beautiful letter, told me to relax, to take time, to think with my ears. He knows, & the letter spoke to my condition. I <u>must</u> take at least five years on *The Chestnut Rain*! I have a chance to get <u>everything</u> in!

5/22/78

Amen to that last sentence.

Wish I could remember the stanza that came to me yesterday while I was breaking sod in the garden—it had the refrain "Come back to the poem," and was good, despite that line.

Al called 3-4 times while I was working outside. I returned his call in the evening. Nothing new, really. Just back from Athens, he leaves tomorrow for a NYS Council meeting in New York. Go! I've had chances to join such groups.

Han's birthday tomorrow. And a dentist appointment for me.

Am planning a party for Rook Press and Ernie Stefanik on June 11th. Hope some good folks can make it. We'll drink, cook hamburgers, talk. That's on a Sunday evening.

Lovely letter from Werner Merten today. He says he mentioned us at old Mr. Pietsch's funeral in Hannover. Otto was a good old man, so kind & loving to Billy & Kristen. Maybe we'll meet again. What is it about that year in Germany?—when I think of it, the people & places & ourselves younger, I feel sad, and blessed, at the same time. We will see the Mertens again, I pray, and trust. They may get to this country before we get there.

May 29, 1978

I'm outside, under the silver maple. It's been over 90 degrees the past couple of days, and will be again today. How beautiful everything is—Han's flowers, the honeysuckle bushes now flowering, the hundreds of ash trees around the property. Such a lush year, too. Despite the recent heat, the ground is still wet around here.

The garden is in now, and my corn plants are already an inch high. Peppers & tomatoes have taken. We should have good vegetables this year. I've cooked out three days in a row now, too. There is nothing deadly about this supposedly deadly suburban life. What gives it meaning is the ground, the plants, the presence of so much alive around us.

I've been typing up the finished sections of *CR*—added some lines about our native Americans yesterday to the light section. Today, sitting out here, I finished the poem "Blackbirds," or "Redwings," which I'd rather call it, except for the Wright poem—but, what the hell, I'll call it "Redwings" anyway. I'd like to do a companion piece called "Pines," if I can. Have the first stanza.

Billy is off to play soccer, despite the heat. Han is painting the trim in Kristen's room. I will be lazy today. I look forward to Ernie's visit, & then to my folks' visit later in June…. Just to be, on a day like this, is plenty.

June 1, 1978

Day follows beautiful day. I've had a nice balance, reading/writing, & doing garden work. Have also played basketball to stretch. It's odd, though: sometimes the more poetry I write (drafted another section—burr oak—of *CR* today), the more I feel driven to write & even irritable when I have to/want to (as contradictory as this sounds) do something else. Maybe it's just this business of the single, ongoing poem—an experience I've never had.

Straightened the ten pines along the fence today. Winter beat the hell out of them. Maybe I should screen them next year.

Am reading a wonderful book called *The Near Woods*.

Bill Elkins called. We'll visit next month. Buena Vista, Va.

Kristen's room about done. Food order comes tomorrow. We're busy.

Suburbia, this pause in history, unreal peace. Happiness, Hegel said, is sterile, does not contribute to progress of the race.

6/4/78

The fine days continue. Much sweat & work, then (as this evening) basketball with the kids, & a shower, & puttering around. Don't want to get to the letters I should.

Al called today about literary things, & I was just in from outside, & was just in a different world, & that shit is all he ever thinks about.

So much poison ivy where I mowed in the woods out back today—I'm making a path I can use to walk the circumference (or jog it!) of the whole property. Will kill the poison ivy little by little. The grapevines!: they never cease to amaze me, stringing 30-40-50 feet along the ground & into trees…. Worked hard a couple days along the Mosher line, planting more ash, then about 20 tiny pines Wicks gave us, and making a small rock wall in the corner. And spent some time clearing where I'll have my little shed. Have a perfect place. It has been a great life…. And this morning's headline was that a million people are starving in Ethiopia, & that gangrene is rampant.

Ernie arrives Thursday. I look forward. So much to show him & to talk about.

Have the CAPS application ready to go in, just for fun. Made me gather & xerox *CR*, & that's good, & now I have proof of outside application when I look for a SUNY summer grant.

6/13/78

Just back from my 3rd, and final (for a while) dentist appt. My front teeth now look decent, if still dingy.

Ernie left yesterday already, & I'm glad. We had a fine time, talking & drinking & planning. He is, too, as Han said, "a good man," considerate & gentle. I'd like to get together with him in New York for a few days some time, hitting the book shops.

Our big party Sunday went well. The weather blessed us, & 30-40 people were here, and all had a good time. The Shuffeltons showed up, & the Rosenblums, and Jerry Mazzaro even showed up. He's the same, wears blinders, is a sad/pathetic person, but I'm fond of him & feel sorry for him. He mentioned he was thinking of selling his books. I want to be there, when that happens. And Bob Mondy was there & excited to meet Ernie & Jerry, & I took groups around the property a couple of times. Now we are all tired, of course…. My folks arrive in a few days, but that will be no problem. And Allen Hoey called & might show up with *The Ash* this weekend…. And Brian Johnson is here with Billy this week…. But I already feel relaxed again, & can get back to puttering with my poems & doing some reading.

Tony & Sandi came to the party, left around 11, & Tony came back, very drunk, & sat in his arm-crossed daze, & made a phone call somewhere (probably to Charles Napravnik) & Han overheard "I'm so lonely," and then leaned his head into our air conditioner for fifteen minutes, & then took off in his van. If Tony doesn't have serious trouble before too many years go by, it will be a miracle.

6/16/78

I just spent a long time reading over the completed sections of *CR*. Some movement upstairs, Brian Johnson visiting, kitchen noises, etc., and I couldn't concentrate except in brief patches, but *CR* is impressive, so ambitious. I know that in the back of my mind I'm planning to work on it in my little shack out back once it's built, hopefully by next spring. I have to be <u>alone</u> with the poem in ways never before necessary. But what made me happy just now was my realization that I am indeed having trouble getting inside *CR* to the point where I can make meaningful progress precisely because I now do definitely conceive of it as and consider it to be a <u>single</u> long poem. Yes, and it knows, too, that it is one poem. There will still be rearrangements of sections until I have the flow I need, inevitable transitions, balances of dream/waking, etc. I <u>hope</u> that teaching will not interrupt the poem to the point where even a summer won't bring it back to me. I'll be all right, but must spend periods with it regularly, I think, if only to read over what I've already written.

I have a hunch my folks will be here today.

6/21/78

My folks have been here, will leave tomorrow. Eddie & Cheryl—8 months+ pregnant—were here Sunday. We've had a good time, but hectic. My mother talks <u>all</u> the time; Pop is <u>always</u> finding something wrong with a window or bookcase or carpet. True story: we were walking across a field to Kristen's soccer game, a nice lawn, and there was a worn spot a couple inches wide in the lawn, and it bothered Pop!... He's told me how we'll build my shanty, & it should be good. 8' x 12'—that will be a good size, and an attached shed for the lawn mower etc.

Nothing, of course, new with my writing.... Sid Gold just called, and I'm glad my folks were here and that I'll miss him. Nice kid, but—the same old story.... I know that Barry Leeds & David Fraher & Allen Hoey and others will show up.... We don't really want to go to the Island, but probably will. Gulp. And the flight alone will be maybe $340.

6/28/78

Dave Fraher leaves today. He's been staying with us for several days, when I thought he'd be staying with Poulins or Picciones. He's just a fine fellow, but I've had enough visitors, surely, and no sense lately of summer calm. But when Boo picks him up for the airport today, I'll take a long shower and then work relaxed and steady on that inverview that that goddamned Rubin finally dropped off.

We had Picciones & Poulins over a few nights ago, and Picciones have made no effort since to get into touch with David. Very strange. They were so close. Poor David remarked without thinking the other night that all his friends had gotten slimmer since he'd seen us years ago, and all eyes turned to Tony, who looks like a baby whale, & Sandi patted his great big gut and said she liked it. I did not laugh, as everyone else did. I <u>know</u> Tony, who just smiled.

Allen Hoey & wife will visit and stay over Saturday, but just this one night. Pshew. Again, a nice fellow, but enough is enough. I want my study back.

I see that I haven't noted here that *The Ash* arrived. It's <u>very</u> handsome, and with Kristen's hand-colored drawing is a lovely item. I wish Ernie's work were letterpress like this.... Long letter from Ernie about many projects. *Lord Dragonfly* due any day, and then we'll do *Swastika Prose* in 1979. But right now my priority is my little peace-place and writing place out back.

We fly to the Island July 7th. It will be good to get away for ten days, and once back I'll have the rest of the summer clear.

We had Lynne Studier over yesterday for dinner with David. First time we've ever played matchmaker.

Kristen is playing goalie this summer, and doing a good job, and Billy is playing soccer and basketball. Kristen's report card was her best ever, and Billy got a 98 on the biology regents and a 100 on the geometry. I flunked my geometry regents in high school, and that's a fact.

6/30/78

Woke up at seven this morning & dressed and walked around out back within the trees near where my shack will be. It's so beautiful there, everything giving of bird and bush.

Wrote a little poem the other day that might be finished.

<u>The Buffalo</u>

Had the herds roamed the moon,
we could have seen them
in the clear night sky,
rivers of black light
flowing and emptying
into the sea.

7/20/78

    Brockport Sidewalk Sale Days began today. I went to see the Twig books—found nothing terribly special, but a humorous novel by Frank Sullivan inscribed to Dorothy Parker. But last night, at the Book Rack on Ridge, I found a Vachel Lindsay, inscribed and with a holograph poem. For two bucks!
    Our Island vacation went quickly. In general, it was fine, though Werner's hard-to-believe laziness (naps all day) and their chain-smoking got me down.... In Riverhead, came across a cache of Vanguard books in a junk store, no doubt stolen from the Commack warehouse, and I have Tom Woll in touch with Werner.
    Boston University sent a check for $2,000. Gotlieb has been good to me. I was just getting depressed about how our money just flew away, when the check came. I didn't even know the deal had gone through. Yesterday, I got the package of manuscripts ready to send off. More money for manuscripts than for royalties. Maybe before I die there will be a catalogue of Boston's Heyen holdings. I'd like that.
    Reading Donald Hall's new book, *Kicking the Leaves*, which he had sent to me. Some very moving poems.... Got Sandy McClatchy's Sexton book just before we left for the Island.... The first copy of *Lord Dragonfly* arrived. I like it very much. Ernie did a fine job. Now he's sliced off part of his thumb working on the book (as has Allen Hoey working on *The Ash!*), and other copies won't be around for a while.
    Nice afternoon at Clementes, & Krapfs were there too. We all walked to the Lubbers Oak. I'm glad Han got a chance to see it. I hope to add a short prose piece about it to *Long Island Light*, the contract for which, says Tom, is in the mail.
    The bastards Hine & Parisi did take a poem, "The King's Men," for the upcoming Houghton-Mifflin *Poetry* anthology.... Check for $141 from *Poetry*, too, for July issue, to which I look forward because of "Lord Dragonfly," etc. Maybe I'll win a prize this year.
    All in all, I feel fine. Brockport is <u>baking</u>, but I've moved the downstairs air conditioner into my study. Got much done, cleaning files etc., yesterday, and hope to turn to *Long Island Light* again this evening when Han & both kids are away playing ball.
    Saw Petroskys before we left; all's well with them. But Tony Piccione was surly & dead drunk, & threatening, their whole visit, & they got the hell out of there a day early. Now the word is that Sandi is off pot & Tony off booze again. Both were close to the edge. Anything can happen. Can he stop drinking?
    We'll go to Nashville & Han's 20th reunion Saturday. After that we're staying put for the summer. Do I actually look forward to teaching?

7/25/78

    Enjoyed the reunion very much. Felt close to many of Han's classmates before the evening was over. 22 of the 36 in her class returned, and from Kentucky & Minnesota & Washington State. They will have another reunion in five years.
    I haven't felt quite right since we got back. I was on edge for a couple of days, and couldn't sleep, & feel now sort of sluggish & bloated. But one more night's sleep & I might catch up.
    Poetry (July) arrived, & I have a good spread. Also, the contract for *Long Island Light* arrived, and I signed it and sent it in. Can't quite believe that I'll have another book, and this one a big one. I'll try to help them sell it, but who knows what will happen. But this time, I think selfishly, if they drop me after this book it won't really matter. I'll take years on *Chestnut*, and by then will be able to find a publisher anyway. <u>But</u>, I just hope *Light* does well enough to please Vanguard. Mainly, I will have that big book to hold.... Have added a prose piece on Lubbers Oak to *Light*, and "To a Warplane."
    Got the package in the mail to Boston. When I get a note saying it arrived safely, I'll feel as though the money is mine. What luck! Bill Ewert will be sending me some money, too (I sent him the Mss. for "Witness" & some books), & there will be $375 from Vanguard. Maybe I can pay for the shack my father will build for me without using the $2,000 from Boston. I get a kick out of building up my writing account.

7/31/78

    Picked up the ticket for Pop today. August 21st he'll arrive, and we'll get busy. I look forward.

I don't know how there can be so much to do, but for days I've been working with my books, making my roll-top and the bookcase above it my collector's center, with bibliographies & trading stock & catalogues. Also, I've tried to arrange my own publications, three of everything for the family, and two extra of everything else, for the "hall collection." So many different sizes, so this becomes difficult. What am I doing already, preparing for my death?

I think, when I get a chance, I'll try to get 5 or 10 of certain things to put away, like the new Stafford from Croissant. For trading, or for a little retirement mail-order business. I've often been too generous, giving good items away for little in return. I'll be a little more alert in the future.

No poems lately, but, what the hell, everyone is worried that I'm writing too much or, at least, publishing too much. It's true, too, and I have an awful lot of time. Hey, maybe once I have that shack back there, I can write that novel.... I have, lately, though, been looking through *Long Island Light*. Made a couple of perfect changes in the prose piece on the cardinal yesterday.

8/6/78

Han & I are off to her softball picnic in a half-hour.

The copies of *Lord Dragonfly* are all signed & holographed with poems & packaged & ready to send to Ernie.

$175 from Bill Ewert again.

Decided to get an electric, rather than wood, stove for my shack in back. Cleaner, quicker, more convenient.

Han & I will have a week alone, for the first time ever, when Kris goes to Kelly's & Billy to Kurt's beginning next Friday.

We all enjoyed the parade & carnival & *Jaws II* in recent evenings.

8/13/78

Han returned from dropping the kids off yesterday. Sunday morning now, and we're alone, and the silence is deafening. We played a little tennis last evening, the kids not on our minds or whizzing around the block on their bikes, and it was like a second honeymoon.

I spent a few hours over at Bill Andrews' yesterday sorting a font of type with him. He's going to do a chapbook of five poems that I'll call *Brockport's Poems*. Each one mentions the town. He works on an 1871 press. He'll call his press—the name escapes me—but it was the name of a newspaper he printed when he was a kid in Colorado. So he thinks of the press as being founded in 1944! I like Bill. My kind of man: a dean who has a printing press in his garage. He'll do a postcard advertisement first, and I'll send them out, and should be able to sell at least a hundred copies for him.

I haven't slept well lately, and part of it is my excitement, elation over these small-press things!

Ernie called to talk over the advertising brochure he'll print. He had the excellent idea of making everything available through Spring Church Books, Ed Ochester, and talked to Ed. That booklet will be good for my ego.... I had to laugh the other day when *APR* rejected "Mantle" (how could they?—It's a beauty!), and a reading series in Connecticut decided on Plumly & other poets instead of me (I hedged about money, and this didn't help). Things have been going so well for me that some rejections are fine, reminding me of how things always were, and will be.

Signed the Vanguard contract for *Light*. And Tom said how about an edition of a thousand hardbacks, & the rest in paper, and I said <u>sure</u>. Will see if I can get some boxed and signed. What a book. I keep skimming it & seeing how big it is.

Peter Dzwonkoski and wife and child visited the other day, and we had a fine time. He was knocked over by my collection, and said that if they had it at Rochester it would put them on the map. And I'll keep building.

Duane Schneider wrote and told me not to forget our project for the spring, his first hardback! I'm rich with such things. Have to guard against this getting in the way of new work.

8/17/78

Letter inviting me to read at Columbia! I asked for April. Will see. A good center for the group of readings I hope to give after *Light* comes out. Big deal!—so I'll sell 50 copies.

Card from Joyce Oates, on her way to Princeton for a year. She liked *Lord Dragonfly*. I also sent her *The Ash* before that. I keep hoping, of course, that she'll package up a bunch of her things, Black Sparrow etc., and send them to me.

I'm making progress on my Whitman essay. Don't have anything of interest to say, but hope to be distracting enough to cover a few pages.

We called the kids yesterday. They're fine. Han will pick them up Sunday.

Foundation blocks & floor lumber delivered today. Look forward to building my 8' x 12' palace, and Pop looks forward to coming.

Good letter from good Jack Matthews. He's sending me another package of contemporary books he doesn't want.

I bet Bill Andrews is working like hell on the press right now. It's dark, and Han's at a meeting, and I haven't taken a bike ride in the dark in a long time, so maybe will drop in on Bill for fun.

8/20/78

Han will return with the kids today. Han and I had a great week, kept one another company, snuggled a lot while watching television. I love her.

Sunday today. I exhausted myself sealing the driveway in 90° heat yesterday, will rest today. Pop called to say Mom is ill (her scalp problem) and he can't fly in tomorrow to begin my shack. I have the blocks out back (which I'll dig in) and some lumber in the garage for the floor.

The *Poetry* anthology arrived. I'm glad for even my tiny part in it, am sentimental about the magazine, remember opening the envelope with my first acceptance there, from Henry Rago.

Have finished, I think, my little "Essay Beginning and Ending with Poems for Whitman" for Vince Clemente's magazine. I'm thinking of adapting parts of it for a section of *Long Island Light*.

8/25/78

A gloomy morning. Kurt is visiting, and drives now, and took our car golfing with Billy. (What a sentence!)

My correspondence this past week has been amazing—my attempt to clear off my desk, meaning clear my mind of obligations, etc. Long letters to Ernie about projects, and my realization that this has to stop, that it takes time from other work I might do, and is too easy, and even clutters up the world with ephemerae. I want to slow that down. I said I'd put together *Handbook of Heartbreak*, and then changed my mind—I want that giant catch-all of a book in my cabin for many years in a box!—and said no to a reprinting of *Eighteen Poems and a Story* and yes to a special little item of my Bartleby poem, etc., etc., etc., & this has to stop. And will surely slow down. Volumes of other correspondence. I'll get back to just sending an occasional postcard for most things. Pshew, it's the price of writing. It's even pleasant in a way, but not this back-breaking volume & pace. No. Even Han says she is amazed with the mail that comes in every day. And I don't even answer everything.

I've about finished my poem "The Sunflower." It's damned interesting. Its sounds. I still hope to do a *Sunflower Journal* some day.

Party (going-away for Gemmetts) this evening. No, at Gemmetts for Tanksley.

Mailman just pulled in!—a package from Ernie for sure.

Afternoon now. Kristen & I just back from a bike ride to the school.

Yes, packages of books to sign & send back to Ernie. And he asked for poems written out in all. I don't think I'll do this in copies of *Swastika*. Pshew, and I'm tired, right now, of signing things. Bob Phillips sent me a wonderful Updike story. Poor Bech, at the end, couldn't even sign his name.... Ernie, too, has a bad habit of doing too many extra copies of things. I know there were 19 out-of-series copies of *Son Dream/Daughter Dream*, but now he just found another twenty! I'll mention this to him.

Nice letter from Emmanuel in Greece. Letter from Peter Dzwonkoski.

8/27/78

Sunday. Ernie called about several things, mainly the possibility of his coming to exhibit during the SUNY Creative Writing Conference. I hope it can work out. I was feeling bugged for several days about all the action & correspondence. I have my head above the water, now.

The year is closing down. Since Pop & Werner might arrive the 6th, I'd better prepare handouts, etc., for classes before school begins.

I've gotten lazy about outside work, but otherwise have been playing tennis & basketball & feeling strong.

Kristen did a crane drawing for the Christmas card. Should be a nice one.

Saw Bill Andrews. I should have stayed more on top of the project. His taste is abysmal. He's chosen the college colors for *Brockport's Poems*, and the green for the cover is all right, but the yellow paper is lousy. Again. Will I ever learn. Depressed me for a while. He'd bought $110 worth of paper, so the damage was done. Also, I have to put all these small-press things in perspective (not to mention <u>all</u> my publications). They amount to little, and, hell, no one around here will be able to read those five poems anyway, and most people will think the paper attractive!

8/28/78

I might just include part of my Whitman piece in *Long Island Light*. Put together the piece I might use this morning. Will see. Looked over *Light*, and it looks/sounds strong to me, both sections of poems.... Also read over "Redwings" and "The Sunflower." They're stronger than I'd thought. And "The Pines" is about finished, I think.

Piccione just pulled in, left something in the garage, and left. I'll peek out to see what's there.

Dropped off Kurt & Billy at the golf course this morning, despite the rain. I think they'll get eighteen in, anyway.

One of the things Ernie mentioned was that Rochester had ordered even one of the $50 *Lord Dragonfly*s. I'm glad. They'll have a nice collection there, and I'll have the feeling that a whole run of my things is safe.

8/30/78

I'm missing the first meetings & President Brown's remarks over at the College this morning. I'm stretching my Guggenheim year, literally, for all it is worth.

Today, this afternoon, I'll try to put down my eight chimney blocks out back for my shack. Will borrow Al Studier's level. Will go to an auction this evening in Holly—books advertised (usually this turns into absolutely nothing, of course) and two wheelbarrows. I need one badly.

Han still going through hell with her certification. They keep changing the rules on her.... And she is still waiting to hear about a part-time teaching job.

Kurt is still here. Three days in a row I've gone for a long bike ride and then have played tennis for about an hour-and-a-half. And when I play tennis, I run constantly for loose balls, etc. So, I've had great workouts.

I see that *Kenyon Review* is starting up again. Just for fun, I sent them the four finished poems I have on hand.

Han says that at the dentist office she saw Joycie in *People* again.

I look forward to classes, but I have a hunch that there will be a big mess over books—only 15 of each seem to have been ordered, and my classes are always bigger. And there will be the pressure of Pop & Werner here as I get started. But that shack out back will be worth everything!

8/31/78

Played soccer yesterday after supper with about twenty boys up at the high school. Played better than I thought I could. Made some fine traps, and even scored a header. Four days straight now I've run like hell. Today, I think, it would be best if I gave my old muscles and bones a rest.

I put out the saw-horses yesterday and brushed creosote on the dozen floor beams for my shack. Will brush more on the ends again today. And I'll work with the blocks again. Getting them level & exactly the right distance is the hardest part.

Threat of rain today. Kurt & Billy are off playing golf. I actually beat both of them in miniature golf last evening. Shot a 40. They'd beaten me twice in a row this week.

Last day of my Guggenheim year………………………………………

9/1/78

I didn't take the day off. Again last night I played soccer for about two hours. Fun! My feet hurt, but I'm otherwise fine, and today I'm going to rest for sure. I want to keep this up, this running.

Letter from Tom Woll. I have the *Light* Mss. back with queries (at the perfect time—I've wanted to write him about some small changes), and I'll work on it all weekend. Also, he says that *Noise* is now out-of-stock! Made it. 2,500 copies made their way around. The last thousand were slow. It seems the country library- and bookstore-system pick up 1,500 in a hurry. After that, it's a struggle. I will push & bust my ass with mailings & ideas to get *Light* around. It should become a permanent part of the Island's literature.

Called Ernie for a long talk about lots of things. He's doing fine with sales of *Lord Dragonfly*, even the $50 one! Does my heart good.

Beautiful day today. I might work for an hour or two with the cement blocks & the creosote job. Otherwise, the body, old elm, has earned a rest.

9/2/78

Another perfect day. I mowed the back, spread creosote on the 4' x 8' plywood sheets, and finished digging in the cement blocks with Billy. A good workout. The place where the cabin will be is wonderful. It will not only be peaceful, but beautiful back there. The cabin will be seen, during winter, though snow may drift deep against it, but it will be about completely hidden in summer. Werner & Pop arrive in four days.

I'm going over the *Light* Mss. Many queries from Tom in the new prose, but I'm erasing/ignoring most. He wants to change some of my best rhythms. Well, with Vanguard I've always been able to do just what I want. Tom is forgetful, lets things slide, did not even enter the changes I'd spent so much time sending him a month or two ago. But they're with me, and *Light* will be quite a book, one to hold to, whatever, if anything, the world says about it!... Am taking the evening off, watching Alabama/Nebraska football.

9/5/78

The foundation is in. Pop & Werner arrive tomorrow. I hope the shed goes up fast. And once I have it the way I want it, I will not clutter it, will keep it simple and clear, a place for quiet reading and for writing poems, a place for getting away, for being in the trees while I write. I hope I can get the electric line down, too. Pop is bringing me a heater that they don't need.

So, I'm in an inbetween-time now, waiting for school—must do some preliminary work tonight—and for my cabin.

Three bee stings yesterday when I hacked into another nest, the second in a month. My bee-dream poem will be one of my first projects back there.

Picciones called from Poulins' yesterday and wanted us over, but we were happy doing things outside. It has been excellent, especially, being away from Alfred for so long. I just don't want to know what he's up to.

Worked all weekend on the Mss of *Light*. Sometimes I lose my confidence in it, and sometimes I wade through thinking it's one goddamned interesting voice. In a way, many styles, yes, but this is maybe to be expected in a book that has grown the way it has.

Kids begin school tomorrow, and they're excited.

I bicycled up around the college today, saw the cars unloading, the kids moving in. Twenty-one years ago I was one of them. Twenty years ago Han was. So many emotions flowing as I ride around the campus.... Sunday is a varsity vs. alumni soccer game, and I'll show up and see what happens.

Mirko called yesterday. I'm glad they're back safely from Ukraine. Look forward to the first poker game. Maybe it will be at Chuck's on the lake.

Eddie & Cheryl & the baby, we hear, will visit Sunday.... I sure hope for good weather so that I can get this project finished.

Will I have a cabin by the next time I write in this diary?

9/16/78

Saturday. I'm relaxing a little after a frantic ten days.

Pop left Thursday. I dropped him off at the airport early in the morning, and made it back for my eight o'clock class. Wern left two days before that in his pickup. The three of us worked like hell getting the cabin up. I had no idea what a job it would be. We often got on one another's nerves—Pop is a hard man to work with/for—but ended each day in good spirits. And now the little place is up. I love it. It's <u>solid</u>, and feels right, from floor to peaked roof to picture window that will be to my left as I sit at the oak table. It's well insulated, and even the electric line is down—I'll have to dig it under a little at a time. Yesterday I cleaned up back there, and have more to do. Every once in a while I look behind me and make sure it's there. Al Studier helped out a little, too, and he'll install the ceiling tiles and paneling, the only things left to do. The place is so tight, that the small heater, probably on low, will warm it right up. It has a rolled-tarpaper roof, green, and a nice grooved plywood called Texture III outside. Three windows screened, and the door. And the comfort of the century will be there when I carry my air conditioner back and buy a shag-rug remnant. It's not that I'll be roughing it at all, I know. I don't give a shit. The paneling has already given me a line for the "Light" section of *Rain*.... The Lord allowing, I'll spend a great deal of time back there over the years. Bless Wern & Pop for my little 8' x 12' place for poetry.

At the same time, school began for me. I got very little sleep, but now have this weekend to gather myself together. I'm meeting my classes in my room, though the Intro. Poetry class is too large for it.

What else is new? Not much. I'm planning on having Ernie & Vince here for the SUNY conference. It will be hectic, but fun.... I'm sending out the cards for *Brockport's Poems*. Archie at the Lift Bridge ordered 120 of the 300 copies!... *Light* has arrived back at Vanguard & things are underway. That book is <u>something</u>, I do believe.

9/17/78

Rain this morning, but Billy and I worked outside in a drizzle burying the electric wire. This afternoon, I'll read composition papers while watching pro football.

Vince Clemente called. He's applying for a state grant.... Hmmm.... I just remembered that he would have had to apply elsewhere, too. Don't know what he can do. I'd better write him.

I bought seven bound volumes yesterday at the Dickinson house—1 *Atlantic Monthly*, two *Scribner's*, four *Harpers*. Five bucks each, and they always go for fifteen or more. The Harpers may be duplicates. I'll check at school. Also bought, for 50¢, a William Allen White first signed by him & a Henry White—*The Martial Adventures of Henry and Me.* Han bought a beautiful old walnut wall shelf.

9/18/78

Rain all day today. I did get out twice and extend the line underground about twenty feet. It's about half-way now.

An auction this evening. Books advertised. Han will drop me off, pick up Kristen at soccer practice (if it's not called off), and pick me up again.

Al Studier called and will begin soon putting up the ceiling tiles and wall panels in my shack.

Read a set of freshman compositions yesterday. Painful. Sad. Many are basically illiterate. What the hell can I do? Should have planned to teach strictly a grammar course. I do like *The Portable English Handbook* I've adopted.

Evening: Max Wickert just called inviting me to read at Buffalo, for some small not-quoted figure. I said no, that I promised myself I wouldn't read for less than a couple hundred dollars. I'm proud of myself. I will pick my spots, as I promised myself. I'll make some mistakes, but not many. So, I've turned down Buffalo & Bucknell lately.

News last evening & today is Carter/Begin/Sadat. I choked up a few times, in hope. Maybe, just maybe, there can be peace. I'd be pleased if some of the prophecy of *Of Palestine* turned out to be silly.

9/19/78

Tired as I was, I just couldn't sleep last night, and today was a crazy day. In the hours between my classes, I had to deal with Bill Andrews regarding typos (and even missing lines) in *Brockport's Poems*, had to fill out vaguely an application for merit that I thought was due next month, and had to deal with Patti Ross in Albany about the Conference coming up—at <u>last</u> I was told what they wanted me to do (be the sole reader in English of Voznesensky's poems) and I said no thanks! Then, I think, Bob & Patti must have called Al, wanting me to be on the program, somehow, with a reading, and I think he said no. Anyway, they can all go fuck themselves. I will try to pace myself and have a good time. Will see about getting some books signed—John Gardner & others. These things come and go. Eighteen readers, I've heard, and I wasn't invited. They want to have people who didn't read at Binghamton, but this general rule didn't apply to Simpson & Logan. What the hell do I care? You know, though it sounds as though I protest too much, and though I'll feel some twinges those days, I really <u>don't</u> care much.

9/21/78

I am home between classes, trying to catch my breath. It's <u>extremely</u> hot out, and muggy—worse than at any time over the summer. And I have a slight cold. Had to change my shirt.

Al Studier out back finishing the paneling.

Nice talk yesterday with Tom Bartunik at WXXI. They're sending me $100! I'll go in to make the tape in a couple of weeks. Might end up selling a few books.... Today, a woman from Buffalo *Courier-Express* called, wants to reprint "The Mailman" from *Niagara Magazine*, and will send me a check. Egads.

Lovely letter from Bill Ewert. He mentions he was just 35! I thought he was <u>at least</u> ten years older than I am. I suppose he'll be with me all the way.

...Now it is evening. I went to bed at seven, right after the news, and got up a little while ago when Han got home from class. I <u>slept</u>, my first solid hours of sleep, I swear, since Pop & Werner arrived. School was exhausting today, but my classes went well. The kids get a tremendous amount of energy from me.

The paneling is all in. Now I'm looking for decent weather the next four days so that I can dig the electric line the rest of the way in, creosote the ends of the rafters, etc. Today in the mail came a fine afghan from my mother to be used out back. It's thick & warm, brown & yellow & orange. I'll call to thank her. Finally got a thank-you letter into the mail for Pop & Werner yesterday.

9/25/78

Al Studier is out back framing in the air conditioner, the last job, really. Han & Billy put a wood preservative on the whole building, I finished the creosote job, the electric line is about dug in (though the last fifty feet won't be easy). When Al is done today, the place can be swept out. Then I'll pick up a carpet, and move my furniture & poems in!... Many visitors to the place lately: Nora, Irma & Mirko again, Charlie Studier & his Jane, Ross Wicks. I'm pleased by this, and know that once I'm settled in people will leave me alone back there.... I called home the other day, and Mom & Pop are just delighted by the whole place, the whole idea. Pop even drew a sketch of it for Mom.

Wrote to Bill Ewert, inscribed the *Lord Dragonfly*s he sent, wrote out "The Pigeons" for the Audubon project he mentioned, and also wrote out my new "The Sunflower" for him.... He now has a printer/press for the broadside of *The Witness*—woodcut, two-color & all.

All four of us are trying to shake slight colds. Almost.

Sunny & cold today. I've a lot of school work, but have classes underway in decent shape now.

The meadow out back is unbelievable. All blooming together: purple aster, goldenrod, those tiny daisies, and black-eyed Susan. Better than a planned garden. But the trees are losing leaves. In a couple weeks, my cabin will be visible, alas.

9/30/78

I felt fine yesterday, and got a lot done, but today I feel weak & slightly dizzy. Even missed the U. of R. rare book sale. Am relaxing.

Han picked up my carpet today. The place out back is finished. Will carry the carpet out back later. Such a good feeling. The place is ready for some serious writing, when my mood turns, as it will. First things first—school, the recording of *Swastika* in Rochester a week from Monday, and the SUNY writing conference here. Then....

My take-home pay is actually $620 every two weeks now ($24,190 annually). That's a hell of a lot of money. <u>Now</u>, if a bag of potatoes didn't cost twenty bucks in this country.

10/1/78

Feel fine today. Billy & I worked hard this morning and got the rest of the electric line dug in. For the first time today, I sat out back at the table for fifteen minutes. How peaceful! The place is <u>right</u>!

Pulled out the cornstalks.... Next, Han and I want to plant some pine trees.

I want to drop Bob Phillips & Vince notes thanking them for their books. The Phillips book is depressing—cheap paper, weak inking, blah cover. Vince's *Puccini* is all right. My one-page piece sounds good.

If the Yankees lose & Boston wins today, the division ends in a tie, and the playoff will be a single game, tomorrow night. I'm a Boston rooter.

Picked up Ed Murray's *Fellini* for a quarter. Will get him to autograph it.... Peter Dzwonkoski says he did get my two Exley books autographed. So, little by little my library improves.

It's now about 7:30, & already dark. I'm out back, writing my first words in my cabin—Nora & Al will stop back soon for a look. I realize, now, at this second, that the silence here, and being alone here, is astounding. It will be impossible not to write poems here. I've never been alone, within a building, as I am here.... I already have my work-in-progress here, too.

10/2/78

I worked on "The Bees" out here last night. Nora & Al did not drop by. I just kept at the poem, and made some progress.... It is morning now, and I'm out here with my thermos & have just turned the heater on, and the place is warming up. In colder weather, when I leave here I'll just leave the heater on low, turn it off by switch in the laundry room in the house, and then, ten minutes or twenty minutes before I want to come back here, just turn the switch on and warm this place up.

Overcast morning, very still. I can see the Matskos' house about 150 yeards off, through the trees, and just the outline of Moshers', about a hundred yards off. Otherwise, only trees, goldenrod, purple aster and those little daisies, called, I think, "Michaelmas Daisies," always in bloom then, Sept. 29.

Already the chill is off my place.

So, a couple hours to fiddle in peace with a poem; then a bike ride to school, and then the Boston/N.Y. game on television. This evening, while watching football, I'll get to that set of compositions.

10/4/78

I've stopped in just briefly.... After my last entry, that afternoon, Billy broke his leg in a soccer game. All the attendant nervousness & bitterness & sadness. He'll be in a cast for about 3 months, will miss basketball season. Han & I felt like crying. Such a shame & bad luck that this happened to Billy <u>again</u>. The other leg this time. He's comfortable now, and watching ball games on television, but such a shame....

The upcoming SUNY gathering makes me nervous. Poulin calls twice a day. He makes decisions for me, telling Irma & Mirko that I wouldn't want to go to their dinner for Voznesensky because I have guests! Well, maybe I'll call Mirko. It would be a good time to get my books inscribed.

Much school work tonight.

Andrews project off my hands now, thank God. I guess, though, that I'll have to drop Ernie off there for some sewing.... Too soon old, too late smart.

It is so cool & peaceful out here now in the near dark.

10/10/78

Evening, and a warm one. I'm out here just briefly to relax a little while before going in to watch the first game of the Series with Billy.... Pat & Grandma were here today to visit him. Tomorrow, he'll try school & we'll see how he gets along with the cast.

Poulin over yesterday for my help with his bibliography for the 3rd edition of his anthology. And he wants more help, and more. And it's a drag, and, again, I won't get proper credit.

Got that recording over with yesterday, and it went well. Now I'll see if anything comes of it. <u>Next</u>, the really big SUNY show coming up. I'm anxious to get some books inscribed.... Ralph Sipper called & wants to send me some thing, for myself, though I hope to get one or two things signed for him, or for Cordelia.... I'm especially anxious to meet Gardner. Reading *Moral Fiction* now, and hope to get to other things before he gets here, especially *October Light*.

This place back here is, simply, wonderful. Will spend <u>much</u>, <u>much</u> time back here. When time allows!

The past few days I've read Roger Kahn's *A Day in the Sun* & Jim Boughton's *Ball Four*, beating Billy to them.

10/15/78

Sunday morning. I am back in my cabin, where this diary will stay. I was back here several hours yesterday, and will be today. This place is everything I hoped it could be. The little heater is working out fine.

Ernie called to say he couldn't make it here this week. I'm sorry. His district is cracking down on things like sick days/leave days.

Finished John Gardner's *On Moral Fiction*. It's an important book. Am reading *The King's Indian*. What a writer he is! Hope to meet him and not be too shy. Sent him *The Ash* and *Swastika*. Think I'll give him a copy of *Of Palestine*.

About finished "A Story From Chekhov." Am writing "The Bees," which may become a good one. Not much else new. I should, this fall or winter, put together two miscellaneous collections for Slow Loris & Croissant. I think I have enough poems.

10/16/78

I've had in mind for a long time the germ of another of those little *Lord Dragonfly* poems. It would/wanted to have rhymes of "sod" and "toad," playful and perfect. I thought of many variations, but this morning this one: "My sod leaps up: / a toad." What might give this one life is the Wordsworth echo, and it brings romance down to the toad. I like it. Maybe: "My sod / leaps up: / a toad."

Han is off substituting, the kids in school. I expect packages in the mail, and was a little reluctant to come back here this morning, but already I'm glad I did. Cold and clear today. I feel <u>alive</u> back here away from the details to attend to back in the house.

I'm just not interested in the second and third parts of *The King's Indian*. Had to stop reading. But the stories in the first part are magnificent, especially "Pastoral Care" and "The Temptation of St. Ivo." Oh, to have written a story like the last one.... I read, too, yesterday, the children's book *Gudgkin the Thistle Girl*. He's quite a man.

Am reading a nice old edition of *The Oregon Trail* back here, moving with Parkman's party toward the plains of Wyoming that I can still picture.

10/18/78

Finished *Grendel*, a wonderful book.

The big show begins tomorrow. I will try to stay reasonably calm. Gemmett, Rubin, Poulin are going nuts. And I hear that fewer than a hundred students have registered. There will be about fifty faculty "writers," and only a hundred kids. Except for Friday night, when the buses will roll in with high school kids to hear Voznesensky, I understand. What a world.

The package of *William Heyen in Print* arrived. I like it. It will be handy. It is good for my ego. It will help me with a few orders for Ernie.

Most of the leaves are down now. Within a space of only two days, after a killing frost, the big catalpa on the edge of our land over by Moshers' lost all its leaves.

Furious at Gerber yesterday. He said that it was Billy's own fault that he got another broken leg: "If something happens once, kick someone else; if it happens twice, kick yourself." He's a detestable fellow, smug, and stupid without knowing it. I was pleased to see that he was bothered that I'd missed the lecture on Cummings the other night. "Really tremendous," he called it. Ha. Fuck him. He has missed many readings, including mine. I should enter in my diary some of his slimy moves, but won't. He runs the department, not Gemmett. And he no doubt thinks I've been ungrateful to him after the boosts he gave me (which he did) when I came to Brockport. Now I have vowed always to ignore him, as he has ignored me for years, never a word on any of my books like *Swastika*, an occasional cutting word from him (to which I have never replied, but have affected a passivity). But the crack about Billy was too much. If Gerber hurts his back again, as he did once, I will say, "When something happens once, kick someone else; if twice, kick yourself."... I would make <u>many</u> intense enemies if I told people exactly what I thought. <u>That</u> can't be the way to go through life, can it?... Gerber is so limited, has no sense of <u>poetry</u> as anything but biographical/historical trappings. A class like the one I had in British Poetry yesterday (wish I had it on tape) on our failings when we respond to <u>idea</u> in a poem, would be all news to him. And it goes on. What does all this mean? I'd just like to crack his sullen, smug mug once. He's a pretentious ass.

Vincent here tomorrow. I'll show him this place. We'll make him feel at home.... What should I read for fifteen minutes tomorrow night. Gardner will be there. What a mind! What a writer!

10/19/78

Morning. The rush will begin in a couple of hours. So peaceful back here. I've made a list of the things I'll read this evening, and I've finished the little study of *The Cheyennes*.

I drove the Poulins over to Duryea's yesterday evening where they picked up two courtesy cars for the Festival. Al also arranged for 2 for 1 drinks all weekend at Casey's. This ought to save John Logan a couple of hundred bucks. I hope the poor bastard is okay. He is only alive, I think, for these kinds of gatherings.

Looks like snow weather, cold and overcast.

Into the Valley of Death ....

A beautiful, warm Saturday morning. I am back here with a cup of coffee, trying to catch my breath. Vince & Jim Mattimore stayed with us the last two nights, and just left. More festivities today.

My reading went well. Again & again someone comes up to me to say I am wonderful, the best, the best poetry ever heard, etc., etc. I read only fifteen minutes.... Have met John Gardner, talked a little with him, care for him very much, am awed, am hoping he'll inscribe all the books I left with Fergussons, where he's staying.... Talked quite a bit with Simpson & Logan. Simpson: "You know how much I care for your poetry." Well, much of this. Vince told me that Phyllis Thompson told him I was the best poet writing in America now! Egads.... Fine gathering at Mirko's for Voznesensky, who is gentle & smart & honest. I left *Swastika* with him, and he inscribed some books for me. The Voz/Simpson/Logan reading was fine, crowded with people we never otherwise see, people trying to get in on some of the glory, & this can be sickening, these fucking administrators.... Gerber: doing more hateful things.... All in all, much friendship & fun here. Much bad poetry. Much book signing. More readings today (Gardner) & the Voz. panel.

I become calm back here so quickly.

10/24/78

Rain this morning. Perfect back here in my cabin. I am winding down these tense, intense days.... They have all gone away.... I've learned something about how I like to, and how important it is, to sing. My best poems sing. I never understood this before, or at least never felt it. Now (my God could I have believed this would ever have happened to me) people look at me shyly, and many blush and stammer after I read—it's only the poems, but those poems of mine that I love need to be sung.

I have a list of about ten things to do on my desk inside. And I have to get ready for classes that meet tomorrow. But, out here, I am at ease writing here in this journal, or reading, or fooling with a poem. I am settled in here now, and will miss more and more events and consolidate my good fortune.

Gardner read beautifully. He gave of himself here, declared himself a part of SUNY, not like that shit Creeley....

Well, back to my life.... Gulp, Sandra McPherson here Nov. 8th. We'll have a dinner.

10/25/78

My last entry must have been on the 23rd.

A dream this morning about all my old colleagues from Springville. We were in a restaurant. They were having a dinner party for something, and I'd just come in, and was meeting the old teachers I'd known. Aah, now I know that the one woman from Springville, the sort of pretty and witty woman who carried on during our lunch breaks, was also to me Mrs. Wild, my fourth grade teacher in Nesconset, in my dream.

Cold in here this morning. Now 1/ my body 2/ the sunlight & warming day 3/ the heater 4/ the steaming coffee 5/ the electric light over my shoulder warm my little room.

Had excellent & exhausting classes yesterday, and read some journals in the evening. Am literally a little dizzy, dazed, this morning.

Just remembered another dream—Gibbs Pond was now miles of marsh, and opened to the Sound.... If there is ever another edition of *Light* ...

Vanguard finally sent Joyce's *Son of the Morning*. Will get to it this winter. My next novel will be *October Light*.

Some trees were delivered yesterday. I hope to dig them in, or a few of them, this afternoon.

Now, after the Festival and all those people & all that "literature" I am ready for the rhythms & routines of school & my own work & snow.

10/28/78

Fine cool day again. I raked some leaves, and transplanted the bigger of the two horse chestnut saplings. Deep roots. Hope I got enough. Planted the tree about 40 feet to the front-right of my cabin.... Have decided to buy more spruce trees, and put some along the Mosher line. What's money?

Lazy today. And I don't seem to want to get to typing up and sending out poems. Well, this evening or tomorrow.

I was given a $750 merit raise. That will add up over the years.

Looks like we might buy a '78 Ford with 12,000 miles on it. Our old '68 is liable to give out any time. Manny wants to buy it--$300; and the service manager at Duryea's wants it--$400. Hell, everyone wants to buy our old car. It is an unusual one—generally in good shape and only 70,000 miles on it. Maybe we still should push it through another winter. Who knows? I hate worrying about such things.

Reading *October Light*. Enjoying it.

Looking forward next week to a royalty check from Vanguard. If it's not at least $250 I'll be disappointed—*Noise* should be closed out, and this should be the best statement on *Swastika*, the advance paid off last time.

Ernie sent another big package of *Print*. I'm sending it around.

Offered readings in one day at Cayuga CCC & the Auburn Prison--$350—in the spring. YES! That's a day's pay.... Don't want to teach next summer, but how, if I don't get a SUNY grant, can I turn down the money?

Han looked at a soon-to-be-empty store today. She and another woman are toying with the idea of opening a fabric shop. I'd like that. It would be good for her. Maybe it could work out, make out.

Moshers are out in their back yard. It's still private here, but it will be nice to get some evergreens planted. During the summer, the ash & elm & catalpa leaves block those houses.... Next spring/summer, I ought to thin out some of the ash trees between here & my house to make the others stronger. Will see. Will see what it's like back here when the snow is piling up.

11/1/78

38 today. A comfortable age. I have a couple of hours this beautiful morning to relax, and then school work and a meeting.

Jim Mattimore sent me a fine first in jacket of *I Am! Says the Lamb*. It made me write a few nonsense poems for children. Don't know if I'll do any more. Would like to.

Gold is up to about $245 an ounce! And probably going higher. Our 12 ounces have been keeping pace with inflation, like nothing else.

Han got me a hassock for my birthday. I'll carry my old one out here.

The weather this week has been a blessing.

Letter from Vicky Gold. I hope she's okay. I should pick up *Brockport's Poems* from Bill Andrews and send her a copy.

A mind of bits & snippets today. Shell-shocked after exhausting classes yesterday, and some kind of dream about being lost in some gymnasium while trying to get to Syracuse or Cornell to hear Voznesensky read.

Sent out some poems to *Poetry* and to that lovely girl at *Hudson River Review*.

We bought a dozen Norway spruce/white spruce the other day. I hope to get them into the ground this weekend. We accomplished quite a bit around here this year. And now I have this cabin. I suppose, too, that this journal could become more than just chatter out here, but maybe not. Maybe I must save my energy for the poems.

11/2/78

Thurs. evening. Han is off to class. I'm just out here for a minute, and then will go in and keep the kids company.

Meeting in Gemmett's office in the morning to discuss the new literary magazine, *The Brockport Review*, in its planning stages. I really don't want anything to do with it—what else do I need to keep me from writing anything? But, hell, I don't want to seem unfriendly to Fitz Gerald et. al. But, hell, I want to get those trees planted. Another magazine. Why? We worry about everything here except a solid program in creative writing. And it looks as though the MFA will go through. It's a joke. We have no staff for it, for one thing.

Good, solid classes today. Still, I talk too much and exhaust myself.

No poker game this evening. That's all right with me.

I still feel sad about Billy. And he's sad, too, thinking about how his leg is getting thinner every day, and will.

11/10/78

Friday afternoon. I have an hour or so, at last, to spend back here. A cool, beautiful afternoon.

Life seems so full, so exciting, though I am ready for snow and a different, quieter, rhythm, just of Brockport/school/family/my poems.... Sandra McPherson's visit was a good one. We had a nice party for her—about twenty people—and then her reading—add to our party guests about fifteen of my students who came, and she had an audience of about 50. The other bastards, including Piccione, Marchant, Rubin, Piccione, here, who even teach creative writing, do not get their students to readings. It only takes a little urging. Anyway, then a few of us had a few drinks at my house, & the next morning the half-hour videotape went well—I set up the conclusion, her reading of "The Bittern," beautifully. Glad it's all over. The same morning I'd gone in to Monroe CC to meet Hall & hear him read. He was good, though not as good as he should have been, as though his voice were straining to get through his own poems. This all sounds petty & silly; my notes never suggest the sometimes even profound things I experience during these "literary" meetings.

Peter Dzwonkoski will visit Wednesday. I very much look forward, and it isn't often that I do.

Mouganises & Alice from Canada & maybe Pylyshenkos coming to dinner, & then we'll play a little poker. I'd rather just have settled in to watch the fights, but we do owe Alice a dinner & game.

Long letter from Joyce Oates. She mentions that she's upset, brooding about her relationship with Vanguard. Hard for me to imagine, though the stakes/steaks in her world are a lot bigger than they are in mine, I suppose. Maybe I'll write Tom Woll, & talk secretly—I'd hate to see her leave Vanguard.... Herb Yellin sent me Joyce's *The Step-father*, which I've just read. It's okay, a bit plodding. I don't know. I'm anxious to read *Son of the Morning*.

Bob Phillips called from California about nothing special.

Poulin got sick at our McPherson gathering the other night. And Piccione left today on a 10-12 hr. trip to see Mike Waters. Just what the Picciones need during a terribly hectic time, especially for Sandi. Tony is still in trouble.

Almost forgot to mention: John Nims wrote to tell me I'd won the Eunice Tietjens award from *Poetry*. $200. If, years ago, someone had told me that one day I'd win one of those prizes!...

Put in three apple trees last weekend. In three years, with luck, fruit.

At the party the other night Ken Venick mentioned that he's sorted the school mail & had put a postcard from R.P. Warren into my mail box. I never got it. Stolen, no doubt, & I have a feeling that this has happened several times before. I'm sure it has. I have a feeling I have one real enemy at the school.

11/12/78

Cold this morning, and wet. Overcast. The winter begins.

I've a couple hours to spend out here this morning, and then I'll read freshman papers this afternoon and watch football.

Al Studier put the door weatherstripping in back here yesterday. Door is so tight now that it's even a little hard to close.... Poulin stopped by, about nothing special. I made half a mistake & told him who Peter Dzwonkoski was (didn't mention he'd be visiting), and Al began talking about placing his BOA archives somewhere. No doubt Poulin will some day follow me to Rochester, if I work something out there. But I can slow things down by being mum for a while.

Am reading *Son of the Morning*. Am writing "The Bees."

11/15/78

I think I've about finished "The Bees." It's a good one.

Peter Dzwonkoski arriving soon. I'm thinking hard about my whole book collection. It is often distracting, this gathering and caring-for and increasing, as it was yesterday and the day before: I bought a beautiful small antique revolving bookcase, and was placing it in the living room, & deciding which books I'd put in, & rearranging my collection, & calling House of Books for a few items—all this takes time away from writing I could be doing. It is often fun, <u>usually</u> fun, but does sometimes makes me nervous, and maybe makes me feel that I am, essentially, "getting and spending" and frittering my real life away. It is this desire to <u>preserve</u>. That's one motive. It is pleasure in their financial value. That's surely another. Many other things involved, surely.

Joyce said <u>no</u> to writing a ¶ or two as foreword to *Of Palestine*. This surprised me. She is swamped, yes, but I thought our relationship was something special. I understand and don't understand. Well, I'd be disappointed if she were predictable.

Billy had a new cast put on today. We're not sure how fast his leg is healing. He'll be disabled even longer than he thinks. It would be wonderful if he could get rid of the cast by Christmas, but I don't know.

11/17/78

A cold and raining Friday morning. My cabin is warming.

Han is substituting, both kids in school. I'm unwinding from the week of school. Tonight we & the Picciones will go to two art openings. Egads.

Wayne Dodd asked for an essay on Wilbur for *Ohio Review*. I wish I could. But I can't. I really can't. It would take me months of worry. I want to be ready to work on some poems as they surface.

Fine visit Wednesday with Peter Dzwonkoski. We're going ahead in our thinking about a room at U. of R. devoted to my collection. Next, I want to stop in to see his place—maybe a week from next Monday—and then maybe have his boss out here.... On the same subject: called Ralph Sipper after his latest catalogue arrived, and got a fine first of *Praise to the End!*—a scarce book & excellent addition to my collection. Today I sent him a note about some other items, but I wanted to get to that one, first.

11/18/78

Saturday afternoon. So peaceful back here, but I'm tired, and have things to fool with in the house, and won't stay long. I'm feeling mellow & happy & relaxed.

Bill Andrews dropped off my copies of *Brockport's Poems* this morning. Maybe the whole appearance of the thing is just bad, rather than ghastly, as I've thought. I won't send too many copies to friends.

The openings last night were fun. Tony had a terrible time.... I ended up playing poker at Rock's with him & Mirko & Emmanuel until 4:30 in the morning. It was very relaxing. I lost $27—first time in a long time that I've lost.

Talked with Jack Wolsky for a while about *Swastika*, which he's now read, & his Holocaust series.... Marx: finally, no vision, turning in on himself again & again.... Castle: tremendous talent frittered away on, essentially, jokes.... Stewart: much fun, but will he be a kid all his life?... Paley: impressive, of course, surely a major talent. So ends my cocktail-chatter evaluations.... Starting to have fun watching Alfred operate. Ha, when he heard me mentioning my *Poetry* prize to Atherton, he turned away quickly. I think it pains him. Alfred is a generous and jealous friend.

<u>Much</u> wind here the past two days. My row of spruce stands straight.

11/20/78

First few snowflakes today. I've never watched a season approaching day by day as I have this one.

My cabin is a little too cool for comfort, but it's very cold out and I haven't been inside since Saturday, have not taken the chill off it. I'll have to turn on the heater about a half-hour before I come out here.

A disturbing call this afternoon from Cheryl, who was crying. It seems Eddie is very unhappy with his job, did not sleep all night again, & she's <u>worried</u>, about Ed, about their finances, etc., etc. He needs his family to help him, she says. I wish I knew what I could do in the way of helping Ed find some kind of fulfilling work. I don't know. I don't know him very well, or what happened with his teaching jobs, or his two years with Friendly's, or now with these insurance jobs. And Cheryl might not be giving me the whole story. Maybe he's content, but she isn't: she's brought up this idea that he ought to be in college teaching several times. I don't know. He's had some bad breaks, and he's made some foolish mistakes (these coming out of insecurities going back to a childhood when Mom & Pop were tooth & claw with each other, virtually insane—he got the brunt of it) like getting married so quickly again, & having another child in that way. I don't know. We've never mentioned the $500 we gave Ed, and I'm glad we haven't. If he asks, I'll probably send more. But Ed doesn't seem to have a <u>future</u>. Kenny seemed like that, too, but now has found himself. I hope Ed & Cheryl will get over whatever the problem is right now, the thing of the moment that led to the call. Christ, she was crying the whole time. Han came in from picking Billy up at the end, but I was the only one who talked to her.

I'm a lucky man. Chili for supper coming up, the best possible wife & mother, two great kids, a secure job, this thing of trying to write poems & once in a while managing. My books. Sometimes I feel selfish, but sometimes feel that the feeling is silly.... Mom & Pop are very upset about Ed, of course, but feel helpless, as I do.

11/22/78

It's about eight in the evening. Soon I'll go in & play a game of "Scrabble" with the family and take a hot shower and then the four of us will watch the Steve Martin special at ten. Another family day to look forward to tomorrow.

Proofs of *Long Island Light* arrived and I've been reading. Will finish them tomorrow. It will be quite a book.

Tony came by this morning. He'd just had a two-hour talk with Gemmett. It turns out that the APT Committee nor Gemmett support his promotion application. He's upset, of course. He feels he's gotten a bad deal. I've told him several times that this wouldn't be his year, especially with Gerber as APT chairman, and have told him to treat the whole thing cynically, to put in the same application next year. In fact, he doesn't have the "credentials" for promotion, <u>but</u> our department has many full professors who are a disgrace. Enough. I will not serve on the APT Committee. Tony has been told, for one thing, that he needs another book. It doesn't help him that his friend Al published his other one.

Very cold out, but warm in here. The heater just has to be given a chance.

Maybe I should call Eddie. But maybe not.

I look forward to a few hours out here tomorrow. Hell, it's easier on the family, too, if I don't grumble around the place nervously. I am calm out here. Hard to believe I have this place.

11/25/78

A lazy Saturday. I did go for a bike ride in the very-cold, to stay a little bit in shape, and did clear my desk inside a little bit. And I've been reading the Gospel of Matthew, and just read the first wonderful section of

Gardner's *Jason and Medeia*. Finished *Son of the Morning* yesterday and wrote Joyce to tell her I think it's a great book. I think it is. At least, if I don't read much, I am reading enduring things.

It's almost dark out, the neighbors' houses disappearing. It was easy to imagine myself in Kreon's company.

Sent back the *Light* proofs. The new work struck me as very strong. Some of those little prose pieces have everything, go down, down and out.

Called Ed & Cheryl yesterday. Things seem normal over there. Maybe they'll visit for a couple of days over Christmas.

I look forward to seeing Peter's world Monday.

11/26/78

The world is always the same, always relative. It's early Sunday afternoon, a few snowflakes floating down, the sun shining. Han & I & Billy felt miserable after a call from Dr. Sansocie saying Billy would have lab work tomorrow & then Tuesday would have his break, in effect, reset, pushed closer together by the Rochester orthopedic man—we should have gone to this man <u>first</u>, I know, and the kid would have healed much quicker. So, there's this. But it will pass. Still, I hope, by Christmas he'll be close to getting rid of the cast—maybe a couple weeks past that. But just now, before I came out, television news of a fire in a Rochester Holiday Inn—at least ten dead. Terrible. And to think of the 900 suicides at Jonestown in Guyana. Trust to good verses?... "I don't know about those other things. / I only know about Wenzel." I think I'll work on that poem for a while, & then go back to King Kreon.

11/27/78

Spent a few hours this morning with Peter at his rare book dominion. Like it there. I'm impressed. If they ever want to convert that one room they have to a room to house my collection, so be it. I'll draw up a list of what I want done, all in all, should it come to that. Peter's enthusiasm increases.

Snowing fairly heavily right now. How wonderful to be out here!

We're worried, but things are all set for Billy tomorrow.

My *Praise to the End!* arrived in the mail. Also, a sad letter from John Brinnin. Also, a disturbing letter about Joyce from Tom Woll. Looks like, for her next five books, she's skipped away to another publisher. And she seems to have done it in an underhanded way, though probably not intentionally, and this is no contradiction, for the woman imagines all sorts of things, no doubt, probably hears voices. A blow to Vanguard. I'm glad I wrote to Tom, telling him what I knew.

Weather allowing, I'll go into Tom Freeman's class tonight & talk & read some poems.

Too cold out here. I must turn the heater on earlier.

Food order comes Thurs. We'll hunker in for winter. Only worried about Billy.

11/29/78

Crazy day, crazy day. But I've just walked out here through a foot of snow with my flashlight, and now will relax.

So relieved about Billy's leg. The bones were set <u>close</u> together this time, & he was given a shorter cast—now his knee is free & will loosen up. We're all in good cheer about this now. If only this doctor had set the leg to begin with.

This time I turned on the heater a half-hour before I came out here, and it's warm enough. I can't get over being out here like this. It's perfect. The kids and Han are about 200 feet away, watching television, enjoying the evening, and I am, too, knowing they're safe. And here, now, it is absolutely quiet, and I need this.

The Freeman class was all right. I talked too fast. After this semester I think I'll make the general rule for myself that I won't go into another class unless it is using one of my books.

Went Christmas shopping this morning with Han. And renewed my license, standing in many lines. Oh, what junk in the stores. Literally, standing next to tables of awful glassware & knick-knacks & false "art" I feel sick, wd. vomit if I had to stand there long. And the stores are packed. Bought a dress for Kristen that Han picked out, & golf balls & a golf glove for Billy.

Talked for an hour with Tony yesterday about his rejection by APT Committee & Chairman for promotion. Did him a <u>big</u> favor, going over his 5-page rejoinder with him, suggesting changes, necessary clarifications.

I've carried out here to ponder a letter from Evelyn at Vanguard. She thanks me for my letter, talks about their "suddenly changed world." I'm very sorry about their loss of Joyce. Sorry for her, too. She's losing a family, and may miss it, never mind the money or fame that might come her way with a bigger (I assume) outfit. I'm sure Joyce had already made the change by the time she sent me that letter. She is always complex & sometimes cold.... I probably don't even realize the extent to which Vanguard was carried by Joyce. Wish I could do something that would make money for them.

I've not been sleeping well. Too nervous about too many things, but should be able to unwind this weekend.

Fitz Gerald's Forum meeting just dreadful today. All priorities backward.... Rodney stopped over. We'll have some fun at Forum parties, though.

12/1/78

I came out here again without giving this place a chance to warm up. The last time! It's just a matter of giving the little heater twenty minutes.

Out here, writing, I should be more aware of weather.

I want, over Christmas break, to spread *Chestnut Rain* out in front of me on the desk here & feel it again & nudge it forward. I still have those hundreds of pamphlets to read for the long section. Have them here, waiting.

Food order came yesterday; the house is filled with boxes. This fits my siege mentality.... Mirko & Irma, & Nora, & the Kaysers will pick up their things today.

Got a beautiful copy, uncut! (& therefore unread), of *Nobodaddy* in the mail yesterday. 1926. I'll read it this weekend.

I think a lot of the possibilities of that room at U. of R. Maybe something will work out. No hurry. My collection needs no apologies. And what will it be like in 20 years?

It's already warm enough in here for me to be comfortable. Will fool with a poem or two for an hour or two.

Five in the evening now, almost full dark. I've come out again to relax. Just finished *Nobodaddy*, and like it, as old-fashioned as it is of me to like it. It is so much like so much of his poetry, in some ways: mellifluous, flowing, but lacking jolt & charge, dramatic tension. Romantic rhythms & emotions rather than intensity. But I like the play, and am happy to have the lovely book.

Nice letter from Peter again. Maybe, just maybe, something will work out, and in years to come I'll be spend a day or two a week at Rochester building the collection, cataloguing it. Maybe teaching a course once every couple of years on contemporary poetry? Well, I don't know, but something rewarding, & even important, could be worked out. The University of Rochester seems <u>permanent</u>.

I wrote a stanza today of what could turn into a real poem—about the speaker's finding, in 1990, a ragged copy of *Swastika*. I don't know right now what the rest of the plot will be.

12/2/78

Judy Minty called last evening to say she'd stop by on her way from Yaddo back home to Michigan, and, this morning, she did. We like her, enjoyed her visit. She told, ha, of her argument with Diane Wakoski in Hawaii. Diane as dumb as ever, and as bloated with herself.

I still have hanging over my head all those damned freshman papers to read. Keep putting them off, but will do some tonight, if I don't play poker.

Our bird seed arrived with the food plan. Time to put it out. Will do it now! Am only killing time before the karate matches are on television at five.

A curious, poised time of day, darkness not quite setting in, but, of course, setting in.

12/3/78

Sunday morning. Some snow last night, and a light, but freezing rain this morning.

Read some freshman papers last evening, and will again this afternoon. Should be a good day. A couple of good football games on, too.

I must be getting lazy, for better or worse. In the old days, in Cortland, I'd begin a poem & keep working on it, losing sleep over it, until I'd finished it. Now, back here, I have two or three going that could be good ones, but even avoid turning to them. Maybe because I know it's hard work; or because I believe that being away from them while they work on me subconsciously helps them; or because the big book is appearing in the spring and I'm just marking time until then; or ...

Will put together the group for Duane Schneider. Will call it, maybe, *The City*....

Letter from Bob Phillips the other day—I seem to think of Katonah on Sundays—outdid his others. Much of Mazzaro in Phillips. Mazzaro & Poulin. I will write to Bob about everything but literature!

Two white pigeons just flew by overhead as I was gazing and dreaming.

I've been in touch with Martin Booth lately. A driven man, but cause to be driven.... He's going to do "The Children" as a Sceptre pamphlet. Ha, my English publisher.

Andrews, Gemmett, dept. Christmas parties coming up soon. Secure in this life, I love this season.

12/4/78

Terrific winds today, but my new pines seem to be holding up.

Reading poems over thinking of possibilities for the little book Duane Schneider wants to do. I see that "A Manuscript" (maybe to be called "From the Ukraine") is a real poem.

Han working very hard on various papers.

Nice letter from Bets Vondrasek at Walt Whitman House. Looks like I'll read there on Sunday, April 22.

Tony stopped over yesterday afternoon. I kept watching football & grading papers. Gave him some coffee & chatted in between. Hope he didn't mind. I didn't want to throw away the whole afternoon again. I do think I made him leave early, I'm afraid. Oh, shit, so goes the world.... Alfred back yesterday.

Wonderful solitude back here.

Gardner's *Jason & Medeia* becomes more & more impressive day by day.

Sent a book about Isadora Duncan to Vicky Gold. Looked through it, especially the parts about her & Essenin. The last time she saw him he was staggering off from her apartment bearing a wooden bust of himself he'd wanted.

I've seen a few gulls lately, but <u>no</u> small birds, not <u>one</u> the past few days. Hard to understand. Not <u>one</u> junco or chickadee or sparrow or cardinal. I even filled the feeder yesterday. What's going on? There doesn't seem to be a bird in the whole neighborhood.

More mimeographed letters from PSA bearing charges & counter-charges. Poets, indeed. In deed.

It's quarter-to-three. Will see if I can stay out here until signaled for supper, today. Back to Kreon's feast, Jason about to hold forth....

Friday

Don't know the date. The world a buzz. It's four in the afternoon. Seems like a long time since I've been out here.

Yes, the SALT talks are in the air, & the Egyptian-Israeli Camp David agreements. But I picked up Billy from school today, and my thoughts are all with him.

Raining now, gloom, but the first basketball home game tonight, and he'll be going to watch, but is now inside listening to music, & is sad. I know the almost overwhelming feelings of being an adolescent, full to bursting with the excitement of an impending ball game. He can see himself as he might have been, coming out to warm up, shooting some in, playing, the cheering, this year surely a winning team, maybe a girlfriend. It hurts. And the music now is so poignant to him. He misses his whole sophomore year. I hope he is blessed after this, injury free. He'll never forget the way he feels right now. And he would have been the best player on the team. Still, he has other good friends to watch the game with. Han will probably go, too. I'll stay home.

Spent all morning clearing off my desk. Six letters to law schools for Bill Clauss alone. Many other details, crap.

The Christmas cards came from Ernie. Lovely, but no envelopes. Tried to order some today. No dice. Almost more trouble than it's worth. Don't know why Ernie couldn't have taken care of this.

Today in the mail from Ximenes a copy of *Streets in the Moon*, a beauty, the first book to print "Ars Poetica." Twenty bucks. What's money?

Day after day memos at school about Fitz Gerald's Forum activities/bullshit, & about the creative writing track & courses, & about the cognitive skills-freshman composition thing. Christ! All I can do is do a good job in my classes. Screw all the administrative fol-de-rol. Next week I'll be buried in journals & papers, but that then will end the semester, one that somehow seemed to lack unity. Or something.

12/11/78

Good letter from Tom Woll, with a photocopy of jacket design for *Long Island Light*. A yellow emanating from the bottom. I like it. Charcoal-gray lettering. And there will be 276 boxed copies. It will be a beauty. Maybe best of all, Tom says there's a Long Island salesman who is anxious to get started selling the book.... I know the issues & prices now, & will have a postcard made up. Much excitement. Another book! Amazing. I just hope they will sell enough to be happy. Then I can settle back for two or three years with *Chestnut Rain* and maybe with the introduction to poetry text I'm hoping to write.

Haven't been out here in 3 days. And the rest of this week will be lost. But I'm counting on a couple of good weeks in January........... Ewert's *Witness* cards arrived. Nice. And I got in the mail today about 40 of the 1978 Christmas cards that Ernie did such a beautiful job with. Han & Billy & I made the envelopes the other night. A nice project, satisfying.

The next three days in school will be an absolute whirl, and then there will be days of reading papers & grading.

Han & I went with Mirko & Irma to Andrews' gathering yesterday. A drag. But we then picked up Manny & went to Rocks' and played cards. I lost $30, but it was still much fun.

Han seems to be surviving her course work. And Billy & Kris are doing fine.

Supposedly Oswego just had four feet of snow, Buffalo two; just missed us, but won't forever. Just scattered flakes sifting down now.

Tonight I want to work on dust-jacket & back cover (paperback) stuff for *Light*. Hmmm ... yellow, upwelling. I like it. It's quiet, will last.

12/13/78

Wednesday morning. I've come out back for a couple of hours before the day's whirl begins.... Meetings this afternoon. I should attend. It's just before Christmas break and I'll stay current before disappearing.

Worked on the jacket blurbs etc. for *Light* Monday night and sent the stuff off to Woll. I'm going to love the look of the book.

It would be nice to memorize "The Crane" and begin readings with it. I know about the first half. I must learn by heart more of my poems.

12/18/78

    I'm back here only for a half-hour. Inside, I have ten journals more to read—I'm shell-shocked with papers & journals—and then will be off.... We're all so busy.
    I still feel sane, though, and ready to come back here to read & write soon. Even look forward to holiday parties & such.
    Han <u>almost</u> done. One more exam. What a semester she's had.
    Much mail today. Dan Gerber sent some good books. Dave Smith, etc., wrote.
    A <u>chance</u> I'll go to Picciones' tonight, with Ken Venick, if Schiff & Eddy arrive. Am not crazy about this.
    Billy & Kris okay. Kris missed school w. menstrual pains, will be fine tomorrow.

12/21/78

    Haven't turned in grades yet—a couple of dilemmas—but might tomorrow. In any case, I'm about done. And Han has finished the last shopping, so we can settle in. <u>Much</u> wind today, and some snow, so it is good to be home. I haven't been back here for three days. My little place is holding up nicely.
    Good news: 95% of a chance that Billy's cast will come off in two weeks.
    Tony dropped over night before last with Jeff Schiff & Gary Eddy—the boys are publishing things now, attractive things by Sandi & Tony, etc. Good to see them, but I really wanted that evening alone with the family—we'd just returned from Kristen's Christmas concert. Jeff threatens to drop by again! And Ken Venick. But, no sweat, I'll spend much time out here in January.
    Aaron Kramer called from Dowling. I'll read there April 23rd. Just hope nothing holds up *Long Island Light*. I plan to be away about two weeks in the spring.
    Proof of *Witness* broadside arrived. It's beautiful, as I knew it would be. I think I'll get three framed—home, office, & here.
    Cheryl & Eddie having trouble. I've talked with Wern, & with Mom & Pop. Long story. Ed & family are to visit us Sunday.
    I may have scratched out a little Christmas poem this morning, about a suicide after seeing the Christ child, but a suicide to be with God, one of faith. Will work on it.

12/28/78

    Place warming nicely. I'm just out here this morning to relax a little. Just finished another book of *Jason & Medeia*. Enjoying it.
    Got one of the SUNY fellowships for the summer--$2,000. Tony didn't, though I didn't think he could miss, with Dick Frost one of the two readers. Al got $1,300, all he was eligible for. I've worried for a week about the effect the rejection would have on Tony.
    Poetry took four poems, including "Mantle."
    Jeff Spuck was here day before last, showing me pictures of the 10' x 12' place he's built himself on 40 acres in California. And we went for a little gathering in the evening for Elaine Taylor.
    About a foot of snow. But the sun is out. A beautiful day. Han is picking up her cross-country skis today.
    I'm just screwing around these days, doing an NEA application, writing a few letters, fooling with my books. But will work on poems soon, maybe for a few hours this afternoon even.

    Later.... It's 4:30 now. I've been out here a while. Have finished a poem called "The Child," a strange poem of suicide and Christmas.... Was just thinking that I guess the first poem I wrote back here was "A Story from Chekhov," one of the four taken by *Poetry*. Surely, this is a good, comfortable, quiet place to work. It does remain slightly chilly here, but this may be a good thing. The windows do fog up a bit, but even this is generally pleasant.... So, I've finished another poem out here.
    Was reading from my first book of this diary last night. I seem to have had a prose style, even years ago, that still speaks with my rhythm.... And it's interesting to listen to the person I was, to be listening to the person I am becoming.... The quality of my entries has not improved, but it's much fun for me to be writing

here. Maybe it's an evasion. In any case, this book fills up much quicker than did the other.... There are still, of course, the point-of-view & sincerity problems here. Can I shake off the notion, completely, that this will be read by someone eventually? If I can't, will I still write truly—I don't mean just about events, but naturally, my own body flow rather than that of the poet I imagine myself, during my worst moments, to be.... Did I just mean <u>that</u> sentence, or was it a defense, a manipulation of my reader-to-come. Enough. I doubt that this will resolve itself. But I'll keep writing all the way from here on in, I'm sure, even if I stop writing poems.

 Bob Phillips sent a review by Hayden Carruth from *The Nation*. He singles out *Swastika* as the single strongest book he read this year. A nice surprise, that review, & it will please the folks at Vanguard.

1/2/79

 Today I begin what will be, hopefully, a couple of weeks of much time spent back here. The holiday parties and football games were a pleasure—we were up singing with the neighbors & playing our player piano until 3 a.m.—and now I want to work at some writing and reach the ease that comes from it.

 Read Robert Penn Warren's *A Place to Come To*. Enjoyed it. Some very interesting characters & plotting, a very moving conclusion (old Perk); also, somehow, some major things wrong with the book as a whole. It just doesn't sit right. But it is a good read.

 Just read over my new poem "The Child." It's done, and it seems to me to be <u>strong</u>. And I just wrote a piece about Karen, about that evening of two orgasms against her. It is a piece about the ponds. I think I wish it was in time to go into <u>Light</u>, but maybe not. Maybe I feel the need to have other pieces on hand to add, eventually, to the book, & this one is the first. It <u>does</u> deepen an already-subtly-stated theme. Glad I wrote it. Hope that ten years from now there will be another edition of *Light*.

 We're supposed to get a lot of snow today.

 Some boy called from East High last evening, a cute voice, saying he's read *Swastika* ("I liked it very much") and asked me if I'd come into his English class. I thanked him and said I couldn't, and feel sort of sad about it. I <u>hate</u> the idea of driving into Rochester, got the idea that maybe the kid's class could come to <u>me</u>, my room, & maybe see a little of the College at the same time. Maybe I'll drop a note or something.... Same old news. I sometimes wish I were more outgoing, wd. just say sure & rush off to East High & see the kid, etc., etc, but I always know that I would write less or not at all if I began to live the Peter Marchant life. "Perfection of the life or of the work"—I won't perfect either, but hope for some sort of human balance. At least *Swastika* touched the kid a little. I won't, in any case, always be on hand, and the poems will have to do. <u>Still</u>, I'd like to see that kid, Sam, with the squeaky voice.

 Billy's cast comes off in two days, we trust.... Han will register for her last course today.... Kristen had a wonderful vacation, loved the party the other night.

 Picciones have their place on the market, hope to sell & move to town. A long & complex story. Tony will go nuts, I know it.

 Time of crisis for our Dept. We'll even be looking for a new Chairman, an internal search, no doubt. Declining enrollments, loss of majors, etc., etc.

 I'm still getting used to my little place back here. I love it, will love it even more during the summer, I think, though I'll be back here during some beautiful snowfalls soon.

 Vince will look into reviewing *Light* for *Newsday*. I'm going to work up & have printed a mailer. A couple of breaks, a couple of strategic ads, & it could sell a few thousand copies right off the bat.

 Witness should arrive any day. And *Manassas Review*. Simple pleasures.

 In the news: Iran, and Castro denouncing the Chinese as traitors to Communism.

1/3/79

 We missed most of the snow which buried Han's Mom again, but it is extremely cold here, the windows in my cabin patterned with frost though I've had the heater on for a half hour. My palm, or side of my hand, <u>cold</u> on this page. I will want to remember this—can I <u>feel</u> it?—in August. It's almost too cold out here to work. I could easily just get a little bigger heater. But I think I like this sense of roughing it, my coffee cup steaming.

Walked to the school yesterday and stopped into my office to water the plants. Then wrote a poem, as yet untitled, about a baby snapper. Might be a good one. Why these things, Karen & ponds, have been so much on my mind these days I don't know. Maybe a defense: when friends on the Island read *Light*, I'll be able to say, "Well, I have some new, better pieces about the old Island."

We'll have a nice gathering tomorrow evening for Floy DeLancey & some German/Polish friends of hers. Mirko & Irma, etc., the Winnicks, will be here. I look forward. I have plenty of liquor on hand, & should pick up some brandy.

1/4/79

Billy just got back from the hospital—he'll miss school today—feeling low because his leg is so thin, but the cast is <u>off</u>! Now he'll have to be especially careful for a few weeks while the bone continues to fill in and strengthen. He's about to take his first tub bath in three months. I wanted to get out of the house, out of the way.

It strikes me again & again: how amazing that I have this little house back here. It's terribly cold today, & the picture window I face is frosted up, but beautifully, & the cold field, brown & white, lies before me, the bare ash trees scattered, the row of pines about a hundred feet away. This morning I was reading my old diary again, the days of Cortland & Athens. I am lucky that I came out of the degree mill when I did, when the economy wanted me and would eventually give me this home & this acre of land & this little place back here.

1/5/79

It's three in the afternoon. Still extremely cold. The cabin temperature keeps me awake.

We had a perfect party yesterday. The more I drank, the better my German became. Mrs. DeLancey & Mirko & Irma & the Winnicks & Lynne & Nora & Charlie & Jane & Chris Kayser etc. all had a fine time. Our main guests, Eva & Richard, felt at ease—he's an agricultural economist working on a farm here for a year, a Pole. Joe talked me into playing basketball today, and I did, and did all right, and didn't get hurt. So I cashed the $100 check I got from WXXI, and bought a decent pair of sneakers, & hope to play again Monday & the whole week.

Wrote some tiny poems yesterday, including a couple of beauties. I'd love to do a sort of winter "Lord Dragonfly," with one added character, this cabin. Which is better?: "Across the white field / a crow's black squawk." or "Across the white field / a crow's squawk."? But here's a perfect one!

> Under my cabin,
> field mice
> and China.

1/6/79

Wonderful long letter from Bill Ewert this morning about the care and signing of *Witness*, soon to arrive.... And a card c/o *Poetry* from May Sarton who liked "The Field."

We called Mom to thank her for the box of hats & scarves she knitted.

A little warmer today, and, so far, the sun is out. I'll be out here an hour or two and then go in to watch a couple of basketball games on television.

Sparrows around by the dozens—don't see <u>many</u> other birds, but have seen cardinals & starlings & juncos lately. Things are back to normal.... Well, I'll go back to fooling with those tiny poems.

1/7/79

Sunday. This evening Han & I will go to Mirko's for their Christmas. This morning I'm out here to fool with my sequence of little poems. This afternoon, like everyone else in the country, I'm going to watch the NFL playoffs.

These have been idyllic days. Billy walking around without his cast or crutches now, though he says he'll still use the crutches in school for a couple of days. Han has been crocheting, Kristen skating in our flooded back yard with Lorraine & Antoinette Vallone. And I can come back here any time I like. In about ten days I'll begin worrying about/preparing for school again.

Snow warning again, but no snow, but it will find us out soon enough. In the mind of my tiny poems, the snow is six feet deep back here, as it soon will be.

1/8/79

I'm out here just for an hour or so before going over to play some basketball. Hope not to get hurt!
Wonderful time with about 30 Ukrainians at Mirko's last evening.
An inch or two of snow, but the brunt of another storm missed us. I don't miss the snow shovel.
Hannelore has the Twig meeting here tonight. Excellent time for me to be back here, and I will be.... Billy went to school without crutches today, so he's almost off my mind in that way.
Will look over my little poems. Wish I had a title. I wrote one yesterday that may end the sequence. So important that I get it right. I <u>intuit</u> what it says, but have to make <u>sure</u> that it does.
Such a pleasure sipping coffee here and writing. This is inside the first poem: "A crow's black squawk-- / the white field lost again." The little poems will not be forced and, so far, I haven't.

1/9/79

I'm out here just for an hour or so before going over to play some basketball. Hope not to get hurt!
Spent three periods out here yesterday working on the tiny poems, which keep coming, the sequence almost rounded out.
One of Han's friends got hung up in the snow on our big rock out front—I had to jack her station wagon up & sort of push the car forward off the jack & off the rock. Cold work.
And it's too cold in here. The day deceived me—sun shining, little wind, but COLD, and I didn't have the heater on long enough.
Billy going to school & returning by bus now. It's a load off our minds after about 200 extra trips with our old car, and lately, often, in uncertain weather.
Not much else new, I'm happy to report, in my literary life. The days slide by. It seems I've taken up the tiny poems instead of the long one, a good rhythm. I did this two summers ago, too, in a kind of preparation for the long one.... Picciones & Poulins have not visited or called. Poulin will never bother me again in the ways that he did. I will be out here in my cabin.

Afternoon: no injuries! A fine work-out. I ran hard for about 45 minutes.
Well, I'll be smart and let it sit for a time, but I think I've about finished the sequence of tiny poems. There are now 32. It's called, for now, *Evening Dawning*. I think it's at least as good as *Lord Dragonfly*.
Han & Bill will go to a high school basketball game tonight. I'll be home with Kristen. I think I won't come out here. I should work on that projected flyer for *Light & Swastika*. I feel written out right now. Somehow, it happened again.... I don't think I'll write a little preface or afterword for the book this time. I suspect Ernie will want to do it. I should, after I give it some time & space & a fresh look, send it to magazines first.
No distractions out here. It takes much of the strain out of writing.... Don't know, though, when I'll have the courage to spread *Chestnut Rain* out & begin again. But I've just this moment decided that I don't want to, that maybe I'll gather a little collection together for Schneider, first.

1/10/79

It's 3:30 in the afternoon. I'm wonderfully relaxed. Played ball over an hour today, running pretty steadily the whole time. Then stopped at Mary Marchant's and got that brief interview over with. And now it is snowing, & the kids & Han are home, & we don't have to go anywhere the rest of the day.

Last night, just when I was relaxing, Frank Judge stopped in. I ended up at Fitz Gerald's with Rod & Frank until about 3 this morning. But I'm at ease, after finishing, except for fine-tuning, the *Evening Dawning* sequence.

Will come out here again this evening & fool with a table of contents for Schneider.

I have everything. Still cannot believe this little cabin.

1/11/79

I've been out here about two hours this morning. I've left my hat & coat on, but don't mind. Now, the place is warm. But, what the hell, it's about a record cold outside.... Have been fiddling again with the new sequence, adding to it. Once in a while a little poem just comes along. It's done by sound association, usually, it seems. 37 poems now.

Called Ernie last night. He sounds okay, but different, as though he has become very religious lately?... Woman called from New School for Social Research--$175 for April 19th—perfect. Day after I'll be at Columbia. I should have a few good days in the city. Maybe will meet Bill Ewert there?... I think I'll write Burt Britton, come to think of it.

(Later.) I've just changed these last several dates to 1979! Wonder if I'll ever catch up with the world.

Well, I played <u>three</u> games of basketball today, and am still in one piece. Will play again tomorrow. Nothing like it.

That *Bear* anthology came today. It's handsome. And some books from Dan Gerber, including *Departure*, not very good, but something he had to work through, I guess. Some strange grammar & spelling, too!?

I'm about ready to maybe type up my new sequence this evening, especially if a title declares itself. Will stare at it for a while.

1/12/79

Friday, and after a fifth session of basketball this week, I'm fine.

Billy will be going to an away game tonight, & Han to the soccer dinner for Frank Sherman. Kristen will spend a nervous evening practicing for some kind of clarinet competition tomorrow. I've got several items of busywork to accomplish, unless my sloth & disinclination get the best of me.

I typed up, for the first time, *Evening Dawning*. Will now stare at it again. Drafted a letter to Tom Woll— don't know if this is what I want to do—about the possibility of making *LD* & *Evening Dawning* into a small book. The idea sounds right to me. Will see.

Boo stopped by, is not feeling well, has a doctor's appt. And she said that Tony & Sandi rushed daughter Sarah to the hospital at 4 the other morning w. possible appendicitis—don't know what happened. A flu is going around, Han says, that strikes with severe stomach cramps.

Several male cardinals flying around. Don't seem to see any females.

I'm very much enjoying *The Oregon Trail*. I know that Wyoming country Parkman is presently suffering through.

1/14/79

Sunday morning. I've come out back for a couple hours. Pleasantly warm here. This perfect, quiet place is still unbelievable to me.... Cleared this old oak table yesterday and read *Chestnut Rain* and worked on the new section beginning with Edwards' "Images and shadows of divine things." Am pleased to be inching ahead again in no hurry.

Drizzle outside just turned to sleet, much snow expected.

1/15/79

It's down around zero again, still a little chill back here, but I've about finished the section of *CR* that begins "Old man Wenzel, try to forget"—I'm glad I came up with the idea of making this a Wenzel piece.

Call from Al yesterday afternoon, our first contact in weeks, and kind of a low-voltage shock again: did I know who won the Pulitzer & did I see *People* with Burt Britton's store in it & did I see *New Republic* with James Atlas' attack on contemporary poetry & what should BOA's series of young poets be called, etc., etc., etc., etc., ... And Al coughing periodically. I was listening & looking out the window. I can get caught up in that crap, too, I know, that disease, that ambition. Hope to avoid it. My chances have improved immensely because of this cabin. Al is a thousand miles away.

I look forward to playing ball later.

Evening Dawning just sitting around, aging a little. I drafted a letter to Tom Woll about my two sequences, & will think that over, too. *Long Island Light*, a few months away, makes me feel relaxed about having to do something now.

1/16/79

Han substituted today. I worked out here this morning, and then biked up through snow & ice & slush to the gym, played too many games, and then biked home. My legs are tired. But I'm getting into shape & soon should be able to play with a kind of steady intensity that I haven't managed. I had one fine game today, about 8 for 10 from all over.... Even Bill Stewart showed up.

Found a way this morning to begin a piece about old soldiers, reunions, that I've wanted/needed for *CR*. So far, so good.

Billy's last appt. today for his leg. He's doing fine.

I eat too much junk just before going to bed and haven't been sleeping well. Need a little discipline.

Witness still hasn't arrived, but will, any day. Did get some copies of *Lord Dragonfly* from Ernie, and the hardback of *On Turtle's Back*. Spent the evening a few days ago rearranging all my books in the hall, getting all my things up to the top shelf—much room to expand downwards now.

It's 4 o'clock, my cabin nice & warm now.

Picciones visited yesterday. They're desperately broke, somehow, despite the thirty grand they've been pulling in for a few years.

1/17/79

It's noon. Han & kids are in school. I had some typing to do this morning (*Lord Dragonfly / Evening Dawning*) and have just got out here. Decided to skip basketball one day to allow my muscles to get over their shell-shock.

Had to laugh at myself a minute ago. I am a damned picture postcard, coming out here in the snow with my old black ski-hat, setting my thermos down on my oak table, hanging up my coat. I am a living stereotype of the "poet."

Yesterday a section (needing work) of *CR* came along quickly—auction & chestnut leaf section. I think it's going to be a beauty.

Noon whistle blowing, dogs' painsongs soon to begin, and their howls are pain, not accompaniment. They're howling now, but distant, muffled. I'm going to spend all afternoon out here!

Han's Permanent Certification came today. At last! She'll be very happy, as I am. It was a struggle for her.

1/18/79

It's eight in the morning. I let the place warm up an hour before coming back, and it's okay here. Much snow overnight, and it's cold. The kids were hoping for a snow day, but were not in luck. Han is inside catching up on a little sleep. I'll fiddle around here for a few hours, and then go over to play basketball. Bottom of right foot hurts a little, but my body seems otherwise ready.

... After a good workout, & lunch, I'm back again. It's still snowing. Again, I'm so relaxed after hustling around the gym for an hour.

Just about finished, this morning, by remembering something I'd read about Tacitus, my soldiers section of *Chestnut Rain*. What the hell is that whole book coming to? If I ever do that one very-long section I have in mind, I'm going to be in business.

Nice letter from Bill Ewert again. He's sold 25 copies of *Witness*, which should arrive any minute. Letter from Peter Dzwonkoski, too, that I can't quite make out. He isn't even <u>dreaming</u>, I hope, that I'd <u>donate</u> my collection to U. of R.? Anyway, Peter & his friends will visit in 2-3 weeks.

Basketball again tomorrow. I already look forward.

1/19/79

Friday at 4. I've had a good day, working out here this morning—have I finished that poem called "The Voice"?—playing ball at noon. I think Han & the kids will go to a high school game tonight. I'll try to start in on schoolwork.

Heard from several faculty today—Ray Duncan, John Catan, Mike Osier, Paul Curran—that registration has been a disaster. The students are simply not here. Surely we're all going to be jolted here in the next year or two by budget cuts, cuts of faculty lines. I think I'll have a small enrollment this semester. Brockport will shrink.... I don't know what it will all mean to me over the years. My job should be secure. I'm one of the old-timers, for one thing.

I've xeroxed some copies of *Lord Dragonfly/Evening Dawning*. Not sure what I'll do with them. Maybe one to Vanguard, one to Harry Duncan? Herb Yellin?—he'd go broke on me. Maybe this should be the book for Duane Schneider?

There's a painting of the Red Buttes in my *Oregon Trail*!

I happened to see a new poem by Richard Wilbur in *New Yorker* today. No, it just is too artificial, I'm afraid, for me, for now.

Han said Jack Palombella stopped by today. Sorry I missed him.

Haven't seen the card-players for quite a while. Maybe next week. Certainly before Mirko leaves, once or twice, but there will be little or no poker this semester, I'm sure, with Mirko gone.

1/20/79

Saturday, quarter-to-six in evening, dark out, & a freezing rain. I'm only out for a few minutes, to get a little air. Unexpected poker game this morning until 4 a.m.—I lost $28, but had much fun.... Worked all afternoon inside on a syllabus for my 112 class. Gulp. So, the winter break has wound down, but last day of classes is already May 3rd. Hard to believe. I'm the first one to want to be off, but these semesters are just too squeezed for adequate course development. Oh, shit, what am I saying—a few moments of real intensity make any semester, & for the rest, well, it's just a pleasant social occasion.

If I get some work done tomorrow morning, maybe I'll come out here early afternoon for a couple-three hours before the big game. I'll root for Dallas, but Pittsburgh will win.

Sent *Lord Dragonfly/Evening Dawning* to Vanguard & to Herb Yellin at Lord John Press.... *Witness* arrived, is beautiful. I'll search for proper ink & pen to sign it.

Now back inside for coffee & an evening of stupor with couch pulled out, & warmth of it.

1/21/79

Dallas got screwed. Several times, but most notably in the 4th quarter on an interference call.

About two inches of snow since yesterday. 3-6" more predicted by tomorrow.

I've managed some schoolwork. Just have to plan, now, the Transcendentalism course, and am screwed up because the most important book, the Emerson, was out-of-print. Hope the other arrives <u>soon</u>.

Walking out here toward my cabin light in the snow, outlines of houses lit around me, I had to smile again. What a place this is.

1/23/79

Ink a peculiar color because I had a thick brown in my pen for the signing of *Witness*, & now have gone back to blue-black. I may have messed up the tip by pressing, too.... Anyway, that job is done & the package is ready to be picked up by UPS. Will drop Bill Ewert a note tonight.

First day of classes over. I'm tired. Should have some good classes. Comp class is the biggest, too big. I'll have about 60 students, fifteen of which are graduate, this semester, I think.

Here I am again in this quiet, this complete contrast.

1/25/79

Well, I think my cabin is high & dry enough, but this weather makes me nervous. Rain all day yesterday, sleet all day today. A foot of slush across the whole back property, & I had a heck of a time just walking back here. The bottom of my building is in the slush. This is no big deal, I think; the floor beams stand on their edges, & the whole floor must be 10" above the bottom of the outside plywood. All of the back drains down the ditch well enough when it just rains. It's the slush that has clogged everything up. It's still sleeting now. Under my rug is a piece of ¾" masonite under which is the plywood under which, stapled on the beams, is a solid piece of plastic sheeting. I hope everything is dry. The rug & masonite are. Another lesson in the fragility of all things.

Classes went all right. About 20 people, including several teachers, in the Wednesday evening workshop; eighteen or nineteen in the transcendentalism class. I'm tired, as I will be every Thursday evening, but this is the place to recuperate. Never thought the weather wd. be a worry back here. Six feet of snow would be all right, or six days of rain. The slush is terrible. Maybe I'll shovel some paths in it, or shovel around the cabin, tomorrow, if it seems as though that might do any good.

Han is pushing the gift cart at the hospital, Kristen off to band concert, Billy inside playing chess. I would like to keep him company, but do want to calm down out here. Lord, it is wonderful out here in this small lit place in the darkness. Thank you.... Will take Billy to play ball tomorrow, his first time since his accident. He's excited.

I might be getting close to an order for the poems for the Croissant book. No real hurry. Fun shuffling. Does any of this make even the slightest sense, this business of putting poems into a thematic order, or what I see to be an order? It satisfies. It sometimes disguises weaknesses? It is a way of bringing together old and new poems into a pattern seen at the time of gathering, anyway.

1/26/79

Sunday morning, 9:00. I shoveled yesterday a small sluiceway from the south corner of the cabin about five feet to the path in front, and the water has run out & the cabin is high & dry now, though water is running fast through the ditch. So, I'm up plenty high enough, but just had to let the water out from under. We had very unusual conditions, anyway, inches of ice <u>under</u> a foot of slush & then rain, everything blocked from flowing through the ditch.

Wrote a poem about Ryōkan yesterday. Judy Minty sent me a book of the old beggar and priest. I want him with me, too, here, in this place.

Still working on table of contents for the Schneider book.
Billy played ball again yesterday and is doing fine.... Now for coffee, & tomfoolery w. poems.

Monday

Colder today, all the slush frozen. I'll be out here two hours and then, if the falling snow allows, go over to play ball.
Thought of a little poem this morning that may be finished:

> Woodpecker, red
> buddha-head hammering
> *heart, heart, heart, heart, heart ...*

Saw a huge woodpecker yesterday morning in the biggest ash, and guess the little poem came from that. That last word could be almost anything, but not something soft as "love" or "live." Would "flame-red" be too much? An uncapitalized "Buddha" seems more myriad to me. How many "hearts"? The head-heart gathering is best, I think.
UPS picking up *Witness* today. When they're off to Bill, I'll be glad.
Peter Dzwonkoski and friends arriving Friday. I just don't think I'm ready to do anything with my books right now?
This cabin has changed my life. I write more, read more. I write fewer letters and fuss with my books less. I'm less nervous.
From where I sit at this table I can see all twelve pines along the Mosher side. They look like they're doing all right.
School tomorrow, but I feel, again, as though I've been off for a long time. The freedom will lessen when I start bringing home, next weekend already, papers and journals.

***

Afternoon: I had a good workout. I'm starting to rebound. My team won all four games.... I'm lazy about getting to schoolwork, & Manny & Helen & Alice want us over for cards again this evening. We played with them Friday night until 4:30 Saturday morning; then they played in Rochester all day Saturday; then the Greeks from Rochester came out Sunday to play all day, & the Rocks joined in at midnight and they played until 7 this morning! Now, tonight. We'll quit by 1:00, latest, Han & I. We won about $30 last time.
Herb Yellin can't do *Lord Dragonfly/Evening Dreaming*. Too bad. Maybe for the best, since he'd do only 200-300 copies. I'd like to try, maybe, Black Sparrow, or some other fine press that does hardbounds.

Tues.

Evening. About a dozen women gathering inside for Han's Tupperware party. An American institution. In fact, Tupperware is good stuff.
We played poker until 2 a.m., won about $35. I'm tired today after my two classes. It would definitely be better to have the composition class 3 times a week instead of twice for 1½ hrs. I end up lecturing, I'm afraid. <u>How</u> to make the connection between writing that they read and their own writing. Well, I'll get their first papers Thursday.
Sent a batch of poems off to *Ohio Review*. Don't know where to send things. Can't send more to *Poetry* until the four he has on hand are used.
Reading *The Puritan Oligarchy*, have prayed that in another life, but with the knowledge of this one and others to come!, that I'll be part of a colonial village.
Had coffee with Al today. General, pleasant talk of entanglements of literature, politics.
Somehow, Bobbs-Merrill reports twice as much usage of *AP '76* in 1978 as in 1977. I'm still far from making any money on the book, but happy it's getting around as much as it is. I'm glad I decided to use it in

the workshop this semester, and will again next fall. Is it <u>possible</u> that it will pick up sales again for '79? If so, I'm going to be in business!

Sat. Feb. 4 (?), 1979

Haven't been out here in a couple of days. So quiet, again, after days of rush. I'll stay out here until lunch, and then come back again for a few hours.... Deep snow now, and an overhang of snow on my cabin roof.

Margaret Perry, Peter Dzwonkoski, & Alan Taylor came over yesterday afternoon. I showed a little of my collection for a couple of hours. Don't know what will come of it all. I'll go over to see them in the spring, by which time I'll make some decisions, by which time I'll know what they have in mind.

Corrected all but six of my freshman compositions last night. Feel free. Have much correspondence to take care of. This evening.

Called home last night. The folks are fine, worried only about Eddie's ongoing uncertain future.... Mrs. Terlik is in a Polish old folks' home in Huntington. Mrs. Wenzel has just had an operation on both arthritic kneecaps. And Mr. Rogas, Junior's father, died about a month ago of lung cancer. I liked that man so much, have only the happiest and warmest memories of him. He was a detective in the city, but spent every summer weekend in Nesconset at Mrs. Terlik's, his mother-in-law, playing pinochle out back & drinking beer. A strong, red-headed man. I can hear his voice now.... Junior is now working in California, I hear. That Nesconset life a part of the light rays now, a part of time, but still vivid. Eddie Rogas.... My folks sound healthy. I look forward to spending several days with them in April.

We're having a farewell gathering for Mirko tomorrow afternoon. He leaves Wednesday, and will be in Russia until June. We'll miss him, though the time between now and then will go by in a blink. Irma will be lonely.

Played ball again yesterday with Billy. He's doing fine. He's at the center of a circle of friends who are at the center of their whole world right now.... Kristen had a crisis, a "D" on her report card in social studies. We're trying to get her to improve her powers of attention. Her social life blooms & booms, but not her studies. She is the best with her clarinet, though, and this gives her much assurance.

Han's father having an operation on his foot Thursday—he has some kind of clot. He's in bad shape in many ways, and this winter has been rough on them, ice storms on days they've had doctor appointments, etc.

?

Still don't know the date. It's Monday, the 6th or 7th?

We had a fine dinner for Mirko last night. Men played cards later on. I won $152, a welcome win, since we surely won't play much if at all while Mirko is away. Joe Winnick & Chuck Lang came over, too.

Public schools closed because of all the blowing & snow. Billy & I went over to the college gym & played ball. He's coming along nicely. I am, too.

Just wrote letters to Vince, Norbert, & Karl Elder. Didn't really feel like working on a poem, I guess.... Actually got a letter today from <u>the</u> Leonard Bernstein about *Swastika* which, apparently, Bernice Woll gave to him. Exciting. Wish he'd compose a piece based on the book & make me famous. Or, better still, rich?... I want to send him *Palestine*. Only have a few copies left.

79 adoptions in 1978 for *AP '76*. There were only 45 in 1977. Could it be catching on. One more leap like that, and I'll <u>know</u> something is happening. I think I'd like to do another edition. Could improve it quite a bit.... I just feel so rewarded, so welcomed these days. Tom Woll says *Light* is being ordered by stores in <u>fives</u>, unheard of for poetry, as he says. <u>Now</u>, if the book can get a little attention in *Newsday* or wherever, and catch on in a slight way, Vanguard will be happy, and that alone will make <u>me</u> happy.

I feel all ready for school again. There is always much time to recuperate, despite the compositions I brought home, even.

Guess I'll call it an afternoon & go in.... I'm afraid of what the news will be from Iran today. Meanwhile, the snow falls.

Fri., the 8th or 9th?

I vow that the next time I write here, I'll know the date!

Haven't been back here since Monday. It seems as though months, or no time at all, have gone by.

Classes went well this week. One student cried and left the workshop early, saying I'd insulted her. She should have felt chastised (for babbling illogically) and not insulted, I hope. The Transcendentalism class has been a joy, thanks to the transparent and bottomless book that is a pond, *Walden*.

Archie Kutz tells me that Vanguard had 2 pages in *Publishers' Weekly*, & featured *Light*, used the Stafford picture of Heyen. I wouldn't be surprised if they had a decent advance sale.... Ha, now that Joyce is gone, I am their literary star!... They should tie the book to the author of *Swastika*.

Han's father's leg too far gone, somehow, for the operation they'd wanted to do. Will have to wait and see if amputation is necessary.... Sandi's mother had a rough time in Florida, too. I talked to Tony—less and less will we have open spaces of time, now that we are early-middle-age, when someone close is not sick.

Good workout in basketball today.

Very cold out, & deep snow. Both kids out this evening, Kris to her band/play, & Billy to a ball game. I'll have to do some driving.

Bob Phillips says I have <u>2</u> poems in Field's anthology. Hope I'll be sent a copy.

I'm sort of marking time until *Light*. Why shouldn't such a book sell a few thousand copies right away? (The first printing will be 2,500.) No bound proofs, I guess. Don't know if I'll get another look at it before I see the finished book.... Well, maybe I'll fiddle with a poem before going in to supper.

Saturday

Another resolution (happily?) (am I becoming contentious?) down the drain: I still don't know the date. I will begin my next entry with the proper date.

Very cold, and still snowing. I've left my hat and coat on, but the cabin is warming.... Finished the shadowless Suzuki book. May just have the beginning of a short section for *Chestnut Rain*.

I think maybe I don't feel particularly ambitious this weekend.... Han going to the play this evening. I'll watch the Syracuse-Bonaventure game on television.

This will be a petty paragraph, but a true one—already beginning with apology (am I talking to myself, or a future [come to think of it, had some thoughts about my audience the other day: next¶]). In some ways, I feel like an enlightened man, part of the mind of the finest Zen literature I read. This declaration, in these terms, of course, speaks for itself, and badly, betrays, but I do not have around me the enlightened community that the monk-in-training has. He has the knowledge that those around him know & will know when he has become. Family, western teaching, anchor me much of the time to another mind, but the anchor shifts in the mud, the ropes sway in the water. Between these two sentences, minutes of attentive dreaming went by. It just happened again. I will pass to another mind.

I was thinking that my audience for *The Chestnut Rain* is myself, but myself living another life, myself as a farmer on the prairie in South Dakota or north of here along the lake—I am too busy in this other life to write, but I can, sometimes, after the wearying day of planting/feeding/washing manure out of the stalls, read, and what I want to read is a language, a rhythm that knows the intense beauty & strain of my life & what I see around me. I will write *CR* for myself in this other life. I will write it for the farmer who needs not only his own life but the poetry of words to tell him, to deepen for him, his own life.

Noise was, & *Light* is, in many ways, various, diffuse. *CR* is to this point all of a piece, & so satisfying to me, a single work, an extended "Witness."

2/11/79

Sunday. I have the date!

A new government in Iran, probably, by now.... U.S. inflation rate 16% a year now.... Brockport in a deep freeze & will be for at least a few more days.... UCLA-Notre Dame basketball on television later. Regarding television: the more we <u>witness</u>, the less we want to become involved in. Yes, except basketball.

Letter from Tom Woll yesterday saying Vanguard "might well" want to publish *Lord Dragonfly/Evening Dreaming*! They have the Mss. out for estimates. What a lovely little book it could be. I'm somehow afraid that they will publish it—those little defenseless things—but.... Maybe the rhythm is perfect—after *Light*, a tiny book, a <u>book</u> only about 250 lines long.

I have, no doubt, a bladder infection again, and I have a pain in my right side, which could be a muscle strain, but which could possibly be of some connection with the infection. I'm trying to drink a lot and wash it out, but maybe it can't work this way & needs medication. I'd hate to take ten days of sulfur again. Knocks the hell out of me. I wish the pain in my side would go away. Don't even notice it when I'm playing ball, & it does seem superficial, but ... Han has a touch of the flu. A good Sunday for the family to get some rest. Kristen exhausted from 3 days of the school play.

Regarding Zen time & western old age & health—I have the feeling that I just want to finish *The Chestnut Rain*, get it to what I want it to be. Then I will have done the writing work I was supposed to do on this planet. Then, any years or decades left to me will be extra blessing.

I want the weather to break. I want to garden and work on *CR*. By mid-May that life will begin. Now, I will blink my eyes....

2/12/79

Nothing, nothing is as cleansing as the kind of workout and then hot shower I had today. I ran pretty good for more than an hour.

Fiddling with the *LD/ED* sequences. <u>Would</u> like to see Vanguard do it. It's a good book. I will not kill it with small word changes that impose meanings, but do want it to have an ongoing energy.... If Vanguard takes it, I figure, they'll publish it for next Christmas. I'll use it for presents, will keep it a secret from most people until it appears, my precious secret.

The groundhog on my sill sees his shadow every day, I'm afraid, but in another month or so I'll point him into the sun—he's so stiff that he won't be able to turn around. I just had a thought. I'd love to have my polar bear out here. I will! If a thief comes, it will turn into a poem.

2/16/79

Friday, 3 in afternoon. What a day. Happy as a lark this morning, I was leaving for basketball when I got stuck in the driveway. Took me 2 hours of hard work to get out. Put me in a stupid angry mood. I'm all right again. My little cabin is surprisingly warm. Good letter from Bill Ewert today. Classes went well this past week. I've missed this place. The weather was brutal, five days in a row of record cold. Time flying toward May, but these, too, are good days, but the cold will not let up.... Billy gets dropped off in two hours for his bus to an away game. Student readings at the college this evening—don't know if I'll go over. I'd be smart not to.... Auburn next Thursday....

2/17/79

All five Great Lakes are just about frozen over for "the first time in meteorological history," as the weatherman puts it. And more arctic air is bearing down on us. I will get a little bigger heater for this place for next winter.... I see that the ink in my inkwell is frozen!

Dropped Billy off at basketball practice this morning, & will be back here for an hour or two, just to taste the quiet & aloneness.

Han still not feeling well, penicillin maybe not working. We'll see.

Have a hunch Picciones will stop by today.

I want to keep working on the selection for Duane Schneider, maybe get it down to poems I really believe in, if I can tell which ones they are. Often even misshapen ones have something about them that I care for.

A Geography of Poets made its way to the Lift Bridge & I picked it up. I like the feel of Bantam books.... I sent Ed Field some chapbooks.... Also sent out *In Print* to about 20 libraries with special collections. Trying to prime the pump just a little.... Bill Ewert says he's sold 37 copies of *Witness* to date. This is good, I think, for a $15 broadside. He wants to do a little book, maybe of Wenzel poems. If he does arrange for this, it will be a beauty, I know. Maybe Christine Bertelson would take it on. Ewert, I learn more all the time, has dough, and upper-class taste, which feels good to this farm boy.

2/18/79

It's 6 in the evening. Just had a great spaghetti dinner. Spent the day doing nothing—watching basketball on television, reading the newspapers. Now I'm out here in this other world. Freezing out, but not too bad in here—I had the heater on for 45 minutes before I came out.... Only thing I'd like to get done is the brief introduction for Dan Stryk. Don't know if I'll turn to it, or fiddle with my own things....

.... Two-and-a-half hours later, time that went by in a blink, and I have a draft of the piece for Dan Stryk. I think it may be okay. I'm glad, now that it's over, that I was asked.... This place is fairly warm now, at 8:00, in freezing weather.... I look forward to watching "Marathon Man" tonight, and I'm <u>anxious</u> to play basketball tomnorrow.

2/19/79

Morning. I have 1½ hrs. before I'll go in and shave and then drive up to play some ball. Billy will meet me there after his practice at the Middle School.

Today and tomorrow the cold snap is supposed to break a little.

Kristen just this moment came to the door & told me she's going shopping with Vallones. For just a second I didn't recognize her!—her hair pulled back as she's had it lately, she looks like a young boy.... Han and I think often of how lucky we are with Billy & Kristen. Thank you, Lord.

2/22/79

It's 7:30 in the evening. I got back this afternoon from Auburn. Just came out here to check on my shack in all this rain & snow—it's high & dry—and to write this.

Reading at CCC was the usual sort of thing. It was all right. Kind people. Eddie & Cheryl were there, sort of lost. Good meeting Howard Nelson, who turns out to be 32 & a beginning poet, a <u>fine</u> one to my way of feeling.... But at the center of my trip was the reading last evening at the prison, to about sixty prisoners, mostly black. Anything could have happened, I could have lost them completely, but I didn't, & recited poems & read some & talked & tried to answer questions. At the end, several came up and shook hands and said "thanks" and said they were glad I'd come, & were happy. It was moving to me, too, at the beginning of the 2½ hr. session, to watch these men stand up and struggle with the recitation of a poem from their texts, a poem they chose—their assignment. Frost, Dickinson, L. Hughes, Blake, Dunbar. They applauded one another, and applauded me after each poem. I was afraid, at first, but came through, and will always remember some of those faces.

2/23/79

Back yard a pond when I woke up this morning. I shoveled for an hour, opening the ditch. Water is flowing through pretty good right now. Same thing every year. Nothing to worry about. Still, there's ice, thick ice against the ground, over which the water flows. This keeps the water level high.... My place out here is perfect. I'll come out here for a few hours this evening. Right now I'm just puttering.

Got a check today for $46.50 from Bantam for "The Children." Was paid $350 for the Auburn readings. It's this extra money that keeps us afloat & gives us hope of saving for college for the kids. $2,000 from the State Research Fdn. this summer, & money for spring readings.

Spoke with Tom Woll. Vanguard will probably do the short poems. I'll suggest 750 copies. This is the kind of thing they have in mind, a collector's item. I hope they could make a little dough on such a thing. It will make me happy, I know.... I hope *Light* is on the Island by the time I get there in April.

Folks called this morning. Mom has heavy sinus—otherwise they're okay.

--- 6:30 now. Back out for a couple of hours. Getting cold again, & snow tomorrow, the weatherman says.... Lazy day—took care of a few notes I had to write. Tomorrow, I'll type & work on *Lord Dragonfly/Evening Dreaming* & write Tom Woll.... Somehow, don't feel like doing anything right now, & keep doodling in this journal. Well, will put it down. Now.

2/27/79 (Tues.)

"Blueprints" for *Long Island Light* arrived Monday, and I called Tom this morning about one or two small things. All's in order, & the book is in the works. It's supposed to be done by March 30. I hope it is, that copies can make it to SCCC by the 25th of April. Tom described the slipcase—if it isn't too gaudy, it should be wonderful. I'm excited about this book.

I had two good classes today. Tomorrow, basketball and the workshop.

I typed *LD/ED* and have it ready to send to Tom.

Much snow yesterday, much melted today.

Saw Tony & Al briefly.

I keep imagining this place in spring & summer. In spring it will disappear into these woods. And brambles and bushes will grow around the outside. I had to cut so much away when we were building the place.

Stryk sent *The Duckpond*, & Jack Matthews sent his *Tales from the Ohio Land*, two nice additions to my collection.... I'm sending several Dickey items to Ben Franklin for his colleague's inscription.... Sent another Mss. to Bill Ewert, & expect he'll be sending me a check.... The *Light* blueprints make a fine item. Maybe I'll have it bound....

3/2/79

It's been a good afternoon out here. I've just read Jack's book. A few of the stories are very deep. What a man he is....

In the 40s today, the whole world melting. Still there are ice shelves above our land and I walk about a foot above the ground. But the ditch is running through, and I hope tomorrow is the same kind of day.

My classes this past week were excellent. After the Transcendentalism sessions—one whole period spent on Thoreau's artist of Kouroo—and after the workshop, the kids, or several of them, just sort of stayed around, wanting to talk.

Played basketball today (& yesterday & the day before) but only two games. I quit early because down under both groins feel tense, ache, as my right one did a few summers ago just before I really injured myself. I hope I can play comfortably again Monday.

Light is not far away now. I'm looking forward. I think I'll see it before I get to New York.... Sent off the revised *LD/ED* Mss. to Tom. Maybe they'll send me a contract! If not, no real disappointment.

I'm waiting for the signal to go inside for some hamburgers & fries.

Han has the long paper hanging over her, & very much wants to find a job for next September. I hope something fine will work out for her within the next few years.

Will pass up the student reading tonight. I think it's wise for me to clear my head after a few days of reading journals & poems. Will have to do a set of comps tomorrow & Sunday, but that's a mechanical thing.

Dan Stryk liked the note I did on him.... *Buffalo Evening News* sent $20 out of the blue for use of my poem in the White Pine anthology.... I'll want to get back to work on the selection for Duane Schneider before too long.... Will turn down request again for essays for books Donald Greiner is doing. Wish I could knock these things off, but I can't & they'd kill months....

Found out that Kristen will need much dental work. It's the metaphysical parental pain, not the physical or financial that hurts. Always something. But all these things pass.

3/4/79

Sunday evening: warm all day today and, at last, a substantial amount of ice and snow has melted. All day the ditch ran high. Poor Wicks had their basement flooded. They don't know why.

Cabin is high & dry, & ready for much work. After Thursday I'm off for ten days, & will finish the line-up for Schneider.... Bill Ewert called yesterday about several things, most notably about doing a little book of sections of *The Chestnut Rain*—Christine Bertelson will print it. Well, yes, I want to do this. It will certainly be a beauty, if *Witness* is any indication.

Kristen doesn't feel well & may miss school tomorrow. Han might substitute. My groin muscles are tender, but I might play basketball.

Wrote Mirko today. And wrote thanks to Jack Matthews & Dan Gerber for books.... Seem to have misplaced my fountain pen. Hope it's not lost.

Sunday morning news, of all kinds from all sources (television, newspapers) especially depressing. Acid rains & gas cutbacks & Middle East. It will all connect with me soon enough. I feel like not going to meet it, but like waiting for it in my cabin. It's all coming, and soon, as the space probe cameras have just come to the moons of Jupiter, even!

3/5/79

Found the pen.... Decided to skip basketball today & rest whatever muscles or tendons in my groin that declare themselves when I walk.... Kristen is home with a cold, or something, & Han is substituting. It's one of those vaguely restless days, but the ice is still melting away and maybe this will be the year when all my muskrats are drowned out.

... Later.... I took a bike ride to the school. The exercise makes me feel better. Billy is home now with Kristen. I'll go in in two hours to give Billy a ride up to the school... Now, will fool with the group of poems for Bill Ewert. I have 7 Wenzel & country poems in mind.

3/9/79

Friday. Played ball today. School out for ten days. Sun shining, Brockport in the 40s. Went to town & arranged for my flights for my trip next month. Look forward. The book dealers will be exhibiting for a few days at the Americana & maybe I'll stay there. Will see. Will probably meet Ralph Sipper, among others. Talked to him on the phone. New big 1400-item poetry catalogue in mail.

Have a hunch I should be doing more to promote *Light*, but don't know what. It's up to Vanguard, I guess. Archie at Lift Bridge told me he ordered 25 cloth, 25 paper, & 5 specials. He's a good man. I'm sure Tom Woll is pleased by this, even if it's small potatoes.... Dave Hale is using "Carrie White" in a centennial booklet (sesquicentennial?) this summer. The town will pay Vanguard $25.

Oh, it's so nice out here now. Heater pops on for a minute in every five or so. My place weathered the winter.... Snow expected Sunday.... Melting fast for a week around here, but still ice is 6-8 inches deep in some places in the back. I know now how ice "grips."... Many grackles around these last two days.... As I walked back here, I could hear worms slurp back down into the wet high ground.

Stopped to see Al today. He was still in bathrobe at 3:00. Tony was there from afternoon to midnight yesterday, drunk, worried about the MFA proposal. The whole deal, it's true, is so shoddy, a big lie, but I don't plan to become ruffled about it. Will do what I can in my own classes, and that's all.

Need this vacation. Have lots of little items to clear from desk. Will watch much basketball this weekend. Will write a few days.... Han & Kris not quite well, but will be, soon, I trust.... Hope to play basketball a few times next week, too.

3/10/79

I seem to be able to do very little constructive when plans for a trip, arrangements, are hanging over me. yesterday I arranged for plane tickets; today I'm trying to make hotel reservations, after deciding which & how many nights, but no luck yet. I tried to call Bob, but he's not in, and Judith was terrifically distant, sounded lost, as if she didn't know me. Well, anyway, things will work out. I just want to make sure that I clear things away so that I can have some good sessions back here next week.

Ed Kumar, Manny, Joe, Ed Culbertson & I played poker at Joe's last night. I won $84.

Sipper's big catalogue came. Am I jaded? Nothing too exciting, but then I don't know if I'm looking for anything special.

Picciones stopped in today. They'd love for me to get involved with out MFA planning. I can't, am unable and selfish and lazy. Whatever comes, I will just do the best I can in the courses given me.

3/11/79

Sunday. I've only been out here a short time. Snow blowing, but not much sticking.... Guess I've about finished the poems "Gardener" and "Here." The latter might be best, some day, for an edition of my Island book. "Gardener," if it's good enough, will go into the Schneider book. It's another poem with sunflower motif.

Called the Roosevelt in NYC & reserved a room for two days. It's closest to where I want to be. Decided to head for the Island on Friday, not Saturday.

Want to do two things this next week: type up the 7 *CR* poems for Bill Ewert, & put together, finally, the Schneider book.

Look forward to the city trip. Will take a cab right from LaGuardia to the Vanguard offices on a Tues., & hope to train to Katonah with Bob that evening. Will drop Tom Woll a note. Is my Columbia thing Tues. afternoon? 4:15 comes to mind.

Basketball tomorrow and, with luck, all week. My damned groin muscles are so stiff. Don't know if I'm hurt or not! Have to avoid little quick turns & play fluidly.

3/12/79

Monday, 2:30. Did it: played ball, had fun, didn't get hurt, played well. Even avoided arguments, & there were many. The older we get, the weaker our skills, the more we argue. But I've learned just to shut up & run.

Han seems better today. This illness of hers, post-flu, has lingered on. And Kris is back in school.

Fairly cold today. A little blowing snow, nothing sticking.

Copies of *The Children* arrived from Martin.

I've stared at the 7 *CR* pieces for Bill Ewert. They seem set, except for typing. Will work on the Schneider gathering today.

Carter still in the Middle East. Look forward to the news tonight. How will it all work itself out over the next 25-50 years?

Bob Phillips called yesterday. Looks as though all plans are working out. I'll meet him at Vanguard for lunch with the bunch on the Tuesday I fly in. I'll have a good time, though rushed, but good.

3/13/79

Evening.... Haven't done a damned thing today, except play ball and hose out the garage, but I feel fine, relaxed. What's a vacation for?

50° today, the ditch still trickling. Colder weather on the way.

Can't get over this cabin, how it sort of waits for me. I'm alone here in this lit space in mid-darkness. It's drizzling now.

Toni Dempster called from GCC. I'll go there morning of April tenth, and will make $200. Will use the money for my New York trip.

Still have the feeling that I'd like to do something to help *Light* sell, but I don't know what. I keep sending *In Print* out to bookdealers w. a xerox of the *Publishers' Weekly* ad for *Light*.

3/15/79

I don't think I'll ever take this place for granted: walked back over the frozen field, opened the door, and here I was again, in a quiet world inside the outside. Sunlight flooding in. Winter is having its last gasp, & the birds know it. They woke Han up at 5 this morning—there's been a whole pool of starlings, redwings, grackles under the feeder all day. That color of the grackle's neck—unreal!

Kristen is 13 tomorrow. I remember writing in this journal on the day she was born.

Played ball today. Three good games, little arguing. Will play tomorrow. My legs are in very close to excellent shape.

Letter from Jon Collett at Old Westbury. I <u>will</u> read there in April, and for about $400. This is a lift, will be all profit on an otherwise skinny trip. I hope *Light* is out & makes it to these readings.

Finished "The Poet in the Heavens" for *Wallace Stevens Journal*, I hope. The phrase "seventy years of poems" maybe trouble, for some.

Poulin called yesterday about the nonsense of the editorship of Brockport's interviews for SUNY Press. I just don't care about the machinations & politics & don't care if the books are ever published.

Letter from Vince with his *Times* Woodbox piece. What a rare man he is!

While I've been writing this, the light snow has increased to a thick fall. As Vince says, <u>not yet</u>, <u>not yet</u>.

I've had a wonderful vacation of playing ball & fiddling with small things. Still several days to go. Then I'll work <u>hard</u> in school before my trip begins on the 17th.

Billy & Kris fine. Han has a cold, but is feeling better day by day.

3/16/79

Kris's friends arriving soon for supper/party, and then I'll drive them up to the school for a dance. Billy will be staying at a friend's tonight.

Played ball, and then came out here for a couple hours. Shuffled around the poems for *The Sunflower Parables* again, and I think the 31 poems are in about as good & meaningful & various order as I can give them.

Just stopped for a minute after basketball to check my mail at the school, & Ken Venick cornered me with some poems, & then Sandi Piccione. Jesus, I'm on vacation, and just want to read & work on my own. Hard not to have the head & tongue turn into mush in the hearing of so much poetry by other people whose poems are all so different & generally unrealized. I like those folks, & I guess I'm paid to encourage & humor them along, and maybe to tell them how to make their poems more like mine! <u>This</u>, it seems to me is what has to happen, not the ideal of my being able to help them into the voice natural for them. But, I only listen with half my head, and this is right. These students will need years by themselves, working alone. Sooner or later they have to make up their own minds about whether or not they care for & believe in their own poems.

Sun is out, the world is warming. I plan to have a fine weekend watching basketball & maybe typing. Monday I'll get busy on schoolwork.

3/17/79

I'm just plain excited. Jacket of *Long Island Light* arrived today, and I've folded it around an old book, and have been admiring the heft & look of it. The lettering is black, rather than gray, but all-in-all I like the whole thing. Does it at first seem too gaudy? I don't know. Another book out soon. Amazing. CAPS grant rejection today, but no matter. The chestnut sapling's buds are stick with spring, & the book is on its way quickly now.

Looking forward to being in the Vanguard offices on the 17th—just a month from today.

Good use of quotations on the jacket. Tom decided on the Carruth one, and I'm glad.

I feel like running, but I'll just watch basketball today & yell at the refs.

3/19/79

It seems as though spring is here. Bright sunshine today, & the wet and soggy world is draining. Only a few chunks of ice left back here. Buds on the five pink honeysuckle bushes along the Vallone line in the back yard. They've survived the coldest winter we've ever had around here, survived the two feet of solid ice they were buried in.

I played ball, took Han to lunch, & then Tony stopped over. He'd been down to Michael's place, making connections & circles for all of us.

Tony mentions that Al will have a BOA party at Lift Bridge in April. Again, I'm glad I won't be here.

Letter from Big Jim Dickey today. He's signed/inscribed the things I'd sent to Ben Franklin, & is returning them, along with a couple of gifts.

Once in a while I do some constructive work—on a poem or some schoolwork—but it's true that my whole being is marking time for the book to appear & for my trip & for end-of-semester.

3/23/79

Friday, close to 70°. What a day! Rain coming, but what a day. Only trouble is that Han isn't feeling too well—she's been ill, really, for months. Gradual improvement lately, maybe.

Basketball today. Jim Newton hurt his ankle badly.

Went to a faculty-at-large meeting about new administrative set-up. Couldn't understand a word.

Wonderful items from MacLeish & Dickey have arrived in the mail lately. Holograph poems in books ("Ars Poetica") from both of them, e.g. I feel rich & enriched.

I have windows open to screens in here now, first time since last summer.

David St. John read here the other night. Good man & good poet. Long party afterward. Etcetera.

Long letter from Bill Ewert; proofs from *Poetry*; invite from Gregor to read at Hofstra next year. My literary life booming. Only important thing is that I work steadily reading for & writing on *CR* this summer.... Today is almost balmy.... Billy shot a 78 yesterday.... Fights on television tonight.... Al Studier & Lisa coming over for dinner in 15 minutes.

Wrote out, quickly, a strange poem this morning about Belsen in blue light.

3/24/79

It's been a long day. I've dropped notes to Dickey & Franklin & Blessing & Toni Dempster & Arthur Gregor, etc., to catch up on thank-you's etc. And then I spent a couple of hours reading a couple of journals. After a shower, later, & with a cup of coffee, I'll read some compositions.

Much wind, but rain did not come today as predicted.

Han still not 100%.

The peepers are singing.

3/25/79

Interesting day, filled with shit and with some true moments, the deadness of finishing the set of compositions, the depth of looking at Han and loving her for whole moments as we looked at the footnotes for her paper, and the time spent reading a few poems in Dickey's *Drowning With Others*, the wonderful "Armor" and (is it called?) "Changes," which sang to me, whose rhythms I felt & wanted to catch, and I've just written a poem that might be called "The Eyes" or "The Sandshark," 40 lines that might be a good one. The death of a greasy call from Poulin worried about what Gemmett was going to do about Poulin's latest deception, and the pleasures of being back here now alone in the evening with everything out there in the cool dark beginning its budding. And my first dactylic poem on my oak table.

3/26/79

    Big flakes driving against my window, and it's cold again.
    Just looked at "This Night" again. Seems finished, and interesting.
    Played ball, had a good workout.
    Han not 100% yet, has some bad times I managed several errands for her today.
    Note from the fellow at Columbia. Things are all set.
    Today was the Egyptian-Israeli signing in Washington. My prayers with it.
    Chili for supper in about an hour—perfect for this weather.
    Rearranged a bit the order of the beginning poems for the Schneider book. I may change my mind, but right now I feel a little rushed and wish I weren't doing it? I want it to be tight, and good.
    I remember snow on the hyacinths last spring, too.

3/31/79

    Nuclear plant at Three Rivers near Harrisburg, Pa., in the news—even the possibility of a melt-down. And the other night, too, a television special on the poisoned land made me sick and angry.
    Haven't been back here in a few days. A wild week. And even this morning, when, at last, I was making my thermos to head back here, Picciones dropped in with kids & Sandi went shopping and I was stuck with the other three. They are all on the edge. Tony had the crazy idea of going to study with John Hollander under the NEA program. He's nuts. They're broke.
    Did get for a few hours to some thinking about the Ewert project. I'm going to propose to him not one but 5 books that would print the sections of *The Chestnut Rain* in order. Will see. Will keep thinking. Wrote a "Preface" & will type it tonight and send it to him.
    Maybe I shouldn't quite hope yet, but I'm hoping that a copy of *Light* will arrive next week. I certainly hope one arrives before I leave on the 17th.
    Tony & I wrote a letter saying we think <u>no one</u> should edit the Forum interviews right now. I'm not 100% sure this is the right move, but maybe it is. A copy to all in the department, one to Bretton, one to Eastman at SUNY Press—I'm not sure about this last—this admits we are divided & up to our necks in mud around here.... Crossed my mind that <u>I</u> could edit the whole series. But why? Oh, what headaches!
    My new poem "This Night" is a beauty.
    Nice letter from Rev. Schoon at Nes Amiin in Israel. I'd sent him *Swastika*.

April 1, 1979

    Sunday evening. I just finished reading and skimming the blueprint copy of *Light* for about an hour. Away from it (and with the stronger ((or closer to me now)) *Chestnut Rain*) I find myself doubting it, especially its first section. No need. It's quite a book, one I don't think I'll ever have to be embarrassed about.
    Looks as though Han's father will have to have that bad leg amputated. Han might head home soon.... I'll just try to stay on top of things as I get ready for my big trip.
    A little nervous this evening about all that. Look forward to basketball tomorrow.... The nuclear plant is still making up its mind on what to do.

4/6/79 (Fri)

    Han & car dealer just about some mud flaps & a side strip apart on a 1978 Buick. Hope it works out. I'll probably accept the deal tomorrow if the dealer doesn't call first.

Played ball today. Felt wonderful.... Also went over *The Sunflower Parables*, knocking out two poems. Am determined to type it this evening.

Unbelievable weather, wind gusts up to 60 mph. The cabin stands <u>solid</u>.

Long unwanted call from Henry Bretton yesterday. Bah! He's protecting his ass, but Tony & I declared in a letter that we want nothing to do with the project.

Light not here yet, alas. Maybe tomorrow, as the song goes.

Almost every day some little news surfaces that makes me more & more happy that I won't be around for the Alumni Writing Weekend here.

I keep thinking about the five-book proposal I made to Bill Ewert. The idea continues to feel right, for many reasons. There would be so few copies that it would be almost like not publishing the sections. I'd just salt my copies away. I wouldn't be distracted by having my sections in magazines here & there. Will see what Bill says.... Have to remember to pick up my plane ticket Monday.... Many things to do this weekend. The wind is frightening.

4/13/79

It's before eight in the morning. I haven't slept much lately, anticipating the trip today to Han's folks for Easter, & my trip to the big city & L.I. next Tuesday. And I've been working hard at school.

Haven't gotten back here in several days. Suddenly, it's a new world again. Most of the snow melted, robins scrapping for territory, a bluejay giving the world hell.

Our new car is in the garage. Do we really own all this metal now?

Card from Duane Schneider telling me to take life easy. He's right. Still, I want to get *The Sunflower Parables* to him before long. Something in me doesn't want to let it go. It must be strong.

Han & the kids are fine these days.

I'm glad to be missing all the parties & readings here the 21-23.... Vince called to say he'd be staying with me for readings at Dowling and Old Westbury.

In just about one month, trips & classes over. My summer will begin.

4/16/79

Well, the time is almost here. Will leave early tomorrow morning.... Bob Phillips called today to say he'd be away the whole time I'm in NYC, so I called the Roosevelt & reserved my room for tomorrow night, too. Should actually be a little less hectic for me this way.... So, tomorrow morning I'll see *Light*!

Our Easter at Han's folks & then at Wolf & Pat's was fine. Our new car, too, rides like a fucking dream. No wonder America is car crazy: I forgot what it could be like not to hack around in the noisy, cold, worried ten-year-old Ford of ours.... Han will go to Nashville again tomorrow, & her pop will have the bottom half of his right leg amputated Wednesday. No fun at all. They're up against a lot living out there in the country like that, & ill half the time, & the big dog & property & very old house to take care of, & the awful weather to contend with.

I walked to the cemetery about a mile up the road, & walked around it. People buried there who lived during the Revolution. It's high on a hill, and a moving place in that stark country.... And then we went to church again—about twenty people were there this time. It rained, and Han's mom was sort of in a bad mood, but it was a beautiful service. Maybe, here or there in a stanza or a poem, I'll get past words like "moving" & "beautiful" and say what it is like there.

I wish myself luck, & my little cabin goodbye, for now. Green will be shading around it when I get back.

April 29, 1979

Is it possible that I'm back? It was a long trip, beginning badly when I couldn't sleep in New York & promised myself never again, ending on high notes at readings at Dowling & Old Westbury & Suffolk when *Light* sold. Will remember walking Times Square again a couple of nights—saw "Deep Throat"--& the readings at Columbia & New School, & Halpern, & Aaron Fischer, & Pearl London's class at the New School, & the Whitman House in Huntington where Bill Ewert showed up with his wife & two kids & mother, & traveling the old Island with Vince & even stopping in at 3 bookstores & showing them my book, & walking to the Americana with Tom Woll, & the Book Fair, & finding the *October Light* firsts remaindered at Barnes & Noble, & seeing *Light* for the first time in the Vanguard offices, & a late talk there about Joyce with Bob Phillips & Evelyn, & spending 2-3 days with my folks who seem better than ever. Will go to Fredonia tomorrow, & see Han's mom & her pop in the hospital, & will come back & finish school up & get to the garden & the poems. Thank you, Lord: the bushes are turning green & beginning to hide this cabin.... Saw Poulin for first time in a month yesterday & heard from him, & had heard from Han, about all the goings-on during the alumni weekend.... Han & Billy & Kristen are fine, wonderful.... I've been clearing off my desk, getting ready for the final week of school & the pile of journals & papers & bookwork.... My summer back here in this perfect cabin is beginning. I'll drive carefully tomorrow, & get back to this lucky life I have made & found.... Met Florence Anthony (Ai), who was very friendly & read her excellent poems in her bad singsong at Suffolk. I saw her write out a check for *Swastika!*... Graham Everett was good, & others at Suffolk. A Dutch poet drove me nuts with his rudeness & self-promotion, bugging me while I was trying to listen to readers.... Tom Woll gave me one of the first issue of *Son of the Morning*—I'll try to get him & Ralph Sipper together on the others.... Met Ralph briefly & Charles Seluzichi, & saw Marge Cohn briefly.... Will watch two basketball games on television today.... To be here again, scribbling in this journal.... I have only one hardback *Light* and one paperback here, & look forward to sending many out when I get them.... Heard that Tony was sick, as Al was/is.... Han will substitute all next week.... I guess I made, profit, about $800 on the trip, & have made $200 at GCC & have a $52 check from *Harper's* & will get royalties & $375 more advance from Vanguard, & will make $250 tomorrow. So, the money is good & will set us up for the summer, but I will continue to be careful about picking my spots, as I promised myself, for readings: feeler for a reading at Indiana: I asked $1,000. Gulp. Will see. Lost readings in Connecticut & at Kenyon asking a lousy $300. That's okay.... Hope Vanguard gets *Light* around.... Am reading Jimmy Kunstler's first novel.... The birdsong background & silence out here is amazing—part of me is still walking on Madison Ave & driving the Jericho with Vince.... Sold about 80-100 books at readings.... Warm today, the ground drying, the leaves unfolding from buds. Am I really here? My brain buzzes with City & Island, but is slowing. A nice light here at the old oak table. I'm very happy, even looking forward to reading tomorrow & this last week at school.... Found/bought other books in the City, too, but, as always, didn't have enough time, but pounded the pavements <u>enough</u>.... My first project in May, besides gardening, will be to get *Sunflower* to Duane, & my second, in May I think, to show a sequence of sequences to Tom Woll—I don't think I want to, though would, do the *LD/ED* by itself. Am I home? A lovely day. I'm a lucky man.

.... Just read the April 27, 1978 entry. A year ago. I'm a little closer to becoming the spirit I want to be. Will now read the 4/28/78 one again! It makes me happy, now, to read this one.... I should be able to call my own shots. I've been getting <u>much</u> better. After tomorrow, <u>months</u> away from "the circuit." I have a couple of weeks to go before I can really begin my writing routine, but the ash buds are slow coming, too, & we'll move in back here together.

5/3/79

And I am back from Fredonia. And I have taught (today) my last class until September—a fine 1½ hrs. on Whitman. A pile of papers & journals, and then my vacation will begin.

Piccione & Poulin mistreat students to such an extent that they make me sick. They themselves are sick, as many students around here know. I want distance from them, & lately there pretty much <u>has</u> been adequate distance, and the summer will, hopefully, increase it.

Went to MCC last evening to hear & see Stan Plumly. He's a good old boy, was happy to see me, too. He's full of shit in many lovable ways, but he's a <u>friend</u>, and I care for him, & like the way he reads. He'll be at Houston in the fall, at Ann Arbor in the summer.

So nice back here. Will spend <u>long</u> hours reading & writing. Have the books *The Third Reich of Dreams* & *New Lives* here—picked them up on remainder. Have more feelings about the Holocaust that want saying.

Sort of a disappointing report on *Swastika* sales today. The $ is nothing, but I want that 3,500 printing exhausted so that I can talk them into a paperback. No hurry, I guess, and, as usual, reports are slow & the book has probably sold several hundred more copies. $189 royalty check, which ain't hay.

So peaceful & beautiful back here.

Poulin called tonight, but Han fended him off. I'm strong now—the fuck himself doesn't bother me: it's the terrible disservice he does to his students.

I don't quite understand what it means, but Archie MacLeish sent a note to me from John Cheever to him saying that my name wd. go on the list for the Order of Merit or Award of Merit for the (is it?) American Academy, & that Wm. Meredith agreed. Could be something, & may not be, but I'm warmed & thankful.... Wish copies of *Light* would arrive.

5/5/79

Got the lawnmower going with Billy—he mowed the front—and walked the property with him and straightened a few trees, but mostly I've been reading papers & journals. A ways to go yet, but the end is almost in sight. I hope to turn in grades end of next week, and be free, to till for the garden & to work on my poems and things. I'm glad that it's still cool & a bit too wet to get too serious.... Cold out already now (at six o'clock) but this cabin is nice & warm, without the heater, holding on to the day's sunlight. It hasn't disappeared from view yet, except in the back. The ash trees leaf late, but there's a green tinge on everything, and I like the hovering inevitability of my cabin's disappearance.

5/6/79

Reading papers all day. A pleasure to read the good journals, and physical pain, aggravation, anger to read the lazy or deceitful ones. And all sorts of problems as I bend this way and that with individual cases. I'm nearing the end--2½ more journals here, & a couple late, & a couple freshman research papers, and that's going to be about it. I could have promised away my whole summer with incompletes & individual meetings, etc., etc., but I've kept it clear & would be kicking myself if I hadn't.... Han nearing the end with her paper, too.

Picked up Billy at Danny's at midnight, and when we got home he threw up, was very sick, & said he'd been drinking--1½ beers. He's been grounded for a couple weeks. He feels badly about the whole thing & says it won't happen again. He's a good boy, the best possible son.... And Kristen had such a good weekend.

I'm anxious for copies of *Light* to arrive. Must get it to MacLeish, Wilbur, etc. Gave my one hardback to Stan, & am anxious to have one for the cabin, too.

Cold again today, but 70° tomorrow, we hear.

Oh, I'm close to being a full-time gardener & writer. Have one or two lit-er-ar-y projects—Mss. to read for Illinois, stuff for *Contemporary Poets*—and then I'll be free to spend much time back here, much time.

Ash leaves are afraid to take a chance on the weather. I so much look forward to reading some new books back here, too, during warm summer evenings....

Will play ball tomorrow—after dropping off many journals in my office.

Campus is moody when school is closing. Hartwell echoes, & seems dark.

5/8/79

I've made it. One missing journal, and then the grades are ready to go in.... It's about 85° outside, & too hot in here, but I want to feel this heat. I've just opened the windows & the place is airing out beautifully. How lucky can I be? Now I am sitting in perfect comfort back here where a year ago I stood dreaming of a little place like this.

Am meeting Rod & Greg for drinks tonight in celebration of year's end.

Also have Bellow's *To Jerusalem* back here, and will read.

First real green tinge on the ash trees. No more reversals. The winter is broken at last!

5/9/79

    Grades turned in. That's it.
    Hot day. Too hot to mow or begin garden. Will relax, read, goof around.
    Got $100 from the Whitman House people today. Thanks, Walt.
    Ken Venick's thesis about taken care of. Need Tony's signature.
    Went out drinking with Parshall & Fitz Gerald last night. Fun. Much bullshit. Enough. Now home for a good long time.... Must do St. James Press thing. Did Illinois Press report on Bellamy volume. Played their game & have $75 coming.
    Dropped off old Ford at garage for tire-changing, oil-change, tune-up. Will pick up later.
    Han had long talk with Irma about various problems. I wrote a good letter to Mirko. Miss him. Look forward to seeing him.... Helen leaving for Greece today. Manny juggling & juggling things as time for his trip comes. So, friends are gone or going. It will be a long & hot & probably boring summer before it's done. Wonderful. Look forward to school in the fall, or will, but now, oh, I need long periods back here, need to fiddle with the book for Croissant, etc., etc.
    Reading *To Jerusalem and Back* now.
    Wrote Stan Rubin a letter after getting his fine one from San Francisco.
    Birdsong all around me, & the air getting greener by the hour. Put screens in door yesterday, & took air conditioner cover off. Once the leaves are out fully around here, the late afternoon sun, very hot yesterday, will be filtered. Cabin direction perfect, & my reading corner.

5/10/79

    I'm tired, but the time I've waited for is here. It's 8:30 on a beautiful cool-to-muggy morning. Noises of commerce in the distance, lawn-mowing, road-crews. Back here there is much bird-song, and the folks in back actually have a rooster that celebrates the morning. Leaves are still unfurling. Our back meadow is a carpet of dandelions. We have a lot in this little space.
    Saw "The Deer Hunter" last night. Close to a great movie—I choked up at some of the wedding scenes, the friendship & small-Pennsylvania-ethnic-friendship scenes—but it's too "fantastic."
    Such fatigue sets in at the end of the semester. I just sit here dazed these days.
    The temperature back here now seems to me to be perfect. I have two screened windows open. No thought of heater or air conditioner.... I wonder if I'll ever do a spring or fall sequence of tiny poems.
    Well, I'll read, or fool with a poem.

5/11/79

    A perfect morning. Getting hot. I'm back here sipping coffee, listening to the birds & watching them zip by my windows. Day by day the ash leaves unfold and grow.
    I can't seem to get at desk work, letters & such. Don't care. Just a few things I <u>must</u> do, like write old Archie a letter. It will be a while before my copies of *Light* arrive & I can get them into the mail like long letters.
    Dropped Duane Schneider a note saying I'd send out the Mss. in a few days.
    Han & Boo taking Sandi to lunch today—Sandi leaving for Greece very soon.
    Got much mowing done yesterday after starting the mower miraculously. So I can relax about this for a week, and try to get the mower's recoil fixed soon. I hate mowing the rich clover & dandelions back here, and wouldn't, except for Han. We'll compromise, & I'll let part of it alone.
    Finished Peter Davison's *Half Remembered*.
    Won't play basketball today. Will Monday. Had some good games yesterday.
    There's an auction tomorrow morning in Clarendon, "many books," and I look forward. Haven't been to one in a long time.
    Haven't heard from Bill Ewert in a while, since my trip. I'm sure he's making arrangements for the first sections of *Chestnut Rain*.

.... Later.... There's no question but that I'm still tired from the semester. I'm mentally washed out from all the papers & journals. I just went over *The Sunflower Parables*, and couldn't focus very well, couldn't get involved. There's still a yawn in back of my throat & behind my eyes.... Tonight there's a playoff basketball game on TV.... I'll watch.

For a couple hours now—as it was here yesterday—a bumblebee has been chewing wood above the big window outside. He makes tiny creaking sounds. He's upside down, working like hell.... And I stared before at a male red-wing, about fifty feet away, and singing/warning. His sound was something like *pou-pou-pourrii, pou-pou-pourrii*, and he kept turning on his branch so that he sounded out his territorial claim (if that was what it was) in all directions.

Sun., 13th

8:30. So nice back here in the last light. Wonderful day today. Went over the Mss. for Schneider, dropped a poem, changed title to *The City Parables*, wrote a little poem that may be called "The Catbird," worked outside 2-3 hrs. digging around the garden, expanding it, getting it ready to till. Planted the lovely flowering crab that Han bought.... Will watch a film this evening, & type over a few pages of *The City* ... & get it ready for the mail. This is the balance of poetry & outdoor work that I love & need. Han <u>happy</u> again now that her last paper is turned in.... I see that same plant outside that led to my poem about "which way the root & which the tip of the bramble" this winter, when it was half buried in snow. And now, half buried in weeds & other bushes, I still can't tell.... Minute by minute now as I write the light leaves.

5/14/79

Came out here this morning, too, & now it's mid-afternoon. Have been reading *New Lives*. Powerful book.... Have several poems to do another draft of.... Sent off *The City Parables* to Duane at last.... Played ball today—ankle sore.... Hardback copies of *Light* (not the boxed specials) finally arrived. I'll send some out, or package them up, this evening.... Billy has a golf match today, & Han has a softball scrimmage. I'll dig for an hour or two, and keep working toward getting the garden ready.... It's perfect back here. How did I get to be this lucky?... Once the garden is in, etc., I'll spend <u>much</u> time back here.

5/16/79

Played ball yesterday, and then worked hard mowing, and spading the garden, and then Ken Venick came over and stayed late. Today I'll work back here & then do some tilling (if the machine starts & my muscles hold out). Tomorrow we'll drive to Forestville for Mrs. Waxham's funeral. That good woman was very dear to Han for years. One of the last of the farm women. So, tomorrow we'll see Han's Mom & Pop, too. A return

I'm pretty much at ease. Have written "The Hair: Jacob Korman's Story" and "Dark in the Reich of the Blond." And my "Catbird" poem. Once the garden is in & my mower is fixed so that I can depend on it, I'll have a summer of writing.

Letter from Martin Booth, who will unload himself on Bill Ewert for a couple of weeks in July. I have a hunch they'll want to visit here, too.... I've many letters to answer on my desk, and will. I'm close to clearing away.

5/18/79

An extremely tiring day yesterday. I hope to write a poem about Mrs. Waxham's funeral.

This morning I slept until past 10:30, woke up with that feeling of deep calm in my lungs that comes to me only a couple times a month after deep sleep. Poetry was on my mind. I felt clear. And then like an ass I put the phone on the hook & right away got a call from Henry Bretton. Hard to ignore him. I said "no" again to the SUNY Press reading thing, etc. Well, but now I'm back here where I belong and plan to spend all afternoon here & till in the early evening, & then come back again.

Much good news. Checks & books coming in. I'll stop writing here & have coffee & be <u>glad</u> back here for this peaceful & beautiful place.

5/20/79

A perfect morning back here. My throat tightens when I think of how lucky I am, after years of tension trying to find a good place to write.... Yesterday evening Han and I sat back here and a scarlet tanager came close. And I've seen several warblers, hard to tell apart. Birds weaving past all the time, & the mewling of nestlings right behind the cabin.

I've written to Bill Ewert saying yes, let's go with the 5-volume *Chestnut Rain*. And I've touched up the preface. Exciting, and little pressure on me, especially if I have a good summer & begin to draft the one long section I yet want to do. Smaller sections will fall into place by themselves.

Just about finished "The Host" yesterday. It may be that eventually I'll add some good poems to *The City Parables* for a sort of miscellaneous book, the closest to *Depth of Field*, since I began.... Gulp, so many poems & projects that it's almost unsettling. Still want to do something with *Evening Dawning*.

Vanguard is actually sending me 250 remaindered Oates books (5 titles) @ 40¢ each, or a total of a hundred bucks! I'll use them for gifts & trades for years.... Evelyn sent Kristen a beautiful Brahms clarinet record, too.

Al Studier will rebuild our back porch next month. We're lucky. Only other thing I'd like to do is get a small shed out back over by Wren's for mower, etc.

It's so pretty back here, so downright lovely that it's almost distracting. I will waste my life.

May 21, 1979

It's 8:30 in the morning. It's cool out, and raining, a lush spring rain. The leaves seem to be growing by the second.

Kristen has a dental operation this morning. Han will take her.

Can't believe how much I did yesterday. Wrote drafts of the poems "The Shy Bird" and one about Wenzel on his back in his meadow. Got an idea for one for *CR* on the catbird. (The Wenzel one will be a *CR* section, too). Even retyped the preface for *The Snow Hen* for Bill Ewert. I feel ready to roll with that 5-volume project now. Even finished "The Host," I think. Even wrote Vince, and sent poems to *Upstate*. Even did some garden work. It's the being free from school that does it, and having this place, and having *Light* behind me.

Han got in her strawberry plants yesterday.... Wednesday she'll be 39. Kristen picked up a $39 gift certificate for me to give Han from Frieda Weber's. Next year, as a joke, I'll get her another $39 one.

Rain. Not even the sound of a mower anywhere.

I've been reading *Local Lives* back here. It may have set me off on my own track once or twice.

May 22, 1979

I've been working on "The Psalm." It's going to be a good one. My stanza form of lengthening & shortening lines is complicating it for me. I have to get its reading rhythms right. When <u>I</u> begin a line with "will", say, or "we"—a helping verb or a pronoun, when I read it/feel it, I stress that syllable, for many reasons, but because of the power of line beginning. And this is why I don't like lines to begin with a preposition, e.g.

Anyway, "The Psalm" is about, in part, time. Again it comes out of my feeling, I suppose, that what poems do, what they are are spans of timelessness, of even stopped time, that poetry gives us what life does not, a time warp, a relief from the inexorable <u>passing</u> of this palpable substance time. It may be that we can only be happy in the acceptance of a fast-flowing, changing nature. <u>Still</u>, to appreciate the beauty of this entity, maybe, the poem can stop it, so that we can see it, so that we know the beauty of the billions of scintillations in nature around & within us. And this, I think, is my answer to this rage against "anthology pieces" by the Beats, & one part of an answer to all these poems "in process," these poems even <u>dated</u> (for chrissakes) by their authors to show a consciousness growing, part of the flow. Fuck that. And something important about the moral nature of poetry in the appreciation, without the destruction, of fast-moving nature is caught in "The Cardinal," e.g.

And at the root of this is my feeling that that beautiful complexity out there, that harmony (and maybe in here, inside (another decade's, lifetime's work)) is enough, will serve for happiness. It won't do any good to feel any other way, anyway, but I believe I do happen to feel this way. And often my poems want to stop for a second that beautiful blur. And why not?

...

It is now about four in the afternoon. I wrote the above, and then was relaxing, dreaming out the window, when Tony Piccione came back here with Jeff Schiff, and that was nice, but, and then I had to drive Poulin to the airport, & then Andrews had called & I called him & then post office & then dropping Billy off at a golf course, etc. So, the day became very nervous ... but at least I had the time back here this morning. People will interrupt me back here very seldom, I'm sure.

Jeff leaves tomorrow. I might go out to Tony's tonight for a while.

May 23, 1979

1:00 in the afternoon. I've just come back here for a minute. Have been keeping Kristen company. Maybe she can to to school tomorrow. Han went to sewing & lunch, this afternoon will go around with real estate woman to see possible places for her mother, tonight will have a softball game. This is not an easy age as men get used to liberated women. I want so badly, now, to spend great blocks of time back here.... Today is Han's birthday. I still love her. Very often lately she has felt depressed, too, & loses herself in many frenetic activities, and many unnecessary ones. Then, because she's sad, I'm thrown way out of whack. I just want to try to write, & begin to feel sorry for myself because of things that distract me. But all this life, & truth, the real world, no doubt tempers the poems I do write in a good way. There should still be some good long weeks back here this summer.

The specials of *Light* arrived today, and I'll be mailing them out. The slipcase is a cheap one, but, all in all, *Light* is a handsome production. Official publication is July 2, they tell me. I'm hoping for a little fuss about it, maybe especially in *Newsday*, so that it will sell. Have I mentioned here that Tom Woll said that the *Times* Island section will print "The Traffic," and maybe another, this coming Sunday?

It's in the 60's today. Wonderful weather lately.

Went out to Tony's last evening with Venick for an hour. Jeff left this morning.

Should I give Bill Andrews "The Bees" for a pamphlet? I've been working the poem over. It may be a good one.

May 24, 1979

About 50° out, & drizzle. I have the heater on, to take the chill off. Didn't think I'd need it this time of year.

Cashed a couple of readings checks. Han & I will go to Harris Seeds tomorrow. Mailed out about a dozen copies of *Light*, so all that is about done with. And played ball today, & felt pretty good.

Kristen much better today, though still swollen.

I've been sitting here just daydreaming. Would like to think of a few things to finish this page.

Look forward to the arrival of the 250 Oates remainders from Vanguard.

I've decided on the little tool shed that I'll buy soon. Chase-Pitkin has it. With that, and with the rebuilt porch, we'll be done around here!

May 25, 1979

Morning. Cold again, raining. I have the heater on again to take off the chill, as Mom & Pop used to say.

Lush green back here now, everything dripping.

Drafted part of a piece on a cross-section of chestnut yesterday.... I know that what I want to do, maybe June 1, is to get down to serious reading & drafting for the long section. I'll want no other distractions, then, &

will want to work 8-10 hrs. a day for a few weeks on end, engrossing myself in the poem, only *The Chestnut Rain*. After that, polishing individual sections, I can drag my feet for a long time. That reading will lead to a few other, smaller sections, too.... Maybe I'll finish *Local Lives* this weekend, and then get down to it.

May 26, 1979

Cold & dreary today, but wonderful back here.... Kids are in the house, Han is out getting our meat order at the butcher's, the world is too wet for me to work outside.

A sudden call from Mirko yesterday, and he's home for a couple of weeks. I went to the Rochester airport to pick him up, but he ended up in Buffalo, but it was an experience for me to enter the world of the "city" again for an hour.... Mirko looks good.

Long talk with Bill Ewert yesterday. Hard to believe, but we're going ahead with six volumes, the five *CR* ones and, I think, *Evening Dawning*. Wow! Years ago I so much wanted a small press to do some things, and Ernie came into my life luckily, and now Bill Ewert, who knows, it seems, all the small presses in America, has come along. A very exciting time to look forward to. Imagine five small volumes of *CR* in a slipcase!... Now that Ernie is off his feet for a while, Bill might arrange for "The Snow Hen" Christmas card. I'm a lucky man. And poems & fragments of poems keep coming. I want to send some things out, including sections of *CR*. I keep thinking that *APR* gets a much bigger audience than *Poetry*, and should try there, but then realize that people who read *APR* don't buy books anyway, so what's the difference. I am still, I guess, a jumble of conflicting desires, wanting to mind my own business & write, wanting to impress the locals (hell, it's true that I don't care if nobody in California has heard of me) by being on the cover of *APR*, or some such thing.

Letters from Vince Clemente & from Snodgrass today.

I carried the typewriter out here yesterday for the first time, & will type some poems up again today. "Evening Dawning" ready to go to Bill Ewert & to a magazine. And "Catbird" and "The Shy Bird."... I woke up this morning looking for the Sunday paper, though it's Saturday. Feel as though I have an extra day.

May 27, 1979

Have thought <u>hard</u> for a few days about whether or not to send <u>any</u> sections of *CR* to magazines. Decided, for a dozen reasons, <u>not</u> to. It will cost me a little money & some publicity—I think Nims at *Poetry* would have taken some—but this way I <u>almost</u> can mind my business completely, & work on the poem (and not even send out my own free copies), & still look forward to a handsome set of books that Bill Ewert will have published. I'll be glad I did it this way.

Mom called to say that "The Traffic" <u>is</u> in the *Times* Island section today.

I've just wandered around sticking in some giant sunflower seeds here & there, including 6 or 8 around the cabin. Will love watching what happens. Incredible numbers of mosquitoes around, & this wet weather will bring on zillions more. But, I read this morning, they're helpful in pollinating smaller grasses & meadow flowers. May their tribes increase.

I found a dead catbird beside the cabin. Yes, I do see the rusty tailfeathers, or rumpfeathers. Buried it with some sunflower seeds.

Such a still afternoon, and overcast right now. I feel on the verge of the flowing, quatrained poem, one with touches of dusky colors, I want to write.

May 28, 1979

This morning I've cleared away the table out here, and have been reading *CR* again, getting a sense of it, making a tiny change here & there in completed sections. Reading 1-7, *The Snow Hen*, I feel the unity, the introduction of themes that will be with me. I think my own pace will be this: to wait until the completed volume is in front of me, to stare at it for a few days, and then to send the next volume, *The Ewe's Song*, to Bill. This will slow the whole thing down nicely. I feel at ease—several fine drafted sections to work on. I need long hours with the poem if I'm going to do a good job of entering it & having it before going on. It has to stop somewhere—say at 35 sections, & this is another reason that this 5 volume Ewert project is a good idea. When he has the prospectus ready, I'll send him a long list of all possibilities, and then back away completely, & he can do the selling. I will send my free copies to only 3 or 4 people. I have to make *CR* my best book.

May 29, 1979

A glum day again, but radiant because I am at ease. Played ball again. Have puttered & read back here. I keep going over the first 15 sections of *CR*, getting senses of how it holds together.... Nothing much new.... I wait for the Oates books to arrive. Made a makeshift bookcase in a corner of my study to hold maybe ¼ of them. It's going to be <u>fun</u> to have them.... I'm still reading *Local Lives*.... Kristen getting her stitches out today.... Letter from Norbert. They're adopting a child, a Colombian child.... Postcard from Sandi Piccione from Greece.... Told Winnick I'd help him move tomorrow. Will spend the morning back here & then help out after lunch, I think.... Han teaching these days, but only for two weeks this summer....

May 30, 1979

If the solar system isn't careful, a little bit of sunshine is going to spill into my cabin this morning.

Took Billy practice driving a little yesterday after supper. I like being older, going through the cycle. I will enjoy being a grandfather, too. Being young—there were always so many intense pressures.... Billy and Kristen—they're perfect kids, and doing beautifully, getting through hard times (Kristen with her teeth, Billy with his leg), adjusting, having <u>fun</u> in their lives.

Out here, for the rest of the summer, it's going to be *The Chestnut Rain*. My decision <u>not</u> to send sections to magazines was the right one. No fuss & bother & distraction & diffusion. And the 5-volume scheme with Ewert is the right one. "Song of Myself" may be too long, & my poem has to end somewhere, & the 35 section (approximately) scheme feels right. Everything about the whole limited-edition-first project seems right.

May 31, 1979

I've made the start on the long "that," "how," "when," "why," catalogue section. Am set now to read the farm journals & remember & jot down lines. Should end up with wonderfully long & raw sections for working over & over for about a year. Feel good right now about the whole project. The <u>language</u> of the whole long section has to be interesting, always, and sometimes charged.

Began a section yesterday about being in the room where Whitman was born.

Sunshine today, at last. I'll play ball, and then hope to get the mower started and running all day before rains, we hear, tomorrow.

June 1, 1979

Perfect morning. Will spend much time out here today.

Drafted a nice 6-line "muse" section for *CR* yesterday. Will come at the end of one of the books.... Letter from Ernie with Rook Press close-out sheet. I've sent a check for 20 copies of *Lord Dragonfly* & 15 of *XVII Machines*, all @$1.20. They make nice gifts. He sounds better, & was on the phone with Bill Ewert, discussing projects.

My skin tingles a little. There's a mosquito or two loose in here—one or two always come in when I do. They've never been as thick as this year. Standing water everywhere.

An auction this evening. Hope at least one of the books is a good one. Guess I'll have to shave today, too, for a change.

I planted a pussy willow about 20 feet from the cabin, toward Moshers, yesterday, and Han put in, below my picture window, one or two of those tiger lilies I like so much. They are part of my old Island.

... [later, 8 p.m.] ... It turned into quite a day. The hassle with Patti Ross on the phone & turning down another committee; then I tried to finish raking the garden & ran out of time; this evening Han & I went to an auction, & were joined at home later by Irma & Mirko, great people.... Smelled another old barn. No smell like it. I always think of & remember catching mice when I smell that old straw & manure & dust & dry boards smell.

... a perfect evening, but I'll only sit out here an hour & then watch the 5th Seattle/Washington NBA game. It might be the last one, alas.

Lovely note from Archie today about *Light*.

Another auction tomorrow morning. I'll take a quick look for books.

6/4/79

One of those days suddenly, almost bafflingly sad for me. Beautiful weather, and Billy & I did put in the corn this morning, and I did make a start on what could turn out to be a good Brockport poem.... I was out of sorts, to begin with, when a kid I'm not crazy about was suddenly staying overnight, a boorish kid, and he kept me up until 4 in the morning—so, that was one thing, and I yelled at poor Billy this morning. But then, just as I came back to my cabin, Mosher started mowing the closest spot to me he could, and I hated on such a perfect morning to close the door & windows & turn on the fan on the air conditioner to drown him out, so I figured what the hell, Sunday morning, I'll do some garden work myself, & did. But then, at 1:30, the minute I came back here, he began mowing in the same spot again. I did use the fan, but I was glum. I've become, no doubt, more sensitive to noise than anyone else in town, & become frustrated. Right now, 9:30, it's quiet, except for distant dogs & traffic.... But all of this doesn't explain my melancholy. Maybe it's that I can't get into a work routine: tomorrow the lumber for the back porch will be delivered, & Al Studier will be banging & sawing back there for a week or two, & I'll have to help here & there. There's <u>always</u> something. Of <u>course</u> life is like this, but still I should be able to find a few clear weeks just to work back here two or 3 stretches a day. I'll come back here tomorrow morning, but with too much on my mind? Fuck it. I'll work until 11 or so & then go play basketball.... And now I can't find my pen.... This is all petty, but it's true that good work takes quiet, or, at least, the kind of work <u>I</u> want to do takes quiet.... More beautiful here in the trees now, but quieter in winter. But things will still settle down before the whole summer—not yet begun!—runs through the glass.... Well, enough of that. It's hard to grow up.

Reading of those pamphlets is going well, & my scheme for the section they'll go into is a good one.

I've got a few bits of busywork to take care of inside on my desk—recommendations, etc., & will get to them.

How well off I am. I don't have a <u>job</u> this summer.... The canal bridge just rang. My new poem is so far titled "1829-1979: The Bells."

Cleaned out here today—vacuumed. And sprayed the sills to keep out ants.

Finished *Local Lives*.

My mother called while I was outside & talked to Kristen. The demonstration against the Shoreham Nuclear Plant may have been a big one & may be in the news tonight. I hope the Island people can stop that project.

Quiet back here now, a moth or two against the screens. Everything is all right.... Ha, come to think of it, some of the distraction seems more acute now than in the past, though I didn't have a cabin & office & study in the past as I do now, because I'm tangled up with the beast known as "a long poem"!

6/5/79

I've had a fine morning, sipping tea, doing a little with *CR*, working on my new Brockport poem, writing a letter to Wm. Stafford. Got out here before eight. Now, at 10:30, Al Studier is banging away at our house/porch at sufficient distance so that the sounds are muffled back here. I'm relaxed again. Even pissed out my cabin door so I wouldn't have to go into the house & talk to Al & worry about a lumber delivery, etc., etc. Now, in a half hour or so, I'll go in and shave & then leave for the gym.

Invited Stafford to stay here between his Buffalo & Rochester stints next month. It will be a happy time if he does—I think he'd like to—and if he doesn't I'll see him in Rochester.

Light in the trees all around me, but the cabin beautifully shaded.... Again it's true that once I work for a solid hour or two, I'm relaxed after that.

[Later] ... Had a good workout. My team won 3 out of 4 games.... Fine letter from Dick Wilbur today, and a collector's item from Wm. Stafford, and other nice things—a Braille *Lord Dragonfly* from a student of Vince's. And it must be about 75° out, and sunny. Al is making progress on the porch. The treated lumber is handsome & this time will last for decades. All's right with the world.

6/6/79

10 a.m.—have just worked a couple of hours on a section of *CR* begun a year ago, one about the dusty miller plant holding the sandgrains in. Made good progress. It's a matter, again, of wanting easy-to-follow rhythms, & convincing ones.

It has started to rain, is beautiful back here, cool—I have put on the flannel shirt I keep back here. Only thing on my mind is Al Studier working by the house, probably in a hurry now to close up the hole, the repair job where the side of the house had rotted where the old porch was attached.... How could there not always be something? But this has been, again, a fine morning.... I look forward to playing ball again, later.

Dave Smith called yesterday to praise *Light* & say he was going to review it in *APR*, & ask if I wanted to teach at Utah for a year. He called the book a "magnificent achievement." I'm awkward on the phone, and he was so smooth—how say anything like that without embarrassment. I guess I don't know him very well, but I'm selfishly <u>glad</u> for any attention.... Will write Tom Woll about an ad for *APR*, I think.... I keep skimming *Light*: I need to get <u>more</u> into it!

Next day....

Maybe my dates have been off again. Today, Wednesday, may be the 6th?

It's only nine in the morning, but I've had a good session already with the poem I've called "The Bark." Sometimes I'm excited by *CR*, by the body it will eventually have. It's <u>good</u>, I believe.... I have other leads to follow into other sections, and also will keep reading & making notes toward the long section. All in all, the scheme with Bill will give me plenty of time. *Light* will hold me, hopefully, in good stead for a while. Meaning?

There's a small auction this evening just outside of town—mainly tools & farm machinery. I'll take it in.

Will try, now, to have a couple more good hours back here before I head to the house & keep Al Studier company.

Buttercups blooming around the cabin. Always something.

June 7, 1979

Thursday. It has been a good day. This morning I finished the new Brockport poem.... I see lines of ants, & will pause to spray.... Did.... Should spray around the whole building, I guess.

Al Studier has finished all but the stair to the back porch. A fine, solid job. He won't be coming over tomorrow morning, so I'll be back here with a clear mind.

Serendipity Catalogue #38 (fiction of the 60s) came today, & I've had fun with my collection. $22.50 for Gardner's *The Crow*! He must have gotten it from Sipper or Lepper.

Muggy, again, after a too-brief shower.... The mosquitoes are elephants.

Played ball, & had fun, though there are always minor disputes. Soon, maybe, I'll quit for the summer. It will be hard getting back in shape in the fall, though.

Nice letters from Tom DeLigio & Vince.

Quick trip to an auction this evening. Nothing.

Sandi Piccione home from Greece. Called this evening. Said Mike Waters might be around this weekend.... It's been peaceful here, without Al Poulin & Tony et. al. around.... Mirko leaves on the 10th again, & we'll probably get together with them once more. In the fall, hopefully, there will be some good poker games again, when the old gang is back together. Ed Culbertson has moved south, but Ed Kumar will be a player to join the usual 5 or 6.

6/8/79

Raining. I have the door open to the screen door, and one of the windows open. Of all the times I've been back here, this is the most perfect, lush green & private & quiet except for rain and birdsong. It's 8:00 a.m. I'll just dream & write & read the day away.

[afternoon] This morning I saw a large bird—at first I thought it was a gull or maybe some kind of hawk—sweeping this way erratically. It came close and stood in a tree in the neighbor's lot behind me, apparently. He made one loud squawking note about every second.... This afternoon, back here again reading a farm journal. I heard the loud squawk again, but this time over by Wicks, just past our garden. I went over there quietly, and got very close, got a good look at it. Now, I see from my guide, it is a flicker, the first one I've identified. It is described as having an undulating flight. And the one I saw was a male, with a bar of red behind its head. It had the dark crescent across the breast, to me the most noticeable feature.... It almost seemed to be distressed, maybe lost. A flicker, the third kind of woodpecker we've seen around here....

Just about finished a beauty of a section for *CR* this morning, the one on the cross section that I'd half-drafted a week or two ago. It works in lots of ways.

6/9/79

It's only 8:30 in the morning, and I've been out here an hour-and-a-half after a good sleep. Have gone over more farm journals, getting some possible lines down on my catalogue sheets. It will actually be fun, eventually, to work those lines and that whole section into shape.... And getting some serious "entering" done this morning will relax me for the whole day, I know.... I even look forward to seeing the Piccones, maybe Mike & Robin, maybe Irma & Mirko, later.... Will stay out here, now, 2-3 more hours.

One of the trees I keep a close watch on is the Colorado blue spruce about 15 feet past my big window. Put it in last fall, I believe. Was worried about it, but now see its new growth pushing its little brown caps off. It's a beauty, and song sparrows have a nest in it, though it's only about 4 feet high, but it's thick & its needles sharp & protective.

The weather is such, shower & sun & shower & sun, that everything grows visibly. On the spur of the moment last evening, I got out & did all the mowing. Am glad I did. And am glad I've left the meadow I have in strips along the back. The clover & buttercups et. al. are having a great year.... Only one acre. I wish more land were available around me. I'd sell my whole library to buy it.

Sunday, June 10th, 1979

Mirko leaves today for a couple months in the Soviet Union, this time to do some traveling out of Moscow. I sent along a copy of *Swastika* for him to give to Voznesensky, if he can get it through—Mirko is sure that the box of books we gave Andrei here at Brockport will never reach him.... Also gave Mirko five copies of *Lord Dragonfly* to use as gifts. Han & I stopped out there last evening for a half hour to say goodbye. Irma & Katja not terribly happy about the whole thing.

I sat back here reading for a half hour, wanting to do without the air conditioner, but it got very stuffy & I closed the windows & door & now have it on low. I can breathe deeply now. Cool air is such a luxury. Is it a sin to be this comfortable?

We could use some rain today, and may get it.

I watched a damselfly land on the tip of an ash leaf, and then fly maybe five feet away, & come back to the same exact leaf tip again, & keep doing this. I'll check the leaf later for eggs.... And I read that soon after the song sparrow hatches her clutch of eggs & the babies are out of the nest, she'll lay more eggs.... My knowledge of all these processes is very imprecise, but back of my brain are precise colors & textures, & sometimes these find words & rhythms.... I'm watching a morning glory climbing the ash right in front of me—it's been circling upward quickly this past week.... The wild blackberries about fifty feet away are blooming.

June 12, 1979

    Good day yesterday. Worked back here, then played ball (as I will today, I guess), then had lunch with Picciones & Boo & the Waters at Casey's. Then a short gathering at Picciones last evening. Han & I came home <u>tired</u>, but we had a nice time & peaceful drive.... Note from Billy that he'd shot 79 & his team had won. Quite a team.... Invitation to read at Library of Congress with Peter Viereck on Nov. 5th for $1,000! Good old William Meredith. That's his answer to the copy of *Light* I sent him. Also in the mail an answer from the fellow at Lordly & Dame—I wrote him in December—who <u>will</u> take me on as one of the poets he'll arrange readings for. I'll have to think this all over again.... Mike Waters seems fine, settling in at his school. BOA will publish his next book, & he'll meet with Al about this today.... cool back here, heater on to take off chill, but a perfect morning.

June 13, 1979

    Managed to mow the ditch just now, no easy job the first or second time each spring.... About the only constructive thing I've done today. Did hang up a couple of nature/pastoral/sheep scenes bought at auction last evening—hung them in my office. And did mail out a few more copies of *Light*: Schiff, Gold, Stafford, Zimmer, Gregor. That about takes care of that. Will save one for Turco, & others for folks like him who give me their things.... Letter from (rather card from) Joyce today saying thanks for *Light*.... Kept rewriting the first stanza of my song sparrow poem, looking for the line rhythms it wants. Don't know.... Will go briefly to another auction tonight, just a few miles from here.... Will get up early tomorrow morning & put in some solid hrs. back here before basketball, which was fun again yesterday & the day before.

June 14, 1979

    I just finished working for about an hour-and-a-half on my song-sparrow poem. It could end up being a good one. It's at that happy stage, in any case, where I know it will be finished, will be a part of the poem. Lots of things emerging in it—the speaker mentions the knot of chestnut almost offhandedly, but then in the end will return to it as a central theme.... The bringing in of the cabin, though, will be a problem for *CR*—so far, for better or worse, there is no such grounding. Maybe I can prepare for it with a line or two in the "light" section?... A few days ago, finding a third source referring to the chestnut as a ghost, I thought maybe of an "Epilogue" called "The Ghost"—I like the idea. I like the whole traditional music of muse, and "marrow," & epilogue, etc.... I'm about ready to sit down & take another batch of notes from farm journals I've gone through.... And from *Whose Woods These Are*, which will open up some things.
    Perfect here now. Han & kids in school, beautiful weather, no worries, pleasant anticipation of basketball in a couple hours, not even any mowers at work. Only birdsong. How busy the rest of the world is. Bill, never complain about this almost anonymous work you're doing. You could not have a better life. You suspect you're doing something that matters, anyway. And you are among trees & birds in a little cabin built by a friend & by a brother & your father. And your whole being is being preserved in books. And you are loved, and love.
    I keep thinking of the traffic, now, in Brockport, in NYC, the trains, the airports at Rochester & Chicago & Seattle. All of that, of course, through the air & rain, is touching this acre every day, as it touches me, and everything I write. I hope I have decades more, here, on this acre, & someone—maybe a grandchild?—has this cabin after I'm dead.

June 15, 1979

    It's about noon. I'm back here just to relax after a hectic morning. At 8:30 the nine boxes of Oates books came. A pleasure to have them. I unpacked & stacked. *Marriages & Infidelities* is not a first, but the others are, except for a few copies of *Do With Me What You Will*. Gifts & trades for years.... Then Monika Andrews dropped by with a copy of *Light* to inscribe for Bill.... Then Bill Ewert called—he & his family will visit next Friday already! I'll be nervous, but happy about this.... Well, quite a morning.... Hot today, & windy.... All's well.... Bill moving fast, I guess, on *Evening Dawning*. There are to be, he thinks, 76 hardbound copies on special paper, and 200 others. Wonderful....

June 16, 1979

    A lazy Saturday. I decided not to go to either of the auctions. Worked out here on my "Diary Entry: Nocturne" section. If I can get its melody, & its ending, it's going to be a good one.
    Han & Kristen are out shopping & to Kristen's clarinet lesson. Han might buy a small air conditioner, for downstairs, for use especially when she's canning later on in the summer, & making strawberry jam, soon.
    Ken Venick stopped over yesterday evening and we talked for a couple hours. Then Han & I went to see *The China Syndrome*, which was not as exciting as we thought it would be. It was nice to go out, though. It was the film's first night in town, & not many people at the movie—this is a great town when college is out. And the summer sessions have certainly gotten <u>much</u> smaller here recently.... Gave Ken a copy of each Oates title. Fun passing them out.... Will watch some baseball today, & clean up in the yard a little, & maybe turn back to my song sparrows poem this evening. I need a session with it in starlight, in which it is set.

6/17/79

    A fine morning this morning, with Father's Day gifts & love, & I called home. But then I fucked up trying to fix the outside faucet, was fooled, & broke a solder seal on a copper pipe, & we've been without water all day, & I've been depressed, weighed down, again, with another thing going wrong like that. There's always something on the blink—like the furnace in the house right now, though we don't need it. Like the lawn mower's recoil. Like the dryer that was busted, & the fuel line in the car, etc., etc. It hurts, it disturbs my equilibrium, & a day like today is sort of lost. I'm not grown up enough to adjust to these things, I know. But also, somehow, we're involved in a life that can no longer be simple. How to cut ourselves away from these possessions & the constant drain of money? We spend too much & don't get our money's worth. Well, my day, & last evening wrestling the air conditioner in (seeing today, that it will be <u>very</u> hard to oil it once a year, to get inside it) has been a strain. This is all petty & stupid, but also serious. Can't quite grab hold of the problem, & it's not just us, but everyone. Can't go back to the begging bowl & candle, but there must be, will be, some way to simplify. We <u>will</u> get back to one car. And we will get down to one television. So beautiful & simple back here in my cabin, and I don't often enough have the peace of mind to enjoy it. Al Studier is in the house putting in a new coupling, I think. Again I feel stupid, not knowing how to do things, not knowing how things work.... God, what I sound like (am) here, a spoiled American suburbanite worried about oiling an air conditioner when the SALT talks are going on and thousands of refugees are being cast out of Malaysia, & Nicaragua is bloody. I'm such an ass. But I hate needing other people all the time to do these mechanical things. What a fine feeling it would have been for me if I could have done the porch, or fixed the damage I'd done to the plumbing. Well, Han even bought a book. We'll learn to do more such things.
    Present from Han was a framing of *Witness*. It hangs out here now.
    I'm more high strung this year than other years. Swings of elation & sadness. Well.... I needed this place back here. I pull myself together again, talk myself around to being human. I feel better right now.
    Talked to Ernie yesterday. The poor bastard was hospitalized again, is recovering again, spends much of his time in bed. I'll try to write him often this summer.
    I hope to have a good week, working back here in the mornings, playing ball three days, & preparing for the Ewerts in the evenings. Han teaching until Thursday, alas.... Kristen & Billy will be taking their last tests, and getting out of school. They're had fine years.

Our garden doesn't seem to have much zip this year. I've got to water more. The corn seems to be coming best.... So goes another weekend. With luck, I'll have a solid week's work beginning tomorrow, but Al will be fucking around by the porch again, etc., etc., & it goes on like this. But I hope to push all that out of my mind. The damned summer flies by. Slow down, slow down, for the garden's sake along the fence!

6/18/79

An overcast morning. I feel at ease again. The water line fixed by Al, other things in perspective. The root problem remains, of course, but for now the distractions are gone. How to simplify?—to begin with, by needing & wanting less.

I'm ready, again, to add to the catalogue lines of the big section of *CR*. Maybe will wait for a session until after the Ewerts visit. I touched a section here & there this morning, but didn't really enter one. Unwinding, I guess, from yesterday.

My most constant companion back here is that spruce I planted last fall. I keep looking over at it, following the sparrows into and out of it. It's about 5 feet tall now, I guess, and thick with new growth. It has lost its blue tinge, missing something in the soil, but is healthy. It's about 18 feet, I'd guess, from where I sit in my easy chair, & even closer when I sit at the table in front of the window. It won't be as easily buried by snow next winter.

6/19/79

Fine day today. Some solid work out here this morning—on the "notes" to what will be the long catalogue for *CR*, and I drafted a new section, the "tumbleweed" section—then basketball, and now I'm just coasting. A beautiful day, maybe 70-75°, & sunny. Beginning tomorrow, will straighten up here & there & do yard work & generally get ready for the Ewerts' visit. I look forward.... Sunday, we'll have to leave them to go to Kurt's graduation party....

Have been reading some stories, like "Happy Onion" & "The Sacred Marriage" (both very close in theme) in Joyce's *Marriages & Infidelities*. Jesus!

A letter today from a Robert Heyen in Joliet, Illinois, wondering if we're related! We must be. I'll show it to Pop.

The garden is looking better.

End of another page of chestnut paper.

6/20/79

Worked 1½ hrs. taking notes, refining lines, etc., and then, on this perfect morning, took a walk around the property, seeing. The big catalpa over by Moshers is blooming, a few blooms already down. They have a delicate smell, & their white frilled edges are rusted—tiny streaks of purple & yellow inside. Can't be described, of course. It has so many whites, alone.... So much going on—a little of everything here, from meadow with its clover & daisies & grasses, to wetter ground with ferns & different saw grasses. And as one level of weed gives way after blooming, another moves into the light....

Nothing at the auction last night I couldn't live without, but there was a garage sale next door & I bought a beautiful leatherbound 1843 Philadelphia Coleridge for 50¢.

Will stay very busy today—driving kids (must pick up Kristen in Hamlin), cleaning garage, going to post office & bank, etc.

Couldn't sleep well last night. Those thoughts keep coming back, because, it's true, I'm so often lonely around here because Han is so busy. Not just the teaching, but her library board meetings, Twig meetings, softball practices and games, etc., etc. She works hard & gets everything done, but there's not much time for me, and I feel it, & sometimes feel lonely & sorry for myself. I have everything, but sometimes, still, immature as it may be ...

6/23/79

Pshew. The Ewerts just left. I shaved & showered. In an hour we'll leave for Kurt's graduation party.

That fucking Kunstler woke us up early Fri. morning, & dropped in, & I entertained him and said goodbye!, & he dropped in again for hours in the afternoon before Ewerts came, so I was nervous, & then the buzz began. Their kids are nice but a pain in the ass. Mary is quiet & doesn't seem to have much of a personality but is pleasant. Bill is wonderful. We laughed & schemed & talked a blue streak. Christ, he wanted to buy manuscripts & write checks, etc., etc., but I slowed him down. Have sold some things I don't want—to him & to Bert Babcock & to U. of N.H. Library by way of Bill—2 Oates broadsides, etc., and was glad to do it. Sold the Lowell postcard about Frost, too, that I bought for $5 from Ned Grade. I'll get $75 for it! So, fun & profit.... Only regret is that I missed the auction of thousands of books just a mile away.... Ducked in & ducked out of Kunstler's Lift Bridge party.... I actually look forward to all the driving today. The new car is clean & has a full tank of gas.... Oh, the projects Bill & I are scheming....

6/24/79

Fine time at Pat & Wolf's yesterday. I got the prize as the recreation director, Wolf said.... We got home about midnight.... It's afternoon now—I'm back from playing ball, & feel lazy & good.

Fine letter from Norbert, and I called them a little while ago to say thanks and wish them a happy trip. Good friends. They'll spend three weeks in Germany. He's done an effusive essay on me for *Contemporary Poets*. And a letter today from BC Research—guess they'll have an essay on me, with photo & facsimile, etc., in a research book. And Bob Phillips says *PR* will run, now, his review of *Swastika*. And I got the *Newsday* review, which is as nice as could be.... All this attention: now if only *Light* begins to sell a little... Projects on my mind: will begin by sending Ewert "Mantle," for a possible broadside by Rara Avis, again.

6/25/79

One of those mornings when I am content & happily lazy back here, unable or unwilling to push forward on anything, & unvisited by anything new. One or two tiny poems for a spring sequence might have asserted themselves.

Got a holograph of "The Leaves" into the mail for Bill Ewert. Kristen drew two fine chestnut leaves on it. And I got the letter to Jack Hagstrom into the mail. Ewert told me all about him.

The summer begins to feel like a wide space again.... Brockport's International Summer Special Olympics in the news every day now, & the excitement is just beginning. A couple of big sculptures by a Russian are going up over at the college—all sort of a mini-scandal which seems to have been instigated by Mirko!

6/26/79

I've been working, but without much enthusiasm, on "Wenzel's Death." Something has to take hold of the poem at the end. Meanwhile, I'll keep drafting for the right rhythms in the first few stanzas.... I guess I was just extremely hurried, when school was out at last, to get to *CR*, and I did, early mornings when kids & Han went to school. Now I don't feel as driven. Will begin a cycle of reading again, in those bulletins, for the long section.

Upstate called yesterday. They'll use "Carrie White." I hate phone interviews, and what they'll print in the way of a profile will be half-truth & shit, but I tell myself something true, that it doesn't matter to anyone who might see it, it is only a surface matter & folks will be impressed no matter how wrong or stupid or misquoted the thing is.

I'm still excited after Bill Ewert's visit. The man appreciated my collection, & made me feel that my own things are important, even valuable. Digging around last evening, I even found many broadsides I didn't know I had.

It bothers me to see, for a few reasons, *Brockport's Poems* in the Lift Bridge, the only place that has any. Maybe, once and for all today, I'll buy them all out? I'd get my money back, eventually. I will. (I think!)

Gave Billy a ride to his job at the high school this morning. He's becoming a man. What a great son.... Went to Kristen's soccer game yesterday. She did fine. She's a little beauty—had braces put in yesterday, too, as, it seems, have all of her friends. It doesn't interfere with her clarinet-playing. She was worried about this.... She & Han will go strawberry picking today, I think, & Han will do preserves, enough to last a year.

6/27/79

I did buy out *Brockport's Poems*. Cost me $248. This hurt, & bothered me yesterday. Today already my brow clears, and I realize it was smart. Ha, I now have the only copies generally available. I think there's one copy left in back at Lift Bridge. I'll buy that too.

Poulin called up about some scheme to get Logan an NEA grant—Bill Claire, it turns out, is NEA head. So, I anticipate Poulin will & I won't get a $10,000 grant next April. Paranoid? After my argument with his sweetheart Toby Hewitt about the "C" she got in the workshop this spring?

Decided on "From the Ukraine" as a Christmas card, if it's okay with Bill & Ernie.

Went to Han's softball game last evening. They lost.... Now I'll pull in a bit & spend much time back here in the cabin.... Read *CR* this morning, & now have a sense of the opening sections of Book III—so, all is well. I spend about a half-hour reading *CR* before going ahead with any work, it seems.... Despite all the projects in the works (*Evening Dawning* & broadsides & *CR* with Ewert, & Christmas card & maybe *Swastika Prose* with Ernie, & *City Parables* with Schneider), these are all small press things and I can just stay low and mind my business. Will send out very few *Evening Dawning* when it's out.... Basketball today, & maybe an auction this evening.

Fri., 6/28/79

Oh, what swirls of activity around here the past 24 hrs. or so. But I've been ducking back here to read or write a letter.

Bob Koch called yesterday to ask me to conduct a workshop for seventy-five bucks during U. of R's creative writing week. I called back to say no thanks. Then Poulin called to ask me to read, again for $75, in Rochester at some small-press gig next month. Again, no thanks. I'm proud of myself. Usually the phone spooks me into promises I detest. Each thing would have been a good day's pay, but no, no, no, to these sorts of things.

Ernie called, says Rook is "in the black" largely because of me and Bert Babcock, & is aglow with ideas for projects: *Swastika Prose*, *Abortion* as a broadside, *Redwings/Pines* (which I sent him today), & even *The Handbook of Heartbreak*—Jesus, he proposed this as 26 pamphlets! I've told him to slow down, but am pleased Rook will get its second wind.... Lately, I'm not worrying about all these small-press things pouring out (maybe 3 from Ewert & *Chestnut Rain*; 2-3 from Ernie; 1 from Croissant). Fuck it. Let the chips of sales & collectors fall where they may. I'll just write, & see that I believe in the things being published.... Ernie may have even found a better printer. We'll see. I just want to keep my desk & mind cleared for writing, so will continue, this afternoon, writing letters & doing other necessary busywork.... But right now maybe I'll finish Carl Carmer's *Dark Trees To the Wind*....

July 2, 1979

I just realized that today is the official publication date of *Long Island Light*. Congratulations, Bill!

A long, good, generally lazy weekend. I did clear away some of the crap, course outlines & such, on my desk, & finally did write to Charles E. Merrill Co. to see if I could get the last copies of the Roethke profile.

Ernie called to say he'd fly in for a visit on the 17th. I really look forward. We'll exhaust ourselves talking about books, projects.... For a couple of days I've been staring at *The Handbook of Heartbreak* again. I guess I will. In one way, my publishing it will allow in that whole other world, the aesthetic that calls attention to process & creator rather than just relying on its own excellence, and I may be wrong to publish so many pieces that are not very good, but in this case ... Will limit it pretty strictly to 126 or 176, and some of the pieces—D & V—are good & should see light. Am writing an "apology" for it.... I hope Ernie stays healthy now.

July 4, 1979

203rd year. A beautiful day, sunny & about 70°. Today even the sounds of lawn-mowing are pleasant, and neighbors off from work are talking & gardening. Han and I had a cup of coffee on the back porch.

Jerry called. I'll pick up Stafford at his place Saturday. John Nims may be around, too. I'd love to meet him. Will take *The Iron Pastoral* along for signing. Will carry copies of *Light* for Jerry & Nims, and maybe a *Witness*. Then we'll have a little gathering for Stafford here in the evening. Next day, we'll get him to Rochester, and we'll go to brother Ed's for a party. Busy. All fun. We'll have to be watchful of the gasoline situation.... There's a copy of Stafford's *Collected* at the Lift Bridge that I'll pick up and get inscribed, I think, for Cis & Ernie.

7/8/79

We got back from Ed's party a couple hours ago. Sort of a dismal affair. We drove about four hours to be there two hours. His relatives didn't offer us a drink or make room for us at a table. Nice folks, but sort of off the wall.

Venick & Nolan drove Stafford over to Rochester this morning. My time with him in Buffalo & here was perfect. My feelings about him continue to deepen. He is complex & warm & genuine.... Jerry was the same he's always been.... John F. Nims—we had a long lunch, the four of us—was nice. I feel somehow fulfilled, and arrived. These poets accept me as a poet, a respected one. Amazing.... Our gathering for Stafford last evening was filled with excellent stories—of Stafford & Jeffers, Stafford & Bukowski, & Bly, & Hugo, & Haines, & Levertov, & Rich.... Only Tony again acted odd & silent. I know he's resentful of Al at such meetings, and, apparently, Al had never sent Stafford Tony's book, as he was supposed to, said Tony.... Stafford & Nims again & again kind to me, insisting on saying nice things, though I hemmed & hawed.... Jerry still a sad, lost soul.... I'm ready now for a few days of relaxed writing & basketball. Just picked a jar of big raspberries, & more are on the way. I'm very tired, but the pressure is now off.... Stafford: he sat in this chair, and will now be present in this cabin, always.

7/9/79

I've come out here this morning, and after a good night's sleep, but I'm still too wound up to get down to any work on my poems. This is okay, too, though I know the summer is just waving, flowing, cycling (the cycles of plants outside) by. I'll get down to, or plan to, one more extended period of work on *CR* this summer—after Ernie's visit. We'll have other visits, too.

This place keeps giving gifts. This morning, I look out to hundreds of rose blossoms, wild roses. What a world. And the tiger lily's stalk now rises higher than the bottom ledge of my window—looks as though it will have at least three separate flower heads. It's taking its time.

Han called a dealer this morning & got me 3 signed Viereck 1sts for $15! I'll have them inscribed, I hope, in November.... Long letter from Bill Ewert with news of money & publications.... 20 copies of *The Ash*, about the last, from Allen Hoey.... Again, I look up, & life is so full, so beautiful with these roses & birds that I'm just sort of dazed. Maybe, yes, memory will concentrate into song this winter. Wordsworth was essentially right.... But that would mean that I would write of winter now? But I don't yearn for it!

7/11/79

It's 8:00, the family still sleeping. I plan to be out here for a long time today for two or three sessions. Ground wet again this morning—we've had a couple of showers lately, anyway.

New Yorker arrived with "Stories." I'm glad it's in print, and it's nice to have ½ a page of that magazine, in the hands of hundreds of commuters right now. "If my friends could only see me now," and they can.

T'will be hot & humid today. Skylab fall around noon. The news has had a lot of fun with it.... Watched a 1½ hr. debate on SALT II last night. Better than nothing. I guess. Maybe. Yes.

Han's folks coming tomorrow, Billy off to Kurt's for a week on Saturday, Wolf & Pat & Kurt & Kelly coming back with Billy then, Ernie here between, and I look forward to all, & *CR* is in good shape to enable such a life. Now I'll turn to it.

7/12/79

Han's folks here, bringing much excitement with them. They'll stay until just about when Ernie arrives. I'll try to relax. Glad I have this place.

Mosher keeps unloading materials. He's putting up a garage, or barn, or shed, or something. Hell, if I don't like its looks, I'll slap up a tall fence over that way. Wish there were a few more trees in key places. Time, & my pines, will do it.... He's got a mixer over there. Maybe he's just cementing in his kennel—the dog kept digging his way out.... So comfortable in here. I have the air conditioner on low right now. I'm spoiled.

Played ball today, after a good short session out here with *CR*. Changed some of the sections of *The Ewe's Song* around. Have the right order now, though I'd like to put something between "Foals" & "The Ewe's Song" at the end, some short piece pointing to the ruination clearly. "Foals" shows perfection, witnessing & helping. "The Ewe's Song" shows what we've lost. Something between them, something short, maybe a few lines of "light" images, would be a good thing. Bill Ewert has lined up the printer he's wanted for *The Snow Hen*. It feels <u>right</u>, this business of doing *CR* in five books, right in many different ways.

God, I just bathe in this cool air!

Disturbing news the other night about the two bastards at Nesconset Woodworking objecting to Pop's working where he does. That job is keeping Pop young, and both the folks happy.

Well, guess I should go in & check on the in-laws.

Reading Oates' *The Assassins*. It just keeps going & going. Sort of interesting, though the staccato narration—true to its narrator as it is—is disconcerting, even boring sometimes.

7/14/79

Just dropped Billy off at the bus. Had a little breakfast with him at the diner, & waited a little while with him in the center of our 150-year-old town, and dropped him off. Good for him to get away from us for a week. He'll have a fine time. Such pleasure to slip the kid an extra $25 for golf & fishing & all. He's on the bus right now, thinking & dreaming.

Han & Nora Studier & Han's folks & I went into the Stafford reading at U. of R. We liked it. Delivered a letter to him that Dorothy had sent here.... All the Rochester poetry crowd there, all.... Stafford is the one man I could write a book about. Heard some fine things last night, & some weak ones, of course. "I love feeble poems," he says.

We'll let the folks <u>be</u> today. Han will be able to stay home all day. *Jaws* tonight?

7/20/79 (I think)

Friday. Ernie gone last evening. Such a hectic but good time. He seems all right again. We talked & hunted books, schemed, took pleasure in our small-press fortune. He's putting finishing touches on the Heyen bibliography coming up in *Bulletin of Bibliography*. I gave him about 15 copies of *Brockport's Poems*, & the Mss. of *Handbook of Heartbreak*. So, he has that & *Swastika Prose*—he felt a little bad that he'll publish none of *CR*.... Anyway, years ago I so much wanted some small-press publications. Now, look!... Ernie gave me a beautiful (redwood, I think) woodburned sign reading "The Elm's Home" that I think one of his students did. I have it inside the cabin, above the back window.

Bill Stafford sent a lovely letter saying his Brockport visit was the highlight of his trip, & mentioning "Stories"—Dorothy (& folks at Rochester) had told him to read it. He also sent along 5 Wang Hui Ming woodcut broadsides of his poems. What treasures!

Overnight the tiger lily opened. I'll watch it for a long time.

The giant food order arrives from Buffalo today. And Wolf & Pat & Kurt & Billy & Kelly. I look forward. I'm so happy right now I could bust. This family, this circle of love, & so much a part of it are these poems of mine coming up in lovely editions, & these trees around me. Unreal. But, anyway: long letter from Bill Ewert, with another check, & with news of *Evening Dawning*, *The Snow Hen*, and, it looks like, *Mantle*, which he read over the phone to Christine, who had just seen "Stories" & was thinking of us & loved "Mantle." So, another beautiful broadside, too, within the year. *New Yorker*: Jesus, everyone sees it. A postcard out of the blue from Charles Wright, too. That is the one magazine where there is a great deal of response to a piece. Will try some poems again this fall.... Almost forgot to mention: Ernie brought with him the broadside *Abortion*, a nice item, though not nearly as spectacular as *Witness*, of course. Rook Press, we said, is in a new stage, slower, smarter, less megalomaniacal. *Abortion* is strictly 96 copies; we x'd out the extras. No more fooling around.

With luck, I'll miss Barry Leeds, visiting Picciones beginning today. Tony seems tense. Ernie & I visited for a half-hour, picked raspberries, walked back to the pond. Poor Tony, so much on his mind, can't relax, visits, wife frenetic, etc., etc.

... News that Al will actually travel back from Maine a couple of times to go to this book fair in Rochester. I'm happy to miss it.... This journal gets little of what I feel in it, the dozen tangents & questions & dilemmas & yearnings behind each sentence. My life is unreal. I have to be careful sometimes that I'm not too happy. And....

Sunday 22nd July

Wolf, Pat, Kurt gone. We all had a fine time, Lancers game, play, etc. Leeds/Piccione may or may not visit tonight. Kelly here with Kristen for several days.

Norbert just called—he'd gone up to Concord to see Ewert & Booth. Quite a circle this is all getting to be. Some of my things were read & passed around. All this is good, these friendships, if I can still keep to myself, the secret at the center.

Han & I are very tired.... My folks called—all's well.

I've been reading *Wonderland*.

7/24/79

Finished *Wonderland*. Stretches when I was interested, engaged, but, in general, too much odd psychology, madness, disorientation in Oates. Never the simple & primal sanities of nature. Reading her becomes less rewarding all the time. And her books are too long.... And the musical the other night, *Carousel*, enjoyable sometimes (the beautiful romantic song "If I Loved You"), but, in general, I feel, silly, "the antics of dancers," not earnest enough to be beautiful, often boring. And the house was packed, again making me realize the tiny audience for poetry.

Wrote, about an hour ago, prose section XXXVI of the memoir, a good piece that will enable it to begin again.

Good day yesterday—a little writing, basketball, even a little tennis with Han & Kris & Kelly. I do want to & will enter *CR* seriously again for a couple of weeks before summer's end. There is still time.... Letters from Vince & Ernie & Bill E.—those 3 keep up a small swirl of Heyen activities around me & make me feel, well, important? My silliness.

With *CR* I just may be doing something important, though. Sometimes I look for something in one of the finished "books," and it's there, all right, in several ways.

I'm looking up & over at the framed *Witness*. Just lines of type, a poem, lines of type, but once spoken, voiced, set blooming, a whole world—as though the lines of type were seeds & the voice a water-music. Black lines of type, but all of a boy's & man's world waiting in them.

7/26/79

It's afternoon. I'm back from playing ball. Han is at her mother's, with Kristen. This evening, I'll see "The Omen," & meet Rod & Greg at a bar. Billy hurt his neck slightly yesterday playing ball, but he's okay.

Rain the last couple of days, & the sky seems ready for more.

Manassas Review arrived. It's okay. I've been enjoying it. The articles sort of make me scrunch down. I don't really want to pay too-close attention. My immediate sense of Ernie's on *XVII Machines* is that if he is right then most of the time the poems don't carry the emotions I thought I felt while writing them.... Vince's is personal & romantic, some fine ¶s showing *Swastika* as an outgrowth of the nature poems. And the one by Kenneth MacLean is sharp & clear, & zeroes in on things I sensed, worked toward.... Well, it's a good issue, all in all, as far as such things go. Will it find me another reader, or a few, who will buy the books? Then it will be worth it.... With paperwork here & there, I put off turning to poems. This ain't right.

7/28/79

Last evening, scything out back, I was stung by four or five yellowjackets. I burned out their nest, and burned it and hoed it up again today. My poem "The Bees" aside, I can't live with them back here in the half of the property we'll use as garden and lawn.

I don't seem to be doing much. I'm sort of uninspired these days. Summer is muggy, and I'm lazy. Maybe it's that when there's no sense of pressure I don't do much. This is often the case. And the weather, too, seems right for a bike ride, or picking beans, or a game of tennis. *CR* bides its time. It knows its whole body will come together.... Bill Ewert tried to call twice yesterday, but I missed him.

I'm missing the Book Fair in Rochester. Proud of myself for avoiding, in general, that whole scene.... Read the Olson/Pound book.... Chopped back all the wisteria on the garage.... Wrote out all of *Evening Dawning* on one of those extra sheets of paper from *Abortion*. Want to do Lord Dragonfly the same way, too. Should be worth fifty bucks each to the kids when I die.

As I was drinking with Rod & Greg, Poulin walked in. He's back from Maine just for the Book Fair. He looks like hell.... Many rumors around regarding just what the College & our jobs are coming to. It doesn't sound good.

7/31/79

Back from Jerry's last evening. Oh, what a day. Listening, listening, to his strange talk all day—"Who is going to write the Mazzaro biography?"—"People are trying to solve the Mazzaro enigma."—etc., etc. He's so unbalanced, but means well, but.... He gave me four or five bags and boxes of books, many for the collection, many to read, like the Allen biography of Whitman that I've brought back here. Runs of several magazines. We stopped in a couple of bookstores in Buffalo. One even had a paperback of *Light*. Mazzaro. Right down to the "one" of the inscription in my '76 book! One would have to know him.

Humid & gloomy right now. Might rain.

Cleaned my cabin the other day, and sprayed for ants. Winter has its virtues, too.

One more month, with a few things to do here and there. I'd still like to spend some extended time on *CR*, and will.

8/2/79

I've just worked on *CR* for a couple of hours. I make new discoveries often. First I spent an hour just going over Book I, making tiny changes (that will not be in the Ewert book), and then entered Book II again. It has a new, better arrangement (maybe its final one!). Finished, I think "The Amber" for Book II. Wrote, yesterday, the one about Li Po's girl, another beauty, I think. The whole rhythm of preparing these books for Ewert, seeing them in cold print, and then large spaces to prepare them for Vanguard, is right. Each book will need deep, substantial time. I don't want *CR* flitting from section to section. And I want certain overt themes to come up in each book in a direct way. 5 books still seems just right.

Reading Allen's biography of Whitman, and will be—it's a thick one. Wrote to those folks having a Whitman conference on L.I. next spring. I'd like speaking or reading there, at Hofstra, & maybe Gregor will work something out with them.

Mom 65 yesterday. The folks are picking up their new car today, a Chrysler LeBaron. I hope it's good-sized: Pop is not a good driver these years.

Very muggy today. I'll spend much time back here—maybe all evening, too, because Han & Kris will be at a play, & Billy at a ball game. Han works 10 hrs. a day at Special Olympics.... I watched Billy's basketball game last night. He's slick, the best on the court.... Later I played a little tennis with Kris, who now can hit some good shots back.... Saw the Picciones yesterday. We're <u>all</u> girding our sore loins for school again. *CR* will preserve me.

Sunday

Billy leaves this morning for a week at basketball camp. We'll miss him. Somehow, he's on his own there, though with several friends, more than when he was with Wolf & Pat.... Billy & Kristen had good times at the Brockport carnival the past couple of nights. Han & I went one night, too, took a Ferris wheel ride again—those years, those rides once a year, go by like blinks.... Han will be busy with Special Olympics all day. Next week, for the Games, Brockport will be a madhouse. I look forward. I'll be one of the volunteers with a special shirt, and should be close to the action. Will hold the finish-line string for the 50-yard dash heats for a couple hours.

Foul-up with *Georgia Review* & "The City"—I'll write Lindberg an apology today. It's Bizzaro's fault.... Will try to have a productive day today back here, writing & reading.

Fellow called yesterday who is doing a John Gardner bibliography. He needs *The Crow*, & I'll trade him for a copy of the book! I love this. I have a whole stack of *The Crow*—those programs lay around the mail room for months for the taking, so when no one else wanted them, I grabbed them.

I bid $140 for a box of books at auction yesterday, but gave way, in the end, to Doug Calhoun. Mainly it was for a book called *Views of Louisiana* (1845) by Breckenridge. Maybe 1813. Probably worth $500-1,000. I just can't give myself over to the time & trouble of making money.... Must call off Dzwonkoski for next week.

Read a book by Charles Boer on Olson. More confirmation.... Still reading Allen's Whitman, and learning.

Hard rain yesterday afternoon. Hot & muggy today. Will stay back here most of the day. Do I begin to look forward to fall busyness, cold, classes? Not quite. I should dig in for a couple weeks of serious work after Special Olympics, and will. Will keep working on *CR* II, & get back into reading the agricultural bulletins.

Got his Schwartz from Bob. All in all, it's a sad story, & there's no denying it. I don't think there are any real poems there.... I was reading an *Unmuzzled Ox* from (was it) the late '50s, surprised how dated those poems by Daniel Hoffman & others are already. A simple, straight unaffected speech is the only way. Those poems were so labored and artificial—oh, yes, too, I was reading the 1958 Borestone that Jerry gave me. Poet after poet forced, & with stilted music. Instinctively, I think, I can avoid this.

8/9/79 (Thurs)

A big day for Brockport today. Release of the U.S. Special Olympics stamp, and the official opening of the games. Han & Kris & I will spend all afternoon & evening over there. Kris & I bicycled around there yesterday—a moving sight to see the hundreds of red-shirted volunteers & the groups of athletes/chaperones coming in. I'll see Ted Kennedy today, I think. Have finished Allen's *Whitman*, and followed Whitman & his Lincoln. Kennedy will be President, and I'll have seen him, & now, with Walt's help, *CR* will become a real poem. The five books will help me to see, too, where it might be too jagged. There is something in modern speech & methods more jagged than Walt's eddying romantic language, less unity somehow in utterance.

Peter Dzwonkoski & another librarian visited yesterday. We had a good talk. Peter will write something up, and I'll begin to deposit things for safe-keeping at Rochester. I'll make room for myself in my study. I'll be able to save things at Rochester that I'd otherwise have to sell—I have packages, e.g., of the magazines *Padeuma*, *Prose*, *Fubbalo*, *Rapport*, *Tennessee Poetry Journal*, *John Berryman Studies*, *Boundary II*, *The Far Point*, etc., & wd. like these to be a part of my whole collection eventually, & wd. have to get rid of them if I had to keep them at home. And I will begin to put many of my better books there. They will be safe. And correspondence. Still, in 20-30 years, Rochester will have to give the collection its own room, or I'll find a place that will—this is the way I feel now, anyway. Anyway, I'll be able, once the proper paper regarding insurance etc. is written up, to make some space in my study.

A perfect day today, sunny & cool. Bless all the Olympians.

....

Later.... Well, back again in my cabin. I had a fine time with Kris & Han, but decided to come home & relax & miss the spectacle tonight. Saw Kennedy, Ali, so many others. So many thoughts whirling in me. A very emotional afternoon for me. Pride in Brockport; joy for all the kids experiencing this. Also, the trembling sense of the power of these celebrities, the expectant crowd. Their fame levels me, makes me nothing, makes my pursuit of the poem silly & inconsequential—I feel some of these things even as I love Ali.... Tent City excellent. So much happiness. A full day at the track for me tomorrow.

8/10/79

Pshew, back after five hours in the sun, holding the finish-line string, wandering around. I'm wiped out. A long day. And for Han it began much earlier, & will go on much later.... Watched a volleyball game. Players included Jim Chones, Phil Donohue, Ethel Kennedy, Scott Wedman, Phyllis George.... Saw Frank Gifford et. al. Fun. Tiring. The celebrities, I'm happy to say, wear off quickly. The kids racing & jumping—they were beauties. I watched some basketball. Didn't see swimming or soccer. Too much. Tomorrow, though things are still going on, Han will pick up Billy and, hopefully (if the old car starts) I'll go to a big auction in Albion. Next week Brockport will return to normal. Pshew.

Our garden, these woods, this cabin—does this all really exist about a mile from that spectacle? I'm myself again, resting here, restoring myself, myself.

So many strange dreams last night. I'll try to finish the poem I began on one, about being in a tree in the middle of the ocean. In my dreams, I'm a survivor.

Monday 13th

I almost drowned in the Canal At Adam's Basin last night after our outing. I thought I was walking along some kind of dock, stepped into a dark space, and went straight down—it was the space between two flat boats of some kind. I had on pants & sneakers & T-shirt, shirt, sweater, & jacket filled with keys, a wine bottle opener, etc. I came up between the boats, dogpaddled to the side, but the bank was perfectly smooth, no place to hold. I was heavy, & it was almost pitch dark. I went ten or fifteen feet along the side, between the concrete & the boat, & saw a rope dangling down. I tried for it once & missed it, then tried again & just got it with my right hand. It was a cable, & saved me. A minute later I was hauled up. It was all unreal, & so sudden. I'd had some wine, but was nowhere drunk. If I hadn't been an athlete, I'd have drowned. The second I went down, that moment at Seaford flashed into my mind. I hope to write about this. Han almost fell in, too—we were holding hands—but jumped across that black space to another flat boat.... I was never frightened—didn't have time to be—but wonder now if my mind would have gone on, as though in a dream, if I'd have drowned, or if I'd have blacked out, extinguished. Somehow, I feel there still would have been a voice inside me saying/seeing the whole thing. Yes, a seeing voice, somehow.... One moment walking along, two seconds later under the water, <u>way</u> under. Much to think about. It puts everything else into perspective. I'd <u>heard</u>, before, of the suddenness possible in our leaving, but this brought me close to a sensible apprehension of it.

8/16/79

    Beautiful afternoon. Played ball again today—Billy came along too—and feel good. Have a little quirk in my neck, but feel strong & healthy. Han & I will go to an auction this evening. This morning, I had a <u>good</u> hour with *CR*, entering it, touching a poem here and there. I feel good about it.... Tony Petrosky called last night. An uncomfortable talk. He'd wanted to print some of *CR* (I'm rich with small presses!), & I'd written him to explain my Ewert project, so there would be no misunderstanding, but there was.... I'll next think about a small book for Slow Loris, though. Maybe my small-press sequences?
    Nice review of *Light* in *Library Journal*, stupid one in *Booklist*, mentioning "the Long Island town of Brockport," and comparing my prose to Merwin's, when my prose is a reaction, in a way, to that misty & surreal stuff. Can't satisfy all the people.

8/21/79

    Good days going by—time in my cabin, basketball & tennis, auctions, eating our own corn & tomatoes. I feel lazy, but have been working on a couple of poems. May have finished one called "Off the Expressway."
    Han is feeling better, Kristen is very busy with band practices in Greece, and Billy is having a great summer. All four of us, too, look forward just a little to school.
    Yesterday a backhoe rumbled at Wicks', & today an electric saw. They're having a back porch built—can't complain: much noise here from ours a couple months ago. If I get serious about some writing, I'll close up & turn on the fan.
    Have all the materials ready to send to L. of Congress.... Want to type a batch of poems to send to *New Yorker* in a couple weeks. Richard Blessing at *Seattle Review* wrote for something. I'd like to send him something good. I sent a few things to Martin Booth.... Am toying with the idea of putting together an expanded *Swastika* & trying to get a paperback done of it, maybe in England. Maybe this is just a pipe dream. Mainly, in my writing & collecting life right now I'm looking forward to *Evening Dawning*, which I should be seeing any day. And I spend time planning how I'll begin my own "safe-deposit collection" at U. of R. Crazy, but in the back of my mind I think of retiring to the kind of place my folks have retired to. My books & papers could buy that for us, some day.
    I keep thinking of more sentences to add here so that I won't have to get to that unfinished poem. I'm not as reluctant to enter *CR*, I'm glad to say.
    Later (evening). It's been a long, good day. I've spent much time back here, typing up poems that I'll send out early next month, touching up a poem here and there.... Mirko & Irma stopped by. They're going through hell trying to stop smoking.... Han & I & Billy & Kris played tennis for an hour.... I took a bike ride, talked to Archie at Lift Bridge who showed me Bill Ewert's postcard announcement for *Evening Dawning*—Bill hasn't sent it to me yet.... I haven't received the batch of *Manassas Review* Pat Bizzaro promised, and am anxious to send some out—Stafford, Simpson, MacLeish, etc.—just to keep a correspondence going. I'm too lazy & uninspired to write decent letters.... Kris off to play her clarinet, Billy at basketball, Han at a Library Board meeting....

8/22/79

9:30 in evening. I came out back to finish a letter to Bert Babcock. Am sending him the drafts of "The Children" for the collection he's selling—will trade him for a few *Evening Dawning* & some copies of the special *Light*. I'm sure he'll be willing.

Perfect evening. Only the crickets singing with their legs. I like to have my screen door open, & the outside light on, moths fluttering around, a few ash trees lit up around me.... Mowed the lawn this evening, too, and there's that green smell. "I have come to have/everything...."

Finished the poem "The Conspiracy" today. As I noted on a draft, a good book called *The City Parables* with Vanguard is becoming a possibility. It wd. be a nice touch, maybe, after *Light* & before *CR*. Will see. I shouldn't rush anything, maybe should develop & work on the idea of getting something substantial published in England, a *Selected* or an expanded *Swastika*—hmm. I've a couple weeks to fool around yet, & then schoolwork, but I should have an easy semester, anyway.

8/26/79

Rained all night, drizzling now. Good day to spend much time back here.

Another fine letter from Tom Woll. He's sold the "bad" copies of *Son of the Morning* for $90 each to Ralph Sipper.... Received the $375 in advance for *Swastika*.... Tom says Vanguard "would love" to see my five sequences, so I'll type that book up this week. I've been playing with the order of the sequences.... So many ideas for books.... No hurry.

Received a first copy of *Evening Dawning*. I like it. Maybe it could have used another color, or the drawing that's on the title page could be on the cover, but it's nice, a match for *Lord Dragonfly*, and I look forward to the hardbacks. All these small-press projects, the angle of collecting & adding to the list of A items, excites me irrationally. If Heyen becomes much collected (& thanks to Ewert & Ernie & a few others he may be, relatively, for a poet), then he would be in a great position to trade his things for books he wants. So far, so good. I'm way past most like Plumly, Matthews, Simic in this way—only a collector could understand my greed here, greed that doesn't have much to do with money.

8/30/79

Gloomy yesterday, even some leaves falling already, the foliage thinning. I actually felt, well, a little fear—that summer was over, school beginning, that I'd be leaving my cabin womb, that the warmth & sun were going. Fear. Hmmm ... Today, warmth again, sun, & I'm back here after a bike ride after a good morning's work here. Oh, I've loved this last month of summer.

Long talk just now with Bill Ewert. He's thinking of offering his collection to Ohio. No sweat to me. That collection of Bill's is the best around, except for Boston's, and mine, eventually, wherever that goes.

Well, I've typed up the five-sequence Lord Dragonfly. Will sit on it for a few days, and stare, to mix a metaphor.

Wonderful letter from Mike Stephens yesterday.... I hope *Light* is still getting around.

Nothing good at two auctions last night. Han & I will take a ride to Batavia this evening.

Well, today the foliage is still thick & the sunlight is warming my legs in here.

Bibliomania gobbles my days too often, I'm afraid.

(later—9:30 in evening). Han & I went to an auction near Batavia. Amazing prices--$950 for an oak bookcase that was nothing special, $675 for a round glass oak china cabinet. We have better things in the house. I looked through a couple thousand books, but they were all junk.

Bill Ewert called & missed me & I called back: on the spur of the moment, he said, he wondered whether Ohio wd. want to buy his collection of Heyen. Don't know how I feel about this. It wd. be the best, but maybe it's a bit soon for this. Maybe his collection would have been the one for Brockport, some day. Well, what the hell do I care about all these machinations? If Ohio gets his collection, I'll be pleased, I'm sure, to know it's safe there. Ewert must have accumulated a ton of stuff by now, every issue, holographs, manuscripts. So far as I know, he has everything except the Lauderdale book, & even has things I don't have. Just as long as Jack Matthews doesn't think there's any screwing around. Bill said he'd sell cheap, too, to give Ohio a break. Maybe this wd. all be best. Then the collection that Burt Britton is building, much smaller, could be a separate issue in a catalogue. Well, we'll see.

9/5/79

Haven't felt right lately—stomach pressure. I've tried to eat little. Something doesn't agree with me—milk? tomatoes?—but I don't know what.

First meeting tomorrow. Will do some school work this evening.

I work a half-hour or hour each day out back, leveling & raking. It gets done. Planted some grass seed yesterday, & it rained this evening. Perfect.

Read Raymond Carver's stories yesterday. Very strong.

The cabin is just about a year old now.

9/16/79

Monday morning, 8 o'clock. I'm going to begin my routine now of getting out here in the morning to work on my writing. Han leaves just before eight. I'm all set. I've even cleaned this place up the last couple of days.

All's well, nothing much new. My stomach seems better, but Han now has the trouble I had. The kids are fine.... A cool but sunny day.... I skipped an MFA meeting Friday, will skip one today with SUNY Press man. Let Gerber have that project. I dislike him more all the time—he's so secretive & selfish about all things, and hard. I hope to ignore him and series of volumes of Writers Forum interviews. They might be a mess. The transcribers, most of them, have had no ear.

Too much correspondence. I try to keep up with letters to Bob & Vince & Ernie, but even these pile up, and it's a weight. Now I owe Norbert. But I want mail, and it goes both ways.

Tony's back is bad, much pain.... Poulin is the same, upset that he has to teach at all for his salary.... My classes are off and running. I'm aiming for a nice balance of writing, teaching, basketball this semester.

Awaiting proof of *The Snow Hen*. Some sections will be hard to just let go by as they are, except for typos, because I've made changes—these will be in the eventual Vanguard book.

Sent Vanguard the book of five sequences. They rejected Bob's book of stories.

Well, Bill, despite the Los Angeles fires, the abortion debate now on the *Today* show, local worries (meeting with Clevenger Wednesday about possible book on Special Olympics), get down to the writing, your poems, even if they matter, and will, mainly to yourself.

9/21/79

So much to enter here, & won't.

Meeting with Clevenger—possible year off to work on Special Olympics book, if a grant comes through for which the college will apply. That would be something, the right thing for me now, I think.

Margaret Atwood reading okay. Judy Minty showed up, is sweet & loving & distracted as always.

Teaching going well, even my experimental composition class.

Will play ball again today, 4th time this week.

So, Gerber will edit the SUNY interviews, many volumes. He's the only applicant. Let the bastard go. I hope the details smother him.... Rubin wild-eyed yesterday about the project. Wild. Gerber has shit on people for years. Let him go.

I want to write my schlock novel, a sure $-maker, *The Elvis Presley Room: A Novel of the Fifties*. It couldn't miss, would sell to the movies. I've a dynamite scheme in mind, could write it, under <u>Haines</u>, in a week or two.

Proofs of *The Snow Hen* came. I'm on top. When that whole book, *CR*, gets done, hell, I'll rest easy, fuck the world, I'll have said it.

Nov. trip coming together. Johns Hopkins, too, I guess, though it will all be a race. Why not. I'll clear a grand, anyway.... Invitation from Bowling green, too. Never know whether I really want to go, or how much dough to ask.

Have I mentioned that I sent my book of sequences to Vanguard?

Auction tomorrow, I think. Will skip Ron Matsko's wedding.

Han & kids fine.... Much excitement over the two gold/diamond rings I got in a box of costume jewelry—oh, they were so well hidden—for five bucks in Shortsville. Kris & Han so excited! Me, too. $600-$800 worth of rings, or more, for $5, & even a nice little sterling silver ring.

Many letters & books coming in. Too much to stay up with all the time. But I <u>do</u> answer, and then, of course, there's return mail. Over the years of the five Ewert books, though, maybe, I'll get lost & be out of the small poetry community's thoughts.

Annette Shapiro visiting today. Murph has left her sad. Four kids. I don't know. My life happy, fulfilling. All because of the ego-satisfaction of poetry & family. Christ, we love those kids, & they amaze us—so mature & strong & popular & independent kids. We must have done something right. They are truly unusual.

What is the purple weed outside now making the gloomy fall more pleasant?

No poker game yet. Soon, I hope.

9/24/79

I did go to that auction, all the way to south of Penn Yan. I'm glad I did. I spent $220 ($235 with taxes) for about 30 boxes of books, then sold $80 to folks hanging around. Mainly I wanted, badly, the fine copy of *The Pioneer History of Orleans County*, but there were other things. But, most important, I was there early, at that Gleason farm above Keuka Lake, and walked through grapefields, seeing the light in the lake and in the hills on the west side. And I listened to farmers later. A memorable time. Even drove through Geneva twice, which brought back parts of my old life.

I've just been reading what I have of *The Chestnut Rain* for a couple of hours. It's very good. So much there, and more coming. It's the central work of my life. God be with me.... Going at it one slim volume at a time is best. Good luck that this came up for me.

Threw out many books yesterday, & crated some maybe to sell at auction. Upgrading the ones in the garage a bit.

Han & the kids are off to school. I'll play ball later.... I just have to keep finding quiet times for *CR* so that it will stay together despite all the distractions of teaching. <u>Auctions</u> are a part of my feelings about that poem, are time spent <u>with</u> the poem, reinforce everything about it.... Came home with a railroad magazine with a picture of a chestnut tie, too.

10/1/79

I just made good progress (maybe have <u>finished</u>) *The Ewe's Song*. Went over "The Amber" again, and think I have what I want now. Also, I managed to hold all the 9 sections in mind for a little while, and have now the order that seems just right. It's funny how it happens, how there are a few moments of clarity within all the reading of all the poems when I feel everything at once.... Now, for my own sake, I'll be holding all first 16 sections in mind together as I go on. With Book III, *American Time*, things will begin to get harder? Maybe not—I've got some awfully good sections. But I'll want to think of it at the center, <u>as</u> the center of my poem.

I've been thrown off my ease by 1/thinking about the Clevinger business, 2/ thinking about & planning the trip to Washington. A lesson there somewhere again. Stay home & stick to school and writing. But, again ...

Han hasn't been well, stomach problems—has a doctor's appointment in a week. What a woman she is. I love her and need her.

Played a little tennis with Billy & Kristen yesterday. I'm trying to stay loose, and it isn't easy.... Will play ball today.... Good auction a week from today, Monday, and I'll make a day of it. Any other profession might have stopped my writing.

No word that Vanguard has received *Lord Dragonfly*. The "book" doesn't matter, but I wouldn't want the lady's watercolor lost.

My new swastika poem, "The Holocaust Songs," is <u>strong</u>.

10/2/79

Had a half-hour to kill yesterday before picking up Kristen, and was a little restless, so stopped in to see Al. He was at his own xerox, at home, running things off for one of seventeen projects! I was dizzied by the whole thing again. Well, I'll stop in like that once in 6 months, I guess.... I was thinking that in many ways his world gives him more reinforcement than mine does—the world of committees & angling & rushed translating & publishing BOA opposed to, now, for me, work on a long poem very few people might ever care about. But I'm going to persevere with *CR*. Drafted "The Tie" yesterday, and will turn to it this morning. I love the idea of being out here a few hours in the morning even on the day when I have 6 hrs. of classes. It's eight in the morning. I'm alone. It's an overcast day. Ash leaves fall one by one in front of my windows. Not the slightest breeze. There's no question but that Poulin still bothers me, but not in any way that can really, from here on in, really bother me.... It's still this cabin that makes the poem possible that has me at ease, much work ahead, confidence it will become what I want it to be.

10/3/79

Two classes didn't (to my mind) go well yesterday, and a rejection from *The New Yorker* (nothing I ever dwell on), and rushing off for cider/doughnuts when I just remembered minutes before the evening course, and seeing (before I could stand no more and shut it off) the worst film I've ever seen—*Once By The Pacific*—well, yesterday was not my best day, though I had a good morning back here, and have had a good one again today. *CR* continues to grow & take shape. I thought I had a tentative arrangement for III, but I think I'll just put all the finished sections in a grab-bag & begin again. I know I need <u>strength</u> at the center of III. Maybe a dark section or two should begin it, & then my "Li Po" section could work out of it. Anyway, I'll be glad to work on it. II is just about completely finished, I think. I can give it my best with III, because IV will consist largely, the way it looks, of the <u>long</u> catalogues. Yes, I must keep this in mind.

Will meet with Tim Hearsum today, after I play ball. I need that workout.

Haven't been sleeping at all well lately. Don't know why.

The sun has come out, at least for a few minutes, after the rain!

Milton Kessler here today. I guess I'll go to dinner & the reading.

Oct. 9 (I think).

Pen lost. Think I let Milton Kessler use it, and that was the end of it.... No writing in this journal lately, but much attention to *The Chestnut Rain*. Work most mornings. Joy at the way it is going, joy from Ewert's letter with descriptions of *The Snow Hen*, joy that *The Elm's Home* is about as good as I can make it. What a project! 5 books, two bound in red, two gray, one green, and all to be slipcased, eventually. Best of all, the poem comes along. I'll have to work on the reading/writing of the long poem sort of deliberately; otherwise, the sections will take care of themselves, as they have.

Long day tomorrow. I'll skip a morning back here & go to my office for several things, including turning in the application for a discretionary raise that kept me busy last evening & this evening.

Mainly, school, those 2-3 busy days of mid-week, has <u>not</u> distracted me from *The Chestnut Rain*. I feel close to the poem.... "The Tie" is the latest new piece. Interesting.

Han having stomach tests tomorrow. Trust it's nothing serious. Otherwise we are all fine.... We look forward to a party for basketball players & wives the 26th.

Saw Peter Dzwonkoski & Betsey & Frank Shuffleton at U. of R. Also, saw Tony Hecht, who jumped up from a chair & told me that I'd been doing a lot lately and wonderful work! Wonder what he has up his sleeve. Why do I think he would never support me for anything?

I've no right to be as happy & fortunate as I am. Again & again, this cabin, this space so important. Without it I'd be jumpy, on edge, unkind to the family, unable to keep *CR* going…. Dark out now. A little steam on the windows for the first time this year. The little heater perfect for this weather, 30's & 40's.

Sleeping better.

Christine Bertelson mailing me *Mantle* tomorrow. Should be a little beauty.

Bert Babcock's catalog #4 arrived, with all the Writer's Forum programs I passed on to Bill Ewert. I bet there will be many inquiries over the years for those items. I'll trade like hell. Have very few, if any, extras of the good ones.

Will watch a football game starting in about a half-hour, & putter.

Washington trip falling into place.

Next day.

A few more minutes & I'll go inside & get ready to go play ball. I haven't been out here long, but did about finish "The Tie" section. It could have gone so many different ways.

Cold this morning. Beginning today, I'll have to start turning the heater on from the house 10 or 15 minutes before I come back here.

Classes went very well yesterday, especially the 3-hour evening session on Stevens. I played & heard him read for the first time the recording of "The Idea of Order at Key West." A beautiful, perfect voice for his own poem. And the poem lifted for me again. I'd sort of gotten tired of its … well, sort of evasive meditative style … but I loved it again last night. Thank God for the great poems—they make teaching possible year after year. The eleven graduate students were all moved by "The World As Meditation," too.

Han feeling a bit better. We wait for the results of her tests. Kristen & Billy fine. Billy came back here yesterday to type his Hemingway paper. What a boy he is. A <u>much</u> better student than I was, not only smarter, but more conscientious. And Kristen is doing well this year, too, goalie, clarinetist, student, little Miss Popular.

Snow predicted for tomorrow or Friday. I'm not ready.

10/12/79

Friday evening. It's been a long, good day. Series game on in an hour…. Played ball, got some books, in trade, from Archie at Lift Bridge…. Raining, and going to rain…. Did a couple hours on *CR* this morning. Looking ahead I see that I might have to make book III a pretty big one if I'm going to get everything in in five…. *Mantle* didn't arrive today, as I thought it might…. Still no poker games this fall. I'm not anxious. Ed & Charlie gone, that circle of friends is sort of cool, Rock especially. I look forward to our party on the 26th— it can't help but be a great one, with a dozen or more rusty old ballplayers & their wives. I'd like to see us all get together a couple times a year…. Letter from Ken Venick at Cincy, card from Donald Hall. Maybe will go to Monroe to see Marvin Bell next Wednesday…. Bob called to say that E. Bishop had died….

10/13/79

A couple hours at a time—8-10:00 this morning—is about all the concentrated work I can do on *CR*. Then I begin to drift. Worked mainly on that pesky section 4 again this morning. I have it, now, I think.

Monday. Another week begins. I look forward to basketball, the mail (*Mantle*, maybe). Didn't sleep well last night. Ridiculous, but I made myself nervous thinking about my trip to Wash. next month. Too many details. Will clear about $1,000—that's important, though it is good to see, too, many folks, & to **hear** my own poems, & to sell a few books.

Very lazy yesterday, & watched much football & baseball. Game #6 of the Series is tomorrow night, back in Baltimore.

Curious to see how my application for merit fared within the dept. Not well, I'd guess.

The folks called yesterday—they'll arrive the day before Thanksgiving, & stay for about a week. I'm glad.... They're happier than they've ever been.

Han has a cold. Otherwise, we're fine. I eat too much crap, get belly aches, & should mend my ways, develop some discipline. And I will.

... later.... evening.... found out that today is the 15th!

10/19/79

Time goes by very quickly back here.... I sort of drafted a good preface for *The Ewe's Song*, better than my last draft. It does a couple of things.... Both *Mantle* (I like it more & more the more I study it) and *Evening Dawning* (the hardbounds) arrived. Exciting. And the best is yet to come from Ewert.... Thursday evenings I'm tired. Friday, today, is my best day. Sun shining, too. I'll play ball in about an hour.

I was rated by APT & Curran satisfactory in teaching & 4 in one category & 5 (highest) in "Scholarly Activity." The teaching was a bad deal—I'm surely the best in our dept.?—but hard to document. I thought of sending a letter along with the application, disagreeing, but then decided not to, and a weight lifted from my soul. Screw it. I'll probably get some merit money anyway, and this way I feel free of it all. We'd all cut our throats for a dime around here.

Many letters to answer. Will probably make a start this afternoon.

Old Ford terminally ill—frame breaks. We'll junk it this weekend.

Called Ernie—Cis in hospital again, but improving.

10/20/79

Letter from Vicky Gold saying she's got two years, at most, to live. I've just written her a long letter. So sad. She wants to leave money to her friends, including me! I wouldn't mind, but told her I'd rather she used it up herself, e.g. on a book of her poems. We'll see. This is all lousy, & terrible. I can't quite believe it.

Indian summer here, in the 70's today. I'm deepening the ditch line beside the cabin so that maybe I won't have water around the cabin this winter & spring.

It's so nice back here now—fresh air, & sounds of leaves scraping by. There's something about a couple of days of Indian summer that is helping me get ready, psychologically, for winter.

Went over the preface for *The Ewe's Song* again. Just about have it. And the sections are about ready. I'll see page proofs next week of *The Snow Hen*, & then it won't be long. Duane Schneider, too, says he's making a beautiful book of *The City Parables*. How can I be this lucky? What more could I want from my writing life than for these collector's items to keep coming out? Imagine the five volumes of *The Chestnut Rain* boxed!

Han's feeling fine again.... Kristen heartbroken over some boy & angry at some girl after her football game outing last evening. I know about "heartbreak." Maybe she'll learn a lot earlier than I did.

I haven't mentioned here that last Wednesday I went to Monroe CC to hear Marvin Bell. I was 15 feet from him during his reading, & he looked at me many times, but I guess he didn't recognize me, and I left early, while he was still signing books, and didn't get a chance to say hello. But someone told him I'd been there, & the next morning he phoned, & we talked about a half-hour. Petty of me, but I feel I've arrived, and always think of what I was thinking as I walked up that hill in Athens every day.

Talked to Tom Woll briefly yesterday. Want him to rush that indication of interest in the Olympics volume to me.... No indication of interest regarding *Lord Dragonfly: Five Sequences*. No matter. I will try to find another publisher, if Vanguard won't do it. Maybe that would be best, anyway.

Not a bad pen for a buck and a half. The cartridges seem to last a long time, & this pen doesn't leak, as my other did.

10/21/79

A few minutes ago Mirko came back here to the cabin. I said "Good to see you my friend," and I <u>was</u> glad, he's such a friend. He said that I wouldn't be glad to see him when I knew why he came. He had the most terrible news he could bring, he said. I was stunned, fearful, <u>cold</u>. I thought of Hannelore, Billy, Kristen. "Rocks lost Linda," Mirko said. She was killed in an auto accident, with her boyfriend, yesterday. Terrible, terrible news. She was a wonderful girl, the best in everything. Oh, what a grievous loss, the Rocks having to bury their oldest child. Unimaginable. How to survive it? Oh, God. No funeral. A memorial service Wednesday at Rocks. They want no one around, Mirko says—just Emmanuel. Terrible. I'll tell Han this afternoon. Unimaginable. <u>Relief</u>, at first, and still, after what Mirko first said. To bury your own child—no worst there is none.

10/24/79

Han & Helen & I went over to Rocks' last evening, about ten. Bill and I cried most of the time. True grief. When I think of it, it hurts me—the Rocks' pain must be intense, and moments of emptiness. Maybe that emptiness, that hollowness, is a motion of the soul, a desire to join the dead, but the body has a hold on it still. Today, a memorial service, this evening. Mirko, Manny, Bill and I brought close again over this, another of dead Linda's gifts.

10/29/79

The memorial service for Linda was beautiful & sad. I stayed late, got drunk, sick later. That's over now, the pain, for <u>me</u>. I'll stop over today & drop a little gift off, *Lord Dragonfly*, for Bill's birthday. Then, if he ever wants to, he knows where Mirko and I are.... Han & I <u>did</u> have the party Friday night for the basketball gang, & it was wild, & good. It was a long, long week.... I leave next Saturday, so will want to prepare this week for my trip.

Page proofs of *The Snow Hen* arrived. It will be a beauty. And this morning I went over books 2 & 3, both strong. Book 3 will be long, and will declare the poem's qualities once & for all....

I haven't raked a single leaf yet, but had better before I leave.... So much to do.... This cabin, though, keeps my writing life in necessary summary & order, & available to me.

Nov. 1, 1979

I'm 39 today, and a long way from Brooklyn, in some ways.

Sun this morning, and some wind. Rain on its way. It's in the fifties, but after this last warmth ...

I've worked hard at schoolwork & form-filling-out to get ready for my trip. Will fly to Washington Saturday. Things are all arranged. I'll fly back the following Friday and have time to catch my breath again before classes. Han & the kids will visit the folks in Nashville for a day or two while I'm gone. And then we'll settle in for the long winter. I should clear about $1,200 on the trip, & maybe sell a few books, if they're at the readings. I belong here, within my routine, deepening into *The Chestnut Rain*, but this will be a good trip.

I'm in touch with Vicky Gold/Ernie, about that predicament & sorrow.

Linda Rock's photo on front page of *Brockport Post* yesterday. I dropped off, for Bill's birthday, a card & copy of *Lord Dragonfly*, but didn't see them. Now it will have to be up to them, if they want to, to move toward their friends again.

Han, Billy, Kristen are fine, healthy & happy. The kids lead full and exciting lives.

I was thrown off track a little last evening by going to listen to Nick Meyer, who is at the center of ... popular entertainment. That's some world, next to my world of 126 copies of *The Snow Hen* or 2,500 of *Light*. Makes me want to write *The Elvis Presley Room*. But *CR* is what I want. I want to make it as moving & beautiful as the feelings I have for its subjects inside me.

11/12/79

How do I feel? After the trip, I have a head-cold, have been tired, unwinding. Did play ball today, the body playing out of habit. L. of C. reading went well—Viereck was like Berryman, nervous & talking non-stop, and not well. Meredith warm and kind again, enjoying his part, also sort of sad, as he increasingly will be, I think, once out of the spotlight. I did a good job for that half-hour, & Tante Elfriede was at the reading, & Liz, & cousin Anke. My visit with Henry & Liz was a good one. Matt was sick that Sunday. Henry & I visited the nuclear plant south of his place, & walked the Chesapeake shore later on.... My visit with Mike & Robin was good, too, & exhausting. I read well. The one downer was Hopkins. I didn't like my reading. No one even smiled when I recited "The Emperor of Ice Cream" after telling that "brick-a-brack" story. David St. John didn't seem to go to any trouble for me, & that's for sure. John Irwin—I took a quick ride with him to his apartment. He talked a blue streak about his upcoming book(s). Worse than Mazzaro at his worst. No time for the world while ideas flood the mind.... Reading at Manassas was maybe my best ever. Good time with Pat Bizzaro. Met a real artist, Wes Porter, who, if his life allows him to paint, will do wonders, as he already has.... Came home with a strange sense of power over a few people—it must be like the way Kinnell affected me—a few people who could hardly talk after the reading and would say, using this word & unable to look in my eyes, they were "awed." I don't know. Now, I just want to get my teaching in order again, get over my cold, and get back to a routine of working on *CR*. I look forward to having my folks here, but just don't want to go anywhere else.... Look forward to *The Snow Hen* & *The City Parables*.... All my feelings/knowledge reaffirmed in those situations: the ambition of the Waters/Poulin connection, Mike showing the projected dustjacket everywhere we went; the small audience, all in all, only a few folks genuinely interested in the poetry under the performance, a few who will look up the books; the sadness of all these students, including the workshop people at Hopkins, who want to be "poets," who envy me, as they should, but not because of any mark I have made in the infinitesimal poetry world, but because of the joy I find in collecting, the small-press/fine-press publications, and in the work itself on *CR*. Well, I'm home to the kids, and Han—she is just a wonderful woman, and I love her more all the time.

Read "Mantle" and "The Girl" a few times. Beauties. I must keep memorizing sections of *CR*.

It's not right to be anxious for summer already, as I am. I must live day by day. But it's no wonder: the warm summer, the garden, the ease of the cabin, no classes. If that Special Olympics grant does not come through, that will be all right, too. It will not be on my mind, then, over the summer. If it does, fine: I'll roll up my sleeves this winter already.

Dave Smith sent the hardback *Goshawk, Antelope*, & I added the cloth *Heisenberg* & *Hush* & a beautifully inscribed *Hazard, the Painter*, etc.... Saw Allen Hoey, too, who will do *The Bees* after doing a Smith thing. So goes my life in the midst of my corny melancholy today—even saw a funeral while driving home today! I'm no Werther.

11/17/79

Saturday. Relaxing. Caught up with my life again, after a hectic week. Few students will show up Tuesday. In effect, I'm on vacation. Look forward to having the folks here, beginning Wednesday.

Rara Avis, says Bill, wants to do a little book, maybe, so I'll type up & arrange the 6-8 new "swastika" poems I have. Need copies for other people, too.... I've many odds & ends & thank-you notes to take care of. Judy Minty's new book came yesterday, e.g.

The 1979 Christmas card, Almond, came. Han & I like it a lot. I've finished folding it now, & in 2-3 weeks will send them out.

I want to get back, after Thanksgiving vacation, to steady staring at *CR*.

So peaceful this afternoon.

12/3/79

Monday. Life so fast. My folks' visit hectic, & ended in argument. My mother is sick, & five or six days wore me down. She promises never to talk to me again. Again Pop is caught in the middle. Again. It's boring. I'm disappointed that I couldn't just shut up for a week as she raved of blacks & Jews & said she wouldn't have had children if she'd known any of them would lose their hair, etc., etc., etc., etc., etc., but I'm human too.

Ewert will have the Bixlers print *My Holocaust Songs* (9 poems) too. It will be beautiful, I'm sure. Rara Avis wanted too much money, $3,000 for 126 copies.... *The Snow Hen* shouldn't be long now, as long as the signed sheets I sent got back to Bill & Emily Rizzo all right. The announcement arrived—elegant. It should, though, have been more explicit about the 5-volume project? Anyway, I hope enough folks can afford it so that Bill gets his dough back right away. Now this morning, after a weekend of catching up on correspondence, I'm going to read over *The Ewe's Song* & see if it's ready to go.

A picture of *Light* in a *NYTBR* ad that many have seen.

Sipper bought 13 copies of *Mantle* from Ewert!

Looks like Ohio will buy the Babcock Heyen collection. My fingers are crossed. I should write Bert for a list of what he's selling. $1,750.

Agreed to a week next Nov. at U. Wisconsin-Milwaukee. A grand. O America.

12/5/79

Word from Tom Woll yesterday that Vanguard almost certainly will do my book of sequences. I just read it over again and like it, its various textures. Well, what the hell, why not—it will keep my name out there and warm until *The Chestnut Rain* (though this is all my imagination, as though more than a few people care, or will). Tom mentions "a small edition," with maybe 100 limited. Sounds great to me. This book will not have the kind of "hook" that *Swastika* & *Light* have, even. But publication by Vanguard will get it around. I'll think about what I'll suggest regarding a hardback, paperback split. Maybe 1,500 paperback, 500 hardback, 100 of which are numbered & signed & slipcased?... Also, I typed up and have ready to send to Bill Ewert *The Ewe's Song*. I lost sleep last night excited about the *CR* project especially. So much happening. *The City Parables* upcoming, too, and *My Holocaust Songs*, and *The Bees*, and *The Snow Hen* will be on its way to me soon. I believe in my poems, care for them, still spend enough time with each before letting it go—and I guess what I want is to be considered one of the 25 necessary poets of my generation, for the sake of anthologies in the future, etc. Half of this is public relations, staying around until the work is seen as a whole. These concerns are petty, of course, but *CR* will have something to say, and I'll want an audience for me. I love it, and am confident I'll finish it up beautifully.

12/7/79

Friday morning, and all's well. I just dropped Han off at work, made a thermos of coffee, and am back here for a couple hours or so. Classes were good yesterday. Han had 11 women here for bridge last night. Billy's first game is tonight, away—Han will go, but I'll wait for the first home game, Wednesday. So, we're busy. But I feel fine about *CR*, beyond everything else.... Made out some Christmas cards last evening—filled in a little chalk in the almond blossoms. A nice card.

Talked to the boys of Mammoth Press about Vicky Gold in case Stefaniks can not do her collection.

Judy Minty came over for Mary Elsie Robertson's reading the other night. We had a good talk. She's leaving Syracuse after this semester. Carruth is permanent there, she says.... Rod Parshall has the Forum next year. Must get ... Carruth, MacLeish.

12/13/79

Last two classes today. For part of one, while the students talk to one another, I'll visit Parshall's class & read from *Light*.

December *Poetry* out. Nice. Nims put me as lead name again. He also sent me his translation of St. John of the Cross, which I've been reading. He also sent a letter saying Han & I would soon be invited to the White House to a reception honoring American poetry & poets! Amazing. Aw, what the hell, I told Poulin to get

Dickey to get him an invitation, & maybe the four of us from Brockport would go together. I thought that would be nice. Han thinks I was stupid even to mention it to Al.... My first reaction was, no, I don't want to leave here during the winter, Jan. 3rd; then I realized this is a once-in-a-lifetime thing, that Han & I would be able to be at the White House without standing in a tourists' line. We'll go.

Had my class in my study Tues. night. It went all right. We had some wine. At 9:30 Ken Venick & John Stigall dropped in, too.

Last night's ball game was wonderful. Billy's team won. He had 18 pts., and played beautifully. I choke up when I watch him play.

12/20/79

Haven't been back here for at least several days. I've been reading student journals steadily. Finished the last at two this morning. Relief. Now, back here, the snow, hot coffee, the heater warming this place, I'm breathing deep again. The semester is over. Relief.

Bulletin of Bibliography is out with Ernie's checklist. I especially like the list of poems first appearing in magazines. Many memories.

Long talk with Bill Ewert the other night. All's well. Don't know if I'll see a copy of *The Snow Hen* by Christmas.

I still play ball every M-W-F. Love it.

Official invitation from the White House came. Han & I are going! Weather allowing.

Billy has scored 18 pts. in his last two ball games. He's shooting the lights out: 7 for 10, 8 for 10 from the field, and some long ones. Kris had her last volleyball game yesterday, and played well. We're proud parents.

Just some rabbit tracks around my cabin this morning. My coffee cup still steams, but it's warm enough in here now. Everything is just as I left it, a life within a life.

Jeff Spuck & Rich Holowka will visit tomorrow afternoon. Good chaps.

My head is already clearing, after all those journals. I'm all right. Half the school year is over. Soon it will be summer & I'll be working on the long section of *CR*.

I'm getting the 2 gold coins made into necklaces for Han & Kris. It should be a real surprise—each will cost about $70 with the gold band & chain. They should be completely surprised. Next best thing I could have done to saving those rings I got by luck at auction.

We'll go to another of Billy's games tomorrow evening.

We stood at Parshall's party until about two in the morning. Fun, but the next day was tough, especially for Han.

Enough chatter. I'm alive again.

12/24/79

Raining/fog, and we've decided to stay here and not surprise Han's folks with a visit. We'd have been on the road 4 hours in uncertain conditions. We'll have a fine Christmas Eve by ourselves.

Picked up the necklaces today. They're nice.

Drafted a Zimmer poem for a "Festschrift" Rod Jellema is doing. Sending a poem for a *Tendril* anthology. One or two other miscellaneous things going.

This cabin—still unbelievable to me, so perfect.... I hung two Christmas bulbs back here, wildlife bulbs, one marked 1978 (the year the cabin was built), and will each year.

Still haven't turned in grades. Will on the 26th.

I've finally just about caught up on answering mail.

Alas, I'll not see a copy of *The Snow Hen* before Christmas. Soon after, I'm sure.

Tomorrow Han & I will stop for a drink at Winnicks', at four; otherwise, we'll just enjoy being home. Guess I won't call the folks tomorrow, or, ha, maybe I should—that would surprise them, & disappoint my mother, who would have a hard time staying angry.

12/27/79

Out here this morning, out here this afternoon. Reading: *Specimen Days*. Writing: "Zimmer in Sunshine," another version of section 9, "A Letter," of *The Ewe's Song*. Coasting. Looking forward to Billy's game tonight. Without this cabin, it would be impossible to enter the calm circle where I can read and write: when I went in a while ago to have a sandwich, one of Billy's friends was in the garage, and Sandi Piccione called, and the mail came, and ...

My windows are clouded up. It's not as much fun here during winter as during summer when the leaves surround me and fresh air wafts in. Summer is when I can tackle the very long section of *CR*. But this place is warm and necessary, now, on a cold, wet day.... One or two other miscellaneous poems close to being finished.

12/28/79

Complex emotions—call from Poulin: he did get himself invited to the White House, and in the way I advised him to. Han angry—she wanted us to do one thing on our own, away from the manipulator Poulin. I got over my bad feelings in a hurry, then felt bad again when I told Han. It's nothing, in the true run, all capitols/capitals already the dust they'll be. I've nowhere near the bitterness I'd have felt a couple years ago. Did I tell him about all this hoping he'd be punished by not getting an invitation? or curious to confirm my view of poetry politics? or to punish myself somehow? No matter. What isn't politics? I feel pretty good about myself really caring very little. Han has a new dress/shoes/bag. Next Thursday it is.

Billy had 24 pts last night, was 9 for 10 from the field. An amazing shooter. Tournament final tonight. Wolf/Pat/Kurt might come.

Debacle at Han's folks Christmas Eve—Grandma slapped one of Kenny's wild kids & Marty started screaming & they left without opening presents, etc. Grandma heartbroken, of course. Life is a series of soap operas. For me, the main thing is to make *The Chestnut Rain* a major poem. I have the makings. It's on its way.

12/30/79

I've slept very well the last two nights, waking up once or twice, going back to sleep until about eleven, waking with such a relaxed feeling in the lungs, ease. A blessing.

The Poulin thing still on my mind, but in different lights. Han & I are now almost glad for the company. My "honor" may be "diminished" locally, but who cares, among the people who don't care themselves, don't know any of my poetry or anyone else's?... Al reports that *Poetry* may have a party after the White House reception. Al has been on the phone, now, steadily finding things out.

Seem to have finished my "Spring Song to Kenji M...." today, and my "December 31, 1979: The Candle"—both take many chances.... Sometimes I seem to me to have so many poems that I really don't know what will become of them all. The book *The City Parables* could be expanded for Vanguard—hell, maybe *Lord Dragonfly: Five Sequences* in 1980, *The City Parables* in 1981, & maybe *CR* the next in line after that. The glut is a pleasant problem, I suppose, and the worry that my books will wear out non-existing readers has always been an illusion, I suppose. When I feel the books are ready, I should try to publish them. I suppose I'll <u>never</u> feel complete: even when/if a *Collected* appears, I'll have poems handy that didn't make it in.

Han is happy/healthy these days, as are the kids. Billy is playing poker inside now with Dennis & Allen & Danny. Kris stays in touch with her friends by phone.... I'm living the good life. Tomorrow night is the neighborhood dinner & party.

Idea yesterday & tentative lines for a section of *CR* for fifth volume maybe to be called "The Binding."

1/1/80

The new decade, but the overcast air the same as yesterday. I did finish my Dec. 31, 1979 poem yesterday. Don't know if it's any good.... Party around the neighborhood, ending at #142 Frazier St. at 2:30 a.m., was fun—too much smoke, especially Pete DeToy's fucking pipe. Anyway, all's well that ends well, as even the world's decade has, for Americans at least.

I still think about the Poulin business, sometimes bothered, sometimes not. But such petty feelings will not be a part of my whole life. I'm too lucky: Han & the kids—this morning all three waking up warm and healthy—my cabin—this morning a pair of woodpeckers (I thought, but couldn't find them in my guide & don't really know what they were) in the big ash, and the doves behind the cabin, as I walked back; and my upcoming books, and the luck, yesterday, of finishing the new Wenzel poem, a beauty, 16 tight lines—it might be called "The Socket" though I use the phrase "that socket" within & this title wd. be awkward. This will be my 40th year. What do I want, as Russia invades Afghanistan & thousands starve in Cambodia & people die of cancer & heart disease & fire & accident? I want, still, now, to finish CR & for it to be, for me, a very beautiful, even major, poem. And I guess I do want, whatever the reality & depth of the larger world, some enduring & undeniable kind of fame or recognition, and even as I write this I know that this is not only abysmally bleak & stupid & pretentious & literally neurotic of me (and ask Snodgrass about the enduring benefits of even a Pulitzer, e.g.), but also very human. The crux of it, this ongoing (but, in truth, I think), diminishing disease of mine is that I want to impress local people (people even who would never buy a book or care about a poem), & this is so dull & dumb. And do I think I will do this by outstripping Poulin (even as I know that we are two entirely different men)? How boring I'm becoming to myself as the new decade begins. I'll grow up. I swear that right now fifty sparrows are in the small Colorado spruce where I emptied a bag of sunflower seeds the other day. The primal sanity.

Among these creatures calling themselves "poets" on this earth, I have so much.... I did not know myself well enough to know that I wanted the White House thing for myself, not for Poulin. There, I said it. The sentence was so simple. This may be the hope of the new decade for me, maybe to struggle against those parts of myself I don't like, but at least to know myself, at least to be able to avoid the unnecessary distraction & even hurt that my big mouth led to—and I say this even as I know that good things will come of the very fact that 4 of us are going on the trip, & not just two. Fuck it. I can't even find a way to end this entry so that I like myself well enough to get on with my work. It's all a goddamned joke. I'll laugh at this entry, and before very long. On to *The Chestnut Rain*. Amen.

1/2/80

Late afternoon, cabin warm, slight snow falling outside, just beginning to cover the ground.... I won't even read over my last entry. I'm an ass. So hard to grow up, though.

Long call from Bill Ewert last night. He'll be picking up *The Snow Hen* in Boston any day now, and I should get my first copy in a week or two. And then the others. Not much else new. He has orders so far for about 50.... Today I reworked (after going through many drafts yesterday) the dangerous 9th section of CR, and sent it, & a revised #17, off to Bill. That's it on *The Ewe's Song*, as far as I can see now.... Finished & typed up the section for book 3 on Wenzel called (picked this title today) "Blackberry Light." I know, intuitively, this piece is right, important, deep, though I can't put my mind on what it's about besides what it's obviously about. It does a great deal. I'm very happy with it. Am leaning toward naming book 3 *Blackberry Light*. Close to Warren, but not too close.... Listed titles of CR's first 29 sections. What a hell of a fine book it's going to be. Nothing like it. Looks like there will be just about 45 sections. I hope I'll still know what I've done (a damned fine & important poem, & more: the poem of my generation) when the Vanguard book just sort of appears with little notice....

So, Washington tomorrow. There will be thrills, but the great joy will be in being back home, having survived, & being in the stands at Billy's game Friday night, with memories.

Still reading *Specimen Days*, and the Berry book. No hurry on such things.

Those birds I couldn't identify are definitely tufted titmice, at least the pair back here today. Many birds around after the sunflower seeds I scattered about.

My next entry will flow with the pleasure of being home.

1/4/80

I've just brought in this diary from the cabin. I want to enter the whole Washington experience, get it behind me, and begin my work, my life again.

Han & I just back from Billy's game. A rough one. Brockport beat Churchville by two. Billy had a good game. Exciting. A sweet win.

I'm tired, will sit in my study bed in pajamas & watch *The Sea of Grass* & write here. Eyes tired. So glad to be home. Many memories. More education regarding this life as one of the so-called "poets."

So glad it's over. In about 30 hrs. Han & I visited Ford's Theatre (a moving experience, this time, to have time to see the exhibits—I'll dream on a few things for a long time), the Capitol, the Library of Congress, the National Gallery, the Wash. Press Club, and took in the White House readings. I met Phil Levine, Peter Klappert, Lisel Mueller, Alfred Corn, Archie Ammons for the first time (I may have met Ammons briefly in Cortland), saw Lucien Stryk, John Ashbery, Sandra McPherson, Dave Smith, Peter Stitt, Diane Wakoski, Jim Dickey—he was very cordial, & even recognized me after all these years—Richard Eberhart, Stanley Kunitz, David Ignatow, Karl Shapiro, Daniel Hoffman, John Nims, Richard Hugo, Bill Matthews, Henry Carlisle long enough to say hello to & exchange pleasantries. Saw Louis Simpson, De Snodgrass, Donald Hall, Bill Claire long enough for good conversations. And Marvin Bell. Mike Waters around later. Saw Ai again. Etc. Etc. Ciardi, Gwendolyn Brooks, Jonathan Williams, others I didn't meet. A plethora of "poets." Wish they'd taken a big goddamned picture of everyone there. So, there was that. The misery of shaking hands with Parisi before I knew who he was. The dross of seeing McClatchy gain. The good talks with Hall & Snodgrass. So much more. Simic.

I heard Wright was there, with Annie, but Han & I didn't see him. Others did, & said he was very sick, cadaverous, was having a lung operation soon. This morning, in the hotel bathroom, unconsciously, I was saying fragments to myself—"fired his gun across the gray autumn where now his life is done," "where now his life is done"--& then realized they were phrases of Wright's, & realized that that news had struck me hardest of all.

Rod McKuen was there, and Bill Bradley, and, recognized later, William Cohen of Maine. For the reading period, Han & I sat in the back of the Green Room, stunned by the whole place. Later, we all went to the East Room. Mrs. Carter said a few words. Then, a log jam for the reception line. When Han & I got about thirty feet away, I saw that President Carter was there. I readied myself, and looked right into his eyes, was very moved. We spoke a sentence or two back and forth. I've always cared for him, was thinking, my God, what must have been on his mind as he stood there—Iran & Afghanistan especially. And Mrs. Carter spoke to Han & me, too. And Mrs. Mondale. And then I drank much wine & stood around with all the poets. For about a half hour Han & I went back through several rooms, pausing long in the Blue Room, knowing we'd always remember being there, our age, the beautiful soft lights in those historic rooms, having just met the President. Wish we'd had a photograph of the four of us together.

Poulin had a party until late. It was good. Half the time I was glad he was around—Boo, though, is such a pain in the ass—and half the time I was still sorry. All in all, I'm so glad it's over, that I'm back. A heady experience. Poets I hadn't met before really knew my name. So what? But it felt good. Now to the real work of *CR* again. My cabin a steady place in the whirling universe. Home, home. I want to pull in my head & stay within my warm shell, and remember Wenzel from sleep to shed to stall.

Snow in Washington right now. Mirko waiting for daughter at airport, & the flight keeps being postponed from Wash. Our luck held up.

I'd like to finish this page, and soon this blank book, & then begin again. This book began in October of 1975, I see. It's only worth what memories are worth.

Han happy to be back, & with a weekend to rest up.

Where's *The Snow Hen*? Next week, I believe, for sure.

Norbert's chapbook here, Mike Waters' book on the way.

Okay, all that bad juice & crap & distraction is just about behind me now. As always, it helped me to write its outlines down.

1/5/80

Morning. I'm out back again. It's cold, my coffee steaming, but warming. I just emptied a bag of sunflower seeds on and around the small spruce outside my window. An inch or two of snow on the ground, and we're supposed to get more this weekend.

For about ten days, now, this best time of year, I won't have to worry about school or travel or anything else. Home. Will work on some of the almost-finished pieces for book 3 of *CR*—*Blackberry Light* still seems like a good title.

Wilbur, MacLeish, Stafford not at the White House, alas—nor Meredith, away on a reading tour. And contrary to what Al and I thought, Berryman did not show up.

Even some of my poorest friends want to buy/are buying the $35 *Snow Hen*. I can't help it, can't give mine all away, won't think of mailing even one & worrying about lettered/numbered sets being broken until all five are in my hands, and the slipcases. Then, maybe, a set to Vince Clemente, maybe Ernie, etc.

Fairly warm in here now.... Do I have my first touch of arthritis, in my right hand? No pain quite like it.

1/7/80

Monday. I've read over *The Ewe's Song* a little—impressed with it—but can't really get down to work this morning. Look forward to basketball at noon—first time in 17 days. Hope I won't collapse.

White House vivid but fading away. I keep thinking of poets I met there but didn't mention here: Ann Darr, Roland Flint.

Vanguard has a big add for *Light* in *APR*, not the kind of ad I'd have designed, but much better than nothing. For *Poetry* it will be right.

Seems to be getting very windy. Storm warnings. Clear blue sky, so far.

Night before last Han & I went over to Pylyshenkos' and talked until about two in the morning. Mirko & I finished a whole bottle of cognac. There was some real talk for a change. Today, come to think of it, is their Christmas?

I must come back here this afternoon & maybe evening too and get down into a section or two of *CR*. All in all, it's coming beautifully.

1/8/80

Tuesday. I've decided to skip basketball today. Maybe will go for a long walk later, up by the winter canal.

Working this morning on the *CR* section called "The Poem." It's going to be good, when I get it done. I don't want to overdo the catalog effect.

Cold in the cabin this morning. Could use a little bigger heater, but this winter I'll get by with this one.... We've had nice cozy family evenings lately. Billy has a home game Friday, and that will be fun again, though we'll all feel bad if Brockport loses, but not for long.

1/9/80

Had a good morning, bringing "The Poem" section of *CR* forward. It's going to be a strong one.... Played basketball & had a good time despite hurting my right knee, on the fleshy part just above the knee.... A couple of irritations regarding Poulin worming his way into two notices, the one in the *Post* particularly disgusting—I've made a resolution, after, twice now, nothing has come of the press notices I've done, not to bother again with inquiries/interviews here or in Rochester, ever; so much good will come of this.... Bad news is that our 1978 tax return is being audited—this will upset Han—and we have an appt. in Rochester on Feb. 7th. I'm debating whether or not to show her the letter now, or wait a couple of weeks. Han does the return too honestly. Why doesn't the fucking government look into these bastards like Reagan & corporations like Ford that don't pay a cent in taxes and leave us the hell alone. All we're trying to do is save a little money for Kristen & Billy for college.... Really, all's well, otherwise. There's distancing between us & the White House business—at least the irritating part of it—and I know my whole mind now, and what I'll be like regarding Poulin, through the '80's!

Got Martin Grossman's review of *Swastika* in *Skywriting*. He says it may be the best book of the decade, that it will last. It will, I know. I still want to see an expanded paperback version. And Vanguard wd. do it, if they could sell the rest of the hardbacks, I know.

The four of us are healthy. The kids are back in school & working hard. Billy has been in a terrific mood the last few days. Kristen is still busily practicing her solo for competition, & practicing with the play band. I'm practicing learning to mind my own business. It isn't easy.

1/10/80

Just wrote Michael about *Not Just Any Death*. It's a nice book, readable, interesting, and I could honestly write Mike that it's a whole book. I also see many lines that do nothing, and some bad (it seems to me) similes—like Plumly's "like water"—and other things that manage to sometimes kill off a poem's promise. Well, may Michael flourish. He's in Poulin's stable now, too, and like Tony, may find it a bit confined. I think Mike sent out about a hundred review copies. The lessons about reviews come hard & late. Michael <u>wants</u>. We all do, but his wants take the shape of Poulin's. Let it be. I have resolutions for myself for the '80s. Distance from the kinds of crap that bothered me in the five years of this journal. There may be darker things to deal with, the inevitable life-things coming to us all, but I'll be damned if I don't grow up regarding my wavering on some things. I'll be entering some of my triumphs of distance here, a progress report.

Section #24 coming along, becoming 3 16-line stanzas.

Reading the Boyer book on John Brown.

Heating pad on my pained right knee. Still hope to at least shoot a little tomorrow & work up a sweat.

Han took the news about the tax audit in stride.

News of Iran & Afghanistan still seems to be building up every day.

1/11/80

Just now, in the middle of reading a section from book 3 of *CR*, I heard the background rain & looked out the cabin window and realized again how lucky I am, thought of the struggles & insecurities of graduate school again, the pressures, and now have all this, a wife & daughter to go with tonight to see a son play ball, a home & cabin in the woods behind it, books to my name and one, *CR*, the best one, building. Can't play ball today because of my knee. Happy to be here, arriving in the year when I'll be 40.

Wind increasing, & will.

Maybe *The Snow Hen* will arrive today. This is worth watching for the mail for.

1/12/80

Billy's team won last night. A good game. He had about a dozen points. Kristen feels she did well in her clarinet competition this morning.

I don't know why, but I read carefully & slowly Hecht's "Venetian Vespers" this morning. It's not the kind of poem I could or would want to write, but it's a real poem, & intelligible, & often beautiful in its music—things I had not thought his poems were. I wrote him about it, and about us at the White House. I wonder if my general sense of him (guarding his position as <u>the</u> poet of Rochester) is a right one. He did write me kindly & has spoken kindly of my books. As I was writing him, I kept hearing Piccione's derision, e.g., but I won't be scared off from speaking what I feel. It's a beautiful poem, though I yearned for a bit more affirmation, which I felt the speaker earned & deserved, at the end.

Still reading, & will be for a long time, the book on John Brown. Brown, apparently, occasionally passed through Brockport on Canal barges with his sheep.

Very windy today, the cabin solid & warm enough.

1/13/80

    Bill Ewert called last night, said he'd picked up *The Snow Hen* (100 copies, anyway) from Emily Rizzo, would mail me a copy first class tomorrow, that I should have it by Wednesday. Wonderful. Also, that he'd written Kinnell & Kinnell sent him a batch of poems & Bill believes he can get a book into print by March! I might not only get several copies, but also the Mss. for my collection. Bill makes all the right moves. I told him to go after Richard Wilbur next. We just bubble when we talk over the phone. So, this coming week I'll get *The Snow Hen*, the first one. Thinking ahead of the whole set ... stunning.... Bill says Ernie had been in the hospital again for two weeks—I don't know what the deal is. Poor guy. I'll write Ernie today.... Bill read all of *The Ewe's Song* to his mother, even #16, & she loved it!...
    Kristen finally at ease, received an A- on her tough grade #6 (the highest) competition. This will mean All-County to her.
    The larger world swirls with news of Carter & Russia & Iran & Afghanistan.

Tues. (15th?)

    Unbelievably poisonous & sick letter from my father yesterday, sent to the school, as though I wouldn't show it to Han! I'll have to answer. Probably tomorrow. Made me ill.
    Letter from collector Michael Broomfield. I'm digging out a few things for him (promised him *The Train* some time ago, one of my last 2 extras), but really don't want to part with copies, though extras, of the lettered *Light* and the special *XVII Machines*. Maybe I'm a hoarder, or maybe waiting for important collections at libraries in the future, but the 2 extras of *XVII Machines* that I have in the hall give me pleasure. I don't even want to sell one for a hundred, or two hundred bucks.
    Letter from Duane Schneider, who is going ahead now with *The City Parables*. I'm writing him & will jam in 3 more poems, I hope. It's gotten to be a full-sized book. Some <u>excellent</u> poems in it, though I'm worried about some weaknesses, "The Bridge," e.g., & poems at the end. Will be out during the summer, probably.
    I'll spend much time back here today. The vacation seems as though it's been a long one.
    I've found something in *Specimen Days* that will be a perfect epigraph for *CR*. Also, I've always loved & wanted to use that quotation about "deadly earnestness that makes beauty" in Jeffers "Boats in a Fog." To use Whitman & Jeffers like that would be, well, perfect!

Wednesday

    Wrote the letter to my folks. Will xerox for my brothers. That's going to be about the end of it. They're too sick to deal with, & Han does not have to live with what the stupid old man wrote. Enough. Too much.
    Dug up those 3 "ghost" quotations today. Something might come of it.
    Almost certain that *The Snow Hen* will arrive tomorrow.
    I've <u>dropped</u>, once & for all, that 9th section of *CR*, "A Letter," that was driving me nuts. "At West Hills" will more than take its place.
    Sun again today, & about 40°! Record warm spell, and to continue.
    No ball today, but definitely Friday. Knee is 80% back.

Thursday

    The Snow Hen did not arrive yesterday, but will today, I'm almost sure.
    Billy's team won last night—a great game. Billy scored 14 or 16 pts. Han and I are almost <u>too</u> excited by these games. Great pleasures in life—sex, poetry, books—but nothing for me is quite like watching my son play ball. He's 16, the age I was when I played for the Smithtown Indians in that small gym filled with screaming people, and I was one of the starters, after years of struggle & <u>heartbreaking</u> disappointment. Now Billy is back from a broken leg, & is skillful. And the aesthetics of basketball—his great wrist release, the arc of the ball. American reporters were just thrown out of Afghanistan, too, & thousands are starving in

Cambodia, and I am thrilled watching my son in this rich & safe suburban world play basketball. The contraries, again.

Again in the 40s today. Chores to do later, after lunch. Will turn to *CR* now.

1/18/80

The Snow Hen did arrive yesterday, my first five copies. I feel a deep glow about everything about it. I'm in Bill's debt. He'll make very little money on the project, but has chased around & worked his ass off to publish it. I don't want to get too anxious about *The Ewe's Song*, 8-10 months away.

Played ball today, painlessly, and felt in decent shape.

Much schoolwork to do this weekend and Monday. Tonight, though, another of Billy's games.

Most of my work the rest of the winter will be polishings of 3 or 4 sections from *Blackberry Light* that are not completely finished. Next summer I'll finish reading the farm journals, & will finish the draft of the long section, and then will have an idea, a better idea, of the shapes of the last two books.

1/20/80

It's Monday, & school things have started, though I'm having a hard time starting myself. Will type up syllabi this evening, etc. Dropped Han off this morning, & spent an hour in my office, but <u>left</u>, & came home, & wasn't going to come back here, but have, if only for a little while. Snow falling, birds feeding, wish I could retire. But the semester will be all right, once started. It's hard for me each time to get into touch with 75-100 new students.... Will play basketball today, & then begin in earnest. Two classes tomorrow.

1/23/80

Thursday morning. Am prepared for courses this afternoon. Will steal a few hours back here this morning. It's cold & snowing. I just spread bread & bird seed around.... Classes so far okay, though registration in composition is a mess.... Han & kids fine, both kids doing well in many recent tests.... I look forward to playing ball tomorrow, & to Billy's game in the evening.... Managing to mind my own business as school gets underway.

2/1/80

Very cold, but basketball to warm my bones in a couple hours. Billy has a game tonight, too.... Not bad back here, though I can still see my breath.

Have my classes sort of settled now. Shouldn't be a bad semester.

Haven't been sleeping well, but will. Haven't been back here for a few days.

I've entered changes in the copy of *The Snow Hen* I keep back here.... Judy Minty called about the book, and said nice things, and invited me to read at Interlaken. Guess I will.... Card from Bob Phillips—the fellow is always insensitive, calling the sections "poems," saying the light section is too Whitmanian. Bob just doesn't have a sharp mind or taste.... No word from Vanguard on the sequence book. No hurry.... I'm reluctant to finish this volume of my journal.

2/8/80

So much, regarding the disease, that I'll not be able to express here, or anywhere. A good week. Good basketball & some good moments in classes. Some slothful moments because of dead students.... Strange pressures from Curran regarding a telephone in my office & other things in memos without tact. This leading to doubts about teaching again, & Emerson making me think again of challenging myself by quitting and taking a chance on writing for a living. But the family, kids' college, and all.... But back here again, for an hour or two, health seeps back into me, balance, patience. My life is privileged, of course. Maybe it's the fault of this cabin, which makes me yearn to be here all the time that is not family time.... Now to *CR* for an hour.

[#3: February 9, 1980-December 31, 1981]

2/9/80

This was the only thing I could find in the way of a journal. Hope it holds up. The paper seems thinner than in the last two.

Just about finished a new Wenzel section of *CR*, maybe to be called "Science Fiction." I had to send Wenzel to another world, as science wants to send man, but he says no, and the chestnut rain begins again. I sense the rightness, the morality of this. This world is all we'll have.... My faith in *CR* grows. All I want is summer & some heat & green shadows & some evenings in the cabin.

Billy scored 21 in a win last night. His team is 10-5 now, a fine season.... Tonight Han & I will go to the school play—Kris is in the band. Tomorrow night, dinner at Mirko's.

Judy Minty writes that Pitt will do her 3rd book. I'm happy for her.

I've just carried this book out back. Its red looks good back here, and it feels comfortable on my lap as I write.

2/10/80

Right after I wrote that last line, Han clicked my heater off, as signal. The Picciones visited. We had a nice hr. bitching about the world.... The play last evening, "Fiddler ..." was good. I was moved, again, in parts—the "Tradition, oi" gestures, & the "sunrise, sunset" melody again.... Later, Han & I spent a couple of hrs. at Pylyshenkos, where we'll have dinner tonight.

It's ten in the morning, the cabin cold but warming, my family asleep inside. I'll read & write until one, and then watch some basketball.

Good thoughts about how the machine is working in *CR*, especially the Wenzel sections, beginning with "The Snow Hen."

I've seen Poulin twice, & he called once—trying to finagle for BOA with Parshall & getting me to intervene. But I shied off. And didn't tell him so many things I ordinarily would have—the Ewert *Kinnell* (Poulin wd. jump in on the ones Ewert won't do), etc., and didn't even show him *the Snow Hen*, etc. It's a new decade. No more. No more.

I stared down at Kristen often last evening. Her face was illuminated by her music stand light. Such a beautiful, sensitive, vulnerable girl, but in many ways strong and able to take care of herself. With a little luck, like finding a good man to love & to love her, past adolescent craziness, and with her music, she'll be fine.

2/11/80

Much talk of antiques, silver, gold, old Brockport, at Mirko's last night. Great dinner, much cognac.... Still cold, but the cabin is okay.... Will work on *CR* (that word "work" always makes me flinch), and then play basketball, no doubt badly, after all I've eaten this weekend.

2/17/80

Sunday morning. Have spent days on busywork, mail. And still much on my desk inside waiting for me. I don't know. Know how to avoid it, but don't yet have the courage. Maybe age 40 will call for even stronger resolutions.

Peaceful here, though. Restoring. After the Thursday afternoon gathering with Erik Steele & Greg Scarborough & Mirko—I must not become a regular part of that, as they'd like me to—after Billy's ball game (he had 22 pts.), and drinking after the faculty reading last Wednesday (the kid forgot about me though I disrupted my class to be there), and driving the kids back & forth, etc., etc., it's just good to sit here. And at this second I realize I'm saved: I feel fresh & new in this place, & receptive, after only a half-hour of sipping coffee & reading whatever is at hand. Inside, the pressure would just build. Thank you, Lord, for this cabin. What can I give to you from back here on this acre? Not much room for more trees.

Tom Woll called to definitely accept *Lord Dragonfly: Five Sequences*. Another book! I'm glad. It could be handsome, & it's an "original" gathering. Hmmm ... yes ... it's a good thing, the right thing for me now.... First *The City Parables* will appear. I'll drop Duane a note today in answer to his good letter. I'll probably read at Ohio in the fall.

I did not go to the dept. meeting. I'll resist Curran's poor taste & power hunger.... I joined the Union.

Han & kids off from school for a week. They all need a vacation.

I like this long red journal.

Pot-luck dinner at Van Gundys' this evening for basketball parents.

Scratched out a couple ¶s on Vicky Gold. Gave Bruce Agte a copy of *Witness*. Have six journals to read. Hear a cardinal behind the cabin. Barry Leeds called—I'm so tired of him. Ken Venick wrote & I answered. Brother Henry sent me *Snow Hen* to inscribe & wondered if he could get things at cost. The sun is out & in. My cabin warm now. Will look at *Lord Dragonfly* & *City Parables* & maybe *CR*.

2/18/80

Beautiful afternoon back here, but I've profaned it. Last night I didn't want to give Billy's friend Al a ride home—a long story—and today I had an argument during basketball with Barry Schultz. Neither a big deal, but I feel guilty—oh, and I guess Curran, since I missed that meeting on purpose, hangs over my head, too. All this minor shit passes, but how to live a gracious, truthful live so that I have no regrets, no guilt? Maybe it's enough to have the low times come further & further apart, as they do. I waste my time whining. My diary might not believe it by now, but I am growing up. Most of most days I'm inside myself, and content.... I'll say no to the reading here March 19th. Fitz Gerald asked me to fill in for [unintelligible name] that evening. Sounded like it might be fun, & fulfilling, but I don't really want the strain right now, the local strain. Nice title for my *Love & Fame* disease book: *Local Strain*. Perfect opposite of *Local Lives*, too.... It helps to write out my discontents here, helps clear them away....

2/22/80

It's hard even to recount how real life has slipped away these days—the upset I've felt about Curran, the trip to Rochester for the tax audit, etc. But it's Friday, and I have the afternoon to unwind. I responded to Curran's demand for a written explanation on why I missed the last meeting by saying that meetings make me ill, literally depressed and nauseous, and that I did not plan to attend any future meetings, either. I don't know how this brilliant & truthful approach could backfire on me. I always want to settle things forever, get them behind me forever.

My classes have been good. I like the young people, most of them trying to wake up, as I am.

At last today the 10 cloth copies of *Light* arrived. Now I can tie up some loose ends.

Billy plays 1st sectional game, against Batavia at Churchville, Monday night. Hope they can win. Then they'll play in the War Memorial.... Russia-U.S. Olympic hockey match tonight.... I played ball today, and feel in good shape.

I've dawdled over this entry a half-hour or so, looking around, placing myself back here in this land—a few hundred feet clearance on each side, all the ash trees ready to leaf again. I had a dream last night that the trees around the cabin, especially in front & in front of the picture window, especially the spruce I spend so much time looking at, had been uprooted, that there were ditches & muddy excavations back here. I was angry. But the real world is making it, apart from my fear for it. I need this place. Just to know it's here keeps me sane.

2/25/80

I've brought this diary inside, for no special reason, for a while; also have brought inside several books I've been reading out back—want to concentrate on writing when I'm back there. This morning I read *CR* for an hour, & then moved ahead with a section in *Blackberry Light*.

Ewert announcement for two Kinnell items came today. I feel like buying out the edition!... I have to decide if we want to visit Bill in N.H. this summer. Right now all the presidential candidates are bugging him.

Hockey victory for U.S. yesterday lit up everybody in the country. Soul-stirring and, of course, stupid.... Billy's play-off game tonight. I have my fingers crossed. Just want one more win for him so he gets a chance to play in the War Memorial. Billy seems ready to go. He's a winner. I'm sure, mentally, I wasn't.

2/28/80

I was out until 6 this morning—a late class, Casey's bar, & then Bruce Agte's party with many students & Poulin & Parshall, then the diner. Physically, I feel fine now, ready to walk up to school in a half-hour and teach. But I feel wary, guilty, somehow. Part of it is just the drinking & the noise I made, & part of it the extra money I threw around (maybe $15 in all, which is nothing), & part of it the times of deep feeling spread around loosely regarding poetry at the 10-12 sessions in my office (though these times are fun, and good for the class); but there's something else I feel: somehow I've offended an inner-economy that wants me nearer to home and family, wants me mainly to mind my own business and go about my poetry. That's what it is, and I'm glad to know it.

3/2/80

Spent all day yesterday reading journals & doing other schoolwork. Have more to do today. Record cold outside. Not cabin weather, though maybe I'll go out back this evening for a couple hours. I seem to have a slight sinus cold, though.

Debating what manuscripts to trade/sell Bill Ewert for multiple copies of the Kinnell things he's doing. I'd like to be smart about this for once in my life. Was thinking of sending him a notebook marked #14 with "Anthem" & "Stories" etc. in it. But, little as I think of my own drafts, maybe it's silly of me to want ten copies of a Kinnell item, and maybe in 20-30 years when I set up the Heyen collection somewhere I'd want to have such a notebook.

Card from Joyce Oates saying maybe she could read here in October. Suggested I call her. I hate the phone for such things, but will.

Actually got $1 back, yesterday, from someone in Michigan, on that "chain letter." Might even break even, and get another $5!

Later: I did call Joyce, and it was a fairly relaxed talk. Looks like she'll be here Oct. 29 to read. I hope it works out.

I'm sending Ewert the drafts of "The Ewe," "Off the Expressway," and my Sexton review. It should cover the $200 for all the nice things he'll be sending.

The Attica movie is on television tonight.... I saw *Apocalypse Now* the other night. It wasn't as good as I thought it would be.

Kristen is not well & won't go to school tomorrow. Guess I won't get out in the cabin as I'd hoped. No big deal. I'm in a lull, anyway, when it comes to *CR*—but, I just remembered, I'm close to a week's vacation!

3/3/80

Bill Ewert called last night to report that Ernie Stefanik had a bad car accident, was in hospital. I've written Cis this morning. What a streak of terrible luck the Stefaniks have had.

We talked of Bill's Oates/Kinnell/Heyen projects, too. I wish I could become wiser and not want many copies of things & not become excited about these fine-press things to the point of losing sleep. After the Kinnell, and except for my own things, I'll just want one of each for my collection. It's good that Bill is building a fine Heyen collection, & I appreciate this, but I don't want to keep digging up manuscripts to send him for trade.... Next, I want to find something for Bill to have Rara Avis do next summer, maybe.

I've been feeling low lately—Han's busyness & our relationship lately, the weather, schoolwork so piled up that I can't get back to the cabin. But, vacation next week, and I should be able to keep it clear so that I can work on *CR* (or what rises) out back.

Kristen home today, but will be okay by tomorrow.

I look forward to basketball later.

Phil Donohue show debating paddling in schools right now. For the first time, this year, I've had to ask my freshman class to be quiet a few times!... What is Brockport coming to? It will take a few years for the smoke to clear.

Later: evening: I feel better this evening after a good workout, and with the news that the temperature will shoot up to 40s & 50s the next couple of days. I might even get back to the cabin in the morning.... Kristen is better, too.

Contract for the book of sequences came in the mail. Ha, guess I'll sign it though no cost of living increase is built into it, as Joyce complained about one of her Vanguard contracts some time ago.... Two more dollars came in from that chain letter!... Letters from Ralph Sipper (& his catalogue #17) & Peter Stitt, with Stitt's upcoming review of *Light* in *Georgia Review*. He's not a sharp critic, but he's complimentary. I'm reviewed with Phil Levine again.

Bill Ewert says he's sending me a 200 pp. blank book bound by Emily Rizzo. Don't know what I'll do with it. Maybe a hand-written *CR*, or maybe Volume 4 of my diary?... I realize that this diary will always be banal, non-literary, and only for me to look back on curiously. No energy now, e.g., to talk about what Stitt says, at first, echoing the "pure description" comment in the Thesing essay & echoing part of the Vernon Young review: these people cannot hear the reverberations in what appears to them to be just a simple or straight-forward poem. I can't help them to read. Anyway, these sorts of things, often on my mind, will never find their way in here. Just glimpses of mood, reports of what I've finished or what was published. But, for me, hosts of memories surrounding any poem, e.g., that I complete.

3/5/80

I'm back in the cabin, for the first time in about a week, more.

Couldn't sleep again, though I went to bed around ten. I know what I need. To be beyond worries of school details, beyond Oates & Parshall, beyond the upcoming trips I have, beyond my teeth, beyond Poulin, beyond the Vanguard contract & the letter in the *Times* that Tensil Clayton called me about, beyond my mother & father, beyond Gerber and Curran, beyond Stefanik & Ewert & Sipper and all that—just to be with my own poem again, *The Chestnut Rain*, and to be minding my business—beyond Thesing & Young & Bob Phillips who 3 or 4 times has said he hopes my sequences will retain their original dedications (they won't), beyond Colombia & Iran hostages & the primaries & Peter Stitt & Helmut's April visit—just to be back here minding my business with my poem is what I need.

In the 30s now, the cabin warming, the year warming. All's well, actually. Another month or so & that pale green tinge will appear around me.

3/7/80

I wrote (having a few lines toward something I thought would be much different) "The Fourth Dream" yesterday. It's a beauty, complex and subtle. It will take a good reader, but it's a beauty. It comes, if anywhere, out of the *Uphanishads*.

Out drinking last night. Fun. To celebrate this 12-day vacation which begins today. I slept late & decided not even to play ball today. The weather is milder, the weather warmer (I meant to say "the cabin warms"—I drift away as I write in this journal).

Rod (and maybe Greg) will go with me to Bowling Green.

Three more dollars came in on that chain letter today. Total of $12 now. Billy is getting a terrific kick out of this.

Emergency meeting of the English Dept. this afternoon about our losing positions, the chairman search, etc. I won't go. Too unsettling. I suppose I'm a fat cat here, too, with seniority. Mainly, though, such a meeting would ruin my weekend.

Tony & Jeff Schiff here last night. Maybe I'll drive out to Tony's place tomorrow, or Sunday.

3/9/80

Sunday. A couple hours back here this morning. Tony & Jeff will probably stop by this afternoon.

Han & I drove to Fairport yesterday through hail & snow & rain to Kristen's all-county concert. Kris was in the front row. We were very proud. I dreamed backward & forward. She's a lovely girl.

Spoke to Cis, & then Ernie, the other night. What awful luck they keep having. Now daughter Kerri is in the hospital, too, with an ear infection. Maybe, at least, Ernie will not have to teach the rest of this year. They have money problems, too.

Read the news this morning. This cabin, the soft hum of the heater, the rectangles of sunlight coming in, the snow-laden spruce outside the window, the thousands of small ash trees toward the front—almost otherworldly. I think of the same things back here that I would think about in church this morning.

Got out of bed to write down this piece last night!: "Proposal for the Safe Disposal of Nuclear Waste": "Bury/the stuff/in bad/poetry."

Letter from Vince yesterday. No one else like him. Lord, let him live long, & longer, and then always.

From the looks of the tracks around the cabin, the sunflower seeds I spread are feeding as many rabbits, mice, squirrels as they are birds.

3/10/80

I've been reading books II & III of *CR* this morning, glancing up from time to time at the many birds around. And just now the first redwing flew down beside the cabin. Just this morning I've been ten feet from the redwing, a bluejay, sparrows, goldfinches, a mourning dove couple, a starling, black-capped chickadees, a male cardinal, juncos—almost the whole range of birds we have here. Sunny, and warming. Spring.

3/11/80

Two dreams last night, or one dream with transitions lost. Students and I on a cart or flat wagon passing what I pointed out as the house I was building—land graded, the house modern, wood, yellowish. Then this cabin in a lot next door to it. Then, same dream or another, when I looked for my cabin on the other wide of the lake where I'd placed it to be away, it wasn't there, or was, and people had told me it was and visited it. Then three or four men had carried it to this side of the lake—it had floated like an ark—and were playing cards in it. They were friends, but I wanted my cabin left alone, over there, where it was, so I could get to it when I could. I've not written this well, and have dim apprehensions of all but a few places in the dreams, but this cabin & my time back here have obviously become extremely important—my life of thought & poetry, my spirit is held together here.

Windy and colder today. Later, I'll walk to town and arrange for my Michigan trip. Except for the money, this time I'd stay home, though, again, it will be pleasant except for the class arrangements here & the damned airports & travel.... Talked to Judy Minty again last night.

Six dollars came in the mail yesterday on that chain letter. What a lark.

3/12/80

Looks like the dates above are a day fast? Today is Thursday.

For two days I've lived in the Third Reich again. Read the non-fiction *Walls* by a woman who'd helped a great deal with Scandinavian prisoners in Germany during the war, and read the diary-novel *The Confessions of Elizabeth Von S.* by Gillian Freeman. That was some world, again & again unbelievable.

Long letter from Bill Ewert yesterday. Today a beautiful letter about wasps from his mother.

Very relaxing day today. Now I'll turn to the Mss. of sequences; I'm reading it through to see if some small changes are wanted.

Quite a bit of snow already today, and maybe much more on the way.

Kristen excited about her dance tonight. Her friend Christine will be staying over.... Billy & Han are fine these days.

A starling banged into my picture window & perched dazed on a nearby branch.

Next I'll read Teale's *A Naturalist Buys An Old Farm*.

Will make all plans this weekend for my classes & trips.

Have I mentioned here the $2,200 tax bill Han & I received? A heartache & headache. MIT tuition is now over $9,000 a year, & the government wants 20% of the money we've saved. Maybe we can get the amount knocked down.... $4 in mail from chain letter today.

Looks like Werner & Debbie will visit this spring. He's called twice.... Ongoing sadness about the situation with my folks, & bitterness.

3/14/80

Friday. Maybe my date yesterday was off.

I've begun reading *A Naturalist*.... It makes me think and dream about this place of mine, less than an acre, here in a suburb. Birds are zipping in and out of the small clearing between my picture window and lthe spruce for the sunflower seeds I've thrown about. I can see, a few hundred feet away, the backs of the Matsko and Mosher homes. Maybe, with those houses & the street looming so close, I can better appreciate these birds & the bushes & trees around me. Also, I know that those houses will disappear as the leaves come out, and my pleasure then will be intensified. I believe I could write a book like Teale's based just on my small land—the woodpile I've made over there, the white spruces growing along the line, the one mountain ash, the huge ash, the ferns along the path, the stone wall in back, the two horse chestnut saplings, the different birds, the silver maple beside the cabin, the rotting tree trunks behind me, the berry bushes, the light coming in to me at different times of the year, the tracks in the snow, the movement of water, the grapevines and poison ivy vines, the beech trees with cable embedded, the apple tree stump, the morning glory vines climbing the fence, the teasel and black-eyed Susan & honeysuckle & dying elms & the toads & butterflies & squirrels, the different soils in different corners, the new fast-growing shoots of the box-elder trees, the sunflowers we plant and the garden, the one white pine and the sun-starved maple, the two rocks—one a boulder & one a slab of flat stone—the moonlight filtering in, the sounds of summer & winter, the butterflies and moths, the insects, clouds of flies, invasions of ants, thumps under the floorboards, the snow in summer and the leaf-shadows of winter, the red-twig dogwood red summer and winter. I am part of something here.

3/16/80

As I write, two squirrels are eating sunflower seeds on the snow outside my window. They're about six-feet away, making herky-jerky movements as they burrow, and sit up with a seed in their paws, or leap up on an ash trunk for a few seconds when a movement makes them nervous. Goldfinches & chickadees & sparrows are also getting seed. Why don't I like the squirrels? Maybe because they're small hogs. Teale describes his own fruitless efforts to move one bird-feeder to where a squirrel couldn't get every damned last seed. Maybe, but there's something more. I shot a dozen squirrels when I was a kid, knocked them out of the Nesconset pines with 22's, but still I don't feel like feeding them, as I do like feeding the bird species I also killed. Maybe part of it is the old legends of squirrels burying nuts for weather like this. Have they lost their old instincts, their self-reliance, these squirrels? Maybe they seem too much like rats—they are rodents, I think. Maybe they are frightening in their own way—I netted one when I was a boy, in a crab-net, and it chewed & ripped its way out in about two seconds. The cute little thing could have killed me easily. Maybe I don't like them because of the stories of squirrels getting into attics, raising hell, being impossible to get rid of. They seem furtive and sneaky, the little bastards, twitching around to the opposite sides of tree trunks. If snakes remind us of our intestines, maybe squirrels are more deeply sexual, muffs with teeth and claws. I can see a brown spot in the snow where apparently one just urinated. It is the color of sunflower oil. Now the squirrels are gone, as are the birds, afraid of something I can't even see, maybe afraid of me as I looked up and looked right through them as l hunted this paragraph.

3/17/80

It's up to 50° today. The snow is melting fast. Bob Mosher has taken his new red Dodge from out of the backyard and will drive it, now that he doesn't have to worry about salt. Ron Matsko's blue Camaro left my view about a week ago. So, spring improves my view around here.

I read and wrote back here for a couple hours last evening. Walking back to the house, I stopped every few feet and could smell the slight spring tinge of skunk on the air. Then I had a thought and doubled back to check, by flashlight, the horse chestnut I transplanted to about 30 feet. This will be its second year in that spot. It's only about 4-ft. high now, but some day will dominate the other trees near the cabin.

3/22/80

I was at Bruce Agte's last night, with Rod and a dozen kids, listening to my rock-and-roll tapes, drinking in the spring. Much fun. Came in at about 4 in the morning, slept well, decided not to play ball today. I feel very strong and healthy these days, and my new short spring haircut seems to make me feel young.

Raining now, but it must be 45° or 50° out. I have the inner door of my cabin swung open for the first time this year, so I can see another section of ash trees toward the house. I've never felt a spring come on as I have this one. I have little schoolwork this weekend, and will spend much time back here. Reading Teale, I often think I want to do a book like his but based on just this acre. His knowledge is astounding, pouring forth in simple wisdom of things seen. But I could write a little, too, about the grackles *I* see, and the spring branches swelling with *Brockport* rain. But, no, no such project, except in poems as they come.

I fixed and finished "The Wool" section of *CR* a couple days ago. It came out better than I thought it could. Maybe I should think of adding another section, a Wenzel section to *Blackberry Light*? Don't know. I just don't want any of these good sections left over, left out. It all depends on the eventual long catalogue, I guess.

I'm struck, again, by the silliness of this pen, <u>my</u> silliness and, somehow, inability here over a few paragraphs again to write down the <u>depth</u> of my field the last couple of days. The prose pen is a kind of mind that skims. It's not evasion. It's just that my times, in diary language, become just notations, can't begin to suggest the richness of my world—in a notable class, in talking with Bruce or Marianne Burke, in learning something about grackles, in <u>seeing</u> the kids & Han & feeling such love for them, in working with a poem—the last couple of spring days.

3/23/80

Blizzard conditions last night. Wind and snow this morning. The world says "be wary"!
Yesterday I drafted a beauty, Teale's story of the steer that loved flowers.
Dropped Billy off at his SATs this morning. Han & Kris asleep.
Tom O'Donnell died. His last years seemed very sad to me.

3/24/80

I just this moment discovered how *Blackberry Light* will get to the fourth volume. I was listing the first 30 sections, & their lengths, just to get an overview. When I read section #30 ("The Muse"), which rests, I wondered how to get on, this time, from one of these rests—transition from 7 to 8, & from 18 to 19, work nicely. But this stop had me stopped until I thought of my long catalog-in-process, "Family Tree," that begins with a "But," almost sending the sleepers out of sleep: "But their children, and theirs, / and theirs out to the blight-struck chestnut branches, feel / something missing, almost / past remembering.... Yes, this will do it. And this means, then, that much of volume 4 (will it be called *Family Tree*?) will consist of this long section, that after that *The Chestnut Rain* will wind down.

3/25/80

I've finished John McPhee's *Encounters With the Archdruid*—a wonderful book. As rational as Dominy sounds, finally, he's a menace. The Archdruid knows doom when he sees it coming, in silt and in a landscape so tame that water skiers above what were once canyons won't know who they are, and won't know God.
Typed up the section of *CR* to be called "The Poem." Just about have it. *Blackberry Light* is going to be, well, heavy, or thick, or—I can't think of the word—there won't be much skirting away. It will be an insistence. It will be at the center, less jumpy, swirling into itself.
Mom wrote such a sad letter, sent it to me at school, told me not to write again. I'm glad I didn't enclose the note I wrote to send along with Kristen's. If the folks want to go on believing that we are nasty bastards, that they can attack Han indiscriminately and for no reason forever, then that's it, goodbye, though this is sad, and though their cries of martyrdom will hurt me in the future, and though I am disappointed in myself (am I, really, or was my relationship with them based on lies & my forever putty-like forbearance?) that I didn't, somehow, keep the lid on everything when they were here? Now, I just want years to go by. Poor people. And every day their ridiculous belief that they are the injured party will deepen. Oh, Lord. Nothing, nothing to be done. I swear that even should Han die tomorrow, I want nothing to do with them. Too much bitterness & nastiness & sickness, & it finally boiled over.

3/28/80

Haven't been back here in a few days.
Had a gathering last evening for James Wright from 8-10 in my office. The Marchants were there, and eight or ten students, and I. I played the album of Wright reading, and then we talked and read things. I had a dozen Wright books spread out in the center. At first, I felt, well, wrong to be doing this, ill at ease—Tony nor Al nor Sandi showed up—but then it went nicely, and I felt fine later. If I'd been in NYC I'd have gone to the memorial service Bob mentioned. This was a little thing in my office, but it was nice, but, again, I see how few people care about what I deeply care about. James Wright, Berryman, Sexton, Hayden already dead of the poets I've met, and Wright the closest, most important to me.
Had a dream last night that there were piles of letters at a neighbor's at an auction, and shuffling through, looking for stamps on the envelopes, I saw one addressed to me—addresses on the envelope had tried to find me. I'd never received it. It was written in German. It was from Yale & offered me a spot there, years before. I woke up with a deep feeling of relief, knowing that because I never got that letter I was saved from the kind of deadening life it would have led to. I realized that I would never have written any poems if I'd gotten the letter.
Billy's basketball banquet this evening. Han has done a great deal of the planning for it, & the work. I usually wish she wouldn't, & wd. let others do it for a change.
Galley proof for *My Holocaust Songs* came a couple of days ago. I'm pleased that it, too, will be hardbound.
I've finished, now, "The Fourth Dream." It's a good one, but it takes/needs a good reader.... I want to send a batch of poems to *Poetry*.

3/30/80

Sunny day today, and warmer than it's been. It was supposed to rain all day, so we've been lucky. I washed out the garage, and then we visited Mirko & Irma for a half-hour. Han is working outside in her raspberry patch, cutting canes & raking through. All's well. I typed up a batch of poems yesterday, & will pick out ones to send to *Poetry*, I think.... Worked long on the "Auction" section of *CR* the other day. I'm having a hard time getting it just right.

Werner & Debbie arriving for a visit on Thursday, we think. I sure don't want to spend much time talking about my rupture with the folks.... I'd better do much schoolwork this evening & tomorrow to get ready for my trips.

3/31/80

Worked back here this morning—sent some poems off to *Poetry* & worked on the "Auction" section of *Blackberry Light* (might have it about right now), then played ball & ate lunch & am back here for a couple hours before supper. Raining all day, but just a slow, seeping spring rain. Boxing on this evening—I'll do school work while I watch the four bouts.

Tomorrow, April, and it should go very quickly, especially with my trips.

Glad I missed the dept. meeting again Friday. They seem to have come to no agreements regarding major revisions, tracks, etc. All the depts. except for business & nursing are crying " a student, a student, my kingdom for a student."

Read over *The Ewe's Song* this morning. It's finished. Haven't heard from Bill about whether we can get "The Steer" in.

Day after Easter

Debbie & Werner have left. I miss them, but the past few days were a whirlwind. I feel close to Werner, and we had good talks, and went to a coin shop twice—he's become a fanatical collector—and saw old slides twice. I managed to do some journals while watching television a few times. Werner has gained much weight since we last saw him, and smokes all day, and sits around. He doesn't enjoy life much, keeps saying how the world is going to hell and how he doesn't care, constantly talks about money. In many ways we've grown far apart, but I don't say much, and love him. He's sort of puzzled by my life, my poetry-writing. He's a good guy, a solid brother. Ed didn't make it here yesterday. Kris & Debbie had a wonderful time together. Billy has been playing golf & poker & basketball with his friends. Han has worked hard. We'll visit her folks tomorrow, right after my classes. So many things to do, details, details. My upcoming trips have been on my mind for a long time, too long. But the money sure will come in handy.... Vanguard sent me $250 (½ advance for *Sequences*) today, just in time for me to pay for plane tickets.... I hate always to look ahead, but I'll be in great shape about May 15th!

Put one screen in my cabin door just now. Will wait a few days for the other. A beautiful, warm day, much bird-chatter around me.

Ewert sent me proof copies of *The Shy Bird*. It's a beauty, the illustration by Craig Towers hand-colored. I'll want to frame one for back here.

4/11/80

What a week. Schoolwork every minute, even while we were in Nashville. Getting ready for my jaunts next week. Most things in order now. I'll play ball today, and then keep planning and getting things ready.

Han will pick out a garden storage shed for us today. Al Studier will put it in while I'm on Long Island.... While I'm away, all sorts of things will be going on—poets coming to Poulin's doings and all. I'm glad to miss most of that. I'll come back feeling fulfilled, and ready to finish the semester.

Lovely letter from Archie yesterday. I'll <u>tell</u> Rod Parshall to get MacLeish here next year & to give him the International Award we give. Maybe MacLeish will stay several days. Lord, keep him.

It's the time of the year when the light is a little too strong coming in toward me from the picture window. I think of a shade, and then the leaves come.

No word from Ernie Stefanik at all. Maybe I'll call again.

Vicky Gold's chapbook should be ready soon.

The word is that out MFA in creative writing is about to go through around here. I'm not sure what this will mean to me. More work, certainly. Some better students, maybe.

Is it possible that I'm back, that I'm through with trips and readings for now? Spring sunlight in small patches on this page as I write. I've just vacuumed back here, and later will go over the desk & bookcase and sills with some lemon wax, will get this place ready for my soon-to-be summer.

Bowling Green trip was exhausting. Things went generally well. Got into touch with a few people who cared.... Michigan trip was excellent. Judy Minty and I walked and talked. Some young people cared, and a few other people—Jack Driscoll & Nick Bozanic—were around. Jack and his lady Lois made a great dinner and Jack gave me his book of poems and about 10 pounds of trout to take home. Han looks forward to our meals of fresh trout. I owe many thank-you notes.

Back yesterday from LI & NYC. Things went well—one disappointing turn-out. Good experiences with the Clementes, with the folks at Vanguard, and with Bob Phillips, though Judith is in sad shape. I have 17 pounds of poetry books on their way to me from the Strand, & others from Barnes & Noble. It's so delicious, now, to be home, walking my own life. Even now Poulin's big show is going on in Rochester, too, and I'm glad to be missing it.

Stopped in to see Marge Cohn at House of Books & she drove me nuts.... Sat on a boulder at Stony Brook Harbor with Vince one perfect morning.... Spent a few hours with Norb & Katherine, who will get their baby, a girl, from Colombia soon, & will spend next year in Freiburg.... Have many thank-you notes to write.... Signed a book for Lars Svanberg's daughter at SCCC!... LIRR & the city were almost intolerable for me this time. I have a new light line about the one smiling commuter reading the *Ramayana*.... Am I really back? My whole body needs to unwind. A few last days of classes, and then a week of reading papers, and I'll be done. Al will be putting up the garden shed this next week.... Han & the kids are fine. I love & need them, and this home, & this lucky peacefulness. That city: oi weh! I have checks (not all profit) totaling $1,400 in my drawer now, for all this work. So it goes.... My mind is mud, and it will be a couple of weeks before I can move into *CR* again.... I'm home again!

May 4, 1980

Perfect spring weather these past few days. My journal-reading is going along, and I've been relaxing. In a few days my grades will be in and my summer will begin.

Al Studier has just about finished our garden shed. It looks good. Billy & I uncluttered the garage this morning, and mowed. Everything becoming orderly.... I gave Han $765 in checks from my readings to take care of the shed bill & to pay Al.... One more house expense—replacing the sliding doors at the back of the house—and we'll be caught up with everything we've wanted to do.

Went to Pyramid Gallery in Rochester last night for Frank Judge's conference. First Joseph Bruchac read, for about a damned hour and a half—he tried to disguise it but he's a horse's egotistical ass—and then <u>ten</u> others at an open reading. It went on and on—awful stuff: a high school student reading "roses are red / violets are blue" poems, a poor lisping fellow reading love poems filled with lines like "I love you oh my dearest darling"—and I felt <u>low</u> when I got out. I didn't even meet Bruchac, or Lynn Lifshin, though there were only about 20 of us in the place. American poetry.

I'm so dazed, that it will take me a few days of resting and writing back here to get back with any intensity into *CR*.

I've been in touch with Bill Ewert about MHS. 30 copies to be quarter-bound in leather, blue leather!

My new one-word poem: Frogress.

5/8/80

I've been exhausted, unable to sleep well, head swirling with journals and book orders and a pile of mail needing answering. But I am already, now, back here (and will stay up late to watch the Philadelphia-LA game), beginning to unwind. Still some chores, grades still not turned in, but behind my eyes the tension eases. Tomorrow morning I'll come back here early, and poke into a section or two of *CR*, and steady myself again.

I've just finished—it helped me keep my balance these past days—May Sarton's *Journal of a Solitude*. Many of her themes reach me here. The burden of the mail (and she has many times more readers and subsequent busy work than I do), the lack of time after a trip to think over just what has happened, the relation of the work and of the social life, the people and events that drain us while as Roethke says "great nature has another thing to do." I enjoy so much reading testimony.... I guess she'll use my poem in another of her journals. I want to write her a note (insisting she not think of answering) and send her *Swastika* & *Light* & maybe *The Ash*. Yes, I will.

The bushes have leaved around me, the cherry trees behind me are white. The ash & maples begin. The Vallones' home, the Moshers', Heyens' disappear day by day. I have a cabin crowded only under ash and silver maple beauty. There is a tanager moment in Sarton, too!

Han is fine, has found some time here and there to work in her flowers. The beds behind the house are beautiful, hundreds of tulips & hyacinths & daffodils in bloom right now. Tonight we'll attend Kris's concert. Kris is becoming more beautiful & sensitive day by day, is becoming a musician.... Billy had his driver's test yesterday. I stood there in a daze waiting for him, remembering myself at sixteen in Smithtown, and my own test.

Al Studier finished our garden shed out back. So good to have it—at last, now, we have room in the garage. My whole life has a new order to it.

Dinner with Picciones the other night, a good feeling of friendship over many years. Tony will soon spend two weeks by himself in a cabin at Letchworth. He knows what he needs. More power to him.... I don't see Poulin, who is off to Yaddo, with Mike Waters & Mary Marchant, etc. I'm glad I missed all the hoopla in Rochester when I was away.

My projects with Ewert are exciting, deeply satisfying. He keeps finding me new readers, collectors.

I'll be close to my soul again very soon, I know. It only takes me a few days back here to stand at ease again, composed. The ash trees know this, and keep time with me.

I'll walk to school later, slowly, and breathe deep.

5/10/80

I've been reading for a half-hour May Sarton's *I Knew a Phoenix*. Our lives are so full/too full—what to do with time?

My mind is still trying to unglue itself from school. I'll try to turn in grades and the last book orders on Monday. Bruce Agte's journal is holding me up. He may be the best student I've ever had, but is pushing it, this time.

I signed all the colophon sheets for *My Holocaust Songs* yesterday—they arrived from McCurdy at Penmaen Press—and called Bill to make sure where to send them. Han is mailing them to Bill for me this morning, and also sending to him the copies of *The Shy Bird*, which I also signed. *MHS* will be stamped on the spine, as I hoped it would be. My work is all done on it now, and I need only wait for the finished copies. Just two issues: I-XXX w. holograph poem, bound in leather; 1-150 bound in cloth & boards. It will be a beauty. Bill is single-handedly making me eminently collectible.

I want to begin reading *CR* again, from the beginning, bringing it inside me again for the summer, but today isn't the day, but soon.

Cool & sunshine right now. Behind my eyes I'm still shell-shocked from end-of-semester, wounded, but the shrapnel is rising to the surface of my brain and will work its way out.

Mon—5/12?

I read for an hour from my 1852 *Transactions of the American Institute*—the world of farms and machines when America was booming as never before (I want to find out if Whitman attended the fair that year), then read in May Sarton's autobiography for a while, but now I've been sitting at my cabin desk just sort of dazed. Sunlight and green all around me. A pleasure just to watch the honeysuckle bushes moving in a soft wind, the blackbirds sailing past me, the "feeding spruce" soaking up bright light, the small elm in front of me, and the almost fiery dandelion heads, and the tiny blue forget-me-nots, and the red-twig dogwood bushes, and the ash trees just beginning their unfoldings, and the white cherry blossoms off to my left. Now, for the first time this year, the occasional screen-ping of a bee. Many letters still to answer, and some jobs at school. I breathe deep. My mind is tired. I <u>feel</u> my mind, and it's tired. A day or five of farm-reading and tilling, and I'll be able to begin reading CR again.... I just saw—was it an oriole?—in the ash line to my left. I hope many birds nest around me.

Mother's Day yesterday—the four of us had dinner uptown on the Canal. And yesterday morning I attended Brockport's 113th Commencement. I came close to tears, often, sitting there in the sun, in the middle of the stadium, all those young people in front of me, the crowd in the stands behind me. I felt a part of something long, and good. I also felt as though my life were passing fast. I'm 39 / evening dawning. Spring is so emotional, all that reawakening. I've never felt another one like this one.

I've no contact now with my own mother and father. It's all very sad. I think it's up to them. I can't move toward them with their attack on Han still hovering in the air. This all must hurt them very much, too. If they would just once realize what they've done and have been doing since about 1960....

5/15/80

I've been back here five-six hours, reading (Bly's anthology), typing ("The Whistle" & the prose piece on the box turtles), writing (finished in a draft or two, I think, "The Emblem"). I've enjoyed this, and count my blessings, but still, for no reason, feel nervous, anxious, tight under my breastbone and between my temples. That will all pass, day after day, as I write. Maybe there's a tense desire, right <u>now</u>, to do something perfect, write something that will last a thousand years. Bill, slow down, relax, you just turned in grades two days ago.

Still cool, door closed, heater on intermittently. Wish it would get hot. I want the door & windows open. But leaves are hiding me fast back here.

Look forward to Kristen's concert tonight.

5/16/80

The door and windows <u>are</u> open. Perfect day today. I tilled—the garden is ready—and worked back here. It's dusk now, birds singing around me. Four students stopped by a while ago—Tony Vallone, Bruce Agte, John Stigall, Keith Hafford—we took a couple pictures & played a game of basketball. John is leaving tonight. Bruce is dropping by later, "to talk," no doubt about his journal.

Got a few letters written this morning. Have almost caught up. Want to write Dave Smith about the *APR* review of *Light*.... Bob Phillips called to say his review of *Swastika* just came out in *Partisan Review*!... Wrote what might become a poem about finding an arrow. A strange piece. It began, really, with a rhythm from Robert Hayden's "Night-Blooming Cereus."... Monday morning I'll read *The Snow Hen* & *The Ewe's* Song & enter *Blackberry Light* again.... I look forward to pleasure to the finished MHS, & Duane Schneider says I'll receive proofs of *City Parables* by month's end. So it goes. And I want to send Tom Woll some notes on the sequence book.

Kristen was wonderful yesterday.

May 19th?

My fingers are sticky with spruce gum—I just straightened a tree.... Mowed all three lawns today again. A lush spring. Everything growing almost visibly now.... So much on the property. I just piled up a few rocks over there by the Mosher corner, and there's a good-sized pink honeysuckle over there. I should clear the weeds from around such things, but don't want to be that sort of undemocratic caretaker, but do admit to clearing space around some nice little maples.... In the middle of writing this I keep looking up and out into the trees and bushes—a hum of lawnmowers in the distance, and kids playing, and the coo of (I guess) a mourning dove somewhere. About an hour ago loud rock radio music from the Wrens, and the intolerable pounding, pounding of a punching bag. I get angry, but then things settle down, as now, into green quiet.

Played poker last night with Mirko, Manny, Manny's brother Ike—I won $70. It was good, after so long a time without a game, to play again.

Have written a few things. Mainly, have tried to render Paul Celan's "Mandorla," a poem that at first seemed to me empty, sketchy, but kept getting deeper, more haunting and complex. With my little German and small understanding, it's presumptuous of me to do this, and maybe even wrong for me to appropriate Celan like this, but I do love the poem, and it would be a strong addition to *Swastika*, especially near "The Liberation Films," for example, with its talk of knowing the Lord.

Wrote to Bly, Stafford (at last), Dave Smith. Am about caught up on correspondence. MacLeish says tentative yes to October 1st reading here.

Volcanic dust drifting over the whole country from Mt. St. Helens in Washington State. A pin-point on the map that affects the whole world. Our life is so fragile, so delicately balanced.

Next I'll get to the busywork of a letter to Tom with corrections for *Sequences*. Then I'll stay with *Blackberry Light* for a while.

May 23, 1980

Han's 40th birthday today. Hard to believe. Thanks to my poetry money, I got her a hundred dollar gift certificate at Frieda Weber's—she'll get several nice things with it. We've been through a great deal together, have been many places together. I love her.

These mornings have been perfect back here in the cabin. This is what I've always wanted. Leaf shadow & sunlight in here, and only *CR* on my mind—I'm able to get the big picture now. A morning with poems, an afternoon of gardening/reading/writing a letter maybe, and a long evening of puttering.... Bill Ewert sent the *MHS* ads, and a copy of unbound signatures for me. He's planning on maybe 10 *hors commerce* copies of the special, and I've written him to say let's stick pretty closely to the colophon.

Dinner tonight at Mirko's for Irma's & Han's birthday. Always a great time there.

Saw Bill Rock at auction the other night. I don't know. I feel sorry for him. He's had a rough year, as he says, and it's not over for him yet. I think he'll pull out.

Got four rows of onions in yesterday, and planted some sunflowers here and there.

I seem to be losing weight—194 now. Feel healthy.

Keep thinking of typing up the much-revised *Snow Hen* to send to *APR*, maybe. Maybe not. I keep rejecting my ambition. I'll stay with *CR*. Read over the as-yet untyped "Diary Entry: Nocturne" section again last evening—it's a beauty. And my ghost epilogue has great potential. Unfold it, then, again, Bill.

May 24, 1980

Just cleaned up and washed the garage, vacuumed back here, did other yardwork. Showered. Have come back here with a cup of coffee and have flipped on the air conditioner. Will spoil myself this hot afternoon.

Good dinner & talk at Irma & Mirko's yesterday. We were there until almost midnight. Tonight Han & I will drive out to Picciones' to see Jeff Schiff & others. Should be generally pleasant.

Billy is finishing the mowing. Much to do around here to achieve the look of country ease. Han is good at & enjoys planting, and will probably put in the tomatoes & lettuce & maybe beans today. Must be about 90°. <u>Seems</u> as though frost is past.

Worked on the section of *CR* called "The Poem" this morning. It's coming. The ending is hard to get.

Monday 30th?

  Bill Andrews here yesterday morning—picking up corn husks for his paper! Then Irma & Mirko & Irma's mother in afternoon. Then Tony Vallone & Keith & Bruce & Mike Waters & the Picciones till after midnight. Much fun playing basketball and showing & giving books, but now I've had enough people & will spend much of the day back here. <u>Fine</u> day. Billy off to golf, & Kristen will have Christine here today, & for supper (our first cookout), & Bill will have Brad. I look forward. Han in high spirits, too, with some extra time. I'm just plain happy, would not trade my life with anyone's…. Piles of Oates books left here last night, & many other things…. Came back here with Mike last night & showed him the sequences Mss. & some of the *CR* Mss. He's at Yaddo & chasing here & there. No thanks. But he's young, of course. Sandi & Tony were pleasant. Tony quit smoking and started again. This makes him unhappy, I know. Enough. A perfect day. I'll read the BOA Stafford, & maybe the Carver *Salmon* for fun, & then turn to a section or two of *CR*.
  Later: As I was reading, Bill Andrews came back here! To show me the spacing for the corn poem he'll be printing. He can be a pain in the ass, though he means well. I'll force him to do a decent job this time or the broadside won't be released.
  Put in 4 rows of corn, cleaned up the dumping ground in the middle of the property, dug a couple barrows of topsoil out of the ditch for Han, watered my acorns and sunflowers, cleaned the grill, ate lunch, am now back here for coffee. Just saw, as I checked the calendar to be able to answer Peter Dzwonkoski about his visit, that it's only the 26th today. I feel like I've just been given extra spring.

5/28/80

  Worked many hours yesterday in the yard trying to clear & level the center where we've thrown leaves & clippings & brush & rocks for years. A cool, sunny, perfect day to work, & I was surprised at how much I got done. Will begin building a low rock wall over by Moshers, too.
  Came back here this morning blessing the world & my luck. Thought it would be a perfect morning for work on *CR*, but it was the morning that comes once a month for town trucks to lumber & grind up & down the streets picking up junk. The noise was just terrible, even back here. I'll survive all this—there are enough peaceful times between—but (the noon siren whines as I write this) noise increases all around. A neighbor ruined our hour's visit with Irma & Mirko & Oma here the other day—we were sitting in our back yard—by having the nerve to mow & mow as close as 20 ft. from us. I never would have done that to him, but now will, & will clear out over on his side the first time I see he has some company, as we did. He'll probably be too dumb to get the message…. And yesterday, the <u>minute</u> I sat down back here, Bob Mosher started pounding on steel drums…. At this moment, a lull….

May 31, 1980

  A peaceful Saturday morning. In about an hour I'll go in for something to eat, and then head for an auction in Holley.
  Took care of some letters yesterday. Feel clearer by the day. Have a couple more weeks, now, while Han & the kids are in school, and I'll be back here with *CR*. After that, I hope to get my teeth taken care of, and, maybe—I don't even want to mention it here!—try that junk '50s novel that could make me, under the name Haines, rich. I probably won't have the courage to try it—one of my illusions about riches would be broken if I had to abandon it. Still … Ha.
  I looked up from my desk yesterday and a hummingbird was buzzing in front of me, trying the white blooms of the red-twig dogwood. What a bit of beauty. I hope it nests near here…. Several different yellow warblers around, one with black eye patches yesterday.
  I've got to learn not to be upset by noise, to count my blessings back here. Just read Henry Smith's essay on Gertrud Kolmar in *Dark Soliloquy*, the terrible conditions endured while writing certain things, and I feel

like a whiner. The problem here is that surrounded by trees I'm so <u>close</u> to perfection? So quiet now, only birdsong & wind in the leaves.

6/2/80

Bombings on the West Bank this morning—mayors losing their legs. Violence in South Africa, and in Fort Chaffee, Ark., where Cubans want <u>out</u> of the processing center. Mass starvation, still, in Cambodia. I'm drinking my coffee this morning form a mug marked "Chu Lai/RVN", brought back from Viet Nam by Kenny. It's not easy to write or want to write or even to believe in poetry. Maybe it has never been, and maybe that is what it is for. I'll type up, again, the "bark" section of *CR* and enter that poem again.

6/4/80

This was to be a week for me with only writing on my mind. We weren't going to have the glass doors put in the house until maybe July, but I said (did I?) what the hell, & Han had them delivered, & Al started working, and not in the afternoon as we sort of asked but he didn't hear. And of course he needs me for this or that. So this morning I was in a foul mood when he arrived before eight & started banging. I helped for a half-hour pulling out & carrying down the old doors, and then had breakfast, and then headed back here with a cup of coffee. Al called down from the porch things about having to cut through a header & measurements & such. I like him very much, & his work gets other things off my mind, and we're lucky to have him do these things (the back porch, the garden shed, now these doors, not to mention work on this cabin wherein I now write this entry), but he has no conception, nor does anyone else here in Brockport, nor do people in this country in general, of the quiet & peace of mind it takes for poetry to get written. I stood there with a cup of coffee in my hand and nodded and listened, beginning to swirl again with things I'd managed to dissipate while eating a bowl of cereal. I was discouraged & angry, at Al, at Han for not forgetting about the fucking doors until July or so, at the world. Just read more of Ellman's *Yeats*, and there's no question that W.B. couldn't have done all that screwing around and experimenting (with a "psaltery" where I am now) had he not been part of a culture (and out of a family) that exalted art & poetry. So, here I am, and have mainly myself to make me believe in what I'm doing. So be it. <u>But</u>, the point, or conclusion, or event that confounds this paragraph is the fact that when I did get back here, an hour or so ago, I sat down with the line I had from a week ago ("Blackie was her dog that roamed the dark / while Mrs. Terlik slept") and in about 15 minutes wrote "Blackie," a beauty in twelve rhymed lines. Despite everything, a poem came along, a good one, and I'm grateful for it.... If I could just grow up enough to take things in stride ... Maybe I will. It just occurred to me that maybe in part this will involve sort of being distracted with my own work, not really hearing or listening to these other phantoms of the world as they call down from the porch.

6/6/80

The hardest rain last evening, for about an hour, that I've ever known in Brockport. Han & I picked up Kristen and Christine from their dance, and sailed home.... At home, Billy and five friends playing cards, then all of us up until midnight talking of high school and making jokes. A moving evening. I kept looking at Kris & Billy as they are now, wanting to stop time, but told myself (and it's true, too) that I will have as much joy in them (will I, or be so sad that they will age and die?) when they are middle-aged. Well, with luck they will have children, too. In all this <u>I</u> feel strong, am not (now) sorry for myself.

The world so fresh and green back here this morning. I typed a few sections of *CR* and have just read the "Right Mastery of Natural Things" chapter in Ellmann's *Yeats*. I feel such a fullness, right now, in my own life, and want to go on with confidence filling out *CR* as though it were a masterpiece. Could it be? It will be <u>my</u> masterpiece, the best <u>I</u> can do, at any rate.... I have a sense of wide time right now, too, am even ready to expand my Whitman essay for an anthology, & maybe write some kind of lecture for Wisconsin.

Dan Stryk writes that Dave Smith will be at SUNY Binghamton next year.

A call last night from Bernie Quetchenbach who was drinking at Bruce Agte's with Tony Vallone & Tony Piccione—they'd been there for about eight hours since their class, I'm sure. I first said I'd go over, and thought I would, but decided to stay home, and am glad I did. Am I growing up? At least the inner-economy speaks more and more often. I really have fun with them, but have nothing to gain from them for my writing. I hope Tony Piccione is not going overboard again with his drinking. His rhythms are all excesses, one way and then the other.

Rich letters from May Sarton and Bill Stafford.

A baby robin, speckled and fat, fluffing on an ash branch about six feet from me.

6/12/80

I went into Tony's class yesterday, and was generally sorry I did, and have learned another lesson. It went okay, but I did all the talking for an hour and a half, and felt I was back at mid-semester. That's enough poetry talk for the rest of the summer.... And later, Tony tried to see polarities in his view of poetry and mine, and I was just too tired to listen. I'll make him talk more, always, in the future.

Spent about three hours moving rocks to the wall by Moshers yesterday, and this felt good. I like prying them from the wet ground, and lifting them, & trying to fit them together in some semblance of solidity. I like the way my wall is growing. It will protect my row of ash, & to some extent the pines, too.

48° now, and warming, at last. Just now, walking back here, I got to no more than six feet away from one of two rabbits that like it back here. The sun was shining through its ears and I could see the vein-patterns.

Felt like some talk last night, and called Bill Ewert. I'm to get a long letter from him today about all sorts of things. Orders coming in for *MHS*. I have to keep telling myself to think more about Vanguard & wider things, but do feel happy to hear an Ewert thing is selling.... Ernie, Bill says, wants to sell all his Heyen letters & manuscripts—Bill will work with him in finding an institution. Rochester?... This whole rhythm in my life will pass, too, I think, this rhythm of collecting, archives, limited editions. It will be something that happens naturally, while I write poems and build books, but won't be at the center of my interests, as it often is now.

I just took a deep breath. Peaceful back here. No more classes and such the rest of the summer, just pure work on *CR*, and work on the wall.

Later: I read over my new poem "Blackie," about Mrs. Terlik, and began to think about Joe Terlik, called "Black Joe," the drunk of my childhood I seldom saw but heard much about. I scratched out a first draft of what might be called "The Ground." It could turn out to be a good one. Good to be back here in the cabin. Minor poems, yes, and I'd rather be writing great, major, magnificent poems of life and death and time and history, but right now I'll take what I can get.

6/13/80

How obliging can a bird be? He's still in front of me, as I write, and I've identified him clearly, I believe. I've been looking at him, a male yellow-throated warbler, for about fifteen minutes. He's still there, in an ash branch, about fifteen feet away and ten feet from the ground. Distinctive black mask with white above it, and the dandelion-yellow throat.... He just sprung away and I've lost sight of him. About ten feet in front of me some tiny birds are obviously building a nest in a small honeysuckle bush—I think I've only seen the female. She may be the yellow-throat's mate. I get just tiny glimpses and trembles as she approaches the bush from the other side.

June 13th, a Friday, and the moon's pull maybe did it again, and Mt. St. Helens has erupted, covering Portland and vicinity with ash. A sad thing—I think of people waiting to get their gardens going, as we do—and an awesome one. Maybe the fertilizing effects will balance the damage, but around that mountain is muddy-gray wipe-out. The earth has time, speaks in eons, but people only have a few score springs and only if they're lucky.

6/14/80

It's almost ten in the evening. It's raining, but after two full days of sun. Only the sound of the rain back here, only the light over my left shoulder.

Found/wrote the poem, in fourteen lines, "Post Mortem: Literary Criticism." Much fun. Don't know if it's for *CR*.

Han and I were at an auction this morning in Chili when a deer's head was sold and passed back. I began to write on my bid-card, in a trance for a minute or two, and have a hunch that the poem I'll make from this writing—I've been afraid to look at it all day—will be a beauty. I swear, consciously I didn't even think of the deer theme in *CR* and how perfectly this trophy sold at auction will work in the last book. Thank you, Lord.

I answer letter after letter, still clearing away. I am also writing the bullshit thing for Kord-Lüdgurt in Germany (will finish it Monday night while watching baseball, relatively painlessly this way), then will do the activity/merit form for the college, & the parking business, and then will be free. It's not easy. But the poems, and *CR*, keep coming. It's all working out just the way I'd hoped. *The Ewe's Song* is close to proof stage, *Blackberry Light* will be finished probably by the time we drive to New Hampshire, but if not, no sweat.

Brother Ed actually sent us the $500 he borrowed 2-3 years ago. We were surprised. Hope it signals a new prosperity for him, and not machinations by my mother.

The stone wall is coming nicely.

Kristen came home yesterday with an engraved trophy. She was picked as best performer in select band. She deserved it.... Billy was reading the catalogue from MIT today.

6/17 (I think)

I still haven't looked at what I wrote on the auction bid-card. I will when the time is right, some evening. I'm probably completing it inside me now.... Last evening I drafted a poem that begins being about a pair of yellowthroats. Could be a fine one. Many things underway now, as always when school is not on my mind, apparently.

Record low again last night, but a few days of sun upcoming, supposedly.

Han's picnic for her ten "poor-learners" was fun & exhausting yesterday. I took them for a "nature walk" back here, cooked the hamburgers and hot dogs, and played soccer with them on the back lawn.

I'm looking forward to a package of *MHS* from Bill Ewert. Another week or two, I'd guess. And proofs for *City Parables* are overdue.

"Post Mortem" is for *CR*, and *CR* knew it all the time, was waiting for it to follow "The Poem."

A perfect day to be back here, as I will be, for 8-10 hrs. today.

6/21/80

A long, perfect day. I actually slept until about ten, after being up my usual couple of hours of tossing and turning at 3 & 4. My best night's sleep in months. Warm & sunny today, and the family at home. Picciones stopped in for an hour. Only dim note: rabbits have gotten to my last two sunflower seedlings, alas. I'd have enjoyed them all summer.

Bill Ewert says *MHS* won't be done until end of July. No sweat, though I was starting to watch the mail. Allen Hoey, meanwhile, doing a little broadside, which he'll drop off July 2. "Our Light" in a portfolio of five things, nicely printed.... Martin Booth doing "...: The Candle" as a pamphlet. Let it go, what the hell.

My poem that holds the boy in the fold with the pail of blood for a while is getting there.

I said no to judging a contest for PSA.

Han's nest of baby rabbits still seems undisturbed. The four little ones seem fat & healthy. Such big eyes looking upward through the hair-nest when I look in.

Han & I played poker for a couple hrs. at Bruce Agte's last evening.

All at once, just now, two robins, a cardinal, a catbird (until chased by the cardinal) feeding in the cherry tree behind the cabin.

The summer is going too quickly. Maybe it will slow down the next month or two.

Han can't believe she's through with school.

Letter on *Swastika* from a Robert Jay Lifton at Yale. Quite a letter.

I did send the revised *Snow Hen* to *APR*. Wd. be nice if they'd do the 7 sections. Then, in a year, I'll do *The Ewe's Song* with them or another magazine, etc.

I like the bits & pieces rhythm of this entry.

Vicky Gold's chapbook dropped off by Tony Vallone the other day. It looks good. I'll drop her a card.

I should make dentist appointments for the summer.

Still haven't looked at the auction card. I know it will be good.

"Yellowthroats" just about done.

Sprayed against ants again out here yesterday.

Pretty close to finishing "The Poem" section of *CR*.

Ewert now reading all my 150-200 letters to Ernie. I don't know. Are we all trying to clear everything away so that we can die?

6/22/80

I came back here this morning just to sip coffee for an hour and maybe to turn to a poem, probably the one on Wenzel and the ram, but picked up the auction card where I haven't looked at my "Trophy" poem, on purpose, for a week or two. I started to work on it, worried that I could ruin it, apprehensive, and began to find it again, when the tractor noises began, & loud rock noises, from neighbors, and Cindy Mosher yelling for the dog, & then for her father to come to the phone, & I was in and out of my poem in an effort to concentrate, and began to smile, because I lost the neighborhood for stretches of 15 seconds maybe, and the poem will be okay!

Later:

The Trophy

The deer's head is sold at auction for a few dollars,
    carried by its antlers to a bidder in the back row.

He is so old, ten-pointed buck who'd lived on mast
    in the chestnut hills and valleys of this county,

that his brown neck- and forehead fur have gone gray,
    moths have notched the edges of those ears

that once heard wind speak through long grasses where he lay
    as the night awoke with what were godly eyes to him

before he slept, dreamless, or, if this is the way things are,
    dreamed of passing over a crowd of people,

saw himself not as he was that day, but bodiless,
    eyeless, or with other eyes, depthless,

something other-than-himself, ghost over this same land,
    as human noise goes on,

as he floats within this nimbus, the last bone
    and fur vestige of the being he once was.

6/23/80

I've done in June "Trophy" (for *CR*), "Ram Time," "Yellowthroats," and "Blackie," and probably one or two others. I'm glad about these. They come from being away from school work, I'd guess.

Han and Kris are picking strawberries—not enough here in our patch yet…. Billy just finished mowing two of our three lawns. I like to do the back one myself.

Summer couldn't be much more than this. Such fullness, so much here now, and to look forward to.

At last I am able to sit back here with windows & door open, and in a T-shirt. About 70° now, and sunny.

High school graduation today. Billy will be one of the two junior marshals.

I've been soaking the chestnut burs Bill Ewert sent me some time ago, and will plant them where the rabbits ate my sunflower seedlings, and hope one or two will sprout.

6/24/80

I was finding rocks outside last evening—Han was inside making strawberry jam—when Mirko called. He had Bill with him to play cards. They came over, and what was to have been an evening of watching Yankees-Red Sox & getting that school form out of the way, was wasted in cards. I had to play, as a kind of therapy for Bill, his first time, in his two year strangeness now that I've felt, since Linda's death last fall. I lost $90 (almost on purpose?) and Bill won $135. It may be, after all is said and done, that I just don't like him much, despite his terrible pain since Linda's death. Joe came over to play, too, for the same reason. But now that's been done, and we'll feel free to say no. It's all complex, but one simple part of it is that I'm growing up and surely don't want poker over a beautiful summer evening. I was going to write this entry right away when I got back here this morning, because I was bothered by the whole thing and writing it would get it behind me, but turned to reading (*Zen in the Art of Archery* again), and to the poem "Ram Time," which found a new line (the "It" sensed that my other version was too cluttered). This is another stage of my growth, this entry here to record not the overall poor time/situation, but the turning to my own life again after the nonsense blows by. Yes, I'm becoming, growing in the right direction.

90° today. I'll take a bike ride, maybe mow the back, & settle into the cabin again after a shower.

6/27/80

Storm last night while I was back here typing Bill Ewert a letter. At one point, and I didn't mention this to Bill, water poured in on my desk. It must have blown up & under the roof where there is a space above the side plywood that I'll have to caulk, and will. A five-second leak in here.

Sort of an unpleasant note from Bob Phillips after I'd pointed out a few things in his review of *Swastika* that were maybe misunderstandings. He's so defensive, and seems ready for an argument. The truth is that he does not have a sharp critical intelligence, that his was a pedestrian review to say the least. Issues he takes for granted are beyond him—as though, e.g., one poem or three can stand to say what a book's consciousness as a whole articulates, and then almost unintelligibly…. And then the way he moans and says that the moral may be not to review books by friends (ha, he recalls no doubt my run-in with Mazzaro about *Noise* years ago)! The brain puddles up when it tries to think when hearing these sorts of things. I give up…. Also in the mail some wacky poems from poor Paul Gaylord…. But also in the mail a fine letter from Bill Ewert about, in part, his visit with Kinnell. He enclosed as a gift the inscribed copy "P" of *Angling, A Day*. Bill is the most important person in my writing life. What sort of sad & fragmented shape would I be in with the long poem now if it weren't for his project? And with other things: he'll have beautiful books made for me whenever I have something worthy. I can't ask for more. And he keeps getting my name around…. I meant to say, regarding Phillips/Gaylord et. al. (it was Poulin & Rock who got to me for years), that I'm calm & through with that. I've been thinking a lot of changing my life at my 40th birthday, of no longer saying things I don't believe in, if this is possible, especially about poetry. It won't be easy. I keep trying to make people happy, and may be spending my own soul when I do.

Decided, this morning, to leave "The Trophy" (think I truly finished it yesterday, that the buck declared himself still existing to me), "Yellowthroats," "Ram Time," and even *CR* alone for a few days. I've read & read finished & new things over for a week, & now will rest for a few days. Maybe I'll stop in at Tony's workshop today. Then the auction this evening. Some odds & ends to take care of this weekend.... Maybe I'll turn to the Whitman essay to see if I can come up with something.

Han & the kids are fine. Billy at the school working this morning, Han out picking strawberries again, Kris just rousing herself up by now. We're having a fine summer.... I'm just in no hurry on *CR*. *BL* is about done, & I have <u>many</u> excellent pieces for the last two books.

Read Wagoner's *Whole Hog* & loved it.

6/30/80

Proofs arrived from Duane Schneider of *The City Parables* a few minutes after my last entry. The book is such a change of pace that I've been glad to work on it. Maybe Duane will be unhappy, but I've been making ruthless cuts & changes. Have knocked out eight of the poems already set. Will add several others. The book is coherent to me now, and the individual pieces are good. I'll stare at it for about another ten days, & then send it back to Duane with apologies.

I bought a pair of binoculars at the auction the other day, for $15, and love having them back here. 10x50 power. They're marked "Dienstglas" and I have a feeling they were German army issue, maybe WWI? I hope I'll never look out on a line of approaching tanks with them. Commander Heyen wants only to focus in on trees and birds, and on little beauties like the dragonfly whose eyes I could see clearly yesterday.

7/2/80

I've been working fairly steadily on *The City Parables*. It's getting very tight. Its movement is complex. Allen Hoey to visit today, & probably the two Tonys will stop in, and probably Sandi. Oi weh.

Rain again the last few days. Some sun in between, but the ground is soaked as it has been all spring.

Han & I had an argument yesterday over the same old things. Nothing too serious. Nothing that can be resolved! The writing life <u>is</u> a selfish life, and maybe has to be. An hour here or there between family activities won't work, will not lead to any intensity. Also, visits with friends & small-talk is boring to me next to the drama of working with a poem or book. I place demands on Han & the kids to adjust to me.... Oh well, the years slide by without serious ruptures, and with love, and the poems & books get written.

7/5/80

Just walked back here, sat down at my desk, and was going to type up my revised "The Fourth Dream" for *The City Parables* when I saw that the whole top of my typewriter was covered with a spiderweb! I just used it yesterday, but overnight a spider built an intricate web, anchored on the return lever and the carriage knobs. I'm not ready yet, spider. Grant me a few decades more!

Had a fine breakfast this morning with Han on the back porch, which she's finished staining.... Tomorrow she & I & Kris will visit the Studiers on the St. Lawrence four hours from here for a couple days.

Allen Hoey visited and dropped off the broadside portfolios, which are attractive. He's not very lively, and it becomes a long day with him.

City Parables rounding into final shape. It now knows which poems it wants where, and will not abide intrusions.

Later: finished Paul Theroux' *Picture Palace*. The lessons keep coming back to me. An important book. I will someday make my own retrospective. It will not need me. It will be apart from me; at the same time, it will include all of me. The poems will stand for themselves, but behind many of them, when I look through the book when I'm very old, will be memories.

The last day or two, for no reason I can think of, I've been remembering Cortland—my heart just skipped a beat when I realized, again, that the bookcase a few feet to my left was with me there—our 3rd floor apartment, my fear about teaching, my easy chair with a few books in a table/trough to my right, a table with my aquarium on my left, the television eight or ten feet in front of me, and the bookcase/cabinet with its white hardware past the television on the left wall. The nice rug, and the couch to the right, and the wide doors to the porch in front, my desk in that porch overlooking Church Street. Han so young and vibrant, little Billy there—we have one particular picture of him in a red sweater that just made me choke up when I thought of it. Now he's seventeen, and Han is still beautiful but as old as I am, and I am here, and have two fine children who are themselves getting old, and what do I have to show for the years, what of consolation & substance?—the books, the poems, I think, always to be in collections, at least, and cared for, even if no one reads them. They say I was alive. I just thought of that *SHR* poem "In a Mortal Country"—I live that life now, do I? That Cortland world is now a series of photographs for me.

7/10/80

    Back from Clayton. It was a four-hour drive each way. We had a good time, but it's tiring being so close to others and talking all day. The river and islands were beautiful.
    Much to do. Right now, I'm just going to sit back and get my bearings again. I'll get *CP* to Duane probably tomorrow.
    Auction last evening. For $12.50 I bought a box of books on Shakespeare (3 variorum volumes & Bradley & Stoll & Kittredge, etc.) & hundreds of folders and guide books for various places—for gifts, etc.
    Picked about a quart of raspberries last evening, and the bushes are still full.... I feel like I've been away from my little cabin for six months.

Mon: 7/14/80

    Friday evening Han & I drove to the book auction in Leroy (I bought *Records of Southampton* ($30) (1874) for myself, and am reading it now, and a 4 volume *Geneology of New Hampshire* ($74) (1908) to sell up in New Hampshire, hopefully) and hated to leave early, but did, to get to Stafford's reading in Rochester. It was good to see him, and the Kochs & Kitchens and Stafford and Han & I spent a couple hours with him later in Kitchens' greenhouse in Pittsford. Much talk flowing, Judith babbling too much, but I did edge a question in to Stafford about how tiring these workshops must be for him, and he said something I'll treasure. Wish I had it word for word. He said that on Sunday morning he'd be on a plane, and the cities would go by, and then the towns, and then he'd still be flying. Then he'd be home, and late, before bed, he'd be in his working room behind the garage, and all Rochester would fade, the whole workshop scene, and he'd have in mind only Bill Heyen, in his cabin, writing, a "globe of thought" shaping itself in that cabin.
    Strange meeting, again, with Marvin Bell.
    Great letter from William Ferguson inviting me to give him a Mss. of 6-8 poems for his new Metacom Press. What luck. I've come a long way. Such pleasure in these limited edition fine press things.
    Perfect weather here. I've gotten a full quart of raspberries each of the last three or four days, and many more are ripening.

7/15/80

    Feeling sort of tired, lazy, disinclined to get on with *CR*. Did manage to find the ending that "Arrows" wanted this morning.
    Han got herself several nice things on sale for the gift certificate I got her for Christmas—a suit, some blouses, a skirt.
    I've dug out some Mss. for Ewert, and some books to sell to Babcock. Allen Hoey called to say Babcock ordered <u>30</u> of the folio!
    We had a little rain this morning, and could use more. Hot & muggy now. The air conditioner back here is a blessing. I'm spoiled. I can imagine what farm work is like in weather like this.
    Saw Picciones' car at Poulins, but missed them all praise the Lord.
    Dropped a note to Bob Phillips, not even mentioning his stupid reply to my reaction (even <u>faked</u> in its enthusiasm) for his review of *Swastika*. Bob just doesn't have it, the intensity, the poetic intelligence. No use

ever trying to talk with him.... I keep thinking that maybe when I turn 40 I'll begin telling the truth, when I speak at all. Best not to respond at all, most of the time.

I wasn't going to pick raspberries today, but I think I will.

Two bad dreams last night, one about the White House, and maybe they tired me out.... Maybe brought on by the Republican Convention, which I've been watching. Such a circus. So silly & so <u>free</u>.

7/21/80

Nine in the evening. I cam in to watch *Is Paris Burning*, which I've never seen. Have been wanting to enter a dream in this diary, and haven't had a chance.

Han is with the kids at her folks' and returns in two days. It feels odd to be alone, but I like it, for this short time. Friday we leave for Wolf's, & the next day for Canada.

I thought I would spend all this alone time on *CR*, but I've been reading. Finished Erdstein's book, finished *On the Other Side*, am reading Crankshaw's *The Gestapo*; have done a poem called "The Trains" and rough-drafted a poem about Himmler, a poem of chaos I want to make very chaotic & get much into.... I won't force *CR*. I've learned, at least, to do what I want to do. Can't force. No hurry on the *CR* volumes.

The dream was long. I'll make it short. Han and I drove out in the country, to an auction, at a farmhouse. A dinner there, too. A man's body was being auctioned off—I was surprised and a bit sick in my dream—the privilege of dismembering it with an ax. I stood in a doorway, not really wanting to see, but seeing—the body on a table, a black-haired man wearing cowboy boots. Then someone striking the corpse, first at the very top of the skull, then in the back where the whitish embalming fluid spurted out. A horrible dream, & it bothered me for a couple of days. I told Han in the dream that it was good she stood in the other room. Craig Wilcox was the auctioneer. The man had murdered someone, a girl, and the man first to strike the body was a relative of the girl. The body looked like no one I knew.

I haven't spoken one word to another human being today.

About 85° today. Comfortable in the cabin, of course.

Thunderstorms the past couple of days.

My world unreal as I go back to the days of the Reich. Endlessly fascinating, unbelievable. Did it all really happen? I keep learning. There is something indefinable inside me, soul sickness, sympathy, as I read of the death, the *Einsatzgruppen*, as though, after the first terrible death, I want all of it over with, <u>want</u> the world to go through a complete horror until all are dead but one race & color & religion. What is inside me. But my sentences here don't touch this either. These men like Hoess & Himmler & Heydrich. Animals, but out of a climate. But could it all have happened? And what is it to me? Much disgust inside me. Much <u>recognition</u> of the bastards doing the killing.

7/22/80

Yes, will not fight it. Worked this morning on the Himmler poem, now called "Poem Touching the Gestapo," and a couple of very interesting things happened to it. It will be a good one, eventually. So I will stay with this now, want to begin Waite's *The Psychopathic God: Adolf Hitler* now. The "Poem Touching ..." may enable me to pour everything into it. I will swim with this inclination, now, to keep feeling the Reich's light, and not worry about *CR*. If I don't take *Blackberry Light* up to Ewert with me, that's fine, too. If at the end of the summer, before the distractions of school, I get back to *CR*, that might be best anyway, so I can keep the poem close during the semesters, as I did last year.... Raining today, and I'll spend it with Hitler again.

Later: I am on page 107 in *The Psychopathic God*. For days I have been learning about myself, facing inhuman sympathies rising, my anti-Semitism, my hate & fear of, is it?, impurity, wondering what is wrong with me. Revelation after revelation. My inclination to be a Nazi, my thoughts of my racially pure children, my desire even to finish the job of the *Einsatzgrupen*, get it over with once and for all and then die, feelings of sickness rising in my breath, basic questions as to the possible <u>truth</u> behind the Nazis and their racial programs. But I now know, despite my questions (not put down clearly here) and feelings, what I'm up against: it is a pathology within myself, going back to my childhood, especially with my anti-Semitic extremely sick mother. Hitler, Wagner—what do we have but pathological cases, infantalism, interesting, even "genius," but finally unbalanced in unhealthy ways, as I am, when these feelings arise. I want to be whole, and mature. Probably my writing of all the *Swastika* poems is an effort to balance the sickness inside me with declarations, in poetic ways, or morality. I can believe, I think, thank God, in the morality of the poems as a whole. Language, music never lies, but whatever is found in my book eventually, it will mark a man trying to struggle upward out of his own sickness. How the infection of my childhood stays with me! So much more to this than I can begin to surround here.

Later: maybe I can never reconcile myself with my parents without giving myself to that anti-Jewish sickness again and again. Even to <u>humor</u> them and their feelings is to die a little inside. Even to <u>listen</u> is to make it harder for me to free myself and become human, whole.

7/23/80

Wednesday morning. Han & Kris & Kelly return today.
Disturbing call from Cheryl early this morning. She says that she & Ed will probably split up, that things have not been right for a long time, that Ed needs help & won't get it. I don't know.
I'm still reading the Waite book & will be, today. Robert Jay Lifton's name has come up, now, and I feel doubly warmed now by his letter, trebly!... When I finish the book, I'll finish my Gestapo poem, which, like "Darkness," will be a receptacle, everything poured into it.
Overcast today. A pleasant day. Out west, Mt. St. Helens has blown again.

8/3/80

Back from Canada—an exhausting, fine week. Many memories.
Found a few books in Lindsay, including *The Murderers Among Us* by Simon Wiesenthal. I keep learning. Am now reading Olga Lengyel's *Five Chimneys*. I must read these things. At the same time, I cannot help feeling like a voyeur. Also, when some of this comes out into poetry, it is as though I am appropriating the experiences of which I've read. But prose accounts, in the end, are somehow barely, only rationally (consciously) believable; maybe poetry of pounding rhythms (or what is needed for the particular subject) and deep images could be made a permanent part of the reader. Well, I seem to be with all this instead of *CR* now. Let it be.
My Holocaust Songs waiting for me at the post office. I'll pick it up in the morning.
Han & I have decided to <u>fly</u> to Ewerts, never mind the money.
Call from Tom Murphy this morning about readings in Pittsburgh. My fall will be filled up.
Good to be home again.

8/4/80

Have *MHS* in hand at last. It's handsome in both issues. I read over the whole collection this morning again, and my throat tightened up in a few places.
Call from Monroe CC this morning for a fall reading. What's happening? Am I arriving? The extra money ($250 for an evening this time) puts us at ease here. All's well as long as it doesn't interfere with my poems. So far, so good. I seem naturally to work hard at something and then leave it alone.
Our flights to Manchester and back will be $255 each! I was hoping it would be about $150. But, we're going to fly. And I look forward, though Bill seems to be setting up a couple of too-formal occasions.
I still feel worn out, maybe from the Canada trip. Did get a haircut today. Will now make some notes from my reading and see if any things want to get into my "Gestapo."... Don't think I'll be carrying along the Mss. of *Blackberry Light* to New Hampshire. A few loose ends need attention, and there seems to be no hurry. Bill is having a hard time prodding Bixler to get busy on *The Ewe's Song*... I have a free week now before New Hampshire.

8/5/80

Well, I have just typed up "The Trains" and "Poem Touching the Gestapo"—the latter poem has again exhausted me, emptied me, and left me free again for other work. It is an important poem, I believe. Someday there will be one big book containing all of *Swastika*, *MHS*, these two new poems, and two or three others I've done. And then I will have done what I was able to do.... Over the next days, now, I'll work on *CR* and maybe the little book for Fergusson's Metacom Press.

8/8/80

Extremely hot & humid these past couple days. I mowed the back lawn yesterday in 95° temperature.... Han & I are excited about the upcoming trip. Bill Ewert called to say that next Wednesday we'd be having lunch with the Halls, and that Annie Wright would be there.... Began last night and continued this morning drafting an article on collecting. Will talk about it with Bill.... Picciones maybe stopping by this afternoon. We might visit Pylyshenkos this evening—Irma returned early from Europe.... Billy went to see the first round of the PGA yesterday in Rochester, and loved it.... I've been very happy the past couple of days. Part of it, certainly, is getting "Gestapo" behind me, once again, for now. I believe my lecture in Wisconsin will be about my German poems.... My little air conditioner here in the cabin is a tremendous luxury....

8/18/80

So much to enter here, but I'll just scratch a few memories in.
Back here catching my breath again. The New Hampshire trip was exciting, exhausting. All in all, we got along well with the Ewerts. Things were hectic, and the constant book talk wore Han & me down. I contributed my share, but this was my first true exposure to terminal bibliomania—Ewert, Broomfield, Babcock. Now I want to rest, and write, and get away from the mania of collecting. My reading went well, & there was an autograph party. An artist by the name of Sig Abeles drew me. Many bookstores. A perfect visit to see Don Hall & Jane Kenyon & Annie Wright. A visit to the Boston Aquarium and, also on the way to Ewerts, the Old Manse, where I stood in the room where Emerson wrote *Nature*.
Kristen flew back today. Glad to have the kids home, to have all of us here—Billy decided at the very last minute that he didn't want to go to the basketball camp—Han & I found out a lot about our son. And when we passed MIT, I sure felt that that place was not for him.
I've sent out seven or eight copies of *MHS*, and am done with that. I want to tone down this whole business of busyness past the writing of poetry itself.... Ewert wheels & deals, to my advantage, but turns a corner here & there I don't care for.
Elizabeth Woll is designing *Lord Dragonfly* now. *The City Parables* is in the works, and *The Ewe's Song*. I want to get a Mss. to Fergusson. Then, I just want to work on *CR* & forget even about publishing for a while. In the end, only the poems will matter. I keep seeing this in so many different ways, if I'll only get the message.
A couple of golden weeks, now, before school. I'll hold them in hand, and not let them fall, for a long time.

8/19/80

Yesterday and today I managed to revise and type up my "Essay Beginning & Ending With Poems for Whitman" for that anthology I wanted to be in. Another thing off my mind.
Billy and I came back here for an hour yesterday and cleaned & vacuumed. All's in readiness. I'm even lugging into the house some extra books I'd accumulated back here.
Hot today, but the air conditioner is on. I'm spoiled & glad to be. Han's been putting up our pickles & making blackberry jam. I look forward to picking more blackberries today.
Next, my project for Fergusson, and then on to *CR*, to get it in heart & mind before school takes over.

8/20/80

Last evening and this morning I decided on and typed up a manuscript for Fergusson. It's called *The Trains*, and consists of 1/ "The Legacy," 2/ "Poem Touching the Gestapo," 3/ one part of the 71-72 journal, 4/ "The Trains." Also, I wrote a preface. A good group, and I think I'm doing the right thing. What is it that I want?—this is the question. I think I want this, now—to get it behind me again.

Just back from a bike ride to the school. For the second time this summer, a great sadness came over me, and I even cried a little. I find myself mainly thinking about the kids, Billy & Kris & Kurt & Kelly, in Canada, the swift vacation, the years going by, only one more short year, so short, for Billy in high school. I'm the one always preaching to the kids about the main life later on, and now these bouts of melancholy. Maybe it's myself I mourn for, but it's more than this. The children get older, the togetherness disappears. I would like to live on a farm, with my kids & grandkids, the generations together, for everything.... I guess the trouble is that I'm getting old—the kids are ready to go on with their lives. My poem, a beauty, "Ram Time," anticipated all of this in me. My life will go on. I'll lift the pail. Maybe next summer the eight of us will head to Canada again.

Memos for meetings, etc., now coming in. Still, I want to work on *CR* from now until studying for classes again.

I guess some sad things have been adding up: Archie MacLeish unable to come, Vicky Gold's sweet & courageous call last night, school coming on, the elm in front of the cabin dying & dropping brown autumn leaves already, the news about Kris's friend's soon-to-die father, the again immediate knowledge of the Holocaust during my writing of "Poem Touching ...", the auction the other night of the run-down mean farm....

8/21/80

Have been typing up *Blackberry Light* this morning. Won't send it to Ewert until I send proofs of *The Ewe's Song* back to him, but I want it typed up before school begins. Am just about done.

When Bill Ewert visited Kinnell, Galway told him a funny story, one that shows how much attention people are really paying—and one that may show many other things, in fact. It seems that after the conference in Michigan some years ago, after I'd read some of the *Swastika* poems for the first time, and after Galway had read the next night, someone came up to him and said that that was a wonderful reading he'd given of those swastika poems. He had to say, well, that it wasn't him, but, er, someone else....

My melancholy of yesterday has passed by.

I dropped my folks a note a couple weeks ago, saying we were sorry about Mom's broken ankle, and we are. We've heard nothing, and I don't in truth care. My next move will be to send a Christmas card. Then, the next thing will be to send a Christmas card the next year. The poison has never dissipated since Han visited Nesconset in about 1960, that unbelievable poison that poured out of them. A weird connection keeps coming up in my mind: someone wrote in *New Yorker* that one visiting Germany has the feeling of a whole nation that has not yet admitted or come to grips with its crimes, and my folks are filled with hatred for all minorities, all poor, all other races, and have never faced the truth about themselves. They are my parents, but again & again my silence has been a kind of tacit approval & I become a walking lie & I'm sick of it, sick of it to death. They have damned me & my family. I'll send an occasional card—this will give them the chance to think they're hurting me, punishing me, and also make them convince themselves beyond the shadow of a doubt that they of course are right about everything—but don't really care if I talk to them again. My father is the pity. He could have been a gentle and understanding man. He had so much to give people. My mother has turned him against the world. My emotion, now, as I write, becomes anger. I know what I feel, and will.

8/22/80

Was just reading over this journal, looking especially for the entry of how Book IV of *CR* would begin, and saw so many little things (Billy's driver test, my trip to Michigan) that call up details to me that I'll always remember. I'm glad I keep this journal, as thin as it is.

That bastard Gerber is going ahead with the books of interviews now. A note wanting response in my mailbox yesterday. I ripped it up, deciding to wash my hands completely of the whole thing.

Stopped in to make a dentist appt. yesterday, and there was an immediate opening & he fixed my cavity where a filling had washed out. I'll go back in a couple weeks for x-rays & cleaning.

Finished typing *Blackberry Light* yesterday. Want, still, to assemble, even in barest form, Book IV before school begins. I'll have to draft, again, the long catalogue section. First, I have more notes/images to transcribe.

Cool today, but warming. Autumn blowing our way.

8/24/80

Han & the kids and I are going off in fifteen or twenty minutes for a game of miniature golf. I'll have a good time just watching the family.

This evening I said Billy wasn't allowed to go off with his friends, that he had to stay home for a change. He and I went for a long walk, & talked: I told him about my worries about him, his sports obsessions, and our hopes for him, told him he was a perfect son and that he had a chance to make something of himself, that I knew it was summer but that maybe it was time for some more serious things. A good talk, a great boy.

This afternoon I worked hard for a couple of hours chopping down, with my dull hatchet, three dead elms. I'm so ignorant when it comes to DED, even after reading *World Without Trees*, that I don't really know if I've done any good. I've dragged the trunks to the road for the town to take away tomorrow. The trunks may not be buried or burned, and may lead to disease elsewhere, but here they surely would be harmful in the beetle & fungus cycles. I poured lighter fluid on & burned the stumps. Maybe some of the remaining elms will survive. We've one very big one near the house. It appears as healthy as can be. If this is the elm's home, I'll at least watch over them.

This morning I had one of my best sessions ever with *CR*. I've begun drafting "Family Tree," and it's coming together nicely. I've got enough material so that I can keep only the strongest lines.

This evening, this afternoon, this morning. Such a rich day.

8/25/80

Excellent progress again today on the "Family Tree" section. Decided to weave in the light refrain. Some excellent effects. To the "that" part next.... I have *BL* ready for Ewert. Just read it over. It seems finished, and strong, to me.

Played basketball at noon today for the first time since May. My locker had been broken into, ruined, but my sneakers weren't taken! Must get a different locker.

Guess I'll go in and fiddle around in the study. Will work on *CR* in the morning.

8/27/80

Things are happening quickly regarding my storage of books & papers & Mss. at U. of R. Peter & Mary Huth coming Tuesday to cart many things away. I've set aside & made a list of 150 good books, all inscribed, ones I have other copies of in collected poems, or won't need, etc. I will get my study in reasonable order, clear out correspondence files, pack away anthologies I'll want for my eventual collection, etc. I'm glad about all this. It will enable me at one and the same time to collect more and to focus on my own writing. So, I'll stay busy this evening getting things ready again. I was ready to let *CR* be for a few days, anyway.

Played ball & felt fine today. Meeting tomorrow morning, alas.

Yes, I'm really doing it. I want to build a tremendous contemporary poetry collection, & can't build it in my study!—that's the whole story. Now, I'll be able to store things, & maybe get some filing help. They're going to bring along acid-free storage boxes.

Lovely letter from MacLeish about *MHS*.

Nice back here, & I'm drawn here, but am drawn to keep working in my study to clear things away.

8/29/80 ?

Just typed up a list of another 75 books to store at U. of R. I'm loving this clearing away. It will change my life!

Saw Bill Andrews today. My poem (in brown) on his paper, doesn't look bad. The drawing will no doubt kill the whole thing. In any case, never again. Too many appointments with Andrews—I'm supposed to see him again tomorrow.

Terrible day yesterday, all in all. Han nervous about her job (that's all settled) & my meeting at school (awful beyond expectation or belief again) & then Bruce Agte came over, which was okay, but then Poulin did, & he made me sort of anxious, vaguely anxious again. Glad to be quit of him. He gave me a xerox of "A Nest of Sonnets" he wrote while at Yaddo. They're juvenile, a joke, badly-written silliness. This affirms a great deal for me. He can't live the life he lives and expect to be a writer. Lord, how embarrassing they are. And when he sends them off to people!! Now I do know what I knew before.... And there's an odd dimension to them, an attempt to write poems against the long poem, CR, he thinks I'm writing? Han noticed this. I don't know. It's strange, though, to be sure.... This journal, my soul, has been free of him for a long time, and will be, now, again.... Did play basketball, yesterday, and ended a couple of close games with some long jump shots.

Nice penguin broadside from Stafford today.

9/1/80

Have worked steadily inside on getting letters & books & manuscripts ready for U. of R. They visit tomorrow. I haven't minded being away from CR. It's all part of the rhythm.

Have spent much time thinking about how, at 40, I would like to become a man, free from anxieties about petty things, and, when I have to speak, telling the truth. This means to Phillips & Poulin, e.g., whatever the consequences, & to someone like Bill Andrews. Silence in most cases, but straight talk when—is "necessary" the word?—called for, when it would make me feel better. No more lies about poetry & what I believe. I haven't expressed any of this here with the intensity with which I feel it. It's time to grow up. Why do I flow along trying to be (am I?) every asshole's friend? Misguided loyalty. The business of my (too-gentle) letter to Phillips regarding his review, & his one nasty and another maudlin reply. Poulin & his sense of himself as he cheats & abuses our students. Such things. I don't have to countenance or ignore everything. I have been afraid that honesty in such cases wd. lead to reciprocal anger that would (as it would) disrupt my writing. I'll get over this, become a human being. 40 seems to me an important age. Time to grow up.

By my last entry I'd only skimmed a couple of Poulin's sonnets. The other evening, I really read a few (still can't read them all—too painful). It's almost unbelievable how bad they are. This confirms what I've wanted to believe: that that kind of business wheeling & dealing entrepreneurship hype life leads to great distortion & dishonesty in the language. It does. Can't wait for Tony to see them. Hope Poulin sends them out to all the poets he knows. And here's maybe my chance to begin: when Phillips tells me how wonderful Al's poems are.... Ha....

Good to be back here again.... Now the largest elm near the cabin has died. After I chop it out, & another ash or two, I'll put in a pine, this fall.

Just to teach truly, and love the family truly, and write truly, and read truly. Just to ignore the memos, & newsletters, and congress of stinks that most of the contemporary poetry scene is....

Getting these materials to Rochester is a real help. I'll preserve my collection for whatever I want to do with it, and will empty some shelves here & make room & simplify. I feel very happy—hope everything goes well tomorrow—about the whole thing. Just sorting loosely through correspondence, pulling hundreds of letters from books, I feel the rich life of fellowship in poetry I've led. Wilbur, MacLeish, Stafford and others. Yes, there is still something genuine in some of the humanity behind some of our poetry.

9/3/80

Peter and Mary were here. They left with a station wagon full, and called me from U. of R. Everything arrived safely. They will be putting the boxes on shelves today. My study now has some room. I'm so relieved, and will continue to deposit things with U. of R. 275 inscribed books went yesterday, and a box of criticism, and a box of anthologies, and my Mss. & correspondence, and a box of Heyen items for storage, including the scarce issues of *Noise* & *Swastika* & *XVII Machines* & *MHS*, etc. A wonderful arrangement. If I live another 30 years, I'm sure (the nuclear world willing) I'll have the room I want, somewhere.... Now I even feel free not only to get on with my life and write, but also to <u>collect</u>!

I've said "no" to committees & Tollers wants to talk with me. I'll humor him, make him feel that by leaving me alone he'll be serving literature!

Many chores today, but I'll look forward to a couple of evening hours back here.

Later: evening now. I'm going over to Mirko's for some poker. He called to say Manny was back, & Bill, & that the Rocks have split up. Hard to believe. What a year they've been through. So much pain.... I'll enjoy the game tonight, and will play tight.

Proofs for *The Ewe's Song* arrived today. I'll get to it tomorrow morning, and send *Blackberry Light* back along while I'm at it.

Han & I walked around several blocks, as we do many evenings, and stopped at Studiers. About a billion starlings have settled into the woods behind & next to them, and have been there for weeks.

9/7/80

The Rochester arrangement feels better and better. Warm letter from Peter, and I've continued to clean out my files—my brain, my life!

Talk with Tollers about my "duties." He couldn't have been nicer. I'll teach and write. No committees. Meanwhile, Poulin has taken on the chairmanship of the APT committee. This makes me happy. Go to it, old buddy, & keep writing poems like those sonnets.

I lost $130 at that poker game, so I have about $250 to make up for after two losses in a row. I will. It's all one game.

Han hasn't been feeling well. Some kind of gastritis.

A beautiful day. I'll have to keep busy with schoolwork.

Sent out a bunch of poems to *New Yorker* yesterday. I really want to send them all to *Poetry*, & will. "Ram Time" is a beauty.

Heard from Richard Wilbur about *MHS*, a warm and caring verdict. His may still be the opinion, if not the poetry, most important to me.

Warm today, but autumn is in the air.

Call from Ed Ochester. I'll read at U. Pittsburgh, too, if only for $100.... I called Bill McTaggart, and will stay an evening with him. <u>That</u> will be fun, my old Lauderdale buddy.

Looking closely at *The Ewe's Song*, I cared for it again. Now, I'll be working on the fourth book—it will be called, simply, <u>Wenzel</u>!—for as long as it takes. I've got plenty of time. Would like to have it done by the time *Blackberry Light* is about ready—by mid-1981, I'd guess.

9/8/80

I've spent a little time, between swatches of schoolwork, reading May Sarton's *The House By the Sea*, and have had the idea (though at the same time I doubt that I'll go through with it) of keeping a journal with publication in mind, a year's journal. Some day, I'm sure, I will, though not now while the poems keep arriving.

What has this journal been like? I suppose, in the recesses of my mind, I sense an audience, but more like a single person in a library some day (someone who has in the back of his or her mind doing a little more work on Heyen before lunch or dinner, someone looking forward to a movie or gathering that weekend) in a rare book room, than any audience of a book. This journal constantly reminds me, as my prose flows or stutters along, how hard it is to write simply. I often regret a previous sentence, one that maybe has a cliché or pretentious phrase, or ambiguity. No scratching out here, though.

Read Ted Hughes' beginning poems in *Moortown* last evening. Some strong things, like the poem on dehorning (which loses itself, though), but he's too fucking noisy all the time, overly dramatic, whatever it is that makes *Gaudette* so awful. This new book, the first part of it, was interesting because I'm doing "farm" things too. That's not the language of sheep.

A little cool in the cabin this morning. My little heater is ready, but I refuse to plug it in this early in the year.

I'll fool with a few poems.

9/9/80

An absolutely crazy evening. Rushed letter of recommendation for Sandi Piccione. Then an unexpected visit from poor, shaking Paul Gaylord. Then a long call from Bill Ewert. So it was about 11:00 before I got to my syllabus for composition.

Classes not bad today, but I'm very tired. Am off until next Tuesday, and now will catch up on everything.

So many things in the mail yesterday: Wilbur's *Bobó* broadside, two broadsides from Stafford, three inscribed books from MacLeish, and May Sarton's new journal, with my poem "The Field." I choked up when I read it in context. She's quite a woman. I love her journals, and want to look for a first of *Journal of a Solitude*.

I'll recuperate this evening, watch a ball game while catching up on a few notes I have to write, including one to Bill McTaggart.

A short in my other lamp, so I just carried another back here.

Think I might enter into that Arvon contest in England with "Poem Touching the Gestapo." Have a hunch it will be used in their anthology, at least.

Heavy rain a little while ago. The world quiet now.

9/11/80

It's early, eight in the morning. I woke up early, and was hoping to sleep an extra hour or two, but couldn't. Often, when I wake up, I begin to dwell on things that worry me, or make me angry. And irritant juices flow into my system, of course, and sleep is over. If I could meditate for a few minutes, or dwell on my happiness, I'd be much better off. Or maybe—and I believe I'll do this when I get older—I don't need more than the four or five hours of sleep I usually get, and I'd be smart to just get up and come back here. I've just spent a half-hour or so on the poem I drafted yesterday, one beginning, "The old masters, in their music ...", and I like what it's become, and it has helped me to feel, as May Sarton says in her *Recovering*, "centered."

Played ball yesterday, and maybe will again today. The fellowship of us ten or fifteen men is important to me, and the workout, the tiredness, the patterns of the games, the shower later, being naked and absolutely unselfconscious in the showers with other men, athletes over the hill but now taking the pleasures I do in my diminishing abilities. I began playing basketball when I was about 8 or ten, dribbled up Gibbs Pond Road to the asphalt court behind Nesconset school. The continuity is deeper than I can get down on this page.

Kristen is home from school today with a cold.

A beautiful, late-summer day.

May Sarton makes me want to keep and publish a journal. Some day, maybe, when I'm 60 or 80, I'll unpack my notebooks, my journals at the U. of Rochester, or wherever, and edit one or more for publication, while I write a current journal, also for publication. That would be interesting. Two parts in each book. To do that for a few or several books, and then to publish, after catching up on the journals, a journal purely in the present of the last year.

9/12/80

I'm back here this morning with nothing special in mind. So many things, business, busyness things I could do, but don't really want to—begin preparing for Tuesday's classes, Guggenheim application, letters to write. I come back here, as I often do, thinking I might get to a poem. This is one of the things about being a poet (is this the first time I've said this straight out, admitted that I'm a poet?) is that the product of the work is so ill-defined ahead of time. Also, it is apparently useless once finished, or so it seems in this age of hype and glitter. Were I to be lucky and soulful enough this morning to write a good poem, this would give certain satisfactions now and lead to others, but I would not feel I had contributed anything to the community or country or, really, even to my family. I saw William Manchester this morning on television. He is leaving for England to begin work on a biography of Winston Churchill. It is easy for him to feel good about himself and what he is doing. He will, in the end, be welcomed. How different it is for me to work back here on a poem.

An hour later: And now, worse even than finishing a poem, I've just pored over one for an hour, one that won't take shape or define itself. What have I been doing? Indulging myself? Could/should I have spent the hour at schoolwork, or raising money for starving Asians, or teaching some backward child to read. Working on the poem, I am enjoying the balances & tones I feel and see, as it shapes itself, but what's that? It's everything. It's nothing. It's almost the end of my journal page. This is the elm's home.

9/15/80

I profaned the day, yesterday, sort of waited around nervously, doing nothing, until time to go to Tollers' department party. I feel so creepy around most of those people that I was nervous all day. I could have/should have come back here and gotten to work. I could have done so much, completed the whole Guggenheim application, e.g., but I'm not mature enough to get those people off my mind. Maybe what started the bad juices flowing was my answering, early in the morning, of two memos from Tollers. There are hundreds to come, and I'd better begin to ignore him and them, or I'll despise myself. He didn't really understand when I told him I could not fritter away my life on details and still stay open for writing.

I keep thinking of my upcoming 40th birthday. It's silly for me to think I can change from one day to another. I did stop smoking from one day to another, and on another birthday, but ridding myself of certain distractions is of course a mental thing. But I look forward to November 1st, & my trip to Wisconsin at that time. I hope to do much walking & thinking while I'm away for that week.

Saw John Logan at Poulin's the other night. A very sad man, pale and so quiet. He's quit drinking, been forced to. Maybe this was the first time I've ever seen him sober, and that makes all the difference.

So, the last few days filled with Poulins, Picciones—I must stop talking about the department with Tony, tell him we must stop—Tollers, thoughts of Gerber, Gemmett, Curran, et. al.

In a few minutes just now, my little heater took the chill off in here. Now the sun is out. It's a beautiful morning. I'll see if I can be true to myself here for a couple hours. Then basketball, and soon after the dentist. Schoolwork this evening. My trip to Louisiana & Pittsburgh begins Friday.

Ewert called the other night—about nothing special, about May Sarton's journal, which he'd just picked up.... All my publishing projects are moving along. Signed the contract for *The Trains*. This element enters in, too: I keep thinking that I'm about 40, and am able now, all in all, to write a lot, and should while I can, because in 15 years, when I retire, I might not be able to. Or, in other terms: I have to hold on to my soul, as I had to in graduate school, or the poetry in me will dry up.

It's always back here in my cabin where these battles are won. I breathe deep back here. I should learn to leave the dept. & other irritations behind me on the desk in my study, & spend more & more time here. I don't want to be lulled into mistakes just because I know this place is back here and waiting for me at any time.

I sent "Poem Touching the Gestapo" to the Arvon contest in England, and sent eight poems to *New Yorker* & will next send them to *Poetry*. "Ram Time" is a wonderful poem.... I was looking through my notebook of submissions last night, and saw, e.g., that *Antaeus* had rejected "Witness," and another magazine, I forget which, had rejected "Mantle" & "Redwings." Those are real poems, and that's the way it goes.

Goldenrod up high around the cabin windows now.

Han & Kris home from school with colds.

I think more & more about Cornell for Billy.

9/17/80

I leave in two days for La. & Pittsburgh, and am at the point where I'm nervous about the trip, not sleeping well and not doing much. But I'm about set to go.

Han & neighbors will have a big garage sale Saturday when I'm gone.

Rain today, but I managed to bike up to the school and play ball.

Letter from a man in Sweden who has read my books & will translate a few things for a magazine.

Han got a weeping call from Cheryl, who is in hospital in Syracuse. She said she checked herself in, was worried about a nervous breakdown. When I talked to Ed, he said he'd checked her in, that she had had a nervous breakdown. It's all sad. Ed said he'd be okay. Things are not going well for him at work, either.... And I got a strange, long call from a woman from U. South Carolina, who had been a student of James Dickey. She, too, was crying, had lost her assistantship, had apparently offended Dickey, who'd once given her *Depth of Field* to read. She was, she said, a diagnosed manic-depressive. How could I help her? I told her to write me and we'd talk by mail and that things would work out for her if she'd stay calm and had faith. What the hell could I say to this stranger. I'm sure there was a lot more to her story....

Sent back proofs of *The City Parables*. It's going to be a good book, and a handsome one. I'm glad it's upcoming.

I look forward to my next entry in this journal, when I'll be back, a little richer, and wiser, as always, after trips. Some day, maybe, I'll be so wise that I'll almost always decide to stay home.

9/27/80

It's Saturday. Margie Palombella was a surprise visit this morning—Han's college roommate—and our godson Alan showed up this afternoon. I took him & his friend around the campus, and showed them the cabin. We had a nice visit. Han filled them with good soup. They're at a party in Rochester this evening, & will head back to Oswego tomorrow.

As May Sarton mentions, it's hard to write in a journal about the recent past. This kind of writing is interested in me, my own process, and is an inquiry, and is prophecy. I'm back. It was an exhausting week, Louisiana to Pittsburgh to Wells College the day after I got back. I met some people, enjoyed Herb Fackler and his friends, liked the young poet Jeannie Weaver & her husband Richard, disliked the pushy & frenetic young poet Sue Owens, enjoyed Tom Murphy & Ed Ochester & the Doblers & Bill McTaggart, & I read especially well in Pittsburgh. I'm back. Made some money. Am getting some rest, praise the Lord. This cabin is light years from all that.

A perfect letter, regarding Poulin et. al., from Peter Dzwonkoski. Colophon pages to sign for *The Ewe's Song*. Books from May Sarton & John Woods. School details to take care of, and yard work to do here. Long letter from Judy Minty, who may never be happy, dear woman.

I'm back to being who I am. Relieved that that trip is over with. A reading at MCC in a couple of weeks, & a week in Wisconsin in November. I may not take on such readings again.

From the sounds of it, Duane Schneider has asked Wilbur & Stafford for blurbs for *The City Parables*. I didn't want this at all, don't want to bother them. Maybe I'm not sure enough of that book, as I will be sure of *CR* when done. I'll write Wilbur, especially, and say sorry, forget it!

Just read my last entry. I am richer & wiser.

I look forward to basketball on Monday, & getting my classes rolling again. Han & the kids are my center. I love them very much. Han is not content with her job, and that's no surprise, but things will work out.... This evening & tomorrow I'm going to watch television (football & *The Boys From Brazil* & *Marathon Man*) while doing schoolwork.

Al & Tony & I might just put a little unpleasant heat on Gerber about the Forum interviews. I can't make up my mind on things.

Poems rejected by *New Yorker* including "Ram Time" & "Yellowthroats" & "Arrows," and now off to *Poetry*.

10/1/80

First day of October. It's in the 60s, and sunny, and beautiful back here around the cabin. A big clump of black-eyed Susan is in bloom. The ash leaves are browning and curling, but I'm still hidden back here. I'd planned to read student journals this morning, but will have enough time this evening, so have given myself the gift of the morning back here. Again, just now, I realized how much this place means to me. I hadn't stepped foot back here for a couple of days, and when I stepped inside just now, everything had been waiting for me.

Werner called to say Pop is in the hospital with appendix and gall bladder trouble, and an aneurysm. Maybe an operation this morning. My relationship with the folks is a very sad one. I can't see into the murk enough to see anything clearly. They are so, well, hopeless in their hates and prejudices. Now, their old-age martyrdom may make them strangely happy regarding their alienated son. So it goes.... Old Roy Dooks is in the hospital, too, and probably beyond repair.

The poetry goes on. Sent the signed colophon sheets for *The Ewe's Song* to Emily Rizzo. *The City Parables* is in the works now and just about ready for printing and binding.

10/13/80

Hartmut Merten and his friend Istvan Ella, a Hungarian organist, were with us, unexpectedly, for five days. They were not easy guests to have on hand, took and took and seldom said thanks. We'll deflect them next year. A very trying time ... in the middle of which continued the saga of Gerbergate, which would make for an academic novel, too long to set down here, but unforgettable anyway. In short, he actually had the nerve to negotiate a <u>personal</u> contract with SUNY Press for the editing of the tapes. I could not respond to requests of his (an odd one to sign away my name, e.g.) without seeing the contract, and then the outrageous story began to break. I've gone to Tollers, Gemmett, will go to President and Chancellor if I have to to make my case for a new, clean contract. Gerber's last ploy, yesterday, was to tell Tollers he'd give all monies to the Forum, that his lawyer would draw up an amendment to the contract. No to this. If we're setting out for a decade or two to edit tapes, we have to begin with a clean & clear contract. Tollers admits that this is a "face-saving gesture" by Gerber. No. And now Han has received one and I've received another threatening phone call. Gerber terribly upset, and should be: his greed got the better of him. I <u>hate</u> all this, have lost touch completely with my writing (will read at MCC tomorrow night and hear my own poems again), but have to go through with this. I am just a dept. member, have only talked with Vince a few times and now Bob once. They are all jumping, & jumpy, because they know I'm right. Much more to this story, and Gerber may find ways to become very nasty. He worries me, but I'd have been upset for decades if I didn't state my case. Imagine the nerve: he was to profit from the community effort the Forum has been, wanted to make money, e.g., from MacLeish's words. <u>No</u>. And the amendment he proposed to the contract may be, it occurred to me this morning, a tax benefit device for him. No.

Otherwise, here I am. A wet, cold day today. First time I've been back in the cabin in about a week. Not clear enough for writing, but I wanted to assure myself of this place.... It was a rough week for all of us.

I did call my father in the hospital. Hope he's home by now.

I'll have Gerber pop up in this ¶ the way he pops up everywhere. I can't jump into the mail room at school for ten seconds without seeing him, and Saturday morning, at the Rochester book fair, there he was, right in front of me, at one booth. He does this sort of thing on purpose, but will not spook me.

I did get the Guggenheim application in, and am glad I did. Small chance, but I took it.

Tony & Al & I actually brought close through this Gerber business.

My last ¶ a brilliant one, the way that ghost showed up again, as he does in this one!

I owe letters to Vince Clemente, Martin Booth, and others. Letter from Tess Gallagher inviting me to read at Syracuse. Maybe, oh well, I will.

It won't be long before *TES* is out, I think. Then, *The City Parables*.... I want to send a few poems to sweet people down in Lafayette for their magazine.

Two-day auction Friday and Saturday, to which I look forward.

Safe back here, not a friend in sight.

Must write Len Fulton to thank him for the book.... Have much reading for classes to do today, but will get back on my feet, maybe even play basketball today.

10/15/80

Many more developments in Gerbergate. I just spent two hours drafting a long letter to the President. I'm proud of myself for staying with this. Because of me, monies, one way or the other, will go to the Dept. I may never send the letter, but may. I'll see what happens. I have a couple other aces in my hand. Vince tells me that Gerber has to save face, that he is worried about being embarrassed. I can't help that. If he'll rip up the contract and begin fresh, okay. If not, my letter will go to the President. When that happens, he will be embarrassed. He'd better not wait long to rip up his contract with SUNY.

Read at Monroe last night. I read well, they sold maybe ten books, I made $250. A good evening, but I am tired of reading & still debate the Syracuse thing in the spring.

Inside, my phone is probably ringing—Gemmett, Tollers. I've stirred up a bees' nest, and hell, I'm no one, just a single Dept. member. Tollers called yesterday asking me to meet with him and Phil! No!... When will this all be over? It has probably cost me some poems, but will be worth it, I hope, and maybe already has been.... Second World Series game on tonight. And in an hour I'll go up to play some basketball, which should relax me.

I think I'll turn to some happier things for a few minutes, maybe look at *The Ssnow Hen* & think of *The Ewe's Song* to come.

10/18/80

It seems to be about 70°. A perfect fall day. I've chopped out some grapevines, now more easily seen, and have chopped out some twisted ash seedlings, wanting to thin out a little, but mainly I spent the morning back here typing the letter (or draft of it) to Brown. I still haven't heard from Gemmett, and am not sure he means to get into touch with me at all. I have another step in mind, regarding the editing of the MacLeish tape, after this one. Don't know what, altogether, is best. Will dwell on it for the weekend.

"This Night" appeared in *Harper's*.... I talked to Bill Ewert last night, about various things. All's well.... Went to book auction yesterday. Bought a signed 1st in fine jacket of R.P.T. Coffin's *Golden Falcon* for one buck.... Fourth Series game today. So far, the Phillies are up 2-1 in games....

10/19/80

Sunday evening. Dark outside, and a cold drizzle. I've come out back for the last time to consider things before going ahead with delivery of the long letter to Brown & English Dept. members. I decided last night that I must, whatever could happen next—perhaps some serious charges thrown back at me that could cost me months of worry. But Gerber should not get away with his silence and greed without people knowing about it. I worked long and hard on the letter, sent it through a few drafts. Also, I believe, I'll work on another letter regarding the MacLeish tape after delivering this one—i.e., go further on the offensive while Gerber least expects it, while he is readying his reply to the first letter. I have strategies in mind. I'll see. I might talk to Al & Tony tonight yet. I'd much rather that none of this had ever occurred, but it has, and I can't let it float by. I must get out the first letter tomorrow, too, or some sort of vacuous excuse & evasion will take place. My letter is the absolute truth as I see it. To hell with Gerber, then: let him sue.... Maybe, though this is all draining and stops me from getting to any poems, it is an experience that will enter poems in the future. This is all a city parable.... He made two threatening phone calls to us. He has been underhanded in several ways. I must send the letter. I will. That's the only outlet for my anger. Yes. The letter goes out in the morning. Vince Tollers comes off as an oaf. I can't help it. He's been intimidated by Gerber who, no doubt, himself suggested that he be our nominee for Distinguished Teaching Professor, he of the slow dryness and thirty-year-old notes! It's a farce, and Tollers has perpetuated it. Gerber even tore Tollers to shreds when Tollers was interviewed for department chairman. Tollers has no backbone. He could have been a man about all this, and wasn't, and now will be the fool.... What a fucking life this is I lead. I just want to write poems & be an athlete and live life with my family. I'm involved with shits like Gerber and Tollers, the kind of men who, when they were boys, were the kind of boys I never had anything to do with. Now these types are all around me. I've never thought about it in this way before, but it's true. The men I play ball with are my friends and know (not all of them) something about the body, and growing old gracefully, and real speech. These English teachers I associate with, these prissy and smug shits I'm supposed to feel close to ... Tollers is stupid, dogged but stupid. Gerber is smug, secretive, dishonest. They asked for it.

10/20/80

The long letter is xeroxed and sent out or delivered. Now I will be nervous, of course, waiting for Gerber to do something wild. And I will not be looking forward to passing him and Tollers in the halls. So be it. Now, some things to think about: 1/ my letter regarding the MacLeish tape, etc.; 2/ my lecture for Wisconsin—probably on *Swastika*; 3/ planning classes for when I won't be here. I'll have to stay on the ball now, for sure. And <u>always</u>. Gerber will be waiting until one of us dies for me to slip up. So be it.

10/22/80

About midnight last night I stood here in my cabin with two old Chinese gentlemen, Feng Yidai (associate editor of a magazine in Peking called *Dushu*) and Pien Chih-lin, a major poet. Al had picked them up yesterday and driven them around. Then, there was a short reading and reception in the library—Al, Tony, and I read a couple translations each. Later, I met the two men again at a party at Bruce Agte's. I talked for hours with the poet. He told me of the turmoil he'd lived through. We spoke of Chinese and American poetry. They have a long itinerary in front of them, but at 11:30 or so, when we were thinking they should get some sleep, I had the bright idea that I'd show them my cabin. Six of us came over here and walked through the moonlight to this place. I think the two men will always remember, as I will. I told them: "Under my cabin, / field mice, / and China." And I had the good luck to remember to show them *Noise in the Trees* with its 11th century epigraph. Such gracious men. I felt in the presence of wisdom, experience. I gave them both several books, and hope they and the books get safely back to Peking. They return around Thanksgiving.
It seems profane to enter here other matters. I've written a letter just to Gerber regarding his phone calls here. And I've written a letter to the whole department regarding a letter Vince Tollers sent to the editor of SUNY Press. Tollers will not get the message. He does seem to be dumb, even incompetent.... I have a feeling that Gerber may still press some sort of charges against me. I hope not, of course, and keep trying to deflect all of these concerns to the Department, where they should be.
So much work—classes, Gerbergate, preparations for Wisconsin, book orders & annual reports. But I'll get everything done, in time. I'll ride my bike up today, even if it's raining, to play ball.... Gerber might ruin my year yet, but I'll go through with all of this, as I have to. It is more than a little help that I've been reading/teaching Emerson.

10/24/80

It's been cold back here this morning, but it's just about comfortable now.
I'm writing at the oak table, crowded, this journal propped on piles of poems haphazardly. The sun is pouring in now, dappled by leaves. Such a feeling of profusion here. *Poetry* accepted four poems, including the beautiful "Ram Time," and I'm glad, and will get 20 extra copies to give to friends. *APR* rejected the first seven sections of *CR*. What do I care. So rich back here with the world warming.
I've typed a letter to Tollers on Gerbergate, and will xerox and mail it today. It protects me, as it should in a few ways, and comes back to my point about the need for a new contract, not just any sort of letter or amendment.... I sent the letter to Gerber, just to him, on his phone calls.

I need this weekend and will have to keep busy. Joyce here next week, and soon after that I'm off. I think I'll be able to put together the Wisconsin lecture without much trouble.... Basketball party tomorrow at Mancuso's. Go slow, Bill, go slow!

Many birds around my cabin now. Such a beautiful October day, though leaves are floating down around me.... Han & the kids are more a part of me every day.

Called Vince Clemente last night, and miss him.

Later: delivered my letter to the Department today. <u>Now</u> Tollers will have to inform the Department as to what is going on.... Got a fine letter from President Brown. The letter takes my fear of a lawsuit away. Spoke with Al Poulin. All is going well. I must say, he has come through for me, generously, courageously, and I won't forget it.... I'll call Tony and read the President's letter to him.... I don't want to be hurt & jolted in case Gerber goes ahead with some sort of lawsuit, so I don't want to feel too confident. But things look good, and I hope, now, I can just step away from the whole thing.

10/25/80

Saturday. Raining. I have a slight sinus cold. Han & I look forward to the basketball party at Mancuso's tonight.

Finished my little prose piece, "The Dragonfly," for Karl Elder at *Seems*.

Talked to Rod Parshall about Gerbergate.... Things seem okay, but there will be some mortar fire coming my way, I'm sure.

10/26/80

Great party last night. I laughed so hard, during Bill Stewart's award presentations, that my scalp hurt. Didn't drink too much, and the clock went back an hour, so I feel okay today. Much schoolwork to take care of, but much football on TV: it's easiest for me to do schoolwork while sports are on.... Have to call Joyce later about details of her visit.

Just wrote Bill Ewert & Bob Phillips.... Oh, when the snow comes, and this Gerbergate crap is off my mind, I'll be happily buried back here within my real life.

Pushed ahead my *Swastika* lecture yesterday. Wrote for a concentrated hour yesterday. It should be an interesting talk.... And I typed up that little (slightly petulant) piece for Karl Elder. And I finished that odd poem about being the last one alive. It's fun to publish. I should keep up that bibliography that Ernie did. I'm glad he did it when he did. No word from Ernie for so long. He seems to have changed completely. Ewert trying to sell my letters to Ernie to Peter Dzwonkoski.

My little dragonfly poem ("a blue lord...") makes me wonder if I have another spate of tiny poems in me. That would be a perfect one in a sequence, the circling, altered state of consciousness it implies. Maybe it should be in present tense!

10/27/80

Gerber did it again, put another stupid & insulting letter in my mailbox. I drafted an answer. He's just going to brazen the whole thing out, it appears. He keeps making it possible to me to write letters to give to the whole Dept. & administration that make a fool of him. <u>Still</u>, I must be very careful and not underestimate him and must worry about some sort of lawsuit.... For the first time the thought crossed my mind that I should give the whole file of letters to Joyce to read on Wednesday night. She's tough enough to give a good interview despite the problem. All in all, I'm nervous again (though not as agitated as I have been) and look forward to basketball later.

Nov. 1, 1980

I'm forty today. Part of me is still that boy who waded those ponds. It's somehow hard for me to think of myself as a man. Thank you, Lord, for the gift of another decade. I want to deepen in the ability to tell the truth and act truthfully. Maybe by fifty!...

Met with the Provost & Dean & college lawyer yesterday. We all fumbled around a while, and then I read them my two-paragraph prepared statement. One paragraph says what the clean & honest thing to do would be; the second says what might happen (all writers becoming involved) if we don't. I was satisfied, in the end, by the meeting. Then Tony & Al & I got together. Al had just gone through a horror of a scene with Gerber in Tollers' office, Gerber yelling & demanding & wild. Pshew. It shows what the Grinch is feeling. He is up against it, between a rock and a hard place, because he will not back up a step, will not admit any mistake, will not slow down until questions are answered. Hard to feel sorry for him. It's not over yet.

Ray & Joyce & her folks were here. A perfect visit, which I won't recount. Han & I care for the four of them very much. Joyce inscribed an embarrassing number of books for us, and this time often with "love." We all came back here to the cabin for a few minutes, took a couple of pictures I hope come out. Joyce's reading was excellent, funny & sharp. We had a great dinner here, and they even forced me to say a few poems. Joyce gave us the leather first edition of *Bellefleur*. She is still so frail & tough at the same time. Tour of the Morgan-Manning House—she even took a couple notes that will no doubt be in the novel she's doing. So many images in my mind from that rich day.

Saturday today. Monday morning I'll head for Wisconsin. I'll be glad to get away, will enjoy it there, will be glad to get back to classes.

A sudden realization just now. There seems to be at the center of my mind some kind of calm, a peacefulness, maybe just the morning here in the cabin, but maybe more. Some slight anxiety in the lungs & chest, but some kind of serenity at the center of the brain. In some ways, and there were many digressions, I've worked for this since the trauma of about my freshman year in college.

Bill is taking achievement tests this morning. Kris has her friend Christine with her. And Han is getting some extra sleep, I'm glad to say.

Call from D.D. Stine of Antic Hay books the other night, and then two calls from Bill Ewert who continues to be my angel.

I hope there's some decent weather in November so that I can still plant 2-3 pines. If not, I'll do it in the spring.

I need to work on my *Swastika* lecture a bit this weekend. That's about it.

Only a few straggling leaves left. I've more leaves left in me than the trees.

11/2/80

I've just finished my notes for what I think could be an interesting lecture on *Swastika* tomorrow. I must go slowly, that's the important thing.

Tony Vallone & Bruce Agte stopped in yesterday evening. Richard Ehrlich stopped by in the afternoon. A busy day. Might see the Picciones today. I should rake leaves for an hour and get some air in my lungs.

A woman called about a new club of book collectors in Rochester. Doubt that I'll join.

I've begun *Bellefleur*, & will probably be reading it for a long time.

My next journal entry will have me home again. I hope to have a peaceful winter. Regarding the whole Gerber & contract business, it won't be pleasant or fun, but I plan to conduct myself like a man, and tell the truth, and take a part, if need be, in contract discussions.

Think I'll go inside pretty soon, after a chapter or two of Joyce's book, and take a good hot shower. Or maybe I'll rake before the shower. Anyway, I'll be ready to leave early in the morning. On Wisconsin.

11/10/80

Home again, and relieved to be back here in the cabin. A dust of snow this morning.

Tony Piccione brought over a tree for my birthday. I might get a chance to plant it today. Hope it will make it.

All in all, a good stay in Wisconsin, though the time dragged. Some good folks there—Betty Williams, Bill Harrold, and especially Bob Siegel. I lectured well, read decently, enlivened a couple of classes.

Wild developments in Gerbergate. Gerber accused, in effect, Al & Tony & me of breaking into his office and stealing a file. He sent a calculating/irrational (that weird mixture of the sick mind) letter to the President & Provost & Dean & Tollers on this. Tollers gave us copies! Al has gotten us a lawyer, & it looks like we'll press libel charges. Gerber also sent a nutty note titled "Lost & Found" to the Dept.! I laughed when I read the two pieces, and don't take all this seriously, but guess I'll have to press charges, with Tony & Al, on this. It's absurd! Big, dramatic meeting today at 5:15, Dean & Provost to be there. Wild.

Billy's trip to Cornell went well, & Kristen's concert. Han still has stomach trouble. Otherwise, we're fine.

Roy Dooks died, another of those old Island spirits for me.

Nice note from Joyce, and a card already from Ray. He's going to feature *The Snow Hen* in his spring issue. Well, I'm embarrassed about friends publishing me, but they kept asking, and those seven sections of *CR* are <u>good</u>.... Now I'll think about a magazine for sections 8-18, out any day from Ewert now.

I found some nice books in Milwaukee, bargains. Kinnell's *The Snow Rabbit*, Nemerov's *The Image & the Law*, a book by Mark Van Doren signed by him & Waldo Pierce, the illustrator. So, another dozen books added to the collection.

Will play basketball later to get back to my life. Aside from the Gerber business, I'm fine & happy to be back. All that stuff, too, will finally wash clean. Some good things have already come of it.

11/15/80

Gerbergate taking up all my time and energy.... Al & Tony & I had our first meeting with our lawyer in Rochester this morning, & long meetings with Dept. committee tomorrow, & Dept. meeting Monday, etc. So it goes. In the end, everything will come out in the way it has to.... This is a whole chapter of my life! The things down in writing will tell it all.

Nice talk with Bill Ewert last night. When I <u>do</u> get back to the center of my life, it will be deeper, due to Gerbergate, than it is now. It is like entering the lion's mouth & walking out again.

11/17/80

Sunday. Some rest at last. An amazing day yesterday.

Four or five hours of meetings, and on a Saturday, on Gerbergate. In the end, all went well. Gerber's trump card, it turned out, was a vicious personal attack on me centering on my use of the Sexton interview in *AP '76*. When I deflected him, told the members present (14) that I'd told the Dean & Provost of my own four uses of interviews, when I said Gerber had just given the wrong impression, that Brockport & the videotape <u>were</u> mentioned, that, in fact my use of this interview in 1976 <u>was</u> another instance of the "haphazardness" of all prior publications (Gerber has used about 20), I felt cleared. Gerber had even written to Bobbs-Merrill! He is not getting away with all of this. On one front, the ballot for the Dept. tomorrow will embarrass him all the way. On the other front, Al & Tony & I will meet in Rochester with our lawyer regarding the libel suit. The lawyer will first draft a letter asking Gerber to apologize.... So many developments in all this that it would take Chekhov a thousand pages to get it down.... Must still be afraid of and not underestimate the man. He could do something extremely sick. Apparently the investigation regarding Poulin's keys is still going on.... Tollers actually admitted showing his 12-page letter to Brown to Gerber on Oct. 25 & not to me until a few days ago! I told him, in front of everyone, that this was the worst thing anyone had ever done to me, and I wouldn't forget it.

Then, I came home and heard my folks had called. My mother & father both apologized for everything to Han. My God, they are changed people. I called home later on, and could almost not recognize my mother's voice. I didn't think she could ever say what she said, & with no accusations or strings attached. It's as though she has found her soul. I can hear her voice, beginning <u>Listen, Bill</u>, and her words. I told them that we loved them, and I tried to give Pop a pep-talk on all his health problems. I am relieved that I have parents again. I do love them, whatever awful things happened.

Well, here I am then, no longer an orphan. That's one thing. On the other, my poetry has been disrupted, for now, but must deepen into thankful peace as the struggle resolves itself.

Nov. 21, 1980

Gerbergate still in full heat, but things are going well. The ballot went heavily our way, was more than I could have hoped for. 15 voted to void the current contract & negotiate a new one (I'd hoped for 7 or 8). 5 voted to amend, five to keep the contract as is. In the second part of the ballot, if the contract was to be amended, only 2 of 25 people said to keep royalties as they are. So, Gerber and one other.... Stan called, Rod & Greg visited before that Monday meeting. I'm not isolated.

It's a Friday afternoon. I just finished a 3-page letter to all on Gerber's "Statement to the Committee...." I feel good.... Al & Tony & I at lawyer's yesterday regarding the libel suite. First, each of us, by certified letter, will ask Gerber to apologize.

So it goes on. We all wonder what the administration will do now after the Dept. vote. Gerber will fight tooth & nail. He's ill, too. His 3 points demanding remuneration in his "Statement" are something to behold. But he's so nasty, so vicious, it's hard to feel sorry for him.

Played ball today against a basketball class. The faculty lost by about six. I scored about 30, I think.

Two games at the College tonight. Han & I will go and look forward.

Last evening from 8-12, Al & Tony & I & 15 or so good students met in my office for a reading & wine party. It was fun, even though Al read several interminable and awful confessional pieces.

Don't know what madness Gerber is perpetrating now. He might be getting in touch with writers & twisting the issues, though first he'll have to protect his contract? I don't know. Anyway, our lawyer says that if he doesn't apologize, he's got a real problem.

Male cardinal in the feeding cup in the blue spruce. Will stare with my binoculars.

11/29/80

I've brought this journal inside for an entry or two.

It's Saturday. We were in Nashville over Thanksgiving. I loved every minute, the food & family love & wine & sleeping up in that cold room under my thick comforter. I feel far away from any Brockport problems when I'm there.

The letters went out to Gerber. We'll see what happens next.

Rod Parshall had a heart attack last Tuesday. He's lucky to be alive. I've seen him twice. He'll be at Lakeside for a few weeks, at least.

Bizarre encounters for me and Tony with Gerber near the school. He keeps baiting us, saying wild things. He scares us. No telling what he'll do next.

The City Parables arrived. I like it very much, and look forward to the trade edition. Other things arriving soon, including the Christmas card.

We've watched Billy & team in a few scrimmages. First game next Friday.

Semester winding down. Only Gerbergate in the way of freedom, but I still enjoy some good hours out back. Have been working the past couple days over the proofs of *Lord Dragonfly*. That's going to be a nice book. I feel lucky about all these publications.

Han & the kids are fine.... Snow flurries & rain the last few days. I've enjoyed lounging around early in robe and pajamas after a hot shower.

I owe so many people so many letters.

11/30/80

A quiet morning back here in the cabin. Sunny, and warm. A pair of cardinals, and three black-capped chickadees around.

I took some notes from the Fénelon book. Then Giff Mosher started chainsawing. Without getting upset, I turned on my electric typewriter—this drowns out outer noise—and typed a letter to Vince Clemente. That's the kind of useful deflection of disturbance I need to practice more often.

Will walk with Han up to Poulins soon to say goodbye to Al, who will be in Greece for a few weeks. We'll see Picciones there too.... Then I'll busy myself with paperwork the rest of the day.

Proofs for *Lord Dragonfly* ready to go back to Tom Woll. *The City Parables* ready to be picked up by UPS tomorrow. Looking forward to *The Ewe's Song* and to the Christmas card. Finally received my copies of *The Candle* from Martin.

The blessing of this little cabin just doesn't wear thin. It's what Stafford calls my "little house behind [my] big house" where I have a window "that looks out in the right direction."

12/3/80

Unexpectedly, the day has become a special blessing. The phone rang early: no school for Han & the kids. Wind and blowing snow. The game I was supposed to play in tonight, parents & faculty vs. a television station team, was also called off, and with my bad ankle (sprained Monday) I'm glad of this. A family morning, Han so glad to be home. I worked with Billy on an essay application for a scholarship—actually he'd done an excellent job writing it and I just added a phrase or two and typed it up. Kristen ecstatic to be home, too. Now I have the whole evening for schoolwork, and this afternoon of winter sunlight in my cabin. I just put kitchen scraps & sunflower seeds out for the birds.

The Ewe's Song arrived. It is simple & beautiful & perfect. I believe the whole poem, when finished, will be an important event for American poetry. When the Vanguard book does appear, in 3-4 years, I must have flyers, etc., sent everywhere, to the whole directory of poets list, to people I've met wherever I've read, etc.... And the little *Christmas 1980* card is a beauty, too. I spoke with Bill & thanked him. This morning my package went off to him filled with signed proofs, *The City Parables*, a *Ewe's Song*, etc. He never stops, is going ahead with *The Steer* broadside!

The bad news is that Pop is in the hospital with clots on his lung. Apparently, though, these clots stem from his appendectomy, and medicine should clear them up. I'll call him this evening. Mom will visit him today, and Werner tomorrow. Maybe I'll fly to the Island for a couple days over Christmas break?

The Gerber business still bothers me—he's doing all sorts of strange things (like meeting with APT Committee & saying he's worried he & his wife will be insulted, in the light of registered letters he's received, at the Christmas party!) and lobbying & working constantly behind my back, but we backed him up, stopped his money-grabbing (though he'll somehow, claiming expenses, drain off the money for the first volume), and I have a feeling I can back away myself from the whole sordid mess (except for, maybe, the libel suit, which is another matter), and still feel good about the vote against Gerber and other accomplishments. We'll see if he apologizes & retracts his Nov. 3 letter to Brown. If not, as the lawyer says, Gerber's got troubles, real troubles.

I've the *hors commerce* copy of *The Ewe's Song* back here with a few revisions, for the eventual Vanguard book, to enter. And I guess I can start thinking of a magazine for sections 8-18, though I wouldn't want them to appear before *Ontario Review* with sections 1-7. How many sections in "Song of Myself"? Maybe, playfully, I'll make *CR* the same.

12/5/80

My cup of tea is steaming. I can see my breath. It's cold out here, at the point where it takes the little heater an hour to warm things up, but I'd hate to get another heater, but could, but not this winter.

Billy's team won by one point last night. A great win, after two losses to this team last year. Han & I are very excited by these games. Billy is very skillful. He had 14 pts., and will do much better often this year.

I have occasional thoughts/worries about Gerber (e.g., Tollers said at the Dept. meeting yesterday that negotiations are continuing between Phil and the administration, and I wonder why the English Department shouldn't be privy to these negotiations), but want to let all that shit go away—except for what will happen regarding our certified letters, of course.

I've spoken to Pop twice. He's feeling much better. I'll call again this evening…. Visited Rod Parshall yesterday. He's nervous, won't slow down, and I wish he would.

Will poke at a poem or two this morning, and then go in for a hot shower and tackle all sorts of things that need doing. Maybe I'll do some Christmas shopping with Kristen this evening. I want to stock up on some wine, too. I want to see the Kentucky-Indiana game this afternoon, too. The poetry needs time to simmer. Enough of it gets done, all I have in me, despite everything else. At least I think so.

12/6/80

Warmer today, and it's comfortable back here. It's about 9:30 on a Sunday morning. A sabbath hush around me.

Talked to Pop again. He's getting better, his spirits on the upswing.

Worked yesterday on "Yellowthroats," which wants to be longer. Something in me kept it back here until I turned to it again. It's a matter, now, of a flowing, concluding music.

My ankle still aches, but I'd like to get back to a little ball, maybe tomorrow. At least I could lurch around a little on the outside?

I think often of the Gerber business—things are in a state of settled unsettlement—but I'm not nervous in the same way I was.

Dan Stryk's little book has appeared. I like the sound of my little note. I had a hard time saying anything about those poems, but I like him very much and am glad I did the little piece.

I feel lazy this morning, but will spend a couple hours back here. Later, I want to work with Billy on his Princeton application. He has two ball games next week. Before the Friday one, there's that spooky department Christmas party that we'll go to with the Picciones, though we're not exactly looking forward. Such pettiness to be concerned about, and all because of one bastard no one will face up to!

12/7/80

Worked a little on "Yellowthroats" this morning, and read over *CR*. Played ball, sliding around, my ankle no worse off than when I began. Went to two very stupid & useless meetings. Will spend a couple hours back here this afternoon.

Will have 7 hrs. of classes (with Poulin's) tomorrow. No journals coming in this week, though.

Invitation from Hofstra to be their poetry workshop leader July 6-17th. I'll no doubt say no, as I did to Brockport. So, it does happen this way: when I badly wanted such things to do, no dice; now, I want to stay home and write, and the invitation comes. I'll see. I could sell some books, etc. No fee mentioned. Maybe I'll inquire.

Raining most of the day. Gray day. I feel subdued, and settled.

12/13/80

Sunday. Cold & blowing snow. Warm enough back here. A good day.

Billy's team 3-0 after last night. He had 13 pts. in 1st quarter, but only 15, in the slaughter…. I took Billy & two of his friends out for pool and pizza last night…. Yesterday, went Christmas shopping with Kris & Billy. Kris a great help, knowing exactly what Han needs & wants in the way of a dress, purse, wallet-combination.

Another call this morning at 6. No one on the other end. I suspect Gerber, of course. We'll just take the phone off the hook from here on in…. Things in a good state. Letter from Gerber not apologizing & wanting us to prove our innocence—I've sent it to the lawyer and we'll see what's next on that front. I'm not nervous about that at all…. Meanwhile, a letter, asking the administration to inform us of what the hell is going on regarding Gerber-administration negotiations, is about ready to go to everyone from the creative writing sub-committee. That will jolt Gerber hard. All in all, all's well…. I'll see Boo today, & drop the letter off to Rubin.

Last day of classes coming up Tuesday. Then, some days of reading/grading and I'll be through.

Duane Schneider called about a couple of things. It was good hearing form him. He's selling *The City Parables* well enough.

Sparrows in the cup of the spruce where I put sunflower seeds.

I played poker the other night at Squeak's and won about a hundred and bought much wine & liquor with it yesterday. I left the game at four in the morning. Mirko reports that Rock won $700 from Squeak head-to-head.

Saw Rod at home with Greg yesterday. He's okay. We all spoke mainly of Gerbergate, of course..

Buffalo on television at New England today.

My father at home now & recuperating…. Mirko's father in hospital.

We & Picciones decided not to go to Dept. Christmas party. Screw it. We had dinner and went to the ball game. When all this crap is over with, I might, or might not, feel part of the Dept. again.

One wall of the living room now looks beautiful (to my prejudiced eye) with framed *Witness*, *The Pigeons*, *The Shy Bird*, & the little Rook Press *Pickerel*. Han had them all framed.

Some arctic air on its way to Brockport, we hear.

We'll go out with Picciones on their anniversary Wednesday.

Will get out the last of the Christmas cards today.

12/18/80

Another ugly meeting yesterday, an "emergency" meeting of the Creative Writing/Writers Forum sub-committee. Gerber, apparently, going through the roof on Rubin's letter. A long story. Confrontations again. Some information: the contract, it appears, will be amended, not scrapped, etc. All of this more upsetting than I hoped it would be by now. Don't know what is down the line. I could drop everything now, or keep pushing. I get angry, just plain angry when I think of that bastard Gerber, and that underhanded Tollers. If I ever (and I will) get free of this, I might withdraw from this department virtually always.

Went out to dinner with Picciones to a place in Albion for their 13th anniversary.

Am reading journals now, a long & slow time, but at least classes are over with for a month.

Carried my new/old desk organizer—got it from Mrs. DeLancey—back here today. It comes from Berea, Kentucky, about 40 years ago, she tells me. If I ever find the perfect table for back here, the organizer will fit better than it now does.

Thursday night, and I guess I'll go up & play a little ball with Mahan's tonight. My ankle is very tender, but getting there…. I played two whole games yesterday without a thought of Gerber, I realized, despite that upcoming meeting. Basketball may save me yet…. No more fear of him, Tony & I realize. Just anger. Confrontations yesterday between Marchant & Gerber, Rubin & Gerber, Fitz Gerald & Gerber, but minor ones, but they're all learning…. I might write to Joyce, or maybe first to Mary Elsie, about the Oates tape and this dirty first volume.

Letter from Lynne (Studier) Williamson at Oxford again. This time, I'm going to go, either in May or June…. Long letter from Martin Booth today, and many Christmas cards from people I hadn't planned to send cards to…. Bill Ferguson writes that I'll receive proof of *The Trains* in January…. Trade edition of *The City Parables* came, and I like it…. Billy has a game tomorrow night…. I sat between Billy & Han at Kristen's concert the other night, and just soaked in the warmth and sense of well being…. I want to apply for the NEA & Ingram-Merrill grants—no great hurry, but soon after grades are turned in.

12/23/80

Played ball with Mahan's last Thursday night and did very well despite bad ankle. Got about 15 pts., & helped the team. Terry & Dale & all glad to have me aboard, and I'm glad…. Played yesterday, and will again, with faculty old-timers, and Billy has a game tonight we'll look forward to. So, basketball very important lately.

Yesterday, a 2 pp. report from Provost regarding Gerbergate. Gerber got his way here and there, but I trust my feelings, and I was relaxed yesterday, and slept well (until another phone call, with no one at other end, woke us at 5:30), and believe that if I were Gerber I'd be upset, again, by the memo and some of its implications. Some loose ends, still, but I feel like I'm becoming disentangled, surely less worried.

Finished, I think, "Jesus" yesterday and will type it today. Chilly back here, but I can still work. Will warm my bones in the gym later.

A man here last evening to interview Billy for an engineering scholarship. So proud of Billy—the manly and calm way he answers questions, his intelligence.

Al back today. I'll stop & see him later & drop off his grade sheets.

Many black-capped chickadees & a couple of juncos darting in and out of the spruce I've thrown seed on.

Have been reading *The City Parables*, making slight changes here and there, maybe for eventual *Collected Poems*, maybe for something else, with added poems like "Jesus," before. Who knows.

I like Mrs. DeLancey's organizer back here—it seems now to me to fit.

I've got final grades about ready to go in. Spring semester will pass quickly, I know.

They're amazing, these little fluttery things we call birds!

12/27/80

On the 23rd I went to school after writing the above, received a terrible memo attack in the mail from Gerber, and then had a rough, upsetting confrontation with him in the hall. His memo was unstable, I think, but I felt I had to answer it right away, went to my office to write an answer, and am glad the answer got too long for me to take care of right away. Al called our lawyer, the lawyer called me to say try to resist answering until we all speak, and we'll all see him Monday morning. I have drafted an answer, one that will knock Gerber on his sick ass again! I think my answer will get him off my back, too, though he's wild enough to do anything. My Christmas was not free and clear, and I've been thinking/worrying a lot about all this, but I feel certain now that all this will turn out all right, however long it takes.

Many nice things. A good family Christmas, and visits from many friends. The past two days I've been wrapping my books in the new stuff, and I'm happy as hell with protecting the books this way.

I'm inside. It's been so cold that I haven't wanted to work in the cabin, but I'll get out there for a couple hours tomorrow to type a draft of that letter. Must turn in grades Monday, and then see the lawyer, and then our nephew Kurt is coming and there will be two days of Billy's tournament games to look forward to. Han and the kids are off for another week.

The four of us went to Piccionès for a few hours last night. Billy played pool. Jeff Schiff & his brother Ken and Gary Eddy were out there. I'll probably get a visit from them soon, too.

Life has great potential. Once this Gerber crap is over with, I'll be a new man.... Oh, I did write Joyce and think she'll pull out of G's book. We'll see.

I'm going to fix something to eat. I've been eating for days.

12/30/80

Al and I visited Braunsdorf yesterday—Tony couldn't make it. We're going ahead with the libel charge. Paul says it will cost 5-10 grand for the three of us, will take a year at least. We will. From Paul's tone, I'm optimistic. He's very sharp.

A jolt yesterday. Received a transcript of the MacLeish tape (Al received the Ashbery) from Gerber who, "in conformance with the Provost's etc.," plans to use us. Was this the Provost's intention? Probably. Can we stop Gerber? We'll see. A long struggle ahead, perhaps even in the Faculty Senate.... No fooling myself. This drains me, costs me sleep, keeps me from poetry, diminishes my pleasure with the family and even watching Billy play last night (they won); but, I will see this all through and become a better man because of it. Most of the work, after the letter regarding Gerber's Christmas letter that I must send, will be Paul's. I'll (and Tony & Al) just have to deal with the anxiety. I'll feel better once Gerber, and the college community, knows we're pressing libel charges. I think we'll win. Paul is closing off the loose ends. We'll see. I <u>must</u>, soon, get back to my real work, *The Chestnut Rain*.

1/4/81

Walked out back just long enough to feed the birds and pick up this journal for a couple of entries here in my study. Bitter cold, wind chill factor about 35 below, and snow. It's good to be inside, watching football & taking care of letters & sending out some books. I'll work on the NEA application today.

Gerbergate in back of my mind, but, unless I'm wrong (and there will be flare ups from time to time), diminishing for me, something I think I'll be able to put in perspective increasingly as the semester goes by. The worries will be Gerber's.

I wrote to the people at Hofstra and says yes for July. I should enjoy it.... Got letters written to Sarton, Oates, Clemente, Ewert.... Look forward to basketball tomorrow, a workout, sweating and running.... Will go ahead with plans to spend a week in England in May.... Billy has a cold; otherwise, we're fine. Han & Kris & Billy are not exactly anxious to begin school again tomorrow.... Very much enjoyed wrapping my books— used up a whole roll of Milar and sent for two more and a dispenser.... I've packed a couple more boxes of books away for storage at U. of R.... I'm so happy at home with the family. We all played a game of cards at midnight last night.... Cleveland playing Oakland in terrible weather in Cleveland right now....

1/6/81

I did get out back this morning and worked a couple hrs. on *CR*, into it and then out of it (distracted by Gerbergate), but all in all a decent session.

Call from lawyer this morning about my letter. I'm ready to go. Will not pass it out until next week. We'll give Gerber plenty to worry about.

Will watch Billy's scrimmage today, and will play with Mahan's this evening myself. And will play tomorrow at noon, if I'm not too sore.

Call from Wesleyan University today asking if I'd run a workshop there in July this summer, but it's one of the weeks I'll be at Hofstra. Maybe the summer of '82.

Still reading Golenbock's *Dynasty*. Wish I'd been underlining things from the beginning.

I've finished the NEA application & just have to xerox it off, at least the poems, seven copies of each.

Long letter from Bob Phillips, who is the same. Allen Hoey writes to say *The Bees* is on his mind. Soon I'll be getting proof for *The Trains* and the Vanguard book. Soon, school again, but I've got a couple of good weeks yet before classes begin. May is almost here!

I sent off *The City Parables* to Martin, and got to some other letters and things.

Bill Rock has divorced Sis, and married Nadine Synneskvet. Mr. Chorney has died of cancer. Betty Marx not in good shape. That's the news from the college community lately.

Look forward to the U. of R. announcement about my deposit.

Billy found out today that he'll be given the Bauch & Lomb medal at graduation for the highest science average. What a kid.

I look forward to wrapping more books when the materials arrive.

Not <u>quite</u> as cold, but it's not swimming weather.

1/7/81

Gemmett called. Everything came down the wrong way. He is a shit, a fence-sitter, has never taken a stand one way or the other. Anyway, I've made an appointment, and Al and I will talk to the Provost on Monday. I must stay calm when I talk with him.

I think a lot about my body, and how I'm doing through this time of stress. I feel strong, and maybe the anxiety I feel is about the same degree of anxiety I often feel about other things. I played ball last night, ran hard for about an hour of four on four. I'm proud of the condition I'm in at 40. The only emotion that keeps welling up in me is anger/frustration, not the fear I once felt about all this. Maybe I'm getting used to being under fire.

Wrote Bill Ewert this morning. I've been fiddling around in the house—it's too cold for the cabin. One of these years, I'll get another heater. Generally, I'm glad to be in the house during this very rough weather.

Han & I might go over to Mirko's this evening for their New Year. Probably the weather will keep many of the Rochester "Ukies" away.

I like this journal. Maybe when I do no other writing all day, I feel as though I've added a few ¶s of evidence that I was alive, innocuous as my reporting here is.... Maybe this journal, which seems to me just jotting, is more unusual than I've thought it to be. Maybe not many people these days keep such a journal, for better or worse, at all.... It's a pleasure to watch the ink-flow.

I'm reading the Yankee book, *Dynasty*. Feel stirrings of poems inside me. To have been part of that whole story, say, in a roll like even Bob Grim, or John Kucks—that would have been something to smile about in old age, to dream about. Meanwhile, Grim & Kucks would probably trade places with me.

1/11/81

Sitting inside on a below-zero day watching football.

Meeting tomorrow with Provost. Those problems less on my mind the last few days than at any period since September. But things will flare up again, no doubt.

Billy's team now 8-0. He played a fine game the other night.

I'll play ball again tomorrow. Played Thurs.—not one of my better efforts—and we lost.

Martin Booth called from England. I'll spend a weekend with him at his place, and we'll read here and there together. He might make it to New Hampshire over the summer, too.

1/12/81

Meeting with Provost/Gemmett settled nothing, but was important for public relations & openness, if nothing else. Next, Gemmett will try to talk Gerber out of including Tony & Al & me in his book. I feel relaxed this evening. I may never send out the letter I was going to send.

Bruce Agte visited for a few hours last evening, and we talked books. He'd had a two-hour phone conversation with Bill Ewert!

Played ball today. Am tired. Will stay home tomorrow and spend time out back in the cabin. It may get all the way up to ten above zero.

1/14/81

Tony & I went to Curran's Enl. 112 meetings this morning, then cut out. I played ball, & then picked up Han. Am relaxing at home a couple hrs., & then there's Billy's game tonight.

Turco called me last night about Nims' anthology with that odd "Galaxy." Got my copy today. Wonder what that's all about! It's fun, anyway.

Letters from Aaron Kramer, Vicky Gold, Clemente today, and a card from John Nims. My life is pleasant, except for the Gerber business, which tempers it toward what it is for most people.

Worked on *CR* yesterday morning. Will again tomorrow. Not <u>quite</u> as cold now. Much schoolwork this weekend, but I don't mind, as long as I can stay at home.

1/15/81

2-3 good hours in the cabin this morning. Went over, typed up the "Family Tree" section again. It's still forming. Now, I'll do more reading in the farm journals for more possible lines. I'll be going over that section for a long time.

Have a ball game tonight; hope I survive.... Billy's team won last night. He played a fine game. 9-0 now. Hilton tomorrow night. Schoolwork looming.

I'm actually enjoying Bob Siegel's *Alpha-Centauri*, and want to write him.

1/17/81

Billy's team lost to Hilton. No big deal. 9-1 now.

I had two good sessions in the cabin today. Drafted what might become two sections of *CR*, both Wenzel/farm ones.

Both kids out to the school play tonight. Feels funny for Han & me to be alone. We went to bed with enough energy, for a change, and it was good. Now we're up again, & will wait up for the kids.

I'll drive Billy to RIT tomorrow for an interview. Then, schoolwork for me. I've been putting it off.

Two books, nicely inscribed, back from May Sarton today, one with a holograph poem.

1/18/81

Just back from RIT where Billy was interviewed by a bunch of engineers. Maybe he'll come up with some college money.

I finally got around to writing Bob Siegel. I enjoyed *Alpha Centauri*, and admire him as a writer. I'd have changed some sentences here & there, and some repetitions, but it's quite a book, and one I couldn't have written. I'll actually look forward to reading his next book of poems.

Am putting off all schoolwork until the last minute.

Kristen had trouble yesterday with her band teacher, who is bad news. She'll be okay.

Won about $50 the other night playing cards.

Dear diary, here comes another semester.

1/21/81

First day of classes went okay. About 28 showed up for the Transcendentalism course. I'll have much work reading papers and journals, but May is not far away, but I want to live within this semester, too.

I was out back only an hour or so this morning—too cold. I did type up and touch up my new beauty, maybe to be called "The Heart," probably a section of *Wenzel* in *CR*. "The Scrapple" looks good now, too.

I played ball at noon Monday, and played well, relaxed, shot very well. Will play again today, and warm up.... Blocks of ice build-up in the driveway, and the car almost gets stuck each time out or in.

Hostages freed yesterday, Reagan inaugurated.

1/23/81

Friday. Classes went very well yesterday, but tired me out, too. Getting organized is difficult, and establishing the spirit of the classroom. That's done now, and I'm on my way.

I have a list of about eleven things to do this weekend, some pleasant and some not. This evening, one of Billy's home games.... I played ball last night and did okay—Billy watched me for a while, as I missed my first two foul shots but then made four. Later, I played poker and won about $125. Card games have kept me in cash lately.

Al ill again with phlebitis. I don't know why this comes on him on occasion. I hope he'll recuperate and be strong as the year goes on with our suit.

I'll write to Ed Ochester & Jack Matthews this weekend to tell them why I'll be scarce when they visit. Package of books in the mail from Jack yesterday.

About finished "The Heart" the other day. It's a beauty, one of my best.

Judy Minty sent her letters poems. I look forward to reading the chapbook. I like her. She's a warm, true friend.... Nice letter from Duane Schneider, too, who will be sending more copies of *The City Parables*.

Renee Ganassi wrote to say she's still working on a program—some kind of dance/song program?—on *The Swastika Poems*. Hmmm. I wonder what my reaction will be if/when I see it.

Lately, these have all been short, winter entries, written inside. My journal will be more lush once the weather breaks. I lose most touch with trees and growing things, but the Christmas cactus in my office at school is budding.

1/26/81

A good day. Kurt & his girlfriend & Billy & Julie are playing cards upstairs. I've begun to do schoolwork, have just read a few papers. Warmer today, up to 40°, but now getting cold again, but the ice has at least melted from the driveway.

Looks like I finished "Yellowthroats" this morning. Looks like I wrote another poem called "The Berries," which came from the walk Han & I made to Lucille Raleigh's the other night. With "The Scrapple" and "The Heart," I've had a good week or two.

Saturday and yesterday I got many things done, alternating things I didn't want to do with things I did, like wrapping books. Now, a few rushed days, and I'll have a great long weekend off again.

Long letter from Ewert on various collecting things. Fun.

Tony and I will visit Al in hospital tomorrow after school.

Feb. 1, 1981

Sunday morning. I'm out back with my journal again. It's drizzling and cold out, but I'm comfortable, enjoying coffee. Han & the kids are inside, and fine. Birds are sailing in to my feeding spruce.

Two games for Billy last week. His team now 10-3. He's had 26 (double-overtime win over Hilton) and 17 (loss to Roth) the two games, and has made about a dozen free throws in a row. Han & Billy & I also went to the College's win over St. John Fisher last night. The Van Gundys are having a happy day, I'm sure.

I've had some nice days wrapping books & writing letters, and will again today, with some schoolwork thrown in.... I'm drafting a brief essay on collecting Heyen for Bert Babcock's Heyen catalogue—so far, so good.

Played well Thursday night myself. We beat an undefeated team. I was 5-6 from the field, and 2-2 on the foul line.

Looks like Al won't teach this semester, but I wouldn't trade places with him.... Nothing new in all the Gerber business....

Stan Lindberg is here tomorrow, come to think of it. I guess I'll stop over to listen to him.... Matthews & Ochester are here around the middle of the month. Ed called the other day, after he got my letter, and we had a good talk.

I thought this morning of not coming back here. I'm always glad when I do. The wind is blowing by, and the rain is hitting the snow crust around me, and the birds are zipping in and out—including, just now, a male cardinal. I'm at ease back here. I promise myself, now, that I will not again profane this place with departmental/Gerber business, as I did when typing/writing some of those letters back here. No more.

2/6/81

No more, except brief mentions, which tidy up & move things behind me: a few hours just now, Friday afternoon, regarding Gerbergate. Calls/talks with lawyer & Tony & Al. Lawyer will speak with President Brown, etc. Unbelievable letter to me from Provost yesterday, etc.

Al still in hospital, now in Rochester, for tests.

Billy's team won a beauty away the other night.

Classes going very well. Some wonderful students, who buoy me up.

Game tonight, Arcadia, the big one.

I played ball yesterday and did well—about 6 for 11 from the field, in a loss. Then I played poker and won about $50. Great release for me Thursday nights—classes done, then basketball & poker.

Snowing now. This place gives me back to myself.

Saw a nuthatch again this morning.

I've been thinking of a short Zen book of some sort. Presumptuous, of course, but I could. The master could be back here in my cabin, always, and I could talk with him. I think I'd need more time than I have now to make a start. Someday, maybe, I'll be reading another testimony (I've just read *The Empty Mirror*) and will begin.

I'll go in to eat in an hour, and then spend a great evening, win or lose, at Billy's game. He was wonderful the other night, deadly from the field, & running his foul shots to 23 in-a-row before he missed one, over four games.

I <u>will</u> fill up this page.

Abeles' ugly but good drawings arrived.

Good letter from Jack Matthews.

I'll read over some of my poems.

I didn't go to see Lindberg, didn't go to see Edward Albee. I'm growing up.

2/7/81

A loss last night to Arcadia. Billy had 15, and played very well. An emotional evening, for lots of reasons—this guy (I didn't know who he was at first) came to me after the game in the bleachers & said the trouble with the team was Heyen, etc.! He didn't know who I was. A few minutes later I went to this fellow, Sodoma, President of the school board, and told him off. I was a hero! A dozen teachers came to me later and said it was about time someone did it. Sodoma was very apologetic, etc. What a nerve he has. Instead of praising the team after a tough, honorable loss, he pulls that, singling out one of the best ballplayers, a senior, class valedictorian, like that, and <u>wrongly</u>. Billy held that team together. I thought of holding my tongue, but was glad, and all were glad, I didn't.

My only decision now regarding Gerber is whether or not to send the long letter. It will make the Provost my enemy, for sure.

I will spend a long time back here today, Saturday. I feel fine. Life is somehow tense, though, even here in the superficial suburbs.

2/15/81

Sunday morning, after an exhausting (but all in all good) week. My 3-page letter to the President on Gerbergate went out; teaching and journal reading; two games for Billy; Thursday evening dinner for Matthews & Greg Fitz Gerald & Rod & Tony Vallone; Thursday evening basketball for me (I scored about 20 pts in half-a-game; and then poker (+$100); meetings with Ochester & Matthews Friday & late drinking; correcting papers yesterday; a list of about 15 things for me to do inside. Now, here, it's about 40°, and the sun is shining. All is well. Patches of brown stubble appearing through the snow and ice for the first time in months.

Al had a lung biopsy, and is just not in good shape. The doctors suspected cancer, but it wasn't, but he's still in intensive care and uncomfortable. If he makes it home and this time does not change his life, stop smoking and get some regular exercise, it will mean he wants to die.

Matthews is the same wonder.

Han & the kids are fine. Billy had a touch of flu or something, and he has orders to stay home all day today and get in shape again for the last stretch of the season. Last regular-season game Tuesday evening.... Jack Palombella showed up at Olympia Friday night. Han & I have so many friends.

Wild Martin Booth wrote & is orchestrating my whole England trip. He's quite a chap.... I want to get some poems maybe to him, & Bill Meredith, and Bruce Agte, and maybe send "Yellowthroats" & "The Berries" to *New Yorker*, just for fun.... Diary, I'll only see you in bits & starts until about May 20th.

2/20/81

    A Friday morning. Warm for this time of year, and raining, the ditch flowing, the cabin high and dry.
    What days lately. Tues. was Billy's game, a win, and then pizza party afterwards for players & cheerleaders & coaches & parents. It went perfectly, right down to the wine we adults toasted ourselves with after the season. Wednesday Billy & I went to U. of R. for his tour and interview. I also dropped off seven more boxes of books & correspondence for safekeeping with Peter Dzwonkoski. When Billy got home, his mail included an acceptance from the engineering program at Cornell. Much schoolwork Wednesday night for me, and then a long day of teaching yesterday. No basketball or poker last night, thank God, and I slept. I'm back here for a couple hours before going up to play a little ball. And tomorrow at noon is our big faculty game preceding the college game.
    Call from Bill Ewert last night. I should be getting a package today. A new broadside of *Bean*, I guess. Ewert's Oates book will be dedicated to Han and me!
    Nothing wild from Gerber yet. I'm relaxed. President Brown sent me a copy of his letter to Provost. All those administrators will meet again. A couple of angles I can't figure, but I am relaxed about this stuff, and wish our lawyer luck.
    Talked to Al by phone yesterday. He seems in good spirits, and may be home by early in the week. He <u>must</u>, now, stop smoking and drinking so much coffee, must get exercise & rest.
    I have to finish the report on the Wright book this weekend; otherwise, just pleasant things to do.
    So many young & aspiring writers stopping by, treating me like a guru of some sort. All my life I've just stumbled forward. As far as writing goes, it's only with *CR* that I feel I've really found something.
    I sent some books to Martin Booth, who is looking for an English publisher for me.
    I do not get back to this cabin for several days, and then do, and it is the same, just waiting for me. It would be impossible for me to try to do everything inside, to decompress & to write.
    Kristen is in love with this senior, Mike, a nice fellow. Billy still going with Julie. Han & I still happy after all these years.
    Dustjacket for *Lord Dragonfly*, though yellow again, is a beauty.

2/22/81

    I woke up this morning a little restless, thinking of going to book store and post office, of playing ball. I've had to kick myself, remind myself that this kind of morning is what I've always wanted. I'm back here, and free. Dan Stryk sent a card to say that after months and months of work at Utah, he'd passed his exams and was free. I know, from my life in Athens, what that is like. Now it is a warm morning, overcast, the cabin comfortable. I will settle down, and read (*Black Sun*, the story of death-haunted Harry Crosby), and write.
    I scored 27 of our 40 pts in our 2-pt. win over the administration. The game was much fun.
    Bean arrived, attractive, a pleasure.
    I finished the report on Smith's *Wright* for Illinois.
    Some schoolwork this evening.... Mouganises had us over twice for poker. The second time, we didn't want to go at all, but they needed us. Bill Rock played with them all weekend, too.... I hope he's okay. And Poulin. I almost said and Gerber, but he deserves much unhappiness for a while....
    Billy's playoff game against Franklin at Hilton tomorrow. I hope we win. If we can get the ball to Felipe, & if Billy plays like he can, we will.
    Ewert says he'd like to do *Blackberry Light* by October. That should give me plenty of time for *Wenzel*.... I look forward to *Lord Dragonfly*, and wish I could help Vanguard sell it, but that's up to them. I should, must just keep the poems coming. If Vanguard abandons me, I'll find someone else to do, e.g., *Chestnut Rain*.

2/28/81

    Oh, what a week again. Thursday, teaching & then basketball & then poker. Friday morning, meetings with lawyers over Gerbergate—nothing settled, & Tony & Al more upset than I am, and this is all costing us money, but now Gerber will have some legal fees, too, since our lawyer will contact his, once more, for an apology—and then Friday night, last night, the War Memorial. The boys not only did beat Franklin to get to the War Memorial, but won last night, too, a great thrill, and will play there again next Wednesday. So, we're still a little basketball crazy here. Four buses of spectators from Brockport yesterday.... Today I have some free time and space for the first time in a long time. The Gerber business is the only thing on my mind, and what, in the end, is it to me but some money? It has been a long mental & spiritual test for me. If our lawyer can work something out that satisfies, maybe this can be over with by the time school breaks for summer.... Much in my writing life to look forward to, including *Lord Dragonfly*.... This cabin has its own life, abides here with part of me when I'm away.... I have a little poem going about the blue spruce.... Such happiness from parents of players yesterday, happiness for our good boys and girls, cheerleaders, too, who made it as far as they did, and then played so well. We play Arcadia, 19-1, Wednesday (their only loss this year, early, was to us, and then they beat us ((by 3)) later), and we'll be underdogs, but even a loss would end a wonderful season, all Han & I hoped for for Billy for years, since that sophomore broken leg, since that 2-17 year he had as a freshman with the J.V. What solid kids on Billy's team this year, maybe the smartest starting five in the nation, and no dissention all year, a joy for their coach, who went through hell many years with disruptive players and parents.

2/29/81

Sunday morning, after a restless night—I couldn't sleep much. It would be nice to learn to empty my mind. Some of the reading I do, the scattershot Zen texts I love, nudge me toward this. Fifty years of not wanting, says Rumi, too, is what it would take, maybe. But this morning and this cabin make me happy. My thoughts have been half on basketball & half on Gerber. I want to get back to steady sessions of writing. Many good things back here. The cabin sequence, untitled, might become something fine. Yesterday, too, I finished a little piece, "The Spruce," that, as it turned out, wanted to follow my "Nocturne" piece in *CR*. I also want to work on the collecting essay for Babcock. And.... Flocks of geese have been heading to Canada already. Tomorrow is March.

3/2/81

Yesterday was March—I had the date wrong.
Decided, this morning, not to attend either the Curran or Department meetings this afternoon. Much involved in this. I mean to drop away, and if these bureaucrats someday decide to press the issue, well, that will be that. I am 40, now, and will live my life.... Part of this will involve my never receiving merit money again (attendance at meetings, says Tollers, is governance), for example, but what is money in this matter? I so much want to be strong, to allow all that crap to swirl around me, to be oblivious to it, while I keep working on poems, keep building my writing life. When I consider that I am probably the best teacher in the Department, the center of the Department's student writing activities, and that others have gotten & keep getting the paperwork awards for excellence in teaching, I'm bothered. I will become a man. Let these people buzz and do.
Sent my "Collecting Heyen" through another draft yesterday.
"You must change your life" comes to my mind. I wonder if there is another job, another life out there for me somewhere. In about five years, anything can happen.
Tony says that if we're fired we can first collect about 18 months of unemployment! It's a thought. These people here, I think, do not have the courage ever to press us, no matter how angry they become over our dropping-out. How to reach "detachment" over these things?—this is the question.

Later: it's about 3:30 in the afternoon now. I feel very relaxed, after playing ball, after picking up Han & Fran Setter, after missing two meetings. Also, I stopped in to see Al for twenty minutes about that other business. We'll be all right, even if it takes time.... But it's the running and sweating, and then the hot shower, and then the cold air, that clears the mind/body. I'll turn to *CR* or some other writing for a couple of hours, and then Han will click my light, and I'll go inside for some supper (franks & beans & a salad tonight) with the family.

3/4/81

I just finished going over that new dragonfly/cabin sequence again. It may or may not ever come to anything.

Martin Booth called yesterday. He's arranging & wheeling & dealing. He must be a dynamo, Poulin & Turco & Dave Smith put together. I bet he has his enemies over there. I'll have a good, exhausting week, and will try not to get nervous anticipating it.

Billy's game tonight. Han & I are basketball crazy in Brockport, but are not alone, but it might be all over today.

Cold again, but it won't be long now, but snow is on its way to us again.

I'll turn to *CR* for a while, & then go play a little ball.

Sunday (the 8th?)

Morning. I'll be back here 3-4 hours.

Dream last night of Gerber, a strange one, Gerber getting me, subtly, to agree to something I didn't want to. And Emmanuel was standing on my back with his hard shoes, hurting me, until I gasped for help.

Billy's team lost the big game by 1 pt. It was awful the way Dennis Crawford threw it away. The kid will never forget it. Billy played a fine, solid game, scored a dozen points, kept his head.

Long calls from Ewert. I mentioned Jack Matthews had sent me a *Lauderdale*. Ewert went nuts, kept proposing trades & deals. I'll send the damned thing to him, and will get about $250 in credit!... Steve Claeson's Swedish anthology arrived. He's quite a man. Again, from time to time I just get lucky and the right person comes upon my poems.... I spent yesterday, and will spend today, once I go back in, catching up on mail. Now I'm going to have a long session with *CR*.

Won $240 at poker the other night.

Monday (3/9?/81)

It's almost eleven in the morning. I've been back here working with various things—"The Cabin" sequence (still don't know about it), and *Wenzel* of *CR*, which has fallen into place. Looks like it will mainly be a matter of finishing the "Family Tree" section.

I took care of much correspondence yesterday. It's the price I pay for being in literary touch with so many people, and for liking mail.

Han's stomach still hurts her. She's been to the doctor & in for tests more than once. I don't know.... My folks called, too, & Pop will have his operation in about a month. Meanwhile, of course, they're edgy & worried.

A light snow drifting down.

Soon I'll head inside, drink some fruit juice and take some vitamins, and go up to play ball.

3/12/81

Right now, as I write back here in my cabin, thousands of young people around the country are in workshops and classes, working toward degrees, worried about jobs, writing term papers, wanting to be poets. They are where I was back in Ohio: I can see myself against that bedroom wall on Wolfe St., working on a poem, worried meanwhile about a dozen things. Right _now_, while I'm in this miraculous place (and I just finished ordering the sections of *Wenzel*), thousands of people are going through that dismal strain. I've been so lucky. This is mid-semester, a Wednesday, and I still have some time to be back here like this.

Dentist today, and car to drop off for wheel alignment, and Kristen to pick up later on, but *CR* comes along, a wonder.

I see that amazing Dave Smith has four books upcoming this year (a book of poems & the Wright book from Illinois, a book of poems and a novel from LSU). More power to him. I want to stay within his energy-field.

Bits & snippets: I sent Ewert *What Happens in Fort Lauderdale* for about $250 in trade!; hardback of her new book came from Judy Minty with a holograph; Philip Appleman's new novel came gratis; I'll approach Washington Square Press on an expanded paperback *Swastika*; Warren Slesinger from U. Pa. Press called, and I suggested a book idea to him, but don't care much about it; Pop will have his operation in about a month; Eddie is out of work, apparently, and Cheryl is sort of a day patient for mental problems in Syracuse Hospital; I slept hard & woke up happy & early this morning; Gerber business seems to be on hold for the moment; MFA reports from Ochester & Matthews appeared and it's as though they were written by me & Poulin & Piccione.

3/14/81

I feel happy this Saturday morning, whole somehow, complete. I just finished typing up my new sequence, so far called "The Cabin," and it will be a good one, when done, but it isn't just that that makes me happy. The Gerber business is only a slight under-the-surface irritation now (though I've had two dreams about him: twice I've twisted his nose!), and my life is otherwise so rich, with books coming up, and trips, and my sense that deep things are swimming into my poems lately. Also, Han had her tests at the hospital yesterday, and they were hard on her, the doping up & the tube-swallowing, but she doesn't have an ulcer. (As I understand it, she does have some kind of herniation that can be treated with medicine and diet.) Also, the kids are fine. Also, trivial as this should be to me, I played a good game Thursday night and we won; then I won $275 at poker (won $240 the week before). Also, about one more month and I'll be back from England, with only papers & journals to read before a free summer. I even look forward to doing the Hofstra thing and am glad I said yes.

Tony and I went to the Dept. meeting on the MFA yesterday. He yelled at everybody once or twice, about wanting <u>writers</u> in our dept., not rationalists, to write proposals, etc. But he was okay. In the evening, Boo called to report that Tony's mother had died the night before, that Tony hadn't wanted to burden any of us with this yesterday. In so many ways, that Tony is the most profoundly human of us all.

3/15/81

And after my entry yesterday, I went inside and Han and I had as bad an argument as we've ever had. It had to do, again, with my not doing enough around here in the way of chores and errands, etc. It's true. I'm lazy about those things. Also, I don't care about those things because they never diminish, are always there to do, and will not give me pleasure in old age as any poems I manage to write will, will be a consolation. Also, I have not done so many of these things because Han has always taken it upon herself to do them. It is all more complex than this, having to do with her job and mine, her interests and mine. And with the weather. And with so much on our minds.

I have a slight sinus cold—all that smoke irritation at cards the other night, and the walking up to school on Friday.

Kristen's 15th birthday tomorrow. A special dinner for her today, I think, and some girlfriends coming over.

I'll spend a couple hours back here, go in, finish my freshman papers, watch basketball while I answer a letter or two, and stew.

One of the pressures against poetry now is the constant pressure on the poet to "grow up." I just looked at a few of my "word things," and the old worry intrudes: what do they have to do with the real world this Sunday morning? Do they only clear some kind of childish and egotistical space for <u>me</u>? Family inside, and world of politics past that, and time wiping us all out past that, and I spend my time and mental/emotional energies in writing poems.... A dream last night of trying to connect with a certain trolley, and I did, earlier than the others.

3/21/81

Second day of spring. It's been cold, and snowing an inch or two every day, but melting.... I haven't been back here since my last entry. Busy with school and all, and the cold keeps me from coming back here more often, but it doesn't matter much: this place keeps me steady even when I'm not here.

A quick flurry of activity—letters to SUNY Press & to the Dept. Committee—on Gerbergate. Maybe some space/time to relax before other actions are necessary again.

I won $214 at poker. Again, over $200. A bad drunk at the last game made things unpleasant, but the money coming in for me has eased everything.

Ewert's Wright item appeared. Not much for $30. I don't know. A work of art, yes, but the poem already published, etc. I don't know. But, what's the difference?

Kristen's 15th birthday went by. She had a fine time, and has a date tonight with her new boyfriend. Billy has been in good spirits. Han still has esophagus aches, but the medicine & diet should be taking effect soon.

I finally got around to writing Pocket Books about an expanded version of *Swastika*, in paperback, and will try other places later on.

I threw seed into & under the spruce in front of me. Already sparrows, a pair of cardinals, juncos, chickadees are with me.... I'll turn to *CR* for a couple hours.

3/22/81

I just saw my first robin of the year. I think it was an arrival, too, the way she (a very large one) ruffled her feathers, as though it had been a long trip.

Tony over yesterday. We talked over the lawyer's letter, which just arrived. We feel okay. We're ready to sue by April 1st if no apology or retraction form Gerber.

I was looking over the materials for Book V of *CR*. It's going to be a knockout. I look forward to working on sections like "The Ghost" & "The Binding."

Much family fun over Kristen's strange double date last night.

My father goes into the hospital today, Sunday, for his Wednesday operation. I hope he'll be okay and will have another decade or two.

3/25/81

Pop's operation is this morning. He'll be in surgery at least two hours. Werner will call me later. Somehow, I feel sure it will go okay.

Last town-team game last night. We lost. I should have shot a little better, but did decently, and didn't get hurt in that league all season—so, maybe I'll play again next year.... Thursday night, since there's no play-off game for me, I'll go to Dave Smith's reading at U. of R. Will miss the Waters/Oliver reading here, but see them late at Casey's, where my basketball teammates will also be for our league party. All I need now is a poker game to go to, too.

Long call from Ewert last night. I guess my letter about the Wright publication disturbed him, though I didn't mean to. I still have reservations about such things. I sure don't want to hurt Bill, though, who is generous and loyal, a true friend.

The sun is shining down on my cabin. The temperature is supposed to inch up toward 60° over the next week. I'm spreading the last of the birdseed around.

I had a good session the other morning with the "Family Tree" section of *CR*. Will turn to *CR* again for a couple of hours now.

3/28/81

Blackberry Light will be bound in a muted green. I think I'll sign it in this color, which I get by mixing the blue-black ink I usually use with the bottle of emerald green I bought. I might darken it even a bit more.

Pop is recovering after a four-hour operation. He's very uncomfortable, but will be okay. I'll write him again today. And I've been calling, & Mom will call again this evening to tell us how he's doing.

A warm, sunny day today. This weekend has been/will be shot with doing things. I went to the Smith reading in Rochester on Thursday, & stopped in at Rubin's party for Waters/Oliver later, & then played cards until six in the morning. Slept until noon—then spent time with Michael yesterday, & drank with the writing gang last night, & will watch basketball today & go to a dance concert tonight to see Bruce Agte et. al., & the basketball banquet tomorrow night, and I'll go to Syracuse Wednesday. And. It's okay, this spring rush. And I'll have many still times back here for Wenzel.

I liked Smith & his reading. I learned how private even his plots can be, the story lines. A good voice. He looked for me, and was glad to see me. He dedicated a poem to me, "Running Back." I'm glad I went, as creepy as that whole crowd can be. Hecht, as usual, almost resented anyone's getting near the poet.

Han's feeling pretty good these days. She & Kristen will do some spring shopping today.... Billy's already played a few rounds of golf.... So many things upcoming that I'm sometimes anxious about them, but I remind myself that there will be long, slow times around here, as there will be.

3/30/81

It's 10:30 in the morning. I'm back in the cabin after driving through rain to Albion for my passport application. A moody day, the sense of all that time past since our year in Germany, the rain & spring fields. On the way there, I picked up a hitch-hiker, a black guy in sneakers and a brown-paper bag, and drove him a few miles. He said he was looking for work. He said he'd just gotten out of the hospital: someone had held a gun on him and forced him to use drugs.... My sense of myself now: a man who uses colons, is a "professor," and picks up down and out hitchhikers. He could have been dangerous. Money is the difference, the reason I can sit here writing now while that poor black bastard is killing that bag of wine wherever he is.... Moody, too, after the basketball banquet last night. So proud of Billy, & sad/happy he's on his way out of high school... I'm drinking coffee from the Chu Lai cup Kenny brought back from Viet Nam. I like to bring it back here, to remind me.... The grinding of town trucks on the roads, doing spring-cleaning pick-ups.

Billy & I worked outside for a couple hours yesterday morning, raking, carrying a few rocks to the Mosher line, thinning out ash saplings here and there.

Pop is recuperating. I talked with Mom, Werner, & Eddie yesterday. Eddie is down, not even working. I'll see him Wednesday in Syracuse, I think.

4/4/81

President Reagan was shot several days ago by a crazy bastard who was even too violent for the American Nazi Party. I'm glad Reagan is recuperating.

I guess the suit against Gerber, as of a few days ago, is going ahead.

It's a Saturday morning. It was 80° yesterday. I smeared some creosote around the cabin's sills and corners yesterday maybe to discourage the ants from massing above me this year.

The Syracuse reading went well Wednesday. I took along Tama Baldwin and Tony Vallone and Li-Young Lee and his wife Donna. We visited Allen Hoey, saw his press. I stopped in at Carruth's class, and then he didn't make my reading. But it was a decent audience, and Ray Carver & Tess Gallagher & Philip Booth were there, and said things to me later that made me glow. Now I'm back, and back to the writing of the poem.... Reading next week at the Seymour Library. Gulp.

I bought Hamburger's translation of Celan in Syracuse. That book is going to hit me. I just know it, though I'm usually averse to poetry that cryptic.

I have a couple of windows open back here. It's warm, but overcast today, and some rain is almost here. Honeysuckle leaves unfolding around me. Han's hundreds of tulips & hyacinths are rising.

Reading sections of CR at Syracuse again convinced me that I've got hold of something very good, and satisfying, and of a whole.

I've decided not to do the Festschrift for U. Pa. Press that I believe I could have talked them into doing.

Billy has shot the best qualifying rounds of golf for his team. Kristen is in some sort of local beauty contest tonight. I went for a walk with her last evening. She's a mature kid, and knows what makes her happy and unhappy, and just wanted to do this thing once.... Pop is recuperating nicely. I spoke with him yesterday. He's out of intensive care. Werner & Henry will visit him today. Mom is of course relieved.

My life is all anyone could ask a life to be. I need only purify myself of the feelings I have regarding a few people—Tollers, Gerber, Gemmett, Douglas, Wolfe, Bird—develop a true disinterest, and I'll be free. The summer vacation comes on. Before that, in just two weeks, come to think of it, our trip to Myrtle Beach. Then my week in England. This 40th year of mine has been/will be the fastest.

4/5/81

Turned to schoolwork details yesterday, and came to the Rubin note asking for support for the MFA, & became upset again over Gerbergate. If I could only reach a calm, disinterested wisdom, a state of mind and being where I could truly not care about what anyone in this town or school thinks of me. I spoke with Rod & Tony & Al yesterday. Provost has apparently forbidden the special Forum committee to deal with current problems!... What is the bottom line? Am I afraid I will not be given sabbatical? Am I afraid of being fired?... I realize that it's the making of <u>decisions</u> about these things that often bothers me the most, not the things themselves. I might still have to become a man. It might have to begin today. I will <u>not</u> circulate the letter I wrote yesterday. But I can't decide whether or not to call Rubin and/or Fitz Gerald. If I could just ignore, ignore, and lose myself in work and family. It's sad how all of this tinges the spring.

Kristen didn't win the contest last night, but handled herself beautifully. We're very proud of her. She has courage, and she's been learning so much.

I drafted the letter to the man at Vintage, and will get to that today. I've some papers to read, but there are some playoff NBA games to correct them by.

Bill Ewert called yesterday about Abeles' drawing, etc. I love talking to him. Maybe he'll join me in NYC on the 27th.

Cooler today, the temperature here in the cabin just right.

Poulin has a touch of pleurisy & pneumonia. I don't know. Unless he stops smoking, he's a dead man.

I'll read at Seymour Library Wednesday evening. I'll talk, more than read, probably.

Talked with Marie Mosher along the line yesterday when I was piling rocks. I like her, and she's been through hell, has mental problems, and will. She loves the woods, trees, flowers, has probably kept Giff from allowing even more houses to be built behind them.... She's lost two peach trees to the winter.

Several song sparrows flitting around back here. I hope they nest close again.

Some day, I will recollect all these academic-inspired emotions in tranquility & write a sequence on *Graver, the Professor*.

I don't have it in me to turn to *CR* now, but will glance maybe at "The Cabin." Maybe I'll think of a poem or poems to embroider stories around for the Wednesday reading.

4/6/81

Thoughts of Gerber & lawyers & Dept. affairs keep interrupting my life, but I am otherwise fine. Will avoid a meeting today.

Spoke with Ewert again yesterday about various things, and sent him the new version of the "Blackberry Light" section just now.

Yesterday, Billy and I moved the boulder I've wanted to move to near the cabin, outside my window. I've seen much already. I may finally have a use for that blank book Bill sent me, the one bound by Emily Rizzo to show Bill what *The Snow Hen* would look like. Yes. I think, in fact, I will go inside and get that blank book now.

Han & the kids flourish. I slept fine.

4/8/81

This is spring-green Roethke ink. I like it darker.

Wednesday. I read for local folks this evening at Seymour Library. I'll do fine, though it's a chore picking things to read.

I began *The Boulder*. I won't talk about the boulder in this diary from here on in.

Warm and sunny right now. A perfect day. I'll put in my door screen this weekend.

Have been watching the *Masada* series on television each evening. Will get back, I trust, to watch the conclusion tonight.

Saw Bruce Agte in a short play yesterday.

Got *Poems of a Jew* back from Karl Shapiro with "My Grandmother" in holograph.

A rabbit ran into my middle path when I walked back here, and is still there.

I feel about the way these lines look, drifting. The Gerber business just about in its final stage. He met with his lawyer yesterday. Within the week he'll apologize/retract or we'll sue.... All his career he has gotten away with this kind of thing, and no one has made him accountable. Now he will be.

We leave for Myrtle Beach next week already. I'll concentrate on driving carefully, all the long way. I think it will do me good to get away, will break the spell here of thinking about Gerber and his book.

Those young people I see on teaching days—Tama Baldwin & Tony Vallone & Richard Ehrlich & Li-Young Lee & Keith Hafford—make me happy.

4/11/81

A night of many dreams. One about Gemmett & Gerber showing up at a college auditorium somewhere to read their poems, and then leaving after they found out I was there. And a dream of me purposely bumping into Gerber in the hall in front of Perry. And packages falling apart in the mail room.... But the good dream was one in which Kinnell (we called him "Danway"!) was visiting. And Nesconset & Brockport were somehow combined. When I looked across the old Nesconset property from back where the fish-pond was to over to the corner where the shed was near those two big maples, I saw my Brockport cabin. Such a warm & beautiful & timeless dream.

Kris & her friend Karen & Han & I went to Sandi Piccione's play in Kendall last night. It was based on the tale of the princess & the pea. Fun, but it dragged on.... Han not feeling very well again.

This weekend is clear for me. Much deskwork.

A good gathering at my Seymour Library reading the other night. Bruce & Tony Vallone came over later to watch *Masada*.

Billy actually shot a hole-in-one yesterday while playing with Brad Howe & Jim Cook.

Tony Piccione and Li-Young Lee have been translating Li-Young's father's Chinese poems into English. The man had been personal physician to Chairman Mao, I hear. Some rich things happening around here.... I don't know, but after my reading at Syracuse a woman said to me that I must have read a lot of Buddhism—everything flows together.

Later: I've written in *The Boulder*. And I've just looked over "The Cabin." It reminded me, somehow, of the big project I talked over with Tony Vallone. What if, a few years from now, Vanguard issued *The City Parables* and *The Chestnut Rain* both at the same time, those two worlds. I can see the boxed set now! *CP* wd. be expanded, of course. I want to keep this project in mind.

4/13/81

Henry called this morning, wondering if we could stop in to see him when we go to South Carolina. Maybe.

Tony will stop by later, and we'll go to that Com. Skills meeting. Death.

A long weekend. I slept better last night than I have in a long time.

Have some poems ready to go off to Nims, a schizophrenic submission, not only "The Berries" and "Yellowthroats" and "The Cabin," but my Tower of London "Dream" and my old Wallace Stevens poem.

Had to spray the ants creeping in above me the other day, and the odor lingers. I'm keeping a window open.

I'm always a bit nervous on Monday. No real reason. Even the thought of going over to the school does it.

4/16/81

We'll leave this afternoon for South Carolina. I'll have a good, free week, I'm sure. Must drive carefully. Will stay with Henry tonight in Glen Burnie. Will read Kaplan's biography of Whitman. Love it so far.

Only cloud is the Gerber business. <u>Today</u>, I feel I want it all over with before summer begins. Have drafted a final letter to the President. Will show it to Al & Tony next weekend. Just don't know if the libel suit will go ahead.

Should I take this journal with me on the trip?... No.

I'll be back on Saturday, will fly to New York on that Monday! Will try to buy a riding mower that Sunday, unless our old one starts & we can make do.

4/26/81

Sunday morning. Cool and sunny. Birds around the cabin. The boulder in front of me, honeysuckle on both sides of it. I'm dazed from all the driving. I ran and walked the South Carolina shore, read Kaplan's *Whitman*, swam, ate, missed home, am glad to be back. Han and the kids were in their glory. It was good to see Henry, going & returning. Tomorrow I fly to New York for one fast day. A busy week of teaching & readying for England.... I hope, too, to get Gerbergate behind me. Another letter or two, and out from under lawyers and anger and everything. It can be done. A weary time right now. I'll be exhausted by the time I get final grades turned in. But there will be plenty of time this summer. I've always had the time, have even become restless. So much I want to do/write that I won't become bored this summr.

Long talk with Ewert last night. I've got $1,125 coming from him and Bert for manuscripts & books. I want to get in the clear with money, too. The England trip will be expensive.... Day we left for Myrtle Beach, Billy's letter from Cornell came—good financial assistance, including four grand off the top in scholarships. It will cost us only two thousand or so a semester. That's where he's going. Princeton turned him down. Hard to believe, but a good lesson for him.

I want to relax and enjoy these trips, as I should.

I think I'll pile a few rocks, just to relax. Cabin, boulder, by about May 20th, I'll be back here, and whole.

4/28/81

I've now had about a total of 3 hrs. sleep in two nights.... Rushed back to classes from NYC this morning, after a day there—saw the Vanguard folks & Bob Phillips & Bill Ewert (we shared a room at the Roosevelt), & met William Bronk (who said warm things to me but is an extremely bitter man who feels that the world has never discovered him). Our reading was to about 30-40 people. More important than my reading, I got to the Strand for 32 books, & got a few things at Barnes & Noble. And talked with Ewert, and Evelyn at Vanguard—*LD* not ready for another month.

I hope to sleep deep tonight. Will first watch a little basketball. Getting away for the England trip without bullshit from Tollers bothers me now, but I'll get there, and also, soon, get out from under Gerbergate. It's virtually over. I'm going to write him a letter, forgiving him everything, and thus free myself!

I called Vince Clemente, and it happened to be his 49th birthday. I have to bask in such friendships.

May 1, 1981

It's over. For one thing, I talked with SUNY Press, and Mandel thought Tony & Al & I would <u>not</u> have to be in the volume, if there is one. This was great news, a victory. If we're disappointed, and it goes down the wrong way, the three of us will go ahead with that letter to all the writers. Then we will have done all we could do.

On the second front, I wrote Gerber a personal letter, listing all the things I forgive him for (as I do, that convoluted, inward, nasty personality), and wishing him decades of happiness. If he responds in any hasty way, I'll just tell him I forgive him. I couldn't pretend anger any longer, and pretend being upset by his "break-in letter," etc. It's over. I'm so relieved. I doubt that anything crazy will happen from here on in. It's over. I leave for England in four days. I'll finish the school year, and be off. It's hard to believe. For the first time now, since Sept. or Oct., I can let my mind be free. I was so caught up in all that business for so long. It's over.

May 3, 1981 (Sunday)

Another cool and sunny day, as yesterday. Perfect. I'm back in the cabin, which I cleaned the other day. Also, mowed the lawns the other day with my clunk of a mower. Am marking time, but marking the spring, as I get ready for my trip on Tuesday.

I've been relieved and happy, and not in any way untrue to myself. That shit is all over. At an auction yesterday, Virginia Weiss said we wouldn't have peace in the Dept. until Gerber was committed. <u>She</u> can fight that fight! If I were Tony or Al, I'd feel I had some loose ends. My letter to Gerber forgave all, settled all.... Yesterday I told Han that the reason I'd been so upset the first day or two of our stay in Myrtle Beach was the Gerber business. It's been a weight for so long. Now, every fifteen minutes or hour, I feel inside myself for that conflict, and realize it's over, and breathe like a new man.

Much fun yesterday with the kids on the way to their prom.... Then Han & I had dinner at the diner, and dessert with Poulins. A great evening. Kristen has been at Christine's.

Evelyn Shrift called. She wants to make sure that *Swastika* gets to Oxford, somehow.

End of May and all of June I'll want/need long sessions back here, with *CR*, & with Holocaust reading, such as the Wiesel book Cargas sent.

May 6, 1981

I've been trying to sleep, but haven't been able to. I'm in a room at Saint Peter's College at Oxford. The noises below me of students laughing has reminded me of noises I heard while trying to sleep in that *Gasthaus* at Tübingen so many years ago. And there may be a gas leak in this room, and I have windows open. This reminds me of the time in Connecticut it was so hot in my room I had to leave the cold shower running all night. I'm very tired after getting ready for the trip & then the sleepless flight. I wonder, again, what the fuck I'm doing here. I can't quite figure out my depression. Not finding any books I want to buy. Lugging my damned luggage all over. The indignity of carrying 10 copies of *Swastika* across the ocean, as Evelyn wanted me to, and then seeing that *Light* had not arrived. I forgot my toothbrush. Generally low scene at the readings this evening (Teller/Paulin) and probably only twenty will be there tomorrow for Booth & Heyen. But subtler things I can't quite zero in on. This magnificent city reminds me of all those dreary hours with all those dreary English authors—the collected work of John Lyly is on sale at Blackwells! Lynne Williamson doesn't have a car, and I'm supposed to check out by ten, and have nowhere to go. Everyone talking about Seamus Heaney's upcoming reading—a thousand people will show—and he's just my age and is a fine poet but I'll be fucked if he's more important than I am—and I bet he won't have to worry about what to do with his luggage. In any case, many things I understand and do not understand tell me, again, as I wrote to myself in Wyoming, to, generally, stay at home, but at least pick my spots. If Han were with me, I'd enjoy this city more. I miss her and the kids, indeed I do.... Well, I will see Martin tomorrow, and will be at his place tomorrow night, and we'll walk and talk a lot.... I just don't have the soul to fly all over the planet and have a great time. I don't know who I am here. I want to walk from my home to my cabin, and cabin to home, want to bicycle around Brockport and go to some auctions.... Well, I will give a good reading tomorrow, and maybe get some sleep now, and maybe see a few memorable things, like the Bodleian, tomorrow. As always, it helps to write. As always, I look forward to reading this journal entry when I'm past it, and wiser.... I know that Hofstra will be good for me this summer. I'll be somebody there, and close to home, and will have my toothbrush with me.

May 7, 1981

It's about four, and in about an hour I'll walk over for the reading, and will meet Martin. It's been a full day, and I feel much better. I got some sleep last night for the first time in about three days (rose from the dead again), bought a toothbrush, arranged to stay in this room until the reading. I even bought this little notebook, and jotted down some lines while walking High Street—probably a satirical little piece, self-directed, will come of it.... Bought a beautiful *Leaves of Grass* (1891-92) for five pounds. It's apparently missing a frontispiece portrait, but I'm glad to have it for my collection.... I should think now about what I'll read.... Hit hard in the Pitt Rivers Museum by the American Indian clothes.... Soon it will be goodbye to Oxford, maybe, probably forever.

May 13, 1981

It's 9:30 in the morning. I'm at Heathrow for my 12:00 flight, which has been delayed until at least 17:25 because of a strike here. This will fuck up my flight from Toronto. I'm only worried about Han. Otherwise, the week is over, and I'm glad.

My days with Martin were long, sometimes good, sometimes a pain-in-the-ass with his kids & sick dog & his ordering Helen all about as though she were a slave & his general arrogance about most things & his class consciousness. But he was kind and generous to me, a friend, and all's well. I talked to a class of his at Rushden, and saw him teach a sort-of poet-in-the-schools thing elsewhere. I met a poet by the name of George Surtees (something like this), and liked him. I spent a day in Cambridge with Martin, saw his ancient college—Kings—and many other things. We visited several pubs. We read at a place called Toddington, and yesterday I took an early train to London, walked the Kensington section, read at the sort-of dreary National Poetry Society. All three times, I think, I read very well. I read, in the three readings at Oxford, Toddington, London, to a total of about fifty people. I am surely right to turn inward and find private joy in the kind of uncaring poetry scene I move in, while Martin becomes angry about it & <u>pushes</u> by pumping himself in various ways, even lying about himself in things he says. He has many enemies here, I've found out, and this has not helped our audiences.... Saint Margaret's was a place I'll remember, and maybe write something about.... Martin gave me many Sceptre Press pamphlets. It's amazing what he gets away with charging for them, and he <u>does</u> sell them.... It's going to be a very long day & perhaps evening & night & day here and in the plane & in Toronto. Maybe, to begin with, I'll buy a paperback on Elvis that I glanced at.... I might have to let time take care of itself while I think of the boulder outside my cabin.... Lynne Studier (Williamson) was a real friend, even journeyed to London for the reading last night.... Didn't manage to buy any good books, really, since Oxford.... I long for home—will correct journals all weekend, and really won't even mind. <u>Joy</u>—I'm going home, and will <u>stay</u> home, until Hofstra in July.

May 19, 1981

I'm back in the cabin as the sun is falling on a perfect day and evening—well, a perfect day except for the Communications Skills meeting I attended all afternoon. I just pasted in my England diary notes. I'm home, at last. I'm a bit dazed—spent days recuperating, and then days of journal reading, and then got final grades in—and happy. So much seems cleared away, and my summer off begins.

A new riding mower in the shed. I'll run it tomorrow or next day.

Al Poulin off to Greece.

The word from SUNY Press via MacLeish is that the interview book is "shelved," "scratched." If it is, a wonderful, satisfying victory. I feel very little anger inside me for Gerber, but at the same time am not sorry that he is tense and suffering these days, "crushed," as Manny said. If ever a man deserved it. He tried once too often to make us eat shit. Fuck him. Now he is angling to be on Writers Forum committees, etc., but it doesn't matter at all. There's not a thing he can do, I think, at this point. I don't think SUNY Press will be pushed around. Diary, if there are more chapters in this, you'll hear from me again. But I hope it's over. Gerber will strain to put the best face on this, but—how can he? Most people will be glad he's stopped, <u>been</u> stopped. Who knows what he'll do? For all I know he'll find some way to go ahead. But for now, he's stopped.

Very encouraging letter from Random House editor on *The Swastika Poems* as a Vintage paperback. <u>That</u> would be something. I sort of have my fingers crossed.

My Whitman <u>does</u> have the portrait, opposite p. 29. The book is a beauty. It's not the "Death Bed Edition," I think, but close.

Went to afternoon graduation ceremony Sunday. Said goodbye to Richard Ehrlich & parents, Stephanie Coulson & mother, Jill Norberg and parents. We were out in front of Hartwell, where I stood at graduation just twenty years ago.

Evening sun pouring into the cabin, & deep-scented air through screen door, and sound of robins and squawking blackbirds, and my pen just flowing as I begin to relax again. Many books to put away, and letters to answer, and tilling to do and.... But I am home with Han—I love & need her so much—and children, lucky, lucky. Will get back to some reading and writing over the next few days, and have a summer, I hope, that blesses and stays long. Am I really home, and about done with school? Yes.

May 23, 1981

A very emotional day or two for me. Han's 41st birthday today, and we went to the small Memorial Day observance and parade, from downtown to Morgan-Manning House to High Street Cemetery. Kristen in the high school band. This small town, so central, so moving, so many friends around us.... A perfect day today. Will till and rake a little.

Disconnected or connected things. I saw a German shepherd kill a raccoon yesterday over on East Avenue. It disturbed me. I didn't sleep much, if any, last night.... And I've been reading the Cargas/Wiesel book.

I'm in the cabin, birdsong and honeysuckle bloom and millions of spring-green leaves around me. I'm done with school now, and those other problems, and feel in my chest joy and thanks. There will be time, now, for everything. I still have some letters to write.

My mind was so tangled with the Gerber business for so long, that I habitually (though less and less often now) go back to thinking about it. But spring growth is in my brain and covering over the dead matter.... I wrote to Al in Greece to tell him the project seems to be dead. He'll laugh and have a drink to celebrate.

I want to write to Henry Carlisle, Harry Cargas, others. I want to look at the expanded *Swastika*, to have it firmly in mind in case Vintage says yes & takes the book. And I want to get back to *CR*. And I want to garden. And I will do all these things, knowing I have forever now.

May 25, 1981 (Tues.)

Tomorrow, Han and I will drop Kristen off at Rundells, and she'll go with them to Kelly's graduation. Friday, Han & Billy will leave, too, and I'll be here in the cabin for a couple of days by myself.

Rain expected today. Right now, sun, and I have all the screens open back here.

Allen Hoey has called a couple of times. *The Bees* comes right along.

I worked on my new Jesus poem yesterday. It did me good, again, to get back. Wrote a little one called "Carnival," too, after reading a book of Zen wisdom.... Finished the Cargas book, and wrote him, and wrote Snodgrass and others. My desk is just about cleared. Have to do that year-end report.... I just took a deep breath. My chest feels free, relieved.... A pleasure, again, to look out at so much green.... Elm leaves reaching across my picture window.... I have Sarah Appleton's *The Plenitude We Cry For* to read....

5/28/81

I've just tried to write in *The Boulder*, and found that I kept wanting to enter topical, too-personal things in it, the things for here. So, in the future, I will write here first, or move to *The Boulder* when I am ready to write something.

Back and glad to be from Nashville yesterday. Han's folks glum. Now, I am free for days. Dinner with Picciones, then poker at Squeak's, later today. Friday & Saturday I'll be alone when Han & Billy leave. I'll be back here.

Nims took two poems, one good, for *Poetry*.... I'll pick up Hoey's colophon sheets at the post office today.... Will send poems to *Georgia Review*.

Wet and lush back here.

Reading Ray Carver's new book of stories. Dark and brilliant. Must write to him, and to Emily Borenstein.

Finished "Collecting Heyen" yesterday before the trip. I think it's okay.... Yes, this weather reminds me of the visit to Little Gidding. I want to read "Four Quartets" again.

5/29/81

Dinner with Picciones last evening. We're all fine. Tony called this morning to read me a MacLeish letter he just got. The Gerber project is <u>dead</u>.

Played poker last night until 5 this morning and won $220. Also, the boys paid me the $70 they owed me, so I feel rich. Threw Billy 15 & Han 50 & bought the new Hall book, etc.

After finishing the Carver book, hell, I wrote a story about baseball. Han & Billy are gone, too, and it's a Friday evening, and I plan to stay back here until midnight, and would like to write another story.

Have some important letters to write, too: Borenstein, Shrifte, etc.

Well, cabin, here I am for several hours of a May evening. I'll enjoy just watching the darkness fall around me.

5/30/81

Wrote my little poker story last night. I think it turned out okay. I like this thing of having written a couple of stories!

It's odd being alone, not even having the usual "good mornings."... I'll have a full day today: work back here this morning, then some letters while watching baseball this afternoon, then several hours back here this evening again. Looks like rain today.... Wonder if I can do that German shepherd story....

Guess I'll type up the baseball story and see what I have.

Also wrote out "Night Flight from England" last night, & worked on the Jesus poem.

Later: I just typed up "Forestville vs. the Indians," and know again now one of the reasons I stopped writing stories in graduate school. Typing prose is a pain-in-the-ass. The story is only five pages long, but it was still a drag to type.

Yes, looks like rain coming up.

Later: <u>another</u> letter from MacLeish today on the Gerber business. It seems Gerber is trying to sell the MacLeish interview to *Mass. Review* without asking anyone's permission! I almost sent a letter to Gerber et. al. reaffirming our position, but don't want to get caught up in all <u>that</u> again, and will just let Archie take care of it. Still, I'm tempted!

I'm <u>lonely</u> without the family here. What a different existence this is here at home without Han & Billy & Kris around. I walk around the house & look out windows and talk to myself a lot.... I did write to Evelyn Shrifte, Emily Borenstein, Stan Lindberg, & Archie.... I don't think I have the guts this evening to begin the story I'd like to do. Maybe tomorrow morning. Maybe I'll watch Kirk Douglas tonight in that cowboys & Indians flick.

June 1, 1981

 Han & the kids back safely last evening.
 I got so much done yesterday—all the lawns mowed, and even that pain-in-the-ass-of-a-year's end-report. A new month begins, and I'm free.... Thursday afternoon, Peter Dzwonkoski will visit. I'm getting some books packed up for him now....
 I'd like to do a third story before I type up my second one. Bill Ewert will be surprised to hear I've written a couple of stories.
 A whole month off, and then two weeks on the Island, and then a month off. I'm blessed.

6/3/81

 Yesterday, the first copy of *The Bees* arrived. Allen took some chances—it's a "busy" book, as Han said—but I like it and look forward to the hardbound copies. Also, three boxes of *Lord Dragonfly* arrived for numbering and signing. It's a damned handsome book. I just read it over again, & have all my old reservations, but I'm glad these sequences are in print again.... Almost too much fucking around with books the past few days—am also getting boxes ready for Peter Dzwonkoski to pick up tomorrow—but it's a pleasure, usually, & parcel post will pick up *LD* tomorrow, & my study will be clear, & I'll begin, I think, to turn to *CR* again.
 Wish I had just the germ of an "idea" for a fourth story.
 Oates' *Nightless Nights* arrived from Ewert, dedicated to Han and me. The hardback is a <u>beauty</u>, though at $75 I wouldn't have bought it. I also have one of the four proof copies, thanks to Bill.... And the MacLeish *Collected Poems* that Han got me for Christmas came back from Archie with "Memory Green" written out in it. It's all just too much. I'm way past—in the way of books myself, & knowing authors—what I imagined or hoped for for myself.... Maybe I'm not ambitious enough. Instead of screwing around with limited editions, I could be pushing *LD* in various ways, e.g., getting review copies out, making sure copies go to contests, and all that. I just don't have much of an interest, and maybe I think the prizes will come to me, maybe after *CR*, of their own accord.
 Overcast this morning, still, rain predicted. Only a day or two more of school for the kids. We're having a pretty big graduation party on the 21st for Billy—in-laws and teachers and all. I hope we have good weather for it.
 I feel too at ease, happy, fulfilled somehow, to write. Almost every day the mail brings some good news or a treasure for my collection. I feel like a little kid today, and this diary entry reflects it. Why not?—it will be dark soon enough.
 Just read over a couple of months of entries in this journal when Gerbergate was in full swing. It was a <u>miserable</u> time for me, more miserable than I'd even admit to myself here. From here on in, there may be little incidents connected with the whole business, but it's over. I haven't thought about it at all for several days. Thank God I didn't go ahead with a letter & tangle myself up emotionally again regarding the *Mass. Review* business.
 Am reading & enjoying McPhee's *Giving Good Weight*. Want Billy to read it, too.

6/5/81

 June, go slowly!
 Such a busy, and clearing, day yesterday. Dzwonkoski visited, and I sent along boxes of stuff. Now I can dust my study.... In the evening, Ewert called, & we talked a long time. Then, poker until 5:30 in morning—I won $85.... The Rochester storage is a great help.... Also, I donated some stuff (17 volumes, heavy, of *Contemporary Literary Criticism*, e.g.), & we'll get a tax break.
 Finished McPhee's *Giving Good Weight*. Want to read *Coming Into the Country*. Am reading Dick Hugo's detective novel now. Good so far.
 Auction tomorrow morning, & some gardening. Hope to get the riding mower Monday.

6/9/81

I was just writing out the revised contents for an expanded *Swastika*, and got to "A Voice from the Night at Belsen." I remembered the day when Klaus Burmeister asked Han & me if we wanted to go to Bergen-Belsen. I didn't know about, hadn't heard of the place, as I remember now. I was abysmally ignorant. I know that I hadn't heard of the "Horst Wessel Lied" until that evening of drinking in Bad Godesberg. I had written some German background poems, but maybe the situation (half before & half after the 1971-72 year) wasn't as I described it in the *Manassas Review* interview. I'm not sure. In any case, the shock, maybe, of the Holocaust coming to me emotionally all at once, as it were, rather than gradual immersion & time to adjust to the horror, maybe gave me *Swastika* in the end. I came to the central materials when I was thirty or so.

Worked on "Death Fugue" again last evening. My version is as finished as I will finish it.

6/12/81

Played poker until 5:30 this morning. Fought my way back from $180 down and ended up winning $19....

Gerbergate flared for me again an hour ago when I biked to school and learned the bad guy was reporting on status of project & urging, I guess, some sort of action from the Provost, & wanting to talk to Tollers, etc. But I'll not tangle, no matter what. No more of those nights of being afraid. I can do things obliquely to foul up the villain. And, from outer perspectives, all that is over and not a contest any longer between Gerber and me. The burden is on him, and if he does manage to edit a book, I'm sure I won't have to be in it, and I don't/shouldn't care.

Drizzling now, lush back here. This cabin—I just have no words for it.

Dick Hugo called today. Such a warm & friendly man. He said that he'd had cancer, had had one lung removed, was okay now. He sounded strong. I'll send him some books for inscription.

Worked on the essay for Peter Klappert yesterday.

Ontario Review arrived with "Snow Hen" done attractively.

Random House, alas, turned down *Swastika*.... Peter Marchant might follow up my suggestion and have a WF Holocaust Remembrance week....

Though I've written some things, June is slipping away without any very concentrated work back here for me, especially on *CR*. But I know there's no urgency.... Maybe I'll come back here for a few hours later, before the Holmes/Spinks fight on TV.

6/13/81

Holmes, fairly easily.

A shining and cool Saturday morning. I feel on top of things, after the minor Gerbergate spook. I slept fine.

I was thinking of typing up one of my stories just now, but I think I'll turn to *CR*, send a group to *Georgia Review*, and look at *Wenzel*.

Han's feeling better again.... I played tennis in a drizzle yesterday against Han & Kristen.... The three of us go to a band dinner tonight.... A cardinal is whooping it up outside the window at the back of the cabin.

Later: typed up "The Mills," and I like the story, though I know I'm clumsy, mainly because I can't decide who the speaker is, & what his speech is like. Maybe he can't decide what his language is like, now, in the present, as he looks back on himself, and how he wants to talk and tell that story.

Wrote Lindberg, & will send *Ewe's Song*.

Watched a groundhog through my binoculars for a half-hour. It has its burrow under our garden shed. I read about them just now, their general surliness, but at least they don't congregate in societies (just a family in one place). A tunnel, no doubt, 20-30 ft. obliquely. And they're rough on corn in its milkstage—hope our garden 18" fence will stop them! Anyway, neighbor, welcome, but please behave yourself. I remember going outside Springville with Hank Joslin & watching him shoot your distant relatives hundreds of yards away.

6/14/81

Sunday, almost one in the afternoon. Rain last night, hot sun today. I just stood over by the garden with Han. Such a bountiful day. Much to do, but pleasure in it. I'll wash out the garage, clean the shed, vacuum back here. The big gathering coming up next weekend.

Read over *Wenzel* this morning. It's going to be something. Should I read the rest of those journals & even expand "Family Tree"?

I think I'll write to Bill Ewert, and then get on with different things.

Went to band dinner last night with Han & Kris. Kris is a beautiful daughter.

6/15/81

I swing back and forth about whether I'll be able to take a full-year sabbatical year after next, or will have to go with a half-year. Money, money.

Rain again last night. Muggy today. I feel fine, but in one of those moods where I wonder what the hell I'm devoting my life to poetry for. No one is out there. The magazines that come in the mail on occasion with my poems, the books that don't sell and that even when bought sit on shelves like the books in my own study—these things disguise the nature of the effect. The thing is, then, again and again, the meaning to be found in the process, the act. Part of that meaning is in the realization of that which is art, so the "product" is important, but not the reception. I want to make *The Chestnut Rain* a beautiful thing in its own right. And, I am enjoying turning to it and nudging it forward, or following it, especially when it's at the stage where it is now.

6/16/81

Just now, cup of coffee in hand, as I walked back here past the garden, the first bird I saw was a male redstart. I got to within about twenty feet of him as I walked by.

Will spend the morning on *Wenzel*.

Clementes definitely coming July 3.

Hot again today, maybe tending to rain.

I actually played some basketball at the college yesterday. 16 of us!

Kristen all done with school now, too. Han done Thursday. I'm glad.

Watched the CBS special on nuclear arms last night. Frightening.

Later: I had a fine morning back here on *CR*, working my way all the way through up to *Wenzel*, making a slight change here and there. It's a wonderful poem, I must admit. It can't miss, no matter what I do from here on in on the uncompleted parts.

Spent $150 on liquor & beer & mixers & wine for Billy's party.

Dropped off my year-end report to Tollers, with a note saying, in effect, I'd be dropping away if I didn't receive merit again. We'll see.... I hate even going over to the Department.... Am also having some copies of *The Snow Hen* xeroxed from *The Ontario Review*.... Saw Tama Baldwin, a friendly face, and she passed a new poem on to me....

Hot today, but I couldn't feel better, or happier. I even got a haircut today. Short hair makes me feel clean and handsome, and makes me look less bald. Vanity o vanity.... Ewerts can't come July 4th weekend. Letter from Bill today. UNH will buy Martin's correspondence/manuscript Sceptre Press archives. And it sounds as though Martin has sold his house. I'm glad for his whole family....

6/17/81

I was just ready to come back here when I got a long phone-call from Bill Ewert. He wants to do "The Cabin" sequence, which *Georgia Review* and *Poetry* didn't take. I guess so. I love such little things. Still, it's the same story about unnecessary "A" items.

I had a good few hours back here yesterday evening. Am reading *The Artists of Terezin*. Drafted a discursive sort of a poem called "The Census." I swing back & forth, according to my mood, from the concerns of *CR* to the concerns of *Swastika*.

Today, totally free to do as I please. No errands, no nothing. I'm going to stay back here all day.

Later: rode my bike up and played ball. Enjoyed it. I quit, again, before knocking myself out. I'm smart just to play a game or two and call it a day.

Grapevine has it that Gerber has been told by SUNY Press that he can 1/ use other interviews than the Poulin/Piccione/Heyen ones and they will publish his book; 2/ leave out our names altogether, and put all our questions in his own words[!] and they will publish his book. The three of us, apparently, are the bad guys. I feel like wading in and making trouble for SUNY Press, asinine Mandel, but <u>must</u> remember to be cool, to keep the whole thing separate from me, distanced, not to get involved <u>personally</u> here on campus with Gerber & the Provost et. al. I must not forget what a misery it all was. Really, only pride is involved. If G. uses all my interviews, & changes them around—how awful, & unhistorical & unprofessional & garbled & deceptive—but what have I lost? If my name is not in the book, wonderful! I could just butt out, and the three of us could make fools of the editor & book later on. But, I feel the urge to write Mandel, & tell him how unprofessional he is, and to tell him that SUNY Press will be the laughing-stock of the industry if Gerber takes him up on #2.... I wish I had the energy to write a full-length exposé of this whole matter. I'd publish it in *Coda* or *Georgia Review*, or somewhere.... But, I must remember that I am essentially free of Gerber & his few henchmen with vested interests, & must do nothing to entangle myself again & lose my summer & next year & maybe even a sabbatical over what, in terms of my life, amounts to nothing. The only emotion I feel right now is anger.

Emotional energy still goes into this, but none of the fear from previous months. A different dimension now, and I can go on with my life, Billy's party & graduation & maybe even some poems.... Come to think of it, it looks as though, even with new recommendations coming along from the advisory committee, that Gerber will be the one editing books in the future. I sure still wouldn't want to, except to deny him. No, even that is nothing, or shouldn't be, anything, to me. <u>Shouldn't</u>, but my pen keeps moving across the page, of course.... The biggest differences are 1/ I'm not personally involved in a public way with confrontations, etc., and 2/ I'm not in school, and don't have to see Gerber & think of his dirty machinations while I'm trying to teach.

I look forward to poker tomorrow night. It would help to <u>win</u>, what with my big Visa bill now (lawnmower, Kristen's clarinet, etc.).

6/18/81

Okay. That stuff is over with again, and I won't be bothered by it this summer. So much of this is stupid of me: as though it mattered a tinker's damn to any of the people who matter to me, or to my career, whatever the fuck Gerber does with those tapes! The bottom line, I'm afraid, is that I hate him. He stands to me for the Nazi. But life is wide and good. So many friends. So many poems and projects. He's not dangerous. The English Department is not a prison camp. My children & wife are safe!

Ron Luce visited yesterday evening. He's doing fine at Ohio U., after a rocky start. He'll begin Ph.D. work there in the fall.... He made up just 13 copies of a chapbook of poems, and gave me one yesterday.

Today, at last, is Han's last day of school, and it's an easy one. She deserves and <u>needs</u> a rest.

Raphael Rudnik & Neil Baldwin have sent me manuscripts for comment/advice. Why? I don't know RR & know NB so slightly.

Henry had his rupture operation yesterday. I tried twice just a while ago to call the hospital number Mom gave me, but no answer? I'll try later.

I should type up my third story one of these days.... I find myself not wanting to send Ewert the "Cabin" sequence for a separate publication. Even if there's a cheap issue, I hate to see people spend even five bucks for the slight thing. I don't know. He can make some money on it, he says.

I've been caring for Bob Siegel's new book, and am anxious to write him. He's a kindred spirit.

Card from Lynne Studier, who found me another Heaney 1st. She'll be here for Charlie's wedding in the fall with my Heaney books. My collection is becoming priceless.... I look forward to sending hardcover *The*

Bees to MacLeish, Wilbur, Stafford when the books are ready. Won't send any of my copies of *The Trains* to anyone.

Ron Luce is already 32. I was 27 when I finished at Ohio, and exhausted. I'm absolutely rich, with secure job, home, property, books, and this cabin. He's with his wife & kids in a small apartment, as we four were. Well, he'll survive, but the biggest difference is that when he finishes in two years or so he'll have a hell of a time finding a job.

Perfect weather, and I've all day to read my poems, write friends, and then play poker.

Later: I washed out the garage, and mowed the lawns. I feel pleasantly tired.... Earlier, wrote to Bob Siegel. That's a fine book he's made.... Han & Kristen getting some sun on the back lawn.... I'm going to write to Ewert and tell him to forget about "The Cabin." Enough little things for a while.... Odd letters from Bob Phillips & Bob Hauptman today. Some of my correspondents. Gulp!

6/19/81

It's ten in the morning. I'm in a half-sour mood, because I lost about $80 at poker—played tight but had lousy luck—and only got about 2-3 hrs. sleep. But it's a perfect day back here.... I got the bright idea to do my rock-and-roll novel as a <u>story</u>, instead, & have my tapes back here & the tape recorder for background music for if and when I feel I can make a start. Maybe I cherish that plot because it's my get-rich-from-writing fantasy, and once I've written it, even published it, and it comes to nothing, I'll have lost a dream. Anyway, maybe I'll do that, or stay with the expanded *Swastika*. A new poem, "The Census," became more and more interesting.

Daphne Poulin staying with us for a week beginning tomorrow. Han's folks & Kurt will stay over Sunday & Monday. I'm glad to be having the house full. Some good writing sessions back here today, and a good night's sleep, and I'll be a new man & have a great weekend.

It's interesting that when I don't get much sleep, and then lose money (even when I have plenty) I feel fears & nervousnesses the next day, and guilty somehow. It's good to know this about myself. This cabin in the trees, almost hidden, almost a womb, and as close to my best friends as a letter is.... *Swsastika*, or "The Elvis Presley Room"?...

Later: went over "The Census," and worked on notes to be added to *Swastika*. What I'm going to do this summer, maybe even by the time I fly to the Island, is put together the whole expanded book, & xerox a few copies. Then, that will be behind me (the "marketing" to Vanguard or wherever something I can do with a tiny corner of my brain), and I can get on solidly with *CR*, & maybe the silly story mentioned above.

I feel fine. I'm listening to rock & roll music back here, the Flamingos right now. Supper with Han soon. Bert Babcock sent me the $600 he owed me, so I'll pay off the Visa card to this point, & then owe only about two grand more! I'll strain next year to save money to help finance my full-year sabbatical, if it comes through, the following year.

6/20/81

Preparations & excitement. Brother Ed & family will be here by noon tomorrow, as will Han's folks & Pat. Fifty others arriving. Vinnie Lista will be bringing over the food about five in the evening. I'm really looking forward, and sure do hope for some sunshine—that would make everything perfect.

I had a good night's sleep last night, so caught up, after my poker game.

Finished Gardner's *Freddie's Book*. A good one.

Nice letter from the woman at Hofstra. I look forward. Will make plane reservations Monday.

I mowed the paths & edges today. And I played some volleyball with Daphne & Kris, & tennis with Billy. Feel fine.

6/22/81

What a party it was! Weather luck, darkening and cooling at 3:30 yesterday, after rain in the morning, and then sun & warming at 4:00, when the party began. So all 60 of us were outside for drinks & food. Perfect mixture of people. People wandering back here to the cabin. Ed & family, Wolf & family, Han's folks, Johnsons & Beanys & Setters & Piepkes & Malaks & Wickses & Millers & Vallones & Picciones & Bruce Agte & Tony Vallone & Mrs. Raleigh & Mrs. Corbin & Studiers & the Matskos & many of Billy's friends & Kristen's floating around. And I actually slept until ten this morning. Windy today, sun in and out. Graduation tonight. It just felt, feels good, and warm, to be around so many friends. It puts everything in this Brockport place that bothered me into perspective.... Kurt & Daphne & Han's folks still here.... I just heard thunder.... Tony & Bruce have become real collectors. I gave them a bunch of broadsides yesterday.... Billy got many fine presents.... Such a rich life we're leading here. I want it to go on forever.

Evening of the 20th, I was back here in the cabin with Bruce & Tony & Bernie Quetchenbach until 2:30 in the morning drinking brandy & reading poems & then listening to rock & roll.

6/23/81

4:30 in the afternoon. Relaxing, sipping coffee back here.... Just played some tennis with Billy. I win only one or two games in eight or ten from him now....

What a great evening. At graduation, Billy spoke beautifully. He won the $25 Valedictorian Prize, the $50 math prize, the Bauch & Lomb Science medal, and a $500 Lee Award. What a kid. Han & I have never been so proud.

Han's folks & Kurt left this morning. Daphne here until Friday. She was supposed to show up by 4:30 yesterday, & no word from her until 10:30. We called Boo, etc. A pain in the ass. Last time.

My 3 volumes of Traubel arrived. Some good summer reading.

Flight arrangements made for L.I. trip. $118. I'll profit, all in all, by about $800, I guess. Will be gone 2 weeks. Will be able to see the folks.

Will get back into the swing of some writing. Will get the revised *Swastika* together.

Saw John Maier & Stan Rubin uptown today, & had pleasant talks. From here on in, I'm just going to float along in the department. They're okay, & I've many friends. My hang-up is extreme dislike for Gerber—for good reasons, yes, but nevertheless my world is much bigger than all that, and enough was enough.

6/26/81

Friday. Won about $230 last night. Got enough sleep, but look forward to a good sleep again. Daphne gone, at last—what a sneaking pain-in-the-ass! She's at Picciones.... I'm still doing the expanded Ms. of *Swastika*.... Very cool today.... Billy in Rochester watching the LPGA.... Han hoeing!... We'll see Picciones & Leeds one of these days......... Billy just stopped back here, and is off to get burgers & fries for supper, so I'll head inside when I've used this page up.... Ewert publication called *Auction* should be in the mail soon. I look forward to seeing what it's like.... I guess Werner called & had a long talk with Han yesterday.... Saw Gerber at school, that ghost!.... Will do some television watching and reading this evening....

6/30/81

Time going too quickly. It's Tuesday evening. Mirko's party & poker Thursday, Clementes here Friday, I leave Monday.... Pshew.... Xeroxed 4 copies of the expanded *Swastika*. Will drop one off at Vanguard when I visit the city, maybe next week. I hope they'll do the paperback....

Damned woodchuck, apparently, ate our sunflowers & lettuce. Lifted up our wire fence & got in. Glad we're not depending on our crops for our winter's food.

Mail from Poulin in Greece, Norbert in Germany, Richard Ehrlich & Emily Borenstein in Israel, Mike Waters in Yellowstone. Still, I'm glad to be home.

Have an idea for one more story about a tennis game?

Trees dripping after a rain.

Haven't really gotten to work on *CR* this summer. Wanted to finish work on *Swastika*. Must remind myself, as I do every summer, that there's plenty of time. August even drags on.

Might call Ewert tonight to say hello.... Am trying to clear off my desk inside before I leave.

July 5, 1981

We had a couple of great days with the Clementes, and they took off early this morning. Yesterday, the Morgan-Manning House activities, and a walk uptown for ice cream cones, etc. A cook-out. They're *so* easy to get along with. Vince and I had some nice talks. Brian Johnson's party the night before—Annie & Vince loved that, too.... I'll see them again Friday on the Island.... I think I'd rather not be going anywhere, but it will be a good experience, and I'll have plenty of time once back here for writing.... Raining today, perfect here in the cabin.... We picked about five quarts of berries yesterday.... Tony Vallone stopped in last night.... Tony & Vince have seen the paperback *Lord Dragonfly* in bookstores on L.I. and Rochester, but I don't have a copy yet.... Well, diary, see you in a couple of weeks. Be well back here in the cabin.

7/6/81

Well, Ollie, here you are again. It's the same place, this time called Hempstead, on the Island.... I'm in a small dormitory room, seven floors up. Sort of a dreary place. Busy workshop today, but I still feel lonely. Many nice folks around, but I still feel lonely. But I walked over to see a lacrosse game just now, and called my folks to tell them I'll see them on the 17th, and from now on there will be events during the evenings, and Friday Vince will pick me up and I'll spend the weekend with him, so I'm well off. And I can squeeze in a trip to NYC if I want. And. But I feel out of place, as always, Wyoming or England or wherever, and wonder what the fuck I'm up to. Well, money is involved this time, anyway. Might even do a little writing this evening. And I'll get up early for breakfast and do some coffee drinking and scribbling over in the cafeteria.

The flight was quick & uneventful, though I slept little last night. Sat next to Burt Wolin on the plane, of all people. Limousine service to Hofstra for eight bucks.

What courage it would take to stay in this room and study.... Here, I think of my cabin, the evening smells of Brockport. My workshop room # is 142!

My reading here is Wednesday evening. Probably, not many of my workshop people will be able to make it—commuters.... Good folks here, but ...

7/7/81

Again, I'm in better spirits today. Exhaustion almost always leads to depression, the only exception being, maybe, the day after a poker game when I've won a lot of dough. But these trips—it's always the same. I think of some poets who compounded this sleepless bullshit with booze on these trips.... Anyway, the workshop begins in a half-hour, and I'm all set. I even worked on a couple of *CR* sections for a couple of hours this morning.... And I realized that today is my 19th anniversary. Han & I don't worry about such occasions or make a big deal of them, but I'll call her this evening.... Found a very fine little room to work in over here near the workshop activities.... Ate breakfast amid about 200 black/Hispanic "Upward Bound" students this morning.... Lecture on writing for television at 5:00 today. Hell, maybe I'll take it in.... Look forward to staying with Vince & Annie this weekend. Vince & I will visit Nesconset, maybe, and Gibbs Pond and all. Walking the pavement here yesterday on this big pavement, I kept thinking that my Island was underneath it all. This Nassau County—*oi weh*!... I meant to write "campus" for the second pavement above, but my sentence holds true.... Billy & Han & Mackie are painting the house this week. I hope they have good weather and don't fall off ladders....

Later: workshop went very well.... Connected with Bob Sargent about books, and we'll visit a shop or two tomorrow if things work out.... Will eat a good dinner tonight, for a change.... Have a couple of ideas about marketing the expanded *Swastika* in paperback.... Appointments with students tomorrow, etc., so I'd better plan my reading this evening....

Later, evening: I called to tell Han I love her on our 19th. She's connected with Stan Plumly & Bill Meredith, & will see them again.... Also, a long letter from MacLeish to the provost & Gemmett & Tollers & all, one that exposes Gerber & puts him down. That dumb son-of-a-bitch never learns. So, he follows me to Wisconsin & England & Myrtle Beach & Hofstra, but he must be reeling. How he has lost face again!... Painting of house going fast. Kristen's clarinet lessons going well. Oh, I miss home, but the Gerber business would have made me nervous again, so I've gotten more writing done here, and Han & I draw even closer when I'm away, as in the Donne "Valediction: Forbidding Mourning."
Tomorrow will be extremely busy, will go quickly. I think, in fact, I'll think about my reading now....

7/8/81

I'm sort of hanging around, waiting for a session with an agent to begin. I'll be glad, all in all, when my reading is over this evening. Roberta from Vanguard might be here with some books, which ones I don't know!... Tired today already.... Will go book-hunting with Bob Sargent Friday morning. Time passes slowly here. I feel sort of <u>dazed</u>, <u>thinking</u> about poetry so much again, instead of just <u>writing</u> it.

Later: the reading was okay—about 30 people. The thing bothering me again, the business of selling books—only 7 or 8 of the batch that Roberta brought in were sold. Now to be lugged back to NYC, and I feel like an under-achiever. Thoughts of books coming to the campus bookstore, & then shipped back. Fuck it. But mainly I was stupid not to grab a few of the paperbacks & tell Roberta to tell Evelyn I'd taken them. I don't even have one, for christ's sake. Why am I so shy and unassertive sometimes?... <u>Then</u>, a surreal hour with the woman who'd called me in Brockport, Melanie Johnson, a wreck, ready to fall apart, shuffling through her poems & talking & reading a mile a minute. Pshew. I was patient, & told her to be happy with her poems, etc., etc., but there I was, poor sap unwinding from a long day, coming down from a reading, and listening to poor Melanie, or trying to. Manic depressive, lithium, the whole thing, and poor Bill just wanting to be away from commerce/reading worlds, workshop worlds, and back in my cabin in Brockport.... God, tomorrow is Thursday: I've a morning meeting with students, & must call Vince, & Evelyn in NYC.... I'm getting tired of trying to be intelligent and insightful around here.

7/9/81

A decent day. After the workshop, I got a ride to Hempstead & hit a couple of bookstores. Bought 5 copies of Hill's *For the Unfallen* for a buck each, and a couple of Holocaust books, etc.... Time flying.... I just heard two agents that I think I'll try to contact about *Swastika* once I'm back home.... Hitched back from Hempstead in about 100° heat, & a kid gave me a ride.... I'll miss a card game tonight in Brockport, alas. With a <u>little</u> luck last time I'd have won a couple hundred, at least.... Vince coming tomorrow, and I'll be <u>happy</u> to be in Setauket by evening....

7/12/81

A whirlwind few days. Just before my class Friday, Vince phoned in a message & had to cancel our whole weekend. He was sick. I hope he's okay. Sort of fucked me up, but I connected with the folks for a day, & then Wern & Barb. Returned this evening, Sunday, so I don't have to worry about getting back for class tomorrow, & so I can relax. Now, I'll be able to sleep tonight.... The folks are the same, so nervous, restless, crazy. Wern & Barb are the same, easy-going. I swam & ate well, & spent today cruising Dune Road with Werner, who is a good cop.... Remember a drunk in Huntington—golf caddy! Remember 350 motorcyclists on Dune Road....

Debbie & Alan fine.... Now, I'm not sure what I'll do next weekend. Maybe try to arrange to get home sooner. I hate the idea of training back east again. Will sleep on it for a day or so.... Work over breakfast tomorrow.... Spoke with Han, & all's well, though we like being apart less and less. Well, my stay on the Island is at least half over. I don't think it has been less than 90° yet.... So, it's past midnight, and here I am away from home / displaced, again, & I'll wise up more & more....

7/13/81

Just saw Diana, old friend from Cortland. Am killing time now before the workshop. It's Monday. Things winding down. All's well, & the week will pass quickly, and I don't know what I'll do this weekend, but I guess I'll leave the flight, for next Monday, as it is. Now I second-guess myself and say maybe not.... Killed my breakfast by writing letters to two students, alas, instead of being able to work on CR, as I will, maybe tomorrow.... I hate this feeling of marking time until I get home, but that's where my life is....

Later: evening, and I'm scratching here just before the agent (of James Clavell, etc.) talks. 9th floor of library, this time, where I read once a year (?) or so ago. So, now I am here in an audience. I'm more calm this time, for sure.... Time goes quickly here. Tomorrow will be very busy, & Wednesday will be fine, with dinner at Bob's and a long visit to a bookshop, a good one, from the sounds of it.... May have written a little poem, one of my "relations," today. Found a way to end it. Have decided to call Vince Wednesday, & see what's up. If he doesn't come Friday, I'll call my folks to pick me up in Hauppauge. Then, whatever. But I'll stick it all out until my flight a week from today.

Later: I'm about ready for bed again. All's well, but better in Brockport. Maybe I'll find another poem about this Island. I was thinking about something on the "Motorcycle Rally on Dune Road, Quogue, July 1981."... Cops & beach and school kids and 95°....

7/14/81

I'm sitting in the Hofstra cafeteria at 7:30 in the morning. With coffee, I've just been working on "The Trophy" of CR. Next to me, two young blacks are eating and jiving their talk about all their fucked up friends, etc., etc. It occurs to me that I've got to watch out about living a full, contemporary life now, experiencing such things, while I write about deer in the chestnut wood of forever. I am in the middle of a project I want to carry through, but these outward bound blacks ought to get into my poems, too, sooner or later.
Didn't sleep much last night. No good reason. A sense of many dreams, but only a few fragments remembered.... Am reading Wiesel's *Night* now.... Student reading this evening at five. I don't know. I'm just here making the best of it. I keep thinking of the cabin, the rock down in the foliage. I used the word "rock" just now, I see, instead of boulder....
Long talk yesterday with Mrs. Teresa Silber, a lovely woman who talks a mile a minute, but is all soul, dear person.... Have conferences at ten this morning. Will write for a couple hours now, and eat breakfast, if the line of kids disappears.

Later: well, I'm about ready to turn off the light. Another day over with. Tomorrow, in the morning, no appointments—I'll write in the cafeteria.... I still have periods of loneliness—I miss Han & the kids.... Finished Wiesel's *Night*....

7/15/81

Wednesday morning, and all's well. I'm in the cafeteria, after a breakfast of bacon and potatoes and roll, ready to skim CR and see if anything happens. An appointment after class today with a woman who read an awful anti-male poem yesterday, gulp. Her last name is Poe. After that, I'll be off to that bookshop.

Later: another exhausting day. I'm glad I'm back in my room, ready to read a little & sleep.... Out to Sea Cliff with Sargents: Lia's doll business & collection is an eye-opener.... Listened to & met Budd Schulberg, and like him very much—his grace & solidity. Bought his new book, *Making Movies*, & he inscribed it. I'm glad to have it. Will send him a cooupIe of books, I think.... Rich day, but I felt a little carsick coming back from Sea Cliff. Am okay now.... Plans all set for weekend—to Vince's, & folks will pick me up....

7/16/81

So I walked into the University Club a few hours ago and this guy I didn't recognize came up to me and said "I know you, you're Bill Heyen." And he shook my hand and said, "I'm John Gardner." So, it went easily, and we talked a half-hour or so, and he even gave me the name and number of his agent, for my *Swastika* project. And Liz Rosenberg is awfully nice, too, and will probably review *LD*, and wants poems for *Mss*. Etc. A nervous, but rich evening, and I have four more books beautifully inscribed to remember it by.... Tomorrow, will leave this place. I feel as though I've been here six months. Miss Han & the kids, and have so much writing/letters/seeing projects through, to do.... Will read until tired tonight....

7/17/81

So, the day of leaving Hofstra arrives. At last. I don't think I'll leave home for two weeks again, unless with Han.... Gardner makes a place like Binghamton sound awfully good. And he lives in Pennsylvania, in an old farmhouse, on thirty acres. I would be itchy right now, I think—and Gardner suggested I could easily have Dave Smith's job—to move from Brockport, except that it would be heart-breaking for Kristen. No, no chance of moving before she graduates from high school. Until then, I'll just keep writing, and do one or two more good books.... I actually look forward to the workshop today, the last one. Will just listen to people read poems....

7/22/81

Home. Just pasted in the diary-notebook sheets from my trip. Home, back in the cabin, green all around me. It's Wednesday—I got back on Monday, and have been answering mail, signing the sheets for *The Trains*, spending much time with Han, etc. The trip gave me a new sense of myself, of my worth away from this place. I think, again, of leaving in a few years, maybe even to Binghamton, beginning a new life. Brockport going down, away from poetry, in so many ways.... Brought home about 25-50 books I picked up—3 Sarton novels, 3 Wiesel books, a 1st American of *Crow*, etc.... Got letter into the mail to George Borchardt, Gardner's agent, today, with statements on *Swastika*.... Piccione visiting today, Allen Hoey tomorrow. I'll get hardbacks of *The Bees*, & hope to send it and *LD* to MacLeish & Wilbur & Stafford.... Six weeks or so of summer left.... Han & Billy painted the house. Billy broke up with his girlfriend—she's hurt, I'm afraid.... Kristen here last evening with friends from band. She's a live one.... We'll go to Studiers on the St. Lawrence in two weeks for a few days.... *Auction* arrived from Ewert. It's an interesting item.... Last weekend with Vince & Annie, then with my folks. Everything went well.... One poem written at Hofstra: "Released from Dachau, 1939." It seems like a good one, a last addition to *Swastika*.... Once my desk is cleared, I'll devote my time to finishing *Wenzel*. Only need to read the rest of those bulletins, in case a few more lines for "Family Tree" appear. And I might push the writing toward my (I'm afraid to say it) novel ahead, and I must do the essay for Klappert.... The garden is coming along. If there are no more visits from groundhogs, we'll even have sunflowers, which have burst upward again from their cut stems.... I'll mow today. Had no real exercise for two weeks, but walked & played a little tennis with Han, & will mow, & make a bit of a come-back.... Home.

7/23/81

    Thursday. Poker coming up later this evening. I'd like to win. But I'm tired already, after not sleeping much (for no reason) last night. Hope I'm not too knocked out tomorrow.

    Allen & Cid Hoey were here. Dropped off my hardbacks of *The Bees*. A nice item. Buckets of warm spit, these small-press items, but pleasure.... I signed *Auction* for Ewert, & wrote the poem out fifteen times, too. Have a package ready to go to him.

    Billy is fishing, Kristen at a band concert, Han at Vallones' for some sort of jewelry party. Darkening out here in the cabin. I feel lazy, and guess I'm still catching my breath from the Island. I still owe thank-you notes & other letters & stuff.

    Bruce Agte & Tony Vallone were over last evening.

    Reading & enjoying Allan Seager's *A Frieze of Girls*.

    If I'm smart I'll quit around four, the latest, tonight!

7/26/81

    Sunday, cooling, getting ready to rain. Yesterday was a perfect day, and I didn't even step into the cabin, but sat outside, reading Steiner's *Treblinka*.

    Lost $150 at poker—two losses in a row. No cards, and lost with my best hand of the night, a full house in 7-stud, e.g. It will all come back.

    I feel between things. Long talk with Ewert. So, *Blackberry* Light won't be here for signing for a couple months, and *Auction* is signed & in the mail, and *The Trains* is done from this end, and *The Bees* is done with, so I can get on with some writing now, and plan to spend the next ten days or so steadily at it. Yes. <u>Reading</u> slows me down. When I finish Steiner & Untermeyer, I'll finish at last the farm journal readings, & then will finish *Wenzel*. I'm in no hurry, but do feel like forging ahead and finishing CR, in fact. Maybe, in the next stage of my writing life, to do the novel.

    Another element enters our lives. Han & I talk once in a while of leaving this place, when Kristen is out of high school. We always thought we'd always be here, but maybe won't be. Talking to Gardner made me a little itchy, maybe, the idea of 20-30 acres within easy driving distance of a school, e.g., & better students/classes, & away from shits like Tollers & Gerber & Wolfe. But I won't be driven out. That isn't it. But I may be better as a teacher & writer somewhere else. This thought, for about the first time in a dozen years, tinges things a little differently around here. But we'll be here, surely, for at least three years, and who knows if I'll be able to get a job I'd want, anyway, though things look good, what with all the burgeoning creative writing programs around.

    <u>Thick</u> green around me. Leaves pressing against windows & screens.

    I'd like to hear from *Georgia Review* on *ES*. Then I could send it, or *Blackberry Light*, to Liz Rosenberg for *Mss*. Will send Liz & John *The Bees*.

    Billy had a one-day virus of some kind; otherwise, we're all fine. My correspondence is just about caught up & cleared away. I've been home almost a week. Didn't sleep well for a couple of days, & my stomach has been out of sorts, but I still feel strong.

    Later: Bill, you & Han are 40 years old. You have chances to do everything, go anywhere—Sweden, Europe, anywhere—and <u>will</u> go to some of these places, and they will become golden memories. But now, too, it is raining, and back here in the cabin it is peaceful and beautiful. You could be in the Pantheon in Rome now, or in Venice, or seeing—to change the world—Auschwitz or Jerusalem, but this small place in the trees is in its own way as deep. Wherever you are, whatever you do, <u>live</u>, and don't just mark time. <u>See</u>. <u>Now</u>.

    I'm very happy, all of a sudden, again, back here in the cool and rainy air. Han just stopped in and kissed me and told me she & Kris were going shopping. Billy is fine. I'll go inside for lunch soon & some sports on television & some busywork. Now, this place is home again.

7/28/81

A steady rain.... I've been reading Treblinka, as moving a book as I've ever read, and will finish it today. Last summer, too, I seemed to have to work my way through these Holocaust experiences to be able to go on with other work like *CR*....

Long call from Ewert again last night. He'd been at Kinnell's in Sheffield, and got some things inscribed for me, and was lively with details. So, Galway has sold his home in Hawaii and resigned there and is at NYU for 3 years.

Han & I today will sell the gold coins and get one of those short-term 14% certificates. We're trying to get our dough in the best places to see the kids through college through the eighties. Aah, if only we'd sold the gold when it was at $700 or so, instead of the about $410 it is now. But, we did okay for people who know nothing about money.... Even wrapped my jug of saved dimes last night. $300 worth!... Han watches over our money & pays the bills. I'm just trying to feel secure about taking a full-year sabbatical. Have many things I'll want to sell to Ewert/Babcock....

July 31, 1981

It's even too nice a day today to be in the cabin. I'm sitting in the back yard, in shade, with a cup of coffee. I'll write a few postcards and letters, maybe write a little. I'm just glad to be home, not in Greece like Al, or moving like Martin, or. Home.

Tony Vallone & Bruce Agte stopped by last evening. I gave them their copies of the holograph *Auction*.... Han stood overnight at Margie's in Auburn—her Spencer House reunion. I hope she had a great time.

I'm under the big silver maple.... Kristen's Brockport parade tonight, and then Han & I will work the Band Booster's Taco stand, and then I'll play some poker.

Oh, Han & I sold our 10 gold coins at $468 each. We'll pay our two charge bills, and get one of those $2,500 14.5% certificates, and will this way be ahead of the game. We're out of debt, and solid financially, and all set for Billy's first Cornell bill.

August 1, 1981

Won about $170 at poker last night.... Fun heating up the shells and passing them to Han at the Band Boosters' booth at the carnival last night.... Billy going by bus to Hamburg Greiners for a week today. The house will slow down!... Beautiful day today. I'm going to sit for hours in the back yard.... The beautifully-bound Vicky Gold book came yesterday, & some Kinnell gifts from Ewert.... I feel fine....

Aug. 1, 1981

Date above was 7/31....

A nice lazy day today. Sitting & reading & writing a few letters outside. Then Sandi & Tony & Boo came over. Later, Han & Kris will go to a play, and I'll spend some time in the cabin.

Long call from Ewert again last night, about all sorts of things. I guess I'll think about a book of 3-4 stories from him. I hope Han & I will visit him next summer.

This brown ink does not flow easily enough.

Disappointing letter from Gardner's gent. Vanguard should sell the rights to *Swastika*, is the message.

Yes, a nice full evening in the cabin, the first in a long time.

Later: I'm back here, sipping coffee, waiting for the impulse to get to my desk & survey the Holocaust books I've recently read & take the notes & begin the poems, maybe, that I've wanted to. Want to get that behind me for another summer. Will type a letter to the other agent tomorrow, & give that a shot. If they say no, I'll just about be out of luck, and will try Bantam & Avon myself, I guess, and then see about Evelyn at Vanguard.

It's getting dark. I haven't been back here for nightfall for a long time.

Won $170 at poker the other night—glad to be on the winning track. I see I mentioned this before. I'm just spinning my wheels. Diary, it's time for me to work for an hour or two.

August 3, 1981

It's late afternoon. This morning, I got that letter to the Goodmans in the mail (agents), and finished rewriting "The Word," and ate lunch with Han. Then we played tennis, and I mowed the lawns. Here I am, back in the cabin, after a shower. It's been a good day. It's quiet and relaxed around here with Billy in Hamburg.

Check for $335 from Bill Fergusson today. Will wait for the $250 from Vanguard, and will then start a new checking account (one that gives interest) and try to build up my money for my year off, etc.

Air controllers' strike nationwide—I can't believe I'm not stuck in an airport somewhere.

Since I've been back from the Island, I've had a great summer. Han & I have never been closer. This next week will be fine, too, including our trip up to 1000 Islands.

August 4, 1981

Four in the afternoon. I'm back here to read a little of Traubel's Whitman again, & then go in to supper.... All's well, life in a delicious slumber.

Worked back here this morning. Wrote a piece called "A New Bible," a *Swastika* piece. I'm almost at the bottom of all that for the summer. Just have to review *Treblinka*.

Rain again today.... I'm sending *City Parables* to Steve Claeson in Sweden.... Must write Emily Borenstein this evening.... Kristen having a half-dozen friends over for a party.

I was thinking of the soap operas and real opera, which is soap opera set to music and dance. I love the afternoon soaps, though I see only an hour or two a week. Today, a grand dress ball in London....

August 5, 1981

A rainy day, today, after thunderstorms last night. I don't remember this much rain over a summer before. The tomatoes have a long way to go before ripening.

I'll work back here this morning, going over *Treblinka*, watch soaps/write letters this afternoon, go to an auction this evening. Old books advertised. It would be nice if there were some good ones.

The Trains arrived (2 copies in wraps), yesterday. A beautifully made book, and I feel lucky, though I wish I'd had a couple of other things done when I sent the group to Fergusson. But, it's strong, I think. I found an error, "graves" for grave, but the error deepens the poem, enables me to get in the idea that has always haunted me, that when one girl by the name of Sarah died, she died for all Sarahs, and all Sarahs down the line live for her/died with her/must live for her. I'll keep the plural.

Aug. 9, 1981

Back from 1000 Islands. Kristen to return with Studiers today, and Billy back by bus from Buffalo.... Had a good time on the trip. Even visited Duryea's island.... Read H.P. Kraus' *A Rare Book Saga*, but couldn't find any good books on my own, though we went to a huge antiques show and stopped at a dozen garage sales. Did buy a dozen rolls of interesting paper that I'll probably be using for years.... Today, I want to get the *Swastika* manuscript ready for Elise Goodman, agent, who said she wanted to read it, and for Evelyn.... August, but we had rain again, & everything is lush green.... I should have a couple of great weeks now.

Aug. 10, 1981

I think, for now, I finally have *Swastika* behind me. Expanded Mss. are off to Evelyn at Vanguard & to Elise Goodman. Now, I'll just wait & see what, if anything, happens. I'm done (except for some rearranging & retyping should a paperback or hardback deal come up). Fifty pieces in all in the book, now.

Much rain again. I wanted to sit in the back yard all day, & do that crash reading for *CR*, and maybe will be able to this afternoon. I think I am at last done with all letters & packages & small-press stuff, etc., etc., and will use the next few weeks to deepen with *CR*, & maybe my stories, and maybe even pick up the novel again.

Billy & Kris home safely. We all had a picnic with the Studiers for supper yesterday.

Aug 11th, 1981

I'm off with Han & Kris & Julie to work at the Hamlin carnival in an hour—my mind just flashed back to our visit to Hemeln with Werner Merten.... Had a fine day today. Read & took notes on about a dozen of those farm journals, and read more Traubel—about done with volume 1—and mowed the lawns with Billy, and Terry Joseph came to visit. It was a good day for sitting outside. Tomorrow, too, I hope. The journal reading is worth it, a promising idea for a line showing up here & there. When that's done, I'll finish *Wenzel*.

August 12, 1981

A bit restless today, but a poker game tonight, and I hope the game lasts until sunrise.

Some good mail. Duane Schneider will send me some money, etc. But I feel a bit low, for no reason, but a letter from Liz Rosenberg which makes me suspect I was hearing things regarding a job at Binghamton, and a letter from Tess Gallagher calling me Jim. What an off-the-wall chick she is. Makes me wonder if she can pay proper attention at all to what her poems are doing. Miss *faux pas* all the way from her introduction of me at Syracuse to her inscriptions in my books to this. Anyway, as a poet I seem to myself today not to matter. But who <u>does</u> matter? I'm not becoming known, I think, along the channels that Plumly & Matthews & Hass & McPherson are. But I'll go my own ways. Will see about the expanded *Swastika*, & will finish *CR*, and <u>that</u> book I'll push.

Thunder-rumblings & drizzle again.

Stopped at Poulins to check the place. All seems well. Al is no doubt straining to go on permanent disability around here. I'll envy him & be glad for him at the same time. No one knows when he'll be back from Greece.

Good reading progress again today on those journals which yield a line or thought here & there.

8/16/81

I have a sort of sore or strained throat, but otherwise feel fine. Cool again today, but maybe warm enough to sit in the back yard & read Walt later.

I've finished the reading for *Wenzel*, and will wade in and polish up and finish "Family Tree" one of these days.

I came back here at ten last evening and vacuumed and cleaned up. I'm ready for some writing, whenever.

Visited Mazzaro day before yesterday with Tony Vallone and Bruce Agte. Spent some time with John Logan, too.... Boo up in the air about Al's plans.... Billy off to college in about ten days.... Big auction with old books Saturday....

8/19/81

I was walking back here to write in this journal when a cat disappeared into the bushes ahead of me. It had what looked to be a baby cardinal in its mouth. Just the other day Han called me to the window to see a baby cardinal. I hate cats, I admit. I have my BB gun back here and will send a BB into a cat's ass when I get a chance.

Beautiful day. I'm bothered by a sore throat, but I think it's only from sinus drip.... Played tennis with Billy, and read outside. Bill Ewert called about many things. Maybe he'll visit this fall and we'll go to see Logan. I knew he'd be excited about the proof copy of *Noise* I got from Jerry.

I'm still reading and enjoying Traubel's *With Walt Whitman in Camden*. Glad I bought those volumes. I keep having things confirmed for me.

One more week and Billy will be off to Cornell.

Tomorrow night, poker. Friday morning, I'll drive to near Geneva for an auction. Saturday, a big auction in Brockport. Maybe at one of those places I'll come up with some old books.

Want to write Logan, Mazzaro, Matthews this evening. A couple of other things on my desk inside.... Another card from Poulin in Greece. Wonder what he's up to regarding the fall.

No word yet on the copy of *Swastika* I sent to the agent in NYC. Maybe some day out of the blue there will be some good news. Realistically, probably not.

So much goes on in me as I walk with Traubel into Whitman's room ninety-some years ago. Walt is human, and divine.

So nice back here. I'm not in a work rhythm, but no doubt will be, as always, when school comes closer, threatens.

It's pleasant just following this pen across the page, down into the whiteness.

I still think occasionally about Gerber, about whether or not I should xerox the things I have for the Dept., or whether I should now let it all drop. Probably, the latter. I'll be quiet, and scarce as I can be. I'll also, as APT member, see what's going on.... That's all still far away.

Blessed be August.

8/23/81

I've been in sort of a state of semi-exhaustion since the card game Thursday (won $190) until 4:30 a.m., then getting up before 8 Friday to drive to the auction near Keuka Lake, then getting up early yesterday again for another auction, and playing tennis & going to the pro slow-pitch double-header yesterday with the Setters & Billy. But, today is Sunday and I'm catching my breath. Alas. the auctions had no good books. Han & I bought an old oak bucket at the one yesterday, though.

The agent in NYC wants to work with *Swastika*. I'll ready a second manuscript today, I guess. Maybe something will happen.

We drive Billy to Cornell Wednesday.

I have a slight cold that's been hanging on.

Reneé Gorin sent all sorts of flyers & things. I'd like to hear her do *Swastika*.

I feel lazy the last couple of weeks. I did work on *CR* the other day, inserting lines into "Family Tree," so *Wenzel* is just about done except for the typing.

Folks just called. Pshew. They're sending me some buffalo nickels or something. Mom talked herself into breathlessness. They're fairly healthy. Werner may visit us in September. Henry is flying to Florida for a week or two. No word on Eddie.... The folks have received *Paumanok Rising*, though I haven't, and like it.

8/24/81

Received Bob Phillips' *Running on Empty*. Some things in it not so bad, but, in general, it's flabby, and so many pieces go nowhere, are undigested, tell a story and do not manage to get the material into concentrated form. I don't know. It's sad. And Bob will never get the message. I'll write him and say I'm enjoying the book—something like that. Don't want to hurt him. But it's a dreary book, dreary beyond any expectation or wanting of the Heyen style, dreary to Donne or Wordsworth or Karl Shapiro—it's prose, and only mediocre prose.

I'm still lazy. Did get the letter to the agent into the mail. I could be on the verge of a big step, signing with an agency. I hope it proves to be a good thing.

Will do some typing of <u>Wenzel</u> today.

Long letter from Poulin today. He'll be home soon, I guess. We saw Boo yesterday, heard of her Chautauqua week. She's in limbo.

Begun Traubel volume 3—some sameness setting in.

8/25/81

Tomorrow, Cornell. I've been sad, choked up off and on all evening. Well, it has to be, I guess. If I were a farmer, as in the old days, I wouldn't have to lose my son already. Well, we'll look forward to vacations. Oh for a family business, to be close always, like auctioneer Harrris Wilcox & his son.

Watching *The Lion in Winter*, a wonderful movie.

Letter from Ewert today—news of tramping Kinnell's farm. And a list of things I can sell to Babcock. I have a package ready to send off to make about a thousand bucks.

I'll just make believe Billy is at Kurt's for a week or two.

8/26/81

Very hard day for me. The trip to Cornell went well, and Billy's room is fine, and we got him a carpet and small refrigerator, and he has everything he needs. I started crying when we said goodbye, and have been crying or choked up since. A whole new stage in my life, my relationship with Billy. I love him so much, remember him in Athens & Cortland & Athens again, remember playing so much ball with him, admiring him for so long for so many reasons. I'll get used to his being away, and look forward to the times he'll be with us. Right now, it hurts. Han & Kris were weepy, too. I'm taking it hardest, gulp, but will be all right. Hell, he's only a few hours away, and at a major university, and has everything to look forward to. What if we were sending a son to war?... I just always want to be close to Billy, and think, alas, that we've no father-son business, and think of how he'll be away, away, maybe working in a far city. American life. Near or far, love, love.

8/27/81

Stan Lindberg from *Georgia Review*, trying to get Heritage Printers, just called by mistake. We had a nice talk. He has to reject *The Ewe's Song*, for length & for section 17. I don't care, and will send the group somewhere else, maybe to Liz & John Gardner.

I have frequent moments of sadness, but feel better than I did yesterday. I look forward to talking to Billy. I think I'll try to call this evening before I go to play poker. We need his P.O. box #.... I hope he connects with the golf coach.... What the hell, Billy will be home 2-3 times before Christmas, and then for a month at Christmas, and then all summer.

Poulin supposed to maybe show up today.

I don't feel very ambitious today.

8/28/80

Just wrote Billy my first letter to him at college.

Won $50 at poker. I was <u>way</u> ahead, but couldn't hold on.

Fred Poulin home. He looks awful, moves like a 90-yr-old man. Coughed wildly, drinking, smoking, nervous about what his position is. How long can he survive?

Can't/don't want to get down to work—typing the story, application for Imgram-Merrill, etc. Maybe I'm waiting for school pressure. Fuck it. I like floating. Auction tomorrow morning.

8/30/81

 Long talk with Billy, and I've written him again & sent along a few bucks. Miss that kid.
 Long talk with Bill Ewert yesterday. *Blackberry Light* is in proof and on the way already. And he & Bert need more Heyen items, so I'll be raising quite a bit of dough, all in all. The main thing is for me to keep winning at poker.
 Poulin stopped in yesterday. Han said he was shaky. She gave him a couple of scotches, & then I got back from tennis, and we had a nice talk. His meeting with Tollers is tomorrow.
 Have to <u>force</u> myself to clear my desk this morning.

8/31/81

 So, the last day of August is here. I spent the morning going through a pile of school things, throwing most away. I see that my first meetings are Wednesday & Thursday (today is Monday). I see that I missed already this morning the new president's first presentation. I'm sort of pleased by this. I only want to be dimly aware of such things, so that when I miss them, I'll do so easily and naturally.
 Clearing away other things on my desk. Dropped notes to Theresa Silber, Lew Turco, Meredith, Hanson, etc. Did Krapf & Ellen Wood recommendations yesterday. Wrote blurb for David Axelrod. So it goes. I'm beginning to feel clear.... Mainly, if I can get the end of "Family Tree" right, I'll xerox *Wenzel* and send it to Bill.

9/1/81

 Paumanok Rising arrived. It cries for better production, but has a full spirit. Vince keeps making something out of me. His essays convince me that I'm important.
 I take care of a little thing here and there, but don't have the guts or energy to get down to real work.... Proof of *Blackberry Light* was to arrive yesterday or today, but hasn't.... I'm in a kind of limbo before school begins. Will have a few drinks with Rod & Greg tonight....

9/6/81

 Rain again, still. I don't remember weather like this. There's a toadstool six inches high under the silver maple in the back yard.
 I've signed the Goodman Assoc. contract for *Swastika*. Ellen is already knocking on the door at Avon. Maybe I'll get lucky. I'll only get about 50% of any royalties, but I just couldn't market the book myself. Maybe nothing will happen.
 We're off to Pylyshenkos for dinner. My stomach has been bothering me for a couple of days. I'll not eat much.
 Dept. meetings the other day relatively painless, sometimes comic. I'll see, I'll see.... I'm trying to get several other big things done (application for sabbatical—I've drafted the letter—Ingram-Merrill, etc.) before wading into school work.
 Kristen is off on a date to the state fair in Syracuse. We've been trying to call Billy, but he's not in.
 Talk with Al yesterday. Good Dr. report. He'll teach.
 Reneé Gorin to appear here in the spring. I'll read with her. Should be quite an evening.
 Babcock visited Ewert yesterday. I'll get a check for a cool grand this week for the books I sent. It will go into our high-interest account. Good news, good news. Makes me feel secure. Might have to use it during my year off.

9/7/81

Fred stopped over yesterday & gave me a bunch of books he didn't want, mostly small-press, and today I'll go over to his house for more. And he says he has more in his office. I'll take them.

Good fun & dinner at Mirko & Irma's yesterday. George Simmons was there. Turns out he was at Cortland when we were.

Called Billy yesterday. He's doing fine, was puffing from a game of hall-soccer!

I've been watching Jerry Lewis's telethon, which alternately moves me and repels me, but makes me wonder as always what I'm doing for the world. Can't have much faith that my poetry will ever matter. I'll give what I can to my students this semester....

Labor Day. I'll do some typing later but mainly celebrate the day by being lazy.

I'm killing a page of good paper again.

Miss Billy. Guess I can't keep thinking that when I'm doing nothing I'm at least raising a son. He is risen.

Next day.

I think my dates have been off.

Busy, busy day. I'll go to an auction in a half-hour, & then home to some typing of book lists for U. of R.... Then to finish sabbatical application.... Tony Piccione here this morning. I sometimes strain to keep his spirits up.... I did much xeroxing this morning, including the secret documents about which I will some day laugh.... I'm supposed to help at registration tomorrow.... Sent Bill Ewert *Wenzel*.... Rained like hell again today.... Still not sleeping much. Don't know how to shut out the light. For one thing, though, I need more exercise.

9/10/81

Registration generally painless, and I learned a few things.... Note from Mancuso about beginning basketball tomorrow. I've missed that old gang and want to have fun playing ball again.... Poker tonight.... Billy called last night, is doing fine, mentioned "cleaning up in German" and talking quite a bit in his English class. Bless that boy.... I've finished the sabbatical application and have begun the Imgram-Merrill application.... Going to a band boosters' spaghetti dinner with Han & Kris in about an hour.... Wrote to Vince & Reneé Gorin & (at last) Stafford & sent him some books....

Poulin just called to say that Tollers, the walking *faux pas*, just called him to warn that if he was up late doing his own work on BOA, etc., Tollers wd. put him back on governance, etc. Tollers, the fascist rightist Christian steamroller, is so stupid and tasteless. I must quote here his 20 July 1981 memo to the English Department: "Bill Ruff wrote Mark Anderson that Joe Jenks died June 24th—enraged over a problem of a neighbor and his lawn care. Please let me know what you think would be an appropriate memorial that could be given to Shirley." I swear. We will not even be able to die in peace in this Department. But I will outlast this chairman, and the next, and the next, and....

Finally mowed the lawn this morning. It was thick and wet.

I haven't gotten to the cabin for a long while, and won't for another week or two, until syllabi and applications etc. are behind me....

I hope to get some low, low cards tonight for a change....

9/11/81

Won $293 at the poker game. Finally broke through to some good cards. I left at 3:30 in the morning, so I could play a little basketball today. There were still players—Scoppa, Bronk, this guy Simon & Squeak—and I think, playing tight, I could have won more. I hope I don't have slight guilt feelings winning so much! Mirko also won again. He and I have each won 6-7 times running. This is no accident.

Later: just played ball, felt okay, biked back. Beautiful day. Picked up a mailboxful of memos & junk at the school, but I'm undaunted.

Irma is stopping over to have me inscribe a book for Henry Ford, the Henry Ford, with whom her sister is having dinner soon.

A box of *The City Parables* arrived, and I'll have fun wrapping them. Schneider turned out to be okay.

I wrote to Billy.

I could go with Al to Buffalo, but won't. John Logan is having a party for Jerry's new book. No, I don't want to. Yankees-Red Sox on television tonight, and I'll get some work done while watching.... Kristen has her first tennis match today, at Spencerport. I'll wait to see her play at Brockport Monday.

I feel rich & lucky today, O America.

9/13/81

Sunday, Wern & Barb to arrive here maybe about dinner time. The sun is out. I'll cook some steaks outside.

Finished the Ingram Merrill application yesterday. Doing schoolwork today.

Bill Ewert called yesterday about the 1981 Christmas card, which will be *The Wool*. Fine with me.

APT meeting tomorrow morning, alas. Undaunted.

Mirko stopped in yesterday. Good talk.

9/14/81

APT meeting—same shit: Mouganis & Rubin didn't show, and we couldn't do anything.

Wern & Barb here safely, and we're having fun.

I got much schoolwork done yesterday morning, but will still feel rushed tomorrow, but will be all right.

Talked to Billy last evening. He was in the middle of a bridge game. He's all caught up on his work, and doing fine.

Might play ball today. Might drive to Rochester with Wern & drop my books off.

Rain again last night. Local crops a disaster. Snails having much fun with tomatoes in garden.

9/17/81

Thursday, late afternoon, and I'm done with classes until Tuesday. Poker tonight. Sleep. Basketball. Auctions.

Spent 1½ hrs. in dentist's chair yesterday.

Feel fine. Classes off and running. With delivery of letter to Dept., Gerbergate is over for me. Many wounds & lessons, & some abiding anger because of the ongoing secrecy, but I'm now pretty much, almost completely clear of the whole thing.

Kristen played well but lost a 2½ hr. tennis match yesterday. She's been exhausted lately.... Called Billy last night, and he's fine.

Leonard won the big fight with Hearns last night.

So good to be home. Cold & rainy weather. I hope to keep my win streak going tonight.

9/20/81

I'm back in the cabin for an hour or two for the first time in a long time. I've turned on the little electric heater to take the chill out of the place. Sun shining outside at last. Grass high, but too wet to mow. It's been a good weekend. Yesterday, Saturday, I drove to 4 auctions, found no books, but then stopped at the Morgan-Manning annual Peddler's Market and found Richard Drdek selling fine modern firsts. I bought $110 worth, at half-price, of good things that I'll sell to Babcock for about $250 (and have a couple books left over), and found in his "junk" pile a copy of *Forms of Fiction* for a buck. Amazing. And I hope to connect with him on other books. He kept everything in almost mint condition.... Also, thanks to Nora Studier, I'll be able to see the books that the Seymour Library will sell Saturday (when I can't make it) on Friday night! So, here and there I keep connecting, and building my own collection, and even making money.... I made a mistake, though, & paid $25 for what I thought was a perfect first of Fitzgerald's *The Crack-Up*, and read later that the first has some reddish-brown on the title page. But I bought beauties of Lawrence's *Mornings in Mexico*, Capote's *The Grass Harp*, Jones' *From Here to Eternity*, etc.

Won $150 at that last poker game. Have a long win streak going.

Will have an extremely busy week, ending with our visit to Billy Saturday. Classes & June Jordan & Morgan-Manning reception & poker & auction at Willow Creek Auction Barn, etc.... Will do some schoolwork & correspondence today.... Kristen's friend Dave will be over all day....

Life is so rich & full that my writing has come second, but when the cold really comes on I'll be back here with *CR* & the stories and.

Phil Levine in Buffalo today, but I don't have the energy (or desire, I guess) to connect with him.

Saw Poulin yesterday. He told Tollers he wouldn't teach before 11:30, & he won't! Wait until Tony hears that!... BOA slowing down for a while.

I saw Rubin, Hale, Anderson, and then Gerber at the Morgan-Manning House yesterday, the latter getting to the books too late. Yesterday, I think, took the spookiness out of our meetings once & for all. I know it shakes him to see me or Al or Tony, & he sees us at least 3 times more than we see him. That stuff is over for me, no matter what his book looks like when it appears, as I guess it will.

I'm surprised at the good shape I'm in. I've been running & jumping at a good clip during basketball sessions.

Han is fine lately & has put up dozens of jars of pears & peaches, & will get to our grapes soon.

The little heater feels good. I'll read a day or two of Traubel, and maybe read a poem or two.... The colophon sheets of *Blackberry Light* should arrive for signing any day now.

9/21/81

Monday morning, eleven. In a half-hour I'll bike up to play ball.

Wrote notes inside to Dzwonkoski, Mazzaro, Vicky Gold. Reading Traubel back here, the third volume, still.

Peter Marchant called to invite us to dinner with June Jordan, the kind of occasion I hate. I'll be checking out the Willow Creek auction, instead. Then will get to the reading, and to poker.

I just have no real desire to get to any writing. I don't know why. And I have poems & stories to send out, and don't feel like doing that, either. Will not push it. That will all come when it comes. My interest in finding/collecting/selling/saving good books is undiminished. I could spend my life doing it. Maybe I'll do it in retirement.... At the same time, I won't be happy unless I wrote all that should be written. Maybe, some day, a selection from my journals.... Yes, the way I feel now I'll be able to sit back here and write my novel next year. This size journal seems comfortable, and maybe I'll use one like it for the first draft.

All's well, no matter how lazy I am.... We spoke to Billy last evening, & he sounded a bit low, but okay.

9/25/81

Such a long and nerve-wracking day yesterday. First, classes, which went well. Then, I went with Han to the English Dept. gathering at the Morgan-Manning House (met the new President, watched Professor Graver operate, etc.)—a scene that makes me extremely nervous, and one I might avoid other years. Spoke with Gemmett, etc. All in all, prissy & uninteresting people. Then, I went to an auction for an hour or so—didn't find anything, but did not go to dinner with Marchants & June Jordan. That's not where I belong, either. Then went to the Jordan reading, or half of it. She was, generally, a light of a person, but not a very interesting writer. Then, at last, the poker game, where I relaxed again with real men. I lost the $150 I'd won the week before. But I played until 7:30 in the morning, and had four or five bottles of beer, and now feel fine.

I still feel too emotionally involved with the English Dept., and all that. How to cleanse myself of all that? It will come of itself during my 40s, I trust.... This year, I'll wait for the sabbatical to come through, and next year I'll reach inside myself for some discipline, and write, and write, and that may help free me.

Didn't play ball today, but I'm in good shape. Joe & Bill & Dick & John & I, etc., will probably play in an over-30 league on Thursday nights, too.

Letter from Ray Smith today, who accepted "The Ewe's Song," 8-18 for *Ontario Review*. I'm glad.... He also wrote a letter for me to Ingram-Merrill, as did Wilbur, who dropped me a card yesterday. Maybe I've got a shot at the $8,000 I applied for. That would take all the money pressure off for the sabbatical year.

Heard from Klappert.... Did the horse-chestnut exercise in class yesterday, & hope for a good poem for my essay for Klappert. Absolutely nothing interesting came of the poems done by Martin's class in England.

Sat with Poulin at Jordan reading. He left earlier than I did.... I shouldn't be much concerned with worrying about being there for Peter over the next Forum years.... So, the theme, all in all, of this journal, is the same. I'm trying to mature into a man, a centered man who is balanced & self-possessed.

Tomorrow, our day with Billy at Cornell.

Tonight, I'll look over the books at the Seymour Library.

9/27/81

Sunday. Li-Young & Donna & Bruce Agte & Gary Eddy were here this afternoon. Good talk.... This morning I wrote notes to Tollers, Gemmett, Marchant, Parshall, Ferguson about things bothering me. I don't want to stew over such things, but will try to write clear notes, and thus unburden myself. This DTP business in our department has been another of Professor Graver's bailiwicks, a secret one, and it's time some changes were made....

Wonderful, full, emotional day with Billy yesterday. Han loves Billy in the same way I do, of course, but I seem to be hit harder by the whole idea of leaving him at Cornell. Julie went with us. We ate lunch together—then the 3 of them went to a football game while I hunted books. I caught up with them. We had dinner, & talked, & met some of Billy's friends, & went to Freshman Follies for a short time, & walked the campus. We left about 10, got home 12:30, and I slept solid for about 7 hours. God, I love that boy. He's doing fine, & will be home for several days in 2-3 weeks. He's so calm & together. Han and I have such warm feelings in being able to afford Cornell for him.

Kristen has a tennis challenge match tomorrow, and some things about it are unfair. We're weathering the minor middle-class American storms around here. We're lucky to be alive.

Bruce got my Jordan books inscribed. Her reading was so blah the other night that I don't have the guts to read them now.

Much schoolwork to do tonight (if I have the guts) and tomorrow.... Maybe I'll call Bill Ewert & say hello.

9/28/81

I looked over *CR* for a couple hrs. this morning, then biked up to the gym against a heavy wind & played 4 hard games, then biked home & ate & mowed our lawn & the Vallones'. Soon, supper, and then some schoolwork. A busy day. I feel fine.

Letters from Stewe Claeson & Jon Hansen today, & both want to visit next month. Okay.

I've got to go out & pick the grapes....

I did, a big boxful—purple, grapefume, hard tendrils holding the bunches, autumn leaves & blowing sun, & backache....

Want to remember to call Kurt tonight.

Called Bill Ewert last night. All's well.

9/30/81

Busy, good day. A couple hrs. in the cabin, then a bike ride up to school (saw Pete Moser & his big rig along the way), some good basketball, a non-APT meeting again because 2 were absent, and home. The *BL* colophon sheets arrived, and are signed and ready to go. I used this color green to complement the binding.... Some homework this evening, and I'll call Billy, & tomorrow is my favorite day of the week—school done for five days, & poker night.

Record cold last night for this date.

Note from Ferguson saying all I wanted in the Special Writers Forum report wd. be there, and then I saw Parshall, who said the same thing. I want an editor's duty (that voracious Graver, probably) spelled out: he/she must receive permission from all participants. I _hope_ this is indeed in the recommendation. I'll see. Right now I feel assured, and I hope it's not a false alarm.... I feel okay lately about all that stuff....

10/2/81 (Fri.)

I broke out even to the dollar at poker last night.

Didn't play ball today. Han & Kris home from school because of bus vandalism overnight.... Boys coming over this evening to see Kris & friend Stacey....

I've written about a dozen cards/letters this afternoon. Many more to do.

Rain again all day.

I'll shop with Han this evening, & we'll go to the diner.

Billy coming home the 15th already.... October will be a whirl, with many visits.... Peter Dzwonkoski will pick up my boxes on the 28th....

Want to try to look at the Klappert essay again this weekend. Want to stay busy & clear everything away by Tuesday....

10/3/81

Cold & rainy again. I spent a couple hrs. in the cabin this morning, and am inside this afternoon. Will do some schoolwork and clearing away. Maybe spend a couple of hours in the cabin this evening again. I'm starting to turn on its heat from here in the house again.

Won't we have a few shining days yet? Maybe tomorrow.

Kirk Gibson up for Tigers right now. A coming superstar, they say. He just grounded out, but is _fast_.

Not much else new. Hard for me to motivate myself to do _anything_.

10/4/81

Sunday afternoon. Spent 2-3 hrs. in cabin this morning. Sent a batch of swastika poems to *Iowa Review*, and *Blackberry Light* to *Georgia Review*. Will do schoolwork & stuff the rest of the day so that I can get back to the cabin again in the morning before I go to play ball.

Overcast, again, after an hour or two of sun.

Dreamed last night that I was at Cornell. "Lean against the sun," another student's father told me.

I've gone shopping with Han to Wegman's two Friday nights in a row. Filled with all sorts of feelings, images. Can't get over it....

Well, Billy will be home in about ten days.... Then, for Thanksgiving, Pat & Wolf will probably have a big dinner with the folks from Nashville there & all. I look forward already.

Dept. meeting this coming week, w. constitution & WF reports & all. I hope to stay calm, & hope all will be well with the latter.

Still have to get around to typing my story "The Word."

This journal is of notations that will recall images in 20-30 years when maybe I'll get around to some personal writing.

10/5/81

I'm in the Blue Room of Edwards, waiting for a lecture by Samuel Noah Kramer, Sumerian scholar, to begin. This is the first time this journal has left home. I'm in the back, alone. Some English Department members are up front. A surprisingly large crowd here. I wanted to keep rambling along in my journal, while half listening. I must guard this journal with my life. Should I leave it behind by mistake—well, there are no accidents, as Freud says.

Writers Forum report came out today, and it was almost perfect. I've written to the committee to propose an amendment—this has kept me nervous all afternoon. I'm okay. It just might be that all this political stuff will be over soon, though there will probably be so much discussion of the WF thing that passage will be held over for another meeting.... Gulp, I see that bastard the Provost off to my left.... And now John Maier is about to introduce.

Had a couple of good hours in the cabin this morning, and typed up a few more poems that seem finished.

Bill Andrews just sat down, a seat away. All in all, he's a good guy, and I like him.

Played ball today, lousy at first and then fine, shooting beautifully and even passing off like an old all-star. I might fool around here—this Kramer is a fine lecturer.

Before the Bible, before Homer,
tablets in the tablet houses
in the Sumer piled up.
What to do with all these stories,
the boy working in the tablet house wonders.
So much knowledge, so much clay weight.
Spare him! The sky burns blue,
and his young beloved's cheeks blush
in a memory only an hour old....

If I keep this up I'll kill a whole page. I'll just listen. I don't have the desire I had when I was a kid to write poems while listening to lectures....

He has been speaking for an hour, and just asked for another half-hour, and has begun to wipe out his audience. Many have left/are leaving. The dark truth is that, lecture or poetry reading, one should go for 45-50 minutes, get a hand, allow people to leave feeling good about themselves as though they fulfilled a cultural duty for themselves.

I'm afraid that there is no intellectual depth to Kramer's lecture. He has been saying that ancient Sumer had all the problems & conflicts we have. He could have done something much more intense with his material, tell us how these poems work, their sounds, rhythms, etc.... I haven't said it right, but I know what I mean. He knows everything & gives us little but pabulum.... It's one of those talks we could just as well have read. Such a lecture does not have the several validities of a poetry reading.

Hope to talk to Billy tomorrow evening. Hope his tests went okay. I talked to my folks last evening, and they said they sent Billy fifty bucks!

Yes, I become happier in my decision to take the full year off next year.... A grant from Ingram-Merrill wd. solve all financial problems. Postcard from Meredith today saying he wrote to I-M for me. I feel I have a shot at the award.

10/6/81

Classes went well today, but I'm nervous in anticipation of tomorrow's meeting, when my amendment, guaranteeing the right not to participate, comes up. I've no idea what will happen.

Billy called 11:00 last night. He's working hard for hard tests, and is going okay.

10/7/81

I was all primed for the meeting today, and it was changed, without explanation, to next Wednesday. This could turn out to be a good thing: I'll put in writing my feelings about my amendment, and give one to each Dept. member, and be on record, whatever happens.... Burke beat Gerber in the election for Executive Committee, hoorah!

Terrible day today—high winds, & rain. A struggle to bike up to play ball, but I did, and had fun. Have to catch a second wind for some schoolwork this evening. A playoff ballgame on, & it's easy to do schoolwork while baseball is on. Tomorrow, Thursday, is my favorite day—finish off the week & play poker.

Spent two hours in cabin, moving ahead with "The Name," or whatever it will be called.

Agent wrote to say Avon said no to *Swastika*. It's still in the works. So fine to have an agent working like this.... Two letters from good old Vince Clemente today.

More & more I enjoy just chatting in this journal. Fuck its future as, ahem, "literature."

Tony Piccione was over, & had much scotch in a short time. And he said that Al was pretty well shot yesterday early afternoon....

Kristen just got home. Dinner soon. Only Billy missing from my life.

10/9/81

Won exactly twenty bucks at poker last nigh. Played until five in morning, got up at eleven, biked up for a haircut and for basketball, am settled in for weekend now. Some sunshine today. I had a slight argument at basketball with that whiner Barry Schultz, and don't like such squabbles, but it's better to speak straight and feel good about myself than to stew.... Wrote my amendment letter for the Department, and will type it up. I feel mellow/relaxed/lazy, but will do a few busywork things while watching two baseball playoff games today.

Tomorrow is the Sadat funeral in Cairo.

Spoke with Al & Tony yesterday about the usual things, Dept. bullshit—it is all fast entering another dimension for me, sort of an impersonal one. I hope! If that amendment of mine sticks, that will take care of future worries.

Excellent classes yesterday, if I say so myself—a great outpouring of energy, a building toward realizations & intensity in each 1½ hr. session. Yes, 3 classes a day on two days a week are enough. I earn the money I receive.

10/10/81

All day I've been getting things done—typed WF letter, & Clemente letter, & wrote Siegel & Pitchford, etc.—while watching baseball.... I'll see Al this evening & do some xeroxing on his machine so I can deliver my letters to Dept. Mon. morning. I feel pretty good about things. I'm still clearing away things, emotionally & vocationally, and with luck will be able to get back to writing & a good routine in a week or two.... Next week & weekend with meetings & Billy home & Kurt here & Hansen visit & Jane & Charley's wedding, etc., will be busy....

10/11/81

Had a good morning and early afternoon in cabin, reading Klappert's interview & writing him & looking over my chestnut essay, then looking over a few poems including "The Unborn," one I'd forgotten.... Tony stopped over for an hour. Right now I'm trying to work up the courage to start typing up my 4th story.

Han & I stopped at Poulins yesterday & had some laughs.

A fine Sunday it is. Even a good film on this evening that I've wanted to see: Al Pacino in *With Justice For All*. Now, if the Yankees wd. only lose today....

I'll play basketball tomorrow, & mail all my junk at school, etc.

10/12/81

Had a good day, <u>after</u> spending a couple hours reading all those disgusting DSI reports—people taking credit for attending meetings, e.g.!.... But I delivered my letter to Dept., and then had some good games of basketball. It's so good to see Winnick, Stewart, Mancuso, & other ball-playing friends a few times a week.... Tollers so nervous talking to me today that he spilled his coffee. And he can never seem for a second to look me in the eyes.... It's past Christmas in 1888 for Walt.... Important Bills/Dolphins game tonight.... Homework....

Han's been working hard cleaning. She rearranged the living room, etc.... It sure will be fun to have Billy & Kurt here this weekend.

Lynne Studier will drop off my signed Heaney books one of these days.... Stan Rubin invited me to his dinner for Philip Schultz, and I'll have his book inscribed. So, my collecting, associating goes on. Al got my Pitchford books inscribed, & Kenneth sent along two others. Passion—a passionate writer....

Sunshine again today. Wednesday, after the meeting, I'll come home & mow the lawn, maybe.... Kristen wants me to see her tennis match tomorrow.... I have to start reading *Go Down, Moses*, again, for class next week. That's a book I love to teach....

10/14/81

Just finished the last student journal I had to read for tomorrow. In a half-hour I'll leave for basketball, & then there's that meeting. Maybe we won't even get to my amendment.

Tonight, Logan is around. The next few days will be extremely busy, as will the weekend, with Kurt & Billy around.

Had a good day yesterday—good classes.

Sent manuscript of my old Nashville novel off to Bill Ewert for sale. I'm hoping for a solid $500. Will see what Bill thinks.... Waiting for arrival of *Blackberry Light*. Maybe today.... I feel fine knowing Wenzel is done, too.... I've been playing with the idea of a *Selected Poems*, maybe to come out the same time as *CR* from Vanguard?

Sunshine today, perfect for my bike ride to basketball.

10/15/81

It's a little after seven on a Thursday morning. Han drops me off in front of Hartwell for classes in about a half-hour. Classes, then home for lawn-mowing, then a spaghetti dinner at the Vets Club for the Band Boosters.

Out until about 12:30 after Logan's fine reading in Poulin's class. I appreciate him & his poems more than I did. We all went out for drinks later. I spoke with Dale Davis rapid-fire about our collecting passions, about Dr. James Sibley Watson, and much else. I like her.

Well, my amendment went in at the meeting as a kind of friendly amendment. Some obfuscation, but it came out the way I wanted it to. I do think, past the Dept., the Provost will want to scratch the part I've fought to get into the WF document. Then, I'll see if I'll just forget it, or push it up to the President.... Today, I feel fine. I even mentioned at the meeting my feeling about the mysteriousness with which the DTP has been dealt.

Teaching & Dept. business seem to swallow up my time, but that will diminish toward Christmas, I hope, and my soul, my poetry soul feels very strong now, easily able to fly to the sabbatical year which, I trust, unless things get very dirty, will come through.

Logan has applied for the Iowa job, Don Justice's spot.

John gave me copy IX of the special *Bridge of Change*.

I think Al is going to be sick again. He has bronchitis which, he says, is turning into pneumonia, and he's on antibiotics & is smoking up a storm, and has been drinking. I don't know about all this artistic frenzy—I'm caught sometimes myself.

Later: I'll go play poker in an hour or so. It's been a great day, a clearing away. Days without classes now, and anticipation of Billy's visit, and a fine dinner among friends & good kids. I work like hell in classes, & need these long weekends.

I'm down to about $200 in my checkbook & $100 in cash, & could use a win tonight to stay on top in my poker account.

I'm watching baseball now—Yankees-A's—and would love to write a baseball book some day.... There was an inning in a ball game the other day I could do a whole book about....

10/17/81

God, what a couple of days. Billy & Kurt here—great dinner yesterday with them & Kris & her boyfriend Dave. Han made a turkey.... Jon & Jody Hansen here yesterday, too.... Today, the Jane & Charley wedding at Morgan-Manning House (Bruce read a beauty of a poem), & a gathering after that at Studiers.... I mowed the lawns this morning.... Not seen much of Billy & Kurt today. They were at RIT watching Brian Johnson play soccer.... Read a few journals today, & have more schoolwork....

Won $111 in that poker game.

Alas, Heaney only signed, didn't inscribe, my books. I should have asked Lynne to ask him.

Bill Ewert called yesterday & we talked for about an hour about most things.... He's sold about 5-10 copies fewer of *BL*, okay, but says that Bob Phillips has discontinued. In his own way, dear diary, Bob Phillips is a shit, and always has been, a sort of persnickety snip. His poems are all shit, and he doesn't have the critical mind that can whirl into new perceptions. And as a friend he has always been something else, a literary acquaintance playing a game, and a sort of whiner. Anyway, I've given him hundreds of dollars worth of books, not only all the specials of my books, but the bound WF volumes, e.g. He has disappointed me again. He could have lasted out the project for about the last $150. He's got <u>plenty</u> of dough.... If I'd been honest with him about his writing, I'd have lost him as a "friend" long ago.

That is just one of the little things (w. Ewert's mentioning of John Irving's 2.5 million paperback sale for the new novel) that makes me feel nothing, worthless. I <u>know</u> how fine my poems are, but the world, hell—Helen Simpson asking me if I was still writing, e.g.—even Brockport doesn't know I exist. Have to keep the courage <u>within</u> to keep writing, & grow with the aesthetic that writing itself, the process, is the thing, & not what the world makes or doesn't make of the product. Nothing, nothing, nothing.... And then a nice little thing like the letter from U. South Carolina yesterday....

I was good, socially, today, in stiff situations, but then all at once had had enough, and was <u>so</u> glad to get home....

Sun. 18th

Early afternoon. Picciones were just here, talking about money, money. They are driven from post to pillar, and they make about 40 grand a year. I don't know. They're not very happy. And Poulins are not very happy. I don't know.

Finished my last journal, and have to read some of *Go Down, Moses* while watching baseball & football, and will. I'll probably take a drive with Billy to drop Kurt off at RIT this evening.

Han & I will take a walk through this gloomy autumn weather, & then I'll get to work.

10/20/81

Billy's getting picked up in 15 minutes for his ride back to Ithaca. I'm sad already. Han & I have felt, though, a bit dissatisfied. Billy isn't warm, seems distant. But he says he's okay, doesn't have problems. It's true that he's always been quiet. All's well. But Han was very sad before she went to sleep last night.

I'll watch the first Series game tonight, and read journals. I might, just <u>might</u>, get back to the cabin tomorrow morning for the first time in a long time.

APT meeting yesterday was gruesome. Another coming up. But, it's nothing personal, is just generally awful to be ranking, etc. I won't do it again.

10/21/81

We talked to Billy last night. He's back safely. Things going fine for him.

I got back to the cabin for a couple of hours this morning. My two new poems, "Along This Water" and "The Unborn" are close to finished. Peaceful back there.

I have some journals to read, and "Pantaloon in Black" again. Tomorrow, I'll get to that big State Street auction for an hour or two between classes.... Things at school have really calmed down emotionally for me. Just have to get APT business over with now. Another week or two of that crap.

Played ball today. A good, hot workout after the bike ride up there in a cold drizzle.

10/23/81

Won $74 last night. Only 3 players.... Card from Billy: he scored 154 out of 160 on the chemistry prelim.... Worked in cabin a couple hours this morning, then skipped basketball to wash out the garage, rake a little, put away the grill, put the storm windows in the cabin door & the air-conditioner cover on back there.... Have to stay busy, finish schoolwork & all—Stewe Claeson arriving Monday. I look forward to his visit. Very busy next week: meetings & Dzwonkoski coming & all....

10/25/81

Spent a couple good hrs. in cabin this Sunday morning working on "The Unborn" and "Along This Water." Also saw I have 5 nice prose pieces, two untyped, to add to *Light* memoir eventually. Have so much to type up & send out & negotiate into books. Guess I'll never catch up with myself maybe until I publish collected volumes of my own when I'm 70, as Walt did.

Han & I went to the homecoming parade, & then a reception. We saw some people we hadn't seen in 20 years. I don't know. It's all so much. Margie Anderson, that beauty, said to me that she'd heard I'd had some poetry published. That's about what all my books have come to.... Han & I are skipping the soccer game and other activities today. Next year, for Han's class, we'll have a party.

Stewe gets here tomorrow. School & meetings & all will be very hectic, but I'll try to stay calm. I even look forward.

We'll call Billy this evening to say hello.... A World Series game on later.... Pylyshenkos coming for dinner Tuesday....

Just read Faulkner's amazing "The Old People" again.

My freshmen begin their speeches Tuesday. Dreaded APT meeting tomorrow. Must go to school to do some work to prepare for it tomorrow. Will play ball to relax before it.

10/26/81

I cleaned the garden, pulling out corn & sunflower stalks, tomato & pepper plants & bean vines, then tilled. Glad I got to it. Today, it's raining again.

I hope for a fine time with Stewe. Classes & meetings will make it hectic.

Kristen home today with a cold.

Another page of my journals runs down. As the years go by, I continue to enjoy it, find comfort in it, and it may be a source book for me later on. I may, still, want to enter more thoughtful things on more occasions, but don't want to feel any pressure to that end. That worry almost led to my abandoning the journal altogether some years back.

10/30/81

Friday night. The end of what was probably the busiest week in my life. Stewe's visit, our dinner Tues. evening, meetings on Wed. and today, the dinner at Rubin's Wed. evening and then the Philip Schultz reading, Peter Dzwonkoski's visit, etc., etc. But such a rich week:

Claeson is amazing, a light. It was as though we had been friends since childhood. He is as sensitive as I am, and so deeply read & intelligent. He is so charming that people move toward him. He is the handsome sailor! And he knows my poems, really knows them & cares for them. He'll even work on translating a small selection & try to find a publisher. We looked into one another's eyes all week and knew & cared for what we saw there. All week he asked questions & took notes. Han & I made it a fine time for him, too. He's staying in Boston this evening, & then will stay with Don Hall. Stewe Claeson!

Blackberry Light arrived today. Claeson as a book!

Big meeting today. After 1½ hrs. discussion during which I got almost everything said, my amendment passed 15-1 with one abstention. Tony, Al, & I happy, fulfilled today. We sensed warm support. Gerber, again, didn't even show up. Now, should the Provost reverse things, the Department can fight. Some odd & quirky things said by some Dept. members, but all in all they got the message. Peter Marchant was a gem, & Parshall. Anderson & Rubin & Bird—well, I don't know. Fitz Gerald seems to have skipped the meeting altogether. God almighty, my battle may be over. Still, of course, no one knows what is going on with Gerber's book, which interviews will be in it, etc., etc., but I think he'll look like a shit no matter what.

So much work to do, especially correspondence. And I have to read "The Bear." But I'm home, and decompressing, and happy.

11/1/81

41 today. It's been a nice day. I raked some leaves. Picciones stopped in. I've been reading, watching television, that frightening & excellent movie *Farehneit 451*. Han & Kris in Rochester to see "Annie."... Putting off writing letters.... Billy called last night, remembered my birthday, is doing fine....

I feel lazy, content.

Sending four poems off to *Harper's*. Still need to type my 4th story.

11/4/81

I'm about set for school tomorrow—finished about ten journals, and read "The Bear," etc. Want to go to Ashida's lecture this evening on Zen & Judo, and will.

Iowa Review took "The Census." So, poems coming up there & *Georgia Review*, *Poetry*, *Ontario Review*, etc. Not bad for someone with little energy to send poems out.

Last bit of APT business about over with. I had to go over Gerber's long file for DTP. Oh, God, what a bunch of shit & half-lies. He takes credit for the whole Writers Forum! I voted NO. It will be 4-1. We did not discuss, as we were supposed to. I'll write a memo to that effect. Enough.

I have a couple dozen letters to answer. Blessed Thursday arriving, & no meetings, for a change, Friday or Monday. I hope for a good poker game tomorrow evening.

Later: well, this time I am over in Edwards to listen to a lecture I do want to hear: Sashio Ashida will be lecturing on Zen and Judo. I hear he's a great man. I'll know.

Called Billy a little while ago. We had a good talk. He's very conscientious about his classes, & seems to be doing B+ to A work in everything. He's quite a boy. I keep hearing the things that are said underneath the words. He's solid. When I talk to him, or listen to him, sometimes, it's like when I put my arms around Han or Kristen—I just go into sort of a swoon, or daze—I love them so much—that comforting love's mindlessness.

The room is filling. Just talked with a fine friend, Al Peppard. I like the people who will be here at this small gathering tonight. I can tell already.... Peter Marchant, who is in the Judo Club, is passing out programs.... I just moved down about ten rows. I know, already, this is going to be one of the fine hours in my life, at least my life in school buildings.

Simple clothes. Spirit. Isness. Being. Koan & sitting (is meditation & action). Is the frond moving, or is the air moving?... How deep is the river of Zen? [To be what I am within what the world is.] Zen is not religion, not philosophy, but a practical way of self-actualization.... Is our daily life.... 5 steps: 1. absolute/within/relative [who I am]; 2. outer relationships; 3. <u>further</u> recognition of who I am; 4. apprehension of & rejection of dualism: you=I, I=you; 5. dualism completely dissolved.... // Never divorce ourselves from a given society!... <u>Pen it, & erase it</u>!... <u>White</u> paper (erase) or you cannot know somebody!... True human life starts at 60....

To move toward <u>wanting</u> to do, from have to do.... Moon in the flowing water—<u>that</u> kind of serenity....

Zennists accept death, it's a fact, but I can live a <u>long</u> time in terms of social contribution. "Another Zen master may give you a different answer" [yes: eternity is the now].... Master is always with me—a Zen feeling! Move around until you flip him—<u>this</u> is the 3-5 stage, not planning to use such and such a move.... Small satori—ultimate satori. [I've just asked two questions. He knows everything.] "I want to do my best, and that's all I think of before a match."

11/5/81

Thurs. evening. I'm off for five days. In a few hours I'll go to play some poker. I feel good, though nervous today, apprehensive about, in part, my perfect & true letter to Steve Bird—but apprehensive about what else I don't know. I want to play poker all night, and sleep, and wake up a new man & catch up on correspondence, etc.

Good classes today.... I feel I have space in my life now after hectic weeks. Will get out to the cabin for stretches this weekend. Have almost no schoolwork. Will read "Delta Autumn" & "Go Down, Moses." Will rake some leaves. Snow maybe tomorrow.... I feel fine.

11/6/81

Gulp, Tollers just called. I guess I've committed myself to a week-long teaching stint, for $1,000. Okay. We'll need the money. I can invite another poet, too. Maybe I'll get Stafford, or Plumly, or Judy Minty, or Phyllis Thompson, or.... It's okay—a week of worry & a week of work....

Won $173 last night.... Got up early & bicycled up against wind & played ball. Must be in pretty good shape.... Holmes fight on TV tonight, & I'll stay home & relax.

Not much else new.

11/7/81

Spent 5-6 hrs. in cabin today. Finished, at last, the little essay for Peter Klappert. It's not exactly an inspired piece, but it's okay, I think, and may be useful 10-20 years from now in some little gathering of prose pieces.... Wrote MacLeish, Ewert, Clemente.... Have many little things to do inside here this evening. Feel fine.... Han & I actually managed to sleep together down here last night—I fell asleep & woke up about 3 times.... She likes it <u>hot</u>, & I need fresh air. Anyway, we are in love & seem to be closer all the time.... Next, I'll type up that 4th story. Then, I'll do the MacLeish essay. One thing at a time. Then, solid work this winter on *CR*.... Ewert called last night, & we talked long about nothing special....

11/8/81

Sunday. Things clearing away. Typed, at last, my story "The Word." Raked the last leaves I'll rake. Wrote Jack Matthews. About finished the poem "Along this Water"—when the phrase "light-riddled" came to me I had it. Still many little things to do, but I feel about cleared away for the first time in weeks.

11/9/81

Good basketball today.... Got my xeroxing done.... Sent stories to Ewert, & essay to Klappert. Want to send stories to magazines, but don't know where.... About finished "Along This Water" this morning—just one or two rough spots. I want it smooth & simple.... Still no royalty report from Vanguard. Any day now.... Ha, my little APT game continues. Only one or two moves to make, & I'll be done (I hope) with the bothersome part.... Letter from MacLeish biographer today. He'll do a volume of letters, too. I'd love to have one or two in it. May 9th will be a big day.... I just wrote Billy a postcard.... Cold today & tonight.... Han's just getting back from a Twig meeting. I'm watching the end of the Buffalo-Dallas game.... Tomorrow, teaching. I'd like to wise up & not talk so much & exhaust myself so much....

11/10/81

Tuesday evening. Just finished journals. Relaxing, watching "10". Will go to U. of R. tomorrow for MacLeish letters.... I've worked hard & steadily these days, and feel at ease. Will do the MacLeish essay, or draft it, this weekend....

11/11/81

A rich & poignant day. Veterans' Day. I just cried over a news report of a man who built a chapel for his son, dead in Viet Nam, on a New Mexico mountain top....
Played ball, then drove to U. of R. Saw Peter & all. He's enthusiastic about a Heyen room. Saw the "Treasure Room" again, which would be perfect. I think it's going to come to be. The boss will visit some time. Also, Peter's thinking of an exhibition, Heyen as poet & collector, that sort of thing, maybe in March or so.... Picked up my MacLeish letters—about 60! Will xerox a dozen or so tomorrow. What emotions I experienced digging through boxes of things at U. of R., & then this evening reading the letters. He'll always be with me....
Long talk with Billy this evening. Will see him in just two weeks. Good talk with my folks, too. They're doing okay. I like telling them how old Archie is....

11/12/81

Amazing day: conciliatory letter from Steve Bird (he wants to end my little flurry with him), and then a letter from Tollers on merit ranking me 2nd in Dept.—I expected, say, 6th at best. It will be very hard for the Provost, now, to deny me merit. I can't figure Tollers out.
Sleepless last night, mostly, thinking about the room at U. of R. That has driven all Gerber/politics out of my mind. Wonderful. The same old Zen lesson: when I don't look or strain or plan, unhappiness disappears. A lot of that Gerber crap was on my mind even the past few weeks. No more. Victory after victory in the Dept. The collection at U. of R. The MacLeish happenings.
Kristen still has the flu. Maybe she'll see a doctor tomorrow.
Tonight I'll play ball, though tired, and then poker. I hope I'm not in too good a mood to win.

11/13/81

The meeting today should be uneventful.
Kristen home today (Friday) with flu bug.
I lost $72 last night, & even played well. No cards.
U. of R. library called. The big boss will visit Dec. 11. Looks like I'm going to get my own room over there. I don't want to rush things. But maybe it *is* time to assert the importance of my collection & to start

cataloguing it, and to <u>ask</u> for things for it. Still, I believe I'm very right <u>not</u> to be selling now. I will keep gathering.

11/14/81

    Went to Casey's Happy Hour after the meeting yesterday, and drank a lot, and stayed out until two in the morning. Met A.N.
    Did a little work this afternoon, a couple of pages on the MacLeish essay.
    Han & I will go to art opening this evening, probably.
    Space shuttle coming down right now. I don't care.
    Picciones not doing well. Han had a talk with Sandi yesterday.

11/15/81 (Sunday)

    Just about finished the 1st draft of the MacLeish essay this morning. Otherwise, a lazy day. Went to carwash, & stopped at Al's, where Tony was, drinking scotch already....
    Kristen still not well. Dr. tomorrow.
    Student reading tomorrow night. I'll go over, I think.
    Thinking much about something today, he said cryptically.
    Han & Kris talked with Billy, who is fine.

11/17/81

    Only Cal Rich & I showed up for the student reading last night. Fun, but tiring.
    Only two journals to read. I'll be able to catch my breath. My bones feel cold today. School was good, but tiring.... Read my MacLeish paper to the class. It sounded okay. I'll expand it as I type it, too—have a few other ideas.
    Stafford can't make it this summer. Who to ask next?

11/18/81

    Went to Hasha's service today. Ed Murray stricken. Poor guy.
    Very tired, but will go to Rubin's reading.
    Dave Smith sent two new books of poems. I'm glad to have them, especially after I'd just paid eighteen bucks for two books by Liesel Mueller.
    Kristen getting better slowly.... We spoke to Billy this evening. He'll be home in one week.
    Played ball today, & bicycled, & bicycled.
    All's well. Tomorrow is another Thursday to get through. Then several days to catch up on things.

11/19/81

    Thursday evening again. I'm about on vacation again. Soon, I'll go off to play a little ball, & then some poker. Will play <u>tight</u> tonight....
    Fine note from Archie, just enough to solidify a position I have on "Companions," and to give me a fine ¶.
    Poor Kristen will miss her band activities in Honeoye Falls this weekend—she's sitting here as I write—but she's a mature chickadee, and knows she'll blink her eyes, and it will be next year (or month), and she'll be in the clarinet of things again; also, she reminds me of me when I was a kid in Nesconset: I was often sick & home from school. I'd have ice cream & ginger ale, brought home by my father. She has Hershey kisses and

pfefferneuser cookies & Hawaiian punch, and watches the soaps, and talks to her father as he writes in this journal....

Nothing much new in old Brockport. Dinner at Mirko's with President tomorrow, & two ball games at college Saturday, & my MacLeish essay to finish typing the first draft of, and Dave Smith to write, and other correspondence.... Billy home next Tuesday, & we'll head for the wilds west of Buffalo.

Soon, I'll have to hunt for another diary.

11/22/81

A perfect Sunday. Cold/snow outside, and warm inside with Han & Kris & Kris's boyfriend Dave. I'm getting to many things that have been on my desk.

The MacLeish essay is ready for final typing. I'm glad I got it done, and hope they'll accept it for that symposium.

I've written Dick Hugo to ask him if he'd do the summer workshop. I hope so. He's even a friend of the new President. Dinner with Van de Wetering at Mirko's the other evening went very well. I was generally quiet, but not conspicuously so. Mirko insisted I read a poem, so I read "Carrie White." The President was honest, human, let his hair down and said a few things he didn't even have to say. The subject of last year's battles even came up—Ed Kelly & wife were there—and Van de Wetering knew nothing, & wanted to know, but I just said a sentence or two. I gave him *Light*.

Billy called twice yesterday, but I was out both times. He's fine, and will be home Tuesday.... Drop off the car tomorrow for tire-change & oil change to get ready for our Thanksgiving trip.

I won $204 at poker Thursday night. And the team I play on in the "Y" league won Thursday night. I play with kids from Hilton that Billy played against last year. And we've a few old guys, too.

Kristen better.

11/24/81

Billy should be home within the hour!

School tiring today. Now I'm off for a week.

I walked into Tollers this morning and, apparently, he'd heard from Gemmett, & the APT Committee will meet on the DPT. It's okay with me. Then, that stuff will be over with, maybe!... Meeting with Tollers & Peter & Stan on summer business was okay.... I can still do that summer thing without much sweat. The spring, though, will be crazy with readings, etc....

M.L. Rosenthal had his new book, a 1964-1980 collected, sent to me. Yesterday, Jack Matthews' new book of stories arrived. I look forward to the latter.

Long letter from Ewert today about all sorts of junk. I want to pull away from the marketplace & just write for a year or two.

Wonderful basketball game last night against the best team in the league. We won by 5. I calmly made 5 of 6 foul shots at the end. Hurt my right knee a bit, but it's one of those injuries that feels good.

I'll try to play at gym tomorrow, if open....

11/28/81

Friday evening.... We had such a perfect two days away. Wednesday night, up in that cold room—I turned off the heat—at Han's folks, I actually slept from about 11:30 to 10:45, my best sleep in a year. Yesterday, 15 of us at Wolf & Pat's for a 28 lb. turkey, & good talk, & cards with the kids, & pool downstairs. Billy drove back, & I sat in the back seat reading Jack Matthews' stories. I just wrote him, & wrote Judy Minty, and have more mail to catch up on this weekend. Life is full.

Bob Siegel sent *Whalesong*, a beautifully designed book. I'll read it tomorrow. I sure like him. I bet I'll like the book.... And Wayne Dodd sent his new book. And Martin's arrived. All things I want to read.... Meanwhile, I'm finishing Wiesenthal's *Sunflower*....

The same evening I received Ewert's letter, he called, & we spoke for an hour.... All's well.... Christmas card done & arriving soon....

Next week will be wild, beginning Tuesday. It's okay. My writing is building up in me, as it must. My writing soul is whole.

With the Babcock catalogue, & the Rochester exhibition, & the Heyen/Gorin evening, it should be an exciting spring for me. Still, I want to stay serene in important ways, and will....

Letter from Roy Winnick, who likes the MacLeish letters I sent, & will, I'm sure, use at least one.... Letter from Stewe Claeson.... Too much mail.... This family/correspondence/ friendship/Thanksgiving warmth life is not the life of the greater "writer"—I nag myself sometimes with this idea—but it is apparently what I want, with modest success from the non-obsessive style....

11/29/81

Sunday. Just about bedtime. Billy back in Ithaca, & should call any minute. A long good day, with Billy & Dave here for a fine roast beef dinner this afternoon.... I got the MacLeish essay typed, and have kept puttering away at other things.... Am reading Mueller, taking a few notes for the videotapes.... I don't know about contemporary lyric poetry—it begins to sound the same. Something missing. Limits to it. Some bigger conceptions needed. Dodd has no music. Read *Whalesong* yesterday and <u>love</u> it, maybe will review it, if even briefly. Finished *Sunflower*. Now just want to finish the semester gracefully. This will be a mad week, but I will be calm within it, the moon in the water, or rocks themselves in the rapids.... Kristen well again & ready for school.... Han & I stopped at Studiers to drop off Nora's birthday present.... Billy just this second called, & is back safely. Love that boy. The next few weeks will go quickly, and he'll be home again.... Peace....

12/2/81

Wednesday evening.... The past two days have been crazy.... Once & for all, now, the crap is over with (<u>3</u> meetings today including awkward APT one re. the jerk's application for DTP, & I feel <u>clear</u> of it once & for <u>all</u>). Yesterday, teaching & Liesel Mueller's visit & reading & the videotape—up until 1 in bar. Today, a set of papers to read & journals & the meetings. <u>But</u>, tomorrow after teaching I'll actually have time & peace. Classes winding down. I will play ball & poker tomorrow, & go out with Greg & Rod Friday night to dinner & Pyramid Gallery readings, but I'll have time for days to send out Christmas cards & get to the cabin, etc. The APT business had been on my mind, again, at least slightly, for weeks. This was the end of everything that began all conflicts last year. I have raised the consciousness, again, of several members of the Department. Now, I want to avoid all entanglements and spiral into my poems. Hell, maybe I'll even send a pamphlet, including "The Cabin," to Bill Ewert.

Billy home yesterday to see the Arcadia game. It was important to him, but I saw him just for a minute at Casey's yesterday, and he was anxious to get back to Cornell, and I think that now he knows his old high school life is over with. In fact, I'm right now going to write him a card or letter.

Kristen well again. Han's fine. I'll have good classes tomorrow, and then <u>live</u> for a few days of peace.

12/5/81

I want to know things that I can take with me when I die. <u>This</u> is the difference between being a historical critic, and a poet. I want to help my soul make its way, want to learn things that will not be lost.

Reading at Pyramid Gallery (Tama Baldwin, Li-Young Lee, David Bosnick) much fun. Rod & Greg & I had a good evening.

Good letter & book, *Apparitions*, from Dave Smith today.... Spoke briefly to Dick Hugo, who can't do the workshop with me this summer. I called Stan Plumly, and he will. I'm glad.... I've been taking care of mail, mail. Tomorrow I'm getting back to the cabin for sure....

12/9/81

Time going awfully fast. Thursday again tomorrow. I'm staying on top of schoolwork & school details. Han has just pulled in with groceries.
All's well.
Clearing away deskwork. Have a free evening.

12/11/81

Friday morning. Only 3 poker players again last night. I won $20.... I played okay in our ball game. We lost by 6-8.... Library people coming from Rochester today.... Then the Dept. party, and then the dance concert. I'm going to relax & enjoy the day—maybe I'll add a few words when all is over today.

12/14/81

Monday. I was sick yesterday, diarrhea & stomach cramps all day. I seem better now. A one-day virus. Last day of classes tomorrow.
Visit of library people went well Friday. I spent Saturday working on the catalogue already. Much work involved, but it will all be worth it.
Chapbook from Liesel Mueller in mail today.
Two rejections from *Georgia Review* the other day, and one from *New Yorker*.
Okay, a week of reading journals, etc., and then to turn in grades, and then to clear my head for next semester.... Billy will probably be home Saturday.
A silly basketball item in Roch. paper yesterday, with my picture. Everyone has seen the fucking item—but when it comes to getting any attention for serious work! ...

12/16/81

Cold as hell today, and I've got to bike or walk to school for a meeting in about an hour.... Classes done—now, a few days of reading papers, and I'll be done. All's well. Between things, I've been working on the exhibition for U. of R., putting books aside, planning....
Billy called last night when Han & Kris were out, and I had a good long talk with him. He's fine, finishing up tests, will bus to Rochester Saturday evening.... He mentioned his friend Paul Hogue, 17, who just died, wondered if Paul could hear him. It's good that Brad is in Ithaca, too—those two will always be close.... Billy will have over a 3.0 this semester, and that ain't easy. He's very conscientious about studying, etc. I also hope he gets into that fraternity, Sigma Chi, that Rich Booth is in.... Billy saw a copy of *Lord Dragonfly* in the Cornell store, and said he read some things from it. I get a big kick out of it, Billy discovering a different side of his father like this....

12/21/81

Billy and I played some ball today, and had fun.... Many errands. I picked up a few things for Christmas for Han.... I feel fine. Have been working along on things for U. of R. catalogue, & will go in to see Peter on the 29th, with most things done.... I'll turn in final grades tomorrow. Maybe I'll even get into the cabin tomorrow morning!

12/27/81

The days are just drifting by. We've had good gatherings with friends, and family Yahtzee games & dinners. I've not been to the cabin, but have been working on the U. of R. catalogue, which isn't easy to plan.... We all had a perfect Christmas.

Tomorrow, I'll play a little ball. Tuesday, I'll go in to the U. of R.

Cold out, and some snow again today.

12/29/81

Much off my mind after a long day at U. of R. today working with Mary & Peter on display & catalogue.... I've had a great evening at home, writing a few letters, skipping the high school game, sipping tea. Tomorrow I'm supposed to see that fuckstick Gemmett about my books. A waste of time. I'll humor him, and then go play some basketball with Billy.

Some Sarton & Moss books from Davies yesterday—cost me $32—and today a present from Bill Ewert, proofs of Levertov—free & worth about $200. That Bill is a pal.

Kris, Billy, Han fine. I'll go in to U. of R. once next week, but I feel now that my most difficult work on that stuff is done, and my vacation begins in earnest now.

12/30/81

Talk with Gemmett went very well. I said everything. We talked about all of last year, & about the future. Some interesting turns, too long to detail here. The *Provost*, of all people, wants in on discussions about my books & papers. I said to Gemmett I would not talk to the Provost, period. I got other shots in. Gemmett kept saying that with the new president this is a new place, and last year is behind us. I hope so. He also said that the Gerber book is cancelled, so far as he knows. So, when it shows up, he'll be as surprised as anyone else. Anyway, I feel great about everything going on. The U. of R. exhibit, & all this spring, will bury the bad times once & for all. Yes.... After the meeting, Billy & I played ball & had fun. Tonight, I'll go to the high school games.... Steve Bird just called to say there was a freeze on hiring: no APT meeting! Some days everything goes right!

I've bought another journal, one without lines, for when this one is filled, as it almost is.

Last evening, I unwound, wrote Ewert & Phillips & others. This afternoon, I feel like doing nothing. I'll putter. I love that word.

12/31/81

I've carried this journal back here to the cabin to finish it, and to make my last entry of the year. It's not too cold today. Sparrows are on and in the blue spruce looking for seeds.

Tonight is the neighborhood party, which will be okay. Then days of visits and television football. I feel fine, but am anxious at the same time to get back toward some poems, toward building books of poems. The work at U. of R. is always on my mind, and this is not painful, is something to look forward to, but I want times back here with *CR* and other things. There will be so much going on this spring that I'll have to keep my difficult balance. Much publicity on 2-3 happenings, too. I will be locally famous. I wanted to be. I even probably subconsciously arranged all this—the U. of R. exhibition, the Gorin evening at the college, the workshop this summer, the talk to the honors kids at the high school, maybe even the MacLeish symposium—to fight off once and for all the irrational mental crisis that rose from all those events last year. That last one was as honest a sentence as I could write.... The talk with Gemmett yesterday couldn't have gone better. And I don't think I've mentioned here that I got a $1,000 merit raise. I am, quickly, one of the fair-haired boys around here again. I know how petty I am, but emotions are emotions, and I was hurt and low a year ago—the last winter break was miserable because of all those problems. The college, says Gemmett, is now, with the new president, a new world. And I think he's right. Those battles are over. What's left is only what's inside me, a certain lingering but, yes, diminishing bitterness. The year could not be ending in a better way. I feel warm and content. I want to cherish and protect Han & the kids. I want to do some decent writing this next year, and make arrangements for and separate myself from my library a little bit. I want to move toward summer and sabbatical gracefully. I want to spend more hours back here, and will, especially after the day a week from today I'll go in to U. of R. for final work on the catalogue.

I'm glad about these journals of mine. To whom am I talking? After all these years, I'm still not sure. Maybe to myself. Maybe to a future I want to see me in a good light. Maybe I'm justifying myself to God. This journal has a curve of its own, the same figure a poem makes. I'll seal it up, and bury it at the U. of R. for a long time. Some day, it will be beside my other two to its left, and others, hopefully, to its right. This bodiless life, this presence ...

[#4: January 1, 1982-June 29, 1983]

January 1, 1982

Without fuss, another journal begins. Hundreds of blank pages out in front of me. I've come to enjoy this spreading out of ink and words against the paper. I see that ink takes well and dries quickly on this paper.... The other three journals had lined pages, but this shouldn't be any kind of problem.

I just played a game of Monopoly with the family & with Brian Johnson. I'm sipping tea now, and will watch some television and putter.... I visited Freddie Poulin for an hour this afternoon, and we had a couple of scotches and shot the shit. Boo was in the blackest mood I'd ever seen her in.... Tomorrow, maybe a ride out to Kendall. Or maybe we'll wait until Sunday.

I'm still trying to decide what to put in that eighth case of the exhibition. Probably, magazines and anthologies.

Yesterday morning, out in the cabin, I did some writing in *The Boulder*. I've no idea if that project will come to anything. There, of course, I have a much more conscious sense of wanting intensity and good writing than I have here.

The neighborhood party last night was fun, but at one or so in the morning I was <u>tired</u>. No hangover. Found my inscribed *Charisma Campaigns* at Nora Studiers'—it was missing for years.

1/3/82

Han and I just got back from our sort-of obligatory visit to the Picciones. We watched the Buffalo/Cincy football game, and that was okay, but it's so depressing out there, Tony in such hard-to-describe shape (trying to stop smoking & drinking again, etc.), and Lisa in trouble again with weight-loss, etc., and the house a mess & Sandi up against everything. I don't know....

Bruce Agte visited last evening, and we had fun, and he'll spend Thursday with me at Rochester.... I notice that this journal allows/asks for the long line. I wonder if the deep breath will carry over into my poems. I wouldn't mind.

I'm going to have a nice vacation evening, watching "The Boys From Brazil," writing a letter or two, mainly puttering with catalogue descriptions.... Tomorrow, Billy and I will play basketball. Poor Han has to begin teaching again, & Kris will be back to school, too. I want to settle the U. of R. stuff this week, so I can begin schoolwork, & write a little. My last couple of sessions in the cabin have been good ones, if only for the sake of clearing my mind.

1/4/82

Billy & I had a good time playing ball today. Mancuso fingernailed my face bloody on one play—I might end up with a scar. I don't care.

Nice but stiffly-strange and Engfishy note from A.E. Hecht today. And an invitation from American Academy to apply for their annual fellowship to Rome. Hmmm....

I'm just so content sitting in this chair. Kris is watching the soaps with me. Han is upstairs making spaghetti sauce. A cold rain. I'll do a couple letters today, & fiddle with the catalogue again.

Again this morning, I stayed in bed until eleven. My best sleep, after tossing several hours after an initial sleep, is in the morning.... I also spend much time thinking about the catalogue, school, etc. I feel fine.... Cold today, and snowing, and more snow on the way.

Squeak called. Poker begins again Thursday. I'm just about broke and have to win. I have a ball game Thursday night, too. Han & I will visit Mirko & Irma for their Christmas on Friday evening, and will go to Karen Setter's wedding on Saturday.... Last evening Brad stopped in, and we all watched the Providence-Seton Hall game. Such perfect times at home lately. Han is in good spirits, and Kris, too.

I think often that I should be writing more, working on poems more. I did send *Blackberry Light* off to *Ohio Review*, and "The Word."... In any case, I'll try to write some things (i.e. to put myself in a position where some poems might happen) this spring, but I feel as though I'm clearing away and catching up with myself—taking care of my book collection, winding down toward sabbatical, etc.... I did some work last evening, too, on the catalogue descriptions for the 8th & 16th cases, and solved some problems. I don't want any friends feeling left out, though space is very limited, and some feelings are bound to be hurt?

This journal is a little unwieldy, but I like the paper, and the large spaces. I look forward to sitting out in the back yard this summer with it, under the silver maple.

I'm hoping to see that Whitman anthology soon.... I've much other reporting on my Whitman reading to do to my Transcendentalism course. And I think I'll try to read Wagenknecht's *Emerson* before school begins....

Later: The mail came. A letter from Goodman Assoc. saying they've come to the end of their line and no reprint house wants the expanded *Swastika*. Mainly, I feel relieved, as though the whole book is mine again. I can try to convince Vanguard—doing the name-change & transition that I did from *Noise* to *Light*, or try some of the university presses.... A letter from Bill Stafford, with a couple of poems for Marchant's magazine.... A letter from Henry Carlile, a good letter, but filled with a kind of desperation, as though he'd just discovered that books of poems don't sell.

I can't seem to get down to things today, but sit here in front of soaps with a cup of coffee, edging words toward finishing another white page. I feel great, will wrap some books, will fiddle with the exhibition notes, will pluck books from shelves to take over to the U. of R.

Billy is reading Simon Wiesenthal's *The Murderers Among Us*. He needs to read such books once in a while.

Well, what the hell, Bill, do <u>something</u>!

1/6/82

Long call from Bill Ewert last night, about nothing special. He sure wants the manuscript for *The Cabin*, and I <u>should</u> get it to him and let him operate. He's amazing, in so many different ways.

Peter called already this morning about using a MacLeish letter (one I didn't know I had—he found it in a book) as an illustration. I don't know. I'll want to talk to him tomorrow, and look forward to the day there. Also, tomorrow, a ball game in the evening, and then a poker game.... Billy & I played Yahtzee until about one this morning. I think he has sort of broken up with Julie. I don't think he'll be much bothered—if he is, I guess that's a good experience, too. What <u>I</u> went through with Karen about 25 years ago was pretty unusual, I think, and he never needs something like that....

Mancuso will be embarrassed when he sees my scratched-up face today.

Much puttering & thinking & note-taking to do before tomorrow.

1/8/82

It's about noon, and I'm relaxing. Played poker until about three this morning. I won $235, and picked a good time.... My basketball game was called off.... Frigid weather.

Bruce and I worked hard at U. of R. yesterday with Mary & Peter, and the exhibition is just about set. I'll see the catalogue typescript yet, and will be involved later on with things, but I got done yesterday about everything I wanted to. So, 8 cases of Heyen, then one of MacLeish & 3 of misc. & first books, then 10 special shelves (let's see: Wilbur, Wright, Oates, Logan, Kinnell, Snodgrass, Stafford, Meredith, Simpson, & someone else) & a couple of shelves of overspill. Sure wish I'd had several more cases to get in more people. Some literary politics at work—the Hecht & Harrison things—but all's well. The opening will be quite an occasion. I'll hate it & love it. But I used to want to show people my books here at home, & had to handle the books, & felt glum about their not appreciating, etc. Now, things, some things, will be behind glass, & spotlighted.... There will be other displays in years to come, and I've learned much from working on this one....

The Whitman anthology arrived. It's handsome & substantial. I've read the Simpson essay, which is atrocious. Is Simpson's soul all prose? And Bly's is blah. Other things better. I've much more to read. I learn more and more all the time that my Whitman is wider than the Whitman that others read. He has to be taken whole. He knows at the end of his life, making the complete big book, what he's done, and criticism has to begin with that or misses everything. My essay isn't much, but my ability to read Walt is deeper than that thrown around by Simpson & Bly, e.g. Bly doesn't know what the fuck is even going on in *Walden*, e.g., when Thoreau says he's never learned a thing from his elders. Again, a reduction of Thoreau & all of Transcendentalism. And Simpson's pedantic listing of Whitman's "ideas"—such silly generalizations. What the hell is going on? Such ramblings in Bly, too. I don't know. I'll read Ginsberg & others. I sure wish I had an essay of my best moments in class from tape over the last several years.... The Kincaid piece has interesting moments.... What the fuck do I care?

1/9/82

Good party at Mirko's last night—3 Ukrainian singers showed up, and Gemmetts were there (I like Kendra). I drank a bit too much cognac, but got to sleep & felt fine in the morning.... This morning, Han & I went to Kim Setter's wedding, then the reception.... Now, home, & I've been relaxing. Fixed up a package of books to send to Kunitz for inscription.

Al called, a warm call telling me to take the financial pressure off myself for next year by doing a few chapters of my novel & trying to get an advance. Maybe I will.... Maybe I'll buy the set of holograph chapbooks from BOA Editions.

Kurt here for overnight. Billy has had a great vacation.

Waldo Emerson by Gay Wilson Allen arrived free from Houghton Mifflin yesterday—I had that paranoid incident with my mail yesterday at school, too. Glad I caught myself being stupid.

Frigid still, & the report is that we're in for the coldest spell in years.

Will watch football tomorrow, & maybe at least type that manuscript for Ewert.

Still reading the Whitman anthology. Want to read the Allen before school starts.

Poetry East took a couple of pieces.... I wrote Evelyn Shrifte about *Swastika*. And about my damned royalty check again!

The U. of R. exhibition a warm place in my mind.

1/10/82

Absolutely terrible weather. We might not even have a chance to bring Kurt back to RIT this evening.

I visited Al and spoke of the idea I have of putting together a complete BOA collection. It's a good idea for me, for many reasons, and I'm going to pursue it.... I'm going to follow my own rhythms, and if mine are collecting rather than writing rhythms now, so be it. But I keep seeing myself sitting & writing under the silver maple this July & August. Hell, I'll even get around to some cabin-time this vacation.

The Dallas/San Fran game about to begin.

Billy & I will play some ball tomorrow.

1/11/82

A long, good day. No school for Kristen and Han, nephew Kurt still here, a day of games & reading for me. I've gotten to Emerson's sophomore year at Harvard.... I wrote Bill Ewert last night, and put *The Cabin* into an envelope to send him; otherwise, a semi-lazy day. I did go over & over a couple of poems from *The Cabin*, so I stay in that stream. Yes, of course I wish this journal and my writing life were more right now, but these are family times, and the record cold keeps me out of my cabin in any case. And this will go on for at least several more days....

1/13/82

Busy, rich days. I worked all evening on the typescript for the catalogue, & today, & called Peter. All's well.... And Billy & I played ball today, won our games, ran & shot well. I feel very close to that boy. He & Julie—well, it's not good.... Kristen is in love with another boy, Billy Sodoma this time....

Bill Ewert called again—about nothing special. I like chatting with him, of course. He's keeping the faith. It might be hard to bring out *BL*, at least in the same way, with Emily Rizzo going out of business, and Michael Bixler's press broken, etc.

I'm reading the Whitman anthology, and the Allen *Emerson.*

A news report just came on: an airliner crashed in Wash., D.C., into a bridge, into the river—and they have a snowstorm there. Lord, again, why?

Which reminds me, again, of *Swastika* ... and of Hecht's introduction to the catalogue that Peter read to me today. I hope he's right. A generous piece. I owe him.

Al called last night, too. Nothing much new.... I called my folks. They're getting along okay. Pop plays pool every day, I'm glad to hear.

An evening of reading ahead of me. I don't feel very productive, though I did finish once & for all "Along This Water." Will show it to *New Yorker*, then *Poetry* or *Upstate*.

1/15/82

Won $67 at poker last night. Also, played ball last evening, and never shot better—Billy counted 12 of 14 for me from the field.... So, I played again today, and that made it 3 days in a row. I'm back in good running shape now.

The days go by. I keep reading, keep putting off letters I should answer. A good film, *The Hiding Place*, on television tonight.

I treated myself & bought Charles Wright's new book at Lift Bridge today. And Archie will trade me my second printing of Hall's anecdote book for a first.... Saw Peter Marchant today—he chatted about Kizer's visit.... Saw Adam LaZarre today—he chatted about the May 12th program.

My royalty check from Vanguard finally arrived--$216. About 150 books sold in 6 months. I'm not breaking any records. No report on *Lord Dragonfly*. I hope it breaks even & earns the $500 advance by the time of the May royalty report.

Record colds expected this weekend.

At last, my catalogue work is over with. Some worries about leaving some people out, but I did what I could, unless I'd opted, as maybe I should have, for a completely miscellaneous gathering.

Later: A linguistics professor from Bob Jones University said just now on television that the lord created different languages to keep the races apart—she tied it in with natural depravity.

1/16/82

Wrote a few letters, & may even have drafted a poem (about my happiness), & read more in *Waldo Emerson*, but the day went by not very seriously. Billy & I went over to the college game—he kept score. Kris did very well in her clarinet competition today.... Han has a cold, but is okay.

I usually get up at least once in the middle of the night, and I always feel amazed that I am the same person on the same planet. There is a sense of miracle in this, miracle that all my atoms & the atoms of the planet do not go scattering away when I sleep. There is a sense of purpose & direction in this, of God.

The cold is frightening.

1/18/82

It's ten in the evening, and freezing outside, and I'm home from the Brockport loss to RIT watching "Saturday Night Live." I'm a bug in a rug here.... Li-Young was just dropping off a letter and some poems as I got home.... Billy will leave Wednesday, and <u>then</u> I'll have to get down to schoolwork. Meanwhile, some reading, and writing a letter here and there. Han stood home from school today with her cold.

Inscribed books back from David Ignatow, beauties. A book from Paul C. Steele in the mail. Not much else new. This has been, all in all, a wonderful vacation. The first journals of the semester, when they come in, will dizzy me, but May will fly in.

Warm feelings over at the almost-empty gym talking to Mr. Boozer, & Scott Kretchmar, & Chaz Crawford, & Cindy Van Gundy, & Joe Winnick. I feel at home around all those people, and in Brockport. Tollers in the English Dept., & one or two other lost souls, still spook me, but I've little need to be around them.

I'm learning much from the Allen *Emerson*. Read until 1:30 this morning, the house quiet, the family asleep. I will again this evening.

1/20/82

Billy left for Cornell with Brett Wood a half hour ago. I'm alone in the house. I took a shower, and am sitting here with coffee and this journal. It's very quiet.

Reading the Allen *Emerson* makes me keep thinking about what I am thinking about, even what I am seeing as I watch this ink-thread form in my mind and then form on the page. Consciousness is a miracle. From whence?—Alcott's question. It <u>is</u> always as though I'm seeing myself from somewhere else. Is this the soul watching, or my differentiated body-bound being?

I want to do everything: become a scholar & study my three main Transcendentalists all my life; write a book about God/existence; write poems always & steadily (I must soon spend a long time simplifying my beauty "The Unborn"); work with my book collection, & memorize many more poems by others; write only this journal and stay with it. Well, what's new? I've accomplished much ("gleaned" much of myself, in Keats' language), since graduate school while being husband and father, too. Much of this is thanks to Han who not only, in the way of generations of wives took second place to my career for years, but does the financial stuff around here, the taxes, etc. <u>She</u> has kept everything together, or I wouldn't have written more than a miscellaneous book or two, at most.

For a long time now, even when I've been home alone, I've had the television on as a kind of background noise. Right now, I don't, and the silence is loud. I become almost anxious, anticipating the phone, or a car in the driveway, or a knock at the door.

I wrote Evelyn Shrifte and Paul Zimmer about *Swastika*. Dear Evelyn probably won't answer.

Tony stopped by yesterday. He's still off cigarettes. He's so heavy. He's always fighting one battle or another.

Letter from Bill Ewert. Looks like he will do my three poems, *The Cabin*.... And he sent along a letter his 90-year-old grandmother had written after she got the Christmas card, a letter filled with vanished lambs and apple blossoms and farms....

This study of mine—books & desks & comfortable easy chair & couch & shag rug—if I'd known when I was in graduate school that I would someday have a <u>room</u> (not to mention <u>cabin</u> & <u>home</u> <u>*and*</u>), I'd have thought myself blessed and in heaven. Maybe I am in heaven. The recurring feeling, from dreams & snatches of consciousness from somewhere, that in a life immediately previous to this one I taught in NYC, probably in the CUNY system. My memories are somehow filled with dreary halls & desks & papers in marginal buildings, and myself as instructor or assistant professor, very unhappy, unpublished, living in an apartment just with Han (with Han in that other life!) and with little money & trying to finish an article on Henry James or Hawthorne. Where are all these memories from? Did I so much hate the life that someone like Bob Long lived—or Doug Hill or Barry Leeds at Columbia—as I imagined it? Or was there another life. The images are so strong—radiators in hallways outside classrooms where my night class will meet.... Brockport, NY, 1982 years after Jesus' birth, 90 years after Walt's death. I will keep watching my mind, but who is that I?

1/22/82

I just read a sentence from Thoreau about a pine tree: "It is as immortal as I am, and perchance will go to as high a heaven, there to tower above me still." Reminds me a little of "The Unborn," which I finished yesterday. My poem suggests a kind of pool of souls that will not find body on this earth, but which are as real as those that do. Unborn sunflower souls, and my unborn children.

I didn't want to play much last night. I wanted to save my legs for the game tonight at the college, but had to play the whole time. I made my first six or eight shots again, and only missed my last one of the game. Amazing. I've <u>never</u> had two shooting games in a row like that.... Then, at poker, I won $28, but felt almost like a loser. I was up over a hundred once, and it was a big game. But, anyway, another win.

Talked with Billy. He's fine, registered, settled in. His index for the first semester was 3.47.

Tony Vallone came over yesterday. He's okay, but awfully dull, not like Bruce.... I also got over to the school, xeroxed some stuff, got some details off my mind. Will do schoolwork this weekend.... I've an appointment this afternoon with Joyce Busse about her paper on Thoreau.

I'm still reading *Waldo Emerson*, a book I've needed.

Bill Ewert called last night. I missed him. He'll call tomorrow.... I wrote out 3 copies of "The Unborn," and will send him one.

Saw Poulin, who is on some kind of Poulin-high, high even for him. I hope he becomes Al again soon. I still want to go ahead with the BOA collection.

1/23/82

The team I was on won the ball game last night. I worked hard (after playing a full hard game the night before), scored about 15, and was the difference. It's still fun to win, though the game means nothing. Because I have a Thursday night class beginning next week, I won't have to play two days in a row again—my legs need a day's rest. It makes a big difference.

Stopped in at Poulin's, gave him a check for $175, and came home with a whole box of presentation copies and other good BOA things. A good deal for both of us. I now have all 6 issues of the Snodgrass book. Began to do a little listing today in my ledger.

Bill Ewert called today. He's going to do *The Cabin* with Marta Anderson. It's okay with me, even though the thing will be slight & very expensive. I can't worry about Bill's sales.... All's well with him. He'll make quite a bit of money on his Levertov item....

Tomorrow, schoolwork. It shouldn't be difficult getting ready for classes.

Terrible weather. Han & I went shopping this evening, and it's good to be back now & relaxing.

I should check out the cabin tomorrow. Haven't been back there for a week or two.

1/25/82

Got hold of Billy yesterday. He's fine.... He didn't get into that fraternity, but truly doesn't care. As Han says, he has always been his own person, and he has. He's more mature, enlightened in many ways than I am.

First day of classes went okay. Tomorrow, the evening 3-hour grind added. But I feel generally energetic, and can't/shouldn't complain. I just have to think of the traffic to work so early in the morning, and the scenes at airports every minute of my day. I am home, and glad to be, here on Frazier St., or in Hartwell Hall.... Both Tonys, Al, Bruce, students I know, around all day yesterday, so my office is a good place.

Kristen doing fine on tests this week. I'll drive hr to school in a couple of hours for a test, and then I'll play some ball and go to gulp a dept. meeting.

I find myself determined to be a better teacher, softer-spoken, more direct and honest, quieter, allowing more of my inner-light to show, etc.

Ginna nuclear plant in the news after a leak. I wish those fucking places would all go into cold shutdowns.

1/29/82

I expended a terrific amount of energy teaching yesterday, but did a good job, and have the classes off the ground. The intro. to creative writing will go slowly this semester. The other two classes will steam ahead on their own. Last night's class went three hours. Some lively people.... Then I played poker land won $185. Joe Winnick got hit.... I stopped in to see Dick Mancuso in hospital. He's fine.

I feel generally lazy and listless today.... Long letter from Martin Booth—he has a dozen projects going, as usual.... Peter Dzwonkoski writes about a tape of me reading for the exhibition—sounds okay to me.... I'm reading both the Allen *Emerson* & the Cargas Holocaust anthology.

1/31/82

Han & I had a great time last night at the 3rd annual old guys basketball party, this one at Winnicks'. Everybody loose and insulting. Many friends. Han & I started this annual party two years ago. I'm glad we did. There's probably no other party all year in Brockport as wild and friendly as this one, unless the high school kids have it.

Between these two paragraphs, Bill Ewert called. We talked, about everything (Babcock, Simic, some sort of New Hampshire gathering, etc.) for 45 minutes. I turned down $750 to give some sort of talk about something.... All's well—Bill has a package in the mail with some surprises for me, "stellar items," he calls them.

The NBA All-Star game is on.... I'll read today, and enjoy being inside during more snow.

2/5/82

Friday evening. I'm relaxing. Long day yesterday, six hours of classes, all intense. Evening workshop was good, too. No poker game last night, so I played ball today.... Dozens of little things to do to clear my desk.

Card from R.P. Warren today that lit me up! I'll be sending him some books to inscribe. Books back from Kunitz yesterday. Things keep pouring in for my collection. Wish I could afford more of my own books so I could send them to these people.

Drafted a poem yesterday morning that may turn out to be a good one: "At Gibbs Pond."

Kristen has been running herself ragged with all her band activities. I hope she'll be all right. She has to be gone all day tomorrow, too.

Tony Piccione smoking and drinking again. I don't know. He's fat as hell, too. When we see Sandi alone, or Han talks to her on the phone, she sounds desperate.... Al seems in good spirits, but is frail.

Worked on the catalogue proofs today. So, that's about done. Quite a project.

Wednesday night Han & I went to the Arcadia game with the Setters. It was fun. They're good folks.

I'm supposed to call Jamestown CC about a reading. For $150 or more, I'll go, I guess. I wonder why I had so many readings last year, and none this.

Beautiful class on "Crossing Brooklyn Ferry" yesterday, too.

I want to read Stryk's new book this summer, under the silver maple.

2/7/82

Did small jobs all day.... Readied a package to send to R.P.W.... Spoke with Billy this evening, and wrote him a letter.... Brutal weather.... No work with poetry today at all.... Look forward to basketball tomorrow.... I've stay busy, but am not sure where the weekend has gone.... A sense of permanence when a poem is completed, I guess, a book.

Reading Warren has been an experience. Could spend a lifetime inside him. I'll know he's there as a resource should I need someone to help me write. Sometimes, he's too verbose, but he has some range, and writes what he fucking pleases, which ain't easy.

I keep thinking about a book, the expanded *Swastika* or a new book of various poems like "The Berries" & "The Bees" & "Yellowthroats" & "The Unborn," or those in an expanded *City Parables*, or a *Selected* or *Collected*. Bill, go slow. I would like to get some feedback from Evelyn at Vanguard about what they could have in mind for me on my future!

A dramatization of Black Friday, 1929 on television now. Economics addles my brain. It must be something like poetry.... Companies disappeared!...

2/8/82

I'm unbelievably comfortable this Monday evening. I have my couch pulled out, and am watching television (*Lou Grant*), and sipping herb tea. I'm about set for school tomorrow. I just feel like resting here and writing in my journal.

After watching *Brideshead Revisited* & seeing Oxford scenes—the very doorway at J. Thornton Bookseller on Broad St.—I turned to my last journal to read my few words that brought back myriad memories. No matter how skeletal these journals are, they will always be important to me. I look forward to seeing them locked up in a rare books room.

Kristen came home with a good report card.... Han had today off.... A nice postcard from Denise Levertov today, and I'll be reading (skimming) her books for a week or two before sending her some for inscribing.... Package went off to Robert Penn Warren today. I often feel as though I ask for all these inscriptions under false pretenses, and it's true that I don't have the time (or desire?) to read these well-known poets much, but the collection begins to take on a life of its own, important to the future beyond me—ego satisfaction for me now, but that's no matter; an investment for Han & me now, but that's no matter. A collection of poets' books touched by them. The joy will go forth a million-fold in the future for those who use the room of books I see in my dreamy eye....

I've asked for $450 for two readings in Jamestown this spring. Money, money. Don't want to feel money pressure next year. I hope to discipline and deepen myself. Maybe do a single book-length poem, meditative, non-imagistic, that writes itself. Want to do so much. Need maturity, courage, to keep going.

Played ball today. Felt okay.

Began to expand "At Gibbs Pond" today. Don't know what will happen to it.

Just remembered that I have to make a reading tape sometime for the exhibition.

Each of the last three or four times I've seen Al, he's read to me or shown me some note he's gotten from a reader or poet saying nice things, He says, "that's just so nice, you know." I do know, and agree with him, and say he deserves it, etc., etc., and I am glad he's happy in feeling he's becoming known. Yesterday, on the phone, I read to him my Warren card, and he was just silent—I could hear him thinking that he'd better write Warren right away! Al was so cold! Well, we've been close for a long time, but he is still the person he is. He didn't even say "that's nice," though I was of course happy about the card. He has often been insensitive about such things. But I still feel close to him.... Tony & Al, Tony & Al, Tyson & Joe....

Rabbits feed under the bird feeder these cold evenings. I've thrown carrot slices & pieces of lettuce there, too.

Haven't even been back to my cabin in weeks. I should walk back there just to check things, and will, probably tomorrow. Snow storm on its way again.

Read Ryōkan again for a half-hour. He cannot be predicted. He even worries sometimes; and then he offers the tranquility of his hermitage to any visitor.... I often feel I have this hermitage inside myself, too, but its tranquility hasn't really been tested, yet. Or maybe it has, twice—last year, and about 25 years ago....

2/9/82

It's early evening. Classes were okay today, though I felt a bit scattered. Well, they can't all round off with a sense of understanding and accomplishment.

I spent, altogether, before & between & after classes, about an hour with Tony. Oh, he is filled with woe and no—everything so dark & depressing to him, everything too much trouble. I know, at least, what makes me happy. He doesn't/can't be, it seems.

Maybe I'll give myself the evening off from reading journals, and do them before I go to play basketball tomorrow.... Nice letters from Bob Siegel & Stewe Claeson today. Stewe seems to be whirling, wrote one of those odd letters I sometimes write. This one is about Thomas Aquinas—what is Stewe saying?

Bob Phillips wrote that Marya Zaturenska died.

I hear Han laughing upstairs, & hear that Pat Greiner will go with Han & Kris to Myrtle Beach over spring break. I just don't want to go, can't stand the idea of four days on the road. So, my two women will head south. I'm glad Pat will be going. Maybe Han's mother, too, although they'd be better off without her, I think. Anyway, I'll be here, & will spend the time in my cabin, clearing my head, writing, watching the world wake up.... Billy might be here with me for a few days. I'll be worried about all their hours on the road, but feel they'll be okay. Tires, hold on! Never mind my story "The Word."... I love those three women, and hope they have good weather down there. I'll go again another year.... Every time I think that maybe I should go, I say no, no. I'll be glad to be home. Bless those adventurous women!

2/10/82

A good day today. I bought Dave Smith's novel, & Phil Levine's new book, then played ball and picked up Han. She & Kris are off to Eastman.... Peter Dzwonkoski called about illustrations for the catalogue, etc. A sample invitation came. Then, Poulin called and he was extremely upset because Graver had done it again!: published the Ashbery interview in *Michigan Quarterly Review* without Poulin's knowledge or consent. I get pissed off, too, when I think of it, BUT I'm done with that stuff—even though Graver will probably publish that book, even though he will probably publish the MacLeish interview without permission of any of the three people who talked that day. Etc.... Well, let's see what Al does. He must write a strong letter to the President, etc.... Al just called again. He called Tollers, & Tollers was aghast, but of course won't do anything again.... Well, I must relax & give Al a few days to work. Maybe I will write to the President myself.... Ha, maybe here we go again, but I'm much, much wiser, and even passive in important ways....

Later: Fred just called again. He wants the two of us to see the President on this matter of Graver. Yes. We'll go in and speak with him next week, I guess. It might be a good idea.... All in all, I'm relaxed about all this. In the end, what's it to me?...

Vince Clemente wrote to tell me about a windfall of books (Berryman, Wms., Eliot, Penn Warren, etc.) that came his way from A.J.M. Smith's son. That lucky Vince. I envy him. It couldn't have happened to a more angelic person.

I wrote to Stewe.... Tonight we'll call Billy, as we do every Wednesday.... In a few minutes Han & Kris will be back & will have McDonald's for me. They'll both be away again this evening, and I'll get to my schoolwork.... I still haven't gotten back to my cabin to look things over, but I know it's there, like a quiet place in my mind. I want to finish CR this summer & over my sabbatical, want to make it "simple" and beautiful.

Later: I've had a great evening. Called Billy, and we had a long, good talk. Then I called Bill Ewert, as I do once every couple of months, and we chatted happily for about twenty minutes about all sorts of things.... Then I read a few Carver stories for my 210 class, and then read & thought about Ryōkan for my evening class.... Han & Kris home safely now, and I'm winding the day down. I even look forward to seeing Tony in the morning....

I think my new poem, if I make it longer than 32 lines, will take a long while. The third movement could be 16 lines. Yes. And who will begin talking?

Maybe, if Vanguard or Ontario Review Press or someone won't do *Swastika*, Bill Ewert will. I'd even kick in some money to get that book done, all-of-a-piece, the way it should be. Well, many projects to think about & finish once I'm off. I have been feeling awfully ignored—never see my name anywhere, only a single one-paragraph review of *Lord Dragonfly*, etc. As far as being known goes, if *CR* doesn't do it nothing will. A new anthology is out from Longmans-Green, and it looks good, & Plumly & McPherson and a dozen others of my generation are in it, but not me, alas. I feel very happy tonight, though. I love Ryōkan—so human, ultra human, feeling loneliness & melancholy, and sometimes timelessness, and often quiet joy.

I'd like to send copies of *Swastika* to all the contributors to Cargas' new anthology. Wish I could afford a bunch of copies of *LD*, too. I have the money, or Vanguard would deduct it from future royalties, but it's just too much money. Han makes only about thirty bucks a day, I keep thinking. ...

Cold as a bitch outside (silly sexist language) but some warmer air is supposed to be heading our way.... I did walk back to the cabin for a minute. All's secure, and waiting for me. The windows are frosted over. Snowdrifts high around it. Thick crust over the snow, but when I walked by the horse-chestnut, its buds were glinting dark red.

2/12/83

Changed ink color to inscribe Bruce Agte's copy of *Blackberry Light*. He & Tony Vallone & Paula Closson stopped over after class last night for wine & pizza. Good class last night, and all day.

Talked to Gemmett today, & then Poulin. In a way, I've had fun with this Graver business this time. I'm sure Graver's stomach will churn this weekend. Al is in fine fettle, dashing off notes & letters.

Enjoyed basketball today.... Wrote letters to Vince Clemente & Reneé Gorin. Reneé has performed/will perform her Swastika here and there.

Brad Morrow turned down "The Unborn" for *Conjunctions*. I feel generally nowhere. But surely a year or two or three could go by for me without any publications, and I should think well enough of myself to bear it!

Han & Kris just came home to begin their vacations.

Letters from Mike Waters & Karl Elder. I could set up some readings next year with Karl.

Will read Li-Young's thesis this weekend. Will stay home and mind my business. The semester is flying by.

Will send some books to Levertov this weekend, too.

The temperature is up in the 20s, anyway. A heat wave!

2/15/82

Good day today. Temperature in the 40s!, so I actually got back to the cabin for a couple of hours this afternoon after basketball. Schoolwork this evening.

Dinner and movies (*On Golden Pond*) with Poulins & Picciones yesterday. Then cheesecake at Poulins. A warm & friendly evening.... No talk about the Graver business. My only concern is that I'd like the Dept. & the President to know about this piracy; otherwise, I don't care, because it won't/can/t happen again. If I were Graver, I would just feel extremely uneasy about this, even frightened for my job.

I've been reading Lucien's *Encounter With Zen*, and writing some small poems which please me. Lucien's book keeps opening up my eyes to things I know. At heart, I feel more living presence at the center of all things than a Zennist does (at least according to my understanding of Zen) but so much more in Zen is so true and appealing for me, and balanced for my personality. What are my chances over the next ten or twenty years of becoming enlightened? Pretty good, I'd guess. I have a decent start. I'll never reach the inner light (or nothingness) of a master, but I may reach that serenity I've wanted and sometimes have felt close to. A whole year away from school will help quite a bit. I think I'll give Tony & Al the keys to my office for their classes—Al might not want to walk up the stairs, though.

84 men went down with an oil platform in the North Atlantic.... Heavy fighting in El Salvador.... All of that is less real/more real/equally as real as this oasis of Brockport life....

2/17/82

I'm just sort of getting ready for bed. Kristen will sleep at Beth's this evening. Han and I are home alone—she's finishing up the taxes. I'm about ready for my six hrs. of class tomorrow.... It turns out that Daniel Berrigan will be speaking tomorrow, too. Maybe I can meet with him after my late class. I have some books I'd like inscribed. He's a real man—just thinking of him tightens my throat. Wish to hell we'd known he'd be here—a group on campus brings him here suddenly. Grace Paley here tomorrow also. I haven't read her books....

Letter from Ewert today about usual things.

Invitation today to read a poem at the President's inauguration ceremony here May 8th. I'd like to do it, but it's the weekend of the MacLeish gathering, but the important MacLeish day is May 7th. I'll have to see. I might have to write a new poem for the President's occasion.

Poulin will talk with Tollers & Gemmett tomorrow over the Graver plagiarisms. A lot will depend on how much energy Poulin has to pursue this. I must admit that I'm glad it wasn't the MacLeish tape, e.g., that Graver stole—then I'd have to be the main fighter again, as I was during the wars of last year.... I realized last week that whenever Graver is in gravest trouble, he wears his very best suit & walks around, struts, laughing loud. He's in trouble, has something big to worry about now.

Read 6 or 8 student journals today, as I do most Wednesdays.

Great ballgame last night at R.L. Thomas, Brockport High winning by 14. Felipe was devastating.

Han & I talked to Billy tonight. He's fine, will be home next weekend, looks like. I'm glad. The winter is cut in half now. He was especially pleased with the poker twenty bucks I sent him. Maybe I'll drop him a card tonight.

2/19/82

A relaxing morning, anticipating basketball, after a long day of classes after which I went to the reception for Daniel Berrigan and met him briefly—he signed three books & inscribed one for me....

Spoke with Al briefly. Tollers & Gemmett will do nothing, and tell Al he should pursue grievance within the Department if he wants.... I just don't want to fight & fight, I realize (sorry, Father Dan); I do keep thinking of a joke/Junius letter to the Dept. from "Phil" admitting all. Ha. Maybe it's humor/satire needed to combat the megalomania & greed. In any case, I'm relaxed. Poor Al.

Wolf & Pat will visit late this evening after their visit to Kurt at RIT. I'm glad.

I just dropped De Snodgrass a note. He sent us a lovely card, *Star*.

2/20/82

Long, good day. Wolf & Pat here overnight and stayed most of the day. Good people.... Though it's Saturday, I had an editorial meeting with the Marchants, Greg, Rubin—glad I went. Said I was much against including Graver's interview with Algren. They'll use Poulin's Hayden instead! Good. A kick in the ass for Gerber, I mean Graver. The others as angry as I am, too, I'm glad to say, about the Ashbery business. Al calls 2-3 times a day about this & that, but he'll have to decide what, if anything, he wants to do. That so many think Gerber is a despicable shit is almost enough for me.... Then, I got home and in the mail was a letter from the American Academy saying I'd won $1,350 & the Witter Bynner Award. Hey, okay, what the hell, I'll go to New York & their fancy luncheon & pick up the check. I must have had half-a-dozen friends among the voting members. Nice to get something I didn't even try for.... Al just got 14 grand for BOA from NYS Council.... Got a little schoolwork done today.... Peter Stitt here Wednesday, & will go to a class of mine Thursday.... Read another section of the Stryk book, & wrote a tiny poem—<u>something</u> each day, something, until the smoke of busyness all clears. If not too cold, maybe I'll get out to the cabin for a couple of hours tomorrow.... APT Committee meeting Monday.... Student reading in my office Monday.... I said yes to Aaron Kramer about reading with him Oct. 4 in NYC.... Billy coming home next weekend.... Han & Kris & I are at this moment in my study watching a film, couch pulled out.... Catalogue 2 from Davies today with big prices on some things I have.... My desk is filled with letters to answer, even some decisions to make, like whether or not I'll do a poem for the President's inauguration.... Lots of attention this spring for this big-shit poet coasting to summer & sabbatical. I'll have to be very careful I don't fill up next year with too many disruptions from cabin-routine....

2/21/82

Fine day. I kept clearing off my desk, writing letters, sending a book to Norb, doing a recommendation, watching basketball.... Will see *With Justice for All* this evening & keep clearing the desk. We'll call Billy.

I'd like <u>very</u> much to write a beauty of a poem for Van de Wetering's inauguration. If I become political at all, I'll have to be cagey. I <u>almost</u> feel nudged with a beginning. It may begin in our back yard.... I'll call up and agree tomorrow to do the poem, and then just strain like hell to work in the MacLeish conference on the preceding day at least, Archie's birthday....

Yes, Han & I will go together to NYC for the May dinner & Bynner award. It should be a memorable time. Maybe by then I can convince Evelyn to do a paperback of *Swastika*. Anyway, I want Han to see the Vanguard offices, and the Strand, etc. Maybe we'll go to our first Broadway show.

The young millionaires Miller & Watson are in a sudden-death play-off.

2/22/82

Wonderful dream last night of driving in heavy snow, somehow getting into a lane on the left side of the road, unable to get behind the car to my right and in front of me in a clearer lane. I was sure I would go off the road to the left, or be stopped in the higher & higher drifting & crusting snow, but I kept plowing ahead, almost stopped once, but kept going, sluicing through the snow, and came to a place where I went straight ahead to a clear road while the other car went off to the right. Regret, for an instant, that I wasn't going to the right, but realization that the road I was on was the one going to where I was going.

I've many thoughts about the dream's meaning. Mainly, my soul kept moving on.

Later—10:30 p.m.: Good day today of schoolwork & basketball & pizza with Han & Kris. Then, stupidly, I went to that student poetry reading in my office. I usually don't care how <u>bad</u> poems are, but the obscene & spiritless things tonight, that fucking Goffman's interminable mindless strain-for-shock prose, and that new guy Solomon with his endless talk of Ginsberg & Bukowski, and a girl reading a poem about how dead she feels, & then laughing, & Solomon again reading dreary poems about pot parties—one or two good kids/poems among this drivel. I feel <u>old</u>, I guess. Al & Tony wouldn't show up in a hundred years. None of the leavening spirit around of an Agte or Vallone. A diminishing. Pshew. I want still to be <u>present</u>, to be a teacher, but it's awfully dreary. I should teach in Japan or somewhere where students would know things and would teach me.... This ¶ hasn't come close to expressing how dreary it was—it was as awful as Charles Olson's "lecture" that time in Cortland: Turco says he has it on tape for posterity.... Lucien, how the fuck respond to all this? I could easily <u>not</u> respond, but what kind of teacher could I be if I cut myself completely off from this?... Well, I'm home now, & my soul clears....

Saw Al briefly today. He's sending a 10-page letter to a different lawyer. Maybe, just maybe this time, Gerber will be in for a lawsuit.

Han a little depressed about her work-situation, but I cheered her up. She'll be going with Kristen to Nashville soon, and then to Myrtle Beach, & then with me for a few days to NYC.... I just this second realized that the Bynner award makes me happy, but I've not thought much about it. When, on the other hand, 17 years or so ago I heard that I won the Borestone, I couldn't sleep for days, weeks. If a similar thing happens, and I won a Pulitzer or something in 17 years, I'll think almost nothing of it. This is a fine thing....

Justice for All was unbelievable, shitty. It could have been a good film.

My folks called yesterday. They're bored, but okay.... Apparently things are very bad with Henry & Liz. Liz even says Henry has been drinking too much.... I do wish I lived closer to my brothers. I care for all three, & could become very good friends with all three—well, I'm very close to Werner now.... Blood, of course, does not automatically make for kindred spirits.

I've said this before, and will again: I look forward to writing in this big journal when I'm sitting under the silver maple, by Han's flower-beds, this summer.

2/23/82

Just had a long talk with Bill Ewert, about most things, but nothing special.

In touch with *Newsday* today. They'll give me $200 to write a thousand words on Whitman, based on some new book sponsored by the Ford Foundation. I don't mind at all. I'll have 3 weeks to do it. I feel as though money is flying in lately--$600, $1,350, $200 coming this spring.

Peter Stitt here tomorrow and Thursday. I actually look forward. Thursday will be exhausting, but I pretty much feel caught up on my work.

Han in better spirits today after getting some things cleared up at work.

I've sat here a long time dreaming about how to fill another inch of this page.

Let it go.

2/24/82

Last night I dreamed I was walking over by the school when I passed Tollers. He looked extremely old and weary. He had a letter I'd written him about Graver, and he was worried and said he'd get to it right away. I took the letter from him, and said, "Vince, no more," and ripped the letter up. He was very glad. When I walked away I turned back and asked him how his daughter was.

Will leave to play ball in a half-hour.... Read several journals this morning. Anne Berleant's is good. Maybe she'll be a new "young saint" around here.... Li-Young sent me an amazing letter. He thinks I'm a master, I guess. I sure ain't. But I sure have potential. The competitive anger I often feel in games & things—basketball can be a way away from that. I'm trying to get to the point where I don't keep score, but just play.

Should have fun at the gatherings for Stitt today.

2/26/82

Yesterday morning, just before work, Han got a call from the old man in Nashville that her mother was apparently very sick—bed very early, no food, hallucinations. Han rushed home & called an ambulance & apparently her mother had a stroke, is even now worsening, apparently.... Billy will arrive home this evening, & maybe Han, too, just for overnight. Kristen very upset, of course. Anything can happen now. I feel angry about that stupid old man who no doubt let Mom's condition worsen without getting a doctor. He can't drive or talk to people or do anything. No one else like him.

Yesterday was busy & wild in other ways, too: after Stitt's visit the evening before I got about 2-3 hrs. sleep. Bomb scare in Hartwell canceled one class. Lunch in Dailey with Tollers & Gemmett and all. 3 hr. workshop last night—I read part of "Family Tree" and loved it.... Tony Rimore has been an especially good friend lately, and very helpful.... Judy Kitchen around with Stitt, & very emotional.

I'm doing little things to clear my desk. I may end up in Nashville this weekend.

2/27/82

I've been waiting a couple hours for Han to show up from her mother's this Saturday morning. I'm always worried when someone in the family is driving around. Her mother is not well, can't speak. I'll probably go to Nashville tomorrow with Han.

Billy & Ed & Brad here in my study as I write. We're watching the Georgetown/Conn. game.

2/28/82

I went to Nashville yesterday, back today. Kristen & I home alone.... Han's mom in bad shape—can't talk, no reflexes. She seems to see & hear us. Doctors can only wait to see. Kenny & Wolf & Pat and Kurt around. A sad scene, tough on Han, but she's doing okay. She'll probably come home day after tomorrow for at least a day or two.... Billy's back at Cornell—we had very little time with him.... Nora Studier & Mirko called this evening about Han's mom.... I look forward to playing ball tomorrow. Kristen and I will get along. I showed her some old letters Han & I had written to Han's mom before we were married & then when Han was pregnant with Billy & then when Billy was born. Kristen loved the letters.... It's only 9:30, & I'm going to bed soon.

March 1, 1982

Han just called. Her mother in bad shape, not alert today as yesterday, and needing very large amounts of anti high blood pressure medicine. Han may stay there all week, or return home tomorrow for a break, or go over to Wolf & Pat's for an overnight. Kris and I are doing okay, though Kris is very emotional about her grandma, and is bowed down with schoolwork at the same time.... I guess I have a feeling that Mom is not going to get better. Han said that in effect the blood pressure is being kept down artificially, so radical is the medicine she's getting. I think by Friday we'll know what the future is likely to be. Things look bad.

Played ball today. Then Tony & Al stopped over. I made an appointment with the President, will speak with him Friday morning about several things, mainly the Forum & Graver. Al, Tony, & I _won_ completely regarding that struggle. Now, I will tell the President what the struggle, now over, was really about, and it won't do Graver's DTP any good.

I've been working on the May 8th poem every day for a time, and today I drafted part of what might be a little piece for the *Ohio Review* symposium on free verse. Soon I'll be working very hard on the piece on Whitman for *Newsday*. Must take notes on the Perlman anthology, on Kaplan, and on the 3 volumes of Traubel that I've read. I want to do this work for my Transcendentalism course, in any case.

3/3/82

Han went back to Nashville & the Gowanda hospital after being here for a day for a mental break. I'll drive there Friday. Her mother is certainly not improving, & seems to be deteriorating. We've no idea what the situation will be in a few days or in a week or three.

I played ball today, and felt fine. It will be a _long_ day tomorrow, & then I'll have that meeting on Friday morning with the President—then I'll be off to Nashville.

A crazy situation developed between Li-Young & Tony Rimore regarding a, gulp, an obscene phone call. I've never seen anything like this. A bizarre occurrence, and I'll have to stay out of it.

I'll look forward to Han's call this evening, and I'll call Billy late to tell him of the War Memorial game, and of Grandma.

3/6/82

Kris & I back from Nashville, after being there overnight. Han will be home later, too, and begin to teach again. No help/hope for her mother. It's just a matter of time. She's unconscious, has suffered irreversible brain damage. It could be any time, or a matter of months, I suppose. Kristen took seeing her very well, and it was good that she went, and said goodbye.... Wolf & Pat were at the hospital, too. The old man is awfully low, of course, & now will have to spend some time by himself.

I spoke with Van de Wetering yesterday—put it on the line about Graver—and all went well. Now Poulin will speak with him. If Graver gets the DTP, I'll be surprised.... Played ball yesterday, too.... The triple-A final is on TV tonight—Brockport vs. Mooney—and Han & I will watch it. Billy will be at the War Memorial, I guess, but will return to Cornell tonight. Kristen will go to the game.... I've much schoolwork to do, and am tired now from the hospital & driving, but will stay with it tomorrow. Want to do the thousand words on Walt, too.

The Lee-Rimore-Marchant thing got crazier. I'm done with it.

I feel clear, & will feel clearer once I get some things done. A slight headache. I'm anxious for Han to get home safely.

3/7/82

The three of us have been inside today. I touch Han & talk to her & console her often. She's emotionally exhausted. Mom is the same, or a little worse today. It's a rough deal.

We didn't go to the Rock gathering today. I haven't seen Bill for months. I don't want to worry about my relationship with him. We were never really close.

I've been writing letters of recommendation, dropping notes to people, getting my desk cleared away so that I can get to the two things on my mind now: the *Newsday* review and the poem for the inauguration. In some ways, though I've written a few things and done some reading, I've marked time all winter. And the weather is depressing.

3/8/82

Played ball twice today—game against college varsity girls this evening. Went to meeting. Worked on a couple of poems this morning, not getting very far. Now my week of work begins again. I did write another few hundred words on Whitman last evening.

Mirko & Bohdan called. They're making a big deal out of the Rochester exhibition. I'd better plan a good talk.

Poulin happy as shit about the Writers Forum. He called to say that we've now got Graver right where we want him. Al has an appt. with the President in a couple of weeks, too.... Al got a sad note from Archie—Ada's knee, Archie's elbow....

Han's mom same, opened her eyes only briefly today. It was good for Han to go to work today & get her mind off things for a time.

A good film on about Viet Nam.

3/12/82

It's Friday. Some breathing space. I went out with some of the students in my class last night to Barber's. Bill Stewart & Joe Winnick & Mirko were there. Much fun. Played ball today. Am relaxing now, & waiting for energy to return so I can get to some things.

I'm down to read my paper at the MacLeish symposium, & have decided to stay there two days, so I won't be reading my poem at the investiture here. Had to make that decision. I hope Archie is well enough to feel very loved at the gathering & that he'll be there to do the things he wants to. I'll fly there, & come back with Piccione & Vallone & Agte, looks like.

Han's mom the same. We'll drive there tomorrow.

I have a copy of the catalogue for the Rochester exhibition. It's a knock-out. And many people will be at the opening.

I'm close to finishing my Whitman review.

Poulin off to North Carolina for a week today.... Letter from Bill Elkins. He & Ro are divorced, and he's to marry again, & is looking for another job.

In the 40s today, the driveway ice melting away.

3/14/82

Finished the Whitman review and have it ready for the mail.

Still blowing and shining today. The old ice is melting & flowing down the ditch.

Talked to Billy today. He'll probably meet me in Rochester Friday.

I find myself marking time until the events of this spring. I'll arrange tomorrow for my May 7 flight to see Archie.

We saw Han's mom yesterday. No change. She's unconscious. Eyes glazed and dead under the closed lids. The trip was a good chance for me & Han to have a long talk about the whole situation. Some of Wolf's hard-headedness & unreason beginning to come through.... Old man Drachowski is an extremely sad case.

3/17/82

I've spent several hours reading student journals the last couple of days. Finally, finished them.... So, I'm all set for school tomorrow, which should be easy—I'm showing the Roethke film, the Ginsberg tape, and the evening class will break early to see Carolyn Kizer.

A woman wrote to use my Bly essay in a U. of Michigan book.... *Upstate* took "Along This Water" and will give me sixty bucks—should be a nice spread.... Mirko will read my poem at the inauguration while I'm at Greenvale.... Nice note from Archie today about the flowers Tony & Al & I sent.... I'm nervous about the big deal of a gathering at Rochester on Sunday. I'll drive in on Friday to see the exhibit & sign catalogues....

Han's mom is the same. So much action here this weekend—U. of R., Billy's visit, Kris's sweet 16 party Saturday—that we feel funny not getting to the hospital, though Mom is completely unconscious. Maybe Han will go Friday, or I'll go with her early next week.

Good letter from Don Justice, cursing Graver, and with some nicely inscribed books. About Graver I haven't thought for 30 seconds in several days.

May have finished a couple of poems the other morning. My other one about my unborn children, and the one about the "Angel Hour."... Would like to finish the inauguration poem....

Beautiful letter from Vince Clemente lately. He is all soul.

Kris 16 yesterday. She's a beauty, & happy, & has a vivid personality.... Will call Billy tonight....

3/20/82

Well, tomorrow is the big day. I was at U. of R. yesterday, signing/writing out poems in catalogues with this ink.... I haven't definitely decided what I'll read/say, but will this evening or in the morning. The leather & cloth catalogues are beauties. The exhibition looks great. Still, I'll be glad when this whole exciting spring becomes a quiet summer.

Han was in Gowanda/Nashville yesterday. Mom is the same, never opened her eyes.

Sat in front with Kizer the other evening. Didn't get much of a chance to talk with her during the evening, but was not anxious to. I like her, despite her dreary influence-tracing paper.

Bob Phillips called to get an address.... Bob Gemmett tells me my sabbatical has gone through. Wonderful. The only worry is money. But I'll raise enough extra here and there to at least pay the mortgage.

3/22/82

It was quite a day yesterday. I'll never forget it. My books shone in their cases. 150-200 people milling around & gawking. And I never read better. Dinner & party later. I've been decompressing all day. I'll always have the catalogue to remind me.

Gerry Stern was there, and I'll see him here Wednesday.... Met George Parsons.... Wolf & Pat & Kurt showed up, & Barbie Rundell. Tony Hecht was there and very nice. Many neighbors. President Van de Wetering, George Ford, Mirko & Irma & Manny & Helen & Greg & Rod & young poets. Many strangers. Katherine Burski (Kearney).

This will be a very busy week, and I'd better see about arrangements for May 7-8, and the South Carolina business.... Monday I drive to Jamestown for a reading, two readings....

Letter from Bill Ewert today.... I owe so many letters. I feel lazy as hell. It's too early to be marking time toward sabbatical!

3/27/82

Billy & Kurt & Mackie here in my study, watching NCAA basketball with me. A good dinner to look forward to later. At last, after busy & crazy days, some breathing space. I've been sending out a few catalogues, catching up on busywork. Will be away reading in Jamestown & Olean Monday & Tuesday, & don't mind, & will clear about $700, and get away from Brockport.... This journal especially vapid lately, but my life has been a surface one. But my sabbatical was approved, and I'll spend a year facing myself. If I don't discipline myself, I'll make myself miserable and be restless all year.

Gerald Stern here the other night. I like him and his poems. He's going to Iowa next year.

I got the letter/vita done for the South Carolina business.

Li-Young & Donna left town.... Gary Eddy stopped in the other night at the workshop.... Tony Piccione drinking much lately.... Al happy as a clam after his talk with the President.... Next, I have to settle my paper & trip to MacLeish. And finish the President's poem (make me feel like a hack, unless I write a good one). I hope Han can get to Myrtle Beach with Kristen. I'll spend a week, if the weather is willing at last, in the cabin.... I'm still decompressing after the ego excitement of the exhibition. Peter sent the other catalogues for signing, and I have a good number as my own now. I hate to give these cloth ones away at all, but will, to some of the writers. I think there will be a piece in the papers by Stephanie Coulsen next week on the exhibition. I said no to having a photographer out here today, and I'm glad I did. Fuck, I'm still nowhere as far as fame goes in this country, and always will be. But, fortunately, I've had a taste of recognition/attention, enough to know that I don't want that but am happiest just working on poems. The exhibition is good, though, and I'm not sorry about it. The catalogue makes it all worth it. Wish, though, I'd had more time—I'd have done more high-spot miscellaneous books.

This is a great day, the house filled up with young people. We went to Kristen's concert. She's wonderful, getting better & better with her clarinet, and through that, happier. We're all so damned fortunate (that oxymoron sometimes makes sense, too, when this good life bores us) here in this time, this place.

3/31/82 (evening)

Bill Ewert just called. Long talk about many things, nothing special. He received his batch of catalogues from U. of R. today, and likes them very much, as I do.

Kristen leaves very early in the morning for her music trip to Nashville, Tenn. Han & Billy & I will leave for Nashville, NY on Friday.... Billy & I played ball today. Dick Mancuso was back.

Snow gone. Rain today. I walked back & checked the cabin, which is in fine shape. Someone walked off with some of the lumber from my little bridge, though.

My readings in Jamestown & Olean went very well. I met good people who will be in touch with me about other readings—Lynn Matson, Charlotte Martines, Doug Carlson took good care of me. That small branch of JCC in Olean—such a cozy & moving & interesting place. They even bought about 15 Vanguard books. A good trip—ate shrimp & red snapper dinners, and am even $650 richer.

4/5/82

    I'm back in the cabin, and will leave this journal back here now for a long time, maybe all the way through my sabbatical year.
    It's Saturday. Kristen is in Nashville. Han and Billy are off to Grandma's. It's raining, and gusting. Water flowing in the ditch, but the cabin is high and dry.
    The inauguration poem is on my mind, and I'll work on it today.
    Everything brown & beaten & sodden back here, but there are birds around, and it's April. I haven't been back here for any writing in several weeks. Today, the year turns for me again. Argentina-England fighting over the Falklands, nuclear fear in the air (I read of a new cloth that can protect us, if we're in a shelter, from the neutron particles during fallout), dioxin at high levels in Lake Ontario, and always the starving countries—still I'm back here in my own life trying, wanting to believe in poetry as a help for someone. I need the widest vision, a religious vision, maybe. This is just talk. Maybe *Swastika*, at least, does something.
    I'll fly to Boston May 5th, & hope Ewert will pick me up. Will miss one day of classes. Class next Tuesday, and then vacation. My life is blessed. Ha, as I wrote that, a cardinal began its song somewhere off to my left, maybe staking the place out.... Well, let's take a look at that poem.

    Later: I went inside for lunch, and now have been back here again, reading *The Chestnut Rain*. This morning, I moved the inauguration poem ahead, made good progress. But mainly I've been thinking that I'm tired, have no real ambition, don't feel like working on *CR*, don't even anticipate wanting to finish it. This is all teaching fatigue, I think. Once school is out, I won't push myself, but will gradually enter the new world. Maybe to begin with this summer, I'll push the novel ahead, as last summer, I wrote those stories to loosen up. Right now, though, I don't feel like doing anything, not even mailing the catalogue to Jack Matthews & Bill Stafford, not even sending the Christmas poem to Bill Ewert. Years ago, I would have jumped to do such things, to send out new finished poems, to correspond & type & review. I'm past 40, yes, but still think this is the fatigue of talking about literature.
    Roy Winnick sent xeroxes of three letters that he'll use in the MacLeish collection.... I just read *Public Speech* and want to write Archie, to show him my soldiers section, Schwartz & Waskow) of *CR*. But I won't. I'm tired. I'll go in now to watch basketball & boxing & to wait for Han & Billy. Will come out here tomorrow again....

4/10/82

    A winter storm hit hard after my last entry. Today, the snow is still melting, and we expect 50°, at last. This has been the worst fucking winter.
    Billy is back at school, and Han & Kris are on their way to Myrtle Beach. I'll be alone for a week, and plan to spend much of the time back here. I *do* feel, now, as though I have some energy, and being alone will be good for me, too. Last evening, as I was just about to come back here, Mirko called for a card game, so I went over—Gary & Inger & Mouganises were there—and won about $30 after being down forty. From here on this next week until I visit Billy for his birthday, I'll play basketball a few times but otherwise don't even want to see anyone else.
    A strip of tarpaper roofing blew off the cabin. No big deal.
    Went book-hunting in Rochester with Bruce & Tony Vallone the other day, & found some good things, including a fine copy in dj of *Five Young American Poets* (1941) for only $7.50!
    Han's mom still about the same. I hope she stays stable the next couple of weeks.
    Now it is time.

    Later: Well, I seem to have managed to finish a first draft of all three sections of the investiture poem. Will type it up, & stare & stare at it over this next week, and then get together with Mirko on it, read it with him several times. He'll glory in the whole occasion!
    Stopped at Al's for a minute after picking up some milk. He seems okay except, as always, for the shaking, & cigarettes, & coughing.

I feel very good about today. Maybe will come out back again this evening. I hope Han calls later to say they've arrived safely.

Seems to be getting windy again.... The pines along the line have weathered the winter well.

We got a call from Germany from Sigrid & Helmuth—well, they'll be here for a week beginning June 2. They're good folks, & we owe them, and will show them a good time.

I've written Bill Ewert & sent him "The Spruce in Winter." I hope he likes it for our next Christmas card.

I keep fooling with those little "Zen" poems that I came to while reading Lucien's new book.

There was an announcement about the American Academy & Institute of Arts & Letters prizes in one of the NYC papers. Elise Goodman sent me a clipping.

Postcard from Billy: he got 120 out of 120 points on a physics exam.

I'll carry the typewriter out here tomorrow, too.... Suddenly, now that that nagging poem is virtually done, I have all sorts of time on my hands, hoorah.

4/12/82

Good talks with Han & Billy last night. Han & Kris made it safely—it's in the 70s there, at least.

Played ball today. Read May Sarton's *The Small Room*—some excellent things in it. Might come back out here to the cabin again after supper. It will be good to be out here at night again, working on poems. Mirko & Al called yesterday, wanted me over, but it's nice to go through days without company.

The Argentina-Britain Falklands affair is on hold, it seems, for now.

A couple inches of snow again yesterday, all of it running off today.... Cardinals, grackles, robins sailing past the cabin.

Looks like I'll visit Billy on Friday. He'll already be home from Cornell, and his first year of college, in about a month. It seems impossible that time has gone that quickly since that sad and happy day that we dropped him off last August.... I've been thinking a great deal lately, too, about what kind of a father I've been for Kristen. She's closer to Han, & naturally so, but we're close, too. She's her own girl, has her own mind, will always comfort us in her thoughtful & loving ways.

Time for dinner. Think I'll drive up for hamburgers & fries today.

4/15/82

Half of April gone! Sun today, warmer, spring here at last, it appears.

Played ball, ate, am back here for 2-3 hours.... Talked books & had a couple of drinks & then breakfast at the diner with Bruce Agte last night. Keith Hafford around.

The investiture poem is done, & sent over to Ginny Studer.... Read May Sarton's *As We Are Now*. It made me choke up a few times, but I didn't like the ending.

Called Pop Drachowski last night. Dr. Hu called him to say that Mom had pneumonia. I still just want the days of Han's vacation to go by. We'll face Mom's situation when Han is back from Myrtle Beach.

4/16/82

Beautiful day, close to 70°.... I had a good couple of hours back here today. This evening, at ten, I'll go over to Mirko's to go over the poem with him. Tomorrow, I'll drive to Ithaca.... Han will call this evening, I suspect.

Letter from AAIAL telling me the $1,350 prize has been upped to $1,500!

I've had stomach pressure for a few days, but otherwise feel fine.

The MacLeish essay is in about as good shape as I can get it. Mainly I'll do schoolwork/Whitman work the rest of the vacation. May closing in on us fast, and I'm glad. School will be nuts the last few weeks. I'll try to be calm.

Sounds of big machines in the background, a grader, a house going up over on Barry Street. And this summer the Mosers will be grinding away next door at Bobby's new home, but leaves will be out and will soften everything.

Once in a while, I add a bit to *The Boulder*. Don't know if that will ever be anything.

My new poem, "At Gibbs Pond," is going to be a good one.... Now and then, I've picked up a section of *CR*. I look forward to working on that. I still have the (maybe) nonsense of a novel in my mind.... I wrote Archie & sent him "The Leaves" section of *CR*.... Letter from Jascha Kessler about some Greek anthology of American poets today. Yes, I'd like to be in that.... Al Poulin leaving May 6th for Greece for a few months.... I haven't yet heard from any of the people I sent the catalogue to.... Sent out a package of things for Bob Siegel today.... A young poet by the name of David Baker sent me his book.... My literary life is bits & pieces, like this paragraph, lately. The extended work will come with the extended year.... Nice note from John Brinnin the other day about the Bynner Prize—so he sold my books, what the hell!....

What should I do for supper tonight? If I were smart, I'd just have some cereal & toast.

4/17/82

Had a good day with Billy in Ithaca yesterday. I was dizzy from the trip, and got a headache while looking for books in the Cornell store & downtown, but felt better after dinner with Billy & Brad. So many thoughts & feeling going through me when I see him there at that place living that life. He's so <u>young</u>, was going to go to a party with friends when they got back at one in the morning, etc. And I become more & more sedentary (restless from time to time, yes, as now, when I think of going to the movies, or ...), and go to bed early.... Bought many books in Ithaca, Georgia Press poetry books on sale at Cornell (& some Ithaca House paperbacks), & various things in town. Got a dustjacket for my last remaining jacketless book in the Poets of Today series. Bought review copies of Knight, Orr, a proof of Booth, a fine copy of Matthews' *Bitter Knowledge* for a buck. Got a little sick of books, know myself enough not to worry much about this—I spend much time on the collection, yes, but <u>can't</u> spend very much steady time working on lyric poems—but I will slow down over the next year. It's wonderful to have books on hand, though, for when I happen to run into people.... Eberhart books back today, two with holograph poems. Those books with holographs are the ones that most stun me now.... May Sarton wrote to say yes—Bill Ewert & I will visit her on May 5th.

Spoke with Han yesterday. They're on their way back, will arrive tomorrow, will be rushed to get ready for school.

So, it's a Saturday evening and all's well. I'll spend a couple hours back here now.

Went to Pylyshenkos' two nights ago for chicken soup, & to go over the investiture poem. Many laughs.... Tomorrow is their Easter.

Poulin dropped in for a minute today about nothing special. He leaves in 2½ weeks, about the same time I leave for Boston & Ewert & Sarton & MacLeish.

Windy, warm—rain much of the day—spring here.

4/19/82

Morning. I'm back here for a couple hours.... Han & Kris back happily & safely, with light tans. All's well. They spent ten days laughing and having fun. It was good for them to get away from me.

Today, spring is <u>truly</u> here. It's warm & sunny. Many birds. The honeysuckle around the cabin is tinged green.

Because both my wrist-watches are broken, and because I want to go play ball at about 11:30, I brought my travel clock back here—the first time I've heard a clock ticking back here, and I don't like it much. I'll put it outside, and glance at it later.... There.

Bruce stopped over last evening, and I dropped him off later & looked at his books. He's now <u>hooked</u> as a collector.... He has many unsettled years in front of him.

Greg Fitz Gerald's party tonight. I'll stop in for a while. Schoolwork this afternoon & evening & tomorrow morning. Now, will look at some poems.

4/21/82
9:30 a.m.

    Bruce just called to say that he'd heard on a Canadian station that Archie died last night. I've come out here with a cup of coffee and my copy of *Riders on the Earth*. My mind's a muddle and I haven't felt grief yet. Relief for him, and, somehow, even for me—hard to explain. Worry about a father who was in pain. I feel free, now, in some way—so rich because I knew him a little and have his books and letters (I'll never receive another of his notes, will never send another package to him). Honeysuckle is unfolding around the cabin. I just read his 1975 letter to me that's in the catalogue. We were part of his journey, as he wrote to me & Han in his *Continuing Journey*. What a life he had (Yale, Paris, Washington, Conway) and now has, in the poems, in the upcoming books of letters & the biography.... You're going to be with me, Archie, when I write, a presence, a gentle & loving & wise presence—as old as I get.... I don't really feel grief. It's not as though he were wrenched away before his time, or unexpectedly. I think now of Ada.... Did I write about Archie in my journal when he visited Brockport some years ago? Probably. I have vivid memories. He rested on the couch in my study, had dinner at our oak dining room table. I remember packing him down with books & jam at the airport. I'm glad I sent him the last letter I did, a week or two ago, with "The Leaves" section of *CR*, & saying I'd been reading *Public Speech*. I hope he got it, had a chance to read it.... The May 7-8 symposium will still be, I'm sure, but will be much different. Maybe, in some ways, less worried and somber. Walt 1819-1892. Archie 1892-1982.... <u>He</u> got me my Guggenheim, probably, and supported me in many ways. That letter about *Swastika* made me weep. Such a large-hearted and -mannered man. I hope I, too, comforted him a little as he was a comfort to me, just by being there, as he still is.

4/23/82

    Friday, time to catch our breath here. Han will travel to Gowanda/Nashville tomorrow to clean for the old man, & check on lost Mom, etc.
    Classes went okay yesterday. I seemed to be less tired after the night class than usual. Not much of the semester left. I look forward to my May 5th flight and connecting with Bill Ewert.
    Archie much on my mind. An article about him & me in the paper yesterday. Wish <u>I</u> could have written it.
    Feel close to Al & Tony with this, too. Al leaving May 6th for 3 months in Greece.
    Strange talks with Tama Baldwin last night about Peter Marchant & Li-Young & that whole bizarre scene.

4/24/82

    Saturday. Han is at her mother's, Kristen is at a dance marathon. I've been floating around today. Did do some work back here this morning, but spend much time killing time during the day. Don't seem to have much stamina for or interest in a long project. Well, spring makes me restless always. Maybe tomorrow, yes, I'll do some raking, & maybe some tilling, to please my soul.
    Someone set several grass fires along the street about 11:30 last night, including one about 50 ft. from the cabin. Han just happened to see it when she was closing the curtains last night. I hate to have to worry about this cabin, my manuscripts—I'd better keep duplicates of the finished *CR* sections inside. I'm not really worried. A kid's prank, like the taking of my "bridge" beams. I'd like to catch the brat, though.
    It's just past seven in the evening now, and darkening. I love it back here.
    Paula Clossen said to me the other night that she was reading Jim Wright's *The Journey*, and got half through it, and got tired of it, and all poets/poetry seem about the same these days. I know what she means. Yes, being ingenious I can talk all day, say, about a good poem, but it <u>is</u> as though poetry's possibilities are limited—MacLeish, Wilbur, Stafford, it doesn't matter. Whitman is wonderful & amazing, but if I truly loved his work wouldn't I be reading <u>it</u> more often, and not things <u>about</u> him and it? And I know I have feelings in the back of my mind (I'll let that stand) that maybe in my own work I won't be able to do something different. The words can get to sound the same, my romantic bent coming out in poems from Agte & Vallone, e.g. (not very good poems yet), the moods & vocabulary. Yes, I keep trying to do more in the same veins, have found words like "intertinged" & "transluminous" to help carry me again to the same place. And, yes, *CR* will be

damned good. But after that what? Am I just in a rut? I have in mind a long & "obscure" poem to be called *1854*. I can always hold to the faith that technique (not prescribed but technique or process) can make everything new always & always.

Telegram from Ohio University saying I'd won a medal for excellence in poetry, an alumni award. Letter to follow. Looks like I'll be in Athens November 4th!

Read Archie's *The Irresponsibles* again last night. I seem to come awfully close in my prose piece in *The Trains* to what he says there.

I shaved today. I had about a two weeks' beard, just for fun. Didn't like the feel of my chin.

The sky is aqua to blue. "Archie, dark falls around my cabin. / Beyond it, a sky of aqua and blue. / Since you died, the world's the same. / My friend, I'm just as close to you." I'll want to write Ada very soon.

May 2, 1982

A Saturday. Overcast today, but in the 60s & no rain.... Very busy lately. I've even done some yardwork & have cleaned up back here, laying the new little bridge on blocks, tilling that bumpy spot off to the right (my poor milkweed may be done for!).... Great class Thursday night, then joined Greg & Rod at Casey's for drinks.... Stopped at Dept. party briefly.... Dropped some textbooks off at Lift Bridge for sale or trade.... Will try to patch cabin roof tomorrow morning.... Played ball Friday, & enjoyed it. Bright new sneaks, the best I've had.... Received $60 from *Upstate*. "Along this Water" to appear in two weeks.... Getting greener back here.... I leave for Boston etc. in four days.... Note from Van de Wetering that he liked the poem.... Britain beginning to hit the Falklands hard.... Property beginning to be beautiful all by itself, grass & flowers covering over the remains of winter.... Very depressed letter from Martin Booth. He says he's giving up writing, period.... A couple of calls from Bill Ewert.... Tony Piccione in such bad shape with his back, that it's doubtful he'll make the MacLeish symposium. I just refuse to worry about my connection home, etc.... I want to be serious, & be inside my poems & the art/music/dancing on May 12th, which increasingly becomes some kind of social circus. I may have to be very anti-social until after the reading.... Kristen missed school all week with a virus. Hope she'll be better by Monday.... Han's mother weighing her down, and her father, of course, that sad old son-of-a-bitch.... My stomach rumbles after a big dinner, but mainly the strawberries for dessert.... Spring is amazing again, the warmth, the new growth on the spruce trees, the honeysuckle leaflets beginning to hide me back here....

May 10, 1982

It's Monday evening. On Wednesday I'll do the Holocaust reading. I've been back here thinking about it. I have a few remarks ready, and a list of poems.

I've written notes about my trip in a small notebook, but want to recollect a few things here.

The Ewert home is a warm and wonderful madhouse. I was constantly looking for cover from the kids and two cats and two dogs. Bill & Mary had a gathering for me one evening—talks with Ed Hendry & Bert Babcock & others. Bill & Barbara White & I visited May Sarton, who received us warmly with champagne. She has a strong & pleasant voice. I bet she gives fine readings. She inscribed books, and spoke of Archie, choking up. I saw her stone phoenix in a corner of the garden, and, miracle of miracles, a hummingbird flew to a branch near us all when we arrived—none of us had ever seen one perch that way.... I'll remember that living room in which we sat, and the daffodil-spotted vista down to the sea. May had just turned seventy a day or two before. She was kind to me. I kissed her twice, told her I was glad she was well now & writing & centered in her life after some very hard years. I like that woman very much.

Tony Vallone & Bruce Agte came to Ewerts', and the three of us drove down to the MacLeish Symposium. I've so many memories, most of them gratifying. The only negative thing was that I thought that fellow Drabek was rude to me a couple of times.... My paper went very well—I don't think it was my imagination that it was received the warmest of any. I was moved when I read it.... Time with Bill Meredith & his sister Kay. A brief & awkward "meeting" with Robert Penn Warren. Sat through some dreadful lectures—Wallenstein the phoniest & worst. Don Hall there, & stars like Schlesinger & Galbreath on the last day, & that beautiful old man Henry Steele Commager. I felt so close to Archie much of the time. Saw the small collection in their library. Saw slides that brought the Conway home home to me. Met Roy Winnick—maybe the happiest thing of the whole gathering was his joy when I gave him the March 14, 1982 letter from Archie: it turns out he needed a 1982 letter, & the book will end on this one to the three Brockport poets.... The editor of the *Mass Review* introduced himself to me via Dick Wilbur. He said he found out Graver was <u>sick</u>.... Paul Mariani, author of a biography of Williams, came up to me, too. So, so many warm things, though my little journal will probably show how nervous I was, mostly over finding the right spot to present our goddamned Forum award. Finally pressed it into the hands of Archie's son, William, who had come up to me the evening before in Old Deerfield and thanked me for what I'd said about his Dad.... Got back at 2 in the morning. Home now. Now to get through the Wednesday reading, the last day of classes, house guest(s), the nervous trip to NYC next week, getting in final grades, etc.

Mowed the lawns yesterday, & everything is lush & beautiful. Han's flowerbeds outdo themselves hour by hour.... Billy is home for a few days before going back for a few days for finals. Han has a cold but is otherwise well. Her mom is the same. Kristen got an A & A+ in her clarinet competitions the other day.

I've been writing letters, a flurry of them to Hall & Wilbur & Meredith & Booth & Ewert. Have many others to do.

Played ball again today. It was good to run again.

Mirko said he "killed them" when he read my poem at the Investiture. Good report from Bill Stewart, too. I'd like to have a first-class broadside done of the poem.

Look forward to "Along this Water" in *Upstate* this Sunday.

Time to go inside. Recording some of my life like this is a good feeling, almost a relief. I'm not sure why. Mainly, I think, the pleasure of writing <u>something</u> each day, and it is sometimes the turn of this journal. I have no ambitions for it. It feels especially good to move this blue ink across the page—it flows nicely on this paper.

May 12, 1982

It's two in the afternoon. I'm in the cabin, & will plan my reading for this evening. Warm, deep talk with Reneé this morning. I'm glad she's staying with us. Tonight will be very special for all of us. I hope to be true to myself & the spirit of the poems. Gwendolyn Watson, too, is alive and unpretentious and good to be with. The theatre will be filled—400. Many people will be there who have never gone to a poetry reading, or dance concert, or art exhibit....

Reneé mentioned that to her "I Dream of Justice & Happiness" is an affirmative poem. I know that for me, intentionally at least, I ended the poem darkly, showing in nature the existence of things thought justifiably dead & gone. For her, the world is alive, & untainted at the end. There are other ways to hear it, too, I suppose.... Reneé <u>does</u> speak the words as she dances. I'm glad.

Drizzling slightly now. I'm glad.... Billy left for his last few days at Cornell.... Jerry Mazzaro will probably show up this afternoon....

The backyard flowers are so beautiful, the tulips rising above the banks of forget-me-nots. The birds all seem so friendly this year, and unafraid, as I walk back here.

Tonight, then, and then last day of classes tomorrow. Journals to stay with, & a trip to Han's mom this weekend. Then our NYC trip. Egads. I want to enjoy these things as I live them, but also want to get through them & get to wide, free spaces this summer, as I will. And to think of the luxury of a sabbatical year.

I'm somehow apprehensive about looking over my poems to see which ones I'll read. I keep dawdling over this journal—another of its uses: allowing me to talk to myself as I find the right inner moments to do things.... Now it is time.

May 14, 1982

Friday, early evening. In a half-hour I'll go inside to read some journals to the accompaniment of a film. Classes done. Grades to get in. I will not now have to teach for about 15 months (except for one week in June). Imagine. Meanwhile, Tony Piccione will go through a bunch of shit to try to get <u>his</u> sabbatical.

The *Swastika* evening went very well. It was all I hoped it would be, and more. I thought Reneé & Gwendolyn were wonderful. I was amazed that someone knew & felt my poems as Reneé did. Still, I've heard many negative comments about the dancing. But Reneé is a wonderful woman, and I was knocked over by the whole thing. The music/dance of "The Tree" & *Ewige Melodien* was "beautiful" & moving. I was stunned.... So many people there, including president, provost, deans. And last night at ten a call from Adam LaZarre, who wants to drum something up to send to SUNY units. I told him of my loyalty to Reneé & Gwendolyn, and of my upcoming sabbatical. Adam's straining to be appointed one of the 3 new deans by June 20th, a spot Gemmett wants, too. I don't want me or my poems to be used by politicians. The president mentioned to Adam how the *Swastika* event should get around, & Adam took the hint quickly, too quickly.

Mazzaro was unbelievable again, could only say, after the performance, that Reneé mispronounced words. He's so sick, in his own way.... Milton Kessler there, gracious & kind. He has problems, too.... The exhibition by Marx/Wolsky strong, very strong. Reneé & I went to see it the next morning again, & Jack was there, and we had a nice talk.

I've read better, but did okay.

Cocktails at Van de Weterings' today. They were both very nice to me. I'd hate to get on Maxine's wrong side. Pshew, she's tough & unafraid. I love her. She cut a poor bastard apart right in front of me, saying she'd heard his joke, telling him to stop dripping his drink on her oriental rug!... Spent my time at the party talking to Warren Fraleigh, Mike Osier, Tom Markussen.

Well, I can breathe again. Will go with Han to Nashville/Gowanda tomorrow, alas.

Uncle Eric had a lung-cancer operation. Don't know how this will affect Helmuth's trip here in a few weeks.

Teaching done, teaching done. Now, journals, grades in, the NYC trip, & I'll be home free. A mountain of mail on my desk to answer. All in good time.

Han saw a scarlet tanager yesterday. I saw an evening grosbeak, I believe.

May 22, 1982 (Saturday)

It's raining. Everything deep green and hidden back here. Cool—I've turned on the heater for a few minutes to take the chill out. I've never been happier. I'm home with the kids after a dizzying & memorable trip.

Han & I arrived in the city on Tuesday at rush-hour, connected with Evelyn at Vanguard, and took busses with her to her apartment at 135 Central Park West. Then we rushed off to Kay Meredith Keast's party over on the East side—only about a dozen people there, but these included the Jacobsens, Francis Steegmuller, Shirley Hazzard, William Maxwell, and the Kennedys (he the Iran hostage, she the woman I'd seen so often on television, spokesman for the "Free the Hostages" movement). William there too, of course, & Richard Harteis.

Next day, the awards gatherings. I met for the first time William Jay Smith, David Shapiro, Richard Lattimore, Howard Moss. Said hello again (sometimes after not seeing them for years) to Nemerov, Wilbur, Kinnell, Merwin, J.J. Sherwin, Hollander, Merrill, Brinnin, etc. Joyce Oates sat between Han & me at lunch, and Josephine Jacobsen was on my left. It was a rich bash. I felt generally comfortable. Arthur Schlesinger, Jr. gave me the $1,500 check. Before going onstage, I saw Wm. Maxwell again—apparently the evening before, after Han & I left, a small group at the party had been reading my poems. What praise! I couldn't believe my ears. He introduced me to Glenway Westcott, who told me to write him & he'd send me his book of poems. Here & there I was close to the big stars—Mailer, Updike, Bernstein, etc.—but didn't go out of the way to meet them. Much talk with Ray Smith, and with Joyce over lunch—apparently she & Evelyn are so uncomfortable in one another's presence that they all avoided the reception later on. I got three stories (Joyce's, Bob Phillips', Evelyn's) about why three of my poems that Joyce selected for an anthology wouldn't be in it. The monies involved & who ignored whose letter I don't know. I got caught in the middle, & I'm sorry, & wd. have liked to have been in the book.... Little talk with Evelyn about future projects. She's a wonderful, generous, eccentric soul, but also a canny businesswoman, & careful. Apparently, she's trying Carcanet press on *Swastika*, or something.

Disappointed in meetings with Wilbur, who was drinking fast, & Brinnin. Warm meetings with others. A million stories milling around among those at the reception regarding their relationships with one another.

I felt more comfortable than I thought I would. So glad Han was there—we'll be remembering always the faces, the scene.... Annie Wright there & seeming fine.... Charlee Wilbur there & very friendly.... Warm chat with Mark Strand—we have Stewe Claeson in common.... Yesterday, a small ad in the *Times* from Vanguard congratulating me on the Bynner award. I don't know the ins & outs of how I got it, but Joyce was mainly responsible, I'm sure.... Harold Bloom acting the ass.... Met Calisher & Curt Hartnack.... Brief meeting with May Swenson.... Claire White there. Brief meeting with Stanley Kunitz, Eberhart. Enough!

Dinner that evening at Evelyn's with Tom & Elizabeth Woll & Tom's folks & Bob Phillips.

Evelyn's huge apartment: well, impossible to describe, its antiquity & run-down warmth & the views of Central Park & Manhattan.

Next day, shopping for books—Strand, a couple of Barnes & Nobles—then Bloomingdale's etc. for Han—a big rush, catching up to Bob at work for tickets to *A Chorus Line*, rushing back to change, catching a lucky cab in the rain at Grand Central after Bob's tip, seeing Broadway & the play (charms for children) & walking Times Square with Han. Bought a $13.50 cheesecake (!) for Evelyn at Lindy's.

Home at last. All that now a part of us. Too much of everything, & too much rush. Glad to be here where I can write & take chances without being self-conscious, as I wd. be in NYC. I've seen enough writers. Back to home & the kids & the honeysuckle in bloom now. Will go to dance concert this evening, & commencement tomorrow, but I feel calm. Grades about ready to turn in.

Billy doing well with his new job in the grocery store.

Boxes of books coming from the City. Chores next week, but I'm home, hoorah.

Must mention that Sandi & Tony Piccione were here. Tony got a letter from China, offering him some sort of spot for next year. He went to see Van de Wetering in a hurry. Much nervousness & confusion. Sandi seems at her wits end. Tony's back painful. Lisa coming home.

I want to write Mike Waters & Al a letter about the MacLeish Symposium, etc. So much mail to answer. I'll keep clearing it away. Haven't even written O.U. yet to say I wouldn't attend the banquet in the fall.

Kristen is fine. Her big election for class president is Monday. I hope she wins.

My cabin roof-patch seems to be watertight.

Must chop the cable out of the ash tree the minute the weather clears.

Terrible news in the Falklands, the party-goer & literary personage & star-fucker adds as an afterthought.

May 26, 1982 (Wednesday)

Perfect day today, low 70s. I got up mid-morning, after drinking last night with Rod & Greg, sat outside a while, went to play basketball with Billy, ate lunch, went to dentist (ran into Graver there!), and came home to sit under the silver maple. Reading Paul Mariani's book. Pulled some weeds out of the raspberry patch. Will do yardwork tomorrow, all sorts of things, weather willing.

Grades in, desk clearing. The boxes of books from Barnes & Noble and The Strand arrived—I've been shelving them. Will putter in the study this evening. Life has arrived.

Turned down $75 to be on an awards panel in Ithaca. Add that to the $750 + $200 turned down for other things. Must stay clear & get to poems. Do have to report on the Dave Smith manuscript. Then, poetry all summer, or enough work on poetry so that I'll also feel comfortable working on the novel & reading a lot.... Helmut & Sigrid coming next Tuesday, we guess.

The cabin completely hidden now.

Kristen got her learner's permit. And she was elected junior class president for next year! What a kid.... Billy's job working out fine.... Han rushed but feeling okay. Yesterday was her mother's 68th birthday. That's all a sad story.

I did get around to writing a long letter to Mike & Al in Ios, Greece.

Dream of MacLeish last night. He was middle-aged & dressed sharply & walking down a hall to go teach. I was sloppy & out of shape & even having a hard time keeping my pants up. Classic dream after my night of drinking & other excess.

Han & Kris should be home soon from shopping. I'll walk back inside.

Saturday:

Memorial day parade today. I choked up again & again. Vivid memories of last year. The soldiers, the sun & shadows, the high school band, the thoughts of all the soldiers in Tacitus.

Finished the report for Illinois on Smith's *Assays*. As I read more & more, the book became more honest & impressive to me. He is some energetic son-of-a-bitch. Weaknesses here & there of thinking, a too-easy dismissal of some things such as surrealism, but a rolling & strong book. It doesn't try to be clever. It is natural. 2-3 mentions of me in there, and this buoys me up. I am competitive about making it into the top 20 or so of my generation, and getting into anthologies, etc. Many reasons: money, ego, anthologies added to the Heyen collection, etc. But because I feel, shit, if I'm ignored it is by accident & others' gamesmanship, & not because of my poetry, which is substantial & important. Why do I sound so dull & mercenary here? Fuck it, no games. I admire Smith, & care for him, though he will be attacked by sophisticates. I have the same worries about him that I have about me.... He's been loyal to me.

Letter from Ewert today, with $400 from Babcock. I'm pleased. I called Bill & we chatted.

I'm back here for only an hour or so. The quiet and isolation again amaze me. A cool evening. Billy at a party, Han & Kris inside baking cookies. Han & Billy will drive to Nashville tomorrow. I'll stay at home & do a few things & watch the Philly-L.A. game.

Letter from Sigrid today. They're coming, & will arrive in Rochester Tuesday evening. We're getting ready for them.

I let Kristen drive around a couple of parking lots at the college this evening.

We saw Boo this morning. She leaves for Greece in 3 weeks. Looks like Sandi will go, too!

I wrote Don Hall about the possibility of a Heyen book for his series. Should he say yes, it will be a thrill, & give me something to work on on the side next year. I'd do/fix up one piece at a time, until all done. Choices about what to put in it. I could make a book that I could use often in classes, too.

Bill Andrews called about the broadside he's working on.... Ewert going ahead with *Wenzel* and *The Cabin*. The latter will be a beauty, too, but damned expensive for one short sequence. Fuck it. Mine not to reason why.

Billy & I played basketball yesterday at the college, & love it.

No ant invasion in the cabin yet. I have my fingers crossed.

We've got to get the garden in soon now.

Smith's book makes me want very much to write true & beautiful poems. No formulas for this, but I must remain myself, I know, and not be afraid to take chances, & trust myself. I am so fucking smart, I know, leap in my mind levels deeper than Smith when he talks or Harold Bloom when I read a paragraph. Some deep balances in my mind, always the compensations of being able to go deeper & deeper feeling/seeing the other facets of any statement, immediately feeling the weakness or inconsequence or limitation of an argument. But I often don't even want to articulate my intuitions, my wordless knowledges. I respond quickly, in an instant, as though with one word in my mind, & know I could track down the thought & set the writer right that I'm reading, but don't want to. I remember reading that Edwards could & would methodically destroy even the simplest arguments—he could be a blunderbuss, dogmatic about the obvious. I won't retreat in what I've said here. My mind is extremely fast. I'm about the most intelligent person I've ever known—not the allusional intelligence of a Mazzaro or the art intelligence of an Ashbery, but a whip of an intelligence that cracks & leaves a cut in the air that closes over it. I know what I mean. So, I need the balls to allow this sort of intelligence to operate in my poems. Not that it does in *CR*. Not that I've let it so far in the other books. But something in the future, maybe.

A paragraph like the preceding raises all my old questions about the audience of my journal. I was half being honest, & half trying out an idea, a line, to see if it would catch somewhere. I swear I feel more godly than my poor words & sentences show. Right now, as this blue ink flows along, there is something round & golden & glorious & whole inside me, something that I am. I am so much rounder than the craggy & angular apparition I see when I look in a mirror, and so much deeper & more saintlike than this journal could make me appear. How could the fucking brutal & stupid writer of the journal have written those wonderful poems? And it's not just that the poems are artifice & this is all just first-draft scratching.... I've lost my thought.

Never mind anything else. It feels good to write here. It's a beautiful May evening during the 42nd year of my life. Some traces of me will exist here in this journal though I go inside & go to sleep.

6/1/82 (Tues.)

Helmut & Sigrid arrive tomorrow evening. We look forward.

Talks with my folks, & Werner, & Eddie the last couple of days. Eddie has been budgeted out of his teaching job—the poor bastard has had some struggle the last ten years.

Letter from Hall today who says, in effect, maybe to a book by me in the Michigan series.

Raining again today. Sat outside with Tony a couple of hours, though. He seems generally okay, but is on hold, & will be, on the China business.

I did draft a little talk for the banquet Sat. night. Will look at it again now. Am not sure how I feel about it.

6/9/82

Israel in Lebanon against P.L.O., & threat of wider war with Syria. English ready for final assault on Fort Stanley.... For better or worse, though, the world news will dissipate back here the next couple of hours. A cardinal is trilling away, & robins chirping.

It's been some week. Helmut & Sigrid here (leave tomorrow) and we've done so much. I took them in to the Rochester exhibition, & we had lunch at the Faculty Club.

We took them to the awards Banquet at the high school (my speech went over about as well as I'd hoped it would), and to Niagara Falls, & to Wolf & Pat's for a cook-out. Yesterday we all went to that great place Genesee Country Village. We've been busier than busy. Stopped at Pylyshenkos' last evening. Today, maybe, a drive to Picciones'. No one has a more carefree personality than Helmut. I can't imagine anyone I could get along with in the house as easy as I do with him. Sigrid is quiet & nice, but Helmut is special. Han & I have been having fun with German, too.... So, it's gone okay, but it's before eight in the morning, & I'm tired, but back here because I'm anxious to begin writing & getting back to the quiet life for a couple weeks before that workshop. There will be time. We don't even have our garden in yet, but still will.... So perfect back here.

Looks like Tony Piccione is definitely going to China.

Call to go to Oakland (Michigan) Writers Conference in the fall. Guess I will.

Billy's job upped to about 30 hrs. a week, hoorah. Han & Kristen just holding on until end of school.... I did play ball Monday & will again today....

6/12/82

Kristen's band banquet this evening. We're hoping Andrews will announce his retirement.

Raining now, mid-afternoon, & green & cool back here. Han & I finally got the garden in over a few hours this morning. I'm pleasantly tired.

Lost $180 at poker the other evening, just about what I'd won the last time. I played badly & got bad cards. I don't care much, & don't care to play much poker over this next year.

Helmut & Sigrid now with Tante Hanni. I miss them!

Letter from Peter Klappert, who likes my essay, more than likes it.

Babcock catalogue today with about 50 Heyen items in it.

I'm getting boxes of books ready again for Peter Dzwonkoski's visit on Tuesday.

This cabin is always as I leave it, always waiting for me when I'm ready.

Elm leaves pressed wet against the picture window.

Tony came over the other day & severed that cable that was killing a big ash tree at the back of the property. Damned nice of him.... Boo dropping over tomorrow for some sewing help from Han on a cloth for her showcase, or something.

Too many people in the summer workshop. What the hell.

Invited to Oakland U. in Michigan for a writers weekend in October. Will go.

Will ignore, for now, the request from Greenfield for my MacLeish paper.

In touch with George Cornell. He'll take over from here, & mount a Heyen exhibit at Brockport in the fall.

Dozens of people telling me & Han & Kristen how much they enjoyed my talk the other night. Hoorah: it's over with, & I did okay.

6/13/82

It's Sunday, eight in the evening. I mowed the paths today just beating the rain. Dripping and green around me now.

Bruce stopped by. I wrote a little of "The Light" in his copies of *The Snow Hen*, wrapped a couple of books. He gave me a copy of Plutzik's *Horatio* that he'd found in Kingston, Ontario. He stayed for pizza. We walked around the property. Bruce has had a good year, as good as my pines. He'll miss Lisa, <u>does</u> miss her already. I love those kids.

Boo was over for a couple hours. Sandi called. I called home, & then we called Sigrid & Helmuth at Kuhnels' to report that we'd found Sigrid's purse. A good day for me, the most free mentally in a long time. I just want things to go on like this, forever. Han & the kids are healthy and happy. I haven't heard the news today from the Falklands & Lebanon. Birds are singing their drizzle-songs around me. I love being back here as Brockport darkens.

Kristen's band banquet was another sentimental time for me last night.... She's a winner, was elected vice-president of the band. Han is the new secretary of Band Boosters. We're part of this town, the more so as we give more to it. I'm glad I did that speech last week.

Brother Eddie has a new teaching job, in Ohio, near Toledo. Wonderful news. He's had some hard knocks. Maybe this job will be his home at last.

I wrote a little entry for *The Boulder* inside last night, the first time I've not written it directly into the red book. I'll transfer it now and see how it sounds.

6/15/82

I just wrote Bill Ewert a decent letter for a change—this takes my journal energy away.... Suggested "The Berries" for the 1982 Christmas card. I think he'll agree.

A good day—Dzwonkoski visit, Kurt Greiner here, etc.—but I am feeling worried that I have no discipline to get down to solid work back here. Hell, I never <u>did</u> have discipline, but the books got finished. Poems/books won't be forced, I keep telling myself. And that's the truth, too. But the good life, this freedom <u>does</u> spoil me.

Like the Wilbur piece, all in all, for the hoped-for Michigan book. And with a change of title the *Death of a Salesman* piece will fit into my scheme. I'll go along slowly on that project. Wish I had a secretary to make some clean copies of things.

Kristen learning to drive, driving a little each day, *Oi Weh*!

6/16/82 (morning)

I sort of pushed myself to come out here last evening, but after writing in this journal did get one or two things done—a note called "Parable" about the ballplayer who is too fast to be effective (don't know if my intentions come through—I had in mind the fact that we can be awfully fucking deft & ingenious as critics as we say how something works, when it doesn't), and a note to accompany my poem "Literary Criticism." I have in mind these things for a section of the prose book I'll keep building.... So, I'm out here again this morning, did <u>not</u> carry *Angel of Light* back here to read, will putter into a paragraph or stanza or two. Do I have in mind to send Allen Hoey my three Jesus poems for a possible pamphlet?... Later, will play ball with Billy. I have a sore thumb from last time. Rainy day again. I don't care.

Han came in late & will be tired. She needs the summer off.

A dream about Kinnell last night. His face was thin and his eyes shone.... That whole week here begins to make me nervous.

6/17/82

Mirko called, and for better or worse there's a card game this evening. I'll give it another shot. I like to play, but not as much in the nice weather. It stops me from doing much the next morning, etc. But I could stand to win some money.

I read over my "Poets of the War" review. It's a good one. The "Poetry of Place" review not as good, but maybe usable.

Letters from Stafford & Claire White. Books from Vanguard—$188 worth of my own.

Tony visited, & we spent a couple good hours together.

Cleaned out the shed, walked & enjoyed the paths.

Kristen done with last test & school. Billy working. Han out with other teachers to celebrate near-end-of-school.

Got some typing paper today—a signal of my good intentions. I don't care. All I want to do is to play poker tonight & basketball tomorrow. I realized, last night as I watched *Night Line* as I usually do, that I'm sick of the news, sick of the Falklands & Lebanon and 10 yr. anniversary of Watergate, etc., etc.

6/21/82

Good day, good rhythm right now. Bruce & Tony Vallone & Ken Frank stopped over last evening. I like those chaps.... Got my annual report done, & it should lead to some merit money.... Books inscribed back from Robert Penn Warren. A thrill. He's corrected some typos in *A Place to Come To*, too. And the inscription in the Jarrell book is especially nice.... Yesterday morning I spent 2-3 hours drafting a quirky introductory talk for my workshop for next Monday.... 3 more days at school left for Han.... Corn, sunflowers, beans beginning to come up.... Terry Joseph here for dinner yesterday.... Fine letter from that angelic spirit Vince Clemente today.... Nephew Kurt coming again tonight.... Played ball with Billy today.... Intermittent showers, sun today.... I hope to have the energy to write a few decent letters this evening.... Card from Greg Orr today, inviting some poems for *VQR*. I'd sort of like to be in that magazine, but don't have much on hand other than *CR* in progress.... Darkening outside again.... I'm tired, and will go inside for my second cup of coffee of the day....

7/5/82

I want to remember this past week or so, but don't know how to begin even talking about it.

Han's mom died Friday evening, late. She was in the last stages, the doctor unable to get the i.v. in, and Han left suddenly on Wednesday. I had to stay here, finishing the workshop, etc., until yesterday morning. So, I had Plumly here, & the exhausting workshop, and about 20 people over every afternoon. Almost no sleep. Drinks until 1 or 2 every night, & up early. Workshop participants coming at me a dozen different ways, & Han not here, & me not there to comfort her as her mother died, when her mother died. I hated that. I tie it in, again, with this poetry business (which made me do the workshop) & drive for money. Stan seemed solid to me sometimes when here—good in workshop, a good friend—and sometimes secretive & slightly dishonest in his relationship with me, especially when he had his eye on a woman. He drank much & slept little & is anxious to come back here next year even though I won't do the workshop again. Kinnell & Wayne Dodd here, Kinnell exhausted & reading vacantly, Dodd reading very well & being warm. I like him. Anyway, I was wiped out, got very little sleep, got support from dear friend Bruce all week. I read well—read the 38th section of *CR*. Played ball 3 times, & chased around, & one evening Kristen got lost at Eastman, and twice I called brother Ed who is in hospital, & Bill Ewert called, and I kept thinking of Han, & Marchant fucked up the conference here & there, etc., etc.

Yesterday, at last, I broke away early with Billy & Kris for Nashville. Bruce took Stanley to airport. 6-9 in evening at funeral parlor, Mom's casket open. She looked fine, and I've become a believer in this kind of viewing, that peaceful image of her being the one we'll have. Billy & Kristen held up well in the presence of Grandma's corpse. Today, the funeral, & a family dinner in the restaurant Mom used to work in. I was glad to be around Wolf & Kenny & Kurt & Marti & Pat & Mary & Frank Press, etc., etc. The ministers & funeral parlor director & all did a good job, were helpful & professional despite the whole "American Way of Death" prejudices I've had. Han doing okay. Pop is our worry now.... Beautiful & sunny at the grave. Often swirling deeply & truly inside myself, being there inside experiences, & not seeing myself in a role-playing poetic way. I hated/hate whatever it was of being a poet that kept me from Han when her mother died. I am not Plumly, who thrives in these workshops & in the role of poet. I learned so much this past week, about myself & others & how I want to spend my life. Fuck the road, the visiting poet syndrome & everything that goes with it, the bed-hopping Stanley was doing despite his avowal that his friend in St. Louis was important to him. Even Kinnell kissing Boo Poulin long & passionately, embarrassingly so said Han who dropped them off Tues. evening, confirming what I was pretty sure of about those two.... Sue Tannehill & Plumly, then Paula Clossen & Plumly, & poor desperate Lynn Martin trying to get Plumly, & remember Christine Caron & desperate Harriet Susskind & my argument with Judy Kitchen.... I have work left over from the week, manuscripts to read. People flowing around my house all week—I was on edge & very tired of it & sad not to be with Han at the end.... Showed the Gorin/Watson tape Saturday morning—it could have been staged better, but is a knock-out, I think. I want to write Reneé.

Home now again at last. The house is ours again. Back to my life—a clearing away, still, for a week or two, but I'm back to my life again.

7/6/82

Even before Stan called this evening to say he loved us, to say he was sending me collecting gifts, to ask if I'd teach at Houston, I was going to write in this journal and say I'd hoped not to give the wrong impression. He's a good friend, and I admire him, and feel close to him. We couldn't really have gotten along any better. I can't expect him, with the wives and life-changes he's been through, to feel the same way about everything that I do. People were charmed by Stanley, his laugh & story-telling & personality. He's okay. We were once in close touch, before he stopped writing letters. Shit, are all his letters to me in Boston? Or do I still have them in a box in Rochester?

Hot today, even sticky, but we're glad.

Thick growth around the cabin picture window.

Han looking very tired today, and in mourning. I watch her closely. Drove in to Rochester to pick up Kristen at Eastman with her. Tomorrow is our 20th anniversary! I do love her more all the time, and want to protect her, and am out of sorts when she's not right.... If she gets the new job she's applied for—Director of Activities at Senior Citizens' Center—it will change her life, and for the better, I think. If not, she still has the summer off to begin to recuperate from four terrible months as Mom died.

I called Tony Piccione. I guess he's okay, I guess.

So many big projects in back of my mind. Found myself fiddling with a table of contents for a *Selected Poems* again.

7/7/82

Han & I did nothing special for our 20th. A good day at home. I did do some errands, and played ball in the hot gym for an hour, but mainly puttered here, cooked out, picked a quart of raspberries—best smell in God's creation—watered the beans (about our only crop, with sunflowers), went over a few manuscripts left here by workshop participants. Now, evening, and I'm here again. I'm at ease because Han is inside sewing & will soon have Terry Joseph's company. Hot, & strong winds blowing around me. I have the windows & door open. Carried my typewriter back to this perfect place. Went over "The Binding" yesterday, & it's coming along.

Saw Tony briefly. He seems okay.... Wrote to Martin Booth.... Keep thinking of sending my 3 Jesus poems to Allen Hoey for a possible pamphlet.

After a letter from editor of *Mass. Review*, I wrote to the MacLeish estate to see if they'd like me to edit that tape that Graver tried to steal. I'll see.

Want to get back to looking at my prose book on occasion, seeing what I have. I'd like to send it to Hall for a look this fall....

Want to read Warren's poem on Chief Joseph in *Georgia Review*.

Want to send books to a few poets for inscription.

Want to keep enjoying this silly-ass journal. The cover of this one is bending, but the paper is good, and I might have it rebound when it's full up.

The robins' night-cluckings have begun.

7/8/82

Not a bad day, but sort of unsettled, uncentered. Han busy and nervous about her upcoming job interview for a spot at Senior Citizens' Center, Kristen in and out of Rochester, and back and forth to band at high school this evening—the whole day planned around her activities. Now Han busy still & again with Kristen's uniform for her parade tomorrow, etc. Things will slow down, I keep telling myself. I will have to slow down inside myself, whatever the outer world is doing.

I'm sipping a strawberry colada back here—tastes like a milkshake.

Read Mary Elsie Robertson's *The Clearing* today. Didn't like it much. It seemed contrived, constantly unbelievable.... Skimmed Warren's poem—didn't like it much, except for the ending. Enjoyed the interview.

Reading the manuscript Lynn Martin left here.... Dropped Kathy Moser a note. Both were back here in this quiet cabin just last week. That was the loudest this cabin has ever been.... I've propped up a photograph of Walt, who gazes steadily at me. He still loves me, unrealized as I've been.

7/9/82

Billy working, Han and Kriss off to a parade. Evening falling again back here. Walt still looking over at me. I think he's reminding me to get to the other Traubel volumes!

I've done a second draft of "Between Flights," and have looked at my poem for/to Dave Smith again. Last night back here I went over sections of *CR*, and then came upon the "Crane in Reeds" poem. These new poems aren't much, if anything.

Played ball today, sent back some batches of poems to workshop students, ate lunch under the silver maple.... Letters from Booth, Plumly, card from Levertov again.... Card from Ray Smith yesterday welcoming an anthology from me for Ontario Review Press! I don't know. I've several ideas and all would take much work, cost much for permissions, and make little money, if any. Maybe I'm underestimating Ray, & his press could really get an anthology of the poets of my generation around? I should think hard on this.... I sent for Joyce's collected poems—*The Invisible Woman*.

7/11/82 (Sunday)

I'm back here in the rain. Rain at last after a long dry spell.

Han & I thought Meredith would be here for dinner today, but Shreela Ray called yesterday afternoon, and by 6:30 or 7:00 yesterday they were here—Shreela & Hedreck, Richard Harteis, William. Much running around for booze, etc., at last minute, but everything went well. I cooked steaks outside. Bruce dropped over. Some boring talk, Shreela talking too much, and some good talk. I asked William questions about Schwartz, Jarrell, Berryman. Discussion of poets' various intelligences. William said that he always felt he was a disappointment to those men, that John wanted him to do something more, a big poem. Richard is easy to be around. He gave me a book of his poems. William inscribed a second copy of *The Cheer* for Han & me, & his Shelley edition. I gave him a cloth-bound catalogue of the Rochester exhibition. I hope to get in to his Rochester reading—Thursday, I think.

Bill Ewert called today as Germany was losing the World Cup final. He'll do a broadside of "The Berries." Yes, I'll like that. And Bill Andrews dropped over to show me a proof of the *At West Hills, Long Island* broadside.

Some paperwork inside, but I haven't felt like getting to it.

Han seems okay today. Her interview is Tuesday night.

I want to keep thinking about an anthology for Smith. How about, for a title, *The Next Generation*, defining it as the one after the Wright, Bly, Kinnell etc. generation?

At Mosers very briefly today for a goodbye party for Vallones.

Gave Bruce my second copy of *Things of This World*.

Will putter for a couple hours and then, if the rain stops, go for a walk with Han.

7/17/82

Back here with just the fan on low—a fine morning.

I've gotten out of the rhythm again, haven't been back here since the last entry. Our two-day visit to Nashville was painful, again. The old man is a pain-in-the-ass, his situation hopeless, the house depressing, etc. We got him groceries, got him a haircut, etc. He'll have to get along. He has no interests, no hobbies, nothing. Does not care for anybody or anything except eating.

Went in to Meredith's reading. His poems are so low-key. His reading was good. I drifted…. Hecht there, and impossible Harriet, who squeezed between me and Scott at the last second as we were about to sit down. I was invited to the party later on, but didn't want to go. Shreela there, and others. I want to go to the Bronk reading at Memorial Art Gallery Tuesday.

Dept. meeting with President. Not much new. What is new for me is the general feeling around here (John Maier, Perry, Mirko) that there will certainly be more retrenchment over the next few years. Dept. meeting Monday to talk about offering 12 hrs. per instructor! I'll attend. I won't say anything, probably. Several in our Dept. very worried about their jobs…. I talked with Tollers for a half-hour yesterday about various things.

Did read Hall's good *Dock Ellis*, & want to write him.

Ewert called. *Tumbleweed* will be the next Christmas card, and this suits me fine. Not much else new. I got some xeroxing done for my prose book.

Good talk with Billy at midnight after his work…. Han & I went to Holley parade to see Kristen as drum majorette last night…. Han has the inside track on that good job at the Senior Citizens' Center. I have my fingers crossed for her. Right now, at ten in the morning, she & Kristen are at the Band Boosters car wash, and Billy is working. I'll turn to a poem or two.

7/18/82

Spent much of yesterday and this morning clearing away, clearing away—letters, a letter of recommendation, cleaning out drawers. The study is getting close to the emptiness & singlemindedness I'll want it to have for the next year.

Called Tony yesterday. He seems okay, & will attend the Dept. meeting tomorrow, as I will. My last one for a long time.

Han & I will go to the movies tonight to see *E.T.*

Hot today, but perfect back here. I'll write Don Hall, & do a couple other things for a couple hours.

7/19/82

Late afternoon, Monday. Han & Kris in Rochester, Billy inside. I played ball, and then went to a 3-hr. meeting. Heard all angles of future firings, what we can do for more FTEs, etc. I hope a 12-hr. load is not coming along. The administration wants each faculty member to have 100 students a semester, gulp. I don't know. I should, over this next year certainly, get my vita in order.

Spent the morning berating myself, wondering how I could change my life. I go through these periods. Now, a bit tired and relaxed back here in the cabin, I can't quite focus on everything that bothered me. I didn't sleep much, and this was, again, in part, because of all the rich food I consume just before bed—two big pieces, e.g., of Han's raspberry pie. Also, I've been reading Bronk's *Life Supports*, but have enjoyed much more reading Targ's *Indecent Pleasures*, though I would want a life more solid & centered & grounded for myself than his. But not really wanting to read poetry, even good poetry, even the poets I love when I do think of poetry, I wonder what I'm up to. Fuck it, then, Bill. Read what you want. Deepen into yourself. But do, goddamnit, find a little discipline so you're not awake with a bellyache half the night.

I'm the only one from the Department on sabbatical next year. Joy. And I must use the time for 2-3 books, and maybe to start in on another project that will carry me for several years. It's going to get miserable teaching at my alma mater before the dust of the 80s clears.

I like many Bronk poems, the carving he does. Without question, Stevens is the voice behind his, sometimes very close behind.... Will see Bronk tomorrow night in Rochester.

7/21/82

9 in the morning. I'll be out here until I go to play ball. A perfect morning. Two cups of coffee with me.

Drove to the Bronk reading. Shook his hand and spoke with him briefly before the reading, and shook his hand again after. He inscribed my *Life Supports*. As he read, I followed most of the poems along in the book with him. He's a very interesting poet, and may help me with *1854*, if that project ever gets underway. I can see how for certain tastes Bronk could be the best poet ever. Often, he's Stevens without the imagistic life. In any case, I like him as a man, like his voice, his "fuck off," no nonsense demeanor. He's filled with bitterness over being so ignored for so long. Maybe the NBA will diminish that, but I doubt it. Ewert publishing a Bronk item this month.

Never noticed the streaks of sunlight on the doorscreen like that—ash shadows wavering across the streaks.

Great day yesterday: Han got the job. We think it will be a good one for her. She'll work 9-3 five days a week at the Senior Citizens' Center, will be away from school papers & problem kids, will run programs for appreciative adults. No summer vacation, but the days won't be the strain for her that others have been. And, her salary goes up from about $4500 to $10,500 a year!

I've been moving ahead steaily on xeroxing pieces, typing pieces of prose for my hoped-for volume with Hall. Don't want to rush that. It must be good, must hold up for me.

7/22/82

I'm under the silver maple. It's just before noon. I finished typing my MacLeish essay, and also typed the little *Seems* "The Dragonfly" piece. The latter is the kind of piece I wish I had more of.... Will probably do some xeroxing again today, and then more typing. I still can't quite believe that I have that little cabin back there where everything is in order, and I can pick right up where I left off writing or reading.

Feels in the mid-70s, perfect to be sitting here. Leaf-shadows and sunlight on this page.... Tomorrow, I think, Sandi Piccione returns from Greece, & maybe Boo Poulin? I'm truly glad I'm not over there trying to get a last night's sleep before heading to the Athens airport. Some year, yes, but not now.

Han & I went to see *Star Trek II* yesterday. I loved it, Han liked it.

Mowed yesterday, my machine humming.

Long letter from Werner yesterday. He's the best brother I could have. With Han's new job, I don't know when we'll get to the Island.... Package of broadsides, including 3 copies of Kinnell's *First Song*, from Bill Ewert yesterday. I need to invest in a big artist's portfolio so I can house the biggest broadsides safely & so they can be seen.

No more Department meetings for me for a year. I promise myself not even to go out of curiosity.

This evening, Kristen's band plays a concert over at the Senior Citizens' Center.

Should the last words of Wright's "Autumn Begins ..." be "each others' bodies" rather than "each other's bodies"? How does this work? Even *The Branch* has this the first way.

Now for a little lunch, & then for a ride to the school for some xeroxing.

A big bumblebee has been buzzing & bumbling in a blossom just over my left shoulder. Involuntarily, it makes my scalp tingle. Only once was I stung by a bumblebee. I was a kid and jumped into huckleberry bushes to hide from a friend—this was just past the fire department in Nesconset—when I must have jumped right on one. Pain.

A locust whirring in the big elm.

7/23/82

It's ten in the morning. I'm in the house, in my study, sipping coffee from my Cornell mug.

Came in at 2:30 after a party at Agtes' for Tony Vallone's going away. Vallone will visit me here today, too. Good party. I drank only half a bottle of wine, and played poker—won about $15 in dimes & quarters.

Tony Piccione was there. He's decided <u>not</u> to go to China, & is now embroiled in paperwork here at the College about just what his status <u>will</u> be here next year. Tony should have gone, after everything. It could have changed his life. Sandi returns from Greece tomorrow, and it will jolt her to hear Tony, after everything, isn't going. After all the talk, all the plans, it comes to this business of paperwork & problems. I hope he can hold himself together.

Tony had a letter from Al. Al is happy—though returning August 1—and John Logan is in the most terrible shape imaginable

Han & I with Kristen at her concert at Senior Citizens' Center. I loved being there. I'm so happy for Han with her new job, and proud of her.

I gave Kristen a check for $100 for her first savings account. Poetry money.

I'll probably play a little ball today, then see Tony Vallone, maybe pick some raspberries, & answer a few letters. I have a clear mind today, and so much time out ahead. I've <u>never</u> been this free, at least not since I was a kid.

7/25/82 (Sunday)

Under the silver maple, sounds of mowers distances to the right and left, sunlight and shadow—sounds like a 19th-century title—on this page, which will someday be read in the semi-darkness of a library by a young person wanting to squeeze in another hour of notes before going off happily to lunch or dinner. I say <u>okay</u>. I lived my time, you live yours. Smell the good air. Read that passage in *The Swastika Prose* (will I ever publish this?) when I'm in Germany & get out of church & love the rainy air. I often think of that passage, and the one when I'm in the living room of the apartment on *Weizenfeldstr.* as the sun is falling. Right now, I picture you reading this—maybe in a library like the old Chubb library at Ohio University in Athens, downstairs, at a carrel maybe, behind the grill-work, the light just filtering in. It's okay with me. I'm glad for you. Be well. There's silver-maple shadow on this page.

I don't know which way I'll chatter when I open this journal. That's mainly why it keeps going.

The Vallones are moving, and are very busy next door, loading a truck.

The Hearns/McCracken fight on television today.

Tony Vallone is on his way to Lake Charles with Ken Frank. We had a nice visit day before yesterday. He gave me copies of Piccione's new Mammoth Press chapbook.

For several days, between things, I've been cleaning out drawers, throwing papers away, filing things, getting years of mess in order. Finished this morning. My filing is anything but precise, but will be a help. I want my study simpler, less cluttered.... Two or three junk jobs on my mind—Etta Ruth Weigl's stuff, the travel voucher, etc. John Leax visiting tomorrow.

Han & the kids are fine. Kristen at a Baptist church with a friend. Billy just risen for brunch. Han just finished a raspberry pie.... I'm joining Billy for brunch!...

Later: Somehow, my memoir has been on my mind a lot lately. I read parts of it again the other day, and whistled. It's damned good. I <u>can</u> carry out the scheme and add sections to it from time to time. Anyway, after brunch with Billy today, I grabbed a notebook and came outside and thought maybe I'd write something, something about Nesconset maybe for the memoir. Instead, I wrote about the deer in *The Chestnut Rain*, a neat little piece. I feel good about it, and will type it up one of these days.

Ross Wicks just came over and told me of the strange lights he's seen in the sky lately. Sounds eerie.

7/26/82

Stomach rumbled this morning, and I didn't get much done, had to come in from the cabin to the bathroom twice!... Played ball and felt strong—maybe the two days of rest is good for me. Good letters from May Sarton & Don Hall. I still can't believe that I know such people. Then John Leax's visit. I'm not sure what was on his mind. He's nice, but kind of slow, kind of a "sapper," and I was drained when he left at seven.

Catalogue from Bert Babcock again today, with about 30 Heyen items. I feel all sorts of ways about this. I think, maybe, it's good in terms of my getting known. I don't like what it seems to suggest, that I publish so much that my poetry must be flaccid. Much repetition in those items.

Now, I have nothing special on my mind for, well, for all the way, except working on the prose. I did do a ¶, "A Note on Romantic Poetry," this morning—maybe a useful page.

7/27/82

Bike ride to school. Ran into Mirko on Main St., & had coffee with him. Saw Felipe Farley, Pete Mosher, and others. Nice, small-town life. Then, Tony & Sandi & kids were over all afternoon. The China business has turned into an unbelievable mess. Days after he sent his cancellation, they sent him the plane tickets he wanted. Things at the college are fouled up as a bad backlash. Tony got drunk on scotch here, and was planning to drink more at home. We feel sorry for Sandi. So, I don't know whether Tony will get to China at all? What a mess, and it's of his own doing.

I'll spend the evening inside, puttering, answering a letter or two. Will type in the cabin in the morning. Vallones coming for dinner tomorrow, just before they leave. We'll miss them.

7/28/82

I was doing fine today until Sue Tannehill came bouncing into my study with her thesis. Then I felt like I was back in the middle of the workshop week. Pshew.

Played ball, did some typing, got some xeroxing done, am doing little jobs with the prose book. Will continue with this this evening, while glancing up at *Blind Ambition*. Reagan news conference right now.

Fucking Israelis are killing hundreds of innocent Lebanese in Beirut.

7/29/82

Under the maple, but probably not for long. It's a little cool, and I'm a little restless. I biked up to school and did more xeroxing, the prose "book" still coming together.... Han has been having meetings, preliminary to her job, which begins Monday already.... I've definitely made up my mind to leave for a week at the end of August & spend a day in NYC at the Strand or so, and then time with Wern & Barb & the folks.... Eddie still not in good shape—kidney problems. Fingers crossed.... Folks called yesterday, & Wern the day before....

Billy bought his stereo outfit yesterday—almost 500 bucks. But he has so seldom wanted anything over the years.

Vallones over for dinner yesterday, & today again.

Piccione going to China, looks like! Poulin back tomorrow from Greece.

Typed my "Walt's Faith" review this morning. Work to do on the interviews for the prose book; otherwise, the gathering is ready, almost. Maybe my goal will be to send it to Hall before I fly to the Island. This gives me a month. With all the nervousness & upset & teaching this summer, I'm glad I've had that project, at least. I don't think I'd have written any poems, in any case.

7/30/82

Very good day today—a couple hours in the cabin this morning, a couple this afternoon (basketball between), and I'll go out this evening from 7-9 after the news. At nine, I want to see *Stalag 17*.

Good weather. Good health. Good summer, now, for all of us.

Archie from Lift Bridge stopped over for his *First Song*.

I feel like calling Bill Ewert, just to say hello. Trouble is, they turn into 5-buck calls.

Worked on my new Island poem, now called "Sleepers," today.... Put away my idea, once and for all, of publishing *The Handbook of Heartbreak*. Put the mss. away. Some good sections, but.... I <u>do</u> like *The Swastika Prose*, & have been thinking of joining <u>that</u> with the new swastika poems & making a book.... Wrote Ray Smith about anthology ideas.... Wrote Vince Clemente about his new chapbook. I love him like a brother, and like his poems—if he could just rein in their sweet romanticism a little....

Big dinner for Vallones yesterday. Those good folks are now gone.

Han getting ready to begin her new job. Much money we didn't count on this summer. A new life for her, and I hope all goes well for her, that no monkey-wrench is thrown in like a Civil Service test, etc.

Poulin on his way.

Tony & Sandi stopped in yesterday. Tony's <u>going</u>! I'm glad—for my own selfish sake, and for his. I hope he'll be all right.

8/2/82

Pen not flowing just right, so I write bigger.

Good days, some work done here and there, and some rest. Summer settling in.

Ed back in hospital. Biopsy today. I don't know. He's been up against it. They have bought a house in Toledo, and he has a good job waiting for him, if he can just get well.

Sending some books off to Howard Moss for inscription.... I spent last evening getting my broadsides in some kind of order, working with the collection, puttering. My holdings are incredible! When I retire, I'll spend years getting things in order. Right now, I should just keep collecting, happily. Dough is tight, but I just have to keep trading & scrambling & begging.

We called Mom on her birthday yesterday. They seem okay.

Billy drove to Hamburg to play some golf with Kurt. He'll be back today.

Han's first day at her new job today.

Al stopped over day before yesterday. On the surface, he looks okay, but so frail. He told horror stories about Logan in Athens.

Kristen goes to Eastman today for her last lesson of the summer.

I'm wrestling with a <u>title</u> for the 20 swastika poems I want to put into a new book. The title so important. Then I'll see if Evelyn wants it—I sort of hope not—& will then try to place it with Ontario Review Press, or someone.... Next work on my prose book—that needs a title too—is with the interviews. I should push myself & do what has to be done and finish the book before I fly to L.I. first week in September or so.

Many strange thoughts & feelings & realizations inside me about this writing life—long range feelings & realizations of the silly anxieties & desires inside me. I don't have to prove anything. I am the family man I am, the teacher, the friend without becoming famous. No one is looking. I must trust to good verses, and mind my business.

Postcard from Stan Plumly (good transition here) saying Peter Marchant has asked him to come back next summer to do the workshop, & he's said yes. For one thing, Peter shouldn't have done this: the local person should be able to invite a poet he/she wants—if I'd have done the workshop, I'd have invited Dave Smith, to get to know him & for variety here. But I don't care. I won't do the workshop here under any circumstances. But Stan is hungry for such things, cannot emotionally get off the road, loves, apparently, what Don Hall calls the "frazzlement." I don't want to want that. Generally, I don't, but I do get restless & don't want to be ignored, certainly. <u>If</u> I worked hard enough, I suppose, the world would come to me. But I would like to work hard <u>without</u> that desire. This is <u>it</u>, the dirty secret, the disease I've talked about in this journal, but, praise the Lord, there has been a definite diminishment of all <u>that</u> stuff. This is all tied in, both ways & six ways, with collecting, which gets me into uncomfortable spots, but does serve as a way of taking other pressures off, and feels like a progress, a building.

This is not a cluttered day, but it's fun writing big & talking big and filling a second page here. Will play ball today. Have to bike up, but the skies are darkening and I might not be able to do it.

Things pretty much cleared away.

An aspiring local actor on television now. And there was a scene from a local play. And I do feel the way Jeffers does: charms for children, but bitter earnestness makes beauty. All the posing & prancing & mugging & false voices. Retch.

Han & I saw *E.T.*, & liked it, a happy fantasy. Spielberg got everything in.... Then we stopped in at Mirko's and helped him count his quarters from his apartments' washing machines.

Beat the hell out of two pages today.

8/3/82

Han gone all day, & now all evening. I find myself feeling lonely, feeling sorry for myself. Either I enjoy such emotions, or I'm stupid. All's well, & I've got time to write, & Han & I have been close. I want her to work her way into her new job without worrying about me.

Finished typing *From the Night at Belsen* today. Xeroxed half of it, and will do the rest tomorrow. Then will think of writing Evelyn & freeing myself to offer the book somewhere else.

Picked & snapped beans for an hour or two.

Vince sent questions & revisions for our interview. That's my next writing choice. At least some creative work is involved as I concoct some new answers. I just glanced at some of his questions, & even they have that too-too quality that Vince—bless his soul—is subject to.

I'm watching a ball game on television—Phillies & Montreal—and the announcer has twice mentioned Phillies coach Bobby Wine. I played against Wine in high school in baseball & basketball. He played for Northport. Shit, I was as good as he was, but 2-3 years younger, immature. What a different life he's had from mine. Would I switch? Shit, I'd like to spend my summers in the Big Leagues—or at lest try it once. Otherwise? I like sitting here & bullshitting in my journal & remembering Bobby, who almost beat us in that A-2 basketball championship game.

8/5/82

Terribly disturbing television show (Donahue) on the Trident submarine & base in Seattle. I got up for coffee saying "God, God, we are all dead and headed for Walt's world."... It could actually happen that in my lifetime I see a nuclear holocaust.... Seen from a great, great distance this earth is a speck with disease, man. One way or another, I'll die, everyone will die. I hope there is consciousness later. I hope I'll know of the presence of billions of peaceful planets.... The show is still on, America speaking: so much illogic & ignorance that it's frightening, both in those for & against. Talking of Pearl Harbor in relation to this!... If we could only really talk to the Russians, and mutually get off this spiral toward annihilation of everything.... Amen.

I wrote Evelyn, & sent *From the Night at Belsen*. I told her no sweat if she doesn't want to do it, but to let me know.

Will go to dinner with Han & Ross & Nete today, then see the Brockport parade & carnival. Entry ends with word "carnival!"

8/6/82

This morning on Donahue, six young men who had been center-folds in magazines like *Playgirl* and *Cosmopolitan*. American culture. But I kick myself for watching such stuff. But, I do learn.

Finished May Sarton's *The Shadow of a Man*, and liked it, though it is what to my mind is a novel of manners and of worlds that don't usually interest me. The woman can write, though.... Beginning to read

Wendell Berry seriously. Woke up at four this morning & read his essay "The Rise." Want to keep reading him, between my other work, the rest of the summer.

Letter from Bob Phillips saying John Logan had won the $5000 *Saturday Review* Lenore Marshall prize. Poor John. The more he's recognized, the more desperately unhappy he is, says Al Poulin. Guilt? I had a dream of guilt last night, involving cops & traffic, etc. I feel all at ease today. Will putter this morning, then play ball, and putter, & go to the big auction in Bergen.

Worked a little on the Clemente essay. Have letters to answer, as always. Heard from Judy Minty & Brendan Galvin, asking for Guggenheim recommendations.

8/7/82

I'm sort of glad to see that I'm distracted as I write in this journal—not distracted, exactly, but drifting along not worried much about anything but drifting along: I wrote, first, "happy" above instead of unhappy, and it should be the Clemente interview, not "essay." That's okay. I know w—— (a yellowjacket just fell down on my wrist & caused that blur—a drone dying already?) know what I mean, & will remember, and this journal will some day find its right interpreter, or it won't.

Have read 70pp. of the Berry. Have made notes on sheets of paper, but keep wanting to underline & write in the book, to make it mine. Have thought & thought about this. Many questions involved. It does seem to be a book I'll keep with me, and turn to from time to time. Usually I mark up only certain books—no hard and fast rules, but not books of poetry, or books whose authors will some day inscribe them. But I'm glad I annotated my Traubel/Whitman, and my Atlas biography of Schwartz, and I have this need to mark up Berry. What stops me? Do I think it's ego to do so? Or do I want to have the book pristine? I <u>want</u> to comment, to talk to him in its pages. I guess I want to leave this record of our dialogue. I will.... He has given me a confidence in myself, in what I've already done in my memoir and in some poems. I'm very glad to have these books, and will stay with them, reading a little here and there.

Han exhausted yesterday, Friday, after the first week of work at the new job. That should improve. Then her father called last night. He'll always be a bitter & helpless sad-sack. We're too far from him to be there much. He upset Han. And when she or one of the kids is upset, I am, too, and can't get on much with anything worthwhile. Things better this morning after a good night's sleep. She & I work at the carnival for Band Boosters this evening, and then we'll do the shopping. This will save her the strain and time today.

Perfect day for sitting back here under the maple. I guess I will.

There aren't many books I really want to talk with and remember, as I do these books of Berry essays. I will because I'll keep feeling uncomfortable if I don't. No, it's not ego, or I'd be marking up all my first editions.

As I began to underline, the first thing, my pen ran out of ink, but I won't be spooked!... Actually, another way of looking at it, just enough ink came out so that I made a beginning that could not be undone.... Years ago, I marked up a copy of Stafford's *Allegiances*, but was so uncomfortable doing that that I never did it again with a book of poetry. On the other hand. I'm glad I marked up Dickey's *Self-Interviews* as I reviewed it, even though I haven't had it inscribed because of that. This concern/dilemma sounds petty, but isn't, is at the center of the library I'm building. At the center of my book-collecting life. Sheets of notes inserted in the Berry book didn't feel right to me. I begin now gain to read & talk to the book, and this time the ink flow will keep going. Lightning won't strike me.

Later: I've done it, have caught up to my notes through "The Long-Legged House" essay. The sun just burst onto this page. It's okay! It's <u>better</u> this way because I can talk to the book more at length, can deliberate, have my notes more securely. I'm ready for real now to talk to Berry.... Want to write a little prose piece on one of his passages. I just remembered the frogs at Gibbs Pond!

8/8/82

I'm watching a television report on asbestos and its diseases. Millions, especially, were exposed to asbestos in the shipyards of WWII. Pop worked in them, but in, thank God, the woodworking shops. Wood dust in the lungs must dissolve naturally. Asbestos dust leads to a lethal cancer.

Worked the taco stand with Han last night. Moved up from shell-warmer to cheese-adder-onner & lettuce & tomato, & money-taker.... Won a hamburger by sinking 5 of 6 foul shots.... Kristen won a big trophy as best drum majorette in the Albion parade, the trophy on display in our booth.... Then Han & I went shopping, at midnight, in Wegman's, and who should come in but Billy & his five friends, for beer. It was funny. This is still a small town.

I'm glad about my decision to write in my Berry books. Saves much fuss of note-taking, etc. Also yesterday I drafted a prose piece on Berry's "The Lilies" and my "The Unborn"—maybe I'll call this poem "Milkweed." Maybe I'll still expand this piece, getting to Hall's "Old Roses."

Materials from the college yesterday about meetings & orientation week, etc. I'm so glad to be off, away from all that for a year. I suppose if I had the guts I could labor <u>intensely</u> & write 2-3 novels this next year & try to establish a base to break away from teaching. But I won't. My sensibility is to build bigger things little by little—as the memoir builds, as *CR* builds.

Later: Spent several hours in the cabin, good hours, reading and writing and poking at things. Stepped outside a couple of times in a drizzle to piss, surrounded by bushes & trees, cool greenness. Then why am I so out-of-sorts? Can't put my finger on it. Reading Berry may make me profoundly dissatisfied with myself— not with my writing & what I've been doing with poetry, but with my self, this unfarmering unecological life. But he quotes *I Ching* which says we'll lose if we struggle against our faults <u>directly</u>! So, to combat my impatience, my desire for fame & attention, <u>work</u> in the field, plant a tree, wax the car. I've even questioned my basketball playing—is it now to be put aside, a thing of my childhood, for other more dignified work? Well, no, not necessarily. The trouble is that Berry is so clear, as though his whole sensibility is an outline, while I am muddled and somehow heir to all sorts of anxieties & distempers (though he admits to the same).

Aside from all that, I do feel I need a change and will be a new man after a trip home to see my folks, & a day or two in NYC.... Aside from all that, I'm happy & lucky. I should have worked outside for an hour or two today. That would have cured all my little nervousnesses. For sure.

8/10/82

I'm inside, in the corner of my study, at the small mission-oak desk. It's heavy quiet. I feel relaxed, but when I think back on my day, I don't know what to make of it. Am I neurotic, or is this jumping from mood to mood the "normalcy" of our times?

I got up this morning & went back to the cabin. Typed the prose piece "Milkweed." Came inside. Decided to take Kristen & Karen to Pizza Hut, & did, but stopped at the school before that to xerox some things. Saw Mirko, good friend. Came home & talked with Billy & Kurt, & said goodbye to Kurt. Began reading more of Berry's essay on the body. Decided to mow the lawns, and did. Yelled at Billy for lazing around and watching the soaps all afternoon. Read more Berry, becoming more depressed. Han came home, and left again—has been gone since 8 this morning and it's 8 now. Grilled a steak for me and Kristen. Took a bike ride up to Muesey's to talk a little with Billy. Feel fine now. But I haven't caught here the anger & confusion & turmoil I felt for several hours. This had mostly, probably, to do with the inadequacy I felt as a person because of Berry, & the extinction I sense of this earth because what he says is true. In any case, I am in the web of a life style that is physically comfortable, but not meaningful. I can't be a farmer. Maybe my poetry can become more meaningful, nurturing.... Thoughts of how we've raised our children—wonderful, lovely, achieving kids who need action & thrills & rock music & don't know a carrot from a turnip.... Now, here, I am myself again. Television is off, and I must more and more leave it off, even as background noise. <u>Noisy</u> street all day again, gas line being laid. Men in the house twice working with gas regulator. Call from Al about doings at school. Scatterings & fragmentations, while the prose piece I typed and xeroxed is all discovery & harmony.

Right now, the quiet & this journal soothe me.... To be whole, and healthy, is to come to at least care for the hard work of gardening. Meanwhile, society has come to make it seem demeaning (I've no problem there) and <u>pointless</u>—I can buy a bushel of beans <u>so</u> easily around the corner. I do keep thinking that I want more land, 20 or 100 acres of woods to walk. I do keep thinking that I don't know what I want. Han is doing good, meaningful work, will keep so many old people happy, bring joy into their lives, help give them a sense of community. But why are so many of the old so dispossessed and lonely and not on the land they grew up on, not looked after by their families? Why should they need such places?

Berry says we cannot improve ourselves by ourselves, that we can only do this through/with nature. It's true that it begins to look as though all my life I'll be lamenting my shortcomings in this journal, and wishing for change. What makes me think I can do/should be able to do what Whitman & Berry couldn't/can't themselves do: become a saint or an animal self-balanced for contingencies? Even at the end, Walt's calmness & equanimity could be shattered. I want to stand straight, stop skulking (as Henry said), unwrinkle my brow, see clearly, write straight, laugh, work, <u>live</u>. 41, my boat still in the reeds.

Still so quiet. I'll probably spend much time right here next year when the cold comes, at least spend mornings here.

Long letter from Tony Vallone. Letter from Jerry Mazzaro.

Yesterday Kristen & I drove out to Picciones for a swim. Tony seems psychologically ready for his China adventure. He looks well. I walked the paths of his land, beautiful but probably worn-out land. I noticed today that the soil in the middle of the garden, around the tomatoes, seems worn out. I better understand now *The Gift of Good Land*.

So many of the poets I've respected I've respected because they've "made it." Before I sent books to Moss for inscription, I read some poems. Nothing there for me. Listen to the diction of Mazzaro's letter! Oates' afterword in her *Invisible Woman*, so stiff. Bronk wrote me that I undervalued myself. Maybe he's right. <u>But</u> I know that many of my poems are beautiful & true ones, maybe even the very best anyone has written in a long time. <u>But</u> I berate myself for my spiritual inadequacies. My poems are curving the right ways while I, in my relationships with people and myself, am niggardly/shy/anxious/uncomfortable. <u>But</u> I <u>am</u> the person who writes those fine things while I'm writing them. I want to be a saint.

I have to learn to let my family be and to go on with my work. I think of Billy at work now, & Han away, & Kristen. When they are all in the nest, I feel at ease, and can do my work. But I must trust to luck & grace & their safe return & get on with writing in this journal, or moving a poem ahead, or writing a letter to a friend.

Thinking of a group of poems for Allen Hoey. Just thought of a good title: *Along This Water*. Maybe "Along This Water," "Yellowthroats," "The Berries," "Arrows"—any Brockport poems—yes, the "1829-1879: The Bells" poems. Yes, I'll shuffle soon & see what group I'll have to type up. I'll want to look at that "Dec. 31: The Candle" poem again, too—two poems with dates like that could be interesting.

Steady sense of relief not to have the television on. But I forgive myself for using it often for background white noise. I have to forgive myself, maybe, as much as I berate myself.

8/11/82

CR: what does it actually do, what is its vision? This is what I must keep in mind as I finish the poem. That last book is so important. "The Ghost" epilogue will be very important, the restoration of the plant speaking for the whole poem, maybe.

Reading a little Levertov. New book of prose & book of poems arrived. Ewert's beautiful Atwood book arrived.

Sent section 38 to Wendell Berry. Hope he likes it.

Typed "Catbird" prose piece this morning.

8/14/82 (Saturday)

Al picking me up in an hour on this fine day. We're driving out to Picciones for swim & sun. Han & Kris are in Nashville, Billy in New Jersey with the cars. Li-Young & Donna are at Picciones. Li-Young & Tony surprised me in my cabin yesterday morning. Tonight Han & Kris & I work in the taco booth at the Hamlin carnival.

Tomorrow niece Debbie arrives. Monday Peter Dzwonkoski visiting, & Lorene Erickson and a friend. Wednesday brother Ed and family arrive for an overnight on their way to their new life in Toledo. I can tell just from his speech patterns on the phone that Ed is very high-strung and nervous.

Have begun typing the Clemente iterview, adding to it as I go along. This morning, I wrote a little memoir piece about the two driveways and the three Nesconset Woodworking shops.

Wrote to Don Hall, and sent him a catalogue of the Rochester exhibition. Then a card arrived from him about Bobbs-Merrill wanting to charge Annie Wright to use Jim's prose. I found the contract Jim signed, and hope that clears that stuff up.

I'm out back in my lawn chair. Haven't spent a tenth of the time here under the silver maple this summer as I did last.

Bought a $3 bookcase-table at a garage sale the other day, and it fits in my cabin just right.

Nice letter from Evelyn Shrifte. She'll be getting back to me on the new manuscript. I have a hunch Vanguard will want to do it. *From the Night at Belsen. The Night at Belsen. Night at Belsen. Belsen Blue: Twenty Poems.* I sure lean toward this last. Is it too ... something? The book sure seems to say to me that I won't be writing more of those poems. Should I add that third relation?... If Vanguard does it, Ewert will write them & see about doing the limited edition.

I just noticed that I skipped a couple of pages in this journal. I'll remember those pages, & take a chance on drafting a poem there, should I feel ready. Or a memoir piece.

8/16/82

I'm in the yard. Peter will arrive any minute now, I'm sure.

Worked on the Clemente interview for a good session this morning. Then took a bike ride to school (my $170 check for the NYC trip arrived, hoorah) and stopped at Al's with the fucking Tannehill thesis. Al talked for a long time about Logan, had just heard from John's Buffalo roommate. John seems now unable to take care of himself, sounds very sick, disoriented, even when not drunk. I'll call Jerry and see if there's anything we can do. It sounds as though John needs hospitalization, but won't hear of it. He'll fall asleep in class, Al says, if school begins & John tries teaching.

I think of Billy often, now on his way back from Jersey.

Debbie arrived safely. She & Kristen went to the movies last night, & will have a hell of a good time together this week.... I'll drive Billy to Cornell on about the 29th.

I did write to Curt Harnack at Yaddo about the possibility of my spending a week there in late November or early December. I'm just thinking about what might be good for me and my writing and finding *CR*.

Peter just pulled in, I think.

8/17/82

Peter arrived. We had a good visit, filled with book talk, plans—maybe I'll do a small exhibition of Christmas cards with him. <u>Maybe</u>. I don't want to give more than a day or two to any such project.

Lorene and her friend Linda Foster, a woman I liked, arrived. Their visit made me very nervous. I filled the time by showing them books & broadsides. We drank wine in the cabin until 2 in the morning. It's 8:30 now and I've eaten and showered and feel so relieved that they're gone. Nice enough people, but basically strangers.

Picciones stopped in briefly.... Billy arrived home safely, got bombed at Atlantic City, losing 6 or 7 $10 games of blackjack in a row! I'm glad he's back. He won't be home for very long now. I want to spend time with him before Cornell begins again.

I'll drive Kristen & Debbie to the Greece Mall today.

Called Jerry about Logan. Same old story. Maybe Al & I will drive to Buffalo one of these days.

8/19/82

Just wrote letters to Vince & Bill Ewert.... I'm laid up with a bum knee. Pshew, a freak collision in the air at ball yesterday & my right knee somehow hit my left & then somehow the left buckled. I thought I'd broken it. Terrific pain. I've jumped outside on one leg & am in a lawn chair. I think rest will fix it. I hope so. I kept thinking of how Gary Skoog went down & needed an operation.... Well, Bill, are you getting too old for basketball? Maybe, but this could have happened to me in this freak way when I was twenty.

I had to miss the Poulin gathering for Piccione, but I'll see Tony at the airport next Wednesday, I hope.... Might have gone in to Buffalo to see Logan with Al, too, today or tomorrow, except for this knee. John in <u>very</u> bad shape right now—accidents, uncleanliness, blotches on his legs, etc., etc. He needs hospitalization, but won't check himself in.

Knee throbs. First basketball injury in about two years, though, except for scrtches here & there. But this is a fairly bad one. I hope all ligaments & whatever recede back into place.

Agreement in Lebanon, thank God, on P.L.O. withdrawal.

Finished the Clemente interview, & xeroxed it. Now for the Rubin interview. Then maybe a short self-interview, or one with Agte? Or maybe the two are enough. I have a hunch, just a hunch, that Hall will do the book.

From the Night at Belsen. I'll stick with that title.

Looking at Mark Strand's *Selected* the other day. A couple of lovely poems near the end, one that prodded the poem about my mother in Nesconset that I began.... Again, I love the idea of a *Selected*, but surely can wait until *CR* has been published for several years. Maybe at 50, at the earliest.

Evening: wrote Bob Phillips. Managed to take a shower. Am in bed with a general dull ache in my knee. Han made a good chicken dinner.

Letters from Allen Hoey & May Sarton.... Tony & Al called to see how I was. I didn't get to the phone.

Supposed to be cooler tomorrow. Don't know if I'll get the chance to sit outside. Maybe I'll hop all the way back to the cabin.... Just saw a documentary on Iwo Jima & Okinawa—a sprained knee doesn't seem like much.

Debbie leaves already tomorrow. Bill will take her to the airport.

A gorilla special on now—National Georgraphics.

8/20/82

Well, it's eight in the morning. Han just brought me some cereal. I'll be nursing my knee again today. It's on the mend, but slowly. I slept okay, not long but okay.

What could be new or worth noting here? The universe is nothing, my knee everything.

I started to find a new order, much better, for the 20 poems of *From the Night at Belsen* the other evening. Maybe I'll go on with that this evening. The book must begin with "A New Bible," & continue with many of the "story" poems.

Later: did make a better, more meaningful order for *From the Night at Belsen....*
Dropped a note to Stan Plumly.... Made it out to a chair in the downstairs kitchen—it's good to be out of bed.

Han drives Debbie to the airport this morning. Debbie is a <u>very</u> sweet girl. I love her, & am glad she's family. Wern & Barb did everything right with this girl. I'm glad to be her uncle, & look forward to helping her out in the future—much love, a little cash.

This pencil moves nicely on this paper. Well, this was a sketch book, I guess.

Maybe I'll call Al later, and/or Tony, long as I've made it to the chair next to the phone.... I hope I get a big book catalogue in the mail....

8/21/82

Knee mending. I'm hobbling around better now.

Al stopped over yesterday. I called Tony, & sent him another letter ahead of him to China.... Last evening, Lisa & Bruce stopped over. I love them. Bruce leaves for Lake Charles tomorrow.... Debbie got home okay yesterday. I talked with Wern for a while.... So, all in all a pleasant day filled with friends. I even got some typing done, & a couple of letters written. Am putting together *Along This Water* for Allen Hoey. Should "Dec. 31, 1979: The Candle" be part of it?

I've fooled again with my old "Letter to Hugo from Brockport," but can't get it to ease its way forward right. Was reading, incidentally, some letter poems. Love this from "Letter to Logan from Milltown":

> that beautiful bar.... God, the ghosts in there.
> The poems. Those honest people from the woods and mill.
> What a relief that was from school, from that smelly
> student-teacher crap and those dreary committees
> where people actually say "considering the lateness
> of the hour."

How could I be happier? It's a rainy day. I can laze around, read, watch TV sports, sip coffee, decide on the contents for a little book, eat a couple of shrimp rolls for lunch, hear Han & Kris move in the house & know Billy is safe at work.

Letters from Lynn Martin, Martin Booth, etc.

I'll keep puttering today with the Hoey gathering.

Knee getting better fast. I get in & out of bed without any trouble now, & shuffle along rather than hop on one foot. I'll take a hot bath tonight maybe & maybe really loosen the thing up.

Kristen got her class ring c.o.d. in the mail today. An old-timer dropped off a record for Han to listen to. I don't mind being in the house, puttering for a change. Sometimes, maybe (yes) I force myself to the cabin when I'd like to be in here maybe just sputtering along in my journal.

Later: Al called to say he's won a $12,500 translation grant from NEA. I'm glad for him, as I wouldn't have been, frankly, a few years ago when his pushiness got to me. I do think of how money like that would take care of Billy's college for 1½ yrs.—but I'm genuinely glad for Al, and I'm glad I'm glad.

I've got a good order for *Along This Water*, I think.

Kristen got me the heating pad out of the cabin, and it feels good on my knee.

I keep thinking of sending "Ram Time" to Perishable, maybe, but why do I want to keep screwing around with these things? Well, I'm laid up, so use the time to push some small-press things ahead, I guess. No sweat. Mainly, I want to finish the prose book now & get back inside *CR*.

8/22/82

I've gimped upstairs with my journal to wait for breakfast. Usually I just fix some cereal, but this morning Han will fix French toast or eggs before she drives Kris to music camp. My leg isn't healing quite as fast as I hoped it would, and I hope there is nothing seriously wrong. Don't know about a Buffalo trip tomorrow.

Cool & sunny today, a beautiful autumnal day.

I lay around in bed so long yesterday that I began to feel sort of sour, planning smell-press projects, wondering why I wasn't famous, etc. That came from so much time in bed. I tried, last night, to <u>think clearly</u> (hard as hell) about <u>exactly</u> what it was I wanted, and exactly where I am now regarding poetry, collecting, writing, fame, life! Bill, be a friend to yourself, and ease off. To build the significant collection you want to build, your own poetry has to be significant. <u>That</u> is what will make everything else fall into place. And guard against these periodic desires to <u>make money</u> selling books, wheeling & dealing.

<u>But</u>, I did call Allen Hoey last night and have about decided to buy the rest of *The Bees* from him. It would cost $400, but I'd then have some to give as presents for years, & the hardbacks as investments. That's a lot of money, & I go back & forth on this, but it would be the right thing to do. Do it, Bill.

Something of what spurs my restlessness to boom along with America is that a couple people have told me of a *Newsweek* article on small fine presses, Janus & Perishable, etc. If all of America is going to get in on these things, well, then, Heyen, American from Long Island where topsoil is brought in by truck and not time, wants to get in on this, too. But Heyen is 41, and has done okay, and should finally be able to convince his reptilian self of this truth!: on the one hand, he <u>has</u> a wonderful collection which includes examples of many fine-presses' books; on the other hand, he's been published himself by some of them; on the third hand, those investors won't even <u>care</u> what the literature within those books is like, and I don't want to join <u>that</u> crowd; on the other hands, all of that will come toward me naturally should I manage to keep writing things I care for.... How to live with the collector's mania?—this is the question. How to <u>temper</u> it. Well, my writing has gotten written. I'll go along as I have (right now I salivate over the books Don Hall will give me, his own first two, etc.), and I guess this will mean that I'll periodically berate myself in this journal. <u>Things</u>, the spiritual battle to be "care less" of <u>things</u>.... But some of these things, these books, <u>are</u> spirit.... Bill, get the hell out into the cabin for a few hours today and work on some poems.... Write Hall, Hoey, Hamady, whomever. Get it all the fuck over with & get on with your life & eliminate brooding & live, yes, hoorah, where's my breakfast?!

Later: downstairs, pausing to write in this journal to laugh at myself: how many of *The Bees* should I buy from Allen? All? Half? Just the hardbacks? Am I trying to speculate on myself? What <u>is</u> the matter with me, all this soul-searching before writing in my Berry book, and now all this? Watching money carefully is one thing, but figuring out what my fucking motives are is another. Do <u>something</u>.

Kris leaving soon. Billy up. Bright sunshine, brighter than ever today. Leg healing.

I did send a letter & catalog to Hamady. Want to spend the afternoon in the cabin—or, at least, writing, away from clerical-collecting-anal-retentive work.

Later: I got off the fence & sent Allen $213.50 for 30 *Bees* in wraps, 10 *Blue Spruce* in wraps, 10 *Blue Spruce* in hardcover. I will sock the latter away. 50 books for such little money. A bargain. Many for gifts & trade.

Can't get hold of Jerry. Don't really want to go to Buffalo tomorrow. Wd. rather keep Billy company & get some chores done.

A bum leg is good for filling journal pages with chit-chat.

Han back safely from dropping our 16-year-old daughter off—it will be the first time Kris is alone with all strangers. A good experience for her. She's sort of in a "roughing it" place, Han says. We'll go to her concert & pick her up Friday.

8/23/82

Good day. Tony visited at 8 this morning & we sat outside on a warm day and drank coffee & talked, then went to the school where I cleared off my office desk, then stopped at Al's. Then I shopped with Billy—he got a sports jacket and other things. Home to some puttering. Proof of *The Berries* arrived. Letters to Ewert & Booth, a couple of good letters in which I talked about my own wondering of what it is I'm up to. <u>I must read my own poems more!</u> <u>That</u> will help me to keep the faith, they're so fucking good.

Reading Bronowski's *Science and Human Values* (1956): "Science is nothing else than the search to discover unity in the wild variety of nature—or more exactly, in the variety of our experience. Poetry, painting, the arts are the same search...." And later: "We re-make nature by the act of discovery, in the poem or in the theorem. And the great poem and the deep theorem are new to every reader, and yet are his own experiences, because he himself re-creates them. They are the marks of unity in variety; and in the instant when the mind seizes this for itself, in art or in science, the heart misses a beat." Yes, the <u>same</u> instant, and this is what it is all about.

Leg healing. Still very stiff and sore, but I don't think anything is seriously wrong. I walked, shuffled quite a bit today.

Maybe tomorrow I'll make plans & reservations for my LI trip. This time I'll take the tape recorder with me, and make it my main business to interview the folks.

8/24/82

I just made use of one of the blank pages—eight pages back. I like my new poem very much. Writing it out, I felt that final word as "no," too.

[<u>Mother and Son</u>

The failing Long Island light
filters through catalpas along our driveway.
It must be May—the trees' white blossoms
do drift down around her, petal after petal
catching a glint of sun before
dying into ground-shadow. My mother,
now younger than I ever knew her,
looks toward me. I am not there
in body, but somehow as an eye
among the blossoms and heart-shaped leaves.
I have never seen such longing before.
She could fall among the dead petals here,
after her moment of light, and disappear
before I'm born.... I worry that thought
and think to speak to her. What could I say,
if I could? This is up to her.

I have awakened again, with one more after-image:
my mother's decision there in that true dream
waited for all the blossom lamps to blacken.
Then, drawing her shawl tighter around her shoulders,
she walked inside to fifty years of women's work
done each day undone. What should they have known,
the husband and four sons? She would live among them
almost as a stranger.... Only once did one
follow her far enough to read her eyes.
He could not speak to her there
where the Long Island light still holds her,
somewhere, in that driveway, wherever that light is now.
If you die before me, try to find her.
It will be a May evening, petals

    glinting the last sun. Tell her, if you can,
    that I have seen her there, and know.   ]

I'm in the cabin, again, and glad to be. Knee <u>slowly</u> getting better.

I should type up whatever unpublished finished poems I have around, and think of sending them off somewhere next month. Will try *New Yorker* first, as always.

Spoke to Tony again yesterday about this thing of keeping some kind of journal. Read him a few paragraphs from this one. We feel our own way along. I talk to this one as honestly as I want to, which is not always in full honesty. There are so many ways to lie, and some of these are true ways.

Let's see what the day brings....

8/25/82

I've been back here a couple hours. Have finished typing up the new poems that have accumulated. I haven't sent any poems out in a long time. I'll get these into the mail in a week or so.

Had a dream last night that Kristen had been kidnapped, probably raped & murdered. Terrible dream, filled with confusion of cops, etc.... I <u>miss</u> that lovely child around here. She called from camp yesterday. We'll get her day after tomorrow.

Tony leaves <u>today</u>. We'll go to the airport with Al to say goodbye.

John Logan in the hospital at last.

When I look up from this chair to the framed photograph of Archie, I see the outline of his face among foliage reflected by the glass. He says that I can see into the sun. When I do, I see him there.

Rained steadily all night, raining now. Will spend the afternoon inside until we go to the airport.... Want to send the long letter to Hall. I've planned to write.

Getting hungry. Will head inside. This cabin—a joy, everything I needed.

8/26/82

Today, I'm worried about my leg again. It woke me up this morning, and I get strange chills, but it's only been 8 days, and I'm moving along okay, and it's no worse than it was yesterday, so I'll just leave it alone for a time.

Sunny & chilly this morning. I've gotten some work done back here. Wrote Bill Ewert—he called last night and we spoke for about an hour; Babcock wants more Heyen, & is <u>anxious</u>. Wrote to Tony Piccione—we saw him off at the airport yesterday. I'm nervous for him. But I think he'll be okay, will at first survive, and then will <u>prevail</u>. Bless him. I wrote him about a dream I had last night that tied him & me & Al together. <u>He</u> was a runner, & pulled up with a bad knee, & it was phlebitis.

Should arrange for my Island flight today.... Tomorrow, bring Kristen home. Saturday, drive Billy to Ithaca.

8/27/82

I was going to putter in the house this morning, but I'm glad I came back here. It's a beautiful morning. I was feeling sour because of my knee, no exercise, but feel better now. Typed drafts of 3 memoir pieces. Soon will go in and wake Billy & get some chores done readying him for his second year at Cornell.

Ewert called again yesterday. It's all about wheeling and dealing with him and Agte on those stenciled 1968 handouts that Bruce found in my old office. I don't feel quite right about this. Bruce, in fact, never came to me with all those and asked about them. I'm uncomfortable about all the institutions that will shell out much dough for them. There are, I hear, 66 of them. Agte owes Ewert money & will clear his bill by selling a bunch of these. I'm supposed to sign 25, which Bruce's father is to drop off, and send them to Bill. He'll get Bruce about $35 each, he says! He'll of course keep the money to pay Bruce's bill. The item <u>is</u> interesting. I don't know. I'll get as many as I can, and just salt them away. The item is A-2!... In general, I'm going to go slowly with sending things to Bert now. I'll wait until I'm broke. I'm a little bitter, too, that Stafanik at Rook unloaded everything on Bert, but items are clearing out now, and I'm glad I have the things I do. I keep throwing odd things into the U. of R. boxes for surprises for myself years down the line. Ewert will keep Heyen collectible, I think.

I wrote Don Hall, and did some other odds & ends last evening.

Met my new neighbor, Vernon, an army man, briefly, yesterday.

Sent Ewert the drafts of "Mother & Son" & the revised Clemente interview. This should keep me above ground for a while, maybe through the Bronk books at least.

We pick up Kristen today.... Han worked 12 hours yesterday.

Tony must be in his hotel in Peking by now. Gulp! There's a real possibility that he might just not be able to stick it out. I hope he does. Fingers crossed. If he does, he'll be a new man.

8/30/82

Sour again, about my leg. If I weren't injured I could play ball today. It's going to be a long time, at least another month, I think, before I can think of getting some exercise. My body was used to running a few times a week. Maybe I'll be able to do some bicycling in another week or so.

Enjoyed seeing Kristen at music camp. She was 1st clarinet again.... Next day, I drove with Billy to Cornell. Choked up a few times on the way home, but it was nothing like last year. He's with friends now, and settled in, & knows the ropes. I think he'll be home for a weekend the end of September.

Han and I up to the Lake for a picnic with some of her co-workers yesterday.

I'm leaving this Friday for the Island. I'm glad I made these plans. Will have 7-10 days to spend with the folks & with Wern & Barb & Debbie. I need the change.

Letter from Evelyn about the new Holocaust book. She's ready to go on a new book, or also willing to combine all the poems. I've spoken with Ewert again, and think the latter is the way to go, and I'll write Evelyn. I'm in no hurry, but just want all that a unity, a completed unity in my mind.

I feel better already, just from talking to the journal. I will drive up to the post office today, and the travel bureau.... I should call Tony Rimore, & talk with him about my mail, etc.

I have the heater on now for the first time this new season.... Without this cabin, I'd often be more tight & restless & anxious than I am.

There's a good chance that with my knee I've gone past something, and won't have it back again, without surgery. I'll go to a doctor, but not before another month goes by and I see how it comes along.

9/2/82

8:30 in the morning back here. As my pen touched this page, I heard a black-capped chickadee chitter.

I feel okay about the way my knee is coming along now.

I leave for the Island tomorrow morning, early. Will be packing today. Fiddled with Kristen's tape recorder last night, and it works fine. I'll do several tapes with the folks.

A nice note back from Wendell Berry with a few remarks on lines in my 38th section of *CR*. I'll change a few things. All sorts of feelings about hearing from him: discomfort about bothering him; green pleasure that he read something I wrote; dislike for me thinking about other motives. Anyway, I'll be glad should my letter to him be plowed under, as in that poem of his, with other paper accumulations. And I do look forward to sending him *CR* when done.

Spoke with Billy last night. He's fine.

Wrote Evelyn Schrifte a good letter, I think.

Han working hard. A bus broke down on the way back from Syracuse, & she was at the Senior Center until 11:30.

Strong Reagan speech on the Middle East. The Israeli psyche says "Never again," yes, as it must, but still must open up its heart for the Palestinian people.

Hectic day yesterday. The heating repair man was here. The car was in for repairs. Then Linda & David Hamilton, now of Finland, were in town and dropped in and David compusively showed me poem after poem. Nice people, but I don't really know them.

Mail back & forth with Ewert. He makes me happy. I think often of *The Berries*.

Have I mentioned here that Ray Smith wrote to say he wanted to do the anthology of poets of my generation, and that Joyce wanted to join me? I've been thinking hard now about whether or not to get Dave Smith as a third editor. I think <u>yes</u>. Will try to contact him. A big job, but it could/would be an important book.

Saw Al briefly yesterday. He was upset about a Department meeting, etc. Thank you, Lord of sabbaticals.

I hope to mow this afternoon, hope the sky clears & the ground dries.

Made some progress on the book of prose. What materials to include in those first two sections (or to have just two sections in the book), and what order?—these are the questions.

Well, journal, I'll be away from you and this cabin for a while. Dream the dream that the boulder dreams.

9/3/82 (Friday)

The folks have gone to bed. We've had a long and good day. I'm tired too, and thought of not writing here, but would like to paste a page or two into my journal back in Brockport about these ten days I'll be away.

A comedy of errors as my limousine to the Island ran out of gas. Then I left my jacket in the first one. Etc. But I met the folks at the bookshop in Port Jefferson.... I bought a few things there that I like, Moss's *Proust*, Yevtushenko's autobiography, a selected Quasimodo (to try another translation after being so disappointed in my other book).

We drove around a little, visited Wildwood Park, but mostly I spent much time interviewing Pop with the tape recorder. We had a couple of good sessions. Tomorrow I'll focus on Mom, her beginnings. Sunday, already, we'll hook up with Werner and Barb.

I don't want my mind on my other projects while I'm here, but will mention that I called Dave Smith yesterday about the anthology and he's eager. I'll write the first letters after returning, suggesting procedures, etc.

It's good to be here. I'm getting along fine. They're fairly healthy, and are glad to have me here.... Pop and I shot pool for a half-hour. I was 12 balls up, and wanted him to beat me, and he did.... Tomorrow, they'll take me to bookstores in St. James & Centerreach, & we'll eat out, etc.

The Island has hit me hard again. I stood a half-hour beside the Expressway this morning, and watched, witnessed.

9/4/82

A <u>long</u> good day. Drives with Pop in the morning, with Mom & Pop in the afternoon. Looked in several book places & picked up things here & there, though the place in St. James was closed. Long walk with Mom this evening, and then I did a 90-minute tape with her. A rich day, and I'm ready for sleep. Will connect with Barb & Wern tomorrow.

9/5/82

Such a full, busy, hectic day. Drove all over with the folks, met Wern & Barb at a restaurant, came back here, talk & talk & talk. Stopped at a Moloch of a place called Tri-County Flea Market in Smithtown, and at a couple of other garage sales. Played pool twice with Pop. More fun with the tape recorder. Tomorrow the folks will drive me to Werner's.

This is such a big change from my Brockport life, and it's good for me. My head is clearing. I feel close to Walt here, strangely, understandably, on this ugly and beautiful Island!

Labor Day tomorrow. Should have a lazy day. I look forward to East Quogue.... Not sure how I'll get all the books I bought back with me. Might leave most of the duplicates here.

I called Han this morning but missed her. Then she called me and missed me. All's well.

I read "Mother and Son" to my mother, an unusual thing to do. My first reading aloud. It's a beauty, a beauty.

Want to remember maybe for a note or two in the memoir: 1/ the irony here in this community of cat screams outside last night as in old Nesconset; 2/ the story about the bomb shelter ideas in Nesconset that my folks had and the Wenzels.

Passed by my old high school, drove down Gibbs Pond Road & saw the pond again & my old grade schools.

Still worried about my knee. I get around fine, but is it improving or has it improved as far as it will? I limp only very slightly now, but there's so often a "crick" in the knee.

9/7/82

I'm at Werner's—he & Debbie are asleep upstairs, and Barb is off to work already. Sounds of blue jays and crows. Another sunny and warm day. I'm glad to be here and will take it easy for several days, probably going in to NYC on Saturday and staying overnight. Here, I'll have a chance to relax a little. Anyone who has not experienced the constant strain of being with Mom could not understand my references to it. Werner and Barbara know. Those folks love me and take care of me but oh brother. Enough. I hope they live for decades more over there in Ridge, and in good health. I just feel sorry for Pop, who would do many more things if Mom allowed him.

Read a section here in *Reader's Digest* called *The Last Jews in Berlin*.... Saw a film called *All the Marbles* that Wern & Barb & I laughed like hell over.

Fixed up a box with all the books I've bought here to mail to Brockport.

No thoughts about school or writing. I did write a few strange lines on a scrap of paper yesterday: "Just walking in the bright white light / I swear to Christ / I saw a tiny white swastika in the sand." And I did....

My knee discourages me because I'm not sure it's going to heal itself. In a few more weeks, maybe, if it's still the way it is now, I'll have to see a doctor.... Crossing streets, or in crowds, it makes me feel very vulnerable, the way women must always feel, or maybe much smaller men. I'm 200 pounds, have always been strong, an athlete, and fast on my feet, and yesterday it wasn't easy for me to find a space in the traffic to limp across the highway. I think often of what it must be like for people with arthritis, handicaps. Life is terrible for so many. Underneath everything in me, and not just because of my own good fortune, there does seem to be some source of joy & affirmation, maybe untested yet, but it seems patient and confident.

Looking to the back of Werner's property here in East Quogue, now, I see another house where he hoped there would always be woods.... Mushrooms are actually erupting up through his asphalt driveway.... I'll help him close down the pool for the winter.... I'm taking home from the folks photographs of me with my class in 6th & 8th grades, & a confirmation picture, etc.

Oh, Lord, such a different pace here. I'm relaxing now as I wasn't able to in Ridge.

Werner & Barbara smoke constantly. I love them but know there are going to be bad endings to all this in a decade or two. They just don't take care of themselves, but who am I to know? Bless this house, bless the house in Ridge, bless this aching Island and the mushrooms pushing up through tar.

Later: just after ten in the evening. Not late, but I'm tired and ready for bed. Barb & Wern & I watched a war film after supper.... Long day today. Wern & I rode around all over—Southampton, Bridgehampton, etc. Found a couple of book stores and I found a few things.... I called Billy at Cornell and we had a nice chat. He's fine.... My knee seemed somewhat better today. I notice it less often.... Nothing much planned for tomorrow. I'm glad just to laze around.... I'm having a fine vacation, but will also be glad to get back to Han & Kris when I do....

Sept. 10, 1982 (Fri.)

I'm on a bus from East Quogue to NYC. We're bumping along the Expressway. I've just read the *Times*, and thought I'd scribble here instead of just looking at cement & scrub oak.

All's well. I'll spend two nights at the Roosevelt, & go to book stores, & go to the massive book show/sale Sunday when they close off ten blocks to traffic. I'll spend much money, but what the hell. Maybe I'll get lucky and find a few things to sell later on. $150 for the hotel, but it's only once every year or two, so what the hell. Will go to the Strand today, & to that Barnes & Noble over by 15th Street.

Everything went okay at Werner's, but things are depressing there. He worries about money every second, is awfully lazy—won't do a fucking thing in the kitchen or pick anything up or go for a walk or anything, or even make himself a cup of coffee, but just smokes all day & eats & gains weight & complains. But beyond that, Debbie is at a crisis time with hating school her senior year & nothing in plain sight for her future. But beyond that, and this is what tears Werner up & may tear up that marriage in the long run, Barbara's mother will move in with them for 3 months a year. Werner can't stand this, is extremely angry about this, needs his privacy, is in a corner. It's a long story, going back to Roy Dooks, who let everybody down. Werner said Mom & Pop were wrong about most things, but have always been right about this Dooks business. Werner goes into a rage just thinking about this. I couldn't take it either.

My knee seems to be improving little by little. This bus seat is uncomfortable, little room for my long legs.

Called Han the other night. We truly love one another.

Traffic picking up. We'll go slower & slower now. I remember when this Expressway was first completed & a car could sail to the city…. My sense of the Island has deepened again, & this trip will lead me to some good lines.

I don't quite feel ready to get back to writing & work, but maybe will be closer to that by next week, especially when I know college is in session…. A letter from Tony arrived, Han said. She also said she checked the cabin, & all's well, and when it is, I am, my writing life is, & I feel no pressure…. Traffic just about stopped now … now picking up again.

A silly thought/line occurred to me a couple of days ago. A nice line for one of those poems out of the 40s. I enter it here, anyway, to have it: "The straw that broke the camel's back was time."… Heavy traffic now, & slow bumping is worse than fast bumping for writing…. I'll no doubt write in this journal in my room this evening….

Later: Pshew. It's about 9:30. I'm in room 840 at the Roosevelt. I just called Han, and feel warm after that. All's well at home…. Here, too, though I'm tired. I walked several blocks with briefcase & suitcase to the hotel, checked in, then walked 35 or so blocks to the Strand, spent a long time there, then walked over to the Barnes & Noble annex on 15th, then walked the 35 blocks back. Rested. Then walked up to Times Square and back. My feet and my groin muscles hurt more than my knee. Tomorrow, I'll take it easier, and even easier on Sunday as I stroll the Book Fair that I just happen to be here for…. Bought about 75-100 books today, a few nice finds, though nothing spectacular…. Didn't call or stop in at Vanguard, and don't think I will…. Maybe will go down to the Phoenix, if I can find it…. Didn't call Bob Phillips. This city is amazing, and I was glad to pass a million people without knowing anybody. Perfect weather. By the time this session of book-hunting is over with, I'll be sick of books, but that's fine…. Two copies of *The City Parables* in the downstairs stacks at the Strand. Doubt I'll see any other of my books anyplace else. I almost wish Vanguard would remainder a book or two…. Maybe I'll write a postcard or two—I promised Bill Ewert—and then call it a night….

9/11/82

It's early, only eight or so, and I'm in my room already with the television for company. I walked all over the place again today, bought books, ate junk food, enjoyed the sunshine & pavement. My legs feel as though I've just been through a triple-session soccer practice…. I'll be glad to get home tomorrow.

I did call Evelyn to say hello, and maybe will see her tomorrow at the Book Fair. She said Vanguard is going to do the big book of Holocaust poems. I'm glad, and will work on the manuscript and get it as "sharp" as I can. Once & for all, I want to be done with that book.

Well, I did what I wanted to do, visited my folks & Wern & Barb & got into the city for book-hunting. Now it's time for some long days in the cabin, time to get that book to Hall for a look, to get the manuscript of *From the Night at Belsen* to Evelyn, to write Joyce & Dave about the anthology, and to work on *CR* & other poems. I'm ready. One thing at a time. I do have time, and will not spend it awaiting my two October trips.

Saw myself so often in store windows. I look different from the person I feel myself to be. Can't define it. And I float around this city like a ghost (albeit with aching legs & feet). At home, I'm heavier, closer to the ground. It's as though I have to venture out once in a while to prove to myself I'm not afraid of the city & wide world, maybe.

9/13/82

Morning. I'm back on cabin time again. Brockport air and light. Made it back yesterday, taking a 2:30 instead of 7:30 flight. Didn't meet with Evelyn, but will see her next month, I'm sure.

I've just pasted in the pages I wrote while away. Now, before beginning work, I write here. This journal keeps me up with myself, somehow, centers me.

Much mail—May Sarton sent her new book, an invitation to read at Old Westbury, letter from Ewert, note from Ray Carver with a chapbook, etc. Tony's good letter from China.

Han & Kris are fine. It was good for them to be out of my conservative presence for a while. They had fun. Two beautiful women.

I want now to begin to find the discipline to sit on my ass and work. First, I want to round off the prose book. In the Evenings, I'll write letters and wrap books, etc.

Yesterday morning at this time I was walking 5th Avenue in NYC. Yellow balloons tied to all the booths for the book exhibition. The antiquarian booksellers on East 53rd were disappointing. I bought a $3 book on the Erie Canal, and bought John McPhee's 1st book (on Bill Bradley), *A Sense of Where You Are*, for $30. Many cartons of books will arive via UPS.

This is the first week of college. I'm lucky to be here, and will breathe deep.

Maybe I'll begin by writing out a poem, any poem, on the blank page some pages back.

[<u>The Berries</u>

My wife already there to comfort,
I walked over icy roads
to our neighbor who had lost her father.
The hard winter starlight glittered, my breath
formed ascending souls that disappeared,
as he had, the eighty-year-old man
who died of cancer.

In my left coat pocket, a jar
of raspberry jam…. I remembered
stepping into the drooping canes, the ripe
raspberry odor. I remembered bending over,
or kneeling, to get down under the leaves
to hidden clusters….

Then, and on my walk, and now, the summer berries
made/make a redness in my mind. The jar
presses light against my hip, weight
to hand to the grieving woman. This gift
to her, to me—being able to bear
the summer's berry light like that, like this,
over the ice.

When I was a boy, the Lord I talked to
knew me. Where is He now? I seem to have
lost him, except for something
in that winter air, something insisting on being

> there, and here—that summer's berries, that mind's
> light against my hip, myself kneeling again
> under the raspberry canes.   ]

... Just wrote out "The Berries." Half the time as I wrote it, my mind was on other things. That's not the half I want to grow into.... A jay is scolding me—from the Island to here. Jay cells so spread out, all One. Sunlight in and out of moving leaf shadows on my desk. Coffee. This life I've found and made again. Thoughts of Athens, Ohio, and studying & trying to write poems. Thoughts of Kris & Billy, the little ones they were then. Wonderful memories. But now is the time I would like time to forget itself, and stay.

    Later: after writing the above, I worked on the arrangement of the prose book for a time, and then went inside for more coffee. I found another pile of mail that Han had left upstairs. Then, on impulse, I decided to go to the gym & try to break a sweat. I did, and am happy my knee let me trot around. Then home for lunch & another pile of mail and a call from Bill Ewert about the Agte-found item, etc. It took will-power for me to come back here again. I'll try to spend the afternoon here, and get to letters, etc., this evening.

9/14/82

    Just spent a concentrated hour on the contents of *The Moon in the River*. It's getting close to where I can show it to Hall. Some fine-tuning now, as the guy at Bobbs-Merrill always said. Glad I did all that xeroxing & typing this summer.
    Hot & muggy out, but I have the air conditioner on low back here, and am in lung-cool heaven.
    Not much discipline to work hard, but, what the hell, maybe what I do is enough and I'm building things inside me all the time. I did write to Bruce Agte & Tony Piccione this morning, dropped a postcard to Axelrod, called Werner, typed a few pages ("The Fish," & "A Dream of Three Poets") for the prose book. And this past hour was a very good one, decisions made, the book improved. What better place for my essay on "Companions" than after "What Do the Trees Say?" Yes, I have the first section of that book in good order. Will try Illinois, and then Ontario Review Press after Hall. The Hall book would look worst & sell best. Will see. I'll aim to be done with it by this weekend and to get it into the mail by Monday. Yes. That will be a good feeling, whatever its fate.
    Han & Kris won't be home until 7 or 8. I'll make myself super, take a shower, & maybe go up to the college's soccer game with Syracuse. Oh, do I have the life now. It's first day of classes today.... Tomorrow, hoorah, I'll go to the gym & trot around & resist playing again. One month ago tomorrow I hurt my knee. I'm not worried now about needing surgery, but have to watch myself.
    So, the Hall book. Then to get the ball started on the anthology by writing Smith & Oates about procedures. Then, somewhere along the line, to turn to the manuscript for final shaping of *From the Night at Belsen*. Everything gets done, especially this lucky year. Lucky. Even the timing for the big antiquarian book fair in NYC is just right for my next trip.
    Letters yesterday from Bizzaro, McKee, DeLigio, Byrnes, etc. Is this all good, bad? Is it my fault? Well, this year I'll keep the flow going. Letter from Martin Booth yesterday, too.
    When I pay my Visa charges from the NYC trip, I'll be almost broke. But Ewert owes me $400, and I'll sell some things to Babcock when I want, so I'm in good shape on all that. I've always used poetry money for all the trips & books, etc. Han keeps track of the rest of our monies.
    Han is fine, her new job fine.... Kristen's driving test tomorrow. I sure hope she passes.

9/15/82

    I was watching the news late last night when I heard that John Gardner was killed in a motorcycle accident in Pennsylvania yesterday. I don't like it at all. I cared/care for that man. So erudite, so warm & human. I'll never forget talking with him at Hofstra last summer. He inscribed about fifteen books for me the few times we met, and I'll cherish them. I don't like hearing that an author I know has died, and then looking over the list of my "holdings," but it's only natural, and what I've done as collector defeats death and time a little. I read over the sketch of John's life in the Howell bibliography—how did he do all that in less than 50 years? Just a month or two ago, after reading that article on him in *Upstate*, I was telling Han that I felt that man needed, well, me, and I wanted to sit back here in the cabin with him & get him to slow down and get himself into a position where he could just write his beautiful books & get off the frenetic highway he was on. But he was a wide soul, dedicated teacher, farmer, poet. I'm going to miss his presence in the world. I'm glad my Gardner books are safe at the U. of R. I'm afraid, the longer I live, there will be more and more paragraphs like this one in my journal.

Alive, I took Kristen for her driver's test an hour ago. She said she bumped a curb backing up during a parallel park, but otherwise did okay. I sure hope she passes.

Letter from Wesleyan U. asking me to read there. I usually have a hard time deciding when. Maybe I can fit it in on my next trip.

Mirko stopped over yesterday. He's harried, as is Irma, but all's otherwise okay.

Spoke with Al briefly. Various complaints.

Will see what I can do back here for an hour or so, and then will drive to the school and try to work up a sweat again.... Drizzling today, cooler, and foliage yellowing and falling.

9/18/82

Haven't been back here. Have been doing not much, I'm afraid, reacting to the world instead of living in it & <u>making</u> it by writing.

Money & keys stolen from me in the locker room yesterday. $35, but the loss of the keys worries me more.... Won $197 at poker the night before.

Two letters from Tony lately. I wrote him again today.... Billy home Friday with his friend Ed.... Kristen failed her driver's test, alas, & I hope she passes it next time.

Doing a little on the manuscript of the prose book. Want to get it into the mail on Monday.

Call from Ewert again about *The Magnifying Glass*.

Yes, from Yaddo for Nov. 29-Dec. 13. I'll go! Will take this diary with me.

Actually look forward to my next trip. Will do a couple of classes at Sayville High School, too, so the money side of the trip should work out to at least break-even, especially if I can stay with Evelyn a couple of nights.

Birds, apparently, stripped all our white grapes. I'll pick the purples tomorrow.... Sunflowers beautiful, leaning their heads down. No natural thing makes me happier than sunflowers. I'd never known their odor before this year.

Last night I helped in the kitchen at the Senior Center for Han's fish fry. 120 people there for the fine meal. My job was to take the just-fried fish from the draining paper & deliver it to the serving line. Everything went fine. This was the first time they'd had such an evening there. A big success for Han.

1000 Palestinians found slaughtered in a camp. Sickening. And perhaps Israel's fault: the Lebanese army says it was in control of the camp before Israel returned after the assassination of Gemayel. Terrible. But more space given on the evening news to the funeral of Princess Grace of Monaco.

9/20/82

John Gardner was on my mind. I called John Maier yesterday, and rode along with him & Helen to Batavia for the memorial service. The church was full, the service moving. Many hymns, including "The Old Ragged Cross" again—I thought of Han's mom—and "Be Still My Soul," which has been with me since. Hardest was seeing John's old mother & father. I'm glad I went. Sometimes I wanted to curse God again, but this gives way to acceptance, which makes more sense.... Helen & John stopped in for coffee later. Good people. Gardner had visited them often, was working on *Gilgamesh* with the other John. Apparently, Gardner finished the translation. I would like to be with all my Gardner books/inscriptions now, but am glad they are safe at U. of R.

Played ball, staying on the ground for the most part. Knee feels tired now.

Got some letters written. Must do others.... Next serious job is the letter to Oates & Smith to get the anthology moving.... Must play & get ready for my trip, too.... Must fool with "A Note on *The Magnifying Glass*," too.

Han & Kristen have been happy these days, as I have. I've had some trouble sleeping, but that's no big deal.

Football game on tonight, and I'll watch while getting things done. Still no real desire to spend long hours in the cabin.

Later: Evelyn called. Vanguard moving upstairs to smaller quarters at #424 Madison.... Looks like <u>she</u> wants to do the limited of *From the Night at Belsen*.... I'll stay with her a couple of nights my next trip.

Wrote the note for *The Magnifying Glass*. Letters to Ewert & Krapf & Fred Byrnes.

Han making grape juice & jam.

NFL players announced a strike. This Giants-Packers game tonight might be the last one for a while.

This morning, quickly, I applied at Ingram-Merrill Foundation for some dough again.

Billy coming Friday, Kristen having a big party Saturday.

Time to call it a night. Tomorrow, I'll draft that letter to Oates & Smith.

9/22/82

I've just about completed plans for the next trip. Am still deciding whether to fly in on a Friday night or Saturday morning. The latter, I think.

Got a good letter written yesterday to Dave & Joyce & Ray to get the anthology underway.

Went to dinner with the 3 Poulins yesterday when Han & Kris were in Rochester. Apparently all's not well with Tony. His letters to me sound generally okay, but he's called Sandi again, wanting medicine, & he's thinking of returning in January, etc. I mailed him a letter yesterday, & will again today.... Should take it easy playing ball today.

My next job will be to get the Mss. in <u>final</u> shape for Evelyn.

Ewert called again last evening, about nothing special.

Han bought me the big portfolio for broadsides that I needed.

Han worried about our money situation, but not overly so. Our savings will be cut in half by about next September, we know. I'd sure like to get lucky with the Ingram-Merrill, or that South Carolina program, or something. I could easily sell $1000-2000 worth of books. I've been looking at my N.C. Wyeth books again.

A small art opening for Bob Marx this evening. I'll go over. Mirko behind this again in his warm & friendly way.

I realized yesterday that in many ways I've never been as happy as I am now, this gift of <u>time</u> given me by the State.

I stopped at school, even saw Graver. That's all over. He was <u>stopped</u>. I couldn't quite believe it, but Tony & Al & I <u>stopped</u> that book cold!

Al <u>very</u> frail. I just bet he'll come down with something before long.

Nice note from Ray Carver yesterday. He's hurt about Gardner.

9/25/82

Saturday morning. Han just made pancakes for us all—Billy & Ed here from Cornell. The two go to Buffalo today to see The Who tomorrow. They'll stay over at Wolf & Pat's.... Kristen's big party is tonight.

I slept well again, hoorah. Makes a big difference.

Will spend some time in the cabin today, but will get to the final Mss. of the Holocaust book next week. A fellow by the name of McFee sent me a copy of a long essay-review of my books that will be in *Parnassus*. I'm pleased by the whole thing, as much as he dislikes *Swastika*. Maybe he'll help me, though, to hammer that book down into something more vivid? But, I don't know. He doesn't like "Darkness," which seems to me very strong, e.g.

Rainy, gloomy today. I don't care. Inside & out in the cabin I can stay busy.

Wrote to Jenkins in Texas about *Putnam's Monthly* with all the Melville stuff I have. I'd like to raise some money from those, or from the Wyeths.

Georgia Review wants to see *Wenzel*, and I'll get that in the mail. I've been reading poets my age, and thinking about my choices for the anthology. The recent St. Martin's anthology of contemporary poets—well, I've looked at the prospectus, seen the people in it & left out of it (even Hecht, Merrill, Ginsberg—and Smith & Matthews & Tate, etc.), and the Heyen/Oates/Smith of <u>one</u> generation may be a better idea. So, I'll go on the offense. I'm glad I'll be doing this anthology, & with Oates & Smith. Yes.

My Long Island/NYC trip is all arranged, readings & all. I'll make about $600, will spend about $500. That's okay. At least this one is paid for. Will fly back from MacArthur on Columbus Day. Will be glad to see my folks & probably Werner & Barbara again.... I've been out of touch with Vince Clemente for so long, & might type him a letter today. And Bruce Agte.

I don't know if I'm doing any solid & extended & deep work this sabbatical year, but I'm enjoying the hell out of this floating I'm doing. I must realize that my desk will <u>never</u> be cleared off, all my life, unless I do not answer letters, etc. So, I should learn to have times/days/even weeks ferchrissakes when I don't care if all I'm doing is being.

I've begun McPhee's book on Alaska. Want to read the short novel Wayne Dodd sent me, too.

Evening: It's about 11:30, Kristen's party winding down. I took a walk and saw Al for a little while, but mostly have been upstairs reading, letting the kids be. Apparently the one boy Kristen wanted to come didn't show. Otherwise, a good crowd.... I was looking over my Wyeth-illustrated books. I read the whole *Courtship of Miles Standish*, if not for the first time, then for the first time in decades.

I wrote to Bruce, sent some poems for a possible broadside to Stone House Press, sent *Wenzel* to *Georgia Review*, etc.

Al's driving up to New England next weekend with his friend Taki. He'll see Donald Hall. Maybe I'll send a few books up with him for inscription.... I still haven't told Al about my anthology. I will once I've signed the contract. For years he had the damndest ways of doing uncomfortable things once his friends had projects going.

"Wet tire tracks like snail shine under the street lamps"—an overdone line that occurred to me on my walk. I like the word "like" less & less over the years. It now seems almost <u>always</u> overdone to me.

Time for the stragglers to go home. I'm tired.

9/26/82

It's about midnight. We just said goodbye to Billy. We let him drive the LeSabre back to Ithaca. It was too late for a bus, & too late for me to take him—5 hrs. altogether. Lord, keep his tires on the road this wet night.

Han typing right now. She also went to the Center for two hours today, Sunday. I'm afraid that what my mother said, that I don't have a wife much anymore, is in some ways true, and sometimes I get depressed, until I count my blessings. Mainly, right now I feel harried, after Kristen's party, & worry about Billy, & arrangements, and everything. I think often about how my need for the orderly life of routine is not exactly a measure of high spiritual enlightenment, may in fact be a kind of death drift, <u>but</u> these thoughts may all be bullshit, too.... I'm tired.

> Five cedar waxwings
>   lined up on a mountain ash branch.
>   The nearest to the orange berry-cluster
>
> plucks one, passes it to the fourth,
>   who passes it to the third,
>   and so on to the first. The next berry
>
> stops with the second waxwing, the next
>   with the third. The first
>   eats the fifth berry, passes the sixth along.

I can't sleep. It's five in the morning. I'm fooling around. This could come to something, Tighten it, & repeat the first line.

9/28/82

It's lunch time. I'm inside, watching junk television, waiting for the mail. Then I'll take another cup of coffee out back, & work on the ordering of *From the Night* again. About two hours at a time (as this morning) on that project is about enough.

Just dropped notes to Waters & Meredith. I'll write Bill Ewert this evening. He sent the ads for *The Berries*, & other things, and a hundred of the four hundred bucks he owes me.

Al called last night to say that Jim Newman, John Logan's young (less than 30) roommate had died, in NYC. No details. A jolt. And Jerry reports to Al that John is going his old way.

I played ball yesterday, and couldn't jump, but ran & shot better than any other time since hurting my knee. Lifted my spirits.

Han put up peaches last night. She works too hard.

Mail's here.

9/30/82

I'm glad I went over to the Derek Walcott reading. He read from a book to be called *Mid-Summer '81*, and the poems were fine, clear and intelligent & echoing. And later I met him at a small party, and we talked. He questioned me about all sorts of things. I gave him *Light* & *Swastika*. He inscribed five books for me. He was warm & friendly, not the bad guy Al had heard he was.

I didn't sleep much, was excited about the evening, but don't mind being tired. I had breakfast with Han. She went to work. I've showered, am watching the Donohue show. Don't have to do anything. Will go out to the cabin for a couple hours, blessing my sabbatical every step of the way.

Evelyn called this morning to check on my arrival, and to invite me to dinner Saturday night.

Sandi Piccione will visit today. I'll go to an auction this evening, & then stop in at Squeak's for poker if there's a game.

10/2/82

It's midnight. I'm at Evelyn's, trying to unwind, hoping to get some sleep after a hectic day. Couldn't sleep at home last night, either.... It's Saturday night, and the city is still noisy, traffic pushing up to the tenth floor here. Being with Evelyn is nice, and saves much money, but is tiring. Vanguard moving into depressingly small quarters.... The book fair was okay, prices out of sight. I connected with a chap who was <u>excited</u> about buying the N.C. Wyeth books, as I described them.... I spoke with Jordan Davies briefly, & Ralph Sipper & Lee Campbell. Bought, for a total of $37, a Berry novel & John Gardner's Lord John Press *Poems*, which I've wanted for a long time.... I have all the usual thoughts, of course, wondering what the hell I'm doing here, etc.... Han & I stopped in to see Irma & Mirko & Irma's mom last evening.... Tomorrow I'll kill time by myself, at the Strand & other bookshops. I won't get a <u>good</u> night's rest until I'm with my folks in 4-5 days, I think.... Talked with Evelyn a little big about my new book, but she's slippery, as always. Somehow, the books get published out of the mess and jumble that is Vanguard. Both Evelyn & I like the idea, however, of sticking with the title *The Swastika Poems*.... Well, I'll turn off the light and at least rest.... Han & Kris are in Nashville tonight. I miss them.

Sunday/Oct. 3, 1982

I'm sitting on a bench at 67th & Central Park West. It's about 6:00, and I'll walk over to Evelyn's soon. I just walked through much of the park, after strolling 5th Avenue while a Solidarity/Polish parade was going on, after being down to the Strand & the 18th St. Barnes & Noble. I bought $200 worth of books today, & they're being sent home. I'm tired, now, of books, want to get the reading tomorrow night over with, and then the other readings, and get out to my folks. But it's been a beautiful day. Between book-hunting I walked in the sun & shade, ate a hot-dog, had a can of Coke. Evening beginning here. I sort of wish Han had been with me all day, at least while I was walking past Sheridan Square & Rockefeller Center & such places. I'd like to stay with her at the Plaza some time for several days. She'd love wandering up & down 5th Avenue. I'll spend the evening with Evelyn, gulp, and "retire" early, maybe read a little & prepare my readings. All's well. I found some nice books, & got my money's worth, & will be glad this long winter to have them around me, though the money right now feels like a lot.... I think of all my friends & family scattered everywhere. Han & Kris are about on their way back to Brockport now....

10/13/82

And then he walked hundreds more blocks & through Central Park, & read with Aaron Kramer & met Kramer's friends, and had lunch with Bob Phillips, and met Harnack & Calisher on the street, and hung around the Vanguard offices a little where Evelyn was nervous he'd get a free book or something, and then he took the train with Kramer to Babylon & Kramer's car to Sayville where he met up with sweet but very uninformed but enthusiastic Addie Sanders & the next morning taught two good classes at the Sayville High School & then got a lift after a shrimp dinner to Old Westbury & met Jon Collett's class & did a fine job & Norbert Picked him up & he stood over in Roslyn & walked with Norbert the next day over Bryant's grave & met Morris Gelfand & read at Post okay among friends like Dan Murray & Bob Sergeant, etc., & Vince & Graham Everett were there & drove him to Setauket & he & Vince had a good book-hunting day the next day, & then days with the folks, a drive with his Pop to Sag Harbor to hear Vince & Graham & then flew home at last for a good day with Billy before that shining son left for Cornell, & is now unwinding, doing this & that, feeling unbalanced somehow, even afraid about he knows not what, but is home in his chair again, and put away the grill & chairs outside, & played a little ball today bum knee and all. Enough.

The Berries arrived. Handsome. I don't like the yellowish paper.

A guy wants to buy my Wyeths badly, and I want to sell them, but don't really know what they're worth.

Han & Kris fine, too. Kris got her license, hoorah.

My folks are whacky as ever, but okay. My mother, especially, has so much <u>shit</u> in her head (I'm afraid I inherited this) that she can't think straight.

Gardner program tonight at the college, but I really don't want to go. I'd better trust my feelings & stay home and watch the Series.

Sent my list of ten poets to Ray Smith. Feel cowardly about including Phillips, but what the fuck.... Wrote Vince, Evelyn, Piccione, etc. Very disappointing letter from Vicky Gold. She even pissed me off. Enough of that.... Desk piled high with books from NYC & L.I.... Proof of Dave Smith's new book arrived.... Cabin waits for my peace of mind. I'll plan on getting back there tomorrow morning to work on *Erika*, my new title for the Holocaust book.... Saw Al, who is sick & missing classes. He brought back my Hall books nicely inscribed.... Yes, I'll watch baseball & wrap books & write a decent letter to Bruce this evening.... Met Helen Plotz, who was a joy.... Yes, Bill, where does this general sourness come from?: weird letters from Phillips & Gold? rejection again by *New Yorker*? bum knee that stops you from playing good basketball? feeling you're getting nowhere (meaning no fame?) in the writing world? Oh, Bill, fuck all that. You're the luckiest son-of-a-bitch you know. Laugh a little & write books & wrap books & kiss wife & daughter when they come in.

10/14/82

Long day yesterday, from a couple of good hours in the cabin to a poker game (lost $56 but Bronk paid me the $60 he owed me). Hall rejected the prose book. I really don't care much, don't have it together in a satisfying way. And two letters from Dave Smith, good letters, though he'll do an anthology with David Bottoms instead of with Heyen & Oates. This might be for the best, too.... Much other mail.

Wrote "The Halo" while reading a memoir of Auschwitz by Isabella Leitner, a memoir that after all these years should have been wiser (he says to himself carefully). I'll type the pages I have to of *Erika* this morning.

Stopped to see Al yesterday. He was in Binghamton, apparently missed classes again.

Still putting away books from my trip.

Will help at the Senior Center fish fry tonight, & then watch Series game #3.

Ewert called, & we had a good talk. Maybe *CR* will end with a bigger 4th book. I'd like to take the pressure off my friends of having to buy a 5th expensive volume. I'll see where I am after the weeks at Yaddo.

Look forward to running & sweating later. Now, to work. In the morning, the book fair in Rochester.

Later: had a good morning on *Erika*. Now, after relaxing from playing ball, to get a second wind and take care of some other things for a couple of hours before going over to the Senior Center.

10/17/82 (Sunday)

It's early evening. I'm watching the Series.

Got many little things done today. <u>Getting</u> ready to spend all morning on *Erika* again. Will make some decisions & type up the "Notes" section.

Han made a great turkey dinner. She & Kris are fine. Billy called yesterday, & he's okay, too.

Cold today. Han got the rest of the plants in. We got the ping-pong table back to Millers at last—it's been here since Kristen's party.

I put the little chestnut seedling in the ground over by the cabin.

Will write Don Hall tonight. I generally agree with him about my prose book.

I think the cases for *The Magnifying Glass* will arrive next week.

I leave Friday for the Michigan weekend.

I've wrapped & shelved the books from NYC.... Got a $450 credit card bill. I'll pay it after my trip next week.

Went to the Rochester book fair. Bought 3 things: McPhee's 2nd book ($15), Cummings' *Poems 1923-1954* ($22), and a review copy of Berryman's *The Dream Songs* ($16)—all nice items for my collection. I think I'll go after all of McPhee's books now.

Wrote to Tony. Called Al to see how he was, & talked to Boo, & she said okay.

Seems cold in the house. Winter in the air. I don't have much desire for the cabin these days. Don't feel like carrying the typewriter back there, for one thing. I take the phone off the hook here weekday mornings, anyway.

10/19/82 (Tues. evening)

Series game #6 about to resume after a rain delay. Cardinals ahead 7-0, so it looks like the last game will be tomorrow.

I typed up the acknowledgments and "Notes" for *Erika* today. Will go over the whole book tomorrow morning in the cabin.

Went to post office to mail Ewert the inserts for *The Magnifying Glass* and the 51 copies of that item he'll deal with. My 15 cases arrived, and they're elegant. Ewert did it again. Fingers crossed that the box gets to him. I mailed it insured, but not registered, gulp, and if those 51 items are lost Bill will be pissed at me.

My favorite days are the days when there's basketball, as tomorrow. Makes it easier for me to work.

Morris Gelfand will do "Ram Time" as a broadside!

Another good letter from Tony, and I wrote him again. I'll be glad when he's around again in January.

Kristen home from school yesterday with her general upset stomach & weakness feelings she gets. Okay again today. She has all the typical & understandable teenage worries about upcoming PSAT tests, college choices, grades, boyfriends, her music. But she's fine, mature and sweet and smart. She's worked hard in her classes this year, and has been getting good grades.... Grades are not a worry with Billy.

10/20/82 (Wed.)

Han & I just had a long, good talk with Billy. He's fine.
Han had a hard, long day at the Center. Some nonsensical complaints from old Mr. McCauley, etc. But her spirits are good, and there are good words from good folks, too.
I actually fell back asleep this morning after Han left. Slept until ten, so only worked an hour or so on *Erika* before playing ball. Will be in the cabin all day tomorrow, though. Then will get ready for my trip to Oakland Fri. morning.
7th game of Series about to start. I'm rooting for the Brewers, who lost 13-1 in the lousy flood of a game yesterday.
Saw Al today. He looks good, is applying for grants, complaining about school, etc.
Etta Ruth Weigel's *Meltwater* arriged. More power to her.

10/24/82

Sunday evening. I'm in bed, ready to watch a war movie. I feel as though I've been away a month. The conference at Oakland University was okay, and I did good work for them—my hour speech especially good and sharp—but I'm *so* glad to be home, away from all that inane talk, away from Lorene Erickson, away from the exhaustion and odd food & discomfort even at the Poe's-dream-of-a-place Meadowbrook Hall.... Went to some book stores in Ann Arbor.... Sunlight so strong along the highways.... Only writer I met that I was interested in was Charles Baxter.
Billy surprised Han & Kris with a visit home this weekend.
Al told Han that Dick Hugo died. He was a good man. I have only warm memories of him and his poems. Again this evening I'll look over lhis books, think of the ones at U. of R. I'm glad again I've collected, for myself, for others. Will the spirits of all the dead poets be present in the room of my books in a library one day? Yes.
Home now for more than a month.

10/26/82

Early afternoon. Peter Marchant just called to see if Carolyn Forché could stay here next week! I begged off. I don't know her, don't have her books, don't want to be swirled up in College things now.
Worked in the cabin this morning. I guess I've finished *Erika* now, and will make the changes on the copy that goes to Evelyn, and send it in. I've got to let go of it sometime, and now's the time. Once I find out when it will be published, I'll get ambitious (force myself) and think of review places, etc. Publicity pamphlet. Push a little. And let it go.
Wrote to Peking Tony. Wrote Billy, and Allen Hoey, and others. But I don't feel I have in me long days of writing and stuff. I guess I'm lazy, and I'm trying not to care, and doing generally okay at that. What the hell, the poems & books get done.
Took a short bike ride.... Have no enthusiasm for raking leaves or working outside. I leave the soaps on for company & mind-drifting.
Ate a handful of autumn raspberries.
Thanked Al for his four new BOA books. I'll give him some money when I get some.

10/30/82

Kristen is upstairs with two girlfriends getting food ready for a couples party this evening. In about an hour, Han & I will pick up the Poulins and drive to Spencerport for dinner.
Got a birthday card from Billy. I love that boy so much. And _need_ him.
Bad scene, pathetic, with Larry Scoppa at poker the other evening.
Ray Carver sent a hardbound lettered copy of *The Pheasant*. Beautiful book & fine story.

All's well. I've played good ball this past week though my knee stops me from getting underneath and mixing it up.

Went to pot-luck dinner at Senior Center two nights ago. Last night I took Kristen over to her Brockport Symphony Orchestra concert. Enjoyed it. "A Night on Bald Mountain" for Halloween.

Letter from Dan Hirsch—he'll pay $800-1100 for my Wyeths. Sounds okay to me.

I wrote John Felstiner after reading his piece on Celan in *APR*.

Will write to Joyce Oates again over the next few days about the anthology.

Couldn't start the riding mower, but got the small one started (barely, & with luck) ((cripes, just realized now that I forgot to prime it!!)) and did the lawns. A good feeling of tiredness from that work in the clean & cool air.

10/31/82

Sandi & kids visited. Saw many photos of Tony in China—on a camel, at the Great Wall, etc.… Much fun with Poulins at dinner yesterday—we went to the Pilot House in Spencerport. Boo loved my punk-rocker & chicken joke.… Kristen's dinner-party went well.

Vicky Gold called. An uncomfortable call. I don't even write the letters to Billy or my folks or close friends that I'd like to write. Have to get to some letters this evening.

Worked outside for an hour this morning. Haunting Halloween weather. This small town western NY autumn life is poignant & reverberating.

Boo talked hard about Bruce last evening. Called him a liar and thief!

Kids will be coming to the door all evening. This is the All Hallows of the poison scare.

11/1/82

This 42nd birthday of mine has been a happy one. Worked in the cabin this morning, pushing that sunflowers-at-night poem ahead (it took me along, actually). Then played ball, and my knee was best yet. It makes me play within myself. Since then I'm not sure what I've done … some letters, some chores, but a good feeling of being inside. An excellent roast beef dinner with Han & Kris. Call from Mirko. Finished that statement for Jerry Ramsey on the Plutzik series. Etc. Wrote Norb & Vince & Ray Carver today, & Pam Conrad.… Went to the bank. Paid off my $450 Visa bill, & am broke now, but no matter. Will kill time watching a film this evening. Nice gifts from Han (another, smaller case for broadsides) & Kris (candy).

Han & I walked down to Nora & Luanne, the two witches, last evening. Spent a friendly half-hour talking to them & Al Studier & Charlie & Jane & Beth & Mark, & Terry & Denny stopped by, etc.… Called Billy last evening, too.

I know that this journal has been all chatter for a long time. To a large degree, that disease I've had has gone away. I have ambitions for my poems, but can't be a star. I'm just trying not to lose too much ground to Matthews & Tate & Plumly & that Halpern gang. But their names are all over the place all the time. Vanguard is a publisher (thank God I have a publisher) but certainly not a good one for getting books around or advertising or promoting or whatever. My poems are fucking good, but the other political & publishers' stuff is beyond me. But I'm more & more comfortable with myself, and maybe it's adversity that makes for a "significant" journal. But I'll certainly put no pressure on myself here. Upcoming: decades of weather reports!

11/3/82

It's maybe three in the morning. I've slept some right away, as always, but have awakened, as usual. I toss and turn for hours, and then usually fall asleep for a short time again. Maybe I should just get up. At these times I'll always think of John Gardner.

Worked a little on the anthology this past evening, and will again in the morning.

Window still a few inches open. Very warm yesterday.

Bill Ewert called twice yesterday about nothing special. The Christmas card—nice poem, "Tumbleweed," but not exactly seasonal, though Bill thinks it is.

Voted yesterday. Straight Democratic. I've never liked Republicans, fat cats, smug, arrived, biased. Narrow of me, but me.

Reading Paul Zweig's *Three Journeys*.

I'm still like a little kid about playing basketball, and look forward each M-W-F, and now will be excited about Thursday nights again. Trotting around in the gym the other day, alone, I was thinking of all the gyms I've been in, all the teams I've been on since 6th grade, and even remembering myself as a little kid who used to go up to Nesconset school to shoot outside, then dribbled my ball back home along Gibbs Pond Road. Freshman, J.V., varsity teams in high school, freshman & varsity in college, town-team at Springville, and the faculty-intramural years here. It's no wonder that it's part of me. Over the years, if I tone my game down and expect less of myself, I can keep playing. I'm still about the best percentage-shooter from 15-20 feet in town!

After that paragraph, I've just sat here in bed drifting and early morning-dreaming. How am I? How/s my soul? Okay. Generally settled. Zweig says, "I don't know about faith. It requires, I think, more trust and vulnerability than I can manage." I myself am, I think, somehow, still faithful, faithful to the things Walt was faithful to. I worry of course (worry is too strong a word) about being deluded, and question my own sources of this faith (am I a coward?), but I actually think it's there, and that some kind of light and life will be with me when I die. Interesting that Zweig uses the word "vulnerable" too. To be faithful & trusting is to be vulnerable. I would have thought the opposite. But I can see a gentleness and unassertiveness and patience emanating from faith, and these qualities do lead to vulnerability. "If I were to assign a category to my life it would be the category of longing, along with its corollary, nostalgia." Certainly much of these is in me too, but the faith-buoy still is anchored in the channel. It is there from childhood.... So many balances, as this entry has wanted to balance, apparently, my apparent anxiety about a journal of pure weather report and chatter.

11/4/82

I was going to get up this morning and just work in the study, write Ray & Joyce, etc. Instead, on impulse, I grabbed this journal and my new poem "The Beam" and came back here to the cabin. It's raining. The little heater hums. My coffee steams on the arm of my easy chair. This pen moves across the page.

Went quietly over to the Forché reading last night, and the minute I was in the door Peter grabbed me and dragged me over to her. She said four or five times how much she loved my poems, etc., etc., kept telling people how good I was, that she'd be nervous because I was in the audience, etc. I felt flattered all night, and her reading was very good—I wonder now why I couldn't <u>feel</u> those poems as I should have?—and she was turned on (she's 32 and I know all those emotions before, during, and after readings), but I also felt she knew how to make all the right moves. I like her. She was kind. I'm jealous (am I?—if so, not much, as the heater purrs and the rain falls) of the 18,000 (!) copies in print she says of her *Country Between Us*.... I didn't have her books, couldn't find first printings in N.Y.... I felt okay at the reading—Tollers & Poulin & Rubin & Rimore & Kitchen & Jack Jones & three or four of my ex-students there. I love this life—they all greet me like a long-lost friend.

The last part of the Zweig book has helped give me back to myself again. I like the little laughs that jump up in me once in a while.

The sabbatical is a blessing. Today is a Thursday, I'd have had 3 classes, and my brain would be foggy, and I'd be straining to stay awake for that last class.

I wrote Li-Young last evening.

First league game tonight. My legs will still be tired from yesterday.

Talked to Billy last night. He's fine.

"The Beam" is dedicated to John Gardner, needs him. The dead help. <u>He</u> knew/knows, of all people, what we will do for a good poem or story. But he <u>was</u> a friend to me, even if he had thousands of friends like me.

Just read the April 3 & April 10th entries in this journal. I like this journal. Everything I say is continuous, connects.

11/8/82

Long, good days.

Finished the Bonhoeffer book. Some things got inside me, under where I'd want to summarize or articulate. An interesting poem, "The Film," came from something he mentioned, and a poem about him is in the works & may become something. Dietrich, you were strong and good, one with your suffering God. I have that photograph in my mind, the steps down to the execution area in Flossenburg, the spring leaves that must have shadowed you as you walked by.

I'll spend much time tomorrow, Tuesday, in the cabin.

Han, Kris, and Billy are fine.

I wrote to Daniel Hirsch & told him to visit, that we could make a deal on the Wyeth books.... Also wrote to my folks.... Wrapped some books.... Am not doing any "sustained" writing, but that won't be forced. There's no time-product relationship in this poetry life, maybe. I could kill all day tomorrow and not finish anything at all to satisfaction. I can't put pressure on myself just because I'm on sabbatical and feel I should be producing, producing, producing during this free time; also, I must keep enjoying, as I have been, the mind- and emotion-work of the process of writing. Raspberries building in me—will turn to "The Snow" and the new raspberry poem tomorrow and try to talk straight & simple & deep.

Played ball today. Much fun. Winnick is 46, Mancuso 44, so I'm not the oldest. My knee quirky, but "okay."

I keep thinking about and hoping Archie's *Letters* will show up.

Got the $100 for the Old Westbury class. $150 to come for the Oakland conference, and a small royalty check should arrive from Vanguard. I'm broke right now, and need $28 for Allen Hoey, & money for Brockport & O.U., etc. But we're afloat. Han's pay and my half-pay are adequate, though our savings go down with Billy's Cornell bills.

Han wrote Tony a long letter. I read it. She's great.

Postcard from Bill Beavers, who will do "The Numinous" as a broadside. So, I still have several small-press things upcoming.... Odd note from Evelyn at Vanguard—couldn't she just let me know that *Erika* arrived?! I want a bit more from Vanguard, in the way of "action," than they've given me.

Ray writes that he & Joyce think we should get a 3rd editor, & suggested McClatchy or Charles Wright. I wrote back to say nix to McClatchy, fine to Wright. I hope he says yes and we get underway on this.... I also wrote Helen Plotz about that other possibility.

11/9/82

Just finished typing up in final copy "The Film," "Over This Winter," "Before Snow," and "The Beam." The last two seem just right to me now.

Spent most of the day in the cabin, and it was good for me. Finished Frank Waters' *Pumpkin Seed Point*, a balanced and wise book. So much spirit in these Zweig, Bonhoeffer, Waters books that I've just read. I try to keep my head open, as Waters was told. I drink them. This is the best kind of reading for me. I move ahead by feeling, and let such things complement my spirit and, hopefully, they'll enter my poems. I cannot <u>study</u> my way toward poems. Something in me wants to take voluminous notes, be a scholar, but I think it's that hateful will to impress. Rather, I want these things to impress themselves on me. I want to keep my spirit malleable, head open as a well-pruned apple tree.

I don't look forward to the extravaganza Friday night. My one and only school obligation of the year, though. I'll read a few Brockport poems.

Death Wish, a Charles Bronson revenge film is on. Something in me responds very strongly to such films. Well, I'm not alone, surely. Our great desire for strength and justice when evil wrongs us—passionate, visceral, bloody <u>need</u>, if "desire" sounds too literary.

11/11/82

It's just before ten in the morning. Cabin warming, coffee steaming. Vet's day. Overcast and drizzling. I've nothing special to do, can just read & write & look forward to a ball game this evening.... Billy called last night, and will be home tomorrow, so the four of us will go to dinner at the Senior Center and then to the art/poetry show.

I stopped in Mirko's office yesterday before basketball to help him with his promotion application.... Saw Mark Anderson, who said the top floor of Hartwell will be closed. If I lose my office, no sweat, so it goes, but I'll look for a good one somewhere.

Rimore stopped over with two weeks of school mail, gulp. Nothing new, the English Department choking in rules and regulations.

Han wrote a long letter to Tony in China.

Reading Daniel Hoffman's *Brotherly Love*. Finishing Bonhoeffer poem.

Brother Henry called yesterday. His divorce has gone through. He sounds fine.

Leonid Breshnev died yesterday.

Later: Mirko just stopped back here, and we went over parts of his application. He's one of the few people I'm happy to have walk in on me back here. Last time, I think, he brought me the terrible news of the death of Linda Rock.

11/13/82

Well, thank god that's over, the art/poetry thing last night, the awkwardly perched reading in the Fine Arts Bldg., all the smiling & being nice. Did have good conversation with Stewarts & Wolskys at Bob Marx' party later on.... Billy made it home fine, is playing ball with Kurt & Mack this Saturday afternoon.... Many friends around last night; but social occasions are generally painful for me.

I'll go to Senior Center with Han for a surprise gathering for Joyce McCullough's 40th today. We had a spaghetti dinner there yesterday.

My two new North Point Press books arrived. I was disappointed both in Wendell Berry's *The Wheel* and Merwin's *Finding the Islands*. Both books filled with mannerisms. Berry's poems pleasant, sincere, but talky and they moon too much about song and dance and the great eternal universal circle. He'll end a beautiful stanza, one of a hummingbird standing in air (standing?) to drink from flowers, with a too-blunt, too-true line like "By sweetness alone it survives." It is not enough that he as grounded man is the solid center of this book. The poems have to stay closer to the world he walks. There has to be <u>less,</u> somehow, a narrowing down. The Merwin three-line poems are sometimes worth the three lines, but often not. He has not taken the time to hear whether or not the pieces reverberate. They are often too long, do not trust us, can be made much better by shortening. He needs connective words often because he doesn't use punctuation. "Old dry banana leaf / one of my aunts / but I can't remember which" could easily be "Dry banana leaf, / an aunt— / which?" Bad example, but while reading I could chop through & get down inside the pieces and shorten them. "As I grow older / the cities spread / over the earth" to "I grow older— / cities spread / the earth." "Suddenly wrinkles appear / on the water / and are gone" to "Wrinkles / on the water / and gone." The poems don't trust me enough, or the language. "One cricket starts up / in the still moonlight / and wakes the refrigerator" to "One cricket / in moonlight / wakes the refrigerator." I dwelled & dwelled over the pieces in "Lord Dragonfly" & "Evening Dawning" (after many of them rushed toward me) to make them lean & vibrating, and even some of them don't make it. *Finding the Islands* is too easy to be a book yet. They needed more time from Merwin. I can't help thinking that he makes $1.10 a book for the $11.00 book & needs the money.

I'm lazy as hell today. Wish I could stay home, but have to go to the Senior Center. Well, there will be a good ham dinner.

11/14/82 (Sunday afternoon)

Billy just left for Cornell. He'll be home in about eight days again, so we let him take the car. It was a good visit.

The gathering for Joyce's 40th at the Senior Center last evening for about a dozen friends was one she won't forget. I gave her one of the lip pieces of a Roman cooking pot.

Richard Ehrlich is going to stop over and then have dinner with us. He's a sweet boy. I wonder what he'll make of his life, what he'll end up doing.... No word from my other sons, Bruce Agte & Tony Vallone in Lake Charles, for a while.

Russians playing Indiana in basketball right now.

I'll drive Han to work in the morning, early, and work a few hours in the cabin.

Upstate took the "Milkweed" prose piece I sent them. I'll be locally famous again.

11/16/82

Nine in the morning. Cabin warming. I think of airports, classrooms, city streets, advertising offices, all the places I don't have to be today.

I've carried the typewriter back here, and thermos, and this journal and notebooks, in a laundry basket to make it in one trip. I've had in mind to connect in this journal a couple of things.

Paul Mariani in a review of Thomas Merton quoting the monk who walked among giant Buddhas at Polonnaruway: "Then the silence of the extraordinary faces. The great smiles. Huge and yet subtle. Filled with every possibility, questioning nothing, knowing everything, rejecting nothing, the peace not of emotional resignation but of Madhyamika, of sunyata, that has seen through every question without trying to discredit anyone or anything—*without refutation*—without establishing some other argument.... I was knocked over with a rush of relief and thankfulness at the *obvious* clarity of the figures.... I was suddenly, almost forcibly, jerked clean out of the habitual, half-tied vision of things, and an inner clearness, clarity, as of exploding from the rocks themselves, became evident and obvious.... I mean, I know and have seen what I was obscurely looking for."... Something in me resists the seeming amorality of this clarity, even as I feel and understand the acceptance, the Whitman beyond argument who witnesses and waits. I like "without establishing some other argument." I haven't the energy or desire for a logical system, but would like my life, my being to be the <u>the</u>. Not always to be the tortured asker of questions (as teacher can I ask questions without asking them?—maybe so), but to be at ease inside myself. <u>As I seem pretty much to be already!</u> Death, my own death, is not something I think much about, and it isn't mental laziness, but perspective and balance, maybe, that gives me ease. But I worry about Han & the kids, my folks, others (even as I feel the human family is all one).... I've been anxious about growing old mentally too fast, losing ambition. There's even a yawn behind my eyes right now as I write. But much of this may be emotional peace, being settled, content. Maybe I force myself to ask questions when I really don't have any.

Merton went looking, and found. In the same way, Paul Zweig locked his eyes "on Muktananda's face, on his wonderful brown hands and his supple legs.... In this man's presence I was cured of a 'nightmare' which I had come to accept as the main premise of my life. At this very moment, I am happy. In that case, why shouldn't I chant, bow, and beg for attention?" Zweig says that he learned "to be a bemused spectator of these silly notions of mine." He describes Muktananda as a life unfolding in the present: "he is himself wholly present. None of his mental energy is reserved for holding onto a past or planning for a future; he is never saving, always spending. Every movement he makes, from beating on a tambourine to scratching himself, is so decisive it rivets our attention. The thought and the act coincide; the want and its fulfillment are the same. Another way to say this is that he has no wants, for nothing in him is incomplete. It is, from this point of view, an existence bathed in magic, a spontaneous existence. Maybe that is the fundamental *siddhi*—or supernormal power—which Siddha masters are said to possess: the magic of unwitholding presentness."... Unity and wholeness. To <u>resist</u> turning our life into meanings all the time. To be. Zweig thinks of Jesus as such a person (I hear many contradictions here, but so what?): "Why do you think the apostles hung around Jesus all the time? Why did noblemen and peasants, during the middle ages, have such awe for hermits meditating in their caves all over Europe? It was because they understood the psychic perfection these holy men had achieved.

They knew that by simply hanging around such men, they too might get their second chance.... Trusting him we trust ourselves, and loving him we love ourselves."

Nothing contradicts. So what if Zweig echoes Whitman (always spending), and Eliot on John Donne, and has to understand Muktananda in Western terms? So what if Muktananda gets angry occasionally, or writes an autobiography (I was thinking that this journal, if I became questionless, would go blank)? "Be, be, Budda said," as Stafford said.

So many things around me now—sounds of clock ticking & of heater purring, gloves on table, coffee cup, Walt to my left-front and Archie within white light, brown rug, thumbnail moon riding above this pen, evergreens outside and a thousand ash. Something, some being is underneath/wiithin everything, something that can't be extinguished, something I'm part of, and will be, though probably not in ways I could anticipate or understand. For now, to live with clarity, the clarity of lines & poems, too. A person who had always been blind and after an operation could see for the first time & said she was amazed at how clear everything was. It is clear despite our eyesight. Clarity.

Did write to Tony last night.... Had much fun playing ball yesterday. Biked up to the gym in the snow.... *Translating Neruda* from John Felstiner in the mail, and I look forward to it.... Finished Harnack's *Under My Wings Everything Prospers*—liked the stories, but the novelette "White Blood" seemed strange & diffuse to me. Will read the novel of his I have on hand, too.... Sort of want to get my poems in order back here, see what I have to send out, etc. Waiting for the batch to come back from *Poetry*, and then maybe I'll send to *APR*. Want to type up the couple of prose pieces I've drafted in my copy of *Light*, too.... Han & Kris away all day at work/school, and then in Rochester at Eastman, so except for an hour or so for lunch, I'll stay back here all day.... I've enjoyed, again, scrawling in this journal. Maybe it's the sense of leaving a trace that Bonhoeffer's friend Bethge talked about. My unfinished poem just now called me!...

Later: It's evening. I'm the same person, watching *The Blue & the Gray*, a melodrama, on television, feeling a little fidgety about not doing "big work" all the time. But it's been a good day—cleaned out the drainpipes, finished "The Vapor," took mower battery down to Studiers', typed a couple of prose pieces for my memoir, wrote a couple of letters—and Han is keeping me company, and all's well. Tomorrow, I'll work here inside for a few hours, and then bike up to play ball. It's supposed to be fairly warm again.

Packing boxes of books for Rochester still, again. Want to talk with Peter Dzwonkoski next month about a room, if only an interim place. [?] Maybe I'll keep status quo & just keep piling up. Some impressive books going over there again.

Evelyn called about a file copy from Vanguard (*Shuddering*) ending up in a book catalogue—I told her to press the dealer & find out where he got it—and about all the specials of *Light* & *Dragonfly*. I'd like to buy the latter. Will see how much she asks.

11/17/82

I've decided to stay home this evening and skip the reading. Maybe will get to answer a letter or two. Did write Stewe Claeson & sent him some poems.

Played ball today. Haven't done much else. Spent an hour with Han at the Senior Center after her meeting.... Saw Freddie Poulin briefly at about 1:30—he was drinking scotch & chainsmoking, as usual.

Began the Harnack novel. It's good.

11/19/82

Damn, I'm in bed with a painful left knee after hurting it again last night in the ball game. I got a rebound, and got clipped from the left. It's going to be at least a month before I can play a little, very little, again. I might have to change my life, shoot baskets by myself, something. I don't know. I slept solid a couple of times, though. So, I'm in bed, and will be for a few days, I think. Will not be able to work at the fish-fry tonight or go to Pittsford to Kristen's concert tomorrow. I feel too uncomfortable to answer some mail I should answer. I'll see.

Invited to do the Hofstra workshop again next summer. $1500. I will. I know the ropes there now. The money will help for Billy's tuition.

Finished Harnack's *Limits of the Land*, alternately caring and not caring for it. The feeling that he pushed, in places, to find something to write about and had to lean toward the unlikely or bizarre. Other times, a musical flow of sentences. I was particularly interested, regarding *CR*, that his character August had to give up his dream of family-succession of the land.

Have begun Elie Wiesel's *A Jew Today*. Will probably finish it today.

I'll even have a hard time getting to the bathroom for a few days. I'll watch television, and read, and count my blessings. Hopefully, I'll be comfortable by next Wednesday when Billy & Kurt arrive, and Thursday when we all head for Hamburg for Thanksgiving…. I'll probably scrawl a progress report in this journal this evening.

11/20/82

It's about three in the morning. I've propped myself in bed, after taking a couple of aspirins for my knee…. I've finished *A Jew Today*, and want to write some things about it. Reading it, I felt often that *Erika* was okay, would not/should not be offensive to Wiesel, to the truth. But I'm worried when he talks about the "contempt" those show who confuse killer with victim or suggest they are or could be the same: "You argued that the boundaries were not clearly defined: that after all, under different circumstances, the victims might have turned into killers…. I consider it an unfair, unworthy and despicable hypothesis, one that slanders the dead posthumously and attempts to dishonor the survivors. Only a man who *has* killed is a killer. The victims killed no one." This comes from a powerful essay, "A Plea for the Survivors." Just where does *Erika* stand (if it stands anywhere) in this regard? I know I've come to feel that depending on circumstances—upbringing, threats against family, education—I could have been an *SS*, or perhaps had the courage of Bonhoeffer. Even if I am right, maybe this is where I am wrong. Wiesel spends much time talking of Jewish history and the Talmud being profoundly <u>against</u> war in ways in which Christianity or Mohammedenism is not. Perhaps the Jew, by and large, could not have killed me as I feel I could have killed him. Yes, it seems to me true that the individual man who has killed no one is not a killer. But yes, it seems to me that somehow humanity is connected, that we are one in this, god help me. Bless the sages and the children who died, innocent and soul-free; curse the racist twisted murderers who made Auschwitz. I'm lost. The speaker of "Simple Truths," when he talks about the luck and fortune that we were not the victims or the murderers, has become hysterical and is just raving, maybe, but essentially I believe this. But perhaps, if a survivor were to read this and become part of the "we," my poem would be guilty, I would be guilty of showing contempt. I don't know. I want to believe that *Erika* as a whole will be wiser than I am, will contain, in about fifteen years of my voices, answers within itself and as a whole is not offensive.

The Holocaust as a theme has become desanctified, says Wiesel, and surely he's right. Every videoidiot thinks he knows all about it. We do not speak of it carefully or in hushed tones, allow it its mystery and opaqueness, but act as though we know its whys and wherefores. Does *Erika* contribute to this watering down? I don't know. "Even those who have not experienced the event may learn to be worthy of it." "But it must be approached with fear and trembling. And above all, with humility." My fear and trembling was genuinely there as I wrote most of those poems. I hope the humility is, too, though I guess I do believe in the book.

"If you have not grasped it until now, it is time you did: Auschwitz signifies death—total, absolute death— of man and of mankind, of reason and of the heart, of language and of the senses. Auschwitz is the death of time, the end of creation; its mystery is doomed to stay whole, inviolate."

Late afternoon: I'm still in bed, nursing my knee. Han is in Pittsford with Kristen…. Al called to say that the New Directions anthology just took a long poem of his, and to say he was going in to Buffalo for Logan's 60th birthday. My knee grounds me. I hope to be able to drive to the mall Tuesday maybe to renew my license.

Wiesel mentions that some Jews, faced with despair, came to believe in assimilation as an option. "Yes, there are Jews who arrive at the conclusion that since Jewishness has forever been linked to suffering, they must give it up to protect themselves and their children." "Self-delusion" he calls it. Surely Oscar Mandel is one of these. I've read closely again his "Being and Judaism" in *The Georgia Review*, one of the most jolting essays I've ever read. It makes so much sense. But just as the human species is revolted, as he says, by such obdurate differences of others, so will the human species form its non-conformist enclaves down through time. How could Wiesel argue—well, he would tell stories, turn to the Talmud, sing. He would bore the freer Mandel, freer but maybe less exultant but maybe not as vulnerable at the next (God help us) Holocaust.

When Mandel mentions Hitler's revulsion the first time he saw an East European Jew, and says he felt the same way, too, I begin to think of the scenes I see on West 47th St. in Manhattan. I'm used to those bearded and pale-faced young and old men in black. But once I saw a chubby and unhealthy-looking father in caftan and black wide-brimmed hat, long curls dangling down from each ear, and he was with his son who looked like a smaller version of his father. I didn't like the look of the two of them. I <u>was</u> sort of disgusted—they were pale as slugs, sort of rumpled, flabby, no strength, seemed like aberrtions there in the street. Of <u>course</u> the world should leave them alone. Of <u>course</u> it probably won't. Their rituals & legends & holy books are for Mandel mumbo-jumbo, superstition, written in blood, even <u>boring</u>. Theirs is not the eccentric self-reliance of the American tradition that means so much to me, but the chained stupid religiousness that Whitman despised. The man, were he free as Mandel, would wake up and begin to free his descendents. He can't, of course. The wheel turns. The arguments go on always, all ways.

11/21/82

I'm back in bed, watching a mindless Clint Eastwood film called "Escape from Alcatraz," but I did get up today, got dressed, wrapped some books for Christmas gifts we'll take with us Thursday, and answered some mail. Wrote Charlotte Martinez, Bob Sargent at Hofstra, others. Small checks to Care & Brockport alumni, and paid my last credit card bill of $80. Felt good to get a few things done. I hobble around now, slowly.... Sent for Norbert's book for thirty-six bucks. Ouch. But he buys my Ewert things.

Keep thinking about the Mandel essay. Clear because of its assumptions, its givens. It moves inexorably from an agnostic or atheist center, through a convincing pragmatism, and even toward an ideal, though not one held with much faith....

Have been reading Merwin's *Unframed Originals*. Have not been very interested, and I'm not sure why. Some good moments, but the family blurs together, at least in "Tomatoes." Maybe I've not <u>wanted</u> to like this book, or feel threatened by it because I want my memoir to be better or because I'm envious of the Princeton star or don't like him much. I'll keep reading. I <u>should</u>, no matter what, be more interested. Merwin himself is so absent? No, that's not it. My own childhood—well, I wasn't concerned much with dreary relatives or how my parents got along. I was always staring at our grape arbor, or the pear trees, or the two maples or three dogwoods, or pheasant feathers, or turtle snouts above the pondwater, or Patac's azaleas in pink bloom. Maybe <u>that's</u> why I don't believe much of his *Finding the Islands* book—maybe it's not the intensity that's lacking, but that all the natural things are used as <u>ornament</u>, are not felt as natural symbol, have not really been experienced and thus cannot give themselves, cannot reverberate in a poem—have not been <u>earned</u>. Am I wrong, or do the catalpas in "Mother and Son" (not to mention something especially dwelled on like the pike in "The Return") find a music that carries deep feeling? If so, it's because those trees along our driveway truly are important to me, lead back to my lost world.... I like the question I came to articulate in this paragraph, but feel too arrogant. I'll keep reading *Unframed Originals*.

11/22/82

It's mid-afternoon and I'm resting in bed. I took a bath to loosen up my knee, listened to some Abba bubble-music feeling sad and happy about my life, ate some lunch. Will now spend the day reading and corresponding.

$172 royalty check from Vanguard. I feel okay about it except that *Lord Dragonfly* has sold virtually nothing.

Letter inviting me to apply for a poet's job at U. of Michigan. I'm filled with so many emotions from ambition to fear to gratitude to confusion when such a letter comes. I'm glad I was in Ann Arbor a short time ago and saw a little of that Big Ten campus. I'd be lost there, wondering why the fuck I'd moved. Anyway, I'm glad that Han & I have decided any move is out of the question until Kristen is at least settled into college, or maybe out. What could I have better than I have here—except maybe better students & classes, a bit less teaching? Another place would have more prestige, but I do seem usually to think enough of myself here. O Brockport, my home. But that Roethke/Seager/Hall country intrigues. I'd be the envy of many in a job like that. And I'd probably be sick-at-heart.

Wrote a little twelve-line poem called "December Snow" and it's a good one. I seem to be in my raspberries stage.

Read the "Mary" section in Merwin last night. It's somewhat more interesting than "Tomatoes," but I may be getting closer to understanding what bothers me. I don't believe what he's saying. So much seems posed. There's so much overly-formal literary talk among the homey details. The writing is self-conscious. I'll keep reading....

Here's where "December Snow" stands:

> December snow covers the canes completely,
> but I know where they are,
> and last night, suspended among them
> in cold sleep, I tasted the answer,
>
> which came to me as a story:
> a man picking the summer berries
> kneels to find a perfect cluster before
> December snow covers the canes completely,
>
> and does, and eats the several soft
> delicious dark-red berries which melt
> on his tongue like snowflakes until
> December snow covers the canes completely.

Later: it's evening, after a long slow day. But a good day, Han & Kris & I close. I'll be home all day tomorrow, and will go for my license the day after, Wednesday, which will be given up anyway to waiting for Billy & waiting for cable TV and packing for the trip to Hamburg for Thanksgiving.

"as a story" above should maybe be "in story."

I like "The Skyline" in Merwin best so far. It's less diffuse than the first two sections.

Bill Ewert just called. We spoke for about a half-hour about this and that. Bill says that the journal of May Sarton's 70th year begins with our visit to her, hummingbird and all.

"on his tongue" should maybe be "on your tongue" & the whole poem will melt away this way.

I think I'll write the Smiths & say McClatchy wd. be okay with me as a 3rd editor. It could be a good thing for the book. Sandy wd. get some poets of the fancy-ass school in it.

Monday night football is back, after the eight-week strike, and I'm watching.

I think today may be John Logan's 60th birthday. Except for my knee, I'd be in Buffalo with Al.

Han & Kris & I were talking about Grandma Irene this evening again. I've thought of that good woman often lately. Han had a couple pictures of her blown up for Grandpa for Christmas—that will lead to some weeping, I know. His leg is apparently acting up, the stump, on him again. We'll see him Thursday, and see.

11/24/82

It's about 2:30 in the afternoon. I'm killing time waiting for Billy, and waiting for the guy who is installing our cable to finish—he'll be here a couple of hours, I think. We'll have two wires in from two poles in the street. It's a pain in the ass, but already tonight, I think, there's indoor soccer and pro basketball.... My knee hurts because I've been on it all day—drove to the Greece mall for my driver's license this morning—and I look forward to pulling out the bed this evening.... Some snow, but not much sticking. Kristen will be home soon and cheering to be on vacation.

I've thought hard the last couple of days about withdrawing from the Ontario Review Press anthology, sometimes feeling it would stunt my growing soul! But I wrote Joyce & Ray to say sure, what the hell, ask McClatchy to edit it with us. Or maybe Mary Oliver or Plumly as the 3rd.

Read a little Whitman in the middle of the night. Read "To Think of Time," slowly, and it brought tears, unexpectedly. Holes in the poem, weaknesses, but it got to me anyway. And it gave me an idea for a threnody. I could call it "Black Lines." The epigraph would be from Walt:

> Slow moving and black lines go ceaselessly over the earth,
> Northerner goes carried and Southerner goes carried,
>   and they on the Atlantic side and they on the Pacific,
>   and they between, and all through the Mississippi country,
>   and all over the earth.

Those lines that haunt me, the concentration camp photographed from above, would come in. And maybe I could follow my own black lines through my idea of death. Not a Holocaust poem, but that would be one of the images.... Walt had central questions, but insisted on being faithful, and it is this quality, the desire & force, that is so moving, even if the pain as <u>artifact</u> sometimes breaks down logically, or ignores its own gullibility. But often, he convinces, just within the power of his speech: "You are not thrown to the winds, you gather certainly and safely around yourself."... Walt says the same thing in this poem, too, questioning extinction, that he does in that conversation with Traubel I referred to in my *Newsday* review.

The bum knee is good for the journal, anyway.

Finished the Merwin book, caring more for its last pieces.

11/29/82

It's 2:30 in the afternoon. I'm sitting in my room at Yaddo. I got here about an hour ago. Rosemary, Curt Harnack's secretary, gave me a short tour. I drove all the way (about 5½ hrs.) in rain, and it's a glum afternoon. I've brought my suitcase & briefcase & laundry basket up, and my big blanket. It's very quiet here—I hear a bluejay off in the distance. I think I'm in what was E. Ames' house, room #16. The two weeks will be a long time here, but I <u>know</u>, just sitting here as relaxed as I am, that this will be a good stay, that I'll work long and long on *CR*, uninterrupted. This room seems right for me. I have everything here I need. I'm glad I brought along this journal, which I'll write in often, I'm sure, maybe even for drafting some sections of *CR*—I have loose paper but no notebooks. I'm anxious to begin my work. Kristen is at the Concord for her All-State orchestra, Billy is back in Ithaca, and Han is alone for a couple of days. I'll write her. There will be long days here of minding my own business—only a few guests around at all right now. Yes, I'm going to have a good stay here. Will move a desk or table or chair around a little to make myself perfectly comfortable.

We had a fine Thanksgiving gathering in Hamburg, and a couple good days at home with the kids after that. Han & I spent Thursday night in Nashville, took Pop to the doctor Friday morning. Hopefully, the swelling of his stump will go down.

The car is right below me on the edge of a circular driveway.... A distant susurrus of traffic.... Black-capped chickadees just made me think of Nesconset. Now I think of Archie who said it's the same place always. Now I think of John Brinnin who just left here. A letter from Bob Phillips was waiting for me.... I have some boxes of cereal, a big bottle of red wine, a quart of peaches. Sounds like the lunches (2 sandwiches, etc.) will be adequate, but I'll probably be looking around for snacks, but I'm glad, right now, I'm here. I'll be uninterrupted from after breakfast until dinner, except for having to return the lunch pail by 4 each day.... This is all chatter. I'm here. I'm not sorry I came. I will keep writing—*CR*, letters, journal.... Will read, if I read, Mariani's biography of Wms., which I've brought along....

Later: I wrote Han, and have gotten settled. Have moved the easy chair, a bookcase. Have made myself a comfortable spot. Could use a footrest. Will come to <u>own</u> this spot in this room, focus the light within me in this spot.

How to get started? Maybe, to catch up with where I am (I was thinking) I should write out all of *CR* to where I am, maybe in this journal. Maybe not.... I've been looking at the first section, deciding on the "losing its leaves" line. Such decisions are not easy.

Later: back from dinner. Curt was there, and four or five others that I don't really know, not even their names.... I carried back here and have been browsing John Haffenden's *The Life of John Berryman*. He quotes my memoir. Henry, where did all the frenzy come from? Why did you talk so much? Was it because you thought if you talked long enough you could come to The Truth?

The other 4 (Curt went to bed) are downstairs drinking wine. I'm tempted to join them, but probably won't. It's 9:00. I'll look at *CR* for an hour or two and call it a night, I guess. I want to write, somehow, and not play the role of a writer. I could drink & carry on & recite poems to those folks (who said at dinner nobody knows any poetry by heart these days), but this isn't my economy. Once or twice I *will* socialize over the next couple of weeks, but that's all. But the way to fame (or a kind of infamy) *is* to carry on, impress and offend and spout. J.B.'s work was wonderful. If he'd been a quiet man who minded his business the Haffenden book wouldn't exist.

It was a spaghetti dinner, and delicious....

Later: okay, it's 10:00. Progress report: I've made a start. I've read over the first 18 sections, brought all changes together, hve begun to get back into touch with my poem. It seems all so naturally one to me, of *a voice*, that I don't even worry the transitions as I once did. I'll go on tomorrow looking at the sections of *Blackberry Light* and *Wenzel*, and then begin to push ahead with the new sections, "finished" and unfinished, that I have along. I haven't brought the typewriter—I was thinking of typing the whole manuscript from the beginning, but that mechanical stuff can wait, and I'm not sorry I don't have the typewriter here. Long as I keep my main manuscript clear enough to read.

I should be tired. All that driving in the rain. And I've done about as much work on *CR* as I have in a long time, and that after driving here & settling in and dinner with strangers. I want to go to bed soon. Want to write Phillips—feel obligated—and Billy.... Good night, journal, you've been a comfort again, receptacle for nervous chatter, for my psyche's pretending to be a writer, for moments of forgetfulness, for manifestation of the assumptions that my life and scribblings matter or will, at least to me.

Berryman said that Roethke thought like a flower. I like that. I hope I can do some of that before my stay here is over.

11/30/82

Didn't sleep much. Went over and had some eggs for breakfast. Have been working on *CR*. Much commotion in halls & rooms around me, but this was the one cleaning day, I think.... It's noon now, and I'm sipping wine.

Made some decisions, changes, in various sections. Have come up against my first real difficulty, and it's been a problem for years. It's the ending of "The Bark"; more specifically, it's the search for an adjective before "body," one that would suggest gathering-against-chaos, or form-finding, or building for the future faithfully. I have the concept inside myself, but not a good word for it. That property and purpose that the dusty miller has, the dream of forest, of land out of/away from chaos and the waves. That section of the poem—I just haven't gotten it right. It's close, though. But it's been close for years. I'll keep reading it.

Dropped Billy a card last night, and Bob Phillips a letter this morning.... It's about time for lunch now. Then I want to go for a long walk. Then a shave & shower. Then, from about 3 or so, as it gets dark here, until dinner, a long session with *CR*. I think I'm going to like those hours of darkness before dinner best.... No one in the room next to me yet. I'd like to keep the bathroom for myself.

Later: 2:00. I went for a walk. Knee hurts, and I have to be very careful to put my foot down flat.... Walked around the mansion, through parts of the garden. Quite a place. All too big for me. I know about myself that I'm secure in small, cozy places, even the way I've arranged this easy chair & bookcase. What living went on here—that view from the mansion's back porch! Most impressive are the trees. Maybe tonight I'll take out from the library that book about Yaddo.... I'm already beginning to get settled in here. So far, I don't feel as I did at Hofstra or on other trips. I know what I'm here for—to work on *CR*. In Brockport, I'd likely be more restless (and certainly less disciplined) than I am here. I'll work for an hour or two now, and then shower. I may have found a good way to end "The Bark". Will write it out again….

    Later: 9:00. I'm back from dinner and good talk with Michael McGuire and Marc-Antonio Consoli. Curt also there again. Roast beef, mashed potatoes, peas and carrots. Delicious again. Tempted again to have some wine with new friends, but I want to put in a couple hours tonight. I will go out once or twice. Will certainly go into the bookshops in Saratoga Friday or Saturday.
    Much progress toward holding in mind all of *CR* again. I'm stopped at the section called "A Voice," which follows "Family Tree." I'm not sure wht I'm up to here, and will write it over this evening. I rewrote "The Psalm," getting rid of a flat spot. All's well. I might just have breakfast in my room tomorrow morning, the cereal & peaches I brought along, and pick up my lunch & thermos later on.
    So, all's well. I tried to call home, but no answer. I may or may not try again later. I did drop a letter to Bill Ewert. Might drop a letter to Evelyn Shrifte, just to stay in touch…. At Hofstra for two weeks, I counted the days before I could leave. Here, if I work steadily and stay lucky, time should be a presence and joy, not something to try to get through.

    Later: 10:30. I may have broken toward something else in "A Voice" (or "The Voice"). Will stare at it tomorrow. I'm anxious (probably too anxious) to get through it and move on. I could probably abandon it altogether forever, but do want some such thing before I get to "The Wool."… Just called Han, and she's fine, and she's heard from Kristen who found out again she's the best clarinetist around. A warm & loving talk. Oh, I love that woman, love my home. Mail from Tony, Mike Waters, etc. Apparently, an invitation to do the Southampton workshop next summer, but it's at the same time as Hofstra, alas. Maybe they'll have me the following summer. Apparently, an invitation from GCC to read. Etc…. I want to write Tony—oh, he's ready to come home, says Han…. Well, another day here winds down. Maybe I'll read a little. Very little sleep the past two nights, and I hope tonight's the night. I won't have to worry about breakfast or the cleaning lady tomorrow, and that will help.

12/1/82

    I finally got some good sleep. Woke up at 9:30, after falling solidly asleep about five. Had breakfast hee, worked an hour or so on what is now the about-finished 39th section—Walt came in and saved me last night—and just now walked over for my lunch-box and thermos. Another dark day. I love it hee. I have to see no one now until dinner. I'll work, eat, work and walk. I'm very close now (I think) to getting with new work on *CR*.

    Later: 5:30. Dinner in an hour. A good, peaceful day. I walked for at least an hour, following the small map of trails, ending up on the far side of two lakes, walking up the slope of the towr studio (once an icehouse) and then coming up, just when I was getting tired (my knee) beside Pine Garde. The walk made me happy. I stopped often just to breathe deep and look upward into the pines. I look forward to a walk each day…. Then, hours of good work. I've begun the unfinished book, have worked on "The Binding" section and hope to end up with a satisfactory ending for it. Maybe it will be the section that opens the 5th book. "The Tree," with its "American Time" phrase (maybe my title if nothing else better shows up), pleased me as I read it over. So, I'm into the fifth book after getting the first 42 sections back in mind, and even improving some of these. Do I feel any pressure to _finish_ while I'm here, pressure because of the Ewert project? I _hope_ not! On the other hand, I'm also tempted psychologically _never_ to finish *CR*—in progress, I always feel involved, can tell folks what I'm doing, do not have to feel written out and dried up and between projects. In any case, there's plenty left to do—I think of "The Ghost" section, and others.

    Later: 9:00. Back from a good chicken dinner, and pleasant talk, especially with Marc. An easy-going group of people here…. I'm sitting in bed, my knee propped up in its most comfortable position. I see myself in the full-length door mirror to my left. My clock ticks away.
    I read a little here and there in Mariani's *Williams*. Will stay with it, and write him in a couple of weeks.

Again, I don't feel like turning to *CR* this evening. It's okay to be tired. I don't have to prove anything to anybody here. I've already done quite a bit, when I think of it, over the past few days, and I'm just settling in here and finding my way around and within the routine.... It occurs to me, too, that it's good if I'm a little tired of *CR* (it's not <u>that</u>, exactly, but that I want to get other kinds of beauty into my poems): it may be plenty long, and it will be good to end it before writing many more sections. Maybe I won't end up with 52. Maybe 50. No matter. I guess I still like the idea of 52.

12/2/82

I just found a whacky poem in the Mariani biography, and like what I did.

<u>On a Trolley to the Hospital</u>

There's a story of Doc Williams on a New York trolley
in 1908 or so with a dead baby in a suitcase.
He was in charge of pediatrics, and found himself
in the middle of an outbreak of gastroenteritis
killing his babies like waterbugs.
Story goes that someone loaned an uptown mansion
for overflow patients, but stipulated <u>no deaths</u>.
When the kid died, Williams wanted it
out of there, packed it into the suitcase,
and took that trolley to the hospital.
What if he'd lost the suitcase, or it broke open,
or began to smell?—this was July!
Never again. If they died uptown, they did,
and that was that. It was the same with poetry.

I don't want to screw with it and make it smarter, or less gross or whatever.
    It's about 4:00. I worked some this morning, just about finishing "The Binding," and puttered with other sections and arranging. I went for a long walk, knee hurting quite a bit, then took a ride to Saratoga, went in three bookstores, and couldn't find a thing. Filled up the car. Am back, resting, after a shave and shower. Feel good about things. One or two more people seem to be moving in up here near me—the echoes are such that I can't really tell which side they're on. I'd like to keep the bathroom to myself, but doubt that I will.
    Very warm today, almost 60. I'll be just as glad if the weather gets miserable for a while—makes more sense being inside working.
    Have worked on the section (if it becomes one) beginning "All his life a man loved elms." It might turn out to be a good one. I keep trying to remember what the Japanese potter said: "It's hardest to make simple things." "Time cannot overwhelm," added Roethke.

12/3/82

Well, it's Friday and I'm still glad to be here. I fell asleep for a couple hours sleep each time three times last night, and feel strong and refreshed. Yesterday morning I thought my knee was getting worse, but it's on the mend slowly again today.... Had wine with the group yesterday evening.... It's just before 9:00 in the morning now—I'm back from some good scrambled eggs and ready to go.... I now share the bathroom with a woman, Anna-Lise someone, but it shouldn't be much of a strain. I'm ready for a full day on *CR*. Not as nice out today, and better for working.... Brought over my two Harnack books for Curt's inscriptions last evening.... It was vegetarian night, eggplant parmesan, not bad. I'd never had it before.... Will finish my letter to Don Hall—saving me that task at least when I get home—and get to work....

Later: 10:30. I believe I'm the only goddamned person in all of Yaddo. Unless there's a watchman around somewhere. Curt in New York, and the other four "colonists" are in town. I'm tired and decided to stay here. I did go into town for coffee and cake with Marc & Michael this afternoon.

Had a good morning on *CR*. Things falling into place.

Dropped Han a note.... Got a letter from Bruce.... Discovered a corridor of great pines and walked it three times. It leads from here to the grave knoll.

On occasional jumpy moments I feel like heading home, but I'll still keep trying to make the best of this place. Maybe I'm just too healthy, not driven enough, but then just Puritanical enough to feel guilty about not doing enough, enough, enough!

12/4/82

An experience this morning that I've never had before, not even with *Erika*, which is a collection, but of individual things. I finished *The Chestnut Rain*. Maybe a few details to work out, but I wrote a strong ending for "Epilogue: The Ghost," and that did it. The sections of the last book are in order. I have the title, *The Ghost*. I have my 52 sections, and I have two ending sections that do all I can do. I walked through the pines getting lighter step by step. Now, I just feel like running, but the knee (& I saw the knee images again in the quotation from Millen Brand—how's that for bringing a poem & the chestnut tree into the body!) won't let me. I feel restless, want to go, even want to go home, but won't until at least next Thursday or Friday. Beautiful, warm, sunny day today, and I'll find some way to fill it. Will make clean copies of some sections of *CR* over the next days, too. Will keep reading Mariani, and will write a few letters. If I knew my way around better, I could travel to some other bookstores, too.... Anyway, even while I smile a little reading of Williams' brash claims for his own greatness, I believe *CR* is a great poem, in my own romantic, non-cynical mode. I did it. It began with that Bicentennial piece I fooled with in 1975 or so, and ended here. It is a book, one book, a thing that coheres. No one has done anything like it. Metaphors of tree-war-deer have room to grow within it for always, and that white light, at last, all light, ghost light, sperm light. My best book, my most satisfying book. How did I do it? I did it. I look at myself in the mirror across from my bed. I give the finger. To whom or what? I don't know. I give the finger. I finished the poem. Fuck all of you who said I couldn't do it or that it doesn't matter, fuck you, I did it, and it's done.

Later: it's an hour after the above ¶. I looked at the few words on deer on turnpikes that I scratched out a week or two ago as a possible beginning for a section of *CR* if I needed one, but don't, with 52, but wrote a poem just now called "The Hunters" and it's a good one, a city parable again, yes, yes, and I'll write it out here it flows like no other of my poems except a section of "The Uncertainty Principle" holding the deer in its body the hunters the neighbors the eyelights the nostrils and fur in the cities—

The Hunters

    tar roads and turnpikes deer
    hurtle through darkness
    on fenders or hoods or truck-beds
    on trailers their eyes—
    strobes of yellow in carlights or
    walleye or crimson from neon they
    enter the cities their bodies
    so lungless and gutted so doe-delicate
    nostrils the lashes the faces the bucks'
    antlers as trees as trophies
    dragged from the woods the neighbors
    in clusters by trailer by car
    touching the fur of the kill
    saying deer from the wild saying deer

The Hunters

tar roads and turnpikes deer
hurtle through darkness
on fenders on hoods on truck-beds
on trailers their eyes
strobes of yellow in carlights or
walleyed or crimson from neon they
lurch into traffic in cities their bodies
so lungless and gutted so doe-delicate
nostrils their lashes their faces the bucks'
antlers as trees as trophies
dragged from the woods the neighbors
in clusters by trailer by car
staring touching the fur of the kill
saying deer from the wild saying deer

Later: walked for over an hour, and it seemed even longer, even though I sat down a couple of times in light of the forest primeval (in my imagination). Knee tires me out. Now I am in bed, knee propped up, the Mariani book to read, other things to putter with. About 65° outside this December day. Crow call coming in over/through pines through open windows. A long walk, and I'm here again, and content. Will read all the way to dinner in three hours.

Later: about four. Right now, as I write, that fucking Kunstler is on his motorcycle downstairs. I'd heard someone run up the stairs twice and down—at least he didn't knock—then looked out and there he was. I'm in hiding. He's a pain in the ass in any case. If I'd wanted to see him I'd have written him—I know he lives near here…. He just, at last, left. And there was supposed to be no chance of being disturbed here. I almost caved in and went downstairs as he was tromping around. I'm glad I didn't. Gulp, will he show up at dinner?

I drafted another Williams poem (thanks to Mariani), will write it out here.

Baroness Elsa von Freytag-Loringhoven

She was some episode in Doc Williams' life, that one,
a real baroness who wanted to meet him.
He'd seen a sculpture that looked like chicken-guts,
and heard of her, how she dressed in purple and yellow
with a coal scuttle on her head or a tam-o'-shanter
with feathers and ice-cream spoons, or vest and kilts
with brass teaballs suspended from her nipples.
Once Wally Stevens saw her in the Village,
applauded (only here and there an old sailor, etc.),
and she'd run after him, chased the portly fellow home.
To meet her, Williams bailed her out of jail and fed her,
baroness of black lipstick, teats dangling with
empty sardine cans, Mother of Dada, 1919,
here in the New World. "Villiam Carlos Villiams,
I vant you," she said, jumping out of shadows
in Rutherford, vanting to giff him syph. He
resisted. She scratched him and ran. He bought
a punching bag and practiced, and when
she came for him again, dropped her with a right.
Maybe he'd played it too safe, but how mate with her?
He had to opt for Flossie, always new, American poetry.

> The Baroness' syph blossomed away in Paris.
> Her boyfriend turned the gascocks on and let her die.

That's another city piece, piece of two cities. It could be called, ha, "A City Piece," in fact. Two pretty good Williams almost-improvisations.

12/5/82

It's Sunday morning. After breakfast, I shaved and showered, and have just skimmed *CR*. It's awfully good. How did I write all that? It makes my music, old-fashioned and romantic as it may be. At home, I'll type the whole thing, backwards to forwards (to get the last two books to Ewert), and then sit on it long enough for another objective look at it down the line somewhere spring or so.

Strange night last night. Kunstler called at dinner, and I felt I had to join him at his place for a while. I brought Marc & Michael & Annaliese along. Kunstler was his old babbling strained-wit self talking of Mencken and manners and nonsense. I was very unhappy. But the four of us got up and left—going to a movie at Skidmore was our excuse—and were relieved. Kunstler & his woman Marianne & Clark Blaise & Liz Innes-Brown were there. Gulp. Sometimes I think my own mind is filled with shit. Jimmy's is the whole Slough of Despond. I can't stand that kind of noise, rapid-fire chatter & smart aleckyness. <u>Then</u>, Marc and I went to the movie, which was cancelled, and a porno-flick called *Bad Girls* was shown by the students instead. Wild. The kids were in masks or had bags over their heads. They let us in because they knew we were not faculty or cops. We stayed a half-hour. I laughed like hell. The art has gone a long way since the stag films I'd seen in Springville, and *Deep Throat* and *The Devil and Miss Jones* in New York. <u>Then</u>, back here to the cottage, a fire and talk and wine, the four of us again, McGuire talking of his hellish year in Saudi Arabia.... I'm going to lie low all day today. We'll have a wine/reading session after dinner. Maybe a poem will appear to me; otherwise, I'll just keep reading the Williams book, and maybe write a letter to Ewert, or Evelyn, and/or Vince Clemente, etc. As of tomorrow, I'm here for a week. I'm glad I came. I'll be glad to head back and spend time watching television. I'll type in my study with the television on for a couple weeks. No obligations, except to go in to U. of R. once before Christmas.

I love my Williams poems. Another short one:

<u>Aroma and Squish</u>

> On his first spring walk in 1921, Doc
> stepped in dogshit. "It brought on,"
> he wrote a friend, "an irresistible desire
> to study French literature."

I just made up that title. I was thinking of "Epiphany" or "Eureka" or "Shazam," or something like that, but like this one. So, I now have pieces mentioning 1908, 1919, 1921, and wouldn't mind a sequence called "Scenes in the Life of an American Poet," but won't want to force it. These grabbed me. I'll stay wide open as I read. I know I take liberties with the stories here and there.

Later: It's late afternoon. Nothing much in the way of writing today (<u>so far</u>, he says, ever hopeful!). Reading, a couple of walks, minding my business. Wrote to Bill Ewert about the finishing-up of *CR*. Called home and spoke with Han and all's well.... Cool in this room and I've put the heating pad on my knee, but I'm not sure that's a good idea.... When I get home I'll be in the midst of tons of mail, so I'd best enjoy these next 6 or 7 days. I want to get involved, even this soon, with another poem, and shouldn't forget my idea for "Black Lines," mentioned some pages back, the lines from Whitman. I'll write a few more decent letters this week, too, even if I have to mail them from Brockport.

Williams makes me worry that I'm too concerned about understanding what I'm doing, and this leads to my neat packaging into books of the kind I do. The more I write, I more and more come down to thinking that the thing is to truly care myself for the work I do, or to throw it out. At the same time, I can too easily become too safe and careful about that work of mine I care for. I want to be ready for any departure, radical or otherwise, from the full-blown lush effusive harmonious music of *CR* and poems like "Yellowthroats," "The Berries," "Mother and Son," and those new raspberry poems. I may be, right now, consolidating, after years of finding my way to learning how to write (how to free myself to write) the poem I've wanted to write. Okay, good enough. But if I change—and maybe must change/should change/won't be able to keep changing—I've got to follow <u>that</u> tide too.

12/6/82

    Woke up about five this morning and almost wrote down a dream. It was maybe the strangest, most intense dream ever, and I woke up body-clenched, red-dog angry, but the dream beyond description, but I was parallel to the ground but above it belly down with hand-appendages somehow (I know it sounds snake-like) and directing energy hatefully toward some kid/child/baby that had done me wrong. I was <u>glaring</u> at it with my mind, my face getting harder & harder. I almost could crush it on a mental beam, could stare it down and pin it with hate, and kept getting harder and angrier, my temples tightening when Han, I think, shielded the child from me and I realized my irrationality and shook myself awake but still intensely angry & spiteful & glaring.... Then, I relaxed and slept again. A dream like that could give someone a heart attack. I feel fine today. Got here one week ago.

    Last night three of us read things downstairs by the fire, and Marc was there, too. Michael read what was for me a boring ennui-filled story with bodiless characters for 45 minutes—God, and he's been writing that bloodless thing his whole month or more here. Annaliese read some nice poems. I recited a few things & read "Ram Time" which was in a *Poetry* downstairs. I'm glad I did not in full enthusiasm start spouting *CR*—I would have rushed and felt depressed later with an audience that couldn't <u>know</u>, etc. I'm wising up. The finished book is still mine. I've told Han & Bill Ewert & Billy, but telling does not diminish the poem's power. I know what I have. Patience and faith, and to bask in *CR*'s completion for a time.

    Before dinner, I read more in Mariani's *Williams* (as I will today), and drafted another poem, the fourth, and might as well enter it here now as I have the others so that I'll have them all in one place. Do I have a title yet? I think I'll want to do something unusual with the stanza-forms, too, but won't attempt it here. Maybe the title should have something to do with the girl, something suggesting an American *La Primavera* music, but I'll give it the other one I just came up with. And I'm pleased that all that stuff about the blind girl is my own invention.

    <u>The Monkey Organ</u>   [The Virgin]   [Virgin Music]

    Doc knew what to expect but still holy
    shit what was it did he even like it

    April evening 1927 Carnegie opening to fog-
    horn electric alarm bells maybe stepped-on

    cats fourteen grand pianos like atonal
    subway screech rush hour nervescape

    imploded onstage—George Antheil's *Ballet*
    Méchanique? Some got the hell out fast, but Doc got

    thinking: going home from Beethoven e.g. he'd
    meditate the harmony to blot out city

    insanity, but Antheil counter-pointed cans
    crashing unoiled metal screeching fish-

    market voices scaling up the spine-
    sax cadenza, allegro-andante

oscillation (not Whitman's Brooklyn ferry
crossing seeing and saying the sublime sea-gulls

"high in the air floating with motionless wings,
oscillating their bodies"),

the city's music of the shears and rotgut coffee here,
but <u>clear</u>, clarity, speaking in edges, Doc

remembering a birthblind girl patient virgin eighteen
accidentally struck on the occipital who

<u>saw</u> for the first time said how <u>clear</u>
the world was how vivid she felt cunt-quiver

chills Jesus now a jazz symphony off-key hit the fenders
again O George my city cunt music poetry machine.

I'm doing these Williams things of course because I'm reading the Mariani book, but also surely as counter-weight to the lush harmonies that <u>CR</u> took on. I don't know how I make these lucky moves.

It's only 11:00 in the morning now and I feel as though I've been up for a long time. Cold in the room the last day or two, and I'm glad I have the heating pad along—it warms my palms and fingertips as I sit here now on the bed writing.... Eggs again for breakfast for about the 4th morning in a row. I like the company, the cup of tea and toast with honey, and have to pick up the thermos and lunch-pail anyway, so what the hell, I don't stay in my room and have cereal for breakfast. Might go for a ride with Marc this afternoon, too, who knows.... Back to some reading....

Later: ten in the evening. Elizabeth Inness-Brown is okay, normal, running off with 2-3 different boys & men since she's been here, typing in-between, generally pleasant and not neurotic. She's a sort of stocky tomboy type with a nice smile. I like her, though we've really not spoken. She bombs in and out with her little red car, and is on the phone often, as she is downstairs now.... Marc Consoli is my friend here, warm and smart, secure in his work. Marriage troubles now, but he knows himself, and has been easy to talk to. I'm close to him quickly, as I was with Stewe Claeson. He gave me a record today. I gave him a couple copies of *The Bees*.... The other two here now, little Annaliese Wagner and Michael McGuire, behave very strangely, have suddenly whispered together and gone off to fuck. She seems about 60, he 45. She's okay, really, but he's got problems, changes moods so quickly, is tight in his actions and in everything he says about writing and art. Marc and I seem to me to be the balanced ones. And, really, the rest of the scene here is dull and depleted if not downright odd and neurotic. If he weren't here (and he leaves Wednesday) I'd spend all day by myself. He's natural, easy, good company, and I use him as insulation from the others. I will get his address and send him some books once I'm home.

Well, I just shaved and showered, am glad I'm in bed rather than out again. Will read Mariani until very tired. Didn't do much of value today except the two drafts of the Williams/Antheil poem, which <u>does</u> need a Kore-like title.

Tuesday tomorrow. Marc leaves Wed. morning. I will have long sessions alone once he's not around—he's been here about six weeks—give it a final push before I leave myself on, I think, Saturday. The Georgetown/Virginia game is on television Saturday night, and I'd like to pull out the couch at home and watch it. I'm still, surely, <u>very</u> glad I came, just for the finishing of *CR*.

12/7/82

It's before breakfast, but I've come over to the library here to read and write a little. It's cold over in my room, and the room is being cleaned this morning, so I'll hang out here until about 9:30, anyway.... I had a good night's sleep, after some reading. I'm keeping my inner-ears open, but no new Williams poems stirring. I'd like one from the 30s.

    Just looked through two photograph albums of Yaddo in the old days until about 1900. Strange, beguiling looks on the faces of the Trasks, especially Katrina, who seems dreamy, beautiful, very sexual. She has blinked her eyes and 50-100 years have gone by, and a fellow is writing about her in his journal. That fellow is the only one on earth thinking about her right now, thinking right now about her in her grave up on the knoll. Sleep well, and waken to speak with Walt, and tell him to stay close to me here. Walt: Doc Williams & I, we're all your sons. He is the city son of cacaphony and I am the son so far of pond-music & lilies. Be with us in our silliness.

    11:00. I'm on the bed in my room, listening to the cleaning lady bang and scrub away on the other side of the bathroom door about ten feet away. All morning, noises of cleaning, car doors, the heating man in and out, his radio in his van buzzing. How to work <u>along</u> with noise, I guess. But maybe the trick is not to be <u>distracted</u>, but to make that noise part of the flow, the sensible traffic. If it ain't quiet here at Yaddo (though it usually is) it ain't quiet nowhere…. Anyway, another poem for my sequence came along, a good one, and I write it out here:

    <u>The Plums, 1935</u>

    Purple-bruise-blue
    plums you
    old canker-
    cancer woman
    with a bag of them
    for solace—

    what world <u>did</u>
    the poet find him-
    self in plumb
    <u>that</u> world <u>not</u>
    the waxy blossom
    of the imagined maybe
    dead one to come she

    spreads her branches she
    tastes good to him she
    tastes good to him …

    I've always liked that Wms. plum poem, can hear Bly say it. "Branches" in the last stanza was "legs," and maybe still should be, but why beat my readers over the head? "Come" does it.

    Now a conversation in the bathroom between the cleaning lady and Annaliese, between a woman like my mother and an art lady cultured and spoiled by this place. So many real losers come here, it seems to me, those who have never really become serious about writing, finding, about <u>work</u>. Annaliese plays the role, not arrogantly but subtly, of the artist/aesthete when she deals with these plain folks here. She and that Michael can go fuck themselves. I've a powerful disinterest in them…. A big truck now idling outside. Garbage cans clanging on tile bathroom floor. All I need are some electric bells and 14 grand pianos hitting the wrong notes. I <u>would</u> be uptight if I hadn't done the plums poem this morning, I think. Good luck keeps finding me, the luck of my taking the Mariani book with me, the luck of having it <u>very</u> quiet here during the days last week when I finished *CR*. And the solace of this journal itself.

    2:00. Ate lunch & went for a long walk around all the lakes. A cold but shining day. Back in my room now, planning on a long afternoon of reading & writing & minding my business…. Nice letter from Bill Ewert, with his new Sarton book, and with *Tumbleweed*. The second color, for our names, should have been in yellow—this wd. have lit up the design itself. I may add a little yellow watercolor. But I like the card, and will sit in my study and send them out....

<u>Still</u> the noises of cleaning around me, this time six feet to my left in the hall. Pine Garde is the only place, maybe, that will be open this winter, and they're getting it ready. I can't berate myself for wanting more silence—even Doc got himself a study in his attic up in the trees. At least the heat has been fixed here, and it's warm in my room.... This is Marc's last day here, and he'll be looking for some action this afternoon, but I'll lie low until supper.

4:15. Just went downstairs for 20 minutes. Had an <u>excellent</u> talk with Marc, about Michael and other things. Marc makes all the right moves: out of a sense of obligation, I thought he'd like to take a ride, but because he'd "opened a can of worms," as he said, in his new work—and this after he wasn't going to work at all today—he wanted to work a couple of hours before dinner, as <u>I</u> did. <u>Yes</u>, to that chap, while I have a natural antipathy to McGuire, and I seldom feel instinctively about anyone as I do about this guy.

Wrote a silly little piece the other day, from something in the Mariani book. It won't be part of the sequence, but <u>might</u> be worth saving. I might as well write it out here.

The Door

Men have souls.
Woman do not have souls.

Okay, okay:
women have souls.
Men do not have souls.

Okay, have it your way,
we should say
men <u>and</u> women have souls,
<u>should</u> say. Okay.

Some men have souls.
Some women do not have souls.

Okay, okay:
some women have souls.
Some men do not have souls.

I said that.
The door's open.
Just let yourself in.

That sure ain't much. But I just had another idea. Maybe I should add the three lines from Wms' letter to Burke, lines that I thought could stand by themselves as part of my sequence, to the "Aroma and Swish" poem. Anyway, I'll put down the thing here as I thought I could use it, and then see if I want to work it into the other piece. I'd have 1921 and 1937 in one poem, preceding a 1935 poem, but that would be okay.

Fragment from a 1935 Letter

"the blight of English literature
under which our cocks have all but rotted away
   into each others' ass holes ..."

I guess I'm enjoying the Wms. sequence because I'm getting all sorts of low-down shit into it that I haven't happened to get into other poems. When the images are as gross as the above, I like that New Jersey Doc more and more. The guy doesn't even blink. He's a fighter, when fighting with other people has made me sick and thrown me off the track—he <u>thrives</u> on anger and personality clashes and vituperation & spite. Hit them hard, Doc!

9:15. After dinner 5 of us went to a bar. Met Elizabeth's young boyfriend there. I had a scotch. Inane chatter about nothing—stupid talk of incest and boat rides at Lake George, even Marc pleased to chatter—and I got steadily more uncomfortable and bored, and came back alone. And just now, as I was writing, I hear a car or two back in the circle below me. I don't know. I don't feel superior to these folks, but I guess I'm just so set in my life now, and know what I like, and if I'm not with my family or real friends—little enough time for that—or wasting time watching a game on television or puttering in my study, then I want to be reading and writing, and am glad to be back here now. Probably Marc was disappointed when I left. Maybe I'll see him at breakfast. Yes, part of it is that I'm a little homesick. Riding back, I felt like packing up and going home. I'll actually be <u>alone</u> with the odd couple tomorrow—I think Rod Jellema comes in a couple of days. I <u>will</u> get down to work tomorrow, know what I'll do—write some letters and write clean copies of many sections from *CR* & of the new Wms. poems. And one day will flow into another. I'd still like to stick it out until Saturday morning, but if I find myself feeling morose, I'll just leave. All in all, though, today has been a very good day.... Maybe the gang is downstairs, and having some wine. I don't know. It depresses me that we don't sit in a circle, when we <u>do</u> get together, & share work or at least serious talk.... No wonder Brinnin got the hell out of here. I can't imagine spending more than 2 weeks here—well, maybe in the summer with some good company after a day's work, evening walks and drinks, a swim during the day.... Back to Wms....

12/8/82

It's 11:30 in the morning. I skipped breakfast this morning, and had a good session writing out poems, and I wrote Mariani a letter at last (not much of a letter but a letter), but I still sort of feel like going home. Not surprising: I'd rather putter at home right now than work here, and Han & Kris are there rather than the odd couple I'm supposed to have dinner alone with this evening here, and the pleasure of the cable television. But, I'm still here, and will stay busy today. Maybe will call Billy this evening. I sure want to stay here because I want to stay here and not because I'm too shy or abashed to leve. Anyway, for today I'm here.
Another Wms. piece underway that might come to something. It could be called "The Mole," the Doc under his porch.

1:30. Already feel okay. Had a little lunch, "The Mole" moved ahead (almost ready to copy it out in here), just shaved and showered, look forward to a long afternoon of reading & writing. Should write Tony Piccione a long letter to mail once I'm home. Such a pleasure reading Mariani's book. Hope I get lucky just once or twice more.

<u>The Mole</u>

Sept. 15, '42,
Doc (59 now)
burrowing under
his office for wire,
batteries, a drive shaft,
bolts, axles, any-
thing coherent,
metal, useful,
gets a snootful
of muck, but it's
not much next
to the boys' warblood.
He finds a cast
iron skillet

for grenades and bullets—
it's rusted here
as long as his vision
of Paterson,
and that's long.
How to get it up
before it disappears
over the edge in un-
written ejaculation?
Got to get lower,
rounder, more self-
enclosed and circular,
be the animal,
tunnel ahead in pitch-
blende, the same
powerful pink
flippers in half-light,
lucky nose-star
to burn the way
to the roots
of radium blossom.
For now, bang,
bang he bangs
the skillet which flakes
and clanks like
old armor or
his dull skull-
bell these days bang
goddamnit
ring bell bang.

5:45. A good long afternoon. Besides "The Mole," I have another piece, this one called "Kore Again, 1945." Will get it down in this journal after I write it out again. Curious how depth pours itself into these pieces. There are some very subtle turns and implications in them.

Wrote Tony Piccione.... Have gotten hungry and eaten cereal a couple of times. Only ate half of one sandwich—corned beef tastes like some kind of mistake—for lunch, and a banana.... I'm going to be here tomorrow, and will work just as hard as I did today, but may go home Friday. Will see. I'm anxious to send out Christmas cards and to take care of a dozen other things. But the Williams sequence keeps coming to me, too, now, and I should finish the Mariani book before I leave. So much bullshit in Williams. This finding of the new measure is like finding a new animal in the oak grain of a bed's headboard. Sure, it's there, and it's always been there for the one who can hear it, and the thing is to hear your own swan or cow or planet or blade of grass or pair of panties or bass drum or comet or chestnut rain.

Maybe I'll go over early, and read a little in the library.

Want to call Billy tonight.

Will escape my fellow colonists right away and spend the evening reading & writing. Will go over for some eggs in the morning, though.

10:15. Shit, I didn't want to, but ended up talking with the odd couple after dinner. They stood at the base of my stairs and then Annaliese asked why we were standing, etc. Anyway, I still have a couple of hours to read & write.

Curt back for dinner today. No, not much of the farmboy left in that ultra-cultured fellow.

Called Billy. We seemed to talk only about whether or not he was coming home Saturday. I thought maybe I could pick him up, but don't want to make plans. I don't want to think much about him on the road, either. But, with luck, we'll all be together for the game Saturday night. Maybe a couple of his pals will be staying over, too.

Letters from Al & Han. First letter from her in many years—there's been no occasion to write. Strange feeling. I miss home, and still don't know when I'll go. If the Williams work keeps coming, I'll stay until Saturday. It's been quite a day. My pen needs ink again.

12/9/82

Breakfast with the two again. I don't know—they're not so bad. I find myself talking too much, and tell them so, and they say they enjoy it.

A dust of snow last night. Cold out. Knowing I'm going home soon, I look forward to a full day of reading and writing here in the room today. Rod Jellema is supposed to show up today, too.... *If*, as I read along and Doc comes up with these heart attacks as he finishes *Paterson* I can come up with a concluding poem of some kind, I'll have a hell of a nice sequence, one *very* satisfying to me. I enter one of the Wms. poems here now, so I'll have them all together.

> Kore Again, 1945
>
> The bombs. A week later,
> the war's over. Wms.,
> his daughter-in-law and kids
>
> home alone that evening when
> horns begin, bells, tin cans,
> shouts, whistles, firecrackers,
>
> dogs barking, people
> calling to one another, but ...
> too much suffering and death
>
> for him to celebrate.
> He sends Jinny to the movies,
> stays home to watch the kids,
>
> reads a play or two. Late,
> upstairs to check,
> he finds little Suzie
>
> sitting up in bed, white
> moonbeams touching her to ghostliness,
> staring quietly into the dark.

Later: 11:30. A good morning of reading. I had a sudden thought to write a letter to Archie, then remembered. I wrote this, which will probably just stay here.

> Archie, I'm at Yaddo. Just now,
> I thought to write you,
> to tell you what I've done;
> but you are dead, I just remembered,
> would not be driving into Conway,
> as you did, for mail.
>
> A dust of snow overnight. The pines

touched white as you were in my mind
in your last years, as you are now.
I want you with me here, where I'm sometimes lonely.
I thought: write to a friend, and thought first of you,
but you were gone into history and mind.

All of us who write—we are sometimes close,
never there though to know what death is.
How could you be dead now? I was so sure
I could write to you, whatever picture I have
of your grave covered with snow.
As long as I live, I'll feel your love.

Not much. A sort of tone-poem. But I cried for just a few seconds and felt the loss of that father I wanted, on the spur of the moment, to write.

Don't know if anything else is forming inside me in the way of a poem. Some jottings regarding Wms.' cloud-death-meditations.

Sun out again, and I'm not anxious, as I was a little this morning, about getting caught over here in a snowstorm.... I seem to be growing into this life of mostly solitude and quiet, of reading and writing, but this may have to do with the upcoming holidays with family & friends & cable television & correspondence.

8:00. Back from dinner. I'll go downstairs later for a drink with Rod Jellema & the others.

Worked all day, drafted 2 not-so-good sections of the Williams sequence, trying to finish up. I've left it where I can pick up again. Still have a hundred or so pages of Mariani to read. Decided to go home tomorrow, said goodbye to Curt, have been packing. So, only a dozen days here, but much work done. I've written out a check for $50 to give to Yaddo. It ain't much, but it's something.... Oh, it will be good to be home.... From 7 this morning until dinner at 6:30, I was out of my room no more than an hour.

I'll drive slow tomorrow, coast along those highways. It's supposed to go down to zero this night, but I think the Buick will start.

It's going to be such a good, full time over the holidays. So much correspondence and that kind of busyness, but that's okay. I've got to try to get some exercise, too, though. Maybe, already, on Monday I can go over and work up a sweat. Leg getting <u>slightly</u> better every day.... Yes, time to go home to Han & Kris. Oh, I love them. That wife of mine—we've gone through much together, are growing old together, becoming closer as the years go by.

Well, Yaddo, so long. I'll probably be back again for a week or two some time, with another journal, another project, another big book to read.... Tires, stay on the road. Car, get me home. Saint Christopher, Walt, be with me.

12/15/82

Wednesday morning. I keep telling myself to get to work, type some poems, send Christmas cards overseas, etc., but I'm lazy, <u>but want</u> to learn to be lazy, too. Even at Yaddo I told myself that when I got home I'd just float around my study and relax. I <u>will</u>. Bill, relax, and get to the things you get to!

On the way back from Yaddo I stopped, at the last minute of deciding, in Ithaca, and I'm glad I did. I'll never forget coming down that dark hall toward Billy's room. He was just coming out, and thinking of taking a bus home. He was so glad to see me. We had lunch there, and he packed, and we drove home. That evening the four of us went to the high school basketball game. Billy took the car back to Ithaca Monday, will return maybe Friday for Christmas vacation.... Han has been <u>busy</u> at the Senior Center. I went to a dinner with all the politicos there Sunday night.

I'm finishing Mariani's *Williams*, and have begun typing the sections of *CR*, working my way from back to front. Did get more than 50 Christmas cards into the mail. Have glutted on television, too, watching basketball & news & *All That Jazz* & *The French Lieutenant's Woman* & *Stir Crazy*.

In the mail was an acceptance of 2 poems from *Poetry*, rejection of *Wenzel* (which was just as well because it may be published by Ewert by mid-year) from *Georgia Review*, and so much else. Made myself a list of 15-20 things to get to. Saw Al briefly last evening—on my way to jury duty, which was again aborted for some reason of chancery—and he seemed okay. Dave Fraher on the phone from Wyoming.... Yaddo is another world.

Heard the wonderful news from Dave Hale the other day that the Provost, Douglas, was fired. Fuck him. He was the main problem all during the Graver problem.

Home. Haven't been back to the cabin yet. Maybe this afternoon.

12/16/82

Cable guy just left. The other television is all hooked up now, too. O America!

Still clearing away correspondence. The pile diminishes slowly.... Took care of some details/errands this morning. Went over to the school to drop off my chairman evaluation, and then mixed-up Stan Rubin called to say that the ballot was invalid, had to be redone, etc. So it goes. Post office. Bank. Library for addresses for the Stephenson essay. Lift Bridge, etc.... Kristen's concert tonight. We'll go with Studiers.... Rain turning to snow today.

Finished the Mariani book. Want to spend another hour or three with it going over some notes and looking at my series of poems. Maybe I'll do that in the cabin in the morning.

Letter from Pearl London at the New School. <u>Yes</u> to a visit to her class in April. Now I'll juggle some dates. Will end up making some money on readings in April. Will probably be away almost two weeks, but will spend several days with the folks.

12/17/82

Because I had some discipline today, I feel content this evening. The work ethic declares itself!... Took the phone off the hook this morning, put the garage door down, left the television off, and worked on the Williams sequence. Nine poems done, and I'm pleased—I haven't done such a thing before. Then I typed for an hour or two, until I got sloppy. Finished *The Ghost*, am working on *Wenzel*.

Read the last couple of chapters in Reed Whittemore's book on Williams to see if there would be anything there to help me on the hoped-for tenth and final poem. No luck. Such a thin book, and not just in the matter of pages, next to Mariani's. Also, read some from *Paterson*, and then from *Pictures from Brueghel and Other Poems*. I do like some of the shorter poems, but just can't get interested in *Paterson*. It's just too scatter-shot & collage-like for me. It gives me a headache. I'm afraid I'll never be modern. The insistence that the <u>word</u> in its shape & music was the thing rather than any meaning, led Williams to say finally that it wouldn't matter to history if the British Isles disappeared so long as the works of Shakespeare survived. The man was driven, furious, using the flow of words therapeutically. It was by force of personality and long life that he won through to such fame, finally. For much of his career, nobody knew what the hell he was writing about. When his poems are understandable they are often thin. When, near the end, a poem like "Of Asphodel" came along, everybody applauded with some relief because it seemed at least to be about something besides itself in its own contours. So, Williams has apparently won the century, and I don't care for his poetry, alas. He is not the son of Walt that I am. Walt would have asked him, finally, to pull himself together and stop acting the bad little boy. He had a fetish-attachment, even in his 70s, for the new, the new, looking for it in the next little magazine, instead of inside himself. I've not taken the time to clarify my feelings about Williams, to set out in order and logically why I don't care for his writing. I just don't, and I know I don't. I love the jumpy son-of-a-bitch as a man, but don't care for the poems. Stuffy Stevens: vice versa.

Han beside me in bed as I write. I am rich in her love, and must not lose it, or hurt her. Thank you Doc for that reminder.

I look forward to the MacLeish *Letters*. Sure hope the book arrives soon.

Billy home in two days.

A murder in Brockort, the nude body of a young woman found in a refrigerator on High Street, an Attica ex-con under arrest.

12/19/82

    Such a fine family day. Billy arrived early in the aftrnoon. We all spent much time together wrapping presents, etc. Watched some football. Watching basketball now.
    My folks & Werner called to say that Pop had a bad accident on Dec. 7th? A head-on collision apparently not his fault. A badly-bruised knee, cracked ribs, seventeen stitches in his forehead. But he's doing okay. Pop, be well. I think about Mom & Pop quite a bit lately, maybe especially since being with Doc & Flossie in their old ages. As long as my folks are alive, somehow, I always have the same number of days still to live.
    Al called, about nothing special. He's doing Writers Forum paperwork.
    Christmas card/poem arrived from Tony in China.
    Kris still has three days of school, and has been doing much schoolwork lately.
    Decided to send Vince a copy of *The Magnifying Glass*.
    We stopped at Studiers' last night. Lynne there, and had my signed Tomlinson & Heaney books.
    I shoveled for about 45 minutes. We'll have a white Christmas.
    Han busy, but fine. At least she has the 24th & 25th off—Christmas on Saturday this year.
    Billy seems happy. He worked very hard this past week. He says his index this semester will be at least 3.5.
    Bud Meade stopped over yesterday with a copy of *Lord Dragonfly* for me to inscribe for his secretary.
    We gave one of the hc copies of *The Berries* to Lynne for Christmas…. I wrapped Nora's pewter thimble in about 6 packages. That will be fun watching her unwrap.
    Billy & I will go over to the gym tomorrow. I'll try to shuffle around and work up a sweat, do some sit-ups, etc., but won't play in a game.
    Will have the phone off the hook in the morning, and maybe see how the last Williams poem wants to talk. I should go through the whole Mariani book again, take notes on my notes, and really get my anti-Williams aesthetic said.

12/22/82

    At four this morning, reading Archie's *Letters*, I began a poem called "The New Poetry" that I'm going to have fun with. It's about the fancy-ass school, and might actually stir up the shit or piss some flies off the toilet seat.
    Got up at ten, got some packages ready for the post office, and then took Billy & Brad to lunch. Ran around a little at the gym. Am home relaxing. So much correspondence to get to. So much time stretching ahead. I'm happy. Dance at Senior Center to go to with Han this evening. I don't mind. So much basketball on television. A season of fullness. Archie's *Letters* a joy. Got packages off to Kicknosway, Consoli, Clemente, Felstiner…. Wonderful letter from Ray Smith & Joyce asking to postpone the anthology. Oh God, yes!… Dave Smith sent a poem dedicated to me, and I'm going to send him *The Berries* & maybe *Mantle*…. Card from Bill Elkins!… Kris done with school today. Billy working occasionally at Muesey's…. Nothing to do tomorrow, e.g., but stay home & read & write letters & maybe shovel a little…. Al called about nothing special last night. Also Bill Ewert…. My serious thinking the last couple of days has gone on while reading Archie, though my marginal comments are particularly inane for some reason this time…. I was thinking again about collecting, how my collecting/gathering/building suggests progress to me, continuity, meaning in ways that wouldn't be there if I did not do what I've been doing. I seem more substantial to myself because of the books that surround me. Collecting keeps me from feeling too deflated…. Speaking of inanity, these two paragraphs.

12/24/82

    Bruce came by last evening. It was great to see him. Much talk of McNeese State and of how all the Brockport students ran into problems there—this John Wood sounds like a sick man, a frustrated writer, a man of crystal and phoned-in bids to Sotheby's who loves/hates poets, especially young ones. Bruce will look for an apartment and job in NYC…. He brought me as a gift from him and Lisa Walt's 3-volume daybook/notebook set from the official collected. Good summertime-under-the-silver-maple reading.

I drank a little too much wine, but feel fine now. Al Studier here for a while, and Monika Andrews. Billy & Kristen out bowling. Studiers to drop by this evening.... It won't be a white Christmas—about 55° today—but will be a happy one.

Again, a dozen or so cards arrived. I sent out 80-90 & still owe so many.

Yesterday, an anazing box arrived from Wes Porter. A bottle of wine—he did the label for some rich family—and four of his things: a silkscreen of a girl's head, an etching, a watercolor of a L.I. scene, and a drawing of John Burroughs' cabin. All framed. Treasures. What a man he is. How can I repay him? I can't.

Wrote Bill Elkins, another Virginian. Want to write Dave Smith. Another.

Reading Archie's *Letters*. A <u>responsible</u> man.

12/28/82

Stopped at Al's last night, and did some xeroxing, and got *Wenzel* and *The Ghost* into the mail to Ewert today. So, the poem exists as a whole somewhere else in case the house burns down. Handy as hell to be able to xerox at Al's.... Stopped at Barbers to see Bruce & Vallone & Ken Frank & Paula Closson & all. Had two scotches, some laughs, and came home. Will have that gang over on Thursday night, though. Tonight, basketball tournament at the high school. They should be good games.

Note from Tollers who wants to assign me an office right next to Graver. I'll still see if I can get one in Hartwell, I guess. No big deal, I guess.

Picked up *PM/AM*, Pastan's *Selected*, at Lift Bridge.

Hard to believe, but it's suddenly about 70° again. I shot baskets in the driveway with Billy & Brad. <u>Biked</u> up to town today.

Next, I want to take notes on Mariani and get to the tenth poem, and I want to work on "The New Poetry" poem of mine. Maybe will type & send to *Crazyhorse* or somewhere the 5 or 6 slight poems from *Erika* that haven't been in magazines. I hope to hear from Evelyn soon with a contract, and a price for the specials of *Light* and *LD*.

Skimming Walt's *Daybooks* now. Not much meat there, but impressions of a life. Jesus and Walt.

12/29/82

I have to laugh as I snatch up this journal for this entry. I feel right on the verge of a breakthrough right now, reading Walt's *Daybooks*, hearing him sell his own books, thinking that I'm too used to thinking about those whelps Tollers & Graver and all, thinking I should/will find some way to retire from teaching or get away from Brockport, some way to work at home all day on poems & publicity & things to free myself from the <u>State</u>, cut down expenses and quit, not at this moment but keeping all this secretly & quietly inside myself as I teach a few more years and then getting away, ha-ha!... Back to Walt, the great spirit shining through the ailments. Just found out how much he liked champagne....

1/1/83

A new year. No special resolutions. I'm comfortable. Worry about my knee and teeth, about the kids' and Han's happiness, about who knows what, but otherwise warm and content here at home. Feel solid in my poems now, and the books building. Wonder whether to keep evolving, or to try to break radically somehow;—the former, of course, the only possible way.

Han and I went to the Senior Center last evening to help set up for the folks' party there, then went ourselves over to Chuck & Jane Studiers' for a fine party. Many young friends around, & Nora & Al.

Each day I type a few sections of *CR*, just to feel productive. Typed the Wms. poems the other day, too, and like them, & still will stare at the last one.

Han just back from hospital visiting.

1/4/83

Much trouble sleeping last night. Fell asleep at last about eight in the morning, so did not get up until past eleven. If I could just sleep from midnight to six or seven in the morning I'd be a dynamo. I don't know if sleep can be learned. I don't know what gets in the way. Mainly, words, words, words keep running through my mind, phrases, sentence rhythms, stupid sentences I'm not even listening to, dialogues ditto. All that semi-conscious drivel seems to be a kind of workshop or thrashing house. Maybe more physical exercise would help, or less food, or tranquilizers. At least I have the luxury of time and <u>can</u> stay in bed until along toward getting-up time I fall asleep. We hear that our bodies get the sleep they need, but this may be in one-second space-outs during the day, for all I know. A solid night's sleep as a matter of course and routine would be a great help for me.

Billy and I went to the diner for lunch. Billy is doing fine. Tomorrow we'll go to the gym.

Al stopped over last evening for a book. He seems fine, even manic.

Two books from Curt Harnack in the mail yesterday.

I wrote Bob Siegel, Phillips, Piccione. Phillips an editor of one of the Norton anthologies. I'd love a poem in it.... No word from Vanguard on contract, on copies of special *Light* & *Lord Dragonfly*, etc. With *CR*, I might look for a change, or at least write Evelyn and expect more.... Wrote Claeson, Harnack.

Marianne (Grade) Pietrachowski's step-son stopping in this evening to have a copy of *Swastika* autographed.

I've typed some pages of *CR* each day. Have only *The Snow Hen* left to type. Will then do some xeroxing at school.... Have gone over "The New Poetry" a couple more times. It's almost there.

Note from Tollers about my teaching the Sports in Literature class. It's okay with me. Will use the Dodge anthology, & maybe Exley's *A Fan's Notes* & *Zen in the Art of Archery*.... Should call Gemmett about the office situation, but don't care much....

A girl from Greece Olympia HS just called & wanted to interview me on *Swastika*, gulp. I said no, but am sending her some things.

1/5/83

It's four or five in the morning. I couldn't sleep, but got up with a phrase on my tongue, "seed-puff time," and wrote "Dandelions," which I sort of like right now. It's like my "Catbird" and "Tumbleweed," just sings and drifts along.

Tried to think hard and straight about God during my sleeplessness. There was no particular instant—just an instant, maybe a tenth of a second—when the absolute truth hit, the truth that of course a god began and is part of everything. In my lazy and habitual body, I take all existence for granted, but no possible explanation for the existence of matter can leave out the beginning in god. And I have feelings of return.

I'm sitting in bed downstairs. A spider floats from the ceiling light fixture half-way down to my blanket, then climbs back along its thread and waits in the air. This is the time it usually comes down, no doubt, but it senses the commotion of my writing, maybe, and is not sure it is safe. I don't want to kill spiders this year. — It floats down again and before I can finish the sentence floats back up again. It has other lines, I now see, stretched from bookcase to desk—all this looming and weaving as I tried to sleep. I don't want to kill it, and spiders are supposed to be lucky—it's just a pale & harmless looking thing writing its lines in the air—but my skin tingles, and Han tells me they bite, so I'll try to tangle it on a sheet of paper and escort it out.

Later/evening: It's been a good day. I even <u>played</u> a little ball. Wd. be satisfied just to be able to do that.

After the entry early this morning, I fell asleep until about eleven. I don't know why I seem to relax by 6 or 7 in the morning.

Filled out the course registration form for Tollers, and will go over to the school tomorrow to drop that off & to xerox, etc. Will even stop in my office, where I'll never have another class.

Wrote Tom DeLigio, Michael McFee. Still catching up. Wrote Judy Minty.

Reading an article on Faulkner in *Georgia Review* (Winter 1982). Elmo Howell concludes: He "seldom realized the full, free expression of the creative mind in a state of health. His work lacks wholeness. Unlike the greatest writers, Faulkner leaves only a series of brilliant fragments of what might have been the great

American epic—tragically aborted, like the civilization which produced him." I'm interested in the idea of wholeness, as expressed by Whitman, by Macleish, both of them using that word, wholeness, as I wrote about it in my essay on Archie.

 Stopped in at Al's. He was on the phone with Bob Phillips, and bustling with grant applications, etc.

 Have kept much company with Billy lately. He & I are freest on this vacation. I keep worrying about Han exhausting herself with the long hours and million details at the Senior Center.

1/6/83

 Last night, since I hadn't been sleeping, I stayed up, and about 10:00 began to write, and by about 2:00 a.m. I'd written 32 ten-line poems, or a single poem, or something. I loosened up once in graduate school by writing 50 or 89 poems in a day or a week (I forget), but this poem or sequence might hold up to be something. I'm happy about it. Archie, you wrote me that I had the nature to keep producing. Yes, I think so. I hope, though, that what I produce is good, as poetry, as something. I'll wait a couple weeks and type up what I wrote. Before then, I'd like to look at & maybe finish the Wms. poems. And finish typing *CR*.

 Went to the school today, armed with my resolution to stand straight, stop skulking around. Xeroxed, saw Tollers, stopped in at my office, then saw Gemmett. Gemmett has come through. Looks like I'll have a small but fine office in Hartwell, in the old Training School wing. No room for classes, but cozier for office privacy & writing. Closer to my personality. I realize that the big classroom office was too much, somehow, of a responsibility for me. I won't be as comfortable during classes, nor will the students, but I'll have my own clean, well-lighted place. Room for books & much storage space in two small attached rooms. Even a sink. Yes, yes, I like it. Easy to move into, too. I look forward. I won't have to feel apologetic, now, for the big space I had.

1/8/83

 Han's asleep. I'm waiting for Kristen to come in. Han & I have had a long and tiring day after the party last night. That was a gas. Maxine, or Madia Van de Wetering is wild, swearing & interrupting & singing & talking about men's bums & calling people stupid & schmucks & crying when I read "The Berries" & "Witness." No arguments, though, or unhappiness, & Han & I are comfortable around John. He's a good guy, solid & balanced & warm, one man in a thousand.

 Didn't do much, if anything, today. Wrote Vince Clemente again. Finally got around to writing Wes Porter. Sunday tomorrow, and maybe I'll spend the afternoon in the cabin with my Williams sequence. Haven't spent any time back there since before Yaddo.

 Han depressed today. Whether about something special or whether just generally low for no reason I don't know. But when she doesn't feel well, or is down, I spend the day just marking time until she's better. She'll have a long night's sleep, I'm sure, and will be okay again tomorrow, I hope.

 I hear Kristen coming in. Billy is out, too, & won't be in for a couple hours.

1/10/83

 It's only 10:00 in the morning but I've been up since 6. Just decided to get up, and not fight for sleep and lose the morning if I did fall asleep.

 Finished going over the Mariani book, taking a few notes that would be good to elaborate on in class, taking some notes in case anything else opened up for me in my sequence. Went over the sequence again, adding a small piece on that cat incident I wanted to do something with. There may be too much measuring of Wms. at the end, but the sequence as a whole is good, consistently interesting. Not much on *Paterson* in it, but I don't want it longer. Will type it up when I get the energy, & probably send it to Nims first.

 Don't think I'll go over to play ball today. I'll get some exercise vacuuming, and not risk the knee today. I'll probably be fighting sleep all day. Was up until 2:00 this morning, too.

I don't want to lose the edge I found with that long sequence the other day. I think I'll write another before I type that one up. For better or worse, I may have a line or two to begin with. That whole thing came so quickly & freely—it makes a curve from being forced, maybe, to some free leaps—that I don't want to dismiss it or take it for granted. "Lord Dragonfly" & "Evening Dawning" came fairly quickly, too (each within maybe a week), and I thought I could do other such things, but it takes a long time to build up to such things.

Han and I had a good walk & talk yesterday afternoon. She's okay again. Mainly, I think, she was thinking about her mother, and about not having visited her father in so long.... Han called Sandi Piccione, who always says odd things on the phone—oh, I don't know, artsy things about Tony, etc. Tony, I know, will be in heaven for a few weeks once he's home, and then the old problems will surface. I miss and love that friend of mine, and hope the drinking problem has abated a little, but I don't think Tony's life will change much.

Not a bit of snow on the ground.

I'm packing up books for my visit to U. of R. in about a week.

Want to begin a Harnack novel.

Billy home for another week. He's good company. He's been making some good money at Muesey's, working every other day or so.

So much to do, mainly typing jobs, and I'm not nuts about typing.

Later: Halftime of the Syracuse-Georgetown game. A good evening after a great dinner of roast beef *and* scallops, corn, mashed potatoes, salad, apple sauce. Billy shooting darts. Kristen in the bathtub. Han calling Myrtle Beach for a spring reservation.

Finished and finished typing the Williams sequence. A chance of a slight change here and there, but it's about done. Will xerox it one of these days & send it out.

The call I didn't want came from *Mass. Review*. Permission from the executor to use the MacLeish tape, so I'll work on it all day tomorrow. Will push the papers through after I hear from *Mass. Review* again. This is a good thing. We honor ourselves.

Did play ball today, and managed not to hurt my knee.

A freezing rain falling.

So much to do. Thank God for the sabbatical.

1/12/83

In my easy chair, relaxing in front of the television. Just had a bowl of vanilla ice cream, something I indulge in once a week or three. Feel relaxed, after typing about 20 pages of the interview with Archie today, after playing ball. Dozens of tiny decisions to make with the interview (punct., etc.), but the decisions will be made & the thing will get done. I feel like cleaning the whole thing up, making it sharp & clear, for Archie & for us, but an interview must stutter along and be as diffuse and uneven as speech.

Billy & I have had fun, playing ball, shooting darts. He's working until midnight tonight. I'll be up when he comes in.

Letters from Bob Phillips and Bruce Agte yesterday. Bruce is working at the Strand (!) and will be getting many books for me, I think, at the price he has to pay. I hope he works there long enough to get on his feet, and long enough to get me many books! I'm not sure how solid things are with him and Lisa.

Note from Gemmett to Tollers & Douglas on my office. Seems okay, though he didn't go about it the right way.... And a crazy note from Tollers saying he understood my 675 class next fall wd. be Transcendentalism. No. But all I want to do is get all this shit behind me and get back to the poems floating around in my folders & in my head.

I feel fine, despite that paragraph. I'm off until September!

Al Peppard looked over my knee. Prescribed all sorts of confusing things from ice and isometrics to aspirin. I don't know. Rest will do it good though, I found out, rest of the knee itself while I build up surrounding muscles.

Terrible murder in the city yesterday, Pete Castle killed by a student.

1/13/83

Good day today. Finished typing & going over the MacLeish interview, writing letters for Writers Forum Committee & *Mass. Review*, etc. Will do much xeroxing tomorrow, I hope, and get that project behind me, and get on with some poems. Will send out the Williams sequence—to *Poetry*, I guess. I like the creative swirl I was in before this interview project & memos from Tollers. I'll get back to it, and <u>stay with it</u>!

Wrote to Tony in Peking and to Bob Phillips. Good letter from Dave Smith.

Kristen baby-sitting & staying overnight. Billy visiting a Cornell friend in Greece. Han tucked in for the night. Tomorrow evening, fish fry, ball game, high school dance—we're chaperoning. Should be fun.

I'm trying to rest my knee. I was straining it on purpose, clicking it into place, thinking I was stretching it & building it up, but I probably have bruised cartilege under the kneecap, and <u>maybe</u> if I rest it the knee will improve. <u>Then</u> I can begin building the leg muscles up. Maybe. Fuck, I may be done as an athlete unless I have surgery. Glad I don't make my living as a dancer.

Will write Joyce next week about her prose anthology. Maybe my Berryman essay (maybe with a postscript?) would make good reading therein?

1/15/83

"The Shine of the World" is off to *Mass. Review*. "The Confesions: Ten on Williams" is off for a try to *Poetry*. As of yesterday. I feel <u>good</u> about that. Am clearing away the permissions & notifications shit as best as I'm able. Once Archie's piece is published, that will be that.... Finished "The Shoe" (which was "The New Poetry"). Ewert called today, about nothing special. Kristen just home from auditions in Brighton. Fish fry last night at the Center, & then a high school basketball game, & then Han & I chaperoned the dance. This evening we'll go with Poulins to see *Tootsie*. Life as lively & scattered as this paragraph. I'm in a good mood. Much pressure on Kristen lately, and I'm glad she's through it. Billy home only a few more days. After Tuesday, when I'll go to U. of R. for lunch & to drop off books, I'll get into long rhythms of reading & writing again. Too much school crap lately: the office stuff, fall 1983 schedule, paperwork on "The Shine of the World." That will all disappear over the next months.... Kristen having a party here tonight....

1/16/83

It's almost 11:00 in the morning. I'm in my easy chair, half-listening to a question-and-answer program on social security. Dizzying. Anyway, today I will stay in my room as the whole house is being cleaned up by Kristen & her girlfriend Karen after last night's party. There were about 40 kids here, and the floors are full of popcorn and cookie crumbs.... So many things passing through my mind that I want to note here. At Yaddo, maybe, or even back in my cabin during a calmer time, I could dwell on them, but I at least want to note them here. Already, as I try to think, the things dissipate.

I was trying to <u>think</u>, really <u>think</u>, the other morning while still in bed. I realized something I hadn't known. I'd thought there could be no thinking without words (and maybe this is true: that a particular <u>kind</u> of thinking goes on only with words); but I realized that with the sudden flash of a picture, a whole complex of intuitive understandings takes place immediately, whole steps of rational discourse being whizzed over without the necessity of filling in the spaces, the mind moving much faster than any possible computer. This is not just the kind of thing that "leaping poetry" has been after. This has nothing, in fact, to do with words. It has to do with the way we come to solutions, or decisions, a trillion times a day without words. It is pre-verbal and miraculous.

I've been playing a related game, hoping to rise from bed in the mornings without, in words to myself, deciding to. Sometimes I just roll out, and don't realize until my feet hit the floor, that I've decided to get up, and I smile at this. It has something to do with Herrigel's release of the arrow in *Zen in the Art of Archery*.

I've been thinking hard, or <u>trying</u> to—it's so fucking hard to <u>think</u> without drifting away—about, gulp, God. This thinking takes place when I'm in bed but not asleep. It's not easy to get down under the day's details of habit, under the things that have been taken for granted for so long (in <u>fact</u> miraculous things—breath, being, consciousness, language, existence of this self called Bill Heyen, meaningless syllables in themselves carried with me for so long) to the bedrock of body & blood within which—I feel it, I feel it, I feel & know it during my moments of clarity—soul abides. My mind imagines itself bouncing from star to star in the Milky Way, and then out further & further. I try to "exercise" in this way so that I don't just live in blur & habit as though self & family & Brockport & my language & this whole planet were not miracles themselves balanced, until I find out more (I hope & pray & believe, I think) at the moment of bodily death.

Two childhood memories, I discover, arise in me often, and I just want to note them here. The first: I'm on a bus—I believe this was when we lived in Hauppauge—on the way home from school, and we pass a bleak place—this seems to be late fall or early winter—of pond and woods. Those few moments of seeing that had a profound effect on me. I see myself, when I have this memory, in the bus as a small boy. I'm on the right side of the bus, am wearing a cap with ear-flaps, and snow pants & jacket. That bleak & forbidding place. The second: I was at the creek, on that sort of concrete pipe, across from Lake Ronkonkoma. I saw 2 or 3 pickerel about ten feet from shore hovering under lily pads. They wouldn't bite at my worm. They weren't big— maybe 10-12" long—and were exceedingly beautiful. The memory of those fish was probably behind my poem "The Return."... There are other recurrent memories, and I want to note them here as I catch myself dwelling on them. The mind is as ultra-sensitive as Thoreau's pond, on which we can see an insect dip its wing a hundred yards away, ripples and water-lights.

I worry that I'm drifting into old age, that it is catching me unawares—I become more & more habitual, forgetful, stupid about petty things, absent-minded. I must eat better, I believe. I eat much too much junk food. This has to be detrimental as I try to remain aware & conscious. I must make a resolution, beginning now and today (can I do it?) to eat better, more balanced meals, than I have. I have a sweet tooth, & like salt. The house is filled with chips & cakes & candy. Even when Han buys fruit & fresh vegetables, I avoid them. It's not at all her fault. If I want to stay awake, I've got to wake up now, today, about this. I don't want to be an automaton, inhuman and iron about this, but want in general to put into my body things that are better for it than the things I've been gulping. I'm 6'5", about 195-200 pounds, not in bad shape and feeling more sluggish than usual because of my fucking knee—still, I can do things for my body that I haven't. Jesus, Bill, drink an occasional glass of wine & stop eating all this salt & candy all the time.

Well, I always feel better after trying to follow some of my thoughts along a few paragraphs in this journal. It is so much of what I am becoming, invisibly, away from the few poems that appear once in a while and are not of any importance to anyone but show in a much more exterior way the "finished products" of what this other underground activity leads to.... I didn't put this very well, but the intuitive leap knows that I know what I mean.

Will shovel a little today, and get Billy to shovel, too. Football playoffs. Basketball on television. I want to type the book lists for U. of R., to get back into touch with Joyce, to get generally organized and ready for work again once Billy returns Wednesday, etc. (U. of R. visit, probably one more course form to fill out).

Should I tell Peter that I'm becoming more & more uncomfortable with not having my books in order, my letters filed, and need a place, even if it's a big closet; or, should I just keep boxing up & storing, as I have been, toward my retirement. I don't know. Both ways have many advantages & disadvantages.

Glanced at a Kinnell interview in *Modern Poetry Studies*. He says that some poets should stop writing. My immediate reaction was to laugh. Then I thought of the whole Stafford aesthetic, and became righteously angry, saying to myself that Kinell abuses the whole fight for the enjoyment of process & life enrichment through poetry that Stafford & others had fought for for so long. But yesterday, before sleep, I imagined stopping writing myself, and could feel the relief it would be. Maybe what keeps me in it, still, is fame-lust, ego. What a relief it would be! I could just become a book-collector and teacher. Christ, I hope I'm writing because I truly care for and believe in it. "The Berries" remains a red spot and beautiful moment of music in my soul. I wish myself others such.

Almost noon now, and the house is still asleep, will wake up and go booming & vacuuming toward order again soon.

Thank you, journal, for listening, even caring, again.

Almost midnight now. A long day, a good day. Billy just got back from work. He'll work for just two hours tomorrow, and then will be done for this vacation. He's earned a couple hundred dollars, and this has helped. Haven't had to give him spending money, and he'll have money to go back to Ithaca with.

Got all the lists and boxes of books ready for U. of R. Six boxes.... Dropped a note to Kathy Moser, and a tired letter to Bill Ewert. Wrote Joyce, and sent along my Berryman memoir. Maybe that was a mistake, and I should have used "What Do the Trees Say" for her book.... Will probably get up fairly early and go over some poems, maybe type up a few. Will go over to the gym with Billy. I don't even like to think about my knee—too depressing. It probably needs surgery if it's going to get better.

Television on most of the day. I think often of the difference between that world of noise & presence & generally inane chatter & activity, and the quieter world that blooms the minute the set is off, the world of time and self and death. The television makes us forget the world and what the world is doing to us, with us.

I wasn't an angel when it came to food today—had a candy bar and too many potato chips—but I did eat a couple of apples and pass up a late snack of the usual sandwich & cake.

Kristen was to go to bed by nine. Billy was not to be home until eleven. So Han & I made a date for ten—so hard for us to go to bed together. But Kris stayed up late. And Han gets up so early. There will be advantages when Han & I are living alone, though we'll miss the kids like hell.

1/18/83

Evening. I'm in bed, the pulled-out study couch. I'm going to take it easy, watch basketball, maybe read a little—I've been wanting to get to *Translating Neruda* for some time.

Busy & nervous day today. Dropped Billy off this morning at the bus station in Rochester, then found my way to U. of R. to see the Plutzik exhibition and for lunch with Peter, Mary, & Jerry Ramsey. Dropped off seven boxes of books, too. Cold & snowing. Han was in the city at Eastman with Kristen, too. Now we're home, and Billy's back at Cornell. Tomorrow, a free day by myself at home. Tonight, a long night's sleep, I hope. Lately, when I wake at 3 or 4 in the morning, I try to think hard about this life of mine. It isn't at all easy not to just drift away. To think, to put the thing back into the dimension of miracle, where it belongs. Five or fifteen minutes of hard thinking several times a week can only be a good thing for me. To be aware. Emerson's "active soul."

Kristen got her Brighton audition scores back today. 27 out of 28 possible pts., and 1st chair clarinet in the county again. Quite a girl.

Will spend the morning looking at miscellaneous poems. I like my new, associative, strange poem "Dandelions". My revision, jumpy as the poem seems now, made it more coherent, more of a, gulp, metaphor machine.

Book & chapbook from Molly Peacock today. Broadside from Bob Siegel. Bought a nice 1st of Jane Cooper's 1st book at U. of R. bookstore. And a cookbook for Han, which I put under her pillow for her to discover later.

1/20/83

Kristen's tooting away upstairs. We're waiting for Han to come home for dinner.

Joe Winnick called to say he'd have a poker game at his house tonight, then called back to say he couldn't find players. Too bad. I'm restless.

I've had a good day of writing and typing today, but have been feeling sort of sour and ungrateful for the gifts of a warm home & all else that I have. I'm bothered by my knee, I know. No pain, but I know I can't play ball on it, can't run on it, and know I should call the doctor, and keep avoiding finding out what's wrong and whether I'll need surgery. A good workout keeps me balanced, I know. I can't go through life with a knee this weak—it could collapse any time, and I can't defend myself or get out of my own way.

I'm typing up all my new unpublished miscellaneous poems. When the batch comes back from *New Yorker*, I'll send a dozen to *APR*, or somewhere.... And I want to finish typing *CR* soon. I feel like I'm marking time, waiting to hear about *Erika* from Vanguard.

Much thinking lately about this whole life of mine and what the fuck I'm doing—writing poetry, literary correspondences, etc. etc. Do I think anyone cares? Do I feel I must write? Am I still straining to become famous? Why this pressing to work at poems each day? Yes, goddamnit, I can write beautiful poems, ones that should be important, but who the hell cares. I keep telling myself that I care, that it's a lonely joy, etc., etc. But, who knows: maybe I'd be happy if I just decided to stop all this shit. I keep thinking I'm not ready, am unfinished, and have to get poems like "The Berries" & "Mother & Son" into books, but who the hell cares?

Well, I made my way toward this life, and here I am. I think, too, that moving & beginning all over at another school might give me a new life.... I'm bored. Winter is a pain in the ass. Enough. It's the knee, and the knee is an emblem of bodily ills to come, so I'd better be ready for this spiritual battle.... Enough.... I wanted long days of minding my business at home, and I've got them.... Vanguard gets me down, too.

Sent *Jesus* (3 poems) to Allen Hoey. Been thinking about that since summer.

Package from Ewert yesterday, Sarton broadside & other things.

Why try to lift this entry. Fuck it. So many in such bad shape, even in this country, and I'm low. Disgusting. Bill, you're a slug, a piece of shit, a dung-ball.

1/21/83

I resisted writing in here last night again after my mood changed.

This morning, after a few hours of heavy sleep, I feel fine. Will drop over to the gym later to hobble around and shower, and then stop in, gulp, at English Dept—maybe I'll just throw that registration form into Tollers' mailbox without comment. I wrote up a Whitman-Williams course instead of the Williams and After scheme.

I've a feeling John Hicks will call today about the MacLeish tape.

I think, right now, to solidify the feelings I have this morning about my life & writing, I'll read Archie's letters to me again.

1/23/83 (Sunday)

Long call from Bill Ewert yesterday morning. I think he's concerned that I'm depressed about my life in poetry (maybe not that, as I see it, but my life as poet, as someone who wants to be known) these days. Well, I have moods, but feel fine again. Excellent letters from Louis Simpson & Paul Mariani yesterday. Louis's good advice on "The Shoe," and Paul's praise for *CR* again—these responses make me feel as though I'm taken seriously. I do spend much time writing letters to people who are pleasant enough but do not help me grow, deepen.... Also, a card from Joyce who will use either my Berryman memoir or my *AP '76* essay in her book; and she said again she and Ray would love to do an anthology edited by me. I'm not sure I know, again, how I feel about this. On the one hand— On the other hand—.

Raining today. I'll write letters, read, watch the Jets-Dolphins game.... Spent a few hours with Kristen last evening watching *Dr. Zhivago*, my favorite movie, explaining something to her here and there. She loved the movie, the love story set against the Revolution. A couple of scenes were cut from the movie version, alas.

Billy called us to tell us his grades for last semester: 4 A's and a B+.

Will type "The Shoe" again, and send it with several others maybe to *APR*.

Spoke with Ewert, and with Han, about Vanguard again. No word from Evelyn about anything again. I'm just going to give the whole thing time. Will see what happens. Maybe, after the May royalty report, when work on *Erika* does or not progress, I'll write Evelyn a long letter about my feelings.... Hearing from Ewert about Gary Hunt's reaction to *The Magnifying Glass*, I wrote Hunt a good letter.... As long as the item exists, and is an "A" item, I'm glad about the way it's packaged. The price tag Ewert & Babcock hang on it—out of my hands.

I like my new resolution of not skulking around. Over at the Department, to xerox or drop off forms, I don't hide or slide around, as I did, as though I were a stranger in the world, but stand up straight, don't hurry, go about my business. I look Tollers straight in the eye, unhurried, and explain simple things to him. No more ducking, anxious moments over at that generally unhappy place. I will stand inside my own light in that sad world.

Visited Freddie briefly. He was at his desk, in his pyjamas, in the middle of a cloud of smoke, at 2:00 in the afternoon, happy as a pig in shit, complaining about Department business, haggling with Houghton-Mifflin. He seems okay, but so frail in body.

1/24/83

Speaking of frail in body: I went over to the gym today, and played, hobbling around, but it's no use. I'll call Dr. Riegler later on and make an appointment. It's not fear of surgery, but just laziness & the vague hope that the knee would get better, that has kept me from seeing him.

I finished "The Shoe," taking out two objectionable lines. I was attempting to define, but Louis Simpson was right about my homosexual line. I came up with an excellent line about Ashbery's changing the title of one book from *Paradoxes and Oxymorons* to *Shadow Train*: this points up much of the bullshit for me, going from an honest title for his poems to an imagistic teasing one that suggests some sort of intelligible center. Found out the first title from a set of proofs advertised in Sipper's catalogue last week.... Changed my New Haven and Princeton line to one about germination in the Ivy League.

Sent the Smith poem into another draft.... Wrote 5 letters of recommendation for Tony Vallone.... Got a huge Dickey broadside, *The Eagle's Mile*, in the mail from Herb Fackler.... Piccione back tomorrow night.... Call from Allen Hoey: looks like he'll do my three Jesus poems as a handsome little pamphlet on rice paper. I'll like that. I think I was thinking of a 4th poem, but abandoned the idea? Anyway, I'll enjoy the little project.... Call from U.T. Summers—she'd like me to come into her poetry class at R.I.T. on Feb. 11-$100— why not?... Billy not in when we called yesterday.... Note from *Mass. Review*. Hicks delayed on West Coast, will call in a day or two.... So, what am I up to these days?—I don't seem to have any writing projects in front of me. Maybe I should type up that long freefall I did. Will probably call it *The Trestle*. I wanted to do another one, a death meditation first, just write one out as I did the other, before typing *Trestle*. A few other things to fool with, too. And, oh yes, I want to type up the rest of *CR*, and work on a *vita*.... Letter from a woman in Patchogue. They can't raise money for a reading there.

My stomach hasn't been right, so I ate just some cereal for supper last night, and had only tea for breakfast, and cereal for lunch. I have only hot water in the cereal. My system needs a rest from all those rich foods. I'm sipping tea & honey now. I'm healthier than this page makes me sound. Worked up a good sweat today, and after a workout I always feel relaxed, easeful.

Card from Bill Beavers. *The Numinous* is coming along as a broadside.... Day after day goes by and I hear nothing from Vanguard.

Snow melted from the driveway again.

I still have no desire to go back to the cabin. On sabbatical, freed from school worries, the writing comes along inside here. I don't need, I guess, the separation of place as I need it when schoolwork is all around me.

1/25/83

Typed all of *The Snow Hen* this morning, and just got back from the school where I did some xeroxing. Every time I xerox, I feel like I've just gotten another grant from the State!

Did a little bit with "The Light" while typing, too.

Got up early. Did not go back to the cabin. Feel very happy, somehow, now, mid-afternoon, with some sorting of poems to do, and a letter or two, and looking forward to Tony's arrival tonight.

Han & Kris will be going into the city, to Eastman.

Strange & desperate call from Vicky Gold this morning. She needs some books on Charles the Bold, something to keep her mind off her 24-hour-a-day ordeal with her mother. I'll write Bruce at the Strand, but I can't believe she doesn't have a friend who can get the books from Syracuse U. or somewhere.

Beautiful letter from Vince Clemente again. He has the MacLeish *Letters* now.

1/26/83

Tony was first through the gate last night. I almost didn't recognize him. He was wearing a long blue coat, and a blue yert's hat. He was dazed. He looks good, has lost much weight. Hectic airport scene. Much fun. He's absolutely exhausted, will sleep for a few days now, I'm sure.

I played a little ball. The knee is the same, doctor's appt. for a week from Friday.

I actually spent an hour this morning fooling with watercolors. I don't know if I'll have the urge to keep it up until I at least learn a few things about water & paint & brushes & paper, but if I do I promise myself I'll never talk about my hobby. What do I think I may be up to?—loosening up, for one thing; a buried desire to do something else "significant" between poems, for another?

1/28/83

It's about eleven in the morning. I warmed up the car for Han at eight, and since then have been writing—well, filling pages with words, but probably not finding anything that will be anything. No product. Was the process enjoyable? I guess so, but maybe largely because product is anticipated? No matter. Nothing finished, but at least I got into those areas of the mind close to writing. And it's important to do that every day, if only for a few minutes, I think.

Haven't seen Tony since he landed. He's still sleeping off his China dream, I'm sure.

Still fooling with watercolors. Even kept a couple of things I did yesterday.

Wolf & Pat will be staying over tomorrow night, and then staying Sunday to watch the Super Bowl. Han & I look forward.

Spent a couple hours last evening adding book prices to cards in my file, making out new cards, etc. I've done nothing with that whole file since I began sending books to Rochester, but should, and will.... I'm still reading Holbrook Jackson's *Anatomy of Bibliomania*, too. Some chapters are fun, some too obvious and heavy-going.

No word from Bruce at the Strand.

Letter from Vicky Gold yesterday, and she sent back about fifteen of my letters to her. Apparently, she's moving back to NYC. I wrote Bill Ewert & am sending him the letters. I don't want files of Heyen letters returning back to me—too dizzying, a house of echoes.

Was juggling money around to take care of Billy.

My pay has been $448 every two weeks.

Kristen didn't do as well on her mid-terms as she'd hoped, but is in no danger of failing anything, anyway. Her clarinet will get her into college.

1/30/83

Sitting downstairs with Wolf & Pat & Han watching the Super Bowl. It's been a fine 24 hrs. Han & I at Maiers' last night for dinner & hours of talk, then back here with Wolf & Pat for cards & talk until 3 a.m.—good sleep & breakfast & heavy dinner. Lazy day. All's well.

I called Pop when Mom happened to be out for a walk, so got a chance to talk to him. He's still recovering from the accident, & doing okay. The New York State winter has given us all a break, and the winter slides by, nobody too depressed.

I like having company. It eases me. I don't think about getting work done. I'll have tomorrow to clear my desk.... Good having other adults in the house, somehow. A comfort, somehow. I don't feel so responsible, & even like going to sleep while others are still up and talking.

2/1/83

Morning. I just finished a little poem called "Mother and Daughter" that I like. I'd heard Han & Kris say goodbye as Kris went off to school, and I thought of how close they are and always, even after Han dies, will be, and the poem came along. I should send it to Vince Clemente. I will.... And I went over the "poem" I'll call "Thought," the second of those long semi-automatic things I've done. It seems okay. I'm a little afraid to look at "Trestle" again. When I was done with "Thought," I didn't think it was a keeper or half as good as "Trestle," but now I like it. I hope I come to like "Trestle" again, too. Haven't gone back over it since I wrote it. Unusual things, both of them, for me.

Al got back from NYC yesterday afternoon and was locked out of his house so stopped in for a couple hours. He's trying, with David Fraher, to raise $2,000,000 for BOA. Yes! And when he outlined that and ten other projects for me, and spoke of other bank loans & taxes & classes & projects he's attending to, I wondered why his head & heart didn't just burst, as mine would. It isn't easy for me even to write a simple poem (<u>especially</u> to write a simple poem) when my head is filled with details. I <u>think</u> this is <u>true</u>, and I haven't just talked myself into this because of laziness or some other motive. I want to keep struggling against this because I'll <u>have</u> to teach & be on committees & make plans for trips, etc., but in general I can't write poems like "The Beam" & "The Berries" & "Mother and Son" & "Mother & Daughter" when the world is too much with me.

I wrote a long letter to Paul Mariani last night, and felt relaxed when I was done, as though I'd accomplished something. Am sending him *The Berries*, too.

Want to write another good letter to someone today. Want to work on my vita. Want to fool a little with watercolors. Today is Tuesday, and would be a very exhausting teaching day for me, and I feel the full blessing of this sabbatical.

Brother, it's only ten in the evening now, but it feels as though it's been a very long day. Tony Rimore stopped in, but otherwise I saw no human being until Han & Kris got back from Rochester a few hurs ago. I stay busy, but my days seem much more enjoyable when there's a basketball break at noon, as there will be tomorrow.

Call from *Mass. Review*. All's well. News that Graver wrote Hicks and asked what was going on! Also, that Graver is fucking around again, working under Tollers' dispensation on the Farrell tape, & not reporting to the committee, etc. I find myself becoming irrationally angry whenever I hear or think of Graver. Mainly, the MacLeish tape will get into print, and that should settle things. Graver has the balls to take his bastardized version of the interview with Archie and to try to place it somewhere else, without anyone's permission, because, ostensibly, he worked on it <u>before</u> the President signed the rules! Bill, Bill, don't fret. Go about your business, and relegate Graver to his true residence in a lower afterworld than the one he began in. He's regressed.

Letter from Vince Clemente. He's well. No other mail to speak of. I wrote Vince, and Bob Phillips. Fooled with my watercolors for a time. Got to that course registration form. Wrote Scott Kretchmar & Peter Marchant on school matters. Tomorrow morning, I'll type a few things and stare at them.

Calls from Vicky Gold. She says she's sending money to me and to Vince! She's moving to NYC tomorrow. I don't know how much money or what's really on her mind. I told her I didn't think I could accept money, but she's insistent. Well, maybe I'll use it for books or something.

Called Tony Piccione at 5:00—he was sleeping, and hasn't gotten back to me. I hope he doesn't drink himself to sleep every day.

Note in Peter Taub's column in the paper today about me & noontime basketball again. A good quote from me about Bud Meade's "wild, sweeping, turnaround hook-shot dunk."

2/2/83

Talked to Billy. He's fine. He's sent in his tax forms and will get refunds.

Played ball, had fun. Will see doctor Friday.

Tony called. We talked about our MacLeish interview. Tony doesn't want to socialize at all, for some time, he says.

Papers filled with news of further cuts in Brockport faculty & staff mandated by Governor's budget. It doesn't look good. Things depressing around school, and will be, for some time.

Wrote something called "Thessalalia" at two this morning. It might turn into something. And have decided to get "The Masters" into *CR*, probably in place of the section on the man who loved elms.

2/4/83

Just back from doctor's office. Had x rays of left knee. Things look okay, the doc said, and said I should avoid jumping. I bought a brace that I like the feel of. Thirty bucks…. This was all a lark for me, but I got a feeling again for these doctors' offices. Smells that I smelled when developing pictures for photography course, or when I dissected frogs in biology class in college. Small cubicles with bleached music piped in. Some people with serious, even terminal problems. The robot-like voice of the x ray technician. The bright colors of carpets and walls that are themselves depressing. The body. The body. I'll be back again, and too soon, no matter when. A joy just to be home, writing, sipping coffee. I'll go over in a half-hour and bounce the ball, sweat & shower and come home.

Didn't sleep at all last night. I went to Mirko's for drinks at 4:30 yesterday with Armand Burke & Ron Watts & Greg Scarborough & Francis Keenan—the talk all about the new round of mandated cutbacks, of course—then came home to eat, then went over to the college game that we won by one pt. in the last two seconds, and then, just as I was going to shower and go to bed, Sandi & Tony stopped over. They seem to have so many problems. Sandi has lost weight, & seems on the verge of a breakdown. They use my presence to talk about things they don't talk about at home. Tony haunted in the same old ways, and Han & I suspect an increased drinking problem since he went to China. They have money problems—Tony being paid <u>nothing</u> until September. Sandi talking fast & non-stop about their problems, her poems, her weight. I don't know…. I gave Tony the copy of MacLeish *Letters* that Bruce sent me.

2/6/83

Long drive to & from Irondequoit—and I got upset in traffic and about getting lost—but we liked Kristen's concert. Heard "Finlandia" again.
Wrote a long letter to Don Hall last night, telling him not to get old! He told me not to send out "The Shoe." He keeps telling me not to publish things!
Good letter from Gary Hunt at Ohio Univesity. I look forward to sending them things, including *The Magnifying Glass*, for their collection. I have a hunch I'll read there, along with an exhibit, this year or next.
I don't feel like getting to anything today, but will. Want to send a batch of poems to *APR*, I think. Need to write Molly Peacock thanks. To write that young poet-Long Islander-editor of *Convergence* at Miami U. of Ohio.

2/8/83

It's about noon. I didn't get up until ten, after not sleeping much until 7 or so, but had a good session with my strange poem "Thought."
It's Tuesday today, no basketball, alas. Played yesterday, and harder than in months. I hope I'm not pushing the knee too much. I don't care about the low-level pain, but just don't want it to give way. I like the new brace a lot.
Sent off 17 poems to *APR*…. Got to the school for some xeroxing yesterday, including that essay in *Parnassus*…. Maybe I should send one to Evelyn. Yes.
I actually did a watercolor last night that I like a lot. I called it "Crows."
Kristen has a cold, but has gone to school. I have the phone on the hook.
Six books arrived from Bruce yesterday, and 2 special Sartons from Ewert.
The noon whistle just blew over snowy Brockport. I haven't eaten breakfast. Will maybe have some shrimp rolls for lunch.
On a very low burner in the back of my mind is the fact that Graver inquired at *Mass. Review* about "his" interview! I think of warning Tollers & Gemmett, but probably won't. The main thing is that the Heyen-Piccione interview with Archie will be in print in a month or so. That should settle things with the MacLeish tape, anyway.
Letter from Bim Angst & Jim Manis about an interview.
Finished a little poem called "The Color" yesterday morning.

Think often of Tony out in Kendall. Sandi not at all healthy. They're both under terrific strain brought on by one another. Sandi still has tremendous drive to be something, a poet, an actress, more than just a teacher, and I feel sorry for her. She's the sole support of the family right now. Tony is, without question, a problem husband, basically very lazy, generally lost, maybe alcoholic. I don't know. Anything I can do but be here as sounding board? I don't think so.

2/9/83

Called Tony today. We spoke briefly. He sounds okay.
Stopped to see Al. Many laughs with him and Boo.
Went over to the College to see us beat Tom Pope's Geneseo team by about 20. I'm glad.
Long day. I went over some lists of new poems this morning, thinking about a collection of poems like "Milkweed" & "Ram Time" & "Yellowthroats" & "The Berries" & "Mother & Son" & "The Beam"—the latter a good title.... Then went over to play ball. I <u>must</u> gain strength through exercises or I'll get hurt again. Will begin <u>tomorrow</u>.... Did a couple of watercolor "keepers."... Cold as hell now but I'm living the great life, have the couch pulled out & the television on.
I spent time yesterday and today working on a letter to Evelyn. Wrote a gentle letter, but told her I felt sort of ignored, that Vanguard never answered questions, didn't seem to care, etc., etc. Will see what she thinks. I hope they do *Erika*, but I think I won't mind looking for other publishers? No distribution at all from Vanguard. No ads, not even one in the special spring *Publisher's Weekly*, says Bob Phillips—it's as though Vanguard is not publishing. God, I don't want her to think me ungrateful, but I should get more attention. If she begins thinking I'm pulling an Oates, she'll just dump me in a hurry—Vanguard has nothing to lose in my case. Vanguard has to work a little harder for me, or I'll do better, I think, somewhere else. I just keep thinking Vangurd won't last long. It certainly won't outlast Evelyn. The family seems to run the business just for her. Maybe I'd be better off if they sold out to Norton, or somebody.
Kristen seems okay again. Han fine, too. Talked to Billy last night and when I asked him how he was doing he said "really great."
Yes, I think I'll enjoy putting together *The Beam*. My only question was whether I wanted to keep certain poems like "Ram Time" for an eventual expansion of *Long Island Light*. That's a very big question. I have memoir sections to add, I know. Or should I let *Light* <u>be</u> now? I don't know. I <u>could</u> avoid the issue for a while, and instead of working on *The Beam*, I could expand *The City Parables* as I've wanted to do. No hurry on any project, but I like to know what I'm up to in the future.
Not doing any serious thinking or intensive writing. Am I waiting for winter to pass? I should at least begin another good book, maybe the one on Edwards I got a couple weeks go. Why can't I get interested in the Felstiner Neruda book? I should read another Harnack novel, too.

2/12/83

RIT visit, all in all, was pleasant. Lunch later with Mrs. Summers and others. She talked, in her office, of her "lucky friendship" with poets Wilbur, Bishop, Merrill over the years.... In the evening, I worked at the fish fry—so, I did an honest day's work, almost, I guess.... Then I drove to pick up Billy at Dave Wolf's in Greece. He's here for the weekend and will pick up Kurt at RIT today. The four of us—Kris is at Oberlin today with a friend—will go out to dinner this evening.
My study is in a general mess. Many little things to do.
My knee worries me a little. It's about as weak as it was before I got hurt the second time. I have been doing some exercises on my own. I don't give much of a damn <u>except</u> I don't want to hurt it again before I get it back into shape.
This will be a wonderful weekend. I don't have to do anything in particular, can watch television and catch up on mail and enjoy the company of family. And will fool with watercolors, as I've been doing. Did one called "The Crane" last week that I like very much. It makes the viewer work a little. I like its rust and wheat colors—and the thing was an accident.
Good letter from Mariani, and the next day a Mariani/Moser broadside—I don't like the poem much.

Call from Richard Holowka—he'll stop by on Monday with a few books to trade, and with a topographical map, or aerial map, or aerial photo of my area of the old Island. He thinks we can spot my house in Nesconset from the air!

Later: did some leg lifts a while ago and got myself dizzy. Feel sort of slow & useless today—why not?... Nims sent my Williams poems back.... Might go to an auction in Spencerport this evening.... Did a little watercolor that I've kept, and threw a couple others away.

Driving yesterday, I pinned down in my mind another memory I keep going back to. Driving to one of those many high schools I visited while at Cortland as supervisor of student teachers in English. Out in the country. In front of the school, outside a big line of poplars along the road, the school back deep across a wide lawn. I seeing this from far away. No other cars, no sight of any people. Why is the scene, the moment, so sharp in my memory? It's as though I am dead there, the school waiting.

2/14/83

Long talk with Kristen this morning about her career plans. She worries too much, but she's mature, and knows she has to do what will make her happy, not what will sound good, like attending a school with a status name, etc. She's been torn about whether or not to attend Saratoga music school this summer for a month. She doesn't want to, and knows she doesn't want to, even though college scouts come looking there. She'll be all right. I don't want her away for a month right now, either.

Stopped at Poulin's for twenty minutes before basketball. He went over all sorts of Tollers stuff again, and told me about the Gerber application for Distinguished Prof, etc. I still hate that latter sneaking bastard, and hating him is a monkey on my back that I'd like to shake off. I had a good day today—Kristen, basketball, Richard Holowka's visit & book-talk—but did think about Graver again, and, at the same time, my relationship with the English Dept. here. I'll want to act, to _be_ in such a way so that I can respect myself—maybe bowing out & away from things, but doing it with a laugh, in good humor. Not going to meetings, any meetings. But being at ease. And when the inevitble confrontation comes, to laugh my way away and say I'm just too incompetent & absent-minded for committees. Do I dare be different? Not just to survive, as Archie says, but to _make_ life. I will not do things because of Graver. By September, or by the time committees are appointed, I'd better have my act together so that I'm not sucked into things that will make me miserable. How stupid I am to keep on caring about Graver, but emotion is a hard thing to turn off rationally. At a good school, I'd be taken care of, given some special consideration. Here, Tollers just wants to push me into the same corners as everybody else...... Diary/journal, I keep _trying_ to grow up, and sound like the same old whiner to you, but I'm getting there believe me. Why, I even sent that letter to Henderson at Pushcart the other day to tell him to forget me now and in the future. I like myself for that. And there will be other such things. And I'll deal with/solve my relationship with the English Department, too. It occurred to me today—well, I'd thought of this before—that Tony & Al will not be with me for always. Both seem always on the verge, Tony mentally & Al physically. I'll have to solve things on my own here. I have to be real, and strong. Resignation, says Thoreau, is really desperation. I won't be resigned to being in a system where I have exactly the same duties as people who do no writing/publishing at all.

Gave Richard many books & broadsides, & got a few things from him. A sunny, good day. I'm happy, and free of all but stupid anxieties about school. Through prayer or willpower or jogging, I'll clear _that_ shit out of my soul, too.

2/16/83

Just back from ball. My knee felt a little weaker than it did Monday, but I survived.

Letter from Joyce yesterday about many things. She urged me again to do the anthology of poets. Yesterday and today I've felt like doing it, as much shit-work as is involved. Every poet my age not in it would dislike me, of course. But it could be/would be a good book. I'd be forced to do much reading. It _could_ make a _little_ bit of money. I'd be on the offense, editing a fucking anthology of my generation instead of waiting to be left out of others. I've begun drafting a preface, and this will be the hardest part of the book. I'll keep working at the preface, and a list of 25-30 poets, for a week or two and then write Joyce & Ray. Meanwhile, I've written Joyce about other things. She actually needs bucking up. So famous, so insecure. She should maybe spend five years between novels. But that could hurt her psychically. She seems to need to write like a flood almost daily. I'm glad she's a friend. She's very loyal to her friends, too. I'm glad she'll be using my Berryman essay in her book.

Kristen feeling better. The pills she was taking to assuage period pains made her feel low & weepy. She's stopped the pills and is already feeling better.

Occurs to me that Joyce might want to use the Berryman interview, too, not just the memoir. It will take some paperwork, but that's no problem.

I didn't sleep well last night. And I didn't watercolor yesterday, and there may be some connection. Will do some now.

2/17/83

Drafted the possible preface for the anthology again. It's shaping up.

News from Al that John Logan is in worse shape than ever, and now is up on charges of cocaine possession and molestation of two 13-yr.-old boys.

Wrote to Billy.

Watercolored last night, and then slept well, twice.

Will see Drdek's books & no doubt buy some Saturday morning, and then Dan Hirsh & Jeff Marks will be here Sat. afternoon. So, I should be raising some money.

Will write a few letters this evening, and watch basketball. Would like to get my Wms. poems into the mail, but have no idea where to send them. *Paris Review*? No, the last poem says no to that whole crowd.

Hard to believe how fast the weeks are going by.

Actually got a good letter from Tollers, explaining & assuring. I'm glad I wrote the private letter I did. He will be on his toes now.

Freddie just called, said that the APT Committee voted 3-2 in favor of Graver's nomination as a Distinguished Prof. Ugh.

2/21/83

Friday night was the old-timers' basketball game. I played well & my team won. Jerry & Kathy David stopped over after that.

Saturday I went to Drdek's and bought about 30 books for $60. Later in the day Jeff Marks & Dan Hirsh were here, and I sold $312 worth ($35 of which were from Drdek) to Marks & $1040 to Hirsh ($1000 for the Scribner Wyeths). So, I'm in the money, and now know that because I have markets I can buy other books that I've passsed up now and then. The extra money sure helps. Han and Kris are impressed. I sold the John McPhee books that I paid a total of $50 for for $175. I only sell books that I don't want for my poetry collection. That's a strict rule.... Han made a good dinner for the booksellers Saturday night. Then, yesterday, I drove in to see them & we went to the Yankee Peddler bookshop in Pultneyville, right on the lake. I bought Chase's *Whitman* & Nelly Sachs' *O the Chimneys*.... From Drdek I have nice copies of Ransom's *The Kenyon Critics*, Aldington's *Lawrence*, Rilke's 2-volume *Letters*, etc.... Tomorrow, I'll drive to Buffalo to see Jerry for an afternoon talk. I'd love to buy some books from him—Flannery O'Connor, etc.—but I don't think he'll sell. We won't be able to see Logan, I think—John has a forehead gash & two black eyes from another accident, Jerry says.

These last couple days were a good break for me from literary things—talk of books with bookmen is something else. In the back of my mind, I'm still worrying that anthology (thinking of Berry, born 1934, etc.), and will this week, but I feel like I've been on a vacation, and it's a good feeling. After a visit with Jerry, I'll be glad to settle in again & get down to work.

I gave Marks a half-dozen of my own books to try to sell at his next show. That was a good idea.

Living life on the surface lately, but that's okay.

2/23/83

Spent the day with Jerry in Buffalo yesterday. He's still the same, sometimes on the ground and sometimes talking in the strangest ways of his literary reputation, his relationships with others who are not even aware he's thinking about them. I got there about 10:00 in the morning, and he drank three bottles of beer in a hurry, drove erratically. A couple of young men living in his house I don't know. From time to time, I just tune out, and this makes the time go by.... I wanted to give him $300 for about ten books, and he just wanted to give them to me, he said, but not just now, and I dropped the subject, and he kept returning to it, and pressed several on me (though not the valuable O'Connors) as I left—2 Warren novels I'm glad to have for my collection, Peter Taylor's 1st book that I'll sell or trade, Daniel Hoffman's book on Crane's poetry. I spoke very frankly with Jerry about what I was up to with books. I'm in his will to receive them all, he says, so would feel funny about selling them to me, and doesn't really want them (wants to be dispossessed of so many possessions) but doesn't quite want to part with them, etc.... Jerry does seem to have gotten older quickly, is less in control of himself. Something. I'm getting old, too.

I haven't really had my own feet on the ground for several days. Will get back to my life. I think I've been brooding the anthology idea, though, over these days. Spoke of it with Jerry. Still will take at least a week to think it over.

Driving back in the Thruway drizzle, I was thinking about the differences in Jerry's life and mine since we met 20 years ago in Cortland. I've felt Han & Kris & Billy, felt home intensely. I'm a very lucky man.

Haven't heard from Evelyn Schrifte. Sure do want Vanguard to do *Erika*, and I hope I didn't say anything to jeopardize that.... Want to write Aaron Kramer about the beautiful little Heine translation of his I'd like to use as an epigraph for the book.

It's ten in the morning. Phone is off the hook. I'll look over some poems for a couple hours and then go play a little ball. Picking up my life again.

2/24/83

It's about noon. I drafted a or the preface for the anthology again, fitting in Berry, giving some focus. This preface truer than my other attempts. I keep going back and forth on whether I want to do it. I'd probably regret it if I gave up on the idea.

Many letters & notes to write. I'll get to many today.

Went to last college basketball game last night. We lost to St. John Fisher. Had a good time playing ball yesterday. Knee seems to be improving. Back sore now!

Pleasure being home and getting to some things again. I did, though, add some very nice books to my collection this past week. And the anthology has been percolating all this time. My own poetry projects sort of wait for a letter from Evelyn to take on direction.

2/27/83 (Sunday)

Sunny today, and warming. No snow or water on the ground. Han & I walked around the block. The three of us are staying busy this afternoon, and will go out for a pizza for supper.

Good letter from Billy yesterday. He says we'll always be close, and we will be.

I typed a draft of the tentative preface for the anthology, and am sending it to Ray. I'm ready to do the book. After the first 15 poets, many decisions.

Bill Ewert called yesterday about nothing special. He'll spend tomorrow with Bronk.

Went to War Memorial the other evening—Brockport lost to Fairport. We went with the Setters, good folks.

Evelyn called. She was her usual distracted self with a selective memory very handy for her, but did say that Vanguard would do *Erika* this fall, that Elizabeth Woll wd. do the jacket again with the same sort of Erika sprig as on *Swastika*, and that it was okay with her if Ewert wanted to buy sheets for a limited. I'm glad, and hope the book will be out by fall. No guarantees. I wrote to Aaron Kramer about using the little Heine poem as epigraph.

Basketball on all day. I'll listen with one ear & write letters & do the course descriptions with the other.

3/2/83

The meter man or somebody woke me up this morning banging on the door. I realized that I'd been dreaming about Robert Penn Warren. He was sitting outside at a writer's conference in a place very much like the front porch of the main residence at Yaddo. I walked away from him. He was old, and all alone, and I walked back to him to tell him I loved him. He had that odd, askance look in his eye that he had when I saw him in Massachusetts. We walked away together. I told him I'd read and cared for his poem on Chief Joseph that I'd seen in *Georgia Review*, but that I didn't have the book yet. We walked away to the right under trees.

I've begun reading Ian Hamilton's biography of Robert Lowell, one of the books Bruce sent me. I discover my own strong opinions, or prejudices, as I read. Walt, you were never haunted. I think of Mazzaro & Mariani, now, Catholic Lowellists. Something <u>very</u> unhealthy about so much modern poetry. It has largely been written by neurotics, even psychotics. Those who become best known do so because of wild behavior. It is always the poetry of excess that gets the ink. And this paragraph is beneath me. And I want somehow to break out and be known, but can't. And I don't seem to have much discipline lately for writing, but will find some. And the sun is shining today and it must be about 50°. And reading of Lowell's life I'm torn in 16 directions. I'd like publicity and would like to be left alone. Maybe being on sattabical has made me "antsy." How do I feel?—happy, and ready to play some ball in a couple hours.... I <u>am</u> sort of discouraged by my weak knee, by my back sprain, by various bodily hurts that make me limp around. Right ankle. Shit, I don't want to lose my body this early. I'm 42 and spend much time here in my study with a fucking heating pad on my back.

Tony over yesterday right after proofs of the MacLeish interview arrived. We have that ready for the mail. Tony seems okay.

Contract for *Erika* arrived. I signed it & sent it back. Nothing new. So, another book this fall. I want to look at the proofs closely, and get the book just right. I read over the "Notes" section. I've many doubts <u>but</u> it's strong and right.... I'm going to push Evelyn for an ad or two, too.

Am to see George Cornell about the library display of my things this spring. I didn't want it to turn into a reading-reception thing, but apparently it has.

Will drive to Nashville with Han Friday.

Later: I just wrote a letter, after all these years, to Sandy McClatchy. I'm not sure of all the reasons, but he's been on my mind.

3/6/83 (Sunday evening)

Just spoke with Billy on the phone—he'd had an ankle injury, but seems okay again. He's got about a one-in-four chance for that scholarship, apparently. Wow, it wd. mean about $15,000 in savings for us. He'd be working in Lockport next summer, though.

Han & I drove to Nashville Friday. I meant to take along this journal, but didn't. We stood overnight. Took Pop Drachowski to dinner, shopping, out for beer, to the cemetery. Han did his laundry and cooked up a storm. Did what we could do. Beautiful weather. His stump seems okay, the swelling down.

I feel happy and at ease this evening. Finished the Hamilton *Robert Lowell*, and have read a hundred or so pages of Haffenden's *John Berryman*. So much I ought to enter here about my thinking on these men, on poetry, on my own desires. There it is, then, for them, <u>fame</u>: and a lifetime of desperation, largely, for each. I keep thinking that I can't please everybody from the Merrill school to the sons of Walt, and I can't be recognized withoug tremendous drive & ambition & energy which in turn would make me unhappy & desperate if I engaged these questionable desires, so I can be myself, edit that anthology myself, e.g., and with confidence & pleasure. These names Tate, Jarrell, Lowell, Berryman—they were young men once, and all were in some ways victims of their own delusions (as I am of mine), and I have as good or better a chance as they to win my way through to peace & clarity in my life. And it may be, in the end, that *Erika* and *The Chestnut Rain* are worth as much or more as anything they did.... I wonder <u>why</u>, e.g., I wrote McClatchy. Well, I know why: in part, out of sentiment for an old friendship; in part, because he has & will have <u>power</u> in those circles that seem impenetrable to me, the rich & privileged Ivy League fancy-asses.... Bill, go about your business. Sure, push for *Erika*, why not, but go quietly about your business, your interests.... Back to J.B....

3/8/83

I'm watching the news and waiting for Han & Kris to return from Eastman.

Billy called to say he didn't get that scholarship. He deserved it. They picked a girl whose record was weak compared to his. But, this means he'll be home this summer instead of away, and I'm glad, and that's worth more than money.

Herb Fackler called about nothing special. He's a good guy, and a friend who stays in touch, but he sounds nervous & hyper & politically involved at his school. Maybe I'm just nervous about him after finishing the Haffenden Berryman.... I am, by the way, anxious to write something about that generation.

Peter Klappert called to say he'd sent a batch of essays to *Poet & Critic* & they wanted to use mine ("The Moon in the River") & James Merrill's.

Al called with the bad (and confidential) news that Tony & Sandi are in bad shape, are going to separate. A disaster for Tony. I'll stop at Al's tomorrow and we'll talk about it. I can't imagine the mess it will be. I pray Tony won't explode. I can't imagine how hard/impossible/heartbreaking this will be for him.

3/9/83

Misery. Tony came by this morning, grief-stricken, with the news that Sandi is divorcing him. We talked for 1½ hrs., and then I saw him later in the afternoon at Poulins', too. Sandi has made up her mind. She told Tony she no longer loves him. Tony says that she cannot find sexual satisfaction with him, has not for two years because he is too strong (whatever that means), and thinks she can "get back" her body with others. She thinks she doesn't love him, but does, Tony says. He says she herself doesn't understand what's wrong with her. Tony sobbed again & again that he loves Sandi, could never love another woman. So hard, and thank God Al & Boo are in this too with Han & me. Nothing we can do except comfort them. Tony says he'll be moving out of the house—don't know to where. Al loaned him $600 today, and I'm sure he'll need money from us before long, too. Misery. I told Tony I hoped things would calm down, but he says Sandi is adamant & there's no chance of that. She was going to call a lawyer today. Months, maybe years of heartbreak out ahead for Tony. Apparently, say Al & Boo, during Tony's stay in China Sandi found out she got along better without him than with him, wrote many poems, etc. Sandi is 44 now, feels she must change her life now. Her relationship with Tony has always been so complex that I know only a little about it, but the heartbreak now and to come is a fact. Ironic that when Tony arrived this morning I was taking notes from Atlas' biography on the generally miserable life of Delmore Schwartz—Tony's experience will somehow temper the piece I hope to write on Schwartz, Lowell, Berryman.... Well, this is not all unexpected, but still has hurt Tony grievously, and will....

I read Nelly Sachs a couple hours last night, then slept hard but with many half-remembered dreams. By 6:30 in the morning I felt refreshed, strong, as though I'd come through something, ready to get up. And I did, and got busy.

Tomorrow I'm off to Genesee CC. Will try to enjoy that, and not just make it a thing to get through. One class, and the reading.

3/10/83

Just back from GCC. All went well. I spoke/read to a class from *Erika*, then read to two classes, mainly from *CR*. Damn, the sections I read sounded good.

Tony much on my mind. If Sandi goes through with the divorce, what heartbreak for him. I'm not sure he'll be able to bear it. I think I'll call Kendall this evening, just to speak with Sandi or Tony, to see if they are okay. Or something. I'm helpless, of course. Han & I have talked a lot about this.

Han has a cold. We're otherwise fine. I want to get back to some work again. Card from Ray Smith. He's about ready to roll on the anthology.

3/13/83

It's afternoon. Han & I just about to leave for Kristen's concert. I'll sit & relax & dream a little. Sunny & cool today.

I typed up the letter to contributors to *2000*. Will show it to Ray, and if okay will go ahead.

Saw Tony yesterday. He & Sandi had gone to a lawyer. A loving separation, as he says, and he's determined to get through this, to stop drinking, to be a good father during the separation. He knows he'll often be hurt, but believes he'll be okay. I feel for him. He & Sandi want to sell the Kendall home & property, and each will get an apartment in Brockport. I hope they don't have too big a problem selling the Kendall place. I'd like to live there myself, but only during the summer. That long walk to the pond & cabin is a joy. But the house would need much work. I hope they can sell—if not, they'll have many more problems. Tony is in trouble for money, money, money.

Han & I went to see *Gandhi* last evening, cared for it. One of the saints.

Will drop off the car tomorrow—$300 worth of work including 4 tires. Will arrange for the 2 week April trip I'll take.… Want to see Renée Gorin do *Swastika* at Hebrew Union College on April 10th.…

Later: Good concert, but long.…

A few minutes before Han & I went over, Al dropped in, upset. Seems like Sandi will be moving in with him and Boo, and Boo said okay without checking with him. I don't know how that will work out. Sandi teaches in Kendall. She is powerfully anxious to be apart from Tony, & that's for sure. The kids, apparently, will be out in the country with Tony.

I think I'll take notes on the Berryman book—don't know if the essay I'd like to do will ever come about, but I'll finish doing the notes. I want to get and read *Poets in Their Youth* first, in any case.

Later: Han has talked with Irma on the phone. The word is that all of Hartwell will be closed. So, I'll probably have an office in Neff. I don't care about that—maybe I'll have Armand Burke's cozy office that looks out over the mall. But it will be a damned shame about the old building. We'll lose it. Maybe we'll lose the alumni house. I don't know about SUNY College at Brockport. The plant is too big. Al Brown is largely responsible for these dilemmas now.… In my own life, I want to pull in a little, have a small space at the school, teach in an organized way and stay within myself next fall as I complete the anthology, see *Erika* through the press, go on with other writing projects. Will block myself in my little office. Will feel less furtive and conspicuous if I'm over with the others of the English Department.

This ties in in odd ways with the rest of my life. Han & I will want a smaller, simpler place, we feel, when the kids are out of the house. And the one possesion I worry about and want to preserve & protect is my library. It must have its own place in a library some day. I think it will. Inside me, this feeling to pull in—not to give myself in any long-range way to a Brockport that could be yanked away from me at any time. Tradition & time being lost & obliterated here. I can't fight it. I can only, myself, make & collect books to leave behind. I don't want to become attached to a place of such upheaval & constant change. This is not Harvard or Princeton. All's a flow here. So be it. But meanwhile, here at 142 Frazier St. in my study, on this acre, in the cabin, in my small office next fall wherever it is, I'll write, put books together, make poems of these very inchoate feelings I have, as though I am going downhill, down the slide of the 2nd half of my life and want to shed possessions and attachments, coil up into the power of a spring.… Something inside me, something, has no faith or, maybe, abiding interest in this school, this place. From a Zen point of view, this is a good thing. Sometimes I wonder if I should fight, write letters, raise money, do something to save old Hartwell & the Alumni House. But, no, a long time ago I chose to do other things, and these other things may yet prove to be more important and long-lasting than those things being lost here now.

All day today I've felt glad about the anthology I'll be doing. I can picture it, all the poets who will be in it, the poems I'll pick, ones I'll care for and will use in my teaching. This is the right thing for me at this point in my life. Maybe, just maybe I'll get lucky and do an anthology that stays in print until 2000! I've got to make it a good one, a big one. I should use Berry & Strand, should go on into some of the younger poets like Waters & Orr & McHugh & Forché. Yes.

I couldn't stay up late enough the other night to watch the end of *Chariots of Fire*. It's on again tonight, and maybe I'll catch the ending.

Another big box of books arrived from Bruce Agte the other day. About 25 books for 60 bucks. I couldn't be luckier.

Han finished the tax returns and they're in the mail.

Poem taken by *Crazyhorse* ("The Halo") & David Wojohn, the editor, is sending me his Yale book.

Will have a busy day tomorrow, and play some ball, too. May do my first letter or three to poets, though I'll hold onto them until clearing things with Ray. May wait for a contract.

3/15/83

Good day yesterday—morning work, basketball, afternoon & evening work that included finishing (except for some xeroxing) the NEA application due in a couple weeks. Today, I want to get to the publicity booklet maybe to go along with *Erika*.

Finished (finally executed) contract came from Evelyn. Also, the first letter I've ever had from her that sounds as though she's actually paying attention to anything I say. Just her mention that she'll place the Heine poem in the manuscript is a big step!

I usually get up before or when Han leaves for work. This morning, I fell asleep again, got up at 10:15, have that lung-deep feeling of rest.

Letter from Sandy McClatchy. He actually has a place in Vermont and loves to garden. He has little money, he says. This means, for the rich, that he just hates to touch any capital, and he's got plenty of that, I'd bet—the talk of thousands of shares of oil stocks years ago, etc.... Call from Pam Conrad on Long Island.... Picked up the car for $343 yesterday, and the other one is in there now. I've never liked the idea of two cars, and we'd never have had two, except for Mom Drachowski's death.... Call from Sandi & Tony, both, to tell us not to worry, that it would be a loving split. I hope so. Tony does sound calm & strong. They are both writers, they say, and need their separate lives, though they will always be dearest friends. Tony is not drinking, I'm happy to say....

I become more & more enthusiastic about wading into the anthology. I especially look forward, I guess, to getting into touch with more poets. This is the rhythm of my life now, at least, maybe a natural one because of the general aloneness of the sabbatical.

Will pay the mortgage today, stop in at the travel bureau to arrange next month's flights, stop in at school to xerox, stop at post office on the way back. Before and after all that, blessings of this study, Kristen & Han, this life of comfort & love & plenty. Talked to Billy last evening & he's fine. I drive to pick him up on the 25th.

3/16/83

Kristen's 17th birthday. I've blinked my eyes and seventeen years have gone by. More: the years since I was seventeen. I'll blink again, and she'll have a seventeen year old child. Lord, we're all on the way to you. Let today move slowly, as your spring comes near.

It's eight in the morning. A few hours of various things, and then some basketball. Want to finish the publicity booklet today, and write Evelyn & Ewert on it.

3/17/83

It's about ten in the morning. I just showered, will have only coffee this morning. Am relaxing here on a Thursday, when I'd otherwise be teaching.

Called Bill Ewert last night to tell him when I'd be visiting, to talk with him about the publicity booklet I'd been working on. All's well. I'll go from NYC to Concord to Middletown to Long Island on my trip, and maybe make a few side trips with Bill.

The booklet, or my part in it, is about done. I hope it works out, and helps. Somehow, I feel the hype, if there's to be any, should focus on *CR* down the line, but I don't want *Erika* lost as *Lord Dragonfly* was.

I'm <u>ready</u> to start contacting poets on the anthology. First, want to hear once more from Ray.

Will bike to the school today for some xeroxing. Will think about and make notes for my reading-talk to teachers at Greece Arcadia tomorrow. Will be glad to do that, and glad to get it over with. Saturday morning I'll go to an auction in Chili.

After playing basketball, showering, getting dressed yesterday, I went to the mirror to comb my hair, stood in front of a sink and remembered something I'd not thought about for decades. I saw myself with my foot in a sink after a high school practice. I'd injured an ankle at the last practice before our big championship playoff game with Northport. Coach Mularz banged angrily on the wall. I scored only four points in that game. Every once in a while over the years I've thought of that game and wondered why I had only 4 pts. (when I had 14 in the next game against Bay Shore, a much better team). Before yesterday, I hadn't remembered that I was hurt, so far had I pushed that injury out of my mind. Yesterday, I stood there smiling in front of that mirror in a half-a-lifetime dream.

The school mail already involves next semester, of course. I'm sometimes worried that I'm not doing enough now, that when I'm teaching again I'll look back on those days with regret. But, what the hell, it's okay, even healthy for me to sit here with coffee writing in my journal about a memory. Mainly, I'll have a book coming out in the fall, and others (*CR*, the anthology hereafter referred to as *2000*, and maybe the book of "city" poems) underway—that's the important thing while teaching: to have projects underway, ones to turn to with a sense of progress at free times.

A year ago today I received that last note from Archie.

3/19/83

Raining most of the day. I went to an auction in Chili—so uncomfortable that I came home even before it started. Graver arriving as I was leaving.

Han & I wanted to see *The Verdict* tonight, but the movie changed.

Even if I say so myself, I was a hit in Grece yesterday. I read some poems, & spoke a little about teaching. About a dozen people bought the books Bill Venis had on hand. Many teachers said very kind things.

Surprise check from *Upstate* in mail today: $200. For "Milkweed."

Picked up *Jesus* at post office yesterday. It's as nice a little item as I've ever had published—paper, printing, linoleum block prints. I'll send just a few copies to friends, and save the rest. Will probably buy more from Allen.

Kristen will have the house filled with girlfriends overnight.

As soon as this UCLA-UNLV game is over, I'm going to take a <u>long</u> walk in the drizzle before settling in for the evening.

3/20/83

I did. My knee is slowly on the mend, I think. As long as I avoid injuring it again playing ball.

It's noon. We've had pancakes, and Kristen is dropping off the girls who stayed overnight. She had a good party. I've cleaned up for an hour.

Han and I went over to Poulins last night. Mike Waters there—he seems pretty well, past his back problem, a little tired and maybe slightly paunchy—and Sandi & Tony & their girls. I helped carry Sandi's vanity into the house and up the stairs. She's moving in on Tuesday. All very sad. Tony, ferchrissakes, got drunk the other night out in his cabin & put some explosive stuff on the wood fire & the explosion burned his beard & nose.

Michael will be coming over this afternoon, I guess.... I gave him a copy of *Jesus*.... I want to write or call Allen Hoey, too, to thank him, and maybe get more copies. Michael says that the Scarab Press broadside of *The Numinous* will be a beauty.... I guess I'll get to his Tuesday reading at St. John Fisher.

I've not really been doing any writing, but poems come when they do. I can putter with the expanded book of city poems any time, and that will keep me busy.

Bill Ewert called yesterday about maybe doing some sort of keepsake for my visit to him next month—maybe my Whitman poem.

I'm in an in-between world these days. Will work hard on the anthology once I hear from Ray. Will have to get clothes etc. ready for my trip April 5-6 to Jamestown, and the trip April 10-24 to NYC & Concord & Middletown & LI.

3/22/83

Spent last evening (and part of the day) with Michael & Al. Talks of school & literary politics, the usual things. I mentioned, carefully, for the first time, to Al, that I was on the verge of agreeing to edit an anthology of the poets of my generation, and he became wide-eyed and excited, telling me "Don't!"... I'd spoken to Michael about it. I got a letter from Ray yesterday and now am 99-100% sure I'm going to do it. (Leo Buscaglia is on Donahue right now telling me to get up & do it! What the hell, a good book of Minty & Mariani & Smith & Heyen & Siegel etc.... Why not?).

Don't know whether or not I'll go to Michael's reading at St. John Fisher today.

Bad weather hit us yesterday, snow & sleet & ice. 1st day of spring.

Embrace all your emotions, Leo says.

Good to be here, on a Tuesday, inside, not having to teach.

Sent $180 to Allen Hoey, to help him, and for 10 copies of *Jesus* & 40 of Smith's *Blue Spruce*, which I'll sock away and smile about when I sell them in 10 or 20 years. Embrace all your emotions!

Later: I feel sort of scared, pale, all of a sudden. Just got a call from a social worker in Syracuse who had opened up my note to Vicky Gold—I'd sent her the announcement about Renée Gorin and marked it "please forward" thinking Vicky had moved to NYC, as she'd said—and called me to say Vicky died last week of a drug overdose, and her mother died this weekend. What a sad story it all is. I was talking about her last night at Poulins, telling of her phone calls [and before I could finish the sentence, Bill Andrews, Jr. called to ask if I could inscribe a copy of *The Berries* for his folks' 14th anniversary, so I drove over in the ice and snow and met him, and signed the thing to Bill & Monika, and on the way back home thought of how I would add this sentence in brackets to what I was writing, making writing again out of real death & tragedy & inexplicability, Vicky's despairing life], poking fun at her and questioning whether what she told me of her leukemia was true. I must learn to shut up, to understand the weak & hurt & maimed & sick, Gerber (I thought of writing Graver) or Gold. *The Berries*, no less, and I went over in snow, thick snow on the windshield as I inscribed the poem, bearing the berry light again, like that, like this, over the ice, as story inside story inside story.

I'll probably never know anything more of what happened to Vicky, or anything more about her. As the speech of consolation always goes, she's at rest now, as is her mother.... My first impulse, when I feel myself not hurting as I think I ought to hurt, is to condemn myself as callous & uncaring, but maybe it is true that I've come to feel what Walt and the other saints have told me, that death is nothing. I swear I know already that I won't be (will I?) terribly sad when my parents die, much as I love them now, as much of a constant comfort they are in their presence on this earth for me. It's all going to happen, and to me, too. Hopefully, my dearest loved ones and I will all take our turns, and the order will not be broken. I want to die first of the four of us here. Walt & Archie & John Gardner & all the others, where are they, what are they? I have this sense of miracle right at this moment, as though Jesus will gather us all to another life.... This evening, Bill Andrews, Jr. will walk with *The Berries* under his arm through the snow to give to his parents. This gift to them, to me, that came out of death.

3/25/83 (Fri.)

Just back from Ithaca with Billy. He's fine. I feel as though I've been in a time-warp today, all that grinding along all those highways.

First redwings of the year at the feeder.

Han had a rough day at work yesterday—that bastard Charlie McCullough. I called her a while ago, and she's had a good day today.

I bought several of Robert Morgan's books at the Cornell store. Wd. like to include him in the anthology. Bill Matthews wd. be pleased, too. Was doing okay reading Matthews, until I came to *Flood*. So much flat work in all the books, though, but I guess, still, he should be in *2000*.... I've got letters ready to go out to 7-8 poets now, and want to keep at those initial invitations. Total list of poets not at all definite yet.

Han & Kris leave next Thurs.

Cold today, but most of the ice and half the snow has melted away.

Will watch NCAA basketball games tonight, and read poets, & maybe write Matthews.

I'll stay away from Poulins for a while, let that whole situation catch its breath. Hope it will.

Pshew, good to be off the road, & have the four of us together again. Billy needs a break from school.

We went to Kristen's concert last night with the Studiers.

3/27/83

A <u>long</u> Sunday today. Rain all day, so the four of us have been inside. Good pancake breakfast together, good turkey dinner. All of us staying busy in the kitchen, & getting ready for my trips & the Myrtle Beach trip etc. Han trying to get another calendar done, too. And I've been reading Heather McHugh & Marvin Bell all day, and thinking about the anthology. This one, at first, is much more work than *AP '76*. But once choices are made, & essays are coming in, etc., it should be mainly detail & routine. Many decisions yet about bio-biblio format, etc. I <u>do</u> have months to gather things, write things, decide things, so must tell myself to relax. <u>Still</u>, it won't hurt to choose the 30 poets and contact them as soon as I can. My trip will take a couple important weeks from me. Well, if I'm done with first contacts by the end of May, that will be fine.... A hard time liking Bell. Easy to like McHugh....

Another emotional day for Kristen, this time for lack of a goddamned prom date. I understand all this turmoil. I don't kow. And the boy she liked asked somebody else. She's living the year of my own great heartbreak.... Well, she & Han leave Thursday, and I hope they have a week of sunshine.

Working on the anthology, I do no writing of my own, of course. But enough is upcoming to give me a sense of progress, <u>and</u>, more important, I won't hurt the springs through this anthology work, I'm sure.

Call from Bill Ewert again yesterday. About Vicky Gold.

Billy in fine spirits, and having a good time at home.

A pro game on television soon, and I'll stretch out & watch it.

No contact with Poulins/Picciones for several days. A good respite.

Still look forward to the big box of books from Bruce, & now for the package of 10 *Jesus* & 40 *Blue Spruce* from Hoey, too.

Will play a little basketball tomorrow, staying conscious of my knee. Don't want to get hurt before I leave for 2 weeks. The two weeks without basketball won't hurt it, might improve it.

Much water flowing by outside and around the cabin, but the cabin stays high & dry.

3/30/83 (Wednesday)

<u>Cold</u> days.... I'm working on the anthology.... Han & Kris leave tomorrow morning. Pat to arrive today.... Han's job tense but easing this week—she works with such jerks, grown people who act like babies. Contact with Tony (signed separation papers yesterday) and Al (informs me that Neff-Hartwell are closing, and that Tollers has resigned as Chairman). Billy home, and a little glum about his ankle, but okay. Quiet, thinking about the big questions. I'm glad I'll have a few days by myself with him. Then I'll be here by myself for a week before going on my trip. I must get to U. of R. once or twice for books for the anthology.... I've not been living within the depths I live in when I'm working on my poems—all my time goes into the anthology—but that's okay, maybe even a necessary part of the soul restoration of this sabbatical.... Good letter & books from Herb Fackler & Wm. Pitt Root. Letters from Agte & Greg Fitz Gerald that I've answered.... A desk filled with details today, and not much ambition for much else, except for basketball!...

Later: Was just reading Robert Pinsky's *Sadness & Happiness*. I'd thought he was a poet I might have to include, just from reputation, my sense of that world of opinion out there in the Ivy League. But what awful stuff! So general. And that awful tennis poem. The mannered lines, the posing, the absence of anything necessary and natural. And the blurb from Lowell, and the poem dedicated to Bidart, of course. No, no. Blah.

    Irma stopped over, had a cup of tea with us.

    Pat here, and Kristen's friend arriving.

    Ewert called to tell me we'd drive to Hanover on the 18th. Maybe I can see Eberhart.

    Played ball today. A good session.

    Read C.K. Williams, and want to include him in the book. Read Greg Orr's 2nd & 3rd books, and found some damned interesting poems, and will get his 1st book at U. of R. I'm getting excited: if I can reprint the poems I want to, get the essays & people I want, it's going to be a terrific book. My one worry was Bob Phillips, & I found 4-5 good ones of his that readers <u>will</u> enjoy. His suburban comic voice will be all his in the book, too…. Read Bell, and had a hard time finding poems to care for, & wrote him to invite him, but still have the letter on my desk, and may or may not send it. I don't know. Boring, and I can't remember a single poem once I'm away from it for ten minutes…. Read Turco, and just can't get interested enough (some interesting things in *Still Lifes*) much as I love that poem "The Dream" in *AP '76*….

3/31/83

    Morning. Han & Kris & Pat & Jan left early this morning. Billy is sleeping. I've just had three pieces of rye toast w. jam, and a banana. Sipping tea. Deciding when to go to U. of R. for the books I'll need. So, I'll be on my own for quite a while now, wish I didn't need to go to Jamestown the 5th & 6th, but need the grand…. Billy & I will keep company a few days…. I should stop by Mirko's some evening, and should visit Tony in Kendall some day….

    Anxious for the books to arrive from Bruce, not only for my general mania, but in case some things are there that I need for my anthology, as the new Clifton book, etc.

    Still <u>cold</u>, the Easter flowers shocked, maybe even beaten, daffodil stems flat on the ground, the buds unopened and maybe dead. Give us February again, those warm days.

4/4/83

    Billy back at Cornell last evening. I went over to Mirko's for dinner & a couple shots of brandy…. Han called yesterday, and they're down there safely and having fun.

Played ball…. Saw Al for a few minutes…. Called Tony—I won't be seeing him for a few weeks. He says he's getting stronger. Al says Sandi went out to the farm yesterday, and all they did, says Sandi, was argue.

    Leave early tomorrow for Jamestown. I have to be a teacher, and <u>sociable</u>, for a couple days.

    The snotty letter from Glück has bothered me. I didn't know anything about her third book. Wish I had. I guess I'll look it up, but <u>will</u> say something straight & sharp to her, and will not screw around. Either she'll do the essay, e.g., or she won't. Will get her book in NYC, & Simic's last, etc.

    Houston-NC State game on tonight, the final.

    Had a good couple days with Billy. He's in good shape.

    Nice letter from Pearl London today. That class is really <u>reading</u> me!

    Ewert called. He's worked up a little Ewert-Whitman-Heyen keepsake for my visit.

    Brother Henry called. Looks like he'll visit the Island when I do, that we'll have a nice reunion.

    Lord, keep my wheels on the road the next couple days!

4/5/83   [Castle Inn Motel, Olean]

    Evening. I'm at this place, in a nice room, in bed, after a shower, sucking on an orange lolly-pop, about to watch a Yankees game. It's been a <u>long</u>, but good day. I had two classes, and a reading. In between, a fine shrimp dinner, but, as usual, I was too nervous around strangers to truly enjoy it. I've been given $1000 for this and the one class tomorrow. By about 2:00 tomorrow, I should be sailing home…. Sold half-a-dozen books, too, that Vanguard shipped here.

Castle Inn Motel

Phone (716) 372-1050

Swimming Pool — Par 3 Golf Course

(Across from St. Bonaventure University)

WEST STATE ROAD (ROUTE 17)
P. O. BOX 507, OLEAN, N. Y. 14760

Read only from *CR* tonight. I liked it, feel good about my book, confident.

When I arrived here early this morning, I went for a half-hour walk before reporting in. Glad I did.... A young poet here by the name of Vanessa from Randall Jarrell's school, Greensborough.

This is chatter and I've nothing to say to my journal tonight.

Billy called last night, is fine, must be delighted, as I am, by the last-second North Carolina State win last night.

Hope Han & Kris have good weather.

I called Tony Piccione yesterday. Won't see him for a few weeks. He says he's getting stronger.... Saw Al: "confessed" to him that I'm doing the anthology. So, have that off my back. He didn't react in any special way, unless that was a dance he did when I asked about Glück's 3rd book, Simic's last.... Hope to get a good couple days of work in on that book before I leave Sunday....

Gaylord Perry is 44 years old, & opening pitcher for the Mariners, and he's given up three hits in the top of the first, and I predict he doesn't win ten games this season. I'm 42 & washed up as a basketball player, so I don't need him making me look bad.... He just struck out Don Baylor....

Thank you, Lord, for this day. I look forward to home again. Bless Han & the children & our folks & friends. Save the world from all of us.

4/7/83

Back. All's well. Got some sleep. Raining today again. I'll venture out this afternoon for some xeroxing (did the permissions forms), maybe a haircut, maybe to drop that invitation list for May 1 at the library, maybe to go to the bank, etc.

Good letter from Wendell Berry. I should be in good shape to use his essay & poems.

Han & Kris seem to be having, near as I can tell, the best weather in an otherwise stormy country.

I'm still sort of marking time before my trip, but will do <u>some</u> solid work on the anthology, I hope—maybe read Oates, or Smith, or McPherson.

4/9/83

Very nervous day for me as I get ready for my trip tomorrow. Details: a ride to the airport, a call to Evelyn, etc. Last night I spent some time thinking about what I always think about at such times: changing my life. After the anthology, even while teaching, picking my spots more and more, truly living in a way that would make mortal sense. I often think what a <u>relief</u> it would be <u>not</u> to have this desire to write and to take on everything that goes along with it, even keeping up with people's expectations for me. I wouldn't be nervous now, would be raking the lawn out back, or reading peacefully, or—something. Does my book collection keep me flush against this life? What of my thought not to publish <u>anything</u> for five years after *CR*? Oh, hell, I'm happy as I sit here in my chair, and no matter what life I chose or chose me I'd be nervous some of the time (teacher, bum, book collector), but I think of changing my life. Maybe another home, another job in years to come. Something.

Spoke with Billy & Kris & Han last night. All's well.

Wrote Tess Gallagher last night. Many of her poems unintelligible or uninteresting to me, but once in a while ...

It's <u>real</u>, but absolutely irrational of me to be so nervous, always, about things I have to do: teach, book orders, the anthology, etc. It's as though I live a split life, always worried about obligations. Why? The anthology—I make it into a mountain instead of just getting on with it.... I'm always babbling how Berryman & his friends committed themselves to a false aesthetic that led to unhappiness, even death. Now I know I've come to believe that to <u>write</u> I need long periods of freedom so that work can form itself inside me. Maybe that's my delusion. I should watch it. Maybe <u>that's</u> what makes me nervous, the belief that I can only write something true & beautiful & deep if I do nothing else but let it build in me and keep writing. That's why I resent aspects of teaching, yardwork, housework, the million details of my life that should in some way be pleasureable.... Lately, I've told myself as I've paced around or shot darts, just do something. And I <u>have</u>, have sat down to write a letter or something. And things do get done. It will all get done, all the work on 3 new courses I have to do to teach again, the anthology, the office to move, the trip—all of it. Enough. Yes, I can see myself changing my life!...

4/14/83

I'm sitting in a bus at the Port Authority terminal in NYC, waiting to drive off to Boston and then transfer for the jaunt to Concord & Bill Ewert. I'm tired, but okay. Such a jumble of days and nights since I left. The trip to Newark on Sunday and the long wait at the airport for a bus to this place. The pouring rain that day and finding Hebrew Union College. Seeing Renée Gorin & David Darling (the performance good but somehow noisier & less moving than at Brockport). Hooking up with Bruce and staying at his apt. that night in Washington Heights. Book hunting all day Monday, & staying with Evelyn, and then hooking up with Bob Phillips & the bus to & from Katonah with little sleep, a <u>cat</u> in my bedsprings, and talk, talk, talk. The good Tuesday morning class at the New School, & lunch with Pearl London (the bus is starting) and crew. More book hunting, including a visit to the Phoenix & nervous chat with Bob Wilson. Visit to the new Vanguard orifices. Quick visit with Bruce to Marge Cohen—she <u>gave</u> me two Wesleyan books. Very little sleep in Evelyn's hot & Miss Haversham-like apt. Walked from 72nd to 1st & back & forth most days. Only a couple good meals. Will remember Judy Phillips, & sweet unhappy Katherine who has worked as family maid for weird Evelyn for 40 years. Evelyn miserly & a bag-woman with a million dollars. Good times with Bruce, the walk below the Cloisters. Spent about $300 on books, but have almost all I need for the anthology now. Long loving talk with Han from an outdoor phone on Central Park West. My calves aching from walking. The writing of the prose piece for London's class, and my oncoming poem "The Subway." A pigeon just now flying up to my bus window and backing away. Seeing Harlem. The motionless black bag-lady who scared/startled me. The rich—the limousine lady at the Strand. Buses of whites driving through black neighborhoods, the paradigm of Heyen writing this right at this moment. <u>Seeing</u>: littering/is/filthy/&/selfish/so/don't/do it!—& my decision about composition details that <u>cannot</u> compete with the overwhelming power of megalopolis.... I'm at Madison & 135th now, have just gone through some blasted neighborhoods about 80 blocks from Vanguard. I'll put this sheet away for now, as I leave the city, & read my book on Don Juan & Castenada, the life of happiness, joy, even if there is nothing at the end of the path....

4/15/83

I'm sitting in the Ewerts' living room, relaxing for the first time in a couple days again. Good to be here, though this is the most hectic goddamned place—two wild kids, two wild dogs, two cats, everybody always yelling, Mary & Bill sweet but pursuing phantoms.... Visit to a stone quarry yesterday, and to a place where the stone is cut. I have a sample of Regal Chestnut granite that I'll place in the cabin as a paperweight.... Visited Concord, Mass., today, and came upon the house where Thoreau died, saw the Old Manse again—it's now closed—, etc.... Visited Bert Babcock and came away with some books by Warren, etc.... It was a <u>long</u> bus trip here.... Bill Ewert and I have had many laughs, and will have more time together over the next few years (I mean days). Tomorrow will be Saturday, and even more hectic, with the kids home all day.... All in all, I'm doing okay—2 dogs and a cat at my feet now, the television on, Bill talking, and this is the most relaxed I've been all day!

4/17/83

Extremely busy day yesterday. Two bookstores (Concord & Henniker) where I bought about $100 worth of books that had once belonged to a chap by the name of Settle, now in jail. Some very good things.... Party last night, and I read various poems.... Today is Billy's 20th birthday, and I'll call him later. Just spoke with Han & Kris.... Bill Ewert & I will spend the day in book-talk.... It's Sunday noon, and I've the first moments of peace around here.... I turn the corner today, and it's downhill to home.... Visited Bert Babcock with Bill yesterday, and took $100 of the $175 he owed me in trade.... Sent two boxes of books home from here, and will send one more.... I'm okay, a bit uncomfortable and ragged, but okay. Noise begins here at 5 or 6 a.m.... The little keepsake item Bill prepared is nice, though McCurdy has given Walt a strange & hairy forehead.... Bill just came back, and the action begins....

4/18/83

Just back from Hanover with Bill. I walked around a little during his meeting, met him in the special collections section of Baker Library, visited the Frost room and met Stan Brown, the young curator.... Have a few hours to myself this afternoon, will have dinner out with Bill, and will think of getting to Wesleyan tomorrow.

A typical morning this morning at Ewerts. Scuffling upstairs at maybe five. Clattering and fighting overhead, Mary & Bill shouting orders. The two dogs and two cats coming alive and coming downstairs. Much barking & running around my bed. Mary shouting to the boys to get dressed, get breakfast, brush their teeth. Bill getting his hair washed by Mary—he can't do it himself very well, he's too heavy. Bill yelling at Billy not to get Windex in his orange juice as he cleans his glasses. Mary telling Billy 3-4 times more to brush his teeth. The dogs going nuts because someone is walking along the street. Mark & Billy fighting. The radio on loud & Bill Ewert's special little weather radio on and the television on with one of the video games. Mark punches Billy & Billy cries. Billy vomits. The poodle is having her period and bleeds on the rug. Breakfast cereal knocked on the floor. Running up & down the stairs. Mark coughing & saying he can't breathe. Mary sighing, and then telling family tree after family tree. I am calm in the middle of all this swirl & noise. I look out at a pine tree and think of its serenity opposed to human nuttiness. It's 8:00, and the craziness intensifies, all screaming, the kids late for school, the dogs going crazy. Morning at the Ewerts.

I feel fine. Played some ball, baseball, with the kids at a park yesterday. Have had good talks with Bill when we've gotten out on our own for a drive.... Called Billy & home yesterday and my three loved ones are okay. I miss home, but am downhill, and the next few days will go very quickly.... I hear a snow-storm is on the way.

Surrounded even by a Shakespeare first folio and an Audubon elephant folio this morning, I thought of the vanity of this life of collector, and the wasted time. But.

4/19/83

I've left Ewerts, am on a bus between Boston & Middletown, bouncing along. Slept little, am tired, will be glad to get to the Island tomorrow. It's raining. I did plan my reading for tonight, beginning with p. 160 in the Castaneda book & going through my poems by way of that. The Ewert household is Bedlam itself, and I'm relieved to be away.... Sex much on my mind lately. Sure do look forward to Sunday night with Han. I can feel her on me as I jounce along in this bus.... Heard Bill & Mary screwing last night in their room above me, in fact. Bill must weigh 350, and it can't be easy.... Have one sore spot in the back of my throat from sinus drip, but I seem otherwise to be okay.... Read this morning in the *Times* that Galway won the Pulitzer for his *Selected*. My library just went up a grand or two in value.... I've just thought of Poulin & Piccione for the first time in a long time—it is good to be away from Brockport routine for a change. Wonder if my basketball knee is getting better.... The bus is stopped in Worcester, Mass., home of Metacom Press.... Bus filled up when I wasn't looking, & I have a seat-mate, a young black guy.... Next stop is Hartford, I hear.... Jesus, I need a bath: I must stink. Hope I have some time at the Wesleyan guest house later.... Snow storm in Vermont this morning made my bus in Concord 1½ hrs. late.... Bill gave me a set of Oates proofs for the next item he's doing.... Saw a part of Boston through the bus window that I hadn't seen before: the Public Gardens, a bit of Arlington St. & Bleeker St.... Oriental kid in front of me just told a woman he ran in the Boston Marathon yesterday....

4/20/83

I'm on a train from Meriden, CT., to Penn Station, where I'll take LIRR to Stony Brook. It's early, and the car is packed. I'm fighting a cold, after sleeping little, after a reading to 11 people, including the Maynards, then a drink with Jean & John at their home. Fuck Alpha Delta Phi, the insensitivity of the young who do not know how to treat a guest—I wasn't even introduced, and the room was noisy, etc. Pick your spots better, Bill, as you told yourself to do in Wyoming years ago.

Jean told me that McClatchy only had 12 in his audience for his Connecticut Poetry Circuit reading. "O to be a star. Or, stay home until you are, if ever. And don't care if never." Catchy.

4/25/83

Home again. Decompressing. The two flights yesterday were dizzying, and my head is still a little plugged up. Surprise was that I had to drop Kristen off at train station at 2 a.m. for a trip to Northwestern she's making. Sleep before & after, and Han & I together. <u>Very</u> happy and content to be home.

Piles of mail, and I'm anxious to get going on the anthology again, but will not rush. Just glancing at some letters from Matthews & McHugh & others, I see that things are going along nicely. Here at home, hopefully calm and unhurried, I have time for everything.

Good gatherings the past couple days with Henry & his new Janice—I like her very much. A shadow hanging over her—she'll have an exploratory operation next week... Big dinner at Werner's Saturday, a dozen of us at the table.... And a couple nights ago, Pop in bed, I listened to Mom for two hours, and for the first time emotionally truly felt for her, her struggle—news of Pop's impotence for 20 years now, his alcoholism & the troubles it brought on for her, her inability to get her sons to <u>understand</u> her plight as they identified with the father. And more and more. I wish I had had a tape of the whole thing so that I could listen to it again. My mother, still suffering and trying to come to terms with memories of mistreatment, constant lack of tenderness & sensitivity.... Pop getting old fast, but the folks generally get along. They both drive too fast & erratically.

So, back from NYC, & Concord, & Middletown, & L.I., & stops in between. Home.... Settle in now, Bill. Enjoy.

Will run a little today at the gym—it's actually <u>snowing</u> here now. Will go to the College book sale in the morning, & see my library display. Will unpack some of the boxes of books that arrived here. Will watch some basketball playoff games. So glad to be home.

4/27/83

Took me a couple of days to clear away other correspondence, and get new books out of the way, but I finally broke through this evening and got back to the anthology. Have to work on it steadily the next few weeks. I want all invitations out by May's end.

Played ball, and shot better than in months.

Called Mike Waters. He'll have Joyce (I hope) and me to Salisbury for a "festival" next fall.

We picked up Kris at the train station at 6 this morning. It's been a long day.

Tomorrow evening I'll see Carolyn Forché again.

Will no doubt write very little in this journal over the next few weeks as I keep up work on the anthology.... Did sit in the cabin for a half-hour. Honeysuckle leafing again. I dozed off while reading a new book on Zen koans. 70° today, at last.

Talked to Billy last night. He went to a lacrosse game at Syracuse today. I hope Cornell won, but ... Billy will be home in a week or so to pick up the car.

I'll be able to sleep late tomorrow morning, hoorah. I need it. First chance in about three weeks. Tonight, I'll stay up late watching an NBA game.

In the back of my mind, worry that I'm not staying with my poems. But *Erika* is upcoming, & the last *CR* books from Ewert, and I keep telling myself something that I actually think is true: it's okay to spend these next months on the anthology.

Spent $32 for about 20 books, including a 1st of Emerson's *Representative Men*, at the College sale. I was first one there. Many other good things. Maybe I'll stop in again tomorrow, last day, for some real cheapies—prices reduced on everything. Yes, will bike up there for some exercise, and then get to work on the anthology for a few hours.

May 1, 1983

It's noon. In a couple hours I'll go with Han & Kris to pick up Mrs. DeLancey & head over to the library for my reading. I am nervous, being at the center of so much local attention. Important that it go well for George Cornell and others. I think there will be enough people there. If it weren't for the peace walk going on about the same time, there wd. be many more. But there's seating for only about 50 in the Kiefer Room, in any case.... So, here I go again.... I hope to spend the evening at Mirko's, drinking brandy & playing poker.

I'm pleased at how calmly & steadily I'm going about the details of *2000*. Will stay with it consistently all May, and should have it pretty well under control by month's end. Still have to invite Smith, Oates, Charles Wright, etc.

Spent two evenings with Forché and husband, though we didn't have much of a chance to talk. After reading her inscription to me in *The Country Between Us*, I passed on copies of *Swastika* and *The Bees*.... Dave Smith sent his new book, too, with another inscription that makes me happy on several levels....

After the big El Salvador meeting, I went with Bob Marx & Mirko to Mirko's where we had butter pecan ice cream with pear halves, and brandy. It was the first anniversary of the death of Betty Marx. We talked of her, of afterlives, of our lives in time. I dropped Bob off at his apartment later on.

Heard so much Department politics in two days at dinners with Perry & Rubin, and at Tollers' party for Burke & Ferguson. Proud of myself at last at how calm & distanced I felt/feel. Am I growing up? Have I learned to go about my business?

May 8, 1983 (Sunday)

No desire to write anything much here. Am waiting to watch two NBA play-off games. Billy home, studying. He's fine. Mother's Day, and Han & I think of her mom, that Forestville hillside where she's buried. Raining today. My reading went well last Sunday, the President there again. Kristen's orchestra concert last night, Sibelius' "Finlandia" played again. I've John Gardner's *Michelson's Ghosts* from Bruce, and about 50 other books in the mail. Work on *2000* goes well, some hard decisions to be made down the line. I've only heard from about a dozen of the poets, but things will catch up. Will make a selection from Smith next. Dave sent me a beautifully inscribed *In the House of the Judge*.... I washed out the garage yesterday, and turned in my fall book order at Lift Bridge.... Word is that Picciones have their house sold.... Al leaves next week for 6 weeks away with his mom. I don't envy him the trip. I want to get the lawn cut, the garden tilled, etc.... Kristen had a great time at the prom, but we're all glad that's over!... I've scratched beginnings of a few prose pieces & maybe poems, but literary work is on *2000*.

May 10, 1983 (Tuesday)

It's mid-afternoon, and I'm back in the cabin for the first time in a long time. This past year, I've forgotten too much about this place, have forgotten it too much. I've maybe been complacent about having written enough, done enough, so spend the time inside.... It's cold out, and dark and blowing, so I've the small heater on and it's warming this place. Small leaves out in the small elm to the left of the picture window, and in the honeysuckle bushes. Ash leaves just starting, but the visible outer world of houses a few hundred feet away disappears.

Billy left about an hour ago. His stay here was short but warm and good. A week of tests and he'll be done.... Han & Kris go in to Eastman today, so I'll be alone, as I have been on Tuesdays, until 8:30-9:00 this evening. Anthology work to do, but it's good to be back here, the cabin warming, coffee steaming.

Han not completely happy with her job—the work is just too much, and her staff is entrenched & overly-sensitive & immature, I think. But there are many good moments.... I saw Tony yesterday. He's okay, but different, needs/wants to get settled, find an apartment or house, begin again.... I tried for an hour to do something with the small mower yesterday, but couldn't, so will throw it away. Bought for $50 a trimmer, a Toro, and hope <u>that</u> and the big mower, once Al fixes it for me, will do the job.... Wrote Janice, Henry's friend, wishing her good recovery.... Ed <u>did</u> call Mom on Mother's Day, and I'm glad that heart-ache is over.

I've made a few line-starts & plot-starts the past couple weeks, getting out of sleep. Will turn to them now and see if anything happens. It's kind of an in-between time in my life.

$1000 merit raise, hoorah, and a $400 invitation from Milt Kessler to read at Binghamton. Billy didn't get the work-study job he'd applied for at Cornell....

But I just started reading journal entries from last May at about this time. I've gotten around in the past year, and have made circles—trips to the Ewerts, book-trips to the Strand. Now, right now and here, I have the wide-open time spaces I always yearn for.

Will leave this journal back here now, until I finish it.

May 19, 1983

It's mid-morning, Thursday. I have the heater purring away back here. Overcast today. All's well, Billy home, Kristen & Han fine. Lawns mowed, half the garden tilled, my life orderly and free as can be hoped for.

Richard Ehrlich & his friend Richard, a pleasant man of 65 or 70, visited the other day. I showed them this cabin, the row of pines, my acre world.

Flurry of excitement with a call from Evelyn Schrifte the other evening, and then my call to Ewert—a call in which I didn't hide my disappointment that he hadn't gotten back to her when she'd written him a month or so ago, and didn't tell me he'd heard from her (about the publicity booklet)—and his calls next day to me about that and about the Gemmett/Investiture broadside. All a drag. But I want *Erika* to get around, want cheap Evelyn to put a little money into selling it for a change. Not one ad for *Lord Dragonfly*. She <u>does</u> seem to be doing some things on this book, sent me a xerox of the proposed jacket front, sent me catalogue copy on the book.

Mainly, work on the anthology. Good progress. Heard from Simic, Carver, Gallagher. Wrote Smith. Heard from Oates. Wrote Glück again. Need to invite 3 or 4 more poets, at least. Read Wakoski last evening and this morning. I liked 2 or 3 poems in 2 or 3 books but she's usually embarrassingly bad. I blush. She mentions that she has a Boswell! Her lutes are insipid. No.... Call from Stan Plumly, who just got back to Houston. Final selection on Kicknosway, etc. Want to make a selection of my own poems one of these weeks, write the essay, draft my preface again, adding a couple other things.

Massachusetts Review appeared with the MacLeish interview. It looks fine.... I did a very short prose piece about Archie's last (maybe) letter, but my own writing waits for anthology's-end.... Norbert's handsome *Heartwood* arrived—an extra "in" in his prose afterword. And how careful he & Morris have been. Only God could make a perfect book....

Ash leaves half out, the houses around me almost completely vanished now.

Much fun playing basketball lately. I've bicycled up to the gym. Very physical life lately, bicycling & basketball & tilling & mowing. I've even had my shirt off & gotten some sun.

Good call from Mom—Pop working part-time & making $10 an hour with Richie in his shop. I <u>know</u> how useful this makes Pop feel. It will prolong his life. And bringing in that money is <u>very</u> important to him.... Werner depressed about his live-in mother-in-law.... Henry ready to ship to England.... Letter from Ed's Cheryl. They seem to be doing okay. So, the planet still buoys up the four Heyen boys & their families.

The Ewe's Song and *Blackberry Light* to appear soon in *Ontario Review* and *Ohio Review*, and two poems in *Poetry*, so I'll feel extant, though I've not written a real poem in a while (a 3-line Stonehenge thing the other evening, gulp).

Got a $1000 merit raise.... Bash June 9th for Coach Parker, my old soccer coach, at the College. I actually look forward to seeing all the old players who will be on hand. I'm glad to have been a Brockport co-captain & All-American, to be, now, one of the ghosts.

Have seen Tony a couple of times. Frantic & tense decisions for him as closing on his farm comes near (July)—decision of where to move, what to do with the 3 dogs & several cats so that his kids' hearts are not broken. Han had a long talk with Sandi the other day—two sides to all their stories & problems. But, mentally, Tony seems to be holding up.... Al in Paris now, and I hope his body doesn't let him down (as he has abused it) the next five or so weeks as he travels with his mother.

Great NBA games last night, Philadelphia closing out Milwaukee, Jabbar & Co. losing to San Diego so having to travel to Texas while the '76ers rest. Rings going to Malone/Erving/Toney/Cheeks/Jones/Iavaroni/Richardson this year, I hope.

May 21, 1983

Back here in the deepening green with my Viet Nam cup of coffee. Birdsong all around me. Han at the Senior Center Bazaar, Kris & Billy still in bed.

Heard two scientist-atheists on television yesterday with as bleak and hard-nosed a view of our existence here on earth as I've heard. One said he had a pact with his wife that if either of them, as they grew older, ever came to believe in God or any kind of afterlife, the other would get psychiatric help for the victim. I keep gauging how I feel (knowledge of history inside me, seeming abandonment by God, uncaring power if there is any central power), and keep feeling, in odd but undeniable wordless glints of intuition, that it's not only definite that there is something for us beyond and underneath (during all the moments of quotidien reality) all this right now and later, but that it's illogical not to know this as a fact. This amazing body, and consciousness, the earth as one organism, the galaxies, the beginning some time & somehow & somewhere, time toward which I always feel tending. Well, this is all a floundering, of course, and has no chance against the "prove it" school. Is it defensive, or do I truly feel/believe in the transcendental consciousness? The latter. I second-guess myself even as I say that, but the latter, I believe. Or else there is nothing, as Walt says. Or else, at least, there is not enough, not enough in beauty for only its own time-bound sake.

Working on the anthology, do I feel, somehow, that I'm losing a sense of my own poetry?—not because of all the voices I'm reading, but simply because I'm not staying with my own poems—shuffling & reading & getting inside them—day after day as I usually do? It's okay, there's time, do this in your life now, I keep telling myself.

Billy & I played ball yesterday. Much fun. Saw Tony over at the gym. He's been playing handball.... Billy worked 5-6 hrs. yesterday at Muesey's new store in Clarendon.

Negative review of *Lord Dragonfly* in *Poetry*. I'm glad I don't care much. A professor who can't hear much, and who calls "Lord Dragonfly" haiku & then judges it against haiku tradition, gulp.... I've come a long way since my despair over the Parisi review of *Noise* in *Poetry* years ago.

Will till later if it doesn't rain.

May 22, 1983

Just this minute rushed a mowing of the back lawn to beat the rain, which has begun again. Have to do some raking one of these days.... It's almost noon. The four of us had a good pancake breakfast this morning. The strawberry freezer jam always lights up a Sunday morning.

Pat, Kurt, Pop Drachowski, Mary Press, and Florence Press stoped by on their way back from Kurt's R.I.T. graduation yesterday. Good to see them all. Mary & Florence had never been to Brockport. I took them back to the cabin, too.

Card from Al in Paris yesterday. He seems okay.

Trying to think about thinking again. Thinking needs language, apparently—at least superficial & conscious speech—and language spoken only as fast as the tongue (even when the tongue is still) allows. Unless I experience this because as poet for so many years I've tried out any thoughtful language on my tongue.

Thinking about my day-to-day concern with poetry, too. I could be content to change my life. Could it be?

Green increasing around me, the cabin its own space again.

I'll work inside a couple hours before the ball game, 1st of the final NBA playoffs, Philly vs. L.A.

Stopped at Senior Center yesterday with Han for their bazaar.

Birds squawking. Must be a cat around.

May 26, 1983

Good days, and good sessions in the cabin. I just went over a notebook, touching up about five or six things I can give a first typing to, slight things, maybe (prose ¶s about Han's mom, & about MacLeish; poems about Li Po and blackberries), but things I'm glad I wrote.

Xeroxing & shuffling work on the anthology, but no progress on the final list of contributors. I won't panic, & will keep hoping to hear from Ai, Clifton, Strand, Oliver—and will invite a few more poets.... A letter from Turco that hurt, but I'm over it. A good letter, on the other hand, from Jerry Mazzaro. The book itself that I'm putting together xerox by xerox is going to be awfully good....

Never had as much fun playing basketball as I have this week. I want to keep laughing and having fun as I play.

Good to have Billy home. He's put in many hours at Muesey's already.

I got around to writing Martin. Also, Jerry.

Spent a couple hours reading over *Erika*. Feel good about it, though I'm thinking of adding one more note, on the "obscenity" of the form of some of the pieces, the nails-on-the-blackboard effect I've aimed for. Maybe not.

Overcast today. I want to work outside a couple hours this afternoon.

Tony stopped over, and I broke the news to him about the anthology, and that he wouldn't be in it. Don't know if it was a good time to tell him—he'd asked me what all the xeroxing was that I'd been doing—but there could never be a good time. He said he didn't care. I showed him Turco's letter, with the gratuitous insult, then was sorry I did, but Tony said he was glad I did. He'd no longer have to be polite to Turco.

Thinking this morning about how local & self-involved my thought is. Thinking about politics in Rome or about sequoias in California would be local, too. Have to send the mind <u>way</u> out and <u>way</u> deep into things to escape pettiness.

Houses completely blocked from my view now.

May 27, 1983

Good note from Simic yesterday. Selections all set. And he said it's good there will be this anthology because there isn't a good one on the market!... And Morgan sent his essay already, a beauty. He's keyed it in directly with his poems.... And I xeroxed more yesterday, so the book is a-building.... Right now I feel I won't answer Turco at all.

Only have about an hour back here this morning before Billy & I go over to the gym. I don't know whether it was the two beers I drank last night, or the adrenalin from watching the NBA game (Philly took it again), but I had the hardest time sleeping that I've had in a long time.

Overcast & cold today. Heater purring.

I mowed yesterday, and cleaned out the raspberry patch for a while, the old canes and the (dodder?) creeping plant that wants to take over. And Han & I walked around the property, as, I remember, Mom & Pop did back in old Nesconset, looking at trees, imagining future growth, seeing the growth since last year.

Right now, looking around me, I feel as though I always want to stay in Brockport. A semester here or a year there, but always in Brockport.

Memorial Day, 1983

Relaxing back here before going in for a shower. Did some mowing, some tilling, some hacking away to clear a few trees & bushes from undrgrowth. A perfect day today, cool & shining.

Walked along with the small parade again Saturday, choked up again at all that remembrance. To think of such ceremonies in thousands of small towns & big cities across the country. Found a few lines for a poem again. Wd. like to write a companion piece for the other Memorial Day poem.

Have most of the garden in now—beans, sunflowers, corn.

Good day yesterday. Billy had Brian Johnson for supper. I cooked steak & hamburgers outside. Good family days. A blessed life.

Called Vince Clemente the other evening. Just to send love. Called my folks. I'd forgotten Pop's 73rd birthday.... Bruce called to say he'd been in Oyster Bay in an old schoolhouse Walt had once taught in, that he'd held in his hands a 1st issue of *Leaves of Grass*, that he might work on repairing the place this summer. Suppose, just suppose, that Bruce the carpenter, & like Walt & Jesus, could break free of his own boundaries like a star and write something true & real & new? If he does, I hope I can recognize it. He's serving his long foreground now.

Not hearing from several people I've invited, and not getting around to the last invitations, makes me nervous about the anthology, but it will come together. Robert Morgan sent his prose piece already, a good one.... I see that I've said this already.... And I probably won't answer Turco.... Okay, on with the day.

June 1, 1983

About to go in and get Billy & head up to the gym.

Read some few weeks of Vol. 6 of Traubel's Whitman that Bruce sent me. And pushed a raspberry sequence ahead a little. It may come to be something after all.

Much mail yesterday. And I sent an invitation to Piercy.

Some garden work & rock-moving yesterday. Overcast days & we need some heat for seed germination. Philly swept the series, hoorah.

All's well. Just have to settle on all anthology contributors. Should call Poets & Writers for addresses of Ai & Lucile Clifton & Mary Oliver & Ishmael Reed.... Good letters from Gallagher & Carver yesterday....

Transplanted another honeysuckle bush over to the right of my cabin where it will block me in back her more and more.

Han & the kids fine.

June 2, 1983

It's seven in the morning. I decided to change my life a little and to get back here early. Read a few days of October-1889 in Walt. Walt is not one thing, but everything—champagne & anger & laughter & politics. I want to accept myself, the scrambling the anthology makes me do from day to day, the book-collecting, the worrying, the evading, the basketball playing. I'm okay. Not a Zen purity, an emptiness inside, and maybe, certainly, never, but more and more an acceptance of self.

Will maybe pick my own poems for the anthology this morning, and work on the prose piece. I have in mind to do something on "Ram Time"—at least to begin with it.

Reading Dave Smith again last night. I don't know. At bottom, an unnecessary lack of clarity. I'll find enough poems I believe in for the anthology, and I like <u>him</u>, his warmth & loyalty, but poem after poem grinds on without ... something ... some music & form that will sustain & clarify it. Years from now so much of his work is going to seem awfully posed & antiquated & ungainly & contrived. The poem of mine to set next to his, maybe, to what he would like to do (though Dickey & Warren seem mostly to have generated his work) is "Fires."

Well, then, it's early and I want to have a full day. Green around me. White honeysuckle blossoms. Up to my left, green cherries. The boulder in front of me. Blue sky through the leaves. Quiet back here, and I think now of the airports & bus stations & city streets I'm glad to be away from.

June 3, 1983

Almost time to leave to play ball. Yesterday morning & this morning I've had good sessions back here. Have just sent my own essay for *2000* through a second draft, and it feels okay. I've chosen 8 poems to include, will not be a shrinking violet. I teach, or act like a teacher in my essay. I've called it "Glad to Be a Fool."

This is the cabin season. Perfect back here right now.

Permissions problem w. Harcourt on Berry. Will work it out. Will clear things up all month, little by little.... Wrote Smith for his new poems.... Need more women in the book, but want to write Norman Dubie—many poems made me whistle.

Han & kids fine.... Tony P. called last night—we'll move him on Sunday the 12th.

June 5, 1983 (Sunday evening)

Wrote Stewe Claeson a long letter yesterday, wrote a short one to Vince just now. Have been back here steadily the last couple days, between stints of mowing and raking. Have typed up the 2 new memoir pieces, the new brief essay for the anthology, the batch of shorter poems that showed up in my notebook by and by. Have been reading Traubel's 6th volume, and enjoying Walt again. Feel pretty much at ease about things as June picks up speed.

Bill Ewert called this morning. He's sending a letter on the publicity pamphlet to Evelyn. He mentioned that 3 teachers from Greece ordered *The Berries*—they must have seen the one I gave Bill Veenis. He also mentioned that his new Oates just isn't selling. Hmmm.... I got a letter from Bert Babcock who may visit this summer. He says he's in a buying mood. I sure would like to raise some money, and have some nice things I don't want.

I never did answer Turco, and won't.

Mock-up of *The Numinous* arrived—Beavers played a joke on me & it was titled *The Numerous*, and I thought it had gone to press that way. It's going to be a handsome item, one I'll be glad was done. Some day, a display of broadsides, maybe mine alone, or maybe of many poets.

Was just daydreaming. Sort of wish I had my old journals with me so that I could look back & read the life as it is lived. Also, am glad they're packed away. When I retire, I'll have them, maybe will read them with Han in our old age.

I've got to get on the ball & try to make contact with the anthology people I haven't heard from. Then, line-up set, the book will fall into place. Push might come to shove on certain permissions.

June 8, 1983

It's 8 in the morning, the heater purring to warm up the cabin a little. I've read a little in Volume 6 of the Traubel. I'm blessed to be here, among the trees, rather than in an office, or classroom, or airport.

I've stayed busy, but have to make another push to get into touch with a few people on the anthology. Have been typing the preface again.

Han & Kristen extremely busy, even dizzy. Nothing I can do but stand back and watch them exhaust themselves. Billy has been doing fine. He won't play ball today, but will work some extra hours for Muesey.... Tomorrow night, come to think of it—thought of because when I played soccer little Bobby Muesey was around—is the reception for Huntley Parker at the College. That will be fun. Many old ghosts, including Bill Heyen, will be around.

June 9, 1983

Received an invitation yesterday—it was first sent to Athens, Ohio, and then c/o Wern & Barb on Long Island—to "The Last Prom," a reunion of the classes of the old Smithtown Branch High School. It will be held mid-August in my old gym. The news somehow has disrupted me, made me feel ... incomplete, maybe, for not writing the novel I've always wanted to write; … yearning, somehow, for that world lost, lost. Can I <u>not</u> go to that thing? I think that school is closing. I'd see that gym, maybe my classrooms for the last time. Han wd. see my school. Maybe Wern & Barb wd. go. It wd. be the weekend we'd be visiting Kristen in Saratoga Springs, in any case. Will see…. And tonight is the gathering for Huntley Parker. What to do with all these memories, all this nostalgia? What would be wisdom in dealing with it? It saddens, and it brings joy and a sense of self at the same time. Animals & plants are apparently free of it.

I played ball twice yesterday. The second time was at the playground with five of Billy's friends. Even my basketball playing is connected with that boy who played the middle of the 2-1-2 zone for the Smithtown Indians, no doubt…. I think of Walt who, at the end of Kaplan's book, sails into the past, reminisces—the Walt in the Traubel I'm reading—and finds mostly pleasure and a sense of accomplishment in doing so. A poem like my "Boatman & Boy" doesn't get anywhere, come to think of it, but just rounds off on itself, and this must be because, too, of this dilemma of what to do with those kinds of materials. In "Ram Time" I bring the two worlds together and then do go on.

6/13/83

9 a.m. I'm in the cabin this Monday morning. Several aches and pains from helping Tony move yesterday. It was <u>hot</u>, and the three boys & I & Tony & Ken Lillibridge worked hard. Tony's whole life a clutter. The dirt & the mess & the tons of possessions, nothing ever thrown away. Minute by minute a lesson. Tony under terrific strain, with the kids & little money & all that crap to try to pack into a small apartment. And the two girls, Rachel & Sarah, under strain & confusion, too. Sandi staying far away, apparently…. At the end, we couldn't get the big oak davenport into the apartment, and had to leave it on the landing, where it is now. Possessions, possessions.

The moving day did knock me out, and now that's one thing I won't do in the future, help friends move. It's too strenuous. I have running muscles, not lifting muscles. Moving is for the young. I'll move myself, slowly, if I have to, or help Billy & Kristen out, but no more days like yesterday. Walt is staying put in Camden, too, amidst the things of his life.

Later: just saw my first rose-breasted grosbeak. A male. I stood at the cabin door and it went from branch to branch close to me.

6/14/83

9 a.m. Just read Traubel's account of the party for Walt's 71st birthday. That was some circle of men. Was I there in that life?… Was I <u>Walt</u> in that life?…

Right after my grosbeak sentences yesterday, Tony was back here at the cabin & we spoke for about an hour about his situation, Sandi, the divorce. He has to swallow so much—Sandi's abandonment, the young men in her life, the fact that she's the only one on salary now, etc. But he's holding up, seems mentally strong to me. I would have broken under all the strain, probably.

Han just jumped back here a second to tell me she was taking the other car to Rochester…. She had a confrontation with Charlie at work again yesterday—he's a paranoid, & threatened by a woman, etc.—but Han is doing okay….

I keep having regrets about not getting those two other boxes of books at the auction the other day—though my buy of the 23 volume Wessex edition of Hardy for one dollar was amazing.

In the 90s these days. I want to work on the anthology this afternoon & evening.

Billy & I had fun playing ball again yesterday.

Letters from Tom Murphy & Renee Gorin & Martin & Vince & Ewert lately. Ewert's new Levertov arrived, & samples of what will be his Hall. Unnecessary items, beautiful as they are…. *The Numinous* arrived from Bill Beavers. I touched my copies slightly with gray-blue watercolor. I like the item very much.

I may be feeling a poem building in me.

6/15/83

It's been a good morning. I've finished Traubel's 6th volume, and have gone over "This River" a few times and thought of where to put it in *Chestnut Rain*—it should be part of the book, should take the place of a weaker section, maybe #20.

Hot & balmy today, but I'll still head up to the gym with Billy for a little basketball.

Saw my first possum back here yesterday. It was in the space in front of the picture window, ambling by, sniffing the day lily stalks.

Wrote Glück again yesterday, and Root…. Definitely need to settle on my contributors by the time I leave for Hofstra—July 11th.

6/16/83

Not much shaking today. I'm back here killing a couple of hours after supper. I'll watch some television later and putter with the anthology. Want to write Goldbarth…. Note from Ai today. I doubt she'll do an essay or end up in the anthology. Same story as with the *AP '76* book.

Cleaned back here yesterday, 1st time since last summer. Comfortable here now.

Reading *Bloodsmoor* little by little.

Was thinking today about my days of stupid discontent: some things so deeply engrained in me I won't get rid of them until I die.

Han & I will travel to Nashville either tomorrow evening or Saturday morning. We'll take the old man shopping, and then the two of us will go to Han's reunion.

Did some cutting & gathering of my city poems.

Got the limited of Carver's *Fires* today.

Wish I had more Traubel to read now.

Hoed the beans & sunflowers this afternoon. It was about 90° again.

6/17/83

Han and I will leave for Nashville in a couple hours. It's been a good day—work in the cabin this morning, then basketball—and I look forward to the ride.

Sort of a pinching letter from Mary Oliver today, and I've written her back, but her letter was offset by a good one from Sandy McPherson. So, now I've lined up seven women for sure, and maybe Ai, and hope to hear from others. Permissions from Capra yesterday, Godine today. Little by little.

Still reading (of course) *Bloodsmoor*. Joyce is amazing.

6/18/83

Saturday morning. I'm sipping apple juice and sitting in the old kitchen in Nashville. Things the same around here. Pops said ten times yesterday how he needs "a good woman." This doesn't please Han much. The old bastard is still so selfish & insensitive, & always will be…. He stood up washing his hands for about two hours last night after Han & I had gone to bed…. She'll take him shopping, and to lunch. Then, later, we'll go to the reunion.

Did what I've wanted to do for years yesterday and drove through Springville on the way here. Found the block where I lived, but couldn't at first find the old Academy where I taught. Then realized it had been where there was now an empty lot. Walked across the grass with Han to a sign that said the old building, built in 1830, had had its last classes in 1970. So, that old subject keeps looking for me, though I'll never have the guts to write it, probably. *Time* on our minds as Han & I return here. And then there's the Smithtown reunion. And then there's the fact that Han's mom died just about a year ago and we're back in this place now surrounded by everything that's here, again…. I keep thinking of wisdom and the cosmic smile.

Kristen & Billy at home, 17 & 20 now. Adults.

I'll read *Bloodsmoor* today, snoop around a little, <u>bear</u> the old man who will say 20 times that he needs "a good woman."

6/20/83

Things a little out of order back here in the cabin, with a peanut on the floor & my slippers pushed into a corner, etc. So, the kids, or Billy & Julie, must have been back here. Good for them. Let them have some fun, and some memorable evenings.

Han's reunion gathering was all the things those things are. We listened to the speeches, the entertainment, saw the 50 & 60 year grads, toured the old high school, ended up at the old main hotel with her 25-year class, good folks. An unusual town—to have that reunion every year. And there were a few moments when all time got iside me again—when the Salzman girl sang to her brother's guitar accompaniment, when that 50-year grad played those two songs on his trumpet.

Han cooked the old man a Father's Day meal. She was depressed, coming home and last evening—a combination of things: that impossible old bastard, her mother a year dead now, the 25 years gone, maybe other things.... I do find myself spending a lot of time worrrying about Han's & Billy's & Kristen's happiness. I have to allow them to live, too. Somehow, most of the time I'm very content, am only upset when they are. Kristen will have a crisis this summer when she leaves for a month, but she's 17—I was 16 when I went away to college—and the experience will be a good one for her, and it is time for her to have that kind of experience. It will make going away to college much easier for her.

My letter to Ishmael Reed was returned again.... Atheneum said okay to the use of the Strand poems @ $15, even including the long "Elegy to My Father."

Bloodsmoor (I'm only 200 or so pages into it) is a tremendous book. Joyce makes me feel a part of that whole 19th-century American genteel world of the Kiddemasters. I feel the landscape inside me. The book is a time machine. She is amazing. It's hard for me to imagine anyone able to write such a book.

Will play ball today after a couple hours back here this morning.

Later: I'd just stood up from this journal to sit at the table and work on the city book when I heard yelling over at the neighbors—I don't know their name—past the raspberry bed. Anguished voices. They have a small white dog—not the other pain-in-the-ass of a white dog next door to them—and something had happened to it in the house. I don't know what. Maybe it ate poison, or was killed by the bigger dog that they have inside, or maybe it strangled itself. Something. But he came out with the white thing, and the woman was crying. He tried & tried & tried to resuscitate the thing, moved with it into shade, tried & tried again. I watched, a voyeur but hurt for him, through binoculars through leaves, getting glimpses of that misery, his back moving up & down as he pumped the dog's chest. No use. They were so attached to the little thing, and death came from nowhere, has ruined his day, his vacation from work. He's hurt now for her, and she for him. I watched. People go through these things for their <u>children</u>, something I can't even imagine, that grief.... I hope that other dimension is there, Walt, or the powers that be shouldn't have given us these feelings, this knowledge that, apparently, trees & insects & animals don't have. Still, luckily, it's impossible to say that that impossible heaven I think of, one in which I'll know everything at once, everyone's story, & the story of the land, is not possible. I'm sorry for those neighbors I don't know. They've always been silent, even when I'd say hello when gardening. They resented my buying the land, and our fence, and their raspberry bed that moved over our way. I'm sorry for them, and all of us. Our bodies are dying, however slowly, and that's the problem. There's nothig we can have forever, at least not in these earthly terms.

6/21/83

Sid Gold and his friend Susan visited yesterday just before supper and then in the evening. I had some things I wanted to get to—permissions & decisions on Berry, etc.—but it was good to see Sid again. I like him. Hadn't seen him for 5-10 years.

Perfect day again today. It's 9 a.m. now and about 75°.... I've a slightly sprained back from gardening a half-hour yesterday, but feel fine. Right <u>now</u>, as I sit here surrounded by green, people are rushing around streets & airports all over the country.

Good letter from Bruce. Another box of books on the way.

Will read a little *Bloodsmoor* and will then get back to shuffling poems for the *Between Flights* book, or whatever I call the extended *City Parables*. Things fall into place when I work on it, but it's hard to get back inside it when I'm away from it.

Han feeling better yesterday.... We had a nice family dinner. I grilled a steak. The 4 of us seem to be together for dinner only a couple times a week.... Good time at basketball yesterday....

Wayne Dodd called about a gathering at O.U. next Nov. with Plumly & Smith for Hollis & Jack.

Enjoy these weeks, Bill, before you head to Hofstra.

6/23/83 (Thursday)

It's early afternoon on a hot day. I was back here this morning—wrote a letter to Joyce about *Bloodsmoor*, read some, fooled with *Dandelions*—and plan to spend all afternoon back here. Just got a reply from Harper on the anthology, and a letter from Morgan (more & more I think he's very much like me), and a note from Reneé Gorin with a long letter from the fellow who will tape *Erika*, and a note from Richard Ehrlich along with a *Newsday* special on Suffolk's 300th (and I'm not even mentioned, hoorah). All's well. My back is sore, but I'm otherwise fine. Couldn't sleep much, and the ice cream I ate sent me to the bathroom three times, but I'm otherwise fine.

Big box of books arrived from Bruce yesterday, with Gardner, Wilbur, Haines, Oates items, etc. He should be in town next week. A good, loyal friend. As is Mirko, who stopped by yesterday afternoon. Irma is in Hannover on a research trip—I hope she calls the Mertens.

Not sure what I'm up to putting together *Dandelions*. I'm still trying to catch up with myself before putting out *CR* as a whole. I'm already, gulp, thinking of an expanded *Long Island Light*, but that wd. be years down the line.... Hofstra looms....

Wrote a longish letter to Bob Phillips & Ray about permissions costs for the anthology, & the letter from Doubleday. <u>Much</u> work still on the anthology, but the main thing is to settle on contributors. Getting close. Have 27 definite now, and other letters out.

6/28/83

Cool & raining, after several hot days.... Tony & I picked up Plumly at the airport last night, his plane 1½ hrs. late from Chicago. He looks good, has the proofs & dustjacket of *Summer Celestial* with him. The three of us had Han's pea soup at midnight. Tony seems tired already, and the workshop is going on now as I write. I won't see Stan today, I think, but will gather him up for dinner tomorrow.

Joyce & Ray coming Saturday. Nice letter from her & her essay for *2000* yesterday.

I've had a slight stomach ache for several days but am otherwise fine.

"Yesterday's Youngsters" dinner the other night. Han's cheese distribution for a couple days.... Kristen began her first real job yesterday.... Billy & I having fun playing ball.

Cathy Moser stopped in.... Call from Allen Hoey.... Letter from Goldbarth, and did I mention Piercy? Anthology building. <u>Clifton</u> is the one poet on my mind. If she & Ai wd. come through, I'd have the balances I'd like. Still want to get Ishmael Reed's address. The book is going to be <u>used</u>, I know.... I suppose I could write Oliver again, and could convince her—especially after Ray's letter mentioning how she'd be happy, he's sure, to be in the book—but she made her decision, & a curt one, & made me write her twice. If she changes her mind, okay, but I don't think I'll write her. Most important, she's good, but not someone who will last—though a selected poems could be awfully good. The early work seems mannered to me now, and there's a sameness to the last two books. <u>But</u>, I'd still be glad to have her in the anthology. Ha, maybe I <u>will</u> write her.

Except for Friday night, I'll avoid the workshops this week. Tonight, Rich Setter's graduation party.... Anthology work for me this afternoon.

6/29/83 (Wednesday morning)

I feel great back here on this perfect morning. Came in last night at one from the bar w. Plumly & Piccione & Vallone but with J. Kitchen (we argued about Lowell ferchrissake) & other assorted jerks, and berated myself & felt the offense again against my own inner economy, but I feel wonderful this morning, even, somehow, elated, and more sure of all I know. I have to be willing to let some of the world go—why <u>didn't</u> I let the brooding Harriet just go home last night instead of trying to make her part of the circle?—let people pass in and out of my life—why did I feel I had to say hello to the agents Goodman? Well, I hadn't been in a bar (except at Han's reunion) in many months. That is death in life, the spending of the life force into smoky air.... What I like is the opportunity over the next few days to redeem myself! Bruce is coming today, and I'll have Stan here for supper, and I <u>will</u> go to Barber's again this evening, but I'll be the inner self I truly am except when I'm not in possession of myself because I'm around so many scattered personalities. I like the sound of that phrase, its meanings: self possessed, self possession. Will dwell on it today & the next days.... I have family who love me, have many <u>true</u> friends. Why lose life giving of myself to people so lost I can't do anything for their spirits?... Plumly is okay, a friend, but somehow selfish, left with Cathy Moser, so that unhappy girl will fuck a poet this week & stave off her breaking marriage maybe for a while.

Han left a note that Bill Ewert called last night about a couple of things. I'll call him back this evening.

It will be in the mid-70s today. I look forward to biking up to the gym in an hour or so for some ball. Billy has to work today.

I took a bike ride yesterday to do some xeroxing, and on the way back through town stopped to see Kristen for a second at work in Card & Candle, & Billy in Muesey's. I'm a lucky man to have such children, and to know that they love me, and always will.

I couldn't end this journal in a better way.————

[#5: June 30, 1983-April 27, 1984]

6/30/83

Picked up this new journal yesterday, the only thing of its kind in town. I wanted a shorter one, but this will do, won't be any trouble to take along to Hofstra.

Stan was over from five to ten yesterday. Han made a terrific chicken dinner and strawberry pie. Good talk. We met folks at the bar later on. I spoke mostly with Christian McCrudden, boxer & writer. Stan left early with Cathy Moser. I left early soon after—left the two Tonys behind—stopping at Raleigh's for a look at the pool table the boys got moved over there. My life yesterday was <u>much</u> more economical. Today, I'll stay home all day. Bruce will drop by this evening. I <u>won't</u> go to the Kitchen-Susskind reading this evening, maybe will spend a few hours back here. I feel fine.

Han has a cold and will come home early from work today. The Smiths will visit Saturday, and as soon as they leave we'll drive to the Studiers in Clayton.

Saw a groundhog back here yesterday, but my sunflowers and beans are still coming along.

Reading over the first two sections of *Dandelions* yesterday, I was impressed.

Road crew at it <u>again</u>. I've turned the fan on low for white noise.

Read Han my diary entry from a year ago, the recapitulation of the Forum week, her mother's dying, etc.

Kristen doing fine at her new job. Both kids having a good summer. Kristen worried about Saratoga, but she'll be okay.

Well, I've begun another of these diaries. I wonder if they can embody even a slight curve toward serenity. I think so, so far.

7/1/83

As always, I was up this morning when Han left, but I fell asleep again for the first time in a month, and it's 11:15 now. A half-hour back here and then off to the gym.

I had a dream that the Smiths arrived. I met Joyce in the garage, and she collapsed, crying, into my arms. I comforted her for a long time—she'd had a terrible visit with her parents, and I said I knew what those were like. Her hair was black, and done short in a new and attractive way. Just now as I write I remember the pleasant pressure of her shorter body against my belly and thighs. Then I saw Ray sort of slumped in the corner of the garage. Then I saw that the Smiths had three sons, and all looked very much like Ray. I was thinking of saying this, but connected in my mind the sons' uncanny resemblance to Ray with women's oppression. I don't remember anything more. A dream of being at a golf course and unable to play—forgot my clubs—wasn't about the Smiths, I think.

Bruce over last evening with books & tales of the Strand. We went out for drinks, and met up with Tony Piccione at his apartment later, but didn't find Stan or Tony Vallone. But the gang will be together tonight.... This afternoon I'll want to make sure all is ready for Ray on the various anthology businesses.

I can hear the kids playing soccer next door. I should go over there & show them my tricks.

Tomorrow, after Joyce & Ray leave, we'll drive up to Clayton—wish it could be for a few days, but we'll only have one overnight. Or will we have two? I think Han is off Monday. Yes, that makes a big difference.

July 4, 1983

I'm sitting in the front porch at Studiers' cabin. Had a good breakfast of fruit, juice, toast, coffee. It's almost 90° again in the shade, but it's generally comfortable. Han & I went swimming in the river twice yesterday, and we will again today. Kristen & Lisa are on a picnic on an island somewhere. I've slept very little if at all the past couple nights, and I have a sunburn, a slight one, caught on a boat ride yesterday, but I feel fine. We'll head home later this afternoon. Billy is holding the house down.

The visit with Joyce & Ray was a good one. They were with us only 2-3 hrs., but we talked & walked back to the cabin & ate. Bruce & Stan dropped by for the last half hour. Joyce still looks just like Olive Oyl. She & Ray seem to be in great shape, slim & strong from jogging & bicycling. Literary chatter here & there, Joyce saying that the anthology won't miss Mary Oliver because what Oliver does others are doing, saying she met Clifton once & Clifton seemed "sullen," etc. She inscribed the four books I had ready for her, and two for Bruce as a gift. I like the Smiths. I think they'd be good friends if they lived next door, too—though of course we wouldn't see Joyce often. Her presence, as at dinner, is one thing, and her writing presence—the woman I know is behind the woman I chatter with—is another and amazing one.

The evening before was the Piccione-Plumly reading. Tony did better than Stan, who would gulp water even before finishing the last line of a poem. Both voices were hard to hear over the drone of the room. Bar scene later. Reunion with Greg & Rod—many laughs.

Right after the Smiths left, Han & Kris & I zipped up here. I've finished Kunstler's *The Life of Byron Jaynes*, fun to read but a kind of child's play after *Bloodsmoor*.

We ate at a place called Foxy's in Clayton last evening. We sat forever in that crowded place, but the food was good. Nora & Al are good folks, & Al, especially, flourishes up here.

I leave a week from today for Hofstra. I suppose I'll draft an introductory piece before then, as I like to do, for ice-breaking.

Two of the cutest kids I've ever seen, Nikki & Heather, cousins, came over to give me candy this morning. We all get a big kick out of their antics. Wish I had that Nikki on film—I could sell it.

Will go to a flea market, and then jump in the river.

July 5, 1983

Back safely, and I got some sleep last night for a change.
Started writing to my workshop people, my usual chatter.
Stopped in to see Al today. He seems okay, though he has a touch of phlebitis and is on medication.

I'm doing little things for the anthology, writing for permissions, etc. Will write Joyce tonight about her essay.... Might be able to do some work in the Hofstra library on a few poets.

Rain hovering all day. Wish it wd. fall. I did some watering.

I've nothing for this journal.

Was thinking that it's strange how warm & sentimental my correspondence with Al is when he's away, and how dull and reserved it is when we're together, as today. Why the deep friendship of correspondence, and the cool reunion? My anthology does make him nervous, I know. I try to fill him in on things, and can feel his computers clicking away when I mention anything.

Han called the cops on a strange heavy box left for the seniors. They got it open and it had a roll of quarters inside!

Nice note from Marge Piercy today. I need her prose book.

7/6/83

I've just been shuffling & shuffling the 10-12 poems that will be the first section of *Dandelions*. An order suggests itself & then breaks up. I feel holes or uncomfortable jumps. Then a shape forms in my mind and I shuffle again. I try to read & remember all sides of the poems—voice, theme, tone—and how groups within groups work. The poems so fluid.... I think that I now have (I've thought this before) a good, meaningful order for the ten poems for the first section: opening with the title poem, which is meant to send seed-puffs of all sorts of themes & concerns out; then the plague sermon, not a complex poem but one that urges the bringing out of the dead, and my other 8 poems <u>do</u> bring the dead (dead people, deathly ideas, dreams of death) out; then "The World Cup," the English connection, & the poem itself like a seed-puff, and I want to break in with it into too serious a progression right away; "Dream" traces the competition, and worries of an apocalypse; "The Host" introduces the ecological crisis which is a concern of the book directly & indirectly throughout; "The Sunflower" is a poem of fear, and the next 3 poems flow out from it from where voices/people have run, into religions of death; "Dresden Gals" is sardonic. No relief in this sequence. I keep thinking of the shape of this book in terms of what Wilbur said about *The City Parables*.

So cool in the cabin this morning that I was uncomfortable and plugged in the little heater.

I look forward to basketball. Will meet Billy up there in an hour.

Tomorrow is our 21st wedding anniversary. Han & I will go out the next night, to an auction & to dinner.

Took care of some anthology business—Oates, Piercy, Waters—yesterday.

Actually got a check for $76 from *Iowa Review* for "The Census" yesterday. Seems like a lot of money for me now. Shows how little *2000*'s contributors are being paid for poems, too.

No rain yesterday, though dark clouds rolled by for hours.

All-Star game on television tonight, so maybe I'll spend a few hours back here this afternoon. Yes.

Haircut, plane tickets, anthology xeroxing tomorrow.

7/9/83

Evening. Han & I just came back here together for an hour. She'll do her "granny squares" and I'll putz, getting ready for my trip the morning of the 11th. I keep writing sections of my introductory spiel to the workshop group. It will be okay, though it doesn't seem so far quite to have the intensity other such pieces have had.

I'll take this journal along on my trip. Also, I hope to do a <u>little</u> constructive work on the anthology in the Hofstra library. Maybe on Clifton, maybe will read Robin Morgan? Maybe will take along the book of interviews with Robert Penn Warren, too. Maybe will not go to all the evening readings, but will mind my business and write, if I have the energy. Well, I know the two weeks will go <u>fast</u>. No doubt, I'll see some lacrosse games again, too.

Han & I took a bike ride this evening. Saw Poulin for a few minutes. He's sort of dull & withdrawn these days. Then we biked up by Hartwell. She fell off her bike into a bramble bush where she'd once stood in the Daisy Chain line (!), but wasn't hurt.... So, my wife of 21 years is just a few feet away as I write....

We've just had a long talk about things, goods, how we want to live more simply in the future, and we will. We generally feel the same way about most things.

7/11/83

Hofstra, 8:30 in the evening.
Flight to Newark, shuttle to Kennedy, limousine to Hempstead, taxi to Hofstra, I made it here. Things are just as I expected: glum, sort of lonely. Nothing interesting to do, and days of general exhaustion to look forward to. Two conferences in the morning, then the 2½ hr., class, then my reading in the evening.... I didn't bring towels, and they're not provided. Alice will bring me a couple tomorrow.... Patti Renna-Tana around, & wants me out to dinner some night.... Pam Conrad stopped by, very nice & intelligent woman, and we talked for an hour, about her separation & my *The Elvis Presley Room*, mostly.... I ate a good roast beaf dinner in the cafeteria. I put on shorts this afternoon & took off my shirt and went for an hour's walk in the sun. It already seems days ago that Han dropped me off at the Rochester airport.
I'll get along. Good folks in the workshop. I'll get a good night's sleep tonight, I think. Only one blanket. Hope it isn't too cold in here tonight, too noisy with dormmates. I must keep in mind that I'll clear about $1100, and that I'll see Wern & Barb & the folks on this trip. Also, it was good to get away from Brockport routines. Maybe I could even do a little writing after things settle down....

7/12/83

Two conferences with students just now, two women, one about 55 & one about 20. Everything I say always has to be from the beginning.
I got a few hours sleep last night, anyway. Could use an extra blanket—have been using my jacket.... Much banging around in the halls by the Upward Bound kids until 11:00 or so.
Class in an hour, and three hours after that is my reading. I want to take an hour's walk in the sun again this afternoon.
Want to get the two books by Elizabeth Cullinan, too, if the college store will take my Visa card.
I feel okay about things today. I don't need much sleep to feel balanced, but I do need some.
I want to give the kind of reading (today, especially) that will make the conference seem worthwhile—language & music & emotion. That damned air-conditioning drone all the while, though. It kills nuance, forces my voice to the same level all the time.
Yes, I want sun. Will go out now.

Later: 10:00. It's over. I read well (to about 15 people), and then had drinks with the Patersons & Bob Sargent & Diane (Kunzweiler, from Cortland) Ben Meer, and then Diane and I had dinner. Her treat! She's a sweet & smart woman, a very nice person. We spoke of Jerry & the old days. I saw her here two years ago, too.
I'm relieved, breathing deep. Easier days ahead. Hope even to get to a bookstore or two with Bob Sargent.
Spent only $5 today. Free dinner tomorrow night, too.
Believe I'll sleep better tonight. Not so cold in the room. Much off my mind. Seems to be quieter around here, too.
The workshop today went very well. Remember Dominic, who speaks freely of horrible Viet Nam experiences. He was a POW.
Saw the Hofstra gym today. Big.
Black cop next room over is listening to opera. He's a good man.
And Muriel Hendrix, teacher, such a nice woman. Good people in workshop.

7/13/83

At about 5:00 I was relaxing, talking to Bob Sargent, when Alice Paterson came to us about an urgent matter. She said we'd soon be joined by security people. It seems that when Alice met Marilyn French she mentioned that Marilyn's nephew was here at Hofstra for the conference and looked forward to seeing her. French said no, she had no such nephew, and both women became worried & Alice called security. Dominic, the Viet Nam veteran with terrible experiences and bad dreams who is in my workshop, an ex POW, was the one who told Alice, at registration, that he was French's nephew. Security was worried. Alice told him there was no more room at dinner. No one wanted to confront the poor guy, who seems likeable enough and honest enough to me—he's suffered more than enough—but anything could have happened, and a "nice fellow" killed Jon Lennon, as French said.

    On the way to the reading I fell into step with Dom. I don't know what it was inside me, but we talked and I kept him company—he carried an ominous black bag—and sat in the middle of the audience with him. I was to his left. When we sat down, he told me how bad French's books were, then told me, twice, that he was her nephew but that she didn't own up to it. He seemed to become agitated, started sweating. I was scared, thinking what I could do if he pulled a gun. He's a big man. I'd had a couple glasses of wine at dinner, and when he reached in his bag and brought up a notebook and began writing, only then did I notice he was lefty. I sobered up fast, had planned on grabbing his right wrist, knew I could easily be killed if something happened and I wasn't ready. I hardly heard a word French said. A security guard was stationed to my left about 60 feet away, and was watching Dom. I'd hoped they'd put someone in plain clothes right behind him, but only several old women were near us. What had possessed me to sit with him? He was scrawling fast, in slashes, in his notebook. I made out two phrases: "My head is killing me" and "would shoot him." I didn't know what he was doing. Each of the several times he reached into the bag at his feet I tried to be ready. He told me twice he had to leave at 8:30 to see his sister, his sister, 8:30. At last, at 8:30, he got up, said he'd see me tomorrow, limped away. I saw the security guard to my left tense & then follow him. Dom left, but looked back at me as he did. When he went out, another plain clothes security man followed him, nonchalantly. I began to relax, but five minutes later I looked back and he was back in the audience. A youg girl was with him, probably his sister. A uniformed state cop with a big gun was in back of the room now. I don't think Dom knew he was being watched, or knew how afraid I was. Poor, innocent kid, probably. <u>Maybe</u>, even, it's French who is lying about this familial connection. But when I sat next to him for 45 minutes or so, when he wrapped a red bandana around his left hand, I thought I was in for it. Once he reached down & pulled a thick copy of *Divine Comedy* from his bag. There were only a half-dozen in the whole room who knew what was going on. I was afraid. I still <u>am</u> apprehensive, and will be when I'm around Dom. Who coulda thunk such a thing would happen? I truly thought I was the moth who couldn't resist the flame when I found myself sitting next to him…. When French was done, I watched Dom leave with his sister, and watched the guards watch him leave.

    Then, to make the evening even more surreal, when I left the auditorium there was Pam Conrad who invited me to Jones Beach. It's past midnight now, and I just got back. We walked along the boardwalk & beach, had a hot dog and coke, talked, laughed. She's in the process of divorce, is a beautiful woman, and even asked me if I danced—as we passed the band shell on this perfect evening—and I said I couldn't in front of all these people. A hundred feelings swirling in me, friendship (going back two years) to sex, as we walked or leaned against the railing facing the waves on this perfect evening of moon & breeze & mid-70s temperature. It's definitely best that nothing happened. A man has to learn to be a woman's <u>friend</u> in a sexually uncomplicated way. I hope to keep growing up. I like her, and she's been through a lot this past year. We had good talks. And oh what a night it was there at Jones Beach. I hadn't been there since I played soccer there in a night league about 25 years ago, and never really saw the beaches.

    From an hour of death fear, to a romantic & memorable evening.

    Workshop went well today. Meetings with Dom & Sharon Stein in the morning, then Rose in the afternoon, and then, at 3:15, Bob & I will go to the Hempstead book store.

    I spent only 3 or 4 bucks again today, got a free dinner.

    Will make some calls tomorrow night & see what I'm doing this weekend. Want to call Han, too, & say so long to Billy who is heading to Atlantic City for a week.

    I'm tired, but glad I picked up this diary tonight.

7/14/83

A long day, but nothing much new, especially nothing regrding Dominic. We spoke for an hour this morning. I urged him to do his book. I'm wary but generally comfortable. Will speak to Alice about what she says were other strange happenings last night.

I walked over to watch some lacrosse. And just now I watched ten black kids playing playground basketball. An education. Mainly, I see more and more how men on a court or field just need to earn respect, keep their dignity.

Picked up a few books—nothing special—in Hempstead.

Hve tried to call home, and will again. No answer.

Workshop very intense today.

Looks like I have a ride out to near Quogue tomorrow. Wern will be home & waiting for my call. I look forward to spending much time in the pool.

One good thing. Until I just happened to think again of calling home, the anthology has been far from my mind.

Later: called Han, and all's well. Good news on anthology from Clifton (!) and others. Her inclusion will make the book I want. Will have to do a week's hard work on the book after I get back.... Kris & Billy fine.... Some sicknesses and a death (Wayne) at the Senior Center.... Apparently a letter from Joyce that will make me glow....

7/16/83

It's 6:30 in the morning. I'm in my favorite easy chair in Wern's living room. Hot in my room, and I couldn't sleep much—did have a dream about being on the bottom floor of old Smithtown High School—but I feel fine anyway, and when I'm done writing here I'll jump into the pool, or maybe wade in to keep things quiet.

Remarkable workshop yesterday again, emotional and intense, Bess's piece on her daughter, Dominic's recitation of Viet Nam horror, and in-between some good talk. A ride right to this door by Rose & Susan—I drove, actually—in a little Chevette—and they'll pick me up again on their way back from East Hampton on Monday morning.... Will take Wern & Barb to breakfast, and then we'll go to several garage sales.... Wern has given me their copy of *Lauderdale*! It's in fine shape. I'll send him some silver coins in return—I've about 50 Mercury dimes. Don't know if I'll keep this copy (it wd. be my 3rd) or wheel & deal with it with Ewert or Babcock.

Wern, Barb, Debbie, Alan, seem fine, typical Long Islanders. They have four vehicles now, and four jobs, and have come to be on this Island what this Island has become.... Wern & I sitting by the pool plunge immediately into the deepest talks, about the folks' obsessions with their court cases, about Wern's adjusting to the 3-month mother-in-law stay (things changed much for the better there), etc. He's my best friend. We share long memories, were closest of the four sons. Barb, too, is from old Nesconset and old SHS, so we have warm talks. I like it here. It's easy-going.... Same old story with their smoking. I hope something terrible doesn't happen before a ripe old age....

7/17/83 (Sun.)

Wern & I just back from buying $209 worth of coins for him from a nice old couple we'd met at their garage sale yesterday. Werner made out, & will have much fun with the coins—$38 face value in wheat pennies, a roll of quarters (silver), and five silver dollars and about a dozen Mercury dimes....

I'm on the pool deck in the shade. Seems cooler today. We sat here last evening while a bat fluttered around us. I'll swim today, and the folks will visit, and then I'll start thinking of Hofstra again.... Am reading Pam's *Prairie Songs*.... Pushed my "The Shore" poem through another draft.... Wern at work today, but will be home for lunch and then off at four.

Found an issue of *Verve* at a flea market yesterday. Not in good shape, but ...

A pair of swallows nests in Werner's garden shed. They take turns skimming the pool & slicing off a beakful of water.

I look forward to seeing Mom & Pop though they are these days obsessed by their court cases. I understand how consuming that kind of thing can be....

7/18/83

The two women, Rose S. & Susan Warm, will pick me up in about an hour. Werner just left for work, & Barb will leave soon. So, it's back to Hempstead today and that class at noon for me.

Turned out that twenty rolls of the pennies were not wheat, so we went back, and the old guy, pacemaker & all, was upset. His wife & grandkids found other pennies & silver to make up the difference. Sort of a sad scene, but so it went.

Finished *Prairie Songs*, a good little book Pam has made.... Don't know where my "The Shore" poem is now.... I may have improved my little "The Red Gun" poem with "pot shoot" at the end. Yes.

Later: I'm in my room at Hofstra. The women picked me up at about 11:00 for an hour & half drive for my 12:00 workshop. A pain in the ass. I took the waiting time, and some of the driving time, to write a letter to Bill Ewert. The shorter workshop was the weakest of the 6 so far, I think.

Heard Elizabeth Cullinan read a story & answer some questions. I'm not much interested in that kind of writing. The centuries may not have time for it. She stood there with a handbag slung over one shoulder and read, pleasantly enough, from a copy of the *New Yorker*, a slow-developing story called "Idioms." Not enough voltage for me, but pleasant enough reading, I suppose, on the subway or train on the way home.

Watched the rookies & free agents & early veterans work out at Jets' training camp today. When the defensive backs did their backing-up drills, I was impressed with the speed. Then cutting drills. Awesome. I'll watch a few more workouts this week. Wish some of the name players were here. They probably will be as the week wears on.

No appointments with workshop people tomorrow.

Did not get to Fellins, those rich folks, this evening. He's ill, says Alice.

It's just a matter of hanging on the rest of this week, and not wasting it, and connecting with the folks this weekend, and then getting the hell home. Han called yesterday, and all's well at home.

Jogged around a little this evening. Sure don't have much ambition for that. If I had a basketball I'd get a good workout, probably, but I'm glad to be giving my weak knee and ankle a rest.

Guess I won't buy the two Cullinan books. I haven't had a chance to meet her, and she didn't go to my reading in any case, and I'd rather have the twenty bucks, I guess.... Tomorrow, Patti Renna-Ranna is picking me up after class for dinner.

Should I or shouldn't I walk over for a doughnut before I call it a night?

7/19/83

It's actually the 20th, I guess, 12:30 a.m. I'm tired, but haven't been able to sleep, but will. I've used this journal to block out light at the bottom of the venetian blinds, but now take it up to receive, again, the ink-flow.

Long day today. Dominic this morning. Saw the exhibit of summer authors' books. Saw the exhibit of Eastern religious art—it gave me, deep down, the creeps. Wrote in library for an hour, pushing my new Whitman poem ahead. Richard Ehrlich showed up out of the blue. Class for 2½ hrs. Talk, talk, then more talk, talk with Patti Renna-Tana who picked me up & drove me to Long Beach for dinner & talk, talk with her & her husband John. Walked along the boardwalk in drizzle. The ride back here. Reading things by Rose & Sue. Ready for class & talk, talk tomorrow.... I plan on a big breakfast—eggs, potatoes, and all. Ate a supper of steak & corn-on-the-cob, but could hardly experience it with all that talk, talk. I truly like Patti, but women like her are going to be the death of me. She pressed yet another copy of her "book" *How Odd This Ritual of Harmony* on me.

Richard will pick me up tomorrow after the banquet, and I'll spend a few hours with him. The day will rocket by again. I'm beginning to miss home & Han a lot. Will call her tomorrow night or Thursday night.

Walt, the traffic along Hempstead Turnpike—can you?
The heron over the Long Beach dunes—did you?
Waves swelling in against the shore—are you?
Me jogging Hofstra parking lot cement—will you?

7/21/83

I'm a little high now at midnight on a few glasses of wine. One more night's sleep here, and then away. Just had a gathering a couple doors down with Sharon & Dominic & Philip & Rhoda. Dominic telling horrible stories of being paid $50 each to waste peasants, cutting off ears, etc., while the Beatles are singing "A Day in the Life."... The people in the workshop feel very close to me. Sue Warm brought in a magnum of champagne today, & another bottle I haven't unwrapped. Last session tomorrow, and it will be a good one, I'm sure. Wish I had a volume of Whitman with me.

Last evening with Richard Ehrlich & his folks in Woodmere. We all walked a Rockaway boardwalk.... Saw Budd Schulberg yesterday, listened to him again. Laurel Lee this evening was wonderful. What a woman!...

Watched the Jets practice, saw their new back-up quarterback. An arm like a gun.

Will get a ride from Sea Cliff to Pt. Jeff or Stony Brook tomorrow, and spend tomorrow night at Vince's. The folks will pick me up there Saturday afternoon.

I'm tired. I'm about packed. I'm ready to end all this. The two weeks went <u>very</u> fast, as I look back on them now.

Saw Pam Conrad. She gave me the book of her poems that her father published for her when she was 11 or 12.

7/23/83

I'm at Werner's. It's Saturday evening. Hooked up with Vince Friday night, & stayed with him. The folks picked me up there today, and after a good dinner brought me here. They'll take me to the airport tomorrow.

Vince & I hit bookstores. I bought a first of Eliot's *Notes...* for $5 (Am. first). Got a 1st of Stevens' *Collected* from Vince in trade! Bought Joyce's *Edge of Impossibility* at the Sea Cliff store Bob Sargent took me to. Bought a bunch of good books, including an illustrated 1914 in dj. at a sale in Setauket this morning: 16 books for a total of four bucks. So, I'm going home with all sorts of things again.

Last days of workshop went very well. Tears by Sharon & Gail at end, and I was weighed down by presents. I wrote a poem for them & read it for them. I'll swim tomorrow, and then will get <u>home</u> to Han & children. I feel fine. I'm heading for <u>home</u>.

7/24/83

I'm sitting at MacArthur in Islip, an hour before flight time. The folks just dropped me off here, as they have many times before. I'm at the end of another stay away from home, and look forward to getting back to Han & Billy & Kris, if not to the mailwork & homework & schoolwork. I can't complain about my life…. Stayed last night with Wern & Barb. Worked with Werner on his penny collection for a couple hours this morning. We then went to a barn sale, and I found a nice 1st ptg. in dj of Warren's *World Enough & Time*, not a rare book but a nice one, and the first non-book club copy I've seen. It was good to see Wern again. We watched a bad film on television last night and ate the shrimp rolls Barb went out for…. The folks look and sound good, seem to have stopped worrying about those lawsuits pending for and against them after Pop's accident…. Right now, it doesn't seem to have been 13 days since I left. The Hofstra workshop already seems far away, though…. I took a swim last evening…. Wern might drive to Brockport in August for a few days…. I did send a card to Bob Sargent with the workshop grades already, so that's off my mind…. A little kid that reminds me of Billy 17-18 years ago is racing around in front of me…. I hope Han & I get a chance to go to bed together tonight. It's always touch & go, with Kristen & Billy coming in and out, and with Han having to get up so early, etc. Years down the line, the kids gone, there won't be this problem. Lord, let me still be able to get it up once Han & I have the time & space we've wanted!… I've been conscious of the fact that I've not talked about sex in my journals. This is proof that I think someone will be reading them someday, I suppose, though I try (though I find myself posing in different ways) to talk & think straight here. I still do, after all these years of journal-keeping, often feel unnatural here, my mind racing way in front of my pen, as even, I suspect, my slurred handwriting shows, especially the ends of my words—my mind is already on the next phrase…. Sex: my pecker tingles, and I keep picturing Han & me in various positions. Each trip, I masturbate several times, though try not to a few days before coming home. I've felt about myself for some time that I have a generally unclouded sex sensibility. I could report some colorful non-marital indiscretions here, but am embarrassed by them, and hope there won't be a single other one, though there may be. I do remember clipping out from my first journal a report of a trip to a "house" in buffalo I went on with Baldy Hall & Jim Muck that long ago. No, ha, all in all I don't have to be any more honest in this journal than I have been. It's sort of the same dance between autobiography & various personae that goes on in the different poems. I think.

7/27/83

Back in the cabin again for the first time since getting home…. Han & the kids fine, Billy back from Jersey safely…. Cheese day at the Center for Han again today…. Kristen with her old flame and heartbreak Mike last evening…. The world is dry here, no rain for so long, record low rainfall (43/100") so far in July.

I played ball Monday & will again today…. I've made a good start clearing off my desk, and have much work still to do catching up with the anthology. Want to have it pretty much taken care of by the time school begins….

TriQuarterly took 3 poems, including my "The New American Poetry" piece. I'm more pleased by this than by any magazine acceptance in a long time. I'd read editor Reginald Gibbons' 2 books for the anthology, but was not really impressed. Maybe I'll read them again. Still want to write Dubie, I think.

Kristen's concert at a Clarkson church last night. She leaves Sunday already for Saratoga Springs. Han will take her.

Spent most of the afternoon yesterday with Tony talking about the whole world. Saw Al, too. And Boo & Sandi…. Saw Hale at the concert, my new chairman-to-be, alas. He won't grow any younger in the job…. Mirko & Irma were at the airport waiting for Katja the other evening, too….

Made $1100-1200 profit on my trip, and just sent half of it to Cornell—it was a good feeling having made that money from poetry. A check from *Poetry* for $32.50 waiting for me here, too. I like these small checks from magazines, and have many more poems to send out, and will.

Perfect back here this morning as I float with the morning. Green smells and bird sounds, the hum of town far off, time and space away….

No word from Vanguard or Bill Ewert on anything.

My life doesn't have to stop once school begins. I have to keep reminding myself of this. I make so much money for what I do. Also, though, I'm worth it. I'm the best teacher of literature I know. I wish I had, too, the first half-dozen Hofstra workshop sessions on tape.... Word around here is that enrollment for fall is a disaster. Maybe more firings down the line. I've little worry about being let go, though maybe the English Department would be hit, though John Crowley just retired, Hale tells me, and Armand Burke has only one more year—so, the Department shrinks, and the Indians are circling the Brockport circle of wagons.

Sent Vince books & Werner coins....

7/23/83

Couldn't find my journal for a minute. Thought somebody had lifted it out of the cabin.... So far, so good back here. I just leave the door open in case some marauder comes by....

I feel fine, though don't know exactly what to do. Many new poems floating around. An order for the poems of *Dandelions* will take some concentrated work. I do the anthology work inside, and got much done yesterday—will write Dubie today. Maybe I'll type up some new poems and get them all ready to send out the beginning of September.

Ewert called. Long talk about not much. He hasn't heard a word from Vanguard, of course. Maybe I should write Evelyn, and not play it cool: my pride could hurt *Erika*. Yes, I should write her.

Played ball & had fun yesterday. Tried to play outside myself, & will have to contain myself better—some bad passes & shots—etc.

Vague feeling of discontent, I guess, because summer is again disappearing, and I have to move out of my school office, and prepare classes, and Kristen will be gone a month, and both cars will need mufflers, and money is scarce, and we've had no rain for so long that everything is parched & cracked. Something inside me smiles at me. Here I am in this blessed cabin. I could be in Beirut, or San Salvador. I could be a laborer from Turkey in Hannover. I could be a terminal cancer patient. I sip coffee here & try to get myself moving to do something.

Basketball tomorrow, auction tomorrow evening.

Told Ewert I'd send a box of stuff for him to sell Babcock. Bill will do "Mother and Son" or "Ensoulment" as a broadside. Maybe Meadow Press.... He's still wheeling & dealing, has the only 10 copies of a Heaney broadside otherwise destroyed. He's sending me a couple blank books to write poems in—one copy for each of us—and is having a box made for *XVII Machines*, the first of many more that he'll do over the years.

I seem to be in a page-at-a-sitting rhythm in this journal lately.

Yes, I should write Evelyn, and get her ass moving on some things.

Two hours later: I feel as though I've accomplished something: typed up ready to send out about ten new poems. Have run out of good paper, and have more new things to type up, so will get to them maybe tomorrow morning. What has happened is that I've written so much that I feel ahead of myself, or something. The *Dandelions* book should be able to gather many of these, but I shouldn't (should I?) publish a miscellaneous book before I do *CR*? Fuck it, Bill, just keep writing. It wouldn't be a catastrophe if no book came out for five years or ten until you saw where you are. Get the poems written, & typed, and in folders, and let time take care of the rest.

Did write a note to Evelyn.

Will go inside now for lunch, and maybe a longish bike ride to library & school & post office. May come back here again later.

Why this urge to record life? This human creature in his cabin deluded in thinking the future will care about such scribbling? That's part of it, but part of it, too, is the pleasure of forming sentences, as I've formed this one.

Later: evening. Raining out, at last, as though my journal were a prayer for it and it was answered.

Perfect back here now. Han & Kris going to a play, & Billy is with friends. I'll spend a couple hours back here, and then go in maybe to watch *Helter Skelter*. The book knocked me over a couple/few years ago.

I stayed very busy today. Heard from Root, & xeroxed his & Ai's poems for anthology. Still need to write Dubie.

Brett has his pine-tar home run back. Hoorah!

I was thinking about this life as "poet." The trouble is, nothing is ever really finished. Always the next thing to be done, to be written, the next book to be gathered together. I <u>do</u> want to be what I do, do what I am—there is a blessing in this ongoingness, yes, and I'd like to be natural about writing, but there are always so many loose ends in the doing of it that maybe the past keeps cluttering up the present. Maybe if I <u>only</u> kept a journal, & kept hauling myself up to the present moment—rain in the leaves around me—there wouldn't be that feeling of hurry & incompletion. Or if I truly learned not to hurry, to finish things when they got finished. That's the real answer, and only my flawed personality holds me back from being an artist of the beautiful.

July 29, 1983 (Friday morning)

Still raining, or, rather, raining again, and I'm glad. I feel fine this morning, have basketball to look forward to, and then the auction this evening. Books mentioned in the ad. It's in Hamlin. Han will go, too. And Billy will play ball today. And Kristen and I have had good talks about her first boyfriend, Mike, she's still hung up on in ways as complex as my old relationship with Karen Gregersen. She has seen Mike twice this week, and they've talked, and he isn't the boy who first awakened all those feelings in her.

Will type "This River" this morning, a piece I'd sort of forgotten about, a good one. It reaches the movement of "The Trophy," the kind of ongoingness that feels so right in certain pieces.

Between paragraphs here I've looked up through my picture window & windows & screen door to the trees and bushes dripping. Rain keeps kids & dogs inside, mowers in their garages, and muffles other distractions. Maybe I should live somewhere where it rains often, Seattle or London or, rather, a small town on Puget Sound or a village in Bedfordshire.

Coffee from my Viet Nam mug today.

July 31, 1983

Rainy Sunday afternoon. I'll be back here a couple hours, but want to get back inside to sort of keep things together as I always I feel I must when Han & kids are in "limbo" somewhere: Billy at work, & Han is dropping Kristen off for her month at Skidmore. A terrific amount of driving for Han, and my fingers are crossed. The car was <u>so</u> filled up with Kristen's things that there would have been little room for me, so I feel less guilty about not going. I can't stand those long trips, and back-and-forth in one day from past Yaddo wd. be torture for me.

Bought a great old Royal typewriter at auction yesterday for five bucks, and have it back here.... Also, for $20, bought an album of 75 photographs of Colorado at turn of the century by one Otto Westerman—could be worth nothing, or a lot. Will find out. Scenes of landscape, mountains, mining, snowscapes, people dwarfed.

Han & I walked down to the graduation party for Mark Wadhams yesterday.... Al & Phyllis Matsko moving to Tennessee in 4 weeks, too. Memories of the neighborhood kids I played so much ball with.

Siegel's essay came in. I wrote Dubie. Need to read Harper's *Images of Kin* now and get back to him.

8/2/83

Two mornings in a row now I've come back here and when I've closed the cabin's screen door behind me have seen that I've brought in a deer fly with me. All summer as I come back here one of these bastards lands on my head, and I swat at it with my free hand and usually spill my coffee. Once inside, it apparently is afraid of the darkness of the closed-in space and buzzes against the screen. I let it out. I heard that a deer fly always lands on the very highest tip of man or beast, and that's why Indians wore the single feather up from a headband. They <u>are</u> maddening. I wanted to kill the one this morning, but let it out to do whatever it does in the great scheme besides spill Heyen's coffee.

Call from Kristen. She's doing fine, has found a girlfriend just like her. Electricity was off in her dorm after a storm, & the kids were baking.

Tony stopped over. His closing went through, and he paid me the $400 he owed me. He's eight grand in the clear after everything. I'm glad for him.... I had a dream last night that he was surly and wanted in on my anthology.

I'll probably drop by Poulin's today. Wd. like to get Charles Wright's *Bloodlines* from him. Owe him for some BOA titles.

Wrote to Dubie & Harper. Need to write Siegel back, and choose Plumly poems. Bob Hass called & missed me, and I called California twice & missed him. He has some questions about the essay.... I started reading his intro. to the Mitchell Rilke. My intuitions about Rilke are being borne out. He's not my poet, for many reasons. Nor is he poetry for me.

Much fun with my new old typewriter.

8/3/83

Was going to spend the morning at my desk inside, but changed my mind and have come back here—one of those perfect times.

A woodchuck lives under the cabin. Billy surprised it when he came back here yesterday.

Went to Greg Fitz Gerald's last night for drinks with him and Rod Parshall. I like them both a lot. We love raging about Department politics once in a while—Hale's chairmanship grilling is tonight, & Rod & Greg will attend. I'll go to an auction in Bergen, but will see them at Casey's later on.

Worked on the Siegel selection, found beauties that made me happy, again, to know him & have him in the book. Will now go over his essay closely.

Finished "The Coffin" yesterday, a 15-pt. sequence that turned into a good one, I think.

Birds have stripped most of our grapes. The corn is stunted and there won't be edible ears. Only the sunflowers thrive.

Mowed yesterday for the first time in about 6 weeks.

Did get *Bloodlines* from Poulin for $10.

Just watched a young bluejay flutter for food from parent.

Summer rushing by, but all's well. I want to get everything regarding the anthology caught up, and then I'll be set to get to some schoolwork & worry about office moving, etc.

Billy spent $12 on greens fees yesterday, & lost $5 playing, & spent $3 for food, and was depressed about it. I know that sick-at-heart feeling of blowing a day's pay like that.... I hope he catches onto something regarding his career that will keep him more meaningfully busy, somehow, than he's been. He sort of wonders, I think, what happened to his summer, now that his much-anticipated trip to Atlantic City is past him.

Kristen called again to report, happily, that though she'd done poorly on her audition, she'd gotten 2nd chair (of 5). There shouldn't be much competition from here on in. She's occasionally homesick, but doing fine.

8/4/83

It's eight in the morning. I'm back here early, in a slow rain, with my new view: to my right, through the screen door, I can see the birdbath I bought at the auction in Bergen last evening. It's stone, not the plastic ones I've seen at stores lately. It has a yellowish cast. It looks like it's been back here for a long time. Haven't seen a bird in it yet. Paid $22. Nothing else I wanted at the auction.

At Casey's & then the Ale House until midnight, big softball celebrations going on. Rod & Greg & I are talked out for now. I'm back here in the rain in this idyllic place. I can hear a plane overhead, and I'm not on it. Robin squawks from the treeline to my left.

I'll putter with poems. Began one at the auction about a cherry tree. Don't know if it will come to anything.

Parade this evening if the rain lets up.

Just heard Han start the Buick to head up to the Center.

Billy inside sleeping, Kristen at Skidmore.

8/12?/83 (Sat.)

So much seems to be going by so fast. Mainly, I'm cleaning up & getting into order my study inside. Bill Kenny from the auction barn picked up a dozen items yesterday, including my 3-door oak bookcase & my 2-door china cabinet I'd been using for books. And the smallest of the 3 desks in the study. Now, I can breathe a little. And sent 2 boxes of things for sale to Ewert/Babcock. And have 10 boxes ready to go to U. of R. And will be shipping magazines—about 10 boxes—to UNH. So it goes on. Good for the soul. I must begin school again feeling free. This cabin is always simple & clean & clear. I am not, I feel, getting things into order because I'm getting ready to die, but because I'm getting ready for various writing projects and for years of teaching again with all teaching's details.

Han fine. She's cleaning my study windows right now.... Billy is at work. I'll drive him back to school in just about two weeks.... Kristen calls us every couple of evenings from Skidmore where, it turns out, she's having the time of her life with friends and learning a great deal about music & her instrument.

I saw Barry Leeds at Tony's one night last week.... Bruce & Lisa will visit tomorrow or Monday.... Billy & I had much fun playing ball yesterday.... Lee Frisbee stopped in after the auction last evening, and I gave him a bunch of books.... Have seen a catbird & a bluejay in my birdbath.... Cooler today after much heat these past 2 weeks.... Here & there something gets done on the anthology. The Matthews & Plumly essays have come in.... Not a word from Vanguard. Evelyn will probably let lme down on the brochure.... I hope to raise about two grand from Ewert-Babcock on the things I sent.... Working on the MacLeish manuscript.... A very poignant time of year again, my life racing by, but I do not have to end this life of the spirit just because school begins gain. I think I know, now, how to say no.... Ewert called to say Meadow Press will do *Ensoulment* as a broadside. It will be a beauty, I know....

8/15?/83 (Tues.)

The other day I saw the neighbor's cat up on its hind paws drinking from my birdbath, and just now I came back here and saw that the basin had been knocked off. Don't know what to do about it. It could have been one of the neighbors' dogs, too. Would it help to move the birdbath to in front of my picture window?

Bruce & Lisa & Charlie & Jane over last night. Many laughs. They're off on a camping trip for a week, and then I'll see them again. Bruce will carry my album of Otto Westerman photographs to NYC for sale—20 % commission, I told him.

Good day yesterday. Office key mess taken care of, for now, and I got the literary magazines out & ready for UPS shipping to Ewert/UNH. The month is closing in on me too fast! Tomorrow, Han & I will see Kristen in Albany. Billy is at cousin Kurt's until tomorrow.

I keep pecking away at the MacLeish, a few poems at a time. Wonder if McAdoo looked at the uncollected poems listed in Mullaly.... I keep clearing out the study & house. Have a couple packages of books ready to mail Vince Clemente.... Want to get to schoolwork, but want to complete office move first. Shouldn't be too hard. Will have Billy to help with the few big things....

Much fun playing basketball yesterday. Another big (6'7") young graduate student around. I play guard now, and hit the jumper when I can....

Feel a little scattered back here this morning.

Sent my MacLeish/Whitman proem and "The Horse Chestnut" off to Aaron Kramer for *West Hills Review*.

8/18/83

A long, long day of driving to Albany & back for Han & me yesterday, but in-between some golden time with Kristen. There she was on Rocky's Plaza, in front of the old Capitol, playing in that orchestra of gifted young people. Then we strolled down the State Street hill in sunlight—Kristen held my hand—to a place for lunch. We were with her friend Audrey & sister & mother. Kristen is fine, growing & learning & storing up an experience she'll never forget. We're all so glad she had the chance to go, and went.

I saw/felt <u>traffic</u> again, crowds, gasoline clouds again. My cabin back here sometimes seems otherworldly. I am lucky in this life, <u>must</u> keep that other death-in-life in mind when I'm teaching, whenever I feel pressed or anxious or sorry for myself.

I didn't sleep at all the night before we left, but did last night, and today feel much better.

Packages arrived at Ewert's, are on their way to the UNH library.

Dark today, rain in the air. I'll work on the MacLeish poems a while, maybe move a bit more over at school, clean up the downstairs & vacuum, catch up on anthology mail, etc.

Billy home from Kurt's. He had a fine time.

So, here I am again, lucky & glad to be. I thank the Lord, always, for keeping our tires on the road.

8/21/83 (Sunday)

Curious, scattered days lately as approaching-school restlessness builds up in me. Went to two auctions yesterday, spending a total of $1—and this for a box of books including 3 by Edwin Way Teale that I'll be reading back here.

Mowed the lawn this morning. Then Han & I had breakfast—Billy still slept. Kris called. I drove Billy to Ithaca Friday, & Han picks up Kris Saturday. Won't have the whole family together for even one day.

I've filled the birdbath again—it was knocked over by some fucking cat or dog—and hope it won't get busted.

Very uncomfortable talk with Bill Ewert about the price of manuscripts I sent him. I tried to explain to him how I felt. It's okay. I just don't want to have <u>business</u> dealings with friends.... I'll get about $300 from Bill and about $1100 and some books from Bert. This is <u>big</u> money for us right now. With my Hofstra money, I paid 2 $590 tuition installment bills for Billy, and $85 for a muffler, and the plane fare to the Island & back.

Just about moved into my office in Neff. Billy much help.

Keep working on anthology here and there.

Talk with Evelyn, who is a pain in the ass but will eventually get *Erika* published. She keeps saying she'll do something, & does nothing. Bless the old gal. But with *CR* I'll probably look for another publisher.

Cooler today.... I just heard Han sneeze in the distance.... I've never loved her more.

Still typing Archie's poems. Should try to finish today, and will, unless I go to that auction in North Rose, wherever that is.

Despite all the clearing away & cleaning, I still have thoughts of changing my life radically, getting out from under all the books, all the habit. I think of a different kind of journal, one holding all and the only writing I'll do, entries & drafts of poems & everything. And that's all. Maybe it could become all I would need. The collector's impulses are all against this, of course, and the feelings I had last night when I saw my bookcases in the auction barn ready for next month's auction—they seemed like my children, but forlorn & out of place. But they'll be sold, & that's that. I'm not hopeless. My life <u>is</u> changing!

Mowing the lawn this perfect autumn-cool August morning I was thinking of this western New York State, my place here and now. It's a good place to be on this planet in this galaxy.

Richard Lautz was in Rochester & called yesterday, but I wasn't here.

The Ewe's Song is out in *Ontario Review* and looks good.... Long letter from Reginald Gibbons about my Wms. sequence, which he returned. His Wms. is not mine. I'll be glad though, to keep staring at it this fall during my Wms. class.... *Blackberry Light* will be out in *Ohio Review* any day.

8/24/83

I'm sitting with Earl Ingersoll & other Dept. members at the opening meeting of the school year. Seymour Union ballroom. Van de Wetering introducing speakers & new vice presidents, etc.

On the way over here I thanked the Lord for the year off, its safety and health for family and writing and freedom, and prayed to do well, to stay calm, be of help over the next years.

Han & I worked hard getting the carpet from my office down in my study, & cleaning, and moving the rolltop back & forth. Am now settled, & happy in that clean & comfortable room.... Then, a wonderful dream of peace and joy, one that probably connected with teaching. I was flying a kite that became, high, high over Brockport, a sparkler in the sky that I had on a string, felt its tug & curves & swerves as it showered sparks from high above the town. Then there were two boys beside me on the grass, & my sparkler above showered down through the night sky golden slips of paper that slid down in little rushes, & there were chocolates in foil on some of the papers, & the boys gathered them up. To describe this dream makes it all of course seem silly & corny, but I woke as I do only once or twice a year with that deep sense of peace under my breastbone, and with a smile, and rested. Showers of spark-gold papers sliding down in curves like water lily stems.

So, I'm here, and surrounded by friends—Mirko to my right, John Maier behind me—and will have a good year. Will drive Billy to Cornell tomorrow, Kristen home the next day.

I'm ready, even, for the necessary initial meetings.

Voices sliding above me. I thought of not having a journal here, and don't want to play a role of any kind, but do want to carry my writing activities right into school. It's okay. But I wish this blank book were shorter.

All's well. In an hour I'll play ball with Billy.

8/25/83

I'm back from Ithaca, sad in my usual way without Billy around. No desk or curtains or dresser in his room, but he's happy as a pig in shit with his friends roughing it. He does have a big & generally clean carpeted place, and a big double bed.

I'm tired, but promised to meet Greg & Rod tonight. I'll break away soon as I can.... Also didn't eat too well today & my stomach is bloated & gurgling from pop & doughnuts & such.

Found a nice copy of Goldbatth's *Opticks* in the Bookery in Ithaca.

Lost Billy's address!

I think I broke the damned typewriter instead of being patient with it & shaking out the razor blade that was somehow stuck down inside it.

Long talk with Bill Ewert last night after a long letter from him. I want to get off the business relationship with him. And I won't send any more books to Babcock. He can travel here if he wants any more. Simplify, simplify. So far, so good, here in the study.... Maybe I'll keep this journal inside for a while now. Don't know why I feel like that, but will. Will see. So comfortable here now, psychologically & physically—the "new" light green carpet, the cleanliness, the room now that 3 pieces of furniture & innumerable books are out of here.

8/26/83

Long & brusque letter from Ewert today. After a while, I sat down & typed an answer, but something in me just doesn't care about so much of that trivial stuff, so I won't send the letter. I want to change my life, and it will be little by little, and the little by little with Ewert will have to do with slowing down projects—once he's done with the current spate—and not doing certain kinds of business with him.

Much fun playing ball today with Felipe Farley et. al. I'm so glad I'm still able to compete.

Typed & xeroxed sabbatical report. Took care of one or two anthology details. Must get to some solid schoolwork tomorrow. Need to do at least one syllabus.

Berry & Wesleyan books from Babcock today.

Saw Greg & Rod at Casey's yesterday. Many laughs.

Praying for a safe trip for Han & then Han & Kris tomorrow. I will be glad to have my little live wire home gain.

Think I'll have some watermelon.

8/30/83

My meeting this morning with the ten freshmen went well. Two hours went by in easy talk & introductions. I was of use, I think. And I went back in the afternoon to help one young man. I <u>know</u> I was of use there. I meet the ten again tomorrow.

Peter Dzwonkoski coming tomorrow, too. I'll want to talk long-range with him. I've two more boxes for deposit ready for him, and many things for donation.

I'm about set for classes Thursday. Then, an auction Thurs. evening, and I'll go with Bill Stewart to a 400-booth antique show in Buffalo Friday morning. <u>Then</u>, I'll begin the semester in earnest.... Basketball tomorrow, too, and I've missed it, though only away from it for five days.

Drinks with Tony & his friend Frank & Rod & Greg today.

I feel scattered but okay.... I do have a batch of poems ready to send to *New Yorker*.... Wrote Ewert telling him to scratch the Christmas card & the special of *Erika*. Will be firm on some things. Our relationship is changed. Okay. So be it.

I've heard from several people that I'll be asked to write a poem for the 150th anniversary of Rochester & read it at some big deal ceremony. Hecht will be slighted? The poem won't come easy, I'm afraid. Well, I'll wait to hear officially about all this.

Kristen adjusting to being back. She's really missing that boy she met & became friends with in Saratoga.

I brought the little bookstand in from the cabin to be alongside my chair here. It has a trough for books. It reminds me so clearly of when I sat in the easy chair in Cortland alongside the same type stand and studied for classes the next day. I was quietly terrified as I tried to learn enough, organize enough, to fill out class periods. I remember so vividly the several Wadsworth Co. critical guides, the one on "Young Goodman Brown"—I read the whole thing & <u>still</u> couldn't fill 50 minutes. Now my 1½ hr. classes go by quickly. I just didn't know anything, & had the wrong idea, in any case, about what teaching was.... Anyway, that 3rd floor apartment, the flowered rug, Billy an infant, the first years of marriage.

9/3/83

Saturday evening. Ten minutes ago, after typing & reading & writing most of the day (a poem on Scanella called "After the Wars" came along), I was bored as hell, complaining to Han about being bored. Now I'm content to be sitting here. Will watch the season's 1st NFL game on television, & putter.

Typed Siegel's essay. Edited down & typed Root's. Will do a few more anthology things tomorrow, but have to get to schoolwork: comps to read for comp, syllabus for the Wms. class & a journal description, etc. But, after classes Tuesday I'm off for a week again. Blessings on my job.

Peter & another staff member came over, picked up some more books. I was awfully rushed, but we had a good talk. He says the Library & English Dept. at Rochester are very much in favor of a poetry room for me.

I did get a letter from the Sesqui-Centennial Committee in Rochester. The woman is to call me, too. Maybe I won't have to slave to do an "important" poem for the occasion, and can get away with something maybe slight & cryptic, or something.

What quickly broke my boredom, maybe, was just a few minutes poking among my books, finding a plastic jacket for a Kinnell item, looking at my paperback copy of Wright's *Moments of the Italian Summer*, etc. I always have to remember this, must not sell all my books before I retire, or I might twiddle my thumbs until death.

I'm watching a segment of "Great Railway Journeys of the World," this one about what 1st class European travel used to be like. Han & I must see some of those places, France & Switzerland, etc. Belgium. But in my mind I feel, at least today, so lazy & blurred—no interest in learning French, e.g. And I'm 42. I often think how different, how much more energetic my life wd. be, if I could sleep 6-8 solid hrs. a night. I slept maybe 4 hrs. last night—a good night—and maybe 1 or 2 the night before. I hear that the body gets enough rest, somehow, but if I could get that lung-deep sleep more often ...

Russia shot down a South Korean jumbo jet carrying about 265 passengers—the jet had strayed over Russian territory. A <u>terrible</u> story, even unimaginable. I counted 200 people at an auction the other night & tried to imagine.... And the numbers of the Holocaust?... I don't know all of what I mean, but god is still in nature & nature doesn't lie, and men are perverting places.... About 225,000 more people on the planet every day....

Labor Day, 1983

I haven't been able to sleep much lately, and couldn't this morning, so was smart enough to come back here with my journal and a cup of tea. It's before 8:00, and there's a light here that is a true gold because it touches the woods of bookcase and panelling that darken it. Walt and Archie are in the eastern light this morning, too. The sun, then, comes up over my left shoulder in this cabin.

Schoolwork noises in my mind, noise of the Monday garbage pick-up on Frazier Street. I want my life to be seamless, want to think and write about those things, yes, but not this morning. I feel a small poem coming on about Walt's face.

Later: I did. I wrote a piece called "The Way" that I love. Thank you, Walt, again. I've sent the poem to Vince, have it in my shirt-pocket over my heart right now.... And on the spur of the moment I've put "The Beam" into an envelope to send to *Upstate*.... And I've been thinking and staring at my 1854 paperweight, the one thing in my life I don't want to lose. Right at this moment the eerie feeling that I've written this same thing down somewhere, underlining thing, but I don't know where. Maybe my thoughts were so centered & compressed that I believed I was writing them down.... Over the last couple of hours, I've lived a long time, have added to my store of time. Now, into the day, but Walt's portrait and the paperweight are with me....

Spoke with Billy yesterday. Kris & Han fine, too. I did the syllabus for the Wms. class yesterday, found my way around the *Selected Poems*.... Han & I watched *Reds* together last night, ate popcorn, attended the movies at home..... I'll leave this journal back here now again.... It is the deepening back here that will enable me to be a teacher of soul, to keep my life seamless, somehow, so if it seems to be a split, my distancing myself back here, it isn't: but I must learn to speak & think in class as I do back here. It's probably happening, in fact. Often when I feel I'm acting very normally & not unusually at all, speaking naturally, others give me that quizical look—but one of friendliness and understanding.

In for some breakfast now, then to school for xeroxing, mimeographing, & basketball.

9/6/83

And this morning it's earlier, only 7:00. I'm back here with a cup of tea. Long day today of 3 classes, including the 3-hr. graduate class, but I'm better off here than tossing in bed worrying about sleeping. I can never tell wht an hour back here will give me. I'm back here, too, I know, to keep saving myself by making myself into a person of character whose life is of a whole, whether I'm following a poem or, as I did last evening, reading a set of freshman compositions.

I'll write out "The Way here and hope I feel it as I did yesterday.

The Way

The Sun rises over the left shoulder of my cabin,
grazes a photograph of Walt,
portrait of the middle-aged illuminate.

I am middle-aged, and not one,
except in sun from our first Island,
except in eastern light again,

as here. Or this is that moment from when
I'll never be the same,
or one of them.

The way the sun enters my cabin,
shoulder to heart, heart
to self-portrait.

The way the sun returns.
The way he always waits.
The way the sun stays.

I still like it. The word "grazes" is an odd one. The "one" could refer to age, and that ambiguity wd. be okay. The "or one of them" goes both ways, too. The poem <u>does</u> seem like the beginning of a sequence. I could maybe come to the second one by long-staring.... When I looked up just now, the sun was reflected in the glass just above Archie's head. That inscription, that sun, the foliage outside my cabin in the glass with him. The sun, as I look up again, almost risen out of the frame.... Now gone.

9/7/83

The cabin is here again, waiting for me. Rather, it's <u>still</u> here—there is a world that keeps existing beyond <u>me</u>.

It's nine in the morning, and I feel rested for the first time in a long time. I went to bed about 11:30, was up at 2:00 for maybe a half-hour and watched television, but then fell asleep until Han & Kris left at eight. And I may have even slept for a half-hour after that. I rose with that lung-deep restfulness I feel only seldom.

I haven't stayed inside for the Donahue show He has children from Belfast, El Salvador, Thailand, Israel—kids who have seen war and suffered. And where am I in all that? I have a chance, as teacher, to do a <u>little</u>. First my own character....

I keep backsliding into pettiness, worrying about typing paper, saying something sharp & impatient to a student. Ever since I was a freshman in college, I've been trying to change my personality which, at that time, I think, became twisted. I'm still trying to make myself over, now trying to carry the life of this cabin & journal & poetry right into my office and classroom <u>or</u> the years until the next sabbatical won't be happy or productive ones.... My prose in these paragraphs, my diction, are sloppy & insincere, even, and maybe this has something to do with my 6 hrs. as teacher yesterday, as straight as I tried to be. I must learn to stop lying, to stop striving for effect. I will

A good-sized seminar last night. By reading Mariani again & Wms., I'll be learning—maybe learning what I don't like, but learning.

Stopped in to see Al last night—his new bookcase, etc. Didn't see Tony at all, and was surprised not to.

Only the composition course will be a hard one. 26 or 27 students.

I just noticed that my 3rd stanza of "The Way" has to be

as here. Or this is that moment,
or one of them, from when
I'll never be the same.

or the "one of them" would refer to the company of illuminates. So, again, my language did not lie, and I was trying to fool myself. Maybe. But the way I had it had it both ways, too, but I want it the one way....

I've been noticing that this year my bed of sunflowers has hardened against me! The sunflowers' necks have stiffened now, and they all face away from the cabin and yard. Yesterday morning when I left the cabin I found the first line of the poem I finished in my office at school yesterday. I think, maybe, seeing Fred Burelbach, who lost his father to cancer a few years ago, brought this one on, too.

<u>The Family</u>

They must be ashamed of me,
the sunflowers,
the way they face away,

this year,
for the first time.

Along the fence, only
the backs of their heads,
their halos winging in gold light
across the neighborhood,
but not to me,

and last night,
when I stood behind them,
I heard my dead father
sobbing, saying
tell me you love me,

until the moon of this dream
filled out and faced me,
like a sunflower,
the tallest one,
my father.

    I may not have it quite right. The 5th line may not make sense in terms of the emotional set of the poem, and the first words of the last two paragraphs may go back & forth, but I'm glad the little poem came, and in my office at school.

9/9/83

    Played poker at Mirko's with Ed Kelly & Bud Meade & Joe Winnick—lost $40 after being ahead $100. Stupid. But a beautiful morning, and I'm anxious to get to my new Bryant poem. Have a banana & two cups of coffee back here.... Sounds of jackhammer in background—will turn on fan....
    Bought at auction a small painting of rabbits for Han for Christmas. She'll love it, as I do. It was $50.
    I feel full with life, only thrown off the track yesterday by seeing the trees the town killed right behind my cabin as they put a useless ditch in. Can't I have a little peace all the way back here, secluded as I am? I'll plant a few honeysuckles behind me this fall. This was all a result of a distant neighbor's backyard filled with junk cars.
    Many little things to mention here, but I want to get to that poem, and then basketball later.

    Later: back from basketball, which was much fun. My knee seems generally okay again, though I don't play as hell-may-care as I used to.
    Pushed the Bryant poem forward. It just <u>could</u> become the sesqui-centennial poem for Rochester. I'd love that. I'd still want to do much reading before finishing the last sections. I'm way ahead of myself here: what I have is one 44 line section (11 quatrains) and a lot of maybes about where the poem can go from there.
    I'm very tired, keep dozing for a few seconds every now and then as I write this. Want to read about 50 pages in Mariani tonight to get a jump on my seminar reading.
    Good letter from Steve Claeson today. Disappointing postcard from Joyce, who has too many limited editions going to do one with Scarab. But no big deal.... I wrote Strand & Mariani about their essays for the anthology.... Package for me at the post office, which will either be colophon sheets from Allen Hoey to sign, or Ewert package with blank books & a box for *XVII Machines*.... How cool has my relationahip gotten with Ewert now? Up to him. I'll keep writing him every week or so, and see what happens. I <u>will</u> slow way down on publishing small things, anyway.

9/11/83

It's 11:00 in the morning. I'm sitting in an auction tent in Naples, about 90 minutes from Brockport. The auction begins in an hour, disperses the Widmer family's possessions. I haven't seen any stunning books. Want to get a look at the stereopticon and cards before long. It will be hot today. I've got a good aisle seat. Hope I see something I want, so I don't go home empty-handed. Glad I brought the journal.... A big crowd here. The home, too, is to sell today....

Made another tour, have seen enough.... Have lost my aisle seat, but am comfortable, listening to this Gansz character in derby & black gloves.... Looked through the mansion.... About the most stuff I've ever seen, and all the furniture was auctioned off yesterday!...

Yesterday: I was jolted by a visit from Mazzaro & John Logan & another young man. John—I felt I was in the presence of a dead man. He looks ghostly & fat. He sputters. He's lost. Jerry won't let him drink when with him, and John was straining to hold himself together. I didn't even want to look in his eyes. I spoke with Jerry about John's situation.... A little vase just sold for $500, a little jack-in-the-pulpit vase.... It all scared me in ways I hadn't felt, I think, since Berryman. And there's nothing anybody can do, apparently.... John wanted to stay over, but I told Jerry no, no, please no. Spoke with Al later, and he didn't want anything to do with John, either—he's been through it.... Another vase just went for $375. I don't know what kind they are.... Logan signed three books.... The man to my right just bought a little bud-vase for $350. Maybe I'll talk to him later.... The books here are nothing special, but I'm glad I came. I was <u>haunted</u> last night.... The four of us sat in my cabin for a while, chit-chatting about nothing. Jerry seemed okay, only streaks of his self absorption coming through....

It's now about 2:00. I've bought nothing. The crowd comes back into the tent from the sale outside of books & clothes & junk. I'll hang around for maybe another hour, then drive back home. I have my eye on one picture frame, but they probably won't get to it by the time I leave.... Just had another hot dog.... Am drinking in the spirit here—a pastoral oil painting being sold now, the cows in the pasture oblivious to human noise for about a hundred years now. $225.... A tray of stereoscopic cards that I thought I could get for maybe $20—$125! I'm just dumb.

So, a short time longer, and then the long drive, and a good evening at home.
Logan.

9/12/83

Walking back to the cabin just now, smelling the wet green smells of weeds and spruce trees and grass, I thought again of Walt's "dumb, beautiful ministers" that always wait, always wait for me to waken.

I'm not happy with the voice of my journal lately again. I'm thinking too much of what a reader might think. The journal is mine and has to be as true as I can make it. It is <u>not</u> public and never will be.

A chair was out of place back here just now and reminded me of the Logan visit. He sat in this easy chair.... I've been going through one of those times for a couple days when I can't quite feel grounded, when I wonder about the most common reality: how can this all <u>be</u>? Sometimes I think I could float away, lose myself or become lost. My first thought, then, always, is Han. I'll always keep most of my strangeness to myself, for her sake. And at this moment I think that <u>because</u> of the strangeness, <u>through</u> the strangeness, the oversoul or within-soul is obvious. There's a trill of insects now under the noise of a plane circling from the Brockport airport, under truck noise which always seems heavy Monday mornings. <u>Something</u> under everything. I'll be damned if I don't truly feel and believe something under everything.

If I had to bet on it, I'd bet that I'll never see John again.

I'm glad about my centeredness right at this moment, the centeredness I want to carry into and through my long day at school tomorrow. It is this journal and straight talk to myself that has again given me back to myself.

That rare glassware yesterday was called Quezelle. I keep thinking about that iridescent jack-in-the-pulpit vase—it <u>just</u> hit me!—the john & jack. And the early Catholicism.

    John, the day after I saw you for the last time,
    I drove to an auction in Naples—
    the Widmer family's estate—

no, that detail of vintner is too true to be used, and would make the poem a joke, unless I used it & mentioned it as absurd irony. But no, I'll move to the one object that I'll always associate with Logan.

 A different look in Walt's eyes this morning, because I am different, of course, and because the light is <u>always</u> different.

 Later: I think I've just finished the poem begun this morning. I'll write it out here before typing it up.

<u>Of Wildflower</u>

1.
Each year here on this acre
a single Jack-in-the-pulpit
appears again in woodshade
of early summer.
If you've ever seen one, its single
vertical spadix arched over
by its spathe, a purple-
streaked cowl,
you know the beauty of wildflower.

2.
I've begun there to tell you this,
which is also true:
my alcoholic friend and I
walked from the cabin
past where the flower had been—
I didn't point it out—
only its bent stem left to return
to the world of shades.
Between episodes
of *delirium tremens,*
he was already a dead man.
I knew I'd never see him again.

3.
Believe this: the next day, a hundred
miles away in wine country,
an auctioneer held up a small, iridescent,
amethyst Jack-in-the-pulpit bud vase.
He called it poetry
in black glass.
I don't know how I didn't buy it.
I did. Its hood
leaned over emptiness
that would always hold the need
of wildflower.

    (for John Logan, 1923-)

9/14/83

 I've just read the Logan poem. I feel a few changes coming on, maybe, but it's a good one.

I talked too much in my three classes yesterday, but they were good ones, but I'll try to talk less tomorrow. I don't want to get into the habit of <u>carrying</u> the classes again, as <u>has</u> been my habit…. Even the freshman class was enjoyable, and I began with the simplest questions about how they felt about their assignment and how they'd done…. The 3-hr. Wms. class was good. Down inside myself I feel more and more that Doc is not that good a poet, was never centered enough to be the poet Frost or Stevens or Jeffers was (a <u>dark</u> centeredness in Frost, certainly, and different kinds of centeredness), or at least is not <u>my</u> poet, though there are elements I need…. Have the little "This Is Just To Say" by heart now….

Have office hrs. this afternoon, some papers to read, a meeting with a creative writing group—Gregory's idea—and this evening Han & I will go to Tony's China talk. I'll bike to the gym first for some basketball.

Nothing new on the anthology. I plan (I tell myself) to work hard on it this weekend, write some introductory paragraphs on the poets, get into touch with Reed & Clifton again, etc.

I'm wearing a flannel shirt this cool morning. The heater hums.

Vivid dream two nights ago of Han with another man, me on a mattress on the floor, a dream of hurt and regret. The day always gives me my faithful and beautiful wife back, and she loves me, and that's my center….

I just touched up "Of Wildflower." Yes, I think it's a real poem.

9/16/83

Raining now. Dark & cold around the cabin this morning, but warm in here.

I just wrote Bruce a letter, showed him "Of Wildflower," "The Family," "Here Now"—changed the latter in a couple of ways as I wrote it out. Bruce sent me a story he just wrote, a good one.

Tony's reading the other night was fine. I was on a couch with Han to my right & Greg to her right and Dave Hale to his. I was comfortable, filled with so many thoughts as Tony read his China poems & journal entries & letters to & from me and other friends. He could make a true book out of the whole thing. I hope he does.

These paragraphs are examples of the voice I still don't like in this journal. I'm sort of sappy & blah-blah and don't know why. Audience is the constant problem, but that's not all. Something is in the way. I don't question here the way I do as I move through this shadow world. My sentiments here are trite and predictable—maybe a steadying of personality going on, a grounding and unifying that I shouldn't worry about or tamper with—while my other mind whirls deeper even as I write these sentences. Or maybe that's all bullshit, and I am just this cliché-ridden sucker who can't get out of the way of his own triteness. But it's not that. Am I worried that some entries will be gibberish? Bill, let this journal be <u>anything</u>, anything at all…. My poems are freer, like the "Times Square Meditation" that is almost done, or I think of "The Masters" section of *CR*….

Han & I went to the auction yesterday, saw a dozen of our things auctioned off. The china cabinet went for $180, the bookcase for $210, a big surprise—that mess of a thing. The biggest surprise was that the 2 little sterling platters that I thought wd. sell for maybe $15 together—I bought them for $3 at an auction on Barry St. years ago—sold for $40 & $55! So, we'll get about $500 for stuff we didn't want. And we didn't buy anything! (though maybe I should have bought the 4 pieces of scrimshaw).

Will play ball today. Will answer mail this afternoon, and get started on schoolwork this evening. Classes going well. The sport in literature class may be the easiest & most relaxing one I've ever had. And all my life of reading the sports pages and playing ball prepared me for it.

Haven't heard from Bill Ewert in quite a while. Is he still playing hurt because I balked at the $300 cash & $300 credit for 5 manuscripts? I hope he's over it, and not playing games. Or, it may be that my writing life will be lonelier from here on in—this could have its benefits, too. But I hope he's okay, and over our disagreements.

9/18/83

It's 10:30 of a Sunday evening. I've followed my impulse, tired as I am, to come back here for a time. I'm tired of inside, the schoolwork reminders around me, the full desk. The day turned balmy, and it's cooler back here, too.

The long weekend, the four days, are about gone. I've had fun at auctions, but have done little of substance. Must write several poets about their essays for the anthology, etc. Want to do some of that tomorrow, before evening schoolwork again.

Kristen was in an accident today, was run into from behind while stopped at a light. She and Dawn are unhurt, thank God.... She'll drive to Ithaca next weekend, and we'll have our fingers crossed.

Didn't go to Rod and Greg's party last night. Went to bed early, though I didn't sleep well.

Spoke with Mom this morning. Pop didn't get to the phone. Then spoke with Werner. All's well down there.

What can I turn to for an hour or two?

9/19/83

Morning. I feel rested. Meant to devote the morning to the anthology, but I want the cabin, too.... Didn't do much last night—went over the strange Times Square poem a few times. Just about have it, such as it is.

Very still and warm this morning. Green thinning around me, the blue spruce in sight for the first time in months.

I seem to myself to be more than a little lazy. At least, I'm in no hurry just to jump into busywork. Being in touch with the poets about the anthology is more than that, but still.... I like dawdling back here.... I'm reading Doc's life again, trying to imagine his rhythms. Frenetic doctoring, escaping into writing, driving to make contact with other writers, his sex drive—the life must seem to have gone by awfully fast, faster even than mine seems to be unwinding now. It's back here that time slows almost to nothing. And I don't remember this still a day. I can't see the slightest movement of leaf anywhere around me.

The same old question: how to affirm, why affirm?—experience of human nature (apparently our nature is bloody) and the elements is the history of violent death. There must be a need to affirm. That must be the center line of what I do, or seem to myself to be doing, showing my own need & wishful dreaming, whatever else I do. Such stillness here, the planes over Beirut, the ships in the Sea of Japan looking for wreckage. Most horror can be traced to human causes, but not earthquakes, at least not yet. And cancer seems to have been with us from the beginning.... Where did all this come from this morning? My real thoughts on all this are underneath the words, underneath the qualifications unstated about any statement. I'm here in Brockport on a very quiet Monday morning. The highways and airports are busy all over the county, state, country. Heyen keeps moving his fountain pen to the right margin of his journal, which is real for him, whatever else it is. It's the journal that speaks better than he knows. Underneath anything he says, is what he is really saying. Maybe he doesn't even want to know what that is. He's back in school now, things on his mind, still lamenting without having fully admitted it to himself the passing of his year away from teaching. He has tried talking himself into a wholeness. He has been right (he thinks even now) to do so, and he's a little wiser and closer to that. Discontent beneath these paragraphs. He is still (and maybe always will be) trying to educate himself to his luck. Sometimes the spirit doesn't want to hear.

I just read the paragraph at the end of my July 28th entry. That's about right. And Wms. was saying he could hold only 60 poems or pages or so in the present, somehow, before he had to throw everything away or publish it to get it behind him.... I was just thinking of *City Parables*, excerpting from it in a *Selected* instead of revamping the whole thing for a book called *Dandelions*. Yes, Bill, leave *CP* alone—you've plenty of new poems for a book. Just let the new ones get written.... A little discovery like this, maybe—no more expansions of books (the memoir an easy exception)—can make me feel easy about myself. Yes, let *CP* be what it was. It will be a nice 10 pp. section in a *Selected*, with "Redwings" & "Off the Expressway" and some others.

Well, I've been writing here for almost an hour, looking up around me often, eating a banana and sipping tea, listening to the cheeps and chucks and gurgles of birds I can't identify, thinking a million words more than appear in these paragraphs. Whatever the writing is, I've written myself into a deep-breathing ease.

Haven't heard from him, but I wrote Bill Ewert another letter, about Logan's visit, etc. Will find out before long, in one way or another, whether our friendship meant more to Bill than any disagreement about manuscripts and publishing, or not. I shouldn't have questioned (maybe) the $300 cash & $300 credit he was going to give me for the five manuscripts (2 of them very good ones), and shouldn't have said (definitely) that my credit disappeared so fast on things that in effect cost him nothing (this was mostly true, but I still shouldn't have said it). And he wrote some things he shouldn't have said. But, if he can't get past this, and doesn't realize that the ongoing friendship is fifty times more important than such shit, that our companionship & booktalk & gossiping & growing old together & collection-building is the important thing,... well, that will be too bad. I keep thinking, when I think of Bill, of athletes who struggle & argue but then forget about that and get on with the game the next time—as we at basketball do three times a week. But that part of Bill's personality may be missing. He is pushy, gets his way in intriguing ways (I've seen this often, and not just with me). He weighs about 350, and I connect this with that lack of the athlete's knowledge. That one letter he sent me was in large part nasty. But I'd hurt him, and made him think I was ungrateful. I wrote a strong reply, but did not mail it, sending just a postcard instead (the one in which I told him to forget the special of *Erika* & forget the Christmas card this year and maybe just think about finishing *CR*). Of course in this writing in this journal I try to justify myself to myself, but I've gotten past whatever that squabble with Bill was, and he should have been able to do the same.

Great: my neighbor to my left has started up his chainsaw. That's the end of this entry.

9/21/83 (Wed.)

I'm back here on a dark and rainy morning. Hobbled back, after hurting the knee again Monday. Had a hard time getting to classes yesterday, but did. The evening Wms. class went especially well.

So, I'm hurt again, and won't be playing ball for a long time, and even then will have to adjust, somehow, and do something different—I can't keep hurting this knee every six months, as I have. I'm lucky I didn't break it. Oh, and I was playing well, too, when Dormann clipped me from behind when I was in the air making a lay-up!

But I already do feel inside myself, at least today, real benefits. I'm aware of my body again, my general good health otherwise. I feel more thoughtful these two days as I struggle against pain to do homework or try to get some sleep. And today I don't have to think of the 11:30-2:00 time period when I'm off to play ball.... I might do what I've wanted to do for many years, but have been too lazy to: work on upper-body strength, sit-ups and push-ups, once I'm mobile again. I don't want to cripple myself, want to be able to walk easily with Han around the places we visit when we retire.

No word from Ewert. I did write him again Sunday evening.

Kristen seems okay, the neck stiffness disappearing.

Don't know if I've mentioned the long letter from R.P. Warren the other day. A pleasure to have it. I'm sorely tempted to break my promise to him and to send him a few books for inscription. I have *Brother to Dragons* back here for reading—the new version.

Yes, rain is my favorite weather back here. It keeps all chainsaws and mowers at bay.

Richard Ehrlich good company yesterday evening. He's a good friend.

Postcard from Bruce. That photograph album is apparently worthless.

I linger over this journal, not sure what I'll turn to when I put it down.

9/26/83

I must not get knocked off-center just because I came back here this morning and a truck was parked 20 feet behind my cabin, or because another truck has joined it and men are working back there. It is hard to believe that there is all this action back here behind two properties, and the reasons for all this noise. And all they've done is make a mess and kill trees, for no good reason whatsoever. That land behind me will flood again, and any jerk can see that it will and why it will: because water, even during this crazy century, will not flow uphill. Sounds like they're lengthening the ditch now. Well, a move, if worst comes to worst, may not be the worst thing for Han & me. I could get ten or twenty acres and plop the cabin in the middle of it.

I did not work Saturday—went to the U. or R. book sale with Richard Ehrlich, and then to an auction at the barn in Hamlin in the evening—and worked all day yesterday at the anthology, with a break for lawn-mowing. Didn't get any good books in Rochester, but Bruce sent me a box from NYC including 2 of the 55 copies of Charles Wright's 1st book that he bought on remainder.

Mail arrived early this morning, throwing me off-kilter. That's how used to the afternoon mail rhythm I've become.

If my knee allows, I'll bike to town for a haircut and to get to the travel bureau. I'd like to do one or two worthwhile things back here this morning—somehow, writing in this journal is <u>always</u> worthwhile, at least in terms of focussing my thoughts and emotions—before getting to busywork & anthology work & schoolwork inside.

Essay arived from Ai, praise the Lord, and it will do nicely.... I wrote Ray Smith, listing the poets and catching him up on things.... Want to write Clifton, and maybe Dave Smith, today....

Kristen's visit to Ithaca went nicely. Han and I glow when we think of the kids getting together like that, too.

Sounds of trees being bulldozed down a hundred feet away. More and more I think I've got to use my money, such as it is, to save some acreage for plants & animals somewhere.

More of Archie's poems arrived from McAdoo.... Rejections from *New Yorker* & *Upstate*.... Revision of his essay from Mariani.... I feel, at this minute, with clanging going on from the backhoe as it backs up, well, okay. This one acre here, except for the noise slicing across it, remains. But if they pave the world ...

Have I mentioned here the letter I got from Robert Penn Warren in which he talks about the freaks and smells at Stonehenge?

Later: It's about three hours later. I've written RPW a long letter. I feel good about it. I would like him to be for me what Archie was—a note now and then, a few books inscribed now and then. And I feel abashed at this. But I also may be the only one who knows how deserving I am. I must feel right about this, must give myself to his books in honest ways. I want him to live to be 100. I love my father, but guess I must need another kind of father, too, one who reads and writes books. RPW is one of my temperament, I know and feel. And I may be able to be of <u>some</u> comfort to him as he grows older.... What's all this about? All I did was to write him a letter, not the first or the last.

I'll go inside for some lunch, and maybe take a bike ride for a haircut & travel bureau.

Later: It's seven in the evening. I'll spend an hour or so back here, and then go in to see Han & Kris who usually get back from Kris's lessons in Rochester at 8:00 or 9:00.... I'm about ready for classes tomorrow, though have to review my notes on Mariani.

Bill Beavers called.... He'd like to do a chapbook by Wilbur, too. I'll wait until I get *Along This Water* before writing Wilbur.

Stopped in to arrange for the flights for my two trips. That second one will make me nervous as I worry about connections. The Long Island one will be easy—back & forth to Islip by way of Syracuse.

I should send out 2-3 batches of poems. Hardly knew where. Meant to send to *Poetry*, but Nims is off for a year, and that bastard Parisi is in charge. Greg Orr asked to see something for *VQR*. Maybe I will. And an invitation from *Iowa Review*. I don't like all the patty-cake. Maybe I should try *Atlantic* again. Truth is, I guess, there are not many magazines I'd like to be in, and the thrill is largely gone.

Stopped in briefly to see Al. He looks okay.... My knee held up during the bike ride, but I'm a long way from the ball court.

Wrote Billy a letter.... No word still from Bill Ewert. I guess it <u>must</u> be because of our tiff. <u>Always</u>, disagreements have to do with money. Surely, though, all in all our bad feelings were about something unimportant, and for the sake of friendship he should be able to shake all that off. If not, what <u>was</u> the thing I thought was our friendship? No doubt I'll write him one more letter, about this and that, and then that will be it. And my life will be changed, for the worse in that I'll have lost a friend, for the better in that I won't piss away my time anticipating small-press projects so much as I have since the Ewert phase of my life began.

I'll walk back to the house, maybe eat a few more grapes along the way.

9/28/83

Wednesday. A hazy morning, overcast and cool. Quiet back here, the work behind the cabin maybe done until spring when there will be a flood and the town will come around scratching its collective head again.

Wms. class went very well last night. Because of noise in Hartwell, we moved to my small office in Neff. Good discussions. Fifteen minutes from the end, I had them write down a quick poem. Gave them the title:

"To A Young Woman In An Easy Chair." We heard a dozen different voices and strategies, and that made the point. Tonight I'm to do Peter Marchant's "Writer's Craft" class. Will talk about "Ram Time," etc.

9/30/83 (Fri.)

It's just before seven in the morning, dark back here. I slept several hours, and this time, instead of straining to sleep again, I upped and walked back here. It will be a long day. A few phrases about the river's manicured (or pedicured) embankments and the modern city's skyline were on my mind when I woke up, and this was maybe a message to turn to the sesqui-centennial poem. I <u>could</u> get lucky and it <u>could</u> finish itself off beyond the strain of research. Anyway, I'm glad to be back here now, with a thermos of tea and an apple, the heater humming. I'll watch the morning come on.
   Did Peter's class the other night. Spoke two hours. Turned down Sally Helf's class at the high school—maybe in the spring.
   Later this afternoon, I'll drive to that auction in Sodus.
   Long letter a couple days ago from Bill Ewert. That morning I'd sent him another letter, and after reading his, sent him another. I had Han read his letter, too. Hard to describe. He's a driven man, seems to think that all this shit we've been involved in is the be-all & end-all of life. My friend needs to calm down, get off the train. He's obsessed. I've written the best letters I could, clear in what they say, giving Bill all the space he needs to do nothing but get out of the traffic.... He weighs probably 350 pounds, and in my mind his weight is connected with the way he hurtles around, pushing himself and other people, killing himself. He does have problems. A sweet and good and generous man, and I want him for a friend always, but he's got to look around himself and shed some of that world that's killing him.
   Spoke to my folks last night. They have their pre-trial hearing on Pop's accident a year ago, and they are still understandably frantic about it. I'll be very glad when that's all past them.
   Okay, I'm ready to begin the day. Also want to get a haircut later. For now, a few hours or more back here just seeing what will come to me. The dumb and beautiful ministers always wait. I'm surely one of the luckiest over whom the sun is rising now. If I don't learn to talk clearly, naturally, truly from myself, it will be my own fault.

   Later: my Rochester poem pulled me ahead. It's almost ten now, and I feel fine. When I wake up in the morning, I should get up, and that's about all there is to it.
   Han stopped back here before she went to work at eight. What would I do, where would I be without that woman?
   Herb Fackler called a couple days ago. Looks like I could teach at Lafayette a semester—maybe in '85. They've a house and all. I'd like for Han & me to spend a few months there. The change, and break from work, would be good for her.
   Dare I, should I go over to the gym today and trot around a little?
   I will go inside now. Want to make a selection of Smith poems this weekend, and maybe drop Simic a note, etc. I'll finish that fucking book, too, over the next few months. My Christmas present to myself.

Oct. 1, 1983

Nothing at the auction I wanted, so I was back early. Han & I had a good evening together. Kris was at a dance. Billy called, and we had a long talk, and all's well with him.
   Called the folks again yesterday. Their court hearing on Pop's accident a year ago was a kind of hell for them—they were being grilled as though they were the guilty parties. I hope they can get over it all without heart attacks.
   I actually played ball yesterday. The knee is bad, but I slid around. That improved my spirits.
   Beautiful little book, *Willows*, in the mail from Lucien. And John Stigall's crazy book, *In Avant Gardens*, that I blurbed without seeing!
   I think I'll begin this morning by writing out again all I have of my Rochester poem. It's still looking, as it just begins to round off, for its center.

Oct. 2, 1983

    Call from Bill Ewert yesterday. I was glad to talk with him again. Our friendship is on an even keel again, hoorah, but he just won't change, just about insists on doing a special of *Erika*, still wants to do the Christmas card. It will take me a year or more to untangle myself from that wild pace of his, but I'll do it. For now, he can have his head and run with these things, if he insists, but beyond *Erika* (and I might curtail this one still), the Christmas card, *Ensoulment*, *The Cabin*, and the last volume of *CR* (if it ever comes to be) nothing for a while. I still want Bill and me to be on a different footing. He sure doesn't want to hear what I'm trying to tell him.
    I'm out here early this Sunday morning, am trying to get out of bed once awake. A fucking plane has been circling overhead again for about an hour; otherwise, the world is peaceful.
    Proof of *Ram Time* arrived from Morris Gelfand on Long Island. Oh, what a broadside it's going to be. I wouldn't at all mind one such broadside every year or two.
    Han & I went shopping late last evening, stocked up on things.
    Stan's *Summer Celestial* arrived, and a little beauty from Lucien called *Willows*.... I'm reading the new poems Dave Smith sent, have focused on a few for the anthology. I wonder, though, if my lines so often lack clarity the way his do. All in all, I'm glad with the materials I'm gathering for the anthology, but I keep seeing sloppy writing, both in the prose and poetry. Maybe I miss such things when I read over & over my own poems, too. But maybe not, and I may be, I confess here self-consciously to whatever this journal is, a better writer all around than almost all of the poets I'll have in *2000*.
    The bright idea came to me this morning that I'd read my story "The Scar" to Scott Kretchmar's class on Wednesday. That should round off the session.
    I'll turn to the sesqui-centennial poem. <u>Very</u> hard to stay inside the poem, following it, and not drift away to thoughts of the occasion.
    All sorts of strange dreams last night that I can't quite remember fully enough even to mention here. <u>High</u> above water where I say to someone, a friend, I'll never be able to dive that dive, as he does.
    Much schoolwork this afternoon.
    I like the move to black ink.
    Slipcase for *XVII Machines* arrived from Ewert, and new Kinnell & Hall items. He pushes and pushes. I honestly want to get off that expressway. He's impossible to say <u>no</u> to—I've a feeling he'd be terribly hurt. But I'll find ways to get us back to a non-business thing. I just don't want items from him that make me feel in his debt. Yes, this will take some time to work out, but it will.

Oct. 3, 1983

    I've been back here for a couple hours just reading over miscellaneous poems, making notes to myself on what I could possibly eventually do with them, etc. Some beauties. Don't know how they'll fall into place. Well, I'd like to do *Erika*, then *CR*, then maybe a selected that does not include anything from those two books. Yes, a *Selected and New Poems*. It will be time, then, and the <u>new</u> poems could draw so many of the themes together: Long Island & Brockport & city poems—yes, in the general order of poems taken from preceding books. Yes, this is what to think about. The prefatory note wd. say I've not included poems from *Erika* or *CR*. Hmmm.... Yes, and this whole scheme wd. slow me down. Bill, relax. 1st, *Erika*, then *CR*, then the *Selected* that will satisfy your soul. Those 3 books wd. then have everything I'd like to keep in print & have read for a long time.
    I've decided not to have classes Thursday, and to go to an estate sale, the sale of a whole library.
    Chose the Smith poems for the anthology last night. A good selection, poems that will be good to read aloud and talk about in classes
    Homework tonight, & Kretchmar's class to think about for Wednesday. I'll read "The Scar" to kill some time, and "The Stadium," "Mantle," & "After the Wars." Maybe contrast the latter with Dickey's "The Bee."
    Will stop at post office, at school, and then try to play a little ball. Should call Doris Clune, too, for a look at books for library sale ahead of time. I can drop off a box of books for <u>her</u>, too. Yes, I'd be smart to get a look at the books ahead of time.

Oct. 5, 1983

It happened again this morning. I've worried for a few days about the Kretchmar class today—100 phys. ed. majors—put together a lesson/readings last last night, and then got up this morning and began a poem, one about Bobby Wine & Wicks & Yaz & me. Finished a third draft back here just now. Will read it to that class today. Am very happy about it. Some of those things on my mind as long as Mickey was on my mind before I wrote his poem. "Bobby Wine and the Championship Game" is longish, too. I love it. Now, I shouldn't have any trouble doing that class, making it the kind of class I want it to be.

Very much look forward to that auction tomorrow.

All three classes were excellent yesterday. And I was so tired that I got enough sleep.

I'll play ball in an hour, see Doris Clune to see some books, do that class, go out for supper with Han. Overcast today, rain in the air, foliage diminishing around me, but I've added another couple leaves to my collected poems.

Feel rich in other ways, too. The $1000 check came from Bert Babcock, and a $125 check came from *Ohio Review* for "Blackberry Light." Maybe I'll spend it all on books tomorrow!

Bruce will be around this weekend. His letter about Broomfield and Bill Ewert very interesting.

Oct. 6, 1983

Thursday, 5:45 a.m. Decided not to toss in bed, came back here—groped my way in the dark—with a thermos of tea. Han & Kris still sleeping. I'll go in at 7:15 or so and get ready to drive to the auction near Avon.

Stopped in my tracks by the stars, millions of them and so bright. Unimaginable distances, sizes. And here and now this Brockport place is so important to me. There's something in me of those vastnesses, those millions of points of light. I had the dream once, and wrote about it, of a skylight over my bed. I would like to lie in bed looking up at the starry sky. Aggregates of stars, clusters I'd never noticed before, and tonight so distinct, so clear.

I still feel the afterglow from my Bobby Wine poem. I'll write it out again this weekend. Bobby on television last night in the dugout before a playoff game. Phillies lost to L.A.

The class went well yesterday. "The Scar" was a hit!

Bob Fox called. Haven't seen him in a couple of years, I think. Will probably see him Saturday.

Played ball. Hurt a finger, and the knee felt <u>very</u> odd a few times, almost giving way, but otherwise I had fun.

Han putting in a dozen hours a day on Center work these days. Inexhaustible good spirits. Visits to the hospital. We both know we have to watch her, watch she isn't becoming over-tired. We're talking about Louisiana for a semester two falls from now—she'd get a leave of absence from her job. She needs that, will need it.

A week from today I'll read at Binghamton, will pick up Billy on the way back. All in all, I'll be glad when I'm back from Athens, Ohio, and will settle in for the long winter.

Saw Tony & Al yesterday, good friends both.

Oct. 7, 1983

Bruce will be here this morning. Depending on when he gets here, we'll sit back here in the cabin, then drive Kristen to Rochester to the bus station. And maybe we'll hit a book store or three.

The auction yesterday was at a place called Elm Tree Farm. The books were sold all in one lot--$1500—and there just wasn't enough there for me, and it would have meant days of lugging. A thirty-room farmhouse, packed in ways I'd never seen before. I came home only with $40 worth of picture frames, two Lincoln and Washington prints.... There's an auction today I don't know if I'll get to. I'll skip the Dept. meeting, surely. Will also miss basketball today, but the rest will be good for my knees.

Have another "sports" poem going, on that javelin throw of mine. The "Bobby Wine" poem waits for me like a cherished memory to enter again.

Display is down at the College. Virginia will drop off the books & things today, if I'm around later on. Will turn to javelin.

Later: after about an hour, I've just about finished the javelin poem, to be called "The Body-Bow." I'm going to like it. The gimmicky shape maybe makes me nervous (does it?) but I like it. And now I see—I see I'm running out of ink—I've done "After the Wars," "Bobby Wine ...," and "The Body-Bow" since this sport in literature class began, and probably because of it. It was about time. I'm glad. So many new poems. Bill, just keep writing them and don't worry now about making a book or books out of them.

What a good day to look forward to seeing a good friend. Bruce always makes me happy, never disappoints, will bring me news and gossip of the big city, of Michael Broomfield, of remaindered books and action at the Strand. I just selfishly hope he finds his life's work, that things work out with him & Lisa. Selfishly, because I don't want him moving to Houston, or losing his soul at some shit job, I wish he could start his own bookstore somewhere, Agte's Poetry Bookstore, and get along, build his own collection and mine, keep on writing at the same time, and be happy. I don't want to lose him. He's a friend, but also a second son.

Han, Kristen, Billy, Mom & Pop, Werner & Ed & Henry & their families, Ken & Marti & kids, Wolf & Pat & Kurt, Mirko & Bruce & Richard Ehrlich & Al & Tony, the men at basketball, other friends, Vince Clemente & Norb, Bill Ewert, Bob Phillips, Joyce & Ray, others, Walt & Archie & John G. & Dick Hugo & Jim Wright— all friends, all part of my world—Stafford & Warren & Stryk & Jerry Mazzaro & John Logan & Dave Smith & Martin Booth & Judy Minty & Pam Conrad & the poets who have been with me on the anthology & Peter & Greg & Rod & Peter Dzwonkoski, my world of friendships & love & circles.

Oct. 8, 1983

[3½ pp. drafts of "Bobby Wine and the Championship Game" in journal here. Here is the poem as it eventually appeared in *Confrontation* (November 1985):

Bobby Wine drove into the lane
into the middle of our 2-1-2 zone
for another of his jumpers.
This was 1957, and we were both seniors.
He'd wind up with thirty points, but losing by one,
the Smithtown Indians over the Northport Tigers at the buzzer
when our worst shooter heaved a desperation
two-handed-hook
into a lucky arc he'd remember his whole life.
Dave Wicks was his name, but my mother would always call him
"the-boy-who-made-the-last-basket." I picture him
idling at night somewhre in heavy traffic,
or reading an evening paper on the light-rocking subway,
when he looks up to see that shot again,
the miraculous way it dropped in over the right side of the rim
as though falling into the only place in the whole Milky Way
made for it. It may be that on his deathbed,
just before joining the shooting stars forever, he'll be there
in that neutral gym during the moments Vic Marin
passes him the ball on the right baseline,
and he spins, and the ball leaves his palms, amen....

I heard that Vic was killed in Viet Nam,
came home in a sealed aluminum casket.
Hubie Callahan sells insurance down in Georgia.
Lars Svanberg, our sweet gun, is in construction,

still in Smithtown. I haven't seen him in all this time, but met his
daughter once when I visited her college.
She introduced herself and asked me
could I remember Lars, her father.
She has his eyes. I couldn't blink mine dry....

But I began by thinking of Bobby Wine
who went up over me in the center of our zone
to swish that jumper, the next-to-last shot of the game.
There were maybe only five seconds left, and Bobby
should have been the hero. Instead,
he must have had a long busride home, Wicks' shot
dropping into every pothole in the winter road.
Maybe, too, of course, there was the melancholy joy
which losing deepened into his whole reason for being.
I've watched for him and his name: four or five seasons
of Triple-A baseball in Buffalo,
a decade at shortstop with the Phillies,
traded to Montreal when the league expanded.
He won a golden glove, or three, but I've wondered
if even occasional big-league homers could erase
Wicks' basket—this may sound ridiculous,
but if you'd played on Long Island then,
you'd know what I mean: Wicks redeemed
the fallen world for me. His shot made me
a better husband and father this far later,
made it easier for me to get along, as though the world
were scheming toward perfection in the end.
I played four years of college basketball. In soccer,
I was a first-team All-American at center-half.
There were some good wins, but they went by in a blur,
while, in the bright and deafening air
of that old gym, Wicks' transluminous shot still hangs
over the vivid orange rim....

There was another senior at the time,
playing east of us, over in Bridgehampton.
He's the one who made me remember Bobby Wine.
I never met him or played against him,
though now sometimes I say I did,
trying to keep my past smoky,
as a Yaqui wise man says we should.
Anyway, Yaz stood up from the Island's potato fields
to play for Boston for twenty-three years.
I was at Fenway his last game, in 1983, when he retired.
He played left field, went one-for-four,
a single uncorking another stadium-shaking ovation.
All this adulation, yes, but I most remember,
as he probably does, as you probably do
if you remember anything about him, his pop-up
to Nettles, Boston's final out against the Yankees
during the playoffs in '78. He could fill a gym with trophies,
and not be able to clean and jerk in ten tries
all the gold and silver that's come to him,

but his ring-finger must ache....

Bobby Wine has his. His boys Tug McGraw, Mike Schmidt
and the rest, won it for him. I still see him,
clipboard in hand, when the camera scans the Phillies' dugout.
I hope something, by now, deflects Wicks' shot for him,
that never once as he looks into his ring
does the awkward ass-backwards two-handed baseline hook
of-the-boy-who-made-the-last-basket appear,
or if it does, it misses.
I hope Carl Yastrzemski, whose name I still can't spell
without looking it up in the top ten
of any of three dozen columns in the record book,
I hope—what do I hope for someone who has everything
but one bauble? I hope for his happiness when he's alone,

as I am, here, now, wanting to connect with them,
with my old team and their children, with Bobby Wine
who floats in the air above my area of the zone
until he must come down, with Yaz who wore
Fenway's walls out, the lefty dream ballplayer
jogging around the field to wave goodby,
springing to a box seat to flip a boy his cap,
having the time now for an easy walk to Cooperstown.
You knew all along who my main character was,
as I did, why he unravelled so much line in the telling.
He was the one who threw the pass to Vic Marin
who threw the ball to Wicks.
There were only seconds left. After all these years,
I still believe that shot went in.]

    Well, that's about it. The poem makes me happy. Still several things to check on, from the spelling of Bridgehamton & Yaz's name to the Series & play-off pictures for him & Wine. But I've made the moves I want to make here. This draft, I tried to keep the line movements flowing. I do have a tendency to make them strain too much. I'm not sure why.
    Han leaving soon for Pop's in Nashville. I want to stay here & get schoolwork & letters done this afternoon & go to the Hamlin auction tonight. I don't feel just right, either, have been constipated for days.
    Dropped Kris off yesterday, had a few good hours with Bruce. He brought me some books from New York again.... Want to see Han off—want to write more here later....

    Later: Han left. I took a shower & shaved, watched 2 minutes of the Baltimore-Chicago game, am back here. I've no inclination at all for letters or schoolwork, will read my poems back here, read more of Warren in the book of interviews.
    How we make our lives to allow for writing. And how many of our poems are "tricks," though poems, are poems but not the ones we most want to write that are central to us. These thoughts in Warren right down the middle of things I've realized. I just wrote to Vince, describing "Bobby Wine" as one of the real poems I've always wanted to write, was meant to write. Yes. And much to dwell on regarding this idea and an eventual *Selected*. I'd like to put together a <u>thin</u> selected, those poems that came to me truly and almost all-of-a-piece. Yes. A prefatory note to this effect & mentioning Warren, and then a thin sheaf of poems from <u>all</u> the books, poems that are not "tricks."
    A rare letter from Li-Young yesterday, describing life now with his new son. I'm glad for him.... And a letter from poor May Sarton. <u>If</u> she is not desperate for money, she should stay home and write.... And a

letter from Vince with his Robert Cushman Murphy piece from the *Times*, a solid and moving piece of writing. Vince calls me his best friend. I love him and need him to be around.

Fellow called from J.N. Bartfield yesterday to offer me $500 for the set of Hardy books I bought for $1 in Kendall this summer! I have the box ready to ship off. When the check is in hand, I'll celebrate with Han. Also hoping to sell the 19 volumes, some in poor shape, of *British Theatre* to him.

Hundreds of sparrows in the weeds outside the cabin today. The flocks moving south. I'm glad about the millions of seeds on this property.

Billy called last night. He's fine. Julie visiting Cornell for the weekend.

Well, lazy as I am, I'll turn to something. Trouble is that when I'm doing what I want to do, working on a poem, say, or reading Warren, there are never <u>tangible</u> results. Bill, the thing is in the thing itself.

Just had a notion to come back here late tonight after the auction, too. Maybe I will. But I'm going to sit out at that place and enjoy, in the stream of life.

Oct. 9, 1983 (Sun.)

Just wrote to Richard McAdoo about the second batch of Archie's poems he sent me. I think I'll pass the whole package on to Tony, now. Tony will spend some quiet time with Archie alone again.

I spent $7.50 at the auction for what I thought was a whole box of *American Heritage*, but the bottom of the box had the *Time-Life* series on countries, including a bright copy of Elizabeth Bishop's *Brazil*, so I got a good book for my collection. I had only a dirty copy.

I skulked yesterday. No other way to describe it. Because I was trying to avoid Bob Fox & killing several hours with him, I didn't answer the phone, and hid out. I should have handled it differently, but I'm not sure how. I can't be bluntly honest, can I?, and tell him that we're not in touch and he's in Africa and we're not really friends and I hate disrupting whatever I'm doing just to sit around and shoot the shit and listen to his mile-a-minute complaints even once every couple of years. I didn't want to entertain him—he said, when I said maybe I'd stop over at Rubin's where he's staying, "or I could stop over at your house," and I got the message—and just wanted to have Saturday to myself. So there I was hiding in my study last night and letting the 3 or 4 calls ring on. And this pisses me off, and I won't do it again no matter what, because Han or Kris or Billy or a friend might be trying to reach me. I hate to lie, but could say I don't feel well. Or could say I'm just too busy. Or something. I don't know. It <u>is</u> a dilemma. I'd much rather be reading or writing or doing schoolwork or taking out the garbage than murdering time with Bob Fox.

Will go to an auction in LeRoy tomorrow morning, Columbus Day.

Will pick up Kristen this evening at the bus station in Rochester.

Will watch Buffalo-Miami while reading a few course journals, and doing some other schoolwork. I hope. I hope Fox leaves town!

My stomach hasn't been right. I have decaffeinated tea back here now, and will see if staying off caffeine will help. I didn't eat much yesterday, but the two pieces of pecan pie did not help.

Well, I saw Bobby Wine on television last night as the Phillies won the pennant. Maybe he'll win another ring. My poem will adjust to it. It's more about the speaker than about Wicks or Bobby or Yaz, in any case. I need to type it up again to take with me to Binghamton on Thursday.... Reminds me that I should call Sandi.

Well, on with the day. I'll read over "Bobby Wine" again and then probably go inside.

10/10/83

Long day. I got up 5:30 this morning and sat in bed thinking about a *Selected Poems* in terms of Warren's injunctions. Then went to an auction past LeRoy—many books, but nothing I wanted. Then played ball (carefully, with my knee). Had a sandwich, and have come back here for a couple hrs. before supper. Han & Kris are in Rochester at Eastman & Hochstein. I just typed up "Bobby Wine" again. I still love it, keep discovering things in it.

I've not had <u>any</u> caffeinated tea or coffee in two days. My stomach seems more settled.

Long day of classes tomorrow, and I'll have a ton of journals and papers, and have to think about the Binghamton trip & reading on Thursday. Maybe will begin by developing the Warren idea as I've been thinking about it.... Want to remember to take along my poem for John Gardner.... Well, Bill, stop dozing—get on with something.

10/12/83

Just planned the Binghamton reading. Now for a day of grading papers and journals. Will play ball, though—<u>easily</u>!

Good class on Wms. last night. I talked too much again. Will shut up, from the beginning, next time, and make <u>them</u> strain a little.

Raining. This cabin—what <u>luck</u> that I have it.

So much mail yesterday. Invitation to do the Southampton conference next summer. I will. Card from Turco saying I'll be invited to read in Albany in the spring at the SUNY conference. Must answer other mail. First, though, to get to Binghamton & get that over with, to pick up Billy & get back home. Will worry about one thing at a time, one trip at a time.

10/11/83 [dates confused in journal]

It's 5:30 a.m., and I just hunted for a notebook here inside but can't fine one. I slept a few hours, then woke up and for some reason began thinking of changing the essay I've done on myself for *2000*, and the selection of poems to include only those, in Robert Penn Warren's terms, I <u>had</u> to write: maybe only including "Witness," "Ram Time," "The Snow Hen," "Mother and Son," "The Berries." Could write briefly about Warren's terms, and keep the paragraphs I've written on "Ram Time." Well, I'll keep thinking about this. But that thinking got me to thinking in those terms about a *Selected Poems* again, one with a preface about what Warren is talking about, and then a <u>very</u> selected run of poems. Let me see what comes to mind right now:

[pages of a list of poems from several books, comments & notes to myself alongside these choices, including these:]

    —came quickly, or essential parts came quickly
    —when I narrowed down to poems that I knew in my heart to be central
      to me, I noticed, too, imagery clusters and other connections of voice and belief

I made a list quickly, and then hard-headedly cut it down

a *Collected* an act of ego, maybe, but I'd like to gather all my poems together
some day. The books were put together carefully and I'd like to see the person
I was as he attempted to see movements and patterns.

—obviously, something is going wrong here? I'm caring for & believing in
too many of my poems? Or, I'm wanting to show off too much?

—I <u>care</u> for many of the poems I've cut out—I may never do a *Collected Poems*
and these may be lost in their out-of-print books—but wanted to pick those I'd want
to have handy in case I found myself in a circle of poets in heaven and was asked to
read something, maybe to Walt or Archie. No doubt I've included too many poems
here, but wanted to err on the generous side to myself.

Decided not to excerpt from *Lord Dragonfly: Five Sequences* (1981) or to include
any of *The Chestnut Rain*, the 52-section poem I now have about finished after
beginning it in 1975. (74? check mss.)

10/11/83

I woke up about 5:30 again, after going to bed at ten, but didn't get right up because I wasn't nervous and was resting, breathing in and feeling easeful in the lungs. It's 7:15 now. So, that's the key: if I find myself making myself nervous, to get up.

Warren uses the metaphor "mainline" and "sidetrack" to describe the poems that are central or just tricks, diversions. At least the former ones are those that (as I think of them) came naturally, unforced, got into the flow of themselves. So, I did the list yesterday and kept paring it down. Maybe now, without glancing at a book, I'll just think of the poems, without being too smart about it, that I'd hate to lose. Never mind the chronology. And I was thinking of *Watermarks: [25 Selected Poems]* as a title. Well:

1. The Berries
2. Mother & Son
3. Bobby Wine
4. Witness
5. Mantle
6. Darkness
7. Simple Truths
8. The Tree
9. Ewige Melodien
10. The Children
11. The Trains
12. The Numinous
13. Tonging at St. James Harbor
14. Memorial Day
15. Carrie White
16. Off the Hamptons
17. The Way
18. Ram Time
19. The Cat
20. Cat and Star
21. Redwings
22. Off the Expressway
23. The Shore
24. Of Wildflower
25. A Story from Chekov
26. Fires
27. The Crane at Gibbs Pond
28. This Father of Mine
29. My Deer
30. Mermaid
31. Son Dream
32. A Voice
33. The Child
34. The Conspiracy
35. This Night
36. Poem Touching the Gestapo
37. The Pigeons
38. The River
39. The New American Poetry
40. Milkweed
41. The Bees
42. Yellowthroats
43. Brockport, N.Y.: Beginning …
44. The Stadium
45. Driving at Dawn
46. Off the Hamptons
47. Dog Sacrifice …
48. The Swan
49. The Return
50. The River
51. The Trench
52. The Swastika Poems

Not counting *CR* or *Lord Dragonfly*. Let me look at my list from yesterday, now, after writing down 26 above, and see what I'd want in the thin book.... Well, maybe that wasn't very helpful, but maybe I see there wd. be about 50 poems. Maybe I'm silly thinking of naming the number in the title, though a number shows how arbitrary and chancey such a selection is. How does *Watermarks: Selected Poems* sound? I hate the *Selected and New* label I see so often: even the <u>new</u> ones are "selected." What can I still knock out of the list above? Is there any other poem that I'd have to have with me at a reading as an example, for me, of one that got down into heartwood, one whose watermarks are mine? Maybe little by little I'll xerox the poems above & begin to look at such a book to see how it holds together, and I'll work on a brief preface on the "mainline" and "sidetrack" idea, together, & on the words in Thoreau (& warning about <u>personal</u>, not autobiographical in any crucial way).... Well, a long day today. A long <u>several</u> days, with Binghamton and all.

10/16/83

Sunday, almost nine in the morning. Billy didn't come home last night. I'm sure he just stayed over at Brian's, and didn't want to wake us up by calling.

Perfect autumn day today, and I'll put away lawn chairs later, clean the gutters, put away the grill, etc. Thought maybe I'd try to follow the bear-dream I had into a poem this morning. Will see what happens. I described the dream to both Bruce and Tony yesterday, and maybe shouldn't have, but I know enough by now so that I left its meanings alone.

Trip to Binghamton and Ithaca and home went okay. I gave one of my better readings. The Kesslers were sweet, and Milton is a memorable man. He told me the whole story of his recent visit to John Logan in Buffalo, the buying of John's new suit, etc.... Saw Gary Eddy, Lisa Piccione, Janet Bixler. Got caught in a rainstorm. So, one trip down and two to go. Want to stop in at the travel bureau tomorrow.

Han and I went to the movies last night for the first time in a long time. Saw *Never Say Never Again*. It wasn't very good, but the popcorn was.

10/17/83

It's six in the morning, dark around the cabin. I'd fallen back asleep this morning, and was just fielding a baseball on my front lawn in a dream and getting ready to throw it across the street where there was a ballgame going on, when the phone rang and woke me up. It was Elizabeth, an old German woman, calling to tell Han that Eddie Marks had died—Han saw old Eddie in the hospital yesterday. Han's job keeps her close, too close, to hospital and funeral parlor in this town.

I have my old belly-ache again, am otherwise fine. Hope to do one or two things back here over the next few hours—maybe draft that preface for a selected, a severely selected selected that I've been thinking about.

Typed Martin Booth a letter back here last night.

Have much schoolwork today, too, and *Paterson 1* to read, as we begin that thing.

This little place I have back here—it's always new to me.

My marble polar bear is sniffing the air, as I am.

10/18/83

It's seven in the morning. I've come back here if only for an hour before getting ready to drop Billy off at the bus and then heading up to school for my long Tuesday. I was thinking that I don't want my cabin life distinct/split from my teaching life and family lives (maybe I <u>do</u>, but I'll save <u>that</u> can of worms for another change in my life maybe), but that I <u>like</u> it back here. I flipped the heat-switch on and in five minutes the place was warm, but in very cold weather I won't get back here for just an hour. Then, I should get up and sit in my easy chair. Well, one day at a time, Bill.... I went to bed at 10:30, slept fairly well. My stomach did not bother me much. I drank many cups of water over the evening.... Billy & I went to the diner for dinner, and had a good talk.

Read *Paterson 1* yesterday. It is what it is and won't be more than that, and what it is is collage, and what it may turn out to be is the best of the five books, such as it is. Interesting reading, yes, and places where a fire is lit, but it is what Wms. was, and this is what our writing should be, <u>has</u> to be if it's going to be any good, if it's going to have a chance to be good and useful. But all sorts of misguided things are honest and sincere. He was a dynamo of a human being, whirlwind, vortex. He was also fucked up, and the whole thrown-together thing (however easy it is to find patterns and movements in it, our minds being what they are) does not satisfy, at least does not satisfy <u>me</u>, as a city does not satisfy me, <u>feed</u> me, as does a meadow. Maybe it's my loss. Maybe not. He has taken over, though, has hold of the present air-waves. When I think of just one thing, that battle over at the Poetry Society of America over the "Williams-faction" as it was called, I know what's happened. In any case, I surely have to stick with myself, be my own voice, romantic as it may be.... This paragraph does nothing, goes nowhere, has nothing of the swirl I feel inside me regarding Wms. He's the brat on the block turning the whole block to turmoil. I like my Wms. sequence.

First gray-blue light over the ash trees.

I read the "Mole" and "The Confessions" parts of the Wms. sequence at Binghamton. They sure have the cadences I want in them. Maybe over Christmas vacation, when the course is over with, I'll read Reginald Gibbons' letter once more, then see my sequence again, and work on it or call it finished, and let that be that.

During the time I wrote that last short paragraph, the sky lightened noticeably. The sun, great force, rising over the whole east. And each one of us down below, from Brockport to Attica to NYC to Ridge to the Hamptons to Concord, Mass., & Concord, NH, to Rutherford has his or her anxieties to carry. I have three classes, and other details to attend to. A sense of darkness just dissipating and lifting away around me.

I thought maybe of typing Li-Young a letter about God this morning. I'll maybe get to it this weekend.

Bus stations & airports & highways & stores & train stations crowded right now, the cities' noise levels and billion intricate motions picking up. It's a wonder there is still this Brockport acre. Maybe it will wear away by ten years, or twenty, and I'll enter the city.

10/19/83

Realize this morning that all in all I'm doing much better teaching/writing/sleeping this semester than other semesters. For the first time in a couple of weeks last night, when I woke up at 3 or 4 as I almost always do, my mind was filled with language-shit, details of school. I watched a half-hour of television, and then slept again. I went to bed early, am back here in the cabin early. And I seem nicely to be floating past meetings & book orders & APS details, etc. And I have many new poems, and long-range plans to gather them.

I did a good job for the 3-hr. Wms. class last night. Some of the students completely lost, I'm afraid, but still their journal assignment should enable them to do what they can.

I've a hunk of banana bread, a banana, and a thermos of tea back here with me. And Teale's *Autumn Across America*. And the thought that I should pound out some kind of answer to all Li-Young's questions about God.

It was almost a year ago, already, that I was at Yaddo.

Billy is back at Cornell. For just a few hours, I felt that old sadness about his leaving.... I don't seem to have much time at all with Kristen, and this is her senior year. She's so busy. But I'll have to spend more time with her, chat for a half-hour at bedtime, etc. With Billy, we kept him company through a whole basketball season; with Kristen, her music is somehow more private. Han has a lot more time with her than I do. They couldn't love one another any more than they do, nor I them. I'm lucky, lucky, to be in this place at this time with them.

[evening] So here I am at another of these Writers Forum readings. I'm listening to Alison Lurie read a fairy tale—"the princess searched through all the rooms of the castle"—in a hot room and trying to make herself heard above the rushing air of the heating system. I'm squeezed in next to Greg Fitz Gerald on a couch. Saw Tony, who asked me, as he seems to want to do, "What's the matter with you?" This time I said it must be something inside him that always has him ask me this at one of these things. I hate the question. I seemed tense, he said.... The story is over. Applause.... Maybe I'll follow a chapter in *Only Children*.... Mercifully short reading.... Got three books signed. She didn't even strain toward "best wishes."... Discussion going on now. This will be one of those evenings—I'm committed to a drink with Greg later—that offends my inner-economy. And it's a shame, because I've been so happy today, fulfilled, at ease. The brief flare-up of an argument just now, too, with Frank Judge. Bill: step back & listen: the quick pointed questions of what is next, is next, now, for me, and his hope I'll say "nothing, I'm dried up." Then his reaction to my decision to put myself in the anthology. So it goes. But my ease & steadiness & centeredness must be a very thin veneer if a silly evening like this can "strip" me to anger and disorientation. This class in craft is now talking about the place of women in the 20th century. It's always the same when we hear novelists here. They read a chapter, and if one hasn't read the book, it's generally out of context and a mess; if one has read the novel, the reading, unlike the reading in most cases of poetry, is a waste. And always the discussion not of the music or the craft, but of ideas, didacticism, the world situation, as though a novelist were an expert. Well, this has now all descended into nervous chatter for me, the comfort, again & again, of moving the pen.... Did write Li-Young a good letter this morning, and typed "The Body-Bow" and "The Corral"—the letter turned into a good one, I think. Well, enough for now. I'll maybe just get the hell out of here and go home. Greg has Frank Judge. Frank, really, since he showed his colors in Rome, always has been an asshole, and that's the truth of it, within the colors of my world....

10/21/83

Back lawn white with the first heavy frost. Leaves clicking down steadily around me.

Alison Lurie reading was generally painful—I'll probably tear out & paste in here my notebook scribblings from that night—and I was knocked out of my feelings of well-being by it. And last night, waking up at 2 or so, I had all sorts of details on my mind, felt as though I was slipping back into the pre-sabbatical funk. But I watched a half-hour of television, fell asleep again, and feel soul-strong and centered again this morning.

Milton Kessler sent my pen back from Binghamton. So this one has been through the mails. It's wearing down to its copper sheath, as I am, I hope.

Drove to U. of R. yesterday afternoon for Hollis Summers' reading. I was uncomfortable, the only one in jeans again, but was glad to hear him and see him. He looks well. No one sounds like him. I was thinking as he was reading of where those poems, that voice, had their sources. He says he meant well as he wrote. The wry peeks, the edges, the wit, the margins of praise. I wonder how it was with him as a boy in Eminence, Kentucky.

It's Friday, and I'll head over to play ball a couple hours from now. I have my desk filled with things to do, and will do them, and will stay busy all weekend with anthology and other stuff.

A gratifying composition class yesterday. The kids actually enjoy class, say it's their favorite. I feel guilty that I don't drill them on basics or something, but we *do* have honest talks about their writing, their lives, and they appreciate this. My classes are going very well, actually.

Went over to Han's Oktoberfest at the Center last evening for a couple hours.

Saw Peter Dzwonkoski in Rochester, too, and he was good company at the reading…. Hollis inscribed *Occupant Please Forward* and the *Poetry in Crystal* for me…. I leave for LI next week already. I'll probably take this journal along. I'll have some quiet evenings with the folks for schoolwork & planning my reading, I hope. Want to see Wern & Barb, too.

Lyric Year '84 came. I may have one or two little things to try to lodge in the next one, too…. Had a dream about Kinnell again last night. I was to his right at a big seminar table (I wrote "seminary" & maybe it was) surrounded by workshop students. He asked me a question about, ferchrissakes, a poetry prize, an Elizabeth Bishop PSA prize I'd been nominated for, and he asked me to tell the group about that all. He pushed his chair away to leave, and left the group to me. That's all I remember.

Dubie called…. Dave Smith essay in…. The book will whirl together now, I think, even if I end up with just 25 poets….

A great deal of creative energy flowing forth into classes. I hear myself saying things I've never said before, and they come up from the center, I'm glad to say. I have to let them go, let lthem fly, too, and not wish I had them on tape. They will lodge in the cells of the students in their own ways and be preserved, or they won't.

So, a shining and cold day, and I'm okay again, after the silly lapses of a couple days. I got so angry at Piccione for, again, saying (even before saying hello), "what's the matter with you?"

I want to dance life, yes, but I also have to be careful of my good moods, when I'm oozing friendship—it almost cost me another long evening of drinking with Greg & Rod yesterday, but it didn't come about, praise my lucky spirits.

Had a dream the other evening about my old Smithtown High School gym again. I was returning for a visit, and could hardly find it—there had been so much building around it, so many renovations.

The page almost completed again, I scan my mind for another line or two.

Began a poem on Pete Rose—don't know if it will ever be.

Haven't begun my thermos of tea yet.

Now it is time….

10/23/83

It's raining. I'm back here for a little while this Sunday morning just to write this down. I have coffee in my Viet Nam cup.

The news a couple hours ago was that 76 American marines had been killed when a truck crashed into their quarters near the Beirut airport and exploded. Again, a terrible tragedy, and my mind becoming numb to it & to the whole spectrum of the world's possible destruction. About 20 French soldiers were killed a few minutes later in the same way. I want to huddle close inside myself, stay in my bathrobe inside, sip warm drinks, turn up the heat in the house. I want to say <u>something</u> in the preface to the poetry anthology about this. I want to leave the earth before what almost seems like inevitable nuclear destruction. Those were suicide missions in Lebanon, men believing in the right & religiousness of what they were doing. I suppose a Zennist's deepest being wd. not be touched—there would be an acceptance of these dust swirls—76 or 6,000,000—on the earth's surface. I find myself calling myself jaded and berating myself for not feeling more. I'm emotionally worn out—media overkill of myriad tragedies—or something in me smiles & thinks of the Milky Way & the million other galaxies where there are planets in the dream of peace. The world is a fucking horror, or an illusion, or something else of vast and unimaginable and miraculous balances, shot through with mystery, bloody and golden, and where is the Lord?

My anxieties, my silliness, again smashed into perspective. School worries? Nervousness about upcoming trips? I'm an ass unless I learn to dance calm within. What agony around this country today, the hundreds of grieving families.

Han & I went to the auction barn last night. She bought a little slag-glass lamp, an oldie, for $80. I like it. I feel like covering up from chin to toe with a blanket and looking into the lamp-glow.

10/24/83

Just drafted the beginning of what might be my talk at the Whitman Birthplace.

Death toll up to about 200 Americans & French in Beirut yesterday.

I have much schoolwork, and other anxieties from the trip, to Sarton's visit, to my poor digestive system, but still feel strong & balanced. Maybe they're <u>not</u> even anxieties, but just things that enter my mind once in a while.... Will play basketball today, & then get to schoolwork for my long day tomorrow.

We called Billy last night. He's fine. He looks forward, as we do, to Thanksgiving in Nashville & Hamburg with our relatives.

More & more this journal becomes a natural part of my life.

I'm reading *The Shroud of Turin*, thanks to Bob Siegel.

10/26/83

The death count of Americans is now 216, and rising....

I'm getting ready for clases and my trip tomorrow. I look forward to seeing the folks, having Mom fuss over me, going to bed when they do at 8:30 or 9:00 and planning my reading & doing schoolwork—will have a set of compositions to grade.... I've already drafted the beginning of my reading.

We'll have a dinner for May Sarton next Wednesday. I just invited the Dzwonkoskis. Should be fun. I hope May will be in a good mood. <u>Surely</u>, something is going to go wrong. In fact, I wonder if she's a vegetarian. I'll have to ask Ewert. I sure don't want to make the videotape, but suppose I have to.

Billy sent a nice poem called "The Suitcase." That golden boy.

Han & I had a quiet dinner again at the Diner. Kris was working in Card & Candle.

Jack Matthews' new *Sassafras* arrived.

I'm nervous thinking about the next few weeks, but a good run at basketball today will help.... I'll take this journal to the Island. As I write, now, I hear the sound of the pen on the paper. It is like the sound of breath. It is something I could get inside as a kind of meditation, the sounds of the words as they are formed in the ink-thread pressed on the page.

[evening] [the journal has a circle in the middle of this paragraph that is filled with layers of words unto unintelligibility] So, I'm here again at a reading, but this time I'm relaxed, waiting to see & hear Gregory read a story. More comfortable here in the Green Room.... Parked across the way, and walked over here in autumn cold & blowing leaves & drizzle, thinking: what if I were where it is happening at the center, at a university, a

real one, and not this dark & windblown and scattered place. Then thought of maybe meeting a class in that bldg. at Johns Hopkins that I remember, or in that sterile seminar room at University of Wisconsin-Milwaukee, or maybe I could be in Ellis Hall in Athens, or in a classroom in New Haven. That's not it, no. It's always where you place yourself, in time. To make life here is the thing. And it's true that I'm no further away here than anywhere else. I could be at the New School in one of those rooms, or somewhere on that flat & windblown Stony Brook campus, or, or, or. That's not it. Bill, you are here, so be here. Okay, Enough. A tea time now, & then Greg's story, during which I won't write here. It means so much to him, and I want to listen.... Greg read the story, "October Blood," and I liked it, though it is overwrought, as he is now saying. He has written, apparently, a long explication & is reading it now. He's entertaining. His ideas are often simplistic, and he protests things too much. But I like the old boy, I sure do.... In 11 years Frank Judge hasn't gotten a bit smarter. He has just asked a disconnected and dumb-ass question, and for the purpose of showing off. He is still the chap in Rome that they yanked out of a class because he wasn't doing what he was supposed to do. And he keeps burying himself, Gregory trying to be gracious. One of the reasons I have stopped writing criticism, I think, is that I've come to intuit the complexity of these issues, and become dizzy trying to say everything at once. I'm keeping this chatter going now just to see what this circle will look like when completely surrounded, as it soon will be, by writing.... There's one beautiful blond woman over to my left. I've seen her before, her cane leaning against her chair. She never says a word, and, of course, seems smarter and smarter this way. I'll skip a line again to get to fill in backward writing space.... This is a nice quiet room, and would be better for the Sarton reading. Let me try, now, given this black, to start in blocking another plane out below the circle. Why am I doing lthis? Stop it. I am listening with one ear, but what that ear is hearing is elementary and banal, the stuff I worked my way through many years ago.... Greg has just said that Anne Sexton ("before she died") gave him some ideas for the story. Enough. My hand is tired, the circle buried.

More and more the feeling that when I die I'll be glad to have lived, to have lived with and through....

The blond woman just said something sweet to Gregory, thanked him for doing all that reading. "I have difficulty in retaining," she said, "and I want to thank you for doing all that reading." Hmmm....?....

10/26/83

[Handwritten journal entry, partially illegible, with text circling around a dense scribbled circular shape in the middle of the page. Approximate transcription follows:]

So, I'm here again at a reading, but this time I'm relaxed, waiting to see & hear Gregory read a story. More comfortable here in the green room... Parked across the way, and walked over here in autumn cold & blowing leaves & drizzle, thinking: what if I were where it is happening, at the center, at a university, a real one, and not this dark & windblown and scattered place. Then thought of maybe meeting a class in that bldg. at Johns Hopkins that I remember, or in that sterile seminar room at University of Wisconsin–Milwaukee, or maybe I could be in Ellis Hall in Athens, or in a classroom in New Haven. That's not it, no. It's always where you place yourself, in time. To make life here is the thing. And it's true that I'm no further away here than anywhere else. I could be at the New School in one of those rooms, or somewhere on that flat & windblown Stony Brook campus, or, or, or. That's not it, Bill, you are here, so be here. Okay. Enough. A tea time now, & then Greg's story, during which I won't write here. It means so much to him, and I want to listen.... Greg read the story, "October Blood," and I liked it, thought it is overwrought, as he is now saying. He has written, apparently, a long explication & is reading it now. He's entertaining. His ideas are often simplistic, and he protests things too much. But I like the old boy, I sure do.... In 11 years Frank Judge hasn't gotten a bit smarter. He has just asked a disconnected and dumb-ass question, and for the purpose of showing off. He is still the hope in Reine that they yanked out of a class because he was... I don't what he was supposed to do. And he becomes garrulous. One of the reasons I have stopped writing criticism, I think, is complexities of the sorts— to say everything at once just to see what this is surrounded, as it can be...

[illegible text around circular scribble]

A blond woman over to my left against her chair. She never seems smarter and smarter, and would be better for the Barton readers in a quiet room. Why am I doing this. Stop it. I am started on blocking another plane out below the circle. Listening with one ear, but what that ear is hearing is elementary and banal, the stuff I worked my way through many years ago.... Greg has just said that Anne Lester ("before she died") gave him some ideas for the story. Enough, my hand is tired, the circle buried. More and more the feeling that when I die I'll be glad to have lived, to have lived with and through....

The blond woman just said something sweet to Gregory, thanked him for doing all that reading. "I have difficulty in retaining," she said, "and I want to thank you for doing all that reading." Hmmm....?....

10/29/83

It's about three in the afternoon. I'm at Werner's, have had good days, have even slept well. The folks will pick me up at six. The reading at Walt's house is tomorrow.

Just fifteen minutes ago, I asked Debbie & Werner if they wanted to hear my Bobby Wine poem; both said yes, & Debbie listened. Werner fell asleep when I was a couple dozen lines into it. I read it through. I was actually bothered, but it was stupid of me to care. He's sleeping/snoring beside me right now. The great repeated lesson all the time: I was reading something important to me, and my brother went to sleep. I'd even mentioned the poem to him earlier. Well, frankly, it was insensitive of him, and I'd never do the same for him, try to be interested in his interests. But, so it goes. I write poetry. It puts my brother to sleep immediately, and it would the same if I were Yeats or Walt.

Delicious dinner here last night of striped bass and bluefish that Werner had caught.... We were at the ocean surf-casting for a half-hour this morning, but the surf was too rough. I had only knee-high boots, and the water came in over them twice, so my shoes got wet.... Then we went to many garage sales—I didn't get anything.... At a Salvation Army store in Riverhead yesterday I bought a set of bookends for three bucks—metal, Art Deco style, and I think I'll like them. Will fill them with something heavy....

Just spoke with Debbie for a half-hour, Werner still snoring away to our right. He's *very* lazy, will never fix himself a cup of coffee, will not stir to get himself a pillow but sends people scurrying all over. He's out of shape, smokes all the time, worries about money all the time. I love the lug, but he's just a sourpuss, has lost all joy, abuses his body, wants to retire but has nothing else to do when he does. Spending very much time with him wd. be depressing. At least this is how I feel on this visit....

A pro basketball game is on the tube soon. I've looked forward to it. Ralph Sampson's first pro game, I think.... Tonight I'll go to bed early at the folks', and spend a couple hours preparing my reading. Walt's house will be bursting, I think.

The folks look good. Mom is *so* happy to be fixing food & making plans. I visited the new shop in Rocky Point where Pop will work. Best thing for him. He is treated like the old master, which he is.

Got the set of compositions graded last evening.

I'll try returning Han's call.... No answer again. Will try in an hour or two.

I'd like to read truly tomorrow, draw the group together, have the house itself help me. So many friends will be there. To stay calm, to look into their eyes in friendship but to be myself & read for the sake of the poems.

Well, nothing much new. I'm glad the folks will be picking me up in a few hours. I left my toiletries at their place, anyway, and will shave this evening, etc.... Bill, remember to mention Stone House Press when reading "Ram Time." Remember, in fact, to remember everything you want to remember....

10/30/83

Well, it's evening, and I'm relaxing with the folks. It was a good afternoon at Walt's place. I had no "quiet time" there to breathe in Walt's spirit, but there were people and people, and this is part of it, too. Pam Conrad & Patti Renna-Tana, Vince & Norb & Morris Gelfand, Shirley Newberger & Carol Goldsmith, my folks & the Ehrlichs & Richard, Max Wheat, Raymond Patterson, Bets Vondrosek, Helen Andrews, Fred Byrnes, Dan Giancola, Mr. & Mrs. Skolsky, Grace Nyssen, Sharon Stein, Bruce & Lisa, and so many others. People in the halls & downstairs rooms & on the stairways as I read. I did a good job, I think, read for a little over an hour. *Many* copies of *Light* and *Lord Dragonfly* sold. Warm introductions. Perfect weather. A good day. Tomorrow, home again.

10/31/83

An airport entry again. Between yawns. The folks just dropped me off here in Islip. A shining & cool day. I doubt that all will be on time and I'll be able to get to the gym today, but that's okay. I slept well again. I'm ready for the two flights home. It's going to be a mad week, Sarton and all, and then a mad week away next week. Once that's all over, I'll settle in for the Brockport winter, yes, yes. But I'll want to take things in my stride, too, the next two weeks, and not lose the life in them.

The pasteurized music coming over the speakers is a little, already, like Christmas music, bells & chimes.

So, Walt's little birthplace was bursting. It was a good day. Probably, once every few years, I'll read there. If I lived near that place, I *would* be active in the activities, and in trying to get national money for a library-auditorium, which is what they need.

Mom & Werner had an argument again—over talk about the court case again—and they'll have to work it out. Werner is a downer, a sourpuss about the whole world. Mom needs constant encouragement about wht a wonderful mother she's been, how smart she is, etc. They never enjoy one another's company. Werner never has a sunny day. Maybe his only real happiness is a couple hours of surf-fishing now and then.

Well, then, my next entry will be from *home*.

Home. Even got here in time to play ball. Saw Han, will see Kristen soon. *Much* work to do to get ready for school.

Had jotted this little poem down on a sheet of paper:

At Walt's Place

Here where it began again,
here again where it began.

A beautiful autumn day. Home for a week. And, this weekend, I should even have some time to type "Bobby Wine" and get some things together.

11/3/83

I head over to the Edwards studio in about a half-hour for the Sarton tape. I sure don't look forward to it, and will be glad when it's over with. I have a bunch of slips of paper with questions. If I can stay calm and listen, I'll be all right. Mary Elsie will be with us.

Dinner went well. May was in a good mood. The Dzwonkoskis were here, & Sandi Piccione, & Peter & Mary Elsie. Han worked hard on the dinner. The Gold Room was filled for the reading. I sense here & there in May a certain lack of graciousness—gulping her food before others begin, not saying any small thanks to Peter or Brockport or the audience at the reading—but she has hard miles on her, and I like the scolding way, too, she handles people. She signed books for dozens of people, was kind enough to do that.... Most of her poems exist, I'm afraid, as though Eliot or Pound or Wms or Stevens or Yeats or, for that matter, John Donne never lived, and are hard to focus on. Critics have beaten the hell out of her, from what I've seen. All she has is readers, many thousands of them.

So, the tape & then a class & then to stop at the travel bureau & then to get the hell home to unwind. Must call Bill Elkins, too, & maybe Mike Waters about next week.

Had a few drinks last night with Rod & Greg & their Brockport Community Players bunch. I joined up, for five bucks, just to be a sport.

Newsday called for me to review Louis Simpson's two new books. Yes, I want to. That and the anthology will be my two main projects once I'm back. My own poems seem to be on a back burner, now; but *Erika* is, I suppose (!) in the works, so I have that feeling of forward motion, anyway.

Spoke with Bill Ewert. Again & again from him I feel mainly a businessman's detachment. But I am going to bear with him through *Ensoulment*, the Christmas card, the blank books, *The Cabin*, whatever, but then things are going to clear. I'll find out about *CR*, once & for all, too.

Maybe some snow tomorrow. I do, after this next trip, want to be snowed in here, to get on with teaching & writing & to stay home. But the money will be welcome.

Well, shit, here I go again.

Later: the tape couldn't have gone better. I think I'll take pleasure in it for years, will see it in class once in a while. It's balanced, and packed, 45 minutes of worthwhile talk. It was good to work with Mary Elsie.... Got several books inscribed, too, including a copy of *Recovery* for Bruce for Christmas—a perfect gift.... I'm tired, and maybe should have said goodbye, but said I'd see her this afternoon when she leads a discussion. She was very warm & gracious on the tape. She is quite a woman, has given great energy to this Brockport visit.

Got my plane tickets. Left a message with Bill Elkins about my arrival there.

Essays not coming in for anthology. After my trip, after my trip everything.

Later: I'm in B-8 of Cooper, and May is holding forth in front of a horseshoe of about 40 students. I'm comfortable, will relax here and listen for an hour, and will then go home. Oh, she's an egotist, yes, but does it in the most grandmotherly (gulp) and sweet way, so is not exactly offensive.... Says she is disciplined about the journal as "life on the pulse," does not go back the next day & change things. *A World of Light* & *Plant Dreaming Deep* are memoirs, of course, as opposed to the journals. The memoirs are much harder, she says.... "I was already beginning to be famous ..." "Now it's a thousand, plus expenses." Hmmm. "In time, like air, is essence stated." "The trouble with most journalists is that they are so dishonest." (Anais Nin, e.g.).... "You have to be at white heat emotionally and intellectually to write a good poem." Something about her comments that seems so watered down. She says the most obvious things, but says them dramatically.

I've noticed that she has not once quoted another poet, e.g.... So, I feel several ways about her, don't really care, of course, for her poems. "Climbed the Acropolis on my 50th birthday."... "I think a lot in bed before I get up."... "I do the journal before anything else."... "Valery: poetry is something between song and speech."... "Ask more of yourselves."... "Why should it be given you for nothing?"... "Prayer before work." "The advantage I have over you is that I never went to college. But I have 11 honorary doctorates."... "Angry free verse which I'm very tired of."... Mind sharp, though, catching herself in a contradiction, or pinning down a memory.... "I worked much harder than most people."...

11/4/83

First snow on the ground. It's mid-morning, and I meant to sleep until noon, but am back here in the cabin. Just saw a new look on the boulder's face, and wrote an odd entry in my boulder journal.

Played cards last night at Squeak's, and won a buck. All that dough flowing around, and I won a buck.

I feel lazy & relaxed. Want to do a few things today to get ready for the trip. Can't play ball—hurt my knee Wednesday, but not badly. Would like at least to type up "Bobby Wine," but maybe won't even do that, since I won't get a chance to xerox it for a week or so anyway.

Most of the leaves down around me, but there seems to be more wood than I've remembered; hundreds of ash saplings have added a fraction of an inch to their girths, and this makes a difference.

Both cars away, one with the sacks of birdfood in its trunk, so I'll have to wait to fill my new feeder, my birthday present.

I find myself feeling glad about this upcoming winter. I want to stay warm in the cave of my study. Once the anthology is done, I'll be able to get to my poems, maybe put another book together, maybe keep poring over *CR*.... No word of any kind in 6-8 weeks from Vanguard again.

So, May Sarton has flown home this morning. She was warm & generous again yesterday afternoon. I'm very glad about the videotape. I was lucky. I also stayed calm, my "serenity" self-training paying off. May was just right, of course, giving answers of just the right length, and dear Mary Elsie to my right. And Peter embracing us when we were done. Yes, it was a good one. I look forward to seeing it....

Well, then, here I am again, just sort of marking time. I'm happy. Maybe Han & Kris & I will go out to dinner this evening. I'm comfortable at the diner. Maybe there will be a basketball game on television. Maybe there will be something in the mail for my collection. Maybe I'll walk uptown for a haircut. Yes.

Should I keep this journal inside or back here? Should I take it on my trip with me?

Between sentences, I've thought of Peter Dzwonkoski, of my whole collection in a special room at U. of Rochester, the joy of this, as I grow old.

Got May to inscribe a copy of *Recovery* for Bruce. Will give it to him for Christmas.... PLO under Syrian fire in Lebanon. I listened when May talked of how she has been of help, as she has. I don't know if I deserve to be as happy as I am now. So much luck. I look over at Walt & he knows, in the darkness of his eyes.

11/5/83

I'm back here in the cold and raining dark for just an hour before going back inside to keep Han company. It's a Saturday night, and we'll just snuggle, watch some television. I have tomorrow to pack. Things are about set for my week-long trip.

Along This Water arrived yesterday. There are some things that could be improved, but I like it. That illustration by Alice Wand of the man in the cabin, the night sky streaming away beyond him, the candle flame raying out—I like it very much. It reminds me especially of the evenings I was writing the "Lord Dragonfly" sequence back here.... I've sent copies to Stryk, Warren, Stafford, Li-Young, Bruce, Vince, Norb, Pam Conrad, Patti Rena-Tana, others. Handy gifts at this time of year. I like the blues Allen chose for cover & end-papers.... So, another of these small-press things. Still, I want to wind things down with Ewert.

$100.03 in royalties from Vanguard for 6 months. 165 copies of *Lord Dragonfly* sold in two years. That's a joke. Half those sold in Brockport, the other half at readings I've given. Well, let Vanguard do *Erika*, and then I'll want to try elsewhere with *CR*. I'm going to keep next summer clear, very clear except for the Southampton weeks, to ready *CR* & maybe put another book together and maybe even a selected together....

Here I am again thinking of such things, while the news is that at least 60 Israeli soldiers were killed yesterday morning in another of those sapper attacks....

Kristen is baby-sitting. I'm marking time until back from the trip. I'll have to get busy on the Simpson review. Then the anthology, maybe even getting on the phone to find some things out. Hell, I'll give myself January, too, to finish the thing. The Simpson, though, I'll have to finish earlier, probably over the Thanksgiving break. Maybe will begin with the war poems, & get to that poem about peacetime shopping, a new poem in both books.

11/7/83

It's twenty minutes before flight time. I'm in the Rochester airport, scribbling here again, on the run again. Just switched, though, my return flight to next Saturday evening instead of Sunday. A three-hour lay-over in Pittsburgh on the way back, but that's okay. I'll be sappy & relaxed & glad to flop out in a spot next to the departure gate and anticipate getting home. And I'd just be nervous spending that extra night in Athens—no doubt Stan & Dave will be gone. Anyway, today I'll see Michael & Robin in Salisbury. Bill, live within the present of this trip, each place as you're there.... Have to write a 10-minute piece for the convocation in Athens. Had something in my mind last night about MacLeish, the Whitman House and Walt, finishing with "The Children." Will try to put it together maybe this morning on the plane or in Baltimore before the Salisbury connection.... Bill Beavers will be at Mike's for dinner.... The disorienting airport hum and smell in here. That "Between Flights" poem of mine is a good one. I'm glad, too, that I have this journal along. The hard thing in a journal is not to lie, Sarton says. I know I erect defenses here, and this mainly because I'm not sure of an audience & don't have the courage or genius to write only for myself. But there can still be a down-the-center honesty amid the dissembling.

Later: I'm relaxing in a Baltimore-Washington airport snack bar. Had some French toast—a good choice with my uncertain stomach—and have a cup of tea beside me. Writing the word "tea" made me think of my cabin, this journal back there. I might spend quite a bit of time back there this winter after all, from the feel of my soul the past few days. In a few minutes I'll make my way to the Piedmont area, and maybe write or take notes for the OU convocation. I have my cap & gown packed, and it takes up about ¼ my suitcase.... The flight here, via Albany, was a good one.... Everybody on the run, between flights, and I have such strange feelings in airports. Seeing the people at tables, the glass wall, the people walking by beyond it, and hearing the piped music, and seeing the orange & yellow wall hangings, I'm sent into questions about god, the being beneath & beyond all this superficial parade. This seems unreal....

11/9/83

I'm at the Salisbury airport, stuck in the fog. I made Michael go home & relax. Looks like I'll miss my connection to Roanoke. Somehow, I'll get to Elkins' place. Right now, at least, I'm relaxed. I'm safe here, at least, and not in Beirut whre we are under fire again.

A good evening yesterday. I read okay, but not as well as I did on Long Island. Hard to put my finger on why sometimes a reading is good and why, sometimes, it doesn't quite come off. But folks enjoyed it, and I earned my money. A gathering at the Waters' later on. Mike was good company all the way. I like him, feel close to him.... Bill Beavers gave me another copy of Carver's *Two Poems* in exchange for a copy of *Along This Water*. I'm way ahead on that deal. I didn't ask him for it.... Dozens of people stuck here in the airport, some with important appointments, no doubt. Yes, long as I get to Elkins' in time for the reading, I'll be all set. And if not, no sweat.... I just feel lazy & tired right now, nothing inside me to note down here.

Later: Baltimore, and I'll get an 11:30 flight & make it to Roanoke by 1:30 or 2:00. Just ate a big apple (red delicious) I had in my pocket from Mike's. Called Elkins. Will probably arrive in Roanoke with no one there, but that's okay. Hope I didn't miss a class I was meant to visit. I can get into a class or two tomorrow, hopefully.... Bright sun outside here. The fog lifted all at once in Salisbury.... I like this airport, clean & "understandable."

"At the airport, / I had an apple in my pocket, / remembered to remember it. // I was between flights, alone, / after a long night. / The apple was a red delicious from a basket // on my friends' kitchen table. / They were glad I took it, / and now, a state away from them, // I ate the juicy and perfect thing, / airport traffic swirling around me, / still too far from home. // In a display case across the concourse / I'd seen a gross of golden / apple paperweights // arranged on a glass twelve- / tiered shelf. I felt / the soul-sickness of kitch & gimcracks / ceramic gimmicks and gaudy multi-colored gifts."...

Well, anyway, maybe a start of sorts. Again, I like my "Between Flights" poem. It grabs hold of something in this between lives atmosphere of airports & bus stations that I'd like to follow up on in another poem. The one started above seems almost too neat & obvious, at least the way it's headed now....

11/12/83

It's Saturday, about an hour before my flight. I'm in the Columbus airport, was just dropped off by Duane Schneider & Susan Crowell. What days here! So much to mull over, since Bill Elkins dropped me off at the Roanoke airport & Dave Smith, by chance, was there, and we flew into Columbus together. The readings, the talks with Dave & Stan & Wayne & Jack & Hollis & Tama & Paula & Bob DeMott, the convocation today, Stan & Dave & I talking ten minutes each. I felt part of something here, and did well at my sessions. Impossible to set much down here, and the boredom in doing it after the fact. Something in me wants <u>so</u> much to belong, to be part of my generation of poets, and there was this pleasure with Dave & Stan. And the pleasure of being with Jack & Hollis & giving something back to them in the way we did. Joyce Dodd warm & kind, & Laura Summers & Barbara Matthews. Jack an amazing man, unlike any other personality or wit I've known, or intellect. We had <u>close</u> talks several times. And now, after the press of people & joy of friendships, I'm <u>glad</u>, too, to be alone again, & glad I switched to today's return instead of hanging around until tomorrow. I'll have a long wait in the Pittsburgh airport, but that's okay. Tonight, a hot shower, and being with Han, & seeing Kristen, & mail, & catching my breath. Dave's poems—I'm no closer to them than I was. Stan's poems—no new ones since his last reading in Brockport. No matter.... Seeing Gary Hunt & the rare book archives at OU. The good meals. Wayne's party. The set of pamphlets that will be coming from Duane. Got books inscribed by Dave & Stan.

I'm in a cocktail bar, a loud & good-looking woman at the bar. Quiet now, though, in my head, and I'm unwinding.... Tama & Paula doing well at OU, I'm glad to say, & kept us all company these days, even in Cutter Hall & Baker Center today.... Well, enough for here & now. I'll unwind all the way to Rochester.

Later: it's evening, and I'm in the Pittsburgh airport. Just called Han to tell her my flight will be delayed at least a half-hour, that she should check later on.... I ate a surprisingly good dinner here and for only bout five bucks.... I was so tired that when I got off the plane and looked up at the arrival/departure screen, I forgot for a moment where I was, and even thought for a second that I'd gotten off the plane when I shouldn't have. About four hours of restless sleep last night, maybe less than that the night before. And the night before that, at Elkins', maybe five hours. The night before that, at Waters', maybe 3 or 4 hours. The night before that, at Waters', a good night's sleep, probably six hours. So, let's see, about 20 hours of sleep the last five or six days.

Almost no sleep the night before I left. Tonight, <u>sleep</u>.... Maybe I'll dredge up *Onliness* from my bag & begin it?

11/14/83

    Monday evening. I'm in my bathrobe, in my easy chair, ready for an evening of schoolwork & television. Content, resting, after the 3 trips. And now <u>done</u> with trips except for the Thanksgiving trip which I look forward to. So, I've traveled, made some money, connected with dear friends again.
    Bruce is at Yaddo! Hoorah.
    Beautiful letters from Stryk & Carruth about *Along This Water*. Must write Hayden, send him something. An unforgettable letter, and to my center.
    So much to do. I wrote to Ray to say *2000* won't be done before end of January. This weekend, already, I'll get on the phone to Carver, McHugh, Gallagher, others.... It has crossed my mind that maybe my anthology could include <u>some</u> poets who did not have a prose piece. Must think more about this.
    May Sarton sent *Encounter in April*, her first book. And Dick Hugo's *Sea Lanes Out* arrived.
    Played ball today, and felt fine, despite the layoff. The knee very weak.... I'm so content sitting here. *The Chosen* about to start. So warm & content. Han & Kris fine. Spoke with Billy yesterday. Saw Al & spoke with Tony. Saw Rod. I'm back.
    Letter from Frank Stewart. Maybe I'll be offered a semester as visiting writer at Hawaii!

11/20/83

    Evening. About to watch *The Day After* with Han & Kris.
    I've been in a sour mood for a couple of days, maybe mainly because of my bubbling stomach, all the pressure and gas. I think, maybe, it was mainly the cup of ice cream I had the other night at the fish fry.
    John Leax coming here with a class on alternative publishing. I'll show them some books & things, and talk a little.
    Reading Simpson for two days, too. Impressive.
    Long walk in the rain, and I stood out back in the darkness.
    Billy home Wednesday.... Good days to look forward to.
    Once I'm done with the Simpson review, I can get to anthology work. <u>That</u> hangs over my head & keeps me from my own poetry.

11/22/83

    Had a class today, and only 4 students showed up.... Have been calm, & feeling well—my stomach settling down?—most of the day. Began the Simpson review, and hope to finish it tomorrow morning.... Billy coming home tomorrow.... Spoke to my folks: they've made up with Werner, & their court case is settled at last: they've been awarded $12,500. They're sending each son $1000.
    I'm home in my easy chair. Will watch basketball, & then join Rod & Greg for a pre-vacation drink.... The visit of the Houghton College crew went well yesterday. I'll read at Houghton in the spring.... Kris & Han coming in.

11/26/83

    Evening. I just discovered, a half-hour late, that *The Boat* is on, a film I heard much about when it first came out. I'll watch it the rest of the way.
    All's well. Have had good, family days. Except for Kristen's period and boy problems, we've been happy. Dinner at Greiners' the other day, an overnight in Nashville, home again. Han made another turkey today, and

I've eaten a lot. Billy has had fun, and leaves again tomorrow morning. I've been clearing my desk, and have begun anthology work.

Ram Time arrived. It's beautiful. That woodcut of the medieval farmer in his field, under the moon—it makes me feel connected with a distant past, as though I've been there. I've signed the copies, have kept my five, have mailed the others back, look forward to the portfolios, which will no doubt be held up by Bly or somebody else.... Another chapbook arrived from Lucien, *The Cherries*. And *Arete* has arrived, a fine journal that I'm lucky to have "The Scar" in. And John Leax sent me a second copy of *Bull Island*.

Two weeks of classes, some journal reading, and then winter break. The semester has flown.

Water is rising in the sub, which is on the sea floor off Gibralta!

I feel shallow, on the surface of things. It's been a long time since I've gotten inside my poems.

Later: well, I've redeemed my evening. I've gone over my essay for the anthology (will type over a couple pages tomorrow), have taken out two of my poems & put in "The Children" and "Mother and Son." Will get up early with Billy tomorrow, so will spend a long day on the anthology again, maybe even get to Poulin's for that Poets & Writers address book & make a few calls for essays. Okay, the thing keeps falling into place. I was never quite satisfied with my own essay.... The preface seems okay. I don't have anything to add to it right now. The biographical notes are drab, yes, but I don't really want more in the book than that, even if I felt like pontificating on the poets, which I don't.

Must remember to xerox & send off the Simpson review.

Haven't been in the cabin for a long time.

11/28/83

Late afternoon, and I'm home alone, as I am on Mondays when Han drives Kristen to Rochester for her lessons. I played ball today, got away without injuring the knee, and just now finished typing up the final version of "Bobby Wine and the Championship Game." I still love it. Want to xerox it tomorrow, and show it to Tom Dodge, and send it out, probably pissing in the wind again at the *New Yorker*. I've been putting off schoolwork this afternoon, will get to it this evening.

I couldn't sleep all night, then fell asleep <u>hard</u> after six o'clock when Kris got up, and slept until 10:30. I don't know whether this means I should stay up all night (can't, with classes on Tues. & Thurs.) and hit the sack at 5 or 6, or whether I just don't know how to relax. Sleep is such a blessing.

My stomach has been lousy. I'm constipated, and feel pressure. Am trying to eat fruit & such. Not so bad today.

Worked steadily on the anthology for two days. Typed Dubie's interview, much cut down, etc. I've caught up with things that were on my mind, and now just have to wait for essays to come in.

Tomorrow will be busy, and I'll have the long papers from my freshmen. But I'm ready to finish up the semester.

11/29/83

Managed 2-3 hrs. sleep last night, but was up at 3:30 reading *Life Against Death*. No real <u>news</u> there for me so far, but new terms for some of my own thoughts & assumptions. I want to read the book through, and will.

I have the journal in my office. Have an hour before the sport & literature class. Just saw Peter Marchant who asked me to do a session in his class next semester and to do a session end of June in the Writers Forum class—I think I'll say no to the latter.... Want to do some xeroxing, once the office downstairs is open....

Strange dream last night—of a great fall from space with a whole building into a swimming pool, of riding the crest of a river that reversed itself and rode a stream of itself against itself with Han and me riding in the front until we reached its ending in a tucked-in hem, of my shooting sperm & bits of meat from my cock over the left side of the river to near a car, etc., etc. Some moments of free-flowing beauty in the dream, and then the ugly & clotted & fearful stuff spurted out by my cock. What things I have inside me.

I want to stay calm today & just enjoy the classes.

12/1/83

    5 a.m. I'm inside. Have slept some, will turn out the light again after a while. After school today, I'll have a good long weekend, and will not have the pressure of work I had last weekend.
    Lucille Clifton sent a brief prose piece for the anthology. Looks like I'll be able to include her now—haven't heard from U. Mass. yet—and will have more balance than I'd have had without her. And I want to use that mystical sequence especially.
    Drafted a poem yesterday morning. About a dream of being at Walt's place when he was a boy, just before he moved to Brooklyn. Will turn to it again in a few minutes.
    Bill Ewert called last night to say the Christmas cards are done. And he still wants to do a special of *Erika*. He sounds okay. Has visited Kinnell & Levertov lately. Many projects in the works.
    Felt <u>low</u> after reading most of the freshmen 1000 word papers. Lazy, rushed jobs even after they had 3 weeks or more. For my own sake as writer, I have to be interested in them as people, in their personalities, to keep going and to lead a creative life. At Princeton, I suppose, I could focus on the papers as pieces of writing and for content. I have to keep seeing beyond the badness here, the dullness, the laziness, into … into what?
    Manny Mouganis came into my office Tuesday evening, closed the door behind him, and sat down to tell me that he has prostate cancer. Still having tests. Options on radiation or different operations. He's 65, will no doubt retire soon. This is <u>rough</u>, but life will have some of this for each of us…. We feed our spirits as we can. I'm glad I'll have the Transcendentalism course next semester again…. I hope Manny will be okay, and retire, and have many good years with Helen here or in Greece.
    Snow most of the day, most of it melting. We picked up the second car. Both now repaired. May they run forever. Any decent new car now is at least twelve grand.
    Should I look at my new poem now, or let it deepen in me some more? Since I even have the question, I have the answer.
    Yes, will have a good weekend. Will skip Mirko's faculty art show Friday and go with Han instead to the first high school ball game. And maybe to the college game Saturday.

    Later, evening: made it. Had a good class, then saw 15-20 students for 5 or 10 minutes each. Corrected a few papers. Stopped to see Al. Went to dinner with Han & Kris. Am now free for a few days, free to take care of little things here and there, and maybe even to work on a poem or whatever. Just 5 more classes this semester.
    Faye Kicknosway sent *She Wears Him Fancy…*
    I'm in bed already, ready to watch some basketball. And I can sleep as long as I want.
    Han playing bridge tonight…. Her job at the Center is still perfect for her. Another visit to the funeral parlor for her, but her spirits seem to be solid. She's a happy woman.
    Book from an English poet today, too: David Harsent.
    I did look for a couple minutes at my new Walt poem this morning. It's going to be a good one. I keep choking up when I get to certain rhythms in it.

12/5/83

    I've just been thinking hard again about which courses to put in for for Fall/1984. Nothing looks exciting, actually, and this is a bad sign. Conflicts with other courses taught too close together, etc. I put in for a course on collecting rare books! Will see what happens.
    Had a long and good day yesterday, Sunday. Ate too much, watched television, did a few anthology things. Saturday night Han & I went to the college ballgame—we beat Cortland—and then took Al & Boo to the Ale House. Much fun when we're with those two.
    Call from Glück yesterday. She says she'll come through by month's end. I'll send her a batch of other prose pieces today…. Bob Siegel called the other day, too. And Bob Morgan sent a copy of *The Small Farm*. In these ways, the anthology makes me connect with friends/poets of my generation. By about the 15th of this month, I should be ready to finish the book off, even if some essays aren't in. I can finish the brief biographies, etc. Can't think of a better title than *The Generation of 2000: Thirty Contemporary American Poets*, or vice-versa.

<u>Still</u> mean to send some poems out. Was hoping to hear from *VQR* before I sent other batches out.

Up at five this morning for an hour—read some of Kaplan on Whitman—and then fell back asleep.... Basketball today.... Roads slushy....

12/7/83

I'm in my office at Neff. It's almost 4:00, and I'll head home right after this entry.

Am to serve on augmented Executive Committee tomorrow for DSI, & just went over applications. Read Graver's, and his supporting materials. Things so "organized" that it began to seem sick to me. No one who has not seen it all will believe it. I've never, I think, seen anything like it. I feel in me right now many of the old feelings of hate for the shit. I admit I still think of him once in a while. I wish he were sick instead of Emmanuel. I do.

Life is good. Will read some journals this evening, teach my last two classes of the semester tomorrow, and clear things away. The hardbacks of *Along This Water* arrived today, and they're <u>handsome</u>.

Played ball, got my new knee brace. Wish it was a little tighter, but it's okay. Much snow and wind this morning, but things have cleared up now.... Had last Wms. class last night, and am glad that's all over, though there were some good sessions. The semester went fast.

Note from C.K. Wms. asking me to call, but I'll write. About the essay for the anthology. Maybe I'll even write him tonight.

Han & Kris head for Ithaca on Friday. I hope the weather stays clear for them. Han bought Billy a cabinet for his stereo, and it's in the car—a possession for the boy to have to worry about now.

Yes, during this whole entry I've brooded Graver's style, his intense ambition. Wow. Can his insides be okay, what with all that churning the application & covering materials represent?... Feelings from a couple years ago. Well, I suppose they'll keep diminishing as time goes by around here. He's not real.

Hope for supper and a long warm evening of television & journal-reading.

Don't feel with my poems these days—the anthology hanging above me—but did push "Bread" into another draft. Yes, "pushed" it, and maybe that was the trouble. But it still could be a good one.... Am reading and enjoying Jack Matthews' *Sassafras*.

Might as well finish this page.

Got reimbursed ($278) by Ohio U. for plane trip. That helps. I'll have a big Visa bill soon.

Yes, the world is too much with me. But I have powers within, have not laid them all waste.... Home.

12/12/83

Just read Gail Godwin's good piece on writing a diary/diarists in Oates' *First Person Singular*, which arrived the other day. My own journal/diary gets done, keeps up with me, usually an uninspired paragraph or two at a time. The <u>comfort</u> of the diary is the thing I've felt during bad times, the consolation. Also, I feel worthy, as though I am at least doing <u>something</u> because I'm recording....

Kris & Han back safely from Ithaca, and Billy with them. Billy & I will play ball tomorrow.

I've finished reading course journals. Just a few more papers & late journals and I'll be able to turn in grades for the first semester.

A call from U. of Hawaii the other day. They'll call again. Looks like I'll be spending a semester there. Diary, you'll be along, will be important to me.

I notice a couple blank pages a couple pages back. Will they haunt me? Will I fill them in?

Writing out Christmas cards, 10-20 a day, so it won't be such a big job.

Sent out batches of poems to *New Yorker*, *Iowa Review*, *Bluefish* yesterday morning.

Reading still & enjoying *Sassafras*.

Called home and spoke with the folks. Mom is in a rare mood, won't stop talking, tells Pop what to say every second, etc.

Diary, I think that when the anthology is over & done with, I'll have more time for you. I think you miss the cabin, too, as I do. I'll spend a few snowfalls with you out there this winter, I promise.

12/15/83

Thurs. evening. I'm home alone, at the desk in my study. Han & Kris home soon. Billy on a date in Rochester…. Good days lately, though the details that pile up are almost laughable. Mainly, it's the anthology, and I must finish it and send it out before school begins again. I just want to worry about teaching & my own writing…. For 1½ hrs. just now I've been writing out Christmas cards & post cards & letters to clear the desk. But it's been a long day and I've just run out of steam. Will watch some boxing soon, and then basketball.

Sad day for Kristen yesterday. She was one of 11 (of 30) who won scholarships for classes to Hochstein, but not one of the top 5—& she felt she was better than a clarinetist who won—but then Ithaca College called to say she'd been accepted, and this made up for it. That's where she wants to go. It should only cost about half as much as Cornell, too.

My folks sent us $1,000—from their accident settlement. We'll put it in the IRA account, & lower our taxes thereby, & get more help from Ithaca for Kristen. With 2 kids in college next year, & my salary on the bottom line about the same, we should get good financial-aid packages on both of them.

Finished *Sassafras* & wrote Jack.

Rick Ehrlich stopped by with Irene White today…. Pam Conrad sent me a little Christmas ornament, a camel…. Cynthia Golderman sent me an amazing letter and a packet of bad but passionate poems.

I've eaten too much lately…. Look forward to basketball tomorrow. Billy has played, too. My knee is letting me jump & run, but I'd better smarten up & not try to do so much…. 9 push-ups now…. Billy & I went to a high school game last evening….

Al has had bronchitis. I woke up this morning at nine & felt wonderful after lung-deep sleep. Kept breathing deep & feeling the calm in my lungs & chest. Thought of Poulin, his coughs, his cheese-cloth lungs. And he just keeps smoking. I like that driven son-of-a-bitch, and he's not long for the world…. Boo in NYC at a show selling her jewelry this weekend.

I've a feeling I'm getting a new pen for Christmas.

Haven't been out in the cabin in a century.

Snow melted outside.

Went to Senior Center with Billy & Brian Johnson for lunch today. I love being with those young men. We played a little euchre, listened to Christmas carols, then ate a good lunch of hot turkey sandwiches & peas & boiled potatoes. Brian is about Billy's oldest & best friend.

No second call from Hawaii yet.

Too much candy & cake & junk around, and I've been eating, and then lamenting.

Well, diary, keep skating along, what the hell, it's winter anyway.

12/17/83

I worked on the anthology a few hrs. this morning. It's now mid-afternoon and I'm back in the cabin for the first time in as long as I can remember. In the quiet here for a couple hours, I'll remember my center again, even if I don't do a thing but gaze out the window into the snowscape.

Will do a big shopping with Han this evening.

It's Saturday. Billy home, Kris at work, Han at the mall. Many Christmas cards today, and I must sent to Bob Morgan & Linda Pastan.

The blue spruce past my picture window is weighed down, but now stands 2-3 feet higher than when I used it as the feeding tree back here a couple winters ago. All is white & light & open here this afternoon, and summer dark greenness—was I dreaming? Was reading a Christmas card sent by Jim Mullen. It has a Chesterton quotation saying that we forget many things, but the most important thing we forget is that we're living on a star.

Well, cabin, here's your old tenant again.

An hour later. I've read another interview with Warren, have sipped tea & sucked candy, have read over some of my poems & entered my half-sleep & half-meditation stage with them. My notes & poems & folders are in a mess, still in the clusters I had them in from the readings since Binghamton. I want to put together a book of poems, but must finish the anthology first, & wait for *Erika*. <u>Then</u>, I can get on with it. I <u>am</u> of a different mind-set right now after the semester of teaching. But I'll come back. All's well. Will read more Warren and then go inside....

12/18/83

    Morning. Watching television. Heard a brilliant editorial on the new cynicism & sickness in America, centering on Joan Rivers & a joke about Karen Carpenter. Wish I had a transcript of the reporter's tape.
    Gathering at the Johnsons today, and then the party for town workers—I am the spouse of one—at the Senior Center. I'm going to try, instead of chalking this up as a nervous and wasted day, to <u>see</u> & <u>hear</u> & be <u>present</u> & <u>alive</u> despite these occasions so against my grain. Yes, I live here. These are my walks to the temple, or, maybe in some ways, can be.
    Han and I did our big grocery shopping last evening, $240 worth of groceries, a record for us.
    A record at the bird-feeder: eight mourning doves.
    El Salvador = "saviour of the world."

> There was a Sister,
> Sister Dorothy of El Salvador,
> El Salvador, "saviour of the world."
> This Sister—she would have left, she said,
> would have left many times,
> except for the children, victims
> of adult lunacy. The moon
> over El Salvador, over the trees
> along the roadside where our Sister,
> before her rape and murder,
> cried out in her heart
> to the saviour of the world
> to save the children.

12/19/83

    It's 3:30 in the morning. I just had a dream, a bare outline of a thing, and tried to write it down, but also let some of the details rise into the poem during the writing that were not in the dream. Anyway, it was about Williams, and Billy (<u>Billy</u>, and I'll have to get this into a revision!), and me, and a TV guide filled with listings of films about Williams & his poems. I've felt since Yaddo that I've wanted some other section or sections to finish my sequence, and this could be it, or part of it, or a continuing part of the renunciation. I felt in my dream as I do now, that there's nothing more for me in Wms. that I don't already have from him, and I did in the dream (or in the writing of it—but <u>did</u> think of Han in the dream & think to make sure either we'd have a second car or I'd be home with her or at least nothing wd. interfere with her career—yes, yes— <u>that's</u> true to the dream) say <u>no</u> to that part of me that wants to fuck every woman I meet. That part of Mariani's book hit me hard, and if the whole truth were told, I'd be as goddamned scared & sleepless maybe as I was for nights when I was just a boy after I'd read what was for me that horrifying book *The Scottsboro Boys*, the parts in it of testimonies of blood and sperm and rape: I've often wondered how I could have come to have any sex life, how I could even get it up, so scared was I by that book. I see myself in that bedroom in Nesconset—I may have been ten or twelve—more scared, I think, than I've ever been. And for weeks, at least. I'll never forget that. The gradual and delicate love-at-the-lips sensuality of girls it was, maybe, that pulled me away from all that fear, all that knowledge, so many things mixed up in it. Wms. a reincarnation for me maybe of a feared self I could become. I may be rejecting his poetry from my deepest personal levels, feeling in it that never-satisfied lust and blood and ongoing rape so different from the harmonies and resolutions I love in those poems of mine I most care for. This cannot all be apprehended and sorted out in generalizations. Maybe the poem I need to write, a concluding poem for the sequence, will tell the story of the boy I was there in that bedroom those nights after reading that paperback....

For an hour or so again I've lived deeply. This all has to do with the miracle of the self, his self, my self. Yes, I'm on a star.

Later: now it's past five. I began that other piece on Wms. & the Scottsboro boys. I think it will come to something. It has the potential, finally, of being my last word.... Mariani hit me deeply. Can we imagine what a nightmarish tape it would be if we had all Doc's confessions to Floss? <u>That</u> wd. be a paradigm of the aesthetics of Doc's poetry.... I'm just groping here, but am on to something. In these dregs discovery may lie. That echo of Frost's "such as she wd. become," the republic of Wms' poems.

My <u>self</u> as resource during superficial times. I've learned, too, that I care for myself, even admire myself. That was <u>fear</u> in those months after reading that Scottsboro book. Luck, but also something in me, saved me.

So many ideas, possibilities awhirl in me. And now (and I now welcome these moments) the feelings of strangeness, consciousness & being itself at once wild & unfathomable and, at the same time, some kind of obvious evidence of Emerson's power & order at the center of the universe.... I'm thinking of Jesus now, 2000 yrs. only, in reality, an eye-blink. I will lie down, now, in the Shroud of Turin, and unravel.

12/20/83

Heading back in a few minutes to the Senior Center for the Christmas dance & to help Han close it down. Billy back in Ithaca for a couple days.
<u>Bitter</u> cold today.
I haven't looked at the two Wms. pieces I drafted and wrote about above. Have been doing anthology things. Wrote out a first draft of the table of contents.... Might have an idea so that I can still include Ishmael Reed....
Bluefish took 3 poems but returned the best of the batch, "The Way." I want to keep a run of that magazine for my collection....
Letter from Hawaii.... Portfolios from Stone House Press....
Han & Kris <u>both</u> have colds. Kris missed school. Han putting in another of her 15-hr. days.
I decided not to go to U. of R. today for that collectors' club meeting. Had a roast beef dinner at the Center instead.
Done with all but one or two of the brief bios/biblios for 2000.... I keep thinking of the title, too. Can't think of a better one.
I had an awesome day at basketball yesterday, must have made my last 8-10 shots, but I strained to do too much. Tomorrow will be the last day for a week, so I'll want to take it easy & not hurt my knee....
Diary, I like your hum-drum domestic self, too.

12/22/83

It's five in the morning. I'll write a while, then probably try to sleep again—contradicting myself, the new self I was going to be. <u>Much</u> too cold out to get back to the cabin.
I was thinking of Vicky Gold, then thinking I could some day make a whole book—a sort of narrative poem with parts of her letters to me (and maybe parts of mine to her) out of that strange story. Enough mystery in it. I could just begin, straight out, to tell the story beginning with the first letter I received. I can see myself after I retire, if I have a blank period with no poems coming in, writing <i>Vicky Gold</i>. Some central mysteries there.
Our furnace went out last evening, and I couldn't keep the pilot light lit. Fran Peffer came over and made a <u>quick</u> thirty bucks. I now have a picture of how the "generator," which had slipped loose, works—an ingenious little arrangement.
Terrible weather, icy roads. I'll be relieved when Billy gets back home again.

Package from Duane Schneider with the 13 boxed Croissants, & Dave Smith's *Southern Delights*, which I'm halfway through. The first story, about the driven nature of the writer, with Smith's personality & John Gardner's probably all mixed in, is a good one. The clam rake one—in the southern grotesque genre.

Han's staff over for a little party tomorrow afternoon—today, I mean.

12/23/83

Morning. I'm watching the Donahue show, on capital punishment. A terrible dilemma the human race has. We don't have time on this planet for all the idealistic ways of thinking & acting that we can dream of. When I hear & see a particular victim's story—a daughter testifying of how her mother was shot and killed—then I want the murderer dead. If <u>nothing</u> serves as deterrent, then at least we'd be rid of the worst murderers. It's too late in the time of a crisis planet—compassion fatigue going both ways. If one of my loved ones were murdered, the execution of the murderer wouldn't salve or solve everything, of course, but I'd want him dead in any case. I've even toyed with the idea of doing a radical essay. Why should we punish ourselves, too, with the presence of someone who raped & murdered & butchered fifteen women?... I just get angry, and want to strike back, for all the husbands & kin & suffering children.... This is not a paragraph I can ever be proud of, of course. It would make me sick to think that someone who murdered my wife or father or mother or child was in prison, reading a book, getting art lessons.... The <u>biggest</u> contradiction: my trying to define for myself for years how each of us is in some way responsible, and participant. The Holocaust. Dizzying, and here in peaceful Brockport I'm generally insulated from the violent world. The closest I get to feelings that could make me understand are hearing things via television, or in departmental politics or during a basketball game! But these poor twisted vicious multiple-murderers—even if they are themselves in some ways victims—a quick bullet in the head for them, and a quick burial.

Donahue just said that we'll soon see weekly executions in this country. This is wht the people want. It will make us all sick & guilty.

12/27/83

2 a.m. Dear Journal, Jack Jones of the *Democrat & Chronicle* called yesterday. He was doing a story on journals. I spoke about you, managed to characterize you only roughly.

Haven't slept well for a couple nights.

Glück essay in.

Finished the strange book on Walt by Cameron Rogers.... Am close to getting my desk cleared off.... Double-header tomorrow night at Brockport High School including a match-up of Charlotte w. Murphy & Geneva w. Scott.

I said yes to Hawaii. Looks pretty certain now. Just before leaving, I'll wonder why, maybe, but it will all be an important experience for me, and for Han and me.

Billy & I & Brian Johnson shot some baskets today. We'll play ball again tomorrow.

I keep wishing Al Studier wd. get to my book shelves. He didn't seem well, though, when he was over the other night.

Sent Dave Smith a set of the three volumes of *CR*.

I sure am vacationing these days. I'm idling, if not magnificently.

Haven't seen or heard from Tony Piccione since he canceled out the other evening.

I want to get to that blank book for Bill Ewert. I'll probably save mine a year or three, maybe write out *CR* in it, or something.

Will flip the television on for fifteen minutes. I'm too tired to live deeper than that, right now, as I could by <u>thinking</u>, or working on those Wms. pieces I drafted or another poem. <u>Identity</u> itself is such a miracle & mystery, I sense, for a deep second or three every day. That boy keeps coming to me who bicycled along Gibbs Pond Road. I keep seeing him down just this side of the pond near Zilz's. Now I am in this new body. But it's so easy not to think about these things. I'll flip on the television. I need to get the anthology off my ass before I have another period of writing, putting a book or two together. But, I feel, I still have my soul—Bruce was telling me bout Tony Vallone, how far he feels from poetry these days in his composition program at Purdue.

I still have my writing soul, am here for myself as resource, as I said in that bad poem. Winter is stark and insistent here now, too, somehow, and has its effect. I hunker down inside in my bathrobe, keep my spirit like a coal alive inside me. I'll be okay. I am okay. You are here, journal, for even these nudges.

12/29/83

Played ball for the third time in a row, and will go to high school tournament games again this evening. Only thing of substance I've done is begun doing the copyright shit for the anthology. It's mindless & dizzying, but I'll do a draft of it and type it up.... Have gone over Glück's essay. She needs a good dose of Walt & Stafford so that she doesn't worry & fear the "blank" spaces.

12/31/83

Mid-afternoon of the last day of the year. I'm glad to be home and glad to be staying home this evening. Am watching football & typing my copyright stuff for the anthology, as I can. Have to leave gaps. And my back feels strained. But all's well. For months, though, I have been doing shit I don't want to do, trying to finish the anthology. But that, too, shall pass. Feels like I've been doing the thing forever.

What a wonderful room this study is, as I look around it. And when and if Al Studier gets to the bookshelves, it will be even more of a book-womb for me.

Seattle is beating Miami in the 4th quarter. Can they hang on?

Looked at the 6 slides last evening that Martin sent me. His living room & his study at Draeg House. I think, now, of a few of my books on his shelves so far away, and a few at Mertens' in Hannover, and a few in Sweden at Stewe Claeson's. And a few others scattered around England.

No word of course about anything from Vanguard.

Miami ahead on the interception of a terrible pass.

Life on the surface lately, accepted habit rather than miracle.

1/2/84

Many dreams last night. In one, I was walking out back toward the cabin. The light was very muted orange, rusty, and it was beautiful back there among the trees. A rabbit was at first startled by me, but then went back to nibbling grass as I passed. Then, in the same dream or another one, everything around my cabin was paved, the white cement of a boat ramp, and many kids & Brockport people—I remember Marianne Grace—were around. I was out of place and upset and lost....

Tony Piccione & Sarah stopped over yesterday. I might drop in over there today to see Jeff Schiff.

Got much done yesterday. Typed the rest of the copyright stuff I have ready, did a few letters, etc. I feel very lazy today. Tomorrow, I hope to do some xeroxing, play some basketball, etc.

Kristen had three friends stay over last night. I'm awkward around these teen-age girls, as awkward as I was when I was their age.

I've tried to do some hard thinking again when I wake up for an hour at 3 or 4 a.m. Is it natural that the mind, my mind at least, cannot dwell on important things—I'm trying to place myself in this wooden home on this planet in the Milky Way in the cosmos—or have I learned to be distracted constantly by the trivial? Does the mind protect itself (against what?), or has it gone sappy with the television & fast food over the modern decades? Some poems, maybe, it occurs to me, give in to this "graph," & others don't.

1/3/84

Got home from basketball about an hour ago, opened a nondescript manilla envelope that I thought had an application in it, and saw I'd been given $12,500 by the NEA. Wonderful news, and just when we were really beginning to worry about money, Hawaii, etc. I'd wanted just some kind of grant once more before the kids finished college. This is a big break. It was about ten years ago I got $5000 from NEA. Now this. Right away we'll put $4000 into an IRA account. So much money, as a gift, is almost unreal. Thank you U.S. government, & readers of applications. I'd been rejected 5 or 6 times since the first award. And this is pure gain—I don't have to stop teaching. Called Han to tell her. She said she had goose bumps. This will ease our minds all during our time in Hawaii.... And I was about to apply again, so I'm saved a day or two of shitwork....

Wrote Phyllis Thompson to answer her good letter.... Got some anthology xeroxing done at school. Will stay home to collate while Han goes to a volleyball game tonight.

Began a wishy-washy poem yesterday about getting stuck on the LIE. At least I'm keeping my hand in there.

Visited both Al & Tony yesterday. Jeff Schiff at Tony's. He looks well.

Long, good days, and today lucky as hell. Another "incidental carving" in that old poem of mine.

1/4/84

Tony Vallone over last evening for a few hours. He's at the beginning of what seems to be a 4-year doctoral program at Purdue in rhetoric and composition. It sounds so dreary that I became a little nauseous listening to his descriptions of courses.... I called Bruce Agte while Tony was here—he has more books for me, including Ammons' two latest.... I haven't slept well the past two nights.... Mark Strand called last night but missed me.... Gave Tony *Along this Water* & *The Numinous* and a jar of grape jam. I like him, and feel sorry for him. He's still sort of slow company, but his life now is not all fireworks.

I probably shouldn't play ball today, but probably will. I've been away from the anthology for a couple days, and this evening I'll go with Billy to the RIT-Brockport game.

Told Al about the NEA, but not Tony Piccione or Tony Vallone, or Bruce—though I'll tell Bruce. Too many good things happening all at once: esp. this Hawaii news, and then the money manna dropping down to pay for what would have been a shortfall that year.

Warmer outside these days. I could get back to the cabin, but am not in that world yet, and when I will be, I'll be teaching again. Maybe (almost certainly) I'm too comfortable & settled & satisfied with my life these days, but at least I know the dangers and know what there is for me to do when (as I will) my new rhythms begin.

Vallone says James Atlas mentions my piece on Berryman in his review of Oates: *First Person Singular* in the *Atlantic*. I'm anxious to see it.

1/10/84

Billy & I going over to see the Oneonta-Brockport game in about ten minutes.

Saw Al today. One of his in-bathrobe-all-day days. He seems okay, or at least the same.

Played ball yesterday & today, & will again tomorrow. Much fun.

Still reading the essays in *First Person Singular*.... Reading McClure's *Scratching the Beat Surface*.... Got Hass's essay, & have added it to the anthology manuscript. That book almost done. Missing only Gallagher, Carver, C.K. Williams....

Heard that Mike Waters got an NEA, too.

Han had another run-in at work with asshole Charlie McCullough, but she takes care of herself. It will be wonderful for her to break away for a few months next year.

Should I do the Seamus Heaney tape with Fitz Gerald & Ingersoll, or bow out. Shit, one of them should bow out. No big deal, but maybe I'll hang around & do the videotape.

Notice of *First Person Singular* in the *Times* with good words again on my J.B. memoir.

I'm writing no poetry at all. Will get back to things. Am not worried. Will begin planning classes soon. Will take next semester in stride. Yes.

$62 to get television fixed today. Spent $35 at post office. Bless the NEA.

Ewert says *Ensoulment* arriving soon. Oates' *Small Hymns* very nice.

Did type up the *vita* I've been wanting to get to. Room for improvement, but it's much better than the 2-pager I had. Won't do much with it, but glad I have it.

Going to a ballgame.
All's well.

1/12/84

The bad thing about playing evening games is that I kill time during the day waiting, as I am now. Billy & I played ball, & now I twiddle my thumbs until 9:00. I did get a haircut, & took out an IRA, & arranged to take the car in tomorrow for the busted heater. And called UPS to pick up *Ensoulment*, which came yesterday. At first, I wasn't crazy about it—maybe expected a more realistic illustration—but got to like it as I signed copies.
School begins the 19th, not the 23rd, as I'd thought.
Stitt's mss. arrived from U. Georgia, too.
Mss. from Jeff Schiff.
Call from Don Swaim in NYC. He has a radio program, was calling about a gathering for Jack Matthews. Might be a good connection for *Erika*, too, & as a collector.
Kristen got a card from the motel in Myrtle Beach saying they wdn't rent to the four girls. Kristen sighs & it ruins her day. She seems too often on the edge of silly emotional disasters.
Cold as hell.

1/13/84

Han had another of those upsetting confrontations with Charlie yesterday, but held her own this time without crying. We talked the whole situation over for hours. She has much support from all those around the scene who know Charlie, & the town board will meet Monday to, hopefully, get Charlie the hell away from the Center.... Fish fry there tonight, and I'll help out in the kitchen.... Charlie isn't well, is an obsessive, has a martyr complex. When he cancelled, this time, a mat Han had ordered from her own budget, cancelled it without even consulting her, that was too much. But there have been a dozen other incidents. And I don't want him cornering her again when she's all alone at the Center at 3 or 4 in the afternoon.
My days revolve otherwise around basketball. Played twice yesterday. Much fun. Billy & I in my study at this moment waiting to go play again.
School begins a week from yesterday. I'll get to some syllabi this weekend.
Love Billy. Will also be half-glad to see him go back to Cornell Monday—then I'll be home alone, less television, more work with poems & reading, a different rhythm. And I'll miss him again—he's such good company for me because, really, I don't have the right kinds of friends otherwise—but will sink into classes and literary things again. The Stitt mss. The anthology. Letters to answer, etc.
Supposed to meet Greg & Rod for drinks Sunday night.
For days and days, all in all, I've done nothing of substance. I was 4 for 6 on jumpshots last night. Have to go slow today, Fri. 13th....

1/16/84

It's about an hour before I go up to the gym. I dropped Billy off at the bus in Brockport for his trip back to Ithaca. The house is the quietest it's been in weeks, it seems. I miss him. I'm glad he's back within his school life again, as I will be, now, even as I follow this sentence to its unwinding. Quiet. Cold outside. I just ate three hard-boiled eggs and a doughnut. Coffee. Quiet.
Spent the evening with Greg & Rod & Tony Piccione drinking at Greg's. Many laughs and meandering school-sex-old age talk. Tony had fun, too, and it was good for him to get out. I was surprised to see how heavy he's gotten again. I hope he'll be mostly content this sabbatical.
School work/anthology to finish/report on Stitt's book for Georgia. And have to get the car fixed: $300-350, Carl says.

I hope, during this semester because of the advanced composition course, to write some different kinds of things in this journal, even if they're a bit more posed or self-conscious. I'll see what I can do. I still have to think my way through that course, and only have a few days to do it.

Han's problem at work will resolve itself this week, I'm sure. Charlie could be a good journal entry for me to read to the class, maybe.

1/18/84

Played ball, am watching the soaps with Kristen this cold Wednesday afternoon. She's home from school because she woke up with a headache this morning.

Han's meeting with the town board about that weirdo McCullough is this evening. I hope she gets satisfaction. I think she will. It's all a long story. In general, he's an asshole.

I'm about ready for first classes tomorrow. Am not sure what kinds of writing I want the advanced composition class to do, but I'll be working things out this evening.

Finished my report of the bad Stitt book for Georgia.

Letter from Allen Hoey that his mother died. And he sent his translation of Trakl's "Klage."

Heaney's *Remembering Malibu* arrived from Babcock. I hope Heaney is pleasant next week, and easy to interview. I hope to get him to know me, my name, a little, before he leaves. What the hell.

Plan to mail the anthology to Ray on Monday, whatever holes there are in it.

Date set for Houghton College reading in March.

I've been on the verge, the past couple of days, of getting something besides chatter into this journal, but go to sleep again instead, or turn to something else. Day-to-day busyness becoming day-to-day chatter here. It's okay. I still know what kind of resource I am for myself, and I'm still alive inside.

Got *Gray Soldiers* from Dave Smith.

Bob Fox around at the office today as I was trying to get some things done. He talks so much, and so fast, that it's wearing. He'll be around again tomorrow, I think. I see him once every two or three years when he's back from Africa.

Later: 4:00, can't sleep:

Sheep at Evening

I live on a star
moving at an enormous speed
in the direction of
the constellation Virgo
to which I throw my mind
and beyond, but

sheep at evening
do not. They graze
meadow smells
and nip short the grass
of here so dumb
to the beginning
star-flung sky

that they are themselves
their own cosmos
as the oak shadows
along the meadow
disappear.

1/19/84

I'm in my office—this journal carried here again at semester's beginning, a kind of reminder and challenge to myself—with an hour before first class. I'm about set, except, still, for deciding just what kind of writing I'll ask for in the advanced composition course.

Slept maybe a half hour last night—combination of nerves and sandwiches.

Graver stirs in his cave next office over.

Bob Phillips called last evening wondering if I can make it to Books & Co. end of March for a program on Joyce's *First Person Singular*....

Han had a good meeting w. town board. They heard her, and have all had experiences of their own with that character. Whether they'll be able to do anything is another matter. But at least he'll constantly be looking over his shoulder now, and will not get away with gratuitous insults & undercuttings.

I've thought lately—reading Stitt's interviews brought this on again—of doing a critical/biographical book on myself, speaking in the 3rd person into a tape recorder, centering my talk around one book at a time, just moving ahead as the spirit moves me. It wd. be an experiment in criticism. And I could say in it many things I'd like down there that wdn't come out in shorter interviews. I could do it secretly, under a pen name, if I wanted to, and say in a preface that the book's more private information is based on hundreds of interviews with Heyen and Heyen's family & friends! I could hold my books, one at a time, and talk of what rises to mind as I skim them. Paragraphs could be very long or/and very short. Sometimes there wd. be coherence as I spoke along, sometimes slashes of consciousness. Yes, this is all worth thinking more about. With a tape recorder, Walt probably wd. have done it. And, in part, it wd. be an autobiography, one I'd otherwise not do. Even talking privately to myself here I become self-conscious thinking of such a book—my life has not been "eventful" in outer ways, and I'm an obscure writer—but it could be fun, and I could learn from it, and I could have more of the satisfaction of getting things on record, as my masters (my western ones at least) say we should.

1/20/84

First classes went well. Now I have the weekend to do a few things, read Heaney, etc.

Coldest I ever remember.

Had fun at basketball last night. Made my last shot, and you're only as good as your last shot, as they say. 3 for 3 on the foul line again, and this by concentrating on nothing.

Will soon, maybe this morning already, type the table of contents for the anthology.

Cold. Bird food already running low. What a pleasure, a selfish pleasure there is in feeding birds. Gift-giving that pleasures the giver in the purest way. I like to watch the mourning doves peck rapidly for the small seeds, the black-capped chickadees swoop in for a single sunflower seed and then swoop away, the cardinals split open one sunflower seed at a time, the starlings eating bread or potato rinds, the bluejays bulling in to take over the feeder for themselves. And a rabbit forages under the feeder every night.

Wrote Norton to clear permissions on Dubie.... Wrote a letter to Vince Clemente in my office yesterday.

Drafted the "Sheep at Evening" piece again. I like it. And have drafted another sheep poem in which the same vision enters, the feeling I have about back there where I was and where the planet was when Wenzel's farm in old Nesconset was my learning ground. The light still there in some way in that space where our planet was, the light still holding everything. My two poems can just get to approximations of my feelings about this. And just now, writing the last sentence, I remembered a dream about being back of our Nesconset property along the right side past the sugar maples and shed where there was that low wire fence I'd step over onto Wenzel's property.

Later: 10:00 evening.... Sitting in my study with Han & Kris. Called Billy & he's fine. I've had a good day, will have a good weekend.

Reading Heaney's prose. He's good, deep, sharp. And he makes me want to free myself, drop everything, and let myself fly again into another sheep poem, just let go. Yes, I like his mind. Is he another poet scattering himself around the world, over here conquering America often? With such gifts, I want for him the necessary space & aloneness to keep making the poems.... Wish I had 1sts of some of his early books.... Maybe, if I like him & his reading, I'll have them the next time I see him. He's my age, after all…. He's going to last, like his bog elk….

1/21/84

Have just finished Heaney's lecture on Wordsworth & Yeats. Very fine. I'm envious, wd. like to take several months immersing myself in Dickinson & Whitman and write such an essay. Again, the intensity of Heaney makes me worry how I'm spending my life. I already think of different rhythms for my days once the kids are out of the house, etc., etc. I'll be okay. I'm subconsciously keeping away from *CR* now, too, so that I can take a fresh look at it this summer. But there is something in poetry, the making of it & the finished poem, essential to me. I need badly to keep doing it. Sheep at evening.

Ewert called briefly this morning about nothing special.

Reading Heaney, was struck by certain Yeats lines that seem dragged out to me, surprisingly flaccid, coming from that pounder—"that have to be set up in fifty ways" or "Yet if it does not seem a moment's thought."

Have fed and watched the birds. Could watch them all day. It is like looking into a fish tank, as I did for so long when I was a boy…. Bitter cold out.

All's well. I'm hapy, content, do not have to hurry to get back to what I want to. I know, as I write this, I will always be my own resource. It occurs to me now that this will even intensify for me (meanwhile keep listening, seeing, experiencing) when I can no longer play basketball. I <u>will</u> have to keep my bones & muscles in good enough condition to always be able to go on long walks, though. Bill, don't give yourself up to injury on <u>purpose</u> so that you get back to the torque that leads to writing & this journal!

Scattered entry, close to how the mind works, making perfectly logical leaps of thought but ones not easily followed.

A reminder for later years: Wordsworth is wonderful & reading him can always open many things up.

Will read the Hopkins essay now, but fairly quickly. I think I got from Hopkins years ago, when I used his collected in a modern British poetry class, what would be of use for me. Want to hear Heaney under all.

Later: car cost $416. Bought bird seed. Billy called & all's well.

Reading Heaney all day. Finished the prose. Have read the poems from *The Naturalist* & some from *Door Into The Dark*. He's <u>good</u>, but I'm not as impressed (or won over) as I thought I'd be, or as I remembered from my other reading—on the flight to England, I think. So far, it is <u>P</u>oetry, and excellent early work, and so much like so much early poetry I know, from Roethke's to mine, but it is art language, as Walt wd. say, and I'll look for the flowing….

1/22/84

Super Bowl about to begin. I'm rooting for the Raiders.

Han & I visited Helen & Manny this afternoon. He's done with 9 of a series of 33 radiation treatments. He seems okay, uncomfortable but in good spirits. At the <u>least</u>, excluding other worries, it wd. be like 33 visits to the dentist in a row. Helen is holding up, too, but it's <u>very</u> hard on her. They enjoyed our visit, and a couple hours went very quickly.

Typed table of contents this morning. Have to xerox some stuff tomorrow, and then will package the anthology up, finishing it from a distance.

Will read Heaney off and on all evening.

Called Bob Phillips to say I did want to be at Books & Co. for that party end of March. So, I'll make a trip of that, and have some fun, even if it costs me a few hundred bucks. I'd like to do that radio program with Don Swaim at the same time.

My inner-responses to Heaney are knowing & complex, while my mentions here in the journal are so puerile that I'm self-conscious. I know what I know. I know what he has been coming through to be finding the forms he's finding. And something in me resists some of his strategies, conventional as they may be, as in the "Elegy for a Still-born Child." It is in part his culture that allows him that. I haven't yet gotten to poems that will go on writing themselves. So far, they are pretty much delimited by his control. Several do not lift up at all, are just descriptions with little or no reverberations. Many are very fine in their craft & calculation.

I counted 35 mourning doves at the feeder at one time this morning.

1/23/84

It's before five in the morning. I couldn't sleep much again because of stomach pressure, and, again, this hasn't happened to me since the last time I had pizza. This time, supper last night. I got most but not all of the cheese off the two pieces I ate, and it was the cheese again, apparently, that got me. I just cannot drink milk or eat ice cream or cheese.

But I feel strong. I should probably (no, why even say this?) read more when I'm up like this, but I feel the urge to write in this journal, anything at all—act of ego or testimony or means to another end or habit or whatever it is—or to get to working on a poem, though I don't do that more often these days because I don't have the ease or the block of time. Also, I want to get *Erika* the hell out & then build on it, somehow. So, anyway, here I am, saying nothing but tracing a thought or two.

I want to find out just how many miles our earth does drift (not drift but fly on a plane, I'd guess) each hour, each year. I began thinking of Wenzel's yard again, and the physical distance from it in its light, and that (not even counting time) made me miss it & feel sad about getting further away from it even now as I write. And now, it is essentially still there, not even paved over, Mrs. Wenzel still living & walking there when Wenzel had his chicken gallows, and I saw the headless chickens walking, & saw his terrier fight a rat, and saw those pheasants he kept in a pen between the back of his garage and the first chicken coop. I'm not going to try to push myself out of what seems to be a silly musing on how old Nesconset is back there somewhre in space, the sheep and apple trees still there. It's something in my soul that keeps me there when I'm there. No one knows what dimensions there are. I could find myself back there again.

The next time I visit Nesconset, I'll want to get there alone, and do some walking around, maybe down our driveways again, or in Wenzel's back yard. Maybe around Gibbs Pond, and certainly by Nesconset School again.

Looked at myself in the bathroom mirror as I sometimes do. I often, inside, feel sixteen, young at heart, and then see my scraggly 43-year-old mussed self as I look to others. I'm surprised at how old I've come to be. I seem also to have a good sense of humor about this, am not afflicted with the disease of obsession with staying young. But it's a surprise.

Will turn off the light again.

1/25/84

A windy Wednesday morning. I'm at my study desk, half listening to the news on television—a segment on the Shroud of Turin upcoming—half following what might be on my mind. For the first time in all the years I've kept a journal, I'm conscious of someone overhearing this entry. I may be reading this one to my advanced composition class. I've asked them to keep a journal.

There is a portrait of Jesus on television, reconstructed by a photographer after seven years. The Shroud, I found out by reading a book Bob Siegel sent me, is not just a hyped-up relic. It was probably, is probably the burial cloth of Jesus. And it seems that something extraordinary happened to the body in that cloth. But my own lapsed Christianity isn't really on my mind this morning.

There is nothing in particular I'd want my students to get from my reading of a journal entry—or, if there is, it would only be the following of a thread, sometimes just the thread of ink across the page.

But I woke up this morning—went to bed at midnight, got up at three for a half-hour of silly-ass television to try to relax, and then managed to fall asleep—woke up this morning feeling restored. I don't usually sleep well, and it's only maybe one morning a month I wake up with this lung-deep feeling of ease. I had three 1½ hr. classes yesterday, and did most of the talking (as I hope not to from here on in), and this probably eased my mind and knocked me into the lung-deep sleep. I'm happily married, have two fine children, a warm home and a good job; next to these blessings, certainly, the gift of sleep. Maybe we have to earn it. That was just now a new thought for me. Ever since college when I went to a doctor because I couldn't sleep, I've tried this and that, mainly mental things, to try to sleep. I never noticed that I'd sleep longer or deeper after a day of even very strenuous exercise—sometimes after a hard college soccer game or even now after a basketball game late Thursday night I still don't sleep. But yesterday I worked hard, explained things in three classes as best as I was able, earned my bread, and maybe earned those hours of sleep that made me feel this morning as though I were twenty again.

Maybe not. Maybe I slept because I didn't have my usual late-evening sandwich. Maybe because I have that damned anthology wrapped up and ready to send off after a year of worrying its details into shape. Maybe I'll never locate just what it is that gives me this occasional sleep-ease, but will just say thanks when it happens.

Kristen is home from school today, just came into the study, just as I was going to write something here about Wordsworth's "Ode on Intimations of Immortality," the music of which was running through my mind. Stafford wd. say that we've got to allow the world into our writing. Unity and intensity, yes, the great desire, but sometimes Kristen is home from school and walks into my study, lovely daughter, in her blue bathrobe. She's only a year away from a college composition class herself: I wish for her, vain and self-serving as this may sound, an instructor who keeps a journal and follows his mind within a thread of ink, and not a frustrated writer who tells her exactly how to build exactly a particular kind of paper.

Just thought of a way to <u>force</u> the bonus of coherence on this entry that Stafford talks about: maybe my usual sleeplessness began when Kristen was born and kept waking me up during the night. No, I won't end like that.... I hear your applause.

Dear class, my journal entries are not usually this self-conscious.... I enjoyed this.... Do the same.... This time, I did not come to something that I'd want to do over and place, so to speak, in my course folder, but next time maybe I will. My sleep last night was not, though I almost lied and said it was, dreamless. There was a dream, and I remember parts of it, but it's my secret for now....

Later: I'm in my office for an hour before going over to the gym for basketball. I'm sort of off-balance right now because of the Heaney visit. He's coming, he's not coming, there will be a videotape, there won't be a videotape, etc., etc. So, I'm not sure if tomorrow morning I'll meet my Sport in Literature class, or not. If not, I'll try to phone them. I'd like to live in the present, and often do, but I'll be glad when all the hubbub surrounding the visit of the great Irish poet is over with. I'll read *Field Work* and make a few more notes on possible questions.

Stan Plumly took "December Snow" and "Blackberries" for *Iowa Review*. Keeps my false sense of accomplishment going these days when I'm not within my poems.

There's no question but that my inner defenses are up for this Heaney visit. There will be a crush of hangers-on there this evening, the big Gold Room full, everybody raving, myself a little paranoid feeling people like Kitchen are thinking isn't Heyen envious. I'd draw 50 to a reading, & this poet my age—a real poet, but not yet a poet of the music I most care for, a poet in any case whose five books do not overwhelm mine and whose poems I wouldn't trade for mine—will pack any house anywhere in the world. Yes, he's a star as I'll never be. He's good, but his circumstances make him a media person in ways, say, Richard Wilbur or Simpson or Stafford could never be. Bless the poet Heaney. I'm sure I'll like him as a reader, as a poet, as a person. I hope to get a couple books inscribed. I hope to ask a few good questions, say one or two useful things on the tape. And when he's gone and my classes are done tomorrow, I'll breathe much easier. I can't think, right now, of any American poet who could make me feel so—so unnoteworthy or unremarkable. Were Warren to visit, well he's almost 80, a grand old man. Kinnell is another generation, & Simpson, and the Gold Room wd. yawn. No poet of my American generation. Even Ted Hughes is older. But this man will make me envious, and at the same time make me hunker down inside myself with the faiths I've had, the acceptances I've had. Brockport's going to boom this evening.

... Peter just stopped in to say Heaney wd. arrive at 1:15, that he wanted me to have supper with the man & then get to Peter's class with him & talk, etc. Peter wants me to be a part of all this. I hope to be up to all this.... I don't even hve a copy of *Swastika* to give the man, & want to, will drag one out somewhere. Sunny & cold today. The great Irish poet is on the way. I don't want to hurt my knee today.

1/28/84

Saturday morning. I'm relaxing at my desk. Han & I went to a high school game at Olympia—Brockport won in overtime—last night with the Setters. I'm wiped out after a hectic week, and will regroup this weekend.

Soon after my last entry, Heaney arrived. He wasn't well, but held up graciously all the way, sometimes involuntarily holding his palm to his throbbing cheek. He & Peter & Greg came here for a light supper. It hadn't been planned, but Han put together some soup & tuna fish sandwiches—Seamus, as he insisted we call him, managed to sip the soup and eat his tuna fish sandwich forkful by forkful, then had some peach slices—and everything worked out. I drove him over to the reading, had a couple drinks with him in his room with Earl & Greg later on, made the videotape the next morning, getting in a question or two about poetry while Greg and Earl asked historical questions. He inscribed some books for Han & me, and I gave him a packet of my things. I was satisfied, selfishly, in that he did get to know my name, said he read, getting up early Thursday morning, my Berryman memoir. Yes, this is petty of me, but maybe understandable. Anyone looking at the videotape could see what I was up against. I am the one person in town who has worked as hard at poetry as he has, who has as much faith in it and as much at soul-stake in it as he does. So, there's that. And, of course, my bibliomania draws me to want the kind of closeness that could lead to the moving inscriptions now within my Heaney books. He is famous, besieged, always will be. There will not be chinks in his life for me, for any correspondence or friendship. But there was this warm passing, this mutual caring, and I'm glad for it.

I've agreed to do the videotape with Jane Cooper & Mary Elsie Wednesday. Will read Jane Cooper this weekend.

Big box of good books arrived from Bruce.

Check for $6250 arrived from NEA already. Unbelievable. I already put $2000 into an IRA, sent Billy's $185 rent check in, sent his $590 installment payment in, loaned Al $125—a strange request from him—for an African student, etc. But I feel very rich. Gave Han a check for $2000 too for her IRA, too, so all this is a tax help, money from the government to get tax breaks from the government. It all makes good sense to me.

Much schoolwork. Ehrlich's long Wms. paper. Student names into roll book, etc. But I'm home. I worked book, etc. But I'm home. I worked hard in my classes, and hope from here on in to have students do half, at least, the talking.

Anthology on its way to Ray Smith.

I'm 10 for 12 on the foul line now Thursday nights.

1/29/84

Just called the folks. Pop has a bad cold, and about a week ago he woke up & had lost half the sight in one eye. Had many tests. Probably a cholesterol problem. Mom okay. Maybe they'll come for Kristen's graduation, they say. They are the world's worst travelers, and I'll welcome them, but not encourage them. Also, they may be playing us off against Wern & Barb, & Alan's graduation—they seem to have had some sort of tiff about that.

Getting school things done. And am finishing Jane Cooper's first book. It reminds me of the homogeneous voice in most of the *New Poets of England and America* volumes. I wonder if my own, in *Light*, e.g., will turn out to be this conventional. Well, I'll make the tape. And I'll hopefully like the second book better.

Even though Cooper will be here and I'll do the tape, I should get a chance to catch my breath this week. Have to begin pacing myself while teaching.

Back of my mind, I begin to be a little concerned about that poem for Rochester's 150th. Got a letter the other day from the sesqui-centennial committee. Looks like I'll meet the governor.

1/30/84

What I am not going to do is to start becoming self-conscious about whether or not I'm going to read from this journal to my composition class. I'm still trying to free myself to write truly here, and that other audience-in-mind would sink me completely. So, I did read that other entry the other day, and gave them a sense of what I was up to, but I won't plan to do it again. In fact, I must tell myself that I won't read from this to a class again.

It's mid-morning. Han & Kris are at job & school. I'm definitely more rested, more at ease this morning. I overdid it last week, basketball & tension. The problem at basketball is that I can't take it easy & rest when there are the exact number of players there needed. Even getting there late doesn't help, is sometimes worse. But I'll have to learn to be of my own mind. The extra session Thursday evenings is fun but strenuous, too.

Did get a lot of crap off my desk yesterday—Schiff's mss., reply to Rena-Tana (a good woman but with another of those *The Sixth Sense Quivers* sensibilities), replies to Bill Elkins & Herb Fackler, etc. Wrote a letter to Heaney. Read Jane Cooper for a couple hrs.—she's a very strange case, doublethinking herself most of her life—wrote Tess Gallagher & C.K. Wms., etc. Last semester I seemed to stay with my poems; this semester, all winter, I've done little or nothing. Up for a half-hour at five this morning, I looked over my dream poem about the boy Walt, but am just touching ground, not descending the steps into the sacred rooms.

Already I have commitments to finish the anthology, to give readings and to finish that Rochester poem, etc., but when the flurry of things is over with, I will commit myself again to my center. Only in that way can I possibly become one of the few—I'm groping for the words—who elevate poetry by their lives, whose lives are in turn elevated by poetry. I want to stop scattering myself so much in my readings, want to burrow in and touch the spirit of those I read. I want to read the four books I have on hand by Czeslaw Milosz, e.g., and not just read them, but read them to remember and absorb. Maybe, teaching, all's a scattering, but all can be a coherent shining, too.

So, the phone is off the hook. I haven't snapped on the television. I'm glad in this quiet, which is restorative. I'm glad, again, I have this journal in which to talk to myself.

Later: almost midnight, and I'm almost ready to turn out the light. I thought of reading something, but am too restless to read, and realize that I feel this way when I haven't written anything myself in a long time. When I have finished something, then I'm content to sit back and read a book or three. So my reading now is just a glancing: a few pages of Bly's Machado, a few paragraphs of Gay Wilson Allen's *Emerson*, a few sentences of Jane Cooper's prose, and so it goes.

Long, good day today. Kristen back safely from her competition in Penfield, Han done with her calendar for tomorrow. No mail, and that's fine with me. A note in the paper, though, that Mark Strand will read at St. John Fisher Thursday evening. I'd like to hear him, see him, ask him about his essay, ask him to inscribe a few books.

After writing in this journal this morning, I did spend an hour on my poem "Bread" about dreaming about little Walt. Made some progress. It needs to glimmer at the end.

Sending *Ensoulment* to Cynthia Golderman.

Al Poulin back from NYC tomorrow. His stamina, in his condition, amazes me. He missed a class again today, will surely miss dozens more this semester, as always.

Look forward to getting my Heaney *Field Work* from Earl tomorrow.

Was looking through the lists of books I have at U. of R. A wonderful collection, and I want to drop off a few more boxes there this spring. With luck, with our health, Han and I are going to have good times with all those books when we retire. I still want my own room. Right now, I can't imagine selling them, but could change my mind, I suppose.

Well, then, another page of chatter. In 30 years I'll read this and think how I didn't know how blessed I was at 43. (But I do!)

1/31/84

Morning, an hour before class. I'm in the office. Tramped in deep snow to the cabin this morning to grab the notebook with the sesqui-centennial poem. Have just read quickly over what I have. I think I'll be okay. Difficult not to be self-conscious about this one. So far, so good. I think I'll type up what I have and keep a copy in here, too, to tinker with. It will have three parts altogether, looks like. I want a dreamy, hopeful, prayerful ending—at least this is the music I've felt in me this past week when I think of the poem.

So, another week of classes begins. I'll want to try to stay calm today, talk less than I did last week. Being inside the Herrigel book will help. I don't want to be apologetic about using it, either, in the Sport in Lit. class, though no doubt some of them are finding it heavy going.

2/1/84

In office for a half-hour before basketball & then a quick lunch & then the videotape.

Met Cooper last night at a pleasant gathering at Peter & Mary Elsie's—Greg Fitz Gerald & Judy Kitchen did most of the babbling, and I could sit there & relax, even the Marchants' ten cats & five dogs kept out of the living room. Jane was nice, warm, and should be easy to interview. Read her again this morning, took notes, will turn to a few of her new poems now. Was glad to get *The Weather of Six Mornings* and *Maps & Windows* inscribed.

Apparently, according to Kitchen whose nose is in everything regarding the poetry scene, Poulin didn't get a grant from NYS Council on the Arts for BOA, after getting one eight years in a row. I'm sure it's a jolt to him. Kitchen, apparently, did, for State Street Editions. I saw *CODA* at Marchants, & am glad I don't get it. I'm better able to mind my business when I don't know all that rigamarole, though I no doubt miss out on being in an occasional magazine, or some such thing. Most important now is my relationship with my own poems.

Tonight, Cooper's reading. Long day of classes tomorrow. <u>Then</u> some days off again to regroup. I won't be nearly as exhausted as I was after Heaney's visit, and won't have to worry about another videotape.... Still thinking of Strand's reading tomorrow evening.

2/2/84

I was the first one there in the classroom, but I'd gotten there, somehow, without my books. Then the classroom was outdoors, a backyard, in the country somewhere. I was still alone, walking back there behind a house, thinking about/worrying about the upcoming class. What would I have them write about?

There were five or six very big tanks of water in the backyard. They were all different sized, but each was at least about four or five feet across from any side and they were all square or rectangular. They were made of metal, had been there a long time, came up to almost waist high. They were like big old washtubs back there in the grass, and were filled with water, pondwater. There were chairs scattered around the tanks, and the kind of armed desks that are in the waking world of my classrooms.

I looked into the water of the tank furthest from the house, saw fish in it, golden little darters in the dark but healthy water. I was surprised that they had made it through the winter, this school of fish I could not identify, but saw that there was thick mud down under the water, enough for the fish to have survived the winter, as though they were turtles or frogs.

I walked to the second tank, and thought it was empty, but then saw the water-colored platties, dozens and dozens of them. Each had a tiny red spot on its bottom fin. At least the males did. At this time the phrase "precise observation of nature" came to my mind, and I thought I would just sit my class down around the tanks and have them write down, in precise detail, what they saw. I would tell them they could move from tank to tank, but that there would be absolutely no talking. Then we would hear some of the resulting papers, and some, I knew, would be deeper than the writers knew they could go. But then I thought that I'd better save this wonderful exercise for later in the semester when it would be spring and warmer.

I looked into another tank. Again, it had fish in it. These again were small. They were pale, lemon-colored swordtails. In the next tank, the one closest to the house—then there were many people around me and the tank—were goldfish, a school of them shining. One child sitting by one corner of the tank complained that the fish always moved away from her, that she couldn't see them.

I was behind the back door of the house, listening to a man with a heavy accent talking about the trees in his yard, describing them and their fruit. He had planted them years before. He was laughing with friends as we all looked back over the yard of fish tanks and fruit trees. He said the name, in Latin, of one particular tree we were all looking at, and I said "better known as winter pear." I thought of my Long Island childhood, the pear trees in our backyard. But then I saw that the russet and golden fruit on that tree were already far along, that it was not a winter pear tree. But the main things in all this talk were the shape of that tree—it was slender but full there in what was now dusk in that man's backyard—and the fact that he had himself planted all these trees years before, watched them grow, cared for them. It was a backyard come to a fruition of flourishing fish tanks and trees. Pride in his easy laughter, and this was not an auction. Nothing was for sale here.

It's 5:30 in the morning. I just wrote the above after that lovely dream. Don't know if I really caught any of it. I went from tank to tank and saw, in bits and flashes of color, those fish. Again I was in a dream about what is aparently my deepest sense of the beautiful: pondwater that is murky but healthy, and fish. All this going again back to my childhood in Nesconset....

Jane Cooper's reading generally dull. A sweet but wispy-voiced woman whose poems don't strike me very much. The videotape was a good one, but I was tense throughout, and should avoid them, but will no doubt make more should poets like Simic & Smith & Orr show up here, as Stan Rubin says they might next year or two.

Well, I lay in bed wondering whether just to try to get back asleep or to try to render my dream. I'm glad I wrote it down. Will read it to the class tomorrow, probably. Will now turn out the light.

2/6/84

Monday night, almost midnight. I'm tired, and with a long day tomorrow. I went back and forth about whether or not to pick up my journal.

What have I done? Played ball today, and that was fun. Did some schoolwork. Called Houghton to try to change my reading date so I can make Kristen's concert & hear her Mozart piece. Worked on the sesqui-centennial poem a little, and it's coming. Finished Han's valentine book, which I've called *Meanwhile*. Wrote Martin Booth. Talked with Han about her work problems, trying to get her a little mad instead of sad. It's all going to work out.

Just happened to pick up from my shelves Gary Snyder's book about the origin of a Haida myth—his 1951 thesis. As always, when I see such work I feel like a fraud, shallow, stupid. I should be doing serious work, serious study. But I think of Louis Simpson & <u>do</u> think he's right, that American poets are never again going to be Indians, that poems have to be made from the lives under our noses. No <u>real</u> collision here—if I stare long enough at and make a poem about a Wegman's shopping cart, a real poem, I will have entered mythic dimensions, in western terms maybe Jungian patterns. But those like Bly & Snyder & Ginsberg who study esoteric languages & cultures make me think I've wasted my life. At the same time, I've learned a little about a few things. I've studied the Holocaust, & of course, again, it is the studier who matters & can make depth, & if I'm shallow I'm shallow, but I hope that that immersion of mine is some kind of equivalent for the work that other poets who so often daunt me have done. & I've immersed myself in other things—in basketball, in late-night poker, in closeness to wife and children, in childhood ponds and Wenzel's sheep. I hope that these immersions "earn" for me poems all my life.... Again, the constant feeling as I try to write about something on my mind in my journal that I haven't said just what I mean.

Kept the television off all evening after the news. Quiet, humming in the house now.... I sense more time now since mailing off the anthology....

"Egmont Overture" played very beautifully by Kristen's orchestra the other day. Han & I at Monroe High for the All-County concert. We heard her solo passages clearly.

Another page with just slivers of my life.

2/8/84

I'm in a very good mood this Wednesday morning. No particular reason. Basketball later. A ball game to see tonight—Oswego in town with Richie Setter—and then a poker game at Mirko's. Had good classes yesterday, and have only a few papers to read to be ready for tomorrow.... A morbid fascination with the Beirut wildness, a feeling that in another life I've been through that, the comfort now that I'm not there.... Han & Billy & Kristen fine. And no money worries now, thanks to that grant from NEA.... Progress on the sesqui-centennial poem, and relief that the anthology is in Ray's hands now....

I typed up and dittoed & showed the advanced composition class my little prose piece (for the memoir some day) about the rose I took to Han's mom. The class liked it. I'm self-conscious about going over things in print in front of them, for some reason, as I'm not when I just read them something I've written.

I was thinking that I miss not having my old journals here so that I can look back into them once in a while—I'd like to read some entries now from when I was in graduate school—but it's also good to be away from them for years at a time. They're safe at Rochester.

Greg Orr took 3 poems for *VQR*. I feel like an insider, but he did ask me for poems a few times, and he took good ones, "The Shore" and "The Coffin" and "Cherry." He also sent me a long letter about Hawaii. Good of him. That's all going ahead.

"A major foreign policy setback" for America in Lebanon. I hope so. Will we ever wise up?

Later: a letter from Peter Dzworkoki today about the Heyen poetry room. I'm excited about the idea: a clean, well-lighted place for all my books. I'll go in to talk with Peter & Jim Wyatt early next month. Will think hard about anything I might want. What I don't want is to sell my books or papers now. But I would like a place for everything.

Card game called off for tonight, and I'm glad. Now I can go to the ball game, relax, come back home to get ready for school.

Hard to believe that after classes tomorrow I'll have several days off again. A couple of dinners to go to with Han, though, connected with her work.... Billy might be home Friday for one day.

2/10/84

I'm watching the Phil Donahue show. It features female inpersonators this morning. And what to say?: God knows.

Played ball last night, rushing there after the recreation dinner. Ran hard, began shooting badly & then did better, but seemed to have gotten so much adrenalin in my body that I couldn't sleep much, tired as I was. If I go over to the gym today, I'll want to take it very easy. What a job I have to be able to lead this kind of life! Classes went very well yesterday, and I expended much energy and earned my pay, but what a job I have. How could I be better off? All I need is the discipline to stay with the most important thing: self-deepening.

Will turn to a poem or some desk-work. Will turn off the television. Beirut in smoke. Andropov dead.

2/11/84

Long letter from Ray (and, parenthetically, Joyce, as usual) about the anthology. All's well. Details to take care of. I wrote him a long letter back. It will round off. I become, literally, a little sick, nauseous, about details, as I got physically sick after all our moves years ago when I'd pick up a chair to put it into another room. The anthology offends my sense of inner economy at this point. I want to get to my own work.

Long call from Ewert this morning. It bothered me, and for no particular reason. The sort of breathless & obsessive drive under everything said. And he'd never say, "Bill, I know I only paid fifty bucks for the binding of the blank books and you've given me a $500 item." No, I thank him warmly, and have been grateful for everything. Now, I want out from all this business stuff. He wants to do the little poem "Again" as an item to wheel and deal with, but I feel odd about this again. If the science directors in New Hampshire want to do such a thing, fine. What does Bert Babcock have to do with it? But, there are other angles to all this. I'm just anxious to go about my business, but this has become another weekend filled with activities I'm not crazy about.

Billy here in my study now, clicking away on the television. He leaves for Cornell in a couple hours. He got his lip banged up in a ball game, but is otherwise fine. He came home mainly for the big high school game last night, which we all went to. Brockport still undefeated.

The Carver & Gallagher essays are here. I'll turn to them now.

2/12/84

    Spent a few hours in cabin this afternoon. It was a good feeling to be back there again. Wrote Ewert a letter, Sarton a note, but maybe mainly worked over the first section of the sesqui poem a couple times. Knocked a stanza out.... <u>Much</u> work to do here, but one thing at a time.... I can't quite put my finger on all that bothers me with Ewert. I want some space, want to stop the small items. I want him to do the 4th book of *CR*.

    Han & I had fun at Skoogs' party last night. Played a trivia game for a while. Good dinner.

    Will have a long, full, rest-of-the-day.

2/13/84

    4:30 a.m. I'm writing with the pen Han got me for Valentine's Day. Every once in a while, so far, it seems to skip, as it has a half-dozen times this sentence. I don't know why, but it's got to do better than this for about fifty bucks, or I'll never be able to think about what I'm saying. Nope, this won't do.

    I slept okay for a few hours, then lay awake thinking of all sorts of things: basketball, Hawaii, the poetry room at U. of Rochester, my advanced composition class, Han & her job....

    No, this pen just won't keep flowing, no matter how hard or light I press. I'll have to have Han take it back.

    Evening. It was a long day of teaching. I'm here trying to work this pen again. Nope, it won't do.

    I'll get up early in the morning to head over to Bill Veenis's high school. I'll probably miss basketball, or maybe I can get there about 12:30 for a light workout. Will have many papers to read tomorrow, too.

    Sesqui-centennial poem coming along okay. I'd like to work a line in about Susan B. Anthony, though any forcing will deface the poem, of course.

    Got a call to give a reading to the Friends of the Library at Ashland College in Ohio in April. The $500 is tempting, but I'll call him back and say no, unless I can fly in and out on that Saturday. Jack Matthews recommended me. If I go, I should just talk about "Ram Time" and *Ram Time*, "Witness" and *Witness*, "Ensoulment" and *Ensoulment*, e.g. Or I'll do that talk somewhere some time.

    I think often about that poetry room.

2/16/84

    I'm in my office, a half-hour before my first class, the Sport in Literature class. Leonard's "The Dance Within the Game" today, and I'll bring in "Among School Children"'s last stanza. It will be a good class.

    Why am I so relaxed and content this morning? News, yesterday, of Bob Hass's $212,000 & Simic's $224,000 grants from the MacArthur Foundation. I can't explain it, but my first reaction when I wondered how I'd feel if I got one was fear. I would of course jump for joy, later on, but it would mean a different life, people talking to me in a different way. I'm <u>truly</u> glad for them. I'm glad about myself that I'm glad for them. I need only to keep on doing what I'm doing, maybe growing in my abilities to husband my energies & <u>increase</u> my energies through right eating & right action, and the poems & books will keep coming. Money is <u>time</u>, of course. That's the main thing. There's plenty of transcendental time for me, though, if I can only/<u>will</u> only keep reaching for it. The phrase "Sheep at Evening" keeps coming to me.

    Four classes at Greece Olympia High School yesterday morning. I did a good job, I think, earned that $200. The kids paid very close attention.... Then I played ball, then corrected—or rather read—journals and papers, then played poker at Mirko's until about one in the morning.

    ... Just finished the first class. It went well. Students, some of them, often seem lazy and unexcited by life to me.... Inside a piece of writing, truly inside it, I am dancing—the <u>body</u> can be involved in writing. Viscera, start dancing as I write!

2/18/84

Cabin. Came back here for a few hours yesterday, too. Pushed the sesqui poem along. It's getting there. I need one more unconscious flow for the end, and I'll about have it.

Long call from Ewert again—he's called 3-4 times the past 3-4 days—about various things. He is ready to make a start on the last volume of *The Chestnut Rain*. I'm glad. I've had at least a collector's sense of incompletion without that.

Many poems to think of gathering into books or expanded books, and a sense of disarray now, but mainly *Erika* is out there somewhere, so I'm in no great hurry. I had the anthology to do, and now have the sesqui poem. After this, I'm going to concentrate on making no definite commitments.

All is brown and overcast back here. This place. This place. I feel at ease after a decent night's sleep. Kristen's Billy Sodoma kept her company for television & popcorn & young love. Han & I went to the diner for a snack to leave them alone for a while. I think Kristen is cooking him a meal tonight while Han & I are at the Center for the McCauleys' Golden Wedding dinner.

Haven't seen Al or Tony in a long time.

Mom called yesterday. The folks—despite sinus & Pop's exhaustion because he works too hard when he doesn't have to—are getting along.

Well, I'll turn to the sesqui poem again for a couple hours, maybe read more in my book of Warren interviews, go in for a shower & get to the Hawaii stuff this afternoon.

Two hours later: I almost gave up trying for today to make any progress on the sesqui poem, but then things began to fall into place—especially when I found a way to get that awkward name Susan B. Anthony in (awkward for its sounds), especially when I decided not to get hung up on "Anthony" rhyming with "stupidity" & "duplicity"—and I've just about got it! I also got some good complexity & suggestion in at the end by coming back to Bryant & ending with the refrain of things & the two-handled saw. Maybe I should make it a crosscut saw. Anyway, the poem no longer scares me. My next typing will be close to having it, and then I'll touch it up here and there, and title it, and be done with it. It's okay. Time for some breakfast.

2/19/84

I've been back here for a couple hours in the cabin with the sesqui poem. It's just about done. I need a title, have thought of "Downriver," but would like to do better. How is the poem? I don't know, don't have a sense of it. It may need more mystery. But it's about all I can do right now. It's not a poem, I'd say, that I could use in a book in the future—and I guess that tells all. It remains an occasional poem, maybe a good occasional poem, but an occasional poem. I'll maybe send it to Norb (for his Bryant interest) and Vince & a few other friends just for their looks. All in all, I'm glad I did it, managed to finish it. I must not do this kind of thing again. I like being part of the sesqui, and there may be other such occasions in my life, but then I'll have to dedicate something to them obliquely, use a poem already done, dedicate it, & not try to do something to order…. Yes, I just need a title.

Spread some seed back here by the boulder. Black-capped chickadees have found it.

Many things inside me now from the McCauleys' Golden Wedding celebration at the Senior Center last evening. LaVerne and Lucille & 50 years. Other couples there who have been married even longer…. Spoke mainly with Dr. Victor Schmidt, a wonderful man.

Some schoolwork this afternoon. And I want to write to Charles Simic. I'll putter the day away. Yes, it's a relief to have the poem done.

Stopped to see Tony, who is hunkered down in his cave-apartment. He said he felt abandoned. I must check on him more often. But he could call or stop in here, too. He's not very happy, and it's understandable. Sudden loss of wife & country house & land. The misery of his life in China & after. He spends his time now thinking about/worrying about what he will or won't do at the workshop here end of June. He's gained back all the weight he lost, and is drinking at mid-day. I don't know what the future is going to be for him—well, no kidding, but I mean, in his case, it will be a mental struggle to stay above the water…. Lucien will be reading here, and that should be good for Tony…. Poulin just doesn't give a shit, will not be in touch with either of us except when he needs a favor. And now that he hasn't gotten certain grants he counted on, he might not find it easy to publish Tony's book of translations with Bien. And that will lead to much anger & unhappiness. I can feel it coming.

Want to push down to the bottom of this page. Have nothing much to say. I'm wearing the old black sweater, still, holes and all, that Han's mom gave me so many years ago. I don't want to throw it away. It comes into that longish strange poem, too, that is still in one of my notebooks and that I want to type up some time.

2/20/84

Monday morning. I'm in the cabin with a thermos of tea, my Viet Nam cup. Just ate a banana, one of God's great foods. Didn't really sleep well, but I'm rested. My eye is sore, my cold sore stings my lip, I have that abrasion on my jaw, my back has been bothering me, my knee clucks, but I feel fine, really. Life is beautiful—tea & a banana & the luck to be here and now and not in Viet Nam or Lebanon. And Han & Kristen still sleeping inside. And Billy back in Ithaca after his weekend trip to New York City & New Jersey. And my folks & brothers and their families safe. For now.

Have to re-do my syllabus for the comp. class. Not much else schoolwork.... No mail today, and I'm even pleased by that.

Suddenly I've gone nuts and have readied packages of books for inscription by Kunitz, Simic, & Goldbarth. My room at U. of R. is in back of my mind, and I want the books to justify the space (as surely they do already).

Not cold today, though colder than yesterday, but windy and darker than it's been. We're due for another storm, surely.

Another call from Bill Ewert yesterday—about the 4th volume of *CR*. I really don't care if the printing & binding is done cheaper than with the other three volumes. This is up to Bill. I'd like the set completed. This summer I'll read & read the whole poem. It's just about done. Then I'll see what I can do about publishing it as a whole.... Never a word from Vanguard about anything. Will *Erika* see the light? Well, I guess so.

I'll play some basketball later. It's hard to take it easy, with no subs lately, and with the kamikazes that play there.

Will look at some poems.... "Downriver" a more appealing title to me than it was at first for the sesqui poem....

Later: "Downriver" seems done, except for a final typing.

Did some xeroxing at school. Peter asked if I was going to do the Simpson tape with Al, and I said a definite no. I don't need to get nervous about that already. I want to enjoy Louis's visit and reading.

Have a slight headache, feel more tired than I should, have no desire for schoolwork whatsoever, or for anything else. Maybe I'll just sit in my chair and watch the soaps. Maybe some energy and interest will visit me later.

No word from Bruce in weeks now. Hope he's okay. Ewert received a big box of Ewert items from him, Bruce needing money, but then didn't hear from Bruce or whether or not the offer was accepted. I have no phone # for Bruce.

Details this week: dentist, stuff to drop off at library, post office, should make an appt. with Bud Meade, etc., about Hawaii.... I feel better right now already, thanks to the aspirins.... I should arrange for my plane ticket soon for my trip end of March, too.

Center, & school closed for Kris, so my two women are home.

2/21/84

Office, an hr. before first class. Han dropped me off, and will pick me up about 4:30—so, a long day here with people.... I still find myself looking over my shoulder hereabouts for Graver. Some of that still persists, but not much, and that little mainly because my mail-box is right next to his, my office right next to his.

Some snow back. I brought my lunch. I sit here with a cup of coffee, just pushing the pen along. Why? I know that nothing important will come along here. It's just a comfort, a reaffirmation of what it is that I do, when I thread ink along for a paragraph or three.

I think "Downriver" is done. I should show it to a few people, just for any obvious boners I may have overlooked. It's a long poem, and I don't have all the time in the world to look it over.

["Downriver" as eventually published in *Under Open Sky: Poets on William Cullen Bryant*, ed. Norbert Krapf (NY: Fordham UP, MCMLXXXVI):

I
At the country auction, boxes of books. In one,
Bryant's *Poems*, a gilt-edged, false-leather parlor edition
losing its words, disbound, falling apart
even while I held it.

Under century-old backyard shagbark hickories
in the spread of full summer,
I stood reading "A Forest Hymn" for the first time
in twenty or thirty years.

Do you remember? You probably had it in high school,
as I did. Its hundred-eighteen lines
rocked all us little American scholars into oblivion.
Who cared about trees?

This was the day after a Russian pilot tracked a passenger jet,
locked in his missiles, and shot it down, killing 269.
I tried to imagine that many people in flames,
had counted the auction crowd to half that number.

Bryant rhapsodizes wildflowers growing at the roots
of huge trees. Each one, he says,
"With scented breath and look so like a smile,
Seems, as it issues from the shapeless mould,

An emanation of the indwelling Life,
A visible token of the upholding Love,
That are the soul of this great universe."
There's more in his hymn than heavenly flowers smiling,

but the desperate poet does blame all catastrophe on human pride
his forest could keep us from: "O God," he prays, "when thou
Dost scare the world with tempests, set on fire
The heavens with falling thunderbolts, or fill

The swift dark whirlwind that uproots the woods
And drowns the villages; when, at thy call,
Uprises the great deep and throws himself
Upon the continent, and overwhelms its cities,

Spare me and mine, nor let us need the wrath
Of the mad unchained elements to teach who rules them."
He ends by asking for that quiet wisdom to be found
under the emlematic trees in contemplation:

Be it ours to meditate,
In these calm shades, thy milder majesty,

And to the beautiful order of thy works
Learn to conform the order of our lives."

But I kept brooding the charred fuselage sinking into brine mud
with innocent dead, of limbs washed up on beaches.
I knelt to place the book back into its box.
A long time seemed to have passed.

II
The auction droned into evening, generations-deep possessions
knocked down for the dollars of inflation, spirited
across lawns from home, outbuildings, barns,
into cars and vans.

This was one of the old farmsteads along the Genesee
where the river still glides with Seneca apparitions
past graves of the first settlers. Who could have dreamed
the American city, a glass and steel skyline,

corporate limbs in a hundred countries?
But it was always there, born in the sewn brain-patterns
of homemade quilts, in the first Kodaks giving us back
to ourselves, in flails and scythes,

in pots mended by travelling tinkerers a hundred years before,
in anvils and ogee mirrors, in hand-ruled ledgers,
cast iron stoves, tin candle moulds, a trophy buck whose antlers
branched above this congregation,

in grains of the high-headboard oak beds
whose women bore those who worked this land, in the now
nondescript uniforms of three or four wars,
in shotguns, sheepskin coats, bridal gowns,

coarse overalls, a stereopticon, butter crocks, dovetailed dressers,
a rosewood Aeolian piano, corn shuckers, churns, apple peelers,
cabbage boards, blue-tinged canning jars, a loom,
a spinning wheel, a Currier & Ives of Sam Patch above the river,

a barrel of Depression glassware now fought for by dealers,
oval walnut frames of ancestral faces, redware, sheet music,
an Uncle Sam iron bank, a roll-top desk—the years
cascading forward with yearned-for objects as though

over the river's falls.... And then,
held up by the auctioneer for special admiration,
a single amethyst jack-in-the-pulpit bud vase, its cowl-
like spathe gleaming above dispersal & the emptiness of money....

Did elms once clarify our streets with toothed translucent leaves?
Did we know God because the chestnut hillsides blossomed?
We pray, again, to invest things with meaning, to build a city
within our time but free from the terror of this new world.

III
The others have gone. Will you, now, stay here with me?
We will stand beside the river, watch stars hold still
in the flowing night water. In the same way,
we have come here from everywhere,

and from all time. We, our parents, theirs, theirs,
followed history, dumbly, or beguiled by it.
We were the ones in kitchens, fields, churches
of a thousand villages who heard the repeated dream

until we reached for it, or were handcuffed to it,
or driven toward it by famine, or slavers, or pogroms
of bayonet and flame. In 1834,
as he testifies in his *Narrative*, Frederick Douglass

prepared himself "for a final struggle which should decide
my fate, one way or the other." For Frederick,
for Susan B. Anthony in her and her sisters' life-long passional
against sexist greed and stupidity,

the same city still glows, downriver, over the treeline.
Lord of life and of all things, help us to know,
now, what our struggle is, its human forms
within objects within a world daily

more dangerous. Help us to know ourselves, the motives
of our most secret voices and gestures.
Stars in the river's water move, but stay,
as the river passes away, but stays. May we abide,

but build here the blessed city before we die....
A slag-glass lamp, a book with Bryant's prayer, a two-handled
crosscut saw—let us look into one another's eyes,
imagining flames, imagining love, and decide.   ]

2/22/84

    It's mid-afternoon, a Dept. meeting in a half-hour. Had a dentist appt. this morning—much improvement made on two of my front teeth—and then played ball. Had much fun. Let Mancuso & Kumar do all the arguing. Warm & sunny today. This evening I'll watch a long film on HBO & read journals and papers.
    Sent off the sesqui poem today. Betsey Toole called last night: they may publish it. I hope so.... Bill Ewert called twice yesterday & again today on line breaks & things for *Wenzel/The Ghost*. I'm <u>not</u> terribly fussy right now, just want the book out, and will be fussy later with the single volume I send out maybe next fall or next year.... Ewert likes "Coming," as I do. It has a strange music to it, was written quickly. I might touch it up here and there.... And what of Vanguard & *Erika*? It <u>could</u> be discouraging, but I don't really seem to care much. Just want it out & over with & out of the way & for time to clear past it.
    About time for the meeting.

2/24/84

Well, I'm trying this pen again. I swished ink in & out of the barrel a couple dozen times, and it seems to be flowing now. I'd like to keep this black beauty. Yes, it seems to be doing the job now, only a couple hitches in this paragraph.

Visited Tony again today. He seems okay. Called Al, who missed classes again last week—he says he has a cold that is hanging on, but that he's otherwise okay.

Got back from working the fish fry an hour ago. All went well with Jim Rich, the new cook. & Han's problems there have been diminishing, and this fucking pen is acting up again. It's got to work steadily.

Brockport's boy's team lost to Gates Chili at the War Memorial last night after being 19-0 this season. And they'd beaten Gates twice before this season. A heartbreaking loss for the Brockport boys. Five senior starters.

Just bore down hard on this pen point on another sheet of paper. No, it didn't help.

I just realized that by mistake I've flipped back to this open page for this entry. What's the diff? Anyway, the pen is driving me nuts again. Am I holding it wrong, or what? Should I boil the point or something?... I'll give it one more shot, filling it again, and then give up on it....

Good classes yesterday. Many students, no doubt, are not working hard enough, because of all the freedom I give them, but I don't want to be an overlord.... No, this fucking pen just won't do, handsome as it is. Why won't it just keep going? I can't blame it on the paper, or the angle by which I write. No. Much too distracting for me to keep it. Now I'll try the other pen, stainless steel, that Han brought home.

This one, apparently, will keep writing, but I don't know if I like it much. It seems fine-point. And it has such a brusque barrel. It's damned funny (and maybe stupid) about how hard it is to feel comfortable with a pen. Could I get to like this one? But my personality fits the thicker style above? I think so. When I'm writing a poem, I like the thicker flow.

Now this is a journal page to brag about and hold to. It is filled with soul and centrality.

I should write something opposite & solve the emptiness once & for all.

Don Swaim called today. Looks like he pushed Vanguard a little for *Erika*. Wonderful! Looks like I'll make that radio show end of March.

Robert Marcus, the new Vice President, asked me to join him for lunch. I've no desire to have anything to do with setting up the new MFA that has been breezed about lately.

Played ball today, shot well, had fun.

Billy called the other evening to say he'd been elected to an engineering honor society. Great. He deserves some recognition for his brains & grades.

I'll spend several hours in the cabin tomorrow.

Sent the Carver & Gallagher essays to Ray.

Saw May Sarton's mention of me in the *Paris Review* interview today.

Han & I will go to dinner & movies tomorrow night.

I have new pyjamas & love them.

Can I get to like this pen? Mebbe so. It's unassertive, I guess. Will not stain through when I sign certain things, like the absorbent Vanguard books. Etc. etc.

Louis Orr is doing terrific for the Knicks right now.

I'll go to wash Han's back.

2/25/84

I'm in the cabin. Snow again, after two very warm days. I finally got some sleep last night—tried Billy's room & firmer mattress—after tossing for a couple hours and even getting up to begin reading *1984*. It's awfully good. I promised myself I'd read it this year.

Began a poem in my head inside, and came back here to try to write it down. I need, I think, one more stanza. This is where I am right now.

Long Island Light

It must still be raying out to everywhere, but staying.
How did I return, suspended,
into the Island light where I was born?

On our Nesconset lawn, the same three dogwoods are in bloom
but bare at the same time,
for this is light within light, one season

and I its child, young man, man in all my images at once,
excarnate. This is all so simple—
how could I sometimes not have known?

A single everblue spruce in the eastern corner
draws me into it. We are together
in a shimmer, the light originating here....

Delusion, or a dream? If there is more to say,
to help you, I wish I could. What else
would the light of being have been but this?

I've just pushed out a couple more stanzas in the notebook, but don't think they'll do. But this will find its ending. These poems—"Coming" & "Sheep at Evening" and others—all begin with my feeling for that whole Island life still existing in the light. I <u>can't</u> get all my feelings in, my intimations, but can keep just suggesting. That light does not overlap, but is a fusion of all time.... Some poet said that the "light"—as the "dark"—has become a cliché. Not if I can keep uncovering my senses of this. Well, I have this one going then, and will let it complete itself inside me.

I want to get my study in order today. Am glad I came back here this morning. Am glad to be going back into the house. Will hve a piece of fish for lunch, one I fried myself last night.

2/26/84

This is not going to be one of those entries where I complain about a pen. But I am trying that black beauty again, and will all day, hoping it will work out. I'd like very much to keep this one, keep it here at my desk always. Handsomest pen I've ever had.

Han and I ate at Casey's, then saw Manny & Helen, then saw Boo—Al was conked out on their living-room couch—then went to the movies where "Terms of Endearment" was okay, but not as good as I thought it was going to be. Too unbelievable too often. The comic parts with Jack Nicholson were by far the best.

I just wrote Arnold Edelstein at Hawaii—still have to get to the packet of materials his secretary sent. Decisions about health forms and such.

I'll try to stay busy today. Don't have much discipline. Will read a few papers while watching basketball. <u>Will</u> read Emerson's "Experience" closely—I've had good classes, but have sort of been sliding by in the Transcendentalism course....

Just read over the stanzas opposite, and like them....

We just phoned Pop Drachowski, who has the flu but is hanging on, spiritually, from the sounds of it. Wolf is supposed to visit him today and deliver some anti-biotics & aspirin & stuff.

Later. Trying out the pen again. Maybe I'll do what Han suggests & put the point in hot water. Yes. It's worse now than before, and it was bad then. I'll empty it, wash it out & try a cartridge....

Cartridge in.

Did start filling out Hawaii forms. Han will have to see Bud Meade about questions on health insurance, etc.

I've put no pressure on myself to write anything "significant" in this journal, but I've slushed around too much, really, with quotidien jottings that will put me to sleep when I'm retired and want to take <u>some</u> pleasure and interest in the journal. This <u>fucking</u> pen.

Later: Here I am, 43 years old, and I just watched *That Championship Season*, and it has hit me hard. The old ball team from the Class of 1957, the music, the old coach, my life swirling within me as I watched. How much I've wanted to have written (not to write it but to have written it) my novel about the darkened halls of old SHS, my teammates Lars & Peppy & Dave & Vic & Andy & Bob & Freddie & Gil & Mike, all of us together again, in our 40's, in my imagined world. And it could have been done/could be done, but maybe I won't ever do it.

What is at my center, anyway? How is it that memories of the Northport game, the seconds when it was over when I ran into the locker room missing the center-court celebration, are more central to me than all these fucking poetry books that surround me? I do want to write poems and to hear me say them—it must be that my purest voice in the sheep poems or berries poems or any is of nostalgic yearning for the lost world of those years of awakening sexuality & Karen & basketball & Wicks' shot—but how much poetry by others has ever really moved me?—a poem here & a poem there. So, what of this collecting, my future flowing toward a room? Well, collectors have not always been great readers, have loved books as books. And my collection is of association copies from all sorts of poets. I can still do that, build my collection & stoke my ego, but must always remember that I am my own resource—obsession & return, yes, and that is, for now, through *CR* & later poems, my center. If I've not made the connection in words here now between myself at 16 on the ballcourt and myself at 43 as poet & book-collector, it is inside me, twined deeply—I keep thinking of tendrils of tendon around an artery or vein. God, I wish I could write *The Elvis Presley Room* & get it over with. Can I, ever? It wd. take guts. If I <u>don't</u>, then maybe these emotions will stay more deeply inside me, rising once in a while into something like "Coming" & "Bobby Wine.".... Those poems have their sources back there in the gyms of my childhood—on the farms & fields & at Wenzel's yes—but in the gyms of my childhood, that first shot I remember sinking against Port Jefferson when I was a senior. So much anxiety & heartbreak for years for me, all of it mixed in with first love and friendship and fear and perfume, and then 1957, the championship season. I will never be able to sound it. I hope my old teammates sometimes think of me, as I do of them. I am glad they lived, became part of my life. If they tear down that New York Avenue school, it won't matter. It <u>will</u> exist inside me, much as I doubt my own transcendental sappiness sometimes. If there is an afterlife, a miraculous yearned-for afterlife, maybe I'll be back there again—

I just helped Han with her job description list. This is the world. This is the present. But I will not deny that other world as, e.g., it's trying to objectify itself in my new poem a couple pages back. I'm 43 of your years old, Lord, strata within strata, but not that, either, but all fused, the life as a whole so rich and inexpressible that it will be all right when I come to die so that the sweet and painful yearning will stop. And then someone else can remember....

I have books to build. And I have the poems, written and unwritten, to build them with. And I have to tear away books, too, to get down to the <u>central</u> poems for a *Selected* and a different *Long Island Light* and *City Parables*. I'll keep doing it. And the thing itself will be in that. And this journal will keep me company.

2/27/84

Han has left for work, Kristen for school. I'll stay inside, shuffle through poems. Have the phone off the hook. I have some schoolwork to do, have to arrange for a videotape or two, but will do that this afternoon. I have to at least credit myself this: that the poems have come first. Even when doing other work, it was to get that work out of the way. I could argue the selfishness of that, too, but there is something inside me that keeps fusing me to my sheep at evening and my deer.

.... It's an hour later. Han has dropped Kristen off from school. Kris has period cramps. She is walking around upstairs now. The water is running. I'd gone over three or four poems, was trying to get inside "Sheep One Evening" again.... But that poem, I think, has stopped me anyway. Dealing with light in those poems, my language can't reach the mental picture I have of light all fused from that place where Nesconset was in the heavens when I was a child. There was a light-source there, say the body of a sheep at evening, and the image still exists <u>there</u> and at the same time rays out—doesn't <u>ray</u> but fuses/suffuses outward, all the way to here, if I were sensitive enough still to see it. Somewhere in the brain in hologram.... Maybe I'll just shuffle the poem into the deck and go on to others. I'm seeing what is done and ready for typing to send out.

2/28/84

It's mid-afternoon. I'm home, barely. The worst snowstorm in years. I plowed out of the driveway in hood-high snow this morning, did hold one class, and then, stupid, stuck around. Had to cancel the other two classes anyway, and had a hard time driving home. Han & I shoveled furiously for a while, and then I managed to back the car far enough into the driveway to at least get it off the road. I was too conscientious this mornig, & then after the first class, and should have stayed home.... Han & Kris are home safely—school & Center called off.

What can I do of value today? For now, I'm glad just to have made it to my easy chair & bathrobe.

Later: I'm snug in my new pyjamas & under covers, watching television, reading *1984*, sipping tea, picking up a book here and there. Read a few more MacLeish letters, read his inscription in *Riders on the Earth*—how wonderful to "own" that book that he inscribed to Han and Bill in 1978.

Still snowing. So cozy here inside. We don't know whether Han & Kris will have work and school tomorrow.

Al called, asking & asking me to make the Simpson tape. I just don't want to. Don't know what will happen if Al gets (stays) sick. Why am I setting myself against making the Simpson tape? He's easy to interview. It has to do, I think, more with working with Al than with anything else. I bust my ass and become nervous & sleepless about it. He slides along. But, also, nothing is done with these interviews; also, maybe Atlas is right: there's too much of this talk-talk-talk going on. Louis is himself probably sick of these things.

Why has my handwriting gotten so small? Maybe it's the weather, and I'm hunkering down inside.

Time for a piece of cake with my tea.

The paintings in the caves at Altimira in Spain were only discovered in 1979! No, 1879. Of course. But I just did hear clearly, I think, that the earliest known representation of an animal—all the various important cave paintings seem to date from 15,000-25,000 years—is a stone horse found in Germany thought to be 31,000 years old.... Some of these television shows are amazing.

I thought to write a letter to Bob Phillips or Vince, thought to turn to a poem. I'm particularly lazy and stupid this snowy night.

Had a good talk with Billy. Only an inch of snow in Ithaca.

Leap Day '84

The snow has closed up the town again today. Han & Kris & I inside. I shovelled about two hours this morning, tried to feed the birds. Am watching the soaps now. Finished *1984*. Have a couple journals to read this evening, am otherwise free to watch basketball—couldn't get to the gym today—and think about my visit to the U. of R. March 12th to talk about the Heyen Poetry Room. Marge Barrett called about an hour ago to make the appointment.... No mail delivery again today.

I don't work on any poems when Han & Kris are home like this. I've just sort of been watching the weather. It's still blowing & snowing.

Read that Richard Lattimore died. I regret not sending him a book or two for inscription. Han & I remember speaking with him for a few minutes at that bash in NYC a couple years ago.

Haven't heard about "Downriver"—hope they like it.... Haven't heard from Bruce, and haven't been able to mail the letter I wrote him. Selfishly, I hope he's still at the Strand.

I've wanted to type up and send out some new poems, maybe to *APR*, but haven't been in the mood. Maybe this weekend. Maybe not. That's the level of literary excitement I'm reaching these days.

Many dreams last night. I remembered outlines this morning. Now, nothing.

3/1/84

Office, a half-hour before class. Almost got stuck in the driveway this morning, but made it here, but there were 15-ft. snow piles between parking lots behind Hartwell and Neff Hall. A long trudge around through Security to Neff. Any reasons there haven't been paths plowed from Hartwell to Neff? So, I've bitched & complained for the past half-hour with Greg & Jack Wolf, and it's been fun. But it has been dangerous driving around. Still a very light snowfall. I'll go to the first class—we're talking about Larry McMurtry's wonderful essay on rodeo—but might go home early if it snows more and if there are still head-high pathless drifts around Neff. I'd like to shovel for an hour at home and then work on a few poems; instead, I'm sure, I'll be here all day. The snow broke the school-boredom, anyway.

I've realized that I'm not the same person as I was in September, the one who wanted to integrate, who was determined to write and be writer while in school. I've lost my intensity. To what? Reading bad student journals and papers? Anticipating classes? Being a fat cat with a book coming out—or two? I have lost that edge, despite finishing "Downriver" and the anthology (except for a dozen details). Maybe I'm just marking time until spring, my trip end of March. I do know that I had all the time in the world yesterday, but pissed it away, doing almost nothing when I could have been at my desk at least writing letters. I could have gone out to the cabin for a few hours. I was tired after shovelling, but that was no excuse. Oh, it's good to be a lazy good-for-nothing some times, but I've been perfecting the role, journal, and I hope you're not been aider and abettor. (I suppose, pushing sentences along or following them as though they were brainthreads, I keep learning how to write clearly, as this sentence is clear.) Phone calls and noise in the house, but this isn't enough of an excuse, either, for me not to have cleared my desk.

Just read a couple of Sept. entries in this journal. Well, I'm the same person. And I still do believe that poems like "Long Island Light" (if that remains the title) are finishing themselves inside me while I'm away from them.

I'm a lucky bastard. After classes I'm off until Tuesday again. This weekend I'm going to stay busy—poems & letters & everything, shovelling for good health between.

Later: Home, and glad to be. Much new snow. I did get through those three classes—saw the Gorin/Watson tape in one—and picked up Han, & have seldom been so relieved to get home again. Just got into the driveway again. No basketball tonight, though Han has been picked up for bridge.... I'm resolved to keep busy all weekend, shovelling & reading, writing & shovelling.... Mail today, including the two firsts of *Brother to Dragons* back from RPW. He has signed "Red" this time I think for the first time.... Some book catalogues to have fun with....

3/2/84

Well, I haven't gotten far in the two hours I've been at my desk, but there's no particular place to get to, and at least I've gotten back to myself, have moved "Long Island Light" through a few drafts. It's almost there. I'm trying, maybe, to pack too much in on my ending. Also wrote out "Coming" again. It seems done. I want to feed the birds, want to shovel a little, want to stop at the school, have to cut basketball short so I can pick Kristen up, but at least I've kept busy, as I will all day.

Meant to buy some books, but couldn't really pick any out of the three catalogues that came yesterday. Nothing sems less than $35 now, and the new magic # seems to be $85.

We're not sure whether Billy will be home today. Probably. There seems to be a break in the weather.

Al called Han at work yesterday for a lift to the post office and for some shopping. She couldn't oblige. I'm glad. Let him make arrangements with Boo & Daphne, ferchrissakes. Han is unbelievably busy every minute over at the Center, too. I had the car at school all day, in any case.... Okay, birds, I hear you.

3/3/84

It's eight in the evening. I'm back in the cabin, after making it through the 2-4' drifts. Forced the cabin's outer door back against the snow, squeezed in. The place is warming. The four of us had dinner at the diner, and Billy went off for his Saturday night of poker and bar, & Han is inside with Kris & several of Kristen's friends. I'm glad I decided to come back here, whether or not I accomplish anything going over the folder of poems. Well, of course I will. There's no magic time to finish a poem or poems; the processes have to be gone through, now or on a warm July evening. I've turned the heater right toward me, have the heating pad on my lap, have a thermos of decaffeinated tea, will try to spend time that adds to my store of time.

    Later: I actually accomplished something. I think I've finished "Long Island Light;" and I found a good, flowing form for "Bread." Want to type up the batch of poems that are ready before I keep pulling out more. Also read DeMott's good interview with Warren. It's just overwhelming to think of the years, the man's boyhood, the things he says. I don't want him to die. Not him. <u>He</u> has to read *CR* entire, for Archie, for me, a couple or four or more years down the line.

    Got Howard Nelson's *Bly* yesterday, read some & skimmed some. It looks solid.... Got a book of fiction from Bill Ferguson—read a few pieces that seemed flashy to me. Will read more.... Wish I had the energy now to write Warren & Vince Clemente from back here, but I don't.... I've been warm enough, the house & cabin a bit warmer because of the snow banked around them.... Suddenly, I feel very happy. Walt is still looking over at me, bemused, concerned.... I wrote Dave Smith today, & wrote for Smith permissions again.... Essay in from C.K. Williams. Haven't read it yet.... Billy might leave tomorrow already.... He found out he's 4th in his class of the 66 industrial engineering majors.... Kris had a rough time at her recital today; she was trying for $ or a scholarship of some kind, & played well, but the competition was tough—so many of the kids she runs into now have parents who play in various philharmonic orchestras, or are music profesors, etc. She'll mature on her own, in her own time, and this will be a good and natural thing for her.... Tony called. He's being hounded by that creep Polizzi....

3/4/84

    Just typed "Coming" & "Bread." I like them a lot. I'd typed some others first, and wasn't crazy about them—their line movements seemed strained, no matter how many times I'd gone over them—but these two please me. They seem to "intone." And they have to do with that world I keep feeling. Mainliners.

    Shoveled a couple times today, and pumped up the Regal's flat tire, so I feel as though I've had a good workout. Brian Johnson coming over soon for a game of hearts. Billy will leave already this evening.... But now he just walked into the study and said he might leave tomorrow.... Han & I are going for a walk.

    Dentist tomorrow.... My visit to U. of R. a week from tomorrow. Next weekend I'll get those boxes ready to drop off there.... Look forward to playing ball tomorrow....

3/5/84

    Got Billy back to Ithaca today—played poker until midnight with him & Brian & Kurt & Brad & Aje—and need now to get back to routine. Played ball. Went to dentist and had the one false tooth replaced & a couple of fillings done. Will have another appt. next month.... Card from Mark Strand today—I'll send him some books for inscription—and books back from McHugh, all three with holograph poems. The special Christmas cards arrived from Ewert, and then he called to say that Yankee Typesetters were doing *Erika* for Evelyn. At last. It will still be, I'd guess, late spring before the book shows up. But at least it's now in-process, as is *Wenzel/The Ghost*, which is already set.... A list from Babcock out with over 2 pp. of Heyen. <u>Wish</u> I could scare up about 10 customers for Bert. <u>That</u> wd. tighten the market & make things scarce....

    Billy just called—he's back safely with his haircut and clean laundry.

    Not all that much work to do this evening. A few papers to read. Last week, with the cancellations & snow-mixups, had all classes discombobolated.... In fact, classes Tues. & /Thurs. & then I'm off for ten days. Quite a job.

3/9/84

Friday evening. I'm off for about ten days. Worked hard at classes Tues. & Thurs., corrected papers all day Wednesday. Louis Simpson read here last night, & I spent time with him before and after and again this afternoon. He's easy to be with, unassuming and entertaining and friendly. I like him, care for many of his poems, think often of his life as child, as soldier, as poet. A very complex man, too—the way he slams the Academy of American Poets, talks of the jobs he's been offered lately and the reasons he turns them down—an edge under his voice that says more than his words say. But I like him. A man of integrity, and with an angle in on things that always seems to me sensible and sane.... He looks fine, is a young 60.... He inscribed several books for me, wrote out "Red-avoiding Pictures" in *The Best Hour*.... Many laughs over at Boo & Al's when they gave Louis his sweatshirt....

Han & Kris going to a play this evening. I'll stay home & watch basketball and boxing and putter among my books and maybe write Bruce a letter, etc.... Tomorrow, Han & I will make the planetarium trip with the seniors.

3/12/84

I'm sitting in the lounge at the U. of R. that may become the Heyen room. Just want to muse here for an hour before seeing Peter & Jim for lunch and talk. I saw this room once before, but had forgotten it. It now has about 30 metal chairs in it, has been used for classes.... Seems to be about 20' by 45'. Wonderful courtyard view right across from the main area of Rare Books. Good lighting. The hum of heating system, a white noise that is nice to work in but miserable to speak in. 10'6" to 11' ceilings. Glass on both sides of the entrance door. Warm brick on one wall and in the two columns dividing the 3 huge windows. Could it be that this place will become the place I've dreamed about for my books, for all those poems?... On the one hand, I'd want this room to be of use and, somehow, more than a locked museum; on the other hand, if there were a corner for common poetry books & a sofa & chairs for students and the door were open any time (the good books wd. be locked behind glass), I don't know how the correspondence, etc., could be secure. I'm just floating now, with ideas. In any case, if I work something out here, the room wd. have to be closed for a year or three, anyway, while at least a list of all my books was compiled.... I think I'd want my desk in the brick corner, and was thinking of even having my big roll-top brought over.... In the corner where I'm sitting now, a sofa & chairs. Maybe a table or two in the middle, for work.... Glass front book-cases, poetry broadsides on the walls.... Snow is sifting down in the courtyard as I sit here. This is a wonderful place. And if my books were all here to see & work with!... Peter has mentioned that there wd. have to be drapes to keep the strongest light from the books.... One other person only, a young woman, has been in this room since I came in.... Could the bookcases be floor-to-ceiling, or wd. this be too inconvenient? I estimate that I have at home a hundred feet of books right now, and there are all the books on deposit here, and, with luck, decades of collecting to go, so there cannot be too much shelf-space here.... A small seminar could meet in here, but this would not be a good place for a poetry reading.... Are those laurels in the courtyard?... There will be plenty of color in here, all my gleaming firsts.... Maybe a display cabinet in here so I can show off some things? And one cabinet for a complete collection of my own publications.... Archie, Jim, Dick, Anne, John, Bill Goyen, are you ready for this place? It has the feel of something lasting as long as our world will.... This place could simplify my life, make it easier for me to get out from under the constant urge to collect & worry my collection, make it easier to put my own writing first.... Well, I think I'll walk back over now & meet Peter & Jim.... Fingers crossed we can agree, especially on the big thing: I don't want to sell my books right now, and surely can't donate them right now. Besides other things, it wd. complicate things for me as I went back & forth with books to get inscribed, added letters, added things to my own publications, etc....

Later: Home again. Lunch with Peter & Jim, and good talk. Then the three of us went to the room and talked more. We talked about security, access, book-cases, etc. No problem regarding my ongoing ownership of all materials. Jim Wyatt thinks the incoming president at U. of R. will be very supportive. They are aiming for an opening next fall already. I am, to put it simply, thrilled. My books are worth it, even if I am not. I will keep collecting, keep packing. Yes, will probably send my roll-top desk over there, too. This will all change my life at home, for the better, will give me more time for writing, will put things in perspective. Amazing.

And I will have another place: cabin, study inside, office at school, and now a room at U. of R. Blessings on that room always.

3/14/84

Werner's birthday.
It's morning. I'm at my desk, all shaved and dressed and ready to drive to Houghton in a couple hours. Probably won't get back until midnight. Will drive slowly. Will plan the reading now, and plan the class while driving there. I hope to relax and enjoy this whole thing.
Have spent much time—as I will I think for the rest of my life—quietly excited about the poetry room at U. of R. Some books were on sale at Lift Bridge and I bought things by Bukowski (much more life in him for me than in Merrill and that end of the scale, e.g.), Whalen, Tom Clark (a novel, *Who Is Sylvia?* that I read yesterday) that maybe I otherwise wouldn't have bought. There will be room now for everything. I mentioned the room to Freddie Poulin yesterday and he right away began making plans to store his own archives at U. of R., etc., etc. He had that gleam in his eyes again....

3/15/84

Back safely through cold and patches of thick fog. Had a good day, a good class, a reading that was okay—my voice not at its best—and I'm home sipping coffee and watching boxing on cable. Ruth & Lionel Basney, Linda and John Leax good company. Heard myself read again. Made some money. Unwinding now. I might take a walk later for a haircut and to get to the bank. Warming outside.... I've a feeling that my questioning of Jesus & his father in "Simple Truths" was not a big hit at Houghton.... Kristen's concert tonight. I hope she plays her Mozart piece as well as she wants to.
Thursday already, my vacation shrinking, some schoolwork to do, but I feel fine.... Have been thinking much of the poetry room. And this morning, a thought I've had, truly, for the first time—or at least have made conscious for the first time: the room will be a place where I can preserve my <u>own</u> poems, have them there to be discovered, even studied. I do not have an audience, of course, but the books & all will be there for whenever, if ever, the future wants them: the presence of the work could even <u>encourage</u> attention. There will be a virtually complete Heyen collection, magazines & books & broadsides etc.—and this is <u>something</u>, at least, of course. And there will be the manuscripts. So, I will also take seriously the shelves of my own Heyen collection, will not think of it as the <u>least</u> important part of the room.
Mail came. Things from Spring Church, including the issue of *Cutbank* with Dick Hugo's memoir of the NYS Poetry Circuit. He was a lovable old bear. I've skimmed the memoir, and look forward to <u>reading</u> it and the whole issue.... Also bought a hardback of *Smoke's Way*.... Letter from Norbert. Nothing else.... Maybe I can take a <u>bike</u> ride today!

3/16/84

Last Thursday basketball last night, and I'm glad. Also, the tournament I was going to be in is off. I'm glad. Maybe the thrill of basketball is wearing away while the thrill of the poetry room is on the increase. I want to write Peter about a couple things on my mind. I may not go over to basketball today. I should spend a few hours in the cabin. I should get to some school work later on today, too.
Kristen is 18 today. Her Mozart solo last night was impressive, seven or eight minutes by memory, no music in front of her. She was less nervous than Han & I were. She got to show what she could do, and in front of so many people who mattered to her.
Warmer, the snowbanks melting at last. Should be nice in the cabin, and if I get back there for a good session, I can stop berating myself for this floating I've been doing. I guess I'm marking time until my trips next week & then the week after that. I plan to buy many books in New York, and am now rich enough to do so, especially after the money from Houghton. But I still have to find most of my books in second-hand and remainder dumps.

Later: found my galoshes and walked through sleet back here to the cabin. Water-covered ice across the back yard, rabbit pellets floating above the ice. Perfect back here, the cabin snug, and maybe I should have been back here all day. I didn't play ball, and did get that letter off to Purchase and am ready for the Reddy letter to Columbia, but mainly I spent time with packing books for Rochester again. And the big box of books arrived from Bruce, all sorts of good things including several proofs. So, it's been a day away from my poetry again, but I've been telling myself this is okay. As, damn it, it is! At the same time, I don't want to live life preparing for life or death—the former because I'm trying to get out from under collecting at home so that I <u>first</u> pay attention to my own writing; the latter, maybe, as I go about planning the poetry room so I can die *mit alles in ordnung*, maybe. Just now, I enjoyed putting together that last sentence, was inside it and timeless. At last, then, such moments.... I want to type a letter to Peter on my old banger, then have supper with Han & Kris—we'll give her her presents then. We'll have a cozy evening within this weather. Will definitely come back here tomorrow for a session or two....

3/23/84

7:10. I'm on board for flight to LaGuardia. Billy dropped me off at the airport. Cold this morning, and icy roads. Traffic slow, but I got here in good time. Won't see Billy again for a month or so. My son. Will Kristen, too, be on her way to Myrtle Beach by the time I get home again?

So angry in class yesterday at Howard Edmund. I'd thought he was smart, even enlightened, but it turns out he's, well, dumb, illogical, dense. I'd talked about the homosexual essence of the *Calamus* poems. He didn't want us to use the word. Then, from Tues. to Thurs., he read things & brought them to class, talked ten minutes off the point, said Walt was too moral even to admit that such readings were possible, read that Symonds letter to Walt and then poor Walt's desperate letter back, six children and all. Howard so stupid about everything. His own language, without his knowing it, was anti-homosexual: "Walt would no more write of men having sex with men than men having sex with sheep." So, I was angry, and said so. And I'd thought Howard was a Brockport presence I should get into touch with over the years. I should have known: he reads great books, but plays word games with them, is fascinated that "live" spelled backwards is "evil," etc. I should have known. I look for the light in Brockport, again, and it turns out that Howard's mind is mush.

We're up, above the clouds. I take all this technology for granted now. Saw the canal, the snow-cover below.

The other day in my office I tried to write on some loose paper about Yehuda Amichai's visit. I like him very much. Reading *Amen* I found memorable things. And then listening to him, his quiet wisdom, I knew he was a real poet, one I will read deeply once my life changes, empties of thousands of other books into the room at U. of R. I want to send him *Erika* when it's out—a rabbi, apparently, had given him *Swastika* to read, and he said good things about it to Stan Rubin. Amichai's visit was a sudden one—there was no time to make a tape.

Will meet Bruce at 11:00 in the Gotham, and we'll kick around all day. First, I'll check in with Evelyn in her Dickensian digs.

Good talk with Tony the other day.... Al looks ghostly, seems barely able to walk a couple hundred feet.

Later: it's ten in the evening. I'm in the back apartment at Evelyn's, in bed, resting, planning to write a page in this journal. A big window in front of me—maybe ten feet high—and one to my left. No shades on the windows, so I see the Dacotah to my left and another building straight ahead. The lights go on and off. Shadowy figures. It is like seeing ant colonies, the scurrying from spot to spot against the glass. I've only the night-table lamp on, only the small circle of page and moving hand lit in this room.

Such a good day with Bruce. Several bookshops, lunch and dinner. He's a friend. No one I'd rather kick around with than him, no one who shares my desire for books the way he does. Good talk all day. I've three boxes of books heading toward Brockport from three different stores—the largest shipment is of 23 books ($93) from the Barnes & Noble at 18th St. Tomorrow, I'll visit the Strand & maybe the Phoenix.

There's a restaurant/pub called Blarney's on 8th Ave. near 49th. The best meal I've ever had in NYC, and for $4.50. I love the place—so relaxed & loud, blacks & whites, young & old, beer & food, no waiters to worry about. It's worth taking a cab to any time. 8th Ave. and 49th. I must remember.

Bruce & I stopped in, too, at 424 Madison. Evelyn is the same, deft at changing the subject immediately should I ask about anything having to do with business. But *Erika* will get done. It's in the Vanguard Spring-Summer list now.... I saw *Light* and *Lord* in Gotham, nary a book anywhere else.

Talking to Bruce I further defined for myself how the poetry room would change my life, keep me within some serious reading, keep me within my writing. It's also true that Kristen will be out of the house, her comings & goings, my day-to-day worries about her. More time that I'll be alone, Han at work. Yes, a change in my life from puttering with my book collection to getting down habitually, I hope, into my writing.

3/24/84

10 p.m. A long, full day, too much weighed down by books, book-blur, but a good day. Dinner with Bruce & Lisa & Dave in the same pub. I had turkey & mashed potatoes & green beans & two beers & two slices of rye bread. Bruce will be at Books & Co. tomorrow. Tomorrow night I might head to Long Island.... Called home. My folks called & Don Swaim called & the Hamiltons called, etc. I wish Swaim had been in touch again before I left. Now I don't want to even think of doing the program on Monday, or next Thursday for that matter. Well, it will all turn out for the better if I do the program, say in July, once the book is out.

Haven't thought yet of what to say or read tomorrow. Will, soon as I end this entry. I'll head for the restaurant at about 11:30.

Had a nice chat with Bob Wilson at Phoenix. Many people are going to take me more seriously once my poetry room news gets around. His eyes lit up, as did Evelyn's, when I mentioned it, casually, ahem, of course.... I bought about a hundred bucks worth of books again today, including a few more copies of Archie's *Letters*. Bruce got me a $60 art book edited by Mark Strand for $15. I must have 7-8 packages on their way to Brockport now.

I'm nervous about tomorrow, the meeting with Ray & Joyce, the presentation at Books & Co., the connection out to the Island later, etc.

2 a.m.: anything in this poem?   *The Colony*

    I'm in a dark room on the tenth floor of a building on Central Park West.
    Only a circle of light on this page, like a huge gold coin from El Dorado.
    John Lennon was shot next door. Yoko Ono still lives there
    where she can visit her strawberry field forever.

    Almost midnight, rain gusting against my window.
    Across the way, lights come on, go off, shadowy figures appear,
    vanish. In a few minutes, I remember, it will be spring.
    The city seems to be weeping

    over the building where he sang of love until love
    twisted to kill him. On, off, the cells lit, then dark.
    Then a single room blooms red, awash with flowers,
    as though an ant had dragged a red petal through a tunnel.

I like the poem, will tighten it. More and more the usual 65-70 character line is a pain in the ass. Had to break many lines in *Wenzel/The Ghost*, and this put me off as I read proof. My rhythms were busted, and I'm so glad when I can write longer lines that hang together. Some day I'll lobby for a *CR* of wider format. Haven't seen proof for *Erika* yet, either, and I bet "Poem Touching the Gestapo" will be a mess.

3/26/84

Monday, 10:00 p.m. I'm in bed at the folks'. Quiet here in this secluded retirement place, and trebly quiet because I'm alone and unrushed for the first time in days. A day lost somewhere in Rockville Centre and

Mineola he says to himself in code to remember. Headlong to the Island after the gathering at Books & Co., & the cocktail party at Grace Schulman's in the Village.

Lunch with Renee & Ted Weiss (Ted I called him) & Bob Phillips & the Smiths at a place called The Right Bank. Then that crowded & hectic & high-powered gathering. I sat to Doctorow's right, Grace to my right, then Godwin to D's left & Oates to hers & Ozick to hers & Weiss to hers. I'd made notes for myself, and got up to do my thing second or third, and I did well, am actually proud of myself for holding up as I did. Finished by reading "The Tree" and "The Children" & connecting it with Berryman: "John, at least here / I hold you in mid-air." There I was with the famous, and I did okay. I did it. I'm glad its over.

Ray gave me the info. for the catalogue for Persea on the anthology. Things sure do look good.

I bought a copy of *First Person Singular*—needed a 2nd copy for my collection in any case—and got it inscribed by all six panelists. A beauty of a book to remember that day…. Bruce at that gathering again, that wonderful Agte presence. I have in my duffel bag the big Strand (Mark) book he got me, an art tome…. Many boxes of books will soon begin arriving at #142.

I'm all set now. Will keep Mom & Pop company a couple days, & will get dropped off at Vince's Thursday morning…. Have talked to Billy & Han, & all's well at home.

I'm glad I'm here, diary.

3/28/84

Evening. I'm sitting in the folks' living room in bathrobe & pyjamas. Pop & I are just back from Wern's. A miserable drive in blowing snow. Chicken dinner at Wern's. Pop & I killed the whole afternoon arriving there. We had a beer in the Hampton Bays Diner. A good day all around. In one junk shop, I even bought a new copy of *Deliverance* for a buck…. Tomorrow morning, weather willing, Pop will drop me off at Vince's for a day of book-hunting & poetry talk.

Wern & Barb seem okay. Mrs. Dooks there for the next couple months, too, all three smoking their heads off.

Mom unbelievably nervous, her head filled with anger & frustration & bitterness. Impossible to explain here. Right now, though, after her once-a-month gathering with the neighborhood women, she seems calmer, is reading the newspaper.

I may have added a stanza to "Coming" yesterday. May have to look at it again at Vince's before reading it Friday.

Visited Pop's shop, and somehow we talked about the possibility of having Pop do the table for the poetry room. That wd. be a special touch! I've a feeling it's going to work out…. No energy here for this journal. I'm ready to hit the road again.

Later: 3 a.m. Just bumped into Mom in hallway, Mom in her cap after getting her stomach remedy for eating all that crap all day…. Weather…. Mom just popped into my room to see if I was feeling okay…. Weather miserable, rain & snow blowing against the house. I doubt I'll be able to get to Vince's early in the morning as planned…. Will read for a while from *Shaking the Pumpkin*.

3/29/84

It's past noon, and I'm still with the folks. The weather is terrible. I don't think I'll get to Vince's. Too bad. I'd have enjoyed looking at his books and talking with him. Tomorrow, somehow, I'll get to Roslyn.

Article in *Newsday* on the party at Books & Co. It got everything wrong about what I'd said, but no matter. Interesting how the truth of what is said in any of these kinds of reports is so twisted, and how I couldn't care less really. A good reader would take it for granted that anything any of us said would be mucked up by the reporter.

Mom, especially, so nervous, so fussing all the time. I'm afraid even to be in the bathroom for more than a minute because she'll quiz me about what is wrong. I'm too skinny for her. My hair is too short. It should be comfortable here but I'm on edge all the time, and this weather has stranded me here…. Maybe later, if it's certain (and it looks that way) that I can't get to Vince's, I'll spend a couple hours in my bedroom looking at poems, arranging the reading. Who could have guessed this weather at the end of March? But the timing could have been worse. Looks as though the flight from Kennedy on Saturday, if we can believe the forecasts, won't be affected.... Had a great pork-chop dinner here at about 11:00!... Pop napping now, Mom crocheting.... I just sort of dipped into *God's Grace*, catching the plot & ending. Just doesn't interest me much....

4/1/84

Heard today that I've been given five years off and $250,000 by the MacArthur Foundation. Also, I won the National Book Award and the Pulitzer Prize. Wrote a beautiful book-length poem in one sitting....

<u>Did</u> make it all the way back to Brockport after getting to Vince's, & to Norbert's. Busy, nervous visits, but it was good seeing all of them. Vince's situation still seems strange to me. Norbert was self-centered, but he's a friend, and his Marie Elizabeth & Daniel are little beauties. Catherine sweet as always. In Roslyn I bought firsts of Moore's *La Fontaine* & Warren's *Segregation*, & we visited Morris Gelfand, a great fellow. He wants to do another Heyen broadside. I'll love that. And I wrote him today to tell him I'll take the $292 in royalties he owes me in a portfolio & several broadsides.

This will be a crazy week—Voigt's visit & tape, classes, raffle-party tomorrow night, Han leaving for Myrtle Beach early Thurs. morning, I leaving for Albany Friday, etc.—but I'm going to stay calm through it all. I got 3-4 things done today, & maybe can do 1-2 more things this evening. Wonderful to be home with Han & Kris again. Billy called today, and he's fine, too.

I read <u>very</u> well in Roslyn. Only about 35 people there, but a good audience.

I've unpacked all the books from NYC, have written Peter, am clearing away and <u>will</u> be for a long time before I sit at this desk with just a few books that I want to read & study, a few poems I want to move forward. It looks like the poetry room will be, and it will be a <u>necessary</u> joy for me if I'm going to continue to be a writer.

TriQuarterly here.... Have I mentioned that *Upstate* will do "Downriver"?... I'm so comfortable here at this desk right now.

4/2/84

Waiting for Han to call for a ride home from the Center. At 7:30 we'll meet the Maiers for that buffet at the college, the gambling night.

Talked to *Upstate*. "Downriver" will appear the 29th, & lines will not be broken.

Played ball. Played well. Felt physically strong.... Mailed books to Vince Clemente & to Jay Yost at the Mayo Clinic. Mailed Billy his shoes!

Long lettr from Ray Smith again about anthology details. Will take care of loose ends again over the next week or two.

I'm reconciled to going to Albany this Friday. Might take some anthology work along with me there, and work for several hours, especially on Sunday.

Moved another bookcase out of my study.... I like sitting at this desk reading, as I did for a while, about Bucke & Walt, e.g. Don't need, don't <u>want</u> the crush of my book collection here.

Spoke to Tony. He's fine.

Got the 2 course descriptions written. Will use *2000* in <u>both</u> contemporary literature courses. And in Hawaii.

Yes, yes, journal, I'm all chatter lately. Might take me a while to begin living deeply again. I will. Big changes in my life over this next year. And it wouldn't even hurt me to shut up for a few months now and then. This particular blank book will be filled in before long. With the next one, maybe, a "new" life.

4/4/84

Morning. Have read Voigt again, and noted some questions. Am a little nervous waiting to make the tape. Hate to have it cut into basketball time.

Good classes yesterday. In Transcendentalism, Bill McLean started talking of his suicidal thoughts lately. We made a circle of hands and prayed for him.

Was thinking of Poulin, how he will not be around again for Voigt today, is not around for the younger poets. He devotes himself to that other generation, and will die with them.

I'm pleased with the moves I'm making, the needs I feel to change my life—all this is within the thing itself, the removal of books from here into Rochester, yes. By the summer, already, my world here will be clearer. I have about 20 boxes of books ready to go. Sometimes when I think of that room I think that it can't be for me, because I'm only 43. It's for someone in his 80s. But the books are undeniable. I made a list of 45 poets whose holograph poems I have in one or more books. I've no doubt forgotten some. Probably, the U. of R. will mount a display to go along with the exhibition.

I'll go to dinner at Marchants' this evening, but not Han. She'll be packing for her Myrtle Beach vacation. Voigt reading this evening. I have schoolwork, too, and will be getting up about five to drive Han to the airport. Next day, airport again for my Albany trip. I'll try to make the best of that one.

Called Mom & Pop. They both seem to want a different house, one in New Jersey. No, Pop wd. just as soon stay in Ridge. The work at Richie's is very important to him, too, physically & emotionally. I hope they (Mom makes all the decisions) don't make a big mistake. The wrong move could kill them, I think.

Good being with Irene, Richard, Tricia yesterday. I've some good friends among the older students. They temper the swirling waters over there.... Much thought yesterday about that passage in Berry's "A Native Hill" concluding with the idea that we will not learn from ourselves how to better ourselves.

Between paragraphs the cataloguer, Evelyn, at U. of R. called about the # of items to be catalogued, etc. I said 10,000, but who knows? They do things thoroughly and right there. No doubt she'll be assigned to the job, and Peter is freeing her for it. She wanted to know the percentage of items not on some data base system, broadsides & such. Gulp.... I asked that Peter call—I'd like to have the U. of R. send a truck to pick up about 20 boxes of books I have ready. After this, I can get things to Rochester by myself, a few boxes with each visit. What a relief!

Well, a nervous day ahead, another test for the inner calm I believe I have.

4/6/84

Another airport entry. Flight to Albany in a half-hour. Never have I so much not wanted to go on a trip. Last night, hour after hour, I almost called this thing off, and would have if I thought that woman could be reached in her office. I don't even know all the reasons I'm against this. Han is away, and I've much work to do, and I'm tired still from the last trip and the week of teaching, but there's more to it than this. I've found myself thinking often of that conference in Cortland many years ago. I was nobody, and lost, and didn't have a book, and I wanted only to be home minding my business and trying to write. I don't have these insecurities today, but would like to avoid the crush of hale people heartily met on this once-every-two-years occasion. Do I want to be a star, featured, like Kinnell & Simpson? Truly, I don't think this bothers me. Would I care if I weren't scheduled to read? All this doesn't matter. I just don't want to plod around the Albany campus looking for rooms, looking for rides. And it's such a wind-shitty day again. Sunday, when I can't fly home until 4:00, will be long, but I've brought along some anthology work for the airport.... In the end, I decided to make this trip to see if I could be who I am, could remain centered in the swirl, could stand at ease wearing my hat inside or out. Walt, be with me.... Letter from Cynthia Golderman who will be at the gathering tomorrow night. Oh, what a soul. Her poems are much too messy, but she is all spirit. I'll look into her eyes.

Han called last night. She had a terrible time making it to Myrtle Beach. Her flight to Newark was so wind-bounced that she had to return to Rochester. She then made a couple of lucky connections in Pittsburgh & Charlotte. Anyway, she's well, and she's there, bless her.

Did get around to a letter to Ray Smith last night. And just at this moment I remember that I didn't mail it, and don't know where it is. I probably left it on the downstairs table?

"Branch system," "community line of business," "trainees," "management divisions"—a couple of businessmen are making plans to my right. It is only in airports or on shuttles I hear this language. I think of Billy, the world he is moving into. I'd like to see him teach engineering, instead of being an 8-5 man. But he should have some field experience first, I suppose. Maybe my field of vision is too narrow, but so many of these lives I see lived around me seem dreary. My hand is warm now. This miracle of my life. The good talks in classes, and the times when I am truly at home. "Have the Rochester facility handle the western part of the state. Their space is unrealized. They've got half as many people as the space will allow." "Support of the upstate banking system." My language comes from ponds & trees, at least the language I love. The man talking, though, is excited, even passionate about his business. "Branch integration." "Relationship to the salary base." Briefcases clicking open and clicking shut. "You can see it through the whole organization."... A soldier sitting in front of me. I swear I'd rather be going to boot camp than into a business office. Though maybe, today, I'd rather be going to a business office than to this fucking creative writing conference.

    I have a couple of Galway's books along for inscription maybe, and a couple of Feldman's, a few by Judith Johnson Sherwin.

    I liked Ellen Bryant Voigt. The tape went okay, but not as smooth as others. She & Mary Elsie were late showing up, so I conspired with Martha to make the tape 30 minutes, instead of 45. What the hell, I had to get to the gym!... *Claiming Kin*, the book I couldn't find in NYC, was actually on sale at the reading, so I have both her books. I liked her new poems, flowing ones, including one called "Water Lilies" that she ended with. I'll read her again if I expand the anthology some day. No more tapes for a long time. From here on in, I'll pick my spots. This is what I have to keep learning, as I wrote to myself in that Wyoming motel room years ago....

    Hey, I'm here, at 9:30, and in my room already, and I like this room and will be able to sit at this desk and get some work done. I even have a ride to the campus in a half-hour with a woman whose name I wish I could remember, or where I know her from. Long Island? Jamestown? Anyway, I'm going to sit back within myself and enjoy the day. I don't even have a book of mine with me, just a sheaf of poems to keep in my pocket in case I don't get back here at all today.... Yes, there's something about this room that I like.

4/8/84

    Needless to say, I've done no work. I carried this journal over to breakfast just now thinking no one would be there, but friends were still there.

    I'm in front of a mirror at this desk. I look tired. I am tired. Life goes on outside again, and I am writing in this journal, as though it is real, as it slows into real time, truer to my inner economy—whatever the words and paragraphs come to say—than the flurry of activities these past days.

    David Axelrod has given me books and will send more. Charles Fishman has given me his book, and I know more about him, the selves he still is that I once was, than he knows I know. Late bar talk last night with Turco & Simpson & that fine man Dan Masterson & with new friend John Allman and all. This after the Kinnell reading and reception after dinner with the Brockport crowd—Nancy Kress, Stan, Greg, Gary Eddy (also Charles, David)—at the restaurant where Linda Loranzani works. Missed the Simpson reading, was glad to hear Galway again who, this time, read well. He was behind me alone as we walked the corridor to the reception, and I turned to say hello, then wanted to leave him alone in the press and did. But then he broke away from groups to come over to me later, and this warmed me. We spoke of NYU/Binghamton, John Logan, Bill Ewert, Poulin. He said he'd heard I'd given a wonderful reading. I said I was "tremendous." We laughed.

    I did give a good reading. Cynthia Golderman was there, all soul, called me "Camerado." I guess she'll be my correspondent the rest of the way. I take her on, now.

    Intense talk with Nancy Kress at dinner, about Graver and many other things.

    What is there to say in this <u>welter</u> of the sun (though the weather has been lousy) these days?

    Much confidence in myself, my poems, my abilities in front of a group. Dan Masterson's introduction—well, he called me master, as he did not the others. His introduction floored people, I know, made them listen.

    Nothing, nothing of these past two days makes its way into this journal.... I feel fine, will get to the airport & maybe write some postcards, at least.

    I mentioned my room at U. of R. to Turco. The word got around. People supportive, happy, understanding.

Sinuses dripping from all the smoke these past days.

All's well. I want to get home to Kristen. Han will call tonight, I'm sure. By now she should be hooked up with Wolf & Pat.

Cannot hold all together—dear Dan Murray, Gary Eddy, Vince Clemente, Phillips, all friends everywhere. Cannot hold all together. Except, again, in that room.

No more trips until July, at least no more of these trips. Will settle in to finish the semester. Will catch my breath. Will get some sleep. Will go to the dentist tomorrow morning and then play ball and then get ready for school. And this gathering in Albany will blur into the others, but may the world conspire to bring all of us together again.

I said that in the end I'd make the trip if I could test myself to see if I could remain centered. I did okay. I talked enough to be sociable, was at ease much of the time, was a friend to friends I should be a friend to.... Brockport and home today.

The comfort, for no reason I know of, of this journal again.

Later: I've been here in the airport cafeteria for a good few hours. Have written notes to a dozen of the *2000* contributors, sending along Ray's description. Glad I got this stuff done. I know that, once home, once I get a good night's sleep or three, I'll recuperate quickly.

Just thought of a great title for a couple of the display cases at U. of R. for the exhibition: *Missing Friends Here.* These wd. be cases that showed Hugo/Berryman/Wright/Gardner/MacLeish/Sexton items. Yes, we are missing friends here. Yes, the missing friends are here....

4/11/84

Wednesday evening. I've just finished a few student journals, and am tired. Can't quite catch up with my life. Rushing. Unable to get to mail. Kristen & I missing one another as we rush around. But, I've known I'd be this busy. After classes tomorrow, I'll have my first free weekend in what seems like a long time. Yes, all's well, tired as I am and with this sinus cold. Han's home Friday already, too.

Got the car taken care of for Kristen, snow tires off, oil change, etc. She leaves Sunday or Monday.

Answered another query letter from Ray Smith. Worked a whole mindless morning on questions of date on the copyright page. He won't let anything be, and the truth is that this is an enviable quality in an editor, and the truth also is that no one gives a shit what is on the copyright pages. And who ever stole a poem?... I sure do hope he got that other letter I worked so hard on.

Good talk with Peter the other day. Looks like U. of R. will spend about ten grand on the book cases!

Yes, I plan a long, good weekend. Even want to rake a little, and maybe get the lawnmower battery to Al Studier for charging.

Strand essay not in yet, damn it.

Good talk with Michael Walker today. A rare chap.

Shell box with all sorts of tiny things in it from Cynthia Golderman. And a long letter from her. I'll have to stay with her, now, as I knew. An ultra-romantic spirit, fainting & bleeding, but so loving & warm.

Many letters to answer, & I'd like to send some poems out, and.... A long weekend....

4/14/84

Saturday morning here in small-town western New York State. I'm in the cabin for a few hours for the first time in a long time. Coffee steaming, heater humming, my body buzzing down into the quiet of this place again. Some good sleep last night. Many dreams, one about getting books signed by Ronald Duncan (sic), handing him one & going for two others & then on the way back having to cross a whole golf course.

Han's return a good one yesterday afternoon, but today already she & Kristen are chasing to Niagara Falls for Kristen's $200 prom dress. This life of hurtling around & spending & never sitting still & getting along at home gets me glum. Kristen is a beautiful child, but spoiled, but thoughtful & mature, but spoiled. She shops & buys & spends & there's just never any let-up when she sits in one place and centers herself with a good book or a diary. Phone calls & rushed meals & living on the edge all the time, throwing things around. And

Monday she leaves with 3 friends in our car for Myrtle Beach. Yes, spoiled. And Han's frenetic life—some of it necessary & some of it not—has become a part of Kristen.... I have a wife & daughter & son who love me dearly, and I love them, but there often seems to be an absence of togetherness because of this chasing around, this superficial rush all the time. I know when I'm in that rush, and they don't.... And I still don't have a decent goddamned pen, and I need a pair of shoes, and I buy books and sent $38 to Alvie McWilliams for photographs, and I just made two trips this past month, so I am part of that same whirl.

There's a big Sylvania appliance carton in the middle of my acre. The land is weatherbeaten but coming back quickly.

Inside, I'm still packing away books. Have about 25 cartons ready for U. of R. I know more & more the different economy I want my life to be.

Got around, at last, to a few letters yesterday, including one to Jack Matthews.

Suddenly, I'm happy. My brow unscrews. A long good day to look forward to. Maybe Han & I will go to the play this evening. Maybe I'll wash out the garage today. Maybe I'll go over a poem or three now, or write a new one. Maybe *Erika* will actually be published.

I wrote Cynthia Golderman, too.... Got a book from Edward Hirsch. Owe letters to many others. Lucien here next month. <u>Now</u>, I'm in the cabin. I'll just be in the cabin. The cabin.

4/20/84

A warm late afternoon. Han will be home soon, and we'll go out for a fish fry. Tomorrow, we'll head to Nashville. I suddenly realize that I look forward.

Proofs of *Erika* arrived yesterday. Evelyn did not add the two poems—one by Sachs & one on Bonhoeffer—that she said she'd add, and it might be hard to insert them now because of pagination. I'll get the packet back to her Monday.

Stryk's visit okay. He's still a contradiction, pumping himself while speaking of eternal things. Tony worked hard on dinner & a tape & introduction, etc. Al showed up at Tony's at midnight. I'm a little, just a little pissed at Poulin: for a second time he said every once in a while he thinks of giving me a Simpson book & then says no, decides to tease me. And I reviewed the book for *Newsday* & don't have a copy. So, Al is just Al & I'm not really miffed. But I'll not visit him or call him again until hell freezes over, or until he realizes maybe that some little thing is bothering me.

Sequence, Sometimes Metaphysical arrived from Vince today. I read it over (2 typos, I think!), heard it again, saw how much I'd absorbed of those poems, how many lines I knew even though I'm not nuts about most of the poems. The book is a pleasure to read from, & I like the Roy prints.

The spring, now, feels deep & new. The sunlight & fresh wind today. The honeysuckle leaves appearing. This cabin here & having weathered a hard winter. Lord, may I have some long sessions back here this spring & summer, may poems come along and books fall into place.... More & more I've been thinking about expanding *The City Parables* (whatever it will be called) getting "The New American Poetry" & many other poems into it.

Only two weeks of school left. Then, a week of getting grades in. Then, <u>here</u>, for long hours. I'll do whatever anthology work/*Erika* work is necessary inside in the evenings. Have to decide about whether or not to have a garden this year.... Hope Billy finds a job for the summer. Hope Kris calls this evening to tell us how she's doing.

Guess I'll take this journal to Nashville with me.

Think I hear Han in the garage.

Think I'll have a great dinner with that woman I love and need so much.

Later: phone call just now from Billy: he's hurt his ankle bad, is in a cast, feels miserable, of course, is worried about classes, job interview, etc. He might need surgery next week. <u>Damn</u>. Poor kid. As he said, a broken leg in 5th grade, one in 10th grade, and now this one in 15th grade. Only a couple more weeks of school for him, too. Pain builds character. Adversity builds character. But who needs this? Well, we'll see. We'll have to make a decision, no doubt, about the surgery.... It was one of the worst times in my life when he broke his leg the last time. I don't feel that upset this time. But it's a lousy break. Billy sounded very <u>low</u>. Han is shopping, & will call him later.

4/21/84

Here in Nashville, in my living-room chair. Read much of Arthur Gregor's memoir today.... Han & I had a good trip here. We stopped at Wolf's for a sandwich for lunch. And I stopped in a bookstore near Wolf's & bought $15 worth of poetry books, many (Garrigue, Lieberman, etc., Cooper) @44¢.

Han will probably drive to Ithaca Monday morning to be with Billy & to talk to his doctor. I feel good about that. We'll call him tomorrow night.

I have some student papers/journals with me, but don't feel like getting to them. But I probably will do a few this evening. We just had a good lasagna dinner, though I have to separate out the cheese. Now, I don't want to have a thing before breakfast.

The spring countryside is beautiful. Han & I walked down the dirt road a ways. I'd like to live in the grove of trees back of Waxhams' property, far from everything, able to see anyone coming from a mile away.

We'd come to this place when Billy & Kristen were babies. Now they're 21 & 18, and I'm getting gray. And the Easter flowers keep appearing. A whole way of life passed here when Mom died. I think of her often. Oh, she'd have been irritated by the motorcycle noise from across the way, would have eaten too much & then moaned, would have bitched at Pops for one reason or another, but she was good-hearted, and fun. We miss her. If Han & I get to church in the morning, we'll think of her then, too.... Pops has been acting okay. He's even eaten less than I've ever seen him eat. Tomorrow, Easter, the 3 of us will join the 3 Greiners at Palm Gardens for dinner. Then, I'll be glad to get home and get into touch with Billy.

3 or 4 very long letters & packets of poems from Cynthia Golderman this week.... Good letter from Bob Morgan today.

Kristen enjoying herself in Myrtle Beach. My family is spread out, and will be, but Han is with me here, and will be.

Later: Billy called home. He feels much better, slept nine hours last night, is doing okay, is glad Han will keep him company Monday morning....

I'm watching *King Kong* with Pops.... Have one more journal to go. Church at nine in the morning, maybe....

I've just looked at the beginning date of this particular blank book. I've written all this in less than a year? I'm surprised. Maybe, I'll write less in the next one, but pay closer attention to the more interesting things I think about. Often, I have a realization—realized the other day that during the 15 minutes or so of solitaire I play each day the sounds are <u>iambic</u>: slipping a card from the deck, slapping it down—but then don't note it down. Having a smaller journal will help. It can be handier. I have my eye on an artist's sketch book in the Lift Bridge.... But, hell, I don't want to put any pressure on myself: If I feel like writing about meals and the weather, so be it....

Easter

Just back from the 11:00 service at the Methodist church in Forestville. Pop's been okay. An easy-going, informal service. I thought of services at St. James Lutheran, of the little chapel at Little Gidding, of the church in Hanover, of Saint Margaret's in Knotting, all those reverberating, hallowed places.... In Forestville, they had a "Children's Time," all the little ones skipping or stumbling up to the altar in their new clothes to hear a story about the caterpillar that became a butterfly. Han saw many old friends. I saw Larry Youngberg, Mark Bradigan, Bob Bradigan—old ballplayer friends.... All the feelings that come flooding in, Easter and old friends and our own lives gone/going by so quickly.... Now, dinner in Gowanda with Wolf & Pat & Kurt & the three of us to look forward to. Then, a slow drive back to Brockport.

4/25/84

Argument with Han today because she was late picking me up when I wanted to play ball. Her job still bothers me—she probably averages 12 hrs. a day—but I should grow up, too, and not "rush," not worry about being late. Anyone, as Walt says, whoever has the wind and the air and the sun has enough. She'll be home soon (maybe, that fucking job) and I can apologize. A great woman. I couldn't be luckier. The job is terrible. One of the seniors just now called here for her. Her work goes on with one Center thing or another until she goes to bed, exhausted.

I pick up Billy at the bus station at 7:30. Tomorrow, his appt. with Riegler. Saturday, his job interview. Kristen away, Billy hurt—my life just seems scattered lately.

Ray Smith called last night about Strand's essay, and about raising the price of the anthology to $14.95. The price is completely up to him. Guess I'll have to call Strand. Hate to. Will.

I have my new blank book, a smaller one, so can end this one.

Peter Dzwonkoski called. Guess it's a big hassle, an expensive one, for U. of Rochester to send a truck here for my books, so we'll have to do it a carload at a time. Do I know anybody with a pickup or van?... My study is looking "economical" now, with much shelf space, margins, room for me and my poems now.

Maybe I'll see if I can start some dinner. Too bad I'm so clumsy & ignorant.

I'll be missing Christopher Lasch's lecture on *1984* & today tonight.

Ballgame on tonight, Knicks & Pistons. The games have been very tough ones.... Look forward to gathering Billy, & pray he won't fall down.

4/26/84

Billy home & okay. Han will take him to doctor today. Tomorrow I'll drive him into Rochester for his interview. I might find my way round to a few bookstores while he's busy, or might even come back to Brockport between.

Beautiful day today, as this journal winds down. What kind of year have I had? A couple nights ago I dreamed that I soared up in slow motion and over the defense and dunked a basketball. Last night I dreamed I was on the bow of a ship that re-opened a channel, pushing through low water and grass-clogged and mud-clogged areas, to the sea. On a lawn in front of the sea, I was at first afraid of two wildcats, but then petted them, and a rabbit, and some kind of partridge with almost plastic feathers. Anyway, the dreams were fulfilling, lung-deep, and I am coming close again to a time when I'll open the channels to my poems again.

Han and I have gotten over our tiff. We both agree that her job is too much.

Helen & John Maier will go with us Saturday to the Eastman for those Sesqui activities. I'm glad I'm one of the first on the program, and I hope when I'm done to be able to get back into the audience to sit with Han & Helen & John.

Today should be an easy day. We're going over student work on dittoes in Sport Literature, and Tricia Hess has her period on Margaret Fuller in Transcendentalism. Some good pieces to go over in Advanced Composition, too.

One daffodil from Richard Ehrlich on my desk. Its "vase" is the whale letter-holder made by Kristen 8 or 10 years ago.

Dan Masterson sent me the long poem he read in Albany. It just seems to me that it needs voltage, octane, amps, something.

Read a funny piece from *Esquire* by Peter Nelson—imaginary job applications. I count my blessings here. I'm quiet by nature, would like of course to be walking in the woods now, am a good teacher but not a born one, and there are so many irritations & distractions around school (balanced or even over-balanced by the good moments with students & friends), but I'm at least half-way home here, and make more than enough money, and feel secure. It is not quite life, and I'm not sure I can ever make it life—I began the school year yearning for integration, and still feel that centeredness here at school lacking—but it doesn't stop me from having those other, deeper experiences.

4/27/84

I'm home after dropping Billy off at the Sibley Tower for his interview with Rochester Products. I hope he has a good day and gets back to Ithaca safely. We'll call him this evening.

I have an urge to write, but have all these things unfinished around me—the event tomorrow, the last stretch of school, Kristen's long return, etc.—and this gets in the way. The time will come, and before long.

John Maier's father died, so Mirko & Katja will probably be with us tomorrow, and maybe Nete.

Long letters from Cynthia Golderman yesterday. Once in a while she says something/writes a sentence with poetry in it. Once in a while.

The rhythms of this journal lately are the rhythms of my life, choppy & scattered. Summer amplitude and luck to the next one....